Holmquist

Bus-law Voorhees

COPYRIGHT NOTICES AND ACKNOWLEDGMENTS

AMERICAN LITERATURE

An Anthology and Critical Survey

SELECTED AND EDITED BY

JOE LEE DAVIS

University of Michigan

JOHN T. FREDERICK

University of Notre Dame

FRANK LUTHER MOTT

University of Missouri

FROM 1860 TO THE PRESENT

VOLUME II

CHARLES SCRIBNER'S SONS

CHICAGO   ATLANTA   SAN FRANCISCO   DALLAS

NEW YORK

Contents

VOLUME TWO

BOOK III: AMERICAN LITERATURE 1860-1900

INTRODUCTION   1

PART I: THE REAFFIRMATION OF DEMOCRACY

ABRAHAM LINCOLN   15
Autobiography   15
Farewell Address at Springfield 16
The Gettysburg Address   17
Letter to Mrs. Bixby   17
Second Inaugural Address   17

WALT WHITMAN   19
"Song of Myself"   30
"There Was a Child Went Forth" 70
"Song of the Broad-Axe"   72
"Crossing Brooklyn Ferry"   79
"Out of the Cradle Endlessly
  Rocking"   83
"Once I Pass'd Through a Populous
  City"   88
"I Sit and Look Out"   88
"Beat! Beat! Drums!"   88
"By the Bivouac's Fitful Flame" 89
"Come Up From the Fields Father" 89
"As Toilsome I Wander'd Virginia's
  Woods"   90
"When Lilacs Last in the Dooryard
  Bloomed"   91
"O Captain! My Captain!"   97

"Chanting the Square Deific"   97
"Pioneers! O Pioneers!"   99
"When I Heard the Learn'd
  Astronomer"   101
"Whispers of Heavenly Death"   102
"A Noiseless Patient Spider"   102
"The Last Invocation"   102
"Passage to India"   103
"Prayer of Columbus"   110
"Song of the Universal"   111
"Patroling Barnegat"   113
"Good-bye My Fancy"   114
From the Preface to 1855 Edition
  of *Leaves of Grass*   114
From *Democratic Vistas*   119
From *Specimen Days and Collect*
  "My Passion for Ferries"   132
  "Broadway Sights"   132
  "Battle of Bull Run, July, 1861" 133
  "Abraham Lincoln"   135
  "Spiritual Characters Among the
    Soldiers"   136
  "Boys in the Army"   136
  "The Women of the West"   136
  "Loafing in the Woods"   137

PART II: THE NEW REGIONALISM

SIDNEY LANIER   141
  "Nine from Eight"   142
  "Life and Song"   143
  "A Ballad of Trees and the Master" 144
  "Corn"   144
  "The Symphony"   147
  "The Marshes of Glynn"   152

CONSTANCE FENIMORE
  WOOLSON   154
  "Rodman the Keeper"   155

THOMAS NELSON PAGE   171
  "The Burial of the Guns"   172

OLIVER WENDELL HOLMES   185
  "The Last Leaf"   187
  "My Aunt"   188
  "To An Insect"   188
  "The Deacon's Masterpiece: or, The
    Wonderful 'One-Hoss Shay' "   189
  "Non-Resistance"   190
  "The Two Streams"   191
  "The Voiceless"   191
  From Elsie Venner
  "The Brahmin Caste of New
    England"   191
  From The Poet at the Breakfast
    Table
  "The Scarabee"   194
  "Moral Teratology"   198
  "The Appeal of Darwinism"   202

SARAH ORNE JEWETT   204
  "The Hiltons' Holiday"   205

MARY WILKINS FREEMAN   214
  "The Revolt of Mother"   214

EMILY DICKINSON   224
  "The Snake"   225
  "Success"   225
  "The Bee"   225
  "New Feet Within My Garden Go"   225

"The Chariot"   226
"The Last Night That She Lived"   226
"Exclusion"   226
"I Died for Beauty"   226
"In a Library"   227
"To Fight Aloud Is Very Brave"   227
"Much Madness Is Divinest Sense"   227
"The Lonely House"   227
"The Mystery of Pain"   228
"I Taste a Liquor Never Brewed"   228
"I Had No Time to Hate"   228
"The Brain Within Its Groove"   228
"Suspense"   228
"If You Were Coming in the Fall"   228
"In Vain"   229
"Renunciation"   229
"The Wife"   230
"The Pedigree of Honey"   230
"A Service of Song"   230
"The Grass"   230
"Summer's Armies"   230
"Presentiment"   231
"The Butterfly's Assumption-Gown"   231
"The Wind"   231
"Indian Summer"   231
"There's A Certain Slant of Light"   232
"Setting Sail"   232
"Real"   232
"I've Seen A Dying Eye"   232
"I Never Saw a Moor"   232
"The Bustle in a House"   232
"Death Is a Dialogue"   232
"If I Shouldn't Be Alive"   233
"I Never Lost as Much But Twice"   233
"I Found the Phrase"   233
"I Had Been Hungry"   233
"We Never Know"   233
"And This of All My Hopes"   233

BRET HARTE   234
  "Tennessee's Partner"   235

CONTENTS

SAMUEL L. CLEMENS
(Mark Twain)   241
"The Indignity Put Upon the Remains
of George Holland by the Rev. Mr.
Sabine"   253
From *Roughing It:* Chapters II-IV,
Chapter VIII   256
"The Curious Republic of Gondour"   268
From *Old Times on the Mississippi*
"A Cub Pilot's Experience"   271
"A Daring Deed"   275

"Perplexing Lessons"   278
"Continued Perplexities"   282
From *Tom Sawyer Abroad*
"Speech on the Babies"   285
"On the Decay of the Art of
Lying"   287
From *Personal Recollections of Joan
of Arc:* Chapter III   290
"To the Person Sitting in Darkness"   294
"How to Tell a Story"   304
From *The Mysterious Stranger*   307
From *Autobiography*   311

PART III: CRITICAL REFLECTIONS OF A CHANGING AMERICA

WILLIAM DEAN HOWELLS   321
"A Romance of Real Life"   324
"Somebody's Mother"   331
From *Criticism and Fiction*
"Truth in Fiction"   335
From *My Literary Passions*
"Tourguenief"   338
"Tolstoy"   340
From *My Year in a Log Cabin*   342

HENRY GEORGE   345
From *Progress and Poverty*
"How Modern Civilization May
Decline"   346

HENRY ADAMS   354
From *The Education of Henry Adams*
"The Individual as Primitive
Energy"   355

HAMLIN GARLAND   359
"Under the Lion's Paw"   360

STEPHEN CRANE   368
"The Blue Hotel"   369

FRANK NORRIS   385
"Dying Fires"   386

FINLEY PETER DUNNE   393
"When the Trust Is at Work"   393
"The Union of Two Great Fortunes"   394

O. HENRY   396
"The Voice of the City"   397

JACK LONDON   400
"The Apostate"   401

PART IV: THE INTERNATIONAL THEME

WILLIAM VAUGHN MOODY   415
"An Ode in Time of Hesitation"   415
"Gloucester Moors"   419
"The Menagerie"   420
HENRY JAMES   422
"The Art of Fiction"   438

Daisy Miller   451
"The Lesson of the Master"   484
"Flickerbridge"   520
"The Beast in the Jungle"   532

BOOK IV: AMERICAN LITERATURE SINCE 1900

INTRODUCTION 561

PART I: PERSPECTIVES IN PHILOSOPHY AND CRITICISM

WILLIAM JAMES 585
From *Pragmatism*
  "What Pragmatism Means" 586

GEORGE SANTAYANA 596
Preface to *Realms of Being* 597

MORRIS R. COHEN 604
From *Reason and Nature*
  "In Dispraise of Life, Experience and Reality" 605

IRVING BABBITT 609
From *Democracy and Leadership*
  Introduction: "Democracy and Leadership" 610
H. L. MENCKEN 621
From *Prejudices III*
  "Footnote on Criticism" 622
EDMUND WILSON 630
  "The Historical Interpretation of Literature" 631
JOHN CROWE RANSOM 639
From *The World's Body*
  "Poets Without Laurels" 639

PART II: DIRECTIONS IN FICTION

THEODORE DREISER 651
  "Old Rogaum and His Theresa" 652
WILLA CATHER 663
  "Neighbour Rosicky" 663
JAMES BRANCH CABELL 681
From *The Line of Love*
  "The Wedding Jest" 682
SINCLAIR LEWIS 690
From *Babbitt*: Chapter I 691
SHERWOOD ANDERSON 697
  "Death in the Woods" 697
RING LARDNER 705
  "Ex Parte" 705
F. SCOTT FITZGERALD 711
  "Babylon Revisited" 711
JOHN DOS PASSOS 723
From *U.S.A.—The Big Money*
  "Tin Lizzie" 723
  "The Camera Eye (50)" 728
  "Newsreel LXVII" 729
  "Vag" 730

ERNEST HEMINGWAY 731
  "Big Two-Hearted River," Parts 1 and 2 732
  "A Day's Wait" 743
From *For Whom the Bell Tolls*:
  Chapter XXVII 744
WILLIAM FAULKNER 754
  "Spotted Horses" 754
  "A Rose for Emily" 765
JOHN STEINBECK 770
  "The Raid" 771
THOMAS WOLFE 777
  "The Lost Boy" 778
From *You Can't Go Home Again*
  Chapter XVIII, "The Locusts Have No King" 797
JAMES T. FARRELL 807
  "The Oratory Contest" 807
KATHERINE ANNE PORTER 813
  "The Jilting of Granny Weatherall" 813

PART III: DIRECTIONS IN POETRY

EDWIN ARLINGTON ROBINSON   823
"John Evereldown"   823
"Luke Havergal"   824
"Richard Cory"   824
"The House on the Hill"   825
"An Old Story"   825
"Sonnet"   825
"The Master"   825
"The Town Down the River"   826
"Exit"   828
"Uncle Ananias"   828
"Alma Mater"   828
"For a Dead Lady"   829
"Two Gardens in Linndale"   829
"Eros Turannos"   830
"Bewick Finzer"   831
"The Man Against the Sky"   831
"Mr. Flood's Party"   835
ROBERT FROST   836
"Into My Own"   837
"Mowing"   837
"Home Burial"   837
"The Code"   840
"An Old Man's Winter Night"   842
"Hyla Brook"   842
"The Cow in Apple Time"   842
"Out, Out—"   842
"Brown's Descent"   843
"Stopping by Woods on a Snowy Evening"   844
"To Earthward"   844
"Once by the Pacific"   845
"A Drumlin Woodcock"   845
"A Leaf Treader"   845
"Come In"   846

CARL SANDBURG   846
"A Fence"   847
"Chicago"   847
"The Poor"   848
"Cool Tombs"   848
"Prairie Waters by Night"   848
"Four Preludes on Playthings of the Wind"   849
From The People, Yes: Section 107   850
T. S. ELIOT   851
"The Love Song of J. Alfred Prufrock"   852
"Sweeney Among the Nightingales"   854
"The Hollow Men"   855
"Journey of the Magi"   856
"Animula"   857
From The Rock: Chorus 10   858
EDNA ST. VINCENT MILLAY   859
From Conversation at Midnight   859
WALLACE STEVENS   866
"Another Weeping Woman"   866
"The Worms at Heaven's Gate"   866
"A High-Toned Old Christian Woman"   866
"Anecdote of a Jar"   867
"Architecture"   867
"The Idea of Order at Key West"   868
"Soldier, There is a War"   868
HART CRANE   869
From the Bridge: "Cape Hatteras"   870
STEPHEN VINCENT BENÉT   874
From John Brown's Body: "Invocation"   875
"Ode to Walt Whitman"   878
"Nightmare, with Angels"   884

PART IV: WORLD WAR II AND AFTER

E. B. WHITE   889
From One Man's Meat
"Walden"   889
"Freedom"   893
"Civilian Defense"   896
KARL SHAPIRO   897
From V-Letter and Other Poems
"Troop Train"   897
"The Gun"   898

"Sunday: New Guinea"   899
From Essay on Rime
"The Confusion in Belief"   899
ROBERT PENN WARREN   905
"The Patented Gate and the Mean Hamburger"   905
RICHARD WRIGHT   913
From Black Boy   913
JOHN HERSEY   918
Hiroshima   919

BOOK III

American Literature 1860–1900

I

THE REAFFIRMATION OF DEMOCRACY

II

THE NEW REGIONALISM

III

CRITICAL REFLECTIONS OF A CHANGING AMERICA

IV

THE INTERNATIONAL THEME

BOOK III

American Literature 1860-1900

I

THE REAFFIRMATION OF DEMOCRACY

II

THE NEW REGIONALISM

III

CRITICAL REFLECTIONS OF A CHANGING AMERICA

IV

THE INTERNATIONAL THEME

AMERICAN LITERATURE 1860-1900

I

BARELY a month before Lee's surrender stopped the Civil War, Abraham Lincoln in his Second Inaugural Address besought all Americans, North and South alike, "to bind up the nation's wounds . . . to do all which may achieve and cherish a just and lasting peace among ourselves and with all nations." The national life had to be rebuilt, and with it the national literature.

American literature had suffered injury in many ways, not only during the war itself but also in the years preceding the war. The intolerant and intransigeant sectionalism which had torn the nation asunder had been in part aroused and intensified by the work of writers, both North and South; and that sectionalism had in turn increasingly affected the national literature as a whole. It was needful that intolerance and intransigeance be replaced by open-mindedness and good will, if a true national literature was to be achieved. This could not be accomplished in one generation or in two. But one way toward it lay in the effort of writers of the several regions of the country to record, express, and reveal the life of their own regions—to make it interesting to Americans of other regions, and so to make intersectional understanding and sympathy possible.

The examples of Harriet Beecher Stowe and John Greenleaf Whittier are suggestive. Mrs. Stowe's *Uncle Tom's Cabin* had been the most widely-read and influential individual work in the whole literary war against slavery, both in its serial publication in the abolition newspaper, the *National Era,* in 1851-2, and when it appeared in book form in 1852. She followed it with a *Key to Uncle Tom's Cabin* (1854), in which she attempted to present documentary evidence to refute the violent attacks on the novel by Southern writers, and by a further anti-slavery novel, *Dred, a Tale of the Great Dismal Swamp* (1856). But before the actual breaking of the storm she had done so much to rouse, Mrs. Stowe turned to writing about her own region, which she knew more thoroughly; she produced the quiet, pleasant and sound stories of New England, *The Minister's Wooing* (1859) and *The Pearl of Orr's Island* (1862).

For Whittier the war years were peculiarly painful. As a Friend, his distrust of violence was no less deep-seated than his detestation of slavery; and he could not escape the knowledge that his own fiery poems and his sustained and manifold activities in the abolition cause had had a part in bringing the bloodshed to pass. He turned to the field of regional expression and interpretation of his own New England, which had been his first love (in *Legends of New England,* 1831), and produced during the war years the finest of all pictures of rural New England life, *Snow-Bound* (1866).

II

But before American writers could begin to repair the wreckage they had helped to create, there was—as a century before—the preliminary task of providing the facilities for the building of a unified national literature.

Magazine publishing had entered upon a new era with the founding of *Harper's Monthly* in 1850, for the immense success of this magazine caused others to imitate its larger size, its copious illustration by woodcuts, and its varied and attractive content. The Harper success also caused other book publishers to enter the magazine field, so that for more than half a century there was close association between book and magazine publishing.

Harper's was at first filled with the English fiction on which its publishers founded their success as a book house, though the magazine printed some American short stories and serial histories. The *Atlantic Monthly,* however, was founded in 1857 as a purveyor of distinctively American (or at least New England) writing; and it was natural that when its first publishers got into financial difficulties in 1859, Ticknor & Fields should take it over. Thus this great house published Emerson, Lowell, Holmes, Whittier, Mrs. Stowe, and the other New Englanders both in their books and in the magazine. Putnam's, Appleton's, and Scribner's were other great publishing firms which gave their names and literary support to leading magazines of the period immediately following the Civil War.

Rapidly multiplying periodicals had a tremendous effect in popularizing literature in the 1870's. Twenty-five cent magazines brought the leading American and English writers into American homes as never before. Then in the mid-seventies certain Chicago and New York publishers began to sell books in paper bindings at ten, fifteen, and twenty cents. These were pirated English works, and the novels of Cooper and other books on which the copyrights had expired; as the early works of Emerson, Longfellow and other leading American writers emerged from copyright year after year, they were immediately seized upon as additions to the rapidly increasing numbers of "libraries" and "series" issued by the cheap publishers, whose tribe steadily increased. This episode in our publishing history, forerunner of the modern "pocket book" development, placed millions of cheaply printed, paper-covered volumes in middle-class homes. Some of these books were trash; but some, on the other hand, were classics. By the late eighties some of the cheap publishers were binding their issues in cloth, and hundreds of thousands of sets of Dickens, Cooper, Irving, Bulwer, and others were sold at incredibly low prices, as well as great numbers of single volumes of writers like Emerson, Longfellow, Macaulay, and the popular novelists. This cheap-publishing era lasted for two decades, ending with some bankruptcies in the hard times of 1893.

The International Copyright agreement of 1891 was a severe blow to the cheap libraries. No longer was it possible to republish British works without so much as a by-your-leave to their authors or original publishers. For half a century many American and English writers and some of the publishers had been arguing for International Copyright, against the contention that it would raise bars to free trade in culture. Now American writers could compete on even terms with their brothers from overseas; publishers had to add authors' royalties to the prices of both English and American works.

The last decade of the nineteenth century saw two fairly distinct developments in the American magazine field. *Harper's, Century,* and the new *Scribner's* were the leaders among the great fully-illustrated, general literary magazines. *Harper's* had admitted American serials in the eighties and was now as American as its rivals. The old *Scribner's Monthly* (1870-1881), *Harper's* great competitor in the seventies, had been sold in 1881 and its name changed to *Century Illustrated Monthly Magazine,* and Scribner & Company had promised to stay out of the magazine field for five years. Promptly in 1886, however, they launched *Scribner's Magazine,* beautifully illustrated and an active rival of the two magazines which during the eighties had set such a pace that there was world-wide recognition of the fact that the American illustrated general literary magazine was superior to anything of its kind ever before published. In the meantime, the *Atlantic* kept on its quiet and less prosperous way, without pictures but with careful editing and a conservative insistence on Literature.

To challenge these so-called "quality magazines" there arose in the mid-nineties a group of low-priced magazines selling at ten and fifteen cents, led by *McClure's* (1893-1929), *Munsey's* (1889-1929), and *Cosmopolitan* (1886-   ). These were copiously illustrated and were much closer to current problems and events than the old twenty-five cent magazines. They made an immediate and amazing success, attaining circulations and advertising patronage far beyond anything before known in the monthly magazine field. As the century drew to a close, these lively periodicals were publishing as much good belles-lettres as the older group and had far larger circulations. Also a new medium for mass distribution of literature had been found in the newspaper syndicates, developed in their early stages by S. S. McClure and Irving Bacheller, by which American and foreign novels, short stories, sketches, and poems were sold to many newspapers for republication. Thus within two decades after 1865 American publishers of magazines and books were affording ample facilities for renewed development of the national literature, and these facilities broadened to the end of the century.

III

But one important part of what the Civil War destroyed could never be restored. A very large part of the nation's youth, of the potential writers of a generation, died in battle or in camp, or underwent injuries to body or spirit which blocked creative achievement in later life.

Surprisingly few contributions to the national literature were made by veterans of the Civil War. One of the most substantial of these was the novel *Miss Ravenel's Conversion from Secession to Loyalty* (1867), by J. W. De Forest, of Connecticut, who had seen three years of active service. This novel was markedly in advance of the prevailing taste of its times in realistic treatment of character, and it was also noteworthy for its powerful narratives of battle experience and its presentation of political corruption in the Northern army.

Sidney Lanier was in a sense a delayed casualty of the War: lung infection acquired during his four years of service in the Confederate army caused his death at the age of thirty-nine. His immature novel, *Tiger Lilies,* published in 1867, contains some reflection of his war experience, but his later work was only indirectly affected by it. He became one of the foremost of those writers who, in the decades following the war, were mediators between North and South and labored at the long and difficult task of reconciliation through mutual knowledge and understanding. Lanier spent much of his later life in Baltimore, and contributed his best poems to magazines published in the North. Such poems as "The Marshes of Glynn" and "Corn" were effective contributions to interregional knowledge and understanding.

Other Southern writers who presented the life of their region to wide audiences in the North during this period were Joel Chandler Harris, whose dialect versions of Negro folklore gave new names and characters to the national mythology; Mary Noailles Murfree, who published in the *Atlantic Monthly* and elsewhere her sympathetic studies of Tennessee mountain people under the name Charles Egbert Craddock; and George Washington Cable, whose tales of Louisiana were very popular in the North. A little later Kate Chopin was to give much more honest and effective treatment to some of the material touched by Cable in her *Bayou Folk* (1894). The most discerning and penetrating of all portrayals of the direct effect of the war on the South, however, and the most satisfying artistically, was made by a Northern woman, Constance Fenimore Woolson, who lived for some years in Florida soon after the end of the war. Her stories collected in the volume *Rodman the Keeper* (1880) are marked by unusual comprehension of the inner effects of the conflict as well as its external cost.

It must be noted that not all regional writers of the decades after the war devoted themselves to the task of reconciliation. There were not wanting on either side voices raised in vindication or vituperation—especially in relation to the dark and troubled period of the reconstruction which followed the war itself. Thomas Nelson Page was one of the more competent of the militant spokesmen of the South, and Albion W. Tourgée was a Northern writer whose widely read work was drastically critical of the South's reaction to radical reconstruction policies. These and other writers both North and South contributed to the creation in this period of literary stereotypes which still persist in regional and national consciousness with vicious effects after half a century: varied stereotypes of the Negro and of Southern and Northern whites.

New England's creative energies in the decades following the war were in large part directed toward the task of regional and even of local record and interpretation. Of her great figures of the preceding generation, Thoreau and Hawthorne had died during the war years. Emerson soon fell silent. Longfellow dug into New England's past in his *New England Tragedies*. Whittier followed in the best of his later poems the line laid down in *Snow-Bound*. Oliver Wendell Holmes gave expression in his later *Breakfast-Table* volumes and in his novels to much of the best in the intellectual life of this period. Though he spoke of himself as the voice of Brahmin Boston, his interests were broad and he recognized with especial clearness the rising power of science. The older rural New England was portrayed in the later stories of Harriet Beecher Stowe, notably in *Oldtown Folks* (1869), and that of a slightly more recent period in the many stories contributed by Rose Terry Cooke to the *Atlantic Monthly* from its first volume on, and also to *The Galaxy* and other magazines. Post-Civil War New England was most discerningly and sympathetically portrayed by Sarah Orne Jewett in the fine stories of *Deephaven* (1877) and later volumes, and more critically by Mary E. Wilkins Freeman and others.

The new West of the Pacific coast gave to American literature one of its most popular literary figures of the years just after the Civil War in Bret Harte, nearly all of whose best work was confined to the small volume of his first short stories which made him famous, *The Luck of Roaring Camp* (1870). Harte followed his quickly dwindling popularity to the East and eventually to England; but other writers stayed on the Pacific coast to build a regional literature there, among them Helen Hunt Jackson, author of the popular romance of California Indian life, *Ramona* (1884), and Joaquin Miller, self-styled "poet of the Sierras."

The nearer West of the Mississippi Valley found searching interpretation in a series of novels by Edward Eggleston, beginning with *The Hoosier Schoolmaster* (1871). But Eggleston left the region of which he wrote in order to live near the literary associations and markets of New York and New England, as did the greater midwesterners who were his contemporaries, William Dean Howells and Mark Twain. Twain's greatest books are strongly regional, and regional elements entered into Howells' fiction. But in the work of these men we find the literary expression of America attaining a unified national quality and reflecting issues and problems no longer primarily or characteristically sectional in character.

IV

But all the constructive efforts of those regional writers who sought in the years after the Civil War to create national unity through mutual understanding were outweighed by the negative forces of the times. Their work remains a rich and valid portion of the literature of the period, but its contemporary significance was submerged in the effects of the swift and violent social and economic changes that in the succeeding decades affected the whole life of the politically reunited but still emotionally divided nation.

The vision of a nation reunited that Abraham Lincoln expressed in his Second Inaugural Address all but perished with him, leaving the country spiritually bankrupt. Herman Melville could match Lincoln's understanding, in the noble prose "Supplement" to his *Battle Pieces;* and Whitman's sympathy could embrace South as well as North. But these voices were little heeded, and there were none more resounding to sustain them: even Lowell's eloquent "Commemoration Ode" held little leaven of charity.

Perhaps it was inevitable that a moral collapse in the national life should follow the war and challenge the attention of the nation's writers. The decade after Appommatox saw the reconstruction that Lincoln had hoped for distorted into a ghastly farce, saw riotous speculation followed by crushing depression, saw high political office prostituted to venal ends more flagrantly than ever before in the nation's history. Henry Adams was one of the most discerning and critical observers of this spectacle, entrusting his direct comments to the pages of his journal for publication long after in *The Education of Henry Adams,* but expressing also his dislike of what he saw in his novel *Democracy* (1880). Mark Twain and Charles Dudley Warner made the dishonest politician the object of their most savage satire in *The Gilded Age* (1873).

There was, indeed, little peace and quiet of any kind in the years following the Civil War for the minds of Americans. If some of the questions of the years before 1861 had been answered, others had not; and a host of new problems rose swiftly.

The average thoughtful American of the 1870's and 1880's was likely to be genuinely troubled, for example, by a religious problem. Knowledge of the Darwinian theory and of related scientific conceptions was spreading swiftly in this country during these years. Thomas Huxley and Herbert Spencer were published in the United States and widely read. Controversy concerning the relations of "evolution and revelation" spread from the pulpit and the pages of religious periodicals to the general magazines, even the newspapers. Many writers participated in the debate or were influenced by it. Among the most substantial and penetrating comments were those of Oliver Wendell Holmes, who as physician and teacher of anatomy at Harvard was qualified to speak with authority on scientific matters. Holmes also interpreted in his novels the developing understanding of mental disease and aberration to which he contributed professionally as a scientific observer. The modern science of psychology was developing in this period, and the skill and power of William James as a writer gave lasting literary importance to his pioneer work in this field; while his brother, Henry James, applied psychological knowledge and methods, in his developing work as a writer of fiction, more significantly than any other writer of the time. Also the latter asserted the independence of the creative artist, and examined his purposes, his responsibilities, and his technical problems with forcefulness and insight which give his work continuing significance at the present time.

But while the progress of science was presenting new problems and new resources to the thinking of a minority of Americans in these years, the new practical applications of science were affecting drastically the external lives of almost the whole population. The rise of the modern steel industry and of the petroleum industry, the introduction of electric power and the development of its varied uses: these were only the most striking phases of a general transformation of American life by the machine—a transformation inevitably social as well as economic. Political concepts inherited from earlier democratic thought— to the effect that the best government is the least government—and the established American emphasis on individual rights made it possible in this period for alert and aggressive men to seize control of the new industrial processes and the newly important sources of wealth, to amass huge fortunes swiftly and to attain great political power. The "captain of industry" became a characteristic and in some degree a representative figure of the time. The example of great wealth quickly gained and of great power ruthlessly employed materially affected the thinking of many Americans.

The enormous industrial expansion of this period demanded vast supplies of manpower, in spite of the swiftly increasing mechanization of industrial processes. The demand was met by a marked renewal of immigration from Europe (which had slackened before 1860, and almost stopped during the war), and by a rapid wholesale shift of the native population from rural areas and agriculture to urban industry. The result was a tremendous growth in the size of the industrial cities. The population of Chicago, for a single example, rose from 28,000 in 1850 to over a million in 1890. In the same period the proportion of the total population which was employed in agriculture or lived in small rural communities declined from over seventy per cent to less than forty per cent.

Economic dislocations and maladjustments resulted from these fundamental changes and were brought sensationally to public attention in the railroad strike of 1877, the Haymarket "riot" in connection with the McCormick Harvester strike, and the Homestead steel strike.

It was inevitable that the social stresses created by the monstrous mushroom growth of industry in these years should find expression in the nation's literature. Many writers dealt directly with the times in expository and controversial books. One of the ablest and most lastingly influential of these writers was Henry George, whose demand in *Progress and Poverty* (1879) for tax reform included an eloquent analysis of the economic disorders of the nation. Another favored vehicle for criticism of the period came to be the utopian romance, in which the world as it was could be contrasted with the world as it might be. The most widely read of the books of this type was Edward Bellamy's *Looking Backward* (1888), which presented the future America as one of an elaborate state socialism.

More directly in the main current of our national literary development were the writers who undertook to apply the methods of critical realism, as these had been practiced by Russian and French masters, to the American scene. Foremost among these was William Dean Howells. Howells came very slowly to his full stature as a novelist, through a long period of preparation. Reading of Turgenev and Tolstoi, whose books he commended as a critic, helped Howells to formulate his own aims as a novelist. When finally in *Annie Kilburn* (1888), *A Hazard of New Fortunes* (1890), and other novels he dealt directly with contemporary social and economic problems, though his realism was always tempered and restrained by the literary conventions of his generation, he wrote with insight and with broad sympathy.

One of the many younger writers to whom as editor and critic Howells gave encouragement was Hamlin Garland. Born in the Middle West, Garland became the spokesman, in the short stories of *Main Travelled Roads* (1890) and in his other early stories and novels, of the midwestern farmer in his struggle with the economic inequities of the times. At the century's end the naturalism of Frank Norris, with *McTeague* (1899) and *The Octopus* (1901), succeeded the romanticism of Bret Harte.

As American industry became gigantic and monopolistic, as financial power accumulated in the hands of a few, what had been the adequate horizons of a continental nation seemed no longer ample, and the tone of empire began to enter into the communications of the Department of State. Few American writers were aware that a change in the nation's relation to the rest of the world was beginning; but some saw clearly that to be truly American our national literature could no longer be merely national. This was particularly true of the aging Whitman; in the poems of his last years, he placed increased emphasis on his deepening vision of the common interest of all mankind. The meaning of the brief, one-sided war with Spain was little recognized by American writers in general. But our tentative imperialism was nobly rebuked by William Vaughn Moody in his "An Ode in Time of Hesitation," when the question of annexation of the Philippines as the spoils of war hung in the balance, and scorchingly indicted by Mark Twain in "To the Person Sitting in Darkness" and other essays.

The clearest recognition of the growing necessity of mutual understanding between Americans and the people of other nations was that displayed by Henry James, who devoted his great powers from *The American* (1877) on, very largely, to "the international theme"—to the interpretation of the increasingly frequent and significant sustained encounters of Americans and Europeans, in endless variety and subtlety.

V

Yet as the century rolled to its end, none of these fields of immediate interest and meaning was producing the books which the largest numbers of Americans were reading. In the 1890's American fiction to a marked degree, and drama and poetry in less measure, were dominated—so far as popular favor was concerned—by historical materials, particularly those of melodramatic romance. General Lew Wallace, a veteran of the Civil War, published one of the earlier highly popular books of this type, *Ben-Hur: A Tale of the Christ,* in 1880. Francis Marion Crawford, an American who had expatriated himself to Italy, enjoyed in the 1880's and 1890's a steady popularity based largely on his many historical and cosmopolitan romances. In the last years of the century the favorites came thick and fast, with S. Weir Mitchell's *Hugh Wynne, Free Quaker* in 1896; James Lane Allen's *The Choir Invisible* in 1897; Charles Major's *When Knighthood Was in Flower* in 1898; Mary Johnston's *To Have and To Hold,* Paul Leicester Ford's *Janice Meredith,* and Winston Churchill's *Richard Carvel,* all in 1899; and many others. Many of these popular historical romances were sentimental offshoots of a backward-looking rather than a forward-looking sectionalism. A few may be regarded as expressions of an awakening national self-consciousness. All offered the reader an escape from the social and economic tensions of his time.

American readers showed also, in the last two decades of the century, a seemingly insatiable appetite for memoirs of the Civil War and biographies of leaders in the conflict. The successful publication of Grant's *Memoirs* (1885) by the subscription method stimulated the production of scores of similar works, and the *Century Magazine* for a time specialized in material of this kind.

Perhaps the popularity of the many volumes of memoirs of the Civil War and that of historical romance both encouraged the production of a few examples of historical writing of a very different type: that kind of realistic treatment of the Civil War itself which had been lacking for a generation. Stephen Crane's brilliant projection of the experience of a raw recruit in *The Red Badge of Courage* (1895) was free from false sentiment, marked instead by a precise psychological realism. The Civil War stories of Harold Frederic and of Ambrose Bierce (the latter a veteran of the Confederate army) displayed the same honesty of intention and accuracy of detail.

With these belated interpretations of war experience the decades dominated by the effects of the sectional conflict came to an end. American literature moved on into the new century as unified and national, though somewhat shakily and uncertainly patched together. The stresses of sectionalism had been obscured, where not resolved, by the comparably fierce tensions of economic injustice and class conflict. But our literature was richer for the achievement in this period of three writers of the highest rank: Whitman, who had maintained through the war years and thereafter the steady faith of his democratic vision; Mark Twain, who had matured swiftly from frontier funny man to national satirist and seer, making deathless images of his boyhood's Middle West along the way; and Henry James, absorbed in his patient and elaborate explorations of the social interaction of diverse worlds.

Economic, political, social, and intellectual backgrounds for American literature from 1860 to 1900 may most conveniently be reviewed in Charles and Mary Beard's *The Rise of American Civilization,* Vol. II (New York, 1930); and in Vols. VIII, IX, and X of *A History of American Life,* edited by A. M. Schlesinger and D. R. Fox: these are, respectively, Allan Nevins' *The Emergence of Modern America 1865-1878* (New York, 1927); Ida M. Tarbell's *The Nationalizing of Business 1878-1898* (New York, 1936); and A. M. Schlesinger's *The Rise of the City 1878-1898* (New York, 1933). E. P. Oberholtzer's *A History of the United States Since the Civil War,* in five volumes (New York, 1917-1937), is standard and comprehensive. Merle Curti's *The Growth of American Thought,* R. H. Gabriel's *The Course of American Democratic Thought,* H. W. Schneider's *A History of American Philosophy,* H. A. Myers' *Are Men Equal?*—all previously cited—carry forward the history of ideas to our own century; they should be supplemented by V. L. Parrington's *The Beginnings of Critical Realism* (New York, 1930), which is Vol. III in his *Main Currents in American Thought* and is completed to 1900, H. G. Townsend's *Philosophical Ideas in the United States* (New York, 1934), and Sidney Warren's *American Freethought, 1860-1914* (New York, 1943). Van Wyck Brooks' *New England: Indian Summer 1865-1915* (New York, 1940), and *The Times of Melville and Whitman* (New York, 1947), W. F. Taylor's *The Economic Novel in America* (Chapel Hill, 1942), Franklin Walker's *San Francisco's Literary Frontier* (New York, 1939), and Thomas Beer's *The Mauve Decade* (New York, 1926) are interesting studies of aspects of the literature. F. L. Pattee's *A History of American Literature Since 1870* (New York, 1915) and Granville Hicks' *The Great Tradition* (New York, 1933) are literary histories which still have some value. To comprehensive surveys of literary genres already mentioned, such as Smith's *Forces in American Criticism,* Quinn's *American Fiction,* and the works by Kreymborg and Allen on American poetry, should be added A. H. Quinn's *A History of the American Drama from the Civil War to the Present Day* (New York, 1927), Carl Van Doren's *The American Novel* (revised ed., New York, 1940), Alexander Cowie's *The Rise of the American Novel* (New York, 1948), and H. W. Wells' *The American Way of Poetry* (New York, 1943). Albert Parry's *Garrets and Pretenders: A History of Bohemianism in America* (Chicago, 1933), Floyd Stovall's *American Idealism* (Norman, Okla., 1943), Ferner Nuhn's *The Wind Blew from the East* (New York, 1942), Percy Boynton's *America in Contemporary Fiction* (Chicago, 1940), and Louis Filler's *Crusaders for American Liberalism* (New York, 1939) establish illuminating perspectives toward writers and tendencies before and after 1900. Ernest Leisy's *The American Historical Novel* has been announced for early publication. *American Local-Color Stories*, edited by H. R. Warfel and G. H. Orians (New York, 1941), is an exhaustive anthology, with an informative introduction. F. L. Mott's *A History of American Magazines*, Vols. II and III (New York, 1938), carry its survey to 1885, and his *American Journalism*, previously cited, covers the entire period. Oscar Cargill's *Intellectual America* (New York, 1941) and Alfred Kazin's *On Native Grounds* (New York, 1942), although primarily concerned with 20th Century American writing, contain retrospective discussions of literary tendencies, particularly of naturalism in fiction.

before and after 1900. Ernest Leisy's *The American Historical Novel* has been announced for early publication. *American Local-Color Stories*, edited by H. R. Warfel
and G. H. Orians (New York, 1941), is an exhaustive anthology, with an informative
introduction. F. L. Mott's *A History of American Magazines*, Vols. II and III (New
York, 1938), carry its survey to 1885, and his *American Journalism*, previously cited,
covers the entire period. Oscar Cargill's *Intellectual America* (New York, 1941) and
Alfred Kazin's *On Native Grounds* (New York, 1942), although primarily concerned
with 20th Century American writing, contain retrospective discussions of literary tendencies, particularly of naturalism in fiction.

American Literature 1860-1900

I

THE REAFFIRMATION OF DEMOCRACY

American Literature 1860-1900

I

THE REAFFIRMATION OF DEMOCRACY

1809 ∾ *Abraham Lincoln* ∾ 1865

THE events of Lincoln's public and private life are too well known to justify rehearsal. His development as a writer owed little to formal schooling, but much to the sympathetic interest of one schoolmaster—Mentor Graham, founder of a frontier academy in Lincoln's neighborhood—and to study of the Bible, Plutarch, and the writings of Jefferson. His characteristic style was already apparent in his early speeches as a member of the House of Representatives in 1847-1849, matured rapidly during the controversy over the extension of slavery and especially in the debates with Stephen A. Douglas in the contest for election to the United States Senate, 1858, and reached its highest development in the speeches of his first campaign for the Presidency in 1860, his two Inaugural Addresses, the Gettysburg Address, and the letters and messages of his last years.

[Important biographies are Carl Sandburg's *Abraham Lincoln; The Prairie Years*, 2 vols. (New York, 1926) and *Abraham Lincoln: The War Years*, 4 vols. (New York, 1939); Albert J. Beveridge's *Abraham Lincoln, 1809-1858*, 2 vols. (Boston, 1928); and Ida M. Tarbell's *The Life of Abraham Lincoln* (New York, 1900). *Mentor Graham, the Man Who Taught Lincoln* (Chicago, 1944), by Kunigunde Duncan and D. F. Nickols, gives important information on Lincoln's early education. T. H. Williams' introductory essay in his edition of *Selected Writings and Speeches of Abraham Lincoln* (Chicago, 1943) is recommended.]

AUTOBIOGRAPHY [1]
[1859]

I WAS BORN February 12, 1809, in Hardin County, Kentucky. My parents were both born in Virginia, of undistinguished families—second families, perhaps I should say. My mother, who died in my tenth year, was of a family of the name of Hanks, some of whom now reside in Adams, and others in Macon County, Illinois. My paternal grandfather, Abraham Lincoln, emigrated from Rockingham County, Virginia, to Kentucky about 1781 or 1782, where a year or two later he was killed by the Indians, not in battle,

but by stealth, when he was laboring to open a farm in the forest. His ancestors, who were Quakers, went to Virginia from Berks County, Pennsylvania. An effort to identify them with the New England family of the same name ended in nothing more definite than a similarity of Chris-

[1] This sketch was written by Lincoln late in 1859, at the request of persons who were seeking his nomination as the Republican candidate for the presidency. In the accompanying letter to J. W. Fell, Lincoln said of the sketch: "There is not much of it, for the reason, I suppose, that there is not much of me. If anything be made of it, I wish it to be modest, and not to go beyond the material."

tian names in both families, such as Enoch, Levi, Mordecai, Solomon, Abraham, and the like.[2]

My father, at the death of his father, was but six years of age, and he grew up literally without education. He removed from Kentucky to what is now Spencer County, Indiana, in my eighth year. We reached our new home about the time the state came into the Union. It was a wild region, with many bears and other wild animals still in the woods. There I grew up. There were some schools, so called, but no qualification was ever required of a teacher beyond "readin', writin', and cipherin'," to the rule of three.[3] If a straggler supposed to understand Latin happened to sojourn in the neighborhood, he was looked upon as a wizard. There was absolutely nothing to excite ambition for education. Of course, when I came of age I did not know much. Still, somehow, I could read, write, and cipher to the rule of three, but that was all. I have not been to school since. The little advance I now have upon this store of education, I have picked up from time to time under the pressure of necessity.

I was raised to farm work, which I continued till I was twenty-two. At twenty-one I came to Illinois, Macon County. Then I got to New Salem, at that time in Sangamon, now in Menard County, where I remained a year as a sort of clerk in a store. Then came the Black Hawk War; and I was elected a captain of volunteers, a success which gave me more pleasure than any I have had since. I went the campaign, was elated, ran for the legislature the same year (1832), and was beaten—the only time I ever have been beaten by the people. The next and three succeeding biennial elections I was elected to the legislature. I was not a candidate afterward. During this legislative period I had studied law, and removed to Springfield to practice it. In 1846 I was once elected to the lower House of Congress. Was not a candidate for re-election. From 1849 to 1854, both inclusive, practiced

law more assiduously than ever before. Always a Whig in politics; and generally on the Whig electoral tickets, making active canvasses. I was losing interest in politics when the repeal of the Missouri Compromise aroused me again. What I have done since that is pretty well known.

If any personal description of me is thought desirable, it may be said I am, in height, six feet four inches, nearly; lean in flesh, weighing on an average one hundred and eighty pounds; dark complexion, with coarse black hair and gray eyes. No other marks or brands recollected.

FAREWELL ADDRESS AT SPRINGFIELD, ILLINOIS [4]
[1861]

MY FRIENDS: No one, not in my situation, can appreciate my feeling of sadness at this parting. To this place, and the kindness of these people, I owe everything. Here I have lived a quarter of a century, and have passed from a young to an old man. Here my children have been born, and one is buried. I now leave, not knowing when or whether ever I may return, with a task before me greater than that which rested upon Washington. Without the assistance of that Divine Being who ever attended him, I cannot succeed. With that assistance, I cannot fail. Trusting in Him who can go with me, and remain with you, and be everywhere for good, let us confidently hope that all will yet be well. To His care commending you, as I hope in your prayers you will commend me, I bid you an affectionate farewell.

---

[2] Nathaniel Wright Stephenson says: "Subsequent research has established Lincoln's connection with the New England family."

[3] The rule for finding the fourth term of a proportion when three are given.

[4] An extemporaneous speech, February 11, 1861. Lincoln stood on the rear platform of his train in the rain and spoke to his friends as he was leaving for Washington and his inauguration.

THE GETTYSBURG ADDRESS [5]
[1863]

FOUR SCORE and seven years ago our fathers brought forth on this continent a new nation, conceived in liberty, and dedicated to the proposition that all men are created equal.

Now we are engaged in a great civil war, testing whether that nation, or any nation so conceived and so dedicated, can long endure. We are met on a great battlefield of that war. We have come to dedicate a portion of that field as a final resting-place for those who here gave their lives that that nation might live. It is altogether fitting and proper that we should do this.

But in a larger sense we cannot dedicate, we cannot consecrate, we cannot hallow this ground. The brave men, living and dead, who struggled here have consecrated it, far above our poor power to add or detract. The world will little note, nor long remember what we say here, but it can never forget what they did here. It is for us, the living, rather, to be dedicated here to the unfinished work which they who fought here have thus far so nobly advanced. It is rather for us to be here dedicated to the great task remaining before us,—that from these honored dead we take increased devotion to that cause for which they gave the last full measure of devotion; that we here highly resolve that these dead shall not have died in vain; that this nation, under God, shall have a new birth of freedom; and that government of the people, by the people, and for the people, shall not perish from the earth.

LETTER TO MRS. BIXBY [6]

Executive Mansion,
Washington, November 21, 1864

Mrs. Bixby, Boston, Massachusetts.

DEAR MADAM: I have been shown in the files of the War Department a statement of the Adjutant-General of Massa-

chusetts that you are the mother of five sons who have died gloriously on the field of battle. I feel how weak and fruitless must be any words of mine which should attempt to beguile you from the grief of a loss so overwhelming. But I cannot refrain from tendering to you the consolation that may be found in the thanks of the republic they died to save. I pray that our Heavenly Father may assuage the anguish of your bereavement, and leave you only the cherished memory of the loved and lost, and the solemn pride that must be yours to have laid so costly a sacrifice upon the altar of freedom.

Yours very sincerely and respectfully,
ABRAHAM LINCOLN.

SECOND INAUGURAL ADDRESS
[1865]

FELLOW-COUNTRYMEN: At this second appearing to take the oath of the presidential office, there is less occasion for an extended address than there was at the first. Then a statement, somewhat in detail, of a course to be pursued, seemed fitting and proper. Now, at the expiration of four years, during which public declarations have been constantly called forth on every point and phase of the great contest which still absorbs the attention and engrosses the energies of the nation, little that is new could be presented. The progress of our arms, upon which all else chiefly depends, is as well known to the public as to myself; and it is, I trust, reasonably satisfactory and encouraging

---

[5] At the dedication of the National Cemetery at Gettysburg, November 19, 1863, Lincoln's brief address followed a two-hour oration by Edward Everett, before an audience of 100,000 people. Lincoln wrote the concluding sentences in pencil after his arrival at Gettysburg.

[6] The original letter has not been found. All existing copies appear to be derived from a publication of the letter in a Boston newspaper.

to all. With high hope for the future, no prediction in regard to it is ventured.

On the occasion corresponding to this four years ago, all thoughts were anxiously directed to an impending civil war. All dreaded it—all sought to avert it. While the inaugural address was being delivered from this place, devoted altogether to saving the Union without war, insurgent agents were in the city seeking to destroy it without war—seeking to dissolve the Union, and divide effects, by negotiation. Both parties deprecated war; but one of them would make war rather than let the nation survive; and the other would accept war rather than let it perish. And the war came.

One-eighth of the whole population were colored slaves, not distributed generally over the Union, but localized in the Southern part of it. These slaves constituted a peculiar and powerful interest. All knew that this interest was, somehow, the cause of the war. To strengthen, perpetuate, and extend this interest was the object for which the insurgents would rend the Union, even by war; while the government claimed no right to do more than to restrict the territorial enlargement of it.

Neither party expected for the war the magnitude or the duration which it has already attained. Neither anticipated that the cause of the conflict might cease with, or even before, the conflict itself should cease. Each looked for an easier triumph, and a result less fundamental and astounding. Both read the same Bible, and pray to the same God; and each invokes his aid against the other. It may seem strange that any men should dare to ask a just God's assistance in wringing their bread from the sweat of other men's faces; but let us judge not, that we be not judged.[7]

The prayers of both could not be answered —that of neither has been answered fully. The Almighty has his own purposes. "Woe unto the world because of offences! for it must needs be that offences come; but woe to that man by whom the offence cometh." [8] If we shall suppose that American slavery is one of those offences which, in the providence of God, must needs come, but which, having continued through his appointed time, he now wills to remove, and that he gives to both North and South this terrible war, as the woe due to those by whom the offence came, shall we discern therein any departure from those divine attributes which the believers in a living God always ascribe to him? Fondly do we hope—fervently do we pray —that this mighty scourge of war may speedily pass away. Yet, if God wills that it continue until all the wealth piled by the bondmen's two hundred and fifty years of unrequited toil shall be sunk, and until every drop of blood drawn with the lash shall be paid by another drawn with the sword, as was said three thousand years ago, so still it must be said, "The judgments of the Lord are true and righteous altogether." [9]

With malice toward none; with charity for all; with firmness in the right, as God gives us to see the right, let us strive on to finish the work we are in; to bind up the nation's wounds; to care for him who shall have borne the battle, and for his widow, and his orphan—to do all which may achieve and cherish a just and lasting peace among ourselves, and with all nations.

---

[7] Matt. 7:1.
[8] Matt. 18:7.
[9] Ps. 19:9.

1819 ∽ *Walt Whitman* ∽ *1892*

I

CONSIDERED as a publication venture, Walt Whitman's *Leaves of Grass*, when issued in 1855, was about as flat a failure as a book could be. Probably seven or eight hundred copies were printed, though not all were bound up at once. The first bookseller who undertook to offer the book found lines in it which he considered to be morally objectionable before it had been on sale more than a day or two and told the author-publisher to get it out of the shop at once. Whitman managed to find another firm of publishers and booksellers (Fowler & Wells, specialists in phrenological literature) who were willing to try to sell his book; but they could not force an unwanted product on their trade, though they cut the price in half, and even bound some in paper covers to sell at seventy-five cents. The author eventually gave away a considerable part of the edition, and those that were left were "remaindered," doubtless for a few dollars.

A copy of this edition would sell for at least three thousand dollars today. Moreover, *Leaves of Grass* has become in these days not only a classic but a best seller. One excellent edition of recent years, distributed as a book club "dividend," has had a circulation of 200,000 copies, and eight or ten other editions in popular series continue to pile up large sales. The growth of this book in both critical and popular esteem is not accidental; the reasons for it are to be found, of course, in the book itself and in the character of Walt Whitman as a prophet of modern American democracy.

II

Whitman was born near Huntington, Long Island, in 1819, the second child of a father descended from a New England Puritan line and a mother of Dutch ancestry. Though Walt was born on a farm, his father soon moved to Brooklyn, where he made a living for his large family as a carpenter and builder. There was a strong element of Quakerism in the Whitman home, though the family were not members of "meeting." Mrs. Whitman's parents were Quakers, and Walt spent a good deal of time with them in his boyhood. The customs of Quakerism cling long after the stricter observances fall into disuse, and Walt's mother never dropped the use of the "plain language" and always addressed him with the Friendly "thee." Both the mother and father were partisans of the Hicksite schism, and Walt was once taken to hear that noble Quaker liberal Elias Hicks preach one of his last sermons.

Whitman was always happy to acknowledge this strong Quaker influence, as well as another formative element of his boyhood—his youthful wandering about the fields and shores of his beloved Long Island. "Paumanok" he called the island, after the Indian name. This habit of outdoor loitering and lounging, in which Whitman so markedly resembled Thoreau, became a lifelong characteristic. Both writers were actuated by the same motives—to discover more of themselves in nature. "I loaf and invite my soul," wrote Whitman.

Another boyhood habit lasted throughout his life—the habit of omnivorous and uncritical reading. Walt had little formal education; he had to quit school and go to work when he was ten. But he always managed to read widely—the current English novelists, Shakespeare, Walter Scott, the poets generally, history, philosophy, politics. He was not, of course, a thorough scholar; but he had a remarkable faculty for absorbing ideas and emotions.

Indeed, when we look at some of the leading influences of his youth, we note that he was not a thoroughgoing Quaker, he was not a real naturalist, he was not a scholar; but he was a great absorber of many things. He absorbed much of the spirit of Quakerism, as well as notions and feelings and ideas from many books. As to nature, there is a poem in his first volume which begins:

There was a child went forth every day,
    And the first object he look'd upon, that object he became,
    And that object became a part of him for the day or a certain part
        of the day,
    Or for many years or stretching cycles of years.

Many boys have found the type-case a great educator. So with Whitman, who at twelve (the same age at which Franklin began his apprenticeship) became a "printer's devil" in the shop of the *Long Island Patriot*. Here he absorbed a varied knowledge of the American scene from the stream of news and comment and feature copy that always flows steadily through a newspaper office. From this time forward for nearly thirty years, with one interim of three years' school-teaching and loafing on Paumanok, Whitman was a printer and newspaper editor.

At the age of twenty he set up a little paper of his own at Huntington, the town nearest his birthplace. These were the days when papers were started on shoestrings and discontinued on a little less; Whitman's paper did not last long, and it was after this failure that he made trial of teaching. Journalism is not easily relinquished, however, once it gets a hold on a young man; and by 1842 Walt was in New York working first on one paper and then another. That was the way printers and editorial workers did in those years: to stay in one "sit" very long was unusual, but to change often was to gain experience and to get ahead. In a couple of years Walt was a sub-editor on the New York *Democrat*, a minor political daily. In 1846 he was offered and accepted the editorship of Brooklyn's leading newspaper, the *Eagle*.

The two years which Whitman spent directing this paper and writing its editorials represent his most important contribution to daily journalism. Here he was in direct contact with all the great political and social questions of the country, as well as with local problems and controversies. For him it was a vantage point from which to see the people *en masse,* a great school of Americanism. A Democrat in politics, he was markedly Jeffersonian in his basic principles. He was for fewer laws and less control over such matters as personal habits. "You cannot legislate men into virtue!" he exclaimed. A states-rights man and an anti-abolitionist, he opposed the extension of slave territory and favored the Wilmot Proviso. An enthusiasm for national expansion characterized much of his editorial writing.

Whitman always had the urge to dramatize himself; and in this period he was very much the journalist, somewhat the dandy, quite the man-about-town. He had become very fond of the theater; especially did he frequent the Italian opera (though he thought it not "fitting" for the New World) and Shakespearian productions. A good newspaper reporter becomes acquainted with a very large number of persons, and Whitman found a deep satisfaction in wide acquaintance. Not only was he well acquainted with the "boys" of his own craft, but he came to know men of all occupations and all ranks. He took special delight in his friendship with the drivers of the Broadway "stages" or buses, and the conductors of the horse-drawn streetcars. "I have always had a passion for ferries," he wrote in later years.

Crowds of men and women attired in the usual costumes, how curious
    you are to me!
On the ferry-boats the hundreds and hundreds that cross, returning
    home, are more curious to me than you suppose.

In these years of his work on New York and Brooklyn papers, Whitman also began his long career as a free-lancer; that is to say, he began to write unsolicited pieces to submit to periodicals to be paid for at their "usual rates." This was done in addition to his salaried editorial work and was the effort of an ambitious young man to broaden his audience and increase his income. Several of these contributions were Dickensy short stories, and some were essays not unlike the editorials their author wrote for the *Eagle*. Among the periodicals to which he contributed were the *New World* and *Brother Jonathan*—two miscellanies which, in competition with each other, upset the book publishing business of the early forties by pirating the leading English novels of the time and issuing them in newspaper form as "extras" at 12½ cents. A few novels by American writers appeared in these series, one of which was written by Walter Whitman and entitled *Franklin Evans*. It was a temperance story, telling of a boy who came to New York from the country and fell victim to city vices; it had its good points, but was thin and imitative—and unsuccessful when published.

One evening early in 1848, Whitman attended a play at the Broadway Theater, and in the lobby between acts fell into conversation with a man who was about to start a new daily in New Orleans. The result was an invitation to Walt to join the staff of the New Orleans *Crescent*. Though his stay in the Louisiana city lasted less than six months, the broadening of his American horizon by travel was of great importance to him. Always an interesting and exotic American city, New Orleans just after the Mexican War, with its newly returned soldiers, its busy waterfront, its mixture of races, and its romantic historical backgrounds, made a deep and lasting impression upon Whitman.

After his return to Brooklyn, Whitman for a time edited the *Freeman*, an organ of the new Free-Soil party. But in the early fifties his mind cut its moorings to political partisanship and the more conventional journalism and swung out into deeper waters.

III

It is sometimes said that it was a profound mystical experience like that of Saul on the road to Damascus that made of the political editor and imitative free-lancer a poet of the first importance in our literature. That a change occurred in Whitman's aims—a growth in his idea of his mission and his position in America—there can be no doubt whatever; so much is obvious. But it was a change extending over several years, from about 1847 to 1855. Nor did the growth stop with the year of the first publication of *Leaves of Grass;* Whitman's genius was not static, but continuous in its growth up to the final years of decay.

In 1847 Whitman began a series of notebooks, four of which were filled before 1855. In the notations he set down there we find the emergent poet of "Song of Myself" crowded in with the editor; lines which later reappear in his poems with little change are written out there along with current speeches and editorial utterances. Many things were working within him—the whole complex of his observation of the American scene and his love for people of all kinds, together with ideas out of his reading and the long thoughts of his lounging and sauntering out-of-doors. He had been reading the work of some very stimulating thinkers—Goethe, Hegel, Rousseau, Coleridge, and others. Goethe's *Autobiography* may have influenced Whitman's own work, if a shrewd conjecture based chiefly on a review of the book in the *Eagle* is sound. Whitman reviewed many important books, adding them afterward to his personal library. He was an admirer of George Sand, of Frederika Bremer, and, of course, of Hugo and Dickens. He read Carlyle; and though repelled then and later by certain eccentricities of form and some of the ideas, he was probably influenced more than he ever admitted by the Sage of Chelsea.

But it was Emerson, with his American "applications" of the ideal philosophy, who did more than any other writer in these years to stimulate Whitman's genius. So the poet himself told John T. Trowbridge in 1860. "I was simmering, simmering, simmering," he said; "Emerson brought me to a boil." And in the letter to Emerson printed in the second edition of *Leaves of Grass*, Whitman addresses him as "dear Friend and Master."

Whitman himself set the type for the first edition of *Leaves of Grass*, which was produced with large pages in the shop of two printer-friends. Its failure to sell has already been noted. Its reception by critics was varied: it was praised by some and condemned by others; still others were merely flabbergasted. Many copies were sent to writers and public men. Whittier is said to have flung his into the fire. Alcott and Thoreau appreciated the new poet at something like his true value. Emerson sat down and wrote a letter of enthusiastic congratulation. "Dear Sir," wrote Emerson, "I am not blind to the worth of the wonderful gift of *Leaves of Grass*. I find it the most extraordinary piece of wit and wisdom that America has yet contributed. I am very happy in reading it, as great power makes us happy. . . . I greet you at the beginning of a great career, which yet must have had a long foreground somewhere, for such a start. . . ." Nothing more fortunate could have happened for the career of Walt Whitman than this letter.

For the thirty-seven years following 1855, Whitman's biography becomes basically the history of his great book, *Leaves of Grass*—its growth and change in successive editions as its author's personality grew and his attitudes changed, and the vicissitudes and trials of its publication. How and where its author lived, his circle of acquaintance, personal experiences that modified or motivated his work, his habits and appearance, the growth of his reputation—all these things are important only as they affect the growth of the book. In all literary history there has never been a more striking example of a life-time devotion to the twin objectives of authorship and publication of a book. It is highly significant that Whitman actually set the type for the first edition of the *Leaves:* to him it was all one process—making the poems, making the book, getting distribution, and getting reader reaction. And this process continued until the year and the day of his death.

The second edition was augmented by a score of additional poems, some of them among the best he ever wrote, such as "Crossing Brooklyn Ferry" and "Song of the Broad-Axe." The pages were small this time, but there were 384 of them. Emerson's letter and some reviews, favorable and unfavorable, were

printed in supplementary pages, and low on the backstrip of the binding
appeared a "plug" from Emerson's letter: "I greet you at the beginning of a
great career." Fowler & Wells fathered this edition; but they soon became
frightened at charges of immorality in the book and resigned the entire printing
to the author, who relieved them of responsibility by inserting a new titlepage
and pursuing alone his struggle for acceptance.

Whitman went back to newspaper work to earn his living, editing the
Brooklyn *Daily Times* for about two years and continuing his free-lancing.
But his interest was still centered in the *Leaves;* this was indeed one of his chief
creative periods, when he was in full health, fired with ideas, and bold in experiment. He had more literary friends in Boston, the home of Transcendentalism,
than in Brooklyn or New York; and it was there that he found a young
publishing firm that stereotyped an 1860 edition and sold two printings (about
four thousand copies) before it went into bankruptcy the next year. This third
edition was much increased in size. It included such new poems as "Out of
the Cradle Endlessly Rocking," but the most striking additions were the groups
with emphasis on sex—the "Children of Adam" and "Calamus" poems. Though
it ended in disaster, this Boston episode did much to found a Whitman public,
and it made the author something in royalties.

It also improved (or at least increased) his acquaintance with Emerson.
When Whitman visited Boston to see his publishers, he called on Emerson and
visited with him. One morning the two poets and thinkers walked the paths of
Boston Common for two hours discussing the wisdom and taste of the sexual
passages in the *Leaves,* but nothing the "master" could say persuaded Whitman
to delete a word; indeed this conversation served but to fix him more firmly
in his resolution to "sing the body electric."

IV

The Civil War had deep and lasting effects upon Whitman. Very early in
the war he began visiting the wounded who had been brought back from the
front to recover or die in New York hospitals. Late in 1862 the name of his
brother George, ten years younger than he, appeared in the casualty lists; and
he went down to the Virginia camps to find him. When he discovered that his
brother's injury was not serious, he stayed on to visit wounded Brooklyn boys
in the camp hospitals; and then he drifted back to Washington, where he was
detained to visit other wounded boys, with whom the hospitals of that city were
filled and overflowing. Before long he had made himself a job of importance
which was to last throughout the war. He later wrote that the work of the army
hospital visitor is an art "requiring both experience and natural gifts." Whitman
brought to the frightened, homesick, suffering boys in the crowded Washington
hospitals the steadiness, cheer, understanding, and love of which they had

such desperate need. He worked hard at his job, supporting himself by some writing for local papers, his hospital letters to the Brooklyn *Eagle* and the New York *Times* and *Tribune,* and other part-time labors. The strain of this way of life, and perhaps some blood-poison or malaria contracted in the hospitals, broke Walt's health, so that he had to give up and go home for recuperation in the middle of 1864. This was the beginning of a long series of illnesses leading to partial paralysis in 1873.

But by January, 1865, he was feeling well enough to return to Washington and take a job which his friends had found for him as a clerk in the Department of the Interior. Dismissed after a few months by Secretary Harlan, who disapproved of his poems and got rid of him at least partly for that reason, he was soon settled in another government clerkship, this time in the Attorney General's office. Here he remained for nearly eight years, finding much leisure for literary work, and gaining promotions in his modest clerkships.

In these years he issued two more editions of the *Leaves,* each augmented by new poems. The *Drum-Taps* group, now added to the general collection, had been published first in a pamphlet by themselves early in 1865, and then again later in the year with the addition of the Lincoln elegies. It is clear that a more mature Whitman is writing here, with less of the raucous hoot, less flamboyance—a poet chastened by the experiences of the war. When he came to arrange the *Leaves* as a great composite poem of democracy, Whitman placed *Drum-Taps* "at the hub of the wheel" because of their sharp, realistic depiction of the common people in action.

Whitman's attitude toward Lincoln had at first been the common one of New York and eastern newspaper men in general; he had his doubts about whether this new president, sectional in origins and elected by a minority of the popular vote, would prove to be the great leader the country needed. But having seen him occasionally in Washington and observed his behavior under the terrific burdens of state, Whitman came to respect and love him. It is this love that is spoken so truly in "When Lilacs Last in the Door Yard Bloom'd."

But the editions of the *Leaves* in 1867 and 1871, including the great Civil War poems, were, incredibly enough, publishing failures. Whitman lost money on both of them.

In the summer of 1873, Walt's beloved mother died at the home of his brother George in Camden, New Jersey. The poet was at her bedside. His mother had been the great comfort and dependence of his life; her Quaker steadiness and her unvarying faith in her boy had been of the first importance to him always, and he had reported the details of his life to her after he had reached manhood much as he had when a boy. After her death he decided to resign his clerkship and stay on in his brother's home; he had suffered a partial paralysis early in that same year, and he needed home life.

He became a familiar figure on the streets of Camden and Philadelphia—

his large frame, slightly crippled in movement; his full, flowing white beard; his high-crowned felt hat; his kindly manner as he went about, often with a basket of books on his arm—his own messenger boy as he made a modest delivery to a purchaser. Though he recanted nothing, firmly stood his ground on all that was significant in his early work, and refused to delete "objectionable" lines or poems, Whitman did enter upon a new phase at Camden. Already he had written, in a more humanistic vein, his "Passage to India;" and now progressively his emphasis shifted to such topics as love and death, and the more spiritual aspects of nature and humanity. There was no break with his past; there was only such a change of interests as came naturally with age and illness and a growing public recognition.

The sixth or "Centennial" edition of the *Leaves* was the most elaborate up to that time. Published in the centennial year of 1876, bound in half leather, it sold for five dollars; and an accompanying volume containing his prose works was priced at a similar figure. To the author-publisher's surprise, these books sold rather well.

As a matter of fact, a measure of public appreciation was slowly but surely centering on Whitman and his book. The advance guard of his admirers had begun to gather around him while he was still in Washington; now they multiplied as visitors at his Camden home and defenders and eulogists in the newspapers and magazines. They had to be enthusiasts in order to dent the solid front of respectability which had so generally opposed all that Whitman had stood for. "Whitmaniacs," the anti-Whitman forces called them; and men like Horace Traubel, William D. O'Connor, and even John Burroughs sometimes went to extremes in their laudation of this prophet of democracy. In England, too, Whitman by this time had many devoted followers. W. M. Rossetti, who had come into possession of one of the remaindered copies of the first edition of the *Leaves,* had worked hard to popularize the American poet across the sea—and with no little success.

Toward the end of the seventies Whitman began to do some traveling. He gave his lecture on Lincoln to audiences in various cities, with readings from his elegies. In 1879 he made an extensive tour of the West, visiting Denver and the Rocky Mountains and returning by way of St. Louis to visit there for several months with his brother Jeff. The next year he visited his friend and biographer, Dr. R. M. Bucke, in Canada. In 1881, he revisited the scenes of his childhood on Long Island, and later went to Boston to oversee the new edition of his poems by Osgood, and to greet Emerson for the last time.

But throughout this broadening of the activities of the crippled old poet, the chief object of his life was still the revision and augmentation of *Leaves of Grass* and its publication and distribution to readers. The J. R. Osgood & Company edition of 1881 had sold 1,600 copies at two dollars each, when the

Boston Watch and Ward Society, always vigilant to protect the sensitive conscience of that center of literature and morals, stepped in and threatened to take court action against the book. Osgood surrendered at once and turned over the plates to the author in lieu of royalties; and thus the second Boston edition of the *Leaves* was, like the first, abortive. Whitman thereupon resumed the publication risks of his book, and through Rees, Welsh & Company, of Philadelphia, issued other printings from the Osgood plates in 1882. This edition is said to have yielded the poet-publisher $1,300. A special autograph edition of three hundred, with additional poems, was published at five dollars in 1889.

Whitman was now living in a small house in Mickle Street, Camden, which he had purchased out of his slender savings. Here he was visited by a growing procession of admirers, until the place became a kind of shrine for pilgrims from all over the world. The failing health of the poet did not prevent his enjoyment of his friends; and if he sometimes talked too much, to the confusion of the memoirs which the faithful Traubel was preparing, he was, to the last, the interpreter and the prophet of love and death, of democracy and America.

On his deathbed, Whitman prepared the eleventh edition of the *Leaves*—the eighth to be published by himself. He died in his Mickle Street home on March 26, 1892, and was buried in the Harleigh Cemetery, Camden.

V

Too little thus far has been said of Whitman's prose work. The fiction of his early years is, to be sure, negligible; and his newspaper editorials and early magazine articles are significant chiefly as showing the development of his more important ideas. But the case of *Democratic Vistas*, published in 1871, is different. Two of the three essays which compose this small volume were originally published in that excellent, forgotten New York magazine, *The Galaxy*. Whitman, the government clerk, was fully conscious of the corruptions of the democratic state and the dangers of such a situation; but even though the masses might not be "essentially sensible and good," Whitman believed that "good or bad, rights or no rights, the democratic formula is the only safe and preservative one for coming times." In these essays he gives us, somewhat at random, his ideas of the democratic life—its politics, its literature, its philosophy. Another little prose book, *Specimen Days and Collect*, was issued in 1881. In it we have a kind of journal of Whitman's war experiences, a series of nature sketches, and some brief miscellanies.

But the prose inevitably seems to the reader of Whitman chiefly a commentary on *Leaves of Grass*. We center upon the *Leaves*: the poet's early life seems a preparation for them, and his later life was dedicated to their making and their publication.

How shall the reader approach these poems? Nearly everyone today has read at least a little of Whitman. But let us take the case of the reader who, though he may have read that little, has never plunged into the swirling waters of this verse, never breasted its challenging depth.

He will find Whitman easier than did the readers of the poet's own times. Free verse and free expression of ideas (especially about sex) were both shocking half a century ago, whereas they are now common enough. To both these freedoms Whitman's contribution has been immeasurably important. Whitman's varied and unconstrained rhythms, now in wide sweeping periods, now in staccato drumming, now in dashing phrases, though they need to be read aloud to be appreciated fully, have no difficulty for the average modern reader. The cataloguing which is so prominent—the poet's device to emphasize the immense variety and sum-total of modern man and his life—is scarcely a stumbling-block when once the reader knows what it means. The repetition and parallelism at the line-beginnings is a pleasant and helpful verse conformation. But the total effect is the thing, and this is obtained best by reading freely and aloud.

There has been much discussion of the influences which made Whitman's verse what it became. The Hebrew Scriptures, in the King James version, obviously had a part. Perhaps the tricks of Quaker preaching, with its emotional sing-song overtones, had some effect, though it is doubtful if Whitman ever heard much of this peculiar type of public address. His interest in Italian opera may have brought the recitative into the group of influences on his verse form, and it seems likely that the more rhetorical Shakespearian speeches had their effect. The Ossianic poems, which he pored over in his youth but later disapproved, seem a possible influence.

But it is not the verse-form so much as certain other peculiarities which trouble some of Whitman's readers. What about the use of the vertical pronoun, the omnipresent "I"? "I celebrate myself, and sing myself," begins the great poem set first in the *Leaves*—"Song of Myself." Are you revolted by the tremendous egotism of it all? But remember that in this poem Whitman is dramatizing himself as the completely developed American man. This concept ("I am an acme of things accomplished, and I am an encloser of things to be") runs through all the *Leaves;* it is the central idea, the key, not only to Whitman's poetry, but to much of his life. He dramatized himself as The American—The American of the past, the present, and the future; The American with a soul and with a body, complete, filled with "original energy"; The American of all sections and all classes.

I am of old and young, of the foolish as much as the wise,
    Regardless of others, ever regardful of others,

Maternal as well as paternal, a child as well as a man,
Stuff'd with the stuff that is coarse and stuff'd with the stuff that is fine,
One of the Nation of many nations, the smallest the same and the
    largest the same.

. . . .

I resist anything better than my own diversity,
Breathe the air but leave plenty after me,
And am not stuck up, and am in my place.

At the same time, we must not get the idea that it is not Walt Whitman
speaking. It is indeed "Walt Whitman, a kosmos, of Manhattan the son"; but
he is thinking of himself as no mere clerk or paralytic old man, but as a true
"kosmos" of humanity in all its variety and greatness. Sometimes his utterance
is confused; The American has difficulty in expressing clearly all that he is and
may be. Sometimes he uses slang or tags from foreign speech or queer, tortured
words; sometimes he drops into mere prose. But taken altogether, Walt Whitman, dramatized as the unit of our democracy, tells what he is and what he
feels with eloquence and moving power.

He is the poet of the body as well as of the soul, and it is his celebration
of bodily powers—and especially those of sex—that brought down upon him
the shocked condemnation of an age of evasive modesties. His great sin, in
the eyes of many, was in speaking freely of sex as a part of the life of the
perfectly developed man. The permissibility of free speaking in regard to such
things depends upon custom and taste; and though Whitman's fame was retarded by his boldness, he stuck to it. As he tells us happily in his "Backward
Glance," he "had his say."

Comradeship, or the love of man for man, was also an important part
of Whitman's philosophy of democracy. This is a very personal and intimate
love. It was in the love of men for each other—the attitude of the "friendly
and courageous young men" to whom the poet's heart always went out—that
this poet and thinker saw the salvation for the future of America.

After all, Whitman is for us today more than anything else the poet of
democracy. Many of us have learned more about what that word means by
reading the *Leaves of Grass* than through any other book. It is fundamental
in its democratic doctrine because it gets down to people. In this it is one of
the most modern of books. It is modern also in its internationalism, for Whitman
applied these basic ideas of his to the whole world. "Passage to India," one of
his greatest poems, brings us a vision of humanity united in the merging of
western materialism and eastern wisdom. Whitman is decidedly more a poet
of today and the future than of yesterday.

Thus we are now more than ever inclined to agree with him that his

"foothold is tenon'd and mortis'd in granite," and to be cheered by the final
lines of "Song of Myself":

> Failing to fetch me at first, keep encouraged;
> Missing me one place, search another;
> I stop somewhere waiting for you.

[The most important biographical and critical studies of Whitman are
H. S. Canby's *Walt Whitman, An American* (New York, 1943); Emory Holloway's *Whitman, An Interpretation in Narrative* (New York, 1926); Newton
Arvin's *Whitman* (New York, 1938), and Haniel Long's *Walt Whitman and
the Springs of Courage* (Sante Fé, New Mexico, 1938). Important foreign
studies are by the Danish scholar, Frederik Schyberg (Copenhagen, 1933),
and the French scholar, Jean Catel (Paris, 1929). Horace Traubel's *With Walt
Whitman in Camden,* in three volumes (New York, 1906-14), contains in great
detail the poet's conversations in his old age. Of the early studies of the poet
there are a few which can scarcely be neglected, such as R. M. Bucke's *Walt
Whitman* (Philadelphia, 1883); John Burroughs' *Whitman, A Study* (Boston,
1896), and J. A. Symonds' *Walt Whitman, A Study* (London, 1893). The most
valuable book on all aspects of Whitman scholarship and criticism is Gay
Wilson Allen's *Walt Whitman Handbook* (Chicago, 1946). Challenging shorter
studies are to be found in Floyd Stovall's *Whitman* (revised ed., New York,
1939) in American Writers Series; J. W. Beach's *The Concept of Nature in
Nineteenth-Century English Poetry* (New York, 1936); F. O. Matthiessen's
American Renaissance (New York, 1941); R. H. Gabriel's *The Course of American Democratic Thought* (New York, 1940). The most notable destructive
essays are in George Santayana's *Interpretations of Poetry and Religion* (New
York, 1900); Ernest Boyd's *Literary Blasphemies* (New York, 1927); D. H.
Lawrence's *Studies in Classic American Literature* (New York, 1923).]

SONG OF MYSELF [1]
[1855]

1

I celebrate myself, and sing myself,
And what I assume you shall assume,
For every atom belonging to me as good belongs to you.

I loafe and invite my soul,
I lean and loafe at my ease observing a spear of summer grass.   5

---

[1] This title was first used in the 1881 edition of *Leaves of Grass*. The poem originally had no special title (1855), but in the 1856 edition it was called "Poem of Walt
Whitman, an American," and in the third edition (1860) simply "Walt Whitman."

My tongue, every atom of my blood, form'd from this soil, this air,
Born here of parents born here from parents the same, and their parents the same,
I, now thirty-seven years old in perfect health begin,
Hoping to cease not till death.

Creeds and schools in abeyance, 10
Retiring back a while sufficed at what they are, but never forgotten,
I harbor for good or bad, I permit to speak at every hazard,
Nature without check with original energy.²

2

Houses and rooms are full of perfumes, the shelves are crowded with perfumes,
I breathe the fragrance myself and know it and like it, 15
The distillation would intoxicate me also, but I shall not let it.

The atmosphere is not a perfume, it has no taste of the distillation, it is odorless,
It is for my mouth forever, I am in love with it,
I will go to the bank by the wood and become undisguised and naked,
I am mad for it to be in contact with me. 20
The smoke of my own breath,
Echoes, ripples, buzz'd whispers, love-root, silk-thread, crotch and vine,
My respiration and inspiration, the beating of my heart, the passing of blood and
    air through my lungs,
The sniff of green leaves and dry leaves, and of the shore and dark-color'd sea-rocks,
    and of hay in the barn,
The sound of the belch'd words of my voice loos'd to the eddies of the wind, 25
A few light kisses, a few embraces, a reaching around of arms,
The play of shine and shade on the trees as the supple boughs wag,
The delight alone or in the rush of the streets, or along the fields and hill-sides,
The feeling of health, the full-noon trill, the song of me rising from bed and meeting
    the sun.

Have you reckon'd a thousand acres much? have you reckon'd the earth much? 30
Have you practis'd so long to learn to read?
Have you felt so proud to get at the meaning of poems?

Stop this day and night with me and you shall possess the origin of all poems,
You shall possess the good of the earth and sun, (there are millions of suns left,)
You shall no longer take things at second or third hand, nor look through the eyes
    of the dead, nor feed on the spectres in books, 35
You shall not look through my eyes either, nor take things from me,
You shall listen to all sides and filter them from your self.

---

² From the line beginning "My tongue" to the end of this section, the passage is an
addition dating from 1881. The variants in successive editions will not be pointed out
in the footnotes hereafter, but attention is called to the "Variorum Readings" compiled
by O. L. Triggs and easily accessible in Emory Holloway's Inclusive Edition of *Leaves
of Grass* (Garden City, N. Y., 1926), frequently reprinted.

3

I have heard what the talkers were talking, the talk of the beginning and the end,
But I do not talk of the beginning or the end.
There was never any more inception than there is now,　　　　　　40
Nor any more youth or age than there is now,
And will never be any more perfection than there is now,
Nor any more heaven or hell than there is now.

Urge and urge and urge,
Always the procreant urge of the world.　　　　　　45
Out of the dimness opposite equals advance, always substance and increase, always sex,
Always a knit of identity, always distinction, always a breed of life.

To elaborate is no avail, learn'd and unlearn'd feel that it is so.

Sure as the most certain sure, plumb in the uprights, well entretied,[3] braced in the
　　　beams,
Stout as a horse, affectionate, haughty, electrical,　　　　　　50
I and this mystery here we stand.

Clear and sweet is my soul, and clear and sweet is all that is not my soul.

Lack one lacks both, and the unseen is proved by the seen,
Till that becomes unseen and receives proof in its turn.

Showing the best and dividing it from the worst age vexes age,　　　　　　55
Knowing the perfect fitness and equanimity of things, while they discuss I am silent,
　　　and go bathe and admire myself.

Welcome is every organ and attribute of me, and of any man hearty and clean,
Not an inch nor a particle of an inch is vile, and none shall be less familiar than
　　　the rest.

I am satisfied—I see, dance, laugh, sing;
As the hugging and loving bed-fellow sleeps at my side through the night, and
　　　withdraws at the peep of the day with stealthy tread,　　　　　　60
Leaving me baskets cover'd with white towels swelling the house with their plenty,
Shall I postpone my acceptation and realization and scream at my eyes,
That they turn from gazing after and down the road,
And forthwith cipher and show me to a cent,
Exactly the value of one and exactly the value of two, and which is ahead?　　　　　　65

4

Trippers and askers surround me,
People I meet, the effect upon me of my early life or the ward and city I live in,
　　　or the nation,

---

[3] Tied together.

The latest dates, discoveries, inventions, societies, authors old and new,
My dinner, dress, associates, looks, compliments, dues,
The real or fancied indifference of some man or woman I love,   70
The sickness of one of my folks or of myself, or ill-doing or loss or lack of money, or depressions or exaltations,
Battles, the horrors of fratricidal war, the fever of doubtful news, the fitful events;
These come to me days and nights and go from me again,
But they are not the Me myself.

Apart from the pulling and hauling stands what I am,   75
Stands amused, complacent, compassionating, idle, unitary,
Looks down, is erect, or bends an arm on an impalpable certain rest,
Looking with side-curved head curious what will come next,
Both in and out of the game and watching and wondering at it.

Backward I see in my own days where I sweated through fog with linguists and
      contenders,   80
I have no mockings or arguments, I witness and wait.

5

I believe in you my soul, the other I am must not abase itself to you,
And you must not be abased to the other.

Loafe with me on the grass, loose the stop from your throat,
Not words, not music or rhyme I want, not custom or lecture, not even the best,   85
Only the lull I like, the hum of your valvéd voice.

I mind how once we lay such a transparent summer morning,
How you settled your head athwart my hips and gently turn'd over upon me,
And parted the shirt from my bosom-bone, and plunged your tongue to my bare-stript
      heart,
And reach'd till you felt my beard, and reach'd till you held my feet.   90

Swiftly arose and spread around me the peace and knowledge that pass all the
      argument of the earth,
And I know that the hand of God is the promise of my own,
And I know that the spirit of God is the brother of my own,
And that all the men ever born are also my brothers, and the women my sisters and
      lovers,
And that a kelson [4] of the creation is love,   95
And limitless are leaves stiff or drooping in the fields,
And brown ants in the little wells beneath them,
And mossy scabs of the worm fence, heap'd stones, elder, mullein and poke-weed.

6

A child said What is the grass? fetching it to me with full hands;
How could I answer the child? I do not know what it is any more than he.   100

---

[4] Variant of keelson, longitudinal part of a ship's structure which gives firmness and strength to the whole frame.

I guess it must be the flag of my disposition, out of hopeful green stuff **woven.**

Or I guess it is the handkerchief of the Lord,
A scented gift and remembrancer designedly dropt,
Bearing the owner's name someway in the corners, that we may see and remark,
    and say *Whose?*
Or I guess the grass is itself a child, the produced babe of the vegetation.   105

Or I guess it is a uniform hieroglyphic,
And it means, Sprouting alike in broad zones and narrow zones,
Growing among black folks as among white,
Kanuck, Tuckahoe, Congressman, Cuff,[5] I give them the same, I receive them the same.

And now it seems to me the beautiful uncut hair of graves.   110

Tenderly will I use you curling grass,
It may be you transpire from the breasts of young men,
It may be if I had known them I would have loved them,
It may be you are from old people, or from offspring taken soon out of their
    mothers' laps,
And here you are the mothers' laps.   115

This grass is very dark to be from the white heads of old mothers,
Darker than the colorless beards of old men,
Dark to come from under the faint red roofs of mouths.

O I perceive after all so many uttering tongues,
And I perceive they do not come from the roofs of mouths for nothing.   120

I wish I could translate the hints about the dead young men and women,
And the hints about old men and mothers, and the offspring taken soon out of their
    laps.

What do you think has become of the young and old men?
And what do you think has become of the women and children?

They are alive and well somewhere,   125
The smallest sprout shows there is really no death,
And if ever there was it led forward life, and does not wait at the end to arrest it,
And ceas'd the moment life appear'd.

All goes onward and outward, nothing collapses,
And to die is different from what any one supposed, and luckier.   130

7

Has any one supposed it lucky to be born?
I hasten to inform him or her it is just as lucky to die, and I know it.

---

   [5] Kanuck is slang for French Canadian, Tuckahoe for tidewater Virginian, and Cuff
for Negro.

I pass death with the dying and birth with the new-wash'd babe, and am not contain'd
    between my hat and boots,
And peruse manifold objects, no two alike and every one good,
The earth good and the stars good, and their adjuncts all good.   135

I am not an earth nor an adjunct of an earth,
I am the mate and companion of people, all just as immortal and fathomless as
    myself,
(They do not know how immortal, but I know.)

Every kind for itself and its own, for me mine male and female,
For me those that have been boys and that love women,   140
For me the man that is proud and feels how it stings to be slighted,
For me the sweet-heart and the old maid, for me mothers and the mothers of mothers,
For me lips that have smiled, eyes that have shed tears,
For me children and the begetters of children.

Undrape! you are not guilty to me, nor stale nor discarded,   145
I see through the broadcloth and gingham whether or no,
And am around, tenacious, acquisitive, tireless, and cannot be shaken away.

8

The little one sleeps in its cradle,
I lift the gauze and look a long time, and silently brush away flies with my hand.

The youngster and the red-faced girl turn aside up the bushy hill,   150
I peeringly view them from the top.

The suicide sprawls on the bloody floor of the bedroom,
I witness the corpse with its dabbled hair, I note where the pistol has fallen.

The blab of the pave, tires of carts, sluff of boot-soles, talk of the promenaders,
The heavy omnibus, the driver with his interrogating thumb, the clank of the shod
    horses on the granite floor,   155
The snow-sleighs, clinking, shouted jokes, pelts of snow-balls,
The hurrahs for popular favorites, the fury of rous'd mobs,
The flap of the curtain'd litter, a sick man inside borne to the hospital,
The meeting of enemies, the sudden oath, the blows and fall,
The excited crowd, the policeman with his star quickly working his passage to the
    centre of the crowd,   160
The impassive stones that receive and return so many echoes,
What groans of over-fed or half-starv'd who fall sunstruck or in fits,
What exclamations of women taken suddenly who hurry home and give birth to babes,
What living and buried speech is always vibrating here, what howls restrain'd by
    decorum,
Arrests of criminals, slights, adulterous offers made, acceptances, rejections with convex
    lips,   165
I mind them or the show or resonance of them—I come and I depart.

9

The big doors of the country barn stand open and ready,
The dried grass of the harvest-time loads the slow-drawn wagon,
The clear light plays on the brown gray and green intertinged,
The armfuls are pack'd to the sagging mow.   170

I am there, I help, I came stretch'd atop of the load,
I felt its soft jolts, one leg reclined on the other,
I jump from the cross-beams and seize the clover and timothy,
And roll head over heels and tangle my hair full of wisps.

10

Alone far in the wilds and mountains I hunt,   175
Wandering amazed at my own lightness and glee,
In the late afternoon choosing a safe spot to pass the night,
Kindling a fire and broiling the fresh-kill'd game,
Falling asleep on the gather'd leaves with my dog and gun by my side.

The Yankee clipper is under her sky-sails, she cuts the sparkle and scud,   180
My eyes settle the land, I bend at her prow or shout joyously from the deck.

The boatmen and clam-diggers arose early and stopt for me,
I tuck'd my trowser-ends in my boots and went and had a good time;
You should have been with us that day round the chowder-kettle.

I saw the marriage of the trapper in the open air in the far west, the bride was a red
        girl,   185
Her father and his friends sat near cross-legged and dumbly smoking, they had moc-
        casins to their feet and large thick blankets hanging from their shoulders,
On a bank lounged the trapper, he was drest mostly in skins, his luxuriant beard and
        curls protected his neck, he held his bride by the hand,
She had long eyelashes, her head was bare, her coarse straight locks descended upon
        her voluptuous limbs and reach'd to her feet.

The runaway slave came to my house and stopt outside,
I heard his motions crackling the twigs of the woodpile,   190
Through the swung half-door of the kitchen I saw him limpsy and weak,
And went where he sat on a log and led him in and assured him,
And brought water and fill'd a tub for his sweated body and bruis'd feet,
And gave him a room that enter'd from my own, and gave him some coarse clean
        clothes,
And remember perfectly well his revolving eyes and his awkwardness,   195
And remember putting plasters on the galls of his neck and ankles;
He staid with me a week before he was recuperated and pass'd north,
I had him sit next me at table, my fire-lock lean'd in the corner.

11

Twenty-eight young men bathe by the shore,
Twenty-eight young men and all so friendly;   200
Twenty-eight years of womanly life and all so lonesome.

She owns the fine house by the rise of the bank,
She hides handsome and richly drest aft the blinds of the window.

Which of the young men does she like the best?
Ah the homeliest of them is beautiful to her.   205

Where are you off to, lady? for I see you,
You splash in the water there, yet stay stock still in your room.

Dancing and laughing along the beach came the twenty-ninth bather,
The rest did not see her, but she saw them and loved them.

The beards of the young men glisten'd with wet, it ran from their long hair,   210
Little streams pass'd all over their bodies.

An unseen hand also pass'd over their bodies,
It descended tremblingly from their temples and ribs.

The young men float on their backs, their white bellies bulge to the sun, they do not
    ask who seizes fast to them,
They do not know who puffs and declines with pendant and bending arch,   215
They do not think whom they souse with spray.

12

The butcher-boy puts off his killing-clothes, or sharpens his knife at the stall in the
    market,
I loiter enjoying his repartee and his shuffle and break-down.

Blacksmiths with grimed and hairy chests environ the anvil,
Each has his main-sledge, they are all out, there is a great heat in the fire. 220

From the cinder-strew'd threshold I follow their movements,
The lithe sheer of their waists plays even with their massive arms,
Overhand the hammers swing, overhand so slow, overhand so sure,
They do not hasten, each man hits in his place.

13

The negro holds firmly the reins of his four horses, the block swags underneath on
    its tied-over chain,   225

The negro that drives the long dray of the stone-yard, steady and tall he stands pois'd
    on one leg on the string-piece,
His blue shirt exposes his ample neck and breast and loosens over his hip-band,
His glance is calm and commanding, he tosses the slouch of his hat away from his
    forehead,
The sun falls on his crispy hair and mustache, falls on the black of his polish'd and
    perfect limbs.

I behold the picturesque giant and love him, and I do not stop there,   230
I go with the team also.

In me the caresser of life wherever moving, backward as well as forward sluing,
To niches aside and junior bending, not a person or object missing,
Absorbing all to myself and for this song.

Oxen that rattle the yoke and chain or halt in the leafy shade, what is that you express
    in your eyes?   235
It seems to me more than all the print I have read in my life.

My tread scares the wood-drake and wood-duck on my distant and day-long ramble,
They rise together, they slowly circle around.

I believe in those wing'd purposes,
And acknowledge red, yellow, white, playing within me,   240
And consider green and violet and the tufted crown intentional,
And do not call the tortoise unworthy because she is not something else,
And the jay in the woods never studied the gamut, yet trills pretty well to me,
And the look of the bay mare shames silliness out of me.

14

The wild gander leads his flock through the cool night,   245
Ya-honk he says, and sounds it down to me like an invitation,
The pert may suppose it meaningless, but I listening close,
Find its purpose and place up there toward the wintry sky.

The sharp-hoof'd moose of the north, the cat on the house-sill, the chickadee, the
    prairie-dog,
The litter of the grunting sow as they tug at her teats,   250
The brood of the turkey-hen and she with her half-spread wings,
I see in them and myself the same old law.

The press of my foot to the earth springs a hundred affections,
They scorn the best I can do to relate them.

I am enamour'd of growing out-doors,   255
Of men that live among cattle or taste of the ocean or woods,
Of the builders and steerers of ships and the wielders of axes and mauls, and the
    drivers of horses,
I can eat and sleep with them week in and week out.

What is commonest, cheapest, nearest, easiest, is Me,
Me going in for my chances, spending for vast returns,   260
Adorning myself to bestow myself on the first that will take me,
Not asking the sky to come down to my good will,
Scattering it freely forever.

15

The pure contralto sings in the organ loft,
The carpenter dresses his plank, the tongue of his foreplane whistles its wild ascending
  lisp,   265
The married and unmarried children ride home to their Thanksgiving dinner,
The pilot seizes the king-pin, he heaves down with a strong arm,
The mate stands braced in the whale-boat, lance and harpoon are ready,
The duck-shooter walks by silent and cautious stretches,
The deacons are ordain'd with cross'd hands at the altar,   270
The spinning-girl retreats and advances to the hum of the big wheel,
The farmer stops by the bars as he walks on a First-day loafe and looks at the oats and
  rye,
The lunatic is carried at last to the asylum a confirm'd case,
(He will never sleep any more as he did in the cot in his mother's bed-room;)
The jour [6] printer with gray head and gaunt jaws works at his case,   275
He turns his quid of tobacco while his eyes blurr with the manuscript;
The malform'd limbs are tied to the surgeon's table,
What is removed drops horribly in a pail;
The quadroon girl is sold at the auction-stand, the drunkard nods by the bar-room stove,
The machinist rolls up his sleeves, the policeman travels his beat, the gate-keeper
  marks who pass,   280
The young fellow drives the express-wagon, (I love him, though I do not know him;)
The half-breed straps on his light boots to compete in the race,
The western turkey-shooting draws old and young, some lean on their rifles, some sit
  on logs,
Out from the crowd steps the marksman, takes his position, levels his piece;
The groups of newly-come immigrants cover the wharf or levee,   285
As the woolly-pates hoe in the sugar-field, the overseer views them from his saddle,
The bugle calls in the ball-room, the gentlemen run for their partners, the dancers
  bow to each other,
The youth lies awake in the cedar-roof'd garret and harks to the musical rain,
The Wolverine [7] sets traps on the creek that helps fill the Huron,
The squaw wrapt in her yellow-hemm'd cloth is offering moccasins and bead-bags for
  sale,   290
The connoisseur peers along the exhibition-gallery with half-shut eyes bent sideways,
As the deck-hands make fast the steamboat the plank is thrown for the shore-going
  passengers,
The young sister holds out the skein while the elder sister winds it off in a ball, and
  stops now and then for the knots,
The one-year wife is recovering and happy having a week ago borne her first child,

---

[6] Journeyman; one who has learned the trade.
[7] Nickname for a resident of Michigan.

The clean-hair'd Yankee girl works with her sewing-machine or in the factory or
    mill,   295
The paving-man leans on his two-handed rammer, the reporter's lead flies swiftly over
    the note-book, the sign-painter is lettering with blue and gold,
The canal boy trots on the tow-path, the book-keeper counts at his desk, the shoemaker
    waxes his thread,
The conductor beats time for the band and all the performers follow him,
The child is baptized, the convert is making his first professions,
The regatta is spread on the bay, the race is begun, (how the white sails sparkle!) 300
The drover watching his drove sings out to them that would stray,
The pedler sweats with his pack on his back, (the purchaser higgling about the odd
    cent;)
The bride unrumples her white dress, the minute-hand of the clock moves slowly,
The opium-eater reclines with rigid head and just-open'd lips,
The prostitute draggles her shawl, her bonnet bobs on her tipsy and pimpled neck, 305
The crowd laugh at her blackguard oaths, the men jeer and wink to each other,
(Miserable! I do not laugh at your oaths nor jeer you;)
The President holding a cabinet council is surrounded by the great Secretaries,
On the piazza walk three matrons stately and friendly with twined arms,
The crew of the fish-smack pack repeated layers of halibut in the hold,   310
The Missourian crosses the plains toting his wares and his cattle,
As the fare-collector goes through the train he gives notice by the jingling of loose
    change,
The floor-men are laying the floor, the tinners are tinning the roof, the masons are
    calling for mortar,
In single file each shouldering his hod pass onward the laborers;
Seasons pursuing each other the indescribable crowd is gather'd, it is the fourth of
    Seventh-month, (what salutes of cannon and small arms!)   315
Seasons pursuing each other the plougher ploughs, the mower mows, and the winter-
    grain falls in the ground;
Off on the lakes the pike-fisher watches and waits by the hole in the frozen surface,
The stumps stand thick round the clearing, the squatter strikes deep with his axe,
Flatboatmen make fast towards dusk near the cotton-wood or pecan-trees,
Coon-seekers go through the regions of the Red river or through those drain'd by the
    Tennessee, or through those of the Arkansas,   320
Torches shine in the dark that hangs on the Chattahooche or Altamahaw,
Patriarchs sit at supper with sons and grandsons and great-grandsons around them,
In walls of adobie, in canvas tents, rest hunters and trappers after their day's sport,
The city sleeps and the country sleeps,
The living sleep for their time, the dead sleep for their time,   325
The old husband sleeps by his wife and the young husband sleeps by his wife;
And these tend inward to me, and I tend outward to them,
And such as it is to be of these more or less I am,
And of these one and all I weave the song of myself.

16

I am of old and young, of the foolish as much as the wise,   330
Regardless of others, ever regardful of others,
Maternal as well as paternal, a child as well as a man,

Stuff'd with the stuff that is coarse and stuff'd with the stuff that is fine,
One of the Nation of many nations, the smallest the same and the largest the same,
A Southerner soon as a Northerner, a planter nonchalant and hospitable down by the
    Oconee I live,   335
A Yankee bound my own way ready for trade, my joints the limberest joints on
    earth and the sternest joints on earth,
A Kentuckian walking the vale of the Elkhorn in my deer-skin leggings, a Louisianian
    or Georgian,
A boatman over lakes or bays or along coasts, a Hoosier, Badger, Buckeye;
At home on Kanadian snow-shoes or up in the bush, or with fishermen off Newfound-
    land,
At home in the fleet of ice-boats, sailing with the rest and tacking,   340
At home on the hills of Vermont or in the woods of Maine, or the Texan ranch,
Comrade of Californians, comrade of free North-Westerners, (loving their big pro-
    portions,)
Comrade of raftsmen and coalmen, comrade of all who shake hands and welcome to
    drink and meat,
A learner with the simplest, a teacher of the thoughtfullest,
A novice beginning yet experient of myriads of seasons,   345
Of every hue and caste am I, of every rank and religion,
A farmer, mechanic, artist, gentleman, sailor, quaker,
Prisoner, fancy-man, rowdy, lawyer, physician, priest.

I resist any thing better than my own diversity,
Breathe the air but leave plenty after me,   350
And am not stuck up, and am in my place.

(The moth and the fish-eggs are in their place,
The bright suns I see and the dark suns I cannot see are in their place,
The palpable is in its place and the impalpable is in its place.)

17

These are really the thoughts of all men in all ages and lands, they are not original
    with me,   355
If they are not yours as much as mine they are nothing, or next to nothing,
If they are not the riddle and the untying of the riddle they are nothing,
If they are not just as close as they are distant they are nothing.

This is the grass that grows wherever the land is and the water is,
This is the common air that bathes the globe.   360

18

With music strong I come, with my cornets and my drums,
I play not marches for accepted victors only, I play marches for conquer'd and slain
    persons.

Have you heard that it was good to gain the day?
I also say it is good to fall, battles are lost in the same spirit in which they are won.

I beat and pound for the dead,   365
I blow through my embouchures [8] my loudest and gayest for them.

Vivas to those who have fail'd!
And to those whose war-vessels sank in the sea!
And to those themselves who sank in the sea!
And to all generals that lost engagements, and all overcome heroes!   370
And the numberless unknown heroes equal to the greatest heroes known!

19

This is the meal equally set, this the meat for natural hunger,
It is for the wicked just the same as the righteous, I make appointments with all,
I will not have a single person slighted or left away,
The kept-woman, sponger, thief, are hereby invited,   375
The heavy-lipp'd slave is invited, the venerealee is invited;
There shall be no difference between them and the rest.

This is the press of a bashful hand, this the float and odor of hair,
This the touch of my lips to yours, this the murmur of yearning,
This the far-off depth and height reflecting my own face,   380
This the thoughtful merge of myself, and the outlet again.

Do you guess I have some intricate purpose?
Well I have, for the Fourth-month showers have, and the mica on the side of a rock has.

Do you take it I would astonish?
Does the daylight astonish? does the early redstart twittering through the woods? 385
Do I astonish more than they?

This hour I tell things in confidence,
I might not tell everybody, but I will tell you.

20

Who goes there? hankering, gross, mystical, nude;
How is it I extract strength from the beef I eat?   390

What is a man anyhow? what am I? what are you?

All I mark as my own you shall offset it with your own,
Else it were time lost listening to me.

I do not snivel that snivel [9] the world over,
That months are vacuums and the ground but wallow and filth.   395

Whimpering and truckling fold with powders for invalids, conformity goes to the
          fourth-remov'd,
I wear my hat as I please indoors or out.

----

[8] Mouthpieces of musical instruments.
[9] This second "snivel" is a noun.

Why should I pray? why should I venerate and be ceremonious?

Having pried through the strata, analyzed to a hair, counsel'd with doctors and
    calculated close,
I find no sweeter fat than sticks to my own bones.   400

In all people I see myself, none more and not one a barley-corn less,
And the good or bad I say of myself I say of them.

I know I am solid and sound,
To me the converging objects of the universe perpetually flow,
All are written to me, and I must get what the writing means.   405

I know I am deathless,
I know this orbit of mine cannot be swept by a carpenter's compass,
I know I shall not pass like a child's carlacue cut with a burnt stick at night.

I know I am august,
I do not trouble my spirit to vindicate itself or be understood,   410
I see that the elementary laws never apologize,
(I reckon I behave no prouder than the level I plant my house by, after all.)

I exist as I am, that is enough,
If no other in the world be aware I sit content,
And if each and all be aware I sit content.   415

One world is aware and by far the largest to me, and that is myself,
And whether I come to my own to-day or in ten thousand or ten million years,
I can cheerfully take it now, or with equal cheerfulness I can wait.

My foothold is tenon'd and mortis'd in granite,
I laugh at what you call dissolution,   420
And I know the amplitude of time.

21

I am the poet of the Body and I am the poet of the Soul,
The pleasures of heaven are with me and the pains of hell are with me,
The first I graft and increase upon myself, the latter I translate into a new tongue.

I am the poet of the woman the same as the man,   425
And I say it is as great to be a woman as to be a man,
And I say there is nothing greater than the mother of men.

I chant the chant of dilation or pride,
We have had ducking and deprecating about enough,
I show that size is only development.   430

Have you outstript the rest? are you the President?
It is a trifle, they will more than arrive there every one, and still pass on.

I am he that walks with the tender and growing night,
I call to the earth and sea half-held by the night.

Press close bare-bosom'd night—press close magnetic nourishing night!　　435
Night of south winds—night of the large few stars!
Still nodding night—mad naked summer night.

Smile O voluptuous cool-breath'd earth!
Earth of the slumbering and liquid trees!
Earth of departed sunset—earth of the mountains misty-topt!　　440
Earth of the vitreous pour of the full moon just tinged with blue!
Earth of shine and dark mottling the tide of the river!
Earth of the limpid gray of clouds brighter and clearer for my sake!
Far-swooping elbow'd earth—rich apple-blossom'd earth!
Smile, for your lover comes.　　445

Prodigal, you have given me love—therefore I to you give love!
O unspeakable passionate love.

22

You sea! I resign myself to you also—I guess what you mean,
I behold from the beach your crooked inviting fingers,
I believe you refuse to go back without feeling of me,　　450
We must have a turn together, I undress, hurry me out of sight of the land,
Cushion me soft, rock me in billowy drowse,
Dash me with amorous wet, I can repay you.

Sea of stretch'd ground-swells,
Sea breathing broad and convulsive breaths,　　455
Sea of the brine of life and of unshovell'd yet always-ready graves,
Howler and scooper of storms, capricious and dainty sea,
I am integral with you, I too am of one phase and of all phases.

Partaker of influx and efflux I, extoller of hate and conciliation,
Extoller of amies and those that sleep in each others' arms.　　460

I am he attesting sympathy,
(Shall I make my list of things in the house and skip the house that supports them?)

I am not the poet of goodness only, I do not decline to be the poet of wickedness also.

What blurt is this about virtue and about vice?
Evil propels me and reform of evil propels me, I stand indifferent,　　465
My gait is no fault-finder's or rejecter's gait,
I moisten the roots of all that has grown.

Did you fear some scrofula out of the unflagging pregnancy?
Did you guess the celestial laws are yet to be work'd over and rectified?

I find one side a balance and the antipodal side a balance,   470
Soft doctrine as steady help as stable doctrine,
Thoughts and deeds of the present our rouse and early start.

This minute that comes to me over the past decillions,
There is no better than it and now.

What behaved well in the past or behaves well to-day is not such a wonder,   475
The wonder is always and always how there can be a mean man or an infidel.

23

Endless unfolding of words of ages!
And mine a word of the modern, the word En-Masse.[10]

A word of the faith that never balks,
Here or henceforward it is all the same to me, I accept Time absolutely.   480

It alone is without flaw, it alone rounds and completes all,
That mystic baffling wonder alone completes all.

I accept Reality and dare not question it,
Materialism first and last imbuing.

Hurrah for positive science! long live exact demonstration!   485
Fetch stonecrop mixt with cedar and branches of lilac,
This is the lexicographer, this the chemist, this made a grammar of the old cartouches,[11]
These mariners put the ship through dangerous unknown seas,
This is the geologist, this works with the scalpel, and this is a mathematician.

Gentlemen, to you the first honors always!   490
Your facts are useful, and yet they are not my dwelling,
I but enter by them to an area of my dwelling.

Less the reminders of properties told my words,
And more the reminders they of life untold, and of freedom and extrication,
And make short account of neuters and geldings, and favor men and women fully
    equipt,   495
And beat the gong of revolt, and stop with fugitives and them that plot and conspire.

24

Walt Whitman, a kosmos, of Manhattan the son,
Turbulent, fleshy, sensual, eating, drinking and breeding,
No sentimentalist, no stander above men and women or apart from them,
No more modest than immodest.   500

---

[10] The French "en masse," referring to persons in a body or crowd. The term is
used as democratic symbol.

[11] Figures inscribed on monuments to enclose the names of monarchs.

Unscrew the locks from the doors!
Unscrew the doors themselves from their jambs!

Whoever degrades another degrades me,
And whatever is done or said returns at last to me.

Through me the afflatus surging and surging, through me the current and index. 505

I speak the pass-word primeval, I give the sign of democracy,
By God! I will accept nothing which all cannot have their counterpart of on the
    same terms.

Through me many long dumb voices,
Voices of the interminable generations of prisoners and slaves,
Voices of the diseas'd and despairing and of thieves and dwarfs,   510
Voices of cycles of preparation and accretion,
And of the threads that connect the stars, and of wombs and of the father-stuff,
And of the rights of them the others are down upon,
Of the deform'd, trivial, flat, foolish, despised,
Fog in the air, beetles rolling balls of dung.   515

Through me forbidden voices,
Voices of sexes and lusts, voices veil'd and I remove the veil,
Voices indecent by me clarified and transfigur'd.

I do not press my fingers across my mouth,
I keep as delicate around the bowels as around the head and heart,   520
Copulation is no more rank to me than death is.

I believe in the flesh and the appetites,
Seeing, hearing, feeling, are miracles, and each part and tag of me is a miracle.

Divine am I inside and out, and I make holy whatever I touch or am touch'd from,
The scent of these arm-pits aroma finer than prayer,   525
This head more than churches, bibles, and all the creeds.

If I worship one thing more than another it shall be the spread of my own body, or
    any part of it,
Translucent mould of me it shall be you!
Shaded ledges and rests it shall be you!
Firm masculine colter it shall be you!   530
Whatever goes to the tilth of me it shall be you!
You my rich blood! your milky stream pale strippings of my life!
Breast that presses against other breasts it shall be you!
My brain it shall be your occult convolutions!
Root of wash'd sweet-flag! timorous pond-snipe! nest of guarded duplicate eggs! it
    shall be you!   535
Mix'd tussled hay of head, beard, brawn, it shall be you!
Trickling sap of maple, fibre of manly wheat, it shall be you!
Sun so generous it shall be you!

Vapors lighting and shading my face it shall be you!
You sweaty brooks and dews it shall be you!   540
Winds whose soft-tickling genitals rub against me it shall be you!
Broad muscular fields, branches of live oak, loving lounger in my winding paths, it
    shall be you!
Hands I have taken, face I have kiss'd, mortal I have ever touch'd, it shall be you.

I dote on myself, there is that lot of me and all so luscious,
Each moment and whatever happens thrills me with joy,   545
I cannot tell how my ankles bend, nor whence the cause of my faintest wish,
Nor the cause of the friendship I emit, nor the cause of the friendship I take again.

That I walk up my stoop, I pause to consider if it really be,
A morning-glory at my window satisfies me more than the metaphysics of books.

To behold the day-break!   550
The little light fades the immense and diaphanous shadows,
The air tastes good to my palate.

Hefts of the moving world at innocent gambols silently rising, freshly exuding,
Scooting obliquely high and low.

Something I cannot see puts upward libidinous prongs,   555
Seas of bright juice suffuse heaven.

The earth by the sky staid with, the daily close of their junction,
The heav'd challenge from the east that moment over my head,
The mocking taunt, See then whether you shall be master!

25

Dazzling and tremendous how quick the sun-rise would kill me,   560
If I could not now and always send sun-rise out of me.

We also ascend dazzling and tremendous as the sun,
We found our own O my soul in the calm and cool of the daybreak.

My voice goes after what my eyes cannot reach,
With the twirl of my tongue I encompass worlds and volumes of worlds.   565

Speech is the twin of my vision, it is unequal to measure itself,
It provokes me forever, it says sarcastically,
Walt, you contain enough, why don't you let it out then?

Come now I will not be tantalized, you conceive too much of articulation,
Do you not know O speech how the buds beneath you are folded?   570

Waiting in gloom, protected by frost,
The dirt receding before my prophetical screams,
I underlying causes to balance them at last,
My knowledge my live parts, it keeping tally with the meaning of all things,
Happiness, (which whoever hears me let him or her set out in search of this day.) 575

My final merit I refuse you, I refuse putting from me what I really am,
Encompass worlds, but never try to encompass me,
I crowd your sleekest and best by simply looking toward you.

Writing and talk do not prove me,
I carry the plenum of proof and everything else in my face,   580
With the hush of my lips I wholly confound the skeptic.

26

Now I will do nothing but listen,
To accrue what I hear into this song, to let sounds contribute toward it.

I hear bravuras of birds, bustle of growing wheat, gossip of flames, clack of sticks
          cooking my meals,
I hear the sound I love, the sound of the human voice,   585
I hear all sounds running together, combined, fused or following,
Sounds of the city and sounds out of the city, sounds of the day and night,
Talkative young ones to those that like them, the loud laugh of work-people at their
          meals,
The angry base of disjointed friendship, the faint tones of the sick,
The judge with hands tight to the desk, his pallid lips pronouncing a death-sentence, 590
The heave'e'yo of stevedores unlading ships by the wharves, the refrain of the anchor-
          lifters,
The ring of alarm-bells, the cry of fire, the whirr of swift-streaking engines and hose-
          carts with premonitory tinkles and color'd lights,
The steam-whistle, the solid roll of the train of approaching cars,
The slow march play'd at the head of the association marching two and two,
(They go to guard some corpse, the flag-tops are draped with black muslin.)   595

I hear the violoncello, ('tis the young man's heart's complaint,)
I hear the key'd cornet, it glides quickly in through my ears,
It shakes mad-sweet pangs through my belly and breast.

I hear the chorus, it is a grand opera,
Ah this indeed is music—this suits me.

A tenor large and fresh as the creation fills me,
The orbic flex of his mouth is pouring and filling me full.

I hear the train'd soprano (what work with hers is this?)
The orchestra whirls me wider than Uranus flies,
It wrenches such ardors from me I did not know I possess'd them,   605
It sails me, I dab with bare feet, they are lick'd by the indolent waves,
I am cut by bitter and angry hail, I lose my breath,
Steep'd amid honey'd morphine, my windpipe throttled in fakes of death,
At length let up again to feel the puzzle of puzzles,
And that we call Being.   610

27

To be in any form, what is that?
(Round and round we go, all of us, and ever come back thither,)
If nothing lay more develop'd the quahaug in its callous shell were enough.

Mine is no callous shell,
I have instant conductors all over me whether I pass or stop,   615
They seize every object and lead it harmlessly through me.

I merely stir, press, feel with my fingers, and am happy,
To touch my person to some one else's is about as much as I can stand.

28

Is this then a touch? quivering me to a new identity,
Flames and ether making a rush for my veins,   620
Treacherous tip of me reaching and crowding to help them,
My flesh and blood playing out lightning to strike what is hardly different from myself,
On all sides prurient provokers stiffening my limbs,
Straining the udder of my heart for its withheld drip,
Behaving licentious toward me, taking no denial,   625
Depriving me of my best as for a purpose,
Unbuttoning my clothes, holding me by the bare waist,
Deluding my confusion with the calm of the sunlight and pasture-fields,
Immodestly sliding the fellow-senses away,
They bribed to swap off with touch and go and graze at the edges of me,   630
No consideration, no regard for my draining strength or my anger,
Fetching the rest of the herd around to enjoy them a while,
Then all uniting to stand on a headland and worry me.

The sentries desert every other part of me,
They have left me helpless to a red marauder,   635
They all come to the headland to witness and assist against me.

I am given up by traitors,
I talk wildly, I have lost my wits, I and nobody else am the greatest traitor,
I went myself first to the headland, my own hands carried me there.

You villain touch! what are you doing? my breath is tight in its throat,   640
Unclench your floodgates, you are too much for me.

29

Blind loving wrestling touch, sheath'd hooded sharp-tooth'd touch!
Did it make you ache so, leaving me?

Parting track'd by arriving, perpetual payment of perpetual loan,
Rich showering rain, and recompense richer afterward.   645

Sprouts take and accumulate, stand by the curb prolific and vital,
Landscapes projected masculine, full-sized and golden.

30

All truths wait in all things,
They neither hasten their own delivery nor resist it,
They do not need the obstetric forceps of the surgeon,   **650**
The insignificant is as big to me as any,
(What is less or more than a touch?)

Logic and sermons never convince,
The damp of the night drives deeper into my soul.

(Only what proves itself to every man and woman is so,   **655**
Only what nobody denies is so.)

A minute and a drop of me settle my brain,
I believe the soggy clods shall become lovers and lamps,
And a compend of compends is the meat of a man or woman,
And a summit and flower there is the feeling they have for each other,   **660**
And they are to branch boundlessly out of that lesson until it becomes omnific,
And until one and all shall delight us, and we them.

31

I believe a leaf of grass is no less than the journey-work of the stars,
And the pismire is equally perfect, and a grain of sand, and the egg of the wren,
And the tree-toad is a chef-d'œuvre for the highest,   **665**
And the running blackberry would adorn the parlors of heaven,
And the narrowest hinge in my hand puts to scorn all machinery,
And the cow crunching with depress'd head surpasses any statue,
And a mouse is miracle enough to stagger sextillions of infidels.

I find I incorporate gneiss, coal, long-threaded moss, fruits, grains, esculent roots, 670
And am stucco'd with quadrupeds and birds all over,
And have distanced what is behind me for good reasons,[12]
But call any thing back again when I desire it.

In vain the speeding or shyness,
In vain the plutonic rocks [13] send their old heat against my approach,   **675**
In vain the mastodon retreats beneath its own powder'd bones,
In vain objects stand leagues off and assume manifold shapes,
In vain the ocean settling in hollows and the great monsters lying low,
In vain the buzzard houses herself with the sky,
In vain the snake slides through the creepers and logs,   **680**
In vain the elk takes to the inner passes of the woods,
In vain the razor-bill'd auk sails far north to Labrador,
I follow quickly, I ascend to the nest in the fissure of the cliff.

---

[12] Whitman believed in the theory of evolution, but his conviction that man was not limited by his origins but developed through environment tends to relate his thought to that of the earlier Lamarck (1744-1829) quite as much as to that of Darwin.

[13] Igneous rocks, which, according to the "Plutonic" theory, had been solidified by fire.

32

I think I could turn and live with animals, they're so placid and self-contain'd,
I stand and look at them long and long.   685

They do not sweat and whine about their condition,
They do not lie awake in the dark and weep for their sins,
They do not make me sick discussing their duty to God,
Not one is dissatisfied, not one is demented with the mania of owning things,
Not one kneels to another, nor to his kind that lived thousands of years ago,   690
Not one is respectable or unhappy over the whole earth.

So they show their relations to me and I accept them,
They bring me tokens of myself, they evince them plainly in their possession.

I wonder where they get those tokens,
Did I pass that way huge times ago and negligently drop them?   695
Myself moving forward then and now and forever,
Gathering and showing more always and with velocity,
Infinite and omnigenous, and the like of these among them,
Not too exclusive toward the reachers of my remembrancers,
Picking out here one that I love, and now go with him on brotherly terms.   700

A gigantic beauty of a stallion, fresh and responsive to my caresses,
Head high in the forehead, wide between the ears,
Limbs glossy and supple, tail dusting the ground,
Eyes full of sparkling wickedness, ears finely cut, flexibly moving.

His nostrils dilate as my heels embrace him,   705
His well-built limbs tremble with pleasure as we race around and return.

I but use you a minute, then I resign you, stallion,
Why do I need your paces when I myself out-gallop them?
Even as I stand or sit passing faster than you.

33

Space and Time! now I see it is true, what I guess'd at,   710
What I guess'd when I loaf'd on the grass,
What I guess'd while I lay alone in my bed,
And again as I walk'd the beach under the paling stars of the morning.

My ties and ballasts leave me, my elbows rest in sea-gaps,
I skirt sierras, my palms cover continents,   715
I am afoot with my vision.

By the city's quadrangular houses—in log huts, camping with lumbermen,
Along the ruts of the turnpike, along the dry gulch and rivulet bed,
Weeding my onion-patch or hoeing rows of carrots and parsnips, crossing savannas,
        trailing in forests,

Prospecting, gold-digging, girdling the trees of a new purchase,   720
Scorch'd ankle-deep by the hot sand, hauling my boat down the shallow river,
Where the panther walks to and fro on a limb overhead, where the buck turns furi-
    ously at the hunter,
Where the rattlesnake suns his flabby length on a rock, where the otter is feeding on
    fish,
Where the alligator in his tough pimples sleeps by the bayou,
Where the black bear is searching for roots or honey, where the beaver pats the mud
    with his paddle-shaped tail;   725
Over the growing sugar, over the yellow-flower'd cotton plant, over the rice in its low
    moist field,
Over the sharp-peak'd farm house, with its scallop'd scum and slender shoots from the
    gutters,
Over the western persimmon, over the long-leav'd corn, over the delicate blue-flower
    flax,
Over the white and brown buckwheat, a hummer and buzzer there with the rest,
Over the dusky green of the rye as it ripples and shades in the breeze;   730
Scaling mountains, pulling myself cautiously up, holding on by low scragged limbs,
Walking the path worn in the grass and beat through the leaves of the brush,
Where the quail is whistling betwixt the woods and the wheat-lot,
Where the bat flies in the Seventh-month eve, where the great gold-bug drops through
    the dark,
Where the brook puts out of the roots of the old tree and flows to the meadow,   735
Where cattle stand and shake away flies with the tremulous shuddering of their hides,
Where the cheese-cloth hangs in the kitchen, where andirons straddle the hearth-slab,
    where cobwebs fall in festoons from the rafters;
Where trip-hammers crash, where the press is whirling its cylinders,
Wherever the human heart beats with terrible throes under its ribs,
Where the pear-shaped balloon is floating aloft, (floating in it myself and looking
    composedly down,)   740
Where the life-car is drawn on the slip-noose, where the heat hatches pale-green eggs
    in the dented sand,
Where the she-whale swims with her calf and never forsakes it,
Where the steam-ship trails hind-ways its long pennant of smoke,
Where the fin of the shark cuts like a black chip out of the water,
Where the half-burn'd brig is riding on unknown currents,   745
Where shells grow to her slimy deck, where the dead are corrupting below;
Where the dense-starr'd flag is borne at the head of the regiments,
Approaching Manhattan up by the long-stretching island,
Under Niagara, the cataract falling like a veil over my countenance,
Upon a door-step, upon the horse-block of hard wood outside,   750
Upon the race-course, or enjoying picnics or jigs or a good game of base-ball,
At he-festivals, with blackguard gibes, ironical license, bull-dances, drinking, laughter,
At the cider-mill tasting the sweets of the brown mash, sucking the juice through a
    straw,
At apple-peelings wanting kisses for all the red fruit I find,
At musters, beach-parties, friendly bees, huskings, house-raisings;   755
Where the mocking-bird sounds his delicious gurgles, cackles, screams, weeps,
Where the hay-rick stands in the barn-yard, where the dry-stalks are scatter'd, where
    the brood-cow waits in the hovel,

Where the bull advances to do his masculine work, where the stud to the mare, where
    the cock is treading the hen,
Where the heifers browse, where geese nip their food with short jerks,
Where sun-down shadows lengthen over the limitless and lonesome prairie,   760
Where herds of buffalo make a crawling spread of the square miles far and near,
Where the humming-bird shimmers, where the neck of the long-lived swan is curving
    and winding,
Where the laughing-gull scoots by the shore, where she laughs her near-human laugh,
Where bee-hives range on a gray bench in the garden half hid by the high weeds,
Where band-neck'd partridges roost in a ring on the ground with their heads out,   765
Where burial coaches enter the arch'd gates of a cemetery,
Where winter wolves bark amid wastes of snow and icicled trees,
Where the yellow-crown'd heron comes to the edge of the marsh at night and feeds
    upon small crabs,
Where the splash of swimmers and divers cools the warm noon,
Where the katy-did works her chromatic reed on the walnut-tree over the well,   770
Through patches of citrons and cucumbers with silver-wired leaves,
Through the salt-lick or orange glade, or under conical firs,
Through the gymnasium, through the curtain'd saloon, through the office or public
    hall;
Pleas'd with the native and pleas'd with the foreign, pleas'd with the new and old,
Pleas'd with the homely woman as well as the handsome,   775
Pleas'd with the quakeress as she puts off her bonnet and talks melodiously,
Pleas'd with the tune of the choir of the whitewash'd church,
Pleas'd with the earnest words of the sweating Methodist preacher, impress'd seriously
    at the camp-meeting;
Looking in at the shop-windows of Broadway the whole forenoon, flatting the flesh of
    my nose on the thick plate-glass,
Wandering the same afternoon with my face turn'd up to the clouds, or down a lane
    or along the beach,   780
My right and left arms round the sides of two friends, and I in the middle;
Coming home with the silent and dark-cheek'd bush-boy, (behind me he rides at the
    drape of the day,)
Far from the settlements studying the print of animals' feet, or the moccasin print,
By the cot in the hospital reaching lemonade to a feverish patient,
Nigh the coffin'd corpse when all is still, examining with a candle;   785
Voyaging to every port to dicker and adventure,
Hurrying with the modern crowd as eager and fickle as any,
Hot toward one I hate, ready in my madness to knife him,
Solitary at midnight in my back yard, my thoughts gone from me a long while,
Walking the old hills of Judæa with the beautiful gentle God by my side,   790
Speeding through space, speeding through heaven and the stars,
Speeding amid the seven satellites and the broad ring, and the diameter of eighty
    thousand miles,
Speeding with tail'd meteors, throwing fire-balls like the rest,
Carrying the crescent child that carries its own full mother in its belly,
Storming, enjoying, planning, loving, cautioning,   795
Backing and filling, appearing and disappearing,
I tread day and night such roads.

I visit the orchards of spheres and look at the product,
And look at quintillions ripen'd and look at quintillions green.

I fly those flights of a fluid and swallowing soul,   800
My course runs below the soundings of plummets.

I help myself to material and immaterial,
No guard can shut me off, no law prevent me.

I anchor my ship for a little while only,
My messengers continually cruise away or bring their returns to me.   805

I go hunting polar furs and the seal, leaping chasms with a pike-pointed staff,
    clinging to topples of brittle and blue.

I ascend to the foretruck,
I take my place late at night in the crow's-nest,
We sail the arctic sea,[14] it is plenty light enough,
Through the clear atmosphere I stretch around on the wonderful beauty,   810
The enormous masses of ice pass me and I pass them, the scenery is plain in all
    directions,
The white-topt mountains show in the distance, I fling out my fancies toward them,
We are approaching some great battle-field in which we are soon to be engaged,
We pass the colossal outposts of the encampment, we pass with still feet and caution,
Or we are entering by the suburbs some vast and ruin'd city,   815
The blocks and fallen architecture more than all the living cities of the globe.

I am a free companion, I bivouac by invading watchfires,
I turn the bridegroom out of bed and stay with the bride myself,
I tighten her all night to my thighs and lips.

My voice is the wife's voice, the screech by the rail of the stairs,   820
They fetch my man's body up dripping and drown'd.

I understand the large hearts of heroes,
The courage of present times and all times,
How the skipper saw the crowded and rudderless wreck of the steam-ship, and Death
    chasing it up and down the storm,
How he knuckled tight and gave not back an inch, and was faithful of days and
    faithful of nights,   825
And chalk'd in large letters on a board, *Be of good cheer, we will not desert you;*
How he follow'd with them and tack'd with them three days and would not give it up,
How he saved the drifting company at last,
How the lank loose-gown'd women look'd when boated from the side of their prepared
    graves,
How the silent old-faced infants and the lifted sick, and the sharp-lipp'd unshaved
    men;   830
All this I swallow, it tastes good, I like it well, it becomes mine,
I am the man, I suffer'd, I was there.

---

[14] Polar expeditions in search of the lost Sir John Franklin in 1851-55 had interested
Americans in arctic voyaging.

The disdain and calmness of martyrs,
The mother of old, condemn'd for a witch, burnt with dry wood, her children gazing on,
The hounded slave that flags in the race, leans by the fence, blowing, cover'd with
    sweat, 835
The twinges that sting like needles his legs and neck, the murderous buckshot and the
    bullets,
All these I feel or am.

I am the hounded slave, I wince at the bite of the dogs,
Hell and despair are upon me, crack and again crack the marksmen,
I clutch the rails of the fence, my gore dribs, thinn'd with the ooze of my skin, 840
I fall on the weeds and stones,
The riders spur their unwilling horses, haul close,
Taunt my dizzy ears and beat me violently over the head with whip-stocks.

Agonies are one of my changes of garments,
I do not ask the wounded person how he feels, I myself become the wounded
    person, 845
My hurts turn livid upon me as I lean on a cane and observe.

I am the mash'd fireman with breast-bone broken,
Tumbling walls buried me in their debris,
Heat and smoke I inspired, I heard the yelling shouts of my comrades,
I heard the distant click of their picks and shovels, 850
They have clear'd the beams away, they tenderly lift me forth.

I lie in the night air in my red shirt, the pervading hush is for my sake,
Painless after all I lie exhausted but not so unhappy,
White and beautiful are the faces around me, the heads are bared of their fire-caps,
The kneeling crowd fades with the light of the torches. 855

Distant and dead resuscitate,
They show as the dial or move as the hands of me, I am the clock myself.

I am an old artillerist, I tell of my fort's bombardment,
I am there again.

Again the long roll of the drummers, 860
Again the attacking cannon, mortars,
Again to my listening ears the cannon responsive.
I take part, I see and hear the whole,
The cries, curses, roar, the plaudits for well-aim'd shots,
The ambulanza slowly passing trailing its red drip, 865
Workmen searching after damages, making indispensable repairs,
The fall of grenades through the rent roof, the fan-shaped explosion,
The whizz of limbs, heads, stone, wood, iron, high in the air.

Again gurgles the mouth of my dying general, he furiously waves with his hand,
He gasps through the clot *Mind not me—mind—the entrenchments.* 870

34

Now I tell what I knew in Texas in my early youth,
(I tell not the fall of Alamo,
Not one escaped to tell the fall of Alamo,
The hundred and fifty are dumb yet at Alamo,)
'Tis the tale of the murder in cold blood of four hundred and twelve young men.   875

Retreating they had form'd in a hollow square with their baggage for breastworks,
Nine hundred lives out of the surrounding enemy's, nine times their number, was the
    price they took in advance,
Their colonel was wounded and their ammunition gone,
They treated for an honorable capitulation, receiv'd writing and seal, gave up their
    arms and march'd back prisoners of war.

They were the glory of the race of rangers,   880
Matchless with horse, rifle, song, supper, courtship,
Large, turbulent, generous, handsome, proud, and affectionate,
Bearded, sunburnt, drest in the free costume of hunters,
Not a single one over thirty years of age.

The second First-day morning they were brought out in squads and massacred, it was
    beautiful early summer,   885
The work commenced about five o'clock and was over by eight.

None obey'd the command to kneel,
Some made a mad and helpless rush, some stood stark and straight,
A few fell at once, shot in the temple or heart, the living and dead lay together,
The maim'd and mangled dug in the dirt, the new-comers saw them there,   890
Some half-kill'd attempted to crawl away,
These were despatch'd with bayonets or batter'd with the blunts of muskets,
A youth not seventeen years old seiz'd his assassin till two more came to release him,
The three were all torn and cover'd with the boy's blood.

At eleven o'clock began the burning of the bodies;   895
That is the tale of the murder of the four hundred and twelve young men.[15]

35

Would you hear of an old-time sea-fight?[16]
Would you learn who won by the light of the moon and stars?
List to the yarn, as my grandmother's father[17] the sailor told it to me.

---

[15] The incident here related is the massacre of Fannin and his men at Goliad, Texas,
March 27, 1836, following the Battle of Coleto during the Texas Revolution. Whitman,
of course, "knew" these matters only at second-hand.

[16] This story was probably suggested by a letter from John Paul Jones to Benjamin
Franklin.

[17] Captain John Williams.

Our foe **was no** skulk in his ship I tell you, (said he,) 900
His was the surly English pluck, and there is no tougher or truer, and never was,
    and never will be;
Along the lower'd eve he came horribly raking us.

We closed with him, the yards entangled, the cannon touch'd,
My captain lash'd fast with his own hands.

We had receiv'd some eighteen pound shots under the water, 905
On our lower-gun-deck two large pieces had burst at the first fire, killing all around
    and blowing up overhead.

Fighting at sun-down, fighting at dark,
Ten o'clock at night, the full moon well up, our leaks on the gain, and five feet of
    water reported,
The master-at-arms loosing the prisoners confined in the afterhold to give them a
    chance for themselves.

The transit to and from the magazine is now stopt by the sentinels, 910
They see so many strange faces they do not know whom to trust.

Our frigate takes fire,
The other asks if we demand quarter?
If our colors are struck and the fighting done?

Now I laugh content, for I hear the voice of my little captain, 915
We have not struck, he composedly cries, *we have just begun our part of the fighting.*

Only three guns are in use,
One is directed by the captain himself against the enemy's main-mast,
Two well serv'd with grape and canister silence his musketry and clear his decks.

The tops alone second the fire of this little battery, especially the main-top, 920
They hold out bravely during the whole of the action.

Not a moment's cease,
The leaks gain fast on the pumps, the fire eats toward the powder-magazine.

One of the pumps has been shot away, it is generally thought we are sinking.

Serene stands the little captain, 925
He is not hurried, his voice is neither high nor low,
His eyes give more light to us than our battle-lanterns.

Toward twelve there in the beams of the moon they surrender to us.

36

Stretch'd and still lies the midnight,
Two great hulls motionless on the breast of the darkness, 930

Our vessel riddled and slowly sinking, preparations to pass to the one we have
    conquer'd,
The captain on the quarter-deck coldly giving his orders through a countenance white
    as a sheet,
Near by the corpse of the child that serv'd in the cabin,
The dead face of an old salt with long white hair and carefully curl'd whiskers,
The flames spite of all that can be done flickering aloft and below,   935
The husky voices of the two or three officers yet fit for duty,
Formless stacks of bodies and bodies by themselves, dabs of flesh upon the masts
    and spars,
Cut of cordage, dangle of rigging, slight shock of the soothe of waves,
Black and impassive guns, litter of powder-parcels, strong scent,
A few large stars overhead, silent and mournful shining,   940
Delicate sniffs of sea-breeze, smells of sedgy grass and fields by the shore, death-
    messages given in charge to survivors,
The hiss of the surgeon's knife, the gnawing teeth of his saw,
Wheeze, cluck, swash of falling blood, short wild scream, and long, dull, tapering groan,
These so, these irretrievable.

37

You laggards there on guard! look to your arms!   945
In at the conquer'd doors they crowd! I am possess'd!
Embody all presences outlaw'd or suffering,
See myself in prison shaped like another man,
And feel the dull unintermitted pain.

For me the keepers of convicts shoulder their carbines and keep watch,   950
It is I let out in the morning and barr'd at night.

Not a mutineer walks handcuff'd to jail but I am handcuff'd to him and walk by his
    side,
(I am less the jolly one there, and more the silent one with sweat on my twitching
    lips.)

Not a youngster is taken for larceny but I go up too, and am tried and sentenced.

Not a cholera patient lies at the last gasp but I also lie at the last gasp,   955
My face is ash-color'd, my sinews gnarl, away from me people retreat.

Askers embody themselves in me and I am embodied in them,
I project my hat, sit shame-faced, and beg.

38

Enough! enough! enough!
Somehow I have been stunn'd. Stand back!
Give me a little time beyond my cuff'd head, slumbers, dreams, gaping,   960
I discover myself on the verge of a usual mistake.

That I could forget the mockers and insults!
That I could forget the trickling tears and the blows of the bludgeons and hammers!
That I could look with a separate look on my own crucifixion and bloody crowning! 965

I remember now,
I resume the overstaid fraction,
The grave of rock multiplies what has been confided to it, or to any graves,
Corpses rise, gashes heal, fastenings roll from me.

I troop forth replenish'd with supreme power, one of an average unending proces-
        sion,   970
Inland and sea-coast we go, and pass all boundary lines,
Our swift ordinances on their way over the whole earth,
The blossoms we wear in our hats the growth of thousands of years.

Eleves, [18] I salute you! come forward!
Continue your annotations, continue your questionings.   975

39

The friendly and flowing savage, who is he?
Is he waiting for civilization, or past it and mastering it?

Is he some Southwesterner rais'd out-doors? is he Kanadian?
Is he from the Mississippi country? Iowa, Oregon, California?
The mountains? prairie-life, bush-life? or sailor from the sea?   980

Wherever he goes men and women accept and desire him,
They desire he should like them, touch them, speak to them, stay with them.

Behavior lawless as snow-flakes, words simple as grass, uncomb'd head, laughter, and
        naiveté,
Slow-stepping feet, common features, common modes and emanations,
They descend in new forms from the tips of his fingers,   985
They are wafted with the odor of his body or breath, they fly out of the glance of
        his eyes.

40

Flaunt of the sunshine I need not your bask—lie over!
You light surfaces only, I force surfaces and depths also.

Earth! you seem to look for something at my hands,
Say, old top-knot, what do you want?   990

Man or woman, I might tell how I like you, but cannot,
And might tell what it is in me and what it is in you, but cannot,
And might tell that pining I have, that pulse of my nights and days.

[18] Erench élèves, obsolete as English, meaning pupils.

Behold, I do not give lectures or a little charity,
When I give I give myself.   995

You there, impotent, loose in the knees,
Open your scarf'd chops till I blow grit within you,
Spread your palms and lift the flaps of your pockets,
I am not to be denied, I compel, I have stores plenty and to spare,
And any thing I have I bestow.   1000

I do not ask who you are, that is not important to me,
You can do nothing and be nothing but what I will infold you.

To cotton-field drudge or cleaner of privies I lean,
On his right cheek I put the family kiss,
And in my soul I swear I never will deny him.   1005

On women fit for conception I start bigger and nimbler babes,
(This day I am jetting the stuff of far more arrogant republics.)

To any one dying, thither I speed and twist the knob of the door,
Turn the bed-clothes toward the foot of the bed,
Let the physician and the priest go home.   1010

I seize the descending man and raise him with resistless will,
O despairer, here is my neck,
By God, you shall not go down! hang your whole weight upon me.

I dilate you with tremendous breath, I buoy you up,
Every room of the house do I fill with an arm'd force,   1015
Lovers of me, bafflers of graves.

Sleep—I and they keep guard all night,
Not doubt, not disease shall dare to lay finger upon you,
I have embraced you, and henceforth possess you to myself,
And when you rise in the morning you will find what I tell you is so.   1020

41

I am he bringing help for the sick as they pant on their backs,
And for strong upright men I bring yet more needed help.

I heard what was said of the universe,
Heard it and heard it of several thousand years;
It is middling well as far as it goes—but is that all?   1025

Magnifying and applying come I,
Outbidding at the start the old cautious hucksters,
Taking myself the exact dimensions of Jehovah,
Lithographing Kronos, Zeus his son, and Hercules his grandson,

Buying drafts of Osiris, Isis, Belus, Brahma, Buddha,   1030
In my portfolio placing Manito loose, Allah on a leaf, the crucifix engraved,
With Odin and the hideous-faced Mexitli and every idol and image,[19]
Taking them all for what they are worth and not a cent more,
Admitting they were alive and did the work of their days,
(They bore mites as for unfledge'd birds who have now to rise and fly and sing for
      themselves,)   1035
Accepting the rough deific sketches to fill out better in myself, bestowing them freely
      on each man and woman I see,
Discovering as much or more in a framer framing a house,
Putting higher claims for him there with his roll'd-up sleeves driving the mallet and
      chisel,
Not objecting to special revelations, considering a curl of smoke or a hair on the
      back of my hand just as curious as any revelation,
Lads ahold of fire-engines and hook-and-ladder ropes no less to me than the gods of
      the antique wars,   1040
Minding their voices peal through the crash of destruction,
Their brawny limbs passing safe over charr'd laths, their white foreheads whole and
      unhurt out of the flames;
By the mechanic's wife with her babe at her nipple interceding for every person born,
Three scythes at harvest whizzing in a row from three lusty angels with shirts bagg'd
      out at their waists,
The snag-tooth'd hostler with red hair redeeming sins past and to come,   1045
Selling all he possesses, traveling on foot to fee lawyers for his brother and sit by
      him while he is tried for forgery;
What was strewn in the amplest strewing the square rod about me, and not filling
      the square rod then,
The bull and the bug never worshipp'd half enough,
Dung and dirt more admirable than was dream'd,
The supernatural of no account, myself waiting my time to be one of the supremes, 1050
The day getting ready for me when I shall do as much good as the best, and be as
      prodigious;
By my life-lumps! becoming already a creator,
Putting myself here and now to the ambush'd womb of the shadows.

42

A call in the midst of the crowd,
My own voice, orotund sweeping and final.   1055

Come my children,
Come my boys and girls, my women, household and intimates,
Now the performer launches his nerve, he has pass'd his prelude on the reeds within.

Easily written loose-finger'd chords—I feel the thrum of your climax and close.

---

[19] A gallery of the gods: Jewish (Jehovah), Greek (Kronos, Zeus, Hercules),
Egyptian (Osiris, Isis), Assyrian (Belus), Hindu (Brahma, Buddha), Indian (Manito),
Mohammedan (Allah), Norse (Odin), Aztec (Mexitli).

My head slues round on my neck,   1060
Music rolls, but not from the organ,
Folks are around me, but they are no household of mine.

Ever the hard unsunk ground,
Ever the eaters and drinkers, ever the upward and downward sun, ever the air and
    the ceaseless tides,
Ever myself and my neighbors, refreshing, wicked, real,   1065
Ever the old inexplicable query, ever that thorn'd thumb, that breath of itches and
    thirsts,
Ever the vexer's *hoot! hoot!* till we find where the sly one hides and bring him forth,
Ever love, ever the sobbing liquid of life,
Ever the bandage under the chin, ever the trestles of death.

Here and there with dimes on the eyes walking,   1070
To feed the greed of the belly the brains liberally spooning,
Tickets buying, taking, selling, but in to the feast never once going,
Many sweating, ploughing, thrashing, and then the chaff for payment receiving,
A few idly owning, and they the wheat continually claiming.

This is the city and I am one of the citizens,   1075
Whatever interests the rest interests me, politics, wars, markets, newspapers, schools,
The mayor and councils, banks, tariffs, steamships, factories, stocks, stores, real estate
    and personal estate.

The little plentiful manikins skipping around in collars and tail'd coats,
I am aware who they are, (they are positively not worms or fleas,)
I acknowledge the duplicates of myself, the weakest and shallowest is deathless with
    me,   1080
What I do and say the same waits for them,
Every thought that flounders in me the same flounders in them.

I know perfectly well my own egotism,
Know my omnivorous lines and must not write any less,
And would fetch you whoever you are flush with myself.   1085

Not words of routine this song of mine,
But abruptly to question, to leap beyond yet nearer bring;
This printed and bound book—but the printer and the printing-office boy?
The well-taken photographs—but your wife or friend close and solid in your arms?
The black ship mail'd with iron, her mighty guns in her turrets—but the pluck of the
    captain and engineers?   1090
In the houses the dishes and fare and furniture—but the host and hostess, and the
    look out of their eyes?
The sky up there—yet here or next door, or across the way?
The saints and sages in history—but you yourself?
Sermons, creeds, theology—but the fathomless human brain,
And what is reason? and what is love? and what is life?   1095

43

I do not despise you priests, all time, the world over,
My faith is the greatest of faiths and the least of faiths,
Enclosing worship ancient and modern and all between ancient and modern,
Believing I shall come again upon the earth after five thousand years,
Waiting responses from oracles, honoring the gods, saluting the sun, 1100
Making a fetich of the first rock or stump, powowing with sticks in the circle of obis,[20]
Helping the llama or brahmin as he trims the lamps of the idols,
Dancing yet through the streets in a phallic procession, rapt and austere in the woods
    a gymnosophist,
Drinking mead from the skull-cup, to Shastas and Vedas admirant, minding the Koran,
Walking the teokallis,[21] spotted with gore from the stone and knife, beating the serpent-
    skin drum, 1105
Accepting the Gospels, accepting Him that was crucified, knowing assuredly that He is
    divine,
To the mass kneeling or the puritan's prayer rising, or sitting patiently in a pew,
Ranting and frothing in my insane crisis, or waiting dead-like till my spirit arouses me,
Looking forth on pavement and land, or outside of pavement and land,
Belonging to the winders of the circuit of circuits. 1110

One of that centripetal and centrifugal gang I turn and talk like a man leaving charges
    before a journey.

Down-hearted doubters dull and excluded,
Frivolous, sullen, moping, angry, affected, dishearten'd, atheistical,
I know every one of you, I know the sea of torment, doubt, despair and unbelief.

How the flukes splash! 1115
How they contort rapid as lightning, with spasms and spouts of blood!

Be at peace bloody flukes of doubters and sullen mopers,
I take my place among you as much as among any,
The past is the push of you, me, all, precisely the same,
And what is yet untried and afterward is for you, me, all, precisely the same. 1120

I do not know what is untried and afterward,
But I know it will in its turn prove sufficient, and cannot fail.

Each who passes is consider'd, each who stops is consider'd, not a single one can it fail.

It cannot fail the young man who died and was buried,
Nor the young woman who died and was put by his side, 1125
Nor the little child that peep'd in at the door, and then drew back and was never seen
    again,
Nor the old man who has lived without purpose, and feels it with bitterness worse than
    gall,

---

[20] West Indian Sorceries, probably of African origin.
[21] Aztec temples.

Nor him in the poor-house tubercled by rum and the bad disorder,
Nor the numberless slaughter'd and wreck'd, nor the brutish koboo [22] call'd the ordure of
     humanity,
Nor the sacs merely floating with open mouths for food to slip in,   1130
Nor any thing in the earth, or down in the oldest graves of the earth,
Nor any thing in the myriads of spheres, nor the myriads of myriads that inhabit them,
Nor the present, nor the least wisp that is known.

44

It is time to explain myself—let us stand up.

What is known I strip away,   1135
I launch all men and women forward with me into the Unknown.

The clock indicates the moment—but what does eternity indicate?

We have thus far exhausted trillions of winters and summers,
There are trillions ahead, and trillions ahead of them.

Births have brought us richness and variety,   1140
And other births will bring us richness and variety.

I do not call one greater and one smaller,
That which fills its period and place is equal to any.

Were mankind murderous or jealous upon you, my brother, my sister?
I am sorry for you, they are not murderous or jealous upon me,   1145
All has been gentle with me, I keep no account with lamentation,
(What have I to do with lamentation?)

I am an acme of things accomplish'd, and I an encloser of things to be.

My feet strike an apex of the apices of the stairs,
On every step bunches of ages, and larger bunches between the steps,   1150
All below duly travel'd, and still I mount and mount.

Rise after rise bow the phantoms behind me,
Afar down I see the huge first Nothing, I know I was even there,
I waited unseen and always, and slept through the lethargic mist,
And took my time, and took no hurt from the fetid carbon. [23]   1155

Long I was hugg'd close—long and long.

Immense have been the preparations for me,
Faithful and friendly the arms that have help'd me.

---

[22] A savage of the Ladrones, or Marianne Islands, in the North Pacific.
[23] The "mist" and "carbon" refer to the theory that the earth was originally surrounded by carbonic gas.

Cycles ferried my cradle, rowing and rowing like cheerful boatmen,
For room to me stars kept aside in their own rings,   1160
They sent influences to look after what was to hold me.

Before I was born out of my mother generations guided me,
My embryo has never been torpid, nothing could overlay it.

For it the nebula cohered to an orb,
The long slow strata piled to rest it on,   1165
Vast vegetables gave it sustenance,
Monstrous sauroids transported it in their mouths and deposited it with care.

All forces have been steadily employ'd to complete and delight me,
Now on this spot I stand with my robust soul.

45

O span of youth! ever-push'd elasticity!   1170
O manhood, balanced, florid and full.

My lovers suffocate me,
Crowding my lips, thick in the pores of my skin,
Jostling me through streets and public halls, coming naked to me at night,
Crying by day *Ahoy!* from the rocks of the river, swinging and chirping over my
        head,   1175
Calling my name from flower-beds, vines, tangled underbrush,
Lighting on every moment of my life,
Bussing my body with soft balsamic busses,
Noiselessly passing handfuls out of their hearts and giving them to be mine.

Old age superbly rising! O welcome, ineffable grace of dying days!   1180

Every condition promulges not only itself, it promulges what grows after and out of
        itself,
And the dark hush promulges as much as any.

I open my scuttle at night and see the far-sprinkled systems,
And all I see multiplied as high as I can cipher edge but the rim of the farther systems.

Wider and wider they spread, expanding, always expanding,   1185
Outward and outward and forever outward.

My sun has his sun and round him obediently wheels,
He joins with his partners a group of superior circuit,
And greater sets follow, making specks of the greatest inside them.

There is no stoppage and never can be stoppage,   1190
If I, you, and the worlds, and all beneath or upon their surfaces, were this moment
        reduced back to a pallid float, it would not avail in the long run,
We should surely bring up again where we now stand,
And surely go as much farther, and then farther and farther.

A few quadrillions of eras, a few octillions of cubic leagues, do not hazard the span
    or make it impatient,
They are but parts, any thing is but a part.   1195

See ever so far, there is limitless space outside of that,
Count ever so much, there is limitless time around that.

My rendezvous is appointed, it is certain,
The Lord will be there and wait till I come on perfect terms,
The great Camerado, the lover true for whom I pine will be there.   1200

46

I know I have the best of time and space, and was never measured and never will be
    measured.

I tramp a perpetual journey, (come listen all!)
My signs are a rain-proof coat, good shoes, and a staff cut from the woods,
No friend of mine takes his ease in my chair,
I have no chair, no church, no philosophy,   1205
I lead no man to a dinner-table, library, exchange,
But each man and each woman of you I lead upon a knoll,
My left hand hooking you round the waist,
My right hand pointing to landscapes of continents and the public road.

Not I, not any one else can travel that road for you,   1210
You must travel it for yourself.

It is not far, it is within reach,
Perhaps you have been on it since you were born and did not know,
Perhaps it is everywhere on water and on land.

Shoulder your duds dear son, and I will mine, and let us hasten forth,   1215
Wonderful cities and free nations we shall fetch as we go.

If you tire, give me both burdens, and rest the chuff [24] of your hand on my hip,
And in due time you shall repay the same service to me,
For after we start we never lie by again.

This day before dawn I ascended a hill and look'd at the crowded heaven,   1220
And I said to my spirit *When we become the enfolders of those orbs, and the pleasure
    and knowledge of every thing in them, shall we be fill'd and satisfied then?*
And my spirit said *No, we but level that lift to pass and continue beyond.*

You are also asking me questions and I hear you,
I answer that I cannot answer, you must find out for yourself.

---

[24] The plump part of the palm.

1225

Sit a while dear son,
Here are biscuits to eat and here is milk to drink,
But as soon as you sleep and renew yourself in sweet clothes, I kiss you with a good-by
    kiss and open the gate for your egress hence.

Long enough have you dream'd contemptible dreams,
Now I wash the gum from your eyes,
You must habit yourself to the dazzle of the light and of every moment of your life. 1230

Long have you timidly waded holding a plank by the shore,
Now I will you to be a bold swimmer,
To jump off in the midst of the sea, rise again, nod to me, shout, and laughingly dash
    with your hair.

47

I am the teacher of athletes,
He that by me spreads a wider breast than my own proves the width of my own, 1235
He most honors my style who learns under it to destroy the teacher.

The boy I love, the same becomes a man not through derived power, but in his own right,
Wicked rather than virtuous out of conformity or fear,
Fond of his sweetheart, relishing well his steak,
Unrequited love or a slight cutting him worse than sharp steel cuts, 1240
First-rate to ride, to fight, to hit the bull's eye, to sail a skiff, to sing a song or play
    on the banjo,
Preferring scars and the beard and faces pitted with small-pox over all latherers,
And those well-tann'd to those that keep out of the sun.

I teach straying from me, yet who can stray from me?
I follow you whoever you are from the present hour, 1245
My words itch at your ears till you understand them.

I do not say these things for a dollar or to fill up the time while I wait for a boat,
(It is you talking just as much as myself, I act as the tongue of you,
Tied in your mouth, in mine it begins to be loosen'd.)

I swear I will never again mention love or death inside a house, 1250
And I swear I will never translate myself at all, only to him or her who privately stays
    with me in the open air.

If you would understand me go to the heights or water-shore,
The nearest gnat is an explanation, and a drop or motion of waves a key,
The maul, the oar, the hand-saw, second my words.

No shutter'd room or school can commune with me, 1255
But roughs and little children better than they.

The young mechanic is closest to me, he knows me well,
The woodman that takes his axe and jug with him shall take me with him all day,
The farm-boy ploughing in the field feels good at the sound of my voice,
In vessels that sail my words sail, I go with fishermen and seamen and love them. 1260

The soldier camp'd or upon the march is mine,
On the night ere the pending battle many seek me, and I do not fail them,
On that solemn night (it may be their last) those that know me seek me.

My face rubs to the hunter's face when he lies down alone in his blanket,
The driver thinking of me does not mind the jolt of his wagon, 1265
The young mother and old mother comprehend me,
The girl and the wife rest the needle a moment and forget where they are,
They and all would resume what I have told them.

48

I have said that the soul is not more than the body,
And I have said that the body is not more than the soul, 1270
And nothing, not God, is greater to one than one's self is,
And whoever walks a furlong without sympathy walks to his own funeral drest in his
    shroud,
And I or you pocketless of a dime may purchase the pick of the earth,
And to glance with an eye or show a bean in its pod confounds the learning of all times,
And there is no trade or employment but the young man following it may become a
    hero, 1275
And there is no object so soft but it makes a hub for the wheel'd universe,
And I say to any man or woman, Let your soul stand cool and composed before a
    million universes.

And I say to mankind, Be not curious about God,
For I who am curious about each am not curious about God,
(No array of terms can say how much I am at peace about God and about death.) 1280

I hear and behold God in every object, yet understand God not in the least,
Nor do I understand who there can be more wonderful than myself.

Why should I wish to see God better than this day?
I see something of God each hour of the twenty-four, and each moment then,
In the faces of men and women I see God, and in my own face in the glass, 1285
I find letters from God dropt in the street, and every one is sign'd by God's name,
And I leave them where they are, for I know that wheresoe'er I go,
Others will punctually come for ever and ever.

49

And as to you Death, and you bitter hug of mortality, it is idle to try to alarm me.

To his work without flinching the accoucheur comes,   1290
I see the elder-hand pressing receiving supporting,
I recline by the sills of the exquisite flexible doors,
And mark the outlet, and mark the relief and escape.

And as to you Corpse I think you are good manure, but that does not offend me,
I smell the white roses sweet-scented and growing,   1295
I reach to the leafy lips, I reach to the polish'd breasts of melons.

And as to you Life I reckon you are the leavings of many deaths,
(No doubt I have died myself ten thousand times before.)

I hear you whispering there O stars of heaven,
O suns—O grass of graves—O perpetual transfers and promotions,   1300
If you do not say any thing how can I say any thing?

Of the turbid pool that lies in the autumn forest,
Of the moon that descends the steeps of the soughing twilight,
Toss, sparkles of day and dusk—toss on the black stems that decay in the muck,
Toss to the moaning gibberish of the dry limbs.   1305

I ascend from the moon, I ascend from the night,
I perceive that the ghastly glimmer is noonday sunbeams reflected,
And debouch to the steady and central from the offspring great or small.

50

There is that in me—I do not know what it is—but I know it is in me.

Wrench'd and sweaty—calm and cool then my body becomes,   1310
I sleep—I sleep long.

I do not know it—it is without name—it is a word unsaid,
It is not in any dictionary, utterance, symbol.

Something it swings on more than the earth I swing on,
To it the creation is the friend whose embracing awakes me.   1315

Perhaps I might tell more. Outlines! I plead for my brothers and sisters.

Do you see O my brothers and sisters?
It is not chaos or death—it is form, union, plan—it is eternal life—it is Happiness.

51

The past and present wilt—I have fill'd them, emptied them,
And proceed to fill my next fold of the future.   1320

Listener up there! what have you to confide to me?
Look in my face while I snuff the sidle of evening,
(Talk honestly, no one else hears you, and I stay only a minute longer.)

Do I contradict myself?
Very well then I contradict myself,   1325
(I am large, I contain multitudes.)

I concentrate toward them that are nigh, I wait on the door-slab.

Who has done his day's work? who will soonest be through with his supper?
Who wishes to walk with me?

Will you speak before I am gone? will you prove already too late?   1330

52

The spotted hawk swoops by and accuses me, he complains of my gab and my loitering.

I too am not a bit tamed, I too am untranslatable,
I sound my barbaric yawp over the roofs of the world.

The last scud of day holds back for me,
It flings my likeness after the rest and true as any on the shadow'd wilds,   1335
It coaxes me to the vapor and the dusk.

I depart as air, I shake my white locks at the runaway sun,
I effuse my flesh in eddies, and drift it in lacy jags.

I bequeath myself to the dirt to grow from the grass I love,
If you want me again look for me under your boot-soles.   1340

You will hardly know who I am or what I mean,
But I shall be good health to you nevertheless,
And filter and fibre your blood.

Failing to fetch me at first keep encouraged,
Missing me one place search another,   1345
I stop somewhere waiting for you.

THERE WAS A CHILD WENT FORTH
[1855]

There was a child went forth every day,
And the first object he look'd upon, that object he became,
And that object became part of him for the day or a certain part of the day,
Or for many years or stretching cycles of years.

The early lilacs became part of this child,   5
And grass and white and red morning-glories, and white and red clover, and the song
    of the phœbe-bird,
And the Third-month lambs and the sow's pink-faint litter, and the mare's foal and
    the cow's calf,
And the noisy brood of the barnyard or by the mire of the pondside,
And the fish suspending themselves so curiously below there, and the beautiful curious
    liquid,
And the water-plants with their graceful flat heads, all became part of him.   10

The field-sprouts of Fourth-month and Fifth-month became part of him,
Winter-grain sprouts and those of the light-yellow corn, and the esculent roots of the
    garden,
And the apple-trees cover'd with blossoms and the fruit afterward, and wood-berries,
    and the commonest weeds by the road,
And the old drunkard staggering home from the outhouse of the tavern whence he had
    lately risen,
And the schoolmistress that pass'd on her way to the school,   15
And the friendly boys that pass'd, and the quarrelsome boys,
And the tidy and fresh-cheek'd girls, and the barefoot negro boy and girl,
And all the changes of city and country wherever he went.

His own parents, he that had father'd him and she that had conceiv'd him in her womb
    and birth'd him,
They gave this child more of themselves than that,   20
They gave him afterward every day, they became part of him.

The mother at home quietly placing the dishes on the supper-table,
The mother with mild words, clean her cap and gown, a wholesome odor falling off her
    person and clothes as she walks by,
The father, strong, self-sufficient, manly, mean, anger'd, unjust,
The blow, the quick loud word, the tight bargain, the crafty lure,   25
The family usages, the language, the company, the furniture, the yearning and swelling
    heart,
Affection that will not be gainsay'd, the sense of what is real, the thought if after all it
    should prove unreal,
The doubts of day-time and the doubts of night-time, the curious whether and how,
Whether that which appears so is so, or is it all flashes and specks?

Men and women crowding fast in the streets, if they are not flashes and specks what
    are they?   30
The streets themselves and the façades of houses, and goods in the windows,
Vehicles, teams, the heavy-plank'd wharves, the huge crossing at the ferries,
The village on the highland seen from afar at sunset, the river between,
Shadows, aureola and mist, the light falling on roofs and gables of white or brown two
    miles off,
The schooner near by sleepily dropping down the tide, the little boat slack-tow'd
    astern,   35
The hurrying tumbling waves, quick-broken crests, slapping,

The strata of color'd clouds, the long bar of maroon-tint away solitary by itself, the
    spread of purity it lies motionless in,
The horizon's edge, the flying sea-crow, the fragrance of salt marsh and shore mud,
These became part of that child who went forth every day, and who now goes, and will
    always go forth every day.

SONG OF THE BROAD-AXE
[1856]

1

Weapon shapely, naked, wan,
Head from the mother's bowels drawn,
Wooded flesh and metal bone, limb only one and lip only one,
Gray-blue leaf by red-heat grown, helve produced from a little seed sown,
Resting the grass amid and upon,   5
To be lean'd and to lean on.

Strong shapes and attributes of strong shapes, masculine trades, sights and sounds,
Long varied train of an emblem, dabs of music,
Fingers of the organist skipping staccato over the keys of the great organ.

2

Welcome are all earth's lands, each for its kind,   10
Welcome are lands of pine and oak,
Welcome are lands of the lemon and fig,
Welcome are lands of gold,
Welcome are lands of wheat and maize, welcome those of the grape,
Welcome are lands of sugar and rice,   15
Welcome the cotton-lands, welcome those of the white potato and sweet potato,
Welcome are mountains, flats, sands, forests, prairies,
Welcome the rich borders of rivers, table-lands, openings,
Welcome the measureless grazing-lands, welcome the teeming soil of orchards, flax,
    honey, hemp;
Welcome just as much the other more hard-faced lands,   20
Lands rich as lands of gold or wheat and fruit lands,
Lands of mines, lands of the manly and rugged ores,
Lands of coal, copper, lead, tin, zinc,
Lands of iron—lands of the make of the axe.

3

The log at the wood-pile, the axe supported by it,   25
The sylvan hut, the vine over the doorway, the space clear'd for a garden,
The irregular tapping of rain down on the leaves after the storm is lull'd,
The wailing and moaning at intervals, the thought of the sea,
The thought of ships struck in the storm and put on their beam ends, and the cutting
    away of masts,

The sentiment of the huge timbers of old-fashion'd houses and barns, 30
The remember'd print or narrative, the voyage at a venture of men, families, goods,
The disembarkation, the founding of a new city,
The voyage of those who sought a New England and found it, the outset anywhere,
The settlements of the Arkansas, Colorado, Ottawa, Willamette,
The slow progress, the scant fare, the axe, rifle, saddle-bags; 35
The beauty of all adventurous and daring persons,
The beauty of wood-boys and wood-men with their clear untrimm'd faces,
The beauty of independence, departure, actions that rely on themselves,
The American contempt for statutes and ceremonies, the boundless impatience of
restraint,
The loose drift of character, the inkling through random types, the solidification; 40
The butcher in the slaughter-house, the hands aboard schooners and sloops, the raftsman,
the pioneer,
Lumbermen in their winter camp, daybreak in the woods, stripes of snow on the limbs
of trees, the occasional snapping,
The glad clear sound of one's own voice, the merry song, the natural life of the woods,
the strong day's work,
The blazing fire at night, the sweet taste of supper, the talk, the bed of hemlock-boughs
and the bear-skin;
The house-builder at work in cities or anywhere, 45
The preparatory jointing, squaring, sawing, mortising,
The hoist-up of beams, the push of them in their places, laying them regular,
Setting the studs by their tenons in the mortises according as they were prepared,
The blows of mallets and hammers, the attitudes of the men, their curv'd limbs,
Bending, standing, astride the beams, driving in pins, holding on by posts and braces, 50
The hook'd arm over the plate,[1] the other arm wielding the axe,
The floor-men forcing the planks close to be nail'd,
Their postures bringing their weapons downward on the bearers,
The echoes resounding through the vacant building;
The huge storehouse carried up in the city well under way, 55
The six framing-men, two in the middle and two at each end, carefully bearing on their
shoulders a heavy stick for a cross-beam,
The crowded line of masons with trowels in their right hands rapidly laying the long
side-wall, two hundred feet from front to rear,
The flexible rise and fall of backs, the continual click of the trowels striking the bricks,
The bricks one after another each laid so workmanlike in its place, and set with a knock
of the trowel-handle,
The piles of materials, the mortar on the mortar-boards, and the steady replenishing by
the hod-men; 60
Spar-makers in the spar-yard, the swarming row of well-grown apprentices,
The swing of their axes on the square-hew'd log shaping it toward the shape of a mast,
The brisk short crackle of the steel driven slantingly into the pine,
The butter-color'd chips flying off in great flakes and slivers,
The limber motion of brawny young arms and hips in easy costumes, 65
The constructor of wharves, bridges, piers, bulk-heads, floats, stays against the sea;
The city fireman, the fire that suddenly bursts forth in the close-pack'd square,

---

[1] The roof-plate, laid horizontally on a wall to carry the rafters.

The arriving engines, the hoarse shouts, the nimble stepping and daring,

The strong command through the fire-trumpets, the falling in line, the rise and fall of
    the arms forcing the water,

The slender, spasmic, blue-white jets, the bringing to bear of the hooks and ladders and
    their execution,   70

The crash and cut away of connecting wood-work, or through floors if the fire smoulders
    under them,

The crowd with their lit faces watching, the glare and dense shadows;

The forger at his forge-furnace and the user of iron after him,

The maker of the axe large and small, and the welder and temperer,

The chooser breathing his breath on the cold steel and trying the edge with his thumb, 75

The one who clean-shapes the handle and sets it firmly in the socket;

The shadowy processions of the portraits of the past users also,

The primal patient mechanics, the architects and engineers,

The far-off Assyrian edifice and Mizra [2] edifice,

The Roman lictors preceding the consuls,   80

The antique European warrior with his axe in combat,

The uplifted arm, the clatter of blows on the helmeted head,

The death-howl, the limpsy tumbling body, the rush of friend and foe thither,

The siege of revolted lieges determin'd for liberty,

The summons to surrender, the battering at castle gates, the truce and parley,   85

The sack of an old city in its time,

The bursting in of mercenaries and bigots tumultuously and disorderly,

Roar, flames, blood, drunkenness, madness,

Goods freely rifled from houses and temples, screams of women in the gripe of brigands,

Craft and thievery of camp-followers, men running, old persons despairing,   90

The hell of war, the cruelties of creeds,

The list of all executive deeds and words just or unjust,

The power of personality just or unjust.

4

Muscle and pluck forever!

What invigorates life invigorates death,   95

And the dead advance as much as the living advance,

And the future is no more uncertain than the present,

For the roughness of the earth and of man encloses as much as the delicatesse [3] of the
    earth and of man,

And nothing endures but personal qualities.

What do you think endures?   100

Do you think a great city endures?

Or a teeming manufacturing state? or a prepared constitution? or the best built steam-
    ships?

Or hotels of granite and iron? or any chef-d'œuvres of engineering, forts, armaments?

---

[2] Mizraim was the Hebrew name for Egypt.

[3] French *délicatesse*, delicacy.

Away! these are not to be cherish'd for themselves,
They fill their hour, the dancers dance, the musicians play for them, 105
The show passes, all does well enough of course,
All does very well till one flash of defiance.

A great city is that which has the greatest men and women,
If it be a few ragged huts it is still the greatest city in the whole world.

5

The place where a great city stands is not the place of stretch'd wharves, docks, manu-
    factures, deposits of produce merely, 110
Nor the place of ceaseless salutes of new-comers or the anchor-lifters of the departing,
Nor the place of the tallest and costliest buildings or shops selling goods from the rest
    of the earth,
Nor the place of the best libraries and schools, nor the place where money is plentiest,
Nor the place of the most numerous population.

Where the city stands with the brawniest breed of orators and bards, 115
Where the city stands that is belov'd by these, and loves them in return and under-
    stands them,
Where no monuments exist to heroes but in the common words and deeds,
Where thrift is in its place, and prudence is in its place,
Where the men and women think lightly of the laws,
Where the slave ceases, and the master of slaves ceases, 120
Where the populace rise at once against the never-ending audacity of elected persons,
Where fierce men and women pour forth as the sea to the whistle of death pours its
    sweeping and unript waves,
Where outside authority enters always after the precedence of inside authority,
Where the citizen is always the head and ideal, and President, Mayor, Governor and
    what not, are agents for pay,
Where children are taught to be laws to themselves, and to depend on themselves, 125
Where equanimity is illustrated in affairs,
Where speculations on the soul are encouraged,
Where women walk in public processions in the streets the same as the men,
Where they enter the public assembly and take places the same as the men;
Where the city of the faithfulest friends stands, 130
Where the city of the cleanliness of the sexes stands,
Where the city of the healthiest fathers stands,
Where the city of the best-bodied mothers stands,
There the great city stands.

6

How beggarly appear arguments before a defiant deed! 135
How the floridness of the materials of cities shrivels before a man's or woman's look!

All waits or goes by default till a strong being appears;
A strong being is the proof of the race and of the ability of the universe,

When he or she appears materials are overaw'd,
The dispute on the soul stops,   140
The old customs and phrases are confronted, turn'd back, or laid away.

What is your money-making now? what can it do now?
What is your respectability now?
What are your theology, tuition, society, traditions, statute-books, now?
Where are your jibes of being now?   145
Where are your cavils about the soul now?

7

A sterile landscape covers the ore, there is as good as the best for all the forbidding
        appearance,
There is the mine, there are the miners,
The forge-furnace is there, the melt is accomplish'd, the hammers-men are at hand with
        their tongs and hammers,
What always served and always serves is at hand.   150

Than this nothing has better served, it has served all,
Served the fluent-tongued and subtle-sensed Greek, and long ere the Greek,
Served in building the buildings that last longer than any,
Served the Hebrew, the Persian, the most ancient Hindustanee,
Served the mound-raiser on the Mississippi, served those whose relics remain in Central
        America,   155
Served Albic[4] temples in woods or on plains, with unhewn pillars and the druids,
Served the artificial clefts, vast, high, silent, on the snow-cover'd hills of Scandinavia,
Served those who time out of mind made on the granite walls rough sketches of the
        sun, moon, stars, ships, ocean waves,
Served the paths of the irruptions of the Goths, served the pastoral tribes and nomads,
Served the long distant Kelt, served the hardy pirates of the Baltic,   160
Served before any of those the venerable and harmless men of Ethiopia,
Served the making of helms for the galleys of pleasure and the making of those for war,
Served all great works on land and all great works on the sea,
For the mediæval ages and before the mediæval ages,
Served not the living only then as now, but served the dead.   165

8

I see the European headsman,
He stands mask'd, clothed in red, with huge legs and strong naked arms,
And leans on a ponderous axe.

(Whom have you slaughter'd lately European headsman?
Whose is that blood upon you so wet and sticky?)   170

I see the clear sunsets of the martyrs,
I see from the scaffolds the descending ghosts,

---

[4] Alba is ancient Scotland, north of the Forth and Clyde.

Ghosts of dead lords, uncrown'd ladies, impeach'd ministers, rejected kings,
Rivals, traitors, poisoners, disgraced chieftains and the rest.

I see those who in any land have died for the good cause, 175
The seed is spare, nevertheless the crop shall never run out,
(Mind you O foreign kings, O priests, the crop shall never run out.)

I see the blood wash'd entirely away from the axe,
Both blade and helve are clean,
They spirt no more the blood of European nobles, they clasp no more the necks of
    queens. 180

I see the headsman withdraw and become useless,
I see the scaffold untrodden and mouldy, I see no longer any axe upon it,
I see the mighty and friendly emblem of the power of my own race, the newest, largest
    race.

9

(America! I do not vaunt my love for you,
I have what I have.) 185

The axe leaps!
The solid forest gives fluid utterances,
They tumble forth, they rise and form,
Hut, tent, landing, survey,
Flail, plough, pick, crowbar, spade, 190
Shingle, rail, prop, wainscot, jamb, lath, panel, gable,
Citadel, ceiling, saloon, academy, organ, exhibition-house, library,
Cornice, trellis, pilaster, balcony, window, turret, porch,
Hoe, rake, pitchfork, pencil, wagon, staff, saw, jack-plane, mallet, wedge, rounce,
Chair, tub, hoop, table, wicket, vane, sash, floor, 195
Work-box, chest, string'd instrument, boat, frame, and what not,
Capitols of States, and capitol of the nation of States,
Long stately rows in avenues, hospitals for orphans or for the poor or sick,
Manhattan steamboats and clippers taking the measure of all seas.

The shapes arise! 200
Shapes of the using of axes anyhow, and the users and all that neighbors them,
Cutters down of wood and haulers of it to the Penobscot or Kennebec,
Dwellers in cabins among the Californian mountains or by the little lakes, or on the
    Columbia,
Dwellers south on the banks of the Gila or Rio Grande, friendly gatherings, the
    characters and fun,
Dwellers along the St. Lawrence, or north in Kanada, or down by the Yellowstone,
    dwellers on coasts and off coasts, 205
Seal-fishers, whalers, arctic seamen breaking passages through the ice.

The shapes arise!
Shapes of factories, arsenals, foundries, markets,

Shapes of the two-threaded tracks of railroads,
Shapes of the sleepers of bridges, vast frameworks, girders, arches,   210
Shapes of the fleets of barges, tows, lake and canal craft, river craft,
Ship-yards and dry-docks along the Eastern and Western seas, and in many a bay
    and by-place,
The live-oak kelsons,[5] the pine planks, the spars, the hackmatack-roots for knees,[6]
The ships themselves on their ways, the tiers of scaffolds, the workmen busy outside
    and inside,
The tools lying around, the great auger and little auger, the adze, bolt, line, square,
    gouge, and bead-plane.   215

10

The shapes arise!
The shape measur'd, saw'd, jack'd, join'd, stain'd,
The coffin-shape for the dead to lie within in his shroud,
The shape got out in posts, in the bedstead posts, in the posts of the bride's bed,
The shape of the little trough, the shape of the rockers beneath, the shape of the babe's
    cradle,   220
The shape of the floor-planks, the floor-planks for dancers' feet,
The shape of the planks of the family home, the home of the friendly parents and
    children,
The shape of the roof of the home of the happy young man and woman, the roof over
    the well-married young man and woman,
The roof over the supper joyously cook'd by the chaste wife, and joyously eaten by the
    chaste husband, content after his day's work.

The shapes arise!   225
The shape of the prisoner's place in the court-room, and of him or her seated in the
    place,
The shape of the liquor-bar lean'd against by the young rum-drinker and the old
    rum-drinker,
The shape of the shamed and angry stairs trod by sneaking footsteps,
The shape of the sly settee, and the adulterous unwholesome couple,
The shape of the gambling-board with its devilish winnings and losings,   230
The shape of the step-ladder for the convicted and sentenced murderer, the murderer
    with haggard face and pinion'd arms,
The sheriff at hand with his deputies, the silent and white-lipp'd crowd, the dangling
    of the rope.

The shapes arise!
Shapes of doors giving many exits and entrances,
The door passing the dissever'd friend flush'd and in haste,   235
The door that admits good news and bad news,
The door whence the son left home confident and puff'd up,
The door he enter'd again from a long and scandalous absence, diseas'd, broken down,
    without innocence, without means.

---

[5] See footnote 4 of "Song of Myself," page 33.
   [6] An angled timber used as a brace at the meeting of a beam with the side of the
ship.

11

Her shape arises,
She less guarded than ever, yet more guarded than ever,   240
The gross and soil'd she moves among do not make her gross and soil'd,
She knows the thoughts as she passes, nothing is conceal'd from her,
She is none the less considerate or friendly therefor,
She is the best belov'd, it is without exception, she has no reason to fear and she does
      not fear,
Oaths, quarrels, hiccupp'd songs, smutty expressions, are idle to her as she passes,   245
She is silent, she is possess'd of herself, they do not offend her,
She receives them as the laws of Nature receive them, she is strong,
She too is a law of Nature—there is no law stronger than she is.

12

The main shapes arise!
Shapes of Democracy total, result of centuries,   250
Shapes ever projecting other shapes,
Shapes of turbulent manly cities,
Shapes of the friends and home-givers of the whole earth,
Shapes bracing the earth and braced with the whole earth.

CROSSING BROOKLYN FERRY
[1856]

1

Flood-tide below me! I see you face to face!
Clouds of the west—sun there half an hour high—I see you also face to face.

Crowds of men and women attired in the usual costumes, how curious you are to me!
On the ferry-boats the hundreds and hundreds that cross, returning home, are more
      curious to me than you suppose,
And you that shall cross from shore to shore years hence are more to me, and more in
      my meditations, than you might suppose.   5

2

The impalpable sustenance of me from all things at all hours of the day,
The simple, compact, well-join'd scheme, myself disintegrated, every one disintegrated
      yet part of the scheme,
The similitudes of the past and those of the future,
The glories strung like beads on my smallest sights and hearings, on the walk in the
      street and the passage over the river,
The current rushing so swiftly and swimming with me far away,   10
The others that are to follow me, the ties between me and them,
The certainty of others, the life, love, sight, hearing of others.

Others will enter the gates of the ferry and cross from shore to shore,
Others will watch the run of the flood-tide,
Others will see the shipping of Manhattan north and west, and the heights of Brooklyn
    to the south and east,   15
Others will see the islands large and small;
Fifty years hence, others will see them as they cross, the sun half an hour high,
A hundred years hence, or ever so many hundred years hence, others will see them,
Will enjoy the sunset, the pouring-in of the flood-tide, the falling-back to the sea of the
    ebb-tide.

3

It avails not, time nor place—distance avails not,   20
I am with you, you men and women of a generation, or ever so many generations hence,
Just as you feel when you look on the river and sky, so I felt,
Just as any of you is one of a living crowd, I was one of a crowd,
Just as you are refresh'd by the gladness of the river and the bright flow, I was refresh'd,
Just as you stand and lean on the rail, yet hurry with the swift current, I stood yet was
    hurried,   25
Just as you look on the numberless masts of ships and the thick-stemm'd pipes of
    steamboats, I look'd.

I too many and many a time cross'd the river of old,
Watched the Twelfth-month sea-gulls, saw them high in the air floating with motionless
    wings, oscillating their bodies,
Saw how the glistening yellow lit up parts of their bodies and left the rest in strong
    shadow,
Saw the slow-wheeling circles and the gradual edging toward the south,   30
Saw the reflection of the summer sky in the water,
Had my eyes dazzled by the shimmering track of beams,
Look'd at the fine centrifugal spokes of light round the shape of my head in the sunlit
    water,
Look'd on the haze on the hills southward and south-westward,
Look'd on the vapor as it flew in fleeces tinged with violet,   35
Look'd toward the lower bay to notice the vessels arriving,
Saw their approach, saw aboard those that were near me,
Saw the white sails of schooners and sloops, saw the ships at anchor,
The sailors at work in the rigging or out astride the spars,
The round masts, the swinging motion of the hulls, the slender serpentine pennants, 40
The large and small steamers in motion, the pilots in their pilot-houses,
The white wake left by the passage, the quick tremulous whirl of the wheels,
The flags of all nations, the falling of them at sunset,
The scallop-edged waves in the twilight, the ladled cups, the frolicsome crests and
    glistening,
The stretch afar growing dimmer and dimmer, the gray walls of the granite storehouses
    by the docks,   45
On the river the shadowy group, the big steam-tug closely flank'd on each side by the
    barges, the hay-boat, the belated lighter,

On the neighboring shore, the fires from the foundry chimneys burning high and glar-
      ingly into the night,
Casting their flicker of black contrasted with wild red and yellow light over the tops of
      houses, and down into the clefts of streets.

4

These and all else were to me the same as they are to you,
I loved well those cities, loved well the stately and rapid river,   50
The men and women I saw were all near to me,
Others the same—others who look back on me because I look'd forward to them,
(The time will come, though I stop here to-day and to-night.)

5

What is it then between us?
What is the count of the scores or hundreds of years between us?   55

Whatever it is, it avails not—distance avails not, and place avails not,
I too lived, Brooklyn of ample hills was mine,
I too walk'd the streets of Manhattan island, and bathed in the waters around it,
I too felt the curious abrupt questionings stir within me,   60
In the day among crowds of people sometimes they came upon me,
In my walks home late at night or as I lay in my bed they came upon me,
I too had been struck from the float forever held in solution,
I too had receiv'd identity by my body,
That I was I knew was of my body, and what I should be I knew I should be of my body.

6

It is not upon you alone the dark patches fall,   65
The dark threw its patches down upon me also,
The best I had done seem'd to me blank and suspicious,
My great thoughts as I supposed them, were they not in reality meagre?
Nor is it you alone who know what it is to be evil,
I am he who knew what it was to be evil,   70
I too knitted the old knot of contrariety,
Blabb'd, blush'd, resented, lied, stole, grudg'd,
Had guile, anger, lust, hot wishes I dared not speak,
Was wayward, vain, greedy, shallow, sly, cowardly, malignant,
The wolf, the snake, the hog, not wanting in me,   75
The cheating look, the frivolous word, the adulterous wish, not wanting,
Refusals, hates, postponements, meanness, laziness, none of these wanting,
Was one with the rest, the days and haps of the rest,
Was call'd by my nighest name [1] by clear loud voices of young men as they saw me
      approaching or passing,
Felt their arms on my neck as I stood, or the negligent leaning of their flesh against
      me as I sat,   80

---

[1] First name. Cf. ll. 95 and 109.

Saw many I loved in the street or ferry-boat or public assembly, yet never told them a
    word,
Lived the same life with the rest, the same old laughing, gnawing, sleeping,
Play'd the part that still looks back on the actor or actress,
The same old rôle, the rôle that is what we make it, as great as we like,
Or as small as we like, or both great and small.   85

7

Closer yet I approach you,
What thought you have of me now, I had as much of you—I laid in my stores in advance,
I consider'd long and seriously of you before you were born.

Who was to know what should come home to me?
Who knows but I am enjoying this?   90
Who knows, for all the distance, but I am as good as looking at you now, for all you
    cannot see me?

8

Ah, what can ever be more stately and admirable to me than mast-hemm'd Manhattan?
River and sunset and scallop-edg'd waves of flood-tide?
The sea-gulls oscillating their bodies, the hay-boat in the twilight, and the belated lighter?

What gods can exceed these that clasp me by the hand, and with voices I love call me
    promptly and loudly by my nighest name as I approach?   95
What is more subtle than this which ties me to the woman or man that looks in my face?
Which fuses me into you now, and pours my meaning into you?

We understand then do we not?
What I promis'd without mentioning it, have you not accepted?
What the study could not teach—what the preaching could not accomplish is accom-
    plish'd, is it not?   100

9

Flow on, river! flow with the flood-tide, and ebb with the ebb-tide!
Frolic on, crested and scallop-edg'd waves!
Gorgeous clouds of the sunset! drench with your splendor me, or the men and women
    generations after me!
Cross from shore to shore, countless crowds of passengers!
Stand up, tall masts of Mannahatta! stand up, beautiful hills of Brooklyn!   105
Throb, baffled and curious brain! throw out questions and answers!
Suspend here and everywhere, eternal float of solution! [2]
Gaze, loving and thirsting eyes, in the house or street or public assembly!
Sound out, voices of young men! loudly and musically call me by my nighest name!
Live, old life! play the part that looks back on the actor or actress!   110
Play the old rôle, the rôle that is great or small according as one makes it!

---

[2] Cf. l. 62. Sum-total of phenomena imagined as floating over the universe.

Consider, you who peruse me, whether I may not in unknown ways be looking upon you;

Be firm, rail over the river, to support those who lean idly, yet haste with the hasting current;

Fly on, sea-birds! fly sideways, or wheel in large circles high in the air;

Receive the summer sky, you water, and faithfully hold it till all downcast eyes have time to take it from you!   115

Diverge, fine spokes of light, from the shape of my head, or any one's head, in the sunlit water!

Come on, ships from the lower bay! pass up or down, white-sail'd schooners, sloops, lighters!

Flaunt away, flags of all nations! be duly lower'd at sunset!

Burn high your fires, foundry chimneys! cast black shadows at nightfall! cast red and yellow light over the tops of the houses!

Appearances, now or henceforth, indicate what you are,   120

You necessary film, continue to envelop the soul,

About my body for me, and your body for you, be hung our divinest aromas,

Thrive, cities—bring your freight, bring your shows, ample and sufficient rivers,

Expand, being than which none else is perhaps more spiritual,

Keep your places, objects than which none else is more lasting.   125

You have waited, you always wait, you dumb, beautiful ministers,

We receive you with free sense at last, and are insatiate henceforward,

Not you any more shall be able to foil us, or withhold yourselves from us,

We use you, and do not cast you aside—we plant you permanently within us,

We fathom you not—we love you—there is perfection in you also,   130

You furnish your parts toward eternity,

Great or small, you furnish your parts toward the soul.

OUT OF THE CRADLE ENDLESSLY ROCKING [1]
[1860 (1859)]

Out of the cradle endlessly rocking,

Out of the mocking-bird's throat, the musical shuttle,

Out of the Ninth-month midnight,

Over the sterile sands and the fields beyond where the child leaving his bed wander'd alone, bareheaded, barefoot,

Down from the shower'd halo,   5

Up from the mystic play of shadows twining and twisting as if they were alive,

Out from the patches of briers and blackberries,

From the memories of the bird that chanted to me,

From your memories sad brother, from the fitful risings and fallings I heard,

From under that yellow half-moon late-risen and swollen as if with tears,   10

From those beginning notes of yearning and love there in the mist,

From the thousand responses of my heart never to cease,

From the myriad thence-arous'd words,

---

[1] When this poem was first published in the *Saturday Press*, a New York miscellany, on Dec. 24, 1859, it had the title "A Child's Reminiscence." The first line read: "Out of the rocked cradle."

From the word stronger and more delicious than any,
From such as now they start the scene revisiting,   15
As a flock, twittering, rising, or overhead passing,
Borne hither, ere all eludes me, hurriedly,
A man, yet by these tears a little boy again,
Throwing myself on the sand, confronting the waves,
I, chanter of pains and joys, uniter of here and hereafter,   20
Taking all hints to use them, but swiftly leaping beyond them,
A reminiscence sing.

Once Paumanok,[2]
When the lilac-scent was in the air and Fifth-month grass was growing,
Up this seashore in some briers,   25
Two feather'd guests from Alabama, two together,
And their nest, and four light-green eggs spotted with brown,
And every day the he-bird to and fro near at hand,
And every day the she-bird crouch'd on her nest, silent, with bright eyes,
And every day I, a curious boy, never too close, never disturbing them,   30
Cautiously peering, absorbing, translating.

Shine! shine! shine!
Pour down your warmth, great sun!
While we bask, we two together.

Two together!   35
Winds blow south, or winds blow north,
Day come white, or night come black,
Home, or rivers and mountains from home,
Singing all time, minding no time,
While we two keep together.   40

Till of a sudden,
May-be kill'd, unknown to her mate,
One forenoon the she-bird crouch'd not on the nest,
Nor return'd that afternoon, nor the next,
Nor ever appear'd again.   45

And thenceforward all summer in the sound of the sea,
And at night under the full of the moon in calmer weather,
Over the hoarse surging of the sea,
Or flitting from brier to brier by day,
I saw, I heard at intervals the remaining one, the he-bird,   50
The solitary guest from Alabama.

Blow! blow! blow!
Blow up sea-winds along Paumanok's shore;
I wait and I wait till you blow my mate to me.

---

[2] Long Island.

Yes, when the stars glisten'd,   55
All night long on the prong of a moss-scallop'd stake,
Down almost amid the slapping waves,
Sat the lone singer wonderful causing tears.

He call'd on his mate,
He pour'd forth the meanings which I of all men know.   60

Yes my brother I know,
The rest might not, but I have treasur'd every note,
For more than once dimly down to the beach gliding,
Silent, avoiding the moonbeams, blending myself with the shadows,
Recalling now the obscure shapes, the echoes, the sounds and sights after their sorts,   65
The white arms out in the breakers tirelessly tossing,
I, with bare feet, a child, the wind wafting my hair,
Listen'd long and long.

Listen'd to keep, to sing, now translating the notes,
Following you my brother.   70

Soothe! soothe! soothe!
Close on its wave soothes the wave behind,
And again another behind embracing and lapping, every one close,
But my love soothes not me, not me.

Low hangs the moon, it rose late,   75
It is lagging—O I think it is heavy with love, with love.

O madly the sea pushes upon the land,
With love, with love.

O night! do I not see my love fluttering out among the breakers?
What is that little black thing I see there in the white?   80

Loud! loud! loud!
Loud I call to you, my love!
High and clear I shoot my voice over the waves,
Surely you must know who is here, is here,
You must know who I am, my love.   85

Low-hanging moon!
What is that dusky spot in your brown yellow?
O it is the shape, the shape of my mate!
O moon do not keep her from me any longer.

Land! Land! O land!   90
Whichever way I turn, O I think you could give me my mate back again if you only
    would,
For I am almost sure I see her dimly whichever way I look.

O rising stars!
Perhaps the one I want so much will rise, will rise with some of you.

O throat! O trembling throat!　　　　　　　　　　　　95
Sound clearer through the atmosphere!
Pierce the woods, the earth,
Somewhere listening to catch you must be the one I want.

Shake out carols!
Solitary here, the night's carols!　　　　　　　　　　100
Carols of lonesome love! death's carols!
Carols under that lagging, yellow, waning moon!
O under that moon where she droops almost down into the sea!
O reckless despairing carols.

But soft! sink low!　　　　　　　　　　　　　　　105
Soft, let me just murmur,
And do you wait a moment you husky-nois'd sea,
For somewhere I believe I heard my mate responding to me,
So faint, I must be still, be still to listen,
But not altogether still, for then she might not come immediately to me.　110

Hither my love!
Here I am! here!
With this just-sustain'd note I announce myself to you,
This gentle call is for you my love, for you.

Do not be decoy'd elsewhere,　　　　　　　　　　　115
That is the whistle of the wind, it is not my voice,
That is the fluttering, the fluttering of the spray,
Those are the shadows of leaves.

O darkness! O in vain!
O I am very sick and sorrowful.　　　　　　　　　　120

O brown halo in the sky near the moon, drooping upon the sea!
O troubled reflection in the sea!
O throat! O throbbing heart!
And I singing uselessly, uselessly all the night.

O past! O happy life! O songs of joy!　　　　　　　　125
In the air, in the woods, over fields,
Loved! loved! loved! loved! loved!
But my mate no more, no more with me!
We two together no more.

The aria sinking,　　　　　　　　　　　　　　130
All else continuing, the stars shining,
The winds blowing, the notes of the bird continuous echoing,

With angry moans the fierce old mother incessantly moaning,
On the sands of Paumanok's shore gray and rustling,
The yellow half-moon enlarged, sagging down, drooping, the face of the sea almost
    touching,   135
The boy ecstatic, with his bare feet the waves, with his hair the atmosphere dallying,
The love in the heart long pent, now loose, now at last tumultuously bursting,
The aria's meaning, the ears, the soul, swiftly depositing,
The strange tears down the cheeks coursing,
The colloquy there, the trio, each uttering,   140
The undertone, the savage old mother incessantly crying,
To the boy's soul's questions sullenly timing, some drown'd secret hissing,
To the outsetting bard.

Demon [3] or bird! (said the boy's soul,)
Is it indeed toward your mate you sing? or is it really to me?   145
For I, that was a child, my tongue's use sleeping, now I have heard you,
Now in a moment I know what I am for, I awake,
And already a thousand singers, a thousand songs, clearer, louder and more sorrowful
    than yours,
A thousand warbling echoes have started to life within me, never to die.

O you singer solitary, singing by yourself, projecting me,   150
O solitary me listening, never more shall I cease perpetuating you,
Never more shall I escape, never more the reverberations,
Never more the cries of unsatisfied love be absent from me,
Never again leave me to be the peaceful child I was before what there in the night,
By the sea under the yellow and sagging moon,   155
The messenger there arous'd, the fire, the sweet hell within,
The unknown want, the destiny of me.

O give me the clew! (it lurks in the night here somewhere,)
O if I am to have so much, let me have more!
A word then, (for I will conquer it,)   160
The word final, superior to all,
Subtle, sent up—what is it?—I listen;
Are you whispering it, and have been all the time, you sea-waves?
Is that it from your liquid rims and wet sands?

Whereto answering, the sea,   165
Delaying not, hurrying not,
Whisper'd me through the night, and very plainly before day-break,
Lisp'd to me the low and delicious word death,
And again death, death, death, death,
Hissing melodious, neither like the bird nor like my arous'd child's heart,   170
But edging near as privately for me rustling at my feet,
Creeping thence steadily up to my ears and laving me softly all over,
Death, death, death, death, death.

---

[3] That is, spirit or divinity, from the Greek *daimon.*

Which I do not forget,
But fuse the song of my dusky demon and brother,   175
That he sang to me in the moonlight on Paumanok's gray beach,
With the thousand responsive songs at random,
My own songs awaked from that hour,
And with them the key, the word up from the waves,
The word of the sweetest song and all songs,   180
That strong and delicious word which, creeping to my feet,
(Or like some old crone rocking the cradle, swathed in sweet garments, bending aside,)
The sea whisper'd me.

ONCE I PASS'D THROUGH A POPULOUS CITY
[1860]

Once I pass'd through a populous city imprinting my brain for future use with its
        shows, architecture, customs, traditions,
Yet now of all that city I remember only a woman I casually met there who detain'd
        me for love of me,
Day by day and night by night we were together—all else has long been forgotten by me,
I remember I say only that woman who passionately clung to me,
Again we wander, we love, we separate again,
Again she holds me by the hand, I must not go,
I see her close beside me with silent lips sad and tremulous.

I SIT AND LOOK OUT
[1860]

I sit and look out upon all the sorrows of the world, and upon all oppression and
        shame,
I hear secret convulsive sobs from young men at anguish with themselves, remorseful
        after deeds done,
I see in low life the mother misused by her children, dying, neglected, guant, desperate,
I see the wife misused by her husband, I see the treacherous seducer of young women,
I mark the ranklings of jealousy and unrequited love attempted to be hid, I see these
        sights on the earth,
I see the workings of battle, pestilence, tyranny, I see martyrs and prisoners,
I observe a famine at sea, I observe the sailors casting lots who shall be kill'd to
        preserve the lives of the rest,
I observe the slights and degradations cast by arrogant persons upon laborers, the
        poor, and upon negroes, and the like;
All these—all the meanness and agony without end I sitting look out upon,
See, hear, and am silent.

BEAT! BEAT! DRUMS!
[1865]

Beat! beat! drums!—blow! bugles! blow!
Through the windows—through doors—burst like a ruthless **force**,
Into the solemn church, and scatter the congregation,
Into the school where the scholar is studying;

Leave not the bridegroom quiet—no happiness must he have now with his bride,   5
Nor the peaceful farmer any peace, ploughing his field or gathering his grain,
So fierce you whirr and pound you drums—so shrill you bugles blow.

Beat! beat! drums!—blow! bugles! blow!
Over the traffic of cities—over the rumble of wheels in the streets;
Are beds prepared for sleepers at night in the houses? no sleepers must sleep in those
        beds,   10
No bargainers' bargains by day—no brokers or speculators—would they continue?
Would the talkers be talking? would the singer attempt to sing?
Would the lawyer rise in the court to state his case before the judge?
Then rattle quicker, heavier drums—you bugles wilder blow.

Beat! beat! drums!—blow! bugles! blow!   15
Make no parley—stop for no expostulation,
Mind not the timid—mind not the weeper or prayer,
Mind not the old man beseeching the young man,
Let not the child's voice be heard, nor the mother's entreaties,
Make even the trestles to shake the dead where they lie awaiting the hearses,   20
So strong you thump O terrible drums—so loud you bugles blow.

BY THE BIVOUAC'S FITFUL FLAME
[1865]

By the bivouac's fitful flame,
A procession winding around me, solemn and sweet and slow—but first I note,
The tents of the sleeping army, the fields' and woods' dim outline,
The darkness lit by spots of kindled fire, the silence,
Like a phantom far or near an occasional figure moving,
The shrubs and trees, (as I lift my eyes they seem to be stealthily watching me,)
While wind in procession thoughts, O tender and wondrous thoughts,
Of life and death, of home and the past and loved, and of those that are far away;
A solemn and slow procession there as I sit on the ground,
By the bivouac's fitful flame.

COME UP FROM THE FIELDS FATHER
[1865]

Come up from the fields father, here's a letter from our Pete,
And come to the front door mother, here's a letter from thy dear son.

Lo, 'tis autumn,
Lo, where the trees, deeper green, yellower and redder,
Cool and sweeten Ohio's villages with leaves fluttering in the moderate wind,   5
Where apples ripe in the orchards hang and grapes on the trellis'd vines,
(Smell you the smell of the grapes on the vines?
Smell you the buckwheat where the bees were lately buzzing?)

Above all, lo, the sky so calm, so transparent after the rain, and with wondrous clouds,
Below too, all calm, all vital and beautiful, and the farm prospers well.   10

Down in the fields all prospers well,
But now from the fields come father, come at the daughter's call,
And come to the entry mother, to the front door come right away.

Fast as she can she hurries, something ominous, her steps trembling,
She does not tarry to smooth her hair nor adjust her cap.   15

Open the envelope quickly,
O this is not our son's writing, yet his name is sign'd,
O a strange hand writes for our dear son, O stricken mother's soul!
All swims before her eyes, flashes with black, she catches the main words only,
Sentences broken, *gunshot wound in the breast, cavalry skirmish, taken to hospital,*   20
At present low, but will soon be better.

Ah now the single figure to me,
Amid all teeming and wealthy Ohio with all its cities and farms,
Sickly white in the face and dull in the head, very faint,
By the jamb of a door leans.   25

Grieve not so, dear mother, (the just-grown daughter speaks through her sobs,
The little sisters huddle around speechless and dismay'd,)
See, dearest mother, the letter says Pete will soon be better.

Alas poor boy, he will never be better, (nor may-be needs to be better, that brave and
     simple soul,)
While they stand at home at the door he is dead already,   30
The only son is dead.

But the mother needs to be better,
She with thin form presently drest in black,
By day her meals untouch'd, then at night fitfully sleeping, often waking,
In the midnight waking, weeping, longing with one deep longing,   35
O that she might withdraw unnoticed, silent from life escape and withdraw,
To follow, to seek, to be with her dear dead son.

AS TOILSOME I WANDER'D VIRGINIA'S WOODS
[1865]

As toilsome I wander'd Virginia's woods,
To the music of rustling leaves kick'd by my feet, (for 'twas autumn,)
I mark'd at the foot of a tree the grave of a soldier;
Mortally wounded he and buried on the retreat, (easily all could I understand,)
The halt of a mid-day hour, when up! no time to lose—yet this sign left,
On a tablet scrawl'd and nail'd on the tree by the grave,
Bold, cautious, true, and my loving comrade.

Long, long I muse, then on my way go wandering,
Many a changeful season to follow, and many a scene of life,
Yet at times through changeful season and scene, abrupt, alone, or in the crowded
    street,
Comes before me the unknown soldier's grave, comes the inscription rude in Virginia's
    woods,
Bold, cautious, true, and my loving comrade.

WHEN LILACS LAST IN THE DOORYARD BLOOM'D
[1865]

1

When lilacs last in the dooryard bloom'd,
And the great star early droop'd in the western sky in the night,
I mourn'd, and yet shall mourn with ever-returning spring.

Ever-returning spring, trinity sure to me you bring,
Lilac blooming perennial and drooping star in the west,   5
And thought of him I love.

2

O powerful western fallen star!
O shades of night—O moody, tearful night!
O great star disappear'd—O the black murk that hides the star!
O cruel hands that hold me powerless—O helpless soul of me!   10
O harsh surrounding cloud that will not free my soul.

3

In the dooryard fronting an old farm-house near the whitewash'd palings,
Stands the lilac-bush tall-growing with heart-shaped leaves of rich green,
With many a pointed blossom rising delicate, with the perfume strong I love,
With every leaf a miracle—and from this bush in the dooryard,   15
With delicate-color'd blossoms and heart-shaped leaves of rich green,
A sprig with its flower I break.

4

In the swamp in secluded recesses,
A shy and hidden bird is warbling a song.

Solitary the thrush,   20
The hermit withdrawn to himself, avoiding the settlements,
Sings by himself a song.

Song of the bleeding throat,
Death's outlet song of life, (for well dear brother I know,
If thou wast not granted to sing thou would'st surely die.)   25

5

Over the breast of the spring, the land, amid cities,
Amid lanes and through old woods, where lately the **violets** peep'd from the ground,
    spotting the gray debris,
Amid the grass in the fields each side of the lanes, passing the endless grass,
Passing the yellow-spear'd wheat, every grain from its shroud in the dark-brown fields
    uprisen,
Passing the apple-tree blows of white and pink in the orchards,   30
Carrying a corpse to where it shall rest in the grave,
Night and day journeys a coffin.[1]

6

Coffin that passes through lanes and streets,
Through day and night with the great cloud darkening the land,
With the pomp of the inloop'd flags with the cities draped in black,   35
With the show of the States themselves as of crape-veil'd women standing,
With processions long and winding and the flambeaus of the night,
With the countless torches lit, with the silent sea of faces and the unbared heads,
With the waiting depot, the arriving coffin, and the sombre faces,
With dirges through the night, with the thousand voices rising strong and solemn,   40
With all the mournful voices of the dirges pour'd around the coffin,
The dim-lit churches and the shuddering organs—where amid these you **journey**,
With the tolling tolling bells' perpetual clang,
Here, coffin that slowly passes,
I give you my sprig of lilac.   45

7

(Nor for you, for one alone,
Blossoms and branches green to coffins all I bring,
For fresh as the morning, thus would I chant a song for you O **sane and sacred death.**

All over bouquets of roses,
O death, I cover you over with roses and early lilies,   50
But mostly and now the lilac that blooms the first,
Copious I break, I break the sprigs from the bushes,
With loaded arms I come, pouring for you,
For you and the coffins all of you O death.)

8

O western orb sailing the heaven,   55
Now I know what you must have meant as a month since I **walk'd**,

---

[1] A funeral train carried Lincoln's body from Washington to his home at Springfield,
Illinois. It left Washington on April 21, 1865, and halted at the principal cities along
the route. Burial in Oak Ridge Cemetery, Springfield, occurred on May 4.

As I walk'd in silence the transparent shadowy night,
As I saw you had something to tell as you bent to me night after night,
As you droop'd from the sky low down as if to my side, (while the other stars all
    look'd on,)
As we wander'd together the solemn night, (for something I know not what kept me
    from sleep,)   60
As the night advanced, and I saw on the rim of the west how full you were of woe,
As I stood on the rising ground in the breeze in the cool transparent night,
As I watch'd where you pass'd and was lost in the netherward black of the night,
As my soul in its trouble dissatisfied sank, as where you sad orb,
Concluded, dropt in the night, and was gone.   65

9

Sing on there in the swamp,
O singer bashful and tender, I hear your notes, I hear your call,
I hear, I come presently, I understand you,
But a moment I linger, for the lustrous star has detain'd me,
The star my departing comrade holds and detains me.   70

10

O how shall I warble myself for the dead one there I loved?
And how shall I deck my song for the large sweet soul that has gone?
And what shall my perfume be for the grave of him I love?

Sea-winds blown from east and west,
Blown from the Eastern sea and blown from the Western sea, till there on the prairies
    meeting,   75
These and with these and the breath of my chant,
I'll perfume the grave of him I love.

11

O what shall I hang on the chamber walls?
And what shall the pictures be that I hang on the walls,
To adorn the burial-house of him I love?   80

Pictures of growing spring and farms and homes,
With the Fourth-month eve at sundown, and the gray smoke lucid and bright,
With floods of the yellow gold of the gorgeous, indolent, sinking sun, burning, expanding
    the air,
With the fresh sweet herbage under foot, and the pale green leaves of the trees prolific,
In the distance the flowing glaze, the breast of the river, with a wind-dapple here
    and there,   85
With ranging hills on the banks, with many a line against the sky, and shadows,
And the city at hand with dwellings so dense, and stacks of chimneys,
And all the scenes of life and the workshops, and the workmen homeward returning.

12

Lo, body and soul—this land,
My own Manhattan with spires, and the sparkling and hurrying tides, and the ships,   90
The varied and ample land, the South and the North in the light, Ohio's shores and
    flashing Missouri,
And ever the far-spreading prairies cover'd with grass and corn.

Lo, the most excellent sun so calm and haughty,
The violet and purple morn with just-felt breezes,
The gentle soft-born measureless light,   95
The miracle spreading bathing all, the fulfill'd noon,
The coming eve delicious, the welcome night and the stars,
Over my cities shining all, enveloping man and land.

13

Sing on, sing on you gray-brown bird,
Sing from the swamps, the recesses, pour your chant from the bushes,   100
Limitless out of the dusk, out of the cedars and pines.

Sing on dearest brother, warble your reedy song,
Loud human song, with voice of uttermost woe.

O liquid and free and tender!
O wild and loose to my soul—O wondrous singer!   105
You only I hear—yet the star holds me, (but will soon depart,)
Yet the lilac with mastering odor holds me.

14

Now while I sat in the day and look'd forth,
In the close of the day with its light and the fields of spring, and the farmers preparing
    their crops,
In the large unconscious scenery of my land with its lakes and forests,   110
In the heavenly aerial beauty, (after the perturb'd winds and the storms,)
Under the arching heavens of the afternoon swift passing, and the voices of children
    and women,
The many-moving sea-tides, and I saw the ships how they sail'd,
And the summer approaching with richness, and the fields all busy with labor,
And the infinite separate houses, how they all went on, each with its meals and minutia
    of daily usages,   115
And the streets how their throbbings throbb'd, and the cities pent—lo, then and there,
Falling upon them all and among them all, enveloping me with the rest,
Appear'd the cloud, appear'd the long black trail,
And I knew death, its thought, and the sacred knowledge of deah.

Then with the knowledge of death as walking one side of me,   120
And the thought of death close-walking the other side of me,
And I in the middle as with companions, and as holding the hands of companions,

I fled forth to the hiding receiving night that talks not,
Down to the shores of the water, the path by the swamp in the dimness,
To the solemn shadowy cedars and ghostly pines so still.   125

And the singer so shy to the rest receiv'd me,
The gray-brown bird I know receiv'd us comrades three,
And he sang the carol of death, and a verse for him I love.

From deep secluded recesses,
From the fragrant cedars and the ghostly pines so still,   130
Came the carol of the bird.

And the charm of the carol rapt me,
As I held as if by their hands my comrades in the night,
And the voice of my spirit tallied the song of the bird.

Come lovely and soothing death,   135
Undulate round the world, serenely arriving, arriving,
In the day, in the night, to all, to each,
Sooner or later delicate death.

Prais'd be the fathomless universe,
For life and joy, and for objects and knowledge curious,   140
And for love, sweet love—but praise! praise! praise!
For the sure-enwinding arms of cool-enfolding death.

Dark mother always gliding near with soft feet,
Have none chanted for thee a chant of fullest welcome?
Then I chant it for thee, I glorify thee above all,   145
I bring thee a song that when thou must indeed come, come unfalteringly.

Approach strong deliveress,
When it is so, when thou hast taken them I joyously sing the dead,
Lost in the loving floating ocean of thee,
Laved in the flood of thy bliss O death.   150

From me to thee glad serenades,
Dances for thee I propose saluting thee, adornments and feastings for thee,
And the sights of the open landscape and the high-spread sky are fitting,
And life and the fields, and the huge and thoughtful night.

The night in silence under many a star,   155
The ocean shore and the husky whispering wave whose voice I know,
And the soul turning to thee O vast and well-veil'd death,
And the body gratefully nestling close to thee.

Over the tree-tops I float thee a song,
Over the rising and sinking waves, over the myriad fields and the prairies wide,   160
Over the dense-pack'd cities all and the teeming wharves and ways,
I float this carol with joy, with joy to thee O death.

15

To the tally of my soul,
Loud and strong kept up the gray-brown bird,
With pure deliberate notes spreading filling the night.   165

Loud in the pines and cedars dim,
Clear in the freshness moist and the swamp-perfume,
And I with my comrades there in the night.

While my sight that was bound in my eyes unclosed,
As to long panoramas of visions.   170

And I saw askant the armies,
I saw as in noiseless dreams hundreds of battle-flags,
Borne through the smoke of the battles and pierc'd with missiles I saw them,
And carried hither and yon through the smoke, and torn and bloody,
And at last but a few shreds left on the staffs, (and all in silence,)   175
And the staffs all splinter'd and broken.

I saw battle-corpses, myriads of them,
And the white skeletons of young men, I saw them,
I saw the debris and debris of all the slain soldiers of the war,
But I saw they were not as was thought,   180
They themselves were fully at rest, they suffer'd not,
The living remain'd and suffer'd, the mother suffer'd,
And the wife and the child and the musing comrade suffer'd,
And the armies that remain'd suffer'd.

16

Passing the visions, passing the night,   185
Passing, unloosing the hold of my comrades' hands,
Passing the song of the hermit bird and the tallying song of my soul,
Victorious song, death's outlet song, yet varying ever-altering song,
As low and wailing, yet clear the notes, rising and falling, flooding the night,
Sadly sinking and fainting, as warning and warning, and yet again bursting with
    joy,   190
Covering the earth and filling the spread of the heaven,
As that powerful psalm in the night I heard from recesses,
Passing, I leave thee lilac with heart-shaped leaves,
I leave thee there in the door-yard, blooming, returning with spring.

I cease from my song for thee,   195
From my gaze on thee in the west, fronting the west, communing with thee,
O comrade lustrous with silver face in the night.

Yet each to keep and all, retrievements out of the night,
The song, the wondrous chant of the gray-brown bird,

And the tallying chant, the echo arous'd in my soul,   200
With the lustrous and drooping star with the countenance full of woe,
With the holders holding my hand nearing the call of the bird,
Comrades mine and I in the midst, and their memory ever to keep, for the dead I
          loved so well,
For the sweetest, wisest soul of all my days and lands—and this for his dear sake,
Lilac and star and bird twined with the chant of my soul,   205
There in the fragrant pines and the cedars dusk and dim.

O CAPTAIN! MY CAPTAIN![1]

[1865]

O Captain! my Captain! our fearful trip is done,
The ship has weather'd every rack, the prize we sought is won,
The port is near, the bells I hear, the people all exulting,
While follow eyes the steady keel, the vessel grim and daring;
          But O heart! heart! heart!   5
            O the bleeding drops of red,
              Where on the deck my Captain lies,
                Fallen cold and dead.

O Captain! my Captain! rise up and hear the bells;
Rise up—for you the flag is flung—for you the bugle trills,   10
For you bouquets and ribbon'd wreaths—for you the shores a-crowding,
For you they call, the swaying mass, their eager faces turning;
          Here Captain! dear father!
            This arm beneath your head!
              It is some dream that on the deck,   15
                You've fallen cold and dead.

My Captain does not answer, his lips are pale and still,
My father does not feel my arm, he has no pulse nor will,
The ship is anchor'd safe and sound, its voyage closed and done,
From fearful trip the victor ship comes in with object won;   20
          Exult O shores, and ring O bells!
            But I with mournful tread,
              Walk the deck my Captain lies,
                Fallen cold and dead.

CHANTING THE SQUARE DEIFIC[2]

[1865]

1

Chanting the square deific, out of the One advancing, out of the sides,
Out of the old and new, out of the square entirely divine,

---

[1] Whitman wrote four elegies on Lincoln—"O Captain! My Captain!" "When Lilacs
Last in the Dooryard Bloom'd," "Hush'd Be the Camps To-Day," and "Death Carol."
The last-named is now printed in italics as part of "When Lilacs Last in the Dooryard
Bloom'd."

[2] Whitman proposes not a Trinity but a "square" of four members—Jehovah, Christ,
Satan, and "Santa Spirita."

Solid, four-sided, (all the sides needed,) from this side Jehovah am I,
Old Brahm [2] I, and I Saturnius [3] am;
Not Time affects me—I am Time, old, modern as any, 5
Unpersuadable, relentless, executing righteous judgments,
As the Earth, the Father, the brown old Kronos, with laws,
Aged beyond computation, yet ever new, ever with those mighty laws rolling,
Relentless I forgive no man—whoever sins dies—I will have that man's life;
Therefore let none expect mercy—have the seasons, gravitation, the appointed days,
    mercy? no more have I, 10
But as the seasons and gravitation, and as all the appointed days that forgive not,
I dispense from this side judgments inexorable without the least remorse.

2

Consolator most mild, the promis'd one advancing,
With gentle hand extended, the mightier God am I,
Foretold by prophets and poets in their most rapt prophecies and poems, 15
From this side, lo! the Lord Christ gazes—lo! Hermes I—lo! mine is Hercules' face,
All sorrow, labor, suffering, I, tallying it, absorb in myself,
Many times have I been rejected, taunted, put in prison, and crucified, and many
    times shall be again,
All the world have I given up for my dear brothers' and sisters' sake, for the soul's sake,
Wending my way through the homes of men, rich or poor, with the kiss of affection, 20
For I am affection, I am the cheer-bringing God, with hope and all-enclosing charity,
With indulgent words as to children, with fresh and sane words, mine only,
Young and strong I pass knowing well I am destin'd myself to an early death;
But my charity has no death—my wisdom dies not, neither early nor late,
And my sweet love bequeath'd here and elsewhere never dies. 25

3

Aloof, dissatisfied, plotting revolt,
Comrade of criminals, brother of slaves,
Crafty, despised, a drudge, ignorant,
With sudra [4] face and worn brow, black, but in the depths of my heart, proud as any,
Lifted now and always against whoever scorning assumes to rule me, 30
Morose, full of guile, full of reminiscences, brooding, with many wiles,
(Though it was thought I was baffled and dispel'd, and my wiles done, but that will
    never be,)
Defiant, I, Satan, still live, still utter words, in new lands duly appearing, (and old
    ones also,)
Permanent here from my side, warlike, equal with any, real as any,
Nor time nor change shall ever change me or my words. 35

---

[2] Usually Brahma, the Creator in Hindu theology.
[3] Ancient Roman deity, later identified with the Greek deity, Cronus, named in line 7.
[4] The lowest of the Hindu castes.

4

Santa Spirita, breather, life,
Beyond the light, lighter than light,
Beyond the flames of hell, joyous, leaping easily above hell,
Beyond Paradise, perfumed solely with mine own perfume,
Including all life on earth, touching, including God, including Saviour and Satan,   40
Ethereal, pervading all, (for without me what were all? what were God?)
Essence of forms, life of the real identities, permanent, positive, (namely the unseen,)
Life of the great round world, the sun and stars, and of man, I, the general soul,
Here the square finishing, the solid, I the most solid,
Breathe my breath also through these songs.   45

PIONEERS! O PIONEERS!
[1865]

Come my tan-faced children,
Follow well in order, get your weapons ready,
Have you your pistols? have you your sharp-edged axes?
     Pioneers! O pioneers!

For we cannot tarry here,   5
We must march my darlings, we must bear the brunt of danger,
We the youthful sinewy races, all the rest on us depend,
     Pioneers! O pioneers!

O you youths, Western youths,
So impatient, full of action, full of manly pride and friendship,   10
Plain I see you Western youths, see you tramping with the foremost,
     Pioneers! O pioneers!

Have the elder races halted?
Do they droop and end their lesson, wearied over there beyond the seas?
We take up the task eternal, and the burden and the lesson,   15
     Pioneers! O pioneers!

All the past we leave behind,
We debouch upon a newer mightier world, varied world,
Fresh and strong the world we seize, world of labor and the march,
     Pioneers! O pioneers!   20

We detachments steady throwing,
Down the edges, through the passes, up the mountains steep,
Conquering, holding, daring, venturing as we go the unknown ways,
     Pioneers! O pioneers!

We primeval forests felling,   25
We the rivers stemming, vexing we and piercing deep the mines within,
We the surface broad surveying, we the virgin soil upheaving,
     Pioneers! O pioneers!

Colorado men are we,
From the peaks gigantic, from the great sierras and the high plateaus,   30
From the mine and from the gully, from the hunting trail we come,
Pioneers! O pioneers!

From Nebraska, from Arkansas,
Central inland race are we, from Missouri, with the continental blood intervein'd,
All the hands of comrades clasping, all the Southern, all the Northern,   35
Pioneers! O pioneers!

O resistless restless race!
O beloved race in all! O my breast aches with tender love for all!
O I mourn and yet exult, I am rapt with love for all,
Pioneers! O pioneers!   40

Raise the mighty mother mistress,
Waving high the delicate mistress, over all the starry mistress, (bend your heads all,)
Raise the fang'd and warlike mistress, stern, impassive, weapon'd mistress,
Pioneers! O pioneers!

See my children, resolute children,   45
By those swarms upon our rear we must never yield or falter,
Ages back in ghostly millions frowning there behind us urging,
Pioneers! O pioneers!

On and on the compact ranks,
With accessions ever waiting, with the places of the dead quickly fill'd,   50
Through the battle, through defeat, moving yet and never stopping,
Pioneers! O pioneers!

O to die advancing on!
Are there some of us to droop and die? has the hour come?
Then upon the march we fittest die, soon and sure the gap is fill'd,   55
Pioneers! O pioneers!

All the pulses of the world,
Falling in they beat for us, with the Western movement beat,
Holding single or together, steady moving to the front, all for us,
Pioneers! O pioneers!   60

Life's involv'd and varied pageants,
All the forms and shows, all the workmen at their work,
All the seamen and the landsmen, all the masters with their slaves,
Pioneers! O pioneers!

All the hapless silent lovers,   65
All the prisoners in the prisons, all the righteous and the wicked,
All the joyous, all the sorrowing, all the living, all the dying,
Pioneers! O pioneers!

       I too with my soul and body,
We, a curious trio, picking, wandering on our way,
Through these shores amid the shadows, with the apparitions pressing,   70
       Pioneers! O pioneers!

       Lo, the darting bowling orb!
Lo, the brother orbs around, all the clustering suns and planets,
All the dazzling days, all the mystic nights with dreams,   75
       Pioneers! O pioneers!

       These are of us, they are with us,
All for primal needed work, while the followers there in embryo wait behind,
We to-day's procession heading, we the route for travel clearing,
       Pioneers! O pioneers!   80

       O you daughters of the West!
O you young and elder daughters! O you mothers and you wives!
Never must you be divided, in our ranks you move united,
       Pioneers! O pioneers!

       Minstrels latent on the prairies!   •   85
(Shrouded bards of other lands, you may rest, you have done your work,)
Soon I hear you coming warbling, soon you rise and tramp amid us,
       Pioneers! O pioneers!

       Not for delectations sweet,
Not the cushion and the slipper, not the peaceful and the studious,   90
Not the riches safe and palling, not for us the tame enjoyment,
       Pioneers! O pioneers!

       Do the feasters gluttonous feast?
Do the corpulent sleepers sleep? have they lock'd and bolted doors?
Still be ours the diet hard, and the blanket on the ground,   95
       Pioneers! O pioneers!

       Has the night descended?
Was the road of late so toilsome? did we stop discouraged nodding on our way?
Yet a passing hour I yield you in your tracks to pause oblivious,
       Pioneers! O pioneers!

       Till with sound of trumpet,
Far, far off the daybreak call—hark! how loud and clear I hear it wind,
Swift! to the head of the army!—swift! spring to your places,
       Pioneers! O pioneers!

WHEN I HEARD THE LEARN'D ASTRONOMER
[1865]

When I heard the learn'd astronomer,
When the proofs, the figures, were ranged in columns before me,
When I was shown the charts and diagrams, to add, divide, and measure them,
When I sitting heard the astronomer where he lectured with much applause in the
    lecture-room,

How soon unaccountable I became tired and sick,
Till rising and gliding out I wander'd off by myself,
In the mystical moist night-air, and from time to time,
Look'd up in perfect silence at the stars.

WHISPERS OF HEAVENLY DEATH
[1871 (1868)]

Whispers of heavenly death murmur'd I hear,
Labial gossip of night, sibilant chorals,
Footsteps gently ascending, mystical breezes wafted soft and low,
Ripples of unseen rivers, tides of a current flowing, forever flowing,
(Or is it the plashing of tears? the measureless waters of human tears?)

I see, just see skyward, great cloud-masses,
Mournfully slowly they roll, silently swelling and mixing,
With at times a half-dimm'd sadden'd far-off star,
Appearing and disappearing.

(Some parturition rather, some solemn immortal birth;
On the frontiers to eyes impenetrable,
Some soul is passing over.)

A NOISELESS PATIENT SPIDER
[1871 (1868)]

A noiseless patient spider,
I mark'd where on a little promontory it stood isolated,
Mark'd how to explore the vacant vast surrounding,
It launch'd forth filament, filament, filament, out of itself,
Ever unreeling them, ever tirelessly speeding them.

And you O my soul where you stand,
Surrounded, detached, in measureless oceans of space,
Ceaselessly musing, venturing, throwing, seeking the spheres to connect them,
Till the bridge you will need be form'd, till the ductile anchor hold,
Till the gossamer thread you fling catch somewhere, O my soul.

THE LAST INVOCATION
[1871 (1868)]

At the last, tenderly,
From the walls of the powerful fortress'd house,
From the clasp of the knitted locks, from the keep of the well-closed doors,
Let me be wafted.
Let me glide noiselessly forth;
With the key of softness unlock the locks—with a whisper,
Set ope the doors O soul.

Tenderly—be not impatient,
(Strong is your hold O mortal flesh,
Strong is your hold O love.)

PASSAGE TO INDIA [1]
[1871]

1

Singing my days,
Singing the great achievements of the present,
Singing the strong light works of engineers,
Our modern wonders, (the antique ponderous Seven outvied,)
In the Old World the east the Suez canal,   5
The New by its mighty railroad spann'd,[2]
The seas inlaid with eloquent gentle wires;
Yet first to sound, and ever sound, the cry with thee O soul,
The Past! the Past! the Past!

The Past—the dark unfathom'd retrospect!   10
The teeming gulf—the sleepers and the shadows!
The past—the infinite greatness of the past!
For what is the present after all but a growth out of the past?
(As a projectile form'd, impell'd, passing a certain line, still keeps on,
So the present, utterly form'd, impell'd by the past.)   15

2

Passage O soul to India!
Eclaircise [3] the myths Asiatic, the primitive fables.

Not you alone proud truths of the world,
Nor you alone ye facts of modern science,
But myths and fables of eld, Asia's, Africa's fables,   20
The far-darting beams of the spirit, the unloos'd dreams,
The deep diving bibles and legends,
The daring plots of the poets, the elder religions;
O you temples fairer than lilies pour'd over by the rising sun!
O you fables spurning the known, eluding the hold of the known, mounting to heaven! 25

---

[1] In his preface to the 1876 edition to *Leaves of Grass*, the poet writes about his conception of "Passage to India" (also in *Complete Prose Works*, Philadelphia, 1892). Key sentences: "I am not sure but the last inclosing sublimation of race or poem is what it thinks of death . . . it is no less than this idea of immortality, above all other ideas, that is to enter into and vivify and give crowning religious stamp to democracy in the New World."

[2] In 1869 the first transcontinental railroad was completed when the Union Pacific, built westward from Omaha, joined the Central Pacific, built eastward from San Francisco at Promontory Point, Utah.

[3] Illuminate, clarify.

You lofty and dazzling towers, pinnacled, red as roses, burnish'd with gold!
Towers of fables immortal fashion'd from mortal dreams!
You too I welcome and fully the same as the rest!
You too with joy I sing.

Passage to India!   30
Lo, soul, seest thou not God's purpose from the first?
The earth to be spann'd, connected by network,
The races, neighbors, to marry and be given in marriage,
The oceans to be cross'd, the distant brought near,
The lands to be welded together.   35

A worship new I sing,
You captains, voyagers, explorers, yours,
You engineers, you architects, machinists, yours,
You, not for trade or transportation only,
But in God's name, and for thy sake O soul.   40

3

Passage to India!
Lo soul for thee of tableaus twain,[4]
I see in one the Suez canal initiated, open'd,
I see the procession of steamships, the Empress Eugenie's [5] leading the van,
I mark from on deck the strange landscape, the pure sky, the level sand in the distance, 45
I pass swiftly the picturesque groups, the workmen gather'd,
The gigantic dredging machines.

In one again, different, (yet thine, all thine, O soul, the same,)
I see over my own continent the Pacific railroad surmounting every barrier,
I see continual trains of cars winding along the Platte carrying freight and pas-
          sengers,   50
I hear the locomotives rushing and roaring, and the shrill steam-whistle,
I hear the echoes reverberate through the grandest scenery in the world,
I cross the Laramie plains, I note the rocks in grotesque shapes, the buttes,
I see the plentiful larkspur and wild onions, the barren, colorless, sage-deserts,
I see in glimpses afar or towering immediately above me the great mountains, I see the
          Wind river and the Wahsatch mountains,   55
I see the Monument mountain and the Eagle's Nest, I pass the Promontory, I ascend
          the Nevadas,
I scan the noble Elk mountain and wind around its base,
I see the Humboldt range, I thread the valley and cross the river,
I see the clear waters of lake Tahoe, I see forests of majestic pines,
Or crossing the great desert, the alkaline plains, I behold enchanting mirages of waters
          and meadows,   60
Marking through these and after all, in duplicate slender lines,

---

[4] Two pictures, both of 1869: the opening of the Suez Canal and the completion of
the Pacific Railway.

[5] The Empress Eugénie was on board the first ship to pass through the Canal.

Bridging the three or four thousand miles of land travel,
Tying the Eastern to the Western sea,
The road between Europe and Asia.

(Ah Genoese [6] thy dream! thy dream!
Centuries after thou art laid in thy grave, 65
The shore thou foundest verifies thy dream.)

4

Passage to India!
Struggles of many a captain, tales of many a sailor dead,
Over my mood stealing and spreading they come, 70
Like clouds and cloudlets in the unreach'd sky.

Along all history, down the slopes,
As a rivulet running, sinking now, and now again to the surface rising,
A ceaseless thought, a varied train—lo, soul, to thee, thy sight, they rise,
The plans, the voyages again, the expeditions; 75
Again Vasco da Gama [7] sails forth,
Again the knowledge gain'd, the mariner's compass,
Lands found and nations born, thou born America,
For purpose vast, man's long probation fill'd,
Thou rondure of the world at last accomplish'd. 80

5

O vast Rondure, swimming in space,
Cover'd all over with visible power and beauty,
Alternate light and day and the teeming spiritual darkness,
Unspeakable high processions of sun and moon and countless stars above,
Below, the manifold grass and waters, animals, mountains, trees, 85
With inscrutable purpose, some hidden prophetic intention,
Now first it seems my thought begins to span thee.

Down from the gardens of Asia descending radiating,
Adam and Eve appear, then their myriad progeny after them,
Wandering, yearning, curious, with restless explorations, 90
With questionings, baffled, formless, feverish, with never-happy hearts,
With that sad incessant refrain, *Wherefore unsatisfied soul? and Whither O mocking
    life?*

Ah who shall soothe these feverish children?
Who justify these restless explorations?
Who speak the secret of impassive earth? 95
Who bind it to us? what is this separate Nature so unnatural?

---

[6] Columbus, who discovered America while seeking India.

   [7] Portuguese explorer (1469?-1524) who sailed around the Cape of Good Hope to
India.

What is this earth to our affections? (unloving earth, without a throb to answer ours,
Cold earth, the place of graves.)

Yet soul be sure the first intent remains, and shall be carried out,
Perhaps even now the time has arrived. 100

After the seas are all cross'd, (as they seem already cross'd,)
After the great captains and engineers have accomplish'd their work,
After the noble inventors, after the scientists, the chemist, the geologist, ethnologist,
Finally shall come the poet worthy that name,
The true son of God shall come singing his songs. 105

Then not your deeds only O voyagers, O scientists and inventors shall be justified,
All these hearts as of fretted children shall be sooth'd,
All affection shall be fully responded to, the secret shall be told,
All these separations and gaps shall be taken up and hook'd and link'd together,
The whole earth, this cold, impassive, voiceless earth, shall be completely justified, 110
Trinitas divine shall be gloriously accomplish'd and compacted by the true son of God,
          the poet,
(He shall indeed pass the straits and conquer the mountains,
He shall double the cape of Good Hope to some purpose,)
Nature and Man shall be disjoin'd and diffused no more,
The true son of God shall absolutely fuse them. 115

6

Year at whose wide-flung door I sing!
Year of the purpose accomplish'd!
Year of the marriage of continents, climates and oceans!
(No mere doge of Venice now wedding the Adriatic,)[8]
I see O year in you the vast terraqueous globe given and giving all, 120
Europe to Asia, Africa join'd, and they to the New World,
The lands, geographies, dancing before you, holding a festival garland,
As brides and bridegrooms hand in hand.

Passage to India!
Cooling airs from Caucasus far, soothing cradle of man,[9] 125
The river Euphrates flowing, the past lit up again.

Lo soul, the retrospect brought forward,
The old, most populous, wealthiest of earth's lands,
The streams of the Indus and the Ganges and their many affluents,
(I my shores of America walking to-day behold, resuming all,) 130
The tale of Alexander on his warlike marches suddenly dying,
On one side China and on the other side Persia and Arabia,

---

[8] The doge, or chief magistrate of the republic of Venice, annually threw a gold
ring into the Adriatic Sea in an emblematic wedding of the State and the Sea.

[9] Reference is to the theory that the Caucasus was the original home of man.

To the south the great seas and the bay of Bengal,[10]
The flowing literatures, tremendous epics, religions, castes,
Old occult Brahma interminably far back, the tender and junior Buddha, 135
Central and southern empires and all their belongings, possessors,
The wars of Tamerlane,[11] the reign of Aurungzebe,[12]
The traders, rulers, explorers, Moslems, Venetians, Byzantium, the Arabs, Portuguese,
The first travelers famous yet, Marco Polo,[13] Batouta the Moor,[14]
Doubts to be solv'd, the map incognita, blanks to be fill'd, 140
The foot of man unstay'd, the hands never at rest,
Thyself O soul that will not brook a challenge.

The mediæval navigators rise before me,
The world of 1492, with its awaken'd enterprise,
Something swelling in humanity now like the sap of the earth in spring, 145
The sunset splendor of chivalry declining.

And who art thou sad shade?
Gigantic, visionary, thyself a visionary,
With majestic limbs and pious beaming eyes,
Spreading around with every look of thine a golden world, 150
Enhuing it with gorgeous hues.

As the chief histrion,
Down to the footlights walks in some great scena,
Dominating the rest I see the Admiral himself,
(History's type of courage, action, faith,) 155
Behold him sail from Palos leading his little fleet,
His voyage behold, his return, his great fame,
His misfortunes, calumniators, behold him a prisoner, chain'd,
Behold his dejection, poverty, death.

(Curious in time I stand, noting the efforts of heroes, 160
Is the deferment long? bitter the slander, poverty, death?
Lies the seed unreck'd for centuries in the ground? lo, to God's due occasion,
Uprising in the night, it sprouts, blooms,
And fills the earth with use and beauty.)

7

Passage indeed O soul to primal thought, 165
Not lands and seas alone, thy own clear freshness,
The young maturity of brood and bloom,
To realms of budding bibles.

---

[10] Alexander the Great died in 323 B. C. as he was returning from his invasion of India.
[11] Mongol invader of India in 1398.
[12] Last great emperor of Hindustan (1619-1707).
[13] Italian traveler (1254-1324), who visited India on his way home from China.
[14] Mohammad ibn Abd Allah (1303-1377) called Batutah, traveler in Asia and Africa.

O soul, repressless, I with thee and thou with me,
Thy circumnavigation of the world begin,   170
Of man, the voyage of his mind's return,
To reason's early paradise,
Back, back to wisdom's birth, to innocent intuitions,
Again with fair creation.

8

O we can wait no longer,   175
We too take ship O soul,
Joyous we too launch out on trackless seas,
Fearless for unknown shores on waves of ecstasy to sail,
Amid the wafting winds, (thou pressing me to thee, I thee to me, O soul,)
Caroling free, singing our song of God,   180
Chanting our chant of pleasant exploration.

With laugh and many a kiss,
(Let others deprecate, let others weep for sin, remorse, humiliation,)
O soul thou pleasest me, I thee.
Ah more than any priest O soul we too believe in God,   185
But with the mystery of God we dare not dally.

O soul thou pleasest me, I thee,
Sailing these seas or on the hills, or waking in the night,
Thoughts, silent thoughts, of Time and Space and Death, like waters flowing,
Bear me indeed as through the regions infinite,   190
Whose air I breathe, whose ripples hear, lave me all over,
Bathe me O God in thee, mounting to thee,
I and my soul to range in range of thee.

O Thou transcendent,
Nameless, the fibre and the breath,   195
Light of the light, shedding forth universes, thou centre of them,
Thou mightier centre of the true, the good, the loving,
Thou moral, spiritual fountain—affection's source—thou reservoir,
(O pensive soul of me—O thirst unsatisfied—waitest not there?
Waitest not haply for us somewhere there the Comrade perfect?)   200
Thou pulse—thou motive of the stars, suns, systems,
That, circling, move in order, safe, harmonious,
Athwart the shapeless vastnesses of space,
How should I think, how breathe a single breath, how speak, if, out of myself,
I could not launch, to those, superior universes?   205

Swiftly I shrivel at the thought of God,
At Nature and its wonders, Time and Space and Death,
But that I, turning, call to thee O soul, thou actual Me,
And lo, thou gently masterest the orbs,
Thou matest Time, smilest content at Death,   210
And fillest, swellest full the vastnesses of Space.

Greater than stars or suns,
Bounding O soul thou journeyest forth;
What love than thine and ours could wider amplify?
What aspirations, wishes, outvie thine and ours O soul?   215
What dreams of the ideal? what plans of purity, perfection, strength?
What cheerful willingness for others' sake to give up all?
For others' sake to suffer all?

Reckoning ahead O soul, when thou, the time achiev'd,
The seas all cross'd, weather'd the capes, the voyage done,   220
Surrounded, copest, frontest God, yieldest, the aim attain'd,
As filled with friendship, love complete, the Elder Brother found,
The Younger melts in fondness in his arms.

9

Passage to more than India!
Are thy wings plumed indeed for such far flights?   225
O soul, voyagest thou indeed on voyages like those?
Disportest thou on waters such as those?
Soundest below the Sanscrit and the Vedas?
Then have thy bent unleash'd.

Passage to you, your shores, ye aged fierce enigmas!   230
Passage to you, to mastership of you, ye strangling problems!
You, strew'd with the wrecks of skeletons, that, living, never reach'd you.

Passage to more than India!
O secret of the earth and sky!
Of you O waters of the sea! O winding creeks and rivers!   235
Of you O woods and fields! of you strong mountains of my land!
Of you O prairies! of you gray rocks!
O morning red! O clouds! O rain and snows!
O day and night, passage to you!

O sun and moon and all you stars! Sirius and Jupiter!   240
Passage to you!

Passage, immediate passage! the blood burns in my veins!
Away O soul! hoist instantly the anchor!
Cut the hawsers—haul out—shake out every sail!
Have we not stood here like trees in the ground long enough?   245
Have we not grovel'd here long enough, eating and drinking like mere brutes?
Have we not darken'd and dazed ourselves with books long enough?

Sail forth—steer for the deep waters only,
Reckless O soul, exploring, I with thee, and thou with me,
For we are bound where mariner has not yet dared to go,   250
And we will risk the ship, ourselves and all.

O my brave soul!
O farther farther sail!
O daring joy, but safe! are they not all the seas of God?
O farther, farther, farther sail!   255

PRAYER OF COLUMBUS
[1876 (1874)]

A batter'd, wreck'd old man,
Thrown on this savage shore, far, far from home,
Pent by the sea and dark rebellious brows, twelve dreary months,
Sore, stiff with many toils, sicken'd and nigh to death,
I take my way along the island's edge,   5
Venting a heavy heart.

I am too full of woe!
Haply I may not live another day;
I cannot rest O God, I cannot eat or drink or sleep,
Till I put forth myself, my prayer, once more to Thee,   10
Breathe, bathe myself once more in Thee, commune with Thee,
Report myself once more to Thee.

Thou knowest my years entire, my life,
My long and crowded life of active work, not adoration merely;
Thou knowest the prayers and vigils of my youth,   15
Thou knowest my manhood's solemn and visionary meditations,
Thou knowest how before I commenced I devoted all to come to Thee,
Thou knowest I have in age ratified all those vows and strictly kept them,
Thou knowest I have not once lost nor faith nor ecstasy in Thee,
In shackles, prison'd, in disgrace, repining not,   20
Accepting all from Thee, as duly come from Thee.

All my emprises have been fill'd with Thee,
My speculations, plans, begun and carried on in thoughts of Thee,
Sailing the deep or journeying the land for Thee;
Intentions, purports, aspirations mine, leaving results to Thee. 25

O I am sure they really came from Thee,
The urge, the ardor, the unconquerable will,
The potent, felt, interior command, stronger than words,
A message from the Heavens whispering to me even in sleep,
These sped me on.   30

By me and these the work so far accomplish'd,
By me earth's elder cloy'd and stifled lands uncloy'd, unloos'd,
By me the hemispheres rounded and tied, the unknown to the known.

The end I know not, it is all in Thee,
Or small or great I know not—haply what broad fields, what lands, 35

Haply the brutish measureless human undergrowth I know,
Transplanted there may rise to stature, knowledge worthy Thee,
Haply the swords I know may there indeed be turn'd to reaping-tools,
Haply the lifeless cross I know, Europe's dead cross, may bud and blossom there.

One effort more, my altar this bleak sand;   40
That Thou O God my life hast lighted,
With ray of light, steady, ineffable, vouchsafed of Thee,
Light rare untellable, lighting the very light,
Beyond all signs, descriptions, languages;
For that O God, be it my latest word, here on my knees,   45
Old, poor, and paralyzed, I thank Thee.

My terminus near,
The clouds already closing in upon me,
The voyage balk'd, the course disputed, lost,
I yield my ships to Thee.   50

My hands, my limbs grow nerveless,
My brain feels rack'd, bewilder'd,
Let the old timbers part, I will not part,
I will cling fast to Thee, O God, though the waves buffet me,
Thee, Thee at least I know.   55

Is it the prophet's thought I speak, or am I raving?
What do I know of life? what of myself?
I know not even my own work past or present,
Dim ever-shifting guesses of it spread before me,
Of newer better worlds, their mighty parturition,   60
Mocking, perplexing me.

And these things I see suddenly, what mean they?
As if some miracle, some hand divine unseal'd my eyes,
Shadowy vast shapes smile through the air and sky,
And on the distant waves sail countless ships,   65
And anthems in new tongues I hear saluting me.

SONG OF THE UNIVERSAL
[1876 (1874)]

1

Come said the Muse,
Sing me a song no poet yet has chanted,
Sing me the universal.

In this broad earth of ours,
Amid the measureless grossness and the slag,   5
Enclosed and safe within its central heart,
Nestles the seed perfection.

By every life a share or more or less,
None born but it is born, conceal'd or unconceal'd the seed is waiting.

2

Lo! keen-eyed towering science,   10
As from tall peaks the modern overlooking,
Successive absolute fiats issuing.

Yet again, lo! the soul, above all science,
For it has history gather'd like husks around the globe,
For it the entire star-myriads roll through the sky.   15

In spiral routes by long detours,
(As a much-tacking ship upon the sea,)
For it the partial to the permanent flowing,
For it the real to the ideal tends.

For it the mystic evolution,   20
Not the right only justified, what we call evil also justified.

Forth from their masks, no matter what,
From the huge festering trunk, from craft and guile and tears,
Health to emerge and joy, joy universal.

Out of the bulk, the morbid and the shallow,   25
Out of the bad majority, the varied countless frauds of men and states,
Electric, antiseptic yet, cleaving, suffusing all,
Only the good is universal.

3

Over the mountain-growths disease and sorrow,
An uncaught bird is ever hovering, hovering,   30
High in the purer, happier air.

From imperfection's murkiest cloud,
Darts always forth one ray of perfect light,
One flash of heaven's glory.

To fashion's, custom's discord,   35
To the mad Babel-din, the deafening orgies,
Soothing each lull a strain is heard, just heard,
From some far shore the final chorus sounding.

O the blest eyes, the happy hearts,
That see, that know the guiding thread so fine,   40
Along the mighty labyrinth.

4

And thou America,
For the scheme's culmination, its thought and its reality,
For these (not for thyself) thou hast arrived.

Thou too surroundest all,   45
Embracing carrying welcoming all, thou too by pathways broad and new,
To the ideal tendest.

The measur'd faiths of other lands, the grandeurs of the past,
Are not for thee, but grandeurs of thine own,
Deific faiths and amplitudes, absorbing, comprehending all,   50
All eligible to all.

All, all for immortality,
Love like the light silently wrapping all,
Nature's amelioration blessing all,
The blossoms, fruits of ages, orchards divine and certain,   55
Forms, objects, growths, humanities, to spiritual images ripening.

Give me O God to sing that thought,
Give me, give him or her I love this quenchless faith,
In Thy ensemble, whatever else withheld withhold not from us,
Belief in plan of Thee enclosed in Time and Space,   60
Health, peace, salvation universal.

Is it a dream?
Nay but the lack of it the dream,
And failing it life's lore and wealth a dream,
And all the world a dream.   65

PATROLING BARNEGAT[1]
[1881 (1880)]

Wild, wild the storm, and the sea high running,
Steady the roar of the gale, with incessant undertone muttering,
Shouts of demoniac laughter fitfully piercing and pealing,
Waves, air, midnight, their savagest trinity lashing,
Out in the shadows there milk-white combs careering,
On beachy slush and sand spirts of snow fierce slanting,
Where through the murk the easterly death-wind breasting,
Through cutting swirl and spray watchful and firm advancing,
(That in the distance! is that a wreck? is the red signal flaring?)
Slush and sand of the beach tireless till daylight wending,
Steadily, slowly, through hoarse roar never remitting,

---

[1] Barnegat Inlet, on the south side of which is a lighthouse, connects Barnegat Bay, on the east coast of New Jersey, with the Atlantic.

Along the midnight edge by those milk-white combs careering,
A group of dim, weird forms, struggling, the night confronting,
That savage trinity warily watching.

GOOD-BYE MY FANCY!
[1891]

Good-bye my Fancy!
Farewell dear mate, dear love!
I'm going away, I know not where,
Or to what fortune, or whether I may ever see you again,
So Good-bye my Fancy.   5

Now for my last—let me look back a moment;
The slower fainter ticking of the clock is in me,
Exit, nightfall, and soon the heart-thud stopping.

Long have we lived, joy'd, caress'd together;
Delightful!—now separation—Good-bye my Fancy.   10

Yet let me not be too hasty,
Long indeed have we lived, slept, filter'd, become really blended into one;
Then if we die we die together, (yes, we'll remain one,)
If we go anywhere we'll go together to meet what happens,
May-be we'll be better off and blither, and learn something,   15
May-be it is yourself now really ushering me to the true songs, (who knows?)
May-be it is you the mortal knob really undoing, turning—so now finally,
Good-bye—and hail! my Fancy.

PREFACE TO 1855 EDITION OF "LEAVES OF GRASS"

AMERICA does not repel the past or what it has produced under its forms or amid other politics or the idea of castes or the old religions . . . accepts the lesson with calmness . . . is not so impatient as has been supposed that the slough still sticks to opinions and manners and literature while the life which served its requirements has passed into the new life of the new forms . . . perceives that the corpse is slowly borne from the eating and sleeping rooms of the house . . . perceives that it waits a little while in the door . . . that it was fittest for its days . . . that its action has descended to the stalwart and wellshaped heir who approaches . . . and that he shall be fittest for his days.

The Americans of all nations at any time upon the earth have probably the fullest poetical nature. The United States themselves are essentially the greatest poem. In the history of the earth hitherto the largest and most stirring appear tame and orderly to their ampler largeness and stir. Here at last is something in the doings of man that corresponds with the broadcast doings of the day and night. Here is not merely a nation but a teeming nation of nations. Here is action untied from strings necessarily blind to particulars and details magnificently moving in vast masses. Here is the hospitality which forever indicates heroes. . . . Here are the roughs and beards and space and ruggedness and nonchalance that the soul loves. Here the performance disdaining the trivial unapproached in the tremendous audacity of its crowds and groupings and the push of its perspective spreads with crampless and flowing breadth and showers its prolific and splendid extravagance. One sees it must indeed own the riches of the summer and winter, and need never be bankrupt while corn grows from the ground or the orchards drop apples or the bays contain fish or men beget children upon women.

Other states indicate themselves in their deputies . . . but the genius of the United States is not best or most in its executives or legislatures, nor in its ambassadors or authors or colleges or churches or parlors, nor even in its newspapers or inventors . . . but always most in the common people. Their manners speech dress friendships—the freshness and candor of their physiognomy—the picturesque looseness of their carriage . . . their deathless attachment to freedom—their aversion to anything indecorous or soft or mean—the practical acknowledgment of the citizens of one state by the citizens of all other states—the fierceness of their roused resentment—their curiosity and welcome of novelty—their self-esteem and wonderful sympathy—their susceptibility to a slight —the air they have of persons who never knew how it felt to stand in the presence of superiors—the fluency of their speech —their delight in music, the sure symptom of manly tenderness and native elegance of soul . . . their good temper and openhandedness—the terrible significance of their elections—the President's taking off his hat to them not they to him—these too are unrhymed poetry. It awaits the gigantic and generous treatment worthy of it.

The largeness of nature or the nation were monstrous without a corresponding largeness and generosity of the spirit of the citizen. Not nature nor swarming states nor streets and steamships nor prosperous business nor farms nor capital nor learning may suffice for the ideal of man . . . nor suffice the poet. No reminiscences may suffice either. A live nation can always cut a deep mark and can have the best authority the cheapest . . . namely from its own soul. This is the sum of the profitable uses of individuals or states and of present action and grandeur and of the subjects of poets.—As if it were necessary to trot back generation after generation to the eastern records! As if the beauty and sacredness of the demonstrable must fall behind that of the mythical! As if men do not make their mark out of any times! As if the opening of the western continent by discovery and what has transpired since in North and South America were less than the small theatre of the antique or the aimless sleepwalking of the middle ages! The pride of the United States leaves the wealth and finesse of the cities and all returns of commerce and agriculture and all the magnitude of geography or shows of exterior victory to enjoy the breed of fullsized men or one fullsized man unconquerable and simple.

The American poets are to enclose old and new for America is the race of races. Of them a bard is to be commensurate with a people. To him the other continents arrive as contributions . . . he gives them reception for their sake and his own sake. His spirit responds to his country's spirit . . . he incarnates its geography and natural life and rivers and lakes. Mississippi with annual freshets and changing chutes, Missouri and Columbia and Ohio and Saint Lawrence with the falls and beautiful masculine Hudson, do not embouchure [1] where they spend themselves more than they embouchure into him. The blue breadth over the inland sea of Virginia and Maryland and the sea off Massachusetts and Maine and over Manhattan bay and over Champlain and Erie and over Ontario and Huron and Michigan and Superior, and over the Texan and Mexican and Floridian and Cuban seas and over the seas off California and Oregon, is not tallied by the blue breadth of the waters below more

---

[1] Whitman here uses the noun for "mouth of a river" as a verb for "empty."

than the breadth of above and below is tallied by him. When the long Atlantic coast stretches longer and the Pacific coast stretches longer he easily stretches with them north or south. He spans between them also from east to west and reflects what is between them. On him rise solid growths that offset the growths of pine and cedar and hemlock and liveoak and locust and chestnut and cypress and hickory and limetree and cottonwood and tuliptree and cactus and wildvine and tamarind and persimmon . . . and tangles as tangled as any canebreak or swamp . . . and forests coated with transparent ice and icicles hanging from the boughs and crackling in the wind . . . and sides and peaks of mountains . . . and pasturage sweet and free as savannah or upland or prairie . . . with flights and songs and screams that answer those of the wildpigeon and high-hold and orchard-oriole and coot and surf-duck and redshouldered-hawk and fish-hawk and white-ibis and indian-hen and cat-owl and water-pheasant and qua-bird and pied-sheldrake and blackbird and mockingbird and buzzard and condor and night-heron and eagle. To him the hered-itary countenance descends both mother's and father's. To him enter the essences of the real things and past and present events —of the enormous diversity of temperature and agriculture and mines—the tribes of red aborigines—the weatherbeaten vessels entering new ports or making landings on rocky coasts—the first settlements north or south—the rapid stature and muscle—the haughty defiance of '76, and the war and peace and formation of the constitu-tion . . . the union always surrounded by blatherers and always calm and impreg-nable—the perpetual coming of immigrants —the wharf-hem'd cities and superior marine—the unsurveyed interior—the log-houses and clearings and wild animals and hunters and trappers . . . the free com-merce—the fisheries and whaling and gold-digging—the endless gestation of new states —the convening of Congress every Decem-ber, the members duly coming up from all

climates and the uttermost parts . . . the noble character of the young mechanics and of all free American workmen and workwomen . . . the general ardor and friendliness and enterprise—the perfect equality of the female with the male . . . the large amativeness—the fluid movement of the population—the factories and mer-cantile life and labor-saving machinery—the Yankee swap—the New-York firemen and the target excursion—the southern plantation life—the character of the north-east and of the northwest and southwest —slavery and the tremulous spreading of hands to protect it, and the stern opposi-tion to it which shall never cease till it ceases or the speaking of tongues and the moving of lips cease. For such the expres-sion of the American poet is to be tran-scendent and new. It is to be indirect and not direct or descriptive or epic. Its qual-ity goes through these to much more. Let the age and wars of other nations be chanted and their eras and characters be illustrated and that finish the verse. Not so the great psalm of the republic. Here the theme is creative and has vista. Here comes one among the well-beloved stone-cutters and plans with decision and sci-ence and sees the solid and beautiful forms of the future where there are now no solid forms.

Of all nations the United States with veins full of poetical stuff most need [2] poets and will doubtless have the greatest and use them the greatest. Their Presidents shall not be their common referee so much as their poets shall. Of all mankind the great poet is the equable man. Not in him but off from him things are grotesque or eccentric or fail of their sanity. Nothing out of its place is good and nothing in its place is bad. He bestows on every object or quality its fit proportions neither more nor less. He is the arbiter of the diverse and he is the key. He is the equalizer of his age and land . . . he supplies what wants supplying and checks what wants

_____

[2] "United States" is plural in Whitman.

checking. If peace is the routine out of him speaks the spirit of peace, large, rich, thrifty, building vast and populous cities, encouraging agriculture and the arts and commerce—lighting the study of man, the soul, immortality—federal, state or municipal government, marriage, health, free trade, intertravel by land and sea . . . nothing too close, nothing too far off . . . the stars not too far off. In war he is the most deadly force of the war. Who recruits him recruits horse and foot . . . he fetches parks of artillery the best that engineer ever knew. If the time becomes slothful and heavy he knows how to arouse it . . . he can make every word he speaks draw blood. Whatever stagnates in the flat of custom or obedience or legislation he never stagnates. Obedience does not master him, he masters it. High up out of reach he stands turning a concentrated light . . . he turns the pivot with his finger . . . he baffles the swiftest runners as he stands and easily overtakes and envelops them. The time straying toward infidelity and confections and persiflage he withholds by his steady faith . . . he spreads out his dishes . . . he offers the sweet firmfibred meat that grows men and women. His brain is the ultimate brain. He is no arguer . . . he is judgment. He judges not as the judge judges but as the sun falling around a helpless thing. As he sees the farthest he has the most faith. His thoughts are the hymns of the praise of things. In the talk on the soul and eternity and God off of his equal plane he is silent. He sees eternity less like a play with a prologue and denouement . . . he sees eternity in men and women . . . he does not see men and women as dreams or dots. Faith is the antiseptic of the soul . . . it pervades the common people and preserves them . . . they never give up believing and expecting and trusting. There is that indescribable freshness and unconsciousness about an illiterate person that humbles and mocks the power of the noblest expressive genius. The poet sees for a certainty how one not a great artist may be just as sacred and perfect as the greatest artist. . . . The power to destroy or remould is freely used by him but never the power of attack. What is past is past. If he does not expose superior models and prove himself by every step he takes he is not what is wanted. The presence of the greatest poet conquers . . . not parleying or struggling or any prepared attempts. Now he has passed that way see after him! there is not left any vestige of despair or misanthropy or cunning or exclusiveness or the ignominy of a nativity or color or delusion of hell or the necessity of hell . . . and no man thenceforward shall be degraded for ignorance or weakness or sin.

The greatest poet hardly knows pettiness or triviality. If he breathes into any thing that was before thought small it dilates with the grandeur and life of the universe. He is a seer . . . he is individual . . . he is complete in himself . . . the others are as good as he, only he sees it and they do not. He is not one of the chorus . . . he does not stop for any regulations . . . he is the president of regulation. What the eyesight does to the rest he does to the rest. Who knows the curious mystery of the eyesight? The other senses corroborate themselves, but this is removed from any proof but its own and foreruns the identities of the spiritual world. A single glance of it mocks all the investigations of man and all the instruments and books of the earth and all reasoning. What is marvelous? what is unlikely? what is impossible or baseless or vague? after you have once just opened the space of a peachpit and given audience to far and near and to the sunset and had all things enter with electric swiftness softly and duly without confusion or jostling or jam.

The land and sea, the animals fishes and birds, the sky of heaven and the orbs, the forests mountains and rivers, are not small themes . . . but folks expect of the poet to indicate more than the beauty and dignity which always attach to dumb real objects . . . they expect him to indicate the path between reality and their souls.

Men and women perceive the beauty well enough . . . probably as well as he. The passionate tenacity of hunters, woodmen, early risers, cultivators of gardens and orchards and fields, the love of healthy women for the manly form, seafaring persons, drivers of horses, the passion for light and the open air, all is an old varied sign of the unfailing perception of beauty and of a residence of the poetic in outdoor people. They can never be assisted by poets to perceive . . . some may but they never can. The poetic quality is not marshalled in rhyme or uniformity or abstract addresses to things nor in melancholy complaints or good precepts, but is the life of these and much else and is in the soul. The profit of rhyme is that it drops seeds of a sweeter and more luxuriant rhyme, and of uniformity that it conveys itself into its own roots in the ground out of sight. The rhyme and uniformity of perfect poems show the free growth of metrical laws and bud from them as unerringly and loosely as lilacs or roses on a bush, and take shapes as compact as the shapes of chestnuts and oranges and melons and pears, and shed the perfume impalpable to form. The fluency and ornaments of the finest poems or music or orations or recitations are not independent but dependent. All beauty comes from beautiful blood and a beautiful brain. If the greatnesses are in conjunction in a man or woman it is enough . . . the fact will prevail through the universe . . . but the gaggery and gilt of a million years will not prevail. Who troubles himself about his ornaments or fluency is lost. This is what you shall do: Love the earth and sun and the animals, despise riches, give alms to every one that asks, stand up for the stupid and crazy, devote your income and labor to others, hate tyrants, argue not concerning God, have patience and indulgence toward the people, take off your hat to nothing known or unknown or to any man or number of men, go freely with powerful uneducated persons and with the young and with the mothers of families, read these leaves in the open air every season of every year of your life, re-examine all you have been told at school or church or in any book, dismiss whatever insults your own soul, and your very flesh shall be a great poem and have the richest fluency not only in its words but in the silent lines of its lips and face and between the lashes of your eyes and in every motion and joint of your body. . . . The poet shall not spend his time in unneeded work. He shall know that the ground is always ready plowed and manured . . . others may not know it but he shall. He shall go directly to the creation. His trust shall master the trust of everything he touches . . . and shall master all attachment.

The English language befriends the grand American expression . . . it is brawny enough and limber and full enough. On the tough stock of a race who through all change of circumstances was never without the idea of political liberty, which is the animus of all liberty, it has attracted the terms of daintier and gayer and subtler and more elegant tongues. It is the powerful language of resistance . . . it is the dialect of common sense. It is the speech of the proud and melancholy races and of all who aspire. It is the chosen tongue to express growth faith self-esteem freedom justice equality friendliness amplitude prudence decision and courage. It is the medium that shall well nigh express the inexpressible.

No great literature nor any like style of behaviour or oratory or social intercourse or household arrangements or public institutions or the treatment by bosses of employed people, nor executive detail or detail of the army or navy, nor spirit of legislation or courts or police or tuition or architecture or songs or amusements or the costumes of young men, can long elude the jealous and passionate instinct of American standards. Whether or no the sign appears from the mouths of the people, it throbs a live interrogation in every freeman's and freewoman's heart after that which passes by or this built to remain. Is it uniform with my country? Are its disposals without ignominious distinctions? Is it for the evergrowing communes of brothers and lovers, large, well-united, proud beyond the old models, generous beyond all models? Is it something grown fresh out of the fields or drawn from the sea for use to me today here? I know that what answers for me an American must answer for any individual or nation that serves for a part of my materials. Does this answer? or is it without reference to universal needs? or sprung of the needs of the less developed society of special ranks? or old needs of pleasure overlaid by modern science and forms? Does this acknowledge liberty with audible and absolute acknowledgment, and set slavery at naught for life and death? Will it help breed one goodshaped and wellhung man, and a woman to be his perfect and independent mate? Does it improve manners? Is it for the nursing of the young of the republic? Does it solve readily with the sweet milk of the nipples of the breasts of the mother of many children? Has it too the old ever-fresh forbearance and impartiality? Does it look with the same love on the last born and those hardening toward stature, and on the errant, and on those who disdain all strength of assault outside of their own?

The poems distilled from other poems will probably pass away. The coward will surely pass away. The expectation of the vital and great can only be satisfied by the demeanor of the vital and great. The swarms of the polished deprecating and reflectors and the polite float off and leave no remembrance. America prepares with composure and goodwill for the visitors that have sent word. It is not intellect that is to be their warrant and welcome. The talented, the artist, the ingenious, the editor, the statesman, the erudite . . . they are not unappreciated . . . they fall in their place and do their work. The soul of the nation also does its work. No disguise can pass on it . . . no disguise can con-

ceal from it. It rejects none, it permits all. Only toward as good as itself and toward the like of itself will it advance half-way. An individual is as superb as a nation when he has the qualities which make a superb nation. The soul of the largest and wealthiest and proudest nation may well go half-way to meet that of its poets. The signs are effectual. There is no fear of mistake. If the one is true the other is true. The proof of a poet is that his country absorbs him as affectionately as he has absorbed it.

From
DEMOCRATIC VISTAS
[1871] [1]

. . . TO HIM OR her within whose thought rages the battle, advancing, retreating, between democracy's convictions, aspirations, and the people's crudeness, vice, caprices, I mainly write this essay. I shall use the words America and democracy as convertible terms. Not an ordinary one is the issue. The United States are destined either to surmount the gorgeous history of feudalism, or else prove the most tremendous failure of time. Not the least doubtful am I on any prospects of their material success. The triumphant future of their business, geographic and productive departments, on larger scales and in more varieties than ever, is certain. In those respects the republic must soon (if she does not already) outstrip all examples hitherto afforded, and dominate the world.

Admitting all this, with the priceless value of our political institutions, general suffrage, (and fully acknowledging the latest, widest opening of the doors,) I say that, far deeper than these, what finally and only is to make of our western world a nationality superior to any hither known, and outtopping the past, must be vigorous, yet unsuspected Literatures, perfect per-

---

[1] The text here used is that of the *Prose Works* (1892).

sonalities and sociologies, original, transcendental, and expressing (what, in highest sense, are not yet express'd at all,) democracy and the modern. With these, and out of these, I promulge new races of Teachers, and of perfect Women, indispensable to endow the birth-stock of a New World. For feudalism, caste, the ecclesiastic traditions, though palpably retreating from political institutions, still hold essentially, by their spirit, even in this country, entire possession of the more important fields, indeed the very subsoil, of education, and of social standards and literature.

I say that democracy can never prove itself beyond cavil, until it founds and luxuriantly grows its own forms of art, poems, schools, theology, displacing all that exists, or that has been produced anywhere in the past, under opposite influences. It is curious to me that while so many voices, pens, minds, in the press, lecture-rooms, in our Congress, &c., are discussing intellectual topics, pecuniary dangers, legislative problems, the suffrage, tariff and labor questions, and the various business and benevolent needs of America, with propositions, remedies, often worth deep attention, there is one need, a hiatus the profoundest, that no eye seems to perceive, no voice to state. Our fundamental want to-day in the United States, with closest, amplest reference to present conditions, and to the future, is of a class, and the clear idea of a class, of native authors, literatuses, far different, far higher in grade than any yet known, sacerdotal, modern, fit to cope with our occasions, lands, permeating the whole mass of American mentality, taste, belief, breathing into it a new breath of life, giving it decision, affecting politics far more than the popular superficial suffrage, with results inside and underneath the elections of Presidents or Congresses — radiating, begetting appropriate teachers, schools, manners, and, as its grandest result, accomplishing, (what neither the schools nor the churches and their clergy have hitherto accomplish'd,

and without which this nation will no more stand, permanently, soundly, than a house will stand without a substratum,) a religious and moral character beneath the political and productive and intellectual bases of the States. For know you not, dear, earnest reader, that the people of our land may all read and write, and may all possess the right to vote—and yet the main things may be entirely lacking?— (and this to suggest them.)

View'd, to-day, from a point of view sufficiently over-arching, the problem of humanity all over the civilized world is social and religious, and is to be finally met and treated by literature. The priest departs, the divine literatus comes. Never was anything more wanted than, to-day, and here in the States, the poet of the modern is wanted, or the great literatus of the modern. At all times, perhaps, the central point in any nation, and that whence it is itself really sway'd the most, and whence it sways others, is its national archetypal poems. Above all previous lands, a great original literature is surely to become the justification and reliance, (in some respects the sole reliance,) of American democracy.

Few are aware how the great literature penetrates all, gives hue to all, shapes aggregates and individuals, and, after subtle ways, with irresistible power, constructs, sustains, demolishes at will. Why tower, in reminiscence, above all the nations of the earth, two special lands, petty in themselves, yet inexpressibly gigantic, beautiful, columnar? Immortal Judah lives, and Greece immortal lives, in a couple of poems.

Nearer than this. It is not generally realized, but it is true, as the genius of Greece, and all the sociology, personality, politics and religion of those wonderful states, resided in their literature or esthetics, that what was afterwards the main support of European chivalry, the feudal, ecclesiastical, dynastic world over there—forming its osseous structure, holding it together for hundreds, thousands of years, preserving its flesh and bloom, giving it form, decision, rounding it out, and so saturating it in the conscious and unconscious blood, breed, belief, and intuitions of men, that it still prevails powerful to this day, in defiance of the mighty changes of time— was its literature, permeating to the very marrow, especially that major part, its enchanting songs, ballads, and poems.[2]

To the ostent [3] of the senses and eyes, I know, the influences which stamp the world's history are wars, uprisings or downfalls of dynasties, changeful movements of trade, important inventions, navigation, military or civil governments, advent of powerful personalities, conquerors, &c. These of course play their part; yet, it may be, a single new thought, imagination, abstract principle, even literary style, fit for the time, put in shape by some great literatus, and projected among mankind, may duly cause changes, growths, removals, greater than the longest and bloodiest war, or the most stupendous merely political, dynastic, or commercial overturn.

In short, as, though it may not be realized, it is strictly true, that a few first-class poets, philosophs, and authors, have substantially settled and given status to the entire religion, education, law, sociology, &c., of the hitherto civilized world, by tingeing and often creating the atmospheres out of which they have arisen, such also must stamp, and more than ever stamp, the interior and real democratic construction of this American continent, to-day, and days to come. Remember also this fact of difference, that, while through the antique and through the mediæval ages, highest thoughts and ideals realized themselves, and their expression made its way by other arts, as much as, or even more than by, technical literature, (not open to the mass of persons, or even to the majority of eminent persons,) such literature in our day and for current purposes, is not only more eligible than all the other arts put together, but has become the only general means of morally influencing the world.

Painting, sculpture, and the dramatic theatre, it would seem, no longer play an indispensable or even important part in the workings and mediumship of intellect, utility, or even high esthetics. Architecture remains, doubtless with capacities, and a real future. Then music, the combiner, nothing more spiritual, nothing more sensuous, a god, yet completely human, advances, prevails, holds highest place; supplying in certain wants and quarters what nothing else could supply. Yet in the civilization of to-day it is undeniable that, over all the arts, literature dominates, serves beyond all—shapes the character of church and school—or, at any rate, is capable of doing so. Including the literature of science, its scope is indeed unparallel'd.

Before proceeding further, it were perhaps well to discriminate on certain points. Literature tills its crops in many fields, and some may flourish, while others lag. What I say in these Vistas has its main bearing on imaginative literature, especially poetry, the stock of all. In the department of science, and the specialty of journalism, there appear, in these States, promises, perhaps fulfilments, of highest earnestness, reality, and life. These, of course, are modern. But in the region of imaginative, spinal and essential attributes,

---

[2] See, for hereditaments, specimens, Walter Scott's Border Minstrelsy, Percy's collection, Ellis's early English Metrical Romances, the European continental poems of Walter of Aquitania, and the Nibelungen, of pagan stock, but monkish-feudal redaction; the history of the Troubadours, by Fauriel; even the far-back cumbrous old Hindu epics, as indicating the Asian eggs out of which European chivalry was hatch'd; Ticknor's chapters on the Cid, and on the Spanish poems and poets of Calderon's time. Then always, and, of course, as the superbest poetic culmination-expression of feudalism, the Shaksperean dramas, in the attitudes, dialogue, characters, &c., of the princes, lords and gentlemen, the pervading atmosphere, the implied and express'd standard of manners, the high port and proud stomach, the regal embroidery of style, &c.—Author's note.

[3] Rare word for manifestation.

something equivalent to creation is, for our age and lands, imperatively demanded. For not only is it not enough that the new blood, new frame of democracy shall be vivified and held together merely by political means, superficial suffrage, legislation, &c., but it is clear to me that, unless it goes deeper, gets at least as firm and as warm a hold in men's hearts, emotions and belief, as, in their days, feudalism or ecclesiasticism, and inaugurates its own perennial sources, welling from the centre forever, its strength will be defective, its growth doubtful, and its main charm wanting. I suggest, therefore, the possibility, should some two or three really original American poets, (perhaps artists or lecturers,) arise, mounting the horizon like planets, stars of the first magnitude, that, from their eminence, fusing contributions, races, far localities, &c., together, they would give more compaction and more moral identity, (the quality to-day most needed,) to these States, than all its Constitutions, legislative and judicial ties, and all its hitherto political, warlike, or materialistic experiences. As, for instance, there could hardly happen anything that would more serve the States, with all their variety of origins, their diverse climes, cities, standards, &c., than possessing an aggregate of heroes, characters, exploits, sufferings, prosperity or misfortune, glory or disgrace, common to all, typical of all—no less, but even greater would it be to possess the aggregation of a cluster of mighty poets, artists, teachers, fit for us, national expressers, comprehending and effusing for the men and women of the States, what is universal, native, common to all, inland and seaboard, northern and southern. The historians say of ancient Greece, with her ever-jealous autonomies, cities, and states, that the only positive unity she ever own'd or receiv'd, was the sad unity of a common subjection at the last, to foreign conquerors. Subjection, aggregation of that sort, is impossible to America; but the fear of conflicting and irreconcilable interiors, and the lack of a common skeleton, knitting

all close, continually haunts me. Or, if it does not, nothing is plainer than the need, a long period to come, of a fusion of the States into the only reliable identity, the moral and artistic one. For, I say, the true nationality of the States, the genuine union, when we come to a moral crisis, is, and is to be, after all, neither the written law, nor, (as is generally supposed,) either self-interest, or common pecuniary or material objects—but the fervid and tremendous IDEA, melting everything else with resistless heat, and solving all lesser and definite distinctions in vast, indefinite, spiritual, emotional power.

It may be claim'd, (and I admit the weight of the claim,) that common and general worldly prosperity, and a populace well-to-do, and with all life's material comforts, is the main thing, and is enough. It may be argued that our republic is, in performance, really enacting to-day the grandest arts, poems, &c., by beating up the wilderness into fertile farms, and in her railroads, ships, machinery, &c. And it may be ask'd, Are these not better, indeed, for America, than any utterances even of greatest rhapsode, artist, or literatus?

I too hail those achievements with pride and joy: then answer that the soul of man will not with such only—nay, not with such at all—be finally satisfied; but needs what, (standing on these and on all things, as the feet stand on the ground,) is address'd to the loftiest, to itself alone.

Out of such considerations, such truths, arises for treatment in these Vistas the important question of character, of an American stock-personality, with literatures and arts for outlets and return-expressions, and, of course, to correspond, within outlines common to all. To these, the main affair, the thinkers of the United States, in general so acute, have either given feeblest attention, or have remain'd, and remain, in a state of somnolence.

For my part, I would alarm and caution even the political and business reader, and to the utmost extent, against the prevailing delusion that the establishment of free political institutions, and plentiful intellectual smartness, with general good order, physical plenty, industry, &c., (desirable and precious advantages as they all are,) do, of themselves, determine and yield to our experiment of democracy the fruitage of success. With such advantages at present fully, or almost fully, possess'd —the Union just issued, victorious, from the struggle with the only foes it need ever fear, (namely, those within itself, the interior ones,) and with unprecedented materialistic advancement—society, in these States, is canker'd, crude, superstitious, and rotten. Political, or law-made society is, and private, or voluntary society, is also. In any vigor, the element of the moral conscience, the most important, the verteber[4] to State or man, seems to me either entirely lacking, or seriously enfeebled or ungrown.

I say we had best look our times and lands searchingly in the face, like a physician diagnosing some deep disease. Never was there, perhaps, more hollowness at heart than at present, and here in the United States. Genuine belief seems to have left us. The underlying principles of the States are not honestly believ'd in, (for all this hectic glow, and these melodramatic screamings,) nor is humanity itself believ'd in. What penetrating eye does not everywhere see through the mask? The spectacle is appaling. We live in an atmosphere of hypocrisy throughout. The men believe not in the women, nor the women in the men. A scornful superciliousness rules in literature. The aim of all the *littérateurs* is to find something to make fun of. A lot of churches, sects, &c., the most dismal phantasms I know, usurp the name of religion. Conversation is a mass of badinage. From deceit in the spirit, the mother of all false deeds, the offspring is already incalculable. An acute and candid person, in the revenue department in Washington, who is led by the course of his employment to regularly visit the cities, north, south and west, to investigate frauds, has talk'd much with me about his discoveries. The depravity of the business classes of our country is not less than has been supposed, but infinitely greater. The official services of America, national, state, and municipal, in all their branches and departments, except the judiciary, are saturated in corruption, bribery, falsehood, mal-administration; and the judiciary is tainted. The great cities reek with respectable as much as non-respectable robbery and scoundrelism. In fashionable life, flippancy, tepid amours, weak infidelism, small aims, or no aims at all, only to kill time. In business, (this all-devouring modern word, business,) the one sole object is, by any means, pecuniary gain. The magician's serpent in the fable ate up all the other serpents;[5] and money-making is our magician's serpent, remaining to-day sole master of the field. The best class we show, is but a mob of fashionably dress'd speculators and vulgarians. True, indeed, behind this fantastic farce, enacted on the visible stage of society, solid things and stupendous labors are to be discover'd, existing crudely and going on in the background, to advance and tell themselves in time. Yet the truths are none the less terrible. I say that our New World democracy, however great a success in uplifting the masses out of their sloughs, in materialistic development, products, and in a certain highly-deceptive superficial popular intellectuality, is, so far, an almost complete failure in its social aspects, and in really grand religious, moral, literary, and esthetic results. In vain do we march with unprecedented strides to empire so colossal, outvying the antique, beyond Alexander's, beyond the proudest sway of Rome. In vain have we annex'd Texas, California, Alaska, and reach north for Canada and south for Cuba. It is as if we were somehow being endow'd with a vast and more and more thoroughly-

---

[4] This appears as "vertebrae," the conventional form, in the first edition (1871).

[5] See Exodus, vii, 9-12

appointed body, and then left with little or no soul.

. . . .

As to the political section of Democracy, which introduces and breaks ground for further and vaster sections, few probably are the minds, even in these republican States, that fully comprehend the aptness of that phrase, "THE GOVERNMENT OF THE PEOPLE, BY THE PEOPLE, FOR THE PEOPLE," which we inherit from the lips of Abraham Lincoln; a formula whose verbal shape is homely wit, but whose scope includes both the totality and all minutiæ of the lesson.

The People! Like our huge earth itself, which, to ordinary scansion, is full of vulgar contradictions and offence, man, viewed in the lump, displeases, and is a constant puzzle and affront to the merely educated classes. The rare, cosmical, artist-mind, lit with the Infinite, alone confronts his manifold and oceanic qualities—but taste, intelligence and culture, (so-called,) have been against the masses, and remain so. There is plenty of glamour about the most damnable crimes and hoggish meannesses, special and general, of the feudal and dynastic world over there, with its *personnel* of lords and queens and courts, so well-dress'd and so handsome. But the People are ungrammatical, untidy, and their sins gaunt and ill-bred.

Literature, strictly consider'd, has never recognized the People, and, whatever may be said, does not to-day. Speaking generally, the tendencies of literature, as hitherto pursued, have been to make mostly critical and querulous men. It seems as if, so far, there were some natural repugnance between a literary and professional life, and the rude rank spirit of the democracies. There is, in later literature, a treatment of benevolence, a charity business, rife enough it is true; but I know nothing more rare, even in this country, than a fit scientific estimate and reverent appreciation of the People—of their measureless wealth of latent power and capacity, their vast, artistic contrasts of lights and shades —with, in America, their entire reliability in emergencies, and a certain breadth of historic grandeur, of peace or war, far surpassing all the vaunted samples of book-heroes, or any *haut ton* coteries, in all the records of the world.

. . . .

Did you, too, O friend, suppose democracy was only for elections, for politics, and for a party name? I say democracy is only of use there that it may pass on and come to its flower and fruits in manners, in the highest forms of interaction between men, and their beliefs—in religion, literature, colleges, and schools—democracy in all public and private life, and in the army and navy. I have intimated that, as a paramount scheme, it has yet few or no full realizers and believers. I do not see, either, that it owes any serious thanks to noted propagandists or champions, or has been essentially help'd, though often harm'd, by them. It has been and is carried on by all the moral forces, and by trade, finance, machinery, intercommunications, and, in fact, by all the developments of history, and can no more be stopp'd than the tides, or the earth in its orbit. Doubtless, also, it resides, crude and latent, well down in the hearts of the fair average of the American-born people, mainly in the agricultural regions. But it is not yet, there or anywhere, the fully-receiv'd, the fervid, the absolute faith.

I submit, therefore, that the fruition of democracy, on aught like a grand scale, resides altogether in the future. As, under any profound and comprehensive view of the gorgeous-composite feudal world, we see in it, through the long ages and cycles of ages, the results of a deep, integral, human and divine principle, or fountain, from which issued laws, ecclesia, manners, institutes, costumes, personalities, poems, (hitherto unequall'd,) faithfully partaking of their source, and indeed only arising either to betoken it, or to furnish parts of that varied-flowing display, whose centre was one and absolute—so, long ages hence, shall the due historian or critic make at least an equal retrospect, an equal history for the democratic principle. It too must be adorn'd, credited with its results—then, when it, with imperial power, through amplest time, has dominated mankind—has been the source and test of all the moral, esthetic, social, political, and religious expressions and institutes of the civilized world—has begotten them in spirit and in form, and has carried them to its own unprecedented heights—has had, (it is possible,) monastics and ascetics, more numerous, more devout than the monks and priests of all previous creeds—has sway'd the ages with a breadth and rectitude tallying Nature's own—has fashion'd, systematized, and triumphantly finish'd and carried out, in its own interest, and with unparallel'd success, a new earth and a new man.

Thus we presume to write, as it were, upon things that exist not, and travel by maps yet unmade, and a blank. But the throes of birth are upon us; and we have something of this advantage in seasons of strong formations, doubts, suspense—for then the afflatus of such themes haply may fall upon us, more or less; and then, hot from surrounding war and revolution, our speech, though without polish'd coherence, and a failure by the standard called criticism, comes forth, real at least as the lightnings.

And may-be we, these days, have, too, our own reward—(for there are yet some, in all lands, worthy to be so encouraged.) Though not for us the joy of entering at the last the conquer'd city—not ours the chance ever to see with our own eyes the peerless power and splendid *eclat* of the democratic principle, arriv'd at meridian, filling the world with effulgence and majesty far beyond those of past history's kings, or all dynastic sway—there is yet, to whoever is eligible among us, the prophetic vision, the joy of being toss'd in the brave turmoil of these times—the promulgation and the path, obedient, lowly reverent to the voice, the gesture of the God, or Holy Ghost, which others see not, hear not

—with the proud consciousness that amid whatever clouds, seductions, or heart-wearying postponements, we have never deserted, never despair'd, never abandon'd the faith.

So much contributed, to be conn'd well, to help prepare and brace our edifice, our plann'd Idea—we still proceed to give it in another of its aspects—perhaps the main, the high façade of all. For to democracy, the leveler, the unyielding principle of the average, is surely join'd another principle, equally unyielding, closely tracking the first, indispensable to it, opposite, (as the sexes are opposite,) and whose existence, confronting and ever modifying the other, often clashing, paradoxical, yet neither of highest avail without the other, plainly supplies to these grand cosmic politics of ours, and to the launch'd forth mortal dangers of republicanism, to-day or any day, the counterpart and offset whereby Nature restrains the deadly original relentlessness of all her first-class laws. This second principle is individuality, the pride and centripetal isolation of a human being in himself—identity—personalism. Whatever the name, its acceptance and thorough infusion through the organizations of political commonalty now shooting Aurora-like about the world, are of utmost importance, as the principle itself is needed for very life's sake. It forms, in a sort, or is to form, the compensating balance-wheel of the successful working machinery of aggregate America.

The problem, as it seems to me, presented to the New World, is, under permanent law and order, and after preserving cohesion, (ensemble-Individuality,) at all hazards, to vitalize man's free play of special Personalism, recognizing in it something that calls ever more to be consider'd, fed, and adopted as the substratum for the best that belongs to us, (government indeed is for it,) including the new esthetics of our future.

To formulate beyond this present vagueness—to help line and put before us the species, or a specimen of the species, of the democratic ethnology of the future, is a work toward which the genius of our land, with peculiar encouragement, invites her well-wishers. Already certain limnings, more or less grotesque, more or less fading and watery, have appear'd. We too, (repressing doubts and qualms,) will try our hand.

Attempting, then, however crudely, a basic model or portrait of personality for general use for the manliness of the States, (and doubtless that is most useful which is most simple and comprehensive for all, and toned low enough,) we should prepare the canvas well beforehand. Parentage must consider itself in advance. (Will the time hasten when fatherhood and motherhood shall become a science—and the noblest science?) To our model, a clear-blooded, strong-fibred physique, is indispensable; the questions of food, drink, air, exercise, assimilation, digestion, can never be intermitted. Out of these we descry a well-begotten selfhood—in youth, fresh, ardent, emotional, aspiring, full of adventure; at maturity, brave, perceptive, under control, neither too talkative nor too reticent, neither flippant nor sombre; of the bodily figure, the movements easy, the complexion showing the best blood, somewhat flush'd, breast expanded, an erect attitude, a voice whose sound outvies music, eyes of calm and steady gaze, yet capable also of flashing—and a general presence that holds its own in the company of the highest. (For it is native personality, and that alone, that endows a man to stand before presidents or generals, or in any distinguish'd collection, with *aplomb*—and *not* culture, or any knowledge or intellect whatever.)

With regard to the mental-educational part of our model, enlargement of intellect, stores of cephalic knowledge, &c., the concentration thitherward of all the customs of our age, especially in America, is so overweening, and provides so fully for that part, that, important and necessary as it is, it really needs nothing from us here —except, indeed, a phrase of warning and restraint. Manners, costumes, too, though important, we need not dwell upon here. Like beauty, grace of motion, &c., they are results. Causes, original things, being attended to, the right manners unerringly follow. Much is said, among artists, of "the grand style," as if it were a thing by itself. When a man, artist or whoever, has health, pride, acuteness, noble aspirations, he has the motive-elements of the grandest style. The rest is but manipulation, (yet that is no small matter.)

Leaving still unspecified several sterling parts of any model fit for the future personality of America, I must not fail, again and ever, to pronounce myself on one, probably the least attended to in modern times—a hiatus, indeed, threatening its gloomiest consequences after us. I mean the simple, unsophisticated Conscience, the primary moral element. If I were asked to specify in what quarter lie the grounds of darkest dread, respecting the America of our hopes, I should have to point to this particular. I should demand the invariable application to individuality, this day and any day, of that old, ever-true plumb-rule of persons, eras, nations. Our triumphant modern civilizee, with his all-schooling and his wondrous appliances, will still show himself but an amputation while this deficiency remains. Beyond, (assuming a more hopeful tone,) the vertebration of the manly and womanly personalism of our western world, can only be, and is, indeed, to be, (I hope,) its all-penetrating Religiousness.

The ripeness of Religion is doubtless to be looked for in this field of individuality, and is a result that no organization or church can ever achieve. As history is poorly retain'd by what the technists call history, and is not given out from their pages, except the learner has in himself the sense of the well-wrapt, never yet written, perhaps impossible to be written, history —so Religion, although casually arrested, and, after a fashion, preserv'd in the churches and creeds, does not depend at all upon them, but is a part of the identified soul, which, when greatest, knows not bibles in the old way, but in new ways—the identified soul, which can really confront Religion when it extricates itself entirely from the churches, and not before.

Personalism fuses this, and favors it. I should say, indeed, that only in the perfect uncontamination and solitariness of individuality may the spirituality of religion positively come forth at all. Only here, and on such terms, the meditation, the devout ecstasy, the soaring flight. Only here, communion with the mysteries, the eternal problems, whence? whither? Alone, and identity, and the mood—and the soul emerges, and all statements, churches, sermons, melt away like vapors. Alone, and silent thought and awe, and aspiration— and then the interior consciousness, like a hitherto unseen inscription, in magic ink, beams out its wondrous lines to the sense. Bibles may convey, and priests expound, but it is exclusively for the noiseless operation of one's isolated Self, to enter the pure ether of veneration, reach the divine levels, and commune with the unutterable.

To practically enter into politics is an important part of American personalism. To every young man, north and south, earnestly studying these things, I should here, as an offset to what I have said in former pages, now also say, that may-be to views of very largest scope, after all, perhaps the political, (perhaps the literary and sociological,) America goes best about its development its own way—sometimes, to temporary sight, appaling enough. It is the fashion among dillettants and fops (perhaps I myself am not guiltless,) to decry the whole formulation of the active politics of America, as beyond redemption, and to be carefully kept away from. See you that you do not fall into this error. America, it may be, is doing very well upon the whole, notwithstanding these antics of the parties and their leaders, these half-brain'd nominees, the many ignorant

ballots, and many elected failures and blatherers. It is the dillettants, and all who shirk their duty, who are not doing well. As for you, I advise you to enter more strongly yet into politics. I advise every young man to do so. Always inform yourself; always do the best you can; always vote. Disengage yourself from parties. They have been useful, and to some extent remain so; but the floating, uncommitted electors, farmers, clerks, mechanics, the masters of parties—watching aloof, inclining victory this side or that side—such are the ones most needed, present and future. For America, if eligible at all to downfall and ruin, is eligible within herself, not without; for I see clearly that the combined foreign world could not beat her down. But these savage, wolfish parties alarm me. Owning no law but their own will, more and more combative, less and less tolerant of the idea of ensemble and of equal brotherhood, the perfect equality of the States, the ever-overarching American ideas, it behooves you to convey yourself implicitly to no party, nor submit blindly to their dictators, but steadily hold yourself judge and master over all of them.

What is the reason our time, our lands, that we see no fresh local courage, sanity, of our own—the Mississippi, stalwart Western men, real mental and physical facts, Southerners, &c., in the body of our literature? especially the poetic part of it. But always, instead, a parcel of dandies and ennuyees, dapper little gentlemen from abroad, who flood us with their thin sentiment of parlors, parasols, piano-songs, tinkling rhymes, the five-hundredth importation—or whimpering and crying about something, chasing one aborted conceit after another, and forever occupied in dyspeptic amours with dyspeptic women. While, current and novel, the grandest events and revolutions, and stormiest passions of history, are crossing to-day with unparallel'd rapidity and magnificence over the stages of our own and all the continents, offering new materials, opening new vistas, with largest needs, inviting the daring launching forth of conceptions in literature, inspired by them, soaring in highest regions, serving art in its highest, (which is only the other name for serving God, and serving humanity,) where is the man of letters, where is the book, with any nobler aim than to follow in the old track, repeat what has been said before—and, as its utmost triumph, sell well, and be erudite or elegant?

. . . .

Nor may the genuine gold, the gems, when brought to light at last, be probably usher'd forth from any of the quarters currently counted on. To-day, doubtless, the infant genius of American poetic expression, (eluding those highly-refined imported and gilt-edged themes, and sentimental and butterfly flights, pleasant to orthodox publishers—causing tender spasms in the coteries, and warranted not to chafe the sensitive cuticle of the most exquisitely artificial gossamer delicacy,) lies sleeping far away, happily unrecognized and uninjur'd by the coteries, the art-writers, the talkers and critics of the saloons, or the lecturers in the colleges—lies sleeping, aside, unrecking itself, in some western idiom, or native Michigan or Tennessee repartee, or stump-speech—or in Kentucky or Georgia, or the Carolinas—or in some slang or local song or allusion of the Manhattan, Boston, Philadelphia or Baltimore mechanic—or up in the Maine woods —or off in the hut of the California miner, or crossing the Rocky mountains, or along the Pacific railroad—or on the breasts of the young farmers of the northwest, or Canada, or boatmen of the lakes. Rude and coarse nursing-beds, these; but only from such beginnings and stocks, indigenous here, may haply arrive, be grafted, and sprout, in time, flowers of genuine American aroma, and fruits truly and fully our own.

I say it were a standing disgrace to these States—I say it were a disgrace to any nation, distinguish'd above others by the variety and vastness of its territories, its materials, its inventive activity, and the splendid practicality of its people, not to rise and soar above others also in its original styles in literature and art, and its own supply of intellectual and esthetic masterpieces, archetypal, and consistent with itself. I know not a land except ours that has not, to some extent, however small, made its title clear. The Scotch have their born ballads, subtly expressing their past and present, and expressing character. The Irish have theirs. England, Italy, France, Spain, theirs. What has America? With exhaustless mines of the richest ore of epic, lyric, tale, tune, picture, &c., in the Four Years' War; with, indeed, I sometimes think, the richest masses of material ever afforded a nation, more variegated, and on a larger scale—the first sign of proportionate, native, imaginative Soul, and first-class works to match, is, (I cannot too often repeat,) so far wanting.

. . . .

In the future of these States must arise poets immenser far, and make great poems of death. The poems of life are great, but there must be the poems of the purports of life, not only in itself, but beyond itself. I have eulogized Homer, the sacred bards of Jewry, Eschylus, Juvenal, Shakspere, &c., and acknowledged their inestimable value. But, (with perhaps the exception, in some, not all respects, of the second-mention'd,) I say there must, for future and democratic purposes, appear poets, (dare I to say so?) of higher class even than any of those—poets not only possess'd of the religious fire and abandon of Isaiah, luxuriant in the epic talent of Homer, or for proud characters as in Shakspere, but consistent with the Hegelian formulas,[6] and consistent with modern science. America needs, and the world needs, a class of bards who will, now and ever, so link and tally the rational physical being of man, with the ensembles of time and space, and with

---

[6] Georg Wilhelm Friedrich Hegel (1770-1831) set out in his *Logik* categories used in the interpretation of experience and ordering of life.

this vast and multiform show, Nature, surrounding him, ever tantalizing him, equally a part, and yet not a part of him, as to essentially harmonize, satisfy, and put at rest. Faith, very old, now scared away by science, must be restored, brought back by the same power that caused her departure —restored with new sway, deeper, wider, higher than ever. Surely, this universal ennui, this coward fear, this shuddering at death, these low, degrading views, are not always to rule the spirit pervading future society, as it has the past, and does the present. What the Roman Lucretius[7] sought most nobly, yet all too blindly, negatively to do for his age and its successors, must be done positively by some great coming literatus, especially poet, who, while remaining fully poet, will absorb whatever science indicates, with spiritualism, and out of them, and out of his own genius, will compose the great poem of death. Then will man indeed confront Nature, and confront time and space, both with science, and *con amore*,[8] and take his right place, prepared for life, master of fortune and misfortune. And then that which was long wanted will be supplied, and the ship that had it not before in all her voyages, will have an anchor.

There are still other standards, suggestions, for products of high literatuses. That which really balances and conserves the social and political world is not so much legislation, police, treaties, and dread of punishment, as the latent eternal intuitional sense, in humanity, of fairness, manliness, decorum, &c. Indeed, this perennial regulation, control, and oversight, by self-suppliance is *sine qua non* to democracy; and a highest widest aim of democratic literature may well be to bring forth, cultivate, brace, and strengthen this sense, in individuals and society. A strong mastership of the general inferior self by the superior self, is to be aided, secured, indirectly, but surely, by the literatus, in his works, shaping, for individual or aggregate democracy, a great passionate

body, in and along with which goes a great masterful spirit.

And still, providing for contingencies, I fain confront the fact, the need of powerful native philosophs and orators and bards, these States, as rallying points to come, in times of danger, and to fend off ruin and defection. For history is long, long, long. Shift and turn the combinations of the statement as we may, the problem of the future of America is in certain respects as dark as it is vast. Pride, competition, segregation, vicious wilfulness, and license beyond example, brood already upon us. Unwieldy and immense, who shall hold in behemoth? who bridle leviathan? Flaunt it as we choose, athwart and over the roads of our progress loom huge uncertainty, and dreadful, threatening gloom. It is useless to deny it: Democracy grows rankly up the thickest, noxious, deadliest plants and fruits of all—brings worse and worse invaders—needs newer, larger, stronger, keener compensations and compellers.

Our lands, embracing so much, (embracing indeed the whole, rejecting none,) hold in their breast that flame also, capable of consuming themselves, consuming us all. Short as the span of our national life has been, already have death and downfall crowded close upon us—and will again crowd close, no doubt, even if warded off. Ages to come may never know, but I know, how narrowly during the late secession war—and more than once, and more than twice or thrice—our Nationality, (wherein bound up, as in a ship in a storm, depended, and yet depend, all our best life, all hope, all value,) just grazed, just by a hair escaped destruction. Alas! to think of them! the agony and bloody sweat of certain of those hours! those cruel, sharp, suspended crises!

---

[7] Carus Titus Lucretius (97?-53 B.C.), Roman poet, was the author of *De Rerum Natura*, dealing with basic principles of nature, society, the arts, etc.

[8] With love; with zeal.

Even to-day, amid these whirls, incredible flippancy, and blind fury of parties, infidelity, entire lack of first-class captains and leaders, added to the plentiful meanness and vulgarity of the ostensible masses —that problem, the labor question, beginning to open like a yawning gulf, rapidly widening every year—what prospect have we? We sail a dangerous sea of seething currents, cross and under-currents, vortices —all so dark, untried—and whither shall we turn? It seems as if the Almighty had spread before this nation charts of imperial destinies, dazzling as the sun, yet with many a deep intestine difficulty, and human aggregate of cankerous imperfection, —saying, lo! the roads, the only plans of development, long and varied with all terrible balks and ebullitions. You said in your soul, I will be empire of empires, overshadowing all else, past and present, putting the history of old-world dynasties, conquests behind me, as of no account— making a new history, a history of democracy, making old history a dwarf—I alone inaugurating largeness, culminating time. If these, O lands of America, are indeed the prizes, the determinations of your soul, be it so. But behold the cost, and already specimens of the cost. Thought you greatness was to ripen for you like a pear? If you would have greatness, know that you must conquer it through ages, centuries— must pay for it with a proportionate price. For you too, as for all lands, the struggle, the traitor, the wily person in office, scrofulous wealth, the surfeit of prosperity, the demonism of greed, the hell of passion, the decay of faith, the long postponement, the fossil-like lethargy, the ceaseless need of revolutions, prophets, thunderstorms, deaths, births, new projections and invigorations of ideas and men.

Yet I have dream'd, merged in that hidden-tangled problem of our fate, whose long unraveling stretches mysteriously through time—dream'd out, portray'd, hinted already—a little or a larger band —a band of brave and true, unprecedented yet—arm'd and equipt at every point—

the members separated, it may be, by different dates and States, or south, or north, or east, or west—Pacific, Atlantic, Southern, Canadian—a year, a century here, and other centuries there—but always one, compact in soul, conscience-conserving, God-inculcating, inspired achievers, not only in literature, the greatest art, but achievers in all art—a new, undying order, dynasty, from age to age transmitted—a band, a class, at least as fit to cope with current years, our dangers, needs, as those who, for their times, so long, so well, in armor or in cowl, upheld and made illustrious, that far-back feudal, priestly world. To offset chivalry, indeed, those vanish'd countless knights, old altars, abbeys, priests, ages and strings of ages, a knightlier and more sacred cause to-day demands, and shall supply, in a New World, to larger, grander work, more than the counterpart and tally of them.

Arrived now, definitely, at an apex for these Vistas, I confess that the promulgation and belief in such a class or institution—a new and greater literatus order— its possibility, (nay certainty,) underlies these entire speculations—and that the rest, the other parts, as superstructures, are all founded upon it. It really seems to me the condition, not only of our future national and democratic development, but of our perpetuation. In the highly artificial and materialistic bases of modern civilization, with the corresponding arrangements and methods of living, the force-infusion of intellect alone, the depraving influences of riches just as much as poverty, the absence of all high ideals in character—with the long series of tendencies, shapings, which few are strong enough to resist, and which now seem, with steam-engine speed, to be everywhere turning out the generations of humanity like uniform iron castings—all of which, as compared with the feudal ages, we can yet do nothing better than accept, make the best of, and even welcome, upon the whole, for their oceanic practical grandeur, and their restless wholesale kneading of the masses—I say of all this tremendous and dominant play of solely materialistic bearings upon current life in the United States, with the results as already seen, accumulating, and reaching far into the future, that they must either be confronted and met by at least an equally subtle and tremendous force-infusion for purposes of spiritualization, for the pure conscience, for genuine esthetics, and for absolute and primal manliness and womanliness—or else our modern civilization, with all its improvements, is in vain, and we are on the road to a destiny, a status, equivalent, in its real world, to that of the fabled damned.

Prospecting thus the coming unsped days, and that new order in them—marking the endless train of exercise, development, unwind, in nation as in man, which life is for—we see, fore-indicated, amid these prospects and hopes, new law-forces of spoken and written language—not merely the pedagogue-forms, correct, regular, familiar with precedents, made for matters of outside propriety, fine words, thoughts definitely told out—but a language fann'd by the breath of Nature, which leaps overhead, cares mostly for impetus and effects, and for what it plants and invigorates to grow—tallies life and character, and seldomer tells a thing than suggests or necessitates it. In fact, a new theory of literary composition for imaginative works of the very first class, and especially for highest poems, is the sole course open to these States. Books are to be call'd for, and supplied, on the assumption that the process of reading is not a half-sleep, but, in highest sense, an exercise, a gymnast's struggle; that the reader is to do something for himself, must be on the alert, must himself or herself construct indeed the poem, argument, history, metaphysical essay—the text furnishing the hints, the clue, the start or frame-work. Not the book needs so much to be the complete thing, but the reader of the book does. That were to make a nation of supple and athletic minds, well-train'd, intuitive, used to depend on themselves, and not on a few coteries of writers.

Investigating here, we see, not that it is a little thing we have, in having the bequeath'd libraries, countless shelves of volumes, records, &c.; yet how serious the danger, depending entirely on them, of the bloodless vein, the nerveless arm, the false application, at second or third hand. We see that the real interest of this people of ours in the theology, history, poetry, politics, and personal models of the past, (the British islands, for instance, and indeed all the past,) is not necessarily to mould ourselves or our literature upon them, but to attain fuller, more definite comparisons, warnings, and the insight to ourselves, our own present, and our own far grander, different, future history, religion, social customs, &c. We see that almost everything that has been written, sung, or stated, of old, with reference to humanity under the feudal and oriental institutes, religions, and for other lands, needs to be re-written, re-sung, re-stated, in terms consistent with the institution of these States, and to come in range and obedient uniformity with them.

We see, as in the universes of the material kosmos, after meterological, vegetable, and animal cycles, man at last arises, born through them, to prove them, concentrate them, to turn upon them with wonder and love—to command them, adorn them, and carry them upward into superior realms—so, out of the series of the preceding social and political universes, now arise these States. We see that while many were supposing things established and completed, really the grandest things always remain; and discover that the work of the New World is not ended, but only fairly begun.

We see our land, America, her literature, esthetics, &c., as, substantially, the getting in form, or effusement and statement, of deepest basic elements and loftiest final meanings, of history and man—and the portrayal, (under the eternal laws and conditions of beauty,) of our own physiognomy, the subjective tie and expression of the objective, as from our own combination, continuation, and points of view—and the deposit and record of the national mentality, character, appeals, heroism, wars, and even liberties—where these, and all, culminate in native literary and artistic formulation, to be perpetuated; and not having which native, first-class formulation, she will flounder about, and her other, however imposing, eminent greatness, prove merely a passing gleam; but truly having which, she will understand herself, live nobly, nobly contribute, emanate, and, swinging, poised safely on herself, illumin'd and illuming, become a full-form'd world, and divine Mother not only of material but spiritual worlds, in ceaseless succession through time—the main thing being the average, the bodily, the concrete, the democratic, the popular, on which all the superstructures of the future are to permanently rest.

From
SPECIMEN DAYS AND COLLECT
[1882]

MY PASSION FOR FERRIES

LIVING IN BROOKLYN or New York city from this time forward, my life, then, and still more the following years, was curiously identified with Fulton ferry, already becoming the greatest of its sort in the world for general importance, volume, variety, rapidity, and picturesqueness. Almost daily, later, ('50 to '60,) I cross'd on the boats, often up in the pilot-houses where I could get a full sweep, absorbing shows, accompaniments, surroundings. What oceanic currents, eddies, underneath—the great tides of humanity also, with ever-shifting movements. Indeed, I have always had a passion for ferries; to me they afford inimitable, streaming, never-failing, living poems. The river and bay scenery, all about New York island, any time of a fine day—the hurrying, splashing sea-tides—the changing panorama of steamers, all sizes, often

a string of big ones outward bound to distant ports—the myriads of white-sail'd schooners, sloops, skiffs, and the marvelously beautiful yachts—the majestic sound boats as they rounded the Battery and came along towards 5, afternoon, eastward bound—the prospect off towards Staten Island, or down the Narrows, or the other way up the Hudson—what refreshment of spirit such sights and experiences gave me years ago (and many a time since.) My old pilot friends, the Balsirs, Johnny Cole, Ira Smith, William White, and my young ferry friend, Tom Gere—how well I remember them all.

BROADWAY SIGHTS

Besides Fulton ferry, off and on for years, I knew and frequented Broadway —that noted avenue of New York's crowded and mixed humanity, and of so many notables. Here I saw, during those times, Andrew Jackson, Webster, Clay, Seward, Martin Van Buren, filibuster Walker,[1] Kossuth, Fitz Greene Halleck, Bryant, the Prince of Wales, Charles Dickens, the first Japanese ambassadors, and lots of other celebrities of the time.[2] Always something novel or inspiriting; yet mostly to me the hurrying and vast amplitude of those never-ending human currents. I remember seeing James Fenimore Cooper in a court-room in Chambers street, back of the city hall, where he was carrying on a law case—(I think it was a charge of libel he had brought against some one.)[3] I also

---

[1] William Walker (1824-1860), leader in various Central American revolts.

[2] Several of these were famous visitors from foreign countries, as Louis Kossuth (1802-1894) Hungarian patriot; Charles Dickens (1812-1870), English novelist; the Prince of Wales (later Edward VII), who visited New York in 1860; and members of the Japanese embassy who arrived in the same year to deliver the first American-Japanese treaty.

[3] Cooper sued four New York newspapers for libel—the *Courier and Enquirer*, the *Commercial Advertiser*, the *Evening Signal*, and the *Tribune*.

remember seeing Edgar A. Poe, and having a short interview with him, (it must have been in 1845 or '6,) in his office, second story of a corner building, (Duane or Pearl street.) He was editor and owner or part owner of "the Broadway Journal." [4] The visit was about a piece of mine he had publish'd. Poe was very cordial, in a quiet way, appear'd well in person, dress, &c. I have a distinct and pleasing remembrance of his looks, voice, manner and matter; very kindly and human, but subdued, perhaps a little jaded. For another of my reminiscences, here on the west side, just below Houston street, I once saw (it must have been about 1832, on a sharp, bright January day) a bent, feeble but stout-built very old man, bearded, swathed in rich furs, with a great ermine cap on his head, led and assisted, almost carried, down the steps of his high front stoop (a dozen friends and servants, emulous, carefully holding, guiding him) and then lifted and tuck'd in a gorgeous sleigh, envelop'd in other furs, for a ride. The sleigh was drawn by as fine a team of horses as I ever saw. (You needn't think all the best animals are brought up nowadays; never was such horseflesh as fifty years ago on Long Island, or south, or in New York city; folks look'd for spirit and mettle in a nag, not tame speed merely.) Well, I, a boy of perhaps 13 or 14, stopp'd and gazed long at the spectacle of that fur-swathed old man, surrounded by friends and servants, and the careful seating of him in the sleigh. I remember the spirited, champing horses, the driver with his whip, and a fellow-driver by his side, for extra prudence. The old man, the subject of so much attention, I can almost see now. It was John Jacob Astor. [5]

The years 1846, '47, and there along, see me still in New York city, working as writer and printer, having my usual good health, and a good time generally.

BATTLE OF BULL RUN, JULY, 1861

All this sort of feeling was destin'd to be arrested and revers'd by a terrible shock—the battle of first Bull Run—certainly, as we now know it, one of the most singular fights on record. (All battles, and their results, are far more matters of accident than is generally thought; but this was throughout a casualty, a chance. Each side supposed it had won, till the last moment. One had, in point of fact, just the same right to be routed as the other. By a fiction, or series of fictions, the national forces at the last moment exploded in a panic and fled from the field.) The defeated troops commenced pouring into Washington over the Long Bridge at daylight on Monday, 22nd—day drizzling all through with rain. The Saturday and Sunday of the battle (20th, 21st,) had been parch'd and hot to an extreme—the dust, the grime and smoke, in layers, sweated in, follow'd by other layers again sweated in, absorb'd by those excited souls—their clothes all saturated with the clay-powder filling the air—stirr'd up everywhere on the dry roads and trodden fields by the regiments, swarming wagons, artillery, &c. —all the men with this coating of murk and sweat and rain, now recoiling back, pouring over the Long Bridge—a horrible march of twenty miles, returning to Washington baffled, humiliated, panic-struck. Where are the vaunts, and the proud boasts with which you went forth? Where are your banners, and your bands of music, and your ropes to bring back your prisoners? Well, there isn't a band playing —and there isn't a flag but clings ashamed and lank to its staff.

The sun rises, but shines not. The men appear, at first sparsely and shame-faced enough, then thicker, in the streets of Washington—appear in Pennsylvania avenue, and on the steps and basement entrances. They come along in disorderly mobs, some in squads, stragglers, com-

---

[4] Published weekly from January 4, 1845 to January 3, 1846, and edited by Poe, Charles F. Briggs, and H. C. Watson.

[5] American fur-trader and financier, 1763-1848.

panies. Occasionally, a rare regiment, in perfect order, with its officers (some gaps, dead, the true braves,) marching in silence, with lowering faces, stern, weary to sinking, all black and dirty, but every man with his musket, and stepping alive; but these are the exceptions. Sidewalks of Pennsylvania avenue, Fourteenth street, &c., crowded, jamm'd with citizens, darkies, clerks, everybody, lookers-on; women in the windows, curious expressions from faces, as those swarms of dirt-cover'd return'd soldiers there (will they never end?) move by; but nothing said, no comments; (half our lookers-on secesh [6] of the most venomous kind—they say nothing; but the devil snickers in their faces.) During the forenoon Washington gets all over motley with these defeated soldiers—queer-looking objects, strange eyes and faces, drench'd (the steady rain drizzles on all day) and fearfully worn, hungry, haggard, blister'd in the feet. Good people (but not over-many of them either,) hurry up something for their grub. They put wash-kettles on the fire, for soup, for coffee. They set tables on the sidewalks—wagon-loads of bread are purchas'd, swiftly cut in stout chunks. Here are two aged ladies, beautiful, the first in the city for culture and charm, they stand with store of eating and drink at an improvis'd table of rough plank, and give food, and have the store replenish'd from their house every half-hour all that day; and there in the rain they stand, active, silent, white-hair'd, and give food, though the tears stream down their cheeks, almost without intermission, the whole time. Amid the deep excitement, crowds and motion, and desperate eagerness, it seems strange to see many, very many, of the soldiers sleeping—in the midst of all, sleeping sound. They drop down anywhere, on the steps of houses, up close by the basements or fences, on the sidewalk, aside on some vacant lot, and deeply sleep. A poor 17 or 18 year old boy lies there, on the stoop of a grand house; he sleeps so calmly, so profoundly. Some clutch their muskets firmly even in sleep. Some in squads; comrades, brothers, close together—and on them, as they lay, sulkily drips the rain.

As afternoon pass'd, and evening came, the streets, the bar-rooms, knots everywhere, listeners, questioners, terrible yarns, bugaboo, mask'd batteries, our regiment all cut up, &c.—stories and story-tellers, windy, bragging, vain centres of street-crowds. Resolution, manliness, seem to have abandon'd Washington. The principal hotel, Willard's, is full of shoulder-straps— thick, crush'd, creeping with shoulder-straps. (I see them, and must have a word with them. There you are, shoulder-straps! —but where are your companies? where are your men? Incompetents! never tell me of chances of battle, of getting stray'd, and the like. I think this is your work, this retreat, after all. Sneak, blow, put on airs there in Willard's sumptuous parlors and bar-rooms, or anywhere—no explanation shall save you. Bull Run is your work; had you been half or one-tenth worthy your men, this would never have happen'd.) Meantime, in Washington, among the great persons and their entourage, a mixture of awful consternation, uncertainty, rage, shame, helplessness, and stupefying disappointment. The worst is not only imminent, but already here. In a few hours —perhaps before the next meal—the secesh generals, with their victorious hordes, will be upon us. The dream of humanity, the vaunted Union we thought so strong, so impregnable—lo! it seems already smash'd like a china plate. One bitter, bitter hour —perhaps proud America will never again know such an hour. She must pack and fly—no time to spare. Those white palaces —the dome-crown'd capitol there on the hill, so stately over the trees—shall they be left—or destroy'd first? For it is certain that the talk among certain of the magnates and officers and clerks and officials everywhere, for twenty-four hours in and around Washington after Bull Run,

---

[6] Sympathizers with the seceding states; secessionists.

was loud and undisguised for yielding out and out, and substituting the southern rule, and Lincoln promptly abdicating and departing. If the secesh officers and forces had immediately follow'd, and by a bold Napoleonic movement had enter'd Washington the first day, (or even the second,) they could have had things their own way, and a powerful faction north to back them. One of our returning colonels express'd in public that night, amid a swarm of officers and gentlemen in a crowded room, the opinion that it was useless to fight, that the southerners had made their title clear, and that the best course for the national government to pursue was to desist from any further attempt at stopping them, and admit them again to the lead, on the best terms they were willing to grant. Not a voice was rais'd against this judgment, amid that large crowd of officers and gentlemen. (The fact is, the hour was one of the three or four of those crises we had then and afterward, during the fluctuations of four years, when human eyes appear'd at least just as likely to see the last breath of the Union as to see it continue.)

ABRAHAM LINCOLN

August 12th [1863].—I see the President almost every day, as I happen to live where he passes to or from his lodgings out of town. He never sleeps at the White House during the hot season, but has quarters at a healthy location some three miles north of the city, the Soldiers' home, a United States military establishment. I saw him this morning about 8½ coming in to business, riding on Vermont avenue, near L street. He always has a company of twenty-five or thirty cavalry, with sabres drawn and held upright over their shoulders. They say this guard was against his personal wish, but he let his counselors have their way. The party makes no great show in uniform or horses. Mr. Lincoln on the saddle generally rides a good-sized, easygoing gray horse, is dress'd in plain black, somewhat rusty and dusty, wears a

black stiff hat, and looks about as ordinary in attire, &c., as the commonest man. A lieutenant, with yellow straps, rides at his left, and following behind, two by two, come the cavalry men, in their yellow-striped jackets. They are generally going at a slow trot, as that is the pace set them by the one they wait upon. The sabres and accoutrements clank, and the entirely unornamental *cortège* as it trots towards Lafayette square arouses no sensation, only some curious stranger stops and gazes. I see very plainly ABRAHAM LINCOLN's dark brown face, with deep-cut lines, the eyes, always to me with a deep latent sadness in the expression. We have got so that we exchange bows, and very cordial ones. Sometimes the President goes and comes in an open barouche. The cavalry always accompany him, with drawn sabres. Often I notice as he goes out evenings—and sometimes in the morning, when he returns early—he turns off and halts at the large and handsome residence of the Secretary of War, on K street, and holds conference there. If in his barouche, I can see from my window he does not alight, but sits in his vehicle, and Mr. Stanton,[7] comes out to attend him. Sometimes one of his sons, a boy of ten or twelve, accompanies him, riding at his right on a pony.[8] Earlier in the summer I occasionally saw the President and his wife, toward the latter part of the afternoon, out in a barouche, on a pleasure ride through the city. Mrs. Lincoln was dress'd in complete black, with a long crape veil. The equipage is of the plainest kind, only two horses, and they nothing extra. They pass'd me once very close, and I saw the President in the face fully, as they were moving slowly, and his look, though abstracted, happen'd to be directed steadily in my eye. He bow'd and smiled, but far beneath his smile I noticed well the expression I have alluded to. None of the artists or pictures has caught

---

[7] Edwin M. Stanton (1814-1869), Secretary of War, 1862-1868.

[8] Thomas ("Tad") Lincoln, who died in 1871.

the deep, though subtle and indirect expression of this man's face. There is something else there. One of the great portrait painters of two or three centuries ago is needed.

Spiritual Characters among the Soldiers

Every now and then, in hospital or camp, there are beings I meet—specimens of unworldliness, disinterestedness, and animal purity and heroism—perhaps some unconscious Indianian, or from Ohio or Tennessee—on whose birth the calmness of heaven seems to have descended, and whose gradual growing up, whatever the circumstances of work-life or change, or hardship, or small or no education that attended it, the power of a strange spiritual sweetness, fibre and inward health, have also attended. Something veil'd and abstracted is often a part of the manners of these beings. I have met them, I say, not seldom in the army, in camp, and in the hospitals. The Western regiments contain many of them. They are often young men, obeying the events and occasions about them, marching, soldiering, fighting, foraging, cooking, working on farms or at some trade before the war—unaware of their own nature, (as to that, who is aware of his own nature?) their companions only understanding that they are different from the rest, more silent, "something odd about them," and apt to go off and meditate and muse in solitude.

Boys in the Army

As I walk'd home about sunset, I saw in Fourteenth street a very young soldier, thinly clad, standing near the house I was about to enter. I stopt a moment in front of the door and call'd him to me. I knew that an old Tennessee regiment, and also an Indiana regiment, were temporarily stopping in new barracks, near Fourteenth street. This boy I found belonged to the Tennessee regiment. But I could hardly believe he carried a musket. He was but 15 years old, yet had been twelve months a soldier, and had borne his part in several battles, even historic ones. I ask'd him if he did not suffer from the cold, and if he had no overcoat. No, he did not suffer from cold, and had no overcoat, but could draw one whenever he wish'd. His father was dead, and his mother living in some part of East Tennessee; all the men were from that part of the country. The next forenoon I saw the Tennessee and Indiana regiments marching down the Avenue. My boy was with the former, stepping along with the rest. There were many other boys no older. I stood and watch'd them as they tramp'd along with slow, strong, heavy, regular steps. There did not appear to be a man over 30 years of age, and a large proportion were from 15 to perhaps 22 or 23. They had all the look of veterans, worn, stain'd, impassive, and a certain unbent, lounging gait, carrying in addition to their regular arms and knapsacks, frequently a frying-pan, broom, &c. They were all of pleasant physiognomy; no refinement, nor blanch'd with intellect, but as my eye pick'd them, moving along, rank by rank, there did not seem to be a single repulsive, brutal or markedly stupid face among them.

The Women of the West

Kansas City.—I am not so well satisfied with what I see of the women of the prairie cities. I am writing this where I sit leisurely in a store in Main street, Kansas City, a streaming crowd on the sidewalks flowing by. The ladies (and the same in Denver) are all fashionably drest, and have the look of "gentility" in face, manner and action, but they do *not* have, either in physique or the mentality appropriate to them, any high native originality of spirit or body, (as the men certainly have, appropriate to them.) They are "intellectual" and fashionable, but dyspeptic-looking and generally doll-like; their ambition evidently is to copy their eastern sisters. Something far different and in advance must appear, to tally and complete the superb masculinity of the west, and maintain and continue it.

LOAFING IN THE WOODS

March 8.—I write this down in the country again, but in a new spot, seated on a log in the woods, warm, sunny, midday. Have been loafing here deep among the trees, shafts of tall pines, oak, hickory, with a thick undergrowth of laurels and grapevines—the ground cover'd everywhere by debris, dead leaves, breakage, moss—everything solitary, ancient, grim. Paths (such as they are) leading hither and yon—(how made I know not, for nobody seems to come here, nor man nor cattle-kind.) Temperature to-day about 60, the wind through the pine-tops; I sit and listen to its hoarse sighing above (and to the *stillness*) long and long, varied by aimless rambles in the old roads and paths, and by exercise-pulls at the young saplings, to keep my joints from getting stiff. Blue-birds, robins, meadow-larks begin to appear.

Next day, 9th.—A snowstorm in the morning, and continuing most of the day. But I took a walk over two hours, the same woods and paths, amid the falling flakes. No wind, yet the musical low murmur through the pines, quite pronounced, curious, like waterfalls, now still'd, now pouring again. All the senses, sight, sound, smell, delicately gratified. Every snowflake lay where it fell on the evergreens, holly-trees, laurels, &c., the multitudinous leaves and branches piled, bulging-white, defined by edge-lines of emerald—the tall straight columns of the plentiful bronze-topt pines —a slight resinous odor blending with that of the snow. (For there is a scent to everything, even the snow, if you can only detect it—no two places, hardly any two hours, anywhere, exactly alike. How different the odor of noon from midnight, or winter from summer, or a windy spell from a still one.)

American Literature 1860–1900

II
THE NEW REGIONALISM

1842 ∾ *Sidney Lanier* ∾ 1881

SIDNEY LANIER, dying at thirty-nine, was a delayed casualty of the War between North and South. His native town, Macon, Georgia, declared its secession from the Union even before South Carolina. He enlisted in its first regiment, the Macon Volunteers, as a private soldier, so that he would not be separated from his younger brother; and as a private soldier he served with conspicuous distinction for three and a half years, the last two in the highly dangerous Mounted Signal Service of the Confederate Army. Near the end of the war he was captured, and in Point Lookout prison he developed the disease that eventually caused his death. His few remaining years were a constant fight against tuberculosis. These circumstances of his life, and the affection which he inspired in all who knew him, added to something essentially romantic in the true sense in the man himself, have tended to surround Lanier and his work with an aura of sentiment which has somewhat obscured the character of his actual achievement.

A slender volume holds the poems which constitute the distinctive element of that achievement. His one novel, *Tiger-Lilies* (1867) is an extremely uneven book, discursive and full of talk, wooden in plot and, for the most part, in characterization, though it does contain brilliant battle scenes and penetrating analyses of Southern attitudes before, during, and after the war. *The Science of English Verse* (1880) presents a theory of prosody which is admittedly suggestive and stimulating but not generally accepted. The posthumously published volumes which were by-products of his teaching and lecturing, *The English Novel* (1883) and *Shakespeare and His Forerunners* (1902), are of value only for their occasional penetrating observations and personal reactions. The bread-and-butter work of his last years, the retelling of the famous stories of Malory, Froissart, the Mabinogion, was intended for juvenile readers. But his work as a poet—though the body of that work is very small if compared to the production of most remembered poets—is remarkably consistent in its high quality and in its individual tone.

Lanier was a musician before he was a poet. He showed exceptional musical ability as a child; and when the legal profession proved unremunerative for a Confederate veteran in Georgia after the Reconstruction (and the climate injurious to his health), it was his music which gave Lanier and his family a livelihood and indirectly opened the way to his literary career. He played the flute as a member of the Baltimore Symphony Orchestra, later lectured at the Peabody Institute and at the Johns Hopkins University, and wrote almost all of his best poems during these years in Baltimore. His love and knowledge of music are everywhere apparent in his work.

Lanier was, too, a lover of the earth, the southern American land and landscape. Images and illustrations from nature appear constantly in his poems and are intimately fused with his deepest meanings. It was his love for the Southern land that shaped his expression of concern for his region's economy and social wellbeing, in "Corn" and the earlier dialect poems, with their humor barbing their serious social comment.

Further, Lanier was a religious poet. The earth he loves and celebrates has meaning for him as reflection and expression of God. The human relationships he cherishes hold the same sanction. In the work of no other notable American poet of his century is a religious element so positive and so pervasive.

Finally, Lanier was a discerning and candid critic of his times. He was no more deceived by the pretensions of the Gilded Age than Henry Adams or Mark Twain; and in the terms appropriate to his whole conception of poetry he denounced arrogant materialism and social and economic injustice. Words and images from the mediæval world of knighthood and chivalry are numerous in Lanier's poetry; their usual association with sentimental and romantic attitudes, quite unrelated to today, should not hide the contemporary cogency of Lanier's thinking. In "The New South," an essay first published in *Scribner's Monthly* for October, 1880, and reprinted in his posthumous *Retrospects and Prospects* (1889), he went so far as to advocate a political and economic renovation of the South by "development of small farming" and "obliteration of the color line."

[The standard biography of Lanier is by A. H. Starke (Chapel Hill, 1933). Edward Mims' study in the American Men of Letters Series (Boston, 1905) is still valuable. *The Centennial Edition of the Works of Sidney Lanier*, 10 vols. (Baltimore, 1946), contains critical commentaries on all his books.]

NINE FROM EIGHT
[1884]

I was drivin' my two-mule waggin,
With a lot o' truck for sale,
Towards Macon, to git some baggin'
(Which my cotton was ready to bale),
And I come to a place on the side o' the
    pike   5
Whar a peert little winter branch jest had
    throw'd
The sand in a kind of a sand-bar like,
And I seed, a leetle ways up the road,
A man squattin' down, like a big bull-toad,

On the ground, a-figgerin' thar in the
    sand   10
With his finger, and motionin' with his
    hand,
    And he looked like Ellick Garry.
And as I driv up, I heerd him bleat
To hisself, like a lamb: "Haugh? nine
    from eight
    Leaves nuthin'—and none to carry?" 15

And Ellick's bull-cart was standin'
A cross-wise of the way,
And the little bull was a-expandin',
Hisself on a wisp of hay.
But Ellick he sat with his head bent
    down,   20

A-studyin' and musin' powerfully,
And his forrud was creased with a turrible
     frown,
And he was a-wurken' appearently
A 'rethmetic sum that wouldn't gee,
Fur he kep' on figgerin' away in the
     sand   25
With his finger, and motionin' with his
     hand,
  And I seed it was Ellick Garry.
And agin I heard him softly bleat
To hisself, like a lamb: "Haugh? nine
     from eight
  Leaves nuthin'—and none to carry!" 30

I woa'd my mules mighty easy
(Ellick's back was towards the road
And the wind hit was sorter breezy)
And I got down off'n my load,
And I crep' up close to Ellick's back, 35
And I heerd him a-talkin' softly, thus:
"Them figgers is got me under the hack.[1]
I caint see how to git out'n the muss,
Except to jest nat'ally fail and bus'!
My crap-leen[2] calls for nine hundred and
     more.   40
My counts o' sales is eight hundred and
     four,
  Of cotton for Ellick Garry.
Thar's eight, ought, four, jest like on a
     slate:
Here's nine and two oughts—Haugh? nine
     from eight
  Leaves nuthin' and none to carry.   45

"Them crap-leens, oh, them crap-leens!
I give one to Pardman and Sharks.
Hit gobbled me up like snap-beans
In a patch full o' old fiel'-larks.
But I thought I could fool the crap-leen
     nice,   50
And I hauled my cotton to Jammel and
     Cones.
But shuh! 'fore I even had settled my price
They tuck affidavy[3] without no bones
And levelled[4] upon me fur all ther loans
To the 'mount of sum nine hundred dollars
     or more   55
And sold me out clean for eight hundred
     and four,
  As sure as I'm Ellick Garry!

And thar it is down all squar and straight,
But I can't make it gee, fur nine from
     eight
  Leaves nuthin'—and none to carry." 60

Then I says "Hello, here, Garry!
However you star' and frown
Thare's something fur *you* to carry,
Fur you've worked it upside down!"
Then he riz and walked to his little bull-
     cart,   65
And made like he neither had seen nor
     heerd
Nor knowed that I knowed of his raskilly
     part,
And he tried to look as if he wa'nt feared
And gathered his lines like he never keered,
And he driv down the road 'bout a quarter
     or so,   70
And then looked around, and I hollered
     "Hello,
  Look here, Mister Ellick Garry!
You may git up soon and lie down late,
But you'll always find that nine from eight
  Leaves nuthin'—and none to carry." 75

LIFE AND SONG [5]
[1884 (1868)]

"If life were caught by a clarionet,
     And a wild heart, throbbing in the reed,
Should thrill its joy and trill its fret,
     And utter its heart in every deed,

---

[1] This phrase is explained in a note in
Poems of Sidney Lanier (New York, 1891),
p. 253, in the words of Richard Malcolm
Johnson, author of *The Dukesborough
Tales* and other Georgia stories: " 'Under
the hack' is a well-known phrase among
the country-people, and is applied, generally in a humorous sense, to those who
have been cowed by an accident. . . . The
phrase is possibly derived from 'hackle,'
an instrument used in the breaking of
flax."

[2] A mortgage on the crop, to be paid
when the crop is sold.

[3] Established legal evidence of ownership.

[4] Levied.

[5] This poem is one of a group called
"Street-Cries," all printed as quoted personal utterances.

"Then would this breathing clarionet   5
  Type what the poet fain would be;
For none o' the singers ever yet
  Has wholly lived his minstrelsy,

"Or clearly sung his true, true thought,
  Or utterly bodied forth his life,   10
Or out of life and song has wrought
  The perfect one of man and wife;

"Or lived and sung, that Life and Song
  Might each express the other's all,
Careless if life or art were long   15
  Since both were one, to stand or fall:

"So that the wonder struck the crowd,
  Who shouted it about the land:
His song was only living aloud,
  His work, a singing with his hand!"   20

A BALLAD OF TREES AND
THE MASTER
[1884 (1880)]

Into the woods my Master went,
Clean forspent, forspent.
Into the woods my Master came,
Forspent with love and shame.
But the olives they were not blind to
  Him,   5
The little gray leaves were kind to Him:
The thorn-tree had a mind to Him
When into the woods He came.

Out of the woods my Master went,
And He was well content.   10
Out of the woods my Master came,
Content with death and shame.
When Death and Shame would woo Him
  last,
From under the trees they drew Him last:
'Twas on a tree they slew Him—last   15
When out of the woods He came.

CORN [6]
[1877 (1875)]

Today the woods are trembling through
  and through
With shimmering forms, that flash before
  my view,

Then melt in green as dawn-stars melt in
  blue.
The leaves that wave against my cheek
  caress
Like women's hands; the embracing
  boughs express   5
  A subtlety of mighty tenderness;
The copse-depths into little noises start,
That sound anon like beatings of a heart,
Anon like talk 'twixt lips not far apart.
The beech dreams balm, as a dreamer
  hums a song;   10
Through that vague wafture, expirations
  strong
Throb from young hickories breathing
  deep and long
With stress and urgence bold of prisoned
  spring
  And ecstasy of burgeoning.
Now, since the dew-plashed road of morn
  is dry,   15
  Forth venture odors of more quality
  And heavenlier giving. Like Jove's locks
    awry,
    Long muscadines
Rich-wreathe the spacious foreheads of
  great pines,
And breathe ambrosial passion from their
  vines.   20
  I pray with mosses, ferns and flowers shy
  That hide like gentle nuns from human
    eye
  To lift adoring perfumes to the sky.
I hear faint bridal-sighs of brown and
  green
Dying to silent hints of kisses keen   25
As far lights fringe into a pleasant sheen.
  I start at fragmentary whispers, blown

---

[6] A note written by Lanier's wife, *Poems
of Sidney Lanier*, p. 251, states that this
poem holds special interest as "the first
outcome of his consciously developing art-
life. This life, the musician's and poet's,
he entered upon—after years of patient
denial and suppression—in September,
1873, uncertain of his powers but determined to give them wing." The poem was
written, though not in its final form, in
August, 1874, at Sunnyside, Georgia, where
Lanier spent a happy summer with his
family in the country.

From undertalks of leafy souls un-
    known,
Vague purports sweet, of inarticulate
    tone.

Dreaming of gods, men, nuns and brides,
    between   30
Old companies of oaks that inward lean
To join their radiant amplitudes of green
I slowly move, with ranging looks that
    pass
Up from the matted miracles of grass
Into yon veined complex of space   35
Where sky and leafage interlace
    So close, the heaven of blue is seen
    Inwoven with a heaven of green.

I wander to the zigzag-cornered fence
Where sassafras, intrenched in brambles
    dense,   40
Contests with stolid vehemence
    The march of culture, setting limb and
    thorn
As pikes against the army of the corn.

There, while I pause, my fieldward-faring
    eyes
Take harvests, where the stately corn-
    ranks rise,   45
    Of inward dignities
And large benignities and insights wise,
    Graces and modest majesties.
Thus, without theft, I reap another's field;
Thus, without tilth, I house a wondrous
    yield,   50
And heap my heart with quintuple crops
    concealed.

Look, out of line one tall corn-captain
    stands
Advanced beyond the foremost of his
    bands,
    And waves his blades upon the very
    edge
    And hottest thicket of the battling
    hedge.   55
Thou lustrous stalk, that ne'er mayst walk
    nor talk,
    Still shalt thou type the poet-soul
    sublime

That leads the vanward of his timid time
And sings up cowards with commanding
    rhyme—
Soul calm, like thee, yet fain, like thee,
    to grow   60
By double increment, above, below;
    Soul homely, as thou art, yet rich in
    grace like thee,
Teaching the yeomen selfless chivalry
That moves in gentle curves of courtesy;
Soul filled like thy long veins with sweet-
    ness tense,   65
    By every godlike sense
Transmuted from the four wild elements.
    Drawn to high plans,
    Thou lift'st more stature than a mortal
    man's,
Yet ever piercest downward in the mould 70
    And keepest hold
Upon the reverend and steadfast earth
    That gave thee birth;
Yea, standest smiling in thy future
    grave,
    Serene and brave   75
With unremitting breath
Inhaling life from death,
Thine epitaph writ fair in fruitage elo-
    quent,
    Thyself thy monument.

    As poets should,   80
Thou hast built up thy hardihood
With universal food,
    Drawn in select proportion fair
    From honest mould and vagabond air;
From darkness of the dreadful night, 85
    And joyful light;
    From antique ashes, whose departed
    flame
In thee has finer life and longer fame;
From wounds and balms,
From storms and calms   90
From potsherds and dry bones
    And ruin-stones.
Into thy vigorous substance thou hast
    wrought
Whate'er the hand of Circumstance hath
    brought;
    Yea, into cool solacing green hast
    spun   95

White radiance hot from out the sun.
So thou dost mutually leaven
Strength of earth with grace of heaven;
  So thou dost marry new and old
  Into a one of higher mould;   100
So thou dost reconcile the hot and cold,
  The dark and bright,
And many a heart-perplexing opposite,
    And so
  Akin by blood to high and low,   105
Fitly thou playest out thy poet's part,
Richly expending thy much-bruiséd heart
  In equal care to nourish lord in hall
    Or beast in stall:
  Thou took'st from all that thou mightst
    give to all.   110

O steadfast dweller on the selfsame spot
Where thou wast born, that still repinest
    not—
Type of the home-fond heart, the happy
    lot!—
  Deeply thy mild content rebukes the
    land
  Whose flimsy homes, built on the
    shifting sand   115
Of trade, for ever rise and fall
With alternation whimsical,
  Enduring scarce a day,
  Then swept away
By swift engulfments of incalculable
    tides   120
Whereon capricious Commerce rides.
Look, thou substantial spirit of content!
Across this little vale, thy continent,
  To where, beyond the mouldering mill,
  Yon old deserted Georgian hill   125
Bares to the sun his piteous aged crest
    And seamy breast
  By restless-hearted children left to lie
Untended there beneath the heedless sky,
As barbarous folk expose their old to
    die.   130
Upon that generous-rounding side,
  With gullies scarified
Where keen Neglect his lash hath plied,
Dwelt one I knew of old, who played at
    toil,
And gave to coquette Cotton soul and
    soil.   135

Scorning the slow reward of patient
    grain,
He sowed his heart with hopes of swifter
    gain,
Then sat him down and waited for the
    rain.
He sailed in borrowed ships of usury—
A foolish Jason on a treacherous sea, 140
Seeking the Fleece and finding misery.
  Lulled by smooth-rippling loans, in idle
    trance
  He lay, content that unthrift Circum-
    stance
  Should plough for him the stony field of
    Chance.
Yea, gathering crops whose worth no man
    might tell,   145
He staked his life on games of Buy-and-
    Sell,
And turned each field into a gambler's hell.
  Aye, as each year began,
  My farmer to the neighboring city ran;
Passed with a mournful anxious face   150
Into the banker's inner place;
  Parleyed, excused, pleaded for longer
    grace;
  Railed at the drought, the worm, the
    rust, the grass;
  Protested ne'er again 'twould come to
    pass;
  With many an oh and if and but alas 155
Parried or swallowed searching questions
    rude,
And kissed the dust to soften Dives's mood.
At last, small loans by pledges great
    renewed,
  He issues smiling from the fatal door,
  And buys with lavish hand his yearly
    store   160
Till his small borrowings will yield no
    more.
Aye, as each year declined,
With bitter heart and ever-brooding mind
He mourned his fate unkind.
  In dust, in rain, with might and
    main,   165
  He nursed his cotton, cursed his grain,
  Fretted for news that made him fret
    again,
Snatched at each telegram of Future Sale,

And thrilled with Bulls' or Bears' alternate
    wail—
In hope or fear alike for ever pale.   170
  And thus from year to year, through
    hope and fear,
  With many a curse and many a secret
    tear,
  Striving in vain his cloud of debt to
    clear,
    At last
He woke to find his foolish dreaming
    past,   175
  And all his best-of-life the easy prey
  Of squandering scamps and quacks that
    lined his way
    With vile array,
From rascal statesman down to petty
    knave;
Himself, at best, for all his bragging
    brave,   180
A gamester's catspaw and a banker's
    slave.
  Then, worn and gray, and sick with
    deep unrest,
  He fled away into the oblivious West
  Unmourned, unblest.

Old hill! old hill! thou gashed and
    hairy Lear   185
Whom the divine Cordelia [7] of the year,
E'en pitying Spring, will vainly strive to
    cheer—
  King, that no subject man nor beast
    may own,
Discrowned, undaughtered and alone—
Yet shall the great God turn thy fate,   190
And bring thee back into thy monarch
    state
    And majesty immaculate.
  Lo, through hot waverings of the
    August morn,
  Thou givest from thy vasty sides
    forlorn
  Visions of golden treasuries of
    corn—   195
Ripe largesse lingering for some bolder
    heart
That manfully shall take thy part,
    And tend thee,
    And defend thee,

With antique sinew and with modern
    art.   200

THE SYMPHONY
[1877 (1875)]

"O Trade! O Trade! would thou wert dead!
The Time needs heart—'tis tired of head:
We're all for love," the violins said.
"Of what avail the rigorous tale
Of bill for coin and box for bale?   5
Grant thee, O Trade! thine uttermost hope:
Level red gold with blue sky-slope,
And base it deep as devils grope:
When all's done, what hast thou won
Of the only sweet that's under the sun?   10
Ay, canst thou buy a single sigh
Of true love's least, least ecstasy?"
Then, with a bridegroom's heart-beats
    trembling,
All the mightier strings assembling
Ranged them on the violins' side   15
As when the bridegroom leads the bride,
And, heart in voice, together cried:
"Yea, what avail the endless tale
Of gain by cunning and plus by sale?
Look up the land, look down the land   20
The poor, the poor, the poor, they stand
Wedged by the pressing of Trade's hand
Against an inward-opening door
That pressure tightens evermore:
They sigh a monstrous foul-air sigh   25
For the outside leagues of liberty,
Where Art, sweet lark, translates the sky
Into a heavenly melody.
'Each day, all day' (these poor folks say),
'In the same old year-long, drear-long
    way,   30
We weave in the mills and heave in the
    kilns,
We sieve mine-meshes under the hills,
And thieve much gold from the Devil's
    bank tills,
To relieve, O God, what manner of ills?—
The beasts, they hunger, and eat, and
    die;   35
And so do we, and the world's a sty;

---

[7] Compare *King Lear*, Act IV, Scene
VII.

Hush, fellow-swine: why nuzzle and cry?
Swinehood hath no remedy
Say many men, and hasten by,
Clamping the nose and blinking the
　　　eye.　　　　　　　　　　　　　　40
But who said once, in the lordly tone,
Man shall not live by bread alone
But all that cometh from the Throne? [8]
　　　　　Hath God said so?
　　　　　But Trade saith *No:*　　　　45
And the kilns and the curt-tongued mills
　　　say *Go!*
There's plenty that can, if you can't: we
　　　know.
Move out, if you think you're underpaid.
The poor are prolific; we're not afraid;
　　　　　Trade is trade.'"　　　　50
Thereat this passionate protesting
Meekly changed, and softened till
It sank to sad requesting
And suggesting sadder still:
"And oh, if men might some time see　55
How piteous-false the poor decree
That trade no more than trade must be!
Does business mean, *Die, you—live, I?*
Then 'Trade is trade' but sings a lie:
'Tis only war grown miserly.　　　60
If business is battle, name it so:
War-crimes less will shame it so,
And widows less will blame it so.
Alas, for the poor to have some part
In yon sweet living lands of Art,　　65
Makes problem not for head, but heart.
Vainly might Plato's brain revolve it:
Plainly the heart of a child could solve it."

And then, as when from words that seem
　　　but rude
We pass to silent pain that sits abroad　70
Back in our heart's great dark and solitude,
So sank the strings to gentle throbbing
Of long chords change-marked with sob-
　　　bing—
Motherly sobbing, not distinctlier heard
Than half wing-openings of the sleeping
　　　bird,　　　　　　　　　　　　　75
Some dream of danger to her young hath
　　　stirred.
Then stirring and demurring ceased, and
　　　lo!

Every least ripple of the string's song-
　　　flow
Died to a level with each level bow
And made a great chord tranquil-surfaced
　　　so,　　　　　　　　　　　　　　80
As a brook beneath his curving bank doth
　　　go
To linger in the sacred dark and green
Where many boughs the still pool overlean
And many leaves make shadow with their
　　　sheen.
　　　But presently　　　　　　　　85
A velvet flute-note fell down pleasantly
Upon the bosom of that harmony,
And sailed and sailed incessantly,
As if a petal from a wild-rose blown
Had fluttered down upon that pool of
　　　tone　　　　　　　　　　　　　90
And boatwise dropped o' the convex side
And floated down the glassy tide
And clarified and glorified
The solemn spaces where the shadows
　　　bide.
From the warm concave of that fluted
　　　note　　　　　　　　　　　　　95
Somewhat, half song, half odor, forth did
　　　float,
As if a rose might somehow be a throat:
"When Nature from her far-off glen
Flutes her soft messages to men,
　　The flute can say them o'er again;　100
　　Yea, Nature, singing sweet and lone,
Breathes through life's strident polyphone
The flute-voice in the world of tone.
　　Sweet friends,
Man's love ascends　　　　　　105
To finer and diviner ends
Than man's mere thought e'er comprehends
For I, e'en I,
As here I lie,
A petal on a harmony,　　　　110
Demand of Science whence and why
Man's tender pain, man's inward cry,
When he doth gaze on earth and sky?
I am not overbold:
I hold　　　　　　　　　　　115
Full powers from Nature manifold.
I speak for each no-tonguéd tree

―――――――――――
[8] Luke 4:4.

That, spring by spring, doth nobler be,
And dumbly and most wistfully
His mighty prayerful arms outspreads 120
Above men's oft-unheeding heads,
And his big blessing downward sheds.
I speak for all-shaped blooms and leaves,
Lichens on stones and moss on eaves,
Grasses and grains in ranks and
    sheaves; 125
Broad-fronded ferns and keen-leaved canes,
And briery mazes bounding lanes,
And marsh-plants, thirsty-cupped for
    rains,
And milky stems and sugary veins;
For every long-armed woman-vine 130
That round a piteous tree doth twine;
For passionate odors, and divine
Pistils, and petals crystalline;
All purities of shady springs,
All shynesses of film-winged things 135
That fly from tree-trunks and bark-rings;
All modesties of mountain-fawns
That leap to covert from wild lawns,
And tremble if the day but dawns;
All sparklings of small beady eyes 140
Of birds, and sidelong glances wise
Wherewith the jay hints tragedies;
All piquancies of prickly burs,
And smoothnesses of downs and furs,
Of eiders an dof minevers; [9] 145
All limpid honeys that do lie
At stamen-bases, nor deny
The humming-birds' fine roguery,
Bee-thighs, nor any butterfly;
All gracious curves of slender wings, 150
Bark-mottlings, fibre-spiralings,
Fern-wavings and leaf-flickerings;
Each dial-marked leaf and flower-bell
Wherewith in every lonesome dell
Time to himself his hours doth tell; 155
All tree-sounds, rustlings of pine cones,
Wind-sighings, doves' melodious moans,
And night's unearthly under-tones;
All placid lakes and waveless deeps,
All cool reposing mountain-steeps, 160
Vale-calms and tranquil lotos-sleeps;—
Yea, all fair forms, and sounds, and lights,
And warmths, and mysteries, and mights,
Of Nature's utmost depths and heights,
—These doth my timid tongue present, 165

Their mouthpiece and leal instrument
And servant, all love-eloquent.
I heard, when 'All for love' the violins
    cried:
So, Nature calls through all her system
    wide,
Give me thy love, O man, so long de-
    nied. 170
Much time is run, and man hath changed
    his ways,
Since Nature, in the antique fable-days,
Was hid from man's true love by proxy
    fays,
False fauns and rascal gods that stole her
    praise.[10]
The nymphs, cold creatures of man's colder
    brain, 175
Chilled Nature's streams till man's warm
    heart was fain
Never to lave its love in them again.
Later, a sweet Voice *Love thy neighbor*
    said;
Then first the bounds of neighborhood out-
    spread
Beyond all confines of old ethnic dread. 180
Vainly the Jew might wag his covenant
    head:
'*All men are neighbors,*' so the sweet
    Voice said.
So, when man's arms had circled all man's
    race,
The liberal compass of his warm embrace
Stretched bigger yet in the dark bounds of
    space; 185
With hands a-grope he felt smooth Na-
    ture's grace,
Drew her to breast and kissed her sweet-
    heart face:
Yea, man found neighbors in great hills
    and trees
And streams and clouds and suns and birds
    and bees,
And throbbed with neighbor-loves in loving
    these. 190
But oh, the poor! the poor! the poor!
That stand by the inward-opening door

---

[9] Eider-ducks and ermines.

[10] Nature was not worshipped or loved
directly.

Trade's hand doth tighten ever more,
And sigh their monstrous foul-air sigh
For the outside hills of liberty,   195
Where Nature spreads her wild blue sky
For Art to make into melody!
Thou Trade! thou king of the modern days!
   Change thy ways,
   Change thy ways;   200
Let the sweaty laborers file
   A little while,
   A little while,
Where Art and Nature sing and smile.
Trade! is thy heart all dead, all dead? 205
And hast thou nothing but a head?
"I'm all for heart," the flute-voice said,
And into sudden silence fled,
Like as a blush that while 'tis red
Dies to a still, still white instead.   210

   Thereto a thrilling calm succeeds,
Till presently the silence breeds
A little breeze among the reeds
That seems to blow by sea-marsh weeds:
Then from the gentle stir and fret   215
Sings out the melting clarionet,
Like as a lady sings while yet
Her eyes with salty tears are wet.
"O Trade! O Trade!" the Lady said,
"I too will wish thee utterly dead   220
If all thy heart is in thy head.
For O my God! and O my God!
What shameful ways have women trod
At beckoning of Trade's golden rod!
Alas when sighs are traders' lies,   225
And heart's-ease eyes and violet eyes
   Are merchandise!
O purchased lips that kiss with pain!
O cheeks coin-spotted with smirch and
      stain!
O trafficked hearts that break in twain! 230
—And yet what wonder at my sisters'
      crime?
So hath Trade withered up Love's sinewy
      prime,
Men love not women as in olden time.
Ah, not in these cold merchantable days
Deem men their life an opal gray, where
      plays   235

The one red Sweet of gracious ladies'-
      praise.
Now, comes a suitor with sharp prying
      eye—
Says, *Here, you Lady, if you'll sell, I'll
      buy:*
*Come, heart for heart—a trade? What!
      weeping? why?*
Shame on such wooers' dapper mer-
      cery![11]   240
I would my lover kneeling at my feet
In humble manliness should cry, *O sweet!*
*I know not if thy heart my heart will
      greet:*
I ask not if thy love my love can meet:
*Whate'er thy worshipful soft tongue shall
      say,*   245
I'll kiss thine answer, be it yea or nay:
I do but know I love thee, and I pray
To be thy knight until my dying day.
Woe him that cunning trades in hearts con-
      trives!
Base love good women to base loving
      drives.   250
If men loved larger, larger were our lives;
And wooed they nobler, won they nobler
      wives."

There thrust the bold straightforward horn
To battle for that lady lorn,
With heartsome voice of mellow scorn, 255
Like any knight in knighthood's morn.
   "Now comfort thee," said he,
      "Fair Lady.
For God shall right thy grievous wrong,
And man shall sing thee a true-love
      song,   260
Voiced in act his whole life long,
   Yea, all thy sweet life long,
      Fair Lady.
Where's he that craftily hath said,
The day of chivalry is dead?   265
I'll prove that lie upon his head,
   Or I will die instead,
      Fair Lady.
Is Honor gone into his grave?
Hath Faith become a caitiff knave,   270

---

[11] Trading, merchandising.

And Selfhood turned into a slave
  To work in Mammon's cave,[12]
    Fair Lady?
Will Truth's long blade ne'er gleam again?
Hath Giant Trade in dungeons slain   275
All great contempts of mean-got gain
  And hates of inward stain,
    Fair Lady?
For aye shall name and fame be sold,
And place be hugged for the sake of
    gold,   280
And smirch-robed Justice feebly scold
  At Crime all money-bold,
    Fair Lady?
Shall self-wrapt husbands aye forget
Kiss-pardons for the daily fret   285
Wherewith sweet wifely eyes are wet—
  Blind to lips kiss-wise set—
    Fair Lady?
Shall lovers higgle, heart for heart,
Till wooing grows a trading mart   290
Where much for little, and all for part,
  Make love a cheapening art,
    Fair Lady?
Shall woman scorch for a single sin
That her betrayer may revel in,   295
And she be burnt, and he but grin
  When that the flames begin,
    Fair Lady?
Shall ne'er prevail the woman's plea,
We maids would far, far whiter be   300
If that our eyes might sometimes see
  Men maids in purity,
    Fair Lady?
Shall Trade aye salve his conscience-aches
With jibes at Chivalry's old mistakes— 305
The wars that o'erhot knighthood makes
  For Christ's and ladies' sakes,
    Fair Lady?
Now by each knight that e'er hath prayed
To fight like a man and love like a
    maid,   310
Since Pembroke's life, as Pembroke's
    blade,[13]
  I' the scabbard, death, was laid,
    Fair Lady,
I dare avouch my faith is bright
That God doth right and God hath
    might.   315

Nor time hath changed His hair to white,
  Nor His dear love to spite,
    Fair Lady.
I doubt no doubts: I strive, and shrive my
    clay,
And fight my fight in the patient modern
    way   320
For true love and for thee—ah me! and
    pray
  To be thy knight until my dying day,
    Fair Lady."
Made end that knightly horn, and spurred
    away
Into the thick of the melodious fray. 325

And then the hautboy played and smiled,
And sang like any large-eyed child,
  Cool-hearted and all undefiled.
    "Huge Trade!" he said.
"Would thou wouldst lift me on thy
    head   330
And run where'er my finger led!
Once said a Man—and wise was He—
Never shalt thou the heavens see,
Save as a little child thou be."[14]
Then o'er sea-lashings of commingling
    tunes   335
The ancient wise bassoons,
  Like weird
  Gray-beard
Old harpers sitting on the high sea-dunes,
  Chanted runes: 340
"Bright-waved gain, gray-waved loss,
The sea of all doth lash and toss,
One wave forward and one across:
But now 'twas trough, now 'tis crest,
And worst doth foam and flash to best, 345
  And curst to blest.

"Life! Life! thou sea-fugue, writ from east
    to west,
  Love, Love alone can pore

---

[12] Spenser's *The Faerie Queene*, Book
II, Canto vii.
[13] Probably a reference to Richard de
Clare, 2d Earl of Pembroke, English nobleman and half-legendary hero, d. 1176.
[14] Matt. 19:14. Mark 10:15.

On thy dissolving score
Of harsh half-phrasings,   350
  Blotted ere writ,
And double erasings
  Of chords most fit.
Yea, Love, sole music-master blest,
May read thy weltering palimpsest.   355
To follow Time's dying melodies through,
And never to lose the old in the new,
And ever to solve the discords true—
  Love alone can do.
And ever Love hears the poor-folks' cry-
  ing,   360
And ever Love hears the women's sighing,
And ever sweet knighthood's death-defying,
And ever wise childhood's deep implying,
But never a trader's glozing and lying.

"And yet shall Love himself be heard, 365
Though long deferred, though long de-
  ferred:
O'er the modern waste a dove hath whirred:
Music is Love in search of a word."

THE MARSHES OF GLYNN
[1884 (1879)]

Glooms of the live-oaks, beautiful-braided
  and woven
With intricate shades of the vines that
  myriad-cloven
  Clamber the forks of the multiform
    boughs,—
      Emerald twilights,—
      Virginal shy lights,   5
Wrought of the leaves to allure to the
  whisper of vows,
When lovers pace timidly down through
  the green colonnades
Of the dim sweet woods, of the dear dark
  woods,
Of the heavenly woods and glades,
That run to the radiant marginal sand-
  beach within   10
    The wide sea-marshes of Glynn;—

Beautiful glooms, soft dusks in the noon-
  day fire,—

Wildwood privacies, closets of lone desire,
Chamber from chamber parted with wavering arras of leaves,—
Cells for the passionate pleasure of prayer
  to the soul that grieves,   15
Pure with a sense of the passing of saints
  through the wood,
Cool for the dutiful weighing of ill with
  good;—

O braided dusks of the oak and woven
  shades of the vine,
While the riotous noon-day sun of the
  June-day long did shine
Ye held me fast in your heart and I held
  you fast in mine;   20
But now when the noon is no more, and
  riot is rest,
And the sun is a-wait at the ponderous gate
  of the West,
And the slant yellow beam down the
  wood-aisle doth seem
Like a lane into heaven that leads from a
  dream,—
Ay, now, when my soul all day hath
  drunken the soul of the oak,   25
And my heart is at ease from men, and the
  wearisome sound of the stroke
  Of the scythe of time and the trowel of
    trade is low,
  And belief overmasters doubt, and I
    know that I know,
  And my spirit is grown to a lordly great
    compass within,
That the length and the breadth and the
  sweep of the marshes of Glynn 30
Will work me no fear like the fear they
  have wrought me of yore
When length was fatigue, and when breadth
  was but bitterness sore,
And when terror and shrinking and dreary
  unnamable pain
Drew over me out of the merciless miles of
  the plain,—

Oh, now, unafraid, I am fain to face   35
  The vast sweet visage of space.
To the edge of the wood I am drawn, I am
  drawn,

Where the gray beach glimmering runs, as
   a belt of the dawn,
  For a mete and a mark
    To the forest-dark:—   40
     So:
Affable live-oak, leaning low,—
Thus—with your favor—soft, with a rev-
   erent hand,
(Not lightly touching your person, Lord
   of the land!)
Bending your beauty aside, with a step I
   stand   45
On the firm-packed sand,
    Free
By a world of marsh that borders a world
   of sea.
  Sinuous southward and sinuous north-
   ward the shimmering band
  Of the sand-beach fastens the fringe of
   the marsh to the folds of the land. 50
Inward and outward to northward and
   southward the beach-lines linger and
   curl
As a silver-wrought garment that clings to
   and follows the firm sweet limbs of
   a girl.
Vanishing, swerving, evermore curving
   again into sight,
Softly the sand-beach wavers away to a
   dim gray looping of light.
And what if behind me to westward the
   wall of the woods stands high? 55
The world lies east: how ample, the marsh
   and the sea and the sky!
A league and a league of marsh-grass,
   waist-high, broad in the blade,
Green, and all of a height, and unflecked
   with a light or a shade,
Stretch leisurely off, in a pleasant plain,
To the terminal blue of the main.   60

Oh, what is abroad in the marsh and the
   terminal sea?
  Somehow my soul seems suddenly free
From the weighing of fate and the sad
   discussion of sin,
By the length and the breadth and the
   sweep of the marshes of Glynn.

Ye marshes, how candid and simple and
   nothing-withholding and free   65
Ye publish yourselves to the sky and offer
   yourselves to the sea!
Tolerant plains, that suffer the sea and the
   rains and the sun,
Ye spread and span like the catholic man
   who hath mightily won
God out of knowledge and good out of
   infinite pain
And sight out of blindness and purity out
   of a stain.   70

As the marsh-hen secretly builds on the
   watery sod,
Behold I will build me a nest on the greatness of God:
I will fly in the greatness of God as the
   marsh-hen flies
In the freedom that fills all the space 'twixt
   the marsh and the skies:
By so many roots as the marsh-grass sends
   in the sod   75
I will heartily lay me a-hold on the greatness of God:
Oh, like to the greatness of God is the
   greatness within
The range of the marshes, the liberal
   marshes of Glynn.

And the sea lends large, as the marsh: lo,
   out of his plenty the sea
Pours fast: full soon the time of the flood-
   tide must be: 80
Look how the grace of the sea doth go
About and about through the intricate
   channels that flow
    Here and there,
     Everywhere,
Till his waters have flooded the uttermost
   creeks and the low-lying lanes, 85
And the marsh is meshed with a million
   veins,
That like as with rosy and silvery essences
   flow
In the rose-and-silver evening glow.
    Farewell, my lord Sun!
The creeks overflow: a thousand rivulets
   run   90

'Twixt the roots of the sod; the blades of
　　the marsh-grass stir;
Passeth a hurrying sound of wings that
　　westward whirr;
Passeth, and all is still; and the currents
　　cease to run;
And the sea and the marsh are one.

How still the plains of the waters be! 95
The tide is in his ecstasy.
The tide is at his highest height:
　　And it is night.

And now from the Vast of the Lord will
　　the waters of sleep
Roll in on the souls of men,　　　100
But who will reveal to our waking ken
The forms that swim and the shapes that
　　creep
　　　Under the waters of sleep?
And I would I could know what swimmeth
　　below when the tide comes in
On the length and the breadth of the
　　marvelous marshes of Glynn.　　105

1840 ∽ *Constance Fenimore Woolson* ∽ *1894*

CONSTANCE FENIMORE WOOLSON was not a Southerner, but an accident of family circumstance gave her opportunity for exceptional understanding of the South in the period after the Civil War. She was born in New
Hampshire, but lived most of her early years at Cleveland, Ohio, with summers
at Mackinac Island. Her mother's failing health led Constance to take her, not
long after the end of the war, to Florida. They remained there and in other
Southern states for six years, and Miss Woolson came to love the region. When
she left it permanently, it was to live abroad, chiefly in Italy, for the last fifteen
years of her life.

Miss Woolson's earlier stories, collected in part in *Castle Nowhere: Lake
Country Sketches* (1875), dealt with the region of the Great Lakes and the
specific setting of Mackinac Island. Her sympathetic comprehension of conditions and attitudes in the South after the war was expressed in stories included
in *Rodman the Keeper: Southern Sketches* (1880). Her first novel, *Anne*
(1882), portrays the Mackinac Island of her own early experience. Among her
other novels are *East Angels* (1886), *Jupiter Lights* (1889), and *Horace Chase*
(1894).

[Miss Woolson's writing has not been collected. *Constance Fenimore
Woolson* (London, 1930), edited by Clare Benedict, contains excerpts from
letters and journals, representative stories and poems, and lists of contributions
to magazines. John Dwight Kern's *Constance Fenimore Woolson: Literary
Pioneer* (Philadelphia, 1934) is a biographical and critical study. See also Henry
James, *Partial Portraits* (New York, 1888); F. P. Gaines, *The Southern Plantation: A Study in the Development and the Accuracy of a Tradition* (New York,
1925); Van Wyck Brooks, *New England: Indian Summer* (New York, 1940);
and Alexander Cowie, *The Rise of the American Novel* (New York, 1948).

The text of the following selection is that of the first edition of the volume under the same title (New York, 1880). The story was first published in *The Atlantic Monthly*, March, 1877. An introductory quotation, from a poem by Thomas Bailey Aldrich, has been omitted.]

RODMAN THE KEEPER

"KEEPER of what? Keeper of the dead. Well, it is easier to keep the dead than the living; and as for the gloom of the thing, the living among whom I have been lately were not a hilarious set."

John Rodman sat in the doorway and looked out over his domain. The little cottage behind him was empty of life save himself alone. In one room the slender appointments provided by Government for the keeper, who being still alive must sleep and eat, made the bareness doubly bare; in the other the desk and the great ledgers, the ink and pens, the register, the loud-ticking clock on the wall, and the flag folded on a shelf, were all for the kept, whose names, in hastily written, blotted rolls of manuscript, were waiting to be transcribed in the new red-bound ledgers in the keeper's best handwriting day by day, while the clock was to tell him the hour when the flag must rise over the mounds where reposed the bodies of fourteen thousand United States soldiers—who had languished where once stood the prison-pens, on the opposite slopes, now fair and peaceful in the sunset; who had fallen by the way in long marches to and fro under the burning sun; who had fought and died on the many battle-fields that reddened the beautiful State, stretching from the peaks of the marble mountains in the smoky west down to the sea-islands of the ocean border. The last rim of the sun's red ball had sunk below the horizon line, and the western sky glowed with deep rose-color, which faded away above into pink, into the salmon-tint, into shades of that far-away heavenly emerald which the brush of the earthly artist can never reproduce,

but which is found sometimes in the iridescent heart of the opal. The small town, a mile distant, stood turning its back on the cemetery; but the keeper could see the pleasant, rambling old mansions, each with its rose-garden and neglected outlying fields, the empty negro quarters falling into ruin, and everything just as it stood when on that April morning the first gun was fired on Sumter; apparently not a nail added, not a brushful of paint applied, not a fallen brick replaced, or latch or lock repaired. The keeper had noted these things as he strolled through the town, but not with surprise; for he had seen the South in its first estate, when, fresh, strong, and fired with enthusiasm, he, too, had marched away from his village home with the colors flying above and the girls waving their handkerchiefs behind, as the regiment, a thousand strong, filed down the dusty road. That regiment, a weak, scarred two hundred, came back a year later with lagging step and colors tattered and scorched, and the girls could not wave their handkerchiefs, wet and sodden with tears. But the keeper, his wound healed, had gone again; and he had seen with his New England eyes the magnificence and the carelessness of the South, her splendor and negligence, her wealth and thriftlessness, as through Virginia and the fair Carolinas, across Georgia and into sunny Florida, he had marched month by month, first a lieutenant, then captain, and finally major and colonel, as death mowed down those above him, and he and his good conduct were left. Everywhere magnificence went hand in hand with neglect, and he had said so as chance now and then threw a conversation in his path.

"We have no such shiftless ways," he would remark, after he had furtively supplied a prisoner with hardtack and coffee.

"And no such grand ones either," Johnny Reb would reply, if he was a man of spirit; and generally he was.

The Yankee, forced to acknowledge the truth of this statement, qualified it by observing that he would rather have more thrift with a little less grandeur; whereupon the other answered that *he* would not; and there the conversation rested. So now ex-Colonel Rodman, keeper of the national cemetery, viewed the little town in its second estate with philosophic eyes. "It is part of a great problem now working itself out; I am not here to tend the living, but the dead," he said.

Whereupon, as he walked among the long mounds, a voice seemed to rise from the still ranks below: "While ye have time, do good to men," it said. "Behold, we are beyond your care." But the keeper did not heed.

This still evening in early February he looked out over the level waste. The little town stood in the lowlands; there were no hills from whence cometh help—calm heights that lift the soul above earth and cares; no river to lead the aspirations of the children outward toward the great sea. Everything was monotonous, and the only spirit that rose above the waste was a bitterness for the gained and sorrow for the lost cause. The keeper was the only man whose presence personated the former in their sight, and upon him therefore, as representative, the bitterness fell, not in words, but in averted looks, in sudden silences when he approached, in withdrawals and avoidance, until he lived and moved in a vacuum; wherever he went there was presently no one save himself; the very shop-keeper who sold him sugar seemed turned into a man of wood, and took his money reluctantly, although the shilling gained stood perhaps for that day's dinner. So Rodman withdrew himself, and came and went among them no more; the broad acres of his domain gave him as much exercise as his shattered ankle could bear; he ordered his few supplies by the quantity, and began the life of a

solitary, his island marked out by the massive granite wall with which the United States Government has carefully surrounded those sad Southern cemeteries of hers; sad, not so much from the number of the mounds representing youth and strength cut off in their bloom, for that is but the fortune of war, as for the complete isolation which marks them. "Strangers in a strange land" is the thought of all who, coming and going to and from Florida, turn aside here and there to stand for a moment among the closely ranged graves which seem already a part of the past, that near past which in our hurrying American life is even now so far away. The Government work was completed before the keeper came; the lines of the trenches were defined by low granite copings, and the comparatively few single mounds were headed by trim little white boards bearing generally the word "Unknown," but here and there a name and an age, in most cases a boy from some faraway Northern State; "twenty-one," "twenty-two," said the inscriptions; the dates were those dark years among the sixties, measured now more than by anything else in the number of maidens widowed in heart, and women widowed indeed, who sit still and remember, while the world rushes by. At sunrise the keeper ran up the stars and stripes; and so precise were his ideas of the accessories belonging to the place, that from his own small store of money he had taken enough, by stinting himself, to buy a second flag for stormy weather, so that, rain or not, the colors should float over the dead. This was not patriotism so called, or miscalled, it was not sentimental fancy, it was not zeal or triumph, it was simply a sense of the fitness of things, a conscientiousness which had in it nothing of religion, unless indeed a man's endeavor to live up to his own ideal of his duty be a religion. The same feeling led the keeper to spend hours in copying the rolls. "John Andrew Warren, Company G, Eighth New Hampshire Infantry," he repeated, as he slowly wrote the name, giving "John Andrew" clear, bold capitals and a lettering impossible to mistake; "died August 15, 1863, aged twenty-two years. He came from the prison-pen yonder, and lies somewhere in those trenches, I suppose. Now then, John Andrew, don't fancy I am sorrowing for you; no doubt you are better off than I am at this very moment. But none the less, John Andrew, shall pen, ink, and hand do their duty to you. For that I am here."

Infinite pains and labor went into these records of the dead; one hair's breadth error, and the whole page was replaced by a new one. The same spirit kept the grass carefully away from the low coping of the trenches, kept the graveled paths smooth and the mounds green, and the bare little cottage neat as a man-of-war. When the keeper cooked his dinner, the door toward the east, where the dead lay, was scrupulously closed, nor was it opened until everything was in perfect order again. At sunset the flag was lowered, and then it was the keeper's habit to walk slowly up and down the path until the shadows veiled the mounds on each side, and there was nothing save the peaceful green of the earth. "So time will efface our little lives and sorrows," he mused, "and we shall be as nothing in the indistinguishable past." Yet none the less did he fulfill the duties of every day and hour with exactness. "At least they shall not say that I was lacking," he murmured to himself as he thought vaguely of the future beyond these graves. Who "they" were, it would have troubled him to formulate, since he was one of the many sons whom New England in this generation sends forth with a belief composed entirely of negatives. As the season advanced, he worked all day in the sunshine. "My garden looks well," he said. "I like this cemetery because it is the original resting-place of the dead who lie beneath. They were not brought here from distant places, gathered up by contract, numbered, and described like so much merchandise; their first repose has not been broken, their peace has been undisturbed. Hasty burials the prison authorities gave

them; the thin bodies were tumbled into the trenches by men almost as thin, for the whole State went hungry in those dark days. There were not many prayers, no tears, as the dead-carts went the rounds. But the prayers had been said, and the tears had fallen, while the poor fellows were still alive in the pens yonder; and when at last death came, it was like a release. They suffered long; and I for one believe that therefore shall their rest be long—long and sweet."

After a time began the rain, the soft, persistent, gray rain of the Southern lowlands, and he staid within and copied another thousand names into the ledger. He would not allow himself the companionship of a dog lest the creature should bark at night and disturb the quiet. There was no one to hear save himself, and it would have been a friendly sound as he lay awake on his narrow iron bed, but it seemed to him against the spirit of the place. He would not smoke, although he had the soldier's fondness for a pipe. Many a dreary evening, beneath a hastily built shelter of boughs, when the rain poured down and everything was comfortless, he had found solace in the curling smoke; but now it seemed to him that it would be incongruous, and at times he almost felt as if it would be selfish too. "*They* can not smoke, you know, down there under the wet grass," he thought, as standing at the window he looked toward the ranks of the mounds stretching across the eastern end from side to side—"my parade-ground," he called it. And then he would smile at his own fancies, draw the curtain, shut out the rain and the night, light his lamp, and go to work on the ledgers again. Some of the names lingered in his memory; he felt as if he had known the men who bore them, as if they had been boys together, and were friends even now although separated for a time. "James Marvin, Company B, Fifth Maine. The Fifth Maine was in the seven days' battle. I say, do you remember that retreat down the Quaker church road, and the way Phil Kearney held the rear-guard firm?" And over the whole seven days he wandered with his mute friend, who remembered everything and everybody in the most satisfactory way. One of the little head-boards in the parade-ground attracted him peculiarly because the name inscribed was his own: "—— Rodman, Company A, One Hundred and Sixth New York."

"I remember that regiment; it came from the extreme northern part of the State. Blank Rodman must have melted down here, coming as he did from the half-arctic region along the St. Lawrence. I wonder what he thought of the first hot day, say in South Carolina, along those simmering rice-fields?" He grew into the habit of pausing for a moment by the side of this grave every morning and evening. "Blank Rodman. It might easily have been John. And then, where should *I* be?"

But Blank Rodman remained silent, and the keeper, after pulling up a weed or two and trimming the grass over his relative, went off to his duties again. "I am convinced that Blank is a relative," he said to himself; "distant, perhaps, but still a kinsman."

One April day the heat was almost insupportable; but the sun's rays were not those brazen beams that sometimes in Northern cities burn the air and scorch the pavements to a white heat; rather were they soft and still; the moist earth exhaled her richness, not a leaf stirred, and the whole level country seemed sitting in a hot vapor-bath. In the early dawn the keeper had performed his outdoor tasks, but all day he remained almost without stirring in his chair between two windows, striving to exist. At high noon out came a little black bringing his supplies from the town, whistling and shuffling along, gay as a lark. The keeper watched him coming slowly down the white road, loitering by the way in the hot blaze, stopping to turn a somersault or two, to dangle over a bridge rail, to execute various impromptu capers all by himself. He reached the gate at last, entered, and, having come all the way up the path in a hornpipe step, he set down his basket at the door to indulge in one long and final double-shuffle before knocking. "Stop that!" said the keeper through the closed blinds. The little darkey darted back; but as nothing further came out of the window—a boot, for instance, or some other stray missile—he took courage, showed his ivories, and drew near again. "Do you suppose I am going to have you stirring up the heat in that way?" demanded the keeper.

The little black grinned, but made no reply, unless smoothing the hot white sand with his black toes could be construed as such; he now removed his rimless hat and made a bow.

"Is it, or is it not warm?" asked the keeper, as a naturalist might inquire of a salamander, not referring to his own so much as to the salamander's ideas on the subject.

"Dunno, mars'," replied the little black.

"How do *you* feel?"

" 'Spects I feel all right, mars'."

The keeper gave up the investigation, and presented to the salamander a nicket cent. "I suppose there is no such thing as a cool spring in all this melting country," he said.

But the salamander indicated with his thumb a clump of trees on the green plain north of the cemetery. "Ole Mars' Ward's place—cole spring dah." He then departed, breaking into a run after he had passed the gate, his ample mouth watering at the thought of a certain chunk of taffy at the mercantile establishment kept by Aunt Dinah in a corner of her one-roomed cabin. At sunset the keeper went thirstily out with a tin pail on his arm, in search of the cold spring. "If it could only be like the spring down under the rocks where I used to drink when I was a boy!" he thought. He had never walked in that direction before. Indeed, now that he had abandoned the town, he seldom went beyond the walls of the cemetery. An old road led across to the clump of trees, through fields run to waste, and following it he came to the place, a deserted house with tumble-down fences and overgrown garden, the out-buildings indicating that once upon a time there were many servants and a prosperous master. The house was of wood, large on the ground, with encircling piazzas; across the front door rough bars had been nailed, and the closed blinds were protected in the same manner; from long want of paint the clapboards were gray and mossy, and the floor of the piazza had fallen in here and there from decay. The keeper decided that his cemetery was a much more cheerful place than this, and then he looked around for the spring. Behind the house the ground sloped down; it must be there. He went around and came suddenly upon a man lying on an old rug outside of a back door. "Excuse me. I thought nobody lived here," he said.

"Nobody does," replied the man; "I am not much of a body, am I?"

His left arm was gone, and his face was thin and worn with long illness; he closed his eyes after speaking, as though the few words had exhausted him.

"I came for water from a cold spring you have here, somewhere," pursued the keeper, contemplating the wreck before him with the interest of one who has himself been severely wounded and knows the long, weary pain. The man waved his hand toward the slope without unclosing his eyes, and Rodman went off with his pail and found a little shady hollow, once curbed and paved with white pebbles, but now neglected, like all the place. The water was cold, however, deliciously cold. He filled his pail and thought that perhaps after all he would exert himself to make coffee, now that the sun was down; it would taste better made of this cold water. When he came up the slope the man's eyes were open.

"Have some water?" asked Rodman.

"Yes; there's a gourd inside."

The keeper entered, and found himself in a large, bare room; in one corner was some straw covered with an old counter-pane, in another a table and chair; a kettle hung in the deep fireplace, and a few dishes stood on a shelf; by the door on a nail hung a gourd; he filled it and gave it to the host of this desolate abode. The man drank with eagerness.

"Pomp has gone to town," he said, "and I could not get down to the spring to-day, I have had so much pain."

"And when will Pomp return?"

"He should be here now; he is very late to-night."

"Can I get you anything?"

"No, thank you; he will soon be here."

The keeper looked out over the waste; there was no one in sight. He was not a man of any especial kindliness—he had himself been too hardly treated in life for that—but he could not find it in his heart to leave this helpless creature all alone with night so near. So he sat down on the door-step. "I will rest awhile," he said, not asking but announcing it. The man had turned away and closed his eyes again, and they both remained silent, busy with their own thoughts; for each had recognized the ex-soldier, Northern and Southern, in portions of the old uniforms, and in the accent. The war and its memories were still very near to the maimed, poverty-stricken Confederate; and the other knew that they were, and did not obtrude himself.

Twilight fell, and no one came.

"Let me get you something," said Rodman; for the face looked ghastly as the fever abated. The other refused. Darkness came; still, no one.

"Look here," said Rodman, rising, "I have been wounded myself, was in hospital for months; I know how you feel. You must have food—a cup of tea, and a slice of toast, brown and thin."

"I have not tasted tea or wheaten bread for weeks," answered the man; his voice died off into a wail, as though feebleness and pain had drawn the cry from him in spite of himself. Rodman lighted a match; there was no candle, only a piece of pitch-pine stuck in an iron socket on the wall; he set fire to this primitive torch and looked around.

"There is nothing there," said the man outside, making an effort to speak carelessly; "my servant went to town for supplies. Do not trouble yourself to wait; he will come presently, and—and I want nothing."

But Rodman saw through proud poverty's lie; he knew that irregular quavering of the voice, and that trembling of the hand; the poor fellow had but one to tremble. He continued his search; but the bare room gave back nothing, not a crumb.

"Well, if you are not hungry," he said, briskly, "I am, hungry as a bear; and I'll tell you what I am going to do. I live not far from here, and I live all alone too; I haven't a servant as you have. Let me take supper here with you, just for a change; and, if your servant comes, so much the better, he can wait upon us. I'll run over and bring back the things."

He was gone without waiting for reply; the shattered ankle made good time over the waste, and soon returned, limping a little, but bravely hasting, while on a tray came the keeper's best supplies, Irish potatoes, corned beef, wheaten bread, butter, and coffee; for he would not eat the hot biscuits, the corn-cake, the bacon and hominy of the country, and constantly made little New England meals for himself in his prejudiced little kitchen. The pine-torch flared in the doorway; a breeze had come down from the far mountains and cooled the air. Rodman kindled a fire on the cavernous hearth, filled the kettle, found a saucepan, and commenced operations, while the other lay outside and watched every movement in the lighted room.

"All ready; let me help you in. Here we are now; fried potatoes, cold beef, mustard, toast, butter, and tea. Eat, man; and the next time I am laid up you shall come over and cook for me."

Hunger conquered, and the other ate, ate as he had not eaten for months. As he was finishing a second cup of tea, a slow step came around the house; it was the missing Pomp, an old negro, bent and shriveled, who carried a bag of meal and some bacon in his basket. "That is what they live on," thought the keeper.

He took leave without more words. "I suppose now I can be allowed to go home in peace," he grumbled to conscience. The negro followed him across what was once the lawn. "Fin' Mars' Ward mighty low," he said apologetically, as he swung open the gate which still hung between its posts, although the fence was down, "but I hurred and hurred as fas' as I could; it's mighty fur to de town. Proud to see you, sah; hope you'll come again. Fine fambly, de Wards, sah, befo' de war."

"How long has he been in this state?" asked the keeper.

"Ever sence one ob de las' battles, sah; but he's worse sence we come yer, 'bout a mont' back."

"Who owns the house? Is there no one to see to him? Has he no friends?"

"House b'long to Mars' Ward's uncle; fine place once, befo' de war; he's dead now, an' dah's nobuddy but Miss Bettina, an' she's gone off somewhuz. Propah place, sah, for Mars' Ward—own uncle's house," said the old slave, loyally striving to maintain the family dignity even then.

"Are there no better rooms—no furniture?"

"Sartin; but—but Miss Bettina, she took de keys; she didn't know we was comin'——"

"You had better send for Miss Bettina, I think," said the keeper, starting homeward with his tray, washing his hands, as it were, of any future responsibility in the affair.

The next day he worked in his garden, for clouds veiled the sun and exercise was possible; but, nevertheless, he could not forget the white face on the old rug. "Pshaw!" he said to himself, "haven't I seen tumble-down old houses and battered human beings before this?"

At evening came a violent thunderstorm, and the splendor of the heavens was terrible. "We have chained you, mighty spirit," thought the keeper as he watched the lightning, "and some time we shall learn the laws of the winds and foretell the storms; then, prayers will no more be offered in churches to alter an eclipse. Yet back of the lightning and the wind lies the power of the great Creator, just the same."

But still into his musings crept, with shadowy persistence, the white face on the rug.

"Nonsense!" he exclaimed; "if white faces are going around as ghosts, how about the fourteen thousand white faces that went under the sod down yonder? If they could arise and walk, the whole State would be filled and no more carpet-baggers needed." So, having balanced the one with the fourteen thousand, he went to bed.

Daylight brought rain—still, soft, gray rain; the next morning showed the same, and the third likewise, the nights keeping up their part with lowdown clouds and steady pattering on the roof. "If there was a river here, we should have a flood," thought the keeper, drumming idly on his window-pane. Memory brought back the steep New England hillsides shedding their rain into the brooks, which grew in a night to torrents and filled the rivers so that they overflowed their banks; then, suddenly, an old house in a sunken corner of a waste rose before his eyes, and he seemed to see the rain dropping from a moldy ceiling on the straw where a white face lay.

"Really, I have nothing else to do to-day, you know," he remarked in an apologetic way to himself, as he and his umbrella went along the old road; and he repeated the remark as he entered the room where the man lay, just as he had fancied, on the damp straw.

"The weather *is* unpleasant," said the man. "Pomp, bring a chair."

Pomp brought one, the only one, and the visitor sat down. A fire smoldered on the hearth and puffed out acrid smoke now and then, as if the rain had clogged the soot in the long-neglected chimney; from the streaked ceiling oozing drops fell with a dull splash into little pools on the decayed floor; the door would not close; the broken panes were stopped with rags, as if the

old servant had tried to keep out the damp; in the ashes a corn-cake was baking.

"I am afraid you have not been so well during these long rainy days," said the keeper, scanning the face on the straw.

"My old enemy, rheumatism," answered the man; "the first sunshine will drive it away."

They talked awhile, or rather the keeper talked, for the other seemed hardly able to speak, as the waves of pain swept over him; then the visitor went outside and called Pomp out. "Is there any one to help him, or not?" he asked impatiently.

"Fine fambly, befo' de war," began Pomp.

"Never mind all that; is there any one to help him now—yes or no?"

"No," said the old black with a burst of despairing truthfulness. "Miss Bettina, she's as poor as Mars' Ward, an' dere's no one else. He's had noth'n but hard corn-cake for three days, an' he can't swaller it no more."

The next morning saw Ward De Rosset lying on the white pallet in the keeper's cottage, and old Pomp, marveling at the cleanliness all around him, installed as nurse. A strange asylum for a Confederate soldier, was it not? But he knew nothing of the change, which he would have fought with his last breath if consciousness had remained; returning fever, however, had absorbed his senses, and then it was that the keeper and the slave had borne him slowly across the waste, resting many times, but accomplishing the journey at last.

That evening John Rodman, strolling to and fro in the dusky twilight, paused alongside of the other Rodman. "I do not want him here, and that is the plain truth," he said, pursuing the current of his thoughts. "He fills the house; he and Pomp together disturb all my ways. He'll be ready to fling a brick at me too, when his senses come back; small thanks shall I have for lying on the floor, giving up all my comforts, and, what is more, riding over the spirit of the place with a vengeance!" He threw himself down on the grass beside the mound and lay looking up toward the stars, which were coming out, one by one, in the deep blue of the Southern night. "With a vengeance, did I say? That is it exactly— the vengeance of kindness. The poor fellow has suffered horribly in body and in estate, and now ironical Fortune throws him in my way, as if saying, 'Let us see how far your selfishness will yield.' This is not a question of magnanimity; there is no magnanimity about it, for the war is over, and you Northerners have gained every point for which you fought. This is merely a question between man and man; it would be the same if the sufferer was a poor Federal, one of the carpet-baggers, whom you despise so, for instance, or a pagan Chinaman. And Fortune is right; don't you think so, Blank Rodman? I put it to you, now, to one who has suffered the extreme rigor of the other side—those prison-pens yonder."

Whereupon Blank Rodman answered that he had fought for a great cause, and that he knew it, although a plain man and not given to speech-making; he was not one of those who had sat safely at home all through the war, and now belittled it and made light of its issues. (Here a murmur came up from the long line of the trenches, as though all the dead had cried out.) But now the points for which he had fought being gained, and strife ended, it was the plain duty of every man to encourage peace. For his part he bore no malice; he was glad the poor Confederate was up in the cottage, and he did not think any less of the keeper for bringing him there. He would like to add that he thought more of him; but he was sorry to say that he was well aware what an effort it was, and how almost grudgingly the charity began.

If Blank Rodman did not say this, at least the keeper imagined that he did. "That is what he would have said," he thought. "I am glad you do not object," he added, pretending to himself that he had not noticed the rest of the remark.

"We do not object to the brave soldier who honestly fought for his cause, even though he fought on the other side," answered Blank Rodman for the whole fourteen thousand. "But never let a coward, a double-face, or a flippant-tongued idler walk over our heads. It would make us rise in our graves!"

And the keeper seemed to see a shadowy pageant sweep by—gaunt soldiers with white faces, arming anew against the subtle product of peace: men who said, "It was nothing! Behold, we saw it with our eyes!" —stay-at-home eyes.

The third day the fever abated, and Ward De Rosset noticed his surroundings. Old Pomp acknowledged that he had been moved, but veiled the locality: "To a frien's house, Mars' Ward."

"But I have no friends now, Pomp," said the weak voice.

Pomp was very much amused at the absurdity of this. "No frien's! Mars' Ward, no frien's!" He was obliged to go out of the room to hide his laughter. The sick man lay feebly thinking that the bed was cool and fresh, and the closed green blinds pleasant; his thin fingers stroked the linen sheet, and his eyes wandered from object to object. The only thing that broke the rule of bare utility in the simple room was a square of white drawing-paper on the wall, upon which was inscribed in ornamental text the following verse:

"Toujours femme varie,[1]
    Bien fou qui s'y fie;
    Une femme souvent
    N'est qu'une plume au vent."

With the persistency of illness the eyes and mind of Ward De Rosset went over and over this distich; he knew something of French, but was unequal to the effort of translating; the rhymes alone caught his vagrant fancy. "Toujours femme varie," he said to himself over and over again; and when the keeper entered, he said it to him.

"Certainly," answered the keeper; "bien fou qui s'y fie. How do you find yourself this morning?"

"I have not found myself at all, so far. Is this your house?"

[1] See Verdi's *Rigoletto*, Act III, Scene 1.

"Yes."

"Pomp told me I was in a friend's house," observed the sick man, vaguely.

"Well, it isn't an enemy's. Had any breakfast? No? Better not talk, then."

He went to the detached shed which served for a kitchen, upset all Pomp's clumsy arrangements, and ordered him outside; then he set to work and prepared a delicate breakfast with his best skill. The sick man eagerly eyed the tray as he entered. "Better have your hands and face sponged off, I think," said Rodman; and then he propped him up skillfully, and left him to his repast. The grass needed mowing on the parade-ground; he shouldered his scythe and started down the path, viciously kicking the gravel aside as he walked. "Wasn't solitude your principal idea, John Rodman, when you applied for this place?" he demanded of himself. "How much of it are you likely to have with sick men, and sick men's servants, and so forth?"

The "and so forth," thrown in as a rhetorical climax, turned into reality and arrived bodily upon the scene—a climax indeed. One afternoon, returning late to the cottage, he found a girl sitting by the pallet—a girl young and dimpled and dewy; one of the creamy roses of the South that, even in the bud, are richer in color and luxuriance than any Northern flower. He saw her through the door, and paused; distressed old Pomp met him and beckoned him cautiously outside. "Miss Bettina," he whispered gutturally; "she's come back from somewhuz, an' she's awful mad 'cause Mars' Ward's here. I tole her all 'bout 'em—de leaks an' de rheumatiz an' de hard corn-cake, but she done gone scole me; and Mars' Ward, he know now whar he is, an' he mad too."

"Is the girl a fool?" said Rodman. He was just beginning to rally a little. He stalked into the room and confronted her. "I have the honor of addressing——"

"Miss Ward."

"And I am John Rodman, keeper of the national cemetery."

This she ignored entirely; it was as though he had said, "I am John Jones, the coachman." Coachmen were useful in their way; but their names were unimportant.

The keeper sat down and looked at his new visitor. The little creature fairly radiated scorn; her pretty head was thrown back, her eyes, dark brown fringed with long dark lashes, hardly deigned a glance; she spoke to him as though he was something to be paid and dismissed like any other mechanic.

"We are indebted to you for some days' board, I believe, keeper—medicines, I presume, and general attendance. My cousin will be removed to-day to our own residence; I wish to pay now what he owes."

The keeper saw that her dress was old and faded; the small black shawl had evidently been washed and many times mended; the old-fashioned knitted purse she held in her hand was lank with long famine.

"Very well," he said; "if you choose to treat a kindness in that way, I consider five dollars a day none too much for the annoyance, expense, and trouble I have suffered. Let me see: five days—or is it six? Yes. Thirty dollars, Miss Ward."

He looked at her steadily; she flushed. "The money will be sent to you," she began haughtily; then, hesitatingly, "I must ask a little time——"

"O Betty, Betty, you know you can not pay it. Why try to disguise—But that does not excuse *you* for bringing me here," said the sick man, turning toward his host with an attempt to speak fiercely, which ended in a faltering quaver.

All this time the old slave stood anxiously outside of the door; in the pauses they could hear his feet shuffling as he waited for the decision of his superiors. The keeper rose and threw open the blinds of the window that looked out on the distant parade-ground. "Bringing you here," he repeated—"*here;* that is my offense, is it? There they lie, fourteen thousand brave men and true. Could they come back to earth they would be the first to pity and aid you, now that you are down. So would it be with you if the case were reversed; for a soldier is generous to a soldier. It was not your own heart that spoke then; it was the small venom of a woman, that here, as everywhere through the South, is playing its rancorous part."

The sick man gazed out through the window, seeing for the first time the far-spreading ranks of the dead. He was very weak, and the keeper's words had touched him; his eyes were suffused with tears. But Miss Ward rose with a flashing glance. She turned her back full upon the keeper and ignored his very existence. "I will take you home immediately, Ward—this very evening," she said.

"A nice, comfortable place for a sick man," commented the keeper, scornfully. "I am going out now, De Rosset, to prepare your supper; you had better have one good meal before you go."

He disappeared, but as he went he heard the sick man say, deprecatingly: "It isn't very comfortable over at the old house, now indeed it isn't, Betty; I suffered"— and the girl's passionate outburst in reply. Then he closed his door and set to work.

When he returned, half an hour later, Ward was lying back exhausted on the pillows, and his cousin sat leaning her head upon her hand; she had been weeping, and she looked very desolate, he noticed, sitting there in what was to her an enemy's country. Hunger is a strong master, however, especially when allied to weakness; and the sick man ate with eagerness.

"I must go back," said the girl, rising. "A wagon will be sent out for you, Ward; Pomp will help you."

But Ward had gained a little strength as well as obstinacy with the nourishing food. "Not to-night," he said.

"Yes, to-night."

"But I can not go to-night; you are unreasonable, Bettina. To-morrow will do as well, if go I must."

"If go you must! You do not want to go, then—to go to our own home—and with me"—Her voice broke; she turned toward the door.

The keeper stepped forward. "This is all nonsense, Miss Ward," he said, "and you know it. Your cousin is in no state to be moved. Wait a week or two, and he can go in safety. But do not dare to offer me your money again; my kindness was to the soldier, not to the man, and as such he can accept it. Come out and see him as often as you please. I shall not intrude upon you. Pomp, take the lady home."

And the lady went.

Then began a remarkable existence for the four; a Confederate soldier lying ill in the keeper's cottage of a national cemetery; a rampant little rebel coming out daily to a place which was to her an anathema-maranatha; a cynical, misanthropic keeper sleeping on the floor and enduring every variety of discomfort for a man he never saw before—a man belonging to an idle, arrogant class he detested; and an old black freedman allowing himself to be taught the alphabet in order to gain permission to wait on his master—master no longer in law—with all the devotion of his loving old heart. For the keeper had announced to Pomp that he must learn his alphabet or go; after all these years of theory, he, as a New-Englander, could not stand by and see precious knowledge shut from the black man. So he opened it, and mighty dull work he found it.

Ward De Rosset did not rally as rapidly as they expected. The white-haired doctor from the town rode out on horseback, pacing slowly up the graveled roadway with a scowl on his brow, casting, as he dismounted, a furtive glance down toward the parade-ground. His horse and his coat were alike old and worn, and his broad shoulders were bent with long service in the miserably provided Confederate hospitals, where he had striven to do his duty through every day and every night of those shadowed years. Cursing the incompetency in high places, cursing the mismanagement of the entire medical department of the Confederate army, cursing the recklessness and indifference which left the men suffering for want of proper hospitals and hospital stores, he yet went on resolutely doing his best with the poor means in his control until the last. Then he came home, he and his old horse, and went the rounds again, he prescribing for whooping-cough or measles, and Dobbin waiting outside; the only difference was that fees were small and good meals scarce for both, not only for the man but for the beast. The doctor sat down and chatted awhile kindly with De Rosset, whose father and uncle had been dear friends of his in the bright, prosperous days; then he left a few harmless medicines and rose to go, his gaze resting a moment on Miss Ward, then on Pomp, as if he were hesitating. But he said nothing until on the walk outside he met the keeper, and recognized a person to whom he could tell the truth. "There is nothing to be done; he may recover, he may not; it is a question of strength merely. He needs no medicines, only nourishing food, rest, and careful tendance."

"He shall have them," answered the keeper briefly. And then the old gentleman mounted his horse and rode away, his first and last visit to a national cemetery.

"National!" he said to himself—"national!"

All talk of moving De Rosset ceased, but Miss Ward moved into the old house. There was not much to move: herself, her one trunk, and Mari, a black attendant, whose name probably began life as Maria, since the accent still dwelt on the curtailed last syllable. The keeper went there once, and once only, and then it was an errand for the sick man, whose fancies came sometimes at inconvenient hours—when Pomp had gone to town, for instance. On this occasion the keeper entered the mockery of a gate and knocked at the front door, from which the bars had been removed; the piazza still showed its decaying planks, but quick-growing summer vines had been planted, and were now encircling the old pillars and veiling all defects with their greenery. It was a woman's pathetic effort to cover up what can not be covered— poverty. The blinds on one side were open,

and white curtains waved to and fro in the breeze; into this room he was ushered by Mari. Matting lay on the floor, streaked here and there ominously by the dampness from the near ground. The furniture was of dark mahogany, handsome in its day: chairs, a heavy pier-table with low-down glass, into which no one by any possibility could look unless he had eyes in his ankles, a sofa with a stiff round pillow of haircloth under each curved end, and a mirror with a compartment framed off at the top, containing a picture of shepherds and shepherdesses, and lambs with blue ribbons around their necks, all enjoying themselves in the most natural and life-like manner. Flowers stood on the high mantel-piece, but their fragrance could not overcome the faint odor of the damp straw-matting. On a table were books—a life of General Lee, and three or four shabby little volumes printed at the South during the war, waifs of prose and poetry of that highly wrought, richly colored style which seems indigenous to Southern soil.

"Some way, the whole thing reminds me of a funeral," thought the keeper.

Miss Ward entered, and the room bloomed at once; at least that is what a lover would have said. Rodman, however, merely noticed that she bloomed, and not the room, and he said to himself that she would not bloom long if she continued to live in such a moldy place. Their conversation in these days was excessively polite, shortened to the extreme minimum possible, and conducted without the aid of the eyes, at least on one side. Rodman had discovered that Miss Ward never looked at him, and so he did not look at her—that is, not often; he was human, however, and she was delightfully pretty. On this occasion they exchanged exactly five sentences, and then he departed, but not before his quick eyes had discovered that the rest of the house was in even worse condition than this parlor, which, by the way, Miss Ward considered quite a grand apartment; she had been down near the coast, trying to teach school, and there the desolation was far greater than here, both armies having passed back and forward over the ground, foragers out, and the torch at work more than once.

"Will there ever come a change for the better?" thought the keeper, as he walked homeward. "What an enormous stone has got to be rolled up hill! But at least, John Rodman, you need not go to work at it; you are not called upon to lend your shoulder."

None the less, however, did he call out Pomp that very afternoon and sternly teach him "E" and "F", using the smooth white sand for a blackboard, and a stick for chalk. Pomp's primer was a Government placard hanging on the wall of the office. It read as follows:

IN THIS CEMETERY REPOSE THE
REMAINS OF
FOURTEEN THOUSAND THREE
HUNDRED AND TWENTY-ONE
UNITED STATES SOLDIERS

"Tell me not in mournful numbers
    Life is but an empty dream;
For the soul is dead that slumbers,
    And things are not what they seem.

"Life is real! Life is earnest!
    And the grave is not its goal;
Dust thou art, to dust returnest,
    Was not written of the soul!"

"The only known instance of the Government's condescending to poetry," the keeper had thought, when he first read this placard. It was placed there for the instruction and edification of visitors; but, no visitors coming, he took the liberty of using it as a primer for Pomp. The large letters served the purpose admirably, and Pomp learned the entire quotation; what he thought of it has not transpired. Miss Ward came over daily to see her cousin. At first she brought him soups and various concoctions from her own kitchen—the leaky cavern, once the dining-room, where the soldier had taken refuge after his last

dismissal from hospital; but the keeper's soups were richer, and free from the taint of smoke; his martial laws of neatness even disorderly old Pomp dared not disobey, and the sick man soon learned the difference. He thanked the girl, who came bringing the dishes over carefully in her own dimpled hands, and then, when she was gone, he sent them untasted away. By chance Miss Ward learned this, and wept bitter tears over it; she continued to come, but her poor little soups and jellies she brought no more.

One morning in May the keeper was working near the flag-staff, when his eyes fell upon a procession coming down the road which led from the town and turning toward the cemetery. No one ever came that way: what could it mean? It drew near, entered the gate, and showed itself to be negroes walking two and two—old uncles and aunties, young men and girls, and even little children, all dressed in their best; a very poor best, sometimes gravely ludicrous imitations of "ole mars'" or "ole miss'," sometimes mere rags bravely patched together and adorned with a strip of black calico or rosette of black ribbon; not one was without a badge of mourning. All carried flowers, common blossoms from the little gardens behind the cabins that stretched around the town on the outskirts —the new forlorn cabins with their chimneys of piled stones and ragged patches of corn; each little darkey had his bouquet and marched solemnly along, rolling his eyes around, but without even the beginning of a smile, while the elders moved forward with gravity, the bubbling, irrepressible gayety of the negro subdued by the new-born dignity of the freedman.

"Memorial Day," thought the keeper; "I had forgotten it."

"Will you do us de hono', sah, to take de head ob de processio', sah?" said the leader, with a ceremonious bow. Now, the keeper had not much sympathy with the strewing of flowers, North or South; he had seen the beautiful ceremony more than once turned into a political demonstration. Here, however, in this small, isolated, interior town, there was nothing of that kind; the whole population of white faces laid their roses and wept true tears on the graves of their lost ones in the village churchyard when the Southern Memorial Day came round, and just as naturally the whole population of black faces went out to the national cemetery with their flowers on the day when, throughout the North, spring blossoms were laid on the graves of the soldiers, from the little Maine village to the stretching ranks of Arlington, from Greenwood to the far Western burial-places of San Francisco. The keeper joined the procession and led the way to the parade-ground. As they approached the trenches, the leader began singing and all joined. "Swing low, sweet chariot," sang the freedmen, and their hymn rose and fell with strange, sweet harmony—one of those wild, unwritten melodies which the North heard with surprise and marveling when, after the war, bands of singers came to their cities and sang the songs of slavery, in order to gain for their children the coveted education. "Swing low, sweet chariot," sang the freedmen, and two by two they passed along, strewing the graves with flowers till all the green was dotted with color. It was a pathetic sight to see some of the old men and women, ignorant field-hands, bent, dull-eyed, and past the possibility of education even in its simplest forms, carefully placing their poor flowers to the best advantage. They knew dimly that the men who lay beneath those mounds had done something wonderful for them and for their children; and so they came bringing their blossoms, with little intelligence but with much love.

The ceremony over, they retired. As he turned, the keeper caught a glimpse of Miss Ward's face at the window.

"Hope we's not makin' too free, sah," said the leader, as the procession, with many a bow and scrape, took leave, "but we's kep' de day now two years, sah, befo'

you came, sah, and we's teachin' de chil'en to keep it, sah."

The keeper returned to the cottage. "Not a white face," he said.

"Certainly not," replied Miss Ward, crisply.

"I know some graves at the North, Miss Ward, graves of Southern soldiers, and I know some Northern women who do not scorn to lay a few flowers on the lonely mounds as they pass by with their blossoms on our Memorial Day."

"You are fortunate. They must be angels. We have no angels here."

"I am inclined to believe you are right," said the keeper.

That night old Pomp, who had remained invisible in the kitchen during the ceremony, stole away in the twilight and came back with a few flowers. Rodman saw him going down toward the parade-ground, and watched. The old man had but a few blossoms; he arranged them hastily on the mounds with many a furtive glance toward the house, and then stole back, satisfied; he had performed his part.

Ward De Rosset lay on his pallet, apparently unchanged; he seemed neither stronger nor weaker. He had grown childishly dependent upon his host, and wearied for him, as the Scotch say; but Rodman withstood his fancies, and gave him only the evenings, when Miss Bettina was not there. One afternoon, however, it rained so violently that he was forced to seek shelter; he set himself to work on the ledgers; he was on the ninth thousand now. But the sick man heard his step in the outer room, and called in his weak voice, "Rodman, Rodman." After a time he went in, and it ended in his staying; for the patient was nervous and irritable, and he pitied the nurse, who seemed able to please him in nothing. De Rosset turned with a sigh of relief toward the strong hands that lifted him readily, toward the composed manner, toward the man's voice that seemed to bring a breeze from outside into the close room; animated, cheered, he talked volubly. The keeper listened, answered once in a while, and quietly took the rest of the afternoon into his own hands. Miss Ward yielded to the silent change, leaned back, and closed her eyes. She looked exhausted and for the first time pallid; the loosened dark hair curled in little rings about her temples, and her lips were parted as though she was too tired to close them; for hers were not the thin, straight lips that shut tight naturally, like the straight line of a closed box. The sick man talked on. "Come, Rodman," he said, after a while, "I have read that lying verse of yours over at least ten thousand and fifty-nine times; please tell me its history; I want to have something definite to think of when I read it for the ten thousand and sixtieth."

"Toujours femme varie,
Bien fou qui s'y fie;
Une femme souvent
N'est qu'une plume au vent,"

read the keeper slowly, with his execrable English accent. "Well, I don't know that I have any objection to telling the story. I am not sure but that it will do me good to hear it all over myself in plain language again."

"Then it concerns yourself," said De Rosset; "so much the better. I hope it will be, as the children say, the truth, and long."

"It will be the truth, but not long. When the war broke out I was twenty-eight years old, living with my mother on our farm in New England. My father and two brothers had died and left me the homestead; otherwise I should have broken away and sought fortune farther westward, where the lands are better and life is more free. But mother loved the house, the fields, and every crooked tree. She was alone, and so I staid with her. In the center of the village green stood the square, white meeting-house, and near by the small cottage where the pastor lived; the minister's daughter, Mary, was my promised wife. Mary was a slender lit-

tle creature with a profusion of pale flaxen hair, large, serious blue eyes, and small, delicate features; she was timid almost to a fault; her voice was low and gentle. She was not eighteen, and we were to wait a year. The war came, and I volunteered, of course, and marched away; we wrote to each other often; my letters were full of the camp and skirmishes; hers told of the village, how the widow Brown had fallen ill, and how it was feared that Squire Stafford's boys were lapsing into evil ways. Then came the day when my regiment marched to the field of its slaughter, and soon after our shattered remnant went home. Mary cried over me, and came out every day to the farmhouse with her bunches of violets; she read aloud to me from her good little books, and I used to lie and watch her profile bending over the page, with the light falling on her flaxen hair low down against the small, white throat. Then my wound healed, and I went again, this time for three years; and Mary's father blessed me, and said that when peace came he would call me son, but not before, for these were no times for marrying or giving in marriage. He was a good man, a red-hot abolitionist, and a roaring lion as regards temperance; but nature had made him so small in body that no one was much frightened when he roared. I said that I went for three years; but eight years have passed and I have never been back to the village. First, mother died. Then Mary turned false. I sold the farm by letter and lost the money three months afterward in an unfortunate investment; my health failed. Like many another Northern soldier, I remembered the healing climate of the South; its soft airs came back to me when the snow lay deep on the fields and the sharp wind whistled around the poor tavern where the moneyless, half-crippled volunteer sat coughing by the fire. I applied for this place and obtained it. That is all."

"But it is not all," said the sick man, raising himself on his elbow; "you have not told half yet, nor anything at all about the French verse."

"Oh—that? There was a little Frenchman staying at the hotel; he had formerly been a dancing-master, and was full of dry, withered conceits, although he looked like a thin and bilious old ape dressed as a man. He taught me, or tried to teach me, various wise sayings, among them this one, which pleased my fancy so much that I gave him twenty-five cents to write it out in large text for me."

"Toujours femme varie," repeated De Rosset; "but you don't really think so, do you, Rodman?"

"I do. But they can not help it; it is their nature.—I beg your pardon, Miss Ward. I was speaking as though you were not here."

Miss Ward's eyelids barely acknowledged his existence; that was all. But some time after she remarked to her cousin that it was only in New England that one found that pale flaxen hair.

June was waning, when suddenly the summons came. Ward De Rosset died. He was unconscious toward the last, and death, in the guise of sleep, bore away his soul. They carried him home to the old house, and from there the funeral started, a few family carriages, dingy and battered, following the hearse, for death revived the old neighborhood feeling; that honor at least they could pay—the sonless mothers and the widows who lived shut up in the old houses with everything falling into ruin around them, brooding over the past. The keeper watched the small procession as it passed his gate on its way to the church-yard in the village. "There he goes, poor fellow, his sufferings over at last," he said; and then he set the cottage in order and began the old solitary life again.

He saw Miss Ward but once.

It was a breathless evening in August, when the moonlight flooded the level country; but the mood changed, and climbing over the eastern wall he had walked back

to the flag-staff, and now lay at its foot gazing up into the infinite sky. A step sounded on the gravel-walk; he turned his face that way, and recognized Miss Ward. With confident step she passed the dark cottage, and brushed his arm with her robe as he lay unseen in the shadow. She went down toward the parade-ground, and his eyes followed her. Softly outlined in the moonlight, she moved to and fro among the mounds, pausing often, and once he thought she knelt. Then slowly she returned, and he raised himself and waited; she saw him, started, then paused.

"I thought you were away," she said; "Pomp told me so."

"You set him to watch me?"

"Yes. I wished to come here once, and I did not wish to meet you."

"Why did you wish to come?"

"Because Ward was here—and because —because—never mind. It is enough that I wished to walk once among those mounds."

"And pray there?"

"Well—and if I did!" said the girl defiantly.

Rodman stood facing her, with his arms folded; his eyes rested on her face; he said nothing.

"I am going away to-morrow," began Miss Ward again, assuming with an effort her old, pulseless manner. "I have sold the place, and I shall never return, I think; I am going far away."

"Where?"

"To Tennessee."

"That is not so very far," said the keeper, smiling.

"There I shall begin a new existence," pursued the voice, ignoring the comment.

"You have scarcely begun the old; you are hardly more than a child, now. What are you going to do in Tennessee?"

"Teach."

"Have you relatives there?"

"No."

"A miserable life—a hard, lonely, love-less life," said Rodman. "God help the woman who must be that dreary thing, a teacher from necessity!"

Miss Ward turned swiftly, but the keeper kept by her side. He saw the tears glittering on her eyelashes, and his voice softened. "Do not leave me in anger," he said; "I should not have spoken so, although indeed it was the truth. Walk back with me to the cottage, and take your last look at the room where poor Ward died, and then I will go with you to your home."

"No; Pomp is waiting at the gate," said the girl, almost inarticulately.

"Very well; to the gate, then."

They went toward the cottage in silence; the keeper threw open the door. "Go in," he said. "I will wait outside."

The girl entered and went into the inner room, throwing herself down upon her knees at the bedside. "O Ward, Ward!" she sobbed; "I am all alone in the world now, Ward—all alone!" She buried her face in her hands and gave way to a passion of tears; and the keeper could not help but hear as he waited outside. Then the desolate little creature rose and came forth, putting on, as she did so, her poor armor of pride. The keeper had not moved from the doorstep. Now he turned his face. "Before you go—go away for ever from this place—will you write your name in my register," he said—"the visitor's register? The Government had it prepared for the throngs who would visit these graves; but with the exception of the blacks, who can not write, no one has come, and the register is empty. Will you write your name? Yet do not write it unless you can think gently of the men who lie there under the grass. I believe you do think gently of them, else why have you come of your own accord to stand by the side of their graves?" As he said this, he looked fixedly at her.

Miss Ward did not answer; but neither did she write.

"Very well," said the keeper; "come away. You will not, I see."

"I can not! Shall I, Bettina Ward, set my name down in black and white as a visitor to this cemetery, where lie fourteen thousand of the soldiers who killed my father, my three brothers, my cousins; who brought desolation upon all our house, and ruin upon all our neighborhood, all our State, and all our country?—for the South *is* our country, and not your North. Shall I forget these things? Never! Sooner let my right hand wither by my side! I was but a child; yet I remember the tears of my mother, and the grief of all around us. There was not a house where there was not one dead."

"It is true," answered the keeper; "at the South, all went."

They walked down to the gate together in silence.

"Good-by," said John, holding out his hand; "you will give me yours or not as you choose, but I will not have it as a favor."

She gave it.

"I hope that life will grow brighter to you as the years pass. May God bless you!"

He dropped her hand; she turned, and passed through the gateway; then he sprang after her.

"Nothing can change you," he said; "I know it, I have known it all along; you are part of your country, part of the time, part of the bitter hour through which she is passing. Nothing can change you; if it could, you would not be what you are, and I should not—But you can not change. Good-by, Bettina, poor little child—good-by. Follow your path out into the world. Yet do not think, dear, that I have not seen —have not understood."

He bent and kissed her hand; then he was gone, and she went on alone.

A week later the keeper strolled over toward the old house. It was twilight, but the new owner was still at work. He was one of those sandy-haired, energetic Maine men, who, probably on the principle of extremes, were often found through the South, making new homes for themselves in the pleasant land.

"Pulling down the old house, are you?" said the keeper, leaning idly on the gate, which was already flanked by a new fence.

"Yes," replied the Maine man, pausing; "it was only an old shell, just ready to tumble on our heads. You're the keeper over yonder, an't you?" (He already knew everybody within a circle of five miles.)

"Yes. I think I should like those vines if you have no use for them," said Rodman, pointing to the uprooted greenery that once screened the old piazza.

"Wuth about twenty-five cents, I guess," said the Maine man, handing them over.

1853 ∾ *Thomas Nelson Page* ∾ 1922

THOMAS NELSON PAGE was too young to carry a musket in the Civil War; but as a child in Virginia he saw the fighting, and he inherited a militant Southern tradition. His father was a staff officer in the Confederate army. His family belonged to the plantation-owning aristocracy, and he was related by blood to Thomas Jefferson, John Marshall, and Robert E. Lee.

Page attended Washington and Lee University and the Law School of the University of Virginia during the Rennconstruction period, and then entered the practice of law at Richmond. His first stories were published in magazines in the early 1880's and collected in the volume *In Ole Virginia* (1887). In 1893 he moved to Washington and gave increasing attention to writing. His most popular novel, *Red Rock* (1898), expresses a Southern view of Reconstruction and the "carpet-baggers" in highly dramatic form. Among his best stories are those collected in *The Burial of the Guns* (1894) and *Bred in the Bone* (1904). Although he gained his reputation primarily as a writer of Southern regional fiction, Page also wrote *The Old South* (1892); *Social Life in Old Virginia Before the War* (1897); *The Negro: the Southerner's Problem* (1904); *Robert E. Lee, Man and Soldier* (1911); and *Dante and His Influence* (1922).

As an avowed and ardent apologist for the Old South and the Confederacy, Page contributed to understanding of Southern attitudes in the North, where his fiction was widely popular, in the generation after the Civil War. His regionalism was selective; he sought to portray the better aspects of the ante-bellum South and to commemorate heroic achievements of Confederate soldiers. His method was consciously that of the romancer, but within the limitations imposed by his purpose he was carefully accurate in details of dialect, setting, and other elements of local color.

[Most of Page's work has been collected in the uniform Plantation Edition (17 vols). The only biography which has appeared is that by R. Page, *Thomas Nelson Page* (New York, 1923).

The text of the following selection is that of the first edition of the volume under the same title (New York, 1894). The story first appeared in *Scribner's Monthly*, April, 1894.]

THE BURIAL OF THE GUNS

LEE surrendered the remnant of his army at Appomattox, April 9, 1865, and yet a couple of days later the old Colonel's battery lay intrenched right in the mountain-pass where it had halted three days before. Two weeks previously it had been detailed with a light division sent to meet and repel a force which it was understood was coming in by way of the southwest valley to strike Lee in the rear of his long line from Richmond to Petersburg. It had done its work. The mountain-pass had been seized and held, and the Federal force had not gotten by that road within the blue rampart which guarded on that side the heart of Virginia. This pass, which was the key to the main line of passage over the mountains, had been assigned by the commander of the division to the old Colonel and his old battery, and they had held it. The position taken by the battery had been chosen with a soldier's eye. A better place could not have been selected to hold the pass. It was its highest point, just where the road crawled over the shoulder of the mountain along the limestone cliff, a hundred feet sheer above the deep river, where its waters had cut their way in ages past, and now lay deep and silent, as if resting after their arduous toil before they began to boil over the great bowlders which filled the bed a hundred or more yards below.

The little plateau at the top guarded the descending road on either side for nearly a mile, and the mountain on the other side of the river was the centre of a clump of rocky, heavily timbered spurs, so inaccessible that no feet but those of wild animals or of the hardiest hunter had ever climbed it. On the side of the river on which the road lay, the only path out over the mountain except the road itself was a charcoal-burner's track, dwindling at times to a footway known only to the mountain-folk, which a picket at the top could hold against an army. The position, well defended, was impregnable, and it was well defended. This the general of the division knew when

he detailed the old Colonel and gave him his order to hold the pass until relieved, and not let his guns fall into the hands of the enemy. He knew both the Colonel and his battery. The battery was one of the oldest in the army. It had been in the service since April, 1861, and its commander had come to be known as "The Wheel Horse of his division." He was, perhaps, the oldest officer of his rank in his branch of the service. Although he had bitterly opposed secession, and was many years past the age of service when the war came on, yet as soon as the President called on the State for her quota of troops to coerce South Carolina, he had raised and uniformed an artillery company, and offered it, not to the President of the United States, but to the Governor of Virginia.

It is just at this point that he suddenly looms up to me as a soldier; the relation he never wholly lost to me afterward, though I knew him for many, many years of peace. His gray coat with the red facing and the bars on the collar; his military cap; his gray flannel shirt—it was the first time I ever saw him wear anything but immaculate linen—his high boots; his horse caparisoned with a black, high-peaked saddle, with crupper and breast-girth, instead of the light English hunting-saddle to which I had been accustomed, all come before me now as if it were but the other day. I remember but little beyond it, yet I remember, as if it were yesterday, his leaving home, and the scenes which immediately preceded it; the excitement created by the news of the President's call for troops; the unanimous judgment that it meant war; the immediate determination of the old Colonel, who had hitherto opposed secession, that it must be met; the suppressed agitation on the plantation, attendant upon the tender of his services and the Governor's acceptance of them. The prompt and continuous work incident to the enlistment of the men, the bustle of preparation, and all the scenes of that time, come before me now. It turned the calm current of the life of an old and placid country neighborhood, far from any city or centre, and stirred it into a boiling torrent, strong enough, or fierce enough to cut its way and join the general torrent which was bearing down and sweeping everything before it. It seemed but a minute before the quiet old plantation, in which the harvest, the corn-shucking, and the Christmas holidays alone marked the passage of the quiet seasons, and where a strange carriage or a single horseman coming down the big road was an event in life, was turned into a depot of war-supplies, and the neighborhood became a parade-ground. The old Colonel, not a colonel yet, nor even a captain, except by brevet, was on his horse by daybreak and off on his rounds through the plantations and the pines enlisting his company. The office in the yard, heretofore one in name only, became one now in reality, and a table was set out piled with papers, pens, ink, books of tactics and regulation, at which men were accepted and enrolled. Soldiers seemed to spring from the ground, as they did from the sowing of the dragon's teeth in the days of Cadmus. Men came up the high road or down the paths across the fields, sometimes singly, but oftener in little parties of two or three, and, asking for the Captain, entered the office as private citizens and came out soldiers enlisted for the war. There was nothing heard of on the plantation except fighting; white and black, all were at work, and all were eager; the servants contended for the honor of going with their master; the women flocked to the house to assist in the work of prepara-tion, cutting out and making under-clothes, knitting socks, picking lint, preparing bandages, and sewing on uniforms; for many of the men who had enlisted were of the poorest class, far too poor to furnish anything themselves, and their equipment had to be contributed mainly by wealthier neighbors. The work was carried on at night as well as by day, for the occasion was urgent. Meantime the men were being drilled by the Captain and his lieutenants, who had been militia officers of old. We were carried to see the drill at the cross-

roads, and a brave sight it seemed to us: the lines marching and countermarching in the field, with the horses galloping as they wheeled amid clouds of dust, at the hoarse commands of the excited officers, and the roadside lined with spectators of every age and condition. I recall the arrival of the messenger one night, with the telegraphic order to the Captain to report with his company at "Camp Lee" immediately; the hush in the parlor that attended its read-ing; then the forced beginning of the conversation afterwards in a somewhat strained and unnatural key, and the Cap-tain's quick and decisive outlining of his plans.

Within the hour a dozen messengers were on their way in various directions to notify the members of the command of the sum-mons, and to deliver the order for their attendance at a given point next day. It seemed that a sudden and great change had come. It was the actual appearance of what had hitherto only been theoretical—war. The next morning the Captain, in full uni-form, took leave of the assembled planta-tion, with a few solemn words commending all he left behind to God, and galloped away up the big road to join and lead his battery to the war, and to be gone just four years.

Within a month he was on "the Penin-sula" with Magruder, guarding Virginia on the east against the first attack. His camp was first at Yorktown and then on Jamestown Island, the honor having been assigned his battery of guarding the oldest cradle of the race on this continent. It was at "Little Bethel" that his guns were first trained on the enemy, and that the battery first saw what they had to do, and from this time until the middle of April, 1865, they were in service, and no battery saw more service or suffered more in it. Its story was a part of the story of the Southern Army in Virginia. The Captain was a rigid dis-ciplinarian, and his company had more work to do than most new companies. A pious churchman, of the old puritanical type not uncommon to Virginia, he looked after the spiritual as well as the physical welfare of his men, and his chaplain or he read prayers at the head of his company every morning during the war. At first he was not popular with the men, he made the duties of camp life so onerous to them, it was "nothing but drilling and praying all the time," they said. But he had not commanded very long before they came to know the stuff that was in him. He had not been in service a year before he had had four horses shot under him, and when later on he was offered the command of a battalion, the old company petitioned to be one of his batteries, and still remained under his command. Before the first year was out the battery had, through its own elements, and the discipline of the Captain, become a cohesive force, and a distinct integer in the Army of Northern Virginia. Young farmer recruits knew of its prestige and expressed preference for it of many batteries of rapidly growing or grown reputation. Owing to its high stand, the old and clumsy guns with which it had started out were taken from it, and in their place was presented a battery of four fine, brass, twelve-pound Napoleons of the newest and most approved kind, and two three-inch Parrotts, all captured. The men were as pleased with them as children with new toys. The care and attention needed to keep them in prime order broke the monotony of camp life. They soon had abundant opportunities to test their power. They worked admirably, carried far, and were extraordinarily accurate in their aim. The men from admiration of their guns grew to have first a pride in, and then an affection for, them, and gave them nicknames as they did their comrades; the four Napoleons being dubbed, "The Evangelists," and the two rifles being "The Eagle," because of its scream and force, and "The Cat," because when it became hot from rapid firing "It jumped," they said, "like a cat." From many a hill-top in Virginia, Maryland, and Pennsylvania "The Evangelists" spoke their hoarse message of battle and death, "The Eagle" screamed her terrible note, and "The Cat" jumped as she spat her deadly shot from her hot throat. In the Valley of Virginia; on the levels of Henrico and Hanover; on the slopes of Manassas; in the woods of Chancellorsville; on the heights of Fredericksburg; at Antietam and Gettysburg; in the Spottsylvania wilderness, and again on the Hanover levels and on the lines before Petersburg, the old guns through nearly four years roared from fiery throats their deadly messages. The history of the battery was bound up with the history of Lee's army. A rivalry sprang up among the detachments of the different guns, and their several records were jealously kept. The number of duels each gun was in was carefully counted, every scar got in battle was treasured, and the men around their camp-fires, at their scanty messes, or on the march, bragged of them among themselves and avouched them as witnesses. New recruits coming in to fill the gaps made by the killed and disabled, readily fell in with the common mood and caught the spirit like a contagion. It was not an uncommon thing for a wheel to be smashed in by a shell, but if it happened to one gun oftener than to another there was envy. Two of the Evangelists seemed to be especially favored in this line, while the Cat was so exempt as to become the subject of some derision. The men stood by the guns till they were knocked to pieces, and when the fortune of the day went against them, had with their own hands oftener than once saved them after most of their horses were killed.

This had happened in turn to every gun, the men at times working like beavers in mud up to their thighs and under a murderous fire to get their guns out. Many a man had been killed tugging at trail or wheel when the day was against them; but not a gun had ever been lost. At last the evil day arrived. At Winchester a sudden and impetuous charge for a while swept everything before it, and carried the knoll where the old battery was posted; but all the guns were got out by the toiling and rapidly dropping men, except the Cat, which was captured with its entire detachment working at it until they were surrounded and knocked from the piece by cavalrymen. Most of the men who were not killed were retaken before the day was over, with many guns; but the Cat was lost. She remained in the enemy's hands and probably was being turned against her old comrades and lovers. The company was inconsolable. The death of comrades was too natural and common a thing to depress the men beyond what such occurrences necessarily did; but to lose a gun! It was like losing the old Colonel; it was worse: a gun was ranked as a brigadier; and the Cat was equal to a major-general. The other guns seemed lost without her; the Eagle especially, which generally went next to her, appeared to the men to have a lonely and subdued air. The battery was no longer the same: it seemed broken and depleted, shrunken to a mere section. It was worse than Cold Harbor, where over half the men were killed or wounded. The old Captain, now Colonel of the battalion, appreciated the loss and apprehended its effect on the men as much as they themselves did, and application was made for a gun to take the place of the lost piece; but there was none to be had, as the men said they had known all along. It was added—perhaps by a department clerk— that if they wanted a gun to take the place of the one they had lost, they had better capture it. "By ——, we will," they said— adding epithets, intended for the department clerk in his "bomb-proof," not to be printed in this record—and they did. For some time afterwards in every engagement into which they got there used to be speculation among them as to whether the Cat were not there on the other side; some of the men swearing they could tell her report, and even going to the rash length of offering bets on her presence.

By one of those curious coincidences, as strange as anything in fiction, a new general had, in 1864, come down across the Rapidan to take Richmond, and the old battery had found a hill-top in the line in which Lee's army lay stretched across "the Wilderness" country to stop him. The day, though early in May, was a hot one, and the old battery, like most others, had suffered fearfully. Two of the guns had had wheels cut down by shells and the men had been badly cut up; but the fortune of the day had been with Lee, and a little before nightfall, after a terrible fight, there was a rapid advance, Lee's infantry sweeping everything before it, and the artillery, after opening the way for the charge, pushing along with it; now unlimbering as some vantage-ground was gained, and using canister with deadly effect; now driving ahead again so rapidly that it was mixed up with the muskets when the long line of breastworks was carried with a rush, and a line of guns were caught still hot from their rapid work. As the old battery, with lathered horses and smoke-grimed men, swung up the crest and unlimbered on the captured breastwork, a cheer went up which was heard even above the long general yell of the advancing line, and for a moment half the men in the battery crowded together around some object on the edge of the redoubt, yelling like madmen. The next instant they divided, and there was the Cat, smoke-grimed and blood-stained and still sweating hot from her last fire, being dragged from her muddy ditch by as many men as could get hold of trail-rope or wheel, and rushed into her old place beside the Eagle, in time to be double-shotted with canister to the muzzle, and to pour it from among her old comrades into her now retiring former masters. Still, she had a new carriage, and her record was lost, while those of the other guns had been faithfully kept by the men. This made a difference in her position for which even the bullets in her wheels did not wholly atone; even Harris, the sergeant of her detachment, felt that.

It was only a few days later, however, that abundant atonement was made. The new general did not retire across the Rapidan after his first defeat, and a new battle had to be fought: a battle, if anything, more furious, more terrible than the first, when the dead filled the trenches and covered the fields. He simply marched by the left flank, and Lee marching by the right flank to head him, flung himself upon him again at Spottsylvania Court-House. That day the Cat, standing in her place behind the new and temporary breastwork thrown up when the battery was posted, had the felloes of her wheels, which showed above the top of the bank, entirely cut away by Minie-bullets, so that when she jumped in the recoil her wheels smashed and let her down. This covered all old scores. The other guns had been cut down by shells or solid shot; but never before had one been gnawed down by musket-balls. From this time all through the campaign the Cat held her own beside her brazen and bloody sisters, and in the cold trenches before Petersburg that winter, when the new general—Starvation—had joined the one already there, she made her bloody mark as often as any gun on the long lines.

Thus the old battery had come to be known, as its old commander, now colonel of a battalion, had come to be known by those in yet higher command. And when in the opening spring of 1865 it became apparent to the leaders of both armies that the long line could not longer be held if a force should enter behind it, and, sweeping the one partially unswept portion of Virginia, cut the railways in the southwest, and a man was wanted to command the artillery in the expedition sent to meet this force, it was not remarkable that the old Colonel and his battalion should be selected for the work. The force sent out was but small; for the long line was worn to a thin one in those days, and great changes were taking place, the consequences of which were known only to the commanders. In a few days the commander of the expedition found that he must divide his small force for a time, at least, to accomplish his purpose, and sending the old Colonel with one battery of artillery to guard one pass, must push on over the mountain by another way to meet the expected force, if

possible, and repel it before it crossed the farther range. Thus the old battery, on an April evening of 1865, found itself toiling alone up the steep mountain road which leads above the river to the gap, which formed the chief pass in that part of the Blue Ridge. Both men and horses looked, in the dim and waning light of the gray April day, rather like shadows of the beings they represented than the actual beings themselves. And anyone seeing them as they toiled painfully up, the thin horses floundering in the mud, and the men, often up to their knees, tugging at the sinking wheels, now stopping to rest, and always moving so slowly that they seemed scarcely to advance at all, might have thought them the ghosts of some old battery lost from some long gone and forgotten war on that deep and desolate mountain road. Often, when they stopped, the blowing of the horses and the murmuring of the river in its bed below were the only sounds heard, and the tired voices of the men when they spoke among themselves seemed hardly more articulate sounds than they. Then the voice of the mounted figure on the roan horse half hidden in the mist would cut in, clear and inspiring, in a tone of encouragement more than of command, and everything would wake up: the drivers would shout and crack their whips; the horses would bend themselves on the collars and flounder in the mud; the men would spring once more to the mud-clogged wheels, and the slow ascent would begin again.

The orders to the Colonel, as has been said, were brief: To hold the pass until he received further instructions, and not to lose his guns. To be ordered, with him, was to obey. The last streak of twilight brought them to the top of the pass; his soldier's instinct and a brief recognizance made earlier in the day told him that this was his place, and before daybreak next morning the point was as well fortified as a night's work by weary and supperless men could make it. A prettier spot could not have been found for the purpose; a small plateau, something over an acre in extent, where a charcoal-burner's hut had once stood, lay right at the top of the pass. It was a little higher on either side than in the middle, where a small brook, along which the charcoal-burner's track was yet visible, came down from the wooded mountain above, thus giving a natural crest to aid the fortification on either side, with open space for the guns, while the edge of the wood coming down from the mountain afforded shelter for the camp.

As the battery was unsupported it had to rely on itself for everything, a condition which most soldiers by this time were accustomed to. A dozen or so of rifles were in the camp, and with these pickets were armed and posted. The pass had been seized none too soon; a scout brought in the information before nightfall that the invading force had crossed the farther range before that sent to meet it could get there, and taking the nearest road had avoided the main body opposing it, and been met only by a rapidly moving detachment, nothing more than a scouting party, and now were advancing rapidly on the road on which they were posted, evidently meaning to seize the pass and cross the mountain at this point. The day was Sunday; a beautiful Spring Sunday; but it was no Sabbath for the old battery. All day the men worked, making and strengthening their redoubt to guard the pass, and by the next morning, with the old battery at the top, it was impregnable. They were just in time. Before noon their vedettes brought in word that the enemy were ascending the mountain, and the sun had hardly turned when the advance guard rode up, came within range of the picket, and were fired on.

It was apparent that they supposed the force there only a small one, for they retired and soon came up again reinforced in some numbers, and a sharp little skirmish ensued, hot enough to make them more prudent afterwards, though the picket retired up the mountain. This gave them encouragement and probably misled them, for they now advanced boldly. They saw the redoubt on the crest as they came on,

and unlimbering a section or two, flung a few shells up at it, which either fell short or passed over without doing material damage. None of the guns was allowed to respond, as the distance was too great with the ammunition the battery had, and, indifferent as it was, it was too precious to be wasted in a duel at an ineffectual range. Doubtless deceived by this, the enemy came on in force, being obliged by the character of the ground to keep almost entirely to the road, which really made them advance in column. The battery waited. Under orders of the Colonel the guns standing in line were double-shotted with canister, and, loaded to the muzzle, were trained down to sweep the road at from four to five hundred yards' distance. And when the column reached this point the six guns, aimed by old and skilful gunners, at a given word swept road and mountain-side with a storm of leaden hail. It was a fire no mortal man could stand up against, and the practised gunners rammed their pieces full again, and before the smoke had cleared or the reverberation had died away among the mountains, had fired the guns again and yet again. The road was cleared of living things when the draught setting down the river drew the smoke away; but it was no discredit to the other force; for no army that was ever uniformed could stand against that battery in that pass. Again and again the attempt was made to get a body of men up under cover of the woods and rocks on the mountain-side, while the guns below utilized their better ammunition from longer range; but it was useless. Although one of the lieutenants and several men were killed in the skirmish, and a number more were wounded, though not severely, the old battery commanded the mountain-side, and its skilful gunners swept it at every point the foot of man could scale. The sun went down flinging his last flame on a victorious battery still crowning the mountain pass. The dead were buried by night in a corner of the little plateau, borne to their last bivouac on the old gun-carriages which they had stood by so often—which the men said would "sort of ease their minds."

The next day the fight was renewed, and with the same result. The old battery in its position was unconquerable. Only one fear now faced them; their ammunition was getting as low as their rations; another such day or half-day would exhaust it. A sergeant was sent back down the mountain to try to get more, or, if not, to get tidings. The next day it was supposed the fight would be renewed; and the men waited, alert, eager, vigilant, their spirits high, their appetite for victory whetted by success. The men were at their breakfast, or what went for breakfast, scanty at all times, now doubly so, hardly deserving the title of a meal, so poor and small were the portions of cornmeal, cooked in their frying-pans, which went for their rations, when the sound of artillery below broke on the quiet air. They were on their feet in an instant and at the guns, crowding upon the breastwork to look or to listen; for the road, as far as could be seen down the mountain, was empty except for their own picket, and lay as quiet as if sleeping in the balmy air. And yet volley after volley of artillery came rolling up the mountain. What could it mean? That the rest of their force had come up and was engaged with that at the foot of the mountain? The Colonel decided to be ready to go and help them; to fall on the enemy in the rear; perhaps they might capture the entire force. It seemed the natural thing to do, and the guns were limbered up in an incredibly short time, and a roadway made through the intrenchment, the men working like beavers under the excitement. Before they had left the redoubt, however, the vedettes sent out returned and reported that there was no engagement going on, and the firing below seemed to be only practising. There was quite a stir in the camp below; but they had not even broken camp. This was mysterious. Perhaps it meant that they had received reinforcements, but it was a queer way of showing it. The old Colonel sighed as he thought of

the good ammunition they could throw away down there, and of his empty limber-chests. It was necessary to be on the alert, however; the guns were run back into their old places, and the horses picketed once more back among the trees. Meantime he sent another messenger back, this time a courier, for he had but one commissioned officer left, and the picket below was strengthened.

The morning passed and no one came; the day wore on and still no advance was made by the force below. It was suggested that the enemy had left; he had, at least, gotten enough of that battery. A reconnoissance, however, showed that he was still encamped at the foot of the mountain. It was conjectured that he was trying to find a way around to take them in the rear, or to cross the ridge by the foot-path. Preparation was made to guard more closely the mountain-path across the spur, and a detachment was sent up to strengthen the picket there. The waiting told on the men and they grew bored and restless. They gathered about the guns in groups and talked; talked of each piece some, but not with the old spirit and vim; the loneliness of the mountain seemed to oppress them; the mountains stretching up so brown and gray on one side of them, and so brown and gray on the other, with their bare, dark forests soughing from time to time as the wind swept up the pass. The minds of the men seemed to go back to the time when they were not so alone, but were part of a great and busy army, and some of them fell to talking of the past, and the battles they had figured in, and of the comrades they had lost. They told them off in a slow and colorless way, as if it were all part of the past as much as the dead they named. One hundred and nineteen times they had been in action. Only seventeen men were left of the eighty odd who had first enlisted in the battery, and of these four were at home crippled for life. Two of the oldest men had been among the half-dozen who had fallen in the skirmish just the day before. It looked tolerably hard to be killed that way after passing for four years through such battles as they had been in; and both had wives and children at home, too, and not a cent to leave them to their names. They agreed calmly that they'd have to "sort of look after them a little" if they ever got home. These were some of the things they talked about as they pulled their old worn coats about them, stuffed their thin, weather-stained hands in their ragged pockets to warm them, and squatted down under the breastwork to keep a little out of the wind. One thing they talked about a good deal was something to eat. They described meals they had had at one time or another as personal adventures, and discussed the chances of securing others in the future as if they were prizes of fortune. One listening and seeing their thin, worn faces and their wasted frames might have supposed they were starving, and they were, but they did not say so.

Towards the middle of the afternoon there was a sudden excitement in the camp. A dozen men saw them at the same time: a squad of three men down the road at the farthest turn, past their picket; but an advancing column could not have created as much excitement, for the middle man carried a white flag. In a minute every man in the battery was on the breastwork. What could it mean! It was a long way off, nearly half a mile, and the flag was small: possibly only a pocket-handkerchief or a napkin; but it was held aloft as a flag unmistakably. A hundred conjectures were indulged in. Was it a summons to surrender? A request for an armistice for some purpose? Or was it a trick to ascertain their number and position? Some held one view, some another. Some extreme ones thought a shot ought to be fired over them to warn them not to come on; no flags of truce were wanted. The old Colonel, who had walked to the edge of the plateau outside the redoubt and taken his position where he could study the advancing figures with his field-glass, had not spoken. The lieutenant who was next in command to him had walked out after him, and stood near

him, from time to time dropping a word or two of conjecture in a half-audible tone; but the Colonel had not answered a word; perhaps none was expected. Suddenly he took his glass down, and gave an order to the lieutenant: "Take two men and meet them at the turn yonder; learn their business; and act as your best judgment advises. If necessary to bring the messenger farther, bring only the officer who has the flag, and halt him at that rock yonder, where I will join him." The tone was as placid as if such an occurrence came every day. Two minutes later the lieutenant was on his way down the mountain and the Colonel had the men in ranks. His face was as grave and his manner as quiet as usual, neither more nor less so. The men were in a state of suppressed excitement. Having put them in charge of the second sergeant the Colonel returned to the breastwork. The two officers were slowly ascending the hill, side by side, the bearer of the flag, now easily distinguishable in his jaunty uniform as a captain of cavalry, talking, and the lieutenant in faded gray, faced with yet more faded red, walking beside him with a face white even at that distance, and lips shut as though they would never open again. They halted at the big bowlder which the Colonel had indicated, and the lieutenant, having saluted ceremoniously, turned to come up to the camp; the Colonel, however, went down to meet him. The two men met, but there was no spoken question; if the Colonel inquired it was only with the eyes. The lieutenant spoke, however. "He says," he began and stopped, then began again—"he says, General Lee—" again he choked, then blurted out, "I believe it is all a lie—a damned lie."

"Not dead? Not killed?" said the Colonel, quickly.

"No, not so bad as that; surrendered: surrendered his entire army at Appomattox day before yesterday. I believe it is all a damned lie," he broke out again, as if the hot denial relieved him. The Colonel simply turned away his face and stepped a pace or two off, and the two men stood motionless back to back for more than a minute. Then the Colonel stirred.

"Shall I go back with you?" the lieutenant asked, huskily.

The Colonel did not answer immediately. Then he said: "No, go back to camp and await my return." He said nothing about not speaking of the report. He knew it was not needed. Then he went down the hill slowly alone, while the lieutenant went up to the camp.

The interview between the two officers beside the bowlder was not a long one. It consisted of a brief statement by the Federal envoy of the fact of Lee's surrender two days before near Appomattox Court-House, with the sources of his information, coupled with a formal demand on the Colonel for his surrender. To this the Colonel replied that he had been detached and put under command of another officer for a specific purpose, and that his orders were to hold that pass, which he should do until he was instructed otherwise by his superior in command. With that they parted, ceremoniously, the Federal captain returning to where he had left his horse in charge of his companions a little below, and the old Colonel coming slowly up the hill to camp. The men were at once set to work to meet any attack which might be made. They knew that the message was of grave import, but not of how grave. They thought it meant that another attack would be made immediately, and they sprang to their work with renewed vigor, and a zeal as fresh as if it were but the beginning and not the end.

The time wore on, however, and there was no demonstration below, though hour after hour it was expected and even hoped for. Just as the sun sank into a bed of blue cloud a horseman was seen coming up the darkened mountain from the eastward side, and in a little while practised eyes reported him one of their own men—the sergeant who had been sent back the day before for ammunition. He was alone, and had something white before him on his horse—it

could not be the ammunition; but perhaps that might be coming on behind. Every step of his jaded horse was anxiously watched. As he drew near, the lieutenant, after a word with the Colonel, walked down to meet him, and there was a short colloquy in the muddy road; then they came back together and slowly entered the camp, the sergeant handing down a bag of corn which he had got somewhere below, with the grim remark to his comrades, "There's your rations," and going at once to the Colonel's camp-fire, a little to one side among the trees, where the Colonel awaited him. A long conference was held, and then the sergeant left to take his luck with his mess, who were already parching the corn he had brought for their supper, while the lieutenant made the round of the camp; leaving the Colonel seated alone on a log by his camp-fire. He sat without moving, hardly stirring until the lieutenant returned from his round. A minute later the men were called from the guns and made to fall into line. They were silent, tremulous with suppressed excitement; the most sun-burned and weather-stained of them a little pale; the meanest, raggedest, and most insignificant not unimpressive in the deep and solemn silence with which they stood, their eyes fastened on the Colonel, waiting for him to speak. He stepped out in front of them, slowly ran his eye along the irregular line, up and down, taking in every man in his glance, resting on some longer than on others, the older men, then dropped them to the ground, and then suddenly, as if with an effort, began to speak. His voice had a somewhat metallic sound, as if it were restrained; but it was otherwise the ordinary tone of command. It was not much that he said: simply that it had become his duty to acquaint them with the information which he had received: that General Lee had surrendered two days before at Appomattox Court-House, yielding to overwhelming numbers; that this afternoon when he had first heard the report he had questioned its truth, but that it had been confirmed by one of their own men, and no longer admitted of doubt; that the rest of their own force, it was learned, had been captured, or had disbanded, and the enemy was now on both sides of the mountain; that a demand had been made on him that morning to surrender too; but that he had orders which he felt held good until they were countermanded, and he had declined. Later intelligence satisfied him that to attempt to hold out further would be useless, and would involve needless waste of life; he had determined, therefore, not to attempt to hold their position longer; but to lead them out, if possible, so as to avoid being made prisoners and enable them to reach home sooner and aid their families. His orders were not to let his guns fall into the enemy's hands, and he should take the only step possible to prevent it. In fifty minutes he should call the battery into line once more, and roll the guns over the cliff into the river, and immediately afterwards, leaving the wagons there, he would try to lead them across the mountain, and as far as they could go in a body without being liable to capture, and then he should disband them, and his responsibility for them would end. As it was necessary to make some preparations he would now dismiss them to prepare any rations they might have and get ready to march.

All this was in the formal manner of a common order of the day; and the old Colonel had spoken in measured sentences, with little feeling in his voice. Not a man in the line had uttered a word after the first sound, half exclamation, half groan, which had burst from them at the announcement of Lee's surrender. After that they had stood in their tracks like rooted trees, as motionless as those on the mountain behind them, their eyes fixed on their commander, and only the quick heaving up and down the dark line, as of horses over-laboring, told of the emotion which was shaking them. The Colonel, as he ended, half-turned to his subordinate officer

at the end of the dim line, as though he were about to turn the company over to him to be dismissed; then faced the line again, and taking a step nearer, with a sudden movement of his hands towards the men as though he would have stretched them out to them, began again:

"Men," he said, and his voice changed at the word, and sounded like a father's or a brother's, "My men, I cannot let you go so. We were neighbors when the war began —many of us, and some not here to-night; we have been more since then—comrades, brothers in arms; we have all stood for one thing—for Virginia and the South; we have all done our duty—tried to do our duty; we have fought a good fight, and now it seems to be over, and we have been overwhelmed by numbers, not whipped— and we are going home. We have the future before us—we don't know just what it will bring, but we can stand a good deal. We have proved it. Upon us depends the South in the future as in the past. You have done your duty in the past, you will not fail in the future. Go home and be honest, brave, self-sacrificing, God-fearing citizens, as you have been soldiers, and you need not fear for Virginia and the South. The war may be over; but you will ever be ready to serve your country. The end may not be as we wanted it, prayed for it, fought for it; but we can trust God; the end in the end will be the best that could be; even if the South is not free she will be better and stronger that she fought as she did. Go home and bring up your children to love her, and though you may have nothing else to leave them, you can leave them the heritage that they are sons of men who were in Lee's army."

He stopped, looked up and down the ranks again, which had instinctively crowded together and drawn around him in a half-circle; made a sign to the lieutenant to take charge, and turned abruptly on his heel to walk away. But as he did so, the long pent-up emotion burst forth. With a wild cheer the men seized him, crowding around and hugging him, as with protestations, prayers, sobs, oaths—broken, incoherent, inarticulate—they swore to be faithful, to live loyal forever to the South, to him, to Lee. Many of them cried like children; others offered to go down and have one more battle on the plain. The old Colonel soothed them, and quieted their excitement, and then gave a command about the preparations to be made. This called them to order at once; and in a few minutes the camp was as orderly and quiet as usual: the fires were replenished; the scanty stores were being overhauled; the place was selected, and being got ready to roll the guns over the cliff; the camp was being ransacked for such articles as could be carried, and all preparations were being hastily made for their march.

The old Colonel having completed his arrangements sat down by his camp-fire with paper and pencil, and began to write; and as the men finished their work they gathered about in groups, at first around their camp-fires, but shortly strolled over to where the guns still stood at the breastwork, black and vague in the darkness. Soon they were all assembled about the guns. One after another they visited, closing around it and handling it from muzzle to trail as a man might a horse to try its sinew and bone, or a child to feel its fineness and warmth. They were for the most part silent, and when any sound came through the dusk from them to the officers at their fire, it was murmurous and fitful as of men speaking low and brokenly. There was no sound of the noisy controversy which was generally heard, the give-and-take of the camp-fire, the firing backwards and forwards that went on on the march; if a compliment was paid a gun by one of its special detachment, it was accepted by the others; in fact, those who had generally run it down now seemed most anxious to accord the piece praise. Presently a small number of the men returned to a camp-fire, and, building it up, seated themselves about it, gathering closer and closer together until they were in a little knot. One of them

appeared to be writing, while two or three took up flaming chunks from the fire and held them as torches for him to see by. In time the entire company assembled about them, standing in respectful silence, broken only occasionally by a reply from one or another to some question from the scribe. After a little there was a sound of a roll-call, and reading and a short colloquy followed, and then two men, one with a paper in his hand, approached the fire beside which the officers sat still engaged.

"What is it, Harris?" said the Colonel to the man with the paper, who bore remnants of the chevrons of a sergeant on his stained and faded jacket.

"If you please, sir," he said, with a salute, "we have been talking it over, and we'd like this paper to go in along with that you're writing." He held it out to the lieutenant, who was the nearer and had reached forward to take it. "We s'pose you're agoin' to bury it with the guns," he said, hesitatingly, as he handed it over.

"What is it?" asked the Colonel, shading his eyes with his hands.

"It's just a little list we made out in and among us," he said, "with a few things we'd like to put in, so's if anyone ever hauls 'em out they'll find it there to tell what the old battery was, and if they don't, it'll be in one of 'em down thar 'til judgment, an' it'll sort of ease our minds a bit." He stopped and waited as a man who had delivered his message. The old Colonel had risen and taken the paper, and now held it with a firm grasp, as if it might blow away with the rising wind. He did not say a word, but his hand shook a little as he proceeded to fold it carefully, and there was a burning gleam in his deep-set eyes, back under his bushy, gray brows.

"Will you sort of look over it, sir, if you think it's worth while? We was in a sort of hurry and we had to put it down just as we come to it; we didn't have time to pick our ammunition; and it ain't written the best in the world, nohow." He waited again, and the Colonel opened the paper and glanced down at it mechanically. It contained first a roster, headed by the list of six guns, named by name: "Matthew," "Mark," "Luke," and "John," "The Eagle," and "The Cat"; then of the men, beginning with the heading:

"Those killed."

Then had followed "Those wounded," but this was marked out. Then came a roster of the company when it first entered service; then of those who had joined afterward; then of those who were present now. At the end of all there was this statement, not very well written, nor wholly accurately spelt:

"To Whom it may Concern: We, the above members of the old battery known, etc., of six guns, named, etc., commanded by the said Col. etc., left on the 11th day of April, 1865, have made out this roll of the battery, them as is gone and them as is left, to bury with the guns which the same we bury this night. We're all volunteers, every man; we joined the army at the beginning of the war, and we've stuck through to the end; sometimes we aint had much to eat, and sometimes we aint had nothin', but we've fought the best we could 119 battles and skirmishes as near as we can make out in four years, and never lost a gun. Now we're agoin' home. We aint surrendered; just disbanded, and we pledges ourselves to teach our children to love the South and General Lee; and to come when we're called anywheres an' anytime, so help us God."

There was a dead silence whilst the Colonel read.

"'Taint entirely accurite, sir, in one particular," said the sergeant, apologetically; "but we thought it would be playin' it sort o' low down on the Cat if we was to say we lost her unless we could tell about gittin' of her back, and the way she done since, and we didn't have time to do all that." He looked around as if to receive the corroboration of the other men, which they signified by nods and shuffling.

The Colonel said it was all right, and the paper should go into the guns.

"If you please, sir, the guns are all loaded," said the sergeant; "in and about our last charge, too; and we'd like to fire 'em off once more, jist for old times' sake to remember 'em by, if you don't think no harm could come of it?"

The Colonel reflected a moment and said it might be done; they might fire each gun separately as they rolled it over, or might get all ready and fire together, and then roll them over, whichever they wished. This was satisfactory.

The men were then ordered to prepare to march immediately, and withdrew for the purpose. The pickets were called in. In a short time they were ready, horses and all, just as they would have been to march ordinarily, except that the wagons and caissons were packed over in one corner by the camp with the harness hung on poles beside them, and the guns stood in their old places at the breastwork ready to defend the pass. The embers of the sinking camp-fires threw a faint light on them standing so still and silent. The old Colonel took his place, and at a command from him in a somewhat low voice, the men, except a detail left to hold the horses, moved into company-front facing the guns. Not a word was spoken, except the words of command. At the order each detachment went to its gun; the guns were run back and the men with their own hands ran them up on the edge of the perpendicular bluff above the river, where, sheer below, its waters washed its base, as if to face an enemy on the black mountain the other side. The pieces stood ranged in the order in which they had so often stood in battle, and the gray, thin fog rising slowly and silently from the river deep down between the cliffs, and wreathing the mountain-side above, might have been the smoke from some unearthly battle fought in the dim pass by ghostly guns, yet posted there in the darkness, manned by phantom gunners, while phantom horses stood behind, lit vaguely up by phantom camp-fires. At the given word the laniards were pulled together, and together as one the six black guns, belching flame and lead, roared their last challenge on the misty night, sending a deadly hail of shot and shell, tearing the trees and splintering the rocks of the farther side, and sending the thunder reverberating through the pass and down the mountain, startling from its slumber the sleeping camp on the hills below, and driving the browsing deer and the prowling mountain-fox in terror up the mountain.

There was silence among the men about the guns for one brief instant and then such a cheer burst forth as had never broken from them even in battle: cheer on cheer, the long, wild, old familiar rebel yell for the guns they had fought with and loved.

The noise had not died away and the men behind were still trying to quiet the frightened horses when the sergeant, the same who had written, received from the hand of the Colonel a long package or roll which contained the records of the battery furnished by the men and by the Colonel himself, securely wrapped to make them water-tight, and it was rammed down the yet warm throat of the nearest gun: the Cat, and then the gun was tamped to the muzzle to make her water-tight, and, like her sisters, was spiked, and her vent tamped tight. All this took but a minute, and the next instant the guns were run up once more to the edge of the cliff; and the men stood by them with their hands still on them. A deadly silence fell on the men, and even the horses behind seemed to feel the spell. There was a long pause, in which not a breath was heard from any man, and the soughing of the tree-tops above and the rushing of the rapids below were the only sounds. They seemed to come from

far, very far away. Then the Colonel said, quietly, "Let them go, and God be our helper, Amen." There was the noise in the darkness of trampling and scraping on the cliff-top for a second; the sound as of men straining hard together, and then with a pant it ceased all at once, and the men held their breath to hear. One second of utter silence; then one prolonged, deep, resounding splash sending up a great mass of white foam as the brass-pieces together plunged into the dark water below, and then the soughing of the trees and the murmur of the river came again with painful distinctness. It was full ten minutes before the Colonel spoke, though there were other sounds enough in the darkness, and some of the men, as the dark, outstretched bodies showed, were lying on the ground flat on their faces. Then the Colonel gave the command to fall in in the same quiet, grave tone he had used all night. The line fell in, the men getting to their horses and mounting in silence; the Colonel put himself at their head and gave the order of march, and the dark line turned in the darkness, crossed the little plateau between the smouldering camp-fires and the spectral caissons with the harness hanging beside them, and slowly entered the dim charcoal-burner's track. Not a word was spoken as they moved off. They might all have been phantoms. Only, the sergeant in the rear, as he crossed the little breastwork which ran along the upper side and marked the boundary of the little camp, half turned and glanced at the dying fires, the low, newly made mounds in the corner, the abandoned caissons, and the empty redoubt, and said, slowly, in a low voice to himself,

"Well, by God!"

1809 ∾ *Oliver Wendell Holmes* ∾ *1894*

THE primary interest of Oliver Wendell Holmes throughout his long life was the science of medicine. In that field he was one of the greatest figures of his time, preëminently distinguished and useful to society as physician, teacher, and writer on medical subjects. To him literature was an avocation; he spoke and thought of himself as an amateur in letters. These facts are fundamental in arriving at a fair appraisal of his work.

Some of Holmes' best writing was done in the service of his own profession. As a practicing physician, following graduation from Harvard in 1829 and study of medicine in Boston and Paris, he published at the age of 34 an article on "The Contagiousness of Puerperal Fever," which with the work of the Austrian Semmelweiss (published four years later) ultimately revolutionized obstetrical practice and saved the lives of millions of mothers. In an address on "Currents and Counter-Currents in Medical Science," in 1860, he attacked effectively contemporary dependence on the violent action of powerful drugs as the chief means of treating diseases. These and his many other writings in the field of his profession are admirable in their clarity, force, and human interest—classics of medical literature, and widely appealing to general readers even today. They express the personality which made Holmes, as Professor of Anatomy and Physiology at the Harvard Medical School, America's best loved and most influential teacher of medical students for over thirty years.

Early in his practice Holmes became especially interested in the relations between the body and the mind and in the treatment of mental diseases. He was a pioneer in psychiatry and what would be called today psychosomatic medicine. He came to hold, as a major conviction of his professional life, the view that the mind plays a far larger part in health and sickness than his contemporaries realized, and the related view that much of human conduct ordinarily named as criminal is the result of mental disturbance or disorder which the individual is powerless to control. In his application of these views to actual cases he anticipated with startling precision many of the theories of Freud, and the modern knowledge of the unconscious mind.

To present these views to as wide an audience as possible he resorted to fiction. His three novels, *Elsie Venner* (1861), *The Guardian Angel* (1867), and *A Mortal Antipathy* (1885), are essentially psychiatric case histories. Though they have value in their accurate projection of New England backgrounds, both physical and mental, they are robbed of real effectiveness by their conventional and artificial fictional framework. The most interesting parts of these books to the reader of today are the conversations in which Holmes—thinly disguised as fictional physician or scholar—comments on problems of mental disease, morals and ethics, religion, and life in general.

These conversations are in effect personal essays: and it was as essayist that Holmes made his greatest contribution to American literature. While still a student, he wrote a few conversational essays published in *The New England Magazine* under the title "The Autocrat of the Breakfast-Table." The pattern which he had tentatively laid down at the age of 22 Holmes later carried triumphantly through four books which made him famous in both America and England, and as widely loved: *The Autocrat of the Breakfast-Table* (1858); *The Professor at the Breakfast-Table* (1860); *The Poet at the Breakfast-Table* (1872); *Over the Teacups* (1891). It is a pattern at once simple and rigid, which any other writer would have found intolerable: the table talk of a group of people of varied occupations, tastes, and backgrounds, their conversation dominated by a genial, erudite and tactful "autocrat" who is, of course, Holmes himself.

That talk is unparalleled in American literature and hard to match in any other. Into it Holmes poured the richness of an alert, disciplined, and marvellously retentive mind, not only in the fields of medicine and science in general but in a host of other widely varied interests—theology, horse-racing, literature, photography, history, boating, and many more. In it he expressed the richness of his own nature, the kindly wit, the unfailing sympathy and tactfulness, the infectious courage and common sense which made him great as a physician and teacher and beloved as a friend. In these books Holmes achieved a style at once precise and airy, brilliant and mellow, happy in analogy, extraordinarily responsive to thought and feeling. It is Holmes' own world which we find in these essays—the world of Brahmin Boston, as he called it—a world sharply limited in standards and perceptions as we see it today, but one highly important in the American life of its time and rich in its own right. Nowhere is it revealed so fully as in the essays of Holmes. Though personal preferences among the four volumes of the "Breakfast-Table" series will vary, probably most readers of today will find *The Poet* most to their liking. In *The Poet* the mature Holmes is most fully himself, at once gracious and forthright in his treatment of many questions which are still vital.

Though Holmes is known to every schoolboy as the author of "Old Ironsides," "The Last Leaf," and "The Chambered Nautilus," his voluminous work as a poet holds less lasting interest for the mature reader than his prose. He rarely attempted—and more rarely with success—to use poetic forms for the expression of deep emotion or profound thought; nor did he use poetry extensively as a vehicle for the expression of convictions and ideas, as he did other creative forms. Most of his poems were written simply for the pleasure of his friends and for his own amusement; in poetry, more markedly than in his

novels and essays, he was the amateur of letters, the man whose chief interest
and effort were given to another field. His highest achievement lay in types
of writing not highly valued today: familiar verse, the humorous or sentimental
treatment of small subjects; and occasional verse, that written in celebration
of special occasions—usually to be recited or read. There can be no question
that in both these fields Holmes outranks all competitors in our literature. The
degree of lasting pleasure the individual will find in Holmes' poems—and for
some it is large and genuine—must depend on personal taste. Yet no just
reader will deny their unpretentious excellence of their kind; and the best
of them help us to know one of the most likable men in our literary history.

[M. A. DeWolfe Howe's *Holmes of the Breakfast-Table* (New York, 1939)
and Eleanor Tilton's *Amiable Autocrat* (New York, 1947) are detailed and sympathetic biographies. S. I. Hayakawa and H. M. Jones provide an excellent
introduction in their *Holmes* in the American Writers Series. See also *The
Psychiatric Novels of Oliver Wendell Holmes,* by Clarence P. Oberndorf (New
York, 1943).]

THE LAST LEAF
[1836 (1831)]

I saw him once before,
As he passed by the door,
   And again
The pavement stones resound,
As he totters o'er the ground   5
   With his cane.

They say that in his prime,
Ere the pruning-knife of Time
   Cut him down,
Not a better man was found   10
By the Crier on his round
   Through the town.

But now he walks the streets,
And he looks at all he meets
   Sad and wan,   15
And he shakes his feeble head,
That it seems as if he said,
   "They are gone."

The mossy marbles rest
On the lips that he has prest   20
   In their bloom,
And the names he loved to hear
Have been carved for many a year
   On the tomb.

My grandmamma has said,—   25
Poor old lady, she is dead
   Long ago,—
That he had a Roman nose,
And his cheek was like a rose
   In the snow.   30

But now his nose is thin,
And it rests upon his chin
   Like a staff,
And a crook is in his back,
And a melancholy crack   35
   In his laugh.

I know it is a sin
For me to sit and grin
   At him here;
But the old three-cornered hat,   40
And the breeches, and all that,
   Are so queer!

And if I should live to be
The last leaf upon the tree
   In the spring,—   45
Let them smile, as I do now,
At the old forsaken bough
   Where I cling.

MY AUNT
[1836 (1831)]

My aunt! my dear unmarried aunt!
  Long years have o'er her flown;
Yet still she strains the aching clasp
  That binds her virgin zone;
I know it hurts her,—though she looks 5
  As cheerful as she can;
Her waist is ampler than her life,
  For life is but a span.

My aunt! my poor deluded aunt!
  Her hair is almost gray; 10
Why will she train that winter curl
  In such a spring-like way?
How can she lay her glasses down,
  And say she reads as well,
When, through a double convex lens, 15
  She just makes out to spell?

Her father,—grandpapa! forgive
  This erring lip its smiles,—
Vowed she should make the finest girl
  Within a hundred miles; 20
He sent her to a stylish school;
  'Twas in her thirteenth June;
And with her, as the rules required,
  "Two towels and a spoon."

They braced my aunt against a board, 25
  To make her straight and tall;
They laced her up, they starved her down,
  To make her light and small;
They pinched her feet, they singed her hair,
  They screwed it up with pins;— 30
O never mortal suffered more
  In penance for her sins.

So, when my precious aunt was done,
  My grandsire brought her back;
(By daylight, lest some rabid youth 35
  Might follow on the track;)
"Ah!" said my grandsire, as he shook
  Some powder in his pan,
"What could this lovely creature do
  Against a desperate man!" 40

Alas! nor chariot, nor barouche,
  Nor bandit cavalcade,

Tore from the trembling father's arms
  His all-accomplished maid.
For her how happy had it been! 45
  And Heaven had spared to me
To see one sad, ungathered rose
  On my ancestral tree.

TO AN INSECT
[1836 (1831)]

I love to hear thine earnest voice,
  Wherever thou art hid,
Thou testy little dogmatist,
  Thou pretty Katydid!
Thou mindest me of gentlefolks,— 5
  Old gentlefolks are they,—
Thou say'st an undisputed thing
  In such a solemn way.

Thou art a female, Katydid!
  I know it by the trill 10
That quivers through thy piercing notes,
  So petulant and shrill.
I think there is a knot of you
  Beneath the hollow tree,—
A knot of spinster Katydids,— 15
  Do Katydids drink tea?

O tell me where did Katy live,
  And what did Katy do?
And was she very fair and young,
  And yet so wicked, too? 20
Did Katy love a naughty man,
  Or kiss more cheeks than one?
I warrant Katy did no more
  Than many a Kate has done.

Dear me! I'll tell you all about 25
  My fuss with little Jane,
And Ann, with whom I used to walk
  So often down the lane,
And all that tore their locks of black,
  Or wet their eyes of blue,— 30
Pray tell me, sweetest Katydid,
  What did poor Katy do?

Ah no! the living oak shall crash,
  That stood for ages still,
The rock shall rend its mossy base 35
  And thunder down the hill,

Before the little Katydid
  Shall add one word, to tell
The mystic story of the maid
  Whose name she knows so well.   40

Peace to the ever-murmuring race!
  And when the latest one
Shall fold in death her feeble wings
  Beneath the autumn sun,
Then shall she raise her fainting voice 45
  And lift her drooping lid,
And then the child of future years
  Shall hear what Katy did.

THE DEACON'S MASTERPIECE
OR THE WONDERFUL "ONE-HOSS SHAY"
A LOGICAL STORY
[1858]

Have you heard of the wonderful one-
      hoss shay,
That was built in such a logical way
It ran a hundred years to a day,
And then, of a sudden, it—ah, but stay,
I'll tell you what happened without delay, 5
Scaring the parson into fits,
Frightening people out of their wits,—
Have you ever heard of that, I say?

Seventeen hundred and fifty-five.
Georgius Secundus [1] was then alive— 10
Snuffy old drone from the German hive!
That was the year when Lisbon-town [2]
Saw the earth open and gulp her down,
And Braddock's [3] army was done so brown,
Left without a scalp to its crown.   15
It was on the terrible Earthquake-day
That the Deacon finished the one-hoss shay.

Now in building of chaises, I tell you what,
There is always *somewhere* a weakest
      spot,—
In hub, tire, felloe, in spring or thill, 20
In panel or crossbar, or floor or sill,
In screw, bolt, thoroughbrace,—lurking
      still,
Find it somewhere you must and will,
Above or below, or within or without,
And that's the reason, beyond a doubt, 25

A chaise *breaks down,* but doesn't *wear out.*
But the Deacon swore (as Deacons do,
With an "I dew vum" or an "I tell *yeou*"),
He would build one shay to beat the taown
'n' the keounty 'n' all the kentry
      raoun';   30
It should be so built that it *couldn'* break
      daown;
"Fur," said the Deacon, " 't's mighty plain
That the weakes' place mus' stan' the strain;
'n' the way t' fix it, uz I maintain,
      Is only jest   35
T' make that place uz strong uz the rest."

So the Deacon inquired of the village folk
Where he could find the strongest oak,
That couldn't be split, nor bent, nor
      broke,—
That was for spokes and floor and sills; 40
He sent for lancewood to make the thills;
The crossbars were ash, from the straight-
      est trees;
The panels of white-wood, that cuts like
      cheese,
But lasts like iron for things like these;
The hubs of logs from the "Settler's el-
      lum,"   45
Last of its timber, they couldn't sell 'em.
Never an axe had seen their chips,
And the wedges flew from between their
      lips,
Their blunt ends frizzled like celery tips;
Step and prop-iron, bolt and screw,   50
Spring, tire, axle, and linchpin too,
Steel of the finest, bright and blue;
Thoroughbrace bison-skin, thick and wide;
Boot-top dasher, from tough old hide
Found in the pit when the tanner died.   55
That was the way he "put her through."
"There!" said the Deacon, "naow she'll
      dew!"

[1] George II, king of England 1727-1760.
Born in Germany.

[2] The great earthquake which destroyed
Lisbon, chief city of Portugal, and killed
many thousands, occurred in 1755.

[3] Gen. Edward Braddock, commander of
an expedition which was disastrously defeated near Ft. Duquesne by French and
Indians.

Do! I tell you, I rather guess
She was a wonder and nothing less!
Colts grew horses, beards turned gray, 60
Deacon and deaconness dropped away,
Children and grandchildren—where were
    they?
But there stood the stout old one-hoss shay
As fresh as on Lisbon-Earthquake-day!

EIGHTEEN HUNDRED;—it came and
    found   65
The Deacon's Masterpiece strong and
    sound.
Eighteen hundred increased by ten;—
"Hahnsum kerridge" they called it then;
Eighteen hundred and twenty came;—
Running as usual; much the same.   70
Thirty and forty at last arrive,
And then came fifty, and FIFTY-FIVE.

Little of all we value here
Wakes on the morn of its hundredth year
Without both feeling and looking queer. 75
In fact, there's nothing that keeps its
    youth,
So far as I know, but a tree and truth.
(This is a moral that runs at large;
Take it.—You're welcome.—No extra
    charge.)

FIRST OF NOVEMBER,—the Earth-
    quake-day—   80
There are traces of age in the one-hoss
    shay,
A general flavor of mild decay,
But nothing local, as one may say.
There couldn't be,—for the Deacon's art
Has made it so like in every part   85
That there wasn't a chance for one to start.
For the wheels were just as strong as the
    thills,
And the floors were just as strong as the
    sills,
And the panels just as strong as the floor,
And the whippletree neither less nor
    more,   90
And the back crossbar as strong as the
    fore,
And spring and axle and hub *encore*.

And yet, *as a whole,* it is past a doubt
In another hour it will be *worn out!*

First of November, 'Fifty-five!   95
This morning the parson takes a drive.
Now, small boys, get out of the way!
Here comes the wonderful one-hoss shay,
Drawn by a rat-tailed, ewe-necked bay.
"Huddup!" said the parson.—Off went
    they.   100
The parson was working his Sunday's
    text,—
Had got to *fifthly,* and stopped perplexed
At what the—Moses—was coming next.
All at once the horse stood still,
Close by the meet'n'-house on the hill. 105
First a shiver and then a thrill,
Then something decidedly like a spill,—
And the parson was sitting upon a rock,
At half-past-nine by the meet'n'-house
    clock—
Just the hour of the Earthquake shock! 110
—What do you think the parson found,
When he got up and stared around?
The poor old chaise in a heap or mound,
As if it had been to the mill and ground!
You see, of course, if you're not a
    dunce,   115
How it went to pieces all at once,—
All at once, and nothing first,—
Just as bubbles do when they burst.

End of the wonderful one-hoss shay.
Logic is logic. That's all I say.   120

NON-RESISTANCE
[1861 (1850)]

Perhaps too far in these considerate
    days
Has patience carried her submissive ways;
Wisdom has taught us to be calm and meek,
To take one blow, and turn the other cheek;
It is not written what a man shall do,   5
If the rude caitiff smite the other too!
  Land of our fathers, in thine hour of
    need
God help thee, guarded by the passive
    creed!

As the lone pilgrim trusts to beads and
    cowl,
When through the forest rings the gray
    wolf's howl;   10
As the deep galleon trusts her gilded prow
When the black corsair slants athwart her
    bow;
As the poor pheasant, with his peaceful
    mien,
Trusts to his feathers, shining golden-
    green,
When the dark plumage with the crimson
    beak   15
Has rustled shadowy from its splintered
    peak;
So trust thy friends, whose babbling
    tongues would charm
The lifted sabre from thy foeman's arm,
Thy torches ready for the answering peal
From bellowing fort and thunder-freighted
    keel!   20

THE TWO STREAMS
[1859]

Behold the rocky wall
    That down its sloping sides
Pours the swift rain-drops, blending, as
    they fall,
    In rushing river-tides!

Yon stream, whose sources run   5
    Turned by a pebble's edge,
Is Athabasca, rolling toward the sun
    Through the cleft mountain-ledge.

The slender rill had strayed,
    But for the slanting stone,   10
To evening's ocean, with the tangled braid
    Of foam-flecked Oregon.

So from the heights of Will
    Life's parting stream descends,
And, as a moment turns its slender rill,   15
    Each widening torrent bends,—

From the same cradle's side,
    From the same mother's knee,—
One to long darkness and the frozen tide,
    One to the Peaceful Sea!   20

THE VOICELESS
[1858]

We count the broken lyres that rest
    Where the sweet wailing singers slumber,
But o'er their silent sister's breast
    The wild-flowers who will stoop to
    number?
A few can touch the magic string,   5
    And noisy Fame is proud to win them:—
Alas for those that never sing,
    But die with all their music in them!

Nay, grieve not for the dead alone
    Whose song has told their hearts' sad
    story,—   10
Weep for the voiceless, who have known
    The cross without the crown of glory!
Not where Leucadian breezes sweep
    O'er Sappho's memory-haunted billow,
But where the glistening night-dews
    weep   15
    On nameless sorrow's churchyard pillow.

O hearts that break and give no sign
    Save whitening lip and fading tresses,
Till Death pours out his cordial wine
    Slow-dropped from Misery's crushing
    presses,—   20
If singing breath or echoing chord
    To every hidden pang were given,
What endless melodies were poured,
    As sad as earth, as sweet as heaven!

From
ELSIE VENNER
[1861 (1860)]

CHAPTER I
THE BRAHMIN CASTE OF NEW ENGLAND

THERE IS nothing in New England corresponding at all to the feudal aristocracies
of the Old World. Whether it be owing to
the stock from which we were derived, or
to the practical working of our institutions,
or to the abrogation of the technical "law
of honor," which draws a sharp line between the personally responsible class of

"gentlemen" and the unnamed multitude of those who are not expected to risk their lives for an abstraction,—whatever be the cause, we have no such aristocracy here as that which grew up out of the military systems of the Middle Ages.

What we mean by "aristocracy" is merely the richer part of the community, that live in the tallest houses, drive real carriages, (not "kerridges,") kid-glove their hands, and French-bonnet their ladies' heads, give parties where the persons who call them by the above title are not invited, and have a provokingly easy way of dressing, walking, talking, and nodding to people, as if they felt entirely at home, and would not be embarrassed in the least, if they met the Governor, or even the President of the United States, face to face. Some of these great folks are really well-bred, some of them are only purse-proud and assuming, —but they form a class, and are named as above in the common speech.

It is in the nature of large fortunes to diminish rapidly, when subdivided and distributed. A million is the unit of wealth, now, and here in America. It splits into four handsome properties; each of these into four good inheritances; these, again, into scanty competences for four ancient maidens,—with whom it is best the family should die out, unless it can begin again as its great-grandfather did. Now a million is a kind of golden cheese, which represents in a compendious form the summer's growth of a fat meadow of craft or commerce; and as this kind of meadow rarely bears more than one crop, it is pretty certain that sons and grandsons will not get another golden cheese out of it, whether they milk the same cows or turn in new ones. In other words, the millionocracy, considered in a large way, is not at all an affair of persons and families, but a perpetual fact of money with a variable human element, which a philosopher might leave out of consideration without falling into serious error. Of course, this trivial and fugitive fact of personal wealth does not create a permanent class, unless some special means are taken to arrest the process of disintegration in the third generation. This is so rarely done, at least successfully, that one need not live a very long life to see most of the rich families he knew in childhood more or less reduced, and the millions shifted into the hands of the country-boys who were sweeping stores and carrying parcels when the now decayed gentry were driving their chariots, eating their venison over silver chafing-dishes, drinking Madeira chilled in embossed coolers, wearing their hair in powder, and casing their legs in top boots with silken tassels.

There is, however, in New England, an aristocracy, if you choose to call it so, which has a far greater character of permanence. It has grown to be a *caste*,— not in any odious sense,—but, by the repetition of the same influences, generation after generation, it has acquired a distinct organization and physiognomy, which not to recognize is mere stupidity, and not to be willing to describe would show a distrust of the good-nature and intelligence of our readers, who like to have us see all we can and tell all we see.

If you will look carefully at any class of students in one of our colleges, you will have no difficulty in selecting specimens of two different aspects of youthful manhood. Of course I shall choose extreme cases to illustrate the contrast between them. In the first, the figure is perhaps robust, but often otherwise,—inelegant, partly from careless attitudes, partly from ill-dressing, —the face is uncouth in feature, or at least common,—the mouth coarse and unformed,—the eye unsympathetic, even if bright,—the movements of the face are clumsy, like those of the limbs,—the voice is unmusical,—and the enunciation as if the words were coarse castings, instead of fine carvings. The youth of the other aspect is commonly slender,—his face is smooth, and apt to be pallid,—his features are regular and of a certain delicacy,—his eye is bright and quick,—his lips play over the thought he utters as a pianist's fingers dance over their music,—and his whole air, though it may be timid, and even awkward, has nothing clownish. If you are a teacher, you know what to expect from each of these young men. With equal willingness, the first will be slow at learning; the second will take to his books as a pointer or a setter to his field-work.

The first youth is the common country-boy, whose race has been bred to bodily labor. Nature has adapted the family organization to the kind of life it has lived. The hands and feet by constant use have got more than their share of development, —the organs of thought and expression less than their share. The finer instincts are latent and must be developed. A youth of this kind is raw material in its first stage of elaboration. You must not expect too much of any such. Many of them have force of will and character and become distinguished in practical life; but very few of them ever become great scholars. A scholar is, in a large proportion of cases, the son of scholars or scholarly persons.

That is exactly what the other young man is. He comes of the *Brahmin caste of New England.* This is the harmless, inoffensive, untitled aristocracy referred to, and which many readers will at once acknowledge. There are races of scholars among us, in which aptitude for learning, and all these marks of it I have spoken of, are congenital and hereditary. Their names are always on some college catalogue or other. They break out every generation or two in some learned labor which calls them up after they seem to have died out. At last some newer name takes their place, it may be, —but you inquire a little and you find it is the blood of the Edwardses or the Chaunceys or the Ellerys or some of the old historic scholars, disguised under the altered name of a female descendant.

There probably is not an experienced instructor anywhere in our Northern States who will not recognize at once the truth of this general distinction. But the reader who has never been a teacher will very probably object, that some of our most illustrious public men have come direct from the homespun-clad class of the people,—and he may, perhaps, even find a noted scholar or two whose parents were masters of the English alphabet, but of no other.

It is not fair to pit a few chosen families against the great multitude of those who are continually working their way up into the intellectual classes. The results which are habitually reached by hereditary training are occasionally brought about without it. There are natural filters as well as artificial ones; and though the great rivers are commonly more or less turbid, if you will look long enough, you may find a spring that sparkles as no water does which drips through your apparatus of sands and sponges. So there are families which refine themselves into intellectual aptitude without having had much opportunity for intellectual acquirements. A series of felicitous crosses develops an improved strain of blood, and reaches its maximum perfection at last in the large uncombed youth who goes to college and startles the hereditary class-leaders by striding past them all. That is Nature's republicanism; thank God for it, but do not let it make you illogical. The race of the hereditary scholar has exchanged a certain portion of its animal vigor for its new instincts, and it is hard to lead men without a good deal of animal vigor. The scholar who comes ·by Nature's special grace from an unworn stock of broad-chested sires and deep-bosomed mothers must always overmatch an equal intelligence with a compromised and lowered vitality. A man's breathing and digestive apparatus (one is tempted to add *muscular*) are just as important to him on the floor of the Senate as his thinking organs. You broke down in your great speech, did you? Yes, your grandfather had an attack of dyspepsia in '82, after working too hard on his famous Election Sermon. All this does not touch the main fact: our scholars come chiefly from a privileged order, just as our best fruits come from well-known grafts,—though now and then a seedling apple, like the Northern Spy, or a seedling pear, like the Seckel, springs from a name-less ancestry and grows to be the pride of all the gardens in the land. . . .

From
THE POET AT THE BREAKFAST-TABLE
[1872]

THE SCARABEE

AT MY LEFT hand sits as singular-looking a human being as I remember see-ing outside of a regular museum or tent-show. His black coat shines as if it had been polished; and it has been polished on the wearer's back, no doubt, for the arms and other points of maximum attrition are particularly smooth and bright. Round shoulders—stooping over some minute la-bor, I suppose. Very slender limbs, with bends like a grasshopper's; sits a great deal, I presume; looks as if he might straighten them out all of a sudden, and jump instead of walking. Wears goggles very commonly; says it rests his eyes, which he strains in looking at very small objects. Voice has a dry creak, as if made by some small piece of mechanism that wanted oiling. I don't think he is a botanist, for he does not smell of dried herbs, but car-ries a camphorated atmosphere about with him, as if to keep the moths from attacking him. I must find out what is his particular interest. One ought to know something about his immediate neighbors at the table. This is what I said to myself, before open-ing a conversation with him. Everybody in our ward of the city was in a great stir about a certain election, and I thought I might as well begin with that as anything.

—How do you thing the vote is likely to go tomorrow?—I said.

—It isn't tomorrow,—he answered,—it's next month.

—Next month!—said I.—Why, what election do you mean?

—I mean the election to the Presidency of the Entomological Society, sir,—he creaked, with an air of surprise, as if no-body could by any possibility have been thinking of any other. Great competition, sir, between the dipterists and the lepi-dopterists as to which shall get in their candidate. Several close ballotings already; adjourned for a fortnight. Poor concerns, both of 'em. Wait till our turn comes.

—I suppose you are an entomologist? —I said with a note of interrogation.

—Not quite so ambitious as that, sir. I should like to put my eyes on the indi-vidual entitled to that name! A *society* may call itself an Entomological Society, but the man who arrogates such a broad title as that to himself, in the present state of science, is a pretender, sir, a dilettante, an impostor! No man can be truly called an entomologist, sir; the subject is too vast for any single human intelligence to grasp.

—May I venture to ask,—I said, a little awed by his statement and manner,—what is your special province of study?

I am often spoken of as a Coleopterist, —he said, but I have no right to so com-prehensive a name. The genus Scarabæus is what I have chiefly confined myself to, and ought to have studied exclusively. The beetles proper are quite enough for the labor of one man's life. Call me a Scara-beeist if you will; if I can prove myself worthy of that name, my highest ambition will be more than satisfied.

I think, by way of compromise and convenience, I shall call him the Scarabee. He has come to look wonderfully like those creatures,—the beetles, I mean,—by being so much among them. His room is hung round with cases of them, each im-paled on a pin driven through him, some-thing as they used to bury suicides. These cases take the place for him of pictures and all other ornaments. That Boy steals into his room sometimes, and stares at them with great admiration, and has himself undertaken to form a rival cabinet, chiefly consisting of flies, so far, arranged in ranks superintended by an occasional spider. . . .

We agreed that on some fair night when the Astronomer should tell us that there was to be a fine show in the skies, we would make up a party and go to the Observatory. I asked the Scarabee whether he would not like to make one of us.

—Out of the question, sir, out of the question. I am altogether too much occupied with an important scientific investigation to devote any considerable part of an evening to star-gazing.

—Oh, indeed, said I,—and may I venture to ask on what particular point you are engaged just at present?

—Certainly, sir, you may. It is, I suppose, as difficult and important a matter to be investigated as often comes before a student of natural history. I wish to settle the point once for all whether the *Pediculus Melittae* is or is not the larva of *Meloë*.

[—Now isn't this the drollest world to live in that one could imagine, short of being in a fit of *delirium tremens?* Here is a fellow-creature of mine and yours who is asked to see all the glories of the firmament brought close to him, and he is too busy with a little unmentionable parasite that infests the bristly surface of a bee to spare an hour or two of a single evening for the splendors of the universe! I must get a peep through that microscope of his and see the *pediculus* which occupies a larger space in his mental vision than the midnight march of the solar systems.— The creature, the human one, I mean, interests me.]

—I am very curious,—I said,—about that *pediculus melittae,*—(just as if I knew a good deal about the little wretch and wanted to know more, whereas I had never heard him spoken of before, to my knowledge,)—could you let me have a sight of him in your microscope?

—You ought to have seen the way in which the poor dried-up little Scarabee turned towards me. His eyes took on a

really human look, and I almost thought that those antennæ-like arms of his would have stretched themselves out and embraced me. I don't believe any of the boarders had ever shown any interest in him, except the little monkey of a Boy, since he had been in the house. It is not strange; he had not seemed to me much like a human being, until all at once I touched the one point where his vitality had concentrated itself, and he stood revealed a man and a brother.

—Come in,—said he,—come in, right after breakfast, and you shall see the animal that has convulsed the entomological world with questions as to his nature and origin.

—So I went into the Scarabee's parlor, lodging-room, study, laboratory, and museum,—a single apartment applied to these various uses, you understand.

—I wish I had time to have you show me all your treasures,—I said,—but I am afraid I shall hardly be able to do more than look at the bee-parasite. But what a superb butterfly you have in that case!

—Oh, yes, yes, well enough,—came from South America with the beetle there; look at *him!* These *Lepidoptera* are for children to play with, pretty to look at, so some think. Give me the *Coleoptera,* and the kings of the *Coleoptera* are the beetles! *Lepidoptera* and *Neuroptera* for little folks; *Coleoptera* for men, sir!

—The particular beetle he showed me in the case with the magnificent butterfly was an odious black wretch that one would say, Ugh! at, and kick out of his path, if he did not serve him worse than that. But he looked at it as a coin-collector would look at a Pescennius Niger, if the coins of that Emperor are as scarce as they used to be when I was collecting half-penny tokens and pine-tree shillings and battered bits of Roman brass with the head of Gallienus or some such old fellow on them.

—A beauty!—he exclaimed,—and the only specimen of the kind in this country, to the best of my belief. A unique, sir, and there is a pleasure in exclusive possession.

Not another beetle like that short of South America, sir.

—I was glad to hear that there were no more like it in the neighborhood, the present supply of cockroaches answering every purpose, so far as I am concerned, that such an animal as this would be likely to serve.

—Here are my bee-parasites,—said the Scarabee, showing me a box full of glass slides, each with a specimen ready mounted for the microscope. I was most struck with one little beast flattened out like a turtle, semi-transparent, six-legged, and as I remember him, every leg terminated by a single claw hooked like a lion's and as formidable for the size of the creature as that of the royal beast.

—Lives on a bumblebee, does he?—I said.—That's the way I call it. Bumblebee or bumblybee and huckleberry. Humblebee and whortleberry for people that say Woosses-ter and Nor-wich.

—The Scarabee did not smile; he took no interest in trivial matters like this.

—[Lives on a bumblebee. When you come to think of it, he must lead a pleasant kind of life. Sails through the air without the trouble of flying. Free pass everywhere that the bee goes. No fear of being dislodged; look at those six grappling-hooks. Helps himself to such juices of the bee as he likes best; the bee feeds on the choicest vegetable nectars, and he feeds on the bee. Lives either in the air or in the perfumed pavilion of the fairest and sweetest flowers. Think what tents the hollyhocks and the great lilies spread for him! And wherever he travels a band of music goes with him, for this hum which wanders by us is doubtless to him a vast and inspiring strain of melody.] I thought all this, while the Scarabee supposed I was studying the minute characters of the enigmatical specimen.

—I know what I consider your *pediculus melittae*, I said at length.

—Do you think it really the larva of *meloë?*

—Oh, I don't know much about that, but I think he is the best cared for, on the whole, of any animal that I know of; and if I wasn't a man I believe I had rather be that little sybarite than anything that feasts at the board of nature.

—The question is, whether he is the larva of *meloë*,—the Scarabee said, as if he had not heard a word of what I had just been saying.—If I live a few years longer it shall be settled, sir; and if my epitaph can say honestly that I settled it, I shall be willing to trust my posthumous fame to that achievement.

I said good morning to the specialist, and went off feeling not only kindly, but respectfully towards him. He is an enthusiast, at any rate, as "earnest" a man as any philanthropic reformer who, having passed his life in worrying people out of their misdoings into good behavior, comes at last to a state in which he is never contented except when he is making somebody uncomfortable. He does certainly know one thing well, very likely better than anyone in the world.

I find myself somewhat singularly placed at our table between a minute philosopher who has concentrated all his faculties on a single subject, and my friend who finds the present universe too restricted for his intelligence. I would not give much to hear what the Scarabee says about the old Master, for he does not pretend to form a judgment of anything but beetles, but I should like to hear what the Master has to say about the Scarabee. I waited after breakfast until he had gone, and then asked the Master what he could make of our dried-up friend.

—Well, he said,—I am hospitable enough in my feelings to him and all his tribe. These specialists are the coral-insects that build up a reef. By and by it will be an island, and for aught we know may grow into a continent. But I don't want to be a coral-insect myself. I had rather be a voyager that visits all the reefs and islands the creatures build, and sails over the seas where they have as yet built up nothing. I am a little afraid that science is breeding us down too fast into coral-insects. A man like Newton or Leibnitz or Haller [1] used to paint a picture of outward or inward nature with a free hand, and stand back and look at it as a whole and feel like an archangel; but nowadays you have a Society, and they come together and make a great mosaic, each man bringing his little bit and sticking it in its place, but so taken up with his petty fragment that he never thinks of looking at the picture the little bits make when they are put together. You can't get any talk out of these specialists away from their own subjects, any more than you can get help from a policeman outside of his own beat.

—Yes,—said I,—but why shouldn't we always set a man talking about the thing he knows best?

—No doubt, no doubt, if you meet him once; but what are you going to do with him if you meet him every day? I travel with a man and we want to make change very often in paying bills. But every time I ask him to change a pistareen, or give me two fo'pencehappennies for a nine-pence, or help me to make out two and thrippence (mark the old Master's archa-isms about the currency), what does the fellow do but put his hand in his pocket and pull out an old Roman coin; I have no change, says he, but this assarion of Diocletian. Mighty deal of good that'll do me!

—It isn't quite so handy as a few speci-mens of the modern currency would be, but you can pump him on numismatics.

—To be sure, to be sure. I've pumped a thousand men of all they could teach me, or at least all I could learn from them; and if it comes to that, I never saw the man that couldn't teach me something. I can get along with everybody in his place, though I think the place of some of my friends is over there among the feeble-minded pupils, and I don't believe there's one of *them* I couldn't go to school to for half an hour and be the wiser for it. But people you talk with every day have got to have feeders for their minds, as much as

the stream that turns a mill-wheel has. It isn't one little rill that's going to keep the float-boards turning round. Take a dozen of the brightest men you can find in the brightest city, wherever that may be,—per-haps you and I think we know,—and let 'em come together once a month, and you'll find out in the course of a year or two the ones that have feeders from all the hill-sides. Your common talkers, that exchange the gossip of the day, have no wheel in particular to turn, and the wash of the rain as it runs down the street is enough for them.

—Do you mean you can always see the sources from which a man fills his mind, —his feeders as you call them?

—I don't go quite so far as that,—the Master said.—I've seen men whose minds were always over-flowing, and yet they didn't read much nor go much into the world. Sometimes you'll find a bit of a pond-hole in a pasture, and you'll plunge your walking-stick into it and think you are going to touch bottom. But you find you are mistaken. Some of these little stagnant pond-holes are a good deal deeper than you think; you may tie a stone to a bed-cord and not get soundings in some of 'em. The country boys will tell you they have no bottom, but that only means that they are mighty deep; and so a good many stagnant, stupid-seeming people are a great deal deeper than the length of your in-tellectual walking-stick, I can tell you. There are hidden springs that keep the little pond-holes full when the mountain brooks are all dried up. You poets ought to know that.

—I can't help thinking you are more tolerant towards the specialists than I thought at first, by the way you seemed to

---

[1] Sir Isaac Newton (1642-1727), Eng-lish natural philosopher and mathemati-cian; Baron Gottfried Wilhelm von Lieb-nitz (1646-1716), German philosopher and mathematician; Albrecht von Haller (1708-1777), Swiss anatomist, botanist, and poet. Their discoveries of general principles laid much of the foundation of modern science.

look at our dried-up neighbor and his small pursuits.

—I don't like the word *tolerant*,—the Master said.—As long as the Lord can tolerate me I think I can stand my fellow-creatures. Philosophically, I love 'em all; empirically, I don't think I am very fond of all of 'em. It depends on how you look at a man or a woman. Come here, Youngster, will you?—he said to That Boy.

The Boy was trying to catch a blue-bottle to add to his collection, and was indisposed to give up the chase; but he presently saw that the Master had taken out a small coin and laid it on the table, and felt himself drawn in that direction.

Read that,—said the Master.

U-n-i-ni—United States of America 5 cents.

The Master turned the coin over. Now read that.

In God is our t-r-u-s-t—trust. 1869.

—Is that the same piece of money as the other one?

—There ain't any other one,—said the Boy,—there ain't but one, but it's got two sides to it with different reading.

—That's it, that's it,—said the Master, —two sides to everybody, as there are to that piece of money. I've seen an old woman that wouldn't fetch five cents if you should put her up for sale at public auction; and yet come to read the other side of her, she had a trust in God Almighty that was like the bow anchor of a three-decker. It's faith in something and enthusiasm for something that makes a life worth looking at. I don't think your ant-eating specialist, with his sharp nose and pin-head eyes, is the best every-day companion; but any man who knows one thing well is worth listening to for once; and if you are of the large-brained variety of the race, and want to fill out your programme of the Order of Things in a systematic and exhaustive way, and get all the half-notes and flats and sharps of humanity into your scale, you'd a great deal better shut your front door and open your two side ones when you come across

a fellow that has made a real business of doing anything.

—That Boy stood all this time looking hard at the five-cent piece.

—Take it,—said the Master, with a good-natured smile.

—The Boy made a snatch at it and was off for the purpose of investing it.

—A child naturally snaps at a thing as a dog does at his meat,—said the Master. —If you think of it, we've all been quadrupeds. A child that can only crawl has all the instincts of a four-footed beast. It carries things in its mouth just as cats and dogs do. I've seen little brutes do it over and over again. I suppose a good many children would stay quadrupeds all their lives, if they didn't learn the trick of walking on their hind legs from seeing all the grown people walking in that way.

—Do you accept Mr. Darwin's notions about the origin of the race?—said I.

The Master looked at me with that twinkle in his eye which means that he is going to parry a question.

—Better stick to Blair's Chronology;[2] that settles it. Adam and Eve, created Friday, October 28th, B.C. 4004. You've been in a ship for a good while, and here comes Mr. Darwin on deck with an armful of sticks and says, "Let's build a raft and trust ourselves to that."

If your ship springs a leak, what *would* you do?

He looked at me straight in the eyes for about half a minute.—If I heard the pumps going, I'd look and see whether they were gaining on the leak or not. If they were gaining I'd stay where I was.

MORAL TERATOLOGY

The Master took down a volume from one of the shelves. I could not help noticing that it was a shelf near his hand as he sat, and that the volume looked as if he

---

[2] A system of chronology based on literal interpretation of the Old Testament and for a time widely accepted, which fixed a precise date for the creation of man.

had made frequent use of it. I saw, too, that he handled it in a loving sort of way; the tenderness he would have bestowed on a wife and children had to find a channel somewhere, and what more natural than that he should look fondly on the volume which held the thoughts that had rolled themselves smooth and round in his mind like pebbles on a beach, the dreams which, under cover of the simple artifices such as all writers use, told the little world of readers his secret hopes and aspirations, the fancies which had pleased him and which he could not bear to let die without trying to please others with them? I have a great sympathy with authors, most of all with unsuccessful ones. If one had a dozen lives or so, it would all be very well, but to have only a single ticket in the great lottery, and to have that drawn a blank, is a rather sad sort of thing. So I was pleased to see the affectionate kind of pride with which the Master handled his book; it was a success, in its way, and he looked on it with a cheerful sense that he had a right to be proud of it. The Master opened the volume, and, putting on his large round glasses, began reading, as authors love to read that love their books.

—The only good reason for believing in the stability of the moral order of things is to be found in the tolerable steadiness of human averages. Out of a hundred human beings fifty-one will be found in the long run on the side of the right, so far as they know it, and against the wrong. They will be organizers rather than disorganizers, helpers and not hinderers in the upward movement of the race. This is the main fact we have to depend on. The right hand of the great organism is a little stronger than the left, that is all.

Now and then we come across a left-handed man. So now and then we find a tribe or a generation, the subject of what we may call moral left-handedness, but that need not trouble us about our formula. All we have to do is to spread the average over a wider territory or a longer period of time. Any race or

period that insists on being left-handed must go under if it comes in contact with a right-handed one. If there were, as a general rule, fifty-one rogues in the hundred instead of forty-nine, all other qualities of the mind and body being equally distributed between the two sections, the order of things would sooner or later end in universal disorder. It is the question between the leak and the pumps.

It does not seem very likely that the Creator of all things is taken by surprise at witnessing anything any of his creatures do or think. Men have sought out many inventions, but they can have contrived nothing which did not exist as an idea in the omniscient consciousness to which past, present, and future are alike Now.

We read what travellers tell us about the King of Dahomy, or the Fiji Island people, or the short and simple annals of the celebrities recorded in the Newgate Calendar,[3] and do not know just what to make of these brothers and sisters of the race; but I do not suppose an intelligence even as high as the angelic beings, to stop short there, would see anything very peculiar or wonderful about them, except as everything is wonderful and unlike everything else.

It is very curious to see how science, that is, looking at and arranging the facts of a case with our own eyes and our own intelligence, without minding what somebody else has said, or how some old majority vote went in a pack of intriguing ecclesiastics,—I say it is very curious to see how science is catching up with one superstition after another.

There is a recognized branch of science familiar to all those who know anything of the studies relating to life, under the name of Teratology. It deals with all sorts of monstrosities which are to be met with in living beings, and more especially in animals. It is found that what used to be called *lusus naturae,* or freaks of na-

[3] An account of prisoners in Newgate, famous and ancient London prison, with details of their crimes.

ture, are just as much subject to laws as the naturally developed forms of living creatures.

The rustic looks at the Siamese twins,[4] and thinks he is contemplating an unheard-of anomaly; but there are plenty of cases like theirs in the books of scholars, and though they are not quite so common as double cherries, the mechanism of their formation is not a whit more mysterious than that of twinned fruits. Such cases do not disturb the average arrangement; we have Changs and Engs at one pole, and Cains and Abels at the other. One child is born with six fingers on each hand, and another falls short by one or more fingers of his due allowance; but the glover puts his faith in the great law of averages, and makes his gloves with five fingers apiece, trusting nature for their counterparts.

Thinking people are not going to be scared out of explaining or at least trying to explain things by the shrieks of persons whose beliefs are disturbed thereby. Comets were portents to Increase Mather, President of Harvard College;[5] "preachers of Divine wrath, heralds and messengers of evil tidings to the world." It is not so very long since Professor Winthrop[6] was teaching at the same institution. I can remember two of his boys very well, old boys, it is true, they were, and one of them wore a three-cornered cocked hat; but the father of these boys, whom, as I say, I can remember, had to defend himself against the minister of the Old South Church for the impiety of trying to account for earthquakes on natural principles. And his ancestor, Governor Winthrop, would probably have shaken his head over his descendant's dangerous audacity, if one may judge by the solemn way in which he mentions poor Mrs. Hutchinson's unpleasant experience,[7] which so grievously disappointed her maternal expectations. But people used always to be terribly frightened by those irregular vital products which we now call "interesting specimens" and carefully preserve

in jars of alcohol. It took next to nothing to make a panic; a child was born a few centuries ago with six teeth in its head, and about that time the Turks began gaining great advantages over the Christians. Of course there was an intimate connection between the prodigy and the calamity. So said the wise men of that day.

—All of these out-of-the-way cases are studied connectedly now, and are found to obey very exact rules. With a little management one can even manufacture living monstrosities. Malformed salmon and other fish can be supplied in quantity, if anybody happens to want them.

Now, what all I have said is tending to is exactly this, namely, that just as the celestial movements are regulated by fixed laws, just as bodily monstrosities are produced according to rule, and with as good reason as normal shapes, so obliquities of character are to be accounted for on perfectly natural principles; they are just as capable of classification as the bodily ones, and they all diverge from a certain average or middle term which is the type of its kind.

If life had been a little longer I would have written a number of essays for which, as it is, I cannot expect to have time. I have set down the titles of a hundred or more, and I have often been tempted to publish these, for according to my idea, the title of a book very often renders the rest of it unnecessary. "Moral Teratology," for instance, which is marked No. 67 on my list of "Essays Potential, Not Actual," suggests sufficiently well what I should be like to say in the pages it would preface. People hold up their hands at a moral

[4] Chang and Eng, born in Siam, 1811. Widely exhibited in the United States, where they died in 1874.

[5] See Vol. I, pp. 183-85.

[6] John Winthrop (1714-1779), astronomer and physicist, great-grandnephew of Gov. John Winthrop of Connecticut (1606-76), who was the son of Gov. John Winthrop of Massachusetts (1588-1649).

[7] See Vol. I, pp. 159-61.

monster as if there were no reason for his existence but his own choice. That was a fine specimen we read of in the papers a few years ago,—the Frenchman, it may be remembered, who used to waylay and murder young women, and after appropriating their effects, bury their bodies in a private cemetery he kept for that purpose. It is very natural, and I do not say it is not very proper, to hang such eccentric persons as this; but it is not clear whether his vagaries produce any more sensation at Headquarters than the meek enterprises of the mildest of city missionaries. For the study of Moral Teratology will teach you that you do not get such a malformed character as that without a long chain of causes to account for it; and if you only knew those causes, you would know perfectly well what to expect. You may feel pretty sure that our friend of the private cemetery was not the child of pious and intelligent parents; that he was not nurtured by the best of mothers, and educated by the most judicious teachers; and that he did not come from a lineage long known and honored for its intellectual and moral qualities. Suppose that one should go to the worst quarter of the city and pick out the worst-looking child of the worst couple he could find, and then train him up successively at the School for Infant Rogues, the Academy for Young Scamps, and the College for Complete Criminal Education, would it be reasonable to expect a Francis Xavier or a Henry Martyn to be the result of such a training? The traditionalists, in whose presumptuous hands the science of anthropology has been trusted from time immemorial, have insisted on eliminating cause and effect from the domain of morals. When they have come across a moral monster they have seemed to think that he put himself together, having a free choice of all the constituents which make up manhood, and that consequently no punishment could be too bad for him.

I say, hang him and welcome, if that is the best thing for society; hate him, in a certain sense, as you hate a rattlesnake, but, if you pretend to be a philosopher, recognize the fact that what you hate in him is chiefly misfortune, and that if you had been born with his villainous low forehead and poisoned instincts, and bred among creatures of the *Races Maudites*[8] whose natural history has to be studied like that of beasts of prey and vermin, you would not have been sitting there in your gold-bowed spectacles and passing judgment on the peccadilloes of your fellow-creatures.

I have seen men and women so disinterested and noble, and devoted to the best works, that it appeared to me if any good and faithful servant was entitled to enter into the joys of his Lord, such as these might be. But I do not know that I ever met with a human being who seemed to me to have a stronger claim on the pitying consideration and kindness of his Maker than a wretched, puny, crippled, stunted child that I saw in Newgate, who was pointed out as one of the most notorious and inveterate little thieves in London. I have no doubt that some of those who were looking at this pitiable morbid secretion of the diseased social organism thought they were very virtuous for hating him so heartily.

It is natural, and in one sense it is all right enough. I want to catch a thief and put the extinguisher on an incendiary as much as my neighbors do; but I have two sides to my consciousness as I have two sides to my heart, one carrying dark, impure blood, and the other the bright stream which has been purified and vivified by the great source of life and death,—the oxygen of the air which gives all things their vital heat, and burns all things at last to ashes.

One side of me loves and hates; the other side of me judges, say rather pleads and suspends judgment. I think, if I were left to myself, I should hang a rogue and then write his apology and subscribe to

---

[8] Accursed tribes.

a neat monument, commemorating, not his virtues, but his misfortunes. I should, perhaps, adorn the marble with emblems, as is the custom with regard to the more regular and normally constituted members of society. It would not be proper to put the image of a lamb upon the stone which marked the resting-place of him of the private cemetery. But I would not hesitate to place the effigy of a wolf or a hyena upon the monument. I do not judge these animals, I only kill them or shut them up. I presume they stand just as well with their Maker as lambs and kids, and the existence of such beings is a perpetual plea for God Almighty's poor, yelling, scalping Indians, his weasand-stopping Thugs, his despised felons, his murdering miscreants, and all the unfortunates whom we, picked individuals of a picked class of a picked race, scrubbed, combed, and catechized from our cradles upward, undertake to find accommodations for in another state of being where it is to be hoped they will have a better chance than they had in this.

THE APPEAL OF DARWINISM

What is the secret of the profound interest which "Darwinism" has excited in the minds and hearts of more persons than dare to confess their doubts and hopes? It is because it restores "Nature" to its place as a true divine manifestation. It is that it removes the traditional curse from that helpless infant lying in its mother's arms. It is that it lifts from the shoulders of man the responsibility for the fact of death. It is that, if it is true, woman can no longer be taunted with having brought down on herself the pangs which make her sex a martyrdom. If development upward is the general law of the race; if we have grown by natural evolution out of the cave-man, and even less human forms of life, we have everything to hope from the future. That the question can be discussed without offence shows that we are entering on a new era,

a Revival greater than that of Letters, the Revival of Humanity.

The prevalent view of "Nature" has been akin to that which long reigned with reference to disease. This used to be considered as a distinct entity apart from the processes of life, of which it is one of the manifestations. It was a kind of demon to be attacked with things of odious taste and smell; to be fumigated out of the system as the evil spirit was driven from the bridal-chamber in the story of Tobit.[9] The Doctor of earlier days, even as I can remember him, used to exorcise the demon of disease with recipes of odor as potent as that of the angel's diabolifuge,[10]—the smoke from a fish's heart and liver, duly burned,—"the which smell when the evil spirit had smelled he fled into the uttermost parts of Egypt." The very moment that disease passes into the category of vital processes, and is recognized as an occurrence absolutely necessary, inevitable, and as one may say, normal under certain given conditions of constitution and circumstance, the medicine-man loses his half-miraculous endowments. The mythical serpent is untwined from the staff of Esculapius,[11] which thenceforth becomes a useful walking-stick, and does not pretend to be anything more.

Sin, like disease, is a vital process. It is a function, and not an entity. It must be studied as a section of anthropology. No preconceived idea must be allowed to interfere with our investigation of the deranged spiritual function, any more than the old ideas of demoniacal possession must be allowed to interfere with our study of epilepsy. Spiritual pathology is a proper subject for direct observation and analysis, like any other subject involving a series of living actions.

In these living actions everything is pro-

---

[9] Book of the Old Testament apocrypha.

[10] Preparation used to drive away evil spirits.

[11] Roman god of medicine. His symbol, a staff entwined by a serpent, is still in use.

gressive. There are sudden changes of character in what is called "conversion" which, at first, hardly seem to come into line with the common laws of evolution. But these changes have been long preparing, and it is just as much in the order of nature that certain characters should burst all at once from the rule of evil propensities, as it is that the evening primrose should explode, as it were, into bloom with audible sound, as you may read in Keats' "Endymion," or observe in your own garden.

There is a continual tendency in men to fence in themselves and a few of their neighbors who agree with them in their ideas, as if they were an exception to their race. We must not allow any creed or religion whatsoever to confiscate to its own private use and benefit the virtues which belong to our common humanity. The Good Samaritan helped his wounded neighbor simply because he was a suffering fellow-creature. Do you think your charitable act is more acceptable than the Good Samaritan's, because you do it in the name of Him who made the memory of that kind man immortal? Do you mean that you would not give the cup of cold water for the sake simply and solely of the poor, suffering fellow-mortal, as willingly as you now do, professing to give it for the sake of Him who is not thirsty or in need of any help of yours? We must ask questions like this, if we are to claim for our common nature what belongs to it.

The scientific study of man is the most difficult of all branches of knowledge. It requires in the first place, an entire new terminology to get rid of that enormous load of prejudices with which every term applied to the malformations, the functional disturbances, and the organic diseases of the moral nature is at present burdened. Take that one word *Sin*, for instance: all those who have studied the subject from nature and not from books know perfectly well that a certain fraction of what is so called is nothing more or less than a symptom of hysteria; that

another fraction is the index of a limited degree of insanity; that still another is the result of a congenital tendency which removes the act we sit in judgment upon from the sphere of self-determination, if not entirely, at least to such an extent that the subject of the tendency cannot be judged by any normal standard.

To study nature without fear is possible, but without reproach, impossible. The man who worships in the temple of knowledge must carry his arms with him as our Puritan fathers had to do when they gathered in their first rude meeting-houses. It is a fearful thing to meddle with the ark which holds the mysteries of creation.

I remember that when I was a child the tradition was whispered round among us little folks that if we tried to count the stars we should drop down dead. Nevertheless, the stars have been counted and the astronomer has survived. This nursery legend is the child's version of those superstitions which would have strangled in their cradles the young sciences now adolescent and able to take care of themselves, and which, no longer daring to attack these, are watching with hostile aspect the rapid growth of the comparatively new science of man.

The real difficulty of the student of nature at this time is to reconcile absolute freedom and perfect fearlessness with that respect for the past, that reverence for the spirit of reverence wherever we find it, that tenderness for the weakest fibres by which the hearts of our fellow-creatures hold to their religious convictions, which will make the transition from old belief to a larger light and liberty an interstitial change and not a violent mutilation.

I remember once going into a little church in a small village some miles from a great European capital. The special object of adoration in this humblest of places of worship was a *bambino*, a holy infant, done in wax, and covered with cheap ornaments such as a little girl would like to beautify her doll with. Many a good Protestant of the old Puritan type would have felt a strong impulse to seize this "idolatrous" figure and dash it to pieces on the stone floor of the little church. But one must have lived awhile among simple-minded pious Catholics to know what this poor waxen image and the whole baby-house of *bambinos* mean for a humble, unlettered, unimaginative peasantry. He will find that the true office of this *eidolon* is to fix the mind of the worshipper, and that in virtue of the devotional thoughts it has called forth so often for so many years in the mind of that poor old woman who is kneeling before it, it is no longer a wax doll for her, but has undergone a transubstantiation quite as real as that of the Eucharist. The moral

is that we must not roughly smash other people's idols because we know, or think we know, that they are of cheap human manufacture.

—Do you think cheap manufactures encourage idleness? said I.

The Master stared. Well he might, for I had been getting a little drowsy, and wishing to show that I had been awake and attentive, asked a question suggested by some words I had caught, but which showed that I had not been taking the slightest idea from what he was reading me. He stared, shook his head slowly, smiled good-humoredly, took off his great round spectacles, and shut up his book.

1849 ∽ *Sarah Orne Jewett* ∽ 1909

"GREAT writers don't try to write about people and things; they tell them just as they are," Dr. Theodore Herman Jewett once told his daughter Sarah. Dr. Theodore was a truly distinguished member of his profession and of his community—a general practitioner at Berwick, Maine, but also professor of obstetrics at Bowdoin and for many years president of his state medical society. His was a home of many books and of easy and friendly relationships. Often Sarah rode with him to visit country patients. In later years she was proud when some old resident of Berwick asked, "You're one of the Doctor's girls, ain't ye?"

Writing was an early and seemingly natural choice of occupation for Sarah Jewett, though never an easy one. Her stories, published in *The Atlantic Monthly* and collected in *Deephaven* (1877) and many succeeding volumes, gradually won the admiration of critics and discerning readers, though they never attained pronounced national popularity. Miss Jewett became the friend of successive editors of the *Atlantic*—Lowell, James T. Fields, Howells, and (especially) Thomas Bailey Aldrich. She spent many of her winters in Boston and others in Europe, and her summers regularly in Berwick.

The rural New England of which Miss Jewett wrote had been drained of youth by the Civil War and the demands of the industrial cities. Economically and socially it was deteriorating. Miss Jewett wrote of its people with quiet objectiveness and in a style at once gentle and precise—both qualities that would have pleased the master she studied most earnestly and most sought to emulate, Flaubert. She was much more successful in the short story than in her attempts at the novel, though such a collection of stories as *The Country of the Pointed Firs* (1896) possesses more unity of effect than many novels, achieved through the rich and sensitive rendering of physical background and through method and point of view rather than through ordinary structure. The number of Miss Jewett's stories which deserve to be ranked as her best is not small. Though the reader whose taste is accustomed to the harsher and more inclusive realism of recent writers may find that it requires a little persistence to become adjusted to Miss Jewett's reticence of phrase and frugality of detail, he will be repaid by deepening enjoyment as he realizes the clearness and integrity of her creative vision and the genuine inner drama of her finer stories.

[Much of Miss Jewett's best work is included in *The Best Stories of Sarah Orne Jewett,* 2 vols. (Boston, 1925), with preface by Willa Cather. F. O. Matthiessen's *Sarah Orne Jewett* (Boston, 1929) is an excellent biographical and critical study. See also *The Letters of Sarah Orne Jewett* (Boston, 1911), edited by A. Fields, and *Letters of Sarah Orne Jewett now in the Colby College Library* (Waterville, Me., 1947), edited by Carl J. Weber.]

THE HILTONS' HOLIDAY
[1895 (1893)]

THERE WAS a bright, full moon in the clear sky, and the sunset was still shining faintly in the west. Dark woods stood all about the old Hilton farmhouse, save down the hill, westward, where lay the shadowy fields which John Hilton, and his father before him, had cleared and tilled with much toil,—the small fields to which they had given the industry and even affection of their honest lives.

John Hilton was sitting on the doorstep of his house. As he moved his head in and out of the shadows, turning now and then to speak to his wife, who sat just within the doorway, one could see his good face, rough and somewhat unkept, as if he were indeed a creature of the shady woods and brown earth, instead of the noisy town. It was late in the long spring evening, and he had just come from the lower field as cheerful as a boy, proud of having finished the planting of his potatoes.

"I had to do my last row mostly by feelin'," he said to his wife. "I'm proper glad I pushed through, an' went back an' ended off after supper. 'T would have taken me a good part o' to-morrow mornin', an' broke my day."

"'Tain't no use for ye to work yourself all to pieces, John," answered the woman quickly. "I declare it does seem harder than ever that we couldn't have kep' our boy; he'd been comin' fourteen years old this fall, most a grown man, and he'd work right 'longside of ye now the whole time."

"It was hard to lose him; I do seem to miss little John," said the father sadly. "I expect there was reasons why 'twas best. I feel able an' smart to work; my father was a girt strong man, an' a monstrous worker afore me. 'Tain't that; but I was thinkin' by myself to-day what a sight o' company the boy would ha' been. You know, small's he was, how I could trust to leave him anywheres with the team, and how he'd beseech to go with me wherever I was goin'; always right in my tracks I used to tell 'em. Poor little John, for all he was so young he had a great deal o' judgment; he'd ha' made a likely man."

The mother sighed heavily as she sat within the shadow.

"But then there's the little girls, a sight o' help an' company," urged the father eagerly, as if it were wrong to dwell upon sorrow and loss. "Katy, she's most as good as a boy, except that she ain't very rugged. She's a real little farmer, she's helped me a sight this spring; an' you've got Susan Ellen, that makes a complete little housekeeper for ye as far as she's learnt. I don't see but we're better off than most folks, each on us having a workmate."

"That's so, John," acknowledged Mrs. Hilton wistfully, beginning to rock steadily in her straight, splint-bottomed chair. It was always a good sign when she rocked.

"Where be the little girls so late?" asked their father. " 'T is gettin' long past eight o'clock. I don't know when we've all set up so late, but it's so kind o' summer-like an' pleasant. Why, where be they gone?"

"I've told ye; only over to Becker's folks," answered the mother. "I don't see myself what keeps 'em so late; they beseeched me after supper till I let 'em go. They're all in a dazzle with the new teacher; she asked 'em to come over. They say she's unusual smart with 'rethmetic, but she has a kind of gorpen look to me. She's goin' to give Katy some pieces for her doll, but I told Katy she ought to be ashamed wantin' dolls' pieces, big as she's gettin' to be. I don't know's she ought, though; she ain't but nine this summer."

"Let her take her comfort," said the kind-hearted man. "Them things draws her to the teacher, an' makes them acquainted. Katy's shy with new folks, more so'n Susan Ellen, who's of the business kind. Katy's shy-feelin' and wishful."

"I don't know but she is," agreed the mother slowly. "Ain't it sing'lar how well acquainted you be with that one, an' I with Susan Ellen? 'T was always so from the first. I'm doubtful sometimes our Katy ain't one that'll be like to get married— anyways not about here. She lives right with herself, but Susan Ellen ain't nothin' when she's alone, she's always after company; all the boys is waitin' on her a'ready. I ain't afraid but she'll take her pick when the time comes. I expect to see Susan

Ellen well settled,—she feels grown up now,—but Katy don't care one mite 'bout none o' them things. She wants to be rovin' out o' doors. I do believe she'd stand an' hark to a bird the whole forenoon."

"Perhaps she'll grow up to be a teacher," suggested John Hilton. "She takes to her book more'n the other one. I should like one of 'em to be a teacher same's my mother was. They're good girls as anybody's got."

"So they be," said the mother, with unusual gentleness, and the creak of her rocking-chair was heard, regular as the ticking of a clock. The night breeze stirred in the great woods, and the sound of a brook that went falling down the hillside grew louder and louder. Now and then one could hear the plaintive chirp of a bird. The moon glittered with whiteness like a winter moon, and shone upon the low-roofed house until its small window-panes gleamed like silver, and one could almost see the colors of a blooming bush of lilac that grew in a sheltered angle by the kitchen door. There was an incessant sound of frogs in the lowlands.

"Be you sound asleep, John?" asked the wife presently.

"I don't know but what I was a'most," said the tired man, starting a little. "I should laugh if I was to fall sound asleep right here on the step; 'tis the bright night, I expect, makes my eyes feel heavy, an' 'tis so peaceful. I was up an' dressed a little past four an' out to work. Well, well!" and he laughed sleepily and rubbed his eyes. "Where's the little girls? I'd better step along an' meet 'em."

"I wouldn't just yet; they'll get home all right, but 'tis late for 'em certain. I don't want 'em keepin' Mis' Becker's folks up neither. There, le' 's wait a few minutes," urged Mrs. Hilton.

"I've be'n a-thinkin' all day I'd like to give the child'n some kind of a treat," said the father, wide awake now. "I hurried up my work 'cause I had it so in mind. They don't have the opportunities some do, an' I want 'em to know the world, an' not stay right here on the farm like a couple o' bushes."

"They're a sight better off not to be so full o' notions as some is," protested the mother suspiciously.

"Certain," answered the farmer; "but they're good, bright child'n, an' commencin' to take a sight o' notice. I want 'em to have all we can give 'em. I want 'em to see how other folks does things."

"Why, so do I,"—here the rocking-chair stopped ominously,—"but so long's they're contented"—

"Contented ain't all in this world; hopper-toads may have that quality an' spend all their time a-blinkin'. I don't know's bein' contented is all there is to look for in a child. Ambition's somethin' to me."

"Now you've got your mind on to some plot or other." (The rocking-chair began to move again.) "Why can't you talk right out?"

" 'T ain't nothin' special," answered the good man, a little ruffled; he was never prepared for his wife's mysterious powers of divination. "Well there, you do find things out the master! I only thought perhaps I'd take 'em tomorrow, an' go off somewhere if 't was a good day. I've been promisin' for a good while I'd take 'em to Topham Corners; they've never been there since they was very small."

"I believe you want a good time yourself. You ain't never got over bein' a boy." Mrs. Hilton seemed much amused. "There, go if you want to an' take 'em; they've got their summer hats an' new dresses. I don't know o' nothin' that stands in the way. I should sense it better if there was a circus or anythin' to go to. Why don't you wait an' let the girls pick 'em some strawberries or nice ros'berries, and then they could take an' sell 'em to the stores?"

John Hilton reflected deeply. "I should like to get me some good yellow-turnip seed to plant late. I ain't more'n satisfied with what I've been gettin' o' late years o' Ira Speed. An' I'm goin' to provide me with a good hoe; mine's gettin' wore out an' all shackly. I can't seem to fix it good."

"Them's excuses," observed Mrs. Hilton, with friendly tolerance. "You just cover up the hoe with somethin', if you get it—I would. Ira Speed's so jealous he'll remember it of you this twenty year, your goin' an' buyin' a new hoe o' anybody but him."

"I've always thought 't was a free country," said John Hilton soberly. "I don't want to vex Ira neither; he favors us all he can in trade. 'T is difficult for him to spare a cent, but he's as honest as daylight."

At this moment there was a sudden sound of young voices, and a pair of young figures came out from the shadow of the woods into the moonlighted open space. An old cock crowed loudly from his perch in the shed, as if he were a herald of royalty. The little girls were hand in hand, and a brisk young dog capered about them as they came.

"Wa'n't it dark gittin' home through the woods this time o' night?" asked the mother hastily, and not without reproach.

"I don't love to have you gone so late; mother an' me was timid about ye, and you've kep' Mis' Becker's folks up, I expect," said their father regretfully. "I don't want to have it said that my little girls ain't got good manners."

"The teacher had a party," chirped Susan Ellen, the elder of the two children. "Goin' home from school she asked the Grover boys, an' Mary an' Sarah Speed. An' Mis' Becker was real pleasant to us: she passed round some cake, an' handed us sap sugar on one of her best plates, an' we played games an' sung some pieces too. Mis' Becker thought we did real well. I can pick out most of a tune on the cabinet organ; teacher says she'll give me lessons."

"I want to know, dear!" exclaimed John Hilton.

"Yes, an' we played Copenhagen, an' took sides spellin', an' Katy beat everybody spellin' there was there."

Katy had not spoken; she was not so strong as her sister, and while Susan Ellen stood a step or two away addressing her eager little audience, Katy had seated herself close to her father on the doorstep. He put his arm around her shoulders, and drew her close to his side, where she stayed.

"Ain't you got nothin' to tell, daughter?" he asked, looking down fondly; and Katy gave a pleased little sigh for answer.

"Tell 'em what's goin' to be the last day o' school, and about our trimmin' the schoolhouse," she said; and Susan Ellen gave the programme in most spirited fashion.

" 'Twill be a great time," said the mother, when she had finished. "I don't see why folks wants to go trapesin' off to strange places when such things is happenin' right about 'em." But the children did not observe her mysterious air. "Come, you must step yourselves right to bed!"

They all went into the dark warm house; the bright moon shone upon it steadily all night, and the lilac flowers were shaken by no breath of wind until the early dawn.

II

The Hiltons always waked early. So did their neighbors, the crows and song-sparrows and robins, the light-footed foxes and squirrels in the woods. When John Hilton waked, before five o'clock, an hour later than usual because he had sat up so late, he opened the house door and came out into the yard, crossing the short green turf hurriedly as if the day were too far spent for any loitering. The magnitude of the plan for taking a whole day of pleasure confronted him seriously, but the weather was fair, and his wife, whose disapproval could not have been set aside, had accepted and even smiled upon the great project. It was inevitable now, that he and the children should go to Topham Corners. Mrs. Hilton had the pleasure of waking them, and telling the news.

In a few minutes they came frisking out to talk over the great plans. The cattle were already fed, and their father was milking. The only sign of high festivity was the wagon pulled out into the yard, with both seats put in as if it were Sunday; but Mr. Hilton still wore his everyday clothes, and Susan Ellen suffered instantly from disappointment.

"Ain't we goin', father?" she asked complainingly; but he nodded and smiled at her, even though the cow, impatient to get to pasture, kept whisking her rough tail across his face. He held his head down and spoke cheerfully, in spite of this vexation.

"Yes, sister, we're goin' certain', an' goin' to have a great time too." Susan Ellen thought that he seemed like a boy at that delightful moment, and felt new sympathy and pleasure at once. "You go an' help mother about breakfast an' them things; we want to get off quick's we can. You coax mother now, both of ye, an' see if she won't go with us."

"She said she wouldn't be hired to," responded Susan Ellen. "She says it's goin' to be hot, an' she's laid out to go over an' see how her aunt Tamsen Brooks is this afternoon."

The father gave a little sigh; then he took heart again. The truth was that his wife made light of the contemplated pleasure, and, much as he usually valued her companionship and approval, he was sure that they should have a better time without her.

It was impossible, however, not to feel guilty of disloyalty at the thought. Even though she might be completely unconscious of his best ideals, he only loved her and the ideals the more, and bent his energies to satisfying her indefinite expectations. His wife still kept much of that youthful beauty which Susan Ellen seemed likely to reproduce.

An hour later the best wagon was ready, and the great expedition set forth. The little dog sat apart, and barked as if it fell entirely upon him to voice the general excitement. Both seats were in the wagon, but the empty place testified to

Mrs. Hilton's unyielding disposition. She had wondered why one broad seat would not do, but John Hilton meekly suggested that the wagon looked better with both. The little girls sat on the back seat dressed alike in their Sunday hats of straw with blue ribbons, and their little plaid shawls pinned neatly about their small shoulders. They wore gray thread gloves, and sat very straight. Susan Ellen was half a head the taller, but otherwise, from behind, they looked much alike. As for their father, he was in his Sunday best,—a plain black coat, and a winter hat of felt, which was heavy and rusty-looking for that warm early summer day. He had it in mind to buy a new straw hat at Topham, so that this with the turnip seed and the hoe made three important reasons for going.

"Remember an' lay off your shawls when you get there, an' carry them over your arms," said the mother, clucking like an excited hen to her chickens. "They'll do to keep dust off your new dresses goin' an' comin'. An' when you eat your dinners don't get spots on you, an' don't point at folks as you ride by, an' stare, or they'll know you come from the country. An' John, you call into Cousin Ad'line Marlow's an' see how they all be, an' tell her I expect her over certain to stop awhile before hayin'. It always eases her phthisic to git up here on the high land, an' I've got a new notion about doin' over her best-room carpet sence I see her that'll save rippin' one breadth. An' don't come home all wore out; an', John, don't you go an' buy me no kickshaws to fetch home. I ain't a child, an' you ain't got no money to waste. I expect you'll go, like 's not, an' buy you some kind of a foolish boy's hat; do look an' see if it's reasonable good straw, an' won't splinter all off round the edge. An' you mind, John"—

"Yes, yes, hold on!" cried John impatiently; then he cast a last affectionate, reassuring look at her face, flushed with the hurry and responsibility of starting them off in proper shape. "I wish you was goin' too," he said, smiling. "I do so!"

Then the old horse started, and they went out at the bars, and began the careful long descent of the hill. The young dog, tethered to the lilac-bush, was frantic with piteous appeals; the little girls piped their eager good-bys again and again, and their father turned many times to look back and wave his hand. As for their mother, she stood alone and watched them out of sight.

There was one place far out on the highroad where she could catch a last glimpse of the wagon, and she waited what seemed a very long time until it appeared and then was lost to sight again behind a low hill. "They're nothin' but a pack o' child'n together," she said aloud; and then felt lonelier than she expected. She even stooped and patted the unresigned little dog as she passed him, going into the house.

The occasion was so much more important than any one had foreseen that both the little girls were speechless. It seemed at first like going to church in new clothes, or to a funeral; they hardly knew how to behave at the beginning of a whole day of pleasure. They made grave bows at such persons of their acquaintance as happened to be straying in the road. Once or twice they stopped before a farmhouse, while their father talked an inconsiderately long time with some one about the crops and the weather, and even dwelt upon town business and the doings of the selectmen, which might be talked of at any time. The explanations that he gave of their excursion seemed quite unnecessary. It was made entirely clear that he had a little business to do at Topham Corners, and thought he had better give the little girls a ride; they had been very steady at school, and he had finished planting, and could take the day as well as not. Soon, however, they all felt as if such an excursion were an every-day affair, and Susan Ellen began to ask eager questions, while Katy silently sat apart enjoying herself as she never had done before. She liked to see the strange houses, and the children who belonged to them; it was delightful to find

flowers that she knew growing all along
the road, no matter how far she went from
home. Each small homestead looked its
best and pleasantest, and shared the exquisite beauty that early summer made,—
shared the luxury of greenness and flower-
iness that decked the rural world. There
was an early peony or a late lilac in almost every dooryard.

It was seventeen miles to Topham. After
a while they seemed very far from home,
having left the hills far behind, and descended to a great level country with fewer
tracts of woodland, and wider fields where
the crops were much more forward. The
houses were all painted, and the roads were
smoother and wider. It had been so pleasant driving along that Katy dreaded going
into the strange town when she first caught
sight of it, though Susan Ellen kept asking with bold fretfulness if they were not
almost there. They counted the steeples of
four churches, and their father presently
showed them the Topham Academy, where
their grandmother once went to school, and
told them that perhaps some day they
would go there too. Katy's heart gave a
strange leap; it was such a tremendous
thing to think of, but instantly the suggestion was transformed for her into one of
the certainties of life. She looked with
solemn awe at the tall belfry, and the
long rows of windows in the front of the
academy, there where it stood high and
white among the clustering trees. She
hoped that they were going to drive by,
but something forbade her taking the
responsibility of saying so.

Soon the children found themselves
among the crowded village houses. Their
father turned to look at them with affectionate solicitude.

"Now sit up straight and appear pretty,"
he whispered to them. "We're among the
best people now, an' I want folks to think
well of you."

"I guess we're as good as they be," remarked Susan Ellen, looking at some innocent passers-by with dark suspicion, but
Katy tried indeed to sit straight, and folded

her hands prettily in her lap, and wished
with all her heart to be pleasing for her
father's sake. Just then an elderly woman
saw the wagon and the sedate party it
carried, and smiled so kindly that it seemed
to Katy as if Topham Corners had welcomed and received them. She smiled back
again as if this hospitable person were
an old friend, and entirely forgot that the
eyes of all Topham had been upon her.

"There, now we're coming to an elegant
house that I want you to see; you'll never
forget it," said John Hilton. "It's where
Judge Masterson lives, the great lawyer;
the handsomest house in the county, everybody says."

"Do you know him, father?" asked Susan
Ellen.

"I do," answered John Hilton proudly.
"Him and my mother went to school together in their young days, and were always called the two best scholars of their
time. The judge called to see her once; he
stopped to our house to see her when I
was a boy. An' then, some years ago—
you've heard me tell how I was on the
jury, an' when he heard my name spoken
he looked at me sharp, and asked if I
wa'n't the son of Catharine Winn, an'
spoke most beautiful of your grandmother,
an' how well he remembered their young
days together."

"I like to hear about that," said Katy.

"She had it pretty hard, I'm afraid, up
on the old farm. She was keepin' school
in our district when father married her—
that's the main reason I backed 'em down
when they wanted to tear the old schoolhouse all to pieces," confided John Hilton,
turning eagerly. "They all say she lived
longer up here on the hill than she could
anywhere, but she never had her health. I
wa'n't but a boy when she died. Father an'
me lived alone afterward till the time your
mother come; 't was a good while, too; I
wa'n't married so young as some. 'T was
lonesome, I tell you; father was plumb
discouraged losin' of his wife, an' her long
sickness an' all set him back, an' we'd
work all day on the land an' never say a

word. I s'pose 't is bein' so lonesome early in life that makes me so pleased to have some nice girls growin' up round me now."

There was a tone in her father's voice that drew Katy's heart toward him with new affection. She dimly understood, but Susan Ellen was less interested. They had often heard this story before, but to one child it was always new and to the other old. Susan Ellen was apt to think it tiresome to hear about her grandmother, who, being dead, was hardly worth talking about.

"There's Judge Masterson's place," said their father in an every-day manner, as they turned a corner, and came into full view of the beautiful old white house standing behind its green trees and terraces and lawns. The children had never imagined anything so stately and fine, and even Susan Ellen exclaimed with pleasure. At that moment they saw an old gentleman, who carried himself with great dignity, coming slowly down the wide box-bordered path toward the gate.

"There he is now, there's the judge!" whispered John Hilton excitedly, reining his horse quickly to the green roadside. "He's goin' down-town to his office; we can wait right here an' see him. I can't expect him to remember me; it's been a good many years. Now you are goin' to see the great Judge Masterson!"

There was a quiver of expectation in their hearts. The judge stopped at his gate, hesitating a moment before he lifted the latch, and glanced up the street at the country wagon with its two prim little girls on the back seat, and the eager man who drove. They seemed to be waiting for something; the old horse was nibbling at the fresh roadside grass. The judge was used to being looked at with interest, and responded now with a smile as he came out to the sidewalk, and unexpectedly turned their way. Then he suddenly lifted his hat with grave politeness, and came directly toward them.

"Good-morning, Mr. Hilton," he said. "I am very glad to see you, sir"; and Mr.

Hilton, the little girls' own father, took off his hat with equal courtesy, and bent forward to shake hands.

Susan Ellen cowered and wished herself away, but little Katy sat straighter than ever, with joy in her father's pride and pleasure shining in her pale, flowerlike little face.

"There are your daughters, I am sure," said the old gentleman kindly, taking Susan Ellen's limp and reluctant hand; but when he looked at Katy, his face brightened. "How she recalls your mother," he said with great feeling. "I am glad to see this dear child. You must come to see me with your father, my dear," he added, still looking at her. "Bring both the little girls, and let them run about the old garden; the cherries are just getting ripe," said Judge Masterson hospitably. "Perhaps you will have time to stop this afternoon as you go home?"

"I should call it a great pleasure if you would come and see us again some time. You may be driving our way, sir," said John Hilton.

"Not very often in these days," answered the old judge. "I thank you for the kind invitation. I should like to see the fine view again from your hill westward. Can I serve you in any way while you are in town? Good-by, my little friends!"

Then they parted, but not before Katy, the shy Katy, whose hand the judge still held unconsciously while he spoke, had reached forward as he had said good-by, and lifted her face to kiss him. She could not have told why, except that she felt drawn to something in the serious, worn face. For the first time in her life the child had felt the charm of manners; perhaps she owned a kinship between that which made him what he was, and the spark of nobleness and purity in her own simple soul. She turned again and again to look back at him as they drove away.

"Now you have seen one of the first gentlemen in the country," said their father. "It was worth comin' twice as far" —but he did not say any more, nor turn as usual to look in the children's faces.

In the chief business street of Topham a great many country wagons like the Hiltons' were fastened to the posts, and there seemed to our holiday-makers to be a great deal of noise and excitement.

"Now I've got to do my errands, and we can let the horse rest and feed," said John Hilton. "I'll slip his headstall right off, an' put on his halter. I'm goin' to buy him a real good treat o' oats. First we'll go an' buy me my straw hat; I feel as if this one looked a little past to wear in Topham. We'll buy the things we want, an' then we'll walk all along the street, so you can look in the windows an' see the han'some things, same's your mother likes to. What was it mother told you about your shawls?"

"To take 'em off an' carry 'em over our arms," piped Susan Ellen, without comment, but in the interest of alighting and finding themselves afoot upon the pavement the shawls were forgotten. The children stood at the doorway of a shop while their father went inside, and they tried to see what the Topham shapes of bonnets were like, as their mother had advised them; but everything was exciting and confusing, and they could arrive at no decision. When Mr. Hilton came out with a hat in his hand to be seen in a better light, Katy whispered that she wished he would buy a shiny one like Judge Masterson's; but her father only smiled and shook his head, and said that they were plain folks, he and Katy. There were dry-goods for sale in the same shop, and a young clerk who was measuring linen kindly pulled off some pretty labels with gilded edges and gay pictures, and gave them to the little girls, to their exceeding joy. He may have had small sisters at home, this friendly lad, for he took pains to find two pretty blue boxes besides, and was rewarded by their beaming gratitude.

It was a famous day; they even became used to seeing so many people pass. The village was full of its morning activity, and Susan Ellen gained a new respect for her father, and an increased sense of her own consequence, because even in Topham several persons knew him and called him familiarly by name. The meeting with an old man who had once been a neighbor seemed to give Mr. Hilton the greatest pleasure. The old man called to them from a house doorway as they were passing, and they all went in. The children seated themselves wearily on the wooden step, but their father shook his old friend eagerly by the hand, and declared that he was delighted to see him so well and enjoying the fine weather.

"Oh, yes," said the old man, in a feeble, quavering voice, "I'm astonishin' well for my age. I don't complain, John, I don't complain."

They talked long together of people whom they had known in the past, and Katy, being a little tired, was glad to rest, and sat still with her hands folded, looking about the front yard. There were some kinds of flowers that she never had seen before.

"This is the one that looks like my mother," her father said, and touched Katy's shoulder to remind her to stand up and let herself be seen. "Judge Masterson saw the resemblance; we met him at his gate this morning."

"Yes, she certain does look like your mother, John," said the old man, looking pleasantly at Katy, who found that she liked him better than at first. "She does, certain; the best of young folks is, they remind us of the old ones. 'T is nateral to cling to life, folks say, but for me, I git impatient at times. Most everybody's gone now, an' I want to be goin'. 'T is somethin' before me, an' I want to have it over with. I want to be there 'long o' the rest o' the folks. I expect to last quite a while though; I may see ye couple o' times more, John."

John Hilton responded cheerfully, and the children were urged to pick some flowers. The old man awed them with his impatience to be gone. There was such a townful of people about him, and he seemed as lonely as if he were the last survivor of a former world. Until that moment they had felt as if everything were just beginning.

"Now I want to buy somethin' pretty for your mother," said Mr. Hilton, as they went soberly away down the street, the children keeping fast hold of his hands. "By now the old horse will have eat his dinner and had a good rest, so pretty soon we can jog along home. I'm goin' to take you round by the academy, and the old North Meeting-house where Dr. Barstow used to preach. Can't you think o' somethin' that your mother'd want?" he asked suddenly, confronted by a man's difficulty of choice.

"She was talkin' about wantin' a new pepper-box, one day; the top o' the old one won't stay on," suggested Susan Ellen, with delightful readiness. "Can't we have some candy, father?"

"Yes, ma'am," said John Hilton, smiling and swinging her hand to and fro as they walked. "I feel as if some would be good myself. What's all this?" They were passing a photographer's doorway with its enticing array of portraits. "I do declare!" he exclaimed excitedly, "I'm goin' to have our pictures taken; 't will please your mother more'n a little."

This was, perhaps, the greatest triumph of the day, except the delightful meeting with the judge; they sat in a row, with the father in the middle, and there was no doubt as to the excellence of the likeness. The best hats had to be taken off because they cast a shadow, but they were not missed, as their owners had feared. Both Susan Ellen and Katy looked their brightest and best; their eager young faces would forever shine there; the joy of holiday was mirrored in the little picture. They did not know why their father was so pleased with it; they would not know until age had dowered them with the riches of association and remembrance.

Just at nightfall the Hiltons reached home again, tired out and happy. Katy had climbed over into the front seat beside her father, because that was always her place when they went to Church on Sundays. It was a cool evening, there was a fresh sea wind that brought a light mist with it, and the sky was fast growing cloudy. Somehow the children looked different; it seemed to their mother as if they had grown older and taller since they went away in the morning, and as if they belonged to the town now as much as to the country. The greatness of their day's experience had left her far behind; the day had been silent and lonely without them, and she had had their supper ready, and been watching anxiously, ever since five o'clock. As for the children themselves they had little to say at first—they had eaten their luncheon early on the way to Topham. Susan Ellen was childishly cross, but Katy was pathetic and wan. They could hardly wait to show the picture, and their mother was as much pleased as everybody had expected.

"There, what did make you wear your shawls?" she exclaimed a moment afterward, reproachfully. "You ain't been an' wore 'em all day long? I wanted folks to see how pretty your new dresses was, if I did make 'em. Well, well! I wish more'n ever now I'd gone an' seen to ye!"

"An' here's the pepper-box!" said Katy, in a pleased, unconscious tone.

"That really is what I call beautiful," said Mrs. Hilton, after a long and doubtful look. "Our other one was only tin. I never did look so high as a chiny one with flowers, but I can get us another any time for every day. That's a proper hat, as good as you could have got, John. Where's your new hoe?" she asked as he came toward her from the barn, smiling with satisfaction.

"I declare to Moses if I didn't forget all about it," meekly acknowledged the leader of the great excursion. "That an' my yellow turnip seed, too; they went clean out o' my head, there was so many other things to think of. But 't ain't no sort o' matter; I can get a hoe just as well to Ira Speed's."

His wife could not help laughing. "You

an' the little girls have had a great time. They was full o' wonder to me about everything, and I expect they'll talk about it for a week. I guess we was right about havin' 'em see somethin' more o' the world."

"Yes," answered John Hilton, with humility, "yes, we did have a beautiful day. I didn't expect so much. They looked as nice as anybody, and appeared so modest an' pretty. The little girls will remember it perhaps by an' by. I guess they won't never forget this day they had 'long o' father."

It was evening again, the frogs were piping in the lower meadows, and in the woods, higher up the great hill, a little owl began to hoot. The sea air, salt and heavy, was blowing in over the country at the end of the hot bright day. A lamp was lighted in the house, the happy children were talking together, and supper was waiting. The father and mother lingered for a moment outside and looked down over the shadowy fields; then they went in, without speaking. The great day was over, and they shut the door.

1852 ∾ *Mary E. Wilkins Freeman* ∾ 1930

THE New England of Sarah Orne Jewett was also that of Mary Wilkins Freeman—a New England of the old and the lonely, of work without hope, but also a New England where the power of will, a heritage of the Puritan past, sometimes expressed itself in strange ways. Emphatically Mrs. Freeman wrote of it from within: with a background of Vermont village life, with educational opportunity limited by ill health, she was left after the death of all her immediate family to support an aging aunt. At the town of her birth, Randolph, Massachusetts, she found a home with friends and began to write. Her best stories were those of her early years of authorship, when her own inner revolt against the circumstances of her life was reflected in her recognition of characters and situations in the life about her. These are the stories collected in *A Humble Romance and Other Stories* (1887), *A New England Nun and Other Stories* (1891), and *People of Our Neighborhood* (1898). Of the same stuff are such of her novels as *Jane Field* (1893), *Pembroke* (1896), and *Jerome* (1897). Her powers were not adequate for the successful execution of the more ambitious projects of her later years of writing, although in the novel *The Portion of Labor* (1901) she made a carefully detailed criticism of industrial conditions in her time.

[No adequate critical or biographical study of Mrs. Freeman has yet appeared. Consult F. L. Pattee's *The Development of the American Short Story* (New York, 1923).]

THE REVOLT OF "MOTHER"
[1891 (1890)]

"FATHER!"

"What is it?"

"What are them men diggin' over there in the field for?"

There was a sudden dropping and enlarging of the lower part of the old man's face, as if some heavy weight had settled therein; he shut his mouth tight, and went on harnessing the great bay mare. He hustled the collar on to her neck with a jerk.

"Father!"

The old man slapped the saddle upon the mare's back.

"Look here, father, I want to know what them men are diggin' over in the field for, an' I'm goin' to know."

"I wish you'd go into the house, mother, an' 'tend to your own affairs," the old man said then. He ran his words together, and his speech was almost as inarticulate as a growl.

But the woman understood; it was her most native tongue.

"I ain't goin' into the house till you tell me what them men are doin' over there in the field," said she.

Then she stood waiting. She was a small woman, short and straight-waisted like a child in her brown cotton gown. Her forehead was mild and benevolent between the smooth curves of gray hair; there were meek downward lines about her nose and mouth; but her eyes, fixed upon the old man, looked as if the meekness had been the result of her own will, never of the will of another.

They were in the barn, standing before the wide-open doors. The spring air, full of the smell of growing grass and unseen blossoms, came in their faces. The deep yard in front was littered with farm wagons and piles of wood; on the edges, close to the fence and the house, the grass was a vivid green, and there were some dandelions.

The old man glanced doggedly at his wife as he tightened the last buckles on the harness. She looked as immovable to him as one of the rocks in his pasture land, bound to the earth with generations of blackberry vines. He slapped the reins over the horse, and started forth from the barn.

"*Father!*" said she.

The old man pulled up. "What is it?"

"I want to know what them men are diggin' over there in that field for."

"They're diggin' a cellar, I s'pose, if you've got to know."

"A cellar for what?"

"A barn."

"A barn? You ain't goin' to build a barn over there where we was goin' to have a house, father?"

The old man said not another word. He hurried the horse into the farm wagon, and clattered out of the yard, jouncing as sturdily on his seat as a boy.

The woman stood a moment looking after him, then she went out of the barn across a corner of the yard to the house. The house, standing at right angles with the great barn and a long reach of sheds and outbuildings, was infinitesimal compared with them. It was scarcely as commodious for people as the little boxes under the barn eaves were for doves.

A pretty girl's face, pink and delicate as a flower, was looking out of one of the house windows. She was watching three men who were digging over in the field which bounded the yard near the road line. She turned quietly when the woman entered.

"What are they digging for, mother?" said she. "Did he tell you?"

"They're diggin' for a cellar for a new barn."

"Oh, mother, he ain't going to build another barn?"

"That's what he says."

A boy stood before the kitchen glass combing his hair. He combed slowly and painstakingly, arranging his brown hair in a smooth hillock over his forehead. He did not seem to pay any attention to the conversation.

"Sammy, did you know father was going to build a new barn?" asked the girl.

The boy combed assiduously.

"Sammy!"

He turned, and showed a face like his father's under his smooth crest of hair. "Yes, I s'pose I did," he said, reluctantly.

"How long have you known it?" asked his mother.

" 'Bout three months, I guess."

"Why didn't you tell of it?"

"Didn't think 'twould do no good."

"I don't see what father wants another barn for," said the girl, in her sweet, slow voice. She turned again to the window, and stared out at the digging men in the field. Her tender, sweet face was full of a gentle distress. Her forehead was as bald and innocent as a baby's, with the light hair strained back from it in a row of curl papers. She was quite large, but her soft curves did not look as if they covered muscles.

Her mother looked sternly at the boy. "Is he goin' to buy more cows?" said she.

The boy did not reply; he was tying his shoes.

"Sammy, I want you to tell me if he's goin' to buy more cows."

"I s'pose he is."

"How many?"

"Four, I guess."

His mother said nothing more. She went into the pantry, and there was a clatter of dishes. The boy got his cap from a nail behind the door, took an old arithmetic from the shelf, and started for school. He was lightly built, but clumsy. He went out of the yard with a curious spring in the hips that made his loose homemade jacket tilt up in the rear.

The girl went to the sink, and began to wash the dishes that were piled up there. Her mother came promptly out of the pantry, and shoved her aside. "You wipe 'em," said she; "I'll wash. There's a good many this mornin'."

The mother plunged her hands vigorously into the water, the girl wiped the plates slowly and dreamily. "Mother," said she, "don't you think it's too bad father's going to build that new barn, much as we need a decent house to live in?"

Her mother scrubbed a dish fiercely. "You ain't found out yet we're womenfolks, Nanny Penn," said she. "You ain't seen enough of menfolks yet to. One of these days you'll find it out, an' then you'll know that we know only what menfolks think we do, so far as any use of it goes, an' how we'd ought to reckon menfolks in with Providence, an' not complain of what they do any more than we do of the weather."

"I don't care; I don't believe George is anything like that, anyhow," said Nanny. Her delicate face flushed pink; her lips pouted softly, as if she were going to cry.

"You wait an' see. I guess George Eastman ain't no better than other men. You hadn't ought to judge father, though. He can't help it, 'cause he don't look at things jest the way we do. An' we've been pretty comfortable here, after all. The roof don't leak—ain't never but once—that's one thing. Father's kept it shingled right up."

"I do wish we had a parlor."

"I guess it won't hurt George Eastman any to come to see you in a nice clean kitchen. I guess a good many girls don't have as good a place as this. Nobody's ever heard me complain."

"I ain't complained either, mother."

"Well, I don't think you'd better, a good father an' a good home as you've got. S'pose your father made you go out an' work for your livin'? Lots of girls have to that ain't no stronger an' better able to than you be."

Sarah Penn washed the frying pan with a conclusive air. She scrubbed the outside of it as faithfully as the inside. She was a masterly keeper of her box of a house. Her one living room never seemed to have in it any of the dust which the friction of life with inanimate matter produces. She swept, and there seemed to be no dirt to go before the broom; she cleaned, and one could see no difference. She was like an artist so perfect that he has apparently no art. Today she got out a mixing bowl and a board, and rolled some pies, and there was no more flour upon her than upon her daughter who was doing finer work. Nanny was to be married in the fall, and she was sewing on some white cambric and embroidery. She sewed industriously while her mother cooked; her soft milk-white hands and wrists showed whiter than her delicate work.

"We must have the stove moved out in the shed before long," said Mrs. Penn. "Talk about not havin' things, it's been a real blessin' to be able to put a stove up in that shed in hot weather. Father did one good thing when he fixed that stove pipe out there."

Sarah Penn's face as she rolled her pies had that expression of meek vigor which might have characterized one of the New Testament saints. She was making mince pies. Her husband, Adoniram Penn, liked them better than any other kind. She baked twice a week. Adoniram often liked a piece of pie between meals. She hurried this morning. It had been later than usual when she began, and she wanted to have a pie baked for dinner. However deep a resentment she might be forced to hold against her husband, she would never fail in sedulous attention to his wants.

Nobility of character manifests itself at loopholes when it is not provided with large doors. Sarah Penn's showed itself today in flaky dishes of pastry. She made the pies faithfully, while across the table she could see, when she glanced up from her work, the sight that rankled in her patient and steadfast soul—the digging of the cellar of the new barn in the place where Adoniram forty years ago had promised her their new house should stand.

The pies were done for dinner. Adoniram and Sammy were home a few minutes after twelve o'clock. The dinner was eaten with serious haste. There was never much conversation at the table in the Penn family. Adoniram asked a blessing, and they ate promptly, then rose up and went about their work.

Sammy went back to school, taking soft sly lopes out of the yard like a rabbit. He wanted a game of marbles before school, and feared his father would give him some chores to do. Adoniram hastened to the door and called after him, but he was out of sight.

"I don't see what you let him go for, mother," said he. "I wanted him to help me unload that wood."

Adoniram went to work out in the yard unloading wood from the wagon. Sarah put away the dinner dishes, while Nanny took down her curl papers and changed her dress. She was going down to the store to buy some more embroidery and thread.

When Nanny was gone, Mrs. Penn went to the door. "Father!" she called.

"Well, what is it!"

"I want to see you jest a minute, father."

"I can't leave this wood nohow. I've got to git unloaded an' go for a load of gravel afore two o'clock. Sammy had ought to helped me. You hadn't ought to let him go to school so early."

"I want to see you jest a minute."

"I tell ye I can't, nohow, mother."

"Father, you come here." Sarah Penn stood in the door like a queen; she held her head as if it bore a crown; there was that patience which makes authority royal in her voice. Adoniram went.

Mrs. Penn led the way into the kitchen, and pointed to a chair. "Sit down, father," said she; "I've got somethin' I want to say to you."

He sat down heavily; his face was quite stolid, but he looked at her with restive eyes. "Well, what is it, mother?"

"I want to know what you're buildin' that new barn for, father?"

"I ain't got nothin' to say about it."

"It can't be you think you need another barn?"

"I tell ye I ain't got nothin' to say about it, mother; an' I ain't goin' to say nothin'."

"Be you goin' to buy more cows?"

Adoniram did not reply; he shut his mouth tight.

"I know you be, as well as I want to. Now, father, look here"—Sarah Penn had not sat down; she stood before her husband in the humble fashion of a Scripture woman—"I'm goin' to talk real plain to you; I ain't never complained, an' I ain't goin' to complain now, but I'm goin' to talk plain. You see this room here, father; you look at it well. You see there ain't no carpet on the floor, an' you see the paper is all dirty an' droppin' off the walls. We ain't had no new paper on it for ten year, an' then I put it on myself, an' it didn't cost but ninepence a roll. You see this room, father; it's all the one I've had to work in an' eat in an' sit in sence we was married. There ain't another woman in the whole town whose husband ain't got half the means you have but what's got better. It's all the room Nanny's got to have her company in; an' there ain't one of her mates but what's got better, an' their fathers not so able as hers is. It's all the room she'll have to be married in. What would you have thought, father, if we had had our weddin' in a room no better than this? I was married in my mother's parlor with a carpet on the floor, an' stuffed furniture, an' a mahogany card table. An' this is all the room my daughter will have to be married in. Look here, father!"

Sarah Penn went across the room as though it were a tragic stage. She flung open a door and disclosed a tiny bedroom, only large enough for a bed and bureau, with a path between. "There, father," said she—"there's all the room I've had to sleep in in forty year. All my children were born there—the two that died an' the two that's livin'. I was sick with a fever there."

She stepped to another door and opened it. It led into the small, ill-lighted pantry. "Here," said she, "is all the buttery I've got—every place I've got for my dishes, to set away my victuals, an' to keep my milk pans in. Father, I've been takin' care of the milk of six cows in this place, an' now you're goin' to build a new barn, an' keep more cows, an' give me more to do in it."

She threw open another door. A narrow crooked flight of stairs wound upward from it. "There, father," said she, "I want you to look at the stairs that go up to them two unfinished chambers that are all the places our son an' daughter have had to sleep in all their lives. There ain't a pret-tier girl in town nor a more ladylike one than Nanny, an' that's all the place she has to sleep in. It ain't so good as your horse's stall; it ain't so warm an' tight."

Sarah Penn went back and stood before her husband. "Now, father," said she, "I want to know if you think you're doin' right an' accordin' to what you profess. Here, where we was married, forty year ago, you promised me faithful that we should have a new house built in that lot over in the field before the year was out. You said you had money enough, an' you wouldn't ask me to live in no such place as this. It is forty year now, an' you've been makin' more money, an' I've been savin' of it for you ever since, an' you ain't built no house yet. You've built sheds an' cow houses an' one new barn, an' now you're goin' to build another. Father, I want to know if you think it's right. You're lodgin' your dumb beasts better than you are your own flesh an' blood. I want to know if you think it's right."

"I ain't got nothin' to say."

"You can't say nothin' without ownin' it ain't right, father. An' there's another thing—I ain't complained; I've got along forty year, an' I s'pose I should forty more, if it wa'n't for that—if we don't have another house. Nanny, she can't live with us after she's married. She'll have to go somewheres else to live away from us, an' it don't seem as if I could have it so, noways, father. She wa'n't ever strong. She's got considerable color, but there wa'n't never any backbone to her. I've always took the heft of everything off her, an' she ain't fit to keep house an' do everything herself. She'll be all worn out inside of a year. Think of her doin' all the washin' an' ironin' an' bakin' with them soft white hands an' arms, an' sweepin'! I can't have it so, noways, father."

Mrs. Penn's face was burning; her mild eyes gleamed. She had pleaded her little cause like a Webster; she had ranged from severity to pathos, but her opponent employed that obstinate silence which makes eloquence futile with mocking echoes. Adoniram arose clumsily.

"Father, ain't you got nothin' to say?" said Mrs. Penn.

"I've got to go off after that load of gravel. I can't stan' here talkin' all day."

"Father, won't you think it over, an' have a house built there instead of a barn?"

"I ain't got nothin' to say."

Adoniram shuffled out. Mrs. Penn went into her bedroom. When she came out, her eyes were red. She had a roll of unbleached cotton cloth. She spread it out on the kitchen table, and began cutting out some shirts for her husband. The men over in the field had a team to help them this afternoon; she could hear their halloos. She had a scanty pattern for the shirts; she had to plan and piece the sleeves.

Nanny came home with her embroidery, and sat down with her needlework. She had taken down her curl papers, and there was a soft roll of fair hair like an aureole over her forehead; her face was as delicately fine and clear as porcelain. Suddenly she looked up, and the tender red flamed all over her face and neck. "Mother," said she.

"What say?"

"I've been thinking—I don't see how we're goin' to have any—wedding in this room. I'd be ashamed to have his folks come if we didn't have anybody else."

"Mebbe we can have some new paper before then; I can put it on. I guess you won't have no call to be ashamed of your belongin's."

"We might have the wedding in the new barn," said Nanny, with gentle pettishness. "Why, mother, what makes you look so?"

Mrs. Penn had started, and was staring at her with a curious expression. She turned again to her work, and spread out a pattern carefully on the cloth. "Nothin'," said she.

Presently Adoniram clattered out of the yard in his two-wheeled dump cart, standing as proudly upright as a Roman charioteer. Mrs. Penn opened the door and stood there a minute looking out; the halloos of the men sounded louder.

It seemed to her all through the spring months that she heard nothing but the halloos and the noises of saws and hammers. The new barn grew fast. It was a fine edifice for this little village. Men came on pleasant Sundays, in their meeting suits and clean shirt bosoms, and stood around it admiringly. Mrs. Penn did not speak of it, and Adoniram did not mention it to her, although sometimes, upon a return from inspecting it, he bore himself with injured dignity.

"It's a strange thing how your mother feels about the new barn," he said, confidentially, to Sammy one day.

Sammy only grunted after an odd fashion for a boy; he had learned it from his father.

The barn was all completed ready for use by the third week in July. Adoniram had planned to move his stock in on Wednesday; on Tuesday he received a letter which changed his plans. He came in with it early in the morning. "Sammy's been to the post office," said he, "an' I've got a letter from Hiram." Hiram was Mrs. Penn's brother, who lived in Vermont.

"Well," said Mrs. Penn, "what does he say about the folks?"

"I guess they're all right. He says he thinks if I come up country right off there's a chance to buy jest the kind of horse I want." He stared reflectively out of the window at the new barn.

Mrs. Penn was making pies. She went on clapping the rolling pin into the crust, although she was very pale, and her heart beat loudly.

"I dun' know but what I'd better go," said Adoniram. "I hate to go off jest now, right in the midst of hayin', but the ten-acre lot's cut, an' I guess Rufus an' the others can git along without me three or four days. I can't get a horse round here to suit me, nohow, an' I've got to have another for all that wood haulin' in the fall. I told Hiram to watch out, an' if he got wind of a good horse to let me know. I guess I'd better go."

"I'll get out your clean shirt an'

collar," said Mrs. Penn calmly.

She laid out Adoniram's Sunday suit and his clean clothes on the bed in the little bedroom. She got his shaving water and razor ready. At last she buttoned on his collar and fastened his black cravat.

Adoniram never wore his collar and cravat except on extra occasions. He held his head high, with a rasped dignity. When he was all ready, with his coat and hat brushed, and a lunch of pie and cheese in a paper bag, he hesitated on the threshold of the door. He looked at his wife, and his manner was defiantly apologetic. "*If* them cows come today, Sammy can drive 'em into the new barn," said he, "an' when they bring the hay up, they can pitch it in there."

"Well," replied Mrs. Penn.

Adoniram set his shaven face ahead and started. When he had cleared the doorstep, he turned and looked back with a kind of nervous solemnity. "I shall be back by Saturday if nothin' happens," said he.

"Do be careful, father," returned his wife.

She stood in the door with Nanny at her elbow and watched him out of sight. Her eyes had a strange, doubtful expression in them; her peaceful forehead was contracted. She went in, and about her baking again. Nanny sat sewing. Her wedding day was drawing nearer, and she was getting pale and thin with her steady sewing. Her mother kept glancing at her.

"Have you got that pain in your side this mornin'?" she asked.

"A little."

Mrs. Penn's face, as she worked, changed; her perplexed forehead smoothed; her eyes were steady, her lips firmly set. She formed a maxim for herself, although incoherently with her unlettered thoughts. "Unsolicited opportunities are the guide-posts of the Lord to the new roads of life," she repeated in effect, and she made up her mind to her course of action.

"S'posin' I *had* wrote to Hiram," she muttered once, when she was in the pantry —"s'posin' I had wrote, an' asked him if he knew of any horse? But I didn't, an' father's goin' wa'n't none of my doin'. It looks like a providence." Her voice rang out quite loud at the last.

"What you talkin' about, mother?" called Nanny.

"Nothin'."

Mrs. Penn hurried her baking; at eleven o'clock it was all done. The load of hay from the west field came slowly down the cart track and drew up at the new barn. Mrs. Penn ran out. "Stop!" she screamed —"stop!"

The men stopped and looked; Sammy upreared from the top of the load, and stared at his mother.

"Stop!" she cried out again. "Don't you put the hay in that barn; put it in the old one."

"Why, he said to put it in here," returned one of the haymakers, wonderingly. He was a young man, a neighbor's son, whom Adoniram hired by the year to help on the farm.

"Don't you put the hay in the new barn; there's room enough in the old one, ain't there?" said Mrs. Penn.

"Room enough," returned the hired man, in his thick, rustic tones. "Didn't need the new barn, nohow, far as room's concerned. Well, I s'pose he changed his mind." He took hold of the horses' bridles.

Mrs. Penn went back to the house. Soon the kitchen windows were darkened, and a fragrance like warm honey came into the room.

Nanny laid down her work. "I thought father wanted them to put the hay into the new barn?" she said, wonderingly.

"It's all right," replied her mother.

Sammy slid down from the load of hay, and came in to see if dinner was ready.

"I ain't goin' to get a regular dinner today, as long as father's gone," said his mother. "I've let the fire go out. You can have some bread an' milk an' pie. I thought we could get along." She set out some bowls of milk, some bread, and a pie on the kitchen table. "You'd better eat your dinner now," said she. "You might jest as well get through with it. I want you to help me afterward."

Nanny and Sammy stared at each other. There was something strange in their mother's manner. Mrs. Penn did not eat anything herself. She went into the pantry, and they heard her moving dishes while they ate. Presently she came out with a pile of plates. She got the clothes basket out of the shed, and packed them in it. Nanny and Sammy watched. She brought out cups and saucers, and put them in with the plates.

"What you goin' to do, mother?" inquired Nanny, in a timid voice. A sense of something unusual made her tremble, as if it were a ghost. Sammy rolled his eyes over his pie.

"You'll see what I'm going to do," replied Mrs. Penn. "If you're through, Nanny, I want you to go upstairs an' pack up your things; an' I want you, Sammy, to help me take down the bed in the bedroom."

"Oh, mother, what for?" gasped Nanny.

"You'll see."

During the next few hours a feat was performed by this simple, pious New England mother which was equal in its way to Wolfe's [1] storming of the Heights of Abraham. It took no more genius and audacity of bravery for Wolfe to cheer his wondering soldiers up those steep precipices, under the sleeping eyes of the enemy, than for Sarah Penn, at the head of her children, to move all their little household goods into the new barn while her husband was away.

Nanny and Sammy followed their mother's instructions without a murmur; indeed, they were overawed. There is a certain uncanny and superhuman quality about all such purely original undertakings as their mother's was to them. Nanny went back and forth with her light loads, and Sammy tugged with sober energy.

At five o'clock in the afternoon the little house in which the Penns had lived for forty years had emptied itself into the new barn.

Every builder builds somewhat for unknown purposes, and is in a measure a prophet. The architect of Adoniram Penn's barn, while he designed it for the comfort of four-footed animals, had planned better than he knew for the comfort of humans. Sarah Penn saw at a glance its possibilities. Those great box stalls, with quilts hung before them, would make better bedrooms than the one she had occupied for forty years, and there was a tight carriage room. The harness room, with its chimney and shelves, would make a kitchen of her dreams. The great middle space would make a parlor, by-and-by, fit for a palace. Upstairs there was as much room as down. With partitions and windows, what a house would there be! Sarah looked at the row of stanchions before the allotted space for cows, and reflected that she would have her front entry there.

At six o'clock the stove was up in the harness room, the kettle was boiling, and the table set for tea. It looked almost as homelike as the abandoned house across the yard had ever done. The young hired man milked, and Sarah directed him calmly to bring the milk to the new barn. He came gaping, dropping little blots of foam from the brimming pails on the grass. Before the next morning he had spread the story of Adoniram Penn's wife moving into the new barn all over the little village. Men assembled in the store and talked it over; women with shawls over their heads scuttled into each other's houses before their work was done. Any deviation from the ordinary course of life in this quiet town was enough to stop all progress in it. Everybody paused to look at the staid, independent figure on the side track. There was a difference of opinion with regard to her. Some held her to be insane; some, of a lawless and rebellious spirit.

Friday the minister went to see her. It was in the forenoon, and she was at the barn door shelling peas for dinner. She

[1] James Wolfe (1727-1759), British general who led the successful assault on Quebec which completed the British conquest of North America. He was wounded and died on the field.

looked up and returned his salutation with dignity; then she went on with her work. She did not invite him in. The saintly expression of her face remained fixed, but there was an angry flush over it.

The minister stood awkwardly before her, and talked. She handled the peas as if they were bullets. At last she looked up, and her eyes showed the spirit that her meek front had covered for a lifetime.

"There ain't no use talkin', Mr. Hersey," said she. "I've thought it all over an' over, an' I believe I'm doin' what's right. I've made it the subject of prayer, an' it's betwixt me an' the Lord an' Adoniram. There ain't no call for nobody else to worry about it."

"Well, of course, if you have brought it to the Lord in prayer, and feel satisfied that you are doing right, Mrs. Penn," said the minister, helplessly. His thin gray-bearded face was pathetic. He was a sickly man; his youthful confidence had cooled; he had to scourge himself up to some of his pastoral duties as relentlessly as a Catholic ascetic, and then he was prostrated by the smart.

"I think it's right jest as much as I think it was right for our forefathers to come over from the old country 'cause they didn't have what belonged to 'em," said Mrs. Penn. She arose. The barn threshold might have been Plymouth Rock, from her bearing. "I don't doubt you mean well, Mr. Hersey," said she, "but there are things people hadn't ought to interfere with. I've been a member of the Church for over forty year. I've got my own mind an' my own feet, an' I'm goin' to think my own thoughts an' go my own ways, an' nobody but the Lord is goin' to dictate to me unless I've a mind to have him. Won't you come in an' set down? How is Mis' Hersey?"

"She is well, I thank you," replied the minister. He added some more perplexed apologetic remarks; then he retreated.

He could expound the intricacies of every character study in the Scriptures; he was competent to grasp the Pilgrim Fathers and all historical innovators; but Sarah Penn was beyond him. He could deal with primal cases, but parallel ones worsted him. But, after all, although it was aside from his province, he wondered more how Adoniram Penn would deal with his wife than how the Lord would. Everybody shared the wonder. When Adoniram's four new cows arrived, Sarah ordered three to be put in the old barn, the other in the house shed where the cooking stove had stood. That added to the excitement. It was whispered that all four cows were domiciled in the house.

Toward sunset on Saturday, when Adoniram was expected home, there was a knot of men in the road near the new barn. The hired man had milked, but he still hung around the premises. Sarah Penn had supper all ready. There were brown bread and baked beans and a custard pie; it was the supper that Adoniram loved on a Saturday night. She had on a clean calico, and she bore herself imperturbably. Nanny and Sammy kept close at her heels. Their eyes were large, and Nanny was full of nervous tremors. Still there was to them more pleasant excitement than anything else. An inborn confidence in their mother over their father asserted itself.

Sammy looked out of the harness-room window. "There he is," he announced, in an awed whisper. He and Nanny peeped around the casing. Mrs. Penn kept on about her work. The children watched Adoniram leave the new horse standing in the drive while he went to the house-door. It was fastened. Then he went around to the shed. That door was seldom locked, even when the family was away. The thought how her father would be confronted by the cow flashed upon Nanny. There was a hysterical sob in her throat. Adoniram emerged from the shed and stood looking about in a dazed fashion. His lips moved; he was saying something, but they could not hear what it was. The hired man was peeping around a corner of the old barn, but nobody saw him.

Adoniram took the new horse by the

bridle and led him across the yard to the new barn. Nanny and Sammy slunk close to their mother. The barn doors rolled back, and there stood Adoniram, with the long mild face of the great Canadian farm horse looking over his shoulder.

Nanny kept behind her mother, but Sammy stepped suddenly forward, and stood in front of her.

Adoniram stared at the group. "What on airth you all down here for?" said he. "What's the matter over to the house?"

"We've come here to live, father," said Sammy. His shrill voice quavered out bravely.

"What"—Adoniram sniffed—"what is it smells like cookin'?" said he. He stepped forward and looked in at the open door of the harness room. Then he turned to his wife. His old bristling face was pale and frightened. "What on airth does this mean, mother?" he gasped.

"You come in here, father," said Sarah. She led the way into the harness room and shut the door. "Now, father," said she, "you needn't be scared. I ain't crazy. There ain't nothin' to be upset over. But we've come here to live, an' we're goin' to live here. We've got jest as good a right here as new horses an' cows. The house wa'n't fit for us to live in any longer, an' I made up my mind I wa'n't goin' to stay there. I've done my duty by you forty year, an' I'm goin' to do it now; but I'm goin' to live here. You've got to put in some windows and partitions; an' you'll have to buy some furniture."

"Why, mother!" the old man gasped.

"You'd better take your coat off an' get washed—there's the wash basin—an' then we'll have supper."

"Why, mother!"

Sammy went past the window, leading the new horse to the old barn. The old man saw him, and shook his head speechlessly. He tried to take off his coat, but his arms seemed to lack the power. His wife helped him. She poured some water into the tin basin, and put in a piece of soap. She got

the comb and brush, and smoothed his thin gray hair after he had washed. Then she put the beans, hot bread, and tea on the table. Sammy came in, and the family drew up. Adoniram sat looking dazedly at his plate, and they waited.

"Ain't you goin' to ask a blessin', father?" said Sarah.

And the old man bent his head and mumbled.

All through the meal he stopped eating at intervals, and stared furtively at his wife; but he ate well. The home food tasted good to him, and his old frame was too sturdily healthy to be affected by his mind. But after supper he went out, and sat down on the step of the smaller door at the right of the barn, through which he had meant his Jerseys to pass in stately file, but which Sarah designed for her front house door, and he leaned his head on his hands.

After the supper dishes were cleared away and the milk pans washed, Sarah went out to him. The twilight was deepening. There was a clear green glow in the sky. Before them stretched the smooth level of field; in the distance was a cluster of haystacks like the huts of a village; the air was very cool and calm and sweet. The landscape might have been an ideal one of peace.

Sarah bent over and touched her husband on one of his thin, sinewy shoulders. "Father!"

The old man's shoulders heaved; he was weeping.

"Why, don't do so, father," said Sarah. "I'll—put up the—partitions, an'—everything you—want, mother."

Sarah put her apron up to her face; she was overcome by her own triumph.

Adoniram was like a fortress whose walls had no active resistance, and went down the instant the right besieging tools were used. "Why, mother," he said, hoarsely, "I hadn't no idee you was so set on't as all this comes to."

1830 ∾ *Emily Dickinson* ∾ *1886*

EMILY DICKINSON'S life was outwardly most uneventful. She was born into a home of conscious distinction and respectability, long dominated by a passionate father, a congressman and treasurer of Amherst College, and lived in that home for all but a few months of her fifty-five years. She left it, indeed, only to attend a sectarian school for girls at South Hadley, Massachusetts, and once to visit Washington (with her father) and Philadelphia. She was a lively, talented, and popular girl. But midway of her life she turned away from all contacts outside her family, to live the remainder of her years in increasing seclusion. The deaths within a year of two young male admirers may have had something to do with this. Her meeting and loving a young clergyman, already married, on the visit to Philadelphia was perhaps more important. The immediate influence of emotional tensions in her own home was probably decisive.

During Emily Dickinson's lifetime only a few of her poems were published. But after her death her sister Lavinia found in her room the manuscripts of many hundreds—some copied into little booklets, more scribbled on scraps of paper, newspaper margins and the backs of envelopes—nearly all with corrections and alternative readings. "She did not ask me to destroy them," Lavinia insisted as she tried to persuade her neighbor, Mrs. Mabel Loomis Todd, to undertake their preparation for publication. With the encouragement and advice of Thomas Wentworth Higginson—one of the few persons who had known of Emily's work during her life, through letters she had written him asking for criticism—a small volume was brought out in 1890. It sold well, and two further small collections appeared, in 1891 and 1896, and a volume of letters in 1894, all edited by Mrs. Todd. However, it was not until numerous additional poems were published under the title *The Single Hound* in 1914, at a time when American poetry was alive and sensitive to new impressions and peculiarly responsive to the brilliant and bold figures and the subjective intensity of Emily Dickinson, that her work achieved wide influence and a general recognition of its unique qualities of excellence.

[All of Emily Dickinson's poems published up to 1937 were included in *The Poems of Emily Dickinson* (Boston, 1937), edited by Martha Dickinson Bianchi and Alfred Leete Hampson. The bulk of her published work was approximately doubled by the appearance of *Bolts of Melody* (New York, 1945), edited by Millicent Todd Bingham, daughter of Emily's first editor. A biographical introduction by Martha Dickinson Bianchi appeared in *The Single Hound* (1914), amplified by her in *Life and Letters of Emily Dickinson* (1924, 1930) and *Emily Dickinson Face to Face* (New York, 1932). New facts were presented in Millicent Todd Bingham's *Ancestors' Brocades* (New York, 1945).

Emily Dickinson has been attractive to biographers. Books about her include Josephine Pollitt's *Emily Dickinson: The Human Background of Her Poetry* (New York, 1930); Genevieve Taggard's *The Life and Mind of Emily Dickinson* (New York, 1930); and MacGregor Jenkins' *Emily Dickinson, Friend and Neighbor* (rev. ed. 1939). George F. Whicher's *This Was a Poet* (New York, 1938) is an excellent critical biography. Henry W. Wells' *Introduction to Emily Dickinson* (Chicago, 1947) is an extended critical appraisal.]

THE SNAKE
[1890 (1866)]

A narrow fellow in the grass
Occasionally rides;
You may have met him,—did you not?
His notice sudden is.

The grass divides as with a comb,   5
A spotted shaft is seen;
And then it closes at your feet
And opens further on.

He likes a boggy acre,
A floor too cool for corn.   10
Yet when a child, and barefoot,
I more than once, at morn,

Have passed, I thought, a whiplash
Unbraiding in the sun,—
When, stooping to secure it,   15
It wrinkled, and was gone.

Several of nature's people
I know, and they know me;
I feel for them a transport
Of cordiality;   20

But never met this fellow,
Attended or alone,
Without a tighter breathing,
And zero at the bone.

SUCCESS
[1878]

Success is counted sweetest
By those who ne'er succeed.
To comprehend a nectar
Requires sorest need.

Not one of all the purple host
Who took the flag today
Can tell the definition,
So clear, of victory,

As he, defeated, dying,
On whose forbidden ear
The distant strains of triumph
Break, agonized and clear.

THE BEE
[1890]

Like trains of cars on tracks of plush
I hear the level bee:
Ajar across the flowers goes,
Their velvet masonry

Withstands until the sweet assault   5
Their chivalry consumes,
While he, victorious, tilts away
To vanquish other blooms.

His feet are shod with gauze,
His helmet is of gold;   10
His breast, a single onyx
With chrysoprase, inlaid.

His labor is a chant,
His idleness a tune;
Oh, for a bee's experience   15
Of clovers and of noon!

NEW FEET WITHIN MY GARDEN GO
[1890]

New feet within my garden go,
New fingers stir the sod;
A troubadour upon the elm
Betrays the solitude.

New children play upon the green,
New weary sleep below;
And still the pensive spring returns,
And still the punctual snow!

THE CHARIOT
[1890]

Because I could not stop for Death,
He kindly stopped for me;
The carriage held but just ourselves
And Immortality.

We slowly drove, he knew no haste,   5
And I had put away
My labor, and my leisure too,
For his civility.

We passed the school where children played
At wrestling in a ring;   10
We passed the fields of gazing grain,
We passed the setting sun.

We paused before a house that seemed
A swelling of the ground;
The roof was scarcely visible,   15
The cornice but a mound.

Since then 'tis centuries; but each
Feels shorter than the day
I first surmised the horses' heads
Were toward eternity.   20

THE LAST NIGHT THAT SHE LIVED
[1890]

The last night that she lived,
It was a common night,
Except the dying; this to us
Made nature different.

We noticed smallest things,—   5
Things overlooked before,
By this great light upon our minds
Italicized, as 'twere.

That others could exist
While she must finish quite,   10
A jealousy for her arose
So nearly infinite.

We waited while she passed;
It was a narrow time,
Too jostled were our souls to speak,   15
At length the notice came.

She mentioned, and forgot;
Then lightly as a reed
Bent to the water, shivered scarce,
Consented, and was dead.   20

And we, we placed the hair,
And drew the head erect;
And then an awful leisure was,
Our faith to regulate.

EXCLUSION
[1890]

The soul selects her own society,
Then shuts the door;
On her divine majority
Obtrude no more.

Unmoved, she notes the chariot's pausing   5
At her low gate;
Unmoved, an emperor is kneeling
Upon her mat.

I've known her from an ample nation
Choose one;   10
Then close the valves of her attention
Like stone.

I DIED FOR BEAUTY
[1890]

I died for beauty, but was scarce
Adjusted in the tomb,
When one who died for truth was lain
In an adjoining room.

He questioned softly why I failed?   5
"For beauty," I replied.
"And I for truth,—the two are one;
We brethren are," he said.

And so, as kinsmen met at night,
We talked between the rooms,   10
Until the moss had reached our lips,
And covered up our names.

IN A LIBRARY
[1890]

A precious, mouldering pleasure 'tis
To meet an antique book,
In just the dress his century wore;
A privilege, I think,

His venerable hand to take,   5
And warming in our own,
A passage back, or two, to make
To times when he was young.

His quaint opinions to inspect,
His knowledge to unfold   10
On what concerns our mutual mind,
The literature of old;

What interested scholars most,
What competitions ran
When Plato was a certainty,   15
And Sophocles a man;

When Sappho was a living girl,
And Beatrice wore
The gown that Dante deified.
Facts, centuries before,   20

He traverses familiar,
As one should come to town
And tell you all your dreams were true:
He lived where dreams were sown.

His presence is enchantment,   25
You beg him not to go;
Old volumes shake their vellum heads
And tantalize, just so.

TO FIGHT ALOUD IS VERY BRAVE
[1890]

To fight aloud is very brave,
But gallanter, I know,
Who charge within the bosom,
The cavalry of woe.

Who win, and nations do not see,   5
Who fall, and none observe,
Whose dying eyes no country
Regards with patriot love.

We trust, in plumed procession,
For such the angels go,   10
Rank after rank, with even feet
And uniforms of snow.

MUCH MADNESS IS DIVINEST SENSE
[1890]

Much madness is divinest sense
To a discerning eye;
Much sense the starkest madness.
'Tis the majority
In this, as all, prevails.   5
Assent, and you are sane;
Demur,—you're straightway dangerous,
And handled with a chain.

THE LONELY HOUSE
[1890]

I know some lonely houses off the road
A robber'd like the look of,—
Wooden barred,
And windows hanging low,
Inviting to   5
A portico,
Where two could creep:
One hand the tools,
The other peep
To make sure all's asleep.   10
Old-fashioned eyes,
Not easy to surprise!

How orderly the kitchen'd look by night,
With just a clock,—
But they could gag the tick,   15
And mice won't bark;
And so the walls don't tell,
None will.

A pair of spectacles afar just stir—
An almanac's aware.   20
Was it the mat winked,
Or a nervous star?
The moon slides down the stair
To see who's there.

There's plunder,—where?   25
Tankard, or spoon,
Earring, or stone,

A watch, some ancient brooch
To match the grandmamma,
Staid sleeping there.   30

Day rattles, too,
Stealth's slow;
The sun has got as far
As the third sycamore.
Screams chanticleer,   35
"Who's there?"
And echoes, trains away,
Sneer—"Where?"
While the old couple, just astir,
Fancy the sunrise left the door ajar!   40

THE MYSTERY OF PAIN
[1890]

Pain has an element of blank;
It cannot recollect
When it began, or if there were
A day when it was not.

It has no future but itself,   5
Its infinite realms contain
Its past, enlightened to perceive
New periods of pain.

I TASTE A LIQUOR NEVER BREWED
[1890]

I taste a liquor never brewed,
From tankards scooped in pearl;
Not all the vats upon the Rhine
Yield such an alcohol!

Inebriate of air am I,   5
And debauchee of dew,
Reeling, through endless summer days,
From inns of molten blue.

When landlords turn the drunken bee
Out of the foxglove's door,   10
When butterflies renounce their drams,
I shall but drink the more!

Till seraphs swing their snowy hats,
And saints to windows run,
To see the little tippler   15
Leaning against the sun!

I HAD NO TIME TO HATE
[1890]

I had no time to hate, because
The grave would hinder me,
And life was not so ample I
Could finish enmity.

Nor had I time to love; but since   5
Some industry must be,
The little toil of love, I thought,
Was large enough for me.

THE BRAIN WITHIN ITS GROOVE
[1890]

The brain within its groove
Runs evenly and true;
But let a splinter swerve,
'Twere easier for you
To put the water back   5
When floods have slit the hills,
And scooped a turnpike for themselves,
And blotted out the mills!

SUSPENSE
[1890]

Elysium is as far as to
The very nearest room,
If in that room a friend await
Felicity or doom.

What fortitude the soul contains,   5
That it can so endure
The accent of a coming foot,
The opening of a door!

IF YOU WERE COMING IN THE FALL
[1890]

If you were coming in the fall,
I'd brush the summer by
With half a smile and half a spurn,
As housewives do a fly.

If I could see you in a year,   5
I'd wind the months in balls,
And put them each in separate drawers,
Until their time befalls.

If only centuries delayed,
I'd count them on my hand,   10
Subtracting till my fingers dropped
Into Van Diemen's land.

If certain, when this life was out,
That yours and mine should be,
I'd toss it yonder like a rind,   15
And taste eternity.

But now, all ignorant of the length
Of time's uncertain wing,
It goads me, like the goblin bee,
That will not state its sting.   20

IN VAIN
[1890]

I cannot live with you,
It would be life,
And life is over there
Behind the shelf

The sexton keeps the key to,   5
Putting up
Our life, his porcelain,
Like a cup

Discarded of the housewife,
Quaint or broken;   10
A newer Sèvres pleases,
Old ones crack.

I could not die with you,
For one must wait
To shut the other's gaze down,—   15
You could not.

And I, could I stand by
And see you freeze,
Without my right of frost,
Death's privilege?   20

Nor could I rise with you,
Because your face
Would put out Jesus',
That new grace

Glow plain and foreign   25
On my homesick eye,
Except that you, than he
Shone closer by.

They'd judge us—how?
For you served Heaven, you know,   30
Or sought to;
I could not,

Because you saturated sight,
And I had no more eyes
For sordid excellence   35
As Paradise.

And were you lost, I would be,
Though my name
Rang loudest
On the heavenly fame.   40

And were you saved,
And I condemned to be
Where you were not,
That self were hell to me.

So we must keep apart,   45
You there, I here,
With just the door ajar
That oceans are,
And prayer,
And that pale sustenance,   50
Despair!

RENUNCIATION
[1890]

There came a day at summer's full
Entirely for me;
I thought that such were for the saints,
Where revelations be.

The sun, as common, went abroad,   5
The flowers, accustomed, blew,
As if no soul the solstice passed
That maketh all things new.

The time was scarce profaned by speech;
The symbol of a word   10
Was needless, as at sacrament
The wardrobe of our Lord.

Each was to each the sealed church,
Permitted to commune this time,
Lest we too awkward show   15
At supper of the Lamb.

The hours slid fast, as hours will,
Clutched tight by greedy hands;
So faces on two decks look back,
Bound to opposing lands.   20

And so, when all the time had failed,
Without external sound,
Each bound the other's crucifix,
We gave no other bond.

Sufficient troth that we shall rise—   25
Deposed, at length, the grave—
To that new marriage, justified
Through Calvaries of Love!

THE WIFE
[1890]

She rose to his requirement, dropped
The playthings of her life
To take the honorable work
Of woman and of wife.

If aught she missed in her new day   5
Of amplitude, or awe,
Or first prospective, or the gold
In using wore away,

It lay unmentioned, as the sea
Develops pearl and weed,   10
But only to himself is known
The fathoms they abide.

THE PEDIGREE OF HONEY
[1890]

The pedigree of honey
Does not concern the bee;
A clover, any time, to him
Is aristocracy.

A SERVICE OF SONG
[1890 (1864)]

Some keep the Sabbath going to church;
I keep it staying at home,
With a bobolink for a chorister,
And an orchard for a dome.

Some keep the Sabbath in surplice;   5
I just wear my wings,
And instead of tolling the bell for church,
Our little sexton sings.

God preaches,—a noted clergyman,—
And the sermon is never long;   10
So instead of getting to heaven at last,
I'm going all along!

THE GRASS
[1890]

The grass so little has to do,—
A sphere of simple green,
With only butterflies to brood,
And bees to entertain,

And stir all day to pretty tunes   5
The breezes fetch along,
And hold the sunshine in its lap
And bow to everything;

And thread the dews all night, like pearls,
And make itself so fine,—   10
A duchess were too common
For such a noticing.

And even when it dies, to pass
In odors so divine,
As lowly spices gone to sleep,   15
Or amulets of pine.

And then to dwell in sovereign barns,
And dream the days away,—
The grass so little has to do,
I wish I were the hay!   20

SUMMER'S ARMIES
[1890]

Some rainbow coming from the fair!
Some vision of the world Cashmere
I confidently see!
Or else a peacock's purple train,
Feather by feather, on the plain   5
Fritters itself away!

The dreamy butterflies bestir,
Lethargic pools resume the whir

Of last year's sundered tune.
From some old fortress on the sun 10
Baronial bees march, one by one,
In murmuring platoon!

The robins stand as thick to-day
As flakes of snow stood yesterday,
On fence and roof and twig. 15
The orchis binds her feather on
For her old lover, Don the Sun,
Revisiting the bog!

Without commander, countless, still,
The regiment of wood and hill 20
In bright detachment stand.
Behold! Whose multitudes are these?
The children of whose turbaned seas,
Or what Circassian land?

PRESENTIMENT
[1890]

Presentiment is that long shadow on the
 lawn
Indicative that suns go down;
The notice to the startled grass
That darkness is about to pass.

THE BUTTERFLY'S ASSUMPTION-
GOWN
[1890]

The butterfly's assumption-gown,
In chrysoprase apartments hung,
This afternoon put on.

How condescending to descend,
And be of buttercups the friend 5
In a New England town!

THE WIND
[1890]

Of all the sounds despatched abroad,
There's not a charge to me
Like that old measure in the boughs,
That phraseless melody

The wind does, working like a hand 5
Whose fingers brush the sky,
Then quiver down, with tufts of tune
Permitted gods and me.

When winds go round and round in bands,
And thrum upon the door, 10
And birds take places overhead,
To bear them orchestra,

I crave him grace, of summer boughs,
If such an outcast be,
He never heard that fleshless chant 15
Rise solemn in the tree,

As if some caravan of sound
On deserts, in the sky,
Had broken rank,
Then knit, and passed 20
In seamless company.

INDIAN SUMMER
[1890]

These are the days when birds come back,
A very few, a bird or two,
To take a backward look.

These are the days when skies put on
The old, old sophistries of June,— 5
A blue and gold mistake.

Oh, fraud that cannot cheat the bee,
Almost thy plausibility
Induces my belief,

Till ranks of seeds their witness bear, 10
And softly through the altered air
Hurries a timid leaf!

Oh, sacrament of summer days,
Oh, last communion in the haze,
Permit a child to join, 15

Thy sacred emblems to partake,
Thy consecrated bread to break,
Taste thine immortal wine!

THERE'S A CERTAIN SLANT OF LIGHT
[1890]

There's a certain slant of light,
On winter afternoons,
That oppresses, like the weight
Of cathedral tunes.

Heavenly hurt it gives us;   5
We can find no scar,
But internal difference
Where the meanings are.

None may teach it anything,
'Tis the seal, despair,—   10
An imperial affliction
Sent us of the air.

When it comes, the landscape listens,
Shadows hold their breath;
When it goes, 'tis like the distance 15
On the look of death.

SETTING SAIL
[1890]

Exultation is the going
Of an inland soul to sea,—
Past the houses, past the headlands,
Into deep eternity!

Bred as we, among the mountains,   5
Can the sailor understand
The divine intoxication
Of the first league out from land?

REAL
[1890]

I like a look of agony,
Because I know it's true;
Men do not sham convulsion,
Nor simulate a throe.

The eyes glaze once, and that is death. 5
Impossible to feign
The beads upon the forehead
By homely anguish strung.

I'VE SEEN A DYING EYE
[1890]

I've seen a dying eye
Run round and round a room
In search of something, as it seemed,
Then cloudier become;
And then, obscure with fog,   5
And then be soldered down,
Without disclosing what it be,
'Twere blessed to have seen.

I NEVER SAW A MOOR
[1890]

I never saw a moor,
I never saw the sea;
Yet know I how the heather looks,
And what a wave must be.

I never spoke with God,   5
Nor visited in heaven;
Yet certain am I of the spot
As if the chart were given.

THE BUSTLE IN A HOUSE
[1890]

The bustle in a house
The morning after death
Is solemnest of industries
Enacted upon earth,—

The sweeping up the heart,   5
And putting love away
We shall not want to use again
Until eternity.

DEATH IS A DIALOGUE
[1890]

Death is a dialogue between
The spirit and the dust.
"Dissolve," says Death. The Spirit, "Sir,
I have another trust."

Death doubts it, argues from the ground. 5
The Spirit turns away,
Just laying off, for evidence,
An overcoat of clay.

IF I SHOULDN'T BE ALIVE
[1890]

If I shouldn't be alive
When the robins come,
Give the one in red cravat
A memorial crumb.

If I couldn't thank you,   5
Being just asleep,
You will know I'm trying
With my granite lip!

I NEVER LOST AS MUCH BUT TWICE
[1890]

I never lost as much but twice,
And that was in the sod;
Twice have I stood a beggar
Before the door of God!

Angels, twice descending,   5
Reimbursed my store.
Burglar, banker, father,
I am poor once more!

I FOUND THE PHRASE
[1891]

I found the phrase to every thought
I ever had, but one;
And that defies me,—as a hand
Did try to chalk the sun

To races nurtured in the dark;—   5
How would your own begin?
Can blaze be done in cochineal,
Or noon in mazarin?

I HAD BEEN HUNGRY
[1896]

I had been hungry all the years;
My noon had come, to dine;
I, trembling, drew the table near
And touched the curious wine.

'Twas this on tables I had seen,   5
When turning, hungry, lone,
I looked in windows, for the wealth
I could not hope to own.

I did not know the ample bread,
'Twas so unlike the crumb   10
The birds and I had often shared
In Nature's dining-room.

The plenty hurt me, 'twas so new,—
Myself felt ill and odd,
As berry of a mountain bush   15
Transplanted to the road.

Nor was I hungry; so I found
That hunger was a way
Of persons outside windows,
The entering takes away.   20

WE NEVER KNOW
[1896]

We never know how high we are
Till we are called to rise;
And then, if we are true to plan,
Our statures touch the skies.

The heroism we recite   5
Would be a daily thing,
Did not ourselves the cubits warp
For fear to be a king.

AND THIS OF ALL MY HOPES
[1929]

And this of all my hopes—
This is the silent end;
Bountiful colored my morning rose,
Early and sere its end.

Never bud from a stem   5
Stepped with so gay a foot,
Never a worm so confident
Bored at so brave a root.

1836· ∽ *Bret Harte* ∽ *1902*

ALL of Bret Harte's best work was done in California, within half a dozen years; yet his huge subsequent output was occasionally punctuated by something so close to his best that wholesale condemnation of that later work is unjustified. His was a limited but genuine talent, exercised for a time in a field precisely appropriate to it.

Harte's preparation for writing lay in the precocious and omnivorous reading of his boyhood—perhaps stimulated by the example of his scholarly but impractical father—and in the early days of wage-earning necessitated by that father's death when the boy was nine. The wage-earning began in the East, but at eighteen Harte and a sister followed their mother—who had married a second time—to California, and his education went on there as a country school teacher and perhaps as a miner, drug clerk, and express messenger. The precise extent of his overt participation in the typical occupations of frontier California seems unimportant: that his vicarious participation was ample his stories themselves are proof.

At twenty-one he began sending verses and sketches to the *Golden Era* of San Francisco. The following year he got a job as printer's devil and editorial assistant on the *Northern Californian,* a newspaper newly founded at the town of Union. An editorial vigorously condemning the white settlers of the region for their treatment of the Indians precipitated his departure for San Francisco, where he became a regular contributor to the *Golden Era,* and, in 1864, editor of the newly founded *Californian.*

Harte's first magazine work was conventional and insipid, but growth was apparent in a series of *Condensed Novels* collected in 1867. These are brief parodies of Cooper, Dickens and others, effective both as humor and as literary criticism. In 1868 the *Overland Monthly* was founded at San Francisco and Harte became its first editor. To the second issue he contributed the story "The Luck of Roaring Camp," which with its successors, collected in *The Luck of Roaring Camp and Other Stories* (1870), established his fame. The immediately enthusiastic reception of Harte's stories of the mining camps was in part the fruit of their intrinsic merits of humor, vivid action and effective plot, and in part the result of his introduction of a new region and new materials of American experience into our creative literature. Beneath these factors lay a third: Harte's popularity gives evidence that American taste was beginning to grow tired of "genteel" conventions and hypocrisies. Among the characters of "The Luck of Roaring Camp" are a gambler and a prostitute, and its diction includes profanity.

The humorous poem "Plain Language from Truthful James," better known as "The Heathen Chinee," appeared in the *Overland Monthly* in 1870, and was extravagantly popular. Harte rode the crest of his fame to the East and a $10,000 contract with the *Atlantic Monthly* for a year's output.

Thereafter almost all was anticlimax and disappointment. There were eight years in which he tried lecturing, novel-writing and play-writing, with little success. In 1878 some of his friends—Harte's friends were always numerous and devoted—obtained for him a minor diplomatic post in Germany; and he left the United States and his family to spend the rest of his life abroad. He was an unsatisfactory government employe, both in Germany and later in Scotland. But he was heartily welcome in the social and literary worlds in England, and after losing his consulship in 1885 he stayed in England for his remaining seventeen years. In this period he wrote a few admirable stories and scores that were bad, or merely poor, continuing to portray—to the delight of his British readers—a crude and flamboyant America that had long since ceased to exist.

Harte is interesting as a forerunner of realism and also as an early figure in the migration in reverse which, once American literature had achieved a certain maturity, expatriated many of its most talented writers over a period of fifty years. His best stories contain elements of sound and forceful characterization, and are written with gusto and a certain spontaneity and genuineness of sentiment.

[Earlier biographies and critical studies of Harte were largely superseded by George R. Stewart's *Bret Harte, Argonaut and Exile* (Boston, 1931). An excellent evaluation is found in J. B. Harrison's *Harte* (New York, 1941) in the American Writers Series.]

TENNESSEE'S PARTNER
[1870 (1869)]

I DO NOT think that we ever knew his real name. Our ignorance of it certainly never gave us any social inconvenience, for at Sandy Bar in 1854 most men were christened anew. Sometimes these appellatives were derived from some distinctiveness of dress, as in the case of "Dungaree Jack"; or from some peculiarity of habit, as shown in "Saleratus Bill," so called from an undue proportion of that chemical in his daily bread; or from some unlucky slip, as exhibited in "The Iron Pirate," a mild, inoffensive man, who earned that baleful title by his unfortunate mispronunciation of the term "iron pyrites."

Perhaps this may have been the beginning of a rude heraldry; but I am constrained to think that it was because a man's real name in that day rested solely upon his own unsupported statement. "Call yourself Clifford, do you?" said Boston, addressing a timid new-comer with infinite scorn; "hell is full of such Cliffords!" He then introduced the unfortunate man, whose name happened to be really Clifford, as "Jaybird Charley,"—an unhallowed inspiration of the moment that clung to him ever after.

But to return to Tennessee's Partner, whow we never knew by any other than this relative title; that he had ever existed as a separate and distinct individuality we only learned later. It seems that in 1853 he left Poker Flat to go to San Francisco, ostensibly to procure a wife. He never got any farther than Stockton. At that place he was attracted by a young person who waited upon the table at the hotel where he took his meals. One morning he said something to her which caused her to smile not unkindly, to somewhat coquettishly break a plate of toast over his upturned, serious, simple face, and to retreat to the kitchen. He followed her, and emerged a few moments later, covered with more toast and victory. That day week they were married by a Justice of the Peace, and returned to Poker Flat. I am aware that something more might be made of this episode, but I prefer to tell it as it was current at Sandy Bar,—in the gulches and bar-rooms,— where all sentiment was modified by a strong sense of humor.

Of their married felicity but little is known, perhaps for the reason that Tennessee, then living with his partner, one day took occasion to say something to the bride on his own account, at which, it is said, she smiled not unkindly and chastely retreated,—this time as far as Marysville, where Tennessee followed her, and where they went to housekeeping without the aid of a Justice of the Peace. Tennessee's Partner took the loss of his wife simply and seriously, as was his fashion. But to everybody's surprise, when Tennessee one day returned from Marysville, without his partner's wife,—she having smiled and retreated with somebody else,—Tennessee's Partner was the first man to shake his hand and greet him with affection. The boys who had gathered in the cañon to see the shooting were naturally indignant. Their indignation might have found vent in sarcasm but for a certain look in Tennessee's Partner's eye that indicated a lack of humorous appreciation. In fact, he was a grave man, with a steady application to practical detail which was unpleasant in a difficulty.

Meanwhile a popular feeling against Tennessee had grown up on the Bar. He was known to be a gambler; he was suspected to be a thief. In these suspicions Tennessee's Partner was equally compro-

mised; his continued intimacy with Tennessee after the affair above quoted could only be accounted for on the hypothesis of a co-partnership of crime. At last Tennessee's guilt became flagrant. One day he overtook a stranger on his way to Red Dog. The stranger afterward related that Tennessee beguiled the time with interesting anecdote and reminiscence, but illogically concluded the interview in the following words: "And now, young man, I'll trouble you for your knife, your pistols, and your money. You see your weppings might get you into trouble at Red Dog, and your money's a temptation to the evilly disposed. I think you said your address was San Francisco. I shall endeavor to call." It may be stated here that Tennessee had a fine flow of humor, which no business preoccupation would wholly subdue.

This exploit was his last. Red Dog and Sandy Bar made common cause against the highwayman. Tennessee was hunted in very much the same fashion as his prototype, the grizzly. As the toils closed around him, he made a desperate dash through the Bar, emptying his revolver at the crowd before the Arcade Saloon, and so on up Grizzly Cañon; but at its farther extremity he was stopped by a small man on a gray horse. The men looked at each other a moment in silence. Both were fearless, both self-possessed and independent, and both types of a civilization that in the seventeenth century would have been called heroic, but in the nineteenth simply "reckless." "What have you got there?—I call," said Tennessee, quietly. "Two bowers and an ace," said the stranger, as quietly, showing two revolvers and a bowie-knife. "That takes me," returned Tennessee; and, with this gambler's epigram, he threw away his useless pistol, and rode back with his captor.

It was a warm night. The cool breeze which usually sprang up with the going down of the sun behind the *chaparral*-crested mountain was that evening withheld from Sandy Bar. The cañon was stifling with heated resinous odors, and the decaying driftwood on the Bar sent forth faint, sickening exhalations. The feverishness of day and its fierce passions still filled the camp. Lights moved restlessly along the bank of the river, striking no answering reflection from its tawny current. Against the blackness of the pines the windows of the old loft above the express-office stood out staringly bright; and through their curtainless panes the loungers below could see the forms of those who were even then deciding the fate of Tennessee. And above all this, etched on the dark firmament, rose the Sierra, remote and passionless, crowned with remoter passionless stars.

The trial of Tennessee was conducted as fairly as was consistent with a judge and jury who felt themselves to some extent obliged to justify, in their verdict, the previous irregularities of arrest and indictment. The law of Sandy Bar was implacable, but not vengeful. The excitement and personal feeling of the chase were over; with Tennessee safe in their hands they were ready to listen patiently to any defence, which they were already satisfied was insufficient. There being no doubt in their minds, they were willing to give the prisoner the benefit of any that might exist. Secure in the hypothesis that he ought to be hanged, on general principles, they indulged him with more latitude of defence than his reckless hardihood seemed to ask. The Judge appeared to be more anxious than the prisoner, who, otherwise unconcerned, evidently took a grim pleasure in the responsibility he had created. "I don't take any hand in this yer game," had been his invariable but good-humored reply to all questions. The Judge—who was also his captor—for a moment vaguely regretted that he had not shot him "on sight," that morning, but presently dismissed this human weakness as unworthy of the judicial mind. Nevertheless, when there was a tap at the door, and it was said that Tennessee's Partner was there on behalf of the prisoner, he was admitted at once without question. Perhaps the younger members of the jury, to whom the proceedings were becoming irksomely thoughtful, hailed him as a relief.

For he was not, certainly, an imposing figure. Short and stout, with a square face, sunburned into a preternatural redness, clad in a loose duck "jumper" and trousers streaked and splashed with red soil, his aspect under any circumstances would have been quaint, and was now even ridiculous. As he stooped to deposit at his feet a heavy carpet-bag he was carrying, it became obvious, from partially developed legends and inscriptions, that the material with which his trousers had been patched had been originally intended for a less ambitious covering. Yet he advanced with great gravity, and after shaking the hand of each person in the room with labored cordiality, he wiped his serious, perplexed face on a red bandanna handkerchief, a shade lighter than his complexion, laid his powerful hand upon the table to steady himself, and thus addressed the Judge:—

"I was passin' by," he began, by way of apology, "and I thought I'd just step in and see how things was gittin' on with Tennessee thar,—my pardner. It's a hot night. I disremember any sich weather before on the Bar."

He paused a moment, but nobody volunteering any other meteorological recollection, he again had recourse to his pocket-handkerchief, and for some moments mopped his face diligently.

"Have you anything to say on behalf of the prisoner?" said the Judge, finally.

"Thet's it," said Tennessee's Partner, in a tone of relief. "I come yar as Tennessee's pardner,—knowing him nigh on four year, off and on, wet and dry, in luck and out o' luck. His ways ain't allers my ways, but thar ain't any p'ints in that young man, thar ain't any liveliness as he's been up to, as I don't know. And you sez to me, sez you,—confidential-like, and between man and man,—sez you, 'Do you know anything in his behalf?' and I sez to you, sez I,—confidential-like, as between man and man,—'What should a man know of his pardner?'"

"Is this all you have to say?" asked the Judge impatiently, feeling, perhaps, that a dangerous sympathy of humor was beginning to humanize the court.

"Thet's so," continued Tennessee's Partner. "It ain't for me to say anything agin' him. And now, what's the case? Here's Tennessee wants money, wants it bad, and doesn't like to ask it of his old pardner. Well, what does Tennessee do? He lays for a stranger, and he fetches that stranger; and you lays for *him,* and you fetches *him;* and the honors is easy. And I put it to you, bein' a far-minded man, and to you, gentlemen all, as far-minded men, ef this isn't so."

"Prisoner," said the Judge, interrupting, "have you any questions to ask this man?"

"No! no!" continued Tennessee's Partner hastily. "I play this yer hand alone. To come down to the bed-rock, it's just this: Tennessee, thar, has played it pretty rough and expensive-like on a stranger, and on this yer camp. And now, what's the fair thing? Some would say more; some would say less. Here's seventeen hundred dollars in coarse gold and a watch,—it's about all my pile,—and call it square!" And before a hand could be raised to prevent him, he had emptied the contents of the carpet-bag upon the table.

For a moment his life was in jeopardy. One or two men sprang to their feet, several hands groped for hidden weapons, and a suggestion to "throw him from the window" was only overridden by a gesture from the Judge. Tennessee laughed. And apparently oblivious of the excitement, Tennessee's Partner improved the opportunity to mop his face again with his handkerchief.

When order was restored, and the man was made to understand, by the use of forcible figures and rhetoric, that Tennessee's offence could not be condoned by money, his face took a more serious and sanguinary hue, and those who were nearest to him noticed that his rough hand trembled slightly on the table. He hesitated a moment as he slowly returned the gold to the carpet-bag, as if he had not yet entirely caught the elevated sense of justice which swayed the tribunal, and was perplexed with the belief that he had not offered enough. Then he turned to the Judge, and saying, "This yer is a lone hand, played alone, and without my pardner," he bowed to the jury and was about to withdraw, when the Judge called him back. "If you have anything to say to Tennessee, you had better say it now." For the first time that evening the eyes of the prisoner and his strange advocate met. Tennessee smiled, showed his white teeth, and saying, "Euchred, old man!" held out his hand. Tennessee's Partner took it in his own, and saying, "I just dropped in as I was passin' to see how things was gettin' on," let the hand passively fall, and adding that "it was a warm night," again mopped his face with his handkerchief, and without another word withdrew.

The two men never again met each other alive. For the unparalleled insult of a bribe offered to Judge Lynch—who, whether bigoted, weak, or narrow, was at least incorruptible—firmly fixed in the mind of that mythical personage any wavering determination of Tennessee's fate; and at the break of day he was marched, closely guarded, to meet it at the top of Marley's Hill.

How he met it, how cool he was, how he refused to say anything, how perfect were the arrangements of the committee, were all duly reported, with the addition of a warning moral and example to all future evil-doers, in the Red Dog *Clarion,* by its editor, who was present, and to whose vigorous English I cheerfully refer the reader. But the beauty of that midsummer morning, the blessed amity of earth and air and sky, the awakened life of the free woods and hills, the joyous renewal and promise of Nature, and, above all, the infinite serenity that thrilled through each, was not reported, as not being a part of the social lesson. And yet, when the weak and foolish deed was done, and a life, with its possibilities and responsibilities, had passed out of the misshapen thing that dangled between earth and sky, the birds sang, the flowers bloomed, the sun shone, as cheerily as before; and possibly the Red Dog *Clarion* was right.

Tennessee's Partner was not in the group that surrounded the ominous tree. But as they turned to disperse, attention was drawn to the singular appearance of a motionless donkey-cart halted at the side of the road. As they approached, they at once recognized the venerable Jenny and the two-wheeled cart as the property of Tennessee's Partner,—used by him in carrying dirt from his claim; and a few paces distant the owner of the equipage himself, sitting under a buckeye tree, wiping the perspiration from his glowing face. In answer to an inquiry, he said he had come for the body of the "diseased," "if it was all the same to the committee." He didn't wish to "hurry anything;" he could wait. He was not working that day; and when the gentlemen were done with the "diseased" he would take him. "Ef thar is any present," he added, in his simple, serious way, "as would care to jine in the fun'l, they kin come." Perhaps it was from a sense of humor, which I have already intimated was a feature of Sandy Bar, —perhaps it was from something even better than that; but two thirds of the loungers accepted the invitation at once.

It was noon when the body of Tennessee was delivered into the hands of his partner. As the cart drew up to the fatal tree, we noticed that it contained a rough oblong box,—apparently made from a section of sluicing,—and half filled with bark and the tassels of pine. The cart was further decorated with slips of willow, and made fragrant with buckeye-blossoms. When the body was deposited in the box, Tennessee's Partner drew over it a piece of tarred canvas, and gravely mounting the narrow seat in front, with his feet upon the shafts, urged the little donkey forward. The equipage moved slowly on, at that decorous pace which was habitual with Jenny even under less solemn circumstances. The men—half curiously, half jestingly, but all good-humoredly—strolled along beside the cart; some in advance, some a little in the rear, of the homely catafalque. But, whether from the narrowing of the road or some present sense of decorum, as the cart passed on, the company fell to the rear in couples, keeping step, and otherwise assuming the external show of a formal procession. Jack Folinsbee, who had at the outset played a funeral march in dumb show upon an imaginary trombone, desisted, from a lack of sympathy and appreciation,—not having, perhaps, your true humorist's capacity to be content with the enjoyment of his own fun.

The way led through Grizzly Cañon, by this time clothed in funereal drapery and shadows. The redwoods, burying their moccasined feet in the red soil, stood in Indian-file along the track, trailing an uncouth benediction from their bending boughs upon the passing bier. A hare, surprised into helpless inactivity, sat upright and pulsating in the ferns by the roadside, as the *cortège* went by. Squirrels hastened to gain a secure outlook from higher boughs; and the blue-jays, spreading their wings, fluttered before them like outriders, until the outskirts of Sandy Bar were reached, and the solitary cabin of Tennessee's Partner.

Viewed under more favorable circumstances, it would not have been a cheerful place. The unpicturesque site, the rude and unlovely outlines, the unsavory details, which distinguish the nest-building of the California miner, were all here, with the dreariness of decay superadded. A few paces from the cabin there was a rough enclosure, which, in the brief days of Tennessee's Partner's matrimonial felicity, had been used as a garden, but was now overgrown with fern. As we approached it we were surprised to find that what we had taken for a recent attempt at cultivation was the broken soil about an open grave.

The cart was halted before the enclosure; and rejecting the offers of assistance with the same air of simple self-reliance he had displayed throughout, Tennessee's Partner lifted the rough coffin on his back, and deposited it unaided, within the shallow grave. He then nailed down the board which served as a lid, and mounting the little mound of earth beside it, took off his hat, and slowly mopped his face with his handkerchief. This the crowd felt was a preliminary to speech; and they disposed themselves variously on stumps and boulders, and sat expectant.

"When a man," began Tennessee's Partner slowly, "has been running free all day, what's the natural thing for him to do? Why, to come home. And if he ain't in a condition to go home, what can his best friend do? Why, bring him home! And here's Tennessee has been running free, and we brings him home from his wandering." He paused, and picked up a fragment of quartz, rubbed it thoughtfully on his sleeve, and went on: "It ain't the first time that I've packed him on my back, as you see'd me now. It ain't the first time that I brought him to this yer cabin when he couldn't help himself; it ain't the first time that I and Jinny have waited for him on yon hill, and picked him up and so fetched him home, when he couldn't speak, and didn't know me. And now that it's the last time, why"—he paused, and rubbed the quartz gently on his sleeve— "you see it's sort of rough on his pardner. And now, gentlemen," he added abruptly, picking up his long-handled shovel, "the fun'l's over; and my thanks, and Tennessee's thanks, to you for your trouble."

Resisting any proffers of assistance, he began to fill in the grave, turning his back upon the crowd, that after a few moments' hesitation gradually withdrew. As they crossed the little ridge that hid Sandy Bar from view, some, looking back, thought they could see Tennessee's Partner, his work done, sitting upon the grave, his shovel between his knees, and his face buried in his red bandanna handkerchief. But it was argued by others that you couldn't tell his face from his handkerchief at that distance; and this point remained undecided.

In the reaction that followed the feverish excitement of that day, Tennessee's Partner was not forgotten. A secret investigation had cleared him of any complicity in Tennessee's guilt, and left only a suspicion of his general sanity. Sandy Bar made a point of calling on him, and proffering various uncouth but well-meant kindnesses. But from that day his rude health and great strength seemed visibly to decline; and when the rainy season fairly set in, and the tiny grassblades were beginning to peep from the rocky mound above Tennessee's grave, he took to his bed.

One night, when the pines beside the cabin were swaying in the storm, and trailing their slender fingers over the roof, and the roar and rush of the swollen river were heard below, Tennessee's Partner lifted his head from the pillow, saying, "It is time to go for Tennessee; I must put Jinny in the cart"; and would have risen from his bed but for the restraint of his attendant. Struggling, he still pursued his singular fancy: "There, now, steady, Jinny,—steady, old girl. How dark it is! Look out for the ruts,—and look out for him, too, old gal. Sometimes, you know, when he's blind drunk, he drops down right in the trail. Keep on straight up to the pine on the top of the hill. Thar! I told you so!—thar he is,—coming this way, too,—all by himself, sober, and his face a-shining. Tennessee! Pardner!"

And so they met.

1835 ∾ *Mark Twain* ∾ 1910

I

IT WAS the custom of the publishers of the *Atlantic Monthly* to give occasional "Contributors' Dinners" to bring together the members of their illustrious group. December 17, 1877, the seventieth birthday of Whittier, was fixed upon for one of these distinguished literary events; and Mark Twain, whose *Tom Sawyer* had been published the year before, was invited to make the after-dinner speech. It was a great honor for the western newcomer to be asked to be the spokesman of the nation's affectionate congratulations to the aged poet—and, indeed, to the whole New England hierarchy of American letters, for Emerson, Longfellow and Holmes were there too.

What happened at that dinner is a classic incident in the long, sad history of the tragedies of after-dinner speaking. Mark had conceived a brilliant idea. He had cooked up a story about how one night he knocked at a mountaineer's cabin out in the foothills of the Sierras and asked for food and shelter. But when he said he was Mark Twain, he found the mountaineer hostile because he had recently had some other "liter'y men" there, and they had eaten all his food, drunk all his whiskey, and played euchre all night. They had given their names as Ralph Waldo Emerson, Henry Wadsworth Longfellow, and Oliver Wendell Holmes. Mark provided ridiculous thumbnail caricatures of all three. Of course, it turned out that they were impostors; and the joke was turned on Mark because his host at once decided that he must be an impostor, too. It was a funny story, with the element of hoaxing which Mark and his admirers loved, but it was about as out of place at this dinner as a side-show in a cathedral. These aged leaders of the great period of New England letters were demigods, the guests were their worshipers, and Mark was committing sacrilege. The speech was received in a grim silence which grew heavier as it proceeded doggedly to its end. Mark went home thinking himself disgraced forever, wrote abject apologies to everyone concerned, and never forgave himself.

The episode has some significance in the history of American letters. It was a head-on literary collision which occurred at the Whittier dinner; rough-and-ready western humor there smashed into the dignified and established esthetic standards of the East. The collision was geographical only because it was the wild and woolly West that had afforded Mark Twain a chance to develop that freedom from taboos and restraints and that immense vigor which were to do so much for our literature. But fundamentally the collision was between a new, spontaneous, uninhibited spirit and the old, established standards. It was Mark who retired from this particular encounter defeated, but it was he who triumphed in the end; for Emerson, Longfellow, Whittier, and Holmes had said their say, and Mark Twain was in the full tide of popular production. New England summer was over, and a tumultuous, refreshing gale was blowing out of the West.

II

Samuel Langhorne Clemens (Mark Twain) came of the pioneering stock which had built up the new empire and the new spirit of the West. His mother, whom he seemed to resemble more than he did his father, belonged to a family which had gone with Daniel Boone across the mountains into Kentucky, fighting Indians and raising children. Soon after she and John Clemens were married, they moved out to Fentress County, Tennessee. John had the characteristic energy and optimism of the pioneer: he helped organize the erection of the new courthouse at Jamestown, got himself elected circuit clerk, and invested all the money he could raise in the purchase of 75,000 acres of rich timberland, with some coal and iron on it, at only a few cents an acre. "The Tennessee land" was to play an important part in the family dreams of fortune for years to come, but it was never to make any of the Clemens clan rich.

Meanwhile John Clemens' law practice languished while his family increased. Then one day a letter from a relative in Florida, Missouri, describing the rosy prospects of that region, made him sell everything he could (except the 75,000 acres) and move his family out to the straggling, muddy village of log cabins and high hopes. There the lawyer eked out his income by storekeeping; and there on November 30, 1835, the fifth Clemens child was born and named Samuel Langhorne—the first name after his paternal grandfather and the second after a boyhood friend of his father's.

Sam was a rather frail boy, excitable and full of moods and fancies. He was not yet four when John Clemens made another vain attempt to improve the family fortunes by moving to Hannibal, on the Mississippi. Here the impressionable boy stored up a wealth of observation and childish experience which he was later to share with millions of readers.

Hannibal was not, strictly speaking, on the frontier; but it was essentially a river town in the heyday of river traffic, and on its streets and wharves could be seen all the pioneer and river types—immigrants, Pikes, adventurers, river gamblers, speculators, runaway slaves, bad men, and even Indians. Sam saw terrible fights with bare fists, mobs, murders, posses in action. He heard the "tall talk," the blood-curdling legends, the river lore, and the religious teaching of a typical river town of the pioneer days. He explored the caves nearby, with the other boys; he learned to swim, and was more than once half-drowned. He went to school, too, and to the Presbyterian Sunday School; and he read whatever came to hand, including Davy Crockett, T. B. Thorpe, and Judge Longstreet. He grew up a spare, tough-muscled boy, with a shock of reddish hair, leader of his gang, full of imaginative ideas for pranks and escapades.

Sam was twelve years old when his father died, whispering, "Cling to the Tennessee land; it will make you all rich!" The boy now had to do his part to support the family; play-days were over for him. His elder brother Orion had become a printer and was earning good money in St. Louis and sending some of it home, and it was natural that Sam should be started out on the same road to success. Thus he became "printer's devil" for the local newspaper; and four years later, when Orion started his own weekly (sometimes spelled "weakly") in Hannibal, he worked in his brother's shop. Thus began his career in journalism. For the next twenty-five years Sam Clemens worked for newspapers, except for his four years as a river pilot and one as a miner. Not until 1871 did he decide to cut loose from the papers, and even after he did that his journalistic impulses would seize control of his pen from time to time to the very end of his life.

Sam got his first taste of original journalistic endeavor at the age of sixteen when Orion was out of town and he grasped the opportunity to print some broad satires on the editor of the rival paper. Two years later he left Hannibal for a St. Louis job, still following in his brother's footsteps. But Sam's character was very different from Orion's; Sam longed for travel and adventure and freedom. St. Louis was only the step which took him away from Hannibal. In those days a good typesetter could get a job almost anywhere, and most young printers had their *wanderjahre* which enabled them to see the country while working at their trade. Some liked this way of life so well that they never settled down, but became confirmed "tramp prints" to the ends of their lives. Sam Clemens spent about four years as an itinerant printer, working in New York, Philadelphia, and Cincinnati, as well as in shops which Orion set up at different times in Mississippi River cities in Iowa—Muscatine and Keokuk.

His love for new scenes was about to carry him off to South America; but suddenly when he was on his way down the Mississippi to New Orleans, all the old love of the river and his childhood ambition to occupy the dazzling position of steamboat pilot came back to him so overpoweringly that he gave up his more recent project of exploring the Amazon and Orinoco and devoted himself to the realization of that dream of his boyhood days. For more than a year, with intense application, he labored at his apprenticeship, and then for three years he was a licensed pilot on the Mississippi. Here again at close range Sam Clemens observed types of pioneer character—planters, politicians, gamblers, scouts and adventurers, slave buyers, rowdies, fine ladies, home-

seekers, soldiers, actors, harlots, black and white roustabouts—there was no
end to the variety and interest of the procession. Nor any end to the series
of dramatic incidents with which the future writer of romance and humor
might store his memory—the steamboat races, the fights, the boiler explosions,
and all the tragedy and comedy of the showy, exciting, high-tension life of
steamboating.

In April, 1861, Sam made his last river trip as a licensed pilot. Lincoln
had issued his call for volunteers; the impending war was about to end river
traffic for the duration. Though he seems to have had no strong political
opinions at the time, Sam was a member for three or four weeks of one of
those more or less independent military groups which were organized in the
border states. This one was drawn partly from Hannibal and expected to
serve the Confederate cause; but two weeks of drilling in rain and mud dissolved all dreams of military glory, and the battalion gave the war up as a bad
job and went home. Many years later Mark Twain added a melodramatic
incident or two, embellished the whole episode with humor, and wrote it up
for the *Century Magazine's* series of Civil War histories under the title "The
Private History of a Campaign That Failed."

Orion had received an appointment as secretary of the Territory of Nevada,
and Sam now decided to go west with him in search of adventure, gold,
whatever the West might hold for him. The overland trip was a great experience, the memories of which were to be literary treasure-trove of the first
importance. Arrived in Nevada, Sam was again impressed by the types of
character and the dramatic incidents of the pioneer life.

It was a splendid population (he wrote later) for all the slow, sleepy,
sluggish-brained sloths staid at home—you never find that sort of people
among pioneers—you cannot build pioneers out of that sort of material. . . .
But they were rough in those times! They fairly reveled in gold, whisky, fights,
and fandangoes, and were unspeakably happy. The honest miner raked from
a hundred to a thousand dollars from his claim in a day, and what with
gambling dens and other entertainments, he hadn't a cent the next morning,
if he had any sort of luck. . . .

Sam caught the mining fever himself, as was to be expected; but after
it had run its course, he made a connection with the Virginia City *Territorial
Enterprise.* He was back in a newspaper office once more, and he fitted into
his job as a "local" to perfection.

III

In his itinerant printer days Sam had written letters for Orion's paper, and
in his river days he had done some humorous things for New Orleans journals.
Now, though his main job was news reporting, he had a chance to write a

good deal as he pleased. For two or three decades after 1840 the small-city daily commonly kept one man to look after the local news. He had to be active, to cultivate a very wide acquaintance, to have a "nose for news," and to be able to fill his column on a dull day. As the new "local" of the *Enterprise* wrote:

Our duty is to keep the universe thoroughly posted concerning murders and street fights, and balls, and theatres, and pack-trains, and churches, and lectures, and schoolhouses, and city military affairs, and highway robberies, and Bible societies, and hay-wagons, and a thousand other things which it is in the province of local reporters to keep track of and magnify into undue importance for the instruction of the readers of this great daily newspaper.

This quotation illustrates not only the variety of the reporting, but also the fact that the "local," when he had a turn for humor, was sometimes permitted to give it free rein. That is precisely what occurred on not a few papers in the middle decades of the nineteenth century, and many a city column was the more eagerly read for the coruscations of the "local's" quips and quiddities. Moreover, the system of exchanges among newspapers being still at flood, the watchful editors of journals in other cities, scissors always in hand, would clip the comicalities of their "contemporaries" to enliven their own columns. The spreading fame of his rivals would stimulate the local humorist to greater effort. Thus began the fame of Sam Clemens, soon to be called Mark Twain, on the *Enterprise;* that of Charles Farrar Browne as Artemus Ward on the Cleveland *Plain Dealer;* and that of Orpheus C. Kerr, reporter on several eastern papers, in whose pen name the pun-lover may recognize "orfice-seeker." There were many other newspaper wits less closely connected with local news reporting whose pseudonyms and whose papers became famous in these years, such as Petroleum V. Nasby, of the Toledo *Blade;* Bill Arp, of the *Southern Confederacy,* Rome, Georgia; M. Quad, of the Detroit *Free Press;* and Brick Pomeroy, of the La Crosse *Democrat.*

But it was a story contributed to an eastern periodical that first gave Mark Twain a reputation that was more than local. He had adopted his pen-name for his humorous pieces on the *Enterprise;* and then after a year and nine months in Nevada, he had fled to San Francisco to escape prosecution for sending a challenge to a duel. (They were rough in those times, to be sure!) In his new home he got the police after him again—this time for letters which he had written back to the *Enterprise* attacking the official corruption of the city government. He always had a burning indignation against graft and hypocrisy in office. One reason he lost his job on the San Francisco *Call* was that he had come to be recognized as a rebel and a disturber: it was a lifelong vocation.

At any rate, Mark retreated from the city by the Golden Gate under fire, so to speak; and it was while he sojourned at his hide-out on Jackass Hill, occasionally visiting nearby Angel's Camp, that he heard an old-timer drawl out the story of the "Jumping Frog." It was really an old story, which had been told around many a fire and had been printed at least a dozen years before; but it was new to Mark, and he dressed it up and made it into a little tale which was to become a classic under the title "The Celebrated Jumping Frog of Calaveras County." After some misadventures, it got into print in the New York *Saturday Press* and later became the title-piece in Mark Twain's first published book.

In 1866 Mark made a trip to the Sandwich Islands (as the Hawaiian group was then called), and the twenty-five letters he wrote for the Sacramento *Union* about what he saw there made him such a reputation on the West Coast that he tried his luck at lecturing. Three years before, Artemus Ward had made his famous western trip and had enjoyed memorable high-jinks with Mark and his cronies in Virginia City; it now became evident that Mark had studied the platform techniques of his fellow humorist (whose career of itinerant printer, journalist, humorist, and lecturer had been so like his own) to good effect. The lyceum, which had meant much to Emerson, Thoreau, and many other literary men, was still strong, though it had tended to turn somewhat more to entertainment after the war. Mark Twain became one of the greatest platform men of his times, giving thousands of lectures all around the world.

The rousing success of his early lectures put money in Mark's pockets and made his feet itch again. He went back to New York—not overland but by way of Panama, made a triumphant visit to Hannibal, and then set out on a tour of Europe and the Holy Land. For this last peregrination, Mark joined an excursion party which chartered the steamer *Quaker City;* his passage was paid by the San Francisco *Alta California,* to which he contracted to furnish letters while on the trip. These letters made up somewhat more than half of *The Innocents Abroad,* the book which, when published in 1869, took America by storm. Travel literature had a much greater popular appeal in the latter half of the nineteenth century than it has ever had before or since. Travel was regarded as "improving," and new arts of illustration made such books and articles unusually attractive. Now came Mark Twain's iconoclastic, funny, copiously illustrated book, so fresh and different—it was no wonder that it made its author famous.

But Mark still thought of himself as a journalist, and soon he settled down in Buffalo and bought a half-interest in the *Express* of that city. He married Olivia Langdon, an intelligent, self-poised semi-invalid, sister of one of Mark's fellow-passengers on the *Quaker City*. The Langdons were a cultivated family, socially and financially established, and the ebullient westerner won his bride only after a persistent courtship. After a little over a year of Buffalo, Mark sold his interest in the *Express* and moved to Quarry Farm, near Elmira, to finish his next book.

Also distinctively belonging to the category of travel literature was *Roughing It,* published in 1872, in which Mark tells the story of his journey across the plains to Carson City, his adventures in Nevada and California, and his visit to the Sandwich Islands. The zest of the narration in this book, its vividness and strength, and its free swing of imagination make it a perennial favorite with many of Mark Twain's admirers.

It was shortly after the publication of *Roughing It* that its author realized he was embarked on a definitely literary career. Not that he abandoned journalism or lecturing; but the new book was making his second major literary success, and he resolved to make his home in Hartford, where his publishers were located, and become a writer of books. The subscription book businesss, long a modest success in the publishing industry, had expanded remarkably after the war; and both *The Innocents* and *Roughing It* had been distributed by the American Publishing Company, of Hartford, wholly through book-agents. At Hartford, too, Mark enjoyed a more literary society than any he had known before; among his near neighbors were Charles Dudley Warner and Harriet Beecher Stowe.

IV

The value of the "refining process" to which Mark Twain's reckless and sometimes crude western humor was subjected has long been a subject of dispute among critics, but of the process itself there can be no question. It had begun before Mark came to Hartford. An early influence of the kind was Anson Burlingame, minister to China, whom he met at Honolulu, and whose advice to seek refined companionship greatly impressed him. Another counselor in this direction was Mrs. Mary Mason Fairbanks, wife of the publisher of the Cleveland *Herald,* who was one of the *Quaker City* excursion party, and whose motherly interest followed Mark for many years.

The most important of Mark Twain's literary advisers, however, was his wife. Probably most writers' wives read their husbands' literary output long before it reaches the stage of proof-sheets, and some read it with flattering eagerness but with eyes sharp for slips, errors of taste, aberrations of judgment. Such a "critic on the hearth" was Livy Clemens. Careful studies of the considerable body of data relating to her influence on her husband's work lead to the conclusion that her advice was usually pretty sound and helpful. Mark nearly always worked and reworked his copy, revised, sweat and labored over it, and threw away thousands of words. He knew he was no impeccable genius, and he constantly sought and often deferred to his wife's judgment.

Another major influence was William Dean Howells, editor of the *Atlantic*

Monthly and a close personal friend from the time Mark moved to New England until the end of his life. Howells was an ardent admirer from the first, and a competent literary adviser. It is easy to abuse him for his objection to Huck's complaint, "They comb me all to hell"; but Howells was thinking of the book for which this was written as one designed largely for youngsters—and besides, this was in the 1870's. Mark's growing acquaintance with the cultivated classes, though it never subdued that native buoyancy which is the essence of the Mark Twain spirit, did have its effect upon him. He never lost his contempt for sham and pretence, or his burning indignation against injustice and persecution; but he became a better literary craftsman in matters of fundamental taste, as well as in literary style. His steady improvement as a virtuoso with words is a phase of Mark Twain's career that is often overlooked.

In Hartford the Clemens family made many friends. Mark collaborated with Charles Dudley Warner in *The Gilded Age,* and he formed an intimate and life-long friendship with the Rev. Joseph Twitchell, of Hartford. He became a member of the Monday Evening Club, though when a meeting was too dull and pious (as happens in such organizations) he was apt to complain about the "tiresome damned prayer-meetings." After a year or two in Hartford, the Clemenses built the house which was to become increasingly, as Mark's fame spread, a Mecca for admirers from far and near.

The Gilded Age was a finely conceived novel with a wide sweep, intended to portray the American scene and spirit in the inflated and corrupt era immediately following the Civil War. The masterly character of Colonel Sellers, archetype of the sanguine American speculator whose great schemes never quite come off but whose failures are only springboards to new hopes, does much to redeem a book which, despite its values of realism and satire, must be marked down as one of the misfortunes of unequal collaboration. A play using Colonel Sellers as the central character was successful on the stage; and a second play, in which Sellers pursues an English earldom, was rewritten years later into an amusing novel called *The American Claimant* (1892).

In 1872 and 1873 Mark made trips to England, to lecture and to attend to details of publishing his work there. In 1877 he made a trip to Bermuda with Twitchell, and most of the next two years he spent, with his family, in Germany and Italy. He still had the romantic urge for travel, but now and henceforth there was more than that behind his journeying; he was well on the way to becoming a world figure.

In 1875 *Sketches New and Old* was published. Although very uneven, it represents well the early, spontaneous, journalistic Mark Twain whose reputation was made largely by these short pieces. It contained "The Jumping Frog," "A True Story," some of the newspaper hoaxes, a few after-dinner speeches, and so on. In the same year "Old Times on the Mississippi" appeared serially in the *Atlantic Monthly.* In these papers Mark gave literary form to the spirit of the great river in the fine, robust days of steamboating, with the humor, the vivid recollection of the sleepy river towns, the autocratic rule of the pilots and their complicated art, and all the color and imaginative zest that kept vital his remembrance of some of the happiest years of his life. Here were romance and travel and humor—a strong combination. The papers were included eight years later in *Life on the Mississippi*. In that book the matter was doubled by the addition of a more journalistic account of his observations in revisiting the river and other chapters which were frankly padding.

Tom Sawyer, based on the author's recollections of his own boyhood, was published in 1876. In that year of grace it was a bold thing to write a book about an honest-to-goodness boy, running wild in a little river town, leading a gang of young rapscallions, getting involved in a murder, and displaying what Mark called "the natural cussedness" of boyhood. But the fine unity of the tale, its honesty, and its natural and spontaneous humor gave it an immediate and continuing success. It made Mark Twain's fame secure and was to become the leader of all his books in total sales in America and the world over. The later *Tom Sawyer Abroad* (1894) is in many respects a good boys' travel book, but *Tom Sawyer, Detective* (1896) seems a sad mistake; both are little more than novelettes.

A Tramp Abroad (1880) was based on the author's recent travels in Europe. Some of its comic devices scarcely "come off," but there are excellent humorous chapters and some even more pleasing serious descriptions.

The early months of 1885 brought the American book publication of *The Adventures of Huckleberry Finn*, which had been printed serially (with some expurgations) in the *Century Magazine* and also published in London in 1884. It was a continuation of the vein of boyhood reminiscence opened in *Tom Sawyer*, and is the book upon which critics generally agree as Mark Twain's masterpiece. It is a saga of the Mississippi, full of the inexhaustible charm and fascination of the great river. The conversations of Huck and Jim, the adventures which are so characteristic of the life of the river communities, the descriptions of day and night and life on and along the river combine to give a tone and significance to the story which make it a great American masterpiece.

Mark Twain's first considerable venture into the field of historical romance was *The Prince and the Pauper* (1880). It represents his reaction to the class injustices which he had felt so strongly in England. Perhaps inconsistent with this theme was the design to make it a book for boys and girls, though it is probably better to write a little over the heads of a juvenile audience than to write down to it. The masquerading of the outcast boy as the prince is a good, if not quite original, romantic device; and though some of Mark's reactions to English life may seem naïve, there was certainly reason for his furious indignation against phases of the English penal system and other abuses. *A Connecticut Yankee in King Arthur's Court* (1889), another excursion into

English history, is an extraordinary performance. Sam Clemens, the traveler, had debunked the revered sights and scenes of the grand tour in *Innocents Abroad;* now in this later book he debunks Arthurian romance, using the character of "Sir Boss," a hard-headed American cast into the milieu of early English life. Knighthood was not "in flower" for Mark Twain; he saw too much of its basic filth and cruelty and treachery. The weakness of his thesis is not in his hatred of the evil in King Arthur's court but in his apparent belief that modern industrialism was the cure. Third of Mark Twain's historical romances was *Joan of Arc* (1896), a much more careful and seriously designed work. "I like the *Joan of Arc* best of all my books," wrote the author, "and it is the best; I know it perfectly well." Based on historical facts but embroidered by a multitude of imaginative details, presenting the mystical elements of the life of the Maid with reverence and with an amazing illusion of actuality, lighted by the flame of indignation against injustice, this fictional biography is a masterpiece of its kind.

V

While these books represent the main stream of Mark Twain's career for some two decades now that he had become a man of letters, they by no means comprehend his total effort. His active mind reached out in many directions. He was always excited about some novel scheme, or some new development of an old plan. Inventions fascinated him; he himself patented a new kind of scrapbook and a history game. He put large sums of money into an improvement in engraving which did not work out, and later much larger sums into a typesetting machine which was never successful. He went into the subscription publishing business, setting up a nephew as manager of the Charles L. Webster Publishing Company. But he was no business man, as any reader of his letters to Webster must know. It was not merely that he was too optimistic, but he had no head for figures nor any talent for accounts. But the Webster concern's first book was *Huckleberry Finn,* a pronounced success; and a little later it made another smash hit with General Grant's *Memoirs*. It got into difficulties, however, in connection with its grand project, Stedman and Hutchison's *Library of American Literature,* and in the panic year of 1893 it was forced into bankruptcy.

The firm paid nearly fifty cents on the dollar, but Clemens declared that he would eventually pay every penny of its indebtedness. He plunged into writing, working harder than ever. *Pudd'nhead Wilson* appeared in 1894, and *Joan of Arc* was printed serially in *Harper's Magazine* two years later. This was after he had started on his world-girdling lecture tour. Mark was growing old, and he had come to hate the hardships of lecturing; but to meet his debts he made plans for lecturing around the world, with a book to follow, detailing his experiences. He set out in 1895, with great audiences as he crossed the American continent, and more of them in Australia. He spent his sixtieth birthday in New Zealand, crisscrossed India in tropic heat, toured South Africa, and reached England in the summer of the next year. *Following the Equator,* his last travel book, was written at Guildford, in Surrey, and published near the end of 1897. Early the next year the debt was entirely paid off. Mark's personal friend, H. H. Rogers, Standard Oil and railroad magnate, had managed the bankruptcy and the settlement, and continued thereafter to advise Mark in all financial matters.

After a vacation on the Continent, the Clemenses returned to New York in 1900. All America gave Mark Twain a conquering hero's welcome, with banquets, speeches, laudatory editorials, and an honorary degree from Yale.

Yet it was a sad homecoming, too, for their beloved daughter Susie had died during the absence of the rest of the family; another daughter, Jean, had developed epilepsy, from which she was never wholly to recover; Livy's health had declined; and finally news had come of the death of Orion. The family agreed that they could not return to the Hartford house, with its memories of Susie, and they made their home in New York.

There had always been a cynical vein in Mark Twain: it is summed up in his famous phrase, "the damned human race." Perhaps personal misfortune had something to do with his emphasis on this phase of his thinking and feeling in his later years. Yet such sorrows were not new to him, and he had always reacted almost hysterically to death in his family. He had blamed himself for the tragic death of his brother Henry in a steamboat accident on the Mississippi. He had lost his first-born child and only son in infancy, and his year in Buffalo had been filled with almost unbroken domestic tragedy. Perhaps it was a cumulative indignation against life to which he gave vent in a series of essays, editorials, and stories in the last decade of his career. Or perhaps there was in it something of the old man whose age and position gave him freedom to speak out more loudly than ever before against clearly seen evils, and to be crotchety when he felt like it.

Surely his outbursts against England's war with the Boers, Funston's capture of Aguinaldo, King Leopold's outrages in the Congo, and the Boxer indemnity increase our respect for the intellectual integrity of Mark Twain. In such editorials he became the spokesman for the under-dog in international affairs. In his short story, "The Man Who Corrupted Hadleyburg," he delivered the most stinging rebuke to hypocrisy in our literature. "What Is Man?" was something different—a pseudo-philosophic essay on the mechanistic idea of existence, with a strongly sentimental pessimism. This idea had taken hold of him in the eighties, but he did not write his essay until 1898, and did not allow it to be printed (and then privately) until 1906. His hesitation in writing and printing the essay was due to his feeling that it was shocking.

It suggested a system of belief lacking in the element of faith; and however much he might deny it for argument's sake, he had still a very real residuum of faith himself. The modern reader familiar with the mechanistic philosophy cannot help finding *What Is Man* somewhat too naïve. *The Mysterious Stranger,* published six years after the author's death, is a fable based on an even more thorough philosophy of pessimism.

The Mark Twain of 1900, who walked the streets of New York in his white clothes, with his keen hawklike face, deep-set tragic eyes, and waving white hair, was a figure of great distinction. No American was better known or better loved. He had come a long way from the obscure pioneer village of Hannibal, Missouri. He had brought the life of the great river and of the far-western frontier home to the East. He had performed a literary merger of America; beyond other writers he had become an all-American figure. But he had done more than that: he had become truly a world personality. His famous lecturing trip "following the Equator," his occasional residence in Europe, his outspoken commentary on international affairs, and the honorary degree conferred upon him by Oxford University in 1907 all testified that Mark Twain belonged no more to Hannibal, nor to America, but to the world.

He had also come a long way in mind and spirit. Child of the frontier, his early reliance was upon the burlesque and tall tales and caricature of the rough pioneer literature. His great artistic triumph was his welding of the romantic individualism, the love of nature, and the rebellion against conventionalism characteristic of the pioneer spirit into the great picturesque and picaresque tales of boyhood—*Huckleberry Finn* and *Tom Sawyer.*

Rebellion was an essential part of Mark Twain from the beginning—rebellion against the Sunday School, against an ordered life in one place, against entrenched injustice, against sham and hypocrisy, against graft and the oppression that goes with it. The humorist's weapon against such evils is satire, and Mark Twain was a satirist from his earliest trials in authorship to his last trenchant pages dictated from his death-bed. His writings as a whole do not have the unity of the works of an Emerson. His sails caught too many winds blowing from all quarters, and his craft tacked about too much. His sensitiveness to friendship, his active sympathies, his quick emotional responses made it impossible for him to be the settled spokesman of a philosophy. But in this one aspect he was consistent throughout his life: he was a rebel and a hater of shams. Whatever effect, for good or evil, "refinement" had upon him, he was always a vocal rebel.

And in his quality as satirist, too, Mark Twain had come a long way. His tweaking the noses of the San Francisco police was child's play in comparison with his pleas for the common people in *A Connecticut Yankee* and *Joan.* His attack on the schemes of San Francisco utility companies was sheer buffoonery in comparison with "To the Person Sitting in Darkness."

Livy died in 1904 and Jean five years later. Mark bought a small farm near Redding, Connecticut, and built a house on it, which he called "Stormfield." In his last years he loved to lie in his great white bed, propped up on pillows, smoking his everlasting cigars, talking with his friends, and dictating his prolix autobiography. He died on April 10, 1910. "Death," wrote Howells, "touched his familiar image into historic grandeur."

[Albert Bigelow Paine's four-volume *Mark Twain, A Biography* (New York, 1912), the biography authorized by its subject, leaves much to be desired. The best single-volume comprehensive life is DeLancey Ferguson's *Mark Twain, Man and Legend* (Indianapolis, 1943). It may well be supplemented by Minnie M. Brashear's *Mark Twain, Son of Missouri* (Chapel Hill, 1934) and Ivan Benson's *Mark Twain's Western Years* (Stanford, 1938). Van Wyck Brooks' *The Ordeal of Mark Twain* (New York, 1920) advances the "thwarted genius" theory. The most complete reply is found in Bernard DeVoto's *Mark Twain's America* (Boston, 1932), which is valuable for much more than that reply; De Voto's later *Mark Twain at Work* (Cambridge, 1942) is a continuation of this study. William Dean Howells' *My Mark Twain* (New York, 1910) and Clara Clemens' *My Father, Mark Twain* (New York, 1931) have documentary value. The *Autobiography* (New York, 1924, 2 vols.) is disappointing but not without interest and usefulness. Essays presenting divergent views of Mark Twain's work may be found in F. L. Pattee's *Mark Twain* (New York, 1935), in American Writers Series, and W. F. Taylor's *The Economic Novel in America* (Chapel Hill, 1942). Edward Wagenknecht's *Mark Twain, the Man and His Work* (New Haven, 1935) is well balanced and competent.]

THE INDIGNITY PUT UPON THE REMAINS OF GEORGE HOLLAND BY THE REV. MR. SABINE.[1]

[1871]

WHAT a ludicrous satire it was upon Christian charity!—even upon the vague, theoretical idea of it which doubtless this small saint mouths from his own pulpit every Sunday. Contemplate this freak of Nature, and think what a Cardiff giant of self-righteousness is crowded into his pigmy skin. If we probe, and dissect, and lay open this diseased, this cancerous piety of his, we are forced to the conviction that it is the production of an impression on his part that his guild do about all the good that is done in the earth, and hence are better than common clay—hence are competent to say to such as George Holland,[2] "You are unworthy; you are a play-actor, and consequently a sinner; I cannot take the responsibility of recommending you to the mercy of Heaven." It must have had its origin in that impression, else he would have thought, "We are all instruments for the carrying out of God's

[1] Rev. William F. Sabine had refused to allow an actor's funeral to be held from his church, but suggested "a little church around the corner," which would probably permit the ceremonies. This became the designation of the Church of the Transfiguration on Twenty-ninth Street, New York—long a favorite place of worship for actors. This comment appeared in the *Galaxy.*

[2] George Holland (1791-1871) was an English-born comedian associated chiefly with New York and New Orleans theatres.

purposes; it is not for me to pass judgment upon your appointed share of the work, or to praise or to revile it; I have divine authority for it that we are *all* sinners, and therefore it is not for me to discriminate and say we will supplicate for this sinner, for he was a merchant prince or a banker, but we will beseech no forgiveness for this other one, for he was a play-actor." It surely requires the furthest possible reach of self-righteousness to enable a man to lift his scornful nose in the air and turn his back upon so poor and pitiable a thing as a dead stranger come to beg the last kindness that humanity can do in its behalf. This creature has violated the letter of the gospel and judged George Holland—not George Holland either, but his *profession* through him. Then it is in a measure fair that we judge this creature's guild through *him*. In effect he has said, "We are the salt of the earth; we do all the good work that is done; to learn how to be good and do good, men must come to us; actors and such are obstacles to moral progress." [3] Pray look at the thing reasonably for a moment, laying aside all biasses of education and custom. If a common public impression is fair evidence of a thing, then this minister's legitimate, recognized, and acceptable business is to *tell* people calmly, coldly, and in stiff, written sentences, from the pulpit, to go and do right, be just, be merciful, be charitable. And his congregation forget it all between church and home. But for fifty years it was George Holland's business, on the stage, to *make* his audience go and do right, and be just, merciful, and charitable—because by his living, breathing, feeling pictures, he showed them what it *was* to do these things, and *how* to do them, and how instant and ample was the reward! Is it not a singular teacher of men, this reverend gentleman who is so poorly informed himself as to put the whole stage under ban, and say, "I do not think it teaches moral lessons"?

Where was ever a sermon preached that could make filial ingratitude so hateful to men as the sinful play of "King Lear"? Or where was there ever a sermon that could so convince men of the wrong and the cruelty of harboring a pampered and unanalyzed jealousy as the sinful play of "Othello"? And where are there ten preachers who can stand in the pulpit teaching heroism, unselfish devotion, and lofty patriotism, and hold their own against any one of five hundred William Tells that can be raised up upon five hundred stages in the land at a day's notice? It is almost fair and just to aver (although it is profanity) that nine-tenths of all the kindness and forbearance and Christian charity and generosity in the hearts of the American people today, got thereby being filtered down from their fountain-head, the gospel of Christ, *through dramas and tragedies and comedies on the stage, and through the despised novel and the Christmas story, and through the thousand and one lessons, suggestions, and narratives of generous deeds that stir the pulses, and exalt and augment the nobility of the nation day by day from the teeming columns of ten thousand newspapers,* and NOT from the drowsy pulpit!

All that is great and good in our particular civilization came straight from the hand of Jesus Christ, and many crea-

---

[3] Reporter—What answer did you make, Mr. Sabine?

Mr. Sabine—I said that I had a distaste for officiating at such a funeral, and that I did not care to be mixed up in it. I said to the gentleman that I was willing to bury the deceased from his house, but that I objected to having the funeral solemnized at a church.

Reporter—Is it one of the laws of the Protestant Episcopal Church that a deceased theatrical performer shall not be buried from the church?

Mr. Sabine—It is not; but I have always warned the professing members of my congregation to keep away from theatres and not to have anything to do with them. I don't think that they teach moral lessons.—*New York Times.* [Author's footnote.]

tures, and of divers sorts, were doubtless appointed to disseminate it; and let us believe that *this seed and the result* are the main thing, and not the cut of the sower's garment; and that whosoever, in his way and according to his opportunity, sows the one and produces the other, has done high service and worthy. And further, let us try with all our strength to believe that whenever old simple-hearted George Holland sowed this seed, and reared his crop of broader charities and better impulses in men's hearts, it was just as acceptable before the Throne as if the seed had been scattered in vapid platitudes from the pulpit of the ineffable Sabine himself.

Am I saying that the pulpit does not do its share toward disseminating the marrow, the *meat* of the gospel of Chirst? (For we are not talking of ceremonies and wiredrawn creeds now, but the living heart and soul of what is pretty often only a spectre.)

No, I am not saying that. The pulpit teaches assemblages of people twice a week—nearly two hours, altogether—and does what it can in that time. The theatre teaches large audiences seven times a week—28 or 30 hours altogether; and the novels and newspapers plead, and argue, and illustrate, stir, move, thrill, thunder, urge, persuade, and supplicate, at the feet of millions and millions of people every single day, and all day long, and far into the night; and so these vast agencies till *nine-tenths* of the vineyard, and the pulpit tills the other tenth. Yet now and then some complacent blind idiot says, "You unanointed are coarse clay and useless; you are not as we, the regenerators of the world; go, bury yourselves elsewhere, for we cannot take the responsibility of recommending idlers and sinners to the yearning mercy of Heaven." How *does* a soul like that stay in a carcass without getting mixed with the secretions and sweated out through the pores? Think of this insect condemning the whole theatrical service as a disseminator of bad morals because it has Black Crooks [4] in it; forgetting that if that were sufficient ground, people would condemn the pulpit because it had Cooks,[5] and Kallochs,[6] and Sabines in it.

No, I am not trying to rob the pulpit of any atom of its full share and credit in the work of disseminating the meat and marrow of the gospel of Christ; but I am trying to get a moment's hearing for worthy agencies in the same work, that with overwrought modesty seldom or never claim a recognition of their great services. I am aware that the pulpit does its excellent one-tenth (and credits itself with it now and then, though most of the time a press of business causes it to forget it); I am aware that in its honest and well-meaning way it bores the people with uninflammable truisms about doing good; bores them with correct compositions on charity; bores them, chloroforms them, stupefies them with argumentative mercy without a flaw in the grammar, or an emotion which the minister could put in the right place if he turned his back and took his finger off the manuscript. And in doing these things the pulpit is doing its duty, and let us believe that it is likewise doing its best, and doing it in the most harmless and respectable way. And so I have said, and shall keep on saying, let us give the pulpit its full share of credit in elevating and ennobling the people; but when a pulpit takes to itself authority to pass judgment upon the work and the worth of just as legitimate an instrument of God as itself, who spent a long life preaching from the stage the self-same gospel without the alteration of a single sentiment or a single axiom of right, it is fair and just for somebody who be-

[4] "The Black Crook" was a scandalous light opera burlesque of the 1870's.

[5] This is probably a reference to Flavius Josephus Cook (1838-1901), then attracting attention by his controversial preaching.

[6] Isaac Kalloch (1808-1887) was a notorious clergyman and politician, mayor of San Francisco, 1879-81.

lieves that actors were made for a high and good purpose, and that they *accomplish the object of their creation* and accomplish it well, to protest. And having protested, it is also fair and just—being driven to it, as it were—to whisper to the Sabine pattern of clergyman, under the breath, a simple, instructive truth, and say, "Ministers are not the only servants of God upon earth, nor His most efficient ones either, by a very, very long distance!" Sensible ministers already know this, and it may do the other kind good to find it out.

But to cease teaching and go back to the beginning again, was it not pitiable, that spectacle? Honored and honorable old George Holland, whose theatrical ministry had for fifty years softened hard hearts, bred generosity in cold ones, kindled emotion in dead ones, uplifted base ones, broadened bigoted ones, and made many and many a stricken one glad and filled it brim full of gratitude, figuratively spit upon in his unoffending coffin by this crawling, slimy, sanctimonious, self-righteous reptile!

From
ROUGHING IT
[1872]

CHAPTER I

MY BROTHER had just been appointed Secretary of Nevada Territory [1]— an office of such majesty that it concentrated in itself the duties and dignities of Treasurer, Comptroller, Secretary of State, and Acting Governor in the Governor's absence. A salary of eighteen hundred dollars a year and the title of "Mr. Secretary" gave to the great position an air of wild and imposing grandeur. I was young and ignorant, and I envied my brother. I coveted his distinction and his financial splendor, but particularly and especially the long, strange journey he was going to make, and the curious new world he was going to explore. He was going to travel! I never had been away from home,[2]

and that word "travel" had a seductive charm for me. Pretty soon he would be hundreds and hundreds of miles away on the great plains and deserts, and among the mountains of the Far West, and would see buffaloes and Indians, and prairie-dogs, and antelopes, and have all kinds of adventures, and maybe get hanged or scalped, and have ever such a fine time, and write home and tell us all about it, and be a hero. And he would see the gold-mines and the silver-mines, and maybe go about of an afternoon when his work was done, and pick up two or three pailfuls of shining slugs and nuggets of gold and silver on the hillside. And by and by he would become very rich, and return home by sea, and be able to talk as calmly about San Francisco and the ocean and "the isthmus" as if it was nothing of any consequence to have seen those marvels face to face. What I suffered in contemplating his happiness, pen cannot describe. And so, when he offered me, in cold blood, the sublime position of private secretary under him, it appeared to me that the heavens and earth passed away, and the firmament was rolled together as a scroll! I had nothing more to desire. My contentment was complete. At the end of an hour or two I was ready for the journey. Not much packing up was necessary, because we were going in the overland stage from the Missouri frontier to Nevada, and passengers were only allowed a small quantity of baggage apiece. There was no Pacific railroad in those fine times of ten or twelve years ago—not a single rail of it.

I only proposed to stay in Nevada three months—I had no thought of staying longer than that. I meant to see all I could that was new and strange, and then

[1] Orion M. Clemens was appointed to this office by President Lincoln on the recommendation of Attorney General Edward Bates, in whose St. Louis office Orion had read law.

[2] As a matter of fact, the author had worked in New York and Philadelphia as a printer and had traveled up and down the Mississippi as a pilot.

hurry home to business. I little thought that I would not see the end of that three-month pleasure excursion for six or seven uncommonly long years!

I dreamed all night about Indians, deserts, and silver bars, and in due time, next day, we took shipping at the St. Louis wharf on board a steamboat bound up the Missouri River.

We were six days going from St. Louis to "St. Joe"—a trip that was so dull, and sleepy, and eventless that it has left no more impression on my memory than if its duration had been six minutes instead of that many days. No record is left in my mind, now, concerning it, but a confused jumble of savage-looking snags, which we deliberately walked over with one wheel or the other; and of reefs which we butted and butted, and then retired from and climbed over in some softer place; and of sand-bars which we roosted on occasionally, and rested, and then got out our crutches and sparred over. In fact, the boat might almost as well have gone to St. Joe by land, for she was walking most of the time, anyhow—climbing over reefs and clambering over snags patiently and laboriously all day long. The captain said she was a "bully" boat, and all she wanted was more "shear" and a bigger wheel. I thought she wanted a pair of stilts, but I had the deep sagacity not to say so.

CHAPTER II

The first thing we did on that glad evening that landed us at St. Joseph was to hunt up the stage-office, and pay a hundred and fifty dollars apiece for tickets per overland coach to Carson City, Nevada.

The next morning, bright and early, we took a hasty breakfast, and hurried to the starting-place. Then an inconvenience presented itself which we had not properly appreciated before, namely, that one cannot make a heavy traveling trunk stand for twenty-five pounds of baggage—because it weighs a good deal more. But that was all we could take—twenty-five pounds each. So

we had to snatch our trunks open, and make a selection in a good deal of a hurry. We put our lawful twenty-five pounds apiece all in one valise, and shipped the trunks back to St. Louis again. It was a sad parting, for now we had no swallow-tail coats and white kid gloves to wear at Pawnee receptions in the Rocky Mountains, and no stove-pipe hats nor patent-leather boots, nor anything else necessary to make life calm and peaceful. We were reduced to a war-footing. Each of us put on a rough, heavy suit of clothing, woolen army shirt and "stogy" boots included; and into the valise we crowded a few white shirts, some underclothing and such things. My brother, the Secretary, took along about four pounds of United States statutes and six pounds of Unabridged Dictionary; for we did not know—poor innocents—that such things could be bought in San Francisco on one day and received in Carson City the next. I was armed to the teeth with a pitiful little Smith & Wesson's seven-shooter, which carried a ball like a homeopathic pill, and it took the whole seven to make a dose for an adult. But I thought it was grand. It appeared to me to be a dangerous weapon. It only had one fault—you could not hit anything with it. One of our "conductors" practised awhile on a cow with it, and as long as she stood still and behaved herself she was safe; but as soon as she went to moving about, and he got to shooting at other things, she came to grief. The Secretary had a small-sized Colt's revolver strapped around him for protection against the Indians, and to guard against accidents he carried it uncapped. Mr. George Bemis [2] was dismally formidable. George Bemis was our fellow-traveler. We had never seen him before. He wore in his belt an old original "Allen" revolver, such as irreverent people called a "pepper-box." Simply drawing the trigger back, cocked and fired the pistol. As the trigger came back,

[3] George P. Bemis (1838-1910), financier, later mayor of Omaha.

the hammer would begin to rise and the barrel to turn over, and presently down would drop the hammer, and away would speed the ball. To aim along the turning barrel and hit the thing aimed at was a feat which was probably never done with an "Allen" in the world. But George's was a reliable weapon, nevertheless, because, as one of the stage-drivers afterward said, "If she didn't get what she went after, she would fetch something else." And so she did. She went after a deuce of spades nailed against a tree, once, and fetched a mule standing about thirty yards to the left of it. Bemis did not want the mule; but the owner came out with a double-barreled shotgun and persuaded him to buy it, anyhow. It was a cheerful weapon—the "Allen." Sometimes all its six barrels would go off at once, and then there was no safe place in all the region round about, but behind it.

We took two or three blankets for protection against frosty weather in the mountains. In the matter of luxuries we were modest—we took none along but some pipes and five pounds of smoking-tobacco. We had two large canteens to carry water in, between stations on the Plains, and we also took with us a little shot-bag of silver coin for daily expenses in the way of breakfasts and dinners.

By eight o'clock [4] everything was ready, and we were on the other side of the river. We jumped into the stage, the driver cracked his whip, and we bowled away and left "the States" behind us. It was a superb summer morning, and all the landscape was brilliant with sunshine. There was a freshness and breeziness, too, and an exhilarating sense of emancipation from all sorts of cares and responsibilities, that almost made us feel that the years we had spent in the close, hot city, toiling and slaving, had been wasted and thrown away. We were spinning along through Kansas, and in the course of an hour and a half we were fairly abroad on the great Plains. Just here the land was rolling—a grand sweep of regular elevations and depressions

as far as the eye could reach—like the stately heave and swell of the ocean's bosom after a storm. And everywhere were corn-fields, accenting with squares of deeper green this limitless expanse of grassy land. But presently this sea upon dry ground was to lose its "rolling" character and stretch away for seven hundred miles as level as a floor!

Our coach was a great swinging and swaying stage, of the most sumptuous description—an imposing cradle on wheels. It was drawn by six handsome horses, and by the side of the driver sat the "conductor," the legitimate captain of the craft; for it was his business to take charge and care of the mails, baggage, express matter, and passengers. We three were the only passengers, this trip. We sat on the back seat, inside. About all the rest of the coach was full of mail-bags—for we had three days' delayed mails with us. Almost touching our knees, a perpendicular wall of mail matter rose up to the roof. There was a great pile of it strapped on top of the stage, and both the fore and hind boots were full. We had twenty-seven hundred pounds of it aboard, the driver said—"a little for Brigham, and Carson, and 'Frisco, but the heft of it for the Injuns, which is powerful troublesome 'thout they get plenty of truck to read." But as he just then got up a fearful convulsion of his countenance which was suggestive of a wink being swallowed by an earthquake, we guessed that his remark was intended to be facetious, and to mean that we would unload the most of our mail matter somewhere on the Plains and leave it to the Indians, or whosoever wanted it.

We changed horses every ten miles, all day long, and fairly flew over the hard, level road. We jumped out and stretched our legs. every time the coach stopped, and so the night found us still vivacious and unfatigued.

After supper a woman got in, who lived about fifty miles further on; and we three

---

[4] On July 26, 1861.

had to take turns at sitting outside with the driver and conductor. Apparently she was not a talkative woman. She would sit there in the gathering twilight and fasten her steadfast eyes on a mosquito rooting into her arm, and slowly she would raise her other hand till she had got his range, and then she would launch a slap at him that would have jolted a cow; and after that she would sit and contemplate the corpse with tranquil satisfaction—for she never missed her mosquito; she was a dead shot at short range. She never removed a carcass, but left them there for bait. I sat by this grim Sphinx and watched her kill thirty or forty mosquitoes—watched her, and waited for her to say something, but she never did. So I finally opened the conversation myself. I said:

"The mosquitoes are pretty bad, about here, madam."

"You bet!"

"What did I understand you to say, madam?"

"You BET!"

Then she cheered up, and faced around and said:

"Danged if I didn't begin to think you fellers was deef and dumb. I did, b'gosh. Here I've sot, and sot, and sot, a-bust'n' muskeeters and wonderin' what was ailin' ye. Fust I thot you was deef and dumb, then I thot you was sick or crazy, or suthin', and then by and by I begin to reckon you was a passel of sickly fools that couldn't think of nothing to say. Where'd ye come from?"

The Sphinx was a Sphinx no more! The fountains of her great deep were broken up, and she rained the nine parts of speech forty days and forty nights, metaphorically speaking, and buried us under a desolating deluge of trivial gossip that left not a crag or pinnacle of rejoinder projecting above the tossing waste of dislocated grammar and decomposed pronunciation!

How we suffered, suffered, suffered! She went on, hour after hour, till I was sorry I ever opened the mosquito question and gave her a start. She never did stop again

until she got to her journey's end toward daylight; and then she stirred us up as she was leaving the stage (for we were nodding, by that time), and said:

"Now you git out at Cottonwood, you fellers, and lay over a couple o' days, and I'll be along some time to-night, and if I can do ye any good by edgin' in a word now and then, I'm right thar. Folks 'll tell you 't I've always ben kind o' offish and partic'lar for a gal that's raised in the woods, and I *am*, with the ragtag and bobtail, and a gal *has* to be, if she wants to *be* anything, but when people comes along which is my equals, I reckon I'm a pretty sociable heifer after all."

We resolved not to "lay by at Cottonwood."

CHAPTER III

About an hour and a half before daylight we were bowling along smoothly over the road—so smoothly that our cradle only rocked in a gentle, lulling way, that was gradually soothing us to sleep, and dulling our consciousness—when something gave away under us! We were dimly aware of it, but indifferent to it. The coach stopped. We heard the driver and conductor talking together outside, and rummaging for a lantern, and swearing because they could not find it—but we had no interest in whatever had happened, and it only added to our comfort to think of those people out there at work in the murky night, and we snug in our nest with the curtains drawn. But presently, by the sounds, there seemed to be an examination going on, and then the driver's voice said:

"By George, the thoroughbrace is broke!"

This startled me broad awake—as an undefined sense of calamity is always apt to do. I said to myself: "Now, a thoroughbrace is probably part of a horse; and doubtless a vital part, too, from the dismay in the driver's voice. Leg, maybe—and yet how could he break his leg waltzing along such a road as this? No, it can't be his leg. That is impossible, unless he was reaching for the driver. Now, what can be the thoroughbrace of a horse, I wonder? Well, whatever comes, I shall not air my ignorance in this crowd, anyway."

Just then the conductor's face appeared at a lifted curtain, and his lantern glared in on us and our wall of mail matter. He said:

"Gents, you'll have to turn out a spell. Thoroughbrace is broke."

We climbed out into a chill drizzle, and felt ever so homeless and dreary. When I found that the thing they called a "thoroughbrace" was the massive combination of belts and springs which the coach rocks itself in, I said to the driver:

"I never saw a thoroughbrace used up like that, before, that I can remember. How did it happen?"

"Why, it happened by trying to make one coach carry three days' mail—that's how it happened," said he. "And right here is the very direction which is wrote on all the newspaper-bags which was to be put out for the Injuns for to keep 'em quiet. It's most uncommon lucky, becuz it's so nation dark I should 'a' gone by unbeknowns if that air thoroughbrace hadn't broke."

I knew that he was in labor with another of those winks of his, though I could not see his face, because he was bent down at work; and wishing him a safe delivery, I turned to and helped the rest get out the mail-sacks. It made a great pyramid by the roadside when it was all out. When they had mended the thoroughbrace we filled the two boots again, but put no mail on top, and only half as much inside as there was before. The conductor bent all the seat-backs down, and then filled the coach just half full of mail-bags from end to end. We objected loudly to this, for it left us no seats. But the conductor was wiser than we, and said a bed was better than seats, and, moreover, this plan would protect his thoroughbraces. We never wanted any seats after that. The lazy bed was infinitely preferable. I had many an exciting day,

subsequently, lying on it reading the statutes and the dictionary, and wondering how the characters would turn out.

The conductor said he would send back a guard from the next station to take charge of the abandoned mail-bags, and we drove on.

It was now just dawn; and as we stretched our cramped legs full length on the mail-sacks, and gazed out through the windows across the wide wastes of greensward clad in cool, powdery mist, to where there was an expectant look in the eastern horizon, our perfect enjoyment took the form of a tranquil and contented ecstasy. The stage whirled along at a spanking gait, the breeze flapping curtains and suspended coats in a most exhilarating way; the cradle swayed and swung luxuriously, the pattering of the horses' hoofs, the cracking of the driver's whip, and his "Hi-yi! g'lang!" were music; the spinning ground and the waltzing trees appeared to give us a mute hurrah as we went by, and then slack up and look after us with interest, or envy, or something; and as we lay and smoked the pipe of peace and compared all this luxury with the years of tiresome city life that had gone before it, we felt that there was only one complete and satisfying happiness in the world, and we had found it.

After breakfast, at some station whose name I have forgotten, we three climbed up on the seat behind the driver, and let the conductor have our bed for a nap. And by and by, when the sun made me drowsy, I lay down on my face on top of the coach, grasping the slender iron railing, and slept for an hour more. That will give one an appreciable idea of those matchless roads. Instinct will make a sleeping man grip a fast hold of the railing when the stage jolts, but when it only swings and sways, no grip is necessary. Overland drivers and conductors used to sit in their places and sleep thirty or forty minutes at a time, on good roads, while spinning along at the rate of eight or ten miles an hour. I saw them do it, often. There was no danger about it; a sleeping man *will* seize the irons in time when the coach jolts. These men were hard worked, and it was not possible for them to stay awake all the time.

By and by we passed through Marysville, and over the Big Blue and Little Sandy; thence about a mile, and entered Nebraska. About a mile further on, we came to the Big Sandy—one hundred and eighty miles from St. Joseph.

As the sun was going down, we saw the first specimen of an animal known familiarly over two thousand miles of mountain and desert—from Kansas clear to the Pacific Ocean—as the "jackass rabbit." He is well named. He is just like any other rabbit, except that he is from one-third to twice as large, has longer legs in proportion to his size, and has the most preposterous ears that ever were mounted on any creature *but* a jackass. When he is sitting quiet, thinking about his sins, or is absentminded or unapprehensive of danger, his majestic ears project above him conspicuously; but the breaking of a twig will scare him nearly to death, and then he tilts his ears back gently and starts for home. All you can see, then, for the next minute, is his long gray form stretched out straight and "streaking it" through the low sagebrush, head erect, eyes right, and ears just canted a little to the rear, but showing you where the animal is, all the time, the same as if he carried a jib. Now and then he makes a marvelous spring with his long legs, high over the stunted sage-brush, and scores a leap that would make a horse envious. Presently, he comes down to a long, graceful "lope," and shortly he mysteriously disappears. He has crouched behind a sage-bush, and will sit there and listen and tremble until you get within six feet of him, when he will get under way again. But one must shoot at this creature once, if he wishes to see him throw his heart into his heels, and do the best he knows how. He is frightened clear through, now, and he lays his long ears down on his back,

straightens himself out like a yardstick every spring he makes, and scatters miles behind him with an easy indifference that is enchanting.

Our party made this specimen "hump himself," as the conductor said. The Secretary started him with a shot from the Colt; I commenced spitting at him with my weapon; and all in the same instant the old "Allen's" whole broadside let go with a rattling crash, and it is not putting it too strong to say that the rabbit was frantic! He dropped his ears, set up his tail, and left for San Francisco at a speed which can only be described as a flash and a vanish! Long after he was out of sight we could hear him whiz.

I do not remember where we first came across "sage-brush," but as I have been speaking of it I may as well describe it. This is easily done, for if the reader can imagine a gnarled and venerable live-oak tree reduced to a little shrub two feet high, with its rough bark, its foliage, its twisted boughs, all complete, he can picture the "sage-brush" exactly. Often, on lazy afternoons in the mountains I have lain on the ground with my face under a sage-bush, and entertained myself with fancying that the gnats among its foliage were lilliputian birds, and that the ants marching and countermarching about its base were lilliputian flocks and herds, and myself some vast loafer from Brobdingnag [5] waiting to catch a little citizen and eat him.

It is an imposing monarch of the forest in exquisite miniature, is the "sage-brush." Its foliage is a grayish green, and gives that tint to desert and mountain. It smells like our domestic sage, and "sage-tea" made from it tastes like the sage-tea which all boys are so well acquainted with. The sage-brush is a singularly hardy plant, and grows right in the midst of deep sand, and among barren rocks where nothing else in the vegetable world would try to grow,

[5] The country of the giants, described in Swift's *Gulliver's Travels*.

except "bunch-grass." [6] The sage-bushes grow from three to six or seven feet apart, all over the mountains and deserts of the Far West, clear to the borders of California. There is not a tree of any kind in the deserts, for hundreds of miles—there is no vegetation at all in a regular desert, except the sage-brush and its cousin the "greasewood," which is so much like the sage-brush that the difference amounts to little. Camp-fires and hot suppers in the deserts would be impossible but for the friendly sage-brush. Its trunk is as large as a boy's wrist (and from that up to a man's arm), and its crooked branches are half as large as its trunk—all good, sound, hard wood, very like oak.

When a party camps, the first thing to be done is to cut sage-brush; and in a few minutes there is an opulent pile of it ready for use. A hole a foot wide, two feet deep, and two feet long, is dug, and sage-brush chopped up and burned in it till it is full to the brim with glowing coals; then the cooking begins, and there is no smoke, and consequently no swearing. Such a fire will keep all night, with very little replenishing; and it makes a very sociable camp-fire, and one around which the most impossible reminiscences sound plausible, instructive, and profoundly entertaining.

Sage-brush is very fair fuel, but as a vegetable it is a distinguished failure. Nothing can abide the taste of it but the jackass and his illegitimate child, the mule. But their testimony to its nutritiousness is worth nothing, for they will eat pine-knots, or anthracite coal, or brass filings, or lead pipe, or old bottles, or anything that comes handy, and then go off looking as grateful as if they had had oysters for dinner. Mules and donkeys and camels have appetites that anything will relieve temporarily, but nothing satisfy. In Syria, once, at the headwaters of the Jordan, a camel took charge of my overcoat while the tents were being pitched, and examined it with a critical eye, all over, with as much interest as if he had an idea of getting one made like it; and then, after he was done figur-

ing on it as an article of apparel, he began to contemplate it as an article of diet. He put his foot on it, and lifted one of the sleeves out with his teeth, and chewed and chewed at it, gradually taking it in, and all the while opening and closing his eyes in a kind of religious ecstasy, as if he had never tasted anything as good as an overcoat before in his life. Then he smacked his lips once or twice, and reached after the other sleeve. Next he tried the velvet collar, and smiled a smile of such contentment that it was plain to see that he regarded that as the daintiest thing about an overcoat. The tails went next, along with some percussion-caps and cough-candy, and some fig-paste from Constantinople. And then my newspaper correspondence dropped out, and he took a chance in that—manuscript letters written for the home papers. But he was treading on dangerous ground, now. He began to come across solid wisdom in those documents that was rather weighty on his stomach; and occasionally he would take a joke that would shake him up till it loosened his teeth; it was getting to be perilous times with him, but he held his grip with good courage and hopefully, till at last he began to stumble on statements that not even a camel could swallow with impunity. He began to gag and gasp, and his eyes to stand out, and his forelegs to spread, and in about a quarter of a minute he fell over as stiff as a carpenter's workbench, and died a death of indescribable agony. I went and pulled the manuscript out of his mouth, and found that the sensitive creature had choked to death on one of the mildest and gentlest statements of fact that I ever laid before a trusting public.

---

[6] "Bunch-grass" grows on the bleak mountainsides of Nevada and neighboring territories, and offers excellent feed for stock, even in the dead of winter, wherever the snow is blown aside and exposes it; notwithstanding its unpromising home, bunch-grass is a better and more nutritious diet for cattle and horses than almost any other hay or grass that is known—so stockmen say. [Author's note.]

I was about to say, when diverted from my subject, that occasionally one finds sage-bushes five or six feet high, and with a spread of branch and foliage in proportion, but two or two and a half feet is the usual height.

CHAPTER IV

As the sun went down and the evening chill came on, we made preparation for bed. We stirred up the hard leather letter-sacks, and the knotty canvas bags of printed matter (knotty and uneven because of projecting ends and corners of magazines, boxes and books). We stirred them up and redisposed them in such a way as to make our bed as level as possible. And we *did* improve it, too, though after all our work it had an upheaved and billowy look about it, like a little piece of a stormy sea. Next we hunted up our boots from odd nooks among the mail-bags where they had settled, and put them on. Then we got down our coats, vests, pantaloons and heavy woolen shirts, from the arm-loops where they had been swinging all day, and clothed ourselves in them—for, there being no ladies either at the stations or in the coach, and the weather being hot, we had looked to our comfort by stripping to our underclothing, at nine o'clock in the morning. All things being now ready, we stowed the uneasy Dictionary where it would lie as quiet as possible, and placed the water-canteen and pistols where we could find them in the dark. Then we smoked a final pipe, and swapped a final yarn; after which, we put the pipes, tobacco, and bag of coin in snug holes and caves among the mail-bags, and then fastened down the coach curtains all around and made the place as "dark as the inside of a cow," as the conductor phrased it in his picturesque way. It was certainly as dark as any place could be—nothing was even dimly visible in it. And finally, we rolled ourselves up like silkworms, each person in his own blanket, and sank peacefully to sleep. Whenever the stage stopped to change

horses, we would wake up, and try to recollect where we were—and succeed—and in a minute or two the stage would be off again, and we likewise. We began to get into country, now, threaded here and there with little streams. These had high, steep banks on each side, and every time we flew down one bank and scrambled up the other, our party inside got mixed somewhat. First we would all be down in a pile at the forward end of the stage, nearly in a sitting posture, and in a second we would shoot to the other end, and stand on our heads. And we would sprawl and kick, too, and ward off ends and corners of mail-bags that came lumbering over us and about us; and as the dust rose from the tumult, we would all sneeze in chorus, and the majority of us would grumble, and probably say some hasty thing, like: "Take your elbow out of my ribs!—can't you quit crowding?"

Every time we avalanched from one end of the stage to the other, the Unabridged Dictionary would come too; and every time it came it damaged somebody. One trip it "barked" the Secretary's elbow; the next trip it hurt me in the stomach, and the third it tilted Bemis's nose up till he could look down his nostrils—he said. The pistols and coin soon settled to the bottom, but the pipes, pipe-stems, tobacco, and canteens clattered and floundered after the Dictionary every time it made an assault on us, and aided and abetted the book by spilling tobacco in our eyes, and water down our backs.

Still, all things considered, it was a very comfortable night. It wore gradually away, and when at last a cold gray light was visible through the puckers and chinks in the curtains, we yawned and stretched with satisfaction, shed our cocoons, and felt that we had slept as much as was necessary. By and by, as the sun rose up and warmed the world, we pulled off our clothes and got ready for breakfast. We were just pleasantly in time, for five minutes afterward the driver sent the weird music of his bugle winding over the grassy solitudes, and presently we detected a low hut or two in the distance. Then the rattling of the coach, the clatter of our six horses' hoofs, and the driver's crisp commands, awoke to a louder and stronger emphasis, and we went sweeping down on the station at our smartest speed. It was fascinating—that old Overland stage-coaching.

We jumped out in undress uniform. The driver tossed his gathered reins out on the ground, gaped and stretched complacently, drew off his heavy buckskin gloves with great deliberation and insufferable dignity —taking not the slightest notice of a dozen solicitous inquiries after his health, and humbly facetious and flattering accostings, and obsequious tenders of service, from five or six hairy and half-civilized station-keepers and hostlers who were nimbly un-hitching our steeds and bringing the fresh team out of the stables—for, in the eyes of the stage-driver of that day, station-keepers and hostlers were a sort of good enough low creatures, useful in their place, and helping to make up a world, but not the kind of beings which a person of distinction could afford to concern himself with; while, on the contrary, in the eyes of the station-keeper and the hostler, the stage-driver was a hero—a great and shining dignitary, the world's favorite son, the envy of the people, the observed of the nations. When they spoke to him they received his insolent silence meekly, and as being the natural and proper conduct of so great a man; when he opened his lips they all hung on his words with admiration (he never honored a particular individual with a remark, but addressed it with a broad generality to the horses, the stables, the surrounding country *and* the human under-lings); when he discharged a facetious in-sulting personality at a hostler, that hostler was happy for the day; when he uttered his one jest—old as the hills, coarse, profane, witless, and inflicted on the same audience, in the same language, every time his coach drove up there—the varlets roared, and slapped their thighs, and swore it was the best thing they'd ever heard in all their

lives. And how they would fly around when he wanted a basin of water, a gourd of the same, or a light for his pipe!—but they would instantly insult a passenger if he so far forgot himself as to crave a favor at their hands. They could do that sort of insolence as well as the driver they copied it from—for, let it be borne in mind, the Overland driver had but little less con-tempt for his passengers than he had for his hostlers.

The hostlers and station-keepers treated the really powerful *conductor* of the coach merely with the best of what was their idea of civility, but the *driver* was the only being they bowed down to and worshiped. How admiringly they would gaze up at him in his high seat as he gloved himself with lingering deliberation, while some happy hostler held the bunch of reins aloft, and waited patiently for him to take it! And how they would bombard him with glorifying ejaculations as he cracked his long whip and went careering away.

The station buildings were long, low huts, made of sun-dried, mud-colored bricks, laid up without mortar (*adobes,* the Spaniards call these bricks, and Americans shorten it to *'dobies*). The roofs, which had no slant to them worth speaking of, were thatched and then sodded or covered with a thick layer of earth, and from this sprung a pretty rank growth of weeds and grass. It was the first time we had ever seen a man's front yard on top of his house. The buildings consisted of barns, stable-room for twelve or fifteen horses, and a hut for an eating-room for passen-gers. This latter had bunks in it for the station-keeper and a hostler or two. You could rest your elbow on its eaves, and you had to bend in order to get in at the door. In place of a window there was a square hole about large enough for a man to crawl through, but this had no glass in it. There was no flooring, but the ground was packed hard. There was no stove, but the fireplace served all needful purposes. There were no shelves, no cupboards, no closets. In a corner stood an open sack of flour, and nestling against its base were a couple of black and venerable tin coffee-pots, a tin teapot, a little bag of salt, and a side of bacon.

By the door of the station-keeper's den, outside, was a tin wash-basin, on the ground. Near it was a pail of water and a piece of yellow bar-soap, and from the eaves hung a hoary blue woolen shirt, significantly—but this latter was the station-keeper's private towel, and only two persons in all the party might venture to use it—the stage-driver and the conductor. The latter would not, from a sense of decency; the former would not, because he did not choose to encourage the advances of a station-keeper. We had towels—in the valise; they might as well have been in Sodom and Gomorrah. We (and the conductor) used our handkerchiefs, and the driver his pantaloons and sleeves. By the door, inside, was fastened a small old-fashioned looking-glass frame, with two little fragments of the original mirror lodged down in one corner of it. This arrangement afforded a pleasant double-barreled portrait of you when you looked into it, with one half of your head set up a couple of inches above the other half. From the glass frame hung the half of a comb by a string—but if I had to describe that patriarch or die, I believe I would order some sample coffins. It had come down from Esau and Samson, and had been accumulating hair ever since—along with certain impurities. In one corner of the room stood three or four rifles and muskets, together with horns and pouches of ammunition. The station-men wore pantaloons of coarse, country-woven stuff, and into the seat and the inside of the legs were sewed ample additions of buckskin, to do duty in place of leggings, when the man rode horseback—so the pants were half dull blue and half yellow, and unspeakably picturesque. The pants were stuffed into the tops of high boots, the heels whereof were armed with great Span-ish spurs, whose little iron clogs and chains jingled with every step. The man wore a huge beard and mustachios, an old slouch hat, a blue woolen shirt, no suspenders, no vest, no coat—in a leathern sheath in his belt, a great long "navy" revolver (slung on right side, hammer to the front), and projecting from his boot a horn-handled bowie-knife. The furniture of the hut was neither gorgeous nor much in the way. The rocking-chairs and sofas were not present, and never had been, but they were represented by two three-legged stools, a pine-board bench four feet long, and two empty candle-boxes. The table was a greasy board on stilts, and the table-cloth and napkins had not come—and they were not looking for them, either. A battered tin platter, a knife and fork, and a tin pint cup, were at each man's place, and the driver had a queens-ware saucer that had seen better days. Of course, this duke sat at the head of the table. There was one isolated piece of table furniture that bore about it a touching air of grandeur in misfortune. This was the caster. It was German silver, and crippled and rusty, but it was so preposterously out of place there that it was suggestive of a tattered exiled king among barbarians, and the majesty of its native position compelled respect even in its degradation. There was only one cruet left, and that was a stopperless, fly-specked, broken-necked thing, with two inches of vinegar in it, and a dozen preserved flies with their heels up and looking sorry they had invested there.

The station-keeper up-ended a disk of last week's bread, of the shape and size of an old-time cheese, and carved some slabs from it which were as good as Nicholson pavement, and tenderer.

He sliced off a piece of bacon for each man, but only the experienced old hands made out to eat it, for it was condemned army bacon which the United States would not feed to its soldiers in the forts, and the stage company had bought it cheap for the sustenance of their passengers and employees. We may have found this condemned army bacon further out on the Plains than the section I am locating it in, but we *found* it—there is no gainsaying that.

Then he poured for us a beverage which he called *"Slumgullion,"* and it is hard to think he was not inspired when he named it. It really pretended to be tea, but there was too much dish-rag, and sand, and old bacon-rind in it to deceive the intelligent traveler. He had no sugar and no milk— not even a spoon to stir the ingredients with.

We could not eat the bread or the meat, nor drink the "Slumgullion." And when I looked at that melancholy vinegar-cruet, I thought of the anecdote (a very, very old one, even at that day) of the traveler who sat down to a table which had nothing on it but a mackerel and a pot of mustard. He asked the landlord if this was all. The landlord said:

"All! why, thunder and lightning, I should think there was mackerel enough there for six."

"But I don't like mackerel."

"Oh—then help yourself to the mustard."

In other days I had considered it a good, a very good, anecdote, but there was a dismal plausibility about it, here, that took all the humor out of it.

Our breakfast was before us, but our teeth were idle.

I tasted and smelt, and said I would take coffee, I believed. The station-boss stopped dead still, and glared at me speechless. At last, when he came to, he turned away and said, as one who communes with himself upon a matter too vast to grasp:

"Coffee! Well, if that don't go clean ahead of me, I'm d—d!"

We could not eat, and there was no conversation among the hostlers and herdsmen —we all sat at the same board. At least there was no conversation further than a single hurried request, now and then, from one employee to another. It was always in the same form, and always gruffly friendly. Its Western freshness and novelty

startled me, at first, and interested me; but it presently grew monotonous, and lost its charm. It was:

"Pass the bread, you son of a skunk!" No, I forget—skunk was not the word; it seems to me it was still stronger than that; I know it was, in fact, but it is gone from my memory, apparently. However, it is no matter—probably it was too strong for print, anyway. It is the landmark in my memory which tells me where I first encountered the vigorous new vernacular of the occidental plains and mountains.

We gave up the breakfast, and paid our dollar apiece and went back to our mailbag bed in the coach, and found comfort in our pipes. Right here we suffered the first diminution of our princely state. We left our six fine horses and took six mules in their place. But they were wild Mexican fellows, and a man had to stand at the head of each of them and hold him fast while the driver gloved and got himself ready. And when at last he grasped the reins and gave the word, the men sprung suddenly away from the mules' heads and the coach shot from the station as if it had issued from a cannon. How the frantic animals did scamper! It was a fierce and furious gallop—and the gait never altered for a moment till we reeled off ten or twelve miles and swept up to the next collection of little station huts and stables.

So we flew along all day. At 2 P.M. the belt of timber that fringes the North Platte and marks its windings through the vast level floor of the Plains came in sight. At 4 P.M. we crossed a branch of the river, and at 5 P.M. we crossed the Platte itself, and landed at Fort Kearney, *fifty-six hours out from St. Joe*—THREE HUNDRED MILES!

* * * * * * * *

CHAPTER VIII

In a little while all interest was taken up in stretching our necks and watching for the "pony-rider"—the fleet messenger who sped across the continent from St. Joe to Sacramento, carrying letters nineteen hun dred miles in eight days! Think of that for perishable horse and human flesh and blood to do! The pony-rider was usually a little bit of a man, brimful of spirit and endurance. No matter what time of the day or night his watch came on, and no matter whether it was winter or summer, raining, snowing, hailing, or sleeting, or whether his "beat" was a level straight road or a crazy trail over mountain crags and precipices, or whether it led through peaceful regions or regions that swarmed with hostile Indians, he must be always ready to leap into the saddle and be off like the wind! There was no idling-time for a pony-rider on duty. He rode fifty miles without stopping, by daylight, moonlight, starlight, or through the blackness of darkness—just as it happened. He rode a splendid horse that was born for a racer and fed and lodged like a gentleman; kept him at his utmost speed for ten miles, and then, as he came crashing up to the station where stood two men holding fast a fresh, impatient steed, the transfer of rider and mail-bag was made in the twinkling of an eye, and away flew the eager pair and were out of sight before the spectator could get hardly the ghost of a look. Both rider and horse went "flying light." The rider's dress was thin, and fitted close; he wore a "roundabout," and a skull-cap, and tucked his pantaloons into his boot-tops like a race-rider. He carried no arms—he carried nothing that was not absolutely necessary, for even the postage on his literary freight was worth *five dollars a letter*. He got but little frivolous correspondence to carry—his bag had business letters in it, mostly. His horse was stripped of all unnecessary weight, too. He wore a little wafer of a racing-saddle, and no visible blanket. He wore light shoes, or none at all. The little flat mail-pockets strapped under the rider's thighs would each hold about the bulk of a child's primer. They held many and many an important business chapter and newspaper letter, but these were written on paper as airy and thin as gold-leaf, nearly, and thus bulk and weight were economized.

The stage-coach traveled about a hundred to a hundred and twenty-five miles a day (twenty-four hours), the pony-rider about two hundred and fifty. There were about eighty pony-riders in the saddle all the time, night and day, stretching in a long, scattering procession from Missouri to California, forty flying eastward, and forty toward the west, and among them making four hundred gallant horses earn a stirring livelihood and see a deal of scenery every single day in the year.

We had had a consuming desire, from the beginning, to see a pony-rider, but somehow or other all that passed us and all that met us managed to streak by in the night, and so we heard only a whiz and a hail, and the swift phantom of the desert was gone before we could get our heads out of the windows. But now we were expecting one along every moment, and would see him in broad daylight. Presently the driver exclaims:

"HERE HE COMES!"

Every neck is stretched further, and every eye strained wider. Away across the endless dead level of the prairie a black speck appears against the sky, and it is plain that it moves. Well, I should think so! In a second or two it becomes a horse and rider, rising and falling, rising and falling—sweeping toward us nearer and nearer—growing more and more distinct, more and more sharply defined—nearer and still nearer, and the flutter of the hoofs comes faintly to the ear—another instant a whoop and a hurrah from our upper deck, a wave of the rider's hand, but no reply, and man and horse burst past our excited faces, and go swinging away like a belated fragment of a storm!

So sudden is it all, and so like a flash of unreal fancy, that but for the flake of white foam left quivering and perishing on a mail-sack after the vision had flashed by and disappeared, we might have doubted whether we had seen any actual horse and man at all, maybe.

We rattled through Scott's Bluffs Pass, by and by. It was along here somewhere that we first came across genuine and unmistakable alkali water in the road, and we cordially hailed it as a first-class curiosity, and a thing to be mentioned with éclat in letters to the ignorant at home. This water gave the road a soapy appearance, and in many places the ground looked as if it had been whitewashed. I think the strange alkali water excited us as much as any wonder we had come upon yet, and I know we felt very complacent and conceited, and better satisfied with life after we had added it to our list of things which *we* had seen and some other people had not. In a small way we were the same sort of simpletons as those who climb unnecessarily the perilous peaks of Mont Blanc and the Matterhorn, and derive no pleasure from it except the reflection that it isn't a common experience. But once in a while one of those parties trips and comes darting down the long mountain crags in a sitting posture, making the crusted snow smoke behind him, flitting from bench to bench, and from terrace to terrace, jarring the earth where he strikes, and still glancing and flitting on again, sticking an iceberg into himself every now and then, and tearing his clothes, snatching at things to save himself, taking hold of trees and fetching them along with him, roots and all, starting little rocks now and then, then big boulders, then acres of ice and snow and patches of forest, gathering and still gathering as he goes, and adding and still adding to his massed and sweeping grandeur as he nears a three-thousand-foot precipice, till at last he waves his hat magnificently and rides into eternity on the back of a raging and tossing avalanche!

This is all very fine, but let us not be carried away by excitement, but ask calmly, how does this person feel about it in his cooler moments next day, with six or seven thousand feet of snow and stuff on top of him?

We crossed the sand-hills near the scene of the Indian mail robbery and massacre of 1856, wherein the driver and conductor perished, and also all the passengers but

one, it was supposed; but this must have been a mistake, for at different times afterward on the Pacific coast I was personally acquainted with a hundred and thirty-three or four people who were wounded during that massacre, and barely escaped with their lives. There was no doubt of the truth of it—I had it from their own lips. One of these parties told me that he kept coming across arrow-heads in his system for nearly seven years after the massacre; and another of them told me that he was stuck so literally full of arrows that after the Indians were gone and he could raise up and examine himself, he could not restrain his tears, for his clothes were completely ruined.

The most trustworthy tradition avers, however, that only one man, a person named Babbitt, survived the massacre, and he was desperately wounded. He dragged himself on his hands and knee (for one leg was broken) to a station several miles away. He did it during portions of two nights, lying concealed one day and part of another, and for more than forty hours suffering unimaginable anguish from hunger, thirst, and bodily pain. The Indians robbed the coach of everything it contained, including quite an amount of treasure.

THE CURIOUS REPUBLIC OF GONDOUR
[1875]

As soon as I had learned to speak the language a little, I became greatly interested in the people and the system of government.

I found that the nation had at first tried universal suffrage pure and simple, but had thrown that form aside because the result was not satisfactory. It had seemed to deliver all power into the hands of the ignorant and non-tax-paying classes; and of a necessity the responsible offices were filled from these classes also.

A remedy was sought. The people believed they had found it; not in the destruction of universal suffrage, but in the enlargement of it. It was an odd idea, and ingenious. You must understand, the constitution gave every man a vote; therefore that vote was a vested right, and could not be taken away. But the constitution did not say that certain individuals might not be given two votes, or ten! So an amendatory clause was inserted in a quiet way; a clause which authorized the enlargement of the suffrage in certain cases to be specified by statute. To offer to "limit" the suffrage might have made instant trouble; the offer to "enlarge" it had a pleasant aspect. But of course the newspapers soon began to suspect; and then out they came! It was found, however, that for once,—and for the first time in the history of the republic,—property, character, and intellect were able to wield a political influence; for once, money, virtue, and intelligence took a vital and a united interest in a political question. For once these powers went to the "primaries" in strong force; for once the best men in the nation were put forward as candidates for that parliament whose business it should be to enlarge the suffrage. The weightiest half of the press quickly joined forces with the new movement, and left the other half to rail about the proposed "destruction of the liberties" of the bottom layer of society, the hitherto governing class of the community.

The victory was complete. The new law was framed and passed. Under it every citizen, howsoever poor or ignorant, possessed one vote, so universal suffrage still reigned; but if a man possessed a good common-school education and no money, he had two votes; a high-school education gave him four; if he had property likewise, to the value of three thousand *sacos*, he wielded one more vote; for every fifty thousand *sacos* a man added to his property, he was entitled to another vote; a university education entitled a man to nine votes, even though he owned no property. Therefore, learning being more prevalent and more easily acquired than riches, educated men became a wholesome check

upon wealthy men, since they could outvote them. Learning goes usually with uprightness, broad views, and humanity; so the learned voters, possessing the balance of power, became the vigilant and efficient protectors of the great lower rank of society.

And now a curious thing developed itself —a sort of emulation, whose object was voting-power! Whereas formerly a man was honored only according to the amount of money he possessed, his grandeur was measured now by the number of votes he wielded. A man with only one vote was conspicuously respectful to his neighbor who possessed three. And if he was a man above the commonplace, he was as conspicuously energetic in his determination to acquire three for himself. This spirit of emulation invaded all ranks. Votes based upon capital were commonly called "mortal" votes, because they could be lost; those based upon learning were called "immortal," because they were permanent, and because of their customarily imperishable character they were naturally more valued than the other sort. I say "customarily" for the reason that these votes were not absolutely imperishable, since insanity could suspend them.

Under this system, gambling and speculation almost ceased in the republic. A man honored as the possessor of great voting-power could not afford to risk the loss of it upon a doubtful chance.

It was curious to observe the manners and customs which the enlargement plan produced. Walking the street with a friend one day, he delivered a careless bow to a passer-by, and then remarked that that person possessed only one vote and would probably never earn another; he was more respectful to the next acquaintance he met; he explained that this salute was a four-vote bow. I tried to "average" the importance of the people he accosted after that, by the nature of his bows, but my success was only partial, because of the somewhat greater homage paid to the immortals than to the mortals. My friend explained. He said there was no law to regulate this thing, except that most powerful of all laws, custom. Custom had created these varying bows, and in time they had become easy and natural. At this moment he delivered himself of a very profound salute, and then said, "Now there's a man who began life as a shoemaker's apprentice, and without education; now he swings twenty-two mortal votes and two immortal ones; he expects to pass a high-school examination this year and climb a couple of votes higher among the immortals; mighty valuable citizen."

By and by my friend met a venerable personage, and not only made him a most elaborate bow, but also took off his hat. I took off mine, too, with a mysterious awe. I was beginning to be infected.

"What grandee is that?"

"That is our most illustrious astronomer. He hasn't any money, but is fearfully learned. Nine immortals is *his* political weight! He would swing a hundred and fifty votes if our system were perfect."

"Is there any altitude of mere moneyed grandeur that you take off your hat to?"

"No. Nine immortal votes is the only power we uncover for—that is, in civil life. Very great officials receive that mark of homage, of course."

It was common to hear people admiringly mention men who had begun life on the lower levels and in time achieved great voting-power. It was also common to hear youths planning a future of ever so many votes for themselves. I heard shrewd mammas speak of certain young men as good "catches" because they possessed such-and-such a number of votes. I knew of more than one case where an heiress was married to a youngster who had but one vote; the argument being that he was gifted with such excellent parts that in time he would acquire a good voting strength, and perhaps in the long run be able to outvote his wife, if he had luck.

Competitive examinations were the rule in all official grades. I remarked that the questions asked the candidates were wild, intricate, and often required a sort of knowledge not needed in the office sought.

"Can a fool or an ignoramus answer them?" asked the person I was talking with.

"Certainly not."

"Well, you will not find any fools or ignoramuses among our officials."

I felt rather cornered, but made shift to say,—

"But these questions cover a good deal more ground than is necessary."

"No matter; if candidates can answer these it is tolerably fair evidence that they can answer nearly any other question you choose to ask them."

There were some things in Gondour which one could not shut his eyes to. One was, that ignorance and incompetence had no place in the government. Brains and property managed the state. A candidate for office must have marked ability, education, and high character, or he stood no sort of chance of election. If a hod-carrier possessed these, he could succeed; but the mere fact that he was a hod-carrier could not elect him, as in previous times.

It was now a very great honor to be in the parliament or in office; under the old system such distinction had only brought suspicion upon a man and made him a helpless mark for newspaper contempt and scurrility. Officials did not need to steal now, their salaries being vast in comparison with the pittances paid in the days when parliaments were created by hod-carriers, who viewed official salaries from a hod-carrying point of view and compelled that view to be respected by their obsequious servants. Justice was wisely and rigidly administered; for a judge, after once reaching his place through the specified line of promotions, was a permanency during good behavior. He was not obliged to modify his judgments according to the effect they might have upon the temper of a reigning political party.

The country was mainly governed by

a ministry which went out with the administration that created it. This was also the case with the chiefs of the great departments. Minor officials ascended to their several positions through well-earned promotions, and not by a jump from gin-mills or the needy families and friends of members of parliament. Good behavior measured their terms of office.

The head of the government, the Grand Caliph, was elected for a term of twenty years. I questioned the wisdom of this. I was answered that he could do no harm, since the ministry and the parliament governed the land, and he was liable to impeachment for misconduct. This great office had twice been ably filled by women, women as aptly fitted for it as some of the sceptred queens of history. Members of the cabinet, under many administrations, had been women.

I found that the pardoning power was lodged in a court of pardons, consisting of several great judges. Under the old *régime*, this important power was vested in a single official, and he usually took care to have a general jail delivery in time for the next election.

I inquired about public schools. There were plenty of them, and of free colleges too. I inquired about compulsory education. This was received with a smile, and the remark,—

"When a man's child is able to make himself powerful and honored according to the amount of education he acquires, don't you suppose that that parent will apply the compulsion himself? Our free schools and free colleges require no law to fill them."

There was a loving pride of country about this person's way of speaking which annoyed me. I had long been unused to the sound of it in my own. The Gondour national airs were forever dinning in my ears; therefore I was glad to leave that country and come back to my dear native land, where one never hears that sort of music.

From
OLD TIMES ON THE MISSISSIPPI [1]
[1883 (1875)]

A CUB-PILOT'S EXPERIENCE

What with lying on the rocks four days at Louisville, and some other delays, the poor old *Paul Jones* fooled away about two weeks in making the voyage from Cincinnati to New Orleans. This gave me a chance to get acquainted with one of the pilots, and he taught me how to steer the boat, and thus made the fascination of river life more potent than ever for me.

It also gave me a chance to get acquainted with a youth who had taken deck passage—more's the pity; for he easily borrowed six dollars of me on a promise to return to the boat and pay it back to me the day after we should arrive. But he probably died or forgot, for he never came. It was doubtless the former, since he had said his parents were wealthy, and he only traveled deck passage because it was cooler.[2]

I soon discovered two things. One was that a vessel would not be likely to sail for the mouth of the Amazon [3] under ten or twelve years; and the other was that the nine or ten dollars still left in my pocket would not suffice for so impossible an exploration as I had planned, even if I could afford to wait for a ship. Therefore it followed that I must contrive a new career. The *Paul Jones* was now bound for St. Louis. I planned a siege against my pilot, and at the end of three hard days he surrendered. He agreed to teach me the Mississippi River from New Orleans to St. Louis for five hundred dollars, payable out of the first wages I should receive after graduating. I entered upon the small enter-

---

[1] These *Atlantic Monthly* papers were later included in *Life on the Mississippi*.

[2] "Deck" passage—*i. e.*, steerage passage. [Author's footnote.]

[3] See reference to Clemens' first plan for this trip, p. 243 above.

prise of "learning" twelve or thirteen hundred miles of the great Mississippi River with the easy confidence of my time of life. If I had really known what I was about to require of my faculties, I should not have had the courage to begin. I supposed that all a pilot had to do was to keep his boat in the river, and I did not consider that that could be much of a trick, since it was so wide.

The boat backed out from New Orleans at four in the afternoon, and it was "our watch" until eight. Mr. Bixby,[4] my chief, "straightened her up," plowed her along past the sterns of the other boats that lay at the Levee, and then said, "Here, take her; shave those steamships as close as you'd peel an apple." I took the wheel, and my heartbeat fluttered up into the hundreds; for it seemed to me that we were about to scrape the side off every ship in the line, we were so close. I held my breath and began to claw the boat away from the danger; and I had my own opinion of the pilot who had known no better than to get us into such peril, but I was too wise to express it. In half a minute I had a wide margin of safety intervening between the *Paul Jones* and the ships; and within ten seconds more I was set aside in disgrace, and Mr. Bixby was going into danger again and flaying me alive with abuse of my cowardice. I was stung, but I was obliged to admire the easy confidence with which my chief loafed from side to side of his wheel, and trimmed the ships so closely that disaster seemed ceaselessly imminent. When he had cooled a little he told me that the easy water was close ashore and the current outside, and therefore we must hug the bank, up-stream, to get the benefit of the former, and stay well out, down-stream, to take advantage of the latter. In my own mind I resolved to be a down-stream pilot and leave the up-streaming to people dead to prudence.

Now and then Mr. Bixby called my attention to certain things. Said he, "This is Six-Mile Point." I assented. It was pleasant enough information, but I could not see the bearing of it. I was not conscious that it was a matter of any interest to me. Another time he said, "This is Nine-Mile Point." Later he said, "This is Twelve-Mile Point." They were all about level with the water's edge; they all looked about alike to me; they were monotonously unpicturesque. I hoped Mr. Bixby would change the subject. But no; he would crowd up around a point, hugging the shore with affection, and then say: "The slack water ends here, abreast this bunch of China trees; now we cross over." So he crossed over. He gave me the wheel once or twice, but I had no luck. I either came near chipping off the edge of a sugar-plantation, or I yawed too far from shore, and so dropped back into disgrace again and got abused.

The watch was ended at last, and we took supper and went to bed. At midnight the glare of a lantern shone in my eyes, and the night watchman said:

"Come, turn out!"

And then he left. I could not understand this extraordinary procedure; so I presently gave up trying to, and dozed off to sleep. Pretty soon the watchman was back again, and this time he was gruff. I was annoyed. I said:

"What do you want to come bothering around here in the middle of the night for? Now, as like as not, I'll not get to sleep again to-night."

The watchman said:

"Well, if this ain't good, I'm blessed."

The "off-watch" was just turning in, and I heard some brutal laughter from them, and such remarks as "Hello, watchman! ain't the new cub turned out yet? He's delicate, likely. Give him some sugar in a rag, and send for the chambermaid to sing 'Rock-a-by Baby,' to him."

About this time Mr. Bixby appeared on the scene. Something like a minute later I was climbing the pilot-house steps with some of my clothes on and the rest in my arms. Mr. Bixby was close behind, com-

---

[4] Horace Ezra Bixby (1826-1912), long a pilot on the Mississippi.

menting. Here was something fresh—this thing of getting up in the middle of the night to go to work. It was a detail in piloting that had never occurred to me at all. I knew that boats ran all night, but somehow I had never happened to reflect that somebody had to get up out of a warm bed to run them. I began to fear that piloting was not quite so romantic as I had imagined it was; there was something very real and worklike about this new phase of it.

It was a rather dingy night, although a fair number of stars were out. The big mate was at the wheel, and he had the old tub pointed at a star and was holding her straight up the middle of the river. The shores on either hand were not much more than half a mile apart, but they seemed wonderfully far away and ever so vague and indistinct. The mate said:

"We've got to land at Jones's plantation, sir."

The vengeful spirit in me exulted. I said to myself, "I wish you joy of your job, Mr. Bixby; you'll have a good time finding Mr. Jones's plantation such a night as this; and I hope you never *will* find it as long as you live."

Mr. Bixby said to the mate:

"Upper end of the plantation, or the lower?"

"Upper."

"I can't do it. The stumps there are out of water at this stage. It's no great distance to the lower, and you'll have to get along with that."

"All right, sir. If Jones don't like it, he'll have to lump it, I reckon."

And then the mate left. My exultation began to cool and my wonder to come up. Here was a man who not only proposed to find this plantation on such a night, but to find either end of it you preferred. I dreadfully wanted to ask a question, but I was carrying about as many short answers as my cargo-room would admit of, so I held my peace. All I desired to ask Mr. Bixby was the simple question whether he was ass enough to really imagine he was

going to find that plantation on a night when all plantations were exactly alike and all of the same color. But I held in. I used to have fine inspirations of prudence in those days.

Mr. Bixby made for the shore and soon was scraping it, just the same as if it had been daylight. And not only that, but singing:

"Father in heaven, the day is declining," etc.

It seemed to me that I had put my life in the keeping of a peculiarly reckless outcast. Presently he turned on me and said:

"What's the name of the first point above New Orleans?"

I was gratified to be able to answer promptly, and I did. I said I didn't know.

"Don't *know?*"

This manner jolted me. I was down at the foot again, in a moment. But I had to say just what I had said before.

"Well, you're a smart one!" said Mr. Bixby. "What's the name of the *next* point?"

Once more I didn't know.

"Well, this beats anything. Tell me the name of *any* point or place I told you."

I studied awhile and decided that I couldn't.

"Look here! What do you start out from, above Twelve-Mile Point, to cross over?"

"I—I—don't know."

"You—you—don't know?" mimicking my drawling manner of speech. "What *do* you know?"

"I—I—nothing, for certain."

"By the great Cæsar's ghost, I believe you! You're the stupidest dunderhead I ever saw or ever heard of, so help me Moses! The idea of *you* being a pilot— *you!* Why, you don't know enough to pilot a cow down a lane."

Oh, but his wrath was up! He was a nervous man, and he shuffled from one side of his wheel to the other as if the floor was hot. He would boil awhile to himself, and then overflow and scald me again.

"Look here! What do you suppose I told you the names of those points for?"

I tremblingly considered a moment, and then the devil of temptation provoked me to say:

"Well to — to — be entertaining, I thought."

This was a red rag to the bull. He raged and stormed so (he was crossing the river at the time) that I judged it made him blind, because he ran over the steering-oar of a trading-scow. Of course the traders sent up a volley of red-hot profanity. Never was a man so grateful as Mr. Bixby was; because he was brimful, and here were subjects who could *talk back*. He threw open a window, thrust his head out, and such an irruption followed as I never had heard before. The fainter and farther away the scowmen's curses drifted, the higher Mr. Bixby lifted his voice and the weightier his adjectives grew. When he closed the window he was empty. You could have drawn a seine through his system and not caught curses enough to disturb your mother with. Presently he said to me in the gentlest way:

"My boy, you must get a little memorandum-book; and every time I tell you a thing, put it down right way. There's only one way to be a pilot, and that is to get this entire river by heart. You have to know it just like A B C."

That was a dismal revelation to me; for my memory was never loaded with anything but blank cartridges. However, I did not feel discouraged long. I judged that it was best to make some allowances, for doubtless Mr. Bixby was "stretching." Presently he pulled a rope and struck a few strokes on the big bell. The stars were all gone now, and the night was as black as ink. I could hear the wheels churn along the bank, but I was not entirely certain that I could see the shore. The voice of the invisible watchman called up from the hurricane-deck:

"What's this, sir?"

"Jones's plantation."

I said to myself, "I wish I might venture to offer a small bet that it isn't." But I did not chirp. I only waited to see. Mr. Bixby handled the engine-bells, and in due time the boat's nose came to the land, a torch glowed from the forecastle, a man skipped ashore, a darky's voice on the bank said: "Gimme de k'yarpet-bag, Mass' Jones," and the next moment we were standing up the river again, all serene. I reflected deeply awhile, and then said—but not aloud— "Well, the finding of that plantation was the luckiest accident that ever happened; but it couldn't happen again in a hundred years." And I fully believed it *was* an accident, too.

By the time we had gone seven or eight hundred miles up the river, I had learned to be a tolerably plucky up-stream steersman, in daylight; and before we reached St. Louis I had made a trifle of progress in night work, but only a trifle. I had a note-book that fairly bristled with the names of towns, "points," bars, islands, bends, reaches, etc.; but the information was to be found only in the note-book— none of it was in my head. It made my heart ache to think I had only got half of the river set down; for as our watch was four hours off and four hours on, day and night, there was a long four-hour gap in my book for every time I had slept since the voyage began.

My chief was presently hired to go on a big New Orleans boat, and I packed my satchel and went with him. She was a grand affair. When I stood in her pilot-house I was so far above the water that I seemed perched on a mountain; and her decks stretched so far away, fore and aft, below me, that I wondered how I could ever have considered the little *Paul Jones* a large craft. There were other differences, too. The *Paul Jones's* pilot-house was a cheap, dingy, battered rattletrap, cramped for room; but here was a sumptuous glass temple; room enough to have a dance in; showy red and gold window-curtains; an imposing sofa; leather cushions and a back to the high bench where visiting pilots sit, to spin yarns and "look at the river";

bright, fanciful "cuspidores," instead of a broad wooden box filled with sawdust; nice new oilcloth on the floor; a hospitable big stove for winter; a wheel as high as my head, costly with inlaid work; a wire tiller-rope; bright brass knobs for the bells; and a tidy, white-aproned, black "texas-tender," to bring up tarts and ices and coffee during mid-watch, day and night. Now this was "something like"; and so I began to take heart once more to believe that piloting was a romantic sort of occupation after all. The moment we were under way I began to prowl about the great steamer and fill myself with joy. She was as clean and as dainty as a drawing-room; when I looked down her long, gilded saloon, it was like gazing through a splendid tunnel; she had an oil-picture, by some gifted sign-painter, on every state-room door; she glittered with no end of prism-fringed chandeliers; the clerk's office was elegant, the bar was marvelous, and the barkeeper had been barbered and upholstered at incredible cost. The boiler-deck (i. e., the second story of the boat, so to speak) was as spacious as a church, it seemed to me; so with the forecastle; and there was no pitiful handful of deck-hands, firemen, and roustabouts down there, but a whole battalion of men. The fires were fiercely glaring from a long row of furnaces, and over them were eight huge boilers! This was unutterable pomp. The mighty engines—but enough of this. I had never felt so fine before. And when I found that the regiment of natty servants respectfully "sir'd" me, my satisfaction was complete.

A DARING DEED

When I returned to the pilot-house St. Louis was gone, and I was lost. Here was a piece of river which was all down in my book, but I could make neither head nor tail of it: you understand, it was turned around. I had seen it when coming up-stream, but I had never faced about to see how it looked when it was behind me. My heart broke again, for it was plain that I had got to learn this troublesome river *both ways.*

The pilot-house was full of pilots, going down to "look at the river." What is called the "upper river" (the two hundred miles between St. Louis and Cairo, where the Ohio comes in) was low; and the Mississippi changes its channel so constantly that the pilots used to always find it necessary to run down to Cairo to take a fresh look, when their boats were to lie in port a week; that is, when the water was at a low stage. A deal of this "looking at the river" was done by poor fellows who seldom had a berth, and whose only hope of getting one lay in their being always freshly posted and therefore ready to drop into the shoes of some reputable pilot, for a single trip, on account of such pilot's sudden illness, or some other necessity. And a good many of them constantly ran up and down inspecting the river, not because they ever really hoped to get a berth, but because (they being guests of the boat) it was cheaper to "look at the river" than stay ashore and pay board. In time these fellows grew dainty in their tastes, and only infested boats that had an established reputation for setting good tables. All visiting pilots were useful, for they were always ready and willing, winter or summer, night or day, to go out in the yawl and help buoy the channel or assist the boat's pilots in any way they could. They were likewise welcomed because all pilots are tireless talkers, when gathered together, and as they talk only about the river they are always understood and are always interesting. Your true pilot cares nothing about anything on earth but the river, and his pride in his occupation surpasses the pride of kings.

We had a fine company of these river inspectors along this trip. There were eight or ten, and there was abundance of room for them in our great pilot-house. Two or three of them wore polished silk hats, elaborate shirt-fronts, diamond breastpins, kid gloves, and patent-leather boots. They were choice in their English, and bore themselves with a dignity proper to men of solid means and prodigious reputation as pilots. The others were more or less loosely clad, and wore upon their heads tall felt cones that were suggestive of the days of the Commonwealth.

I was a cipher in this august company, and felt subdued, not to say torpid. I was not even of sufficient consequence to assist at the wheel when it was necessary to put the tiller hard down in a hurry; the guest that stood nearest did that when occasion required—and this was pretty much all the time, because of the crookedness of the channel and the scant water. I stood in a corner; and the talk I listened to took the hope all out of me. One visitor said to another:

"Jim, how did you run Plum Point, coming up?"

"It was in the night, there, and I ran it the way one of the boys on the *Diana* told me; started out about fifty yards above the wood-pile on the false point, and held on the cabin under Plum Point till I raised the reef—quarter less twain —then straightened up for the middle bar till I got well abreast the old one-limbed cottonwood in the bend, then got my stern on the cottonwood, and head on the low place above the point, and came through a-booming—nine and a half."

"Pretty square crossing, an't it?"

"Yes, but the upper bar's working down fast."

Another pilot spoke up and said:

"I had better water than that, and ran it lower down; started out from the false point—mark twain—raised the second reef abreast the big snag in the bend, and had quarter less twain."

One of the gorgeous ones remarked:

"I don't want to find fault with your leadsmen, but that's a good deal of water for Plum Point, it seems to me."

There was an approving nod all around as this quiet snub dropped on the boaster and "settled" him. And so they went on talk-talk-talking. Meantime, the thing that

was running in my mind was, "Now, if my ears hear aright, I have not only to get the names of all the towns and islands and bends, and so on, by heart, but I must even get up a warm personal acquaintance-ship with every old snag and one-limbed cottonwood and obscure wood-pile that ornaments the banks of this river for twelve hundred miles; and more than that, I must actually know where these things are in the dark, unless these guests are gifted with eyes that can pierce through two miles of solid blackness. I wish the piloting business was in Jericho and I had never thought of it."

At dusk Mr. Bixby tapped the big bell three times (the signal to land), and the captain emerged from his drawing-room in the forward end of the "texas," and looked up inquiringly. Mr. Bixby said:

"We will lay up here all night, captain."

"Very well, sir."

That was all. The boat came to shore and was tied up for the night. It seemed to me a fine thing that the pilot could do as he pleased, without asking so grand a captain's permission. I took my supper and went immediately to bed, discouraged by my day's observations and experiences. My late voyage's note-booking was but a confusion of meaningless names. It had tangled me all up in a knot every time I had looked at it in the daytime. I now hoped for respite in sleep; but no, it reveled all through my head till sunrise again, a frantic and tireless nightmare.

Next morning I felt pretty rusty and low-spirited. We went booming along, taking a good many chances, for we were anxious to "get out of the river" (as getting out to Cairo was called) before night should overtake us. But Mr. Bixby's partner, the other pilot, presently grounded the boat, and we lost so much time getting her off that it was plain the darkness would overtake us a good long way above the mouth. This was a great misfortune, especially to certain of our visiting pilots, whose boats would have to wait for their return, no matter how long that might be.

It sobered the pilot-house talk a good deal. Coming up-stream, pilots did not mind low water or any kind of darkness; nothing stopped them but fog. But down-stream work was different; a boat was too nearly helpless, with a stiff current pushing behind her; so it was not customary to run down-stream at night in low water.

There seemed to be one small hope, however: if we could get through the intricate and dangerous Hat Island crossing before night, we could venture the rest, for we would have plainer sailing and better water. But it would be insanity to attempt Hat Island at night. So there was a deal of looking at watches all the rest of the day, and a constant ciphering upon the speed we were making; Hat Island was the eternal subject; sometimes hope was high and sometimes we were delayed in a bad crossing, and down it went again. For hours all hands lay under the burden of this suppressed excitement; it was even communicated to me, and I got to feeling so solicitous about Hat Island, and under such an awful pressure of responsibility, that I wished I might have five minutes on shore to draw a good, full, relieving breath, and start over again. We were standing no regular watches. Each of our pilots ran such portions of the river as he had run when coming up-stream, because of his greater familiarity with it; but both remained in the pilot-house constantly.

An hour before sunset Mr. Bixby took the wheel, and Mr. W. stepped aside. For the next thirty minutes every man held his watch in his hand and was restless, silent, and uneasy. At last somebody said, with a doomful sigh:

"Well, yonder's Hat Island—and we can't make it."

All the watches closed with a snap, everybody sighed and muttered something about its being "too bad, too bad—ah, if we could *only* have got here half an hour sooner!" and the place was thick with the atmosphere of disappointment. Some started to go out, but loitered, hearing no bell-tap to land. The sun dipped behind the

horizon, the boat went on. Inquiring looks passed from one guest to another; and one who had his hand on the door-knob and had turned it, waited, then presently took away his hand and let the knob turn back again. We bore steadily down the bend. More looks were exchanged, and nods of surprised admiration—but no words. Insensibly the men drew together behind Mr. Bixby, as the sky darkened and one or two dim stars came out. The dead silence and sense of waiting became oppressive. Mr. Bixby pulled the cord, and two deep, mellow notes from the big bell floated off on the night. Then a pause, and one more note was struck. The watchman's voice followed, from the hurricane-deck:

"Labboard lead, there! Stabboard lead!"

The cries of the leadsmen began to rise out of the distance, and were gruffly repeated by the word-passers on the hurricane-deck.

"M-a-r-k three! M-a-r-k three! Quarter-less-three! Half twain! Quarter twain! M-a-r-k twain! Quarter-less—"

Mr. Bixby pulled two bell-ropes, and was answered by faint jinglings far below in the engine-room, and our speed slackened. The steam began to whistle through the gauge-cocks. The cries of the leadsmen went on—and it is a weird sound, always, in the night. Every pilot in the lot was watching now, with fixed eyes, and talking under his breath. Nobody was calm and easy but Mr. Bixby. He would put his wheel down and stand on a spoke, and as the steamer swung into her (to me) utterly invisible marks—for we seemed to be in the midst of a wide and gloomy sea—he would meet and fasten her there. Out of the murmur of half-audible talk, one caught a coherent sentence now and then—such as:

"There; she's over the first reef all right!"

After a pause, another subdued voice:

"Her stern's coming down just *exactly* right, by *George!*"

"Now she's in the marks; over she goes!"

Somebody else muttered:

"Oh, it was done beautiful—*beautiful!*"

Now the engines were stopped altogether, and we drifted with the current. Not that I could see the boat drift, for I could not, the stars being all gone by this time. This drifting was the dismalest work; it held one's heart still. Presently I discovered a blacker gloom than that which surrounded us. It was the head of the island. We were closing right down upon it. We entered its deeper shadow, and so imminent seemed the peril that I was likely to suffocate; and I had the strongest impulse to do *something,* anything, to save the vessel. But still Mr. Bixby stood by his wheel, silent, intent as a cat, and all the pilots stood shoulder to shoulder at his back.

"She'll not make it!" somebody whispered.

The water grew shoaler and shoaler, by the leadsman's cries, till it was down to:

"Eight-and-a-half! E - i - g - h - t feet! E-i-g-h-t feet! Seven-and—"

Mr. Bixby said warningly through his speaking-tube to the engineer:

"Stand by, now!"

"Ay, ay, sir!"

"Seven-and-a-half! Seven feet! *Six*-and—"

We touched bottom! Instantly Mr. Bixby set a lot of bells ringing, shouted through the tube, *"Now,* let her have it—every ounce you've got!" then to his partner, "Put her hard down! snatch her! snatch her!" The boat rasped and ground her way through the sand, hung upon the apex of disaster a single tremendous instant, and then over she went! And such a shout as went up at Mr. Bixby's back never loosened the roof of a pilot-house before!

There was no more trouble after that. Mr. Bixby was a hero that night; and it was some little time, too, before his exploit ceased to be talked about by river-men.

Fully to realize the marvelous precision required in laying the great steamer in her marks in that murky waste of water, one should know that not only must she pick her intricate way through snags and blind reefs, and then shave the head of the island so closely as to brush the overhang-ing foliage with her stern, but at one place she must pass almost within arm's reach of a sunken and invisible wreck that would snatch the hull timbers from under her if she should strike it, and destroy a quarter of a million dollars' worth of steamboat and cargo in five minutes, and maybe a hundred and fifty human lives into the bargain.

The last remark I heard that night was a compliment to Mr. Bixby, uttered in soliloquy and with unction by one of our guests. He said:

"By the Shadow of Death, but he's a lightning pilot!"

PERPLEXING LESSONS

At the end of what seemed a tedious while, I had managed to pack my head full of islands, towns, bars, "points," and bends; and a curiously inanimate mass of lumber it was, too. However, inasmuch as I could shut my eyes and reel off a good long string of these names without leaving out more than ten miles of river in every fifty, I began to feel that I could take a boat down to New Orleans if I could make her skip those little gaps. But of course my complacency could hardly get start enough to lift my nose a trifle into the air, before Mr. Bixby would think of something to fetch it down again. One day he turned on me suddenly with this settler:

"What is the shape of Walnut Bend?"

He might as well have asked me my grandmother's opinion of protoplasm. I reflected respectfully, and then said I didn't know it had any particular shape. My gun-powdery chief went off with a bang, of course, and then went on loading and firing until he was out of adjectives.

I had learned long ago that he only carried just so many rounds of ammunition, and was sure to subside into a very placable and even remorseful old smooth-bore as soon as they were all gone. That word "old" is merely affectionate; he was not more than thirty-four. I waited. By and by he said:

"My boy, you've got to know the *shape* of the river perfectly. It is all there is left to steer by on a very dark night. Everything else is blotted out and gone. But mind you, it hasn't the same shape in the night that it has in the daytime."

"How on earth am I ever going to learn it, then?"

"How do you follow a hall at home in the dark? Because you know the shape of it. You can't see it."

"Do you mean to say that I've got to know all the million trifling variations of shape in the banks of this interminable river as well as I know the shape of the front hall at home?"

"On my honor, you've got to know them *better* than any man ever did know the shapes of the halls in his own house."

"I wish I was dead!"

"Now I don't want to discourage you, but—"

"Well, pile it on me; I might as well have it now as another time."

"You see, this has got to be learned; there isn't any getting around it. A clear starlight night throws such heavy shadows that, if you didn't know the shape of a shore perfectly, you would claw away from every bunch of timber, because you would take the black shadow of it for a solid cape; and you see you would be getting scared to death every fifteen minutes by the watch. You would be fifty yards from shore all the time when you ought to be within fifty feet of it. You can't see a snag in one of those shadows, but you know exactly where it is, and the shape of the river tells you when you are coming to it. Then there's your pitch-dark night; the river is a very different shape on a pitch-dark night from what it is on a starlight night. All shores seem to be straight lines, then, and mighty dim ones, too; and you'd *run* them for straight lines, only you know better. You boldly drive your boat right into what seems to be a solid, straight wall (you knowing very well that in reality there is a curve there), and that wall falls back and makes way for you. Then there's

your gray mist. You take a night when there's one of these grisly, drizzly, gray mists, and then there isn't *any* particular shape to a shore. A gray mist would tangle the head of the oldest man that ever lived. Well, then, different kinds of *moonlight* change the shape of the river in different ways. You see—"

"Oh, don't say any more, please! Have I got to learn the shape of the river according to all these five hundred thousand different ways? If I tried to carry all that cargo in my head it would make me stoop-shouldered."

"*No!* you only learn *the* shape of the river; and you learn it with such absolute certainty that you can always steer by the shape that's *in your head,* and never mind the one that's before your eyes."

"Very well, I'll try it; but, after I have learned it, can I depend on it? Will it keep the same form and not go fooling around?"

Before Mr. Bixby could answer, Mr. W. came in to take the watch, and he said:

"Bixby, you'll have to look out for President's Island, and all that country clear away up above the Old Hen and Chickens. The banks are caving and the shape of the shores changing like everything. Why, you wouldn't know the point above 40. You can go up inside the old sycamore snag, now." [5]

So that question was answered. Here were leagues of shore changing shape. My spirits were down in the mud again. Two things seemed pretty apparent to me. One was, that in order to be a pilot a man had got to learn more than any one man ought to be allowed to know; and the other was, that he must learn it all over again in a different way every twenty-four hours.

That night we had the watch until twelve. Now it was an ancient river custom for the two pilots to chat a bit when the

---

[5] It may not be necessary, but still it can do no harm to explain that "inside" means between the snag and the shore. [Author's note.]

watch changed. While the relieving pilot put on his gloves and lit his cigar, his partner, the retiring pilot, would say something like this:

"I judge the upper bar is making down a little at Hale's Point; had quarter twain with the lower lead and mark twain [6] with the other."

"Yes, I thought it was making down a little, last trip. Meet any boats?"

"Met one abreast the head of 21, but she was away over hugging the bar, and I couldn't make her out entirely. I took her for the *Sunny South*—hadn't any skylights forward of the chimneys."

And so on. And as the relieving pilot took the wheel his partner [7] would mention that we were in such-and-such a bend, and say we were abreast of such-and-such a man's woodyard or plantation. This was courtesy; I supposed it was *necessity*. But Mr. W. came on watch full twelve minutes late on this particular night—a tremendous breach of etiquette; in fact, it is the unpardonable sin among pilots. So Mr. Bixby gave him no greeting whatever, but simply surrendered the wheel and marched out of the pilot-house without a word. I was appalled; it was a villainous night for blackness, we were in a particularly wide and blind part of the river, where there was no shape or substance to anything, and it seemed incredible that Mr. Bixby should have left that poor fellow to kill the boat, trying to find out where he was. But I resolved that I would stand by him anyway. He should find that he was not wholly friendless. So I stood around, and waited to be asked where we were. But Mr. W. plunged on serenely through the solid firmament of black cats that stood for an atmosphere, and never opened his mouth. "Here is a proud devil!" thought I; "here is a limb of Satan that would rather send us all to destruction than put himself under obligations to me, because I am not yet one of the salt of the earth and privileged to snub captains and lord it over everything dead and alive in a steamboat." I presently climbed up on the bench; I did not think

it was safe to go to sleep while this lunatic was on watch.

However, I must have gone to sleep in the course of time, because the next thing I was aware of was the fact that day was breaking, Mr. W. gone, and Mr. Bixby at the wheel again. So it was four o'clock and all well—but me; I felt like a skinful of dry bones, and all of them trying to ache at once.

Mr. Bixby asked me what I had stayed up there for. I confessed that it was to do Mr. W. a benevolence—tell him where he was. It took five minutes for the entire preposterousness of the thing to filter into Mr. Bixby's system, and then I judge it filled him nearly up to the chin; because he paid me a compliment—and not much of a one either. He said:

"Well, taking you by and large, you do seem to be more different kinds of an ass than any creature I ever saw before. What did you suppose he wanted to know for?"

I said I thought it might be a convenience to him.

"Convenience! D——nation! Didn't I tell you that a man's got to know the river in the night the same as he'd know his own front hall?"

"Well, I can follow the front hall in the dark if I know it *is* the front hall; but suppose you set me down in the middle of it in the dark and not tell me which hall it is; how am *I* to know?"

"Well, you've *got* to, on the river!"

"All right. Then I'm glad I never said anything to Mr. W."

"I should say so! Why, he'd have slammed you through the window and utterly ruined a hundred dollars' worth of window-sash and stuff."

I was glad this damage had been saved, for it would have made me unpopular with the owners. They always hated anybody

---

[6] Two fathoms. Quarter twain is 2¼ fathoms, 13½ feet. Mark three is three fathoms. [Author's note.]

[7] "Partner" is technical for "the other pilot." [Author's note.]

who had the name of being careless and injuring things.

I went to work now to learn the shape of the river; and of all the eluding and ungraspable objects that ever I tried to get mind or hands on, that was the chief. I would fasten my eyes upon a sharp, wooded point that projected far into the river some miles ahead of me, and go to laboriously photographing its shape upon my brain; and just as I was beginning to succeed to my satisfaction, we would draw up toward it and the exasperating thing would begin to melt away and fold back into the bank! If there had been a conspicuous dead tree standing upon the very point of the cape, I would find that tree inconspicuously merged into the general forest, and occupying the middle of a straight shore, when I got abreast of it! No prominent hill would stick to its shape long enough for me to make up my mind what its form really was, but it was as dissolving and changeful as if it had been a mountain of butter in the hottest corner of the tropics. Nothing ever had the same shape when I was coming down-stream that it had borne when I went up. I mentioned these little difficulties to Mr. Bixby. He said:

"That's the very main virtue of the thing. If the shapes didn't change every three seconds they wouldn't be of any use. Take this place where we are now, for instance. As long as that hill over yonder is only one hill, I can boom right along the way I'm going; but the moment it splits at the top and forms a V, I know I've got to scratch to starboard in a hurry, or I'll bang this boat's brains out against a rock; and then the moment one of the prongs of the V swings behind the other, I've got to waltz to larboard again, or I'll have a misunderstanding with a snag that would snatch the keelson out of this steamboat as neatly as if it were a sliver in your hand. If that hill didn't change its shape on bad nights there would be an awful steamboat graveyard around here inside of a year."

It was plain that I had got to learn the shape of the river in all the different ways that could be thought of—upside down, wrong end first, inside out, fore-and-aft, and "thort-ships" [8]—and then know what to do on gray nights when it hadn't any shape at all. So I set about it. In the course of time I began to get the best of this knotty lesson, and my self-complacency moved to the front once more. Mr. Bixby was all fixed, and ready to start it to the rear again. He opened on me after this fashion:

"How much water did we have in the middle crossing at Hole-in-the-Wall, trip before last?"

I considered this an outrage. I said:

"Every trip, down and up, the leadsmen are singing through that tangled place for three-quarters of an hour on a stretch. How do you reckon I can remember such a mess as that?"

"My boy, you've got to remember it. You've got to remember the exact spot and the exact marks the boat lay in when we had the shoalest water, in every one of the five hundred shoal places between St. Louis and New Orleans; and you mustn't get the shoal soundings and marks of one trip mixed up with the shoal soundings and marks of another, either, for they're not often twice alike. You must keep them separate."

When I came to myself again, I said:

"When I get so that I can do that, I'll be able to raise the dead, and then I won't have to pilot a steamboat to make a living. I want to retire from this business. I want a slush-bucket and a brush; I'm only fit for a roustabout. I haven't got brains enough to be a pilot; and if I had I wouldn't have strength enough to carry them around, unless I went on crutches."

"Now drop that! When I say I'll learn [9] a man the river, I mean it. And you can depend on it, I'll learn him or kill him."

---

[8] Thwartships, or crosswise.

[9] "Teach" is not in the river vocabulary. [Author's note.]

CONTINUED PERPLEXITIES

There was no use in arguing with a person like this. I promptly put such a strain on my memory that by and by even the shoal water and the countless crossing-marks began to stay with me. But the result was just the same. I never could more than get one knotty thing learned before another presented itself. Now I had often seen pilots gazing at the water and pretending to read it as if it were a book; but it was a book that told me nothing. A time came at last, however, when Mr. Bixby seemed to think me far enough advanced to bear a lesson on water-reading. So he began:

"Do you see that long, slanting line on the face of the water? Now, that's a reef. Moreover, it's a bluff reef. There is a solid sand-bar under it that is nearly as straight up and down as the side of a house. There is plenty of water close up to it, but mighty little on top of it. If you were to hit it you would knock the boat's brains out. Do you see where the line fringes out at the upper end and begins to fade away?"

"Yes, sir."

"Well, that is a low place; that is the head of the reef. You can climb over there, and not hurt anything. Cross over, now, and follow along close under the reef—easy water there—not much current."

I followed the reef along till I approached the fringed end. Then Mr. Bixby said;

"Now get ready. Wait till I give the word. She won't want to mount the reef; a boat hates shoal water. Stand by—wait—*wait*—keep her well in hand. *Now* cramp her down! Snatch her! snatch her!"

He seized the other side of the wheel and helped to spin it around until it was hard down, and then we held it so. The boat resisted, and refused to answer for a while, and next she came surging to starboard, mounted the reef, and sent a long, angry ridge of water foaming away from her bows.

"Now watch her; watch her like a cat, or she'll get away from you. When she fights strong and the tiller slips a little, in a jerky, greasy sort of way, let up on her a trifle; it is the way she tells you at night that the water is too shoal; but keep edging her up, little by little, toward the point. You are well up on the bar now; there is a bar under every point, because the water that comes down around it forms an eddy and allows the sediment to sink. Do you see those fine lines on the face of the water that branch out like the ribs of a fan? Well, those are little reefs; you want to just miss the ends of them, but run them pretty close. Now look out—look out! Don't you crowd that slick, greasy-looking place; there ain't nine feet there; she won't stand it. She begins to smell it; look sharp, I tell you! Oh, blazes, there you go! Stop the starboard wheel! Quick! Ship up to back! Set her back!"

The engine bells jingled and the engines answered promptly, shooting white columns of steam far aloft out of the 'scape-pipes, but it was too late. The boat had "smelt" the bar in good earnest; the foamy ridges that radiated from her bows suddenly disappeared, a great dead swell came rolling forward, and swept ahead of her, she careened far over to larboard, and went tearing away toward the shore as if she were about scared to death. We were a good mile from where we ought to have been when we finally got the upper hand of her again.

During the afternoon watch the next day, Mr. Bixby asked me if I knew how to run the next few miles. I said:

"Go inside the first snag above the point, outside the next one, start out from the lower end of Higgins's woodyard, make a square crossing, and—"

"That's all right. I'll be back before you close up on the next point."

But he wasn't. He was still below when I rounded it and entered upon a piece of the river which I had some misgivings about. I did not know that he was hiding behind a chimney to see how I would perform. I went gaily along, getting prouder and prouder, for he had never left the boat in my sole charge such a length of time before. I even got to "setting" her and letting the wheel go entirely, while I vaingloriously turned my back and inspected the stern marks and hummed a tune, a sort of easy indifference which I had prodigiously admired in Bixby and other great pilots. Once I inspected rather long, and when I faced to the front again my heart flew into my mouth so suddenly that if I hadn't clapped my teeth together I should have lost it. One of those frightful bluff reefs was stretching its deadly length right across our bows! My head was gone in a moment; I did not know which end I stood on; I gasped and could not get my breath; I spun the wheel down with such rapidity that it wove itself together like a spider's web; the boat answered and turned square away from the reef, but the reef followed her! I fled, but still it followed, still it kept—right across my bows! I never looked to see where I was going, I only fled. The awful crash was imminent. Why didn't that villain come? If I committed the crime of ringing a bell I might get thrown overboard. But better that than kill the boat. So in blind desperation, I started such a rattling "shivaree" down below as never had astounded an engineer in this world before, I fancy. Amidst the frenzy of the bells the engines began to back and fill in a curious way, and my reason forsook its throne— we were about to crash into the woods on the other side of the river. Just then Mr. Bixby stepped calmly into view on the hurricane-deck. My soul went out to him in gratitude. My distress vanished; I would have felt safe on the brink of Niagara with Mr. Bixby on the hurricane-deck. He blandly and sweetly took his toothpick out of his mouth between his fingers, as if it were a cigar—we were just in the act of climbing an overhanging big tree, and the passengers were scudding astern like rats—

and lifted up these commands to me ever so gently:

"Stop the starboard! Stop the larboard! Set her back on both!"

The boat hesitated, halted, pressed her nose among the boughs a critical instant, then reluctantly began to back away.

"Stop the larboard! Come ahead on it! Stop the starboard! Come ahead on it! Point her for the bar!"

I sailed away as serenely as a summer's morning. Mr. Bixby came in and said, with mock simplicity:

"When you have a hail, my boy, you ought to tap the big bell three times before you land, so that the engineers can get ready."

I blushed under the sarcasm, and said I hadn't had any hail.

"Ah! Then it was for wood, I suppose. The officer of the watch will tell you when he wants to wood up."

I went on consuming, and said I wasn't after wood.

"Indeed? Why, what could you want over here in the bend, then? Did you ever know of a boat following a bend up-stream at this stage of the river?"

"No, sir—and I wasn't trying to follow it. I was getting away from a bluff reef."

"No, it wasn't a bluff reef; there isn't one within three miles of where you were."

"But I saw it. It was as bluff as that one yonder."

"Just about. Run over it!"

"Do you give it as an order?"

"Yes. Run over it!"

"If I don't, I wish I may die."

"All right; I am taking the responsibility."

I was just as anxious to kill the boat, now, as I had been to save it before. I impressed my orders upon my memory, to be used at the inquest, and made a straight break for the reef. As it disappeared under our bows I held my breath; but we slid over it like oil.

"Now, don't you see the difference? It wasn't anything but a *wind* reef. The wind does that."

"So I see. But it is exactly like a bluff reef. How am I ever going to tell them apart?"

"I can't tell you. It is an instinct. By and by you will just naturally *know* one from the other, but you never will be able to explain why or how you know them apart."

It turned out to be true. The face of the water, in time, became a wonderful book —a book that was a dead language to the uneducated passenger, but which told its mind to me without reserve, delivering its most cherished secrets as clearly as if it uttered them with a voice. And it was not a book to be read once and thrown aside, for it had a new story to tell every day. Throughout the long twelve hundred miles there was never a page that was void of interest, never one that you could leave unread without loss, never one that you would want to skip, thinking you could find higher enjoyment in some other thing. There never was so wonderful a book written by man; never one whose interest was so absorbing, so unflagging, so sparklingly renewed with every reperusal. The passenger who could not read it was charmed with a peculiar sort of faint dimple on its surface (on the rare occasions when he did not overlook it altogether); but to the pilot that was an *italicized* passage; indeed, it was more than that, it was a legend of the largest capitals, with a string of shouting exclamation-points at the end of it, for it meant that a wreck or a rock was buried there that could tear the life out of the strongest vessel that ever floated. It is the faintest and simplest expression the water ever makes, and the most hideous to a pilot's eye. In truth, the passenger who could not read this book saw nothing but all manner of pretty pictures in it, painted by the sun and shaded by the clouds, whereas to the trained eye these were not pictures at all, but the grimmest and most dead-earnest of reading-matter.

Now when I had mastered the language of this water, and had come to know every trifling feature that bordered the great river as familiarly as I knew the letters of the alphabet, I had made a valuable acquisition. But I had lost something, too. I had lost something which could never be restored to me while I lived. All the grace, the beauty, the poetry, had gone out of the majestic river! I still kept in mind a certain wonderful sunset which I witnessed when steamboating was new to me. A broad expanse of the river was turned to blood; in the middle distance the red hue brightened into gold, through which a solitary log came floating, black and conspicuous; in one place a long, slanting mark lay sparkling upon the water; in another the surface was broken by boiling, tumbling rings, that were as many-tinted as an opal; where the ruddy flush was faintest, was a smooth spot that was covered with graceful circles and radiating lines, ever so delicately traced; the shore on our left was densely wooded, and the somber shadow that fell from this forest was broken in one place by a long, ruffled trail that shone like silver; and high above the forest wall a clean-stemmed dead tree waved a single leafy bough that glowed like a flame in the unobstructed splendor that was flowing from the sun. There were graceful curves, reflected images, woody heights, soft distances; and over the whole scene, far and near, the dissolving lights drifted steadily, enriching it every passing moment with new marvels of coloring.

I stood like one bewitched. I drank it in, in a speechless rapture. The world was new to me, and I had never seen anything like this at home. But as I have said, a day came when I began to cease from noting the glories and the charms which the moon and the sun and the twilight wrought upon the river's face; another day came when I ceased altogether to note them. Then, if that sunset scene had been repeated, I should have looked upon it without rapture, and should have commented upon it, inwardly, after this fashion: "This sun means that we are going to have wind to-morrow; that floating log means that the river is rising, small thanks to it; that slanting mark on the water refers to a bluff reef which is going to kill somebody's steamboat one of these nights, if it keeps on stretching out like that; those tumbling 'boils' show a dissolving bar and a changing channel there; the lines and circles in the slick water over yonder are a warning that that troublesome place is shoaling up dangerously; that silver streak in the shadow of the forest is the 'break' from a new snag, and he has located himself in the very best place he could have found to fish for steamboats; that tall dead tree, with a single living branch, is not going to last long, and then how is a body ever going to get through this blind place at night without the friendly old landmark?"

No, the romance and beauty were all gone from the river. All the value any feature of it had for me now was the amount of usefulness it could furnish toward compassing the safe piloting of a steamboat. Since those days, I have pitied doctors from my heart. What does the lovely flush in a beauty's cheek mean to a doctor but a "break" that ripples above some deadly disease? Are not all her visible charms sown thick with what are to him the signs and symbols of hidden decay? Does he ever see her beauty at all, or doesn't he simply view her professionally, and comment upon her unwholesome condition all to himself? And doesn't he sometimes wonder whether he has gained most or lost most by learning his trade?

SPEECH ON THE BABIES [1]
[1879]

AT THE BANQUET, IN CHICAGO, GIVEN BY THE ARMY OF THE TENNESSEE TO THEIR FIRST COMMANDER, GENERAL U. S. GRANT, NOVEMBER, 1879

I LIKE THAT. We have not all had the good fortune to be ladies. We have not all been generals, or poets, or statesmen; but when the toast works down to the babies,

we stand on common ground. It is a shame that for a thousand years the world's banquets have utterly ignored the baby, as if he didn't amount to anything. If you will stop and think a minute—if you will go back fifty or one hundred years to your early married life and recontemplate your first baby—you will remember that he amounted to a good deal, and even something over. You soldiers all know that when that little fellow arrived at family headquarters you had to hand in your resignation. He took entire command. You became his lackey, his mere body-servant, and you had to stand around, too. He was not a commander who made allowances for time, distance, weather, or anything else. You had to execute his order whether it was possible or not. And there was only one form of marching in his manual of tactics, and that was the double-quick. He treated you with every sort of insolence and disrespect, and the bravest of you didn't dare to say a word. You could face the death-storm at Donelson and Vicksburg, and give back blow for blow; but when he clawed your whiskers, and pulled your hair, and twisted your nose, you had to take it. When the thunders of war were sounding in your ears you set your faces toward the batteries, and advanced with steady tread; but when he turned on the terrors of his warwhoop you advanced in the other direction, and mighty glad of the chance, too. When he called for soothing-syrup, did you venture to throw out any side remarks about certain services being unbecoming an officer and a gentleman? No. You got up and *got* it. When he ordered his pap bottle and it was not warm, did you talk back? Not you. You went to work and *warmed* it. You even descended so far in your menial office as to take a suck at that warm, insipid stuff yourself, to see if it was right—three parts water to one of milk, a touch of sugar to

[1] The fifteenth regular toast was "The Babies—As they comfort us in our sorrows, let us not forget them in our festivities."

modify the colic, and a drop of peppermint to kill those immortal hiccoughs. I can taste that stuff yet. And how many things you learned as you went along! Sentimental young folks still take stock in that beautiful old saying that when the baby smiles in his sleep, it is because the angels are whispering to him. Very pretty, but too thin—simply wind on the stomach, my friends. If the baby proposed to take a walk at his usual hour, two o'clock in the morning, didn't you rise up promptly and remark, with a mental addition which would not improve a Sunday-school book *much*, that that was the very thing you were about to propose yourself? Oh! you were under good discipline, and as you went fluttering up and down the room in your undress uniform, you not only prattled undignified baby-talk, but even tuned up your martial voices and tried to *sing!* —"Rock-a-by baby in the tree-top," for instance. What a spectacle for an Army of the Tennessee! And what an affliction for the neighbors, too; for it is not everybody within a mile around that likes military music at three in the morning. And when you had been keeping this sort of thing up two or three hours, and your little velvet-head intimated that nothing suited him like exercise and noise, what did you do? [*"Go on!"*] [2] You simply *went* on until you dropped in the last ditch. The idea that a *baby* doesn't *amount* to anything! Why, *one* baby is just a house and a front yard full by itself. *One* baby can furnish more business than you and your whole Interior Department can attend to. He is enterprising, irrepressible, brimful of lawless activities. Do what you please, you can't make him stay on the reservation. Sufficient unto the day is one baby. As long as you are in your right mind don't you ever pray for twins. Twins amount to a permanent riot. And there ain't any real difference between triplets and an insurrection.

Yes, it was high time for a toast-master to recognize the importance of the babies. Think what is in store for the present crop! Fifty years from now we shall all be dead, I trust, and then this flag, if it still survive (and let us hope it may), will be floating over a Republic numbering 200,000,000 souls, according to the settled laws of our increase. Our present schooner of State will have grown into a political leviathan—a Great Eastern. The cradled babies of to-day will be on deck. Let them be well trained, for we are going to leave a big contract on their hands. Among the three or four million cradles now rocking in the land are some which this nation would preserve for ages as sacred things, if we could know which ones they are. In one of these cradles the unconscious Farragut [3] of the future is at this moment teething—think of it!—and putting in a world of dead earnest, unarticulated, but perfectly justifiable profanity over it, too. In another the future renowned astronomer is blinking at the shining Milky Way with but a languid interest—poor little chap! —and wondering what has become of that other one they call the wet-nurse. In another the future great historian is lying— and doubtless will continue to lie until his earthly mission is ended. In another the future President is busying himself with no profounder problem of state than what the mischief has become of his hair so early; and in a mighty array of other cradles there are now some 60,000 future office-seekers, getting ready to furnish him occasion to grapple with that same old problem a second time. And in still one more cradle, somewhere under the flag, the future illustrious commander-in-chief of the American armies is so little burdened with his approaching grandeurs and responsibilities as to be giving his whole strategic mind at this moment to trying to find out some way to get his big toe into his mouth—an achievement which, meaning no disrespect, the illustrious guest of this evening turned *his* entire attention to some

---

[2] Voice from the audience.

[3] David G. Farragut (1801-1870), American admiral, leading naval hero of the Civil War.

fifty-six years ago; and if the child is but a prophecy of the man, there are mighty few who will doubt that he *succeeded*.

ON THE DECAY OF THE ART OF LYING [1]
[1882]

OBSERVE, I do not mean to suggest that the *custom* of lying has suffered any decay or interruption—no, for the Lie, as a Virtue, a Principle, is eternal; the Lie, as a recreation, a solace, a refuge in time of need, the fourth Grace, the tenth Muse, man's best and surest friend, is immortal, and cannot perish from the earth while this Club remains. My complaint simply concerns the decay of the *art* of lying. No high-minded man, no man of right feeling, can contemplate the lumbering and slovenly lying of the present day without grieving to see a noble art so prostituted. In this veteran presence I naturally enter upon this scheme with diffidence; it is like an old maid trying to teach nursery matters to the mothers in Israel. It would not become me to criticize you, gentlemen, who are nearly all my elders—and my superiors, in this thing— and so, if I should here and there *seem* to do it, I trust it will in most cases be more in a spirit of admiration than of fault-finding; indeed, if this finest of the fine arts had everywhere received the attention, encouragement, and conscientious practice and development which this Club has devoted to it, I should not need to utter this lament or shed a single tear. I do not say this to flatter: I say it in a spirit of just and appreciative recognition.

[It had been my intention, at this point, to mention names and give illustrative specimens, but indications observable about me admonished me to beware of particulars and confine myself to generalities.]

No fact is more firmly established than that lying is a necessity of our circumstances—the deduction that it is then a Virtue goes without saying. No virtue can reach its highest usefulness without careful and diligent cultivation—therefore, it goes without saying that this one ought to be taught in the public schools—at the fireside—even in the newspapers. What chance has the ignorant, uncultivated liar against the educated expert? What chance have I against Mr. Per—against a lawyer? [2] *Judicious* lying is what the world needs. I sometimes think it were even better and safer not to lie at all than to lie injudiciously. An awkward, unscientific lie is often as ineffectual as the truth.

Now let us see what the philosophers say. Note that venerable proverb: Children and fools *always* speak the truth. The deduction is plain—adults and wise persons never speak it. Parkman, the historian, says, "The principle of truth may itself be carried into an absurdity." In another place in the same chapter he says, "The saying is old that truth should not be spoken at all times; and those whom a sick conscience worries into habitual violation of the maxim are imbeciles and nuisances." It is strong language, but true. None of us could *live* with an habitual truth-teller; but, thank goodness, none of us has to. An habitual truth-teller is simply an impossible creature; he does not exist; he never has existed. Of course there are people who *think* they never lie, but it is not so —and this ignorance is one of the very things that shame our so-called civilization. Everybody lies—every day; every hour; awake; asleep; in his dreams; in his joy; in his mourning; if he keeps his tongue still, his hands, his feet, his eyes, his attitude, will convey deception—and purposely. Even in sermons—but that is a platitude.

In a far country where I once lived the ladies used to go around paying calls,

---

[1] Essay, for Discussion, Read at a Meeting of the Historical and Antiquarian Club of Hartford, and Offered for the Thirty-Dollar Prize. (Did not take the prize.) [Author's note.]

[2] Charles E. Perkins, of Hartford, a lawyer and a close personal friend of Mark Twain.

under the humane and kindly pretense of wanting to see each other; and when they returned home, they would cry out with a glad voice, saying, "We made sixteen calls and found fourteen of them out"—not meaning that they found out anything against the fourteen—no, that was only a colloquial phrase to signify that they were not at home—and their manner of saying it expressed their lively satisfaction in that fact. Now their pretense of wanting to see the fourteen—and the other two whom they had been less lucky with—was that commonest and mildest form of lying which is sufficiently described as a deflection from the truth. Is it justifiable? Most certainly. It is beautiful, it is noble; for its object is, *not* to reap profit, but to convey a pleasure to the sixteen. The iron-souled truth-monger would plainly manifest, or even utter the fact, that he didn't want to see those people—and he would be an ass, and inflict a totally unnecessary pain. And next, those ladies in that far country—but never mind, they had a thousand pleasant ways of lying, that grew out of gentle impulses, and were a credit to their intelligence and an honor to their hearts. Let the particulars go.

The men in that far country were liars, every one. Their mere howdy-do was a lie, because *they* didn't care how you did, except they were undertakers. To the ordinary inquirer you lied in return; for you made no conscientious diagnosis of your case, but answered at random, and usually missed it considerably. You lied to the undertaker, and said your health was failing—a wholly commendable lie, since it cost you nothing and pleased the other man. If a stranger called and interrupted you, you said with your hearty tongue, "I'm glad to see you," and said with your heartier soul, "I wish you were with the cannibals and it was dinner-time." When he went, you said regretfully, "*Must* you go?" and followed it with a "Call again"; but you did no harm, for you did not deceive anybody nor inflict any hurt, whereas the truth would have made you both unhappy.

I think that all this courteous lying is a sweet and loving art, and should be cultivated. The highest perfection of politeness is only a beautiful edifice, built, from the base to the dome, of graceful and gilded forms of charitable and unselfish lying.

What I bemoan is the growing prevalence of the brutal truth. Let us do what we can to eradicate it. An injurious truth has no merit over an injurious lie. Neither should ever be uttered. The man who speaks an injurious truth, lest his soul be not saved if he do otherwise, should reflect that that sort of a soul is not strictly worth saving. The man who tells a lie to help a poor devil out of trouble is one of whom the angels doubtless say, "Lo, here is an heroic soul who casts his own welfare into jeopardy to succor his neighbor's; let us exalt this magnanimous liar."

An injurious lie is an uncommendable thing; and so, also, and in the same degree, is an injurious truth—a fact which is recognized by the law of libel.

Among other common lies, we have the *silent* lie—the deception which one conveys by simply keeping still and concealing the truth. Many obstinate truth-mongers indulge in this dissipation, imagining that if they *speak* no lie, they lie not at all. In that far country where I once lived, there was a lovely spirit, a lady whose impulses were always high and pure, and whose character answered to them. One day I was there at dinner, and remarked, in a general way, that we are all liars. She was amazed, and said, "Not *all*?" It was before "Pinafore's" time, so I did not make the response which would naturally follow in our day, but frankly said, "Yes, *all*—we are all liars; there are no exceptions." She looked almost offended, and said, "Why, do you include *me*?" "Certainly," I said, "I think you even rank as an expert." She said, "'Sh!—'sh! the children!" So the subject was changed in deference to the children's presence, and we went on talking about other things. But as soon as the young people were out of the way, the lady came warmly back to the matter and said, "I have made it the rule of my life to never tell a lie; and I have never departed from it in a single instance." I said, "I don't mean the least harm or disrespect, but really you have been lying like smoke ever since I've been sitting here. It has caused me a good deal of pain, because I am not used to it." She required of me an instance—just a single instance. So I said:

"Well, here is the unfilled duplicate of the blank which the Oakland hospital people sent to you by the hand of the sick-nurse when she came here to nurse your little nephew through his dangerous illness. This blank asks all manner of questions as to the conduct of that sick-nurse: 'Did she ever sleep on her watch? Did she ever forget to give the medicine?' and so forth and so on. You are warned to be very careful and explicit in your answers, for the welfare of the service requires that the nurses be promptly fined or otherwise punished for derelictions. You told me you were perfectly delighted with that nurse—that she had a thousand perfections and only one fault: you found you never could depend on her wrapping Johnny up half sufficiently while he waited in a chilly chair for her to rearrange the warm bed. You filled up the duplicate of this paper, and sent it back to the hospital by the hand of the nurse. How did you answer this question—'Was the nurse at any time guilty of a negligence which was likely to result in the patient's taking cold?' Come—everything is decided by a bet here in California; ten dollars to ten cents you lied when you answered that question." She said, *I didn't; I left it blank!*" "Just so— you have told a *silent* lie; you have left it to be inferred that you had no fault to find in that matter." She said, "Oh, was that a lie? And how *could* I mention her one single fault, and she so good?—it would have been cruel." I said, "One ought always to lie when one can do good by it; your impulse was right, but your judgment was crude; this comes of unintelligent practice. Now observe the result of this

inexpert deflection of yours. You know Mr. Jones's Willie is lying very low with scarlet fever; well, your recommendation was so enthusiastic that that girl is there nursing him, and the worn-out family have all been trustingly sound asleep for the last fourteen hours, leaving their darling with full confidence in those fatal hands, because you, like young George Washington, have a reputa— However, if you are not going to have anything to do, I will come around to-morrow and we'll attend the funeral together, for, of course, you'll naturally feel a peculiar interest in Willie's case—as personal a one, in fact, as the undertaker."

But that was all lost. Before I was half-way through she was in a carriage and making thirty miles an hour toward the Jones mansion to save what was left of Willie and tell all she knew about the deadly nurse. All of which was unnecessary, as Willie wasn't sick; I had been lying myself. But that same day, all the same, she sent a line to the hospital which filled up the neglected blank, and stated the *facts*, too, in the squarest possible manner.

Now, you see, this lady's fault was *not* in lying, but only in lying injudiciously. She should have told the truth, *there*, and made it up to the nurse with a fraudulent compliment further along in the paper. She could have said, "In one respect the sick-nurse is perfection—when she is on watch, she never snores." Almost any little pleasant lie would have taken the sting out of that troublesome but necessary expression of the truth.

Lying is universal—we *all* do it; we all *must* do it. Therefore, the wise thing is for us diligently to train ourselves to lie thoughtfully, judiciously; to lie with a good object, and not an evil one; to lie for others' advantage, and not our own; to lie healingly, charitably, humanely, not cruelly, hurtfully, maliciously; to lie gracefully and graciously, not awkwardly and clumsily; to lie firmly, frankly, squarely, with head erect, not haltingly, tortuously, with pusillanimous mien, as being ashamed of our high calling. Then shall we be rid of the rank and pestilent truth that is rotting the land; then shall we be great and good and beautiful, and worthy dwellers in a world where even benign Nature habitually lies, except when she promises execrable weather. Then— But I am but a new and feeble student in this gracious art; I cannot instruct *this* Club.

Joking aside, I think there is much need of wise examination into what sorts of lies are best and wholesomest to be indulged, seeing we *must* all lie and *do* all lie, and what sorts it may be best to avoid—and this is a thing which I feel I can confidently put into the hands of this experienced Club—a ripe body, who may be termed, in this regard, and without undue flattery, Old Masters.

From

PERSONAL RECOLLECTIONS OF JOAN OF ARC
[1896]

Chapter III

SPEAKING of this matter reminds me [1] of many incidents, many things that I could tell, but I think I will not try to do it now. It will be more to my present humor to call back a little glimpse of the simple and colorless good times we used to have in our village homes in those peaceful days —especially in the winter. In the summer we children were out on the breezy uplands with the flocks from dawn till night, and then there was noisy frolicking and all that; but winter was the cozy time, winter was the snug time. Often we gathered in old Jacques d'Arc's big dirt-floored apartment, with a great fire going, and played games, and sang songs, and told fortunes, and listened to the old villagers tell tales and histories and lies and one thing and another till twelve o'clock at night.

One winter's night we were gathered

there—it was the winter that for years afterward they called the hard winter— and that particular night was a sharp one. It blew a gale outside, and the screaming of the wind was a stirring sound, and I think I may say it was beautiful, for I think it *is* great and fine and beautiful to hear the wind rage and storm and blow its clarions like that, when you are inside and comfortable. And we were. We had a roaring fire, and the pleasant *spit-spit* of the snow and sleet falling in it down the chimney, and the yarning and laughing and singing went on at a noble rate till about ten o'clock, and then we had a supper of hot porridge and beans, and meal cakes with butter, and appetites to match.

Little Joan sat on a box apart, and had her bowl and bread on another one, and her pets around her helping. She had more than was usual of them or economical, because all the outcast cats came and took up with her, and homeless or unlovable animals of other kinds heard about it and came, and these spread the matter to the other creatures, and they came also; and as the birds and the other timid wild things of the woods were not afraid of her, but always had an idea she was a friend when they came across her, and generally struck up an acquaintance with her to get invited to the house, she always had samples of those breeds in stock. She was hospitable to them all, for an animal was an animal to her, and dear by mere reason of being an animal, no matter about its sort or social station; and as she would allow of no cages, no collars, no fetters, but left the creatures free to come and go as they liked, that contented them, and they came; but they didn't go, to any extent, and so they were a marvelous nuisance, and made Jacques d'Arc swear a good deal; but his wife said God gave the child the instinct, and knew what He was doing when He did it, therefore it must have its course; it would be no sound

---

[1] The fictitious narrator is Louis de Conte, reared in the same village with Joan and later her page and secretary.

prudence to meddle with His affairs when no invitation had been extended. So the pets were left in peace, and here they were, as I have said, rabbits, birds, squirrels, cats, and other reptiles, all around the child, and full of interest in her supper, and helping what they could. There was a very small squirrel on her shoulder, sitting up, as those creatures do, and turning a rocky fragment of prehistoric chestnut-cake over and over in its knotty hands, and hunting for the less indurated places, and giving its elevated bushy tail a flirt and its pointed ears a toss when it found one—signifying thankfulness and surprise —and then it filed that place off with those two slender front teeth which a squirrel carries for that purpose and not for orna-ment, for ornamental they never could be, as any will admit that have noticed them.

Everything was going fine and breezy and hilarious, but then there came an in-terruption, for somebody hammered on the door. It was one of those ragged road-stragglers—the eternal wars kept the coun-try full of them. He came in, all over snow, and stamped his feet, and shook, and brushed himself, and shut the door, and took off his limp ruin of a hat, and slapped it once or twice against his leg to knock off its fleece of snow, and then glanced around on the company with a pleased look upon his thin face, and a most yearning and famished one in his eye when it fell upon the victuals, and then he gave us a humble and conciliatory salu-tation, and said it was a blessed thing to have a fire like that on such a night, and a roof overhead like this, and that rich food to eat, and loving friends to talk with— ah, yes, this was true, and God help the homeless, and such as must trudge the roads in this weather.

Nobody said anything. The embarrassed poor creature stood there and appealed to one face after the other with his eyes, and found no welcome in any, the smile on his own face flickering and fading and perish-ing, meanwhile; then he dropped his gaze, the muscles of his face began to twitch, and he put up his hand to cover this womanish sign of weakness.

"Sit down!"

This thunder-blast was from old Jacques d'Arc, and Joan was the object of it. The stranger was startled, and took his hand away, and there was Joan standing before him offering him her bowl of porridge. The man said:

"God Almighty bless you, my darling!" and then the tears came, and ran down his cheeks, but he was afraid to take the bowl.

"Do you hear me? Sit down, I say!"

There could not be a child more easy to persuade than Joan, but this was not the way. Her father had not the art; neither could he learn it. Joan said:

"Father, he is hungry; I can see it."

"Let him go work for food, then. We are being eaten out of house and home by his like, and I have said I would endure it no more, and will keep my word. He has the face of a rascal anyhow, and a villain. Sit *down*, I tell you!"

"I know not if he is a rascal or no, but he is hungry, father, and shall have my porridge—I do not need it."

"If you don't obey me I'll— Rascals are not entitled to help from honest people, and no bite nor sup shall they have in this house. *Joan!*"

She set her bowl down on the box and came over and stood before her scowling father, and said:

"Father, if you will not let me, then it must be as you say; but I would that you would think—then you would see that it is not right to punish one part of him for what the other part has done; for it is that poor stranger's head that does the evil things, but it is not his head that is hungry, it is his stomach, and it has done no harm to anybody, but is without blame, and innocent, not having any *way* to do a wrong, even if it was minded to it. Please let—"

"What an idea! It is the most idiotic speech I ever heard."

But Aubrey, the maire, broke in, he being fond of an argument, and having a pretty gift in that regard, as all acknowledged. Rising in his place and leaning his knuckles upon the table and looking about him with easy dignity, after the manner of such as be orators, he began, smooth and persuasive:

"I will differ with you there, gossip, and will undertake to show the company"—here he looked around upon us and nodded his head in a confident way—"that there is a grain of sense in what the child has said; for look you, it is of a certainty most true and demonstrable that it is a man's head that is master and supreme ruler over his whole body. Is that granted? Will any deny it?" He glanced around again; everybody indicated assent. "Very well, then; that being the case, no part of the body is responsible for the result when it carries out an order delivered to it by the head; ergo, the head is alone responsible for crimes done by a man's hands or feet or stomach—do you get the idea? am I right thus far?" Everybody said yes, and said it with enthusiasm, and some said, one to another, that the maire was in great form to-night and at his very best—which pleased the maire exceedingly and made his eyes sparkle with pleasure, for he overheard these things; so he went on in the same fertile and brilliant way. "Now, then, we will consider what the term responsibility means, and how it affects the case in point. Responsibility makes a man responsible for only those things for which he is properly responsible"—and he waved his spoon around in a wide sweep to indicate the comprehensive nature of that class of responsibilities which render people responsible, and several exclaimed, admiringly, "He is right!—he has put that whole tangled thing into a nutshell—it is wonderful!" After a little pause to give the interest opportunity to gather and grow, he went on: "Very good. Let us suppose the case of a pair of tongs that falls upon a man's foot, causing a cruel hurt. Will you claim that the tongs are punishable for that? The question is answered; I see by your faces that you would call such a claim absurd. Now, why is it absurd? It is absurd because, there being no reasoning faculty—that is to say, no faculty of personal command—in a pair of tongs, personal responsibility for the acts of the tongs is wholly absent from the tongs; and, therefore, responsibility being absent, punishment cannot ensue. Am I right?" A hearty burst of applause was his answer. "Now, then, we arrive at a man's stomach. Consider how exactly, how marvelously, indeed, its situation corresponds to that of a pair of tongs. Listen—and take careful note, I beg you. Can a man's stomach plan a murder? No. Can it plan a theft? No. Can it plan an incendiary fire? No. Now answer me—*can a pair of tongs?*" (There were admiring shouts of "No!" and "The cases are just exact!" and "Don't he do it splendid!") "Now, then, friends and neighbors, a stomach which cannot plan a crime cannot be a principal in the commission of it—that is plain, as you see. The matter is narrowed down by that much; we will narrow it further. Can a stomach, of its own motion, assist at a crime? The answer is no, because command is absent, the reasoning faculty is absent, volition is absent—as in the case of the tongs. We perceive now, do we not, that the stomach is totally irresponsible for crimes committed, either in whole or in part, by it?" He got a rousing cheer for response. "Then what do we arrive at as our verdict? Clearly this: that there is no such thing in this world as a guilty stomach; that in the body of the veriest rascal resides a pure and innocent stomach; that, whatever its owner may do, *it* at least should be sacred in our eyes; and that while God gives us minds to think just and charitable and honorable thoughts, it should be, and *is*, our privilege, as well as our duty, not only to feed the hungry stomach that resides in a rascal, having pity for its sorrow and its need, but to do it gladly, gratefully, in recognition of its sturdy and loyal maintenance of its purity and innocence in the midst of temptation and in company so repugnant to its better feelings. I am done."

Well, you never saw such an effect! They rose—the whole house rose—and clapped, and cheered, and praised him to the skies; and one after another, still clapping and shouting, they crowded forward, some with moisture in their eyes, and wrung his hands, and said such glorious things to him that he was clear overcome with pride and happiness, and couldn't say a word, for his voice would have broken, sure. It was splendid to see; and everybody said he had never come up to that speech in his life before, and never could do it again. Eloquence *is* a power, there is no question of that. Even old Jacques d'Arc was carried away, for once in his life, and shouted out:

"It's all right, Joan—give him the porridge!"

She was embarrassed, and did not seem to know what to say, and so didn't say anything. It was because she had given the man the porridge long ago, and he had already eaten it all up. When she was asked why she had not waited until a decision was arrived at, she said the man's stomach was very hungry, and it would not have been wise to wait, since she could not tell what the decision would be. Now that was a good and thoughtful idea for a child.

The man was not a rascal at all. He was a very good fellow, only he was out of luck, and surely that was no crime at that time in France. Now that his stomach was proved to be innocent, it was allowed to make itself at home; and as soon as it was well filled and needed nothing more, the man unwound his tongue and turned it loose, and it was really a noble one to go. He had been in the wars for years, and the things he told and the way he told them fired everybody's patriotism away up high, and set all hearts to thumping and all pulses to leaping; then, before anybody rightly knew how the change was made, he was leading us a sublime march through the ancient glories of France, and in

fancy we saw the titanic forms of the twelve paladins [2] rise out of the mists of the past and face their fate; we heard the tread of the innumerable hosts sweeping down to shut them in; we saw this human tide flow and ebb, ebb and flow, and waste away before that little band of heroes; we saw each detail pass before us of that most stupendous, most disastrous, yet most adored and glorious day in French legendary history; here and there and yonder, across that vast field of the dead and dying, we saw this and that and the other paladin dealing his prodigious blows with weary arm and failing strength, and one by one we saw them fall, till only one remained—he that was without peer, he whose name gives name to the Song of Songs, the song which no Frenchman can hear and keep his feelings down and his pride of country cool; then, grandest and pitifulest scene of all, we saw his own pathetic death; and our stillness, as we sat with parted lips and breathless, hanging upon this man's words, gave us a sense of the awful stillness that reigned in that field of slaughter when that last surviving soul had passed.

And now, in this solemn hush, the stranger gave Joan a pat or two on the head and said:

"Little maid — whom God keep! — you have brought me from death to life this night; now listen: here is your reward," and at that supreme time for such a heart-melting, soul-rousing surprise, without another word he lifted up the most noble and pathetic voice that was ever heard, and began to pour out the great Song of Roland!

Think of that, with a French audience all stirred up and ready. Oh, where was your spoken eloquence now! what was it to

---

[2] The guard of honor, or champions (douzepers) of Charlemagne in medieval romance. The *Chanson de Roland* narrates the adventures of the chief of these heroes, and his death at the battle of Roncesvalles in 778.

this! How fine he looked, how stately, how inspired, as he stood there with that mighty chant welling from his lips and his heart, his whole body transfigured, and his rags along with it.

Everybody rose and stood while he sang, and their faces glowed and their eyes burned; and the tears came and flowed down their cheeks, and their forms began to sway unconsciously to the swing of the song, and their bosoms to heave and pant; and moanings broke out, and deep ejaculations; and when the last verse was reached, and Roland lay dying, all alone, with his face to the field and to his slain, lying there in heaps and winrows, and took off and held up his gauntlet to God with his failing hand, and breathed his beautiful prayer with his paling lips, all burst out in sobs and wailings. But when the final great note died out and the song was done, they all flung themselves in a body at the singer, stark mad with love of him and love of France and pride in her great deeds and old renown, and smothered him with their embracings; but Joan was there first, hugged close to his breast, and covering his face with idolatrous kisses.

The storm raged on outside, but that was no matter; this was the stranger's home now, for as long as he might please.

TO THE PERSON SITTING IN DARKNESS [1]
[1901]

"CHRISTMAS will dawn in the United States over a people full of hope and aspiration and good cheer. Such a condition means contentment and happiness. The carping grumbler who may here and there go forth will find few to listen to him. The majority will wonder what is the matter with him and pass on."—*New York Tribune*, on Christmas Eve.

From *The Sun*, of New York:

"The purpose of this article is not to describe the terrible offences against humanity committed in the name of Politics in some of the most notorious East Side districts. *They could not be described, even verbally*. But it is the intention to let the great mass of more or less careless citizens of this beautiful metropolis of the New World get some conception of the havoc and ruin wrought to man, woman and child in the most densely populated and least known section of the city. Name, date, and place can be supplied to those of little faith—or to any man who feels himself aggrieved. It is a plain statement of record and observation, written without license and without garnish.

"Image, if you can, a section of the city territory completely dominated by one man, without whose permission neither legitimate nor illegitimate business can be conducted; *where illegitimate business is encouraged and legitimate business discouraged;* where the respectable residents have to fasten their doors and windows summer nights and sit in their rooms with asphyxiating air and 100-degree temperature, rather than try to catch the faint whiff of breeze in their natural breathing places, the stoops of their homes; *where naked women dance by night in the streets, and unsexed men prowl like vultures through the darkness on 'business' not only permitted but encouraged by the police; where the education of infants begins with the knowledge of prostitution* and the training of little girls is training in the arts of Phryne; [2] where *American* girls brought up with the refinements of *American* homes are imported from small towns up-State, Massachusetts, Connecticut and New Jersey, and kept as virtually prisoners as if they were locked up behind jail bars until they have lost all semblance of womanhood; *where small boys are taught to solicit for the women of disorderly houses;* where there is an organized society of young men *whose sole business in life is to corrupt young girls and turn them over to bawdy*

---

[1] Originally published in the *North American Review* in the number for February, 1901.

[2] Famous Greek courtesan of the Fourth Century B. C.

houses; where men walking with their wives along the street are openly insulted; *where children that have adult diseases are the chief patrons of the hospitals and dispensaries;* where it is the rule, rather than the exception, that *murder, rape, robbery and theft go unpunished*—in short where the Premium of the most awful forms of Vice is the Profit of the politicians."

The following news from China appeared in *The Sun,* of New York, on Christmas Eve. The italics are mine:

"The Rev. Mr. Ament, of the American Board of Foreign Missions, has returned from a trip which he made for the purpose of collecting indemnities for damages done by Boxers.[3] *Everywhere he went he compelled the Chinese to pay.* He says that all his native Christians are now provided for. He had 700 of them under his charge, and 300 were killed. He has *collected 300 taels for each* of these murders, and has *compelled full payment for all the property belonging to Christians* that was destroyed. He also assessed *fines* amounting to THIRTEEN TIMES [4] the amount of the indemnity. *This money will be used for the propagation of the Gospel.*

"Mr. Ament declares that the compensation he has collected is *moderate,* when compared with the amount secured by the Catholics, who demand, in addition to money, *head for head.* They collect 500 taels for each murder of a Catholic. In the Wenchiu country, 680 Catholics were killed, and for this the European Catholics here demand 750,000 strings of cash and 680 *heads.*

"In the course of a conversation, Mr. Ament referred to the attitude of the missionaries toward the Chinese. He said:

" 'I deny emphatically that the missionaries are *vindictive,* that they *generally* looted, or that they have done anything *since* the siege that *the circumstances did not demand.* I criticise the Americans. *The soft hand of the Americans is not as good as the mailed fist of the Germans.* If you deal with the Chinese with a soft hand they will take advantage of it.'

"The statement that the French Government will return the loot taken by the French soldiers, is the source of the greatest amusement here. The French soldiers were more systematic looters than the Germans, and it is a fact that to-day *Catholic Christians,* carrying French flags and armed with modern guns, *are looting villages* in the Province of Chili."

By happy luck, we get all these glad tidings on Christmas Eve—just in time to enable us to celebrate the day with proper gaiety and enthusiasm. Our spirits soar, and we find we can even make jokes: Taels I win, Heads you lose.

Our Reverend Ament is the right man in the right place. What we want of our missionaries out there is, not that they shall merely represent in their acts and persons the grace and gentleness and charity and loving kindness of our religion, but that they shall also represent the American spirit. The oldest Americans are the Pawnees. Macallum's History says: [5]

"When a white Boxer kills a Pawnee and destroys his property, the other Pawnees do not trouble to seek *him* out, they kill any white person that comes along; also, they make some white village pay deceased's heirs the full cash value of deceased, together with full cash value of the property destroyed; they also make the village pay, in addition, *thirteen times* the value of that property into a fund for the dissemination of the Pawnee religion, which they regard as the best of all religions for the softening and humanizing of the heart of man. It is their idea that it is only fair and right that the innocent should be

---

[3] The Boxers were a secret society in China which advocated resistance to foreign encroachments. After the Boxer rebellion in the summer of 1900 the allied powers demanded the execution of the leaders of the massacres of foreigners and the payment of a large indemnity.

[4] This was later shown to be an error for 1.3 times, but Clemens maintained that the wrong was no less even though the "fine" was smaller.

[5] A parable; not veritable history.

made to suffer for the guilty, and that it is better that ninety and nine innocent should suffer than that one guilty person should escape."

Our Reverend Ament is justifiably jealous of those enterprising Catholics, who not only get big money for each lost convert, but get "head for head" besides. But he should soothe himself with the reflection that the entirety of their exactions are for their own pockets, whereas he, less selfishly, devotes only 300 taels per head to that service, and gives the whole vast thirteen repetitions of the property-indemnity to the service of propagating the Gospel. His magnanimity has won him the approval of his nation, and will get him a monument. Let him be content with these rewards. We all hold him dear for manfully defending his fellow missionaries from exaggerated charges which were beginning to distress us, but which his testimony has so considerably modified that we can now contemplate them without noticeable pain. For now we know that, even before the siege, the missionaries were not "generally" out looting, and that, "since the siege," they have acted quite handsomely, except when "circumstances" crowded them. I am arranging for the monument. Subscriptions for it can be sent to the American Board; designs for it can be sent to me. Designs must allegorically set forth the Thirteen Reduplications of the Indemnity, and the Object for which they were exacted; as Ornaments, the designs must exhibit 680 Heads, so disposed as to give a pleasing and pretty effect; for the Catholics have done nicely, and are entitled to notice in the monument. Mottoes may be suggested, if any shall be discovered that will satisfactorily cover the ground.

Mr. Ament's financial feat of squeezing a thirteen-fold indemnity out of the pauper peasants to square other people's offences, thus condemning them and their women and innocent little children to inevitable starvation and lingering death, in order that the blood-money so acquired might be "used for the propagation of the Gospel," does not flutter my serenity; although the act and the words, taken together, concrete a blasphemy so hideous and so colossal that, without doubt, its mate is not findable in the history of this or of any other age. Yet, if a layman had done that thing and justified it with those words, I should have shuddered, I know. Or, if I had done the thing and said the words myself—however, the thought is unthinkable, irreverent as some imperfectly informed people think me. Sometimes an ordained minister sets out to be blasphemous. When this happens, the layman is out of the running; he stands no chance.

We have Mr. Ament's impassioned assurance that the missionaries are not "vindictive." Let us hope and pray that they will never become so, but will remain in the almost morbidly fair and just and gentle temper which is affording so much satisfaction to their brother and champion to-day.

The following is from the *New York Tribune* of Christmas Eve. It comes from that journal's Tokio correspondent. It has a strange and impudent sound, but the Japanese are but partially civilized as yet. When they become wholly civilized they will not talk so:

"The missionary question, of course, occupies a foremost place in the discussion. It is now felt as essential that the Western Powers take cognizance of the sentiment here, that religious invasions of Oriental countries by powerful Western organizations are tantamount to filibustering expeditions, and should not only be discountenanced, but that stern measures should be adopted for their suppression. The feeling here is that the missionary organizations constitute a constant menace to peaceful international relations."

Shall we? That is, shall we go on conferring our Civilization upon the peoples that sit in darkness, or shall we give those poor things a rest? Shall we bang right ahead in our old-time, loud, pious way, and commit the new century to the game; or shall we sober up and sit down and think it over first? Would it not be prudent to get our Civilization-tools together, and see how much stock is left on hand in the way of Glass Beads and Theology, and Maxim Guns and Hymn Books, and Trade-Gin and Torches of Progress and Enlightenment (patent adjustable ones, good to fire villages with, upon occasion), and balance the books, and arrive at the profit and loss, so that we may intelligently decide whether to continue the business or sell out the property and start a new Civilization Scheme on the proceeds?

Extending the Blessings of Civilization to our Brother who Sits in Darkness has been a good trade and has paid well, on the whole; and there is money in it yet, if carefully worked—but not enough, in my judgment, to make any considerable risk advisable. The People that Sit in Darkness are getting to be too scarce—too scarce and too shy. And such darkness as is now left is really of but an indifferent quality, and not dark enough for the game. The most of those People that Sit in Darkness have been furnished with more light than was good for them or profitable for us. We have been injudicious.

The Blessings-of-Civilization Trust, wisely and cautiously administered, is a Daisy. There is more money in it, more territory, more sovereignty, and other kinds of emolument, than there is in any other game that is played. But Christendom has been playing it badly of late years, and must certainly suffer by it, in my opinion. She has been so eager to get every stake that appeared on the green cloth, that the People who Sit in Darkness have noticed it—they have noticed it, and have begun to show alarm. They have become suspicious of the Blessings of Civilization. More—they have begun to examine them. This is not well. The Blessings of Civilization are all right, and a good commercial property; there could not be a better, in a dim light. In the right kind of a light, and

at a proper distance, with the goods a little out of focus, they furnish this desirable exhibit to the Gentlemen who Sit in Darkness:

LOVE,	LAW AND
JUSTICE,	ORDER,
GENTLENESS,	LIBERTY,
CHRISTIANITY,	EQUALITY,
PROTECTION TO	HONORABLE
THE WEAK,	DEALING,
TEMPERANCE,	MERCY,
	EDUCATION,

—and so on.

There. Is it good? Sir, it is pie. It will bring into camp any idiot that sits in darkness anywhere. But not if we adulterate it. It is proper to be emphatic upon that point. This brand is strictly for Export—apparently. *Apparently.* Privately and confidentially, it is nothing of the kind. Privately and confidentially, it is merely an outside cover, gay and pretty and attractive, displaying the special patterns of our Civilization which we reserve for Home Consumption, while *inside* the bale is the Actual Thing that the Customer Sitting in Darkness buys with his blood and tears and land and liberty. That Actual Thing is, indeed, Civilization, but it is only for Export. Is there a difference between the two brands? In some of the details, yes.

We all know that the Business is being ruined. The reason is not far to seek. It is because our Mr. McKinley, and Mr. Chamberlain, and the Kaiser, and the Czar [6] and the French have been exporting the Actual Thing *with the outside cover left off.* This is bad for the Game. It shows that these new players of it are not sufficiently acquainted with it.

It is a distress to look on and note the mismoves, they are so strange and so awkward. Mr. Chamberlain manufactures a

[6] President William McKinley (1843-1901); Joseph Chamberlain (1836-1914), British cabinet minister; William II, emperor (kaiser) of Germany; Nicholas II (1868-1918), czar of Russia.

war out of materials so inadequate and so fanciful that they make the boxes grieve and the gallery laugh, and he tries hard to persuade himself that it isn't purely a private raid for cash, but has a sort of dim, vague respectability about it somewhere, if he could only find the spot; and that, by and by, he can scour the flag clean again after he has finished dragging it through the mud, and make it shine and flash in the vault of heaven once more as it had shone and flashed there a thousand years in the world's respect until he laid his unfaithful hand upon it. It is bad play— bad. For it exposes the Actual Thing to Them that Sit in Darkness, and they say: "What! Christian against Christian? And only for money? Is *this* a case of magnanimity, forbearance, love, gentleness, mercy, protection of the weak—this strange and over-showy onslaught of an elephant upon a nest of field-mice, on the pretext that the mice had squeaked an insolence at him —conduct which 'no self-respecting government could allow to pass unavenged?' as Mr. Chamberlain said. Was that a good pretext in a small case, when it had not been a good pretext in a large one?—for only recently Russia had affronted the elephant three times and survived alive and unsmitten. Is this Civilization and Progress? Is it something better than we already possess? These harryings and burnings and desert-makings in the Transvaal —is this an improvement on our darkness? Is it, perhaps, possible that there are two kinds of Civilization—one for home consumption and one for the heathen market?"

Then They that Sit in Darkness are troubled and shake their heads; and they read this extract from a letter of a British private, recounting his exploits in one of Methuen's [7] victories, some days before the affair of Magersfontein, and they are troubled again:

"We tore up the hill and into the intrenchments, and the Boers saw we had them; so they dropped their guns and went down on their knees and put up their hands clasped, and begged for mercy. And we gave it to them—*with the long spoon.*"

The long spoon is the bayonet. See *Lloyd's Weekly,* London, of those days. The same number—and the same column— contained some quite unconscious satire in the form of shocked and bitter upbraidings of the Boers for their brutalities and inhumanities!

Next, to our heavy damage, the Kaiser went to playing the game without first mastering it. He lost a couple of missionaries in a riot in Shantung, and in his account he made an overcharge for them. China had to pay a hundred thousand dollars apiece for them, in money; twelve miles of territory, containing several millions of inhabitants and worth twenty million dollars; and to build a monument, and also a Christian church; whereas the people of China could have been depended upon to remember the missionaries without the help of these expensive memorials. This was all bad play. Bad, because it would not, and could not, and will not now or ever, deceive the Person Sitting in Darkness. He knows that it was an overcharge. He knows that a missionary is like any other man: he is worth merely what you can supply his place for, and no more. He is useful, but so is a doctor, so is a sheriff, so is an editor; but a just Emperor does not charge war-prices for such. A diligent, intelligent, but obscure missionary, and a diligent, intelligent country editor are worth much, and we know it; but they are not worth the earth. We esteem such an editor, and we are sorry to see him go; but, when he goes, we should consider twelve miles of territory, and a church, and a fortune, over-compensation for his loss. I mean, if he was a Chinese editor, and we had to settle for him. It is no proper figure for an editor or a missionary; one can get shop-worn kings for less. It was bad play on the Kaiser's part. It got this

---

[7] Paul Sanford (Baron) Methuen (1845-1932), commander of First Division of First Army Corps for the British in the Boer War, defeated by Cronjé at Magersfontein in 1900.

property, true; but it *produced the Chinese revolt,* the indignant uprising of China's traduced patriots, the Boxers. The results have been expensive to Germany, and to the other Disseminators of Progress and the Blessings of Civilization.

The Kaiser's claim was paid, yet it was bad play, for it could not fail to have an evil effect upon Persons Sitting in Darkness in China. They would muse upon the event, and be likely to say: "Civilization is gracious and beautiful, for such is its reputation; but can we afford it? There are rich Chinamen, perhaps they could afford it; but this tax is not laid upon them, it is laid upon the peasants of Shantung; it is they that must pay this mighty sum, and their wages are but four cents a day. Is this a better civilization than ours, and holier and higher and nobler? Is not this rapacity? Is not this extortion? Would Germany charge America two hundred thousand dollars for two missionaries, and shake the mailed fist in her face, and send warships, and send soldiers, and say: 'Seize twelve miles of territory, worth twenty millions of dollars, as additional pay for the missionaries; and make those peasants build a monument to the missionaries, and a costly Christian church to remember them by?' And later would Germany say to her soldiers: 'March through America and slay, *giving no quarter;* make the German face there, as has been our Hun-face here, a terror for a thousand years; march through the Great Republic and slay, slay, slay, carving a road for our offended religion through its heart and bowels?' Would Germany do like this to America, to England, to France, to Russia? Or only to China the helpless—imitating the elephant's assault upon the field-mice? Had we better invest in this Civilization—this Civilization which called Napoleon a buccaneer for carrying off Venice's bronze horses, but which steals our ancient astronomical instruments from our walls, and goes looting like common bandits—that is, all the alien soldiers except America's; and (Americans again excepted) storms frightened villages and cables the result to glad journals at home every day: 'Chinese losses, 450 killed; ours, *one officer and two men wounded.* Shall proceed against neighboring village to-morrow, where a *massacre* is reported.' Can we afford Civilization?"

And, next, Russia must go and play the game injudiciously. She affronts England once or twice—with the Person Sitting in Darkness observing and noting; by moral assistance of France and Germany, she robs Japan of her hard-earned spoil, all swimming in Chinese blood—Port Arthur [8] —with the Person again observing and noting; then she seizes Manchuria, raids its villages, and chokes its great river with the swollen corpses of countless massacred peasants—that astonished Person still observing and noting. And perhaps he is saying to himself: "It is yet *another* Civilized Power, with its banner of the Prince of Peace in one hand and its loot-basket and its butcher-knife in the other. Is there no salvation for us but to adopt Civilization and lift ourselves down to its level?"

And by and by comes America, and our Master of the Game plays it badly—plays it as Mr. Chamberlain was playing it in South Africa. It was a mistake to do that; also, it was one which was quite unlooked for in a Master who was playing it so well in Cuba. In Cuba, he was playing the usual and regular *American* game, and it was winning, for there is no way to beat it. The Master, contemplating Cuba, said: "Here is an oppressed and friendless little nation which is willing to fight to be free; we go partners, and put up the strength of seventy million sympathizers and the resources of the United States: play!" Nothing but Europe combined could call that hand: and Europe cannot combine on anything. There, in Cuba, he was following our great traditions in a way which made us very proud of him, and proud of the

---

[8] Port Arthur was captured by Japan in 1894, but restored to China by a coalition of Russia, France and Germany. It was ceded to Russia in 1898.

deep dissatisfaction which his play was provoking in Continental Europe. Moved by a high inspiration, he threw out those stirring words which proclaimed that forcible annexation would be "criminal aggression;" and in that utterance fired another "shot heard round the world." The memory of that fine saying will be outlived by the remembrance of no act of his but one—that he forgot it within the twelvemonth, and its honorable gospel along with it.

For, presently, came the Philippine temptation. It was strong; it was too strong, and he made that bad mistake: he played the European game, the Chamberlain game. It was a pity; it was a great pity, that error; that one grievous error, that irrevocable error. For it was the very place and time to play the American game again. And at no cost. Rich winnings to be gathered in, too; rich and permanent; indestructible; a fortune transmissible forever to the children of the flag. Not land, not money, not dominion—no, something worth many times more than that dross: our share, the spectacle of a nation of long harassed and persecuted slaves set free through our influence; our posterity's share, the golden memory of that fair deed. The game was in our hands. If it had been played according to the American rules, Dewey [9] would have sailed away from Manila as soon as he had destroyed the Spanish fleet—after putting up a sign on shore guaranteeing foreign property and life against damage by the Filipinos, and warning the Powers that interference with the emancipated patriots would be regarded as an act unfriendly to the United States. The Powers cannot combine, in even a bad cause, and the sign would not have been molested.

Dewey could have gone about his affairs elsewhere, and left the competent Filipino army to starve out the little Spanish garrison and send it home, and the Filipino citizens to set up the form of government they might prefer, and deal with the friars and their doubtful acquisitions according to Filipino ideas of fairness and justice—ideas which have since been tested and found to be of as high an order as any that prevail in Europe or America.

But we played the Chamberlain game, and lost the chance to add another Cuba and another honorable deed to our good record.

The more we examine the mistake, the more clearly we perceive that it is going to be bad for the Business. The Person Sitting in Darkness is almost sure to say: "There is something curious about this—curious and unaccountable. There must be two Americas: one that sets the captive free, and one that takes a once-captive's new freedom away from him, and picks a quarrel with him with nothing to found it on; then kills him to get his land."

The truth is, the Person Sitting in Darkness *is* saying things like that; and for the sake of the Business we must persuade him to look at the Philippine matter in another and healthier way. We must arrange his opinions for him. I believe it can be done; for Mr. Chamberlain has arranged England's opinion of the South African matter, and done it most cleverly and successfully. He presented the facts—some of the facts —and showed those confiding people what the facts meant. He did it statistically, which is a good way. He used the formula: "Twice 2 are 14, and 2 from 9 leaves 35." Figures are effective; figures will convince the elect.

Now, my plan is a still bolder one than Mr. Chamberlain's, though apparently a copy of it. Let us be franker than Mr. Chamberlain; let us audaciously present the whole of the facts, shirking none, then explain them according to Mr. Chamberlain's formula. This daring truthfulness will astonish and dazzle the Person Sitting in Darkness, and he will take the Explanation down before his mental vision has had

---

[9] George Dewey (1837-1917), commanding officer of the Asiatic Squadron of the American Navy which destroyed a Spanish squadron in Manila Bay May 1, 1898, and supported the United States Army forces in the capture of Manila.

time to get back into focus. Let us say to him:

"Our case is simple. On the 1st of May, Dewey destroyed the Spanish fleet. This left the Archipelago in the hands of its proper and rightful owners, the Filipino nation. Their army numbered 30,000 men, and they were competent to whip out or starve out the little Spanish garrison; then the people could set up a government of their own devising. Our traditions required that Dewey should now set up his warning sign, and go away. But the Master of the Game happened to think of another plan—the European plan. He acted upon it. This was, to send out an army—ostensibly to help the native patriots put the finishing touch upon their long and plucky struggle for independence, but really to take their land away from them and keep it. That is, in the interest of Progress and Civilization. The plan developed, stage by stage, and quite satisfactorily. We entered into a military alliance with the trusting Filipinos, and they hemmed in Manila on the land side, and by their valuable help the place, with its garrison of 8,000 or 10,000 Spaniards, was captured—a thing which we could not have accomplished unaided at that time. We got their help by —by ingenuity. We knew they were fighting for their independence, and that they had been at it for two years. We knew they supposed that we also were fighting in their worthy cause—just as we had helped the Cubans fight for Cuban independence —and we allowed them to go on thinking so. *Until Manila was ours and we could get along without them.* Then we showed our hand. Of course, they were surprised —that was natural; surprised and disappointed; disappointed and grieved. To them it looked un-American; uncharacteristic; foreign to our established traditions. And this was natural, too; for we were only playing the American Game in public—in private it was the European. It was neatly done, very neatly, and it bewildered them. They could not understand it; for we had been so friendly—so affectionate, even

—with those simple-minded patriots! We, our own selves, had brought back out of exile their leader, their hero, their hope, their Washington—Aguinaldo;[10] brought him in a warship, in high honor, under the sacred shelter and hospitality of the flag; brought him back and restored him to his people, and got their moving and eloquent gratitude for it. Yes, we had been so friendly to them, and had heartened them up in so many ways! We had lent them guns and ammunition; advised with them; exchanged pleasant courtesies with them; placed our sick and wounded in their kindly care; entrusted our Spanish prisoners to their humane and honest hands; fought shoulder to shoulder with them against 'the common enemy' (our own phrase); praised their courage, praised their gallantry, praised their mercifulness, praised their fine and honorable conduct; borrowed their trenches, borrowed strong positions which they had previously captured from the Spaniard; petted them, lied to them—officially proclaiming that our land and naval forces came to give them their freedom and displace the bad Spanish Government—fooled them, used them until we needed them no longer; then derided the sucked orange and threw it away. We kept the positions which we had beguiled them of; by and by, we moved a force forward and overlapped patriot ground—a clever thought, for we needed trouble, and this would produce it. A Filipino soldier, crossing the ground, where no one had a right to forbid him, was shot by our sentry. The badgered patriots resented this with arms, without waiting to know whether Aguinaldo, who was absent, would approve or not. Aguinaldo did not approve; but that availed nothing. What we wanted, in the interest of Progress and Civilization, was the Archipelago, unencumbered by patriots struggling for independence; and War was what we needed. We clinched our opportunity. It is Mr. Chamberlain's case

[10] Emilio Aguinaldo (1870-1948), Filipino insurrectionist.

over again—at least in its motive and intention; and we played the game as adroitly as he played it himself."

At this point in our frank statement of fact to the Person Sitting in Darkness, we should throw in a little trade-taffy about the Blessings of Civilization—for a change, and for the refreshment of his spirit—then go on with our tale:

"We and the patriots having captured Manila, Spain's ownership of the Archipelago and her sovereignty over it were at an end—obliterated—annihilated—not a rag or shred of either remaining behind. It was then that we conceived the divinely humorous idea of *buying* both of these spectres from Spain! [It is quite safe to confess this to the Person Sitting in Darkness, since neither he nor any other sane person will believe it.] In buying those ghosts for twenty millions, we also contracted to take care of the friars and their accumulations. I think we also agreed to propagate leprosy and smallpox, but as to this there is doubt. But it is not important; persons afflicted with the friars do not mind other diseases.

"With our Treaty ratified, Manila subdued, and our Ghosts secured, we had no further use for Aguinaldo and the owners of the Archipelago. We forced a war, and we have been hunting America's guest and ally through the woods and swamps ever since." [11]

At this point in the tale, it will be well to boast a little of our war-work and our heroisms in the field, so as to make our performance look as fine as England's in South Africa; but I believe it will not be best to emphasize this too much. We must be cautious. Of course, we must read the war-telegrams to the Person, in order to keep up our frankness; but we can throw an air of humorousness over them, and that will modify their grim eloquence a little, and their rather indiscreet exhibitions of gory exultation. Before reading to him the following display heads of the dispatches of November 18, 1900, it will be well to practice on them in private first, so

as to get the right tang of lightness and gaiety into them:

"ADMINISTRATION WEARY OF PRO-
TRACTED HOSTILITIES!"
"REAL WAR AHEAD FOR FILIPINO
REBELS!" [12]
"WILL SHOW NO MERCY!"
"KITCHENER'S PLAN ADOPTED!"

Kitchener [13] knows how to handle disagreeable people who are fighting for their homes and their liberties, and we must let on that we are merely imitating Kitchener, and have no national interest in the matter, further than to get ourselves admired by the Great Family of Nations, in which august company our Master of the Game has bought a place for us in the back row.

Of course, we must not venture to ignore our General MacArthur's [14] reports—oh, why do they keep on printing those embarrassing things?—we must drop them trippingly from the tongue and take the chances:

"During the last ten months our losses have been 268 killed and 750 wounded; Filipino loss, *three thousand two hundred and twenty-seven killed,* and 694 wounded."

We must stand ready to grab the Person Sitting in Darkness, for he will swoon away at this confession, saying: "Good God, those 'niggers' spare their wounded, and the Americans massacre theirs!"

We must bring him to, and coax him and coddle him, and assure him that the ways of Providence are best, and that it would not become us to find fault with them; and then, to show him that we are

---

[11] Aguinaldo was captured by American forces under Colonel Frederick Funston in March, 1901.

[12] "Rebels!" Mumble that funny word—don't let the Person catch it distinctly. [Author's note.]

[13] Horatio Herbert (Lord) Kitchener (1850-1916), who commanded British forces fighting Boer guerrillas in 1900-1902.

[14] Arthur MacArthur (1845-1912), military governor of the Philippines 1900-1901.

only imitators, not originators, we must read the following passage from the letter of an American soldier-lad in the Philippines to his mother, published in *Public Opinion,* of Decorah, Iowa, describing the finish of a victorious battle:

"WE NEVER LEFT ONE ALIVE. IF ONE WAS WOUNDED, WE WOULD RUN OUR BAYONETS THROUGH HIM."

Having now laid all the historical facts before the Person Sitting in Darkness, we should bring him to again, and explain them to him. We should say to him:

"They look doubtful, but in reality they are not. There have been lies; yes, but they were told in a good cause. We have been treacherous; but that was only in order that real good might come out of apparent evil. True, we have crushed a deceived and confiding people; we have turned against the weak and the friendless who trusted us; we have stamped out a just and intelligent and well-ordered republic; we have stabbed an ally in the back and slapped the face of a guest; we have bought a Shadow from an enemy that hadn't it to sell; we have robbed a trusting friend of his land and his liberty; we have invited our clean young men to shoulder a discredited musket and do bandit's work under a flag which bandits have been accustomed to fear, not to follow; we have debauched America's honor and blackened her face before the world; but each detail was for the best. We know this. The Head of every State and Sovereignty in Christendom and ninety per cent. of every legislative body in Christendom, including our Congress and our fifty State Legislatures, are members not only of the church, but also of the Blessings-of-Civilization Trust. This world-girdling accumulation of trained morals, high principles, and justice, cannot do an unright thing, an unfair thing, an ungenerous thing, an unclean thing. It knows what it is about. Give yourself no uneasiness; it is all right."

Now then, that will convince the Person. You will see. It will restore the Business. Also, it will elect the Master of the Game to the vacant place in the Trinity of our national gods; and there on their high thrones the Three will sit, age after age, in the people's sight, each bearing the Emblem of his service. Washington, the Sword of the Liberator; Lincoln, the Slave's Broken Chains; the Master, the Chains Repaired.

It will give the Business a splendid new start. You will see.

Everything is prosperous, now; everything is just as we should wish it. We have got the Archipelago, and we shall never give it up. Also, we have every reason to hope that we shall have an opportunity before very long to slip out of our Congressional contract with Cuba and give her something better in the place of it. It is a rich country, and many of us are already beginning to see that the contract was a sentimental mistake. But now—right now—is the best time to do some profitable rehabilitating work—work that will set us up and make us comfortable, and discourage gossip. We cannot conceal from ourselves that, privately, we are a little troubled about our uniform. It is one of our prides; it is acquainted with honor; it is familiar with great deeds and noble; we love it, we revere it; and so this errand it is on makes us uneasy. And our flag—another pride of ours, our chiefest! We have worshipped it so; and when we have seen it in far lands—glimpsing it unexpectedly in that strange sky, waving its welcome and benediction to us—we have caught our breath, and uncovered our heads, and couldn't speak, for a moment, for the thought of what it was to us and the great ideals it stood for. Indeed, we *must* do something about these things; we must not have the flag out there, and the uniform. They are not needed there; we can manage in some other way. England manages, as regards the uniform, and so can we. We have to send soldiers—we can't get out of that—but we can disguise them.

It is the way England does in South Africa. Even Mr. Chamberlain himself takes pride in England's honorable uniform, and makes the army down there wear an ugly and odious and appropriate disguise, of yellow stuff such as quarantine flags are made of, and which are hoisted to warn the healthy away from unclean disease and repulsive death. This cloth is called khaki. We could adopt it. It is light, comfortable, grotesque, and deceives the enemy, for he cannot conceive of a soldier being concealed in it.

And as for a flag for the Philippine Province, it is easily managed. We can have a special one—our States do it: we can have just our usual flag, with the white stripes painted black and the stars replaced by the skull and cross-bones.

And we do not need that Civil Commission out there. Having no powers, it has to invent them, and that kind of work cannot be effectively done by just anybody; an expert is required. Mr. Croker [15] can be spared. We do not want the United States represented there, but only the Game.

By help of these suggested amendments, Progress and Civilization in that country can have a boom, and it will take in the Persons who are Sitting in Darkness, and we can resume Business at the old stand.

HOW TO TELL A STORY
[1897]

I DO NOT CLAIM that I can tell a story as it ought to be told. I only claim to know how a story ought to be told, for I have been almost daily in the company of the most expert story-tellers for many years.

There are several kinds of stories, but only one difficult kind—the humorous. I will talk mainly about that one. The humorous story is American, the comic story is English, the witty story is French. The humorous story depends for its effect upon the manner of the telling; the comic story and the witty story upon the matter.

The humorous story may be spun out to great length, and may wander around as much as it pleases, and arrive nowhere in particular; but the comic and witty stories must be brief and end with a point. The humorous story bubbles gently along, the others burst.

The humorous story is strictly a work of art—high and delicate art—and only an artist can tell it; but no art is necessary in telling the comic and the witty story; anybody can do it. The art of telling a humorous story—understand, I mean by word of mouth, not print—was created in America, and has remained at home.

The humorous story is told gravely; the teller does his best to conceal the fact that he even dimly suspects that there is anything funny about it; but the teller of the comic story tells you beforehand that it is one of the funniest things he has ever heard, then tells it with eager delight, and is the first person to laugh when he gets through. And sometimes, if he has had good success, he is so glad and happy that he will repeat the "nub" of it and glance around from face to face, collecting applause, and then repeat it again. It is a pathetic thing to see.

Very often, of course, the rambling and disjointed humorous story finishes with a nub, point, snapper, or whatever you like to call it. Then the listener must be alert, for in many cases the teller will divert attention from that nub by dropping it in in a carefully casual and indifferent way, with the pretense that he does not know it is a nub.

Artemus Ward [1] used that trick a good deal; then when the belated audience presently caught the joke he would look up with innocent surprise, as if wondering what they had found to laugh at. Dan

---

[15] "Boss" Richard Croker (1841-1922), Tammany Hall leader.

[1] Pen-name of Charles Farrar Browne (1834-1867), humorist and comic lecturer.

Setchell [2] used it before him, Nye [3] and Riley [4] and others use it to-day.

But the teller of the comic story does not slur the nub; he shouts it at you— every time. And when he prints it, in England, France, Germany, and Italy, he italicizes it, puts some whooping exclamation-points after it, and sometimes explains it in a parenthesis. All of which is very depressing, and makes one want to renounce joking and lead a better life.

Let me set down an instance of the comic method, using an anecdote which has been popular all over the world for twelve or fifteen hundred years. The teller tells it in this way:

THE WOUNDED SOLDIER

In the course of a certain battle a soldier whose leg had been shot off appealed to another soldier who was hurrying by to carry him to the rear, informing him at the same time of the loss which he had sustained; whereupon the generous son of Mars, shouldering the unfortunate, proceeded to carry out his desire. The bullets and cannon-balls were flying in all directions, and presently one of the latter took the wounded man's head off without, however, his deliverer being aware of it. In no long time he was hailed by an officer, who said:

"Where are you going with that carcass?"

"To the rear, sir—he's lost his leg!"

"His leg, forsooth?" responded the astonished officer; "you mean his head, you booby."

Whereupon the soldier dispossessed himself of his burden, and stood looking down upon it in great perplexity. At length he said:

"It is true, sir, just as you have said." Then after a pause he added, "But he told me IT WAS HIS LEG!!!!!"

Here the narrator bursts into explosion after explosion of thunderous horse-laughter, repeating that nub from time to time

through his gaspings and shriekings and suffocatings.

It takes only a minute and a half to tell that in its comic-story form; and isn't worth the telling, after all. Put into the humorous-story form it takes ten minutes, and is about the funniest thing I have ever listened to—as James Whitcomb Riley tells it.

He tells it in the character of a dull-witted old farmer who has just heard it for the first time, thinks it is unspeakably funny, and is trying to repeat it to a neighbor. But he can't remember it; so he gets all mixed up and wanders helplessly round and round, putting in tedious details that don't belong in the tale and only retard it; taking them out conscientiously and putting in others that are just as useless; making minor mistakes now and then and stopping to correct them and explain how he came to make them; remembering things which he forgot to put in in their proper place and going back to put them in there; stopping his narrative a good while in order to try to recall the name of the soldier that was hurt, and finally remembering that the soldier's name was not mentioned, and remarking placidly that the name is of no real importance, anyway—better, of course, if one knew it, but not essential, after all—and so on, and so on, and so on.

The teller is innocent and happy and pleased with himself, and has to stop every little while to hold himself in and keep from laughing outright; and does hold in, but his body quakes in a jelly-like way with interior chuckles; and at the end of the ten minutes, the audience have laughed until they are exhausted, and the tears are running down their faces.

The simplicity and innocence and sin-

[2] Comedian prominent on the New York stage in the 1850's.

[3] Edgar Wilson ("Bill") Nye (1850-1896), humorous editor, writer, and lecturer.

[4] James Whitcomb Riley (1849-1916), poet, humorist, and lecturer.

cerity and unconsciousness of the old farmer are perfectly simulated, and the result is a performance which is thoroughly charming and delicious. This is art—and fine and beautiful, and only a master can compass it; but a machine could tell the other story.

To string incongruities and absurdities together in a wandering and sometime purposeless way, and seem innocently unaware that they are absurdities, is the basis of the American art, if my position is correct. Another feature is the slurring of the point. A third is the dropping of a studied remark apparently without knowing it, as if one were thinking aloud. The fourth and last is the pause.

Artemus Ward dealt in numbers three and four a good deal. He would begin to tell with great animation something which he seemed to think was wonderful; then lose confidence, and after an apparently absent-minded pause add an incongruous remark in a soliloquizing way; and that was the remark intended to explode the mine and it did.

For instance, he would say eagerly, excitedly, "I once knew a man in New Zealand who hadn't a tooth in his head"—here his animation would die out; a silent, reflective pause would follow, then he would say dreamily, and as if to himself, "and yet that man could beat a drum better than any man I ever saw."

The pause is an exceedingly important feature in any kind of story, and a frequently recurring feature, too. It is a dainty thing, and delicate, and also uncertain and treacherous; for it must be exactly the right length—no more and no less—or it fails of its purpose and makes trouble. If the pause is too short the impressive point is passed, and the audience have had time to divine that a surprise is intended—and then you can't surprise them, of course.

On the platform I used to tell a negro ghost story that had a pause in front of the snapper on the end, and that pause was the most important thing in the whole story. If I got it the right length precisely, I could spring the finishing ejaculation with effect enough to make some impressible girl deliver a startled little yelp and jump out of her seat—and that was what I was after. This story was called "The Golden Arm," and was told in this fashion. You can practise with it yourself—and mind you look out for the pause and get it right.

THE GOLDEN ARM

Once 'pon a time dey wuz a monsus mean man, en he live 'way out in de prairie all 'lone by hisself, 'cep'n he had a wife. En bimeby she died, en he tuck en toted her way out dah in de prairie en buried her. Well, she had a golden arm—all solid gold, fum de shoulder down. He wuz pow'ful mean—pow'ful; en dat night he couldn't sleep, caze he want dat golden arm so bad.

When it come midnight he couldn't stan' it no mo'; so he git up, he did, en tuck his lantern en shoved out thoo de storm en dug her up en got de golden arm; en he bent his head down 'gin de win', en plowed en plowed en plowed thoo de snow. Den all on a sudden he stop (make a considerable pause here, and look startled, and take a listening attitude) en say: "My lan', what's dat?"

En he listen—en listen—en de win' say (set your teeth together and imitate the wailing and wheezing singsong of the wind), "Bzzz-z-zzz"—en den, way back yonder whah de grave is, he hear a voice!—he hear a voice all mix' up in de win'—can't hardly tell 'em 'part—"Bzzz-zzz—W-h-o — g-o-t — m-y — g-o-l-d-e-n arm?" (You must begin to shiver violently now.)

En he begin to shiver en shake, en say, "Oh, my! Oh, my lan'!" en de win' blow de lantern out, en de snow en sleet blow in his face en mos' choke him, en he start a-plowin' knee-deep towards home mos' dead, he so sk'yerd—en pooty soon he hear de voice agin, en (pause) it 'us comin'

after him! "Bzzz—zzz—zzz—W-h-o—g-o-t
—m-y—g-o-l-d-e-n—arm?"

When he git to de pasture he hear it
agin—closter now, en a-comin'!—a-comin'
back dah in de dark en de storm—(repeat
the wind and the voice). When he git to
de house he rush up-stairs en jump in de
bed en kiver up, head and years, en lay
dah shiverin' en shakin'—en den way out
dah he hear it agin!—en a-comin'! En
bimeby he hear (pause—awed, listening attitude)—pat—pat—pat—hit's a-comin' upstairs! Den he hear de latch, en he know
it's in de room!

Den pooty soon he know it's a-stannin'
by de bed! (Pause.) Den—he know it's
a-bendin' down over him—en he can't
skasely git his breath! Den—den—he seem
to feel someth'n' c-o-l-d, right down 'most
agin his head! (Pause.)

Den de voice say, right at his year—
"W-h-o — g-o-t — m-y — g-o-l-d-e-n arm?"
(You must wail it out very plaintively
and accusingly; then you stare steadily
and impressively into the face of the
farthest-gone auditor—a girl, preferably—
and let that awe-inspiring pause begin to
build itself in the deep hush. When it has
reached exactly the right length, jump
suddenly at that girl and yell, "You've
got it!"

If you've got the pause right, she'll fetch
a dear little yelp and spring right out of
her shoes. But you must get the pause
right; and you will find it the most
troublesome and aggravating and uncertain
thing you ever undertook.

From
THE MYSTERIOUS STRANGER
[1916]

WE SAT UPON a mountain commanding a vast landscape of mountain-range
and gorge and valley and plain and river,
with cities and villages slumbering in the
sunlight, and a glimpse of blue sea on the
farther verge. It was a tranquil and dreamy
picture, beautiful to the eye and restful
to the spirit. If we could only make a

change like that whenever we wanted to,
the world would be easier to live in than
it is, for change of scene shifts the mind's
burdens to the other shoulder and banishes
old, shop-worn wearinesses from mind and
body both.

We talked together, and I had the idea
of trying to reform Satan and persuade
him to lead a better life. I told him about
all those things he had been doing, and
begged him to be more considerate and
stop making people unhappy. I said I
knew he did not mean any harm, but that
he ought to stop and consider the possible
consequences of a thing before launching
it in that impulsive and random way of
his; then he would not make so much
trouble. He was not hurt by this plain
speech; he only looked amused and surprised, and said:

"What? I do random things? Indeed, I
never do. I stop and consider possible
consequences? Where is the need? I know
what the consequences are going to be—
always."

"Oh, Satan, then how could you do
these things?"

"Well, I will tell you, and you must
understand if you can. You belong to a
singular race. Every man is a suffering-
machine and a happiness-machine combined. The two functions work together
harmoniously, with a fine and delicate precision, on the give-and-take principle. For
every happiness turned out in the one
department the other stands ready to modify it with a sorrow or a pain—maybe
a dozen. In most cases the man's life is
about equally divided between happiness
and unhappiness. When this is not the
case the unhappiness predominates—always; never the other. Sometimes a man's
make and disposition are such that his
misery-machine is able to do nearly all the
business. Such a man goes through life
almost ignorant of what happiness is.
Everything he touches, everything he does,
brings a misfortune upon him. You have
seen such people? To that kind of a person life is not an advantage, is it? It is

only a disaster. Sometimes for an hour's happiness a man's machinery makes him pay years of misery. Don't you know that? It happens every now and then. I will give you a case or two presently. Now the people of your village are nothing to me— you know that, don't you?"

I did not like to speak out too flatly, so I said I had suspected it.

"Well, it is true that they are nothing to me. It is not possible that they should be. The difference between them and me is abysmal, immeasurable. They have no intellect."

"No intellect?"

"Nothing that resembles it. At a future time I will examine what man calls his mind and give you the details of that chaos, then you will see and understand. Men have nothing in common with me— there is no point of contact; they have foolish little feelings and foolish little vanities and impertinences and ambitions; their foolish little life is but a laugh, a sigh, and extinction; and they have no sense. Only the Moral Sense. I will show you what I mean. Here is a red spider, not so big as a pin's head. Can you imagine an elephant being interested in him —caring whether he is happy or isn't, or whether he is wealthy or poor, or whether his sweetheart returns his love or not, or whether his mother is sick or well, or whether he is looked up to in society or not, or whether his enemies will smite him or his friends desert him, or whether his hopes will suffer blight or his political ambitions fail, or whether he shall die in the bosom of his family or neglected and despised in a foreign land? These things can never be important to the elephant; they are nothing to him; he cannot shrink his sympathies to the microscopic size of them. Man is to me as the red spider is to the elephant. The elephant has nothing against the spider—he cannot get down to that remote level; I have nothing against man. The elephant is indifferent; I am indifferent. The elephant would not take the trouble to do the spider an ill turn;

if he took the notion he might do him a good turn, if it came in his way and cost nothing. I have done men good service, but no ill turns.

"The elephant lives a century, the red spider a day; in power, intellect, and dignity the one creature is separated from the other by a distance which is simply astronomical. Yet in these, as in all qualities, man is immeasurably further below me than is the wee spider below the elephant.

"Man's mind clumsily and tediously and laboriously patches little trivialities together and gets a result—such as it is. My mind creates! Do you get the force of that? Creates anything it desires—and in a moment. Creates without material. Creates fluids, solids, colors—anything, everything—out of the airy nothing which is called Thought. A man imagines a silk thread, imagines a machine to make it, imagines a picture, then by weeks of labor embroiders it on canvas with the thread. I think the whole thing, and in a moment it is before you—created.

"I think a poem, music, the record of a game of chess—anything—and it is there. This is the immortal mind—nothing is beyond its reach. Nothing can obstruct my vision; the rocks are transparent to me, and darkness is daylight. I do not need to open a book; I take the whole of its contents into my mind at a single glance, through the cover; and in a million years I could not forget a single word of it, or its place in the volume. Nothing goes on in the skull of man, bird, fish, insect, or other creature which can be hidden from me. I pierce the learned man's brain with a single glance, and the treasures which cost him threescore years to accumulate are mine; he can forget, and he does forget, but I retain.

"Now, then, I perceive by your thoughts that you are understanding me fairly well. Let us proceed. Circumstances might so fall out that the elephant could like the spider—supposing he can see it—but he could not love it. His love is for his own kind—for his equals. An angel's love is sublime, adorable, divine, beyond the imagination of man—infinitely beyond it! But it is limited to his own august order. If it fell upon one of your race for only an instant, it would consume its object to ashes. No, we cannot love men, but we can be harmlessly indifferent to them; we can also like them, sometimes. I like you and the boys, I like Father Peter, and for your sakes I am doing all these things for the villagers."

He saw that I was thinking a sarcasm, and he explained his position.

"I have wrought well for the villagers, though it does not look like it on the surface. Your race never know good fortune from ill. They are always mistaking the one for the other. It is because they cannot see into the future. What I am doing for the villagers will bear good fruit some day; in some cases to themselves; in others, to unborn generations of men. No one will ever know that I was the cause, but it will be none the less true, for all that. Among you boys you have a game: you stand a row of bricks on end a few inches apart; you push a brick, it knocks its neighbor over, the neighbor knocks over the next brick—and so on till all the row is prostrate. That is human life. A child's first act knocks over the initial brick, and the rest will follow inexorably. If you could see into the future, as I can, you would see everything that was going to happen to that creature; for nothing can change the order of its life after the first event has determined it. That is, nothing will change it, because each act unfailingly begets an act, that act begets another, and so on to the end, and the seer can look forward down the line and see just when each act is to have birth, from cradle to grave."

"Does God order the career?"

"Foreordain it? No. The man's circumstances and environment order it. His first act determines the second and all that follow after. But suppose, for argument's sake, that the man should skip one of these acts; an apparently trifling one, for instance; suppose that it had been appointed that on a certain day, at a certain hour and minute and second and fraction of a second he should go to the well, and he didn't go. That man's career would change utterly, from that moment; thence to the grave it would be wholly different from the career which his first act as a child had arranged for him. Indeed, it might be that if he had gone to the well he would have ended his career on a throne, and that omitting to do it would set him upon a career that would lead to beggary and a pauper's grave. For instance: if at any time—say in boyhood—Columbus had skipped the triflingest little link in the chain of acts projected and made inevitable by his first childish act, it would have changed his whole subsequent life, and he would have become a priest and died obscure in an Italian village, and America would not have been discovered for two centuries afterward. I know this. To skip any one of the billion acts in Columbus's chain would have wholly changed his life. I have examined his billion of possible careers, and in only one of them occurs the discovery of America. You people do not suspect that all of your acts are of one size and importance, but it is true; to snatch at an appointed fly is as big with fate for you as any other appointed act—"

"As the conquering of a continent, for instance?"

"Yes. Now, then, no man ever does drop a link—the thing has never happened! Even when he is trying to make up his mind as to whether he will do a thing or not, that itself is a link, an act, and has its proper place in his chain; and when he finally decides an act, that also was the thing which he was absolutely certain to do. You see, now, that a man will never drop a link in his chain. He cannot. If he made up his mind to try, that project would itself be an unavoidable link—a thought bound to occur to him at that precise moment, and made certain by the first act of his babyhood."

It seemed so dismal!

"He is a prisoner for life," I said sorrowfully, "and cannot get free."

"No, of himself he cannot get away from the consequences of his first childish act. But I can free him."

I looked up wistfully.

"I have changed the careers of a number of your villagers."

I tried to thank him, but found it difficult, and let it drop.

"I shall make some other changes. You know that little Lisa Brandt?"

"Oh yes, everybody does. My mother says she is so sweet and so lovely that she is not like any other child. She says she will be the pride of the village when she grows up; and its idol, too, just as she is now."

"I shall change her future."

"Make it better?" I asked.

"Yes. And I will change the future of Nikolaus."

I was glad, this time, and said, "I don't need to ask about his case; you will be sure to do generously by him."

"It is my intention."

Straight off I was building that great future of Nicky's in my imagination, and had already made a renowned general of him and hofmeister at the court, when I noticed that Satan was waiting for me to get ready to listen again. I was ashamed of having exposed my cheap imaginings to him, and was expecting some sarcasms, but it did not happen. He proceeded with his subject:

"Nicky's appointed life is sixty-two years."

"That's grand!" I said.

"Lisa's, thirty-six. But, as I told you, I shall change their lives and those ages. Two minutes and a quarter from now Nikolaus will wake out of his sleep and find the rain blowing in. It was appointed that he should turn over and go to sleep again. But I have appointed that he shall get up and close the window first. That trifle will change his career entirely. He will rise in the morning two minutes later

than the chain of his life had appointed him to rise. By consequence, thenceforth nothing will ever happen to him in accordance with the details of the old chain." He took out his watch and sat looking at it a few moments, then said: "Nikolaus has risen to close the window. His life is changed, his new career has begun. There will be consequences."

It made me feel creepy; it was uncanny.

"But for this change certain things would happen twelve days from now. For instance, Nikolaus would save Lisa from drowning. He would arrive on the scene at exactly the right moment—four minutes past ten, the long-ago appointed instant of time—and the water would be shoal, the achievement easy and certain. But he will arrive some seconds too late, now; Lisa will have struggled into deeper water. He will do his best, but both will drown."

"Oh, Satan! oh, dear Satan!" I cried, with the tears rising in my eyes, "save them! Don't let it happen. I can't bear to lose Nikolaus, he is my loving playmate and friend; and think of Lisa's poor mother!"

I clung to him and begged and pleaded, but he was not moved. He made me sit down again, and told me I must hear him out.

"I have changed Nikolaus's life, and this has changed Lisa's. If I had not done this, Nikolaus would save Lisa, then he would catch cold from his drenching; one of your race's fantastic and desolating scarlet fevers would follow, with pathetic after-effects; for forty-six years he would lie in his bed a paralytic log, deaf, dumb, blind, and praying night and day for the blessed relief of death. Shall I change his life back?"

"Oh no! Oh, not for the world! In charity and pity leave it as it is."

"It is best so. I could not have changed any other link in his life and done him so good a service. He had a billion possible careers, but not one of them was worth living; they were charged full with miseries and disasters. But for my intervention he would do his brave deed twelve days from now—a deed begun and ended in six minutes—and get for all reward those forty-six years of sorrow and suffering I told you of. It is one of the cases I was thinking of awhile ago when I said that sometimes an act which brings the actor an hour's happiness and self-satisfaction is paid for—or punished—by years of suffering."

I wondered what poor little Lisa's early death would save her from. He answered the thought:

"From ten years of pain and slow recovery from an accident, and then from nineteen years' pollution, shame, depravity, crime, ending with death at the hands of the executioner. Twelve days hence she will die; her mother would save her life if she could. Am I not kinder than her mother?"

"Yes—oh, indeed yes; and wiser."

"Father Peter's case is coming on presently. He will be acquitted, through unassailable proofs of his innocence."

"Why, Satan, how can that be? Do you really think it?"

"Indeed, I know it. His good name will be restored, and the rest of his life will be happy."

"I can believe it. To restore his good name will have that effect."

"His happiness will not proceed from that cause. I shall change his life that day, for his good. He will never know his good name has been restored."

In my mind—and modestly—I asked for particulars, but Satan paid no attention to my thought. Next, my mind wandered to the astrologer, and I wondered where he might be.

"In the moon," said Satan, with a fleeting sound which I believed was a chuckle. "I've got him on the cold side of it, too. He doesn't know where he is, and is not having a pleasant time; still, it is good enough for him, a good place for his star studies. I shall need him presently; then I shall bring him back and possess him

again. He has a long and cruel and odious life before him, but I will change that, for I have no feeling against him and am quite willing to do him a kindness. I think I shall get him burned."

He had such strange notions of kindness! But angels are made so, and do not know any better.

From
AUTOBIOGRAPHY
[1924]

MY UNCLE, John A. Quarles, was a farmer, and his place was in the country four miles from Florida. He had eight children and fifteen or twenty negroes, and was also fortunate in other ways, particularly in his character. I have not come across a better man than he was. I was his guest for two or three months every year, from the fourth year after we removed to Hannibal till I was eleven or twelve years old I have never conciously used him or his wife in a book, but his farm has come very handy to me in literature once or twice. In *Huck Finn* and in *Tom Sawyer, Detective* I moved it down to Arkansas. It was all of six hundred miles, but it was no trouble; it was not a very large farm—five hundred acres, perhaps—but I could have done it if it had been twice as large. And as for the morality of it, I cared nothing for that; I would move a state if the exigencies of literature required it.

It was a heavenly place for a boy, that farm of my uncle John's. The house was a double log one, with a spacious floor (roofed in) connecting it with the kitchen. In the summer the table was set in the middle of that shady and breezy floor, and the sumptuous meals—well, it makes me cry to think of them. Fried chicken, roast pig; wild and tame turkeys, ducks, and geese; venison just killed; squirrels, rabbits, pheasants, partridges, prairie-chickens; biscuits, hot batter cakes, hot buckwheat cakes, hot "wheat bread," hot rolls, hot corn pone; fresh corn boiled on the ear,

succotash, butter-beans, string-beans, tomatoes, peas, Irish potatoes, sweet potatoes; buttermilk, sweet milk, "clabber";
watermelons, muskmelons, cantaloupes—all
fresh from the garden; apple pie, peach
pie, pumpkin pie, apple dumplings, peach
cobbler—I can't remember the rest. The
way that the things were cooked was perhaps the main splendor—particularly a
certain few of the dishes. For instance, the
corn bread, the hot biscuits and wheat
bread, and the fried chicken. These things
have never been properly cooked in the
North—in fact, no one there is able to
learn the art, so far as my experience
goes. The North thinks it knows how to
make corn bread, but this is mere superstition. Perhaps no bread in the world is
quite so good as Southern corn bread, and
perhaps no bread in the world is quite
so bad as the Northern imitation of it.
The North seldom tries to fry chicken,
and this is well; the art cannot be learned
north of the line of Mason and Dixon,
nor anywhere in Europe. This is not hearsay; it is experience that is speaking. In
Europe it is imagined that the custom of
serving various kinds of bread blazing hot
is "American," but that is too broad a
spread; it is custom in the South, but is
much less than that in the North. In the
North and in Europe hot bread is considered unhealthy. This is probably another fussy superstition, like the European
superstition that ice-water is unhealthy.
Europe does not need ice-water and does
not drink it; and yet, notwithstanding this,
its word for it is better than ours, because it describes it, whereas ours doesn't.
Europe calls it "iced" water. Our word
describes water made from melted ice—
a drink which has a characterless taste
and which we have but little acquaintance
with.

It seems a pity that the world should
throw away so many good things merely
because they are unwholesome. I doubt if
God has given us any refreshment which,
taken in moderation, is unwholesome, except microbes. Yet there are people who

strictly deprive themselves of each and
every eatable, drinkable, and smokable
which has in any way acquired a shady
reputation. They pay this price for health.
And health is all they get for it. How
strange it is! It is like paying out your
whole fortune for a cow that has gone dry.

The farmhouse stood in the middle of a
very large yard, and the yard was fenced
on three sides with rails and on the rear
side with high palings; against these stood
the smoke-house; beyond the palings was
the orchard; beyond the orchard were the
negro quarters and the tobacco fields. The
front yard was entered over a stile made
of sawed-off logs of graduated heights; I
do not remember any gate. In a corner of
the front yard were a dozen lofty hickory
trees and a dozen black walnuts, and in the
nutting season riches were to be gathered
there.

Down a piece, abreast the house, stood a
little log cabin against the rail fence; and
there the woody hill fell sharply away, past
the barns, the corn-crib, the stables, and
the tobacco-curing house, to a limpid brook
which sang along over its gravelly bed and
curved and frisked in and out and here and
there and yonder in the deep shade of overhanging foliage and vines—a divine place
for wading, and it had swimming pools,
too, which were forbidden to us and therefore much frequented by us. For we were
little Christian children and had early been
taught the value of forbidden fruit.

In the little log cabin lived a bedridden
whiteheaded slave woman whom we visited
daily and looked upon with awe, for we
believed she was upward of a thousand
years old and had talked with Moses. The
younger negroes credited these statistics
and had furnished them to us in good faith.
We accommodated all the details which
came to us about her; and so we believed
that she had lost her health in the long
desert trip coming out of Egypt, and had
never been able to get it back again. She
had a round bald place on the crown of
her head, and we used to creep around and
gaze at it in reverent silence, and reflect

that it was caused by fright through seeing Pharaoh drowned. We called her "Aunt" Hannah, Southern fashion. She was superstitious, like the other negroes; also, like them, she was deeply religious. Like them, she had great faith in prayer and employed it in all ordinary exigencies, but not in cases where a dead certainty of result was urgent. Whenever witches were around she tied up the remnant of her wool in little tufts, with white thread, and this promptly made the witches impotent.

All the negroes were friends of ours, and with those of our own age we were in effect comrades. I say in effect, using the phrase as a modification. We were comrades, and yet not comrades; color and condition interposed a subtle line which both parties were conscious of and which rendered complete fusion impossible. We had a faithful and affectionate good friend, ally, and adviser in "Uncle Dan'l," a middle-aged slave whose head was the best one in the negro quarter, whose sympathies were wide and warm, and whose heart was honest and simple and knew no guile. He has served me well these many, many years. I have not seen him for more than half a century, and yet spiritually I have had his welcome company a good part of that time, and have staged him in books under his own name and as "Jim," [1] and carted him all around—to Hannibal, down the Mississippi on a raft, and even across the Desert of Sahara in a balloon—and he has endured it all with the patience and friendliness and loyalty which were his birthright. It was on the farm that I got my strong liking for his race and my appreciation of certain of its fine qualities. This feeling and this estimate have stood the test of sixty years and more, and have suffered no impairment. The black face is as welcome to me now as it was then.

In my schoolboy days I had no aversion to slavery. I was not aware that there was anything wrong about it. No one arraigned it in my hearing; the local papers said nothing against it; the local pulpit taught us that God approved it, that it was a holy thing, and that the doubter need only look in the Bible if he wished to settle his mind —and then the texts were read aloud to us to make the matter sure; if the slaves themselves had an aversion to slavery, they were wise and said nothing. In Hannibal we seldom saw a slave misused; on the farm, never.

There was, however, one small incident of my boyhood days which touched this matter, and it must have meant a good deal to me or it would not have stayed in my memory, clear and sharp, vivid and shadowless, all these slow-drifting years. We had a little slave boy whom we had hired from some one, there in Hannibal. He was from the eastern shore of Maryland, and had been brought away from his family and his friends, halfway across the American continent, and sold. He was a cheery spirit, innocent and gentle, and the noisiest creature that ever was, perhaps. All day long he was singing, whistling, yelling, whooping, laughing—it was maddening, devastating, unendurable. At last, one day, I lost all my temper, and went raging to my mother and said Sandy had been singing for an hour without a single break, and I couldn't stand it, and *wouldn't* she please shut him up. The tears came into her eyes and her lip trembled, and she said something like this:

"Poor thing, when he sings it shows that he is not remembering, and that comforts me; but when he is still I am afraid he is thinking, and I cannot bear it. He will never see his mother again; if he can sing, I must not hinder it, but be thankful for it. If you were older, you would understand me; then that friendless child's noise would make you glad."

It was a simple speech and made up of small words, but it went home, and Sandy's noise was not a trouble to me any more. She never used large words, but she had a natural gift for making small ones do effective work. She lived to reach the neigh-

---

[1] A leading character in *Huckleberry Finn* and *Tom Sawyer Abroad.*

borhood of ninety years and was capable with her tongue to the last—especially when a meanness or an injustice roused her spirit. She has come handy to me several times in my books, where she figures as Tom Sawyer's Aunt Polly. I fitted her out with a dialect and tried to think up other improvements for her, but did not find any. I used Sandy once, also; it was in *Tom Sawyer*. I tried to get him to whitewash the fence, but it did not work. I do not remember what name I called him by in the book.

I can see the farm yet, with perfect clearness. I can see all its belongings, all its details; the family room of the house, with a "trundle" bed in one corner and a spinning-wheel in another—a wheel whose rising and falling wail, heard from a distance, was the mournfulest of all sounds to me, and made me homesick and low spirited, and filled my atmosphere with the wandering spirits of the dead; the vast fireplace, piled high, on winter nights, with flaming hickory logs from whose ends a sugary sap bubbled out, but did not go to waste, for we scraped it off and ate it; the lazy cat spread out on the rough hearthstones; the drowsy dogs braced against the jambs and blinking; my aunt in one chimney corner, knitting; my uncle in the other, smoking his corn-cob pipe; the slick and carpetless oak floor faintly mirroring the dancing flame tongues and freckled with black indentations where fire coals had popped out and died a leisurely death; half a dozen children romping in the background twilight; "split"-bottomed chairs here and there, some with rockers; a cradle —out of service, but waiting, with confidence; in the early cold mornings a snuggle of children, in shirts and chemises, occupying the hearthstone and procrastinating—they could not bear to leave that comfortable place and go out on the windswept floor space between the house and kitchen where the general tin basin stood, and wash.

Along outside of the front fence ran the country road, dusty in the summertime, and a good place for snakes—they liked to lie in it and sun themselves; when they were rattlesnakes or puff adders, we killed them; when they were black snakes, or racers, or belonged to the fabled "hoop" breed, we fled, without shame; when they were "house snakes," or "garters," we carried them home and put them in Aunt Patsy's work basket for a surprise; for she was prejudiced against snakes, and always when she took the basket in her lap and they began to climb out of it it disordered her mind. She never could seem to get used to them; her opportunities went for nothing. And she was always cold toward bats, too, and could not bear them; and yet I think a bat is as friendly a bird as there is. My mother was Aunt Patsy's sister and had the same wild superstitions. A bat is beautifully soft and silky; I do not know any creature that is pleasanter to the touch or is more grateful for caressings, if offered in the right spirit. I know all about these coleoptera, because our great cave, three miles below Hannibal, was multitudinously stocked with them, and often I brought them home to amuse my mother with. It was easy to manage if it was a school day, because then I had ostensibly been to school and hadn't any bats. She was not a suspicious person, but full of trust and confidence; and when I said, "There's something in my coat pocket for you," she would put her hand in. But she always took it out again, herself; I didn't have to tell her. It was remarkable, the way she couldn't learn to like private bats. The more experience she had, the more she could not change her views.

I think she was never in the cave in her life; but everybody else went there. Many excursion parties came from considerable distances up and down the river to visit the cave. It was miles in extent and was a tangled wilderness of narrow and lofty clefts and passages. It was an easy place to get lost in; anybody could do it—including the bats. I got lost in it myself, along with a lady, and our last candle burned down to almost nothing before we glimpsed the search party's lights winding about in the distance.

"Injun Joe," the half-breed, got lost in there once, and would have starved to death if the bats had run short. But there was no chance of that; there were myriads of them. He told me all his story. In the book called *Tom Sawyer* I starved him entirely to death in the cave, but that was in the interest of art; it never happened. "General" Gaines, who was our first town drunkard before Jimmy Finn got the place, was lost in there for the space of a week, and finally pushed his handkerchief out of a hole in a hilltop near Saverton, several miles down the river from the cave's mouth, and somebody saw it and dug him out. There is nothing the matter with his statistics except the handkerchief. I knew him for years and he hadn't any. But it could have been his nose. That would attract attention.

The cave was an uncanny place, for it contained a corpse—the corpse of a young girl of fourteen. It was in a glass cylinder inclosed in a copper one which was suspended from a rail which bridged a narrow passage. The body was preserved in alcohol, and it was said that loafers and rowdies used to drag it up by the hair and look at the dead face. The girl was the daughter of a St. Louis surgeon of extraordinary ability and wide celebrity. He was an eccentric man and did many strange things. He put the poor thing in that forlorn place himself.

.   .   .   .

Beyond the road where the snakes sunned themselves was a dense young thicket, and through it a dim-lighted path led a quarter of a mile; then out of the dimness one emerged abruptly upon a level great prairie which was covered with wild strawberry plants, vividly starred with prairie pinks, and walled in on all sides by forests. The strawberries were fragrant and fine, and in the season we were generally there in the crisp freshness of the early morning, while the dew beads still sparkled upon the

grass and the woods were ringing with the first songs of the birds.

Down the forest slopes to the left were the swings. They were made of bark stripped from hickory saplings. When they became dry they were dangerous. They usually broke when a child was forty feet in the air, and this was why so many bones had to be mended every year. I had no ill luck myself, but none of my cousins escaped. There were eight of them, and at one time and another they broke fourteen arms among them. But it cost next to nothing, for the doctor worked by the year —twenty-five dollars for the whole family. I remember two of the Florida doctors, Chowning and Meredith. They not only tended an entire family for twenty-five dollars a year, but furnished the medicines themselves. Good measure, too. Only the largest persons could hold a whole dose. Castor oil was the principal beverage. The dose was half a dipperful, with half a dipperful of New Orleans molasses added to help it down and make it taste good, which it never did. The next standby was calomel; the next, rhubarb; and the next, jalap. Then they bled the patient, and put mustard plasters on him. It was a dreadful system, and yet the death rate was not heavy. The calomel was nearly sure to salivate the patient and cost him some of his teeth. There were no dentists. When teeth became touched with decay or were otherwise ailing, the doctor knew of but one thing to do—he fetched his tongs and dragged them out. If the jaw remained, it was not his fault. Doctors were not called in cases of ordinary illness; the family grandmother attended to those. Every old woman was a doctor, and gathered her own medicines in the woods, and knew how to compound doses that would stir the vitals of a cast-iron dog. And then there was the "Indian doctor;" a grave savage, remnant of his tribe, deeply read in the mysteries of nature and the secret properties of herbs; and most backwoodsmen had high faith in his powers and could tell of wonderful cures achieved by him. In Mauritius, away off yonder in the solitudes of the Indian Ocean, there is a person who answers to our Indian doctor of the old times. He is a negro, and has had no teaching as a doctor, yet there is one disease which he is master of and can cure and the doctors can't. They send for him when they have a case. It is a child's disease of a strange and deadly sort, and the negro cures it with a herb medicine which he makes, himself, from a prescription which has come down to him from his father and grandfather. He will not let anyone see it. He keeps the secret of its components to himself, and it is feared that he will die without divulging it; then there will be consternation in Mauritius. I was told these things by the people there, in 1896.

We had the "faith doctor," too, in those early days—a woman. Her specialty was toothache. She was a farmer's old wife and lived five miles from Hannibal. She would lay her hand on the patient's jaw and say, "Believe!" and the cure was prompt. Mrs. Utterback. I remember her very well. Twice I rode out there behind my mother, horseback, and saw the cure performed. My mother was the patient.

Doctor Meredith removed to Hannibal, by and by, and was our family physician there, and saved my life several times. Still, he was a good man and meant well. Let it go.

I was always told that I was a sickly and precarious and tiresome and uncertain child, and lived mainly on allopathic medicines during the first seven years of my life. I asked my mother about this, in her old age—she was in her eighty-eighth year—and said:

"I suppose that during all that time you were uneasy about me?"

"Yes, the whole time."

"Afraid I wouldn't live?"

After a reflective pause—ostensibly to think out the facts—"No—afraid you would."

The country schoolhouse was three miles from my uncle's farm. It stood in a clearing in the woods and would hold about twenty-five boys and girls. We attended the school with more or less regularity once or twice a week, in summer, walking to it in the cool of the morning by the forest paths, and back in the gloaming at the end of the day. All the pupils brought their dinners in baskets—corn dodger, buttermilk, and other good things—and sat in the shade of the trees at noon and ate them. It is the part of my education which I look back upon with the most satisfaction. My first visit to the school was when I was seven. A strapping girl of fifteen, in the customary sunbonnet and calico dress, asked me if I "used tobacco"—meaning did I chew it. I said no. It roused her scorn. She reported me to all the crowd, and said:

"Here is a boy seven years old who can't chew tobacco."

By the looks and comments which this produced I realized that I was a degraded object, and was cruelly ashamed of myself. I determined to reform. But I only made myself sick; I was not able to learn to chew tobacco. I learned to smoke fairly well, but that did not conciliate anybody and I remained a poor thing, and characterless. I longed to be respected, but I never was able to rise. Children have but little charity for one another's defects.

As I have said, I spent some part of every year at the farm until I was twelve or thirteen years old. The life which I led there with my cousins was full of charm, and so is the memory of it yet. I can call back the solemn twilight and mystery of the deep woods, the earthy smells, the faint odors of the wild flowers, the sheen of rain-washed foliage, the rattling clatter of drops when the wind shook the trees, the far-off hammering of woodpeckers and the muffled drumming of wood pheasants in the remoteness of the forest, the snapshot glimpses of disturbed wild creatures scurrying through the grass—I can call it all back and make it as real as it ever was, and as blessed. I can call back the prairie, and its loneliness and peace, and a vast hawk hanging motionless in the sky, with his wings spread wide and the blue of the vault showing through the fringe of their end feathers. I can see the woods in their autumn dress, the oaks purple, the hickories washed with gold, the maples and the sumachs luminous with crimson fires, and I can hear the rustle made by the fallen leaves as we plowed through them. I can see the blue clusters of wild grapes hanging among the foliage of the saplings, and I remember the taste of them and the smell. I know how the wild blackberries looked, and how they tasted, and the same with the pawpaws, the hazelnuts, and the persimmons; and I can feel the thumping rain, upon my head, of hickory nuts and walnuts when we were out in the frosty dawn to scramble for them with the pigs, and the gusts of wind loosed them and sent them down. I know the stain of blackberries, and how pretty it is, and I know the stain of walnut hulls, and how little it minds soap and water, also what grudged experience it had of either of them. I know the taste of maple sap, and when to gather it, and how to arrange the troughs and the delivery tubes, and how to boil down the juice, and how to hook the sugar after it is made, also how much better hooked sugar tastes than any that is honestly come by, let bigots say what they will. I know how a prize watermelon looks when it is sunning its fat rotundity among pumpkin vines and "simblins";[2] I know how to tell when it is ripe without "plugging" it; I know how inviting it looks when it is cooling itself in a tub of water under the bed, waiting; I know how it looks when it lies on the table in the sheltered great floor space between house and kitchen, and the children gathered for the sacrifice and their mouths watering; I know the crackling sound it makes when the carving knife enters its end, and I can see the split fly along in front of the blade as the knife cleaves its way to the other end; I can see its halves fall apart and display the rich red meat and the black seeds, and the heart standing up, a luxury fit for the elect; I know how a boy looks behind a yard-long slice of that melon, and I know

how he feels; for I have been there. I know the taste of the watermelon which has been honestly come by, and I know the taste of the watermelon which has been acquired by art. Both taste good, but the experienced know which tastes best. I know the look of green apples and peaches and pears on the trees, and I know how entertaining they are when they are inside of a person. I know how ripe ones look when they are piled in pyramids under the trees, and how pretty they are and how vivid their colors. I know how a frozen apple looks, in a barrel down cellar in the wintertime, and how hard it is to bite, and how the frost makes the teeth ache, and yet how good it is, notwithstanding. I know the disposition of elderly people to select the specked apples for the children, and I once knew ways to beat the game. I know the look of an apple that is roasting and sizzling on a hearth on a winter's evening, and I know the comfort that comes of eating it hot, along with some sugar and a drench of cream. I know the delicate art and mystery of so cracking hickory nuts and walnuts on a flatiron with a hammer that the kernels will be delivered whole, and I know how the nuts, taken in conjunction with winter apples, cider, and doughnuts, make old people's old tales and old jokes sound fresh and crisp and enchanting, and juggle an evening away before you know what went with the time. I know the look of Uncle Dan'l's kitchen as it was on the privileged nights, when I was a child, and I can see the white and black children grouped on the hearth, with the firelight playing on their faces and the shadows flickering upon the walls, clear back toward the cavernous gloom of the rear, and I can hear Uncle Dan'l telling the immortal tales which Uncle Remus Harris[3] was to gather into his book and charm the world with, by and by; and I can feel again the creepy joy which quivered through me when the time for the ghost

---

[2] Cymblings, small summer squashes.
[3] Joel Chandler Harris (1848-1908), author of *Uncle Remus*.

story was reached—and the sense of regret, too, which came over me, for it was always the last story of the evening and there was nothing between it and the unwelcome bed.

I can remember the bare wooden stairway in my uncle's house, and the turn to the left above the landing, and the rafters and the slanting roof over my bed, and the squares of moonlight on the floor, and the white cold world of snow outside, seen through the curtainless window. I can remember the howling of the wind and the quaking of the house on stormy nights, and how snug and cozy one felt, under the blankets, listening; and how the powdery snow used to sift in, around the sashes, and lie in little ridges on the floor, and make the place look chilly in the morning and curb the wild desire to get up—in case there was any. I can remember how very dark that room was, in the dark of the moon, and how packed it was with ghostly stillness when one woke up by accident away in the night, and forgotten sins came flocking out of the secret chambers of the memory and wanted a hearing; and how ill chosen the time seemed for this kind of business; and how dismal was the hoo-hooing of the owl and the wailing of the wolf, sent mourning by on the night wind.

I remember the raging of the rain on that roof, summer nights, and how pleasant it was to lie and listen to it, and enjoy the white splendor of the lightning and the majestic booming and crashing of the thunder. It was a very satisfactory room, and there was a lightning rod which was reachable from the window, an adorable and skittish thing to climb up and down, summer nights, when there were duties on hand of a sort to make privacy desirable.

I remember the 'coon and 'possum hunts,

nights, with the negroes, and the long marches through the black gloom of the woods, and the excitement which fired everybody when the distant bay of an experienced dog announced that the game was treed; then the wild scramblings and stumblings through briers and bushes and over roots to get to the spot; then the lighting of a fire and the felling of the tree, the joyful frenzy of the dogs and the negroes, and the weird picture it all made in the red glare—I remember it all well, and the delight that everyone got out of it, except the 'coon.

I remember the pigeon seasons, when the birds would come in millions and cover the trees and by their weight break down the branches. They were clubbed to death with sticks; guns were not necessary and were not used. I remember the squirrel hunts, and prairie-chicken hunts, and wild-turkey hunts, and all that; and how we turned out, mornings, while it was still dark, to go on these expeditions, and how chilly and dismal it was, and how often I regretted that I was well enough to go. A toot on a tin horn brought twice as many dogs as were needed, and in their happiness they raced and scampered about, and knocked small people down, and made no end of unnecessary noise. At the word, they vanished away toward the woods, and we drifted silently after them in the melancholy gloom. But presently the gray dawn stole over the world, the birds piped up, then the sun rose and poured light and comfort all around, everything was fresh and dewy and fragrant, and life was a boon again. After three hours of tramping we arrived back wholesomely tired, overladen with game, very hungry, and just in time for breakfast.

American Literature 1860–1900

III
CRITICAL REFLECTIONS OF A CHANGING AMERICA

American Literature 1800-1900

III

CRITICAL REFLECTIONS OF A CHANGING AMERICA

1837 ∽ *William Dean Howells* ∽ 1920

HOWELLS was the first writer born west of the Alleghenies to gain a place of major influence in American literature. Though he lived most of his life in Boston and New York and found most of his literary material there, he remained a midwesterner. With his ascendancy, the dominant point of view in American letters was altered decisively. Perhaps his achievement was necessary to mark the coming of age of our national literature.

Howells' boyhood, in the small Ohio communities in which his father conducted local newspapers, affords the substance of some of the most enjoyable reading to be found in all his books, in *A Boy's Town* (1890), *My Year in a Log Cabin* (1893), *New Leaf Mills* (1913), and others. It was a boyhood of little formal schooling and of much hard work. At nine he began to help his father regularly in the newspaper office. But the father had a remarkably well-stocked library, was a lover of books, and saw to it that his son had ample time for reading, and guidance and help when he needed them.

Like Sam Clemens, Howells was earning his own living as a printer in his early teens. At Columbus, Ohio, he was first compositor, then reporter, and before he was twenty, political editor of the *Ohio State Journal*. His work at the State House in Columbus made him known to Republican leaders in the presidential campaign of 1860, and he was chosen to write a campaign life of Abraham Lincoln. In the same year poems of his were accepted by the *Atlantic Monthly*, and with J. J. Piatt he published a small volume called *Poems of Two Friends*.

As reward for his share in Lincoln's campaign, Howells spent the war years as consul in Venice; he kept on writing, and sending poems and essays to American periodicals. Back in America, he worked for a few months under Godkin on the *Nation* and then joined the staff of the *Atlantic Monthly*, to become its editor-in-chief at thirty-five. The years in Italy afforded material for his first important books, *Venetian Life* (1866) and *Italian Journeys* (1867). Entertaining and smoothly written accounts of a young American's observations, they have also an able journalist's acuteness in analysis—especially in his account of Italian attitudes under the Austrian occupation of Venice—and a humanitarian's sensitiveness.

Howells worked his way from book of travel to novel by easy stages. *Their Wedding Journey* (1872) is a fairly acceptable combination of the two. Through the 70's his successive novels showed gradually increasing mastery of form and deepening purpose until in *A Modern Instance* (1882) he attained his full stature as a writer. By this time he had found the duties of his editorial work too exacting for the achievement of his ambitions as a novelist. He took the decisive step of resigning his position with the *Atlantic,* and entered into an arrangement with the Century company which permitted him to devote most of his time to fiction. In 1888 he moved to New York. He conducted for *Harper's Magazine* a department called "The Editor's Study" from 1886 to 1892, and "The Editor's Easy Chair" from 1900 until his death in 1920.

During these decades he wrote and published steadily—novels, plays, criticism, reminiscences, volumes of stories and poems: a total production, from 1860 to 1920, of more than a hundred books. On this ample basis and that of his editorial work he achieved a commanding position in our letters. Many honors were accorded him, and he became acquainted with university halls for the first time in his life as the recipient of honorary degrees from Yale, Harvard, Princeton, Columbia, and Oxford.

But Howells long outlived the literary generation he marked and moulded. His was the not uncommon experience of finding that the procession he once had led in later years passed him by. The same qualities and attitudes that had caused him to be denounced in the 1880's as a radical and revolutionist were by the second decade of the new century laughed at as "old hat." This later attitude toward Howells has carried over in the discussion and criticism of his work, in the quarter-century since his death, to a surprising degree. It is high time that the whole body of his writing be revalued, and the quality of his achievement and the extent of his service to American literature be fully recognized.

The work of Howells as critic, editor, and novelist was the chief channel through which critical realism became naturalized in American fiction and established in the dominating position which it has held for fifty years. Early committed to "fidelity to experience and probability of motive" as his criteria in fiction, he preached and practiced realism against the overwhelming preponderance of contemporary taste and example. His criticism first effectively recognized for American readers the achievement of the Russian novelists, particularly Tolstoi, releasing an influence that has meant much for American fiction. As editor of the *Atlantic Monthly,* he welcomed to its pages the work of Mark Twain and Henry James. Long before anyone else, he saw in Twain something more than a western humorist, and his steady confidence and friendship contributed in no small degree to Twain's ultimate realization of his powers. In later years he gave recognition, encouragement, and in some cases even material help to a whole generation of young realists, among them Hamlin Garland, Stephen Crane, and Frank Norris.

Howells' realism was critical, not unselective or unmotivated. He saw the evils in contemporary American life clearly, and he not only presented them with candor and courage but he tried to go behind the symptoms to their causes. He became converted to the principles of socialism, and set forth the case for radical social and economic readjustments in the Utopian novels *A Traveler from Altruria* (1894) and *Through the Eye of the Needle* (1907), as well as more directly in other novels and in scores of essays and editorials. As a reviewer he emphasized steadily whatever was sincere and authentic in American writing. As a critic, notably in *Criticism and Fiction* (1891), he defined the principles and purposes of realism, affording a foundation on which the writers who followed him in the 90's largely built.

Howells' place in our literature is not, however, dependent on his achievement as an editor and critic. It rests firmly on his own work as a creative writer. Of his total production it must at once be admitted that much is of relatively small value—the plays, nearly all of the poetry, some of the fiction. There remain at least twenty books in which the reader of today will find durable interest and value. Of these perhaps five, all written within a decade, are representative: *A Modern Instance* (1882), *The Rise of Silas Lapham* (1885), *The Minister's Charge* (1887), *Annie Kilburn* (1889), and *A Hazard of New Fortunes* (1890). These novels present his most penetrating analyses of the contemporary social structure and contain most, though not all, of his memorable characters.

Howells has been damned with many adjectives. His realism has been called soft, gentle, and timid; his fiction as a whole indicted as genteel, or effeminate. It is true that whole areas of human behavior familiar in the fiction of today are left untouched by Howells. Most of his characters are respectable middle-class Americans, and their conduct conforms to the conventions of their group and time. Howells did not attempt the presentation of what he did not know; and he did not know the life of city slums, nor did he know much of physical toil or physical violence. But within the limits which his own literary conscience set for him, Howells dealt with a wide variety of characters and a wide range of experience. That his realism is soft and timid is denied by many pages, from the *Suburban Sketches* (1871) to *The Leatherwood God* (1916). That he shrank from portrayal of tragedy, from intense emotion, is untrue of all of his major novels, notably of incidents in *A Modern Instance, The Minister's Charge,* and *A Hazard of New Fortunes.* If the modern reader will meet Howells fairly on his own ground, he will find him far from shallow optimism, and not afraid to face the logical development of his characters and situations.

He will find, with integrity and courage, other virtues in Howells as a writer. It is no small achievement to provide a whole social group and era with documentation in details of life and manners. Howells has done this for the middle-class America of his time: the dress, the food, the recreation, the vehicles and utensils, the speech and thought. Sometimes the documentation gets in the way of his story—the travel writer's habit of lengthy description not quite outgrown. Usually it is smoothly integrated with the action. Frequently it carries with it the play of his very genuine sense of humor, never adequately recognized in criticism of Howells—a humor usually mellow, often pungent, by no means always kind. Sharpened by humor and enriched by detail, Howells' style is in itself a steady source of pleasure. It is unobtrusive, flexible, deft and precise, characteristically light and easy but with abundant reserve of emphasis and impact. Few Americans have written so much so well. The mind it reveals is urbane, friendly, even genial. But these are not vices in a literary companion when they are accompanied, as they are in William Dean Howells, by sincerity and courage.

Among the selections which follow, "A Romance of Real Life," from *Suburban Sketches,* is representative of Howells' earlier realism, while "Somebody's Mother," from *The Daughter of the Storage* (1916), shows the persistence of the realistic temper, ethically and sociologically searching, in his later prose.

[No collected edition of Howells has appeared. The best biographical sources are his own writings and his *Life in Letters,* 2 vols. (New York, 1928), edited by his daughter, Mildred Howells. The best critical examinations are *W. D. Howells, A Study* (Cambridge, 1924), by O. W. Firkins, and *William Dean Howells, A Critical Study* (New York, 1922), by D. G. Cooke. *A Bibliography of William Dean Howells* (New York, 1948) has been prepared by W. M. Gibson and George Arms.]

A ROMANCE OF REAL LIFE
[1871]

IT WAS LONG past the twilight hour, which has been elsewhere mentioned as so oppressive in suburban places, and it was even too late for visitors, when a resident, whom I shall briefly describe as the Contributor, was startled by a ring at his door, in the vicinity of one of our great maritime cities,—say Plymouth or Manchester. As any thoughtful person would have done upon the like occasion, he ran over his acquaintance in his mind, speculating whether it were such or such a one, and dismissing the whole list of improbabilities, before laying down the book he was reading, and answering the bell. When at last he did this, he was rewarded by the apparition of an utter stranger on his threshold,—a gaunt figure of forlorn and curious smartness towering far above him, that jerked him a nod of the head, and asked if Mr. Hapford lived there. The face which the lamp-light revealed was remarkable for a harsh two days' growth of beard, and a single bloodshot eye; yet it was not otherwise a sinister countenance, and there was something in the strange presence that appealed and touched. The contributor, revolving the facts vaguely in his mind, was not sure, after all, that it was not the man's clothes rather than his expression that softened him towards the rugged visage: they were so tragically cheap, and the misery of helpless needlewomen and the poverty and ignorance of the purchaser were so apparent in their shabby newness, of which they appeared still conscious enough to have led the way to the very window, in the Semitic quarter of the city, where they had lain ticketed, "This nobby suit for $15."

But the stranger's manner put both his face and his clothes out of mind, and claimed a deeper interest when, being answered that the person for whom he asked did not live there, he set his bristling lips hard together, and sighed heavily.

"They told me," he said, in a hopeless way, "that he lived on this street, and I've been to every other house. I'm very anxious to find him, Cap'n,"—the contributor, of course, had no claim to the title with which he was thus decorated,—"for I've a daughter living with him, and I want to see her; I've just got home from a two years' voyage, and"—there was a struggle of the Adam's-apple in the man's gaunt throat—"I find she's about all there is left of my family."

How complex is every human motive! This contributor had been lately thinking, whenever he turned the pages of some foolish traveller,—some empty prattler of Southern or Eastern lands, where all sensation was long ago exhausted, and the oxygen has perished from every sentiment, so has it been breathed and breathed again, —that nowadays the wise adventurer sat down beside his own register and waited for incidents to seek him out. It seemed to him that the cultivation of a patient and receptive spirit was the sole condition needed to insure the occurrence of all manner of surprising facts within the range of one's own personal knowledge; that not only the Greeks were at our doors, but the fairies and the genii, and all the people of romance, who had but to be hospitably treated in order to develop the deepest interest of fiction, and to become the characters of plots so ingenious that the most cunning invention were poor beside them. I myself am not so confident of this, and would rather trust Mr. Charles Reade,[1] say, for my amusement than any chance combination of events. But I should be afraid to say how much his pride in the character of the stranger's sorrows, as proof of the correctness of his theory, prevailed with the contributor to ask him to come in and sit down; though I hope that some abstract impulse of humanity, some compassionate and unselfish care for the man's misfortunes as misfortunes, was not wholly wanting. Indeed, the helpless simplicity with which he had confided his case might have touched a harder heart. "Thank you," said the poor fellow, after a moment's hesitation. "I believe I will come in. I've been on foot all day, and after such a long voyage it makes a man dreadfully sore to walk about so much. Perhaps you can think of a Mr. Hapford living somewhere in the neighborhood."

He sat down, and, after a pondering silence, in which he had remained with his head fallen upon his breast, "My name is Jonathan Tinker," he said, with the unaffected air which had already impressed the contributor, and as if he felt that some form of introduction was necessary, "and the girl that I want to find is Julia Tinker." Then he said, resuming the eventful personal history which the listener exulted while he regretted to hear: "You see, I shipped first to Liverpool, and there I heard from my family; and then I shipped again for Hong-Kong, and after that I never heard a word: I seemed to miss the letters everywhere. This morning, at four o'clock, I left my ship as soon as she had hauled into the dock, and hurried up home. The house was shut, and not a soul in it; and I didn't know what to do, and I sat down on the doorstep to wait till the neighbors woke up, to ask them what had become of my family. And the first one come out he told me my wife had been dead a year and a half, and the baby I'd never seen, with her; and one of my boys was dead; and he didn't know where the rest of the children was, but he'd heard two of the little ones was with a family in the city."

The man mentioned these things with the half-apologetic air observable in a certain kind of Americans when some accident obliges them to confess the infirmity of the natural feelings. They do not ask your sympathy, and you offer it quite at your own risk, with a chance of having it thrown back upon your hands. The contributor assumed the risk so far as to say, "Pretty rough!" when the stranger paused;

---

[1] English novelist and dramatist, best known as author of *The Cloister and the Hearth* (1861).

and perhaps these homely words were best suited to reach the homely heart. The man's quivering lips closed hard again, a kind of spasm passed over his dark face, and then two very small drops of brine shone upon his weather-worn cheeks. This demonstration, into which he had been surprised, seemed to stand for the passion of tears into which the emotional races fall at such times. He opened his lips with a kind of dry click, and went on:—

"I hunted about the whole forenoon in the city, and at last I found the children. I'd been gone so long they didn't know me, and somehow I thought the people they were with weren't overglad I'd turned up. Finally the oldest child told me that Julia was living with a Mr. Hapford on this street, and I started out here to-night to look her up. If I can find her, I'm all right. I can get the family together, then, and start new."

"It seems rather odd," mused the listener aloud, "that the neighbors let them break up so, and that they should all scatter as they did."

"Well, it ain't so curious as it seems, Cap'n. There was money for them at the owners', all the time; I'd left part of my wages when I sailed; but they didn't know how to get at it, and what could a parcel of children do? Julia's a good girl, and when I find her I'm all right."

The writer could only repeat that there was no Mr. Hapford living on that street, and never had been, so far as he knew. Yet there might be such a person in the neighborhood; and they would go out together, and ask at some of the houses about. But the stranger must first take a glass of wine; for he looked used up.

The sailor awkwardly but civilly enough protested that he did not want to give so much trouble, but took the glass, and, as he put it to his lips, said formally, as if it were a toast or a kind of grace, "I hope I may have the opportunity of returning the compliment." The contributor thanked him; though, as he thought of all the circumstances of the case, and considered the

cost at which the stranger had come to enjoy his politeness, he felt little eagerness to secure the return of the compliment at the same price, and added, with the consequence of another set phrase, "Not at all." But the thought had made him the more anxious to befriend the luckless soul fortune had cast in his way; and so the two sallied out together, and rang doorbells wherever lights were still seen burning in the windows, and asked the astonished people who answered their summons whether any Mr. Hapford were known to live in the neighborhood.

And although the search for this gentleman proved vain, the contributor could not feel that an expedition which set familiar objects in such novel lights was altogether a failure. He entered so intimately into the cares and anxieties of his "protégé," that at times he felt himself in some inexplicable sort a shipmate of Jonathan Tinker, and almost personally a partner of his calamities. The estrangement of all things which takes place, within doors and without, about midnight, may have helped to cast this doubt upon his identity;—he seemed to be visiting now for the first time the streets and neighborhoods nearest his own, and his feet stumbled over the accustomed walks. In his quality of houseless wanderer, and,—so far as appeared to others,—possibly, worthless vagabond, he also got a new and instructive effect upon the faces which, in his real character, he knew so well by their looks of neighborly greeting, and it is his belief that the first hospitable prompting of the human heart is to shut the door in the eyes of homeless strangers who present themselves after eleven o'clock. By that time the servants are all abed, and the gentleman of the house answers the bell, and looks out with a loath and bewildered face, which gradually changes to one of suspicion, and of wonder as to what those fellows can possibly want of *him*, till at last the prevailing expression is one of contrite desire to atone for the first reluctance by any sort of service. The contributor professes to have observed these changing phases in the visages of those whom he that night called from their dreams, or arrested in the act of going to bed; and he drew the conclusion—very proper for his imaginable connection with the garroting and other adventurous brotherhoods—that the most flattering moment for knocking on the head people who answer a late ring at night is either in their first selfish bewilderment, or their final self-abandonment to their better impulses. It does not seem to have occurred to him that he would himself have been a much more favorable subject for the predatory arts than any of his neighbors, if his shipmate, the unknown companion of his researches for Mr. Hapford, had been at all so minded. But the faith of the gaunt giant upon which he reposed was good, and the contributor continued to wander about with him in perfect safety. Not a soul among those they asked had ever heard of a Mr. Hapford,—far less of a Julia Tinker living with him. But they all listened to the contributor's explanation with interest and eventual sympathy; and in truth,—briefly told, with a word now and then thrown in by Jonathan Tinker, who kept at the bottom of the steps, showing like a gloomy spectre in the night, or, in his grotesque length and gauntness, like the other's shadow cast there by the lamplight,—it was a story which could hardly fail to awaken pity.

At last, after ringing several bells where there were no lights, in the mere wantonness of good-will, and going away before they could be answered (it would be entertaining to know what dreams they caused the sleepers within), there seemed to be nothing for it but to give up the search till morning, and go to the main street and wait for the last horse-car to the city.

There, seated upon the curbstone, Jonathan Tinker, being plied with a few leading questions, told in hints and scraps the story of his hard life, which was at present that of a second mate, and had been that of a cabin-boy and of a seaman before the mast. The second mate's place he held to

be the hardest aboard ship. You got only a few dollars more than the men, and you did not rank with the officers; you took your meals alone, and in everything you belonged by yourself. The men did not respect you, and sometimes the captain abused you awfully before the passengers. The hardest captain that Jonathan Tinker ever sailed with was Captain Gooding; and Jonathan Tinker was with him only one voyage. When he had been home awhile, he saw an advertisement for a second mate, and he went round to the owners'. They had kept it secret who the captain was; but there was Captain Gooding in the owners' office. "Why, here's the man, now, that I want for a second mate," said he, when Jonathan Tinker entered; "he knows me." "Captain Gooding, I know you 'most too well to want to sail under you," answered Jonathan. "I might go if I hadn't been with you one voyage too many already."

"And then the men!" said Jonathan, "the men coming aboard drunk, and having to be pounded sober! And the hardest of the fight falls on the second mate! Why, there isn't an inch of me that hasn't been cut over or smashed into a jell. I've had three ribs broken; I've got a scar from a knife on my cheek; and I've been stabbed bad enough, half a dozen times, to lay me up."

Here he gave a sort of desperate laugh, as if the notion of so much misery and such various mutilation were too grotesque not to be amusing. "Well, what can you do?" he went on. "If you don't strike, the men think you're afraid of them; and so you have to begin hard and go on hard. I always tell a man, 'Now, my man, I always begin with a man the way I mean to keep on. You do your duty and you're all right. But if you don't—' Well, the men ain't Americans any more,—Dutch, Spaniards, Chinese, Portugee,—and it ain't like abusing a white man."

Jonathan Tinker was plainly part of the horrible tyranny which we all know exists on shipboard; and his listener respected him the more that, though he had heart enough to be ashamed of it, he was too honest not to own it.

Why did he still follow the sea? Because he did not know what else to do. When he was younger, he used to love it, but now he hated it. Yet there was not a prettier life in the world if you got to be captain. He used to hope for that once, but not now; though he *thought* he could navigate a ship. Only let him get his family together again, and he would—yes, he would—try to do something ashore.

No car had yet come in sight, and so the contributor suggested that they should walk to the car-office, and look in the Directory which is kept there for the name of Hapford, in search of whom it had already been arranged that they should renew their acquaintance on the morrow. Jonathan Tinker, when they had reached the office, heard with constitutional phlegm that the name of the Hapford for whom he inquired was not in the Directory. "Never mind," said the other, "come round to my house in the morning. We'll find him yet." So they parted with a shake of the hand, the second mate saying that he believed he should go down to the vessel and sleep aboard,—if he could sleep,—and murmuring at the last moment the hope of returning the compliment, while the other walked homeward, weary as to the flesh, but, in spite of his sympathy for Jonathan Tinker, very elate in spirit. The truth is,—and however disgraceful to human nature, let the truth still be told,—he had recurred to his primal satisfaction in the man as calamity capable of being used for such and such literary ends, and, while he pitied him, rejoiced in him as an episode of real life quite as striking and complete as anything in fiction. It was literature made to his hand. Nothing could be better, he mused; and once more he passed the details of the story in review, and beheld all those pictures which the poor fellow's artless words had so vividly conjured up: he saw him leaping ashore in the gray summer dawn as soon as the ship hauled into the dock, and making his way, with his vague sea-

legs unaccustomed to the pavements, up through the silent and empty city streets; he imagined the tumult of fear and hope which the sight of the man's home must have caused in him, and the benumbing shock of finding it blind and deaf to all his appeals; he saw him sitting down upon what had been his own threshold, and waiting in a sort of bewildered patience till the neighbors should be awake, while the noises of the streets gradually arose, and the wheels began to rattle over the stones, and the milkman and the iceman came and went, and the waiting figure began to be stared at, and to challenge the curiosity of the passing policeman; he fancied the opening of the neighbor's door, and the slow, cold understanding of the case; the manner, whatever it was, in which the sailor was told that one year before his wife had died, with her babe, and that his children were scattered, none knew where. As the contributor dwelt pityingly upon these things, but at the same time estimated their aesthetic value one by one, he drew near the head of his street, and found himself a few paces behind a boy slouching onward through the night, to whom he called out, adventurously, and with no real hope of information,—

"Do you happen to know anybody on this street by the name of Hapford?"

"Why no, not in this town," said the boy; but he added that there was a street by the same name in a neighboring suburb, and a Hapford living on it.

"By Jove!" thought the contributor, "this is more like literature than ever"; and he hardly knew whether to be more provoked at his own stupidity in not thinking of a street of the same name in the next village, or delighted at the element of fatality which the fact introduced into the story; for Tinker, according to his own account, must have landed from the cars a few rods from the very door he was seeking, and so walked farther and farther from it every moment. He thought the case so curious, that he laid it briefly before the boy, who, however he might have been inwardly affected, was sufficiently true to the national traditions not to make the smallest conceivable outward sign of concern in it.

At home, however, the contributor related his adventures and the story of Tinker's life, adding the fact that he had just found out where Mr. Hapford lived. "It was the only touch wanting," said he; "the whole thing is now perfect."

"It's *too* perfect," was answered from a sad enthusiasm. "Don't speak of it! I can't take it in."

"But the question is," said the contributor, penitently taking himself to task for forgetting the hero of these excellent misfortunes in his delight over their perfection, "how am I to sleep to-night, thinking of that poor soul's suspense and uncertainty? Never mind,—I'll be up early, and run over and make sure that it is Tinker's Hapford, before he gets out here, and have a pleasant surprise for him. Would it not be a justifiable *coup de theatre* to fetch his daughter here, and let her answer his ring at the door when he comes in the morning?"

This plan was discouraged. "No, no; let them meet in their own way. Just take him to Hapford's house and leave him."

"Very well. But he's too good a character to lose sight of. He's got to come back here and tell us what he intends to do."

The birds, next morning, not having had the second mate on their minds either as an unhappy man or a most fortunate episode, but having slept long and soundly, were singing in a very sprightly way in the wayside trees; and the sweetness of their notes made the contributor's heart light as he climbed the hill and rang at Mr. Hapford's door.

The door was opened by a young girl of fifteen or sixteen, whom he knew at a glance for the second mate's daughter, but of whom, for form's sake, he asked if there were a girl named Julia Tinker living there.

"My name's Julia Tinker," answered the maid, who had rather a disappointing face.

"Well," said the contributor, "your father's got back from his Hong-Kong voyage."

"Hong-Kong voyage?" echoed the girl, with a stare of helpless inquiry, but no other visible emotion.

"Yes. He had never heard of your mother's death. He came home yesterday morning, and was looking for you all day."

Julia Tinker remained open-mouthed but mute; and the other was puzzled at the want of feeling shown, which he could not account for even as a national trait. "Perhaps there's some mistake," he said.

"There must be," answered Julia: "my father hasn't been to sea for a good many years. *My* father," she added, with a diffidence indescribably mingled with a sense of distinction,—"*my* father's in State's Prison. What kind of looking man was this?"

The contributor mechanically described him.

Julia Tinker broke into a loud, hoarse laugh. "Yes, it's him, sure enough." And then, as if the joke were too good to keep: "Miss Hapford, Miss Hapford, father's got out. Do come here!" she called into a back room.

When Mrs. Hapford appeared, Julia fell back, and, having deftly caught a fly on the door-post, occupied herself in plucking it to pieces, while she listened to the conversation of the others.

"It's all true enough," said Mrs. Hapford, when the writer had recounted the moving story of Jonathan Tinker, "so far as the death of his wife and baby goes. But he hasn't been to sea for a good many years, and he must have just come out of State's Prison, where he was put for bigamy. There's always two sides to a story, you know; but they say it broke his first wife's heart, and she died. His friends don't want him to find his children, and this girl especially."

"He's found his children in the city," said the contributor, gloomily, being at a loss what to do or say, in view of the wreck of his romance.

"O, he's found 'em, has he?" cried Julia, with heightened amusement. "Then he'll have me next, if I don't pack and go."

"I'm very, very sorry," said the contributor, secretly resolved never to do another
good deed, no matter how temptingly the
opportunity presented itself. "But you may
depend he won't find out from *me* where
you are. Of course I had no earthly reason
for supposing his story was not true."

"Of course," said kind-hearted Mrs. Hapford, mingling a drop of honey with the
gall in the contributor's soul, "you only
did your duty."

And indeed, as he turned away, he did
not feel altogether without compensation.
However Jonathan Tinker had fallen in
his esteem as a man, he had even risen as
literature. The episode which had appeared
so perfect in its pathetic phases did not
seem less finished as a farce; and this person, to whom all things of everyday life
presented themselves in periods more or
less rounded, and capable of use as facts
or illustrations, could not but rejoice in
these new incidents, as dramatically fashioned as the rest. It occurred to him that,
wrought into a story, even better use might
be made of the facts now than before, for
they had developed questions of character
and of human nature which could not fail
to interest. The more he pondered upon his
acquaintance with Jonathan Tinker, the
more fascinating the erring mariner became, in his complex truth and falsehood,
his delicately blending shades of artifice
and *naïveté*. He must, it was felt, have believed to a certain point in his own inventions: nay, starting with that groundwork
of truth,—the fact that his wife was really
dead, and that he had not seen his family
for two years,—why should he not place
implicit faith in all the fictions reared upon
it? It was probable that he felt a real sorrow for her loss, and that he found a fantastic consolation in depicting the circumstances of her death so that they should
look like his inevitable misfortunes rather
than his faults. He might well have re-
pented his offence during those two years
of prison; and why should he not now cast
their dreariness and shame out of his
memory, and replace them with the free-

dom and adventure of a two years' voyage
to China,—so probable, in all respects,
that the fact should appear an impossible
nightmare? In the experiences of his life
he had abundant material to furnish forth
the facts of such a voyage, and in the
weariness and lassitude that should follow
a day's walking equally after a two years'
voyage and two years' imprisonment, he
had as much physical proof in favor of one
hypothesis as the other. It was doubtless
true, also, as he said, that he had gone to
his house at dawn, and sat down on the
threshold of his ruined home; and perhaps he felt the desire he had expressed to
see his daughter, with a purpose of beginning life anew; and it may have cost him
a veritable pang when he found that his
little ones did not know him. All the sentiments of the situation were such as might
persuade a lively fancy of the truth of its
own inventions; and as he heard these
continually repeated by the contributor in
their search for Mr. Hapford, they must
have acquired an objective force and re-
pute scarcely to be resisted. At the same
time, there were touches of nature throughout Jonathan Tinker's narrative which
could not fail to take the faith of another.
The contributor, in reviewing it, thought it
particularly charming that his mariner had
not overdrawn himself or attempted to
paint his character otherwise than as it
probably was; that he had shown his ideas
and practices of life to be those of a second mate, nor more nor less, without the
gloss of regret or the pretences of refinement that might be pleasing to the supposed philanthropist with whom he had
fallen in. Captain Gooding was of course
a true portrait, and there was nothing in
Jonathan Tinker's statement of the relations of a second mate to his superiors and
his inferiors which did not agree perfectly
with what the writer had just read in
Two Years before the Mast,[2]—a book
which had possibly cast its glamour upon

[2] By Richard Henry Dana (1815-1882);
published in 1840.

the adventure. He admired also the just and perfectly characteristic air of grief in the bereaved husband and father,— those occasional escapes from the sense of loss into a brief hilarity and forgetfulness, and those relapses into the hovering gloom, which every one has observed in this poor, crazy human nature when oppressed by sorrow, and which it would have been hard to simulate. But, above all, he exulted in that supreme stroke of the imagination given by the second mate when, at parting, he said he believed he would go down and sleep on board the vessel. In view of this, the State's Prison theory almost appeared a malign and foolish scandal.

Yet even if this theory were correct, was the second mate wholly answerable for beginning his life again with the imposture he had practised? The contributor had either so fallen in love with the literary advantages of his forlorn deceiver that he would see no moral obliquity in him, or he had touched a subtler verity at last in pondering the affair. It seemed now no longer a farce, but had a pathos which, though very different from that of its first aspect, was hardly less tragical. Knowing with what coldness, or, at the best, uncandor, he (representing Society in its attitude toward convicted Error) would have met the fact had it been owned to him at first, he had not virtue enough to condemn the illusory stranger, who must have been helpless to make at once evident any repentance he felt or good purpose he cherished. Was it not one of the saddest consequences of the man's past,—a dark necessity of misdoing,—that, even with the best will in the world to retrieve himself, his first endeavor must involve a wrong? Might he not, indeed, be considered a martyr, in some sort, to his own admirable impulses? I can see clearly enough where the contributor was astray in this reasoning, but I can also understand how one accustomed to value realities only as they resembled fables should be won with such pensive sophistry; and I can certainly sympathize with his feeling that the mariner's

failure to reappear according to appointment added its final and most agreeable charm to the whole affair, and completed the mystery from which the man emerged and which swallowed him up again.

SOMEBODY'S MOTHER
[1916 (1915)]

THE FIGURE of a woman sat crouched forward on one of the lowermost steps of the brownstone dwelling which was keeping a domestic tradition in a street mostly gone to shops and small restaurants and local express-offices. The house was black behind its closed shutters, and the woman remained sitting there because no one could have come out of its door for a year past to hunt her away. The neighborhood policeman faltered in going by, and then he kept on. The three people who came out of the large, old-fashioned hotel, half a block off, on their way for dinner to a French table d'hôte which they had heard of, stopped and looked at the woman. They were a father and his son and daughter, and it was something like a family instinct that controlled them, in their pause before the woman crouching on the steps.

It was the early dusk of a December day, and the day was very chilly. "She seems to be sick or something," the father vaguely surmised. "Or asleep."

The three looked at the woman, but they did nothing for a moment. They would rather have gone on, but they waited to see if anything would happen to release them from the spell that they seemed to have laid upon themselves. They were conditional New Yorkers of long sojourn, and it was from no apparent motive that the son wore evening dress, which his unbuttoned overcoat discovered, and an opera-hat. He would not have dressed so for that problematical French table d'hôte; probably he was going on later to some society affair. He now put in effect the father's impulse to go closer and look at the woman.

"She seems to be asleep," he reported.

"Shouldn't you think she would take

cold? She will get her death there. Oughtn't we to do something?" the daughter asked, but she left it to the father, and he said:

"Probably somebody will come by."

"That we could leave her to?" the daughter pursued.

"We could do that without waiting," the son commented.

"Well, yes," the father assented; but they did not go on. They waited, helplessly, and then somebody came by. It was a young girl, not very definite in the dusk, except that she was unmistakably of the working class; she was simply dressed, though with the New York instinct for clothes. Their having stopped there seemed to stay her involuntarily, and after a glance in the direction of their gaze she asked the daughter:

"Is she sick, do you think?"

"We don't know what's the matter. But she oughtn't to stay there."

Something velvety in the girl's voice had made its racial quality sensible to the ear; as she went up to the crouching woman and bent forward over her and then turned to them, a street lamp threw its light on her face, and they saw that she was a light shade of colored girl.

"She seems to be sleeping."

"Perhaps, the son began, "she's not quite —" But he did not go on.

The girl looked around at the others and suggested, "She must be somebody's mother!"

The others all felt abashed in their several sorts and degrees, but in their several sorts and degrees they all decided that there was something romantic, sentimental, theatrical in the girl's words, like something out of some cheap story-paper story.

The father wondered if that kind of thing was current among that kind of people. He had a sort of aesthetic pleasure in the character and condition expressed by the words.

"Well, yes," he said, "if she has children, or has had." The girl looked at him uncertainly, and then he added, "But, of course—"

The son went up to the woman again, and asked: "Aren't you well? Can we do anything for you? It won't do to stay here, you know." The woman only made a low murmur, and he said to his sister, "Suppose we get her up."

His sister did not come forward promptly, and the colored girl said, "I'll help you."

She took one arm of the woman and the son took the other, and they lifted her, without her connivance, to her feet and kept her on them. Then they walked her down the steps. On the level below she showed taller than either of them; she was bundled up in different incoherent wraps; her head was muffled, and she wore a battered bonnet at an involuntary slant.

"I don't know exactly what we shall do with her," the son said.

"We ought to get her home somehow," the daughter said.

The father proposed nothing, but the colored girl said, "If we keep walking her along, we'll come to a policeman and we can—"

A hoarse rumble of protest came from the muffled head of the woman, and the girl put her ear closer. "Want to go home? Well, the policeman will take you. We don't know where you live, and we haven't the time."

The woman seemed to have nothing to say further, and they began walking her westward; the colored girl supported her on one hand, and the son, in his evening dress and opera-hat, on the other.

The daughter followed in a vague anxiety, but the father went along, enjoying the anomaly, and happy in his relish of that phrase, "She must be somebody's mother." It now sounded to him like a catch from one of those New York songs, popular in the order of life where the mother represents what is best and holiest. He recalled a vaudeville ballad with the refrain of "A Boy's Best Friend Is His Mother," which, when he heard it in a vaudeville theater, threatened the gallery floor under the applauding feet of the frenzied audience. Probably this colored girl belonged to that order of life; he wished he could know her social circumstance and what her outlook on the greater world might be. She seemed a kind creature, poor thing, and he respected her. "Somebody's mother" —he liked that.

They all walked westward, aimlessly, except that the table d'hôte where they had meant to dine was in that direction; they had heard of it as an amusingly harmless French place, and they were fond of such mild adventures.

The old woman contributed nothing to the definition of their progress. She stumbled and mumbled along, but between Seventh Avenue and Eighth she stubbornly arrested her guardians. "She says"—the colored girl translated some obscure avowal across her back—"she says she wants to go home, and she lives up in Harlem."

"Oh, well, that's good," the father said, with an optimistic amiability. "We'd better help walk her across to Ninth Avenue and put her on a car, and tell the conductor where to let her off."

He was not helping walk her himself, but he enjoyed his son's doing it in evening dress and opera-hat, with that kind colored girl on the other side of the mother; the composition was agreeably droll. The daughter did not like it, and she cherished the ideal of a passing policeman to take the old woman in charge.

No policeman passed, though great numbers of other people met them without apparently finding anything noticeable in the spectacle which their group presented. Among the crowds going and coming on the avenues which they crossed, scarcely any turned to look at them, or was moved by the sense of anything odd in them.

The old woman herself did nothing to attract public notice till they were midway between Seventh and Eighth avenues. She mumbled something from time to time which the colored girl interpreted to the rest as her continued wish to go home. She was now clearer about her street and number. The girl, as if after question of her own generous spirit, said she did not see

how she could go with her; she was expected at home herself.

"Oh, you won't have to go with her; we'll just put her aboard the Ninth Avenue car," the father encouraged her. He would have encouraged any one; he was enjoying the whole affair.

At a certain moment, for no apparent reason, the mother decided to sit down on a door-step. It proved to be the door-step of a house where from time to time colored people—sometimes of one sex, sometimes of another—went in or came out. The door seemed to open directly into a large room where dancing and dining were going on concurrently. At a long table colored people sat eating, and behind their chairs on both sides of the room and at the ends of the table colored couples were waltzing.

The effect was the more curious because, except for some almost inaudible music, the scene passed in silence. Those who were eating were not visibly incommoded by those revolving at their backs; the waltzers turned softly around and around, untempted by the table now before them, now behind them. When some of the diners or dancers came out, they stumbled over the old woman on the door-step without minding or stopping to inquire. Those outside, when they went in, fell over her with like equanimity and joined the strange company within.

The father murmured to himself the lines,

"'Vast forms that move fantastically
    To a discordant melody [1]—'"

with a remote trouble of mind because the words were at once so graphic and yet so imperfectly applicable. The son and daughter exchanged a silent wonder as long as they could bear it; then the daughter asked the colored girl:

"What is it?"

"It's a boarding-house," the girl answered, simply.

"Oh," the daughter said.

Sounds of more decided character than

---

[1] From Poe's "The Haunted Palace."

before now came from the figure on the door-step.

"She seems to be saying something," the daughter suggested in general terms. "What is she saying?" she asked the colored girl.

The girl stooped over and listened. Then she answered, "She's swearing."

"Swearing? What about? Whom is she swearing at?"

"At me, I reckon. She says, why don't I take her home."

"Well, why doesn't she get up, then?"

"She says she won't."

"We can't carry her to the car," the daughter noted.

"Oh, why not?" the father merrily demanded.

The daughter turned to her brother. They were both very respectful to their father, but the son agreed with his sister when she said: "Papa would joke about anything. But this has passed a joke. We must get this old thing up and start her off."

Upon experiment they could not get the old thing up, even with the help of the kind colored girl. They had to let her be, and the colored girl reported, after stooping over her again, "She says she can't walk."

"She walked here well enough," the daughter said.

"Not *very* well," the father amended.

His daughter did not notice him. She said to her brother: "Well, now you must go and find a policeman. It's strange none has gone by."

It was also strange that still their group remained without attracting the notice of the passers. Nobody stopped to speak or even stare; perhaps the phenomena of that boarding-house had ceased to have surprises for the public of the neighborhood, and they in their momentary relation to it would naturally be without interest.

The brother went away, leaving his sister with their father and that kind colored creature in charge of the old woman, now more and more quiescent on the door-step; she had ceased to swear, or even to speak. The brother came back after a time that

seemed long, and said that he could not find a policeman anywhere, and at the same moment, as if the officer had been following at his heels, a policeman crossed the street from just behind him.

The daughter ran after him, and asked if he would not come and look at the old woman who had so steadfastly remained in their charge, and she rapidly explained.

"Sure, lady," the policeman said, and he turned from crossing the street and went up to the old woman. He laid his hand on her shoulder, and his touch seemed magical. "What's the matter? Can't you stand up?" She stood up as if at something familiar in the voice of authority. "Where do you live?" She gave an address altogether different from that she had given before—a place on the next avenue, within a block or two. "You'd better go home. You can walk, can't you?"

"I can walk well enough," she answered in a tone of vexation, and she made her word good by walking quite actively away in the direction she had given.

The kind colored girl became a part of the prevalent dark after refusing the thanks of the others. The daughter then fervently offered them to the policeman.

"That's all right, lady," he said, and the incident had closed except for her emotion at seeing him enter a police-station precisely across the street, where they could have got a dozen policemen in a moment.

"Well," the father said, "we might as well go to our French table d'hôte now."

"Oh," the son said, as if that reminded him, "the place seems to be shut."

"Well, then, we might as well go back to the hotel," the father decided. "I dare say we shall do quite as well there."

On the way the young people laughed over the affair and their escape from it, especially at the strange appearance and disappearance of the kind colored girl, with her tag of sentiment, and at the instant compliance of the old woman with the suggestion of the policeman.

The father followed, turning the matter **over in his** mind. Did mere motherhood hallow that old thing to the colored girl and her sort and condition? Was there a superstition of motherhood among such people which would endear this disreputable old thing to their affection and reverence? Did such people hold mothers in tenderer regard than people of larger means? Would a mother in distress or merely embarrassment instantly appeal to their better nature as a case of want or sickness in the neighborhood always appealed to their compassion? Would her family now welcome the old thing home from her aberration more fondly than the friends of one who had arrived in a carriage among them in a good street? But, after all, how little one knew of Somebody's Mother! It did not necessarily follow from anything they knew of her that she was a mother at all. Her motherhood might be the mere figment of that kind colored girl's emotional fancy. She might be Nobody's Mother.

When it came to this the father laughed, too. Why, anyhow, were mothers more sacred than fathers? If they had found an old man in that old woman's condition on those steps, would that kind colored girl have appealed to them in his behalf as Somebody's Father?

From
CRITICISM AND FICTION
[1891]

TRUTH IN FICTION [1]

IN GENERAL GRANT's confession of novel-reading there is a sort of inference that he had wasted his time, or else the guilty conscience of the novelist in me imagines such an inference. But however this may be, there is certainly no question concerning the intention of a correspondent who once wrote to me after reading some rather bragging claims I had made for fiction as a mental and moral means. "I have very grave doubts," he said, "as to the whole list of magnificent things that you seem to think novels have done for the race, and can witness in myself many evil things which they have done for me. What-

ever in my mental make-up is wild and visionary, whatever is untrue, whatever is injurious, I can trace to the perusal of some work of fiction. Worse than that, they beget such high-strung and supersensitive ideas of life that plain industry and plodding perseverance are despised, and matter-of-fact poverty, or every-day, commonplace distress, meets with no sympathy, if indeed noticed at all, by one who has wept over the impossible accumulated sufferings of some gaudy hero or heroine."

I am not sure that I had the controversy with this correspondent that he seemed to suppose; but novels are now so fully accepted by every one pretending to cultivated taste—and they really form the whole intellectual life of such immense numbers of people, without question of their influence, good or bad, upon the mind—that it is refreshing to have them frankly denounced, and to be invited to revise one's ideas and feelings in regard to them. A little honesty, or a great deal of honesty, in this quest will do the novel, as we hope yet to have it, and as we have already begun to have it, no harm; and for my own part I will confess that I believe fiction in the past to have been largely injurious, as I believe the stage-play to be still almost wholly injurious, through its falsehood, its folly, its wantonness, and its aimlessness. It may be safely assumed that most of the novel-reading which people fancy an intellectual pastime is the emptiest dissipation, hardly more related to thought or the wholesome exercise of the mental faculties than opium-eating; in either case the brain is drugged, and left weaker and crazier for the debauch. If this may be called the negative result of the fiction habit, the positive injury that most novels work is by no means so easily to be measured in the case of young men whose character they help so much to form or deform, and the women of all ages whom they keep so much in ignorance of the world they misrepresent.

---

[1] Title supplied by the present editors.

Grown men have little harm from them, but in the other cases, which are the vast majority, they hurt because they are not true—not because they are malevolent, but because they are idle lies about human nature and the social fabric, which it behooves us to know and to understand, that we may deal justly with ourselves and with one another. One need not go so far as our correspondent, and trace to the fiction habit "whatever is wild and visionary, whatever is untrue, whatever is injurious," in one's life; bad as the fiction habit is it is probably not responsible for the whole sum of evil in its victims, and I believe that if the reader will use care in choosing from this fungus-growth with which the fields of literature teem every day, he may nourish himself as with the true mushroom, at no risk from the poisonous species.

The tests are very plain and simple, and they are perfectly infallible. If a novel flatters the passions, and exalts them above the principles, it is poisonous; it may not kill, but it will certainly injure; and this test will alone exclude an entire class of fiction, of which eminent examples will occur to all. Then the whole spawn of so-called unmoral romances, which imagine a world where the sins of sense are unvisited by the penalties following, swift or slow, but inexorably sure, in the real world, are deadly poison: these do kill. The novels that merely tickle our prejudices and lull our judgment, or that coddle our sensibilities or pamper our gross appetite for the marvellous, are not so fatal, but they are innutritious, and clog the soul with unwholesome vapors of all kinds. No doubt they too help to weaken the moral fibre, and make their readers indifferent to "plodding perseverance and plain industry," and to "matter-of-fact poverty and commonplace distress."

Without taking them too seriously, it still must be owned that the "gaudy hero and heroine" are to blame for a great deal of harm in the world. That heroine long taught by example, if not precept, that

Love, or the passion or fancy she mistook for it, was the chief interest of a life, which is really concerned with a great many other things; that it was lasting in the way she knew it; that it was worthy of every sacrifice, and was altogether a finer thing than prudence, obedience, reason; that love alone was glorious and beautiful, and these were mean and ugly in comparison with it. More lately she has begun to idolize and illustrate Duty, and she is hardly less mischievous in this new role, opposing duty, as she did love, to prudence, obedience, and reason. The stock hero, whom, if we met him, we could not fail to see was a most deplorable person, has undoubtedly imposed himself upon the victims of the fiction habit as admirable. With him, too, love was and is the great affair, whether in its old romantic phase of chivalrous achievement or manifold suffering for love's sake, or its more recent development of the "virile," the bullying, and the brutal, or its still more recent agonies of self-sacrifice, as idle and useless as the moral experiences of the insane asylums. With his vain posturings and his ridiculous splendor he is really a painted barbarian, the prey of his passions and his delusions, full of obsolete ideals, and the motives and ethics of a savage, which the guilty author of his being does his best—or his worst—in spite of his own light and knowledge, to foist upon the reader as something generous and noble. I am not merely bringing this charge against that sort of fiction which is beneath literature and outside of it, "the shoreless lakes of ditch-water," whose miasms fill the air below the empyrean where the great ones sit; but I am accusing the work of some of the most famous, who have, in this instance or in that, sinned against the truth, which can alone exalt and purify men. I do not say that they have constantly done so, or even commonly done so; but that they have done so at all marks them as of the past, to be read with the due historical allowance for their epoch and their conditions. For I believe that, while inferior writers will and must continue to imitate them in their foibles and their errors, no one hereafter will be able to achieve greatness who is false to humanity, either in its facts or its duties. The light of civilization has already broken even upon the novel, and no conscientious man can now set about painting an image of life without perpetual question of the verity of his work, and without feeling bound to distinguish so clearly that no reader of his may be misled, between what is right and what is wrong, what is noble and what is base, what is health and what is perdition, in the actions and the characters he portrays.

The fiction that aims merely to entertain—the fiction that is to serious fiction as the opéra bouffe, the ballet, and the pantomine are to the true drama—need not feel the burden of this obligation so deeply; but even such fiction will not be gay or trivial to any reader's hurt, and criticism should hold it to account if it passes from painting to teaching folly.

I confess that I do not care to judge any work of the imagination without first of all applying this test to it. We must ask ourselves before we ask anything else, Is it true?—true to the motives, the impulses, the principles that shape the life of actual men and women? This truth, which necessarily includes the highest morality and the highest artistry—this truth given, the book cannot be wicked and cannot be weak; and without it all graces of style and feats of invention and cunning of construction are so many superfluities of naughtiness. It is well for the truth to have all these, and shine in them, but for falsehood they are merely meretricious, the bedizenment of the wanton; they atone for nothing, they count for nothing. But in fact they come naturally of truth, and grace it without solicitation; they are added unto it. In the whole range of fiction I know of no true picture of life—that is, of human nature—which is not also a masterpiece of literature, full of divine and natural beauty. It may have no touch or tint of this special civilization or of that; it had better have this local color well ascertained; but the truth is deeper and finer than aspects, and if the book is true to what men and women know of one another's souls it will be true enough, and it will be great and beautiful. It is the conception of literature as something apart from life, superfinely aloof, which makes it really unimportant to the great mass of mankind, without a message or a meaning for them; and it is the notion that a novel may be false in its portrayal of causes and effects that makes literary art contemptible even to those whom it amuses, that forbids them to regard the novelist as a serious or right-minded person. If they do not in some moment of indignation cry out against all novels, as my correspondent does, they remain besotted in the fume of the delusions purveyed to them, with no higher feeling for the author than such maudlin affection as the frequenter of an opium-joint perhaps knows for the attendant who fills his pipe with the drug.

Or, as in the case of another correspondent who writes that in his youth he "read a great many novels, but always regarded it as an amusement, like horse-racing and card-playing," for which he had no time when he entered upon the serious business of life, it renders them merely contemptuous. His view of the matter may be commended to the brotherhood and sisterhood of novelists as full of wholesome if bitter suggestion; and I urge them not to dismiss it with high literary scorn as that of some Bœotian dull to the beauty of art. Refuse it as we may, it is still the feeling of the vast majority of people for whom life is earnest, and who find only a distorted and misleading likeness of it in our books. We may fold ourselves in our scholars' gowns, and close the doors of our studies, and affect to despise this rude voice; but we cannot shut it out. It comes to us from wherever men are at work, from wherever they are truly living, and accuses us of unfaithfulness, of triviality, of mere stage-play; and none of us can escape conviction except he prove himself worthy of his time—a time in which the great masters have brought literature back to life, and filled its ebbing veins with the red tides of reality. We cannot all equal them; we need not copy them; but we can all go to the sources of their inspiration and their power; and to draw from these no one need go far—no one need really go out of himself.

Fifty years ago, Carlyle, in whom the truth was always alive, but in whom it was then unperverted by suffering, by celebrity, and by despair, wrote in his study of Diderot: "Were it not reasonable to prophesy that this exceeding great multitude of novel-writers and suchlike must, in a new generation, gradually do one of two things: either retire into the nurseries, and work for children, minors, and semi-fatuous persons of both sexes, or else, what were far better, sweep their novel-fabric into the dust-cart, and betake themselves with such faculty as they have to understand and record what is true, of which surely there is, and will forever be, a whole infinitude unknown to us of infinite importance to us? Poetry, it will more and more come to be understood, is nothing but higher knowledge; and the only genuine Romance (for grown persons), Reality."

If, after half a century, fiction still mainly works for "children, minors, and semi-fatuous persons of both sexes," it is nevertheless one of the hopefulest signs of the world's progress that it has begun to work for "grown persons," and if not exactly in the way that Carlyle might have solely intended in urging its writers to compile memoirs instead of building the "novel-fabric," still it has, in the highest and widest sense, already made Reality its Romance. I cannot judge it, I do not even care for it, except as it has done this; and I can hardly conceive of a literary self-respect in these days compatible with the old trade of make-believe, with the production of the kind of fiction which is too much honored by classification with

card-playing and horse-racing. But let fiction cease to lie about life; let it portray men and women as they are, actuated by the motives and the passions in the measure we all know; let it leave off painting dolls and working them by springs and wires; let it show the different interests in their true proportions; let it forbear to preach pride and revenge, folly and insanity, egotism and prejudice, but frankly own these for what they are, in whatever figures and occasions they appear; let it not put on fine literary airs; let it speak the dialect, the language, that most Americans know—the language of unaffected people everywhere—and there can be no doubt of an unlimited future, not only of delightfulness but of usefulness, for it.

From

MY LITERARY PASSIONS
[1895]

TOURGUENIEF

IN THOSE YEARS at Cambridge my most notable literary experience without doubt was the knowledge of Tourguenief's novels, which began to be recognized in all their greatness about the middle seventies. I think they made their way with such of our public as were able to appreciate them before they were accepted in England; but that does not matter. It is enough for the present purpose that *Smoke,* and *Lisa,* and *On the Eve,* and *Dimitri Roudine,* and *Spring Floods,* passed one after another through my hands, and that I formed for their author one of the profoundest literary passions of my life.

I now think that there is a finer and truer method than his, but in its way, Tourguenief's method is as far as art can go. That is to say, his fiction is to the last degree dramatic. The persons are sparely described, and briefly accounted for, and then they are left to transact their affair, whatever it is, with the least possible comment or explanation from the author. The effect flows naturally from their characters, and when they have done or said a thing you conjecture why as unerringly as you would if they were people whom you knew outside of a book. I had already conceived of the possibility of this from Björnson,[1] who practises the same method, but I was still too sunken in the gross darkness of English fiction to rise to a full consciousness of its excellence. When I remembered the deliberate and impertinent moralizing of Thackeray, the clumsy exegesis of George Eliot, the knowing nods and winks of Charles Reade, the stage-carpentering and lime-lighting of Dickens, even the fine and important analysis of Hawthorne, it was with a joyful astonishment that I realized the great art of Tourguenief.

Here was a master who was apparently not trying to work out a plot, who was not even trying to work out a character, but was standing aside from the whole affair, and letting the characters work the plot out. The method was revealed perfectly in *Smoke*, but each successive book of his that I read was a fresh proof of its truth, a revelation of its transcendent superiority. I think now that I exaggerated its value somewhat; but this was inevitable in the first surprise. The sane aesthetics of the first Russian author I read, however, have seemed more and more an essential part of the sane ethics of all the Russians I have read. It was not only that Tourguenief had painted life truly, but that he had painted it conscientiously.

Tourguenief was of that great race which has more than any other fully and freely uttered human nature, without either false pride or false shame in its nakedness. His themes were oftenest those of the French novelist, but how far he was from handling them in the French manner and with the French spirit! In his hands sin suffered no dramatic punishment; it did not always show itself as unhappiness, in the personal sense, but it was always unrest, and without the hope of peace. If the end did not appear, the fact that it must be miser-

able always appeared. Life showed itself to me in different colors after I had once read Tourguenief; it became more serious, more awful, and with mystical responsibilities I had not known before. My gay American horizons were bathed in the vast melancholy of the Slav, patient, agnostic, trustful. At the same time nature revealed herself to me through him with an intimacy she had not hitherto shown me. There are passages in this wonderful writer alive with a truth that seems drawn from the reader's own knowledge: who else but Tourguenief and one's own most secret self ever felt all the rich, sad meaning of the night air drawing in at the open window, of the fires burning in the darkness on the distant fields? I try in vain to give some notion of the subtle sympathy with nature which scarcely put itself into words with him. As for the people of his fiction, though they were of orders and civilizations so remote from my experience, they were of the eternal human types whose origin and potentialities every one may find in his own heart, and I felt their verity in every touch.

I cannot describe the satisfaction his work gave me; I can only impart some sense of it, perhaps, by saying that it was like a happiness I had been waiting for all my life, and now that it had come, I was richly content forever. I do not mean to say that the art of Tourguenief surpasses the art of Björnson; I think Björnson is quite as fine and true. But the Norwegian deals with simple and primitive circumstances for the most part, and always with a small world; and the Russian has to do with human nature inside of its conventional shells, and his scene is often as large as Europe. Even when it is as remote as Norway, it is still related to the great capitals by the history if not the actuality of the characters. Most of Tourguenief's books I have read many times over, all of them I have read more than twice. For a

----

[1] Björnstjerne Björnson (1832–1910), Norwegian novelist, dramatist, and poet.

number of years I read them again and again without much caring for other fiction. It was only the other day that I read *Smoke* through once more, with no diminished sense of its truth, but with somewhat less than my first satisfaction in its art. Perhaps this was because I had reached the point through my acquaintance with Tolstoy where I was impatient even of the artifice that hid itself. In *Smoke* I was now aware of an artifice that kept out of sight, but was still always present somewhere, invisibly operating the story.

TOLSTOY

I come now, though not quite in the order of time, to the noblest of all these enthusiasms—namely, my devotion for the writings of Lyof Tolstoy. I should wish to speak of him with his own incomparable truth, yet I do not know how to give a notion of his influence without the effect of exaggeration. As much as one merely human being can help another I believe that he has helped me; he has not influenced me in aesthetics only, but in ethics, too, so that I can never again see life in the way I saw it before I knew him. Tolstoy awakens in his reader the will to be a man; not effectively, not spectacularly, but simply, really. He leads you back to the only true ideal, away from that false standard of the gentleman, to the Man who sought not to be distinguished from other men, but identified with them, to that Presence in which the finest gentleman shows his alloy of vanity, and the greatest genius shrinks to the measure of his miserable egotism. I learned from Tolstoy to try character and motive by no other test, and though I am perpetually false to that sublime ideal myself, still the ideal remains with me, to make me ashamed that I am not true to it. Tolstoy gave me heart to hope that the world may yet be made over in the image of Him who died for it, when all Caesar's things shall be finally rendered unto Caesar, and men shall come into their own, into the right to labor and the right to enjoy the fruits of their labor, each one master of himself and servant to every other. He taught me to see life not as a chase of a forever impossible personal happiness, but as a field for endeavor towards the happiness of the whole human family; and I can never lose this vision, however I close my eyes, and strive to see my own interest as the highest good. He gave me new criterions, new principles, which, after all, were those that are taught us in our earliest childhood, before we have come to the evil wisdom of the world. As I read his different ethical books, *What to Do, My Confession,* and *My Religion,* I recognized their truth with a rapture such as I have known in no other reading, and I rendered them my allegiance, heart and soul, with whatever sickness of the one and despair of the other. They have it yet, and I believe they will have it while I live. It is with inexpressible astonishment that I hear them attainted of pessimism, as if the teaching of a man whose ideal was simple goodness must mean the prevalence of evil. The way he showed me seemed indeed impossible to my will, but to my conscience it was and is the only possible way. If there is any point on which he has not convinced my reason it is that of our ability to walk this narrow way alone. Even there he is logical, but as Zola subtly distinguishes in speaking of Tolstoy's essay on "Money," he is not reasonable. Solitude enfeebles and palsies, and it is as comrades and brothers that men must save the world from itself, rather than themselves from the world. It was so the earliest Christians, who had all things common, understood the life of Christ, and I believe that the latest will understand it so.

I have spoken first of the ethical works of Tolstoy, because they are of the first importance to me, but I think that his aesthetical works are as perfect. To my thinking they transcend in truth, which is the highest beauty, all other works of fiction that have been written, and I believe that they do this because they obey the law of the author's own life. His conscience is one ethically and one aesthetically; with his will to be true to himself he cannot be false to his knowledge of others. I thought the last word in literary art had been said to me by the novels of Tourguenief, but it seemed like the first, merely, when I began to acquaint myself with the simpler method of Tolstoy. I came to it by accident, and without any manner of preoccupation, in *The Cossacks,* one of his early books, which had been on my shelves unread for five or six years. I did not know even Tolstoy's name when I opened it, and it was with a kind of amaze that I read it, and felt word by word, and line by line, the truth of a new art in it.

I do not know how it is that the great Russians have the secret of simplicity. Some say it is because they have not a long literary past and are not conventionalized by the usage of many generations of other writers, but this will hardly account for the brotherly directness of their dealing with human nature; the absence of experience elsewhere characterizes the artist with crudeness, and simplicity is the last effect of knowledge. Tolstoy is, of course, the first of them in this supreme grace. He has not only Tourguenief's transparency of style, unclouded by any mist of the personality which we mistakenly value in style, and which ought no more to be there than the artist's personality should be in a portrait; but he has a method which not only seems without artifice, but is so. I can get at the manner of most writers, and tell what it is, but I should be baffled to tell what Tolstoy's manner is; perhaps he has no manner. This appears to me true of his novels, which, with their vast variety of character and incident, are alike in their single endeavor to get the persons living before you, both in their action and in the peculiarly dramatic interpretation of their emotion and cogitation. There are plenty of novelists to tell you that their characters felt and thought so and so, but you have to take it on trust; Tolstoy alone makes you know how and why it was so with them and not otherwise. If there is anything in

him which can be copied or burlesqued it is this ability of his to show men inwardly as well as outwardly; it is the only trait of his which I can put my hand on.

After *The Cossacks* I read *Anna Karenina* with a deepening sense of the author's unrivalled greatness. I thought that I saw through his eyes a human affair of that most sorrowful sort as it must appear to the Infinite Compassion; the book is a sort of revelation of human nature in circumstances that have been so perpetually lied about that we have almost lost the faculty of perceiving the truth concerning an illicit love. When you have once read *Anna Karenina* you know how fatally miserable and essentially unhappy such a love must be. But the character of Karenin himself is quite as important as the intrigue of Anna and Vronsky. It is wonderful how such a man, cold, Philistine and even mean in certain ways, towers into a sublimity unknown (to me, at least), in fiction when he forgives, and yet knows that he cannot forgive with dignity. There is something crucial, and something triumphant, not beyond the power, but hitherto beyond the imagination of men in this effect, which is not solicited, not forced, not in the least romantic, but comes naturally, almost inevitably, from the make of man.

The vast prospects, the far-reaching perspectives of *War and Peace* made it as great a surprise for me in the historical novel as *Anna Karenina* had been in the study of contemporary life; and its people and interests did not seem more remote, since they are of a civilization always as strange and of a humanity always as known.

I read some shorter stories of Tolstoy's before I came to this greatest work of his: I read *Scenes of the Siege of Sebastopol,* which is so much of the same quality as *War and Peace*; and I read *Policoushka* and most of his short stories with a sense of my unity with their people such as I had never felt with the people of other fiction.

His didactic stories, like all stories of the sort, dwindle into allegories; perhaps they do their work the better for this, with the simple intelligences they address; but I think that where Tolstoy becomes impatient of his office of artist, and prefers to be directly a teacher, he robs himself of more than half his strength with those he can move only through the realization of themselves in others. The simple pathos, and the apparent indirectness of such a tale as that of *Policoushka,* the peasant conscript, is of vastly more value to the world at large than all his parables; and *The Death of Ivan Ilyitch,* the Philistine worldling, will turn the hearts of many more from the love of the world than such pale fables of the early Christian life as "Work while ye have the Light." A man's gifts are not given him for nothing, and the man who has the great gift of dramatic fiction has no right to cast it away or to let it rust out in disuse.

Terrible as the *Kreutzer Sonata* was, it had a moral effect dramatically which it lost altogether when the author descended to exegesis, and applied to marriage the lesson of one evil marriage. In fine, Tolstoy is certainly not to be held up as infallible. He is very distinctly fallible, but I think his life is not less instructive because in certain things it seems a failure. There was but one life ever lived upon the earth which was without failure, and that was Christ's, whose erring and stumbling follower Tolstoy is. There is no other example, no other ideal, and the chief use of Tolstoy is to enforce this fact in our age, after nineteen centuries of hopeless endeavor to substitute ceremony for character, and the creed for the life. I recognize the truth of this without pretending to have been changed in anything but my point of view of it. What I feel sure is that I can never look at life in the mean and sordid way that I did before I read Tolstoy.

Artistically, he has shown me a greatness that he can never teach me. I am long past the age when I could wish to form myself upon another writer, and I do not think I could now insensibly take on the likeness of another; but his work has been a revelation and a delight to me, such as I am sure I can never know again. I do not believe that in the whole course of my reading, and not even in the early moment of my literary enthusiasms, I have known such utter satisfaction in any writer, and this supreme joy has come to me at a time of life when new friendships, not to say new passions, are rare and reluctant. It is as if the best wine at this high feast where I have sat so long had been kept for the last, and I need not deny a miracle in it in order to attest my skill in judging vintages. In fact, I prefer to believe that my life has been full of miracles, and that the good has always come to me at the right time, so that I could profit most by it. I believe if I had not turned the corner of my fiftieth year, when I first knew Tolstoy, I should not have been able to know him as fully as I did. He has been to me that final consciousness, which he speaks of so wisely in his essay on "Life." I came in it to the knowledge of myself in ways I had not dreamt of before, and began at least to discern my relations to the race, without which we are each nothing. The supreme art in literature had its highest effect in making me set art forever below humanity, and it is with the wish to offer the greatest homage to his heart and mind, which any man can pay another, that I close this record with the name of Lyof Tolstoy.

From

MY YEAR IN A LOG CABIN
[1893]

OUR CABIN stood close upon the road, but behind it broadened a cornfield of eighty acres. They still built log-cabins for dwellings in that region forty years ago, but ours must have been nearly half a century old when we went into it. It had been recently vacated by an old Virginian couple, who had long occupied it, and we decided that it needed some repairs to make it habitable even for a family inured to hardship by dauntless imaginations, and accustomed to retrospective discomforts of every kind.

So before we all came out to it a deputation of adventurers put it in what rude order they could. They glazed the narrow windows, they relaid the rotten floor, they touched (too sketchily, as it afterwards appeared) the broken roof, and they papered the walls of the groundfloor rooms. Perhaps it was my father's love of literature which inspired him to choose newspapers for this purpose; at any rate, he did so, and the effect, as I remember it, was not without its decorative qualities.

He had used a barrel of papers bought at the nearest post-office, where they had been refused by the persons to whom they had been experimentally sent by the publisher, and the whole first page was taken up by a story, which broke off in the middle of a sentence at the foot of the last column, and tantalized us forever with fruitless conjecture as to the fate of the hero and heroine. I really suppose that a cheap wall-paper could have been got for the same money, though it might not have seemed so economical.

I was not sure that the use of the newspapers was not a tributary reminiscence of my father's pioneer life; I cannot remember that it excited any comment in the neighbors, who were frank with their opinions of everything else we did. But it does not greatly matter; the newspapers hid the walls and the stains with which our old Virginian predecessor, who had the habit of chewing tobacco in bed, had ineffaceably streaked the plastering near the head of his couch.

The cabin, rude as it was, was not without its sophistications, its concessions to the spirit of modern luxury. The logs it was built of had not been left rounded, as they grew, but had been squared in a sawmill, and the crevices between them had not been chinked with moss and daubed with clay in the true pioneer fashion, but had been neatly plastered with mortar, and

the chimney, instead of being a structure of clay-covered sticks, was solidly laid in courses of stone.

Within, however, it was all that could be asked for by the most romantic of pioneer families. It was six feet wide and a yard deep, its cavernous maw would easily swallow a back-log eighteen inches through, and we piled in front the sticks of hickory cord-wood as high as we liked. We made a perfect trial of it when we came out to put the cabin in readiness for the family, and when the hickory had dropped into a mass of tinkling, snapping, bristling embers we laid our rashers of bacon and our slices of steak upon them, and tasted with the appetite of tired youth the flavors of the camp and the wildwood in the captured juices.

I suppose it took a day or two to put the improvements which I have mentioned upon the cabin, but I am not certain. At night we laid our mattresses on the sweet new oak plank of the floor, and slept hard —in every sense. Once I remember waking, and seeing the man who was always the youngest of his boys sitting upright on his bed.

"What are you doing?" I asked.

"Oh, resting!" he answered; and that gave us one of the Heaven-blessed laughs with which we could blow away almost any cloud of care or pain.

In due time the whole family took up its abode in the cabin. The household furniture had been brought out and bestowed in its scanty space, the bookcase had been set up, and the unbound books packed in easily accessible barrels.

There yet remained some of our possessions to follow, chief of which was the cow; for in those simple days people kept cows in town, and it fell to me to help my father drive her out to her future home. We got on famously, talking of the wayside things so beautiful in the beautiful autumnal day, all panoplied in the savage splendor of its painted leaves, and of the poems and histories so dear to the boy who limped barefooted by his father's side, with his eye on the cow and his mind on Cervantes and Shakespeare, on—

"The glory that was Greece,
And the grandeur that was Rome." [1]

But the cow was very slow—far slower than the boy's thoughts—and it had fallen night and was already thick dark when we had made the twelve miles, and stood under the white-limbed phantasmal sycamores beside the tail-race of the grist-mill, and questioned how we should get across with our charge. We did not know how deep the water was, but we knew it was very cold, and we would rather not wade it.

The only thing to do seemed to be for one of us to run up under those sycamores to the saw-mill, cross the head-race there, and come back to receive the cow on the other side of the tail-race. But the boy could not bring himself either to go or stay. I do not know just how it is with a boy's world now, but at that time it was a very dangerous world. It was full of ghosts, for one thing, and it abounded in Indians on the war-path, and amateurs of kidnapping and murder of all sorts.

The kind-hearted father urged, but he would not compel. You cannot well use force with a boy with whom you have been talking literature and philosophy for half a day. We could see the lights in the cabin cheerfully twinkling, and we shouted to those within, but no one heard us. We called and called in vain. Nothing but the cold rush of the tail-race, the dry rustle of the sycamore leaves, and the homesick lowing of the cow replied.

We determined to drive her across, and pursue her with sticks and stones through the darkness beyond, and then run at the top of our speed to the saw-mill, and get back to take her in custody again. We carried out our part of the plan perfectly, but the cow had apparently not entered into it with intelligence or sympathy.

When we reached the tail-race again she was nowhere to be found, and no appeals of "Boss" or "Suky" or "Subose" availed. She must have instantly turned again, and retraced, in the darkness which seemed to have swallowed her up, the weary steps of the day, for she was found in her old home in town the next morning. At any rate, she had abandoned the father to the conversation of his son, for the time being, and the son had nothing to say.

I do not remember now just how it was that we came by the different "animals of the horse kind," as my father humorously called them, which we housed in an old log-stable not far from our cabin. They must have been a temporary supply until a team worthy our new sky-blue wagon could be found.

One of them was a colossal sorrel, inexorably hide-bound, whose barrel, as I believe the horsemen call the body, showed every hoop upon it. He had a feeble, foolish whimper of a voice, and we nicknamed him "Baby." His companion was a dun mare, who had what my father at once called an italic foot, in recognition of the emphatic slant at which she carried it when upon her unwilling travels.

Then there was a small, self-opinionated gray pony, which, I think, came from one of the saw-mill hands, and which was of no service conjecturable after this lapse of time. We boys rode him barebacked, and he used to draw a buggy, which he finally ran away with. I suppose we found him useful in the representation of some of the Indian fights which we were always dramatizing, and I dare say he may have served our turn as an Arab charger, when the Moors of Granada made one of their sallies upon the camp of the Spaniards, and discharged their javelins into it—their javelins were the long, admirably straight and slender ironweeds that grew by the river. This menagerie was constantly breaking bounds and wandering off; and I believe that it was chiefly employed in hunting itself up, its different members taking turns in remaining in the pasture or stable, to be ridden after those that had strayed into the woods.

---

[1] From Poe's "To Helen." See Vol. I, p. 448.

The origin of a large and eloquent flock of geese is lost in an equal obscurity. I recall their possession simply as an accomplished fact, and I associate their desolate cries with the windy dark of rainy November nights, so that they must at least have come into our hands after the horses. They were fenced into a clayey area next the cabin for safe-keeping, where, perpetually waddling about in a majestic disoccupation, they patted the damp ground down to the hardness and smoothness of a brick yard. Throughout the day they conversed tranquilly together, but by night they woke, goose after goose, to send forth a long clarion alarum, blending in a general concert at last, to assure one another of their safety.

We must have intended to pluck them in the spring, but it never came to that. They stole their nests early in March, and entered upon the nurture of their young before we could prevent it; and it would then have been barbarous to pluck these mothers of families. Some of their nests we found, notably one under the smoke-house, where the adventurous boy who discovered it was attacked in the dark by its owner and bitten in the nose, to the natural gratification of those who had urged him to the enterprise. But he brought away some of the eggs, and had them fried, and I know nothing that conveys a vivider idea of inexhaustible abundance than a fried goose-egg.

1839 ∾ *Henry George* ∾ 1897

THE parents of Henry George were substantial middle-class business people of Philadelphia, engaged in the publication of religious books. Against school and his pious home training the boy rebelled at thirteen, working at various jobs, learning the printer's trade, and spending some time at sea, before he followed the trail of the gold-seekers to California in 1857. His skill as a printer proved his only means of support there, and that precarious. He married in 1861, but lived the next few years in extreme poverty.

As he became a newspaper writer instead of a printer, and eventually an editor, he did much thinking about the effects of the land boom in California, and eventually formulated his theory of man's natural right to live on the earth and of land monopoly and human exploitation through rent as major evils. He presented these ideas in *Our Land and Land Policy* (1871) and *Progress and Poverty* (1879). From 1880 on, he became an active propagandist for his theories and the single tax movement, writing *Social Problems* (1883), and traveling to Ireland and Australia and repeatedly to England. In 1886 he published *Protection or Free Trade* and in 1887 *The Science of Political Economy*. In 1886 he ran for the office of mayor of New York City. He believed he had been defeated only by political trickery and ran again in 1897, but died suddenly during a hard campaign.

George's chief book, *Progress and Poverty*, was one of the most widely read of its time. More than two million copies have been sold, and it has been translated into many languages.

[Volumes nine and ten of George's collected *Works* (New York, 1906-1911) contain the standard biography by his son, Henry George, Jr., originally published in New York in 1900. See also *The Prophet of San Francisco* (1930), by L. F. Post, and *History of the Single Tax Movement in the United States* (1916), by A. N. Young. The best critical study of George's thought is George R. Geiger's *The Philosophy of Henry George* (New York, 1933).]

From
PROGRESS AND POVERTY
[1879]

How Modern Civilization May Decline

THE CONCLUSION we have thus reached harmonizes completely with our previous conclusions.

This consideration of the law of human progress not only brings the politico-economic laws, which in this inquiry we have worked out, within the scope of a higher law—perhaps the very highest law our minds can grasp—but it proves that the making of land common property in the way I have proposed would give an enormous impetus to civilization, while the refusal to do so must entail retrogression. A civilization like ours must either advance or go back; it cannot stand still. It is not like those homogeneous civilizations, such as that of the Nile Valley, which molded men for their places and put them in it like bricks into a pyramid. It much more resembles that civilization whose rise and fall is within historic times, and from which it sprung.

There is just now a disposition to scoff at any implication that we are not in all respects progressing, and the spirit of our times is that of the edict which the flattering premier proposed to the Chinese Emperor [1] who burned the ancient books— "that all who may dare to speak together about the She and the Shoo [2] be put to death; that those who make mention of the past so as to blame the present be put to death along with their relatives."

Yet it is evident that there have been times of decline, just as there have been times of advance; and it is further evident

that these epochs of decline could not at first have been generally recognized.

He would have been a rash man who, when Augustus was changing the Rome of brick to the Rome of marble, when wealth was augmenting and magnificence increasing, when victorious legions were extending the frontier, when manners were becoming more refined, language more polished, and literature rising to higher splendors—he would have been a rash man who then would have said that Rome was entering her decline. Yet such was the case.

And whoever will look may see that though our civilization is apparently advancing with greater rapidity than ever, the same cause which turned Roman progress into retrogression is operating now.

What has destroyed every previous civilization has been the tendency to the unequal distribution of wealth and power. This same tendency, operating with increasing force, is observable in our civilization today, showing itself in every progressive community, and with greater intensity the more progressive the community. Wages and interest tend constantly to fall, rent to rise, the rich to become very much richer, the poor to become more helpless and hopeless, and the middle class to be swept away.

I have traced this tendency to its cause. I have shown by what simple means this cause may be removed. I now wish to point out how, if this is not done, progress must turn to decadence, and modern civilization decline to barbarism, as have all previous civilizations. It is worth while to point out how this may occur, as many people, being

---

[1] Jeng, or Tsin Shï Huangdi, first emperor of the Tsin or Ch'in dynasty, who ruled from 246 to 210 B.C.

[2] Earlier Chinese dynasties.

unable to see how progress may pass into retrogression, conceive such a thing impossible. Gibbon,[3] for instance, thought that modern civilization could never be destroyed because there remained no barbarians to overrun it, and it is a common idea that the invention of printing by so multiplying books has prevented the possibility of knowledge ever again being lost.

The conditions of social progress, as we have traced the law, are association and equality. The general tendency of modern development, since the time when we can first discern the gleams of civilization in the darkness which followed the fall of the Western Empire, has been toward political and legal equality—to the abolition of slavery; to the abrogation of status; to the sweeping away of hereditary privileges; to the substitution of parliamentary for arbitrary government; to the right of private judgment in matters of religion; to the more equal security in person and property of high and low, weak and strong; to the greater freedom of movement and occupation, of speech and of the press. The history of modern civilization is the history of advances in this direction—of the struggles and triumphs of personal, political, and religious freedom. And the general law is shown by the fact that just as this tendency has asserted itself civilization has advanced, while just as it has been repressed or forced back civilization has been checked.

This tendency has reached its full expression in the American Republic, where political and legal rights are absolutely equal, and, owing to the system of rotation in office, even the growth of a bureaucracy is prevented; where every religious belief or non-belief stands on the same footing; where every boy may hope to be President, every man has an equal voice in public affairs, and every official is mediately or immediately dependent for the short lease of his place upon a popular vote. This tendency has yet some triumphs to win in England, in monarchy, aristocracy, and prelacy; while in such countries as Germany and Russia, where divine right is yet a good deal more than a legal fiction, it has a considerable distance to go. But it is the prevailing tendency, and how soon Europe will be completely republican is only a matter of time, or rather of accident. The United States are therefore, in this respect, the most advanced of all the great nations, in a direction in which all are advancing, and in the United States we see just how much this tendency to personal and political freedom can of itself accomplish.

Now, the first effect of the tendency to political equality was to the more equal distribution of wealth and power; for, while population is comparatively sparse, inequality in the distribution of wealth is principally due to the inequality of personal rights, and it is only as material progress goes on that the tendency to inequality involved in the reduction of land to private ownership strongly appears. But it is now manifest that absolute political equality does not in itself prevent the tendency to inequality involved in the private ownership of land, and it is further evident that political equality, co-existing with an increasing tendency to the unequal distribution of wealth, must ultimately beget either the despotism of organized tyranny or the worse despotism of anarchy.

To turn a republican government into a despotism the basest and most brutal, it is not necessary formally to change its constitution or abandon popular elections. It was centuries after Caesar before the absolute master of the Roman world pretended to rule other than by authority of a Senate that trembled before him.

But forms are nothing when substance has gone, and the forms of popular government are those from which the substance of freedom may most easily go. Extremes meet, and a government of universal suffrage and theoretical equality may, under conditions which impel the change, most

---

[3] Edward Gibbon (1737-1794), English historian; author of *The History of the Decline and Fall of the Roman Empire.*

readily become a despotism. For there despotism advances in the name and with the might of the people. The single source of power once secured, everything is secured. There is no unfranchised class to whom appeal may be made, no privileged orders who in defending their own rights may defend those of all. No bulwark remains to stay the flood, no eminence to rise above it. They were belted barons led by a mitered archbishop who curbed the Plantagenet with Magna Charta; it was the middle classes who broke the pride of the Stuarts; but a mere aristocracy of wealth will never struggle while it can hope to bribe a tyrant.

And when the disparity of condition increases, so does universal suffrage make it easy to seize the source of power, for the greater is the proportion of power in the hands of those who feel no direct interest in the conduct of government; who, tortured by want and embruted by poverty, are ready to sell their votes to the highest bidder or follow the lead of the most blatant demagogue; or who, made bitter by hardships, may even look upon profligate and tyrannous government with the satisfaction we may imagine the proletarians and slaves of Rome to have felt, as they saw a Caligula or Nero raging among the rich patricians. Given a community with republican institutions, in which one class is too rich to be shorn of its luxuries, no matter how public affairs are administered, and another so poor that a few dollars on election day will seem more than any abstract consideration; in which the few roll in wealth and the many seethe with discontent at a condition of things they know not how to remedy, and power must pass into the hands of jobbers who will buy and sell it as the Praetorians sold the Roman purple, or into the hands of demagogues who will seize and wield it for a time, only to be displaced by worse demagogues.

Where there is anything like an equal distribution of wealth—that is to say, where there is general patriotism, virtue, and intelligence—the more democratic the government the better it will be; but where there is gross inequality in the distribution of wealth, the more democratic the government the worse it will be; for, while rotten democracy may not in itself be worse than rotten autocracy, its effects upon national character will be worse. To give the suffrage to tramps, to paupers, to men to whom the chance to labor is a boon, to men who must beg, or steal, or starve, is to invoke destruction. To put political power in the hands of men embittered and degraded by poverty is to tie firebrands to foxes and turn them loose amid the standing corn; it is to put out the eyes of a Samson and to twine his arms around the pillars of national life.

Even the accidents of hereditary succession or of selection by lot, the plan of some of the ancient republics, may sometimes place the wise and just in power; but in a corrupt democracy the tendency is always to give power to the worst. Honesty and patriotism are weighted, and unscrupulousness commands success. The best gravitate to the bottom, the worst float to the top, and the vile will only be ousted by the viler. While as national character must gradually assimilate to the qualities that win power, and consequently respect, that demoralization of opinion goes on which in the long panorama of history we may see over and over again transmuting races of freemen into races of slaves.

As in England in the last century, when Parliament was but a close corporation of the aristocracy, a corrupt oligarchy clearly fenced off from the masses may exist without much effect on national character, because in that case power is associated in the popular mind with other things than corruption. But where there are no hereditary distinctions, and men are habitually seen to raise themselves by corrupt qualities from the lowest places to wealth and power, tolerance of these qualities finally becomes admiration. A corrupt democratic government must finally corrupt the people, and when a people become corrupt there is no resurrection. The life is gone, only the carcass remains; and it is left but for the plowshares of fate to bury it out of sight.

Now this transformation of popular government into despotism of the vilest and most degrading kind, which must inevitably result from the unequal distribution of wealth, is not a thing of the far future. It has already begun in the United States, and is rapidly going on under our eyes. That our legislative bodies are steadily deteriorating in standard; that men of the highest ability and character are compelled to eschew politics, and the arts of the jobber count for more than the reputation of the statesman; that voting is done more recklessly and the power of money is increasing; that it is harder to arouse the people to the necessity of reforms and more difficult to carry them out; that political differences are ceasing to be differences of principle, and abstract ideas are losing their power; that parties are passing into the control of what in general government would be oligarchies and dictatorships; are all evidences of political decline.

The type of modern growth is the great city. Here are to be found the greatest wealth and the deepest poverty. And it is here that popular government has most clearly broken down. In all the great American cities there is to-day as clearly defined a ruling class as in the most aristocratic countries of the world. Its members carry wards in their pockets, make up the slates for nominating conventions, distribute offices as they bargain together, and—though they toil not, neither do they spin—wear the best of raiment and spend money lavishly. They are men of power, whose favor the ambitious must court and whose vengeance he must avoid. Who are these men? The wise, the good, the learned—men who have earned the confidence of their fellow-citizens by the purity of their lives, the splendor of their talents, their probity in public trusts, their deep study of the problems of government? No; they are gamblers, saloon keepers, pugilists, or worse, who have made a trade of controlling votes and of buying and selling offices

and official acts. They stand to the government of these cities as the Praetorian Guards did to that of declining Rome. He who would wear the purple, fill the curule chair, or have the fasces carried before him, must go or send his messengers to their camps, give them donations and make them promises. It is through these men that the rich corporations and powerful pecuniary interests can pack the Senate and the bench with their creatures. It is these men who make School Directors, Supervisors, Assessors, members of the Legislature, Congressmen. Why, there are many election districts in the United States in which a George Washington, a Benjamin Franklin or a Thomas Jefferson could no more go to the lower house of a State Legislature than under the Ancient Regime a base-born peasant could become a Marshal of France. Their very character would be an insuperable disqualification.

In theory we are intense democrats. The proposal to sacrifice swine in the temple would hardly have excited greater horror and indignation in Jerusalem of old than would among us that of conferring a distinction of rank upon our most eminent citizen. But is there not growing up among us a class who have all the power without any of the virtues of aristocracy? We have simple citizens who control thousands of miles of railroad, millions of acres of land, the means of livelihood of great numbers of men; who name the Governors of sovereign States as they name their clerks, choose Senators as they choose attorneys, and whose will is as supreme with Legislatures as that of a French King sitting in bed of justice. The undercurrents of the times seem to sweep us back again to the old conditions from which we dreamed we had escaped. The development of the artisan and commercial classes gradually broke down feudalism after it had become so complete that men thought of heaven as organized on a feudal basis, and ranked the first and second persons of the Trinity as suzerain and tenant-in-chief. But now the development of manufactures and exchange, acting in a social organization in which land is made private property, threatens to compel every worker to seek a master, as the insecurity which followed the final break-up of the Roman Empire compelled every freeman to seek a lord. Nothing seems exempt from this tendency. Industry everywhere tends to assume a form in which one is master and many serve. And when one is master and the others serve, the one will control the others, even in such matters as votes. Just as the English landlord votes his tenants, so does the New England mill owner vote his operatives.

There is no mistaking it—the very foundations of society are being sapped before our eyes, while we ask, how is it possible that such a civilization as this, with its railroads, and daily newspapers, and electric telegraphs, should ever be destroyed? While literature breathes but the belief that we have been, are, and for the future must be, leaving the savage state further and further behind us, there are indications that we are actually turning back again toward barbarism. Let me illustrate: One of the characteristics of barbarism is the low regard for the rights of person and of property. That the laws of our Anglo-Saxon ancestors imposed as penalty for murder a fine proportioned to the rank of the victim, while our law knows no distinction of rank, and protects the lowest from the highest, the poorest from the richest, by the uniform penalty of death, is looked upon as evidence of their barbarism and our civilization. And so, that piracy, and robbery, and slave-trading, and blackmailing, were once regarded as legitimate occupations is conclusive proof of the rude state of development from which we have so far progressed.

But it is a matter of fact that, in spite of our laws, any one who has money enough and wants to kill another may go into any one of our great centers of population and business, and gratify his desire, and then surrender himself to justice, with the chances as a hundred to one that he will suffer no greater penalty than a temporary imprisonment and the loss of a sum proportioned partly to his own wealth and partly to the wealth and standing of the man he kills. His money will be paid, not to the family of the murdered man, who have lost their protector; not to the state, which has lost a citizen; but to lawyers who understand how to secure delays, to find witnesses, and get juries to disagree.

And so, if a man steal enough, he may be sure that his punishment will practically amount but to the loss of a part of the proceeds of his theft; and if he steal enough to get off with a fortune, he will be greeted by his acquaintances as a viking might have been greeted after a successful cruise. Even though he robbed those who trusted him; even though he robbed the widow and the fatherless; he has only to get enough, and he may safely flaunt his wealth in the eyes of day.

Now, the tendency in this direction is an increasing one. It is shown in greatest force where the inequalities in the distribution of wealth are greatest, and it shows itself as they increase. If it be not a return to barbarism, what is it? The failures of justice to which I have alluded are only illustrative of the increasing debility of our legal machinery in every department. It is becoming common to hear men say that it would be better to revert to first principles and abolish law, for then in self-defense the people would form Vigilance Committees and take justice into their own hands. Is this indicative of advance or retrogression?

All this is matter of common observation. Though we may not speak it openly, the general faith in republican institutions is, where they have reached their fullest development, narrowing and weakening. It is no longer that confident belief in republicanism as the source of national blessings that it once was. Thoughtful men are beginning to see its dangers, without seeing how to escape them; are beginning to accept the view of Macaulay and distrust that of Jefferson.[4] And the people at large are becoming used to the growing corruption. The most ominous political sign in the United States to-day is the growth of a sentiment which either doubts the existence of an honest man in public office or looks on him as a fool for not seizing his opportunities. That is to say, the people themselves are becoming corrupted. Thus in the United States to-day is republican government running the course it must inevitably follow under conditions which cause the unequal distribution of wealth.

Where that course leads is clear to whoever will think. As corruption becomes chronic; as public spirit is lost; as traditions of honor, virtue, and patriotism are weakened; as law is brought into contempt and reforms become hopeless; then in the festering mass will be generated volcanic forces, which shatter and rend when seeming accident gives them vent. Strong, unscrupulous men, rising up upon occasion, will become the exponents of blind popular desires or fierce popular passions, and dash aside forms that have lost their vitality. The sword will again be mightier than the pen, and in carnivals of destruction brute force and wild frenzy will alternate with the lethargy of a declining civilization.

I speak of the United States only because the United States is the most advanced of all the great nations. What shall we say of Europe, where dams of ancient law and custom pen up the swelling waters and standing armies weigh down the safety valves, though year by year the fires grow hotter underneath? Europe tends to republicanism under conditions that will not admit of true republicanism—under conditions that substitute for the calm and august figure of Liberty the petroleuse[5] and the guillotine!

Whence shall come the new barbarians? Go through the squalid quarters of great cities, and you may see, even now, their gathering hordes! How shall learning perish? Men will cease to read, and books will kindle fires and be turned into cartridges!

It is startling to think how slight the traces that would be left of our civilization did it pass through the throes which have accompanied the decline of every previous civilization. Paper will not last like parchment, nor are our most massive buildings and monuments to be compared in solidity with the rock-hewn temples and titanic edifices of the old civilizations.[6] And invention has given us, not merely the steam engine and the printing press, but petroleum, nitro-glycerine, and dynamite.

Yet to hint, to-day, that our civilization may possibly be tending to decline, seems like the wildness of pessimism. The special tendencies to which I have alluded are obvious to thinking men, but with the majority of thinking men, as with the great masses, the belief in substantial progress is yet deep and strong—a fundamental belief which admits not the shadow of a doubt.

But any one who will think over the matter will see that this must necessarily be the case where advance gradually passes into retrogression. For in social development, as in everything else, motion tends to persist in straight lines, and therefore, where there has been a previous advance, it is extremely difficult to recognize decline, even when it has fully commenced; there is an almost irresistible tendency to believe that the forward movement which has been advance, and is still going on, is still advance. The web of beliefs, customs, laws, institutions, and habits of thought, which each community is constantly spinning,

[4] See Macaulay's letter to Randall, the biographer of Jefferson.—Author's note.

[5] An incendiary who uses petroleum, as in Paris in 1871.

[6] It is also, it seems to me, instructive to note how inadequate and utterly misleading would be the idea of our civilization which could be gained from the religious and funereal monuments of our time, which are all we have from which to gain our ideas of the buried civilizations.—Author's note.

and which produces in the individual environed by it all the differences of national character, is never unraveled. That is to say, in the decline of civilization, communities do not go down by the same paths that they came up. For instance, the decline of civilization as manifested in government would not take us back from republicanism to constitutional monarchy, and thence to the feudal system; it would take us to imperatorship and anarchy. As manifested in religion, it would not take us back into the faiths of our forefathers, into Protestantism or Catholicity, but into new forms of superstition, of which possibly Mormonism and other even grosser "isms" may give some vague idea. As manifested in knowledge, it would not take us toward Bacon, but toward the literati of China.

And how the retrogression of civilization, following a period of advance, may be so gradual as to attract no attention at the time; nay, how that decline must necessarily, by the great majority of men, be mistaken for advance, is easily seen. For instance, there is an enormous difference between Grecian art of the classic period and that of the lower empire; yet the change was accompanied, or rather caused, by a change of taste. The artists who most quickly followed this change of taste were in their day regarded as the superior artists. And so of literature. As it became more vapid, puerile, and stilted, it would be in obedience to an altered taste, which would regard its increasing weakness as increasing strength and beauty. The really good writer would not find readers; he would be regarded as rude, dry, or dull. And so would the drama decline; not because there was a lack of good plays, but because the prevailing taste became more and more that of a less cultured class, who, of course, regard that which they most admire as the best of its kind. And so, too, of religion; the superstitions which a superstitious people will add to it will be regarded by them as improvements. While, as the decline goes on, the return to barbarism, where it is not in itself regarded as an advance, will seem necessary to meet the exigencies of the times.

For instance, flogging, as a punishment for certain offenses, has been recently restored to the penal code of England, and has been strongly advocated on this side of the Atlantic. I express no opinion as to whether this is or is not a better punishment for crime than imprisonment. I only point to the fact as illustrating how an increasing amount of crime and an increasing embarrassment as to the maintenance of prisoners, both obvious tendencies at present, might lead to a fuller return to the physical cruelty of barbarous codes. The use of torture in judicial investigations, which steadily grew with the decline of Roman civilization, it is thus easy to see, might, as manners brutalized and crime increased, be demanded as a necessary improvement of the criminal law.

Whether in the present drifts of opinion and taste there are as yet any indications of retrogression, it is not necessary to inquire; but there are many things about which there can be no dispute, which go to show that our civilization has reached a critical period, and that unless a new start is made in the direction of social equality, the nineteenth century may to the future mark its climax. These industrial depressions, which cause as much waste and suffering as famines or wars, are like the twinges and shocks which precede paralysis. Everywhere is it evident that the tendency to inequality, which is the necessary result of material progress where land is monopolized, cannot go much further without carrying our civilization into that downward path which is so easy to enter and so hard to abandon. Everywhere the increasing intensity of the struggle to live, the increasing necessity for straining every nerve to prevent being thrown down and trodden under foot in the scramble for wealth, is draining the forces which gain and maintain improvements. In every civilized country pauperism, crime, insanity, and suicides are increasing. In every civilized country the diseases are increasing which come from overstrained nerves, from insufficient nourishment, from squalid lodgings, from unwholesome and monotonous occupations, from premature labor of children, from the tasks and crimes which poverty imposes upon women. In every highly civilized country the expectation of life, which gradually rose for several centuries, and which seems to have culminated about the first quarter of this century, appears to be now diminishing.[7]

It is not an advancing civilization that such figures show. It is a civilization which in its undercurrents has already begun to recede. When the tide turns in bay or river from flood to ebb, it is not all at once; but here it still runs on, though there it has begun to recede. When the sun passes the meridian, it can be told only by the way the short shadows fall; for the heat of the day yet increases. But as sure as the turning tide must soon run full ebb; as sure as the declining sun must bring darkness, so sure is it, that though knowledge yet increases and invention marches on, and new states are being settled, and cities still expand, yet civilization has begun to wane when, in proportion to population, we must build more and more prisons, more and more almshouses, more and more insane asylums. It is not from top to bottom that societies die; it is from bottom to top.

But there are evidences far more palpable than any that can be given by statistics, of tendencies to the ebb of civilization. There is a vague but general feeling of disappointment; an increased bitterness among the working classes; a widespread feeling of unrest and brooding revolution. If this were accompanied by a definite idea of how relief is to be obtained, it would be a hopeful sign; but it is not. Though the schoolmaster has been abroad some time, the general power of tracing effect to cause does not seem a whit improved. The reaction toward protectionism, as the reaction toward other exploded fallacies of government, shows this.[8] And even the philosophic free-thinker cannot look upon that

vast change in religious ideas that is now sweeping over the civilized world without feeling that this tremendous fact may have most momentous relations, which only the future can develop. For what is going on is not a change in the form of religion, but the negation and destruction of the ideas from which religion springs. Christianity is not simply clearing itself of superstitions, but in the popular mind it is dying at the root, as the old paganisms were dying when Christianity entered the world. And nothing arises to take its place. The fundamental ideas of an intelligent Creator and of a future life are in the general mind rapidly weakening. Now, whether this may or may not be in itself an advance, the importance of the part which religion has played in the world's history shows the importance of the change that is now going on. Unless human nature has suddenly altered in what the universal history of the race shows to be its deepest characteristics, the mightiest actions and reactions are thus preparing. Such stages of thought have heretofore always marked periods of transition. On a smaller scale and to a less depth (for I think any one who will notice the drift of our literature, and talk upon such subjects with the men he meets, will see that it is sub-soil and not surface plowing that materialistic ideas are now doing), such a state of thought preceded the French revolution. But the closest parallel to the wreck of religious ideas now going on is to

---

[7] Statistics which show these things are collected in convenient form in a volume entitled "Deterioration and Race Education," by Samuel Royce, which has been largely distributed by the venerable Peter Cooper of New York. Strangely enough, the only remedy proposed by Mr. Royce is the establishment of Kindergarten schools. —Author's note.

[8] In point of constructive statesmanship—the recognition of fundamental principles and the adaptation of means to ends, the Constitution of the United States, adopted a century ago, is greatly superior to the latest State Constitutions, the most recent of which is that of California—a piece of utter botchwork.—Author's note.

be found in that period in which ancient civilization began to pass from splendor to decline. What change may come, no mortal man can tell, but that some great change must come, thoughtful men begin to feel. The civilized world is trembling on the verge of a great movement. Either it must be a leap upward, which will open the way to advances yet undreamed of, or it must be a plunge downward, which will carry us back toward barbarism.

1838 ∾ *Henry Adams* ∾ 1918

THE varied literary productions of Henry Adams are spread across the record of forty years. The writing and teaching of American history was a chief interest for most of his life, as well as his occupation insofar as he had one in the usual sense. His first publication was a volume of *Documents Relating to New England Federalism,* which he edited in 1877. He wrote biographies of two American statesmen, *Albert Gallatin* (1879) and *John Randolph* (1882). His *History of the United States, 1801-1817,* covering meticulously the administrations of Jefferson and Madison, appeared in 1889-91.

Another of Adams' major interests was social theory and social criticism. As vehicle for the latter he twice attempted the novel in *Democracy* (1880) and *Esther* (1884), but both are minor works.

The two interests merged in *Mont-Saint-Michel and Chartres* (1904) and *The Education of Henry Adams,* privately printed in 1907 but not published in a general edition until 1918. The first of these is an attempt at analysis of the society and the historical processes which produced the mediaeval cathedrals. The second, by far the most widely read of Adams' books, recounts those of his own observations and experiences which seemed to him, as he looked back in his later years, significant as stages in his search for an understanding of life. The book begins with warm reminiscence of Adams' boyhood in Boston and in Quincy, Massachusetts, and his introduction to his formidably distinguished family tradition through the firm kindliness of his grandfather, John Quincy Adams, always known in the family as "The President." Henry's own father appears also in the *Education.* Charles Francis Adams was distinguished as a member of Congress and as ambassador to England, and in both these capacities he was assisted by Henry as his secretary.

After teaching at Harvard for seven years, Henry Adams spent most of the remainder of his life at Washington, as an observer and sometimes an unofficial participant in political events.

Adams formulated an elaborate theory of human history as a dynamic and deterministic process. On the basis of this theory he predicted that the twentieth century would be one of violent wars and revolutions. He called especial attention to the future of the bomb as an expression of human energy multiplied by science, predicting that it would double in effectiveness every ten years.

[*Henry Adams* (New York, 1933) is a biography by James Truslow Adams. *Letters of Henry Adams, 1858-1891,* 2 vols. (Boston, 1920) was edited by W. C. Ford, and *Henry Adams and His Friends: A Collection of His Unpublished Letters* (Boston, 1947) by H. D. Cater.]

From
THE EDUCATION OF HENRY ADAMS
[1907] [1]

THE INDIVIDUAL AS PRIMITIVE ENERGY

AT LEAST four-fifths of the American people—Adams among the rest—had united in the election of General Grant to the Presidency, and probably had been more or less affected in their choice by the parallel they felt between Grant and Washington. Nothing could be more obvious. Grant represented order. He was a great soldier, and the soldier always represented order. He might be as partisan as he pleased, but a general who had organized and commanded half a million or a million men in the field, must know how to administer. Even Washington, who was, in education and experience, a mere cavedweller, had known how to organize a government, and had found Jeffersons and Hamiltons to organize his departments. The task of bringing the Government back to regular practices, and of restoring moral and mechanical order to administration, was not very difficult; it was ready to do it itself, with a little encouragement. No doubt the confusion, especially in the old slave States and in the currency, was considerable, but the general disposition was good, and every one had echoed the famous phrase: "Let us have peace."

Adams was young and easily deceived, in spite of his diplomatic adventures, but even at twice his age he could not see that this reliance on Grant was unreasonable. Had Grant been a Congressman one would

have been on one's guard, for one knew the type. One never expected from a Congressman more than good intentions and public spirit. Newspaper-men as a rule had no great respect for the lower House; Senators had less; and Cabinet officers had none at all. Indeed, one day when Adams was pleading with a Cabinet officer for patience and tact in dealing with Representatives, the Secretary impatiently broke out: "You can't use tact with a Congressman! A Congressman is a hog! You must take a stick and hit him on the snout!" Adams knew far too little, compared with the Secretary, to contradict him, though he thought the phrase somewhat harsh even as applied to the average Congressman of 1869—he saw little or nothing of later ones—but he knew a shorter way of silencing criticism. He had but to ask: "If a Congressman is a hog, what is a Senator?" This innocent question, put in a candid spirit, petrified any executive officer that ever sat a week in his office. Even Adams admitted that Senators passed belief. The comic side of their egotism partly disguised its extravagance, but faction had gone so far under Andrew Johnson that at times the whole Senate seemed to catch hysterics of nervous bucking without apparent reason. Great leaders, like Sumner and Conkling, could not be burlesqued; they were more grotesque than ridicule could make them; even Grant, who rarely sparkled in epigram, became witty on their account; but their egotism and factiousness were no

---

[1] Privately issued in 1907, the book was published in 1918, immediately after its author's death, by Houghton, Mifflin & Company, Boston.

laughing matter. They did permanent and terrible mischief, as Garfield and Blaine, and even McKinley and John Hay, were to feel. The most troublesome task of a reform President was that of bringing the Senate back to decency.

Therefore no one, and Henry Adams less than most, felt hope that any President chosen from the ranks of politics or politicians would raise the character of government; and by instinct if not by reason, all the world united on Grant. The Senate understood what the world expected, and waited in silence for a struggle with Grant more serious than that with Andrew Johnson. Newspaper-men were alive with eagerness to support the President against the Senate. The newspaper-man is, more than most men, a double personality; and his person feels best satisfied in its double instincts when writing in one sense and thinking in another. All newspaper-men, whatever they wrote, felt alike about the Senate. Adams floated with the stream. He was eager to join in the fight which he foresaw as sooner or later inevitable. He meant to support the executive in attacking the Senate and taking away its two-thirds vote and power of confirmation, nor did he much care how it should be done, for he thought it safer to effect the revolution in 1870 than to wait till 1920.

With this thought in mind, he went to the Capitol to hear the names announced which should reveal the carefully guarded secret of Grant's Cabinet. To the end of his life, he wondered at the suddenness of the revolution which actually, within five minutes, changed his intended future into an absurdity so laughable as to make him ashamed of it. He was to hear a long list of Cabinet announcements not much weaker or more futile than that of Grant, and none of them made him blush, while Grant's nominations had the singular effect of making the hearer ashamed, not so much of Grant, as of himself. He had made another total misconception of life—another inconceivable false start. Yet, unlikely as it seemed, he had missed his motive narrowly,

and his intention had been more than sound, for the Senators made no secret of saying with senatorial frankness that Grant's nominations betrayed his intent as plainly as they betrayed his incompetence. A great soldier might be a baby politician.

Adams left the Capitol, much in the same misty mental condition that he recalled as marking his railway journey to London on May 13, 1861; he felt in himself what Gladstone bewailed so sadly, "the incapacity of viewing things all round." He knew, without absolutely saying it, that Grant had cut short the life which Adams had laid out for himself in the future. After such a miscarriage, no thought of effectual reform could revive for at least one generation, and he had no fancy for ineffectual politics. What course could he sail next? He had tried so many, and society had barred them all! For the moment, he saw no hope but in following the stream on which he had launched himself. The new Cabinet, as individuals, were not hostile. Subsequently Grant made changes in the list which were mostly welcome to a Bostonian—or should have been—although fatal to Adams. The name of Hamilton Fish,[2] as Secretary of State, suggested extreme conservatism and probable deference to Sumner. The name of George S. Boutwell,[3] as Secretary of the Treasury, suggested only a somewhat lugubrious joke; Mr. Boutwell could be described only as the opposite of Mr. McCulloch,[4] and meant inertia; or, in plain words, total extinction for any one resembling Henry Adams. On the other hand, the name of Jacob D. Cox,[5] as Secretary of the Interior, suggested help and com-

[2] New York lawyer (1808-1893). Secretary of State 1869-1877.

[3] Massachusetts politician (1818-1905). Secretary of the Treasury 1869-1873.

[4] Hugh McCulloch (1808-1895). Secretary of the Treasury 1865-1869 and 1884-1885.

[5] Lawyer and army officer (1828-1900). Secretary of the Interior 1869-1870. Later president of the University of Cincinnati.

fort; while that of Judge Hoar,[6] as Attorney-General, promised friendship. On the whole, the personal outlook, merely for literary purposes, seemed fairly cheerful, and the political outlook, though hazy, still depended on Grant himself. No one doubted that Grant's intention had been one of reform; that his aim had been to place his administration above politics; and until he should actually drive his supporters away, one might hope to support him. One's little lantern must therefore be turned on Grant. One seemed to know him so well, and really knew so little.

By chance it happened that Adam Badeau[7] took the lower suite of rooms at Dohna's, and, as it was convenient to have one table, the two men dined together and became intimate. Badeau was exceedingly social, though not in appearance imposing. He was stout; his face was red, and his habits were regularly irregular; but he was very intelligent, a good newspaper-man, and an excellent military historian. His life of Grant was no ordinary book. Unlike most newspaper-men, he was a friendly critic of Grant, as suited an officer who had been on the General's staff. As a rule, the newspaper correspondents in Washington were unfriendly, and the lobby sceptical. From that side one heard tales that made one's hair stand on end, and the old West Point army officers were no more flattering. All described him as vicious, narrow, dull, and vindictive. Badeau, who had come to Washington for a consulate which was slow to reach him, resorted more or less to whiskey for encouragement, and became irritable, besides being loquacious. He talked much about Grant, and showed a certain artistic feeling for analysis of character, as a true literary critic would naturally do. Loyal to Grant, and still more so to Mrs. Grant, who acted as his patroness, he said nothing, even when far gone, that was offensive about either, but he held that no one except himself and Rawlins[8] understood the General. To him, Grant appeared as an intermittent energy, immensely powerful when awake, but passive and plastic in repose. He said that neither he nor the rest of the staff knew why Grant succeeded; they believed in him because of his success. For stretches of time, his mind seemed torpid. Rawlins and the others would systematically talk their ideas into it, for weeks, not directly, but by discussion among themselves, in his presence. In the end, he would announce the idea as his own, without seeming conscious of the discussion; and would give the orders to carry it out with all the energy that belonged to his nature. They could never measure his character or be sure when he would act. They could never follow a mental process in his thought. They were not sure that he did think.

In all this, Adams took deep interest, for although he was not, like Badeau, waiting for Mrs. Grant's power of suggestion to act on the General's mind in order to germinate in a consulate or a legation, his portrait gallery of great men was becoming large, and it amused him to add an authentic likeness of the greatest general the world had seen since Napoleon. Badeau's analysis was rather delicate; infinitely superior to that of Sam Ward[9] or Charles Nordhoff.[10]

Badeau took Adams to the White House one evening and introduced him to the

[6] Ebenezer Rockwood Hoar (1816-1895), Massachusetts jurist. Attorney-general in Grant's cabinet 1869-1870.
[7] American officer (1831-1895), on Grant's staff as military secretary in the last years of the war. He wrote *Military History of Ulysses S. Grant* (3 vols., 1868-1881) and *Grant in Peace* (1887).
[8] John Aaron Rawlins (1831-1869). A fellow-townsman (from Galena, Illinois), he was aide-de-camp to Grant throughout the Civil War. Grant appointed him Secretary of War (1869).
[9] Samuel Ward (1814-1884). Prominent as lobbyist in Washington during Grant's administration.
[10] Writer and journalist (1830-1901). Author of books about the sea and of *Politics for Young Americans* (1875). Grandfather of Charles B. Nordhoff, co-author (with James Norman Hall) of *Mutiny on the Bounty* (1932), etc.

President and Mrs. Grant. First and last, he saw a dozen Presidents at the White House, and the most famous were by no means the most agreeable, but he found Grant the most curious object of study among them all. About no one did opinions differ so widely. Adams had no opinion, or occasion to make one. A single word with Grant satisfied him that, for his own good, the fewer words he risked, the better. Thus far in life he had met with but one man of the same intellectual or unintellectual type —Garibaldi.[11] Of the two, Garibaldi seemed to him a trifle the more intellectual, but, in both, the intellect counted for nothing; only the energy counted. The type was pre-intellectual, archaic, and would have seemed so even to the cave-dwellers. Adam, according to legend, was such a man.

In time one came to recognize the type in other men, with differences and variations, as normal; men whose energies were the greater, the less they wasted on thought; men who sprang from the soil to power; apt to be distrustful of themselves and of others; shy; jealous; sometimes vindictive; more or less dull in outward appearance; always needing stimulants; but for whom action was the highest stimulant—the instinct of fight. Such men were forces of nature, energies of the prime, like the *Pteraspis*,[12] but they made short work of scholars. They had commanded thousands of such and saw no more in them than in others. The fact was certain; it crushed argument and intellect at once.

Adams did not feel Grant as a hostile force; like Badeau he saw only an uncertain one. When in action he was superb and safe to follow; only when torpid was he dangerous. To deal with him one must stand near, like Rawlins, and practice more or less sympathetic habits. Simple-minded beyond the experience of Wall Street or State Street, he resorted, like most men of the same intellectual calibre, to commonplaces when at a loss for expression: "Let us have peace!" or, "The best way to treat a bad law is to execute it"; or a score of

such reversible sentences generally to be gauged by their sententiousness; but sometimes he made one doubt his good faith; as when he seriously remarked to a particularly bright young woman that Venice would be a fine city if it were drained. In Mark Twain, this suggestion would have taken rank among his best witticisms; in Grant it was a measure of simplicity not singular. Robert E. Lee betrayed the same intellectual commonplace, in a Virginian form, not to the same degree, but quite distinctly enough for one who knew the American. What worried Adams was not the commonplace; it was, as usual, his own education. Grant fretted and irritated him, like the *Terebratula*,[13] as a defiance of first principles. He had no right to exist. He should have been extinct for ages. The idea that, as society grew older, it grew one-sided, upset evolution, and made of education a fraud. That, two thousand years after Alexander the Great and Julius Caesar, a man like Grant should be called —and should actually and truly be—the highest product of the most advanced evolution, made evolution ludicrous. One must be as commonplace as Grant's own commonplaces to maintain such an absurdity. The progress of evolution from President Washington to President Grant, was alone evidence enough to upset Darwin.

Education became more perplexing at every phase. No theory was worth the pen that wrote it. America had no use for Adams because he was eighteenth-century, and yet it worshipped Grant because he was archaic and should have lived in a cave and worn skins. Darwinists ought to conclude that America was reverting to the stone age, but the theory of reversion was more absurd than that of evolution. Grant's administration reverted to nothing. One could not catch a trait of the past, still less of the future.

[11] Giuseppe Garibaldi (1807-1882), Italian patriot and revolutionary leader.
[12] Primitive fish, related to the shark.
[13] A genus of primitive mollusks, comprising both living and fossil species.

1860 ∽ *Hamlin Garland* ∽ 1940

H AMLIN GARLAND carried from boyhood days in cornfields and cold barns, in Wisconsin and Iowa, a lifelong distaste for the physical toil of farming. He shone at a prairie academy, taught a rural school, and made his way east to study and then teach elocution in Boston. On a visit in 1887 to his parents—in Dakota now, aging, fighting drouth and a mortgage—he had his eyes suddenly opened to his peculiar literary material. Reacting to his reading of Henry George and to the social unrest of the times, he wrote for the controversial magazine *The Arena* the harshly critical stories of midwestern farm life that were collected in 1891 under the title *Main-Travelled Roads.* His work was praised and encouraged by Howells. He worked as an organizer and orator for the Populist movement, and poured his political experiences as well as his conception of the social and economic injustices of the farmers into four short novels, all published in 1892: *Jason Edwards, A Little Norsk, A Member of the Third House,* and *A Spoil of Office.*

In 1893 Garland moved to Chicago, and became prominent in the literary life there. He set forth his theories of realism and of art in general in a volume of essays, *Crumbling Idols* (1894). After the realism of his most ambitious novel of midwestern rural life, *Rose of Dutcher's Coolly* (1895), had shocked many of his readers, Garland announced the transfer of his literary allegiance from the toilsome farm life of the middle west to more adventurous careers in mountains and cattle country. He also abandoned realism for romance, and wrote a dozen highly romantic novels of the Far West in the next twenty years.

Garland enjoyed a second literary career of importance and influence, inaugurated by the publication of *A Son of the Middle Border* in 1917. This volume of family chronicle and autobiography restates, with perspective and elaboration, the same view of midwestern farm life in the last decades of the nineteenth century that Garland had expressed in his early stories. It is the first and the best of eight volumes of reminiscences, to the writing of which Garland devoted his remaining years.

[Garland was himself so voluminous an autobiographer that it will probably be some time before we have a definitive critical biography of him. Critical evaluation may be found in various books and journals, notably in V. F. Parrington's *Main Currents in American Thought,* Vol. III (New York, 1930).]

UNDER THE LION'S PAW
[1891 (1889)]

IT WAS THE LAST of autumn and first day of winter coming together. All day long the ploughmen on their prairie farms had moved to and fro in their wide level fields through the falling snow, which melted as it fell, wetting them to the skin —all day, notwithstanding the frequent squalls of snow, the dripping, desolate clouds, and the muck of the furrows, black and tenacious as tar.

Under their dripping harness the horses swung to and fro silently, with that marvellous uncomplaining patience which marks the horse. All day the wild geese, honking wildly, as they sprawled sidewise down the wind, seemed to be fleeing from an enemy behind, and with neck outthrust and wings extended, sailed down the wind, soon lost to sight.

Yet the ploughman behind his plough, though the snow lay on his ragged great-coat, and the cold clinging mud rose on his heavy boots, fettering him like gyves, whistled in the very beard of the gale. As day passed, the snow, ceasing to melt, lay along the ploughed land, and lodged in the depth of the stubble, till on each slow round the last furrow stood out black and shining as jet between the ploughed land and the gray stubble.

When night began to fall, and the geese, flying low, began to alight invisibly in the near corn-field, Stephen Council was still at work "finishing a land." He rode on his sulky plough when going with the wind, but walked when facing it. Sitting bent and cold but cheery under his slouch hat, he talked encouragingly to his four-in-hand.

"Come round there, boys!—Round agin! We got t' finish this land. Come in there, Dan! *Stiddy, Kate,*—stiddy! None o' y'r tantrums, Kittie. It's purty tuff, but it got a be did. *Tchk! tchk!* Step along, Pete! Don't let Kate git y'r single-tree on the wheel. *Once* more!"

They seemed to know what he meant, and that this was the last round, for they worked with greater vigor than before.

"Once more, boys, an' then, sez I, oats an' a nice warm stall, an' sleep f'r all."

By the time the last furrow was turned on the land it was too dark to see the house, and the snow was changing to rain again. The tired and hungry man could see the light from the kitchen shining through the leafless hedge, and he lifted a great shout, "Supper f'r a half a dozen!"

It was nearly eight o'clock by the time he had finished his chores and started for supper. He was picking his way carefully through the mud, when the tall form of a man loomed up before him with a premonitory cough.

"Waddy ye want?" was the rather startled question of the farmer.

"Well, ye see," began the stranger, in a deprecating tone, "we'd like t' git in f'r the night. We've tried every house f'r the last two miles, but they hadn't any room f'r us. My wife's jest about sick, 'n' the children are cold and hungry——"

"Oh, y' want 'o stay all night, eh?"

"Yes, sir; it 'ud be a great accom—"

"Waal, I don't make it a practice t' turn anybuddy way hungry, not on sech nights as this. Drive right in. We ain't got much, but sech as it is——"

But the stranger had disappeared. And soon his steaming, weary team, with drooping heads and swinging single-trees, moved past the well to the block beside the path. Council stood at the side of the "schooner" and helped the children out—two little half-sleeping children—and then a small woman with a babe in her arms.

"There ye go!" he shouted jovially, to the children. "*Now* we're all right! Run right along to the house there, an' tell Mam' Council you wants sumpthin' t' eat. Right this way, Mis'—keep right off t' the right there. I'll go an' git a lantern. Come," he said to the dazed and silent group at his side.

"Mother," he shouted, as he neared the fragrant and warmly lighted kitchen, "here are some wayfarers an' folks who need sumpthin' t' eat an' a place t' snooze." He ended by pushing them all in.

Mrs. Council, a large, jolly, rather coarse-looking woman, took the children in her arms. "Come right in, you little rabbits. 'Most asleep, hey? Now here's a drink o' milk f'r each o' ye. I'll have s'm tea in a minute. Take off y'r things and set up t' the fire."

While she set the children to drinking milk, Council got out his lantern and went out to the barn to help the stranger about his team, where his loud, hearty voice could be heard as it came and went between the haymow and the stalls.

The woman came to light as a small, timid, and discouraged-looking woman, but still pretty, in a thin and sorrowful way.

"Land sakes! An' you've travelled all the way from Clear Lake t'-day in this mud! Waal! waal! No wonder you're all tired out. Don't wait f'r the men, Mis'—" She hesitated, waiting for the name.

"Haskins."

"Mis' Haskins, set right up to the table an' take a good swig o' tea whilst I make y' s'm toast. It's green tea, an' it's good. I tell Council as I git older I don't seem to enjoy Young Hyson n'r Gunpowder. I want the reel green tea, jest as it comes off'n the vines. Seems t' have more heart in it, some way. Don't s'pose it has. Council says it's all in m' eye."

Going on in this easy way, she soon had the children filled with bread and milk and the woman thoroughly at home, eating some toast and sweet-melon pickles, and sipping the tea.

"See the little rats!" she laughed at the children. "They're full as they can stick now, and they want to go to bed. Now, don't git up, Mis' Haskins; set right where you are an' let me look after 'em. I know all about young ones, though I'm all alone now. Jane went an' married last fall. But, as I tell Council, it's lucky we keep our health. Set right there, Mis' Haskins; I won't have you stir a finger."

It was an unmeasured pleasure to sit there in the warm, homely kitchen, the jovial chatter of the house-wife driving out and holding at bay the growl of the impotent, cheated wind.

The little woman's eyes filled with tears which fell down upon the sleeping baby in her arms. The world was not so desolate and cold and hopeless, after all.

"Now I hope Council won't stop out there and talk politics all night. He's the greatest man to talk politics an' read the *Tribune*—How old is it?"

She broke off and peered down at the face of the babe.

"Two months 'n' five days," said the mother, with a mother's exactness.

"Ye don't say! I want 'o know! The dear little pudzy-wudzy!" she went on, stirring it up in the neighborhood of the ribs with her fat forefinger.

"Pooty tough on 'oo to go gallivant'n' 'cross lots this way——"

"Yes, that's so; a man can't lift a mountain," said Council, entering the door. "Mother, this is Mr. Haskins, from Kansas. He's been eat up 'n' drove out by grasshoppers."

"Glad t' see yeh!—Pa, empty that washbasin 'n' give him a chance t' wash."

Haskins was a tall man, with a thin, gloomy face. His hair was a reddish brown, like his coat, and seemed equally faded by the wind and sun, and his sallow face, though hard and set, was pathetic somehow. You would have felt that he had suffered much by the line of his mouth showing under his thin, yellow mustache.

"Hain't Ike got home yet, Sairy?"

"Hain't seen 'im."

"W-a-a-l, set right up, Mr. Haskins; wade right into what we've got; 'tain't much, but we manage to live on it—she gits fat on it," laughed Council, pointing his thumb at his wife.

After supper, while the women put the children to bed, Haskins and Council talked on, seated near the huge cookingstove, the steam rising from their wet clothing. In the Western fashion Council told as much of his own life as he drew from his guest. He asked but few questions, but by and by the story of Haskins' struggles and defeat came out. The story was a terrible one, but he told it quietly, seated with his elbows on his knees, gazing most of the time at the hearth.

"I didn't like the looks of the country, anyhow," Haskins said, partly rising and glancing at his wife. "I was ust t' northern Ingyannie, where we have lots o' timber 'n' lots o' rain, 'n' I didn't like the looks o' that dry prairie. What galled me the worst was goin' s' far away acrosst so much fine land layin' all through here vacant."

"And the 'hoppers eat ye four years, hand runnin', did they?"

"Eat! They wiped us out. They chawed everything that was green. They jest set around waitin' f'r us to die t' eat us, too. My God! I ust t' dream of 'em sittin' 'round on the bedpost, six feet long, workin' their jaws. They et the fork-handles. They got worse 'n' worse till they jest rolled on one another, piled up like snow in winter. Well, it ain't no use. If I was t' talk all winter I couldn't tell nawthin'. But all the while I couldn't help thinkin' of all that land back here that nobuddy was usin' that I ought 'o had 'stead o' bein' out there in that cussed country."

"Waal, why didn't ye stop an' settle here?" asked Ike, who had come in and was eating his supper.

"Fer the simple reason that you fellers wantid ten 'r fifteen dollars an acre fer the bare land, and I hadn't no money for that kind o' thing."

"Yes, I do my own work," Mrs. Council was heard to say in the pause which followed. "I'm a gettin' purty heavy t' be on m' laigs all day, but we can't afford t' hire, so I keep rackin' around somehow, like a foundered horse. S' lame—I tell Council he can't tell how lame I am, f'r I'm jest as lame in one laig as t'other." And the good soul laughed at the joke on

herself as she took a handful of flour and dusted the biscuit-board to keep the dough from sticking.

"Well, I hain't *never* been very strong," said Mrs. Haskins. "Our folks was Canadians an' small-boned, and then since my last child I hain't got up again fairly. I don't like t' complain. Tim has about all he can bear now—but they was days this week when I jest wanted to lay right down an' die."

"Waal, now, I'll tell ye," said Council, from his side of the stove, silencing everybody with his good-natured roar, "I'd go down and *see* Butler, *anyway*, if I was you. I guess he'd let you have his place purty cheap; the farm's all run down. He's been anxious t' let t' somebuddy next year. It 'ud be a good chance fer you. Anyhow, you go to bed and sleep like a babe. I've got some ploughin' t' do, anyhow, an' we'll see if somethin' can't be done about your case. Ike, you go out an' see if the horses is all right, an' I'll show the folks t' bed."

When the tired husband and wife were lying under the generous quilts of the spare bed, Haskins listened a moment to the wind in the eaves, and then said, with a slow and solemn tone,

"There are people in this world who are good enough t' be angels, an' only haff t' die to *be* angels."

II

Jim Butler was one of those men called in the West "land poor." Early in the history of Rock River he had come into the town and started in the grocery business in a small way, occupying a small building in a mean part of the town. At this period of his life he earned all he got, and was up early and late sorting beans, working over butter, and carting his goods to and from the station. But a change came over him at the end of the second year, when he sold a lot of land for four times what he paid for it. From that time forward he believed in land speculation as the surest way of getting rich. Every cent he could save or spare from his trade he put into land at forced sale, or mortgages on land, which were "just as good as the wheat," he was accustomed to say.

Farm after farm fell into his hands, until he was recognized as one of the leading landowners of the county. His mortgages were scattered all over Cedar County, and as they slowly but surely fell in he sought usually to retain the former owner as tenant.

He was not ready to foreclose; indeed, he had the name of being one of the "easiest" men in the town. He let the debtor off again and again, extending the time whenever possible.

"I don't want y'r land," he said. "All I'm after is the int'rest on my money— that's all. Now, if y' want 'o stay on the farm, why, I'll give y' a good chance. I can't have the land layin' vacant." And in many cases the owner remained as tenant.

In the meantime he had sold his store; he couldn't spend time in it; he was mainly occupied now with sitting around town on rainy days smoking and "gassin' with the boys," or in riding to and from his farms. In fishing-time he fished a good deal. Doc Grimes, Ben Ashley, and Cal Cheatham were his cronies on these fishing excursions or hunting trips in the time of chickens or partridges. In winter they went to northern Wisconsin to shoot deer.

In spite of all these signs of easy life Butler persisted in saying he "hadn't enough money to pay taxes on his land," and was careful to convey the impression that he was poor in spite of his twenty farms. At one time he was said to be worth fifty thousand dollars, but land had been a little slow of sale of late, so that he was not worth so much.

A fine farm, known as the Higley place, had fallen into his hands in the usual way the previous year, and he had not been able to find a tenant for it. Poor Higley, after working himself nearly to death on it in the attempt to lift the mortgage, had gone off to Dakota, leaving the farm and his curse to Butler.

This was the farm which Council advised Haskins to apply for; and the next day Council hitched up his team and drove down town to see Butler.

"You jest let *me* do the talkin'," he said. "We'll find him wearin' out his pants on some salt barrel somew'ers; and if he thought you *wanted* a place he'd sock it to you hot and heavy. You jest keep quiet; I'll fix 'im."

Butler was seated in Ben Ashley's store telling fish yarns when Council sauntered in casually.

"Hello, But; lyin' agin, hey?"

"Hellow, Steve! how goes it?"

"Oh, so-so. Too dang much rain these days. I thought it was goin' t' freeze up f'r good last night. Tight squeak if I get m' ploughin' done. How's farmin' with *you* these days?"

"Bad. Ploughin' ain't half done."

"It 'ud be a religious idee f'r you t' go out an' take a hand y'rself."

"I don't haff to," said Butler, with a wink.

"Got anybody on the Higley place?"

"No. Know of anybody?"

"Waal, no: not eggsackly. I've got a relation back t' Michigan who's bent hot an' cold on the idee o' comin' West f'r some time. *Might* come if he could get a good lay-out. What do you talk on the farm?"

"Well, I d' know. I'll rent it on shares or I'll rent it money rent."

"Waal, how much money, say?"

"Well, say ten per cent, on the price— two-fufty."

"Waal, that ain't bad. Wait on 'im till 'e thrashes?"

Haskins listened eagerly to his important question, but Council was coolly eating a dried apple which he had speared out of a barrel with his knife. Butler studied him carefully.

"Well, knocks me out of twenty-five dollars interest."

"My relation'll need all he's got t' git

his crops in," said Council, in the safe, indifferent way.

"Well, all right; *say* wait," concluded Butler.

"All right; this is the man. Haskins, this is Mr. Butler—no relation to Ben—the hardest-working man in Cedar County."

On the way home Haskins said: "I ain't much better off. I'd like that farm; it's a good farm, but it's all run down, an' so 'm I. I could make a good farm of it if I had half a show. But I can't stock it n'r seed it."

"Waal, now, don't you worry," roared Council in his ear. "We'll pull y' through somehow till next harvest. He's agreed t' hire it ploughed, an' you can earn a hundred dollars ploughin' an' y' c'n git the seed o' me, an' pay me back when y' can."

Haskins was silent with emotion, but at last he said, "I ain't got nothin' t' live on."

"Now, don't you worry 'bout that. You jest make your headquarters at ol' Steve Council's. Mother'll take a pile o' comfort in havin' y'r wife an' children 'round. Y' see, Jane's married off lately, an' Ike's away a good 'eal, so we'll be darn glad t' have y' stop with us this winter. Nex' spring we'll see if y' can't git a start agin." And he chirruped to the team, which sprang forward with the rumbling, clattering wagon.

"Say, looky here, Council, you can't do this. I never saw—" shouted Haskins in his neighbor's ear.

Council moved about uneasily in his seat and stopped his stammering gratitude by saying: "Hold on, now; don't make such a fuss over a little thing. When I see a man down, an' things all on top of 'im, I jest like t' kick 'em off an' help 'im up. That's the kind of religion I got, an' it's about the *only* kind."

They rode the rest of the way home in silence. And when the red light of the lamp shone out into the darkness of the cold and windy night, and he thought of this refuge for his children and wife, Has-

kins could have put his arm around the neck of his burly companion and squeezed him like a lover. But he contented himself with saying, "Steve Council, you'll git y'r pay f'r this some day."

"Don't want any pay. My religion ain't run on such business principles."

The wind was growing colder, and the ground was covered with a white frost, as they turned into the gate of the Council farm, and the children came rushing out, shouting, "Papa's come." They hardly looked like the same children who had sat at the table the night before. Their torpidity, under the influence of sunshine and Mother Council, had given way to a sort of spasmodic cheerfulness, as insects in winter revive when laid on the hearth.

III

Haskins worked like a fiend, and his wife, like the heroic woman that she was, bore also uncomplainingly the most terrible burdens. They rose early and toiled without intermission till the darkness fell on the plain, then tumbled into bed, every bone and muscle aching with fatigue, to rise with the sun next morning to the same round of the same ferocity of labor.

The eldest boy drove a team all through the spring, ploughing and seeding, milked the cows, and did chores innumerable, in most ways taking the place of a man.

An infinitely pathetic but common figure—this boy on the American farm, where there is no law against child labor. To see him in his coarse clothing, his huge boots, and his ragged cap, as he staggered with a pail of water from the well, or trudged in the cold and cheerless dawn into the frosty field behind his team, gave the city-bred visitor a sharp pang of sympathetic pain. Yet Haskins loved his boy, and would have saved him from this if he could, but he could not.

By June the first year the result of such Herculean toil began to show on the farm. The yard was cleaned up and sown to grass, the garden ploughed and planted, and the house mended.

Council had given them four of his cows. "Take 'em an' run 'em on shares. I don't want 'o milk s' many. Ike's away s' much now, Sat'd'ys an' Sund'ys, I can't stand the bother anyhow."

Other men, seeing the confidence of Council in the newcomer, had sold him tools on time; and as he was really an able farmer, he soon had round him many evidences of his care and thrift. At the advice of Council he had taken the farm for three years, with the privilege of re-renting or buying at the end of the term.

"It's a good bargain, an' y' want 'o nail it," said Council. "If you have any kind ov a crop, you c'n pay y'r debts, an' keep seed an' bread."

The new hope which now sprang up in the heart of Haskins and his wife grew great almost as a pain by the time the wide field of wheat began to wave and rustle and swirl in the winds of July. Day after day he would snatch a few moments after supper to go and look at it.

"Have ye seen the wheat t'-day, Nettie?" he asked one night as he rose from supper.

"No, Tim, I ain't had time."

"Well, take time now. Le's go look at it."

She threw an old hat on her head— Tommy's hat—and looking almost pretty in her thin, sad way, went out with her husband to the hedge.

"Ain't it grand, Nettie? Just look at it."

It was grand. Level, russet here and there, heavy-headed, wide as a lake, and full of multitudinous whispers and gleams of wealth, it stretched away before the gazers like the fabled field of the cloth of gold.

"Oh, I think—I *hope* we'll have a good crop, Tim; and oh, how good the people have been to us!"

"Yes; I don't know where we'd be t'-day if it hadn't ben f'r Council and his wife."

"They're the best people in the world," said the little woman, with a great sob of gratitude.

"We'll be in the field on Monday, sure," said Haskins, gripping the rail on the fence as if already at the work of the harvest.

The harvest came, bounteous, glorious, but the winds came and blew it into tangles, and the rain matted it here and there close to the ground, increasing the work of gathering it threefold.

Oh, how they toiled in those glorious days! Clothing dripping with sweat, arms aching, filled with briers, fingers raw and bleeding, backs broken with the weight of heavy bundles, Haskins and his man toiled on. Tommy drove the harvester, while his father and a hired man bound on the machine. In this way they cut ten acres every day, and almost every night after supper, when the hand went to bed, Haskins returned to the field, shocking the bound grain in the light of the moon. Many a night he worked till his anxious wife came out at ten o'clock to call him in to rest and lunch.

At the same time she cooked for the men, took care of the children, washed and ironed, milked the cows at night, made the butter, and sometimes fed the horses and watered them while her husband kept at the shocking.

No slave in the Roman galleys could have toiled so frightfully and lived, for this man thought himself a free man, and that he was working for his wife and babes.

When he sank into his bed with a deep groan of relief, too tired to change his grimy, dripping clothing, he felt that he was getting nearer and nearer to a home of his own, and pushing the wolf of want a little farther from his door.

There is no despair so deep as the despair of a homeless man or woman. To roam the roads of the country or the streets of the city, to feel there is no rood of ground on which the feet can rest, to halt weary and hungry outside lighted windows, and hear laughter and song within,—these are the hungers and rebellions that drive men to crime and women to shame.

It was the memory of his homelessness,

and the fear of its coming again, that spurred Timothy Haskins and Nettie, his wife, to such ferocious labor during that first year.

IV

" 'M, yes; 'm, yes; first-rate," said Butler, as his eye took in the neat garden, the pig-pen, and the well-filled barnyard. "You're gitt'n' quite a stock around yeh. Done well, eh?"

Haskins was showing Butler around the place. He had not seen it for a year, having spent the year in Washington and Boston with Ashley, his brother-in-law, who had been elected to Congress.

"Yes, I've laid out a good deal of money durin' the last three years. I've paid out three hundred dollars f'r fencin'."

"Um-h'm! I see, I see," said Butler, while Haskins went on:

"The kitchen there cost two hundred; the barn ain't cost much in money, but I've put a lot o' time on it. I've dug a new well, and I——"

"Yes, yes, I see. You've done well. Stock worth a thousand dollars," said Butler, picking his teeth with a straw.

"About that," said Haskins, modestly. "We begin to feel 's if we was gitt'n' a home f'r ourselves; but we've worked hard. I tell you we begin to feel it, Mr. Butler, and we're goin' t' begin to ease up purty soon. We've been kind o' plannin' a trip back t' *her* folks after the fall ploughin's done."

"*Eggs*-actly!" said Butler, who was evidently thinking of something else. "I suppose you've kind o' calc'lated on stayin' here three years more?"

"Well, yes. Fact is, I think I c'n buy the farm this fall, if you'll give me a reasonable show."

"Um-m! What do you call a reasonable show?"

"Well, say a quarter down and three years' time."

Butler looked at the huge stacks of wheat, which filled the yard, over which the chickens were fluttering and crawling, catching grasshoppers, and out of which the crickets were singing innumerably. He smiled in a peculiar way as he said, "Oh, I won't be hard on yeh. But what did you expect to pay f'r the place?"

"Why, about what you offered it for before, two thousand five hundred, or *possibly* three thousand dollars," he added quickly, as he saw the owner shake his head.

"This farm is worth five thousand and five hundred dollars," said Butler, in a careless and decided voice.

"*What!*" almost shrieked the astounded Haskins. "What's that? Five thousand? Why, that's double what you offered it for three years ago."

"Of course, and it's worth it. It was all run down then; now it's in good shape. You've laid out fifteen hundred dollars in improvements, according to your own story."

"But *you* had nothin' t' do about that. It's my work an' my money."

"You bet it was; but it's my land."

"But what's to pay me for all my——"

"Ain't you had the use of 'em?" replied Butler, smiling calmly into his face.

Haskins was like a man struck on the head with a sandbag; he couldn't think; he stammered as he tried to say: "But—I never'd git the use—You'd rob me! More'n that: you agreed—you promised that I could buy or rent at the end of three years at——"

"That's all right. But I didn't say I'd let you carry off the improvements, nor that I'd go on renting the farm at two-fifty. The land is doubled in value, it don't matter how; it don't enter into the question; an' now you can pay me five hundred dollars a year rent, or take it on your own terms at fifty-five hundred, or—git out."

He was turning away when Haskins, the sweat pouring from his face, fronted him, saying again:

"But *you've* done nothing to make it so. You hain't added a cent. I put it all there myself, expectin' to buy. I worked an' sweat to improve it. I was workin' for myself an' babes——"

"Well, why didn't you buy when I offered to sell? What y' kickin' about?"

"I'm kickin' about payin' you twice f'r my own things,—my own fences, my own kitchen, my own garden."

Butler laughed. "You're too green t' eat, young feller. *Your* improvements! The law will sing another tune."

"But I trusted your word."

"Never trust anybody, my friend. Besides, I didn't promise not to do this thing. Why, man, don't look at me like that. Don't take me for a thief. It's the law. The reg'lar thing. Everybody does it."

"I don't care if they do. It's stealin' jest the same. You take three thousand dollars of my money—the work o' my hands and my wife's." He broke down at this point. He was not a strong man mentally. He could face hardship, ceaseless toil, but he could not face the cold and sneering face of Butler.

"But I don't take it," said Butler, coolly. "All you've got to do is to go on jest as you've been a-doin', or give me a thousand dollars down, and a mortgage at ten percent on the rest."

Haskins sat down blindly on a bundle of oats near by, and with staring eyes and drooping head went over the situation. He was under the lion's paw. He felt a horrible numbness in his heart and limbs. He was hid in a mist, and there was no path out.

Butler walked about, looking at the huge stacks of grain, and pulling now and again a few handfuls out, shelling the heads in his hands and blowing the chaff away. He hummed a little tune as he did so. He had an accommodating air of waiting.

Haskins was in the midst of the terrible toil of the last year. He was walking again in the rain and the mud behind his plough; he felt the dust and dirt of the threshing. The ferocious husking-time, with its cutting wind and biting, clinging snows, lay hard upon him. Then he thought of his wife, how she had cheerfully cooked and baked, without holiday and without rest.

"Well, what do you think of it?" inquired the cool, mocking, insinuating voice of Butler.

"I think you're a thief and a liar!" shouted Haskins, leaping up. "A black-hearted houn'!" Butler's smile maddened him; with a sudden leap he caught a fork in his hands, and whirled it in the air. "You'll never rob another man, damn ye!" he grated through his teeth, a look of pitiless ferocity in his accusing eyes.

Butler shrank and quivered, expecting the blow; stood, held hypnotized by the eyes of the man he had a moment before despised—a man transformed into an avenging demon. But in the deadly hush between the lift of the weapon and its fall there came a gush of faint, childish laughter and then across the range of his vision, far away and dim, he saw the sun-bright head of his baby girl, as, with the pretty, tottering run of a two-year-old, she moved across the grass of the door-yard. His hands relaxed; the fork fell to the ground; his head lowered.

"Make out y'r deed an' mor'gage, an' git off'n my land, an' don't ye never cross my line agin; if y' do, I'll kill ye."

Butler backed away from the man in wild haste, and climbing into his buggy with trembling limbs drove off down the road, leaving Haskins seated dumbly on the sunny piles of sheaves, his head sunk into his hands.

1871 ∾ *Stephen Crane* ∾ *1900*

ONE of the numerous, ill-disciplined children of a Methodist minister, Stephen Crane frequently disturbed his father's New Jersey congregation, as he later affronted teachers at Lafayette College and at Syracuse University, by calling Tennyson's poetry "swill." His fragmentary college career was distinguished only in baseball; toward the end of it he was already earning money as a journalist. He was a newspaper man during parts of his few mature years, traveling in the Southwest and Mexico for a newspaper syndicate, to Greece to report a Balkan war, to Cuba to see and write about the Spanish-American War.

Between jobs he wrote fiction and poetry, at first sometimes in extreme poverty which he was too proud to admit to his family. Howells and Hamlin Garland encouraged him, but the pious publishers of the day would have none of the realism of his short first novel of New York slum life, *Maggie, A Girl of the Streets*. Money for its publication was furnished by an older brother, on condition that the honored name of Crane should not be used. *Maggie* appeared in a yellow-paper cover (1893) as written by "Johnson Smith"—and did not sell. But when *The Red Badge of Courage*, which was first published serially in the *Philadelphia Press,* appeared in book form in 1895, Crane suddenly found himself famous and his book a best seller.

Thereafter he wrote rapidly for an eager market. To be sure, two volumes of verse, *The Black Riders* (1895) and *War Is Kind* (1899), unconventional in both form and substance, had to wait twenty years for appreciation; and it has remained for Ben Hecht to speak of *George's Mother* (1896) as constituting, with *Maggie,* "The Great American Novel." But Crane's short stories were eagerly welcomed, most of them appearing in magazines before being collected in *The Little Regiment* (1896), *The Open Boat and Other Tales of Adventure* (1898), *The Monster and Other Stories* (1899), and *Whilomville Stories* (1900). The last-named is a collection of stories about children, reminiscent of Crane's own boyhood. The others contain additional material resembling *Maggie* in vigorous criticism of urban society, or *The Red Badge of Courage* in psychological realistic expression of war experience. Crane also turned his hand to hack work of many kinds in the attempt to maintain a large income. During his last years he lived and wrote in England, where he was the neighbor and friend, and devoted admirer, of Joseph Conrad, then just beginning his literary career. He died only five years after his first success.

[Wilson Follett edited *The Works of Stephen Crane* (1925-7), in twelve volumes. Thomas Beer wrote a biography, *Stephen Crane* (New York, 1923).]

THE BLUE HOTEL
[1899]

THE PALACE HOTEL at Fort Romper was painted a light blue, a shade that is on the legs of a kind of heron, causing the bird to declare its position against any background. The Palace Hotel, then, was always screaming and howling in a way that made the dazzling winter landscape of Nebraska seem only a grey swampish hush. It stood alone on the prairie, and when the snow was falling the town two hundred yards away was not visible. But when the traveller alighted at the railway station he was obliged to pass the Palace Hotel before he could come upon the company of low clapboard houses which composed Fort Romper, and it was not to be thought that any traveller could pass the Palace Hotel without looking at it. Pat Scully, the proprietor, had proved himself a master of strategy when he chose his paints. It is true that on clear days, when the great transcontinental expresses, long lines of swaying Pullmans, swept through Fort Romper, passengers were overcome at the sight, and the cult that knows the brown-reds and the subdivisions of the dark greens of the East expressed shame, pity, horror, in a laugh. But to the citizens of this prairie town and to the people who would naturally stop there, Pat Scully had performed a feat. With this opulence and splendour, these creeds, classes, egotisms, that streamed through Romper on the rails day after day, they had no colour in common.

As if the displayed delights of such a blue hotel were not sufficiently enticing, it was Scully's habit to go every morning and evening to meet the leisurely trains that stopped at Romper and work his seductions upon any man that he might see wavering, gripsack in hand.

One morning, when a snow-crusted engine dragged its long string of freight cars and its one passenger coach to the station, Scully performed the marvel of catching three men. One was a shaky and quick-eyed Swede, with a great shining cheap valise; one was a tall bronzed cowboy, who was on his way to a ranch near the Dakota line; one was a little silent man from the East, who didn't look it, and didn't announce it. Scully practically made them prisoners. He was so nimble and merry and kindly that each probably felt it would be the height of brutality to try to escape. They trudged off over the creaking board sidewalks in the wake of the eager little Irishman. He wore a heavy fur cap squeezed tightly down on his head. It caused his two red ears to stick out stiffly, as if they were made of tin.

At last, Scully, elaborately, with boisterous hospitality, conducted them through the portals of the blue hotel. The room which they entered was small. It seemed to be merely a proper temple for an enormous stove, which, in the centre, was humming with godlike violence. At various points on its surface the iron had become luminous and glowed yellow from the heat. Beside the stove Scully's son Johnnie was playing High-Five with an old farmer who had whiskers both grey and sandy. They were quarrelling. Frequently the old farmer turned his face toward a box of sawdust—coloured brown from tobacco juice—that was behind the stove, and spat with an air of great impatience and irritation. With a loud flourish of words Scully destroyed the game of cards, and bustled his son upstairs with part of the baggage of the new guests. He himself conducted them to three basins of the coldest water in the world. The cowboy and the Easterner burnished themselves fiery red with this water, until it seemed to be some kind of metal-polish. The Swede, however, merely dipped his fingers gingerly and with trepidation. It was notable that throughout this series of small ceremonies the three travellers were made to feel that Scully was very benevolent. He was conferring great favours upon them. He handed the towel from one to another with an air of philanthropic impulse.

Afterward they went to the first room,

and, sitting about the stove, listened to Scully's officious clamour at his daughters, who were preparing the midday meal. They reflected in the silence of experienced men who tread carefully amid new people. Nevertheless, the old farmer, stationary, invincible in his chair near the warmest part of the stove, turned his face from the sawdust-box frequently and addressed a glowing commonplace to the strangers. Usually he was answered in short but adequate sentences by either the cowboy or the Easterner. The Swede said nothing. He seemed to be occupied in making furtive estimates of each man in the room. One might have thought that he had the sense of silly suspicion which comes to guilt. He resembled a badly frightened man.

Later, at dinner, he spoke a little, addressing his conversation entirely to Scully. He volunteered that he had come from New York, where for ten years he had worked as a tailor. These facts seemed to strike Scully as fascinating, and afterward he volunteered that he had lived at Romper for fourteen years. The Swede asked about the crops and the price of labour. He seemed barely to listen to Scully's extended replies. His eyes continued to rove from man to man.

Finally, with a laugh and a wink, he said that some of these Western communities were very dangerous; and after his statement he straightened his legs under the table, tilted his head, and laughed again, loudly. It was plain that the demonstration had no meaning to the others. They looked at him wondering and in silence.

II

As the men trooped heavily back into the front room, the two little windows presented views of a turmoiling sea of snow. The huge arms of the wind were making attempts—mighty, circular, futile—to embrace the flakes as they sped. A gate-post like a still man with a blanched face stood aghast amid this profligate fury. In a hearty voice Scully announced the presence of a blizzard. The guests of the blue hotel, lighting their pipes, assented with grunts of lazy masculine contentment. No island of the sea could be exempt in the degree of this little room with its humming stove. Johnnie, son of Scully, in a tone which defined his opinion of his ability as a card-player, challenged the old farmer of both grey and sandy whiskers to a game of High-Five. The farmer agreed with a contemptuous and bitter scoff. They sat close to the stove, and squared their knees under a wide board. The cowboy and the Easterner watched the game with interest. The Swede remained near the window, aloof, but with a countenance that showed signs of an inexplicable excitement.

The play of Johnnie and the grey-beard was suddenly ended by another quarrel. The old man arose while casting a look of heated scorn at his adversary. He slowly buttoned his coat, and then stalked with fabulous dignity from the room. In the discreet silence of all the other men the Swede laughed. His laughter rang somehow childish. Men by this time had begun to look at him askance, as if they wished to inquire what ailed him.

A new game was formed jocosely. The cowboy volunteered to become the partner of Johnnie, and they all then turned to ask the Swede to throw in his lot with the little Easterner. He asked some questions about the game, and, learning that it wore many names, and that he had played it when it was under an alias, he accepted the invitation. He strode toward the men nervously, as if he expected to be assaulted. Finally, seated, he gazed from face to face and laughed shrilly. This laugh was so strange that the Easterner looked up quickly, the cowboy sat intent and with his mouth open, and Johnnie paused, holding the cards with still fingers.

Afterward there was a short silence. Then Johnnie said, "Well, let's get at it.

Come on now!" They pulled their chairs forward until their knees were bunched under the board. They began to play, and their interest in the game caused the others to forget the manner of the Swede.

The cowboy was a board-whacker. Each time that he held superior cards he whanged them, one by one, with exceeding force, down upon the improvised table, and took the tricks with a glowing air of prowess and pride that sent thrills of indignation into the hearts of his opponents. A game with a board-whacker in it is sure to become intense. The countenances of the Easterner and the Swede were miserable whenever the cowboy thundered down his aces and kings, while Johnnie, his eyes gleaming with joy, chuckled and chuckled.

Because of the absorbing play none considered the strange ways of the Swede. They paid strict heed to the game. Finally, during a lull caused by a new deal, the Swede suddenly addressed Johnnie: "I suppose there have been a good many men killed in this room." The jaws of the others dropped and they looked at him.

"What in hell are you talking about?" said Johnnie.

The Swede laughed again his blatant laugh, full of a kind of false courage and defiance. "Oh, you know what I mean all right," he answered.

"I'm a liar if I do!" Johnnie protested. The card was halted, and the men stared at the Swede. Johnnie evidently felt that as the son of the proprietor he should make a direct inquiry. "Now, what might you be drivin' at, mister?" he asked. The Swede winked at him. It was a wink full of cunning. His fingers shook on the edge of the board. "Oh, maybe you think I have been to nowheres. Maybe you think I'm a tenderfoot?"

"I don't know nothin' about you," answered Johnnie, "and I don't give a damn where you've been. All I got to say is that I don't know what you're driving at. There hain't never been nobody killed in this room."

The cowboy, who had been steadily gazing at the Swede, then spoke: "What's wrong with you, mister?"

Apparently it seemed to the Swede that he was formidably menaced. He shivered and turned white near the corners of his mouth. He sent an appealing glance in the direction of the little Easterner. During these moments he did not forget to wear his air of advanced pot-valour. "They say they don't know what I mean," he remarked mockingly to the Easterner.

The latter answered after prolonged and cautious reflection. "I don't understand you," he said, impassively.

The Swede made a movement then which announced that he thought he had encountered treachery from the only quarter where he had expected sympathy, if not help. "Oh, I see you are all against me. I see——"

The cowboy was in a state of deep stupefaction. "Say," he cried, as he tumbled the deck violently down upon the board, "say, what are you gittin' at, hey?"

The Swede sprang up with the celerity of a man escaping from a snake on the floor. "I don't want to fight!" he shouted. "I don't want to fight!"

The cowboy stretched his long legs indolently and deliberately. His hands were in his pockets. He spat into the sawdust-box. "Well, who the hell thought you did?" he inquired.

The Swede backed rapidly toward a corner of the room. His hands were out protectingly in front of his chest, but he was making an obvious struggle to control his fright. "Gentlemen," he quavered, "I suppose I am going to be killed before I can leave this house! I suppose I am going to be killed before I can leave this house!" In his eyes was the dying-swan look. Through the windows could be seen the snow turning blue in the shadow of dusk. The wind tore at the house, and some loose thing beat regularly against the clapboards like a spirit tapping.

A door opened, and Scully himself entered. He paused in surprise as he noted the tragic attitude of the Swede. Then he said, "What's the matter here?"

The Swede answered him swiftly and eagerly: "These men are going to kill me."

"Kill you!" ejaculated Scully. "Kill you! What are you talkin'?"

The Swede made the gesture of a martyr. Scully wheeled sternly upon his son. "What is this, Johnnie?"

The lad had grown sullen. "Damned if I know," he answered. "I can't make no sense to it." He began to shuffle the cards, fluttering them together with an angry snap. "He says a good many men have been killed in this room, or something like that. And he says he's goin' to be killed here too. I don't know what ails him. He's crazy, I shouldn't wonder."

Scully then looked for explanation to the cowboy, but the cowboy simply shrugged his shoulders.

"Kill you?" said Scully again to the Swede. "Kill you? Man, you're off your nut."

"Oh, I know," burst out the Swede. "I know what will happen. Yes, I'm crazy—yes. Yes, of course, I'm crazy—yes. But I know one thing—" There was a sort of sweat of misery and terror upon his face. "I know I won't get out of here alive."

The cowboy drew a deep breath, as if his mind was passing into the last stages of dissolution. "Well, I'm doggoned," he whispered to himself.

Scully wheeled suddenly and faced his son. "You've been troublin' this man!"

Johnnie's voice was loud with its burden of grievance. "Why, good Gawd, I ain't done nothin' to 'im."

The Swede broke in. "Gentlemen, do not disturb yourselves. I will leave this house. I will go away, because"—he accused them dramatically with his glance—"because I do not want to be killed."

Scully was furious with his son. "Will you tell me what is the matter, you young divil? What's the matter, anyhow? Speak out!"

"Blame it!" cried Johnnie in despair, "don't I tell you I don't know? He—he says we want to kill him, and that's all I know. I can't tell what ails him."

The Swede continued to repeat: "Never mind, Mr. Scully; never mind. I will leave this house. I will go away, because I do not wish to be killed. Yes, of course, I am crazy—yes. But I know one thing! I will go away. I will leave this house. Never mind, Mr. Scully; never mind. I will go away."

"You will not go 'way," said Scully. "You will not go 'way until I hear the reason of this business. If anybody has troubled you I will take care of him. This is my house. You are under my roof, and I will not allow any peaceable man to be troubled here." He cast a terrible eye upon Johnnie, the cowboy, and the Easterner.

"Never mind, Mr. Scully; never mind. I will go away. I do not wish to be killed." The Swede moved toward the door which opened upon the stairs. It was evidently his intention to go at once for his baggage.

"No, no," shouted Scully peremptorily; but the white-faced man slid by him and disappeared. "Now," said Scully severely, "what does this mane?"

Johnnie and the cowboy cried together: "Why, we didn't do nothin' to 'im!"

Scully's eyes were cold. "No," he said, "you didn't?"

Johnnie swore a deep oath. "Why, this is the wildest loon I ever see. We didn't do nothin' at all. We were jest sittin' here playin' cards, and he——"

The father suddenly spoke to the Easterner. "Mr. Blanc," he asked, "what has these boys been doin'?"

The Easterner reflected again. "I didn't see anything wrong at all," he said at last, slowly.

Scully began to howl. "But what does it mane?" He stared ferociously at his son. "I have a mind to lather you for this, me boy."

Johnnie was frantic. "Well, what have I done?" he bawled at his father.

III

"I think you are tongue-tied," said Scully finally to his son, the cowboy, and the Easterner; and at the end of this scornful sentence he left the room.

Upstairs the Swede was swiftly fastening the straps of his great valise. Once his back happened to be half turned toward the door, and, hearing a noise there, he wheeled and sprang up, uttering a loud cry. Scully's wrinkled visage showed grimly in the light of the small lamp he carried. This yellow effulgence, streaming upward, coloured only his prominent features, and left his eyes, for instance, in mysterious shadow. He resembled a murderer.

"Man! man!" he exclaimed, "have you gone daffy?"

"Oh, no! Oh, no!" rejoined the other. "There are people in this world who know pretty nearly as much as you do—understand?"

For a moment they stood gazing at each other. Upon the Swede's deathly pale cheeks were two spots brightly crimson and sharply edged, as if they had been carefully painted. Scully placed the light on the table and sat himself on the edge of the bed. He spoke ruminatively. "By cracky, I never heard of such a thing in my life. It's a complete muddle. I can't, for the soul of me, think how you ever got this idea into your head." Presently he lifted his eyes and asked: "And did you sure think they were going to kill you?"

The Swede scanned the old man as if he wished to see into his mind. "I did," he said at last. He obviously suspected that this answer might precipitate an outbreak. As he pulled on a strap his whole arm shook, the elbow wavering like a bit of paper.

Scully banged his hand impressively on the footboard of the bed. "Why, man, we're goin' to have a line of ilictric street-cars in this town next spring."

"'A line of electric street-cars,'" repeated the Swede, stupidly.

"And," said Scully, "there's a new railroad goin' to be built down from Broken Arm to here. Not to mintion the four churches and the smashin' big brick schoolhouse. Then there's the big factory, too. Why, in two years Romper'll be a met-tro-pol-is."

Having finished the preparation of his baggage, the Swede straightened himself. "Mr. Scully," he said, with sudden hardihood, "how much do I owe you?"

"You don't owe me anythin'," said the old man, angrily.

"Yes, I do," retorted the Swede. He took seventy-five cents from his pocket and tendered it to Scully; but the latter snapped his fingers in disdainful refusal. However, it happened that they both stood gazing in a strange fashion at three silver pieces on the Swede's open palm.

"I'll not take your money," said Scully at last. "Not after what's been goin' on here." Then a plan seemed to strike him. "Here," he cried, picking up his lamp and moving toward the door. "Here! Come with me a minute."

"No," said the Swede, in overwhelming alarm.

"Yes," urged the old man. "Come on! I want you to come and see a picter—just across the hall—in my room."

The Swede must have concluded that his hour was come. His jaw dropped and his teeth showed like a dead man's. He ultimately followed Scully across the corridor, but he had the step of one hung in chains.

Scully flashed the light high on the wall of his own chamber. There was revealed a ridiculous photograph of a little girl. She was leaning against a balustrade of gorgeous decoration, and the formidable bang to her hair was prominent. The figure was as graceful as an upright sled-stake, and, withal, it was of the hue of lead. "There," said Scully, tenderly, "that's the picter of my little girl that died. Her name was Carrie. She had the purtiest hair you ever saw! I was that fond of her, she——"

Turning then, he saw that the Swede was

not contemplating the picture at all, but, instead, was keeping keen watch on the gloom in the rear.

"Look, man!" cried Scully, heartily. "That's the picter of my little gal that died. Her name was Carrie. And then here's the picter of my oldest boy, Michael. He's a lawyer in Lincoln, an' doin' well. I gave that boy a grand eddication, and I'm glad for it now. He's a fine boy. Look at 'im now. Ain't he bold as blazes, him there in Lincoln, an honoured an' respicted gintleman! An honoured and respicted gintleman," concluded Scully with a flourish. And, so saying, he smote the Swede jovially on the back.

The Swede faintly smiled.

"Now," said the old man, "there's only one more thing." He dropped suddenly to the floor and thrust his head beneath the bed. The Swede could hear his muffled voice. "I'd keep it under me pillar if it wasn't for that boy Johnnie. Then there's the old woman— Where is it now? I never put it twice in the same place. Ah, now come out with you!"

Presently he backed clumsily from under the bed, dragging with him an old coat rolled into a bundle. "I've fetched him," he muttered. Kneeling on the floor, he unrolled the coat and extracted from its heart a large yellow-brown whisky-bottle.

His first manoeuvre was to hold the bottle up to the light. Reassured, apparently, that nobody had been tampering with it, he thrust it with a generous movement toward the Swede.

The weak-kneed Swede was about to eagerly clutch this element of strength, but he suddenly jerked his hand away and cast a look of horror upon Scully.

"Drink," said the old man affectionately. He had risen to his feet, and now stood facing the Swede.

There was a silence. Then again Scully said: "Drink!"

The Swede laughed wildly. He grabbed the bottle, put it to his mouth; and as his lips curled absurdly around the opening and his throat worked, he kept his glance, burning with hatred, upon the old man's face.

IV

After the departure of Scully the three men, with the cardboard still upon their knees, preserved for a long time an astounded silence. Then Johnnie said: "That's the doddangedest Swede I ever see."

"He ain't no Swede," said the cowboy, scornfully.

"Well, what is he then?" cried Johnnie. "What is he then?"

"It's my opinion," replied the cowboy deliberately, "he's some kind of a Dutchman." It was a venerable custom of the country to entitle as Swedes all lighthaired men who spoke with a heavy tongue. In consequence the idea of the cowboy was not without its daring. "Yes, sir," he repeated. "It's my opinion this feller is some kind of a Dutchman."

"Well, he says he's a Swede, anyhow," muttered Johnnie, sulkily. He turned to the Easterner: "What do you think, Mr. Blanc?"

"Oh, I don't know," replied the Easterner.

"Well, what do you think makes him act that way?" asked the cowboy.

"Why, he's frightened." The Easterner knocked his pipe against a rim of the stove. "He's clear frightened out of his boots."

"What at?" cried Johnnie and the cowboy together.

The Easterner reflected over his answer.

"What at?" cried the others again.

"Oh, I don't know, but it seems to me this man has been reading dime novels, and he thinks he's right out in the middle of it—the shootin' and stabbin' and all."

"But," said the cowboy, deeply scandalized, "this ain't Wyoming, ner none of them places. This is Nebrasker."

"Yes," added Johnnie, "an' why don't he wait till he gits *out West*?"

The travelled Easterner laughed. "It

isn't different there even—not in these days. But he thinks he's right in the middle of hell."

Johnnie and the cowboy mused long.

"It's awful funny," remarked Johnnie at last.

"Yes," said the cowboy. "This is a queer game. I hope we don't git snowed in, because then we'd have to stand this here man bein' around with us all the time. That wouldn't be no good."

"I wish pop would throw him out," said Johnnie.

Presently they heard a loud stamping on the stairs, accompanied by ringing jokes in the voice of old Scully, and laughter, evidently from the Swede. The men around the stove stared vacantly at each other. "Gosh!" said the cowboy. The door flew open, and old Scully, flushed and anecdotal, came into the room. He was jabbering at the Swede, who followed him, laughing bravely. It was the entry of two roisterers from a banquet hall.

"Come now," said Scully sharply to the three seated men, "move up and give us a chance at the stove." The cowboy and the Easterner obediently sidled their chairs to make room for the new-comers. Johnnie, however, simply arranged himself in a more indolent attitude, and then remained motionless.

"Come! Git over, there," said Scully.

"Plenty of room on the other side of the stove," said Johnnie.

"Do you think we want to sit in the draught?" roared the father.

But the Swede here interposed with a grandeur of confidence. "No, no. Let the boy sit where he likes," he cried in a bullying voice to the father.

"All right! All right!" said Scully, deferentially. The cowboy and the Easterner exchanged glances of wonder.

The five chairs were formed in a crescent about one side of the stove. The Swede began to talk; he talked arrogantly, profanely, angrily. Johnnie, the cowboy, and the Easterner maintained a morose silence,

while old Scully appeared to be receptive and eager, breaking in constantly with sympathetic ejaculations.

Finally the Swede announced that he was thirsty. He moved in his chair, and said that he would go for a drink of water.

"I'll git it for you," cried Scully at once.

"No," said the Swede, contemptuously. "I'll get it for myself." He arose and stalked with the air of an owner off into the executive parts of the hotel.

As soon as the Swede was out of hearing Scully sprang to his feet and whispered intensely to the others: "Upstairs he thought I was tryin' to poison 'im."

"Say," said Johnnie, "this makes me sick. Why don't you throw 'im out in the snow?"

"Why, he's all right now," declared Scully. "It was only that he was from the East, and he thought this was a tough place. That's all. He's all right now."

The cowboy looked with admiration upon the Easterner. "You were straight," he said. "You were on to that there Dutchman."

"Well," said Johnnie to his father, "he may be all right now, but I don't see it. Other time he was scared, but now he's too fresh."

Scully's speech was always a combination of Irish brogue and idiom, Western twang and idiom, and scraps of curiously formal diction taken from the story-books and newspapers. He now hurled a strange mass of language at the head of his son. "What do I keep? What do I keep? What do I keep?" he demanded, in a voice of thunder. He slapped his knee impressively, to indicate that he himself was going to make reply, and that all should heed. "I keep a hotel," he shouted. "A hotel, do you mind? A guest under my roof has sacred privileges. He is to be intimidated by none. Not one word shall he hear that would prejudice him in favour of goin' away. I'll not have it. There's no place in this here town where they can say they iver took in a guest of mine because he was afraid to stay here." He wheeled suddenly upon the cowboy and the Easterner. "Am I right?"

"Yes, Mr. Scully," said the cowboy, "I think you're right"

"Yes, Mr. Scully," said the Easterner, "I think you're right."

V

At six-o'clock supper, the Swede fizzed like a fire-wheel. He sometimes seemed on the point of bursting into riotous song, and in all his madness he was encouraged by old Scully. The Easterner was encased in reserve; the cowboy sat in wide-mouthed amazement, forgetting to eat, while Johnnie wrathily demolished great plates of food. The daughters of the house, when they were obliged to replenish the biscuits, approached as warily as Indians, and, having succeeded in their purpose, fled with ill-concealed trepidation. The Swede domineered the whole feast, and he gave it the appearance of a cruel bacchanal. He seemed to have grown suddenly taller; he gazed, brutally disdainful, into every face. His voice rang through the room. Once when he jabbed out harpoon-fashion with his fork to pinion a biscuit, the weapon nearly impaled the hand of the Easterner, which had been stretched quietly out for the same biscuit.

After supper, as the men filed toward the other room, the Swede smote Scully ruthlessly on the shoulder. "Well, old boy, that was a good, square meal." Johnnie looked hopefully at his father; he knew that shoulder was tender from an old fall; and, indeed, it appeared for a moment as if Scully was going to flame out over the matter, but in the end he smiled a sickly smile and remained silent. The others understood from his manner that he was admitting his responsibility for the Swede's new view-point.

Johnnie, however, addressed his parent in an aside. "Why don't you license somebody to kick you downstairs?" Scully scowled darkly by way of reply.

When they were gathered about the stove, the Swede insisted on another game of High-Five. Scully gently deprecated the plan at first, but the Swede turned a wolfish glare upon him. The old man subsided, and the Swede canvassed the others. In his tone there was always a great threat. The cowboy and the Easterner both remarked indifferently that they would play. Scully said that he would presently have to go to meet the 6.58 train, and so the Swede turned menacingly upon Johnnie. For a moment their glances crossed like blades, and then Johnnie smiled and said, "Yes, I'll play."

They formed a square, with the little board on their knees. The Easterner and the Swede were again partners. As the play went on, it was noticeable that the cowboy was not board-whacking as usual. Meanwhile, Scully, near the lamp, had put on his spectacles and, with an appearance curiously like an old priest, was reading a newspaper. In time he went out to meet the 6.58 train, and, despite his precautions, a gust of polar wind whirled into the room as he opened the door. Besides scattering the cards, it chilled the players to the marrow. The Swede cursed frightfully. When Scully returned, his entrance disturbed a cosy and friendly scene. The Swede again cursed. But presently they were once more intent, their heads bent forward and their hands moving swiftly. The Swede had adopted the fashion of board-whacking.

Scully took up his paper and for a long time remained immersed in matters which were extraordinarily remote from him. The lamp burned badly, and once he stopped to adjust the wick. The newspaper, as he turned from page to page, rustled with a slow and comfortable sound. Then suddenly he heard three terrible words: "You are cheatin'!"

Such scenes often prove that there can be little of dramatic import in environment. Any room can present a tragic front; any room can be comic. This little den was now hideous as a torture-chamber. The new faces of the men themselves had changed it upon the instant. The Swede held a huge fist in front of Johnnie's face, while the latter looked steadily over it into the blazing orbs of his accuser. The Easterner had grown pallid; the cowboy's jaw had dropped in that expression of bovine amazement which was one of his important mannerisms. After the three words, the first sound in the room was made by Scully's paper as it floated forgotten to his feet. His spectacles had also fallen from his nose, but by a clutch he had saved them in air. His hand, grasping the spectacles, now remained poised awkwardly and near his shoulder. He stared at the card-players.

Probably the silence was while a second elapsed. Then, if the floor had been suddenly twitched out from under the men they could not have moved quicker. The five had projected themselves headlong toward a common point. It happened that Johnnie, in rising to hurl himself upon the Swede, had stumbled slightly because of his curiously instinctive care for the cards and the board. The loss of the moment allowed time for the arrival of Scully, and also allowed the cowboy time to give the Swede a great push which sent him staggering back. The men found tongue together, and hoarse shouts of rage, appeal, or fear burst from every throat. The cowboy pushed and jostled feverishly at the Swede, and the Easterner and Scully clung wildly to Johnnie; but through the smoky air, above the swaying bodies of the peace-compellers, the eyes of the two warriors ever sought each other in glances of challenge that were at once hot and steely.

Of course the board had been overturned, and now the whole company of cards was scattered over the floor, where the boots of the men trampled the fat and painted kings and queens as they gazed with their silly eyes at the war that was waging above them.

Scully's voice was dominating the yells. "Stop now! Stop, I say! Stop, now——"

Johnnie, as he struggled to burst through the rank formed by Scully and the Easterner, was crying, "Well, he says I cheated! He says I cheated! I won't allow no man to say I cheated! If he says I cheated, he's a——!"

The cowboy was telling the Swede, "Quit, now! Quit, d'ye hear——"

The screams of the Swede never ceased: "He did cheat! I saw him! I saw him——" As for the Easterner, he was importuning in a voice that was not heeded: "Wait a moment, can't you? Oh, wait a moment. What's the good of a fight over a game of cards? Wait a moment——"

In this tumult no complete sentences were clear. "Cheat"—"Quit"—"He says"—these fragments pierced the uproar and rang out sharply. It was remarkable that, whereas Scully undoubtedly made the most noise, he was the least heard of any of the riotous band.

Then suddenly there was a great cessation. It was as if each man had paused for breath; and although the room was still lighted with the anger of men, it could be seen that there was no danger of immediate conflict, and at once Johnnie, shouldering his way forward, almost succeeded in confronting the Swede. "What did you say I cheated for? What did you say I cheated for? I don't cheat, and I won't let no man say I do!"

The Swede said, "I saw you! I saw you!"

"Well," cried Johnnie, "I'll fight any man what says I cheat!"

"No, you won't," said the cowboy. "Not here."

"Ah, be still, can't you?" said Scully, coming between them.

The quiet was sufficient to allow the Easterner's voice to be heard. He was repeating, "Oh, wait a moment, can't you? What's the good of a fight over a game of cards? Wait a moment!"

Johnnie, his red face appearing above his father's shoulder, hailed the Swede again. "Did you say I cheated?"

The Swede showed his teeth. "Yes."

"Then," said Johnnie, "we must fight."

"Yes, fight," roared the Swede. He was like a demoniac. "Yes, fight! I'll show you what kind of a man I am! I'll show you who you want to fight! Maybe you think I can't fight! Maybe you think I can't! I'll show you, you skin, you card-sharp! Yes, you cheated! You cheated! You cheated!"

"Well, let's go at it, then, mister," said Johnnie, coolly.

The cowboy's brow was beaded with sweat from his efforts in intercepting all sorts of raids. He turned in despair to Scully. "What are you goin' to do now?"

A change had come over the Celtic visage of the old man. He now seemed all eagerness; his eyes glowed.

"We'll let them fight," he answered, stalwartly. "I can't put up with it any longer. I've stood this damned Swede till I'm sick. We'll let them fight."

VI

The men prepared to go out of doors. The Easterner was so nervous that he had great difficulty in getting his arms into the sleeves of his new leather coat. As the cowboy drew his fur cap down over his ears his hands trembled. In fact, Johnnie and old Scully were the only ones who displayed no agitation. These preliminaries were conducted without words.

Scully threw open the door. "Well, come on," he said. Instantly a terrific wind caused the flame of the lamp to struggle at its wick, while a puff of black smoke sprang from the chimney-top. The stove was in mid-current of the blast, and its voice swelled to equal the roar of the storm. Some of the scarred and bedabbled cards were caught up from the floor and dashed helplessly against the farther wall. The men lowered their heads and plunged into the tempest as into a sea.

No snow was falling, but great whirls and clouds of flakes, swept up from the ground by the frantic winds, were streaming southward with the speed of bullets. The covered land was blue with the sheen of an unearthly satin, and there was no other hue save where, at the low, black railway station—which seemed incredibly distant—one light gleamed like a tiny jewel. As the men floundered into a thigh-deep drift, it was known that the Swede was bawling out something. Scully went to him, put a hand on his shoulder, and projected an ear. "What's that you say?" he shouted.

"I say," bawled the Swede again, "I won't stand much show against this gang. I know you'll all pitch on me."

Scully smote him reproachfully on the arm. "Tut, man!" he yelled. The wind tore the words from Scully's lips and scattered them far alee.

"You are all a gang of—" boomed the Swede, but the storm also seized the remainder of this sentence.

Immediately turning their backs upon the wind, the men had swung around a corner to the sheltered side of the hotel. It was the function of the little house to preserve here, amid this great devastation of snow, an irregular V-shape of heavily encrusted grass, which crackled beneath the feet. One could imagine the great drifts piled against the windward side. When the party reached the comparative peace of this spot it was found that the Swede was still bellowing.

"Oh, I know what kind of a thing this is! I know you'll all pitch on me. I can't lick you all!"

Scully turned upon him panther-fashion. "You'll not have to whip all of us. You'll have to whip my son Johnnie. An' the man what troubles you durin' that time will have me to dale with."

The arrangements were swiftly made. The two men faced each other, obedient to the harsh commands of Scully, whose face, in the subtly luminous gloom, could be seen set in the austere impersonal lines that are pictured on the countenances of the Roman veterans. The Easterner's teeth were chattering, and he was hopping up and down like a mechanical toy. The cowboy stood rock-like.

The contestants had not stripped off any

clothing. Each was in his ordinary attire. Their fists were up, and they eyed each other in a calm that had the elements of leonine cruelty in it.

During this pause, the Easterner's mind, like a film, took lasting impressions of three men—the iron-nerved master of the ceremony; the Swede, pale, motionless, terrible; and Johnnie, serene yet ferocious, brutish yet heroic. The entire prelude had in it a tragedy greater than the tragedy of action, and this aspect was accentuated by the long, mellow cry of the blizzard, as it sped the tumbling and wailing flakes into the black abyss of the south.

"Now!" said Scully.

The two combatants leaped forward and crashed together like bullocks. There was heard the cushioned sound of blows, and of a curse squeezing out from between the tight teeth of one.

As for the spectators, the Easterner's pent-up breath exploded from him with a pop of relief, absolute relief from the tension of the preliminaries. The cowboy bounded into the air with a yowl. Scully was immovable as from supreme amazement and fear at the fury of the fight which he himself had permitted and arranged.

For a time the encounter in the darkness was such a perplexity of flying arms that it presented no more detail than would a swiftly revolving wheel. Occasionally a face, as if illumined by a flash of light, would shine out, ghastly and marked with pink spots. A moment later, the men might have been known as shadows, if it were not for the involuntary utterance of oaths that came from them in whispers.

Suddenly a holocaust of warlike desire caught the cowboy, and he bolted forward with the speed of a broncho. "Go it, Johnnie! Go it! Kill him! Kill him!"

Scully confronted him. "Kape back," he said; and by his glance the cowboy could tell that this man was Johnnie's father.

To the Easterner there was a monotony of unchangeable fighting that was an abomination. This confused mingling was eternal to his sense, which was concentrated in a longing for the end, the priceless end. Once the fighters lurched near him, and as he scrambled hastily backward he heard them breathe like men on the rack.

"Kill him, Johnnie! Kill him! Kill him! Kill him!" The cowboy's face was contorted like one of those agony masks in museums.

"Keep still," said Scully, icily.

Then there was a sudden loud grunt, incomplete, cut short, and Johnnie's body swung away from the Swede and fell with sickening heaviness to the grass. The cowboy was barely in time to prevent the mad Swede from flinging himself upon his prone adversary. "No, you don't," said the cowboy, interposing an arm. "Wait a second."

Scully was at his son's side. "Johnnie! Johnnie, me boy!" His voice had a quality of melancholy tenderness. "Johnnie! Can you go on with it?" He looked anxiously down into the bloody, pulpy face of his son.

There was a moment of silence, and then Johnnie answered in his ordinary voice, "Yes, I—it—yes."

Assisted by his father he struggled to his feet. "Wait a bit now till you git your wind," said the old man.

A few paces away the cowboy was lecturing the Swede. "No, you don't! Wait a second!"

The Easterner was plucking at Scully's sleeve. "Oh, this is enough," he pleaded. "This is enough! Let it go as it stands. This is enough!"

"Bill," said Scully, "git out of the road." The cowboy stepped aside. "Now." The combatants were actuated by a new caution as they advanced toward collision. They glared at each other, and then the Swede aimed a lightning blow that carried with it his entire weight. Johnnie was evidently half stupid from weakness, but he miraculously dodged, and his fist sent the over-balanced Swede sprawling.

The cowboy, Scully, and the Easterner burst into a cheer that was like a chorus of

triumphant soldiery, but before its conclusion the Swede had scuffled agilely to
his feet and come in berserk abandon at
his foe. There was another perplexity of
flying arms, and Johnnie's body again
swung away and fell, even as a bundle
might fall from a roof. The Swede instantly staggered to a little wind-waved
tree and leaned upon it, breathing like an
engine, while his savage and flame-lit eyes
roamed from face to face as the men bent
over Johnnie. There was a splendour of
isolation in his situation at this time which
the Easterner felt once when, lifting his
eyes from the man on the ground, he beheld
that mysterious and lonely figure, waiting.

"Are you any good yet, Johnnie?" asked
Scully in a broken voice.

The son gasped and opened his eyes
languidly. After a moment he answered,
"No—I ain't—any good—any—more."
Then, from shame and bodily ill, he began to weep, the tears furrowing down
through the bloodstains on his face. "He
was too—too—too heavy for me."

Scully straightened and addressed the
waiting figure. "Stranger," he said, evenly,
"it's all up with our side." Then his
voice changed into that vibrant huskiness
which is commonly the tone of the most
simple and deadly announcements. "Johnnie is whipped."

Without replying, the victor moved off
on the route to the front door of the
hotel.

The cowboy was formulating new and
unspellable blasphemies. The Easterner was
startled to find that they were out in a
wind that seemed to come direct from the
shadowed arctic floes. He heard again the
wail of the snow as it was flung to its
grave in the south. He knew now that all
this time the cold had been sinking into
him deeper and deeper, and he wondered
that he had not perished. He felt indifferent to the condition of the vanquished
man.

"Johnnie, can you walk?" asked Scully.

"Did I hurt—hurt him any?" asked the
son.

"Can you walk, boy? Can you walk?"

Johnnie's voice was suddenly strong.
There was a robust impatience in it. "I
asked you whether I hurt him any!"

"Yes, yes, Johnnie," answered the cowboy, consolingly; "he's hurt a good deal."

They raised him from the ground, and
as soon as he was on his feet he went
tottering off, rebuffing all attempts at assistance. When the party rounded the
corner they were fairly blinded by the
pelting of the snow. It burned their faces
like fire. The cowboy carried Johnnie
through the drift to the door. As they entered, some cards again rose from the
floor and beat against the wall.

The Easterner rushed to the stove. He
was so profoundly chilled that he almost
dared to embrace the glowing iron. The
Swede was not in the room. Johnnie sank
into a chair and, folding his arms on his
knees, buried his face in them. Scully,
warming one foot and then the other at a
rim of the stove, muttered to himself with
Celtic mournfulness. The cowboy had removed his fur cap, and with a dazed and
rueful air he was running one hand through
his tousled locks. From overhead they
could hear the creaking of boards, as the
Swede tramped here and there in his room.

The sad quiet was broken by the sudden flinging open of a door that led toward
the kitchen. It was instantly followed by
an inrush of women. They precipitated
themselves upon Johnnie amid a chorus of
lamentation. Before they carried their prey
off to the kitchen, there to be bathed and
harangued with that mixture of sympathy
and abuse which is a feat of their sex, the
mother straightened herself and fixed old
Scully with an eye of stern reproach.
"Shame be upon you, Patrick Scully!"
she cried. "Your own son, too. Shame
be upon you!"

"There, now! Be quiet, now!" said the
old man, weakly.

"Shame be upon you, Patrick Scully!"
The girls, rallying to this slogan, sniffed
disdainfully in the direction of those trembling accomplices, the cowboy and the

Easterner. Presently they bore Johnnie away, and left the three men to dismal reflection.

VII

"I'd like to fight this here Dutchman myself," said the cowboy, breaking a long silence.

Scully wagged his head sadly. "No, that wouldn't do. It wouldn't be right. It wouldn't be right."

"Well, why wouldn't it?" argued the cowboy. "I don't see no harm in it."

"No," answered Scully, with mournful heroism. "It wouldn't be right. It was Johnnie's fight, and now we mustn't whip the man just because he whipped Johnnie."

"Yes, that's true enough," said the cowboy; "but—he better not get fresh with me, because I couldn't stand no more of it."

"You'll not say a word to him," commanded Scully, and even then they heard the tread of the Swede on the stairs. His entrance was made theatric. He swept the door back with a bang and swaggered to the middle of the room. No one looked at him. "Well," he cried, insolently, at Scully, "I s'pose you'll tell me now how much I owe you?"

The old man remained stolid. "You don't owe me nothin'."

"Huh!" said the Swede, "huh! Don't owe 'im nothin'."

The cowboy addressed the Swede. "Stranger, I don't see how you come to be so gay around here."

Old Scully was instantly alert. "Stop!" he shouted, holding his hand forth, fingers upward. "Bill, you shut up!"

The cowboy spat carelessly into the sawdust-box. "I didn't say a word, did I?" he asked.

"Mr. Scully," called the Swede, "how much do I owe you?" It was seen that he was attired for departure, and that he had his valise in his hand.

"You don't owe me nothin'," repeated Scully in the same imperturbable way.

"Huh!" said the Swede. "I guess you're right. I guess if it was any way at all, you'd owe me somethin'. That's what I guess." He turned to the cowboy. " 'Kill him! Kill him! Kill him!' " he mimicked, and then guffawed victoriously. " 'Kill him!' " He was convulsed with ironical humour.

But he might have been jeering the dead. The three men were immovable and silent, staring with glassy eyes at the stove.

The Swede opened the door and passed into the storm, giving one derisive glance backward at the still group.

As soon as the door was closed, Scully and the cowboy leaped to their feet and began to curse. They trampled to and fro, waving their arms and smashing into the air with their fists. "Oh, but that was a hard minute!" wailed Scully. "That was a hard minute! Him there leerin' and scoffin'! One bang at his nose was worth forty dollars to me that minute! How did you stand it, Bill?"

"How did I stand it?" cried the cowboy in a quivering voice. "How did I stand it? Oh!"

The old man burst into sudden brogue. "I'd loike to take that Swade," he wailed, "and hould 'im down on a shtone flure and bate 'im to a jelly wid a shtick!"

The cowboy groaned in sympathy. "I'd like to git him by the neck and ha-ammer him"—he brought his hand down on a chair with a noise like a pistol-shot—"hammer that there Dutchman until he couldn't tell himself from a dead coyote!"

"I'd bate 'im until he——"

"I'd show *him* some things——"

And then together they raised a yearning, fanatic cry— "Oh-o-oh! if we only could——"

"Yes!"

"Yes!"

"And then I'd——"

"O-o-oh!"

VIII

The Swede, tightly gripping his valise, tacked across the face of the storm as if he carried sails. He was following a line of little naked, gasping trees which, he knew, must mark the way of the road. His face, fresh from the pounding of Johnnie's fists, felt more pleasure than pain in the wind and the driving snow. A number of square shapes loomed upon him finally, and he knew them as the houses of the main body of the town. He found a street and made travel along it, leaning heavily upon the wind whenever, at a corner, a terrific blast caught him.

He might have been in a deserted village. We picture the world as thick with conquering and elate humanity, but here, with the bugles of the tempest pealing, it was hard to imagine a peopled earth. One viewed the existence of man then as a marvel, and conceded a glamour of wonder to these lice which were caused to cling to a whirling, fire-smitten, ice-locked, disease-stricken, space-lost bulb. The conceit of man was explained by this storm to be the very engine of life. One was a coxcomb not to die in it. However, the Swede found a saloon.

In front of it an indomitable red light was burning, and the snowflakes were made blood-colour as they flew through the circumscribed territory of the lamp's shining. The Swede pushed open the door of the saloon and entered. A sanded expanse was before him, and at the end of it four men sat about a table drinking. Down one side of the room extended a radiant bar, and its guardian was leaning upon his elbows listening to the talk of the men at the table. The Swede dropped his valise upon the floor and, smiling fraternally upon the barkeeper, said, "Gimme some whisky, will you?" The man placed a bottle, a whisky-glass, and a glass of ice-thick water upon the bar. The Swede poured himself an abnormal portion of whisky and drank it in three gulps. "Pretty bad night," remarked the bartender, indif-ferently. He was making the pretension of blindness which is usually a distinction of his class; but it could have been seen that he was furtively studying the half-erased blood-stains on the face of the Swede. "Bad night," he said again.

"Oh, it's good enough for me," replied the Swede, hardily, as he poured himself some more whisky. The barkeeper took his coin and manoeuvred it through its reception by the highly nickelled cash-machine. A bell rang; a card labelled "20 cts." had appeared.

"No," continued the Swede, "this isn't too bad weather. It's good enough for me."

"So?" murmured the barkeeper, languidly.

The copious drams made the Swede's eyes swim, and he breathed a trifle heavier. "Yes, I like this weather. I like it. It suits me." It was apparently his design to impart a deep significance to these words.

"So?" murmured the bartender again. He turned to gaze dreamily at the scroll-like birds and bird-like scrolls which had been drawn with soap upon the mirrors in back of the bar.

"Well, I guess I'll take another drink," said the Swede, presently. "Have something?"

"No, thanks; I'm not drinkin'," answered the bartender. Afterward he asked, "How did you hurt your face?"

The Swede immediately began to boast loudly. "Why, in a fight. I thumped the soul out of a man down here at Scully's hotel."

The interest of the four men at the table was at last aroused.

"Who was it?" said one.

"Johnnie Scully," blustered the Swede. "Son of the man what runs it. He will be pretty near dead for some weeks, I can tell you. I made a nice thing of him, I did. He couldn't get up. They carried him in the house. Have a drink?"

Instantly the men in some subtle way encased themselves in reserve. "No, thanks," said one. The group was of curious formation. Two were prominent local business men; one was the district attorney; and one was a professional gambler of the kind known as "square." But a scrutiny of the group would not have enabled an observer to pick the gambler from the men of more reputable pursuits. He was, in fact, a man so delicate in manner, when among people of fair class, and so judicious in his choice of victims, that in the strictly masculine part of the town's life he had come to be explicitly trusted and admired. People called him a thoroughbred. The fear and contempt with which his craft was regarded were undoubtedly the reason why his quiet dignity shone conspicuous above the quiet dignity of men who might be merely hatters, billiard-markers, or grocery clerks. Beyond an occasional unwary traveller who came by rail, this gambler was supposed to prey solely upon reckless and senile farmers, who, when flush with good crops, drove into town in all the pride and confidence of an absolutely invulnerable stupidity. Hearing at times in circuitous fashion of the despoilment of such a farmer, the important men of Romper invariably laughed in contempt of the victim, and if they thought of the wolf at all, it was with a kind of pride at the knowledge that he would never dare think of attacking their wisdom and courage. Besides, it was popular that this gambler had a real wife and two real children in a neat cottage in a suburb, where he led an exemplary home life; and when any one even suggested a discrepancy in his character, the crowd immediately vociferated descriptions of this virtuous family circle. Then men who led exemplary home lives, and men who did not lead exemplary home lives, all subsided in a bunch, remarking that there was nothing more to be said.

However, when a restriction was placed upon him—as, for instance, when a strong clique of members of the new Pollywog Club refused to permit him, even as a spectator, to appear in the rooms of the organization—the candour and gentleness with which he accepted the judgment dis-armed many of his foes and made his friends more desperately partisan. He invariably distinguished between himself and a respectable Romper man so quickly and frankly that his manner actually appeared to be a continual broadcast compliment.

And one must not forget to declare the fundamental fact of his entire position in Romper. It is irrefutable that in all affairs outside his business, in all matters that occur eternally and commonly between man and man, this thieving card-player was so generous, so just, so moral, that, in a contest, he could have put to flight the consciences of nine tenths of the citizens of Romper.

And so it happened that he was seated in this saloon with the two prominent local merchants and the district attorney.

The Swede continued to drink raw whisky, meanwhile babbling at the barkeeper and trying to induce him to indulge in potations. "Come on. Have a drink. Come on. What—no? Well, have a little one, then. By gawd, I've whipped a man to-night, and I want to celebrate. I whipped him good, too. Gentlemen," the Swede cried to the men at the table, "have a drink?"

"Ssh!" said the barkeeper.

The group at the table, although furtively attentive, had been pretending to be deep in talk, but now a man lifted his eyes toward the Swede and said, shortly, "Thanks. We don't want any more."

At this reply the Swede ruffled out his chest like a rooster. "Well," he exploded, "it seems I can't get anybody to drink with me in this town. Seems so, don't it? Well!"

"Ssh!" said the barkeeper.

"Say," snarled the Swede, "don't you try to shut me up. I won't have it. I'm a gentleman, and I want people to drink with me. And I want 'em to drink with me now. Now—do you understand?" He rapped the bar with his knuckles.

Years of experience had calloused the bartender. He merely grew sulky. "I hear you," he answered.

"Well," cried the Swede, "listen hard then. See those men over there? Well, they're going to drink with me, and don't you forget it. Now you watch."

"Hi!" yelled the barkeeper, "this won't do!"

"Why won't it?" demanded the Swede. He stalked over to the table, and by chance laid his hand upon the shoulder of the gambler. "How about this?" he asked wrathfully. "I asked you to drink with me."

The gambler simply twisted his head and spoke over his shoulder. "My friend, I don't know you."

"Oh, hell!" answered the Swede, "come and have a drink."

"Now, my boy," advised the gambler, kindly, "take your hand off my shoulder and go 'way and mind your own business." He was a little, slim man, and it seemed strange to hear him use this tone of heroic patronage to the burly Swede. The other men at the table said nothing.

"What! You won't drink with me, you little dude? I'll make you, then! I'll make you!" The Swede had grasped the gambler frenziedly at the throat, and was dragging him from his chair. The other men sprang up. The barkeeper dashed around the corner of his bar. There was a great tumult, and then was seen a long blade in the hand of the gambler. It shot forward, and a human body, this citadel of virtue, wisdom, power, was pierced as easily as if it had been a melon. The Swede fell with a cry of supreme astonishment.

The prominent merchants and the district attorney must have at once tumbled out of the place backward. The bartender found himself hanging limply to the arm of a chair and gazing into the eyes of a murderer.

"Henry," said the latter, as he wiped his knife on one of the towels that hung beneath the bar rail, "you tell 'em where to find me. I'll be home, waiting for 'em." Then he vanished. A moment afterward the barkeeper was in the street dinning through the storm for help and, moreover, companionship.

The corpse of the Swede, alone in the saloon, had its eyes fixed upon a dreadful legend that dwelt atop of the cash-machine: This registers the amount of your purchase."

IX

Months later, the cowboy was frying pork over the stove of a little ranch near the Dakota line, when there was a quick thud of hoofs outside, and presently the Easterner entered with the letters and the papers.

"Well," said the Easterner at once, "the chap that killed the Swede has got three years. Wasn't much, was it?"

"He has? Three years?" The cowboy poised his pan of pork, while he ruminated upon the news. "Three years. That ain't much."

"No. It was a light sentence," replied the Easterner as he unbuckled his spurs. "Seems there was a good deal of sympathy for him in Romper."

"If the bartender had been any good," observed the cowboy, thoughtfully, "he would have gone in and cracked that there Dutchman on the head with a bottle in the beginnin' of it and stopped all this here murderin'."

"Yes, a thousand things might have happened," said the Easterner, tartly.

The cowboy returned his pan of pork to the fire, but his philosophy continued. "It's funny, ain't it? If he hadn't said Johnnie was cheatin' he'd be alive this minute. He was an awful fool. Game played for fun, too. Not for money. I believe he was crazy."

"I feel sorry for that gambler," said the Easterner.

"Oh, so do I," said the cowboy. "He don't deserve none of it for killin' who he did."

"The Swede might not have been killed if everything had been square."

"Might not have been killed?" exclaimed the cowboy. "Everythin' square? Why, when he said that Johnnie was cheatin' and acted like such a jackass? And then in the saloon he fairly walked up to git hurt?" With these arguments the cowboy browbeat the Easterner and reduced him to rage.

"You're a fool!" cried the Easterner, viciously. "You're a bigger jackass than the Swede by a million majority. Now let me tell you one thing. Let me tell you something. Listen! Johnnie *was* cheating!"

"'Johnnie,'" said the cowboy, blankly. There was a minute of silence, and then he said, robustly, "Why, no. The game was only for fun."

"Fun or not," said the Easterner, "Johnnie was cheating. I saw him. I know it. I saw him. And I refused to stand up and be a man. I let the Swede fight it out alone. And you—you were simply puffing around the place and wanting to fight. And then old Scully himself! We are all in it! This poor gambler isn't even a noun. He is kind of an adverb. Every sin is the result of a collaboration. We, five of us, have collaborated in the murder of this Swede. Usually there are from a dozen to forty women really involved in every murder, but in this case it seems to be only five men—you, I, Johnnie, old Scully; and that fool of an unfortunate gambler came merely as a culmination, the apex of a human movement, and gets all the punishment."

The cowboy, injured and rebellious, cried out blindly into this fog of mysterious theory: "Well, I didn't do anythin', did I?"

1870 ∾ *Frank Norris* ∾ 1902

LIKE Crane, Frank Norris mixed fiction with journalism; he served as a war correspondent in the Spanish-American War, and in South Africa during the Boer War. To both journalism and fiction he brought an unusually rich and varied preparation. Born in Chicago, he studied art in Paris, attended the University of California, and had a year at Harvard, where his interest in creative writing was stimulated by the teaching of Lewis E. Gates, a brilliant minor literary critic of the period.

As a novelist and short story writer Norris came to hold definite theories of the purposes and values of fiction, which he set forth in the essays collected after his death in *The Responsibilities of the Novelist* (1903). His earlier work was experimental and inconsistent, ranging from the extreme naturalism of his early novel *McTeague,* begun in college days but not published until 1899, to the unabashed sensational romance of *Moran of the Lady Letty* (1898) and *Blix* (1899). But in the last years of his brief life he projected and in part completed an ambitious fictional project which did square fully with his theories. He proposed to tell in a series of three long novels the story of wheat as a part of the world's life—the life of growers, traders, consumers. The first volume, *The Octopus* (1901), portrays the unequal contest of the farmers in a wheat-growing valley of California with the railroad and its oppressive agencies. The second, *The Pit* (1903), dramatizes the trading in wheat on the old Chicago Board of Trade, and the career of one Curtis Jadwin (there were several parallels in actuality) who tries to corner the wheat of the world. The third volume, to have been called *The Wolf* and to have dealt with famine in Europe and Asia, finally relieved by wheat from America, was planned in broad outline only when Norris died. It has since become one of the best known of America's unwritten books!

One of his earliest naturalistic novels, *Vandover and the Brute,* the manuscript of which was recovered from a crate thought lost in the San Francisco earthquake and fire, was published in 1914 and had some direct influence on the revival of naturalistic fiction in the period between the two World Wars. The best of Norris' short stories are found in *A Deal in Wheat* (1903) and *The Third Circle* (1909), from which "Dying Fires" is reprinted.

[The standard biography of Frank Norris is by Franklin Walker (New York, 1932), and the best critical study is that of Ernest Marchand (Stanford, Cal., 1942). An article by W. D. Howells in the *North American Review* discussed Norris's place in contemporary literature immediately after his death (Dec., 1902). W. F. Taylor's *The Economic Novel in America* (Chapel Hill, 1942) contains a discerning essay.]

DYING FIRES
[1909]

YOUNG OVERBECK'S father was editor and proprietor of the county paper in Colfax, California, and the son, as soon as his high-school days were over, made his appearance in the office as his father's assistant. So abrupt was the transition that his diploma, which was to hang over the editorial desk, had not yet returned from the framer's, while the first copy that he was called on to edit was his own commencement oration on the philosophy of Dante. He had worn a white piqué cravat and a cutaway coat on the occasion of its delivery, and the county commissioner, who was the guest of honour on the platform, had congratulated him as he handed him the sheepskin. For Overbeck was the youngest and the brightest member of his class.

Colfax was a lively town in those days. The teaming from the valley over into the mining country on the other side of the Indian River was at its height then. Colfax was the headquarters of the business, and the teamsters—after the long pull up from the Indian River Cañon—showed in-terest in an environment made up chiefly of saloons.

Then there were the mining camps over by Iowa Hill, the Morning Star, the Big Dipper, and farther on, up in the Gold Run country, the Little Providence. There was Dutch Flat, full of Mexican-Spanish girls and "breed" girls, where the dance halls were of equal number with the bars. There was—a little way down the line—Clipper Gap, where the mountain ranches began, and where the mountain cowboy lived up to the traditions of his kind.

And this life, tumultuous, headstrong, vivid in colour, vigorous in action, was bound together by the railroad, which not only made a single community out of all that part of the east slope of the Sierras' foothills, but contributed its own life as well—the life of oilers, engineers, switchmen, eating-house waitresses and cashiers, "lady" operators, conductors, and the like.

Of such a little world news-items are evolved—sometimes even scare-head, double-leaded descriptive articles—supplemented by interviews with sheriffs and ante-mortem statements. Good grist for a county paper; good opportunities for an un-spoiled, observant, imaginative young fellow at the formative period of his life. Such was the time, such the environment, such the conditions that prevailed when young Overbeck, at the age of twenty-one, sat down to the writing of his first novel.

He completed it in five months, and, though he did not know the fact then, the novel was good. It was not great—far from it, but it was not merely clever. Somehow, by a miracle of good fortune, young Overbeck had got started right at the very beginning. He had not been influenced by a fetich of his choice till his work was a mere replica of some other writer's. He was not literary. He had not much time for books. He lived in the midst of a strenuous, eager life, a little primal even yet; a life of passions that were often elemental in their simplicity and directness. His schooling and his newspaper work—it was he who must find or ferret out the news all along the line, from Penrhyn to Emigrant Gap—had taught him observation without—here was the miracle—dulling the edge of his sensitiveness. He saw as those few, few people see who live close to life at the beginning of an epoch. He saw into the life and the heart beneath the life; the life and the heart of Bunt McBride, as with eight horses and much adjuration he negotiated a load of steel "stamps" [1] up the sheer leap of the Indian Cañon; he saw into the life and into the heart of Irma Tejada, who kept case for the faro players at Dutch Flat; he saw into the life and heart of Lizzie Toby, the biscuit-shooter in the railway eating-house, and into the life and heart of "Doc" Twitchel, who had degrees from Edinburgh and Leipsic, and who, for obscure reasons, chose to look after the measles, sprains, and rheumatisms of the countryside.

And besides, there were others and still others, whom young Overbeck learned to know to the very heart of them: blacksmiths, travelling peddlers, section-bosses, miners, horse-wranglers, cow-punchers, the stage-drivers, the storekeeper, the hotelkeeper, the prospector, the seamstress of the town, the postmistress, the schoolmistress, the poetess. Into the lives of these and the hearts of these young Overbeck saw, and the wonder of that sight so overpowered him that he had no thought and no care for other people's books. And he was only twenty-one! Only twenty-one, and yet he saw clearly into the great, complicated, confused human machine that clashed and jarred around him. Only twenty-one, and yet he read the enigma that men of fifty may alone hope to solve! Once in a great while this thing may happen—in such out-of-the-way places as that country around Colfax in Placer County, California, where no outside influences have play, where books are few and misprized and the reading circle a thing unknown. From time to time such men are born, especially along the line of cleavage where the farthest skirmish line of civilization thrusts and girds at the wilderness. A very few find their true profession before the fire is stamped out of them; of these few, fewer still have the force to make themselves heard. Of these last the majority die before they attain the faculty of making their message intelligible. Those that remain are the world's great men.

At the time when his first little book was on its initial journey to the Eastern publishing houses, Overbeck was by no means a great man. The immaturity that was yet his, the lack of knowledge of his tools, clogged his work and befogged his vision. The smooth running of the cogs and the far-darting range of vision would come in the course of the next fifteen years of unrelenting persistence. The ordering and organizing and controlling of his machine he could, with patience and by taking thought, accomplish for himself. The original impetus had come straight from the almighty gods. That impetus was young yet, feeble yet, coming down from so far it was spent by the time it reached the earth—at Colfax, California. A touch now might divert it. Judge with what care such

---

[1] Heavy pestles used for crushing ores.

a thing should be nursed and watched; compared with the delicacy with which it unfolds, the opening of a rosebud is an abrupt explosion. Later on, such insight, such undeveloped genius may become a tremendous world-power, a thing to split a nation in twain as the axe cleaves the block. But at twenty-one, a whisper—and it takes flight; a touch—it withers; the lifting of a finger—it is gone.

The same destiny that had allowed Overbeck to be born, and that thus far had watched over his course, must have inspired his choice, his very first choice, of a publisher, for the manuscript of *The Vision of Bunt McBride* went straight as a homebound bird to the one man of all others who could understand the beginnings of genius and recognize the golden grain of truth in the chaff of unessentials. His name was Conant, and he accepted the manuscript by telegram.

He did more than this, and one evening Overbeck stood on the steps of the postoffice and opened a letter in his hand, and, looking up and off, saw the world transfigured. His chance had come. In half a year of time he had accomplished what other men—other young writers—strive for throughout the best years of their youth. He had been called to New York. Conant had offered him a minor place on his editorial staff.

Overbeck reached the great city a fortnight later, and the cutaway coat and piqué cravat—unworn since Commencement —served to fortify his courage at the first interview with the man who was to make him—so he believed—famous.

Ah, the delights, the excitement, the inspiration of that day! Let those judge who have striven toward the Great City through years of deferred hope and heart sinkings and sacrifice daily renewed. Overbeck's feet were set in those streets whose names had become legendary to his imagination. Public buildings and public squares familiar only through the weekly prints defiled before him like a pageant, but friendly for all that, inviting, even. But the vast conglomerate life that roared by his ears, like the systole and diastole of an almighty heart, was for a moment disquieting. Soon the human resemblance faded. It became as a machine infinitely huge, infinitely formidable. It challenged him with superb condescension.

"I must down you," he muttered, as he made his way toward Conant's, "or you will down me." He saw it clearly. There was no other alternative. The young boy in his foolish finery of a Colfax tailor's make, with no weapons but such wits as the gods had given him, was pitted against the leviathan.

There was no friend nearer than his native state on the fringe of the continent. He was fearfully alone.

But he was twenty-one. The wits that the gods had given him were good, and the fine fire that was within him, the radiant freshness of his nature, stirred and leaped to life at the challenge. Ah, he would win, he would win! And in his exurberance, the first dim consciousness of his power came to him. He could win, he had it in him; he began to see that now. That nameless power was his which would enable him to grip this monstrous life by the very throat, and bring it down on its knee before him to listen respectfully to what he had to say.

The interview with Conant was no less exhilarating. It was in the reception-room of the great house that it took place, and while waiting for Conant to come in, Overbeck, his heart in his mouth, recognized, in the original drawings on the walls, picture after picture, signed by famous illustrators, that he had seen reproduced in Conant's magazine.

Then Conant himself had appeared and shaken the young author's hand a long time, and had talked to him with the utmost kindness of his book, of his plans for the immediate future, of the work he would do in the editorial office and of the next novel he wished him to write.

"We'll only need you here in the mornings," said the editor, "and you can put in your afternoons on your novel. Have you anything in mind as good as *Bunt Mc-Bride?*"

"I have a sort of notion for one," hazarded the young man; and Conant had demanded to hear it.

Stammering, embarrassed, Overbeck outlined it.

"I see, I see!" Conant commented. "Yes, there is a good story in that. Maybe Hastings will want to use it in the monthly. But we'll make a book of it, anyway, if you work it up as well as the McBride story."

And so the young fellow made his first step in New York. The very next day he began his second novel.

In the editorial office, where he spent his mornings reading proof and making up "front matter," he made the acquaintance of a middle-aged lady, named Miss Patten, who asked him to call on her, and later on introduced him into the "set" wherein she herself moved. The set called itself the "New Bohemians," and once a week met at Miss Patten's apartment uptown. In a month's time Overbeck was a fixture in "New Bohemia."

It was made up of minor poets whose opportunity in life was the blank space on a magazine page below the end of an article; of men past their prime, who, because of an occasional story in a second-rate monthly, were considered to have "arrived"; of women who translated novels from the Italian and Hungarian; of decayed dramatists who could advance unimpeachable reasons for the non-production of their plays; of novelists whose books were declined by publishers because of professional jealousy on the part of the "readers," or whose ideas, stolen by false friends, had appeared in books that sold by the hundreds of thousands. In public the New Bohemians were fulsome in the praise of one another's productions. Did a sonnet called, perhaps, "A Cryptogram Is Stella's Soul" appear in a current issue, they fell on it with eager eyes, learned it by heart, and recited lines of it aloud; the

conceit of the lover translating the cipher by the key of love was welcomed with transports of delight.

"Ah, one of the most exquisitely delicate allegories I've ever heard, and so true—so 'in the tone'!"

Did a certain one of the third-rate novelists, reading aloud from his unpublished manuscript, say of his heroine: "It was the native catholicity of his temperament that lent strength and depth to her innate womanliness," the phrase was snapped up on the instant.

"How he understands women!"

"Such *finesse*! More subtle than Henry James."

"Paul Bourget has gone no further," said one of the critics of New Bohemia; "our limitations are determined less by our renunciations than by our sense of proportion in our conception of ethical standards."

The set abased itself. "Wonderful, ah, how pitilessly you fathom our poor human nature!" New Bohemia saw colour in word effects. A poet read aloud:

"The stalwart rain!
Ah, the rush of down-toppling waters;
The torrent!
Merge of mist and musky air;
The current
Sweeps thwart my blinded sight again."

"Ah!" exclaimed one of the audience, "see, see that bright green flash!"

Thus in public. In private all was different. Walking home with one or another of the set, young Overbeck heard their confidences.

"Keppler is a good fellow right enough, but, my goodness, he can't write verse!"

"That thing of Miss Patten's to-night! Did you ever hear anything so unconvincing, so obvious? Poor old woman!"

"I'm really sorry for Martens; awfully decent sort, but he never should try to write novels."

By rapid degrees young Overbeck caught the lingo of the third-raters. He could talk about "tendencies" and the "influence of reactions." Such and such a writer had a "sense of form," another a "feeling for word effects." He knew all about "tones" and "notes" and "philistinisms." He could tell the difference between an allegory and a simile as far as he could see them. An anti-climax was the one unforgivable sin under heaven. A mixed metaphor made him wince, and a split infinitive hurt him like a blow.

But the great word was "convincing." To say a book was convincing was to give posterity the last verdict. To be "unconvincing" was to be shut out from the elect. If the New Bohemian decided that the last popular book was unconvincing, there was no appeal. The book was not to be mentioned in polite conversation.

And the author of *The Vision of Bunt McBride,* as yet new to the world as the day he was born, with all his eager ambition and quick sensitiveness, thought that all this was the real thing. He had never so much as seen literary people before. How could he know the difference? He honestly believed that New Bohemia was the true literary force of New York. He wrote home that the association with such people, thinkers, poets, philosophers, was an inspiration; that he had learned more in one week in their company than he had learned in Colfax in a whole year.

Perhaps, too, it was the flattery he received that helped to carry Overbeck off his feet. The New Bohemians made a little lion of him when *Bunt McBride* reached its modest pinnacle of popularity. They kowtowed to him, and toadied to him, and fagged and tooted for him, and spoke of his book as a masterpiece. They said he had succeeded where Kipling had ignominiously failed. They said there was more harmony of prose effects in one chapter of *Bunt McBride* than in everything that Bret Harte ever wrote. They told him he was a second Stevenson—only with more refinement.

Then the women of the set, who were of those who did not write, who called them-

selves "mere dilettantes," but who "took an interest in young writers" and liked to influence their lives and works, began to flutter and buzz around him. They told him that they understood him; that they understood his temperament; that they could see where his forte lay; and they undertook his education.

There was in *The Vision of Bunt McBride* a certain sane and healthy animalism that hurt nobody, and that, no doubt, Overbeck, in later books, would modify. He had taken life as he found it to make his book; it was not his fault that the teamsters, biscuit-shooters, and "breed" girls of the foothills were coarse in fibre. In his sincerity he could not do otherwise in his novel than paint life as he saw it. He had dealt with it honestly; he did not dab at the edge of the business; he had sent his fist straight through it.

But the New Bohemians could not abide this.

"Not so much *faroucherie*,[2] you dear young Lochinvar!" they said. "Art must uplift. 'Look thou not down, but up toward uses of a cup';"[3] and they supplemented the quotation by lines from Walter Pater, and read to him from Ruskin and Matthew Arnold.

Ah, the spiritual was the great thing. We were here to make the world brighter and better for having lived in it. The passions of a waitress in a railway eating-house—how sordid the subject. Dear boy, look for the soul, strive to rise to higher planes! Tread upward; every book should leave a clean taste in the mouth, should tend to make one happier, should elevate, not debase.

So by degrees Overbeck began to see his future in a different light. He began to think that he really had succeeded where Kipling had failed; that he really was Stevenson with more refinement, and that the one and only thing lacking in his work was soul. He believed that he must strive

---

[2] Wildness or savagery.

[3] From Browning's "Rabbi Ben Ezra."

for the spiritual, and "let the ape and tiger die." The originality and unconventionality of his little book he came to regard as crudities.

"Yes," he said one day to Miss Patten and a couple of his friends, "I have been re-reading my book of late. I can see its limitations—now. It has a lack of form; the tonality is a little false. It fails somehow to convince."

Thus the first winter passed. In the mornings Overbeck assiduously edited copy and made up front matter on the top floor of the Conant building. In the evenings he called on Miss Patten, or some other member of the set. Once a week, uptown, he fed fat on the literary delicatessen that New Bohemia provided. In the meantime, every afternoon, from luncheon-time till dark, he toiled on his second novel, *Renunciations*. The environment of *Renunciations* was a far cry from Colfax, California. It was a city-bred story, with no fresher atmosphere than that of bought flowers. Its *dramatis personae* were all of the leisure class, opera-goers, intriguers, riders of blood horses, certainly more refined than Lizzie Toby, biscuit-shooter, certainly more *spirituelle* than Irma Tejada, case-keeper in Dog Omahone's faro joint, certainly more elegant than Bunt McBride, teamster of the Colfax Iowa Hill Freight Transportation Company.

From time to time, as the novel progressed, he read it to the dilettante women whom he knew best among the New Bohemians. They advised him as to its development, and "influenced" its outcome and dénouement.

"I think you have found your *métier*, dear boy," said one of them, when *Renunciations* was nearly completed. "To portray the concrete—is it not a small achievement, sublimated journalese, nothing more? But to grasp abstractions, to analyze a woman's soul, to evoke the spiritual essence in humanity, as you have done in your ninth chapter of *Renunciations*—that is the true function of art. *Je vous fais mes compliments.*[4] *Renunciations* is a *chef-d'oeuvre*.

Can't you see yourself what a stride you have made, how much broader your outlook has become, how much more catholic, since the days of *Bunt McBride?*"

To be sure, Overbeck could see it. Ah, he was growing, he was expanding. He was mounting higher planes. He was more —catholic. That, of all words, was the one to express his mood. Catholic, ah, yes, he was catholic!

When *Renunciations* was finished he took the manuscript to Conant and waited a fortnight in an agony of suspense and repressed jubilation for the great man's verdict. He was all the more anxious to hear it because, every now and then, while writing the story, doubts—distressing, perplexing—had intruded. At times and all of a sudden, after days of the steadiest footing, the surest progress, the story—the whole set and trend of the affair—would seem, as it were, to escape from his control. Where once, in *Bunt McBride*, he had gripped, he must now grope. What was it? He had been so sure of himself; with all the stimulus of new surroundings, the work in this second novel should have been all the easier. But the doubt would fade, and for weeks he would plough on, till again, and all unexpectedly, he would find himself in an agony of indecision as to the outcome of some vital pivotal episode of the story. Of two methods of treatment, both equally plausible, he could not say which was the true, which the false; and he must needs take, as it were, a leap in the dark —it was either that or abandoning the story, trusting to mere luck that he would, somehow, be carried through.

A fortnight after he had delivered the manuscript to Conant he presented himself in the publisher's office.

"I was just about to send for you," said Conant. "I finished your story last week."

There was a pause. Overbeck settled himself comfortably in his chair, but his nails were cutting his palms.

---

[4] I compliment you.

"Hastings has read it, too—and—well, frankly, Overbeck, we were disappointed."

"Yes?" inquired Overbeck calmly. "H'm —that's too b-bad."

He could not hear, or at least could not understand, just what the publisher said next. Then, after a time that seemed immeasurably long, he caught the words:

"It would not do you a bit of good, my boy, to have us publish it—it would harm you. There are a good many things I would lie about, but books are not included. This *Renunciations* of yours is—is, why, confound it, Overbeck, it's foolishness."

Overbeck went out and sat on a bench in a square near by, looking vacantly at a fountain as it rose and fell and rose again with an incessant cadenced splashing. Then he took himself home to his hall bedroom. He had brought the manuscript of his novel with him, and for a long time he sat at his table listlessly turning the leaves, confused, stupid, all but inert. The end, however, did not come suddenly. A few weeks later *Renunciations* was published, but not by Conant. It bore the imprint of an obscure firm in Boston. The covers were of limp dressed leather, olive-green, and could be tied together by thongs, like a portfolio. The sale stopped after five hundred copies had been ordered, and the real critics, those who did not belong to New Bohemia, hardly so much as noticed the book.

In the autumn, when the third-raters had come back from their vacations, the "evenings" at Miss Patten's were resumed, and Overbeck hurried to the very first meeting. He wanted to talk it all over with them. In his chagrin and cruel disappointment he was hungry for some word of praise, of condolement. He wanted to be told again, even though he had begun to suspect many things, that he had succeeded where Kipling had failed, that he was Stevenson with more refinement.

But the New Bohemians, the same women and fakirs and half-baked minor poets who had "influenced" him and had ruined him, could hardly find time to notice him now.

The guest of the evening was a new little lion who had joined the set. A symbolist versifier who wrote over the pseudonym of de la Houssaye, with black oily hair and long white hands; him the Bohemians thronged about in crowds as before they had thronged about Overbeck. Only once did any one of them pay attention to the latter. This was the woman who had nicknamed him "Young Lochinvar." Yes, she had read *Renunciations,* a capital little thing, a little thin in parts, lacking in *finesse.* He must strive for his true medium of expression, his true note. Ah, art was long! Study of the new symbolists would help him. She would beg him to read Monsieur de la Houssaye's *The Monoliths.* Such subtlety, such delicious word-chords! It could not fail to inspire him.

Shouldered off, forgotten, the young fellow crept back to his little hall bedroom and sat down to think it over. There in the dark of the night his eyes were opened, and he saw, at last, what these people had done to him; saw the Great Mistake, and that he had wasted his substance.

The golden apples, that had been his for the stretching of the hand, he had flung from him. Tricked, trapped, exploited, he had prostituted the great good thing that had been his by right divine, for the privilege of eating husks with swine. Now was the day of the mighty famine, and the starved and broken heart of him, crying out for help, found only a farrago of empty phrases.

He tried to go back; he did, in very fact, go back to the mountains and the canyons of the great Sierras. "He arose and went to his father," [5] and, with such sapped and broken strength as New Bohemia had left him, strove to wrest some wreckage from the dying fire.

But the ashes were cold by now. The fire that the gods had allowed him to snatch, because he was humble and pure and clean and brave, had been stamped out beneath the feet of minor and dilettante poets, and

---

[5] Luke 15:20.

now the gods guarded close the brands that yet remained on the altars.

They may not be violated twice, those sacred fires. Once in a lifetime the very young and the pure in heart may see the shine of them and pluck a brand from the altar's edge. But, once possessed, it must be watched with a greater vigilance than even that of the gods, for its light will live only for him who snatched it first. Only for him that shields it, even with his life, from the contact of the world does it burst into a burning, and a shining light. Let once the touch of alien fingers disturb it, and there remains only a little heap of bitter ashes.

1868 ∞ *Finley Peter Dunne* ∞ 1936

A DECADE of newspaper work in his home town of Chicago prepared Finley Peter Dunne for the creation of his saloonkeeper-philosopher of "Archey Road," Mr. Dooley. At first merely a part of Dunne's editorial stint, the Dooley sketches became a national institution after their publication in book form in *Mr. Dooley in War and Peace* (1898) and *Mr. Dooley in the Hearts of His Countrymen* (1899). Dunne shortly moved to New York, and was prominent in literary circles there for many years, keeping up with some difficulty and loss of power a steady flow of the dialect essays. He was one of the editors of the *American Magazine* during its "muck-raking" period.

Especially in the earlier sketches, Dunne used the humorous monologues of Mr. Dooley for pointed social comment, marked by abundant irony and the emphasis of understatement.

[*Mr. Dooley's America* (New York, 1941) is a biography by Elmer Ellis.]

WHEN THE TRUST IS AT WORK
[1899]

"WHICH d'ye think makes th' best fun'ral turnout, th' A-ho-aitches [1] or th' Saint Vincent de Pauls,[2] Jawn?" asked Mr. Dooley.

"I don't know," said Mr. McKenna. "Are you thinking of leaving us?"

"Faith, I am not," said Mr. Dooley. "Since th' warm weather's come an' th' wind's in th' south, so that I can tell at night that A-armoor an' me ol' frind, Jawn Brinnock, are attindin' to business, I have a grip on life like th' wan ye have on th' shank iv that shell iv malt. Whether 'tis these soft days, with th' childher beginnin' to play barefutted in th' sthreet an' th' good women out to palaver over th' fence without their shawls, or whether 'tis th' wan wurrud Easter Sundah that comes on me, an' jolts me up with th' thoughts iv th' la-ads goin' to mass an' th' blackthorn turning green beyant, I dinnaw. But annyhow I'm as gay as a babby an' as fresh as a lark. I am so.

"I was on'y thinkin'. Ol' Gran'pah Grogan died las' Mondah,—as good a man as e'er counted his beads or passed th' plate. A thrue man. Choosdah a Connock man up back iv th' dumps laid down th' shovel. Misther Grogan had a grand notice in th' pa-apers: 'Grogan, at his late residence, 279 A-archoor Avnoo, Timothy Alexander, beloved husband iv th' late Mary Grogan, father iv Maurice, Michael, Timothy, Edward, James, Peter, Paul, an'

---

[1] Ancient Order of Hibernians.
[2] Catholic lay society.

Officer Andrew Grogan, iv Cologne Sthreet station, an' iv Mrs. Willum Sarsfield Cassidy, nee Grogan' (which manes that was her name befure she marrid Cassidy, who wurruks down be Haley's packin'-house). 'Fun'ral be carriages fr'm his late risidence to Calv'ry cimithry. Virginia City, Nivida; St. Joseph, Mitchigan; an' Clonmel Tipp'rary pa-apers please copy.'

"I didn't see e'er a nee about th' fam'ly iv th' little man back iv th' dumps, though maybe he had wan to set aroun' th' fire in th' dark an' start at th' tap iv a heel on th' dure-step. Mebbe he had a fam'ly, poor things. A fun'ral is great la-arks, f'r th' neighbors, an' 'tis not so bad f'r the corpse. But in these times, Jawn dear, a-ho th' gray hearts left behind an' th' hungry mouths to feed. They done th' best they cud f'r th' Connock man back iv th' dumps,—give him all th' honors, th' A-ho-aitches ma-archin' behind th' hearse an' th' band playin' th' Dead March. 'Twas almost as good a turnout as Grogan had, though th' Saint Vincents had bedther hats an' looked more like their fam'lies kept a cow.

"But they was two hacks back iv th' pall-bearers. I wondhered what was passin' behind th' faces I seen again their windys. 'Twas well f'r himself, too. Little odds to him, afther th' last screw was twisted be Gavin's ol' yellow hands, whether beef was wan cint or a hundherd dollars th' pound. But there's comin' home as well as goin' out. There's more to a fun'ral thin th' lucks parpitua, an' th' clod iv sullen earth on th' top iv th' crate. Sare a pax vobiscum is there f'r them that's huddled in th' ol' hack, sthragglin' home in th' dust to th' empty panthry an' th' fireless grate.

"Mind ye, Jawn, I've no wurrud to say again thim that sets back in their own house an' lot an' makes th' food iv th' people dear. They're good men, good men. Whin they tilt th' price iv beef to where wan pound iv it costs as much as manny th' man in this Ar-rchey Road'd wurruk fr'm th' risin' to th' settin' iv the sun to get, they have no thought iv th' likes iv you

an' me. 'Tis aisy come, aisy go with thim; an' ivry cint a pound manes a new art musoom or a new church, to take th' edge off hunger. They're all right, thim la-ads, with their own porkchops delivered free at th' door. 'Tis, 'Will ye have a new spring dhress, me dear? Willum, ring thim up, an' tell thim to hist th' price iv beef. If we had a few more pitchers an' statoos in th' musoom, 'twud ilivate th' people a sthory or two. Wullum, afther this steak'll be twinty cints a pound.' Oh, they're all right, on'y I was thinkin' iv th' Connock man's fam'ly back iv th' dumps."

"For a man that was gay a little while ago, it looks to me as if you'd grown mighty solemn-like," said Mr. McKenna.

"Mebbe so," said Mr. Dooley. "Mebbe so. What th' 'ell, annyhow. Mebbe 'tis as bad to take champagne out iv wan man's mouth as round steak out iv another's. Lent is near over. I seen Doherty out shinin' up his pipe that's been behind th' clock since Ash Winsdah. Th' girls'll be layin' lilies on th' altar in a day or two. Th' spring's come on. Th' grass is growin' good; an', if th' Connock man's children back iv th' dumps can't get meat, they can eat hay."

THE UNION OF TWO GREAT FORTUNES
[1899]

"THEY'SE WAN THING that always makes me feel sure iv what Hogan calls th' safety iv our dimmycratic institutions," said Mr. Dooley, "an that's th' intherest th' good people iv New York takes in a weddin' iv th' millyionaires. Anny time a millyionaire condiscinds to enther th' martial state, as Hogan says, an', as Hogan says, make vows to Hyman, which is the Jew god iv marredge, he can fill th' house an' turn people away fr'm th' dure. An' he does. Th' sthreets is crowded. Th' cars can har'ly get through. Th' polis foorce is out, an' hammerin' th' heads iv 'th delighted throng. Riprisintatives iv th' free an' inlightened press, th' pollutyem [3] iv our lib-

---

[3] Palladium.

erties, as Hogan says, bright, intilligent young journalists, iver ready to probe fraud an' sham, disgeesed as waithers, is dashin' madly about, makin' notes on their cuffs. Business is suspinded. They'se no money in Wall Sthreet. It's all at th' sacred scene. Hour be hour, as th' prisints ar-re delivered, th' bank rates go up. Th' Threeasury Departmint has to go on a silver basis, there bein' no goold to manny-facther into plunks.

"Inside th' house th' prisints cast a goolden gleam on th' beauchious scene. Th' happy father is seen seated at a table, dictatin' millyion-dollar checks to a stinog-rapher. Th' goold chandeliers is draped with r-ropes iv di'mon's and pearls. Th' hired girl is passin' dhrinks in goolden goblets. Twinty firemen fr'm th' New York Cinthral Railroad is shovelin' di-mon'-stud-ded pickle crutes into th' back yard, among th' yachts an' horses. Chansy Depoo [4] enthers an' thrips over a box iv bonds. 'Ar-re these th' holy bonds iv mathrimony?' he says; f'r he is a wild divvle, an' ye can't stop his jokin', avin on solemn occasions.

"Th' soggarth [5] comes in afther a while, carryin' a goold prayer-book, th' gift iv th' Rothscheelds, an' stands behind a small but valyable pree Doo. To th' soft, meelo-jous chune iv th' Wagner Palace Weddin' March fr'm 'Long Green,' th' groom en-thers, simply but ixpinsively attired in governmint fours, an' fannin' himsilf with a bunch iv first mortgedge bonds.

"Th' prayers f'r th' occasion, printed on negotyable paper, is disthributed among th' guests. Th' bride was delayed be th' crowd outside. Women screamed an' waved their handkerchefs, sthrong men cheered an' wept; an' 'twas not until th' polis had clubbed tin hardy pathrites to death that th' lady cud enther th' house where her fate was to be sealed. But fin'lly she med it; an' th' two happy, happy childher, whose sunshiny youth riprisinted five thousan' miles iv thrack, eight goold mines, wan hundherd millyion dollars' worth iv rollin' stock, an' a majority intherest in th' Chicago stock yards, was r-ready f'r th'

nicissary thransfers that wud establish th' com-bination.

"Th' ceremony was brief, but inthrestin'. Th' happy father foorced his way through di'mon' stomachers; an' they was tears in his eyes as he handed th' clargyman, whose name was Murphy,—but he carried him-silf as well as if he was used to it,—handed him a check f'r tin millyion dollars. I don't blame him. Divvle th' bit! Me own hear-rt is har-rd an' me eyes ar-re dhry, but I'd break down if I had to hand anny wan that much. 'I suppose th' check is good,' says th' clargyman. ' 'Tis certified,' says th' weepin' father. 'Do ye take this check,' says th' clargyman, 'to have an' to hold, until some wan parts ye fr'm it?' he says. 'I do,' says th' young man. 'Thin,' says th' clargyman, 'I see no reason why ye shudden't be mar-rid an' live comfortable,' he says. An' mar-rid they were, in th' same ol' foolish way that people's been marrid in f'r cinchries. 'Tis a wondher to me th' ceremony ain't changed. Th' time is comin', Hinnissy, whin millyionaires'll not be marrid be Father Murphy, but be th' gov'nors iv th' stock exchange. They'll be put through th' clearin' house, me faith, an' securities'll be issued by th' combination. Twinty-year, goold-secured, four per cint. bonds iv mathrimony! Aha, 'tis a joke that Chansy Depoo might've med!

"Th' crowd outside waited, cheerin' an' fightin' th' polis. In this here land iv lib-erty an' akequality, Hinnissy, ivry man is as good as ivry other man, except a polis-man. An' it showed how thrue th' people in New York is to th' thraditions iv Jefferson that divvle a wan iv thim'd move away till th' check'd been passed fr'm father to son, an' th' important part iv th' sacred ceremony was over. Thin a few iv thim wint home to cook dinner f'r their hus-bands, who was previnted be their jooties at th' gas-house fr'm attindin' th' function.

---

[4] Chauncey Mitchell Depew (1834-1928), New York financier, legislator, and lawyer. Renowned in Dunne's time as socialite and wit.

[5] Irish for priest.

Th' rest raymained an' see th' two gr-reat fortunes get into their carredge, pursued by th' guests to th' amount iv five hundhred millyions, peltin' thim with seed pearls."

"Sure," said Mr. Hennessy, "mebbe 'twasn't as bad as th' pa-apers let on. Ye can't always thrust thim."

"P'rhaps not," said Mr. Dooley. "Th' pa-apers say, 'Two gr-reat fortunes united'; an', if that's it, they didn't need th' sarvices iv a priest, but a lawyer an' a thrust comp'ny. P'rhaps, with all th' certyfied checks, 'twas two rale people that was marrid; an', if that's so, it explains th' prisince iv Father Murphy."

William Sydney Porter (O. Henry)

1862　∞　1910

A BAD lung sent William Sydney Porter at 20 from the sleepy North Carolina village of Greensboro, where he had spent leisure hours of his job in an uncle's drugstore drawing sketches and spinning yarns, to a ranch in Texas. Of the jobs he held in the next few years, including work as cowboy, newspaper reporter and columnist, and editor of a humorous magazine, a brief one as a bank clerk proved decisive. Some time after the bank had failed he was charged with embezzlement of a relatively small amount of money. Certainly innocent, as subsequent investigation has proved, and on his way to stand trial, he took the wrong train at a junction, fled to Central America, and spent a fantastic year at sea and on land with smugglers and outlaws. When word of his wife's grave illness reached him, he returned to Texas and gave himself up to the authorities, was with his wife until her death, and then was sentenced to the federal penitentiary at Columbus, Ohio.

Considerately treated by the prison authorities, Porter soon began to write, sending his stories to magazines, through a sister in Pittsburgh, under the assumed name "O. Henry." Editors became interested in him, and in 1902, when he was released after serving a minimum term, persuaded him to come to New York.

In his first years of writing he drew on his adventurous experience of the past for material—especially on his Central American days for the stories which made up his first collected volume, *Cabbages and Kings* (1904). Later he made New York City itself his subject. By preference he lived obscurely in poor sections of the city, and wrote of the men and women he saw and knew. Never so well paid as he deserved, and impulsively generous to the needy whom he constantly encountered in his favorite haunts, he wrote under financial pressure until almost the end of his life, in some years producing more than fifty stories. He became the most widely read short story writer of his time, and the style and structure characteristic of his stories, notably the "surprise ending," were widely imitated. The generous entertainment afforded by his work has blinded many readers to the frequent excellence of his style and his occasional powerful expression of social concern.

[Valuable biographical works are *O. Henry Biography* (New York, 1916), by C. Alphonso Smith; *Through the Shadows with O. Henry* (New York, 1921), by A. J. Jennings; and *The Caliph of Bagdad* (New York, 1931), by R. H. Davis and A. B. Maurice.]

THE VOICE OF THE CITY
[1908]

TWENTY-FIVE years ago the school children used to chant their lessons. The manner of their delivery was a singsong recitative between the utterance of an Episcopal minister and the drone of a tired sawmill. I mean no disrespect. We must have lumber and sawdust.

I remember one beautiful and instructive little lyric that emanated from the physiology class. The most striking line of it was this:

"The shin-bone is the long-est bone in the hu-man bod-y."

What an inestimable boon it would have been if all the corporeal and spiritual facts pertaining to man had thus been tunefully and logically inculcated in our youthful minds! But what we gained in anatomy, music and philosophy was meagre.

The other day I became confused. I needed a ray of light. I turned back to those school days for aid. But in all the nasal harmonies we whined forth from those hard benches I could not recall one that treated of the voice of agglomerated mankind.

In other words, of the composite vocal message of massed humanity.

In other words, of the Voice of a Big City.

Now, the individual voice is not lacking. We can understand the song of the poet, the ripple of the brook, the meaning of the man who wants $5 until next Monday, the inscriptions on the tombs of the Pharaohs, the language of flowers, the "step lively" of the conductor, and the prelude of the milk cans at 4 A.M. Certain large-eared ones even assert that they are wise to the vibrations of the tympanum produced by concussion of the air emanating from Mr. H. James. But who can comprehend the meaning of the voice of the city?

I went out for to see.

First, I asked Aurelia. She wore white Swiss and a hat with flowers on it, and ribbons and ends of things fluttered here and there.

"Tell me," I said, stammeringly, for I have no voice of my own, "what does this big — er— enormous — er— whopping city say? It must have a voice of some kind. Does it ever speak to you? How do you interpret its meaning? It is a tremendous mass, but it must have a key."

"Like a Saratoga trunk?" asked Aurelia.

"No," said I. "Please do not refer to the lid. I have a fancy that every city has a voice. Each one has something to say to the one who can hear it. What does the big one say to you?"

"All cities," said Aurelia, judicially, "say the same thing. When they get through saying it there is an echo from Philadelphia. So, they are unanimous."

"Here are 4,000,000 people," said I, scholastically, "compressed upon an island, which is mostly land surrounded by Wall Street water. The conjunction of so many units into so small a space must result in an identity—or, or rather a homogeneity —that finds its oral expression through a common channel. It is, as you might say, a consensus of translation, concentrating in a crystallized, general idea which reveals itself in what may be termed the Voice of the City. Can you tell me what it is?"

Aurelia smiled wonderfully. She sat on the high stoop. A spray of insolent ivy bobbed against her right ear. A ray of impudent moonlight flickered upon her nose. But I was adamant, nickel-plated.

"I must go and find out," I said, "what is the Voice of the city. Other cities have voices. It is an assignment. I must have it. New York," I continued, in a rising tone, "had better not hand me a cigar and say: 'Old man, I can't talk for publication.' No other city acts in that way. Chicago says, unhesitatingly, 'I will;' Philadelphia says, 'I should;' New Orleans says, 'I used to;' Louisville says, 'Don't care if I do;' St. Louis says, 'Excuse me;' Pittsburg says, 'Smoke up.' Now, New York——"

Aurelia smiled.

"Very well," said I, "I must go elsewhere and find out."

I went into a palace, tile-floored, cherub-ceilinged and square with the cop. I put my foot on the brass rail and said to Billy Magnus, the best bartender in the diocese:

"Billy, you've lived in New York a long time—what kind of a song-and-dance does this old town give you? What I mean is, doesn't the gab of it seem to kind of bunch up and slide over the bar to you in a sort of amalgamated tip that hits off the burg in a kind of an epigram with a dash of bitters and a slice of——"

"Excuse me a minute," said Billy, "somebody's punching the button at the side door."

He went away; came back with an empty tin bucket; again vanished with it full; returned and said to me:

"That was Mame. She rings twice. She likes a glass of beer for supper. Her and the kid. If you ever saw that little skee-sicks of mine brace up in his high chair and take his beer and— But, say, what was yours? I get kind of excited when I hear them two rings—was it the baseball score or gin fizz you asked for?"

"Ginger ale," I answered.

I walked up to Broadway. I saw a cop on the corner. The cops take kids up, women across, and men in. I went up to him.

"If I'm not exceeding the spiel limit," I said, "let me ask you. You see New York during its vocative hours. It is the function of you and your brother cops to preserve the acoustics of the city. There must be a civic voice that is intelligible to you. At night during your lonely rounds you must have heard it. What is the epitome of its turmoil and shouting? What does the city say to you?"

"Friend," said the policeman, spinning his club, "it don't say nothing. I get my orders from the man higher up. Say, I guess you're all right. Stand here for a few minutes and keep an eye open for the roundsman."

The cop melted into the darkness of the side street. In ten minutes he had returned.

"Married last Tuesday," he said, half gruffly. "You know how they are. She comes to that corner at nine every night for a—comes to say 'hello!' I generally manage to be there. Say, what was it you asked me a bit ago—what's doing in the city? Oh, there's a roof-garden or two just opened, twelve blocks up."

I crossed a crow's-foot of street-car tracks, and skirted the edge of an umbrageous park. An artificial Diana, gilded, heroic, poised, wind-ruled, on the tower, shimmered in the clear light of her namesake in the sky. Along came my poet, hurrying, hatted, haired, emitting dactyls, spondees and dactylis. I seized him.

"Bill," said I (in the magazine he is Cleon), "give me a lift. I am on an assignment to find out the Voice of the city. You see, it's a special order. Ordinarily a symposium comprising the views of Henry Clews, John L. Sullivan, Edwin Markham, May Irwin and Charles Schwab [1] would be

---

[1] Henry Clews (1834-1923) was a prominent banker. John L. Sullivan (1858-1918) was American heavyweight champion from 1882 to 1892. Edwin Markham (1852-1940) was a popular poet and lecturer, author of The Man with the Hoe (1899). May Irwin (1862-1938) was a famous actress. Charles M. Schwab (1862-1939) was president of the Carnegie Steel Company from 1897 to 1901, and later held other major positions in American industry.

about all. But this is a different matter. We want a broad, poetic, mystic vocalization of the city's soul and meaning. You are the very chap to give me a hint. Some years ago a man got at the Niagara Falls and gave us its pitch. The note was about two feet below the lowest G on the piano. Now, you can't put New York into a note unless it's better indorsed than that. But give me an idea of what it would say if it should speak. It is bound to be a mighty and far-reaching utterance. To arrive at it we must take the tremendous crash of the chords of the day's traffic, the laughter and music of the night, the solemn tones of Dr. Parkhurst,[2] the rag-time, the weeping, the stealthy hum of cab-wheels, the shout of the press agent, the tinkle of fountains on the roof gardens, the hullabaloo of the strawberry vender and the covers of *Everybody's Magazine,* the whispers of the lovers in the parks—all these sounds must go into your Voice—not combined, but mixed, and of the mixture an essence made; and of the essence an extract—an audible extract, of which one drop shall form the thing we seek."

"Do you remember," asked the poet, with a chuckle, "that California girl we met at Stiver's studio last week? Well, I'm on my way to see her. She repeated that poem of mine, 'The Tribute of Spring,' word for word. She's the smartest proposition in this town just at present. Say, how does this confounded tie look? I spoiled four before I got one to set right."

"And the Voice that I asked you about?" I inquired.

"Oh, she doesn't sing," said Cleon. "But you ought to hear her recite my 'Angel of the Inshore Wind.'"

I passed on. I cornered a newsboy and he flashed at me prophetic pink papers that outstripped the news by two revolutions of the clock's longest hand.

"Son," I said, while I pretended to chase coins in my penny pocket, "doesn't it sometimes seem to you as if the city ought to be able to talk? All these ups and downs and funny business and queer things happening every day—what would it say, do you think, if it could speak?"

"Quit yer kiddin'," said the boy. "Wot paper yer want? I got no time to waste. It's Mag's birthday, and I want thirty cents to git her a present."

Here was no interpreter of the city's mouthpiece. I bought a paper, and consigned its undeclared treaties, its premeditated murders and unfought battles to an ash can.

Again I repaired to the park and sat in the moon shade. I thought and thought, and wondered why none could tell me what I asked for.

And then, as swift as light from a fixed star, the answer came to me. I arose and hurried—hurried as so many reasoners must, back around my circle. I knew the answer and I hugged it in my breast as I flew, fearing lest some one would stop me and demand my secret.

Aurelia was still on the stoop. The moon was higher and the ivy shadows were deeper. I sat at her side and we watched a little cloud tilt at the drifting moon and go asunder, quite pale and discomfited.

And then, wonder of wonders and delight of delights! our hands somehow touched, and our fingers closed together and did not part.

After half an hour Aurelia said, with that smile of hers:

"Do you know, you haven't spoken a word since you came back!"

"That," said I, nodding wisely, "is the Voice of the City."

---

[2] Charles Henry Parkhurst (1842-1933), prominent New York clergyman and reformer.

1876 ∽ *Jack London* ∽ 1916

VIVID pictures of Jack London's boyhood are to be found in the pages of the autobiographical *John Barleycorn* (1913), one of his latest and best books. Born in San Francisco and spending most of his early years on its streets and waterfront and on nearby farms, London saw little more of schools than one year at an Oakland grammar school and part of another at the University of California. His real education came in work on ranches and ships and in roaming much of the United States and Canada as a hobo. Of all prominent American writers, only Melville brought to his literary work so varied and adventurous a background.

Early resolved to be a writer, London found his best material in Alaska during the Klondike gold rush, and a market—after long discouragement—for the stories he made of that experience. His profuse output was soon eagerly sought by popular magazines, and collected in book form. His first volume was *The Son of the Wolf* (1900), followed by *The God of His Fathers* (1901), *A Daughter of the Snows* (1902), *Children of the Frost* (1902), and *The Call of the Wild* (1903). The last of these clinched his fame, and thereafter he was one of the best-paid of American writers.

London's life as a tramp and ordinary workman had made him a rebel and study had made him a Socialist, and for years he carried a red card and served the party as speaker and organizer. Much of his writing expressed the social protest reflected in this activity, notably *The People of the Abyss* (1903), which is based on a stay in London, *War of the Classes* (1905), and *The Iron Heel* (1908). Adding the reading of Darwin, Spencer, and Huxley to his personal observation, London developed a crude personal philosophy of materialism and naturalism, best expressed in what is probably his most powerful novel, *The Sea Wolf* (1904).

Most of London's later work was produced frankly for the money which he used in cruising the South Seas in his own ship, as reported in *The Cruise of the Snark* (1911), and in establishing and maintaining a large ranch in California. However, the autobiographical novel *Martin Eden* (1908) is genuinely interesting, and reveals much both of London's own life and personality and of the literary period in which he wrote. "The Apostate" is reprinted from *When God Laughs and Other Stories* (1911), one of his numerous collections.

[The standard biography of London was written by his wife, Charmian London: *The Book of Jack London*, 2 vols. (New York, 1921). Also of interest are G. L. Bamford's *The Mystery of Jack London* (New York, 1931), Irving Stone's *Sailor on Horseback* (New York, 1938), and Joan London's *Jack London and His Times* (New York, 1939). Philip S. Foner has edited *Jack London, American Rebel* (New York, 1947), a collection of social writings with an extended introduction.]

THE APOSTATE
[1911]

Now I wake me up to work;
I pray the Lord I may not shirk.
If I should die before the night,
I pray the Lord my work's all right.
Amen.

"IF YOU DON'T git up, Johnny, I won't give you a bite to eat!"

The threat had no effect on the boy. He clung stubbornly to sleep, fighting for its oblivion as the dreamer fights for his dream. The boy's hands loosely clenched themselves, and he made feeble, spasmodic blows at the air. These blows were intended for his mother, but she betrayed practised familiarity in avoiding them as she shook him roughly by the shoulder.

"Lemme 'lone!"

It was a cry that began, muffled, in the deeps of sleep, that swiftly rushed upward, like a wail, into passionate belligerence, and that died away and sank down into an inarticulate whine. It was a bestial cry, as of a soul in torment, filled with infinite protest and pain.

But she did not mind. She was a sad-eyed, tired-faced woman, and she had grown used to this task, which she repeated every day of her life. She got a grip on the bedclothes and tried to strip them down; but the boy, ceasing his punching, clung to them desperately. In a huddle, at the foot of the bed, he still remained covered. Then she tried dragging the bedding to the floor. The boy opposed her. She braced herself. Hers was the superior weight, and the boy and bedding gave, the former instinctively following the latter in order to shelter against the chill of the room that bit into his body.

As he toppled on the edge of the bed it seemed that he must fall head-first to the floor. But consciousness fluttered up in him. He righted himself and for a moment perilously balanced. Then he struck the floor on his feet. On the instant his mother seized him by the shoulders and shook him. Again his fists struck out, this time with more force and directness. At the same time his eyes opened. She released him. He was awake.

"All right," he mumbled.

She caught up the lamp and hurried out, leaving him in darkness.

"You'll be docked," she warned back to him.

He did not mind the darkness. When he had got into his clothes, he went out into the kitchen. His tread was very heavy for so thin and light a boy. His legs dragged with their own weight, which seemed unreasonable because they were such skinny legs. He drew a broken-bottomed chair to the table.

"Johnny!" his mother called sharply.

He arose as sharply from the chair, and, without a word, went to the sink. It was a greasy, filthy sink. A smell came up from the outlet. He took no notice of it. That a sink should smell was to him part of the natural order, just as it was a part of the natural order that the soap should be grimy with dish-water and hard to lather. Nor did he try very hard to make it lather. Several splashes of the cold water from the running faucet completed the function. He did not wash his teeth. For that matter he had never seen a tooth-brush, nor did he know that there existed beings in the world who were guilty of so great a foolishness as tooth washing.

"You might wash yourself wunst a day without bein' told," his mother complained.

She was holding a broken lid on the pot as she poured two cups of coffee. He made no remark, for this was a standing quarrel between them, and the one thing upon which his mother was hard as adamant. "Wunst" a day it was compulsory that he should wash his face. He dried himself on a greasy towel, damp and dirty and ragged, that left his face covered with shreds of lint.

"I wish we didn't live so far away," she said, as he sat down. "I try to do the best I can. You know that. But a dollar on the rent is such a savin', an' we've more room here. You know that."

He scarcely followed her. He had heard it all before, many times. The range of her thought was limited, and she was ever harking back to the hardship worked upon them by living so far from the mills.

"A dollar means more grub," he remarked sententiously. "I'd sooner do the walkin' an' git the grub."

He ate hurriedly, half chewing the bread and washing the unmasticated chunks down with coffee. The hot and muddy liquid went by the name of coffee. Johnny thought it was coffee—and excellent coffee. That was one of the few of life's illusions that remained to him. He had never drunk real coffee in his life.

In addition to the bread, there was a small piece of cold pork. His mother refilled his cup with coffee. As he was finishing the bread, he began to watch if more was forthcoming. She intercepted his questioning glance.

"Now, don't be hoggish, Johnny," was her comment. "You've had your share. Your brothers an' sisters are smaller'n you."

He did not answer the rebuke. He was not much of a talker. Also, he ceased his hungry glancing for more. He was uncomplaining, with a patience that was as terrible as the school in which it had been learned. He finished his coffee, wiped his mouth on the back of his hand, and started to rise.

"Wait a second," she said hastily. "I guess the loaf kin stand you another slice—a thin un."

There was a legerdemain in her actions. With all the seeming of cutting a slice from the loaf for him, she put loaf and slice back in the bread box and conveyed to him one of her own two slices. She believed she had deceived him, but he had noted her sleight-of-hand. Nevertheless, he took the bread shamelessly. He had a philosophy that his mother, what of her chronic sickliness, was not much of an eater anyway.

She saw that he was chewing the bread dry, and reached over and emptied her coffee cup into his.

"Don't set good somehow on my stomach this morning," she explained.

A distant whistle, prolonged and shrieking, brought both of them to their feet. She glanced at the tin alarm-clock on the shelf. The hands stood at half-past five. The rest of the factory world was just arousing from sleep. She drew a shawl about her shoulders, and on her head put a dingy hat, shapeless and ancient.

"We've got to run," she said, turning the wick of the lamp and blowing down the chimney.

They groped their way out and down the stairs. It was clear and cold, and Johnny shivered at the first contact with the outside air. The stars had not yet begun to pale in the sky, and the city lay in blackness. Both Johnny and his mother shuffled their feet as they walked. There was no ambition in the leg muscles to swing the feet clear of the ground.

After fifteen silent minutes, his mother turned off to the right.

"Don't be late," was her final warning from out of the dark that was swallowing her up.

He made no response, steadily keeping on his way. In the factory quarter, doors were opening everywhere, and he was soon one of a multitude that pressed onward through the dark. As he entered the factory gate the whistle blew again. He glanced at the east. Across a ragged sky-line of housetops a pale light was beginning to creep. This much he saw of the day as he turned his back upon it and joined his work gang.

He took his place in one of many long rows of machines. Before him, above a bin filled with small bobbins, were large bobbins revolving rapidly. Upon these he wound the jute-twine of the small bobbins. The work was simple. All that was required was celerity. The small bobbins were emptied so rapidly, and there were so many large bobbins that did the emptying, that there were no idle moments.

He worked mechanically. When a small bobbin ran out, he used his left hand for a brake, stopping the large bobbin and at the same time, with thumb and forefinger, catching the flying end of twine. Also, at the same time, with his right hand, he caught up the loose twine-end of a small bobbin. These various acts with both hands were performed simultaneously and swiftly. Then there would come a flash of his hands as he looped the weaver's knot and released the bobbin. There was nothing difficult about weaver's knots. He once boasted he could tie them in his sleep. And for that matter, he sometimes did, toiling centuries long in a single night at tying an endless succession of weaver's knots.

Some of the boys shirked, wasting time and machinery by not replacing the small bobbins when they ran out. And there was an overseer to prevent this. He caught Johnny's neighbor at the trick, and boxed his ears.

"Look at Johnny there—why ain't you like him?" the overseer wrathfully demanded.

Johnny's bobbins were running full blast, but he did not thrill at the indirect praise. There had been a time . . . but that was long ago, very long ago. His apathetic face was expressionless as he listened to himself being held up as a shining example. He was the perfect worker. He knew that. He had been told so, often. It was a commonplace, and besides it didn't seem to mean anything to him any more. From the perfect worker he had evolved into the perfect machine. When his work went wrong, it was with him as with the machine, due to faulty material. It would have been as possible for a perfect nail-die to cut imperfect nails as for him to make a mistake.

And small wonder. There had never been a time when he had not been in intimate relationship with machines. Machinery had almost been bred into him, and at any rate he had been brought up on it. Twelve years before, there had been a small flutter of excitement in the loom room of this very

mill. Johnny's mother had fainted. They stretched her out on the floor in the midst of the shrieking machines. A couple of elderly women were called from their looms. The foreman assisted. And in a few minutes there was one more soul in the loom room than had entered by the doors. It was Johnny, born with the pounding, crashing roar of the looms in his ears, drawing with his first breath the warm, moist air that was thick with flying lint. He had coughed that first day in order to rid his lungs of the lint; and for the same reason he had coughed ever since.

The boy alongside of Johnny whimpered and sniffed. The boy's face was convulsed with hatred for the overseer who kept a threatening eye on him from a distance; but every bobbin was running full. The boy yelled terrible oaths into the whirling bobbins before him; but the sound did not carry half a dozen feet, the roaring of the room holding it in and containing it like a wall.

Of all this Johnny took no notice. He had a way of accepting things. Besides, things grow monotonous by repetition, and this particular happening he had witnessed many times. It seemed to him as useless to oppose the overseer as to defy the will of a machine. Machines were made to go in certain ways and to perform certain tasks. It was the same with the overseer.

But at eleven o'clock there was excitement in the room. In an apparently occult way the excitement instantly permeated everywhere. The one-legged boy who worked on the other side of Johnny bobbed swiftly across the floor to the bin truck that stood empty. Into this he dived out of sight, crutch and all. The superintendent of the mill was coming along, accompanied by a young man. He was well dressed and wore a starched shirt—a gentleman, in Johnny's classification of men, and also, "the Inspector."

He looked sharply at the boys as he passed along. Sometimes he stopped and asked questions. When he did so, he was compelled to shout at the top of his lungs, at which moments his face was ludicrously contorted with the strain of making himself heard. His quick eye noted the empty machine alongside of Johnny's, but he said nothing. Johnny also caught his eye, and he stopped abruptly. He caught Johnny by the arm to draw him back a step from the machine; but with an exclamation of surprise he released the arm.

"Pretty skinny," the superintendent laughed anxiously.

"Pipe stems," was the answer. "Look at those legs. The boy's got the rickets—incipient, but he's got them. If epilepsy doesn't get him in the end, it will be because tuberculosis gets him first."

Johnny listened, but did not understand. Furthermore he was not interested in future ills. There was an immediate and more serious ill that threatened him in the form of the inspector.

"Now, my boy, I want you to tell me the truth," the inspector said, or shouted, bending close to the boy's ear to make him hear. "How old are you?"

"Fourteen," Johnny lied, and he lied with the full force of his lungs. So loudly did he lie that it started him off in a dry, hacking cough that lifted the lint which had been settling in his lungs all morning.

"Looks sixteen at least," said the superintendent.

"Or sixty," snapped the inspector.

"He's always looked that way."

"How long?" asked the inspector, quickly.

"For years. Never gets a bit older."

"Or younger, I dare say. I suppose he's worked here all those years?"

"Off an' on—but that was before the new law was passed," the superintendent hastened to add.

"Machine idle?" the inspector asked, pointing at the unoccupied machine beside Johnny's, in which the part-filled bobbins were flying like mad.

"Looks that way." The superintendent motioned the overseer to him and shouted in his ear and pointed at the machine.

"Machine's idle," he reported back to the inspector.

They passed on, and Johnny returned to his work, relieved in that the ill had been averted. But the one-legged boy was not so fortunate. The sharp-eyed inspector haled him out at arm's length from the bin truck. His lips were quivering, and his face had all the expression of one upon whom was fallen profound and irremediable disaster. The overseer looked astounded, as though for the first time he had laid eyes on the boy, while the superintendent's face expressed shock and displeasure.

"I know him," the inspector said. "He's twelve years old. I've had him discharged from three factories inside the year. This makes the fourth."

He turned to the one-legged boy. "You promised me, word and honor, that you'd go to school."

The one-legged boy burst into tears. "Please, Mr. Inspector, two babies died on us, and we're awful poor."

"What makes you cough that way?" the inspector demanded, as though charging him with crime.

And as in denial of guilt, the one-legged boy replied: "It ain't nothin'. I jes' caught a cold last week, Mr. Inspector, that's all."

In the end the one-legged boy went out of the room with the inspector, the latter accompanied by the anxious and protesting superintendent. After that monotony settled down again. The long morning and the longer afternoon wore away and the whistle blew for quitting time. Darkness had already fallen when Johnny passed out through the factory gate. In the interval the sun had made a golden ladder of the sky, flooded the world with its gracious warmth, and dropped down and disappeared in the west behind a ragged sky-line of housetops.

Supper was the family meal of the day—the one meal at which Johnny encountered his younger brothers and sisters. It partook of the nature of an encounter, to him, for he was very old, while they were

distressingly young. He had no patience
with their excessive and amazing juvenility.
He did not understand it. His own childhood was too far behind him. He was like
an old and irritable man, annoyed by the
turbulence of their young spirits that was
to him arrant silliness. He glowered silently
over his food, finding compensation in the
thought that they would soon have to go
to work. That would take the edge off of
them and make them sedate and dignified
—like him. Thus it was, after the fashion
of the human, that Johnny made of himself
a yardstick with which to measure the
universe.

During the meal, his mother explained in
various ways and with infinite repetition
that she was trying to do the best she could;
so that it was with relief, the scant meal
ended, that Johnny shoved back his chair
and arose. He debated for a moment between bed and the front door, and finally
went out the latter. He did not go far. He
sat down on the stoop, his knees drawn up
and his narrow shoulders drooping forward, his elbows on his knees and the
palms of his hands supporting his chin.

As he sat there, he did no thinking. He
was just resting. So far as his mind was
concerned, it was asleep. His brothers and
sisters came out, and with other children
played noisily about him. An electric globe
on the corner lighted their frolics. He was
peevish and irritable, that they knew; but
the spirit of adventure lured them into
teasing him. They joined hands before him,
and, keeping time with their bodies, chanted
in his face weird and uncomplimentary
doggerel. At first he snarled curses at them
—curses he had learned from the lips of
various foremen. Finding this futile, and
remembering his dignity, he relapsed into
dogged silence.

His brother Will, next to him in age,
having just passed his tenth birthday, was
the ring-leader. Johnny did not possess
particularly kindly feelings toward him.
His life had early been embittered by continual giving over and giving way to Will.

He had a definite feeling that Will was
greatly in his debt and was ungrateful
about it. In his own playtime, far back in
the dim past, he had been robbed of a
large part of that playtime by being compelled to take care of Will. Will was a baby
then, and then, as now, their mother had
spent her days in the mills. To Johnny had
fallen the part of little father and little
mother as well.

Will seemed to show the benefit of the
giving over and the giving way. He was
well-built, fairly rugged, as tall as his
elder brother and even heavier. It was as
though the life-blood of the one had been
diverted into the other's veins. And in
spirits it was the same. Johnny was jaded,
worn out, without resilience, while his
younger brother seemed bursting and spilling over with exuberance.

The mocking chant rose louder and
louder. Will leaned closer as he danced,
thrusting out his tongue. Johnny's left arm
shot out and caught the other around the
neck. At the same time he rapped his bony
fist to the other's nose. It was a pathetically
bony fist, but that it was sharp to hurt
was evidenced by the squeal of pain it
produced. The other children were uttering
frightened cries, while Johnny's sister, Jennie, had dashed into the house.

He thrust Will from him, kicked him
savagely on the shins, then reached for
him and slammed him face downward in
the dirt. Nor did he release him till the
face had been rubbed into the dirt several
times. Then the mother arrived, an anaemic
whirlwind of solicitude and maternal wrath.

"Why can't he leave me alone?" was
Johnny's reply to her upbraiding. "Can't
he see I'm tired?"

"I'm as big as you," Will raged in her
arms, his face a mess of tears, dirt, and
blood. "I'm as big as you now, an' I'm
goin' to git bigger. Then I'll lick you—see
if I don't."

"You ought to be to work, seein' how big
you are," Johnny snarled. "That's what's
the matter with you. You ought to be to

work. An' it's up to your ma to put you to work."

"But he's too young," she protested. "He's only a little boy."

"I was younger'n him when I started to work."

Johnny's mouth was open, further to express the sense of unfairness that he felt, but the mouth closed with a snap. He turned gloomily on his heel and stalked into the house and to bed. The door of his room was open to let in warmth from the kitchen. As he undressed in the semi-darkness he could hear his mother talking with a neighbor woman who had dropped in. His mother was crying, and her speech was punctuated with spiritless sniffles.

"I can't make out what's gittin' into Johnny," he could hear her say. "He didn't used to be this way. He was a patient little angel."

"An' he is a good boy," she hastened to defend. "He's worked faithful, an' he did go to work too young. But it wasn't my fault. I do the best I can, I'm sure."

Prolonged sniffling from the kitchen, and Johnny murmured to himself as his eyelids closed down, "You betcher life I've worked faithful."

The next morning he was torn bodily by his mother from the grip of sleep. Then came the meagre breakfast, the tramp through the dark, the pale glimpse of day across the housetops as he turned his back on it and went in through the factory gate. It was another day, of all the days, and all the days were alike.

And yet there had been variety in his life—at the times he changed from one job to another, or was taken sick. When he was six, he was little mother and father to Will and the other children still younger. At seven he went into the mills—winding bobbins. When he was eight, he got work in another mill. His new job was marvellously easy. All he had to do was to sit down with a little stick in his hand and guide a stream of cloth that flowed past him. This stream of cloth came out of the maw of a machine, passed over a hot roller, and went on its way elsewhere. But he sat always in the one place, beyond the reach of daylight, a gas-jet flaring over him, himself part of the mechanism.

He was very happy at that job, in spite of the moist heat, for he was still young and in possession of dreams and illusions. And wonderful dreams he dreamed as he watched the steaming cloth streaming endlessly by. But there was no exercise about the work, no call upon his mind, and he dreamed less and less, while his mind grew torpid and drowsy. Nevertheless, he earned two dollars a week, and two dollars represented the difference between acute starvation and chronic underfeeding.

But when he was nine, he lost his job. Measles was the cause of it. After he recovered, he got work in a glass factory. The pay was better, and the work demanded skill. It was piecework, and the more skilful he was, the bigger wages he earned. Here was incentive. And under this incentive he developed into a remarkable worker.

It was simple work, the tying of glass stoppers into small bottles. At his waist he carried a bundle of twine. He held the bottles between his knees so that he might work with both hands. Thus, in a sitting position and bending over his own knees, his narrow shoulders grew humped and his chest was contracted for ten hours each day. This was not good for the lungs, but he tied three hundred dozen bottles a day.

The superintendent was very proud of him, and brought visitors to look at him. In ten hours three hundred dozen bottles passed through his hands. This meant that he had attained machine-like perfection. All waste movements were eliminated. Every motion of his thin arms, every movement of a muscle in the thin fingers, was swift and accurate. He worked at high tension, and the result was that he grew nervous. At night his muscles twitched in his sleep, and in the daytime he could not relax and rest. He remained keyed up and his muscles continued to twitch. Also he grew sallow and his lint-cough grew worse.

Then pneumonia laid hold of the feeble lungs within the contracted chest, and he lost his job in the glass-works.

Now he had returned to the jute-mills where he had first begun with winding bobbins. But promotion was waiting for him. He was a good worker. He would next go on the starcher, and later he would go into the loom room. There was nothing after that except increased efficiency.

The machinery ran faster than when he had first gone to work, and his mind ran slower. He no longer dreamed at all, though his earlier years had been full of dreaming. Once he had been in love. It was when he first began guiding the cloth over the hot roller, and it was with the daughter of the superintendent. She was much older than he, a young woman, and he had seen her at a distance only a paltry half-dozen times. But that made no difference. On the surface of the cloth stream that poured past him, he pictured radiant futures wherein he performed prodigies of toil, invented miraculous machines, won to the mastership of the mills, and in the end took her in his arms and kissed her soberly on the brow.

But that was all in the long ago, before he had grown too old and tired to love. Also, she had married and gone away, and his mind had gone to sleep. Yet it had been a wonderful experience, and he used often to look back upon it as other men and women look back upon the time they believed in fairies. He had never believed in fairies nor Santa Claus; but he had believed implicitly in the smiling future his imagination had wrought into the steaming cloth.

He had become a man very early in life. At seven, when he drew his first wages, began his adolescence. A certain feeling of independence crept up in him, and the relationship between him and his mother changed. Somehow, as an earner and breadwinner, doing his own work in the world, he was more like an equal with her. Manhood, full-blown manhood, had come when he was eleven, at which time he had gone to work on the night shift for six months. No child works on the night shift and remains a child.

There had been several great events in his life. One of these had been when his mother bought some California prunes. Two others had been the two times when she cooked custard. Those had been events. He remembered them kindly. And at that time his mother had told him of a blissful dish she would sometime make—"floating island," she had called it, "better than custard." For years he had looked forward to the day when he would sit down to the table with floating island before him, until at last he had relegated the idea of it to the limbo of unattainable ideals.

Once he found a silver quarter lying on the sidewalk. That, also, was a great event in his life, withal a tragic one. He knew his duty on the instant the silver flashed on his eyes, before even he had picked it up. At home, as usual, there was not enough to eat, and home he should have taken it as he did his wages every Saturday night. Right conduct in this case was obvious; but he never had any spending of his money, and he was suffering from candy hunger. He was ravenous for the sweets that only on red-letter days he had ever tasted in his life.

He did not attempt to deceive himself. He knew it was sin, and deliberately he sinned when he went on a fifteen-cent candy debauch. Ten cents he saved for a future orgy; but not being accustomed to the carrying of money, he lost the ten cents. This occurred at the time when he was suffering all the torments of conscience, and it was to him an act of divine retribution. He had a frightened sense of the closeness of an awful and wrathful God. God had seen, and God had been swift to punish, denying him even the full wages of sin.

In memory he always looked back upon that event as the one great criminal deed of his life, and at the recollection his conscience always awoke and gave him another twinge. It was the one skeleton in his closet. Also, being so made and circumstanced, he looked back upon the deed with regret. He was dissatisfied with the manner in which he had spent the quarter. He could have invested it better, and, out of his later knowledge of the quickness of God, he would have beaten God out by spending the whole quarter at one fell swoop. In retrospect he spent the quarter a thousand times, and each time to better advantage.

There was one other memory of the past, dim and faded, but stamped into his soul everlastingly by the savage feet of his father. It was more like a nightmare than a remembered vision of a concrete thing— more like the race-memory of man that makes him fall in his sleep and that goes back to his arboreal ancestry.

This particular memory never came to Johnny in broad daylight when he was wide awake. It came at night, in bed, at the moment that his consciousness was sinking down and losing itself in sleep. It always aroused him to frightened wakefulness, and for the moment, in the first sickening start, it seemed to him that he lay crosswise on the foot of the bed. In the bed were the vague forms of his father and mother. He never saw what his father looked like. He had but one impression of his father, and that was that he had savage and pitiless feet.

His earlier memories lingered with him, but he had no late memories. All days were alike. Yesterday or last year were the same as a thousand years—or a minute. Nothing ever happened. There were no events to mark the march of time. Time did not march. It stood always still. It was only the whirling machines that moved, and they moved nowhere—in spite of the fact that they moved faster.

When he was fourteen, he went to work on the starcher. It was a colossal event. Something had at last happened that could be remembered beyond a night's sleep or a week's pay-day. It marked an era. It was a machine Olympiad, a thing to date from. "When I went to work on the starcher," or, "after," or "before I went to work on the starcher," were only sentences often on his lips.

He celebrated his sixteenth birthday by going into the loom room and taking a loom. Here was an incentive again, for it was piecework. And he excelled, because the clay of him had been moulded by the mills into the perfect machine. At the end of three months he was running two looms, and, later, three and four.

At the end of his second year at the looms he was turning out more yards than any other weaver, and more than twice as much as some of the less skilful ones. And at home things began to prosper as he approached the full stature of his earning power. Not, however, that his increased earnings were in excess of need. The children were growing up. They ate more. And they were going to school, and school-books cost money. And somehow, the faster he worked, the faster climbed the prices of things. Even the rent went up, though the house had fallen from bad to worse disrepair.

He had grown taller; but with his increased height he seemed leaner than ever. Also, he was more nervous. With the nervousness increased his peevishness and irritability. The children had learned by many bitter lessons to fight shy of him. His mother respected him for his earning power, but somehow her respect was tinctured with fear.

There was no joyousness in life for him. The procession of the days he never saw. The nights he slept away in twitching unconsciousness. The rest of the time he worked, and his consciousness was machine consciousness. Outside this his mind was a blank. He had no ideals, and but one illusion; namely, that he drank excellent coffee. He was a work-beast. He had no mental life whatever; yet deep down in the crypts of his mind, unknown to him, were being weighed and sifted every hour of his toil, every movement of his hands, every twitch of his muscles, and preparations were making for a future course of action that would amaze him and all his little world.

It was in the late spring that he came home from work one night aware of unusual tiredness. There was a keen expectancy in the air as he sat down to the table, but he did not notice. He went through the meal in moody silence, mechanically eating what was before him. The children um'd and ah'd and made smacking noises with their mouths. But he was deaf to them.

"D'ye know what you're eatin'?" his mother demanded at last, desperately.

He looked vacantly at the dish before him, and vacantly at her.

"Floatin' island," she announced triumphantly.

"Oh," he said.

"Floating island!" the children chorussed loudly.

"Oh," he said. And after two or three mouthfuls, he added, "I guess I ain't hungry to-night."

He dropped the spoon, shoved back his chair, and arose wearily from the table.

"An' I guess I'll go to bed."

His feet dragged more heavily than usual as he crossed the kitchen floor. Undressing was a Titan's task, a monstrous futility, and he wept weakly as he crawled into bed, one shoe still on. He was aware of a rising, swelling something inside his head that made his brain thick and fuzzy. His lean fingers felt as big as his wrist, while in the ends of them was a remoteness of sensation vague and fuzzy like his brain. The small of his back ached intolerably. All his bones ached. He ached everywhere. And in his head began the shrieking, pounding, crashing, roaring of a million looms. All space was filled with flying shuttles. They darted in and out, intricately, amongst the stars. He worked a thousand looms himself, and ever they speeded up, faster and faster, and his brain unwound, faster and faster, and became the thread that fed the thousand flying shuttles.

He did not go to work next morning. He was too busy weaving colossally on the thousand looms that ran inside his head. His mother went to work, but first she sent for the doctor. It was a severe attack of la grippe, he said. Jennie served as nurse and carried out his instructions.

It was a very severe attack, and it was a week before Johnny dressed and tottered feebly across the floor. Another week, the doctor said, and he would be fit to return to work. The foreman of the loom room visited him on Sunday afternoon, the first day of his convalescence. The best weaver in the room, the foreman told his mother. His job would be held for him. He could come back to work a week from Monday.

"Why don't you thank 'im, Johnny?" his mother asked anxiously.

"He's ben that sick he ain't himself yet," she explained apologetically to the visitor.

Johnny sat hunched up and gazing steadfastly at the floor. He sat in the same position long after the foreman had gone. It was warm out-doors, and he sat on the stoop in the afternoon. Sometimes his lips moved. He seemed lost in endless calculations.

Next morning, after the day grew warm, he took his seat on the stoop. He had pencil and paper this time with which to continue his calculations, and he calculated painfully and amazingly.

"What comes after millions?" he asked at noon, when Will came home from school. "An' how d'ye work 'em?"

That afternoon finished his task. Each day, but without paper and pencil, he returned to the stoop. He was greatly absorbed in the one tree that grew across the street. He studied it for hours at a time, and was unusually interested when the wind swayed its branches and fluttered its leaves. Throughout the week he seemed lost in a great communion with himself. On Sunday, sitting on the stoop, he laughed aloud, several times, to the perturbation of his mother, who had not heard him laugh in years.

Next morning, in the early darkness, she came to his bed to rouse him. He had had his fill of sleep all week, and awoke easily. He made no struggle, nor did he attempt to hold on to the bedding when she stripped it from him. He lay quietly, and spoke quietly.

"It ain't no use, ma."

"You'll be late," she said, under the impression that he was still stupid with sleep.

"I'm awake, ma, an' I tell you it ain't no use. You might as well lemme alone. I ain't goin' to git up."

"But you'll lose your job!" she cried.

"I ain't goin' to git up," he repeated in a strange, passionless voice.

She did not go to work herself that morning. This was sickness beyond any sickness she had ever known. Fever and delirium she could understand; but this was insanity. She pulled the bedding up over him and sent Jennie for the doctor.

When that person arrived, Johnny was sleeping gently, and gently he awoke and allowed his pulse to be taken.

"Nothing the matter with him," the doctor reported. "Badly debilitated, that's all. Not much meat on his bones."

"He's always been that way," his mother volunteered.

"Now go 'way, ma, an' let me finish my snooze."

Johnny spoke sweetly and placidly, and sweetly and placidly he rolled over on his side and went to sleep.

At ten o'clock he awoke and dressed himself. He walked out into the kitchen, where he found his mother with a frightened expression on her face.

"I'm goin' away, ma," he announced, "an' I jes' want to say good-by."

She threw her apron over her head and sat down suddenly and wept. He waited patiently.

"I might a-known it," she was sobbing.

"Where?" she finally asked, removing the apron from her head and gazing up at him with a stricken face in which there was little curiosity.

"I don't know—anywhere."

As he spoke, the tree across the street appeared with dazzling brightness on his inner vision. It seeemed to lurk just under his eyelids, and he could see it whenever he wished.

"An' your job?" she quavered.

"I ain't never goin' to work again."

"My God, Johnny!" she wailed, "don't say that!"

What he had said was blasphemy to her. As a mother who hears her child deny God, was Johnny's mother shocked by his words.

"What's got into you, anyway?" she demanded, with a lame attempt at imperativeness.

"Figures," he answered. "Jes' figures. I've ben doin' a lot of figurin' this week, an' it's most surprisin'."

"I don't see what that's got to do with it," she sniffled.

Johnny smiled patiently, and his mother was aware of a distinct shock at the persistent absence of his peevishness and irritability.

"I'll show you," he said. "I'm plum' tired out. What makes me tired? Moves. I've ben movin' ever since I was born. I'm tired of movin', an' I ain't goin' to move any more. Remember when I worked in the glass-house? I used to do three hundred dozen a day. Now I reckon I made about ten different moves to each bottle. That's thirty-six thousan' moves a day. Ten days, three hundred an' sixty thousan' moves. One month, one million an' eighty thousan' moves. Chuck out the eighty thousan'—" he spoke with the complacent beneficence of a philanthropist—"chuck out the eighty thousan', that leaves a million moves a month—twelve million moves a year.

"At the looms I'm moving twic'st as much. That makes twenty-five million moves a year, an' it seems to me I've ben a-movin' that way 'most a million years.

"Now this week I ain't moved at all. I ain't made one move in hours an' hours. I tell you it was swell, jes' settin' there, hours an' hours, an' doin' nothin'. I ain't never ben happy before. I never had any time. I've ben movin' all the time. That ain't no way to be happy. An' I ain't goin' to do it any more. I'm jes' goin' to set, an' set, an' rest, an' rest, and then rest some more."

"But what's goin' to come of Will an' the children?" she asked despairingly.

"That's it, 'Will an' the children,'" he repeated.

But there was no bitterness in his voice. He had long known his mother's ambition for the younger boy, but the thought of it no longer rankled. Nothing mattered any more. Not even that.

"I know, ma, what you've ben plannin' for Will—keepin' him in school to make a bookkeeper out of him. But it ain't no use, I've quit. He's got to go to work."

"An' after I have brung you up the way I have," she wept, starting to cover her head with the apron and changing her mind.

"You never brung me up," he answered with sad kindliness. "I brung myself up, ma, an' brung up Will. He's bigger'n me, an' heavier, an' taller. When I was a kid, I reckon I didn't git enough to eat. When he come along an' was a kid, I was workin' an' earnin' grub for him too. But that's done with. Will can go to work, same as me, or he can go to hell, I don't care which. I'm tired. I'm goin' now. Ain't you goin' to say good-by?"

She made no reply. The apron had gone over her head again, and she was crying. He paused a moment in the doorway.

"I'm sure I done the best I knew how," she was sobbing.

He passed out of the house and down the street. A wan delight came into his face at the sight of the lone tree. "Jes' ain't goin' to do nothin'," he said to himself, half aloud, in a crooning tone. He glanced wistfully up at the sky, but the bright sun dazzled and blinded him.

It was a long walk he took, and he did not walk fast. It took him past the jute-mill. The muffled roar of the loom room came to his ears, and he smiled. It was a gentle, placid smile. He hated no one, not even the pounding, shrieking machines. There was no bitterness in him, nothing but an inordinate hunger for rest.

The houses and factories thinned out and the open spaces increased as he approached the country. At last the city was behind him, and he was walking down a leafy lane beside the railroad track. He did not walk like a man. He did not look like a man. He was a travesty of the human. It was a twisted and stunted and nameless piece of life that shambled like a sickly ape, arms loose-hanging, stoop-shouldered, narrow-chested, grotesque and terrible.

He passed by a small railroad station and lay down in the grass under a tree. All afternoon he lay there. Sometimes he dozed, with muscles that twitched in his sleep. When awake, he lay without movement, watching the birds or looking up at the sky through the branches of the tree above him. Once or twice he laughed aloud, but without relevance to anything he had seen or felt.

After twilight had gone, in the first darkness of the night, a freight train rumbled into the station. When the engine was switching cars on to the side-track, Johnny crept along the side of the train. He pulled open the side-door of an empty box-car and awkwardly and laboriously climbed in. He closed the door. The engine whistled. Johnny was lying down, and in the darkness he smiled.

American Literature 1860–1900

IV

THE INTERNATIONAL THEME

American Literature 1860-1900

IV

THE INTERNATIONAL THEME

1869 ∾ William Vaughn Moody ∾ 1910

MOODY was born at Spencer, Indiana, and made his way to Harvard and then to Europe. He returned to Harvard for graduate study, taught there briefly, and then joined the English department of the new University of Chicago. He did not like teaching, and his small output of poetry brought little income. He wrote a textbook, *A History of English Literature* (1902), with Robert Morss Lovett, and edited various English classics; in 1906 he achieved financial and critical success with a prose play, *The Great Divide*.

Moody's first book of poetry was *The Masque of Judgment* (1900), a poetic drama which later formed the middle part of an unfinished trilogy. The slender volume of *Poems* (1901) contains his best work, and is marked by deep social sympathy and a profound anxiety for the progress of democracy and mankind in the light of national and international affairs at the turn of the century.

[*William Vaughn Moody* (Boston, 1934) by D. D. Henry is a biographical and critical study. Highly interesting letters are presented in *Some Letters of William Vaughn Moody* (New York, 1913), edited by Daniel Gregory Mason, and *Letters to Harriet* (New York, 1936), edited by Percy Mackaye.]

AN ODE IN TIME OF HESITATION [1]
[1901 (1900)]

I

Before the solemn bronze Saint Gaudens
    made
To thrill the heedless passer's heart with
    awe,
And set here in the city's talk and trade
To the good memory of Robert Shaw,
This bright March morn I stand,   5
And hear the distant spring come up the
    land;
Knowing that what I hear is not unheard
Of this boy soldier and his negro band,
For all their gaze is fixed so stern ahead,
For all the fatal rhythm of their tread. 10
The land they died to save from death and
    shame
Trembles and waits, hearing the spring's
    great name,
And by her pangs these resolute ghosts
    are stirred.

II

Through street and mall the tides of people
    go
Heedless; the trees upon the Common
    show   15
No hint of green; but to my listening
    heart
The still earth doth impart
Assurance of her jubilant emprise,
And it is clear to my long-searching eyes
That love at last has might upon the
    skies.   20
The ice is runneled on the little pond;

[1] After seeing at Boston the statue of Robert Gould Shaw, killed while storming Fort Wagner, July 18, 1863, at the head of the first enlisted negro regiment, the Fifty-fourth Massachusetts.—Author's note. At the end of the Spanish-American War, forcible annexation of the Philippine Islands was loudly advocated. In this poem Moody expressed his opposition to this imperialistic action. Compare Twain's "To a Person Sitting in Darkness," p. xxx.

A telltale patter drips from off the trees;
The air is touched with southland spiceries,
As if but yesterday it tossed the frond
Of pendant mosses where the live-oaks
    grow   25
Beyond Virginia and the Carolines,
Or had its will among the fruits and vines
Of aromatic isles asleep beyond
Florida and the Gulf of Mexico.

III

Soon shall the Cape Ann children shout in
    glee,   30
Spying the arbutus, spring's dear recluse;
Hill lads at dawn shall hearken the wild
    goose
Go honking northward over Tennessee;
West from Oswego to Sault Sainte-Marie,
And on to where the Pictured Rocks are
    hung,   35
And yonder where, gigantic, wilful, young,
Chicago sitteth at the northwest gates,
With restless violent hands and casual
    tongue
Moulding her mighty fates,
The Lakes shall robe them in ethereal
    sheen;   40
And like a larger sea, the vital green
Of springing wheat shall vastly be outflung
Over Dakota and the prairie states.
By desert people immemorial
On Arizonan mesas shall be done   45
Dim rites unto the thunder and the sun;
Nor shall the primal gods lack sacrifice
More splendid, when the white Sierras call
Unto the Rockies straightway to arise
And dance before the unveiled ark of the
    year,   50
Sounding their windy cedars as for shawms,
Unrolling rivers clear
For flutter of broad phylacteries;
While Shasta signals to Alaskan seas
That watch old sluggish glaciers downward
    creep   55
To fling their icebergs thundering from the
    steep,
And Mariposa through the purple calms
Gazes at far Hawaii crowned with palms
Where East and West are met,—

A rich seal on the ocean's bosom set   60
To say that East and West are twain,
With different loss and gain:
The Lord hath sundered them; let them be
    sundered yet.

IV

Alas! what sounds are these that come
Sullenly over the Pacific seas,—   65
Sounds of ignoble battle, striking dumb
The season's half-awakened ecstasies?
Must I be humble, then,
Now when my heart hath need of pride?
Wild love falls on me from these sculptured
    men;   70
By loving much the land for which they
    died
I would be justified.
My spirit was away on pinions wide
To soothe in praise of her its passionate
    mood
And ease it of its ache of gratitude.   75
Too sorely heavy is the debt they lay
On me and the companions of my day.
I would remember now
My country's goodliness, make sweet her
    name.
Alas! what shade art thou   80
Of sorrow or of blame
Liftest the lyric leafage from her brow,
And pointest a slow finger at her shame?

V

Lies! lies! It cannot be! The wars we wage
Are noble, and our battles still are won 85
By justice for us, ere we lift the gage.
We have not sold our loftiest heritage.
The proud republic hath not stooped to
    cheat
And scramble in the market-place of war;
Her forehead weareth yet its solemn
    star.   90
Here is her witness: this, her perfect son,
This delicate and proud New England soul
Who leads despisèd men, with just-un-
    shackled feet,
Up the large ways where death and glory
    meet,

To show all peoples that our shame is
    done,   95
That once more we are clean and spirit-
    whole.

VI

Crouched in the sea-fog on the moaning
    sand
All night he lay, speaking some simple word
From hour to hour to the slow minds that
    heard,
Holding each poor life gently in his
    hand   100
And breathing on the base rejected clay
Till each dark face shone mystical and
    grand
Against the breaking day;
And lo, the shard the potter cast away
Was grown a fiery chalice crystal-fine 105
Fulfilled of the divine
Great wine of battle wrath by God's ring-
    finger stirred.
Then upward, where the shadowy bastion
    loomed
Huge on the mountain in the wet sea light,
Whence now, and now, infernal flowerage
    bloomed,   110
Bloomed, burst, and scattered down its
    deadly seed,—
They swept, and died like freemen on the
    height,
Like freemen, and like men of noble breed;
And when the battle fell away at night
By hasty and contemptuous hands were
    thrust   115
Obscurely in a common grave with him
The fair-haired keeper of their love and
    trust.
Now limb doth mingle with dissolvèd limb
In nature's busy old democracy
To flush the mountain laurel when she
    blows   120
Sweet by the southern sea,
And heart with crumbled heart climbs in
    the rose:—
The untaught hearts with the high heart
    that knew
This mountain fortress for no earthly hold
Of temporal quarrel, but the bastion old 125

Of spiritual wrong,
Built by an unjust nation sheer and strong,
Expugnable but by a nation's rue
And bowing down before that equal shrine
By all men held divine,   130
Whereof his band and he were the most
    holy sign.

VII

O bitter, bitter shade!
Wilt thou not put the scorn
And instant tragic question from thine eye?
Do thy dark brows yet crave   135
That swift and angry stave—
Unmeet for this desirous morn—
That I have striven, striven to evade?
Gazing on him, must I not deem they err
Whose careless lips in street and shop
    aver   140
As common tidings, deeds to make his
    cheek
Flush from the bronze, and his dead throat
    to speak?
Surely some elder singer would arise,
Whose harp hath leave to threaten and to
    mourn
Above this people when they go astray. 145
Is Whitman, the strong spirit, overworn?
Has Whittier put his yearning wrath away?
I will not and I dare not yet believe!
Though furtively the sunlight seems to
    grieve,
And the spring-laden breeze   150
Out of the gladdening west is sinister
With sounds of nameless battle overseas;
Though when we turn and question in
    suspense
If these things be indeed after these ways,
And what things are to follow after
    these,   155
Our fluent men of place and consequence
Fumble and fill their mouths with hollow
    phrase,
Or for the end-all of deep arguments
Intone their dull commercial liturgies—
I dare not yet believe! My ears are
    shut!   160
I will not hear the thin satiric praise

And muffled laughter of our enemies,
Bidding us never sheathe our valiant sword
Till we have changed our birthright for a
gourd
Of wild pulse stolen from a barbarian's
hut; 165
Showing how wise it is to cast away
The symbols of our spiritual sway,
That so our hands with better ease
May wield the driver's whip and grasp the
jailer's keys.

VIII

Was it for this our fathers kept the
law? 170
This crown shall crown their struggle and
their ruth?
Are we the eagle nation Milton saw [2]
Mewing its mighty youth,
Soon to possess the mountain winds of
truth,
And be a swift familiar of the sun 175
Where aye before God's face his trumpets
run?
Or have we but the talons and the maw,
And for the abject likeness of our heart
Shall some less lordly bird be set apart?—
Some gross-billed wader where the swamps
are fat? 180
Some gorger in the sun? Some prowler
with the bat?

IX

Ah, no!
We have not fallen so.
We are our fathers' sons: let those who
lead us know!
'Twas only yesterday sick Cuba's cry 185
Came up the tropic wind, "Now help us,
for we die!"
Then Alabama heard,
And rising, pale, to Maine and Idaho
Shouted a burning word.
Proud state with proud impassioned state
conferred, 190
And at the lifting of a hand sprang forth,
East, west, and south, and north,

Beautiful armies. Oh, by the sweet blood
and young
Shed on the awful hill slope at San Juan,[3]
By the unforgotten names of eager
boys 195
Who might have tasted girl's love and been
stung
With the old mystic joys
And starry griefs, now the spring nights
come on,
But that the heart of youth is gener-
ous,—
We charge you, ye who lead us, 200
Breathe on their chivalry no hint of stain!
Turn not their new-world victories to gain!
One least leaf plucked for chaffer from the
bays
Of their dear praise,
One jot of their pure conquest put to
hire, 205
The implacable republic will require;
With clamor, in the glare and gaze of noon,
Or subtly, coming as a thief at night,
But surely, very surely, slow or soon,
That insult deep we deeply will requite. 210
Tempt not our weakness, our cupidity!
For save we let the island men go free,
Those baffled and dislaureled ghosts
Will curse us from the lamentable coasts
Where walk the frustrate dead. 215
The cup of trembling shall be drainèd
quite,
Eaten the sour bread of astonishment,
With ashes of the hearth shall be made
white
Our hair, and wailing shall be in the tent;
Then on your guiltier head 220
Shall our intolerable self-disdain
Wreak suddenly its anger and its pain;
For manifest in that disastrous light
We shall discern the right
And do it, tardily.—O ye who lead, 225
Take heed!
Blindness we may forgive, but baseness we
will smite.

---

[2] In *Areopagitica*, "Mewing" means "re-
newing."

[3] Battle of San Juan Hill, near Havana,
Cuba, July, 1898.

GLOUCESTER MOORS
[1901 (1900)]

A mile behind is Gloucester town
Where the fishing fleets put in,
A mile ahead the land dips down
And the woods and farms begin.
Here, where the moors stretch free   5
In the high blue afternoon,
Are the marching sun and talking sea,
And the racing winds that wheel and flee
On the flying heels of June.

Jill-o'er-the-ground is purple blue,   10
Blue is the quaker-maid,
The wild geranium holds its dew
Long in the boulder's shade.
Wax-red hangs the cup
From the huckleberry boughs,   15
In barberry bells the grey moths sup,
Or where the choke-cherry lifts high up
Sweet bowls for their carouse.

Over the shelf of the sandy cove
Beach-peas blossom late.   20
By copse and cliff the swallows rove
Each calling to his mate.
Seaward the sea-gulls go,
And the land-birds all are here;
That green-gold flash was a vireo,   25
And yonder flame where the marsh-flags
        grow
Was a scarlet tanager.

This earth is not the steadfast place
We landsmen build upon;
From deep to deep she varies pace,   30
And while she comes is gone.
Beneath my feet I feel
Her smooth bulk heave and dip;
With velvet plunge and soft upreel
She swings and steadies to her keel   35
Like a gallant, gallant ship.

These summer clouds she sets for sail,
The sun is her masthead light,
She tows the moon like a pinnace frail
Where her phosphor wake churns
        bright.   40

Now hid, now looming clear,
On the face of the dangerous blue
The star fleets tack and wheel and veer,
But on, but on does the old earth steer
As if her port she knew.   45

God, dear God! Does she know her port,
Though she goes so far about?
Or blind astray, does she make her sport
To brazen and chance it out?
I watched when her captains passed: 50
She were better captainless.
Men in the cabin, before the mast,
But some were reckless and some aghast,
And some sat gorged at mess.

By her battened hatch I leaned and
        caught   55
Sounds from the noisome hold,—
Cursing and sighing of souls distraught
And cries too sad to be told.
Then I strove to go down and see;
But they said, "Thou art not of us!"   60
I turned to those on the deck with me
And cried, "Give help!" But they said,
        "Let be:
Our ship sails faster thus."

Jill-o'er-the-ground is purple blue,
Blue is the quaker-maid,   65
The alder-clump where the brook comes
        through
Breeds cresses in its shade.
To be out of the moiling street
With its swelter and its sin!
Who has given to me this sweet,   70
And given my brother dust to eat?
And when will his wage come in?

Scattering wide or blown in ranks,
Yellow and white and brown,
Boats and boats from the fishing banks 75
Come home to Gloucester town.
There is cash to purse and spend,
There are wives to be embraced,
Hearts to borrow and hearts to lend,
And hearts to take and keep to the end— 80
O little sails, make haste!

But thou, vast outbound ship of souls,
What harbor town for thee?
What shapes, when thy arriving tolls,
Shall crowd the banks to see?   85
Shall all the happy shipmates then
Stand singing brotherly?
Or shall a haggard ruthless few
Warp her over and bring her to,
While the many broken souls of men   90
Fester down in the slaver's pen,
And nothing to say or do?

THE MENAGERIE
[1901]

Thank God my brain is not inclined to cut
Such capers every day! I'm just about
Mellow, but then—There goes the tent-flap
    shut.
Rain's in the wind. I thought so: every
    snout
Was twitching when the keeper turned
    me out.   5

That screaming parrot makes my blood run
    cold.
Gabriel's trump! the big bull elephant
Squeals 'Rain!' to the parched herd. The
    monkeys scold,
And jabber that it's rain water they want.
(It makes me sick to see a monkey
    pant.)   10

I'll foot it home, to try and make believe
I'm sober. After this I stick to beer,
And drop the circus when the sane folks
    leave.
A man's a fool to look at things too near:
They look back, and begin to cut up
    queer.   15

Beasts do, at any rate; especially
Wild devils caged. They have the coolest
    way
Of being something else than what you see:
You pass a sleek young zebra nosing hay,
A nylghau looking bored and distingué,—20

And think you've seen a donkey and a bird.
Not on your life! Just glance back, if you
    dare.
The zebra chews, the nylghau hasn't stirred;
But something's happened, Heaven knows
    what or where
To freeze your scalp and pompadour your
    hair.   25

I'm not precisely an æolian lute
Hung in the wandering winds of sentiment,
But drown me if the ugliest, meanest brute
Grunting and fretting in that sultry tent
Didn't just floor me with embarrass-
    ment!   30

'Twas like a thunder-clap from out the
    clear,—
One minute they were circus beasts, some
    grand,
Some ugly, some amusing, and some queer:
Rival attractions to the hobo band,
The flying jenny, and the peanut stand. 35

Next minute they were old hearth-mates of
    mine!
Lost people, eyeing me with such a stare!
Patient, satiric, devilish, divine;
A gaze of hopeless envy, squalid care,
Hatred, and thwarted love, and dim
    despair.   40

Within my blood my ancient kindred
    spoke,—
Grotesque and monstrous voices, heard
    afar
Down ocean caves when behemoth awoke,
Or through fern forests roared the
    plesiosaur
Locked with the giant-bat in ghastly
    war.   45

And suddenly, as in a flash of light,
I saw great Nature working out her plan;
Through all her shapes from mastodon to
    mite
Forever groping, testing, passing on
To find at last the shape and soul of
    Man.   50

Till in the fullness of accomplished time,
Comes brother Forepaugh,[1] upon business
    bent,
Tracks her through frozen and through
    torrid clime,
And shows us, neatly labeled in a tent,
The stages of her huge experiment;   55

Blabbing aloud her shy and reticent hours;
Dragging to light her blinking, slothful
    moods;
Publishing fretful seasons when her powers
Worked wild and sullen in her solitudes,
Or when her mordant laughter shook the
    woods.   60

Here, round about me, were her vagrant
    births;
Sick dreams she had, fierce projects she
    essayed;
Her qualms, her fiery prides, her crazy
    mirths;
The troublings of her spirit as she strayed,
Cringed, gloated, mocked, was lordly, was
    afraid,   65

On that long road she went to seek
    mankind;
Here were the darkling coverts that she
    beat
To find the Hider she was sent to find;
Here the distracted footprints of her feet
Whereby her soul's Desire she came to
    greet.   70

But why should they, her botch-work, turn
    about
And stare disdain at me, her finished job?
Why was the place one vast suspended
    shout
Of laughter? Why did all the daylight
    throb
With soundless guffaw and dumb-stricken
    sob?   75

Helpless I stood among those awful cages;
The beasts were walking loose, and I was
    bagged!
I, I, last product of the toiling ages,

Goal of heroic feet that never lagged,—
A little man in trousers, slightly jagged. 80

Deliver me from such another jury!
The Judgment Day will be a picnic to't.
Their satire was more dreadful than their
    fury,
And worst of all was just a kind of brute
Disgust, and giving up, and sinking
    mute.   85

Survival of the fittest, adaptation,
And all their other evolution terms,
Seem to omit one small consideration,
To wit, that tumblebugs and angleworms
Have souls: there's soul in everything that
    squirms.   90

And souls are restless, plagued, impatient
    things,
All dream and unaccountable desire;
Crawling, but pestered with the thought of
    wings;
Spreading through every inch of earth's
    old mire
Mystical hanker after something higher. 95

Wishes *are* horses, as I understand.
I guess a wistful polyp that has strokes
Of feeling faint to gallivant on land
Will come to be a scandal to his folks;
Legs he will sprout, in spite of threats and
    jokes.   100

And at the core of every life that crawls,
Or runs or flies or swims or vegetates—
Churning the mammoth's heart-blood, in
    the galls
Of shark and tiger planting gorgeous hates,
Lighting the love of eagles for their
    mates;   105

Yes, in the dim brain of the jellied fish
That is and is not living—moved and
    stirred
From the beginning a mysterious wish,

[1] The Forepaugh brothers, Adam (1831-
1890) and Charles (1838-1929), were circus proprietors.

A vision, a command, a fatal Word:
The name of Man was uttered, and they
    heard.   110

Upward along the æons of old war
They sought him: wing and shank-bone,
    claw and bill
Were fashioned and rejected; wide and far
They roamed the twilight jungles of their
    will;
But still they sought him, and desired him
    still.   115

Man they desired, but mind you, Perfect
    Man,
The radiant and the loving, yet to be!
I hardly wonder, when they came to scan
The upshot of their strenuosity,
They gazed with mixed emotions upon
    me.   120

Well, my advice to you is, Face the crea-
    tures,

Or spot them sideways with your weather
    eye,
Just to keep tab on their expansive fea-
    tures;
It isn't pleasant when you're stepping high
To catch a giraffe smiling on the sly. 125

If nature made you graceful, don't get gay
Back-to before the hippopotamus;
If meek and godly, find some place to play
Besides right where three mad hyenas fuss:
You may hear language that we won't
    discuss.   130

If you're a sweet thing in a flower-bed hat,
Or her best fellow with your tie tucked in,
Don't squander love's bright springtime
    girding at
An old chimpanzee with an Irish chin:
There may be hidden meaning in his
    grin.   135

1843 ∾ *Henry James* ∾ 1916

I

JESSIE CONRAD, in one of the books devoted to her famous husband, *Joseph Conrad and His Circle*, tells an amusing anecdote about Henry James. It must be an authentic one, for the Conrads knew James intimately. Among their friends, he, like John Galsworthy, could always be relied upon to behave as the perfect gentleman, whatever the occasion or the gathering. The scene of the anecdote is near James' home at Rye, England. "Some three or four little girls," according to Mrs. Conrad, "caught his attention, and in his most ingratiating manner he stopped to talk to them. He began by presenting each with some pence and then proceeded to harangue them far above their understanding. The kiddies at last flung the coins on the ground and burst into loud sobbing before they ran away."

This trivial incident in James' later life has a considerable value as a symbol. The "three or four little girls" may stand for the general reading public with which James tried so hard to establish amicable relations. All his elaborate cajolery to win and hold them seemed unavailing. What he had to say to them, and how he chose to say it, demanded a sustained concentration to which they were unaccustomed and challenged too sharply their stereotypes of thought and feeling and perception. Impatient of his involved and convoluted verbal maneuvers to outflank and trap precision, and frustrated by his elusive intimations of tenuous profundities, they rejected even his slightest bribes to their interest as if these were outlandish bad-luck pieces from the devil's own mint, and turned from most of his major works with an ill-bred hubbub of petulant distrust.

Many average readers today, picking up a short story or novel of James' final phase, such, for example, as "The Beast in the Jungle" or *The Ambassadors,* have reactions comparable to those of the "three or four little girls," but there are other readers who respond quite differently, and their number is increasing. They hold the coins tightly, convinced of their rarity. Having mastered the idiom of the harangue, they do not find it above their understanding. They are impressed by the continuing pertinence of its themes. Instead of running away, they are eager to hear more. They are the discriminating, large coterie that James has won with the passage of time, with the development of a more experimental approach toward the writing of fiction, and with the maturing of contemporary criticism.

II

The James family, of New York State, became a great American family through one ancestor of humble origin who had an eye to the main chance. This ancestor, William James, arrived in Albany, New York, from Ireland, at the age of eighteen; got a job clerking in a store and then kept a store of his own; traveled westward and bought up land; engaged in various enterprises, one of the most lucrative being the salt industry of Syracuse; and at his death in 1832 left a fortune so large that his widow and each of his eleven children were independent for the rest of their lives. One of these eleven children was Henry James, Sr., who married Scotch-Irish Mary Walsh, became a theological philosopher and man of letters, and had five children—William, the psychologist and philosopher; Henry, Jr., the novelist; Garth Wilkinson or "Wilky"; Robertson or "Bob"; and Alice. Henry James, Jr., was born April 15, 1843, in New York City.

Few boys ever grew up in a family atmosphere of such ease and sociability, such freedom and culture, as did this Henry James, Jr. In *A Small Boy and Others,* the first volume of his uncompleted autobiography, he explains that, "thanks to our grandfather's fine old ability," "there was ease, with the habit of ease," and "our consciousness was positively disfurnished . . . of the actualities of 'business' in a world of business." Indeed, they were a family separate, unique, aloof, and special. "I think our fond detachment," he goes on to say, ". . . made us an unexampled and probably, for the ironic 'smart' gods of the American heaven, a lamentable case." There were numerous cousins of young Henry's generation always visiting each other; he was especially attached to "the various brood presided over by my father's second sister, Catherine James, who had married at a very early age Captain Robert Temple, U. S. A."; particularly, he idealized "Mary Temple, radiant and rare. . . ."

His father, Henry James, Sr., cared "for our spiritual decency unspeakably more than for anything else. . . ." This father wrote books such as *The Nature of Evil* (1855), wherein, as he phrased it, he felt himself "obliged to animadvert with some severity upon the prevalent Ecclesiasticism," and *Society the Redeemed Form of Man* (1879), wherein he recorded the influence of Swedenborg upon his thought and yet warned his imaginary correspondent: "I should be greatly mortified if you looked upon this avowal . . . as an ascription on my part of any more dogmatic authority to him than I should ascribe in their various measure to Socrates or John Mill."

This independently minded theological amateur was extremely broad in his interests. Artists and writers were welcome at his New York home, and their work was always being eagerly enjoyed and discussed there. Among young Henry's earliest impressions were those "of the great and urbane Emerson's occasional presence" and of the voice of Thackeray "proceeding from my father's library" and uttering "the formidable words: 'Come here, little boy, and show me your extraordinary jacket!'" and then of Thackeray himself "enormously big" "in the sunny light of the animated room" bending "on my native costume the spectacles of wonder." William Cullen Bryant, Washington Irving, George Ripley, Charles Dana, N. P. Willis—these were but a few of the men of letters who came to the James home.

Above all, that home was haunted by one New York writer who had just died—Edgar Allan Poe. James speaks of "that predominant lustre in him which our small opening minds themselves already recognised" and tells how his elder brother, William, "beckoned on my lagging mind with a recital of The Gold-Bug and The Pit and the Pendulum—both of which, however, I was soon to read for myself, adding to them The Murders in the Rue Morgue," and remarks, "Were we not also forever mounting our little platforms at our infant schools to 'speak' The Raven and Lenore and the verses in which we phrased the heroine as Annabell*ee?*" He concludes: "So far from misprizing our ill-starred magician we acclaimed him surely at every turn; he lay upon our tables and resounded in our mouths, while we communed to satiety, even for boyish appetites, over the thrill of his choicest pages."

Unlike Meredith's Sir Austin Feverel, Henry James, Sr., entertained "so free a suspicion of the unhumanity of Method" that the education he believed in and provided for his children was more of an extravaganza than an ordeal. It resulted in their having what James called a "preponderantly humanised and socialised adolescence." Its main emphases were three—intellectual play, the quest of the ancient, and cosmopolitan experience.

Concerning the first, James points out: "The literal played in our education as small a part as it perhaps ever played in any, and we wholeheartedly breathed inconsistency and ate and drank contradictions." The second emphasis made a very strong impression on his young mind: "I saw my parents homesick, as I conceived, for the ancient order and distressed and inconvenienced by many of the more immediate features of the modern, as the modern pressed upon us, and since their theory of our better living was from an early time that we should renew the quest of the ancient on the very first possibility I simply grew greater in the faith that somehow to manage that would constitute success in life." As a result of the third emphasis—closely related, of course, to the second—James, at an early age, saw more of Europe, had more schooling abroad, than Poe in the previous generation.

Virtually from the cradle, so to speak, James was a cosmopolitan *émigré*, for when he was only a year and a half old his parents had taken him and William on their first European trip. Between 1855 and 1860, save for a year spent back home at Newport, the Jameses were in Europe again, for the express purpose of affording their children the broadest possible education. For Henry, this included a London tutor—the same one who later taught Robert Louis Stevenson; a number of tutors in Paris and a session at the Institution Fezandié, a French school experimenting with the ideas of Fourier; immersement in French literature and art; a session at the Institute Rochette, a scientific school in Geneva, from which he was withdrawn to pursue literary studies in French, Latin, and German; and, finally, a summer in Bonn, where, according to his *Notes of a Son and Brother,* he "rioted" on "the supreme German classics," studied under a German Herr Doktor, and absorbed the culture "which seemed quite to come, come from everywhere at once, with the most absurd conciliatory rush. . . ."

Returned to Newport, young James was still in a cosmopolitan atmosphere, dabbling at art under the eye of William Hunt and John La Farge, reading Browning and Balzac, and making translations of Musset and Merimée that were rejected by New York magazines.

While his younger brothers Wilky and Bob were in the Army, Henry, physically unfit for service because of a back injury, "sat out" the Civil War at Newport and then at Cambridge as a student in the Harvard Law School, where he never finished his course. At this period he was acutely conscious that one of his main personal problems was to become more of an American and less of a European. To make this transition was difficult for him. Miss Upham's boarding house at Cambridge, for example, reminded him of Balzac's Maison Vauquer in *Le Père Goriot.*

When the family moved in 1864 to Boston, he tells us "that the plot began most to thicken for me." Soon after they had come to Ashburton Place, two fatalities occurred that symbolized for him the end of an era—the assassination of Lincoln, the passing of Hawthorne. In *Notes of a Son and Brother* he dwells in detail on what Hawthorne, by this time, had come to mean for him. Although *The Wonder-Book* and *Twice-Told Tales* "had helped to enchant our childhood," it was at Newport that he had "taken in for the first time and at one straight draught the full sweet sense of our one fine romancer's work. . . ." He recalls how, much later, one of his friends at Rome—"the clearest case of 'cosmopolitan culture' I was to have known"—was incredulous that anybody could think highly of *The Marble Faun*. That criticism did not budge James from his desire to keep "the Seven Gables, the Blithedale Romance and the story of Donatello and Miriam . . . somewhere on a shelf unvisited by harsh inquiry." For Hawthorne's work was "all charged with a *tone,* a full and rare tone of prose. . ."; "the tone had been, in its beauty—for me at least—ever so appreciably American. . ."; and "the moral was that an American could be an artist, one of the finest, without 'going outside' about it, as I liked to say; quite in fact as if Hawthorne had become one just by being American *enough*. . . ."

Here, in the Boston-Cambridge and the New York atmospheres, in a post-war world that took a new interest in aesthetic matters, James began to develop rapidly. Such friends and editors as James Russell Lowell, Charles Eliot Norton, William Dean Howells, and E. L. Godkin stimulated him. The *North American Review,* the *Atlantic Monthly,* the *Galaxy,* and the *Nation* were only too glad to receive his contributions. As a writer of both critical reviews and prose fiction, he waged a campaign to improve the "tone" of American letters.

So convinced was he of the need to improve this "tone" that he now and then overreached himself, as he was only too ready to admit later. For example, in the *Nation* for November 16, 1865, he concluded his review of Walt Whitman's *Drum-Taps* with an imaginary lecture addressed to the poet. This lecture contained such passages as the following: " 'To become adopted as a national poet, it is not enough to discard everything in particular and to accept everything in general, to amass crudity upon crudity, to discharge the undigested contents of your blotting-book into the lap of the public. You must respect the public which you address; for it has taste, if you have not. It delights in the grand, the heroic, and the masculine; but it delights to see these conceptions cast into worthy form. It is indifferent to brute sublimity. It will never do for you to thrust your hands into your pockets and cry out that, as the research of form is an intolerable bore, the shortest and most economical way for the public to embrace its idols—for the nation to realize its genius—is in your own person.' "

III

The years 1869 to 1875 constituted a kind of turning point in James' career for several reasons. First, the pull of Europe versus the pull of America in his psyche became marked. In 1869 he was in England, meeting such people as

George Eliot, John Ruskin, William Morris, Charles Darwin, Dante Gabriel Rossetti; then he was in Switzerland, Rome, Naples, Paris; returning to England, he sailed for America in the spring of 1870, to spend two years, primarily at Cambridge. Then he was off to Europe again for two more years—to England, Switzerland, Germany, Italy, France. For about a year, however—from the autumn of 1874 to that of 1875—he was back in Cambridge and New York City. This restless shuttling from continent to continent, from country to country, appealed to him as a way of life because it meant a rich harvest of impressions. He enjoyed the experience of observing contrasts between national cultures. The significance of what he was to call "the international theme" broke into full light in his imagination.

Secondly, the death in 1870 of his cousin, Mary Temple, from tuberculosis, was to affect profoundly his view of both life and art. For himself and William James, he records, her death meant "the end of our youth"—although, in the last fragmentary thin volume of his reminiscences, *The Middle Years,* he makes clear that one's youth, in some senses at least, never comes to an altogether definite end. Her death was something more than the end of his youth; it was the beginning of his tragic sense of life, which eventually must find expression in his writing. "None the less," he tells us at the close of *Notes of a Son and Brother,* "did she in fact cling to consciousness; death, at the last, was dreadful to her; she would have given anything to live—and the image of this, which was long to remain with me, appeared so of the essence of tragedy that I was in the far-off aftertime to seek to lay the ghost by wrapping it, a particular occasion aiding, in the beauty and dignity of art." In his finest women—Isabel Archer of *The Portrait of a Lady,* Milly Theale of *The Wings of the Dove*—lurks the ghost of Mary Temple.

Finally, it was at the end of these six years that he really "arrived" as a novelist. Most of his numerous pieces of fiction thus far published, including his serialized first novel, *Watch and Ward,* had been only apprentice work. But with the appearance of *Roderick Hudson* in the *Atlantic Monthly* for 1875, a greater James unquestionably emerged. Here was a novel richly distilling much of his complex experience of both life and literature—his knowledge of Italy and of Americans abroad, his reading of Hawthorne, Turgenev, Balzac, George Sand, George Eliot, and the *Correspondence de Henri Regnault.*

The next six years, from 1875 through 1881, were spent partly in Paris, but mainly in London, with several short visits to Italy. While the Parisian correspondent of the *New York Tribune,* James became acquainted with the great Russian novelist Turgenev, whose fiction had already considerably influenced his own, and through him gained entry into the circle of the French naturalistic writers—Flaubert, Edmond de Goncourt, Alphonse Daudet, Guy de Maupassant, and Émile Zola. Of Paris, he wrote to William Dean Howells: "The great merit of the place is that one can arrange one's life here exactly as one pleases—that there are facilities for every kind of habit and taste, and that everything is accepted and understood." He told Howells that Flaubert was "the most interesting man and strongest artist of his circle," but confided in Henry James, Sr., ". . . I think I easily—more than easily—see all round him intellectually." Considering "the literary fraternity" there generally, he wrote to Howells: "Turgenev is worth the whole heap of them. . . . He has just gone to Russia to bury himself for two or three months on his estate, and try to finish a long novel he has for three or four years been working upon. I hope to heaven he may. I suspect he works little here."

Feeling "more at home in London than anywhere else in the world," James had more time for work there. He moved in a society that any visiting American would have envied him—the society of Huxley, Lord Houghton, John Morley, Gladstone, Tennyson. Yet he kept the feeling that he was something of an outsider, an aloof spectator. "To tell the truth," he confesses in a letter to Grace Norton, "I find myself a good deal more of a cosmopolitan (thanks to that combination of the continent and the U. S. A. which has formed my lot) than the average Briton of culture—and to be—to have become by force of circumstances —a cosmopolitan is of necessity to be a great deal alone."

These six years, despite all his many contacts, were most productive ones. The wonder is that he found time to do so much. In Paris, he wrote *The American,* which appeared in the *Atlantic* during 1876 and 1877. In London, he wrote *Daisy Miller, The Europeans, Confidence, Washington Square,* and *The Portrait of a Lady,* which some readers consider his masterpiece. Furthermore, his *French Poets and Novelists* and his *Hawthorne,* major contributions to literary criticism, appeared respectively in 1878 and 1879.

In the winter of 1881-1882 and from December, 1882, to August, 1883, James was in America. His mother died during the first of his visits. The second visit was occasioned by his father's last illness, but James did not reach home until after the funeral had been held. His brother "Wilky" died in 1883. Thenceforward, for twenty years, Henry James was to remain in Europe, spending most of this time, up until 1897, in London, although he still followed the practice of making yearly continental visits. His sister Alice came also to live in England. Of delicate health, she had necessarily to remain in retirement, at first in London, and later at Bournemouth and Leamington. James, by now a confirmed bachelor, with no love but the muse of creative writing, was devotedly attentive to his sister's welfare. She died in 1892.

During these years, James felt he had become more of an "insider," a participant in England's life. He could write thus to Grace Norton in 1885: "I am attached to this country and, on the whole, to its sometimes exasperating people. The possible *malheurs*—reverses, dangers, embarrassments, the 'decline,' in a word, of old England, go to my heart, and I can imagine no spectacle more touching, more thrilling and even dramatic, than to see this great precarious, artificial empire, on behalf of which, nevertheless, so much of the strongest and finest stuff of the greatest race (for such they are) has been expended, struggling with forces which perhaps, in the long run, will prove too many for it. If she only will struggle, and not collapse and surrender and give up a part which, looking at Europe as it is to-day, still may be great, the drama will be well worth watching from [such] a good, near standpoint as I have here. But I didn't mean to be so beastly political!" His round of social engagements continued unabated; his friendships with prominent English people were numerous and rewarding. One that was to result in an interesting exchange of correspondence over the years was that with Robert Louis Stevenson.

But James' less tangible relations with the reading public both in England and America began to bother him. With such long novels as *The Bostonians* and *The Princess Casamassima* behind him, he wrote to Stevenson in the summer of 1888: ". . . I propose, for a longish period, to do nothing but short lengths. I want to leave a multitude of pictures of my time, projecting my small circular frame upon as many different spots as possible and going in for number as well as quality, so that the number may constitute a total having a certain value as observation and testimony."

In a letter to his brother William in the same year, he conceives his story-telling function in the most ambitious terms, namely to effect a kind of "Union Now" between America and England: "I can't look at the English-American world, or feel about them, any more, save as a big Anglo-Saxon total, destined to such an amount of melting together that an insistence on their differences becomes more and more idle and pedantic; and that melting together will come the faster the more one takes it for granted and treats the life of the two countries as continuous or more or less convertible, or at any rate as simply different chapters of the same general subject. Literature, fiction in particular, affords a magnificent arm for such taking for granted, and one may so do an excellent work with it. I have not the least hesitation in saying that I aspire to write in such a way that it would be impossible to an outsider to say whether I am at a given moment an American writing about England or an Englishman writing about America (dealing as I do with both countries,) and so far from being ashamed of such an ambiguity I should be exceedingly proud of it, for it would be highly civilized."

What disturbed him, however, was that the literary critics of this Anglo-Saxon world were unable to grasp what he was trying to do. "Criticism," he wrote Stevenson, "is of an abject density and puerility—it doesn't exist—it writes the intellect of our race too low." Too much of it, like that of Andrew Lang, was written "down to the lowest level of Philistine twaddle—the view of the old lady round the corner or the clever person at the dinner party."

Keeping up with the preferences of the American reading public, he was very much depressed when he heard that some trashy book had become a best-seller. The fact, he wrote Howells in 1884, "makes one return upon one's self and ask what is the use of trying to write anything decent or serious for a public so absolutely idiotic." The hope for American letters, he believed, was in the wide acceptance of such work as Howells' *A Hazard of New Fortunes,* which he called "simply prodigious."

It was to rescue his own declining popularity that James tried to write for the theater, producing some seven or eight plays between 1889 and 1894. Only two of these were performed, both in 1891, and the best of them were published in two series of *Theatricals* in 1894 and 1895. Despite James' very wide knowledge of plays, his keen interest in drama as a form, his recognition of Ibsen's "intensity, his vividness, the hard compulsion of his strangely inscrutable art," this adventure into another medium, where concision and lucidity were all-important, did not accord fully with his genius for luxuriant and leisurely expression. In the course of the adventure, however, he was to strike up a lasting friendship with the actress, Elizabeth Robins, and was to become so tantalized with the idea of writing for the stage that he was to try again in 1908, with the same persistent unsuccess.

IV

The final period of James' career may be said to have begun in 1897. The year before, he had spent the summer in a small house on a hill in Sussex, whence he had a view across the valley below to the old town of Rye, with its red roofs and cobbled streets. In the autumn he moved to the Rye vicarage and, while there, became interested in a beautiful 18th Century home, with a large walled garden—Lamb House. To his delight this house was soon without a tenant. He leased it, established himself there in 1897, and was shortly to purchase it and make it his permanent residence.

Although he kept quarters in London and spent considerable time there, and at some intervals was to travel almost as extensively as of old, and was to move to a smaller house in Chelsea several years before his death, Lamb House was the main setting of his great experimental last phase as a creative writer. There, pacing back and forth, drawing freely on all the resources of his richly stored mind and his highly subtilized imagination, he dictated for three or four hours daily to his typist, producing the short stories that were collected in such volumes as *The Soft Side, The Better Sort,* and *The Finer Grain* and such novels as *The Awkward Age, The Sacred Fount, The Ambassadors, The Wings of the Dove,* and *The Golden Bowl.*

For his many friends he maintained a fine hospitality at Lamb House. Above all, he was happy to be reunited with his brother William and to take an interest in the latter's family. In the autumn of 1899 they came to Europe for a visit of two years, and again, in 1902, William James was abroad, to deliver at

Edinburgh the lectures that were soon to appear as *The Varieties of Religious Experience.* The brothers saw as much of each other as possible.

With both Italy and America James was to renew relations deeply during his stay at Rye. His visit to Rome in the summer of 1899 led him to undertake the two-volume biography, *William Wetmore Story and His Friends, from Letters, Diaries, and Recollections.* Here he tried to recreate in detail the career and world of his friend and host of twenty years before. At the outset of the book he remarks: "The old relation, social, personal, aesthetic, of the American world to the European. . . is as charming a subject as the student of manners, morals, personal adventures, the history of taste, the development of a society, need wish to take up, with the one drawback, in truth, of being treatable but in too many lights."

It was to find what had happened to one half of this subject during his long absence that James, at the end of August, 1904, sailed for America, to remain there for ten months, touring the Eastern seaboard from New York to Florida and then venturing westward to California. With lectures on "The Lesson of Balzac" and "The Question of Our Speech," he met in part the expenses of the journey. After his return to Rye in 1905, he wrote *The American Scene,* which recorded his impressions of the Eastern seaboard only. William James, although he praised the book as "supremely great," and showed he had a keen understanding of what Henry was trying to do in his experiment with his involved "third manner," warned him: "But it's the rummest method for one to employ systematically as you do nowadays; and you employ it at your peril."

This "peril" was ever-present during James' labors on the New York Edition of his novels and tales, published by Charles Scribner's Sons. For this edition he selected only what he considered his best work, subjected every inclusion to rigorous critical review, made many textual changes, and for each volume wrote an elaborate preface. He described these prefaces as follows in a letter to William Dean Howells in 1908: "They are, in general, a sort of plea for Criticism, for Discrimination, for Appreciation on other than infantile lines—as against the so almost universal absence of these things, which tends so, in our general trade, it seems to me, to break the heart. . . . They ought, collected together, to form a sort of comprehensive manual or *vademecum* for aspirants in our arduous profession." Yet he also referred to them as "Lucubrations" and spoke of his weariness with them. "This staleness of sensibility, in connection with them," he told Howells, "blocks out for the hour every aspect but that of their being all done, and of their perhaps helping the Edition to sell two or three copies more!"

After a severe nervous illness in 1910 and the loss of his brothers "Bob" and William shortly afterwards, James began to live more in the past in his volumes of reminiscence. Then came World War I, rudely awakening him to what the present of Europe really was. He put the blame squarely, not merely on impersonal forces and conditions or the mysterious "logic of history," but also on evil in men, particularly on "the deep conspiracy for violence, for violence and wrong, of the Austrian and the German Emperors." He thus vented his feelings to Howard Sturgis in a much-quoted letter of August, 1914: "The plunge of civilization into this abyss of blood and darkness by the wanton feat of those two infamous autocrats is a thing that so gives away the whole long age during which we have supposed the world to be, with whatever abatement, gradually bettering, that to have to take it all now for what the treacherous years were all the while really making for and *meaning* is too tragic for any words."

The novels on which he was working, *The Ivory Tower* and *The Sense of the Past,* were left unfinished, along with *The Middle Years.* Regaining something of the indomitable energy of youth, he sought to contribute as much as he possibly could to the winning of the war, talking with wounded soldiers, helping refugees, assisting in several ways to keep the American Volunteer Motor-Ambulance Corps functioning in France, and attempting to bolster morale and influence opinion by writing the essays that were later collected in *Within the Rim.* When Rupert Brooke met death in the service of his country, James wrote: "If there was a stupid and hideous disfigurement of life and outrage to beauty left for our awful conditions to perpetrate, those things have been now supremely achieved. . . ."

He became a naturalized British citizen, explaining the step as follows: "Regard my proceeding as a simple act and offering of allegiance and devotion, recognition and gratitude (for long years of innumerable relations that have meant so much to me), and it remains perfectly simple. . . . I feel all the while too that the tide of American identity of consciousness with our own, about the whole matter, rises and rises, and will rise still more before it rests again—so that every day the difference of situation diminishes and the immense fund of common sentiment increases."

Still holding to this optimistic conviction, James sank into his last illness, following a stroke. He had the satisfaction of receiving from the British government the Order of Merit, and Lord Bryce, his old friend, brought him the insignia. Death came on February 28, 1916, at Chelsea, two months before what would have been his seventy-third birthday.

V

Every writer of fiction who is truly great creates his own special world. Necessarily this world is somewhat limited in its scope and atmosphere, as well as determined in many of its particulars, by the dominant kind of experience, the prevailing quality of the impressions, which his life has permitted him to garner.

The lives of some writers have afforded them wide experience of society's lower depths and of human nature in every condition of thwarted growth. Dostoevsky's Siberian years continued to inspire him in his harried explorations of underground man, of lacerated personality, from *Crime and Punishment* to *The Brothers Karamazov*. Émile Zola amidst the *bourgeois* opulence won by his energy and genius did not forget the Parisian slums of his youth. Theodore Dreiser's imagination never wholly emancipated itself from his reporter's apprenticeship with its daily routine panorama of "the drab and the gross and the horrible," as one of his bosses, H. B. Wandell, the hard-boiled editor of the St. Louis *Republic,* used to describe it.

In contrast with these writers, Henry James led a life that permitted him to wander at will through society's roof-gardens in two hemispheres and to know intimately human nature in all the fineness, all the largesse—as well as some of the pretensions, equivocations, malices, and dilemmas—of its highest growth. The special world of his fiction is not merely a transcription of leisured, cultured, wealthy Albany, New York, Newport, Boston, Cambridge, London, Paris, Rome, Florence, and Sussex as he had known them in mundane reality; rather, it reflects them as in a kind of magic mirror, which heightens here, shortens there, opens vistas yonder, gives Argus-glimpses into the pools and jungles of many minds, and bathes everything in sourceless light.

Quite aware that the world of his fiction was a special world, that the mirror of his art was a magic mirror, James disliked the kind of criticism that sought to define with too glib exactness what good fiction ought to be. The English novelist, Walter Besant, delivered April 25, 1884, at the Royal Institution in London, a lecture on "The Art of Fiction," which was shortly printed in pamphlet form. James' essay commenting upon it, also entitled "The Art of Fiction," is an elaborate plea that the novelist or story-teller should be completely emancipated from a too literalistic respect for formulas, for prescriptions and rules, either on his own part or the part of the critics and the reading public.

Besant, convinced not only that fiction was an art but also that it might be one of the greatest of the arts, had drawn up a list of such rules to help the beginning craftsman. James, praising Besant's general conception of fiction as an art, summarizes these rules, states that he himself finds it difficult "to dissent from any one," adds that "at the same time" he finds it "difficult positively to assent to them," and then proceeds to explain wherein, despite their seeming good sense, they are ambiguous, misleading, and inadequate. Defining the novel as "a personal impression of life," insisting that "Humanity is immense, and reality has a myriad forms" and that "Experience is never limited . . . never complete," James shows the fatuousness and untenability of many of the platitudes, the labels, the neat distinctions dear to the theorist about fiction and to the average reader and reviewer of it.

In the course of his subtle analysis, he makes the point that Émile Zola, "who reasons less powerfully than he represents," thinks "that there are certain things that people ought to like, and that they can be made to like." Although James could appreciate the magnitude of Zola's artistic achievement— as the fine essay on Zola in his *Notes on Novelists* so abundantly shows—, he obviously regarded Zola's theory of the so-called "experimental" or naturalistic novel as another attempt to confine the writer of fiction within pre-established narrow boundaries, to dictate beforehand the life, feeling, observation, vision that ought to go into the making of a fictive world.

Exploring the nature of the novel, Henry James was as much of a radical empiricist and pluralist as William James exploring the nature of the universe, or, more appropriately, the multiverse.

It was during the period when James was in the prime of his still developing powers that the French naturalistic novel—rejecting Balzac's "phantasmatography" but building "experimentally," in the spirit and according to the methods of "science," on his "sense of reality," to use Zola's jargon— achieved wide popularity on the continent and began to exert some influence on both English and American fiction.

The naturalistic novel emphasized environment as one of the factors determining human behavior and conceived environment as including economic forces hitherto usually ignored by writers of fiction in their treatment of given social *milieux*. The naturalistic novel recognized the role of the individual's psychology as a factor in shaping his conduct, but oversimplified this psychology by viewing it as a mechanism of stimulus and response functioning in a pattern of inherited traits and "lesions" of the nervous system. The characters in a naturalistic novel were not morally responsible free agents, but victims of environment, heredity, and circumstance: hence their dramas did not stress inner conflicts and ethical issues, but turned primarily on struggles or half-struggles against disasters largely external and beyond the power of their volition to precipitate, avert, or modify.

The naturalistic novel eliminated supernaturalism of all kinds from its reading of life; no revenants might return from beyond the grave to haunt its glimpses of the slum, the dramshop, the brothel, the mine, the factory, the morgue, the asylum, the battlefield, the rutting pasture, and the barren heath, save in occasional nightmares of the insane or the alcoholic. Finally, the naturalistic novel strove to build its illusion of life by rigorous fidelity to the verifiable external facts of an actual environment, and this method necessarily hampered its author in the use of imaginative symbolism, save of the most rudimentary and obvious sort, and kept him from any real plunge into "the stream of consciousness."

The vast body of fiction which James produced in the course of his long career is generally considered as representing three stages of development: his apprenticeship, his "middle years," his "third manner" or "major phase." Yet in all these stages, and in both short and longer forms, he tended generally to avoid the main emphases found in the naturalistic novel. On the one hand, his kind of fiction looked backward in its reading of life and its technique to the fiction produced before "naturalism" had become a literary conjure-word—to the fiction, say, of Hawthorne and George Eliot and Turgenev. On the other hand, the Jamesian novel and story looked forward, preparing the way for the kind of fiction that would be most prized when "naturalism" had declined into a meaningless label or a spent "movement" or an assimilated "tendency"—the fiction, namely, of Virginia Woolf, James Joyce, Dorothy Richardson, E. M. Forster, Percy Lubbock, and Edith Wharton, all of whom may be regarded as, in varying degrees, his disciples.

VI

Instead of analyzing and dramatizing the economic forces which, from the American Civil War to World War I, were helping bedevil men's relations, James sought to provide in his fiction a wholly different kind of "social signif-icance." By bringing together characters who epitomized in one way or another the national cultures which had produced or most influenced them—English culture or French or Italian or American—he tried to make his novels and stories instruments for better international understanding. To enhance this understanding, he invoked, not only the tragic, but also the comic muse, and peopled his stage so as to portray impartially both the virtues and the defects to be found, say, in either of two given cultures.

The American (1876-7), one of his earlier novels, is an excellent example. Christopher Newman, the American manufacturer and financier who has come to Europe in search of an education and a wife, is the successful self-made man of a democratic society at his best. But two other Americans abroad—the breezily vulgar Mr. Tristram and the portentously serious Reverend Babcock—reveal an incongruous lack of balance in the American environment and psyche. The Bellegarde family, whose charming Claire becomes the object of Newman's suit, represent what is best and what is worst in the French aristocracy. The Nioche family, on the other hand—Papa and Mademoiselle between them—, show that a materialism and an amorality somewhat shocking to the American moral sense may be discovered among the French lower *bourgeoisie*. *Daisy Miller* (1878), James' first widely popular *nouvelle*, should be read as another illustra-tion of what may be called "the international theme."

Instead of oversimplifying the psychology of the individual, James tried to unfold it in all its subtle complexity of reaction and development. He valued characters according to the extent that they had transcended the plane of mere animal existence, as the following passage from his preface to *The Princess Casamassima* makes clear: " . . . the figures in any picture, the agents in any drama, are interesting only in proportion as they feel their respective situations. . . . But there are degrees of feeling—the muffled, the faint, the just sufficient, the barely intelligent, as we may say; and the acute, the intense, the complete, in a word—the power to be finely aware and richly responsible . . . We care, our curiosity and our sympathy care, comparatively little for what happens to the stupid, the coarse and the blind; care for it, and for the effects of it, at the most as helping to precipitate what happens to the more deeply wondering, to the really sentient."

The characters who "matter" to him most are those undergoing inner conflict and confronted by ethical issues. Christopher Newman in *The American* is a character of this kind, as is Claire de Cintré, but the point may be illustrated by another and later novel dealing with "the international theme," *The Portrait of a Lady* (1880-1). Isabel Archer, the American heroine, has the opportunity to pursue in Europe her ideal of self-perfection. Her reactions to her multifarious impressions; the development of her personality under the impact of all this experience, particularly her extreme idealization of Gilbert Osmond, the consummate cosmopolitan *émigré,* and Madame Merle, the woman of cryptically imperturbable poise; her conflict of loyalties after she has plucked out the heart of this woman's mystery; the ultimate, irrevocable, and somewhat surprising decision which she must then make and why she makes it—these are the cruxes on which James lavishes all the resources of his prose.

The Ambassadors (1903), one of the masterpieces of his last phase and another novel wherein "the international theme" has some centrality, is a striking example of his psychological and ethical emphasis. Lambert Strether, sent in his dessicated middle age by his New England patroness, Mrs. Newsome, to bring home her son Chad from the suspected clutches of a hypothetical French siren, recovers gradually much of the youth that was his when he made his one European tour so long ago. There is a French woman with whom Chad is friendly and who has worked wonders with his mind and personality and manner, but she doesn't seem to Strether to have Chad in her clutches or to be at all a siren. So Strether hesitates to command Chad home. The consequence is that Mrs. Newsome sends other ambassadors, her married daughter, Sarah Pocock, and Jim Pocock, and Mamie Pocock, whom she intends Chad to marry. Chad will do whatever Strether tells him. The aggressive Sarah presses Strether for his decision. His cultured expatriate friend, Maria Gostrey, would have him decide quite differently and stands ready to reward him as handsomely as Mrs. Newsome. Here are the codes of Woollett, Massachusetts, and of Paris, France, squarely and bewilderingly opposed! While trying to make his decision, Strether instead makes a discovery—a startling one for him.

What will his decision be now? Thus does James build the reader up to a high point of suspense by keeping the focus upon Strether, the ethical nuances that claim his attention, and the complications introduced by his reburgeoning buried self.

A number of James' stories concern artists and writers—"The Madonna of the Future," "The Author of Beltraffio," "The Lesson of the Master," "The Real Thing," "The Death of the Lion," "The Next Time," "The Middle Years," "The Figure in the Carpet," "The Story in It," "Greville Fane," "Broken Wings," "The Velvet Glove," "The Liar," "The Coxon Fund," "The Private Life," and "The Great Good Place." Some of the characters in these stories are projections of himself or of the kind of artist or writer he might have been; through these characters he poses problems both of the artist's conscience and the artist's sensibility.

Use of the supernatural, of imaginative symbolism, of a presentation very close to "the stream of consciousness" or "interior monologue," or "slow-motion photography"—these possibilities that were shunned or undeveloped in the naturalistic fiction of his day distinguish James' work, especially that of his late "middle years" and of his final period.

In *The Turn of the Screw* (1898) two sinister servants come back from the realm of the dead to entice into their unspeakable possession a boy and a girl who have been entrusted to an unusually intuitive, conscientious, and morally courageous governess. This ghost story with its gothic setting is also a symbolic rendering of the struggle between Good and Evil, with the Evil persisting out of the Past. Poe would have been proud to achieve its effect of terror, and Hawthorne would have admired its ethical suggestiveness and psychological depth.

The Spoils of Poynton (1896) treats two country houses as symbols. Waterbath, the home of the wealthy Brigstocks, who have no taste, is furnished with gaudy junk, with ostentatious rubbish. It symbolizes the world of the new *haute bourgeoisie*. It stands for acquisitiveness, for vulgarity, for modernity. Poynton, on the other hand, the creation of Mrs. Gereth's and her dead husband's impeccable taste, is a kind of "palace of art." It symbolizes the world of a discriminating aristocracy. It stands for beauty, for culture, for tradition. The tale "Flickerbridge," from *The Better Sort* (1903), is rich in a comparable symbolism.

In *The Ambassadors* the whole story is sieved through Strether's thought and feeling and perception, so that the reader has the illusion of being caught in the immediacy of this character's experience. It is experience that can best be described by a passage from James' essay, "The Art of Fiction": ". . . it is an immense sensibility, a kind of huge spider-web, of the finest silken threads, suspended in the chamber of consciousness and catching every air-borne particle in its tissue. It is the very atmosphere of the mind; and when the mind is imaginative—much more when it happens to be that of a man of genius—it takes to itself the faintest hints of life, it converts the very pulses of the air into revelations." "The Beast in the Jungle," another story from *The Better Sort,* illustrates what James can do, in smaller compass, with this method of narrative, this delimitation of the "point of view." Here is a sensibility that is also like a spider-web, but at its center the spider actually emerges, crawling into ken as the irrational always crawls, save where there is Reason or Grace or Irony to exorcise its furtive shadow.

One of the great values of James for the modern reader is that these three—Reason and Grace and Irony—serene, shining, alert, and arm in arm, form "the figure in the carpet" of his immense achievement.

[A standard biography is Pelham Edgar's *Henry James: Man and Author* (London, 1927). C. H. Grattan's *The Three Jameses* (New York, 1932) is the best biographical and critical study of Henry James, Sr., William James, and Henry James as a group. It has been invaluably supplemented by F. O. Matthiessen's anthology, *The James Family* (New York, 1947). Van Wyck Brooks' *The Pilgrimage of Henry James* (New York, 1925) is thesis-ridden but stimulating in its method of presentation. Percy Lubbock's edition of *The Letters of Henry James* (New York, 1920) in two volumes is an indispensable source-book, as is *The Notebooks of Henry James,* ed. F. O. Matthiessen and Kenneth B. Murdock (New York, 1947). Allan Wade has collected James' notes on acting and the drama in *The Scenic Art* (New Brunswick, 1948). Theodora Bosanquet's *Henry James at Work* (London, 1924) is a view of him by his stenographer. Simon Nowell-Smith's *The Legend of the Master* (New York, 1948) is a comprehensive collection of James anecdotes. The best critical studies are Joseph Warren Beach's *The Method of Henry James* (New Haven, 1918), Cornelia Pulsifer Kelley's *The Early Development of Henry James* (Urbana, Ill., 1930), and F. O. Matthiessen's *Henry James: the Major Phase* (New York, 1944). Henry James' *The Art of the Novel* (New York, 1934) is a convenient reprint of his prefaces to the New York Edition and contains a good introductory essay by R. P. Blackmur. Essays are to be found in Ernest A. Baker's *The History of the English Novel,* Vol. IX (London, 1938), in L. N. Richardson's *James* (New York, 1941) in American Writers Series, and in Austin Warren's *Rage for Order* (Chicago, 1948). F. W. Dupee's *The Question of Henry James* (New York, 1945) is an anthology of the best criticism. Clifton Fadiman's edition of *The Short Stories of Henry James* (New York, 1945) contains a popular re-evaluation.]

THE ART OF FICTION
[1885 (1884)]

I SHOULD not have affixed so comprehensive a title to these few remarks, necessarily wanting in any completeness upon a subject the full consideration of which would carry us far, did I not seem to discover a pretext for my temerity in the interesting pamphlet lately published under this name by Mr. Walter Besant.[1] Mr. Besant's lecture at the Royal Institution —the original form of his pamphlet—appears to indicate that many persons are interested in the art of fiction, and are not indifferent to such remarks as those who practise it may attempt to make about it. I am therefore anxious not to lose the benefit of this favourable association, and to edge in a few words under cover of the attention which Mr. Besant is sure to have excited. There is something very encouraging in his having put into form certain of his ideas on the mystery of story-telling.

It is a proof of life and curiosity— curiosity on the part of the brotherhood of novelists as well as on the part of their readers. Only a short time ago it might have been supposed that the English novel was not what the French call *discutable*.[2] It had no air of having a theory, a conviction, a consciousness of itself behind it—of being the expression of an artistic faith, the result of choice and comparison. I do not say it was necessarily the worse for that: it would take much more courage than I possess to intimate that the form of the novel as Dickens and Thackeray (for instance) saw it had any taint of incompleteness. It was, however, *naïf* (if I may help myself out with another French word); and evidently if it be destined to suffer in any way for having lost its *naïveté* it has now an idea of making sure of the corresponding advantages. During the period I have alluded to there was a comfortable good-humoured feeling abroad that a novel is a novel, as a pudding is a pudding, and that our only business with it could be to swallow it. But within a year or two, for some reason or other, there have been signs of returning animation—the era of discussion would appear to have been to a certain extent opened. Art lives upon discussion, upon experiment, upon curiosity, upon variety of attempt, upon the exchange of views and the comparison of standpoints; and there is a presumption that those times when no one has anything particular to say about it, and has no reason to give for

practise or preference, though they may be times of honour, are not times of development—are times, possibly, even a little of dulness. The successful application of any art is a delightful spectacle, but the theory too is interesting; and though there is a great deal of the latter without the former I suspect there has never been a genuine success that has not had a latent core of conviction. Discussion, suggestion, formulation, these things are fertilizing when they are frank and sincere. Mr. Besant has set an excellent example in saying what he thinks, for his part, about the way in which fiction should be written, as well as about the way in which it should be published; for his view of the "art," carried on into an appendix, covers that too. Other labourers in the same field will doubtless take up the argument, they will give it the light of their experience, and the effect will surely be to make our interest in the novel a little more what it had for some time threatened to fail to be —a serious, active, inquiring interest, under protection of which this delightful study may, in moments of confidence, venture to say a little more what it thinks of itself.

It must take itself seriously for the public to take it so. The old superstition about fiction being "wicked" has doubtless died out in England; but the spirit of it lingers in a certain oblique regard directed toward any story which does not more or less admit that it is only a joke. Even the most jocular novel feels in some degree the weight of the proscription that was formerly directed against literary levity: the jocularity does not always succeed in passing for orthodoxy. It is still expected, though perhaps people are ashamed to say it, that a production which is after all only a "make-believe" (for what else is a "story"?) shall be in some degree apologetic—shall renounce the pretension of attempting really to represent life. This, of course, any sensible, wide-awake story de-

[1] English novelist and critic, 1836-1901.
[2] Debatable.

clines to do, for it quickly perceives that
the tolerance granted to it on such a condition is only an attempt to stifle it disguised
in the form of generosity. The old evan-
gelical hostility to the novel, which was as
explicit as it was narrow, and which regarded it as little less favourable to our
immortal part than a stage-play, was in
reality far less insulting. The only reason
for the existence of a novel is that it does
attempt to represent life. When it relin-
quishes this attempt, the same attempt that
we see on the canvas of the painter, it will
have arrived at a very strange pass. It
is not expected of the picture that it will
make itself humble in order to be forgiven;
and the analogy between the art of the
painter and the art of the novelist is, so
far as I am able to see, complete. Their
inspiration is the same, their process (allowing for the different quality of the
vehicle) is the same, their success is the
same. They may learn from each other,
they may explain and sustain each other.
Their cause is the same, and the honour of
one is the honour of another. The Ma-
hometans think a picture an unholy thing,
but it is a long time since any Christian
did, and it is therefore the more odd that
in the Christian mind the traces (dissimulated though they may be) of a suspicion
of the sister art should linger to this day.
The only effectual way to lay it to rest is
to emphasise the analogy to which I just
alluded—to insist on the fact that as the
picture is reality, so the novel is history.
That is the only general description (which
does it justice) that we may give of the
novel. But history also is allowed to represent life; it is not, any more than painting,
expected to apologize. The subject-matter
of fiction is stored up likewise in documents and records, and if it will not give
itself away, as they say in California, it
must speak with assurance, with the tone
of the historian. Certain accomplished novelists have a habit of giving themselves
away which must often bring tears to the
eyes of people who take their fiction seriously. I was lately struck, in reading over

many pages of Anthony Trollope, with his
want of discretion in this particular. In a
digression, a parenthesis or an aside, he
concedes to the reader that he and this
trusting friend are only "making believe."
He admits that the events he narrates have
not really happened, and that he can give
his narrative any turn the reader may like
best. Such a betrayal of a sacred office
seems to me, I confess, a terrible crime; it
is what I mean by the attitude of apology,
and it shocks me every whit as much in
Trollope as it would have shocked me in
Gibbon or Macaulay. It implies that the
novelist is less occupied in looking for the
truth (the truth, of course I mean, that he
assumes, the premises that we must grant
him, whatever they may be) than the historian, and in doing so it deprives him at
a stroke of all his standing-room. To represent and illustrate the past, the actions of
men, is the task of either writer, and the
only difference that I can see is, in proportion as he succeeds, to the honour of the
novelist, consisting as it does in his having
more difficulty in collecting his evidence,
which is so far from being purely literary.
It seems to me to give him a great character, the fact that he has at once so much in
common with the philosopher and the
painter; this double analogy is a magnificent heritage.

It is of all this evidently that Mr. Besant
is full when he insists upon the fact that
fiction is one of the *fine* arts, deserving in
its turn of all the honours and emoluments
that have hitherto been reserved for the
successful profession of music, poetry,
painting, architecture. It is impossible to
insist too much on so important a truth,
and the place that Mr. Besant demands for
the work of the novelist may be represented, a trifle less abstractly, by saying
that he demands not only that it shall be
reputed artistic, but that it shall be reputed
very artistic indeed. It is excellent that he
should have struck this note, for his doing
so indicates that there was need of it, that
his proposition may be to many people a
novelty. One rubs one's eyes at the thought;

but the rest of Mr. Besant's essay confirms the revelation. I suspect in truth that it would be possible to confirm it still further, and that one would not be far wrong in saying that in addition to the people to whom it has never occurred that a novel ought to be artistic, there are a great many others who, if this principle were urged upon them, would be filled with an indefinable mistrust. They would find it difficult to explain their repugnance, but it would operate strongly to put them on their guard. "Art," in our Protestant communities, where so many things have got so strangely twisted about, is supposed in certain circles to have some vague injurious effect upon those who make it an important consideration, who let it weigh in the balance. It is assumed to be opposed in some mysterious manner to morality, to amusement, to instruction. When it is embodied in the work of the painter (the sculptor is another affair!) you know what it is: it stands there before you, in the honesty of pink and green and a gilt frame; you can see the worst of it at a glance, and you can be on your guard. But when it is introduced into literature it becomes more insidious—there is danger of its hurting you before you know it. Literature should be either instructive or amusing, and there is in many minds an impression that these artistic preoccupations, the search for form, contribute to neither end, interfere indeed with both. They are too frivolous to be edifying, and too serious to be diverting; and they are moreover priggish and paradoxical and superfluous. That, I think, represents the manner in which the latent thought of many people who read novels as an exercise in skipping would explain itself if it were to become articulate. They would argue, of course, that a novel ought to be "good," but they would interpret this term in a fashion of their own, which indeed would vary considerably from one critic to another. One would say that being good means representing virtuous and aspiring characters placed in prominent positions;

another would say that it depends on a "happy ending," on a distribution at the last of prizes, pensions, husbands, wives, babies, millions, appended paragraphs, and cheerful remarks. Another still would say that it means being full of incident and movement, so that we shall wish to jump ahead, to see who was the mysterious stranger, and if the stolen will was ever found, and shall not be distracted from this pleasure by any tiresome analysis or "description." But they would all agree that the "artistic" idea would spoil some of their fun. One would hold it accountable for all the description, another would see it revealed in the absence of sympathy. Its hostility to a happy ending would be evident, and it might even in some cases render any ending at all impossible. The "ending" of a novel is, for many persons, like that of a good dinner, a course of dessert and ices, and the artist in fiction is regarded as a sort of meddlesome doctor who forbids agreeable aftertastes. It is therefore true that this conception of Mr. Besant's of the novel as a superior form encounters not only a negative but a positive indifference. It matters little that as a work of art it should really be as little or as much of its essence to supply happy endings, sympathetic characters, and an objective tone, as if it were a work of mechanics: the association of ideas, however incongruous, might easily be too much for it if an eloquent voice were not sometimes raised to call attention to the fact that it is at once as free and as serious a branch of literature as any other.

Certainly this might sometimes be doubted in presence of the enormous number of works of fiction that appeal to the credulity of our generation, for it might easily seem that there could be no great character in a commodity so quickly and easily produced. It must be admitted that good novels are much compromised by bad ones, and that the field at large suffers discredit from overcrowding. I think, however, that this injury is only superficial, and that the superabundance of written fiction proves nothing against the principle itself. It has been vulgarised, like all other kinds of literature, like everything else to-day, and it has proved more than some kinds accessible to vulgarisation. But there is as much difference as there ever was between a good novel and a bad one: the bad is swept with all the daubed canvases and spoiled marble into some unvisited limbo, or infinite rubbish-yard beneath the back-windows of the world, and the good subsists and emits its light and stimulates our desire for perfection. As I shall take the liberty of making but a single criticism of Mr. Besant, whose tone is so full of love of his art, I may as well have done with it at once. He seems to me to mistake, in attempting to say so definitely beforehand, what sort of an affair the good novel will be. To indicate the danger of such an error as that has been the purpose of these few pages; to suggest that certain traditions on the subject, applied *a priori*, have already had much to answer for, and that the good health of an art which undertakes so immediately to reproduce life must demand that it be perfectly free. It lives upon exercise, and the very meaning of exercise is freedom. The only obligation to which in advance we may hold a novel, without incurring the accusation of being arbitrary, is that it be interesting. That general responsibility rests upon it, but it is the only one I can think of. The ways in which it is at liberty to accomplish this result (of interesting us) strike me as innumerable, and such as can only suffer from being marked out or fenced in by prescription. They are as various as the temperament of man, and they are successful in proportion as they reveal a particular mind, different from others. A novel is in its broadest definition a personal, a direct impression of life: that, to begin with, constitutes its value, which is greater or less according to the intensity of the impression. But there will be no intensity at all, and therefore no value, unless there is freedom to feel and say. The tracing of a line to be followed, of a tone to be

taken, of a form to be filled out, is a limitation of that freedom and a suppression of the very thing that we are most curious about. The form, it seems to me, is to be appreciated after the fact: then the author's choice has been made, his standard has been indicated; then we can follow lines and directions and compare tones and resemblances. Then in a word we can enjoy one of the most charming of pleasures, we can estimate quality, we can apply the test of execution. The execution belongs to the author alone; it is what is most personal to him, and we measure him by that. The advantage, the luxury, as well as the torment and responsibility of the novelist, is that there is no limit to what he may attempt as an executant—no limit to his possible experiments, efforts, discoveries, successes. Here it is especially that he works, step by step, like his brother of the brush, of whom we may always say that he has painted his picture in a manner best known to himself. His manner is his secret, not necessarily a jealous one. He cannot disclose it as a general thing if he would; he would be at a loss to teach it to others. I say this with a due recollection of having insisted on the community of method of the artist who paints a picture and the artist who writes a novel. The painter *is* able to teach the rudiments of his practice, and it is possible, from the study of good work (granted the aptitude), both to learn how to paint and to learn how to write. Yet it remains true, without injury to the *rapprochement*,[3] that the literary artist would be obliged to say to his pupil much more than the other, "Ah, well, you must do it as you can!" It is a question of degree, a matter of delicacy. If there are exact sciences, there are also exact arts, and the grammar of painting is so much more definite that it makes the difference.

I ought to add, however, that if Mr. Besant says at the beginning of his essay that the "laws of fiction may be laid down

---

[3] Analogy or likeness (between the two arts).

and taught with as much precision and exactness as the laws of harmony, perspective, and proportion," he mitigates what might appear to be an extravagance by applying his remark to "general" laws, and by expressing most of these rules in a manner with which it would certainly be unaccommodating to disagree. That the novelist must write from his experience, that his "Characters must be real and such as might be met with in actual life;" that "a young lady brought up in a quiet country village should avoid descriptions of garrison life," and "a writer whose friends and personal experiences belong to the lower middle-class should carefully avoid introducing his characters into society;" that one should enter one's notes in a common-place book; that one's figures should be clear in outline; that making them clear by some trick of speech or of carriage is a bad method, and "describing them at length" is a worse one; that English Fiction should have a "conscious moral purpose;" that "it is almost impossible to estimate too highly the value of careful workmanship—that is, of style;" that "the most important point of all is the story," that "the story is everything:" these are principles with most of which it is surely impossible not to sympathise. That remark about the lower middle-class writer and his knowing his place is perhaps rather chilling; but for the rest I should find it difficult to dissent from any one of these recommendations. At the same time, I should find it difficult positively to assent to them, with the exception, perhaps, of the injunction as to entering one's notes in a common-place book. They scarcely seem to me to have the quality that Mr. Besant attributes to the rules of the novelist—the "precision and exactness" of "the laws of harmony, perspective, and proportion." They are suggestive, they are even inspiring, but they are not exact, though they are doubtless as much so as the case admits of: which is a proof of that liberty of interpretation for which I just contended. For the value of these different injunctions—so beautiful and so vague—

is wholly in the meaning one attaches to them. The characters, the situation, which strike one as real will be those that touch and interest one most, but the measure of reality is very difficult to fix. The reality of Don Quixote or of Mr. Micawber is a very delicate shade; it is a reality so coloured by the author's vision that, vivid as it may be, one would hesitate to propose it as a model: one would expose one's self to some very embarrassing questions on the part of a pupil. It goes without saying that you will not write a good novel unless you possess the sense of reality; but it will be difficult to give you a recipe for calling that sense into being. Humanity is immense, and reality has a myriad forms; the most one can affirm is that some of the flowers of fiction have the odour of it, and others have not; as for telling you in advance how your nosegay should be composed, that is another affair. It is equally excellent and inconclusive to say that one must write from experience; to our suppositious aspirant such a declaration might savour of mockery. What kind of experience is intended, and where does it begin and end? Experience is never limited, and it is never complete; it is an immense sensibility, a kind of huge spider-web of the finest silken threads suspended in the chamber of consciousness, and catching every air-borne particle in its tissue. It is the very atmosphere of the mind; and when the mind is imaginative—much more when it happens to be that of a man of genius—it takes to itself the faintest hints of life, it converts the very pulses of the air into revelations. The young lady living in a village has only to be a damsel upon whom nothing is lost to make it quite unfair (as it seems to me) to declare to her that she shall have nothing to say about the military. Greater miracles have been seen than that, imagination assisting, she should speak the truth about some of these gentlemen. I remember an English novelist, a woman of genius, telling me that she was much commended for the impression she had managed to give in one of her tales of the nature and way of life of the French Protestant youth. She had been asked where she learned so much about this recondite being, she had been congratulated on her peculiar opportunities. These opportunities consisted in her having once, in Paris, as she ascended a staircase, passed an open door where, in the household of a *pasteur*,[4] some of the young Protestants were seated at table round a finished meal. The glimpse made a picture; it lasted only a moment, but that moment was experience. She had got her direct personal impression, and she turned out her type. She knew what youth was, and what Protestantism; she also had the advantage of having seen what it was to be French, so that she converted these ideas into a concrete image and produced a reality. Above all, however, she was blessed with the faculty which when you give it an inch takes an ell, and which for the artist is a much greater source of strength than any accident of residence or of place in the social scale. The power to guess the unseen from the seen, to trace the implication of things, to judge the whole piece by the pattern, the condition of feeling life in general so completely that you are well on your way to knowing any particular corner of it—this cluster of gifts may almost be said to constitute experience, and they occur in country and in town, and in the most differing stages of education. If experience consists of impressions, it may be said that impressions *are* experience, just as (have we not seen it?) they are the very air we breathe. Therefore, if I should certainly say to a novice, "Write from experience and experience only," I should feel that this was rather a tantalising monition if I were not careful immediately to add, "Try to be one of the people on whom nothing is lost!"

I am far from intending by this to minimise the importance of exactness—of truth of detail. One can speak best from one's own taste, and I may therefore venture to say that the air of reality (solidity of specification) seems to me to be the supreme virtue of a novel—the merit on which all its other merits (including that conscious moral purpose of which Mr. Besant speaks) helplessly and submissively depend. If it be not there they are all as nothing, and if these be there, they owe their effect to the success with which the author has produced the illusion of life. The cultivation of this success, the study of this exquisite process, form, to my taste, the beginning and the end of the art of the novelist. They are his inspiration, his despair, his reward, his torment, his delight. It is here in very truth that he competes with life; it is here that he competes with his brother the painter in *his* attempt to render the look of things, the look that conveys their meaning, to catch the colour, the relief, the expression, the surface, the substance of the human spectacle. It is in regard to this that Mr. Besant is well inspired when he bids him take notes. He cannot possibly take too many, he cannot possibly take enough. All life solicits him, and to "render" the simplest surface, to produce the most momentary illusion, is a very complicated business. His case would be easier, and the rule would be more exact, if Mr. Besant had been able to tell him what notes to take. But this, I fear, he can never learn in any manual; it is the business of his life. He has to take a great many in order to select a few, he has to work them up as he can, and even the guides and philosophers who might have most to say to him must leave him alone when it comes to the application of precepts, as we leave the painter in communion with his palette. That his characters "must be clear in outline," as Mr. Besant says—he feels that down to his boots; but how he shall make them so is a secret between his good angel and himself. It would be absurdly simple if he could be taught that a great deal of "description" would make them so, or that on the contrary the absence of description and the cultivation of dialogue, or the absence of dialogue and the multiplication of "incident," would res-

---

[4] Pastor.

cue him from his difficulties. Nothing, for instance, is more possible than that he be of a turn of mind for which this odd, literal opposition of description and dialogue, incident and description, has little meaning and light. People often talk of these things as if they had a kind of internecine distinctness, instead of melting into each other at every breath, and being intimately associated parts of one general effort of expression. I cannot imagine composition existing in a series of blocks, nor conceive, in any novel worth discussing at all, of a passage of description that is not in its intention narrative, a passage of dialogue that is not in its intention descriptive, a touch of truth of any sort that does not partake of the nature of incident, or an incident that derives its interest from any other source than the general and only source of the success of a work of art—that of being illustrative. A novel is a living thing, all one and continuous, like any other organism, and in proportion as it lives will it be found, I think, that in each of the parts there is something of each of the other parts. The critic who over the close texture of a finished work shall pretend to trace a geography of items will mark some frontiers as artificial, I fear, as any that have been known to history. There is an old-fashioned distinction between the novel of character and the novel of incident which must have cost many a smile to the intending fabulist who was keen about his work. It appears to me as little to the point as the equally celebrated distinction between the novel and the romance—to answer as little to any reality. There are bad novels and good novels, as there are bad pictures and good pictures; but that is the only distinction in which I see any meaning, and I can as little imagine speaking of a novel of character as I can imagine speaking of a picture of character. When one says picture one says of character, when one says novel one says of incident, and the terms may be transposed at will. What is character but the determination of incident? What is incident but the illustra-

tion of character? What is either a picture or a novel that is *not* of character? What else do we seek in it and find in it? It is an incident for a woman to stand up with her hand resting on a table and look at you in a certain way; or if it be not an incident I think it will be hard to say what it is. At the same time it is an expression of character. If you say you don't see it (character in *that—allons donc!*),[5] this is exactly what the artist who has reasons of his own for thinking he *does* see it undertakes to show you. When a young man makes up his mind that he has not faith enough after all to enter the church as he intended, that is an incident, though you may not hurry to the end of the chapter to see whether perhaps he doesn't change once more. I do not say that these are extraordinary or startling incidents. I do not pretend to estimate the degree of interest proceeding from them, for this will depend upon the skill of the painter. It sounds almost puerile to say that some incidents are intrinsically much more important than others, and I need not take this precaution after having professed my sympathy for the major ones in remarking that the only classification of the novel that I can understand is into that which has life and that which has it not.

The novel and the romance, the novel of incident and that of character—these clumsy separations appear to me to have been made by critics and readers for their own convenience, and to help them out of some of their occasional predicaments, but to have little reality or interest for the producer, from whose point of view it is of course that we are attempting to consider the art of fiction. The case is the same with another shadowy category which Mr. Besant apparently is disposed to set up—that of the "modern English novel;" unless indeed it be that in this matter he has fallen into an accidental confusion of standpoints. It is not quite clear whether he intends the remarks in which he alludes

---

[5] Come, come!

to it to be didactic or historical. It is as difficult to suppose a person intending to write a modern English as to suppose him writing an ancient English novel: that is a label which begs the question. One writes the novel, one paints the picture, of one's language and of one's time, and calling it modern English will not, alas! make the difficult task any easier. No more, unfortunately, will calling this or that work of one's fellow-artist a romance—unless it be, of course, simply for the pleasantness of the thing, as for instance when Hawthorne gave this heading to his story of *Blithedale*. The French, who have brought the theory of fiction to remarkable completeness, have but one name for the novel, and have not attempted smaller things in it, that I can see, for that. I can think of no obligation to which the "romancer" would not be held equally with the novelist; the standard of execution is equally high for each. Of course it is of execution that we are talking—that being the only point of a novel that is open to contention. This is perhaps too often lost sight of, only to produce interminable confusions and cross-purposes. We must grant the artist his subject, his idea, his *donnée*: our criticism is applied only to what he makes if it. Naturally I do not mean that we are bound to like it or find it interesting: in case we do not our course is perfectly simple—to let it alone. We may believe that of a certain idea even the most sincere novelist can make nothing at all, and the event may perfectly justify our belief; but the failure will have been a failure to execute, and it is in the execution that the fatal weakness is recorded. If we pretend to respect the artist at all, we must allow him his freedom of choice, in the face, in particular cases, of innumerable presumptions that the choice will not fructify. Art derives a considerable part of its beneficial exercise from flying in the face of presumptions, and some of the most interesting experiments of which it is capable are hidden in the bosom of common things. Gustave Flaubert has written a story about the devotion of a servant-girl to a parrot,[6] and the production, highly finished as it is, cannot on the whole be called a success. We are perfectly free to find it flat, but I think it might have been interesting; and I, for my part, am extremely glad he should have written it; it is a contribution to our knowledge of what can be done—or what cannot. Ivan Turgénieff has written a tale about a deaf and dumb serf and a lap-dog,[7] and the thing is touching, loving, a little masterpiece. He struck the note of life where Gustave Flaubert missed it—he flew in the face of a presumption and achieved a victory.

Nothing, of course, will ever take the place of the good old fashion of "liking" a work of art or not liking it: the most improved criticism will not abolish that primitive, that ultimate test. I mention this to guard myself from the accusation of intimating that the idea, the subject, of a novel or a picture, does not matter. It matters, to my sense, in the highest degree, and if I might put up a prayer it would be that artists should select none but the richest. Some, as I have already hastened to admit, are much more remunerative than others, and it would be a world happily arranged in which persons intending to treat them should be exempt from confusions and mistakes. This fortunate condition will arrive only, I fear, on the same day that critics become purged from error. Meanwhile, I repeat, we do not judge the artist with fairness unless we say to him, "Oh, I grant you your starting-point, because if I did not I should seem to prescribe to you, and heaven forbid I should take that responsibility. If I pretend to tell you what you must not take, you will call upon me to tell you then what you must take; in which case I shall be prettily caught. Moreover, it isn't till I have accepted your data that I can begin to measure you. I have the standard, the pitch; I have no right to tamper with your flute and

[6] Flaubert's "A Simple Soul" in *Trois Contes* (1877).

[7] Turgenev's "Mumu" (1852).

then criticise your music. Of course I may not care for your idea at all; I may think it silly, or stale, or unclean; in which case I wash my hands of you altogether. I may content myself with believing that you will not have succeeded in being interesting, but I shall, of course, not attempt to demonstrate it, and you will be as indifferent to me as I am to you. I needn't remind you that there are all sorts of tastes: who can know it better? Some people, for excellent reasons, don't like to read about carpenters; others, for reasons even better, don't like to read about courtesans. Many object to Americans. Others (I believe they are mainly editors and publishers) won't look at Italians. Some readers don't like quiet subjects; others don't like bustling ones. Some enjoy a complete illusion, others the consciousness of large concessions. They choose their novels accordingly, and if they don't care about your idea they won't, a fortiori,[8] care about your treatment."

So that it comes back very quickly, as I have said, to the liking: in spite of M. Zola, who reasons less powerfully than he represents, and who will not reconcile himself to this absoluteness of taste, thinking that there are certain things that people ought to like, and that they can be made to like. I am quite at a loss to imagine anything (at any rate in this matter of fiction) that people *ought* to like or to dislike. Selection will be sure to take care of itself, for it has a constant motive behind it. That motive is simply experience. As people feel life, so they will feel the art that is most closely related to it. This closeness of relation is what we should never forget in talking of the effort of the novel. Many people speak of it as a factitious, artificial form, a product of ingenuity, the business of which it is to alter and arrange the things that surround us, to translate them into conventional, traditional moulds. This, however, is a view of the matter which carries us but a very short way, condemns the art to an eternal repetition of a few familiar *clichés*, cuts

short its development, and leads us straight up to a dead wall. Catching the very note and trick, the strange irregular rhythm of life, that is the attempt whose strenuous force keeps Fiction upon her feet. In proportion as in what she offers us we see life *without* rearrangement do we feel that we are touching the truth; in proportion as we see it *with* rearrangement do we feel that we are being put off with a substitute, a compromise and convention. It is not uncommon to hear an extraordinary assurance of remark in regard to this matter of rearranging, which is often spoken of as if it were the last word of art. Mr. Besant seems to me in danger of falling into the great error with his rather unguarded talk about "selection." Art is essentially selection, but it is a selection whose main care is to be typical, to be inclusive. For many people art means rose-coloured windowpanes, and selection means picking a bouquet for Mrs. Grundy.[9] They will tell you glibly that artistic considerations have nothing to do with the disagreeable, with the ugly; they will rattle off shallow commonplaces about the province of art and the limits of art till you are moved to some wonder in return as to the province and the limits of ignorance. It appears to me that no one can ever have made a seriously artistic attempt without becoming conscious of an immense increase—a kind of revelation—of freedom. One perceives in that case—by the light of a heavenly ray—that the province of art is all life, all feeling, all observation, all vision. As Mr. Besant so justly intimates, it is all experience. That is a sufficient answer to those who maintain that it must not touch the sad things of life, who stick into its divine unconscious bosom little prohibitory inscriptions on the end of sticks, such as we see in public gardens—"It is forbidden to walk on the grass; it is forbidden to touch

---

[8] All the more; with the greater force.

[9] A person representing the view of conventional society referred to continually in Thomas Morton's comedy, *Speed the Plough* (1798).

the flowers; it is not allowed to introduce dogs or to remain after dark; it is requested to keep to the right." The young aspirant in the line of fiction whom we continue to imagine will do nothing without taste, for in that case his freedom would be of little use to him; but the first advantage of his taste will be to reveal to him the absurdity of the little sticks and tickets. If he have taste, I must add, of course, he will have ingenuity, and my disrespectful reference to that quality just now was not meant to imply that it is useless in fiction. But it is only a secondary aid; the first is a capacity for receiving straight impressions.

Mr. Besant has some remarks on the question of "the story" which I shall not attempt to criticise, though they seem to me to contain a singular ambiguity, because I do not think I understand them. I cannot see what is meant by talking as if there were a part of a novel which is the story and part of it which for mystical reasons is not—unless indeed the distinction be made in a sense in which it is difficult to suppose that any one should attempt to convey anything. "The story," if it represents anything, represents the subject, the idea, the *donnée* of the novel; and there is surely no "school"—Mr. Besant speaks of a school—which urges that a novel should be all treatment and no subject. There must assuredly be something to treat; every school is intimately conscious of that. This sense of the story being the idea, the starting-point, of the novel, is the only one that I see in which it can be spoken of as something different from its organic whole; and since in proportion as the work is successful the idea permeates and penetrates it, informs and animates it, so that every word and every punctuation-point contribute directly to the expression, in that proportion do we lose our sense of the story being a blade which may be drawn more or less out of its sheath. The story and the novel, the idea and the form, are the needle and thread, and I never heard of a guild of tailors who recommended the use of the thread without the needle, or the needle without the thread. Mr. Besant is not the only critic who may be observed to have spoken as if there were certain things in life which constitute stories, and certain others which do not. I find the same odd implication in an entertaining article in the *Pall Mall Gazette,* devoted, as it happens, to Mr. Besant's lecture. "The story is the thing!" says this graceful writer, as if with a tone of opposition to some other idea. I should think it was, as every painter who, as the time for "sending in" his picture looms in the distance, finds himself still in quest of a subject—as every belated artist not fixed about his theme will heartily agree. There are some subjects which speak to us and others which do not, but he would be a clever man who should undertake to give a rule—an index expurgatorius —by which the story and the no-story should be known apart. It is impossible (to me at least) to imagine any such rule which shall not be altogether arbitrary. The writer in the *Pall Mall* opposes the delightful (as I suppose) novel of *Margot la Balafrée* [10] to certain tales in which "Bostonian nymphs" appear to have "rejected English dukes for psychological reasons." I am not acquainted with the romance just designated, and can scarcely forgive the *Pall Mall* critic for not mentioning the name of the author, but the title appears to refer to a lady who may have received a scar in some heroic adventure. I am inconsolable at not being acquainted with this episode, but am utterly at a loss to see why it is a story when the rejection (or acceptance) of a duke is not, and why a reason, psychological or other, is not a subject when a cicatrix is. They are all particles of the multitudinous life with which the novel deals, and surely no dogma which pretends to make it lawful to touch the one and unlawful to touch the other will stand for a moment on its feet. It is the special picture that must stand or fall,

---

[10] *Margot the Scarred Woman* (1884), by Fortuné Du Boisgobey (1821-1891).

according as it seems to possess truth or to lack it. Mr. Besant does not, to my sense, light up the subject by intimating that a story must, under penalty of not being a story, consist of "adventures." Why of adventures more than of green spectacles? [11] He mentions a category of impossible things, and among them he places "fiction without adventure." Why without adventure, more than without matrimony, or celibacy, or parturition, or cholera, or hydropathy, or Jansenism? [12] This seems to me to bring the novel back to the hapless little *rôle* of being an artificial, ingenious thing —bring it down from its large, free character of an immense and exquisite correspondence with life. And what *is* adventure when it comes to that, and by what sign is the listening pupil to recognize it? It is an adventure—an immense one—for me to write this little article; and for a Bostonian nymph to reject an English duke is an adventure only less stirring, I should say, than for an English duke to be rejected by a Bostonian nymph. I see dramas within dramas in that, and innumerable points of view. A psychological reason is, to my imagination, an object adorably pictorial; to catch the tint of its complexion—I feel as if that idea might inspire one to Titian-esque efforts. There are few things more exciting to me, in short, than a psychological reason, and yet, I protest, the novel seems to me the most magnificent form of art. I have just been reading, at the same time, the delightful story of *Treasure Island,* by Mr. Robert Louis Stevenson and, in a manner less consecutive, the last tale from M. Edmond de Goncourt, which is entitled *Chérie.* One of these works treats of murders, mysteries, islands of dreadful renown, hairbreadth escapes, miraculous coincidences, and buried doubloons. The other treats of a little French girl who lived in a fine house in Paris, and died of wounded sensibility because no one would marry her. I call *Treasure Island* delightful, because it appears to me to have succeeded wonderfully in what it attempts; and I venture to bestow no epithet upon

Chérie, which strikes me as having failed deplorably in what it attempts—that is, in tracing the development of the moral consciousness of a child. But one of these productions strikes me as exactly as much of a novel as the other, and as having a "story" quite as much. The moral consciousness of a child is as much a part of life as the islands of the Spanish Main, and the one sort of geography seems to me to have those "surprises" of which Mr. Besant speaks quite as much as the other. For myself (since it comes back in the last resort, as I say, to the preference of the individual), the picture of the child's experience has the advantage that I can at successive steps (an immense luxury, near to the "sensual pleasure" of which Mr. Besant's critic in the *Pall Mall* speaks) say Yes or No, as it may be, to what the artist puts before me. I have been a child in fact, but I have been on a quest for a buried treasure only in supposition, and it is a simple accident that with M. de Goncourt I should have for the most part to say No. With George Eliot, when she painted that country [13] with a far other intelligence, I always said Yes.

The most interesting part of Mr. Besant's lecture is unfortunately the briefest passage—his very cursory allusion to the "conscious moral purpose" of the novel. Here again it is not very clear whether he be recording a fact or laying down a principle; it is a great pity that in the latter case he should not have developed his idea. This branch of the subject is of immense importance, and Mr. Besant's few words point to considerations of the widest reach, not to be lightly disposed of. He will have treated the art of fiction but superficially who is not prepared to go every inch of the way that these considerations will carry

[11] In Oliver Goldsmith's *The Vicar of Wakefield,* Moses Primrose is sold a gross of green spectacles at a fair.

[12] A religious doctrine promulgated by Cornelius Jansen (1585-1638), Catholic bishop of Ypres in Flanders.

[13] The reference is to her *Silas Marner.*

him. It is for this reason that at the beginning of these remarks I was careful to notify the reader that my reflections on so large a theme have no pretension to be exhaustive. Like Mr. Besant, I have left the question of the morality of the novel till the last, and at the last I find I have used up my space. It is a question surrounded with difficulties, as witness the very first that meets us, in the form of a definite question, on the threshold. Vagueness, in such a discussion, is fatal, and what is the meaning of your morality and your conscious moral purpose? Will you not define your terms and explain how (a novel being a picture) a picture can be either moral or immoral? You wish to paint a moral picture or carve a moral statue: will you not tell us how you would set about it? We are discussing the Art of Fiction; questions of art are questions (in the widest sense) of execution; questions of morality are quite another affair, and will you not let us see how it is that you find it so easy to mix them up? These things are so clear to Mr. Besant that he has deduced from them a law which he sees embodied in English Fiction, and which is "a truly admirable thing and a great cause for congratulation." It is a great cause for congratulation indeed when such thorny problems become as smooth as silk. I may add that in so far as Mr. Besant perceives that in point of fact English Fiction has addressed itself preponderantly to these delicate questions he will appear to many people to have made a vain discovery. They will have been positively struck, on the contrary, with the moral timidity of the usual English novelist; with his (or with her) aversion to face the difficulties with which on every side the treatment of reality bristles. He is apt to be extremely shy (whereas the picture that Mr. Besant draws is a picture of boldness), and the sign of his work, for the most part, is a cautious silence on certain subjects. In the English novel (by which of course I mean the American as well), more than in any other, there is a traditional difference between that which people know

and that which they agree to admit that they know, that which they see and that which they speak of, that which they feel to be a part of life and that which they allow to enter into literature. There is the great difference, in short, between what they talk of in conversation and what they talk of in print. The essence of moral energy is to survey the whole field, and I should directly reverse Mr. Besant's remark and say not that the English novel has a purpose, but that it has a diffidence. To what degree a purpose in a work of art is a source of corruption I shall not attempt to inquire; the one that seems to me least dangerous is the purpose of making a perfect work. As for our novel, I may say lastly on this score that as we find it in England to-day it strikes me as addressed in a large degree to "young people," and that this in itself constitutes a presumption that it will be rather shy. There are certain things which it is generally agreed not to discuss, not even to mention, before young people. That is very well, but the absence of discussion is not a symptom of the moral passion. The purpose of the English novel—"a truly admirable thing, and a great cause for congratulation"—strikes me therefore as rather negative.

There is one point at which the moral sense and the artistic sense lie very near together; that is in the light of the very obvious truth that the deepest quality of a work of art will always be the quality of the mind of the producer. In proportion as that intelligence is fine will the novel, the picture, the statue partake of the substance of beauty and truth. To be constituted of such elements is, to my vision, to have purpose enough. No good novel will ever proceed from a superficial mind; that seems to me an axiom which, for the artist in fiction, will cover all needful moral ground: if the youthful aspirant take it to heart it will illuminate for him many of the mysteries of "purpose." There are many other useful things that might be said to him, but I have come to the end of my article, and can only touch them as I pass. The critic in the *Pall Mall Gazette,* whom I have already quoted, draws attention to the danger, in speaking of the art of fiction, of generalising. The danger that he has in mind is rather, I imagine, that of particularising, for there are some comprehensive remarks which, in addition to those embodied in Mr. Besant's suggestive lecture, might without fear of misleading him be addressed to the ingenuous student. I should remind him first of the magnificence of the form that is open to him, which offers to sight so few restrictions and such innumerable opportunities. The other arts, in comparison, appear confined and hampered; the various conditions under which they are exercised are so rigid and definite. But the only condition that I can think of attaching to the composition of the novel is, as I have already said, that it be sincere. This freedom is a splendid privilege, and the first lesson of the young novelist is to learn to be worthy of it. "Enjoy it as it deserves," I should say to him; "take possession of it, explore it to its utmost extent, publish it, rejoice in it. All life belongs to you, and do not listen either to those who would shut you up into corners of it and tell you that it is only here and there that art inhabits, or to those who would persuade you that this heavenly messenger wings her way outside of life altogether, breathing a superfine air, and turning away her head from the truth of things. There is no impression of life, no manner of seeing it and feeling it, to which the plan of the novelist may not offer a place; you have only to remember that talents so dissimilar as those of Alexandre Dumas and Jane Austen, Charles Dickens and Gustave Flaubert have worked in this field with equal glory. Do not think too much about optimism and pessimism; try and catch the colour of life itself. In France to-day we see a prodigious effort (that of Emile Zola, to whose solid and serious work no explorer of the capacity of the novel can allude without respect), we see an extraordinary effort, vitiated by a spirit of pessimism on a narrow basis.

M. Zola is magnificent, but he strikes an English reader as ignorant; he has an air of working in the dark; if he had as much light as energy, his results would be of the highest value. As for the aberrations of a shallow optimism, the ground (of English fiction especially) is strewn with their brittle particles as with broken glass. If you must indulge in conclusions, let them have the taste of a wide knowledge. Remember that your first duty is to be as complete as possible—to make as perfect a work. Be generous and delicate and pursue the prize."

DAISY MILLER: A STUDY
[1879 (1878)]

PART I

AT THE LITTLE town of Vevey, in Switzerland, there is a particularly comfortable hotel. There are, indeed, many hotels; for the entertainment of tourists is the business of the place, which, as many travellers will remember, is seated upon the edge of a remarkably blue lake—a lake that it behooves every tourist to visit. The shore of the lake presents an unbroken array of establishments of this order, of every category, from the "grand hotel" of the newest fashion, with a chalk-white front, a hundred balconies, and a dozen flags flying from its roof, to the little Swiss *pension* of an elder day, with its name inscribed in German-looking lettering upon a pink or yellow wall, and an awkward summer-house in the angle of the garden. One of the hotels at Vevey, however, is famous, even classical, being distinguished from many of its upstart neighbors by an air both of luxury and of maturity. In this region, in the month of June, American travellers are extremely numerous; it may be said, indeed, that Vevey assumes at this period some of the characteristics of an American watering-place. There are sights and sounds which evoke a vision, an echo, of Newport and Saratoga. There is a flitting hither and thither of "stylish" young girls, a rustling of muslin flounces, a rattle of dance-music in the morning hours, a sound of high-pitched voices at all times. You receive an impression of these things at the excellent inn of the "Trois Couronnes," and are transported in fancy to the Ocean House or to Congress Hall. But at the "Trois Couronnes," it must be added, there are other features that are much at variance with these suggestions: neat German waiters, who look like secretaries of legation; Russian princesses sitting in the garden; little Polish boys walking about, held by the hand, with their governors; a view of the sunny crest of the Dent du Midi [1] and the picturesque towers of the Castle of Chillon.

I hardly know whether it was the analogies or the differences that were uppermost in the mind of a young American, who, two or three years ago, sat in the garden of the "Trois Couronnes," looking about him, rather idly, at some of the graceful objects I have mentioned. It was a beautiful summer morning, and in whatever fashion the young American looked at things, they must have seemed to him charming. He had come from Geneva the day before, by the little steamer, to see his aunt, who was staying at the hotel—Geneva having been for a long time his place of residence. But his aunt had a headache—his aunt had almost always a headache—and now she was shut up in her room, smelling camphor, so that he was at liberty to wander about. He was some seven-and-twenty years of age; when his friends spoke of him, they usually said that he was at Geneva, "studying." When his enemies spoke of him, they said—but, after all, he had no enemies; he was an extremely amiable fellow, and universally liked. What I should say is, simply, that when certain persons spoke of him they affirmed that the reason of his spending so much time at Geneva was that he was extremely devoted to a lady who lived there—a foreign lady—a person older than himself. Very few Americans—indeed I think none—had ever seen this lady, about whom there were some singular stories. But Winterbourne had an old attachment for the little metrop-olis of Calvinism; he had been put to school there as a boy, and he had afterwards gone to college there—circumstances which had led to his forming a great many youthful friendships. Many of these he had kept, and they were a source of great satisfaction to him.

After knocking at his aunt's door and learning that she was indisposed, he had taken a walk about the town, and then he had come in to his breakfast. He had now finished his breakfast; but he was drinking a small cup of coffee, which had been served to him on a little table in the garden by one of the waiters who looked like an *attaché*. At last he finished his coffee and lit a cigarette. Presently a small boy came walking along the path—an urchin of nine or ten. The child, who was diminutive for his years, had an aged expression of countenance, a pale complexion, and sharp little features. He was dressed in knickerbockers, with red stockings, which displayed his poor little spindleshanks; he also wore a brilliant red cravat. He carried in his hand a long alpenstock, the sharp point of which he thrust into everything that he approached—the flower-beds, the garden-benches, the trains of the ladies' dresses. In front of Winterbourne he paused, looking at him with a pair of bright, penetrating little eyes.

"Will you give me a lump of sugar?" he asked, in a sharp, hard little voice—a voice immature, and yet, somehow, not young.

Winterbourne glanced at the small table near him, on which his coffee-service rested, and saw that several morsels of sugar remained. "Yes, you may take one," he answered; "but I don't think sugar is good for little boys."

This little boy stepped forward and carefully selected three of the coveted fragments, two of which he buried in the pocket of his knickerbockers, depositing the other as promptly in another place. He poked his alpenstock, lance-fashion, into

---

[1] Peak in the Swiss Alps.

Winterbourne's bench, and tried to crack the lump of sugar with his teeth.

"Oh, blazes; it's har-r-d!" he exclaimed, pronouncing the adjective in a peculiar manner.

Winterbourne had immediately perceived that he might have the honour of claiming him as a fellow-countryman. "Take care you don't hurt your teeth," he said, paternally.

"I haven't got any teeth to hurt. They have all come out. I have only got seven teeth. My mother counted them last night, and one came out right afterwards. She said she'd slap me if any more came out. I can't help it. It's this old Europe. It's the climate that makes them come out. In America they didn't come out. It's these hotels."

Winterbourne was much amused. "If you eat three lumps of sugar, your mother will certainly slap you," he said.

"She's got to give me some candy, then," rejoined his young interlocutor. "I can't get any candy here—any American candy. American candy's the best candy."

"And are American little boys the best little boys?" asked Winterbourne.

"I don't know. I'm an American boy," said the child.

"I see you are one of the best!" laughed Winterbourne.

"Are you an American man?" pursued this vivacious infant. And then, on Winterbourne's affirmative reply—"American men are the best," he declared.

His companion thanked him for the compliment; and the child, who had now got astride of his alpenstock, stood looking about him, while he attacked a second lump of sugar. Winterbourne wondered if he himself had been like this in his infancy, for he had been brought to Europe at about this age.

"Here comes my sister!" cried the child, in a moment. "She's an American girl."

Winterbourne looked along the path and saw a beautiful young lady advancing. "American girls are the best girls," he said, cheerfully, to his young companion.

"My sister ain't the best!" the child declared. "She's always blowing at me."

"I imagine that is your fault, not hers," said Winterbourne. The young lady meanwhile had drawn near. She was dressed in white muslin, with a hundred frills and flounces, and knots of pale-colored ribbon. She was bare-headed; but she balanced in her hand a large parasol, with a deep border of embroidery; and she was strikingly, admirably pretty. "How pretty they are!" thought Winterbourne, straightening himself in his seat, as if he were prepared to rise.

The young lady paused in front of his bench, near the parapet of the garden, which overlooked the lake. The little boy had now converted his alpenstock into a vaulting-pole, by the aid of which he was springing about in the gravel, and kicking it up not a little.

"Randolph," said the young lady, "what *are* you doing?"

"I'm going up the Alps," replied Randolph. "This is the way!" And he gave another little jump, scattering the pebbles about Winterbourne's ears.

"That's the way they come down," said Winterbourne.

"He's an American man!" cried Randolph, in his little hard voice.

The young lady gave no heed to this announcement, but looked straight at her brother. "Well, I guess you had better be quiet," she simply observed.

It seemed to Winterbourne that he had been in a manner presented. He got up and stepped slowly towards the young girl, throwing away his cigarette. "This little boy and I have made acquaintance," he said, with great civility. In Geneva, as he had been perfectly aware, a young man was not at liberty to speak to a young unmarried lady except under certain rarely-occurring conditions; but here at Vevey, what conditions could be better than these? —a pretty American girl coming and standing in front of you in a garden. This pretty American girl, however, on hearing Winterbourne's observation, simply glanced at him; she then turned her head and looked over the parapet, at the lake and the opposite mountains. He wondered whether he had gone too far; but he decided that he must advance farther, rather than retreat. While he was thinking of something else to say, the young lady turned to the little boy again.

"I should like to know where you got that pole," she said.

"I bought it!" responded Randolph.

"You don't mean to say you're going to take it to Italy."

"Yes, I am going to take it to Italy!" the child declared.

The young girl glanced over the front of her dress, and smoothed out a knot or two of ribbon. Then she rested her eyes upon the prospect again. "Well, I guess you had better leave it somewhere," she said, after a moment.

"Are you going to Italy?" Winterbourne inquired, in a tone of great respect.

The young lady glanced at him again. "Yes, sir," she replied. And she said nothing more.

"Are you—a—going over the Simplon?" [2] Winterbourne pursued, a little embarrassed.

"I don't know," she said. "I suppose it's some mountain. Randolph, what mountain are we going over?"

"Going where?" the child demanded.

"To Italy," Winterbourne explained.

"I don't know," said Randolph. "I don't want to go to Italy. I want to go to America."

"Oh, Italy is a beautiful place!" rejoined the young man.

"Can you get candy there?" Randolph loudly inquired.

"I hope not," said his sister. "I guess you have had enough candy, and mother thinks so too."

"I haven't had any for ever so long— for a hundred weeks!" cried the boy, still jumping about.

The young lady inspected her flounces and smoothed her ribbons again; and Winterbourne presently risked an observation upon the beauty of the view. He was ceasing to be embarrassed, for he had begun to perceive that she was not in the least embarrassed herself. There had not been the slightest alteration in her charming complexion; she was evidently neither offended nor fluttered. If she looked another way when he spoke to her, and seemed not particularly to hear him, this was simply her habit, her manner. Yet, as he talked a little more, and pointed out some of the objects of interest in the view, with which she appeared quite unacquainted, she gradually gave him more of the benefit of her glance; and then he saw that this glance was perfectly direct and unshrinking. It was, not, however, what would have been called an immodest glance, for the young girl's eyes were singularly honest and fresh. They were wonderfully pretty eyes; and, indeed, Winterbourne had not seen for a long time anything prettier than his fair countrywoman's various features—her complexion, her nose, her ears, her teeth. He had a great relish for feminine beauty; he was addicted to observing and analyzing it; and as regards this young lady's face he made several observations. It was not at all insipid, but it was not exactly expressive; and though it was eminently delicate Winterbourne mentally accused it—very forgivingly—of a want of finish. He thought it very possible that Master Randolph's sister was a coquette; he was sure she had a spirit of her own; but in her bright, sweet, superficial little visage there was no mockery, no irony. Before long it became obvious that she was much disposed towards conversation. She told him that they were going to Rome for the winter—she and her mother and Randolph. She asked him if he was a "real American"; she shouldn't have taken him for one; he seemed more like a German—this was said after a little hesitation, especially when he spoke. Winterbourne, laughing, answered that he had met Germans who spoke like Americans;

---

[2] An Alpine pass.

but that he had not, so far as he remembered, met an American who spoke like a German. Then he asked her if she should not be more comfortable in sitting upon the bench which he had just quitted. She answered that she liked standing up and walking about; but she presently sat down. She told him she was from New York State— "if you know where that is." Winterbourne learned more about her by catching hold of her small, slippery brother and making him stand a few minutes by his side.

"Tell me your name, my boy," he said.

"Randolph C. Miller," said the boy, sharply. "And I'll tell you her name;" and he levelled his alpenstock at his sister.

"You had better wait till you are asked!" said this young lady, calmly.

"I should like very much to know your name," said Winterbourne.

"Her name is Daisy Miller!" cried the child. "But that isn't her real name; that isn't her name on her cards."

"It's a pity you haven't got one of my cards!" said Miss Miller.

"Her real name is Annie P. Miller," the boy went on.

"Ask him *his* name," said his sister, indicating Winterbourne.

But on this point Randolph seemed perfectly indifferent; he continued to supply information in regard to his own family. "My father's name is Ezra B. Miller," he announced. "My father ain't in Europe; my father's in a better place than Europe."

Winterbourne imagined for a moment that this was the manner in which the child had been taught to intimate that Mr. Miller had been removed to the sphere of celestial rewards. But Randolph immediately added, "My father's in Schenectady. He's got a big business. My father's rich, you bet."

"Well!" ejaculated Miss Miller, lowering her parasol and looking at the embroidered border. Winterbourne presently released the child, who departed, dragging his alpenstock along the path. "He doesn't like Europe," said the young girl. "He wants to go back."

"To Schenectady, you mean?"

"Yes; he wants to go right home. He hasn't got any boys here. There is one boy here, but he always goes round with a teacher; they won't let him play."

"And your brother hasn't any teacher?" Winterbourne inquired.

"Mother thought of getting him one to travel round with us. There was a lady told her of a very good teacher; an American lady—perhaps you know her—Mrs. Sanders. I think she came from Boston. She told her of this teacher, and we thought of getting him to travel round with us. But Randolph said he didn't want a teacher travelling round with us. He said he wouldn't have lessons when he was in the cars. And we *are* in the cars about half the time. There was an English lady we met in the cars—I think her name was Miss Featherstone; perhaps you know her. She wanted to know why I didn't give Randolph lessons—give him 'instructions,' she called it. I guess he could give me more instruction than I could give him. He's very smart."

"Yes," said Winterbourne; "he seems very smart."

"Mother's going to get a teacher for him as soon as we get to Italy. Can you get good teachers in Italy?"

"Very good, I should think," said Winterbourne.

"Or else she's going to find some school. He ought to learn some more. He's only nine. He's going to college." And in this way Miss Miller continued to converse upon the affairs of her family, and upon other topics. She sat there with her extremely pretty hands, ornamented with very brilliant rings, folded in her lap, and with her pretty eyes now resting upon those of Winterbourne, now wandering over the garden, the people who passed by, and the beautiful view. She talked to Winterbourne as if she had known him a long time. He found it very pleasant. It was many years since he had heard a young girl talk so much. It might have been said of this unknown young lady, who had come and sat down beside him upon a bench, that she chattered. She was very quiet; she sat in a charming tranquil attitude, but her lips and her eyes were constantly moving. She had a soft, slender, agreeable voice, and her tone was decidedly sociable. She gave Winterbourne a history of her movements and intentions, and those of her mother and brother, in Europe, and enumerated, in particular, the various hotels at which they had stopped. "That English lady, in the cars," she said —"Miss Featherstone — asked me if we didn't all live in hotels in America. I told her I had never been in so many hotels in my life as since I came to Europe. I have never seen so many—it's nothing but hotels." But Miss Miller did not make this remark with a querulous accent; she appeared to be in the best humor with everything. She declared that the hotels were very good, when once you got used to their ways, and that Europe was perfectly sweet. She was not disappointed —not a bit. Perhaps it was because she had heard so much about it before. She had ever so many intimate friends that had been there ever so mány times. And then she had had ever so many dresses and things from Paris. Whenever she put on a Paris dress she felt as if she were in Europe.

"It was a kind of a wishing-cap," said Winterbourne.

"Yes," said Miss Miller, without examining this analogy; "it always made me wish I was here. But I needn't have done that for dresses. I am sure they send all the pretty ones to America; you see the most frightful things here. The only thing I don't like," she proceeded, "is the society. There isn't any society; or, if there is, I don't know where it keeps itself. Do you? I suppose there is some society somewhere, but I haven't seen anything of it. I'm very fond of society, and I have always had a great deal of it. I don't mean only in Schenectady, but in New York. I used to go to New York every winter. In New York I had lots of society. Last winter I had seventeen dinners given me; and three of them were by gentlemen," added Daisy Miller. "I have more friends in New York

than in Schenectady—more gentlemen friends; and more young lady friends too," she resumed in a moment. She paused again for an instant; she was looking at Winterbourne with all her prettiness in her lively eyes and in her light, slightly monotonous smile. "I have always had," she said, "a great deal of gentlemen's society."

Poor Winterbourne was amused, perplexed, and decidedly · charmed. He had never yet heard a young girl express herself in just this fashion; never, at least, save in cases where to say such things seemed a kind of demonstrative evidence of a certain laxity of deportment. And yet was he to accuse Miss Daisy Miller of actual or potential *inconduite*,[3] as they said at Geneva? He felt that he had lived at Geneva so long that he had lost a good deal; he had become dishabituated to the American tone. Never, indeed, since he had grown old enough to appreciate things, had he encountered a young American girl of so pronounced a type as this. Certainly she was very charming, but how deucedly sociable! Was she simply a pretty girl from New York State—were they all like that, the pretty girls who had a good deal of gentlemen's society? Or was she also a designing, an audacious, an unscrupulous young person? Winterbourne had lost his instinct in this matter, and his reason could not help him. Miss Daisy Miller looked extremely innocent. Some people had told him that, after all, American girls were exceedingly innocent; and others had told him that, after all, they were not. He was inclined to think Miss Daisy Miller was a flirt —a pretty American flirt. He had never, as yet, had any relations with young ladies of this category. He had known, here in Europe, two or three women—persons older than Miss Daisy Miller, and provided, for respectability's sake, with husbands—who were great coquettes—dangerous, terrible women, with whom one's relations were liable to take a serious turn. But this young girl was not a coquette in that sense; she

---

[3] Misconduct.

was very unsophisticated; she was only a pretty American flirt. Winterbourne was almost grateful for having found the formula that applied to Miss Daisy Miller. He leaned back in his seat; he remarked to himself that she had the most charming nose he had ever seen; he wondered what were the regular conditions and limitations of one's intercourse with a pretty American flirt. It presently became apparent that he was on the way to learn.

"Have you been to that old castle?" asked the young girl, pointing with her parasol to the far-gleaming walls of the Château de Chillon.

"Yes, formerly, more than once," said Winterbourne. "You too, I suppose, have seen it?"

"No; we haven't been there. I want to go there dreadfully. Of course I mean to go there. I wouldn't go away from here without having seen that old castle."

"It's a very pretty excursion," said Winterbourne, "and very easy to make. You can drive, you know, or you can go by the little steamer."

"You can go in the cars," said Miss Miller.

"Yes; you can go in the cars," Winterbourne assented.

"Our courier says they take you right up to the castle," the young girl continued. "We were going last week; but my mother gave out. She suffers dreadfully from dyspepsia. She said she couldn't go. Randolph wouldn't go either; he says he doesn't think much of old castles. But I guess we'll go this week, if we can get Randolph."

"Your brother is not interested in ancient monuments?" Winterbourne inquired, smiling.

"He says he don't care much about old castles. He's only nine. He wants to stay at the hotel. Mother's afraid to leave him alone, and the courier won't stay with him; so we haven't been to many places. But it will be too bad if we don't go up there." And Miss Miller pointed again at the Château de Chillon.

"I should think it might be arranged," said Winterbourne. "Couldn't you get some one to stay—for the afternoon—with Randolph?"

Miss Miller looked at him a moment; and then, very placidly, "I wish *you* would stay with him!" she said.

Winterbourne hesitated a moment. "I should much rather go to Chillon with you."

"With me?" asked the young girl, with the same placidity.

She didn't rise, blushing, as a young girl at Geneva would have done; and yet Winterbourne, conscious that he had been very bold, thought it possible she was offended. "With your mother," he answered, very respectfully.

But it seemed that both his audacity and his respect were lost upon Miss Daisy Miller. "I guess my mother won't go after all," she said. "She don't like to ride round in the afternoon. But did you really mean what you said just now; that you would like to go up there?"

"Most earnestly," Winterbourne declared.

"Then we may arrange it. If mother will stay with Randolph, I guess Eugenio will."

"Eugenio?" the young man inquired.

"Eugenio's our courier. He doesn't like to stay with Randolph; he's the most fastidious man I ever saw. But he's a splendid courier. I guess he'll stay at home with Randolph if mother does, and then we can go to the castle."

Winterbourne reflected for an instant as lucidly as possible—"we" could only mean Miss Daisy Miller and himself. This programme seemed almost too agreeable for credence; he felt as if he ought to kiss the young lady's hand. Possibly he would have done so—and quite spoiled the project; but at this moment another person—presumably Eugenio—appeared. A tall, handsome man, with superb whiskers, wearing a velvet morning-coat and a brilliant watch-chain, approached Miss Miller, looking sharply at her companion. "Oh, Eugenio!" said Miss Miller, with the friendliest accent.

Eugenio had looked at Winterbourne from head to foot; he now bowed gravely to the young lady. "I have the honour to inform mademoiselle that luncheon is upon the table."

Miss Miller slowly rose. "See here, Eugenio," she said. "I'm going to that old castle, anyway."

"To the Château de Chillon, mademoiselle?" the courier inquired. "Mademoiselle has made arrangements?" he added, in a tone which struck Winterbourne as very impertinent.

Eugenio's tone apparently threw, even to Miss Miller's own apprehension, a slightly ironical light upon the young girl's situation. She turned to Winterbourne, blushing a little—a very little. "You won't back out?" she said.

"I shall not be happy till we go!" he protested.

"And you are staying in this hotel?" she went on. "And you are really an American?"

The courier stood looking at Winterbourne, offensively. The young man, at least, thought his manner of looking an offence to Miss Miller; it conveyed an imputation that she "picked up" acquaintances. "I shall have the honour of presenting to you a person who will tell you all about me," he said, smiling, and referring to his aunt.

"Oh, well, we'll go some day," said Miss Miller. And she gave him a smile and turned away. She put up her parasol and walked back to the inn beside Eugenio. Winterbourne stood looking after her; and as she moved away, drawing her muslin furbelows over the gravel, said to himself that she had the *tournure*[4] of a princess.

He had, however, engaged to do more than proved feasible, in promising to present his aunt, Mrs. Costello, to Miss Daisy Miller. As soon as the former lady had got better of her headache he waited upon her in her apartment; and, after the proper inquiries in regard to her health, he asked her if she had observed, in the hotel, an American family—a mamma, a daughter, and a little boy.

"And a courier?" said Mrs. Costello. "Oh, yes, I have observed them. Seen them—heard them—and kept out of their way." Mrs. Costello was a widow with a fortune; a person of much distinction, who frequently intimated that, if she were not so dreadfully liable to sick-headaches, she would probably have left a deeper impress upon her time. She had a long pale face, a high nose, and a great deal of very striking white hair, which she wore in large puffs and *rouleaux* over the top of her head. She had two sons married in New York, and another who was now in Europe. This young man was amusing himself at Hombourg, and, though he was on his travels, was rarely perceived to visit any particular city at the moment selected by his mother for her own appearance there. Her nephew, who had come up to Vevey expressly to see her, was therefore more attentive than those who, as she said, were nearer to her. He had imbibed at Geneva the idea that one must always be attentive to one's aunt. Mrs. Costello had not seen him for many years, and she was greatly pleased with him, manifesting her approbation by initiating him into many of the secrets of that social sway which, as she gave him to understand, she exerted in the American capital. She admitted that she was very exclusive; but, if he were acquainted with New York, he would see that one had to be. And her picture of the minutely hierarchical constitution of the society of that city, which she presented to him in many different lights, was, to Winterbourne's imagination, almost oppressively striking.

He immediately perceived, from her tone, that Miss Daisy Miller's place in the social scale was low. "I am afraid you don't approve of them," he said.

"They are very common," Mrs. Costello declared. "They are the sort of Americans that one does one's duty by not—not accepting."

"Ah, you don't accept them?" said the young man.

"I can't, my dear Frederick. I would if

―――――――――――

[4] Figure.

I could, but I can't."

"The young girl is very pretty," said Winterbourne, in a moment.

"Of course she's pretty. But she is very common."

"I see what you mean, of course," said Winterbourne, after another pause.

"She has that charming look that they all have," his aunt resumed. "I can't think where they pick it up; and she dresses in perfection—no, you don't know how well she dresses. I can't think where they get their taste."

"But, my dear aunt, she is not, after all, a Comanche savage."

"She is a young lady," said Mrs. Costello, "who has an intimacy with her mamma's courier."

"An intimacy with the courier?" the young man demanded.

"Oh, the mother is just as bad! They treat the courier like a familiar friend—like a gentleman. I shouldn't wonder if he dines with them. Very likely they have never seen a man with such good manners, such fine clothes, so like a gentleman. He probably corresponds to the young lady's idea of a count. He sits with them in the garden, in the evening. I think he smokes."

Winterbourne listened with interest to these disclosures; they helped him to make up his mind about Miss Daisy. Evidently she was rather wild.

"Well," he said, "I am not a courier, and yet she was very charming to me."

"You had better have said at first," said Mrs. Costello with dignity, "that you had made her acquaintance."

"We simply met in the garden, and we talked a bit."

"*Tout bonnement!* [5] And pray what did you say?"

"I said I should take the liberty of introducing her to my admirable aunt."

"I am much obliged to you."

"It was to guarantee my respectability," said Winterbourne.

"And pray who is to guarantee hers?"

"Ah, you are cruel!" said the young man. "She's a very nice young girl."

"You don't say that as if you believed it," Mrs. Costello observed.

"She is completely uncultivated," Winterbourne went on. "But she is wonderfully pretty, and, in short, she is very nice. To prove that I believe it, I am going to take her to the Château de Chillon."

"You two are going off there together? I should say it proved just the contrary. How long had you known her, may I ask, when this interesting project was formed? You haven't been twenty-four hours in the house."

"I had known her half an hour!" said Winterbourne, smiling.

"Dear me!" cried Mrs. Costello. "What a dreadful girl!"

Her nephew was silent for some moments. "You really think, then," he began, earnestly, and with a desire for trustworthy information—"you really think that—" But he paused again.

"Think what, sir?" said his aunt.

"That she is the sort of young lady who expects a man—sooner or later—to carry her off?"

"I haven't the least idea what such young ladies expect a man to do. But I really think that you had better not meddle with little American girls that are uncultivated, as you call them. You have lived too long out of the country. You will be sure to make some great mistake. You are too innocent."

"My dear aunt, I am not so innocent," said Winterbourne, smiling and curling his moustache.

"You are too guilty, then!"

Winterbourne continued to curl his moustache, meditatively. "You won't let the poor girl know you, then?" he asked at last.

"Is it literally true that she is going to the Château de Chillon with you?"

"I think that she fully intends it."

"Then, my dear Frederick," said Mrs. Costello, "I must decline the honour of her acquaintance. I am an old woman, but I am not too old—thank Heaven—to be shocked!"

---

[5] Quite simply!

"But don't they all do these things—the young girls in America?" Winterbourne inquired.

Mrs. Costello stared a moment. "I should like to see my granddaughters do them!" she declared, grimly.

This seemed to throw some light upon the matter, for Winterbourne remembered to have heard that his pretty cousins in New York were "tremendous flirts." If, therefore, Miss Daisy Miller exceeded the liberal margin allowed to these young ladies, it was probable that anything might be expected of her. Winterbourne was impatient to see her again, and he was vexed with himself that, by instinct, he should not appreciate her justly.

Though he was impatient to see her, he hardly knew what he should say to her about his aunt's refusal to become acquainted with her; but he discovered, promptly enough, that with Miss Daisy Miller there was no great need of walking on tiptoe. He found her that evening in the garden, wandering about in the warm starlight, like an indolent sylph, and swinging to and fro the largest fan he had ever beheld. It was ten o'clock. He had dined with his aunt, had been sitting with her since dinner, and had just taken leave of her till the morrow. Miss Daisy Miller seemed very glad to see him; she declared it was the longest evening she had ever passed.

"Have you been all alone?" he asked.

"I have been walking round with mother. But mother gets tired walking round," she answered.

"Has she gone to bed?"

"No; she doesn't like to go to bed," said the young girl. "She doesn't sleep—not three hours. She says she doesn't know how she lives. She's dreadfully nervous. I guess she sleeps more than she thinks. She's gone somewhere after Randolph; she wants to try to get him to go to bed. He doesn't like to go to bed."

"Let us hope she will persuade him," observed Winterbourne.

"She will talk to him all she can; but he doesn't like her to talk to him," said Miss

Daisy, opening her fan. "She's going to try to get Eugenio to talk to him. But he isn't afraid of Eugenio. Eugenio's a splendid courier, but he can't make much impression on Randolph! I don't believe he'll go to bed before eleven." It appeared that Randolph's vigil was in fact triumphantly prolonged, for Winterbourne strolled about with the young girl for some time without meeting her mother. "I have been looking round for that lady you want to introduce me to," his companion resumed. "She's your aunt." Then, on Winterbourne's admitting the fact, and expressing some curiosity as to how she had learned it, she said she had heard all about Mrs. Costello from the chambermaid. She was very quiet, and very *comme il faut*; [6] she wore white puffs; she spoke to no one, and she never dined at the *table d'hôte*. Every two days she had a headache. "I think that's a lovely description, headache and all!" said Miss Daisy, chattering along in her thin, gay voice. "I want to know her ever so much. I know just what *your* aunt would be; I know I should like her. She would be very exclusive. I like a lady to be exclusive; I'm dying to be exclusive myself. Well, we *are* exclusive, mother and I. We don't speak to every one—or they don't speak to us. I suppose it's about the same thing. Anyway, I shall be ever so glad to know your aunt."

Winterbourne was embarrassed. "She would be most happy," he said; "but I am afraid those headaches will interfere."

The young girl looked at him through the dusk. "But I suppose she doesn't have a headache every day," she said, sympathetically.

Winterbourne was silent a moment. "She tells me she does," he answered at last—not knowing what to say.

Miss Daisy Miller stopped, and stood looking at him. Her prettiness was still visible in the darkness; she was opening and closing her enormous fan. "She doesn't want to know me!" she said, suddenly. "Why don't you say so? You needn't be

---

[6] Proper.

afraid. I'm not afraid!" And she gave a little laugh.

Winterbourne fancied there was a tremor in her voice; he was touched, shocked, mortified by it. "My dear young lady," he protested, "she knows no one. It's her wretched health."

The young girl walked on a few steps, laughing still. "You needn't be afraid," she repeated. "Why should she want to know me?" Then she paused again; she was close to the parapet of the garden, and in front of her was the starlit lake. There was a vague sheen upon its surface, and in the distance were dimly-seen mountain forms. Daisy Miller looked out upon the mysterious prospect, and then she gave another little laugh. "Gracious! she *is* exclusive!" she said. Winterbourne wondered whether she was seriously wounded, and for a moment almost wished that her sense of injury might be such as to make it becoming in him to attempt to reassure and comfort her. He had a pleasant sense that she would be very approachable for consolatory purposes. He felt then, for the instant, quite ready to sacrifice his aunt, conversationally; to admit that she was a proud, rude woman, and to declare that they needn't mind her. But before he had time to commit himself to this perilous mixture of gallantry and impiety, the young lady, resuming her walk, gave an exclamation in quite another tone. "Well; here's mother! I guess she hasn't got Randolph to go to bed." The figure of a lady appeared, at a distance, very indistinct in the darkness, and advancing with a slow and wavering movement. Suddenly it seemed to pause.

"Are you sure it is your mother? Can you distinguish her in this thick dusk?" Winterbourne asked.

"Well!" cried Miss Daisy Miller, with a laugh, "I guess I know my own mother. And when she has got on my shawl, too! She is always wearing my things."

The lady in question, ceasing to advance, hovered vaguely about the spot at which she had checked her steps.

"I am afraid your mother doesn't see you," said Winterbourne. "Or perhaps," he added—thinking, with Miss Miller, the joke permissible—"perhaps she feels guilty about your shawl."

"Oh, it's a fearful old thing!" the young girl replied, serenely. "I told her she could wear it. She won't come here, because she sees you."

"Ah, then," said Winterbourne, "I had better leave you."

"Oh, no; come on!" urged Miss Daisy Miller.

"I'm afraid your mother doesn't approve of my walking with you."

Miss Miller gave him a serious glance. "It isn't for me; it's for you—that is, it's for *her*. Well, I don't know who it's for! But mother doesn't like any of my gentlemen friends. She's right down timid. She always makes a fuss if I introduce a gentleman. But I *do* introduce them—almost always. If I didn't introduce my gentlemen friends to mother," the young girl added, in her little soft, flat monotone, "I shouldn't think I was natural."

"To introduce me," said Winterbourne, "you must know my name." And he proceeded to pronounce it.

"Oh, dear, I can't say all that!" said his companion, with a laugh. But by this time they had come up to Mrs. Miller, who, as they drew near, walked to the parapet of the garden and leaned upon it, looking intently at the lake, and turning her back to them. "Mother!" said the young girl, in a tone of decision. Upon this the elder lady turned round. "Mr. Winterbourne," said Miss Daisy Miller, introducing the young man very frankly and prettily. "Common" she was, as Mrs. Costello had pronounced her; yet it was a wonder to Winterbourne that, with her commonness, she had a singularly delicate grace.

Her mother was a small, spare, light person, with a wandering eye, a very exiguous nose, and a large forehead, decorated with a certain amount of thin, much-frizzled hair. Like her daughter, Mrs. Miller was dressed with extreme elegance; she had enormous

diamonds in her ears. So far as Winterbourne could observe, she gave him no
greeting—she certainly was not looking at
him. Daisy was near her, pulling her shawl
straight. "What are you doing, poking
round here?" this young lady inquired; but
by no means with that harshness of accent
which her choice of words may imply.

"I don't know," said her mother, turning
towards the lake again.

"I shouldn't think you'd want that
shawl!" Daisy exclaimed.

"Well—I do!" her mother answered,
with a little laugh.

"Did you get Randolph to go to bed?"
asked the young girl.

"No; I couldn't induce him," said Mrs.
Miller, very gently. "He wants to talk to
the waiter. He likes to talk to that waiter."

"I was telling Mr. Winterbourne," the
young girl went on; and to the young man's
ear her tone might have indicated that she
had been uttering his name all her life.

"Oh, yes!" said Winterbourne; "I have
the pleasure of knowing your son."

Randolph's mamma was silent; she
turned her attention to the lake. But at
last she spoke. "Well, I don't see how he
lives!"

"Anyhow, it isn't so bad as it was at
Dover," said Daisy Miller.

"And what occurred at Dover?" Winterbourne asked.

"He wouldn't go to bed at all. I guess he
sat up all night—in the public parlour. He
wasn't in bed at twelve o'clock; I know
that."

"It was half-past twelve," declared Mrs.
Miller, with mild emphasis.

"Does he sleep much during the day?"
Winterbourne demanded.

"I guess he doesn't sleep much," Daisy
rejoined.

"I wish he would!" said her mother. "It
seems as if he couldn't."

"I think he's real tiresome," Daisy pursued.

Then, for some moments, there was
silence. "Well, Daisy Miller," said the elder

lady, presently, "I shouldn't think you'd
want to talk against your own brother!"

"Well, he is tiresome, mother," said
Daisy, quite without the asperity of a
retort.

"He's only nine," urged Mrs. Miller.

"Well, he wouldn't go to that castle,"
said the young girl. "I'm going there with
Mr. Winterbourne."

To this announcement, very placidly
made, Daisy's mamma offered no response.
Winterbourne took for granted that she
deeply disapproved of the projected excursion; but he said to himself that she
was a simple, easily-managed person, and
that a few deferential protestations would
take the edge from her displeasure. "Yes,"
he began; "your daughter has kindly allowed me the honour of being her guide."

Mrs. Miller's wandering eyes attached
themselves, with a sort of appealing air,
to Daisy, who, however, strolled a few steps
farther, gently humming to herself. "I
presume you will go in the cars," said her
mother.

"Yes; or in the boat," said Winterbourne.

"Well, of course, I don't know," Mrs.
Miller rejoined. "I have never been to that
castle."

"It is a pity you shouldn't go," said
Winterbourne, beginning to feel reassured
as to her opposition. And yet he was quite
prepared to find that, as a matter of course,
she meant to accompany her daughter.

"We've been thinking ever so much
about going," she pursued; "but it seems
as if we couldn't. Of course Daisy—she
wants to go round. But there's a lady here
—I don't know her name—she says she
shouldn't think we'd want to go to see
castles here; she should think we'd want
to wait till we got to Italy. It seems as if
there would be so many there," continued
Mrs. Miller, with an air of increasing confidence. "Of course, we only want to see the
principal ones. We visited several in England," she presently added.

"Ah, yes! in England there are beautiful castles," said Winterbourne. "But

Chillon, here, is very well worth seeing."

"Well, if Daisy feels up to it—," said Mrs. Miller, in a tone impregnated with a sense of the magnitude of the enterprise. "It seems as if there was nothing she wouldn't undertake."

"Oh, I think she'll enjoy it!" Winterbourne declared. And he desired more and more to make it a certainty that he was to have the privilege of a *tête-à-tête* with the young lady, who was still strolling along in front of them, softly vocalizing. "You are not disposed, madam," he inquired, "to undertake it yourself?"

Daisy's mother looked at him, an instant, askance, and then walked forward in silence. Then—"I guess she had better go alone," she said, simply. Winterbourne observed to himself that this was a very different type of maternity from that of the vigilant matrons who massed themselves in the forefront of social intercourse in the dark old city at the other end of the lake. But his meditations were interrupted by hearing his name very distinctly pronounced by Mrs. Miller's unprotected daughter.

"Mr. Winterbourne!" murmured Daisy.

"Mademoiselle!" said the young man.

"Don't you want to take me out in a boat?"

"At present?" he asked.

"Of course!" said Daisy.

"Well, Annie Miller!" exclaimed her mother.

"I beg you, madam, to let her go," said Winterbourne, ardently; for he had never yet enjoyed the sensation of guiding through the summer starlight a skiff freighted with a fresh and beautiful young girl.

"I shouldn't think she'd want to," said her mother. "I should think she'd rather go indoors."

"I'm sure Mr. Winterbourne wants to take me," Daisy declared. "He's so awfully devoted!"

"I will row you over to Chillon, in the starlight."

"I don't believe it!" said Daisy.

"Well!" ejaculated the elder lady again.

"You haven't spoken to me for half an hour," her daughter went on.

"I have been having some very pleasant conversation with your mother," said Winterbourne.

"Well, I want you to take me out in a boat!" Daisy repeated. They had all stopped, and she had turned round and was looking at Winterbourne. Her face wore a charming smile, her pretty eyes were gleaming, she was swinging her great fan about. No; it's impossible to be prettier than that, thought Winterbourne.

"There are half a dozen boats moored at that landing-place," he said, pointing to certain steps which descended from the garden to the lake. "If you will do me the honour to accept my arm, we will go and select one of them."

Daisy stood there smiling; she threw back her head and gave a little, light laugh. "I like a gentleman to be formal!" she declared.

"I assure you it's a formal offer."

"I was bound I would make you say something," Daisy went on.

"You see it's not very difficult," said Winterbourne. "But I am afraid you are chaffing me."

"I think not, sir," remarked Mrs. Miller, very gently.

"Do, then, let me give you a row," he said to the young girl.

"It's quite lovely, the way you say that!" cried Daisy.

"It will be still more lovely to do it."

"Yes, it would be lovely!" said Daisy. But she made no movement to accompany him; she only stood there laughing.

"I should think you had better find out what time it is," interposed her mother.

"It is eleven o'clock, madam," said a voice, with a foreign accent, out of the neighbouring darkness; and Winterbourne, turning, perceived the florid personage who was in attendance upon the two ladies. He had apparently just approached.

"Oh, Eugenio," said Daisy, "I am going out in a boat!"

Eugenio bowed. "At eleven o'clock, mademoiselle?"

"I am going with Mr. Winterbourne. This very minute."

"Do tell her she can't," said Mrs. Miller to the courier.

"I think you had better not go out in a boat, mademoiselle," Eugenio declared.

Winterbourne wished to Heaven this pretty girl were not so familiar with her courier; but he said nothing.

"I suppose you don't think it's proper!" Daisy exclaimed. "Eugenio doesn't think anything's proper."

"I am at your service," said Winterbourne.

"Does mademoiselle propose to go alone?" asked Eugenio of Mrs. Miller.

"Oh, no; with this gentleman!" answered Daisy's mamma.

The courier looked for a moment at Winterbourne—the latter thought he was smiling—and then, solemnly, with a bow, "As mademoiselle pleases!" he said.

"Oh, I hoped you would make a fuss!" said Daisy. "I don't care to go now."

"I myself shall make a fuss if you don't go," said Winterbourne.

"That's all I want—a little fuss!" And the young girl began to laugh again.

"Mr. Randolph has gone to bed!" the courier announced, frigidly.

"Oh, Daisy; now we can go!" said Mrs. Miller.

Daisy turned away from Winterbourne, looking at him, smiling, and fanning herself. "Good-night," she said; "I hope you are disappointed, or disgusted, or something!"

He looked at her, taking the hand she offered him. "I am puzzled," he answered.

"Well, I hope it won't keep you awake!" she said, very smartly; and, under the escort of the privileged Eugenio, the two ladies passed towards the house.

Winterbourne stood looking after them; he was indeed puzzled. He lingered beside the lake for a quarter of an hour, turning over the mystery of the young girl's sudden familiarities and caprices. But the only very definite conclusion he came to was that he should enjoy deucedly "going off" with her somewhere.

Two days afterwards he went off with her to the Castle of Chillon. He waited for her in the large hall of the hotel, where the couriers, the servants, the foreign tourists were lounging about and staring. It was not the place he should have chosen, but she had appointed it. She came tripping downstairs, buttoning her long gloves, squeezing her folded parasol against her pretty figure, dressed in the perfection of a soberly elegant travelling-costume. Winterbourne was a man of imagination and, as our ancestors used to say, sensibility; as he looked at her dress and, on the great staircase, her little rapid, confiding step, he felt as if there were something romantic going forward. He could have believed he was going to elope with her. He passed out with her among all the idle people that were assembled there; they were all looking at her very hard; she had begun to chatter as soon as she joined him. Winterbourne's preference had been that they should be conveyed to Chillon in a carriage; but she expressed a lively wish to go in the little steamer; she declared that she had a passion for steamboats. There was always such a lovely breeze upon the water, and you saw such lots of people. The sail was not long, but Winterbourne's companion found time to say a great many things. To the young man himself their little excursion was so much of an escapade—an adventure—that, even allowing for her habitual sense of freedom, he had some expectation of seeing her regard it in the same way. But it must be confessed that, in this particular, he was disappointed. Daisy Miller was extremely animated, she was in charming spirits; but she was apparently not at all excited; she was not fluttered; she avoided neither his eyes nor those of any one else; she blushed neither when she looked at him nor when she felt that people were looking at her. People continued to look at her a great deal, and Winterbourne took much satisfaction in his pretty companion's distinguished air. He had been a little afraid that she would talk loud, laugh overmuch, and even, perhaps, desire to move about the boat a good deal. But he quite forgot his fears; he sat smiling, with his eyes upon her face, while, without moving from her place, she delivered herself of a great number of original reflections. It was the most charming garrulity he had ever heard. He had assented to the idea that she was "common"; but was she so, after all, or was he simply getting used to her commonness? Her conversation was chiefly of what metaphysicians term the objective cast; but every now and then it took a subjective turn.

"What on *earth* are you so grave about?" she suddenly demanded, fixing her agreeable eyes upon Winterbourne's.

"Am I grave?" he asked. "I had an idea I was grinning from ear to ear."

"You look as if you were taking me to a funeral. If that's a grin, your ears are very near together."

"Should you like me to dance a hornpipe on the deck?"

"Pray do, and I'll carry round your hat. It will pay the expenses of our journey."

"I never was better pleased in my life," murmured Winterbourne.

She looked at him a moment, and then burst into a little laugh. "I like to make you say those things! You're a queer mixture!"

In the castle, after they had landed, the subjective element decidedly prevailed. Daisy tripped about the vaulted chambers, rustled her skirts in the corkscrew staircases, flirted back with a pretty little cry and a shudder from the edge of the *oubliettes*,[7] and turned a singularly well-shaped ear to everything that Winterbourne told her about the place. But he saw that she cared very little for feudal antiquities, and that the dusky traditions of Chillon made but a slight impression upon her. They had the good fortune to have been able to walk without other companionship

than that of the custodian; and Winterbourne arranged with this functionary that they should not be hurried—that they should linger and pause wherever they chose. The custodian interpreted the bargain generously—Winterbourne, on his side, had been generous—and ended by leaving them quite to themselves. Miss Miller's observations were not remarkable for logical consistency; for anything she wanted to say she was sure to find a pretext. She found a great many pretexts in the rugged embrasures of Chillon for asking Winterbourne sudden questions about himself—his family, his previous history, his tastes, his habits, his intentions—and for supplying information upon corresponding points in her own personality. Of her own tastes, habits, and intentions Miss Miller was prepared to give the most definite, and, indeed, the most favourable, account.

"Well, I hope you know enough!" she said to her companion, after he had told her the history of the unhappy Bonnivard.[8] "I never saw a man that knew so much!" The history of Bonnivard had evidently, as they say, gone into one ear and out of the other. But Daisy went on to say that she wished Winterbourne would travel with them, and "go round" with them; they might know something, in that case. "Don't you want to come and teach Randolph?" she asked. Winterbourne said that nothing could possibly please him so much; but that he had unfortunately other occupations. "Other occupations? I don't believe it!" said Miss Daisy. "What do you mean? You are not in business." The young man admitted that he was not in business; but he had engagements which, even within a day or two, would force him to go back to Geneva. "Oh, bother!" she said; "I don't believe it!" and she began to talk about something else. But a few moments later,

[7] Dungeons, with openings from the top.
[8] This Swiss patriot, who was imprisoned in the Castle of Chillon from 1530 to 1536, is the hero of Byron's poem, "The Prisoner of Chillon."

when he was pointing out to her the pretty design of an antique fireplace, she broke out irrelevantly, "You don't mean to say you are going back to Geneva?"

"It is a melancholy fact that I shall have to return to-morrow."

"Well, Mr. Winterbourne," said Daisy, "I think you're horrid!"

"Oh, don't say such dreadful things!" said Winterbourne—"just at the last!"

"The last!" cried the young girl; "I call it the first. I have half a mind to leave you here and go straight back to the hotel alone." And for the next ten minutes she did nothing but call him horrid. Poor Winterbourne was fairly bewildered; no young lady had as yet done him the honour to be so agitated by the announcement of his movements. His companion, after this, ceased to pay any attention to the curiosities of Chillon or the beauties of the lake; she opened fire upon the mysterious charmer in Geneva, whom she appeared to have instantly taken for granted that he was hurrying back to see. How did Miss Daisy Miller know that there was a charmer in Geneva? Winterbourne, who denied the existence of such a person, was quite unable to discover; and he was divided between amazement at the rapidity of her induction and amusement at the frankness of her *persiflage*. She seemed to him, in all this, an extraordinary mixture of innocence and crudity. "Does she never allow you more than three days at a time?" asked Daisy, ironically. "Doesn't she give you a vacation in summer? There is no one so hard worked but they can get leave to go off somewhere at this season. I suppose, if you stay another day, she'll come after you in the boat. Do wait over till Friday, and I will go down to the landing to see her arrive!" Winterbourne began to think he had been wrong to feel disappointed in the temper in which the young lady had embarked. If he had missed the personal accent, the personal accent was now making its appearance. It sounded very distinctly, at last, in her telling him she would stop

"teasing" him if he would promise her solemnly to come down to Rome in the winter.

"That's not a difficult promise to make," said Winterbourne. "My aunt has taken an apartment in Rome for the winter, and has already asked me to come and see her."

"I don't want you to come for your aunt," said Daisy; "I want you to come for me." And this was the only allusion that the young man was ever to hear her make to his invidious kinswoman. He declared that, at any rate, he would certainly come. After this Daisy stopped teasing. Winterbourne took a carriage, and they drove back to Vevey in the dusk; the young girl was very quiet.

In the evening Winterbourne mentioned to Mrs. Costello that he had spent the afternoon at Chillon with Miss Daisy Miller.

"The Americans—of the courier?" asked this lady.

"Ah, happily," said Winterbourne, "the courier stayed at home."

"She went with you all alone?"

"All alone."

Mrs. Costello sniffed a little at her smelling-bottle. "And that," she exclaimed, "is the young person whom you wanted me to know!"

PART II

Winterbourne, who had returned to Geneva the day after his excursion to Chillon, went to Rome towards the end of January. His aunt had been established there for several weeks, and he had received a couple of letters from her. "Those people you were so devoted to last summer at Vevey have turned up here, courier and all," she wrote. "They seem to have made several acquaintances, but the courier continues to be the most *intime*. The young lady, however, is also very intimate with some third-rate Italians, with whom she rackets about in a way that makes much talk. Bring me that pretty novel of Cherbuliez's—'Paule

Mérê—and don't come later than the 23rd." [9]

In the natural course of events, Winterbourne, on arriving in Rome, would presently have ascertained Mrs. Miller's address at the American banker's, and have gone to pay his compliments to Miss Daisy. "After what happened at Vevey I think I may certainly call upon them," he said to Mrs. Costello.

"If, after what happens—at Vevey and everywhere—you desire to keep up the acquaintance, you are very welcome. Of course a man may know every one. Men are welcome to the privilege!"

"Pray what is it that happens—here, for instance?" Winterbourne demanded.

"The girl goes about alone with her foreigners. As to what happens further, you must apply elsewhere for information. She has picked up half-a-dozen of the regular Roman fortune-hunters, and she takes them about to people's houses. When she comes to a party she brings with her a gentleman with a good deal of manner and a wonderful moustache."

"And where is the mother?"

"I haven't the least idea. They are very dreadful people."

Winterbourne meditated a moment. "They are very ignorant—very innocent only. Depend upon it they are not bad."

"They are hopelessly vulgar," said Mrs. Costello. "Whether or no being hopelessly vulgar is being 'bad' is a question for the metaphysicians. They are bad enough to dislike, at any rate; and for this short life that is quite enough."

The news that Daisy Miller was surrounded by half-a-dozen wonderful moustaches checked Winterbourne's impulse to go straightway to see her. He had perhaps not definitely flattered himself that he had made an ineffaceable impression upon her heart, but he was annoyed at hearing of a state of affairs so little in harmony with an image that had lately flitted in and out of his own meditations; the image of a very pretty girl looking out of an old Roman window and asking herself urgently when Mr. Winterbourne would arrive. If, however, he determined to wait a little before reminding Miss Miller of his claims to her consideration, he went very soon to call upon two or three other friends. One of these friends was an American lady who had spent several winters at Geneva, where she had placed her children at school. She was a very accomplished woman, and she lived in the Via Gregoriana. Winterbourne found her in a little crimson drawing-room, on a third floor; the room was filled with southern sunshine. He had not been there ten minutes when the servant came in, announcing "Madame Mila!" This announcement was presently followed by the entrance of little Randolph Miller, who stopped in the middle of the room and stood staring at Winterbourne. An instant later his pretty sister crossed the threshold; and then, after a considerable interval, Mrs. Miller slowly advanced.

"I know you!" said Randolph.

"I'm sure you know a great many things," exclaimed Winterbourne, taking him by the hand. "How is your education coming on?"

Daisy was exchanging greetings very prettily with her hostess; but when she heard Winterbourne's voice she quickly turned her head. "Well, I declare!" she said.

"I told you I should come, you know," Winterbourne rejoined, smiling.

"Well—I didn't believe it," said Miss Daisy.

"I am much obliged to you," laughed the young man.

"You might have come to see me!" said Daisy.

"I arrived only yesterday."

"I don't believe that!" the young girl declared.

Winterbourne turned with a protesting smile to her mother; but this lady evaded

---

[9] Victor Cherbuliez (1829-1899), French novelist.

his glance, and, seating herself, fixed her eyes upon her son. "We've got a bigger place than this," said Randolph. "It's all gold on the walls."

Mrs. Miller turned uneasily in her chair. "I told you if I were going to bring you, you would say something!" she murmured.

"I told *you!*" Randolph exclaimed. "I tell *you*, sir!" he added, jocosely, giving Winterbourne a thump on the knee. "It *is* bigger, too!"

Daisy had entered upon a lively conversation with her hostess; and Winterbourne judged it becoming to address a few words to her mother. "I hope you have been well since we parted at Vevey," he said.

Mrs. Miller now certainly looked at him —at his chin. "Not very well, sir," she answered.

"She's got the dyspepsia," said Randolph. "I've got it, too. Father's got it. I've got it most!"

This announcement, instead of embarrassing Mrs. Miller, seemed to relieve her. "I suffer from the liver," she said. "I think it's this climate; it's less bracing than Schenectady, especially in the winter season. I don't know whether you know we reside at Schenectady. I was saying to Daisy that I certainly hadn't found any one like Dr. Davis, and I didn't believe I should. Oh, at Schenectady he stands first; they think everything of him. He has so much to do, and yet there was nothing he wouldn't do for me. He said he never saw anything like my dyspepsia, but he was bound to cure it. I'm sure there was nothing he wouldn't try. He was just going to try something new when we came off. Mr. Miller wanted Daisy to see Europe for herself. But I wrote to Mr. Miller that it seems as if I couldn't get on without Dr. Davis. At Schenectady he stands at the very top; and there's a great deal of sickness there, too. It affects my sleep."

Winterbourne had a good deal of pathological gossip with Dr. Davis's patient, during which Daisy chattered unremittingly to her own companion. The young man asked Mrs. Miller how she was pleased with Rome. "Well, I must say I **am** disappointed," she answered. "We had heard so much about it; I suppose we had heard too much. But we couldn't help that. We had been led to expect something different."

"Ah, wait a little, and you will become very fond of it," said Winterbourne.

"I hate it worse and worse every day!" cried Randolph.

"You are like the infant Hannibal," said Winterbourne.

"No, I ain't!" Randolph declared, at a venture.

"You are not much like an infant," said his mother. "But we have seen places," she resumed, "that I should put a long way before Rome." And in reply to Winterbourne's interrogation, "There's Zürich," she concluded; "I think Zürich is lovely; and we hadn't heard half so much about it."

"The best place we've seen is the City of Richmond!" said Randolph.

"He means the ship," his mother explained. "We crossed in that ship. Randolph had a good time on the *City of Richmond*."

"It's the best place I've seen," the child repeated. "Only it was turned the wrong way."

"Well, we've got to turn the right way some time," said Mrs. Miller, with a little laugh. Winterbourne expressed the hope that her daughter at least found some gratification in Rome, and she declared that Daisy was quite carried away. "It's on account of the society—the society's splendid. She goes round everywhere; she has made a great number of acquaintances. Of course she goes round more than I do. I must say they have been very sociable; they have taken her right in. And then she knows a great many gentlemen. Oh, she thinks there's nothing like Rome. Of course, it's a great deal pleasanter for a young lady if she knows plenty of gentlemen."

By this time Daisy had turned her attention again to Winterbourne. "I've been telling Mrs. Walker how mean you were!" the young girl announced.

"And what is the evidence you have

offered?" asked Winterbourne, rather annoyed at Miss Miller's want of appreciation of the zeal of an admirer who on his way down to Rome had stopped neither at Bologna nor at Florence, simply because of a certain sentimental impatience. He remembered that a cynical compatriot had once told him that American women—the pretty ones, and this gave a largeness to the axiom—were at once the most exacting in the world and the least endowed with a sense of indebtedness.

"Why, you were awfully mean at Vevey," said Daisy. "You wouldn't do anything. You wouldn't stay there when I asked you."

"My dearest young lady," cried Winterbourne, with eloquence, "have I come all the way to Rome to encounter your reproaches?"

"Just hear him say that!" said Daisy to her hostess, giving a twist to a bow on this lady's dress. "Did you ever hear anything so quaint?"

"So quaint, my dear?" murmured Mrs. Walker, in a tone of a partisan of Winterbourne.

"Well, I don't know," said Daisy, fingering Mrs. Walker's ribbons. "Mrs. Walker, I want to tell you something."

"Mother-r," interposed Randolph, with his rough ends to his words, "I tell you you've got to go. Eugenio'll raise—something!"

"I'm not afraid of Eugenio," said Daisy, with a toss of her head. "Look here, Mrs. Walker," she went on, "you know I'm coming to your party."

"I am delighted to hear it."

"I've got a lovely dress!"

"I am very sure of that."

"But I want to ask a favour—permission to bring a friend."

"I shall be happy to see any of your friends," said Mrs. Walker, turning with a smile to Mrs. Miller.

"Oh, they are not my friends," answered Daisy's mamma, smiling shyly, in her own fashion. "I never spoke to them."

"It's an intimate friend of mine—Mr.

Giovanelli," said Daisy, without a tremor in her clear little voice, or a shadow on her brilliant little face.

Mrs. Walker was silent a moment; she gave a rapid glance at Winterbourne. "I shall be glad to see Mr. Giovanelli," she then said.

"He's an Italian," Daisy pursued, with the prettiest serenity. "He's a great friend of mine—he's the handsomest man in the world—except Mr. Winterbourne! He knows plenty of Italians, but he wants to know some Americans. He thinks ever so much of Americans. He's tremendously clever. He's perfectly lovely!"

It was settled that this brilliant personage should be brought to Mrs. Walker's party, and then Mrs. Miller prepared to take her leave. "I guess we'll go back to the hotel," she said.

"You may go back to the hotel, mother, but I'm going to take a walk," said Daisy.

"She's going to walk with Mr. Giovanelli," Randolph proclaimed.

"I am going to the Pincio,"[10] said Daisy, smiling.

"Alone, my dear—at this hour?" Mrs. Walker asked. The afternoon was drawing to a close—it was the hour for the throng of carriages and of contemplative pedestrians. "I don't think it's safe, my dear," said Mrs. Walker.

"Neither do I," subjoined Mrs. Miller. "You'll get the fever, as sure as you live. Remember what Dr. Davis told you!"

"Give her some medicine before she goes," said Randolph.

The company had risen to its feet; Daisy, still showing her pretty teeth, bent over and kissed her hostess. "Mrs. Walker, you are too perfect," she said. "I'm not going alone; I am going to meet a friend."

"Your friend won't keep you from getting the fever," Mrs. Miller observed.

"Is it Mr. Giovanelli?" asked the hostess.

Winterbourne was watching the young

[10] Monte Pincio, a Roman hill within the city's walls.

girl; at this question his attention quickened. She stood there smiling and smoothing her bonnet ribbons; she glanced at Winterbourne. Then, while she glanced and smiled, she answered, without a shade of hesitation, "Mr. Giovanelli—the beautiful Giovanelli."

"My dear young friend," said Mrs. Walker, taking her hand, pleadingly, "don't walk off to the Pincio at this hour to meet a beautiful Italian."

"Well, he speaks English," said Mrs. Miller.

"Gracious me!" Daisy exclaimed, "I don't want to do anything improper. There's an easy way to settle it." She continued to glance at Winterbourne. "The Pincio is only a hundred yards distant, and if Mr. Winterbourne were as polite as he pretends, he would offer to walk with me!"

Winterbourne's politeness hastened to affirm itself, and the young girl gave him gracious leave to accompany her. They passed down stairs before her mother, and at the door Winterbourne perceived Mrs. Miller's carriage drawn up, with the ornamental courier whose acquaintance he had made at Vevey seated within. "Good-bye, Eugenio!" cried Daisy, "I'm going to take a walk." The distance from the Via Gregoriana to the beautiful garden at the other end of the Pincian Hill is, in fact, rapidly traversed. As the day was splendid, however, and the concourse of vehicles, walkers, and loungers numerous, the young Americans found their progress much delayed. This fact was highly agreeable to Winterbourne, in spite of his consciousness of his singular situation. The slow-moving, idly-gazing Roman crowd bestowed much attention upon the extremely pretty young foreign lady who was passing through it upon his arm; and he wondered what on earth had been in Daisy's mind when she proposed to expose herself, unattended, to its appreciation. His own mission, to her sense, apparently, was to consign her to the hands of Mr. Giovanelli; but Winterbourne, at once annoyed and

gratified, resolved that he would do no such thing.

"Why haven't you been to see me?" asked Daisy. "You can't get out of that."

"I have had the honour of telling you that I have only just stepped out of the train."

"You must have stayed in the train a good while after it stopped!" cried the young girl, with her little laugh. "I suppose you were asleep. You have had time to go to see Mrs. Walker."

"I knew Mrs. Walker—" Winterbourne began to explain.

"I know where you knew her. You knew her at Geneva. She told me so. Well, you knew me at Vevey. That's just as good. So you ought to have come." She asked him no other question than this; she began to prattle about her own affairs. "We've got splendid rooms at the hotel; Eugenio says they're the best rooms in Rome. We are going to stay all winter, if we don't die of the fever; and I guess we'll stay then. It's a great deal nicer than I thought; I thought it would be fearfully quiet; I was sure it would be awfully poky. I was sure we should be going round all the time with one of those dreadful old men that explain about the pictures and things. But we only had about a week of that, and now I'm enjoying myself. I know ever so many people, and they are all so charming. The society's extremely select. There are all kinds—English, and Germans, and Italians. I think I like the English best. I like their style of conversation. But there are some lovely Americans. I never saw anything so hospitable. There's something or other every day. There's not much dancing; but I must say I never thought dancing was everything. I was always fond of conversation. I guess I shall have plenty at Mrs. Walker's—her rooms are so small." When they had passed the gate of the Pincian Gardens, Miss Miller began to wonder where Mr. Giovanelli might be. "We had better go straight to that place in front," she said, "where you look at the view."

"I certainly shall not help you to find him," Winterbourne declared.

"Then I shall find him without you," said Miss Daisy.

"You certainly won't leave me!" cried Winterbourne.

She burst into her little laugh. "Are you afraid you'll get lost—or run over? But there's Giovanelli, leaning against that tree. He's staring at the women in the carriages; did you ever see anything so cool?"

Winterbourne perceived at some distance a little man standing with folded arms, nursing his cane. He had a handsome face, an artfully poised hat, a glass in one eye, and a nosegay in his buttonhole. Winterbourne looked at him a moment, and then said, "Do you mean to speak to that man?"

"Do I mean to speak to him? Why, you don't suppose I mean to communicate by signs?"

"Pray understand, then," said Winterbourne, "that I intend to remain with you."

Daisy stopped and looked at him, without a sign of troubled consciousness in her face; with nothing but the presence of her charming eyes and her happy dimples. "Well, she's a cool one!" thought the young man.

"I don't like the way you say that," said Daisy. "It's too imperious."

"I beg your pardon if I say it wrong. The main point is to give you an idea of my meaning."

The young girl looked at him more gravely, but with eyes that were prettier than ever. "I have never allowed a gentleman to dictate to me, or to interfere with anything I do."

"I think you have made a mistake," said Winterbourne. "You should sometimes listen to a gentleman—the right one."

Daisy began to laugh again. "I do nothing but listen to gentlemen!" she exclaimed. "Tell me if Mr. Giovanelli is the right one."

The gentleman with the nosegay in his bosom had now perceived our two friends, and was approaching the young girl with obsequious rapidity. He bowed to Winter-

bourne as well as to the latter's companion; he had a brilliant smile, an intelligent eye; Winterbourne thought him not a bad-looking fellow. But he nevertheless said to Daisy, "No, he's not the right one."

Daisy evidently had a natural talent for performing introductions; she mentioned the name of each of her companions to the other. She strolled along with one of them on each side of her; Mr. Giovanelli, who spoke English very cleverly—Winterbourne afterwards learned that he had practised the idiom upon a great many American heiresses—addressed to her a great deal of very polite nonsense; he was extremely urbane, and the young American, who said nothing, reflected upon that profundity of Italian cleverness which enables people to appear more gracious in proportion as they are more acutely disappointed. Giovanelli, of course, had counted upon something more intimate; he had not bargained for a party of three. But he kept his temper in a manner which suggested far-stretching intentions. Winterbourne flattered himself that he had taken his measure. "He is not a gentleman," said the young American; "he is only a clever imitation of one. He is a music-master, or a penny-a-liner, or a third-rate artist. Damn his good looks!" Mr. Giovanelli had certainly a very pretty face; but Winterbourne felt a superior indignation at his own lovely fellow-country woman's not knowing the difference between a spurious gentleman and a real one. Giovanelli chattered and jested, and made himself wonderfully agreeable. It was true that, if he was an imitation, the imitation was brilliant. "Nevertheless," Winterbourne said to himself, "a nice girl ought to know!" And then he came back to the question whether this was, in fact, a nice girl. Would a nice girl—even allowing for her being a little American flirt—make a rendezvous with a presumably low-lived foreigner? The rendezvous in this case, indeed, had been in broad daylight, and in the most crowded corner of Rome; but was it not impossible to regard the choice of these circumstances as a proof of extreme cynicism? Singular though it may seem, Winterbourne was vexed that the young girl, in joining her *amoroso*, should not appear more impatient of his own company, and he was vexed because of his inclination. It was impossible to regard her as a perfectly well-conducted young lady; she was wanting in a certain indispensable delicacy. It would therefore simplify matters greatly to be able to treat her as the object of one of those sentiments which are called by romancers "lawless passions." That she should seem to wish to get rid of him would help him to think more lightly of her, and to be able to think more lightly of her would make her much less perplexing. But Daisy, on this occasion, continued to present herself as an inscrutable combination of audacity and innocence.

She had been walking some quarter of an hour, attended by her two cavaliers, and responding in a tone of very childish gaiety, as it seemed to Winterbourne, to the pretty speeches of Mr. Giovanelli, when a carriage that had detached itself from the revolving train drew up beside the path. At the same moment Winterbourne perceived that his friend Mrs. Walker—the lady whose house he had lately left—was seated in the vehicle, and was beckoning to him. Leaving Miss Miller's side, he hastened to obey her summons. Mrs. Walker was flushed; she wore an excited air. "It is really too dreadful," she said. "That girl must not do this sort of thing. She must not walk here with you two men. Fifty people have noticed her."

Winterbourne raised his eyebrows. "I think it's a pity to make too much fuss about it."

"It's a pity to let the girl ruin herself!"

"She is very innocent," said Winterbourne.

"She's very crazy!" cried Mrs. Walker. "Did you ever see anything so imbecile as her mother? After you had all left me, just now, I could not sit still for thinking of it. It seemed too pitiful not even to attempt to save her. I ordered the carriage and put on my bonnet, and came here as quickly as possible. Thank Heaven I have found you!"

"What do you propose to do with us?" asked Winterbourne, smiling.

"To ask her to get in, to drive her about here for half-an-hour, so that the world may see that she is not running absolutely wild, and then to take her safely home."

"I don't think it's a very happy thought," said Winterbourne; "but you can try."

Mrs. Walker tried. The young man went in pursuit of Miss Miller, who had simply nodded and smiled at his interlocutor in the carriage, and had gone her way with her companion. Daisy, on learning that Mrs. Walker wished to speak to her, retraced her steps with a perfect good grace and with Mr. Giovanelli at her side. She declared that she was delighted to have a chance to present this gentleman to Mrs. Walker. She immediately achieved the introduction, and declared that she had never in her life seen anything so lovely as Mrs. Walker's carriage-rug.

"I am glad you admire it," said this lady, smiling sweetly. "Will you get in and let me put it over you?"

"Oh no, thank you," said Daisy. "I shall admire it much more as I see you driving round with it."

"Do get in and drive with me!" said Mrs. Walker.

"That would be charming, but it's so enchanting just as I am!" and Daisy gave a brilliant glance at the gentlemen on either side of her.

"It may be enchanting, dear child, but it is not the custom here," urged Mrs. Walker, leaning forward in her victoria, with her hands devoutly clasped.

"Well, it ought to be, then!" said Daisy. "If I didn't walk I should expire."

"You should walk with your mother, dear," cried the lady from Geneva, losing patience.

"With my mother, dear!" exclaimed the young girl. Winterbourne saw that she scented interference. "My mother never walked ten steps in her life. And then, you know," she added, with a laugh, "I am more than five years old."

"You are old enough to be more reasonable. You are old enough, dear Miss Miller, to be talked about."

Daisy looked at Mrs. Walker, smiling intensely. "Talked about? What do you mean?"

"Come into my carriage, and I will tell you."

Daisy turned her quickened glance again from one of the gentlemen beside her to the other. Mr. Giovanelli was bowing to and fro, rubbing down his gloves and laughing very agreeably; Winterbourne thought it a most unpleasant scene. "I don't think I want to know what you mean," said Daisy, presently. "I don't think I should like it."

Winterbourne wished that Mrs. Walker would tuck in her carriage-rug and drive away; but this lady did not enjoy being defied, as she afterwards told him. "Should you prefer being thought a very reckless girl?" she demanded.

"Gracious!" exclaimed Daisy. She looked again at Mr. Giovanelli, then she turned to Winterbourne. There was a little pink flush in her cheek; she was tremendously pretty. "Does Mr. Winterbourne think," she asked slowly, smiling, throwing back her head and glancing at him from head to foot, "that—to save my reputation—I ought to get into the carriage?"

Winterbourne coloured; for an instant he hesitated greatly. It seemed so strange to hear her speak that way of her "reputation." But he himself, in fact, must speak in accordance with gallantry. The finest gallantry here was simply to tell her the truth; and the truth for Winterbourne— as the few indications I have been able to give have made him known to the reader —was that Daisy Miller should take Mrs. Walker's advice. He looked at her exquisite prettiness; and then said, very gently, "I think you should get into the carriage."

Daisy gave a violent laugh. "I never heard anything so stiff! If this is improper, Mrs. Walker," she pursued, "then

I am all improper, and you must give me up. Good-bye; I hope you'll have a lovely ride!" and, with Mr. Giovanelli, who made a triumphantly obsequious salute, she turned away.

Mrs. Walker sat looking after her, and there were tears in Mrs. Walker's eyes. "Get in here, sir," she said to Winterbourne, indicating the place beside her. The young man answered that he felt bound to accompany Miss Miller; whereupon Mrs. Walker declared that if he refused her this favour she would never speak to him again. She was evidently in earnest. Winterbourne overtook Daisy and her companion, and, offering the young girl his hand, told her that Mrs. Walker had made an imperious claim upon his society. He expected that in answer she would say something rather free, something to commit herself still further to that "recklessness" from which Mrs. Walker had so charitably endeavoured to dissuade her. But he only shook his hand, hardly looking at him; while Mr. Giovanelli bade him farewell with a too emphatic flourish of the hat.

Winterbourne was not in the best possible humour as he took his seat in Mrs. Walker's victoria. "That was not clever of you," he said, candidly, while the vehicle mingled again with the throng of carriages.

"In such a case," his companion answered, "I don't wish to be clever; I wish to be *earnest!*"

"Well, your earnestness has only offended her and put her off."

"It has happened very well," said Mrs. Walker. "If she is so perfectly determined to compromise herself, the sooner one knows it the better; one can act accordingly."

"I suspect she meant no harm," Winterbourne rejoined.

"So I thought a month ago. But she has been going too far."

"What has she been doing?"

"Everything that is not done here. Flirting with any man she could pick up; sitting in corners with mysterious Italians; dancing all the evening with the same partners; receiving visits at eleven o'clock at night. Her mother goes away when visitors come."

"But her brother," said Winterbourne, laughing, "sits up till midnight."

"He must be edified by what he sees. I'm told that at their hotel every one is talking about her, and that a smile goes round among all the servants when a gentleman comes and asks for Miss Miller."

"The servants be hanged!" said Winterbourne, angrily. "The poor girl's only fault," he presently added, "is that she is very uncultivated."

"She is naturally indelicate," Mrs. Walker declared. "Take that example this morning. How long had you known her at Vevey?"

"A couple of days."

"Fancy, then, her making it a personal matter that you should have left the place!"

Winterbourne was silent for some moments; then he said, "I suspect, Mrs. Walker, that you and I have lived too long at Geneva!" And he added a request that she should inform him with what particular design she had made him enter her carriage.

"I wished to beg you to cease your relations with Miss Miller—not to flirt with her—to give her no further opportunity to expose herself—to let her alone, in short."

"I'm afraid I can't do that," said Winterbourne. "I like her extremely."

"All the more reason that you shouldn't help her to make a scandal."

"There shall be nothing scandalous in my attentions to her."

"There certainly will be in the way she takes them. But I have said what I had on my conscience," Mrs. Walker pursued. "If you wish to rejoin the young lady I will put you down. Here, by-the-way, you have a chance."

The carriage was traversing that part of the Pincian Garden that overhangs the wall of Rome and overlooks the beautiful Villa Borghese. It is bordered by a large parapet, near which there are several seats. One of the seats, at a distance, was occupied by a gentleman and a lady, towards whom Mrs.

Walker gave a toss of her head. At the same moment these persons rose and walked towards the parapet. Winterbourne had asked the coachman to stop; he now descended from the carriage. His companion looked at him a moment in silence; then, while he raised his hat, she drove majestically away. Winterbourne stood there: he had turned his eyes towards Daisy and her cavalier. They evidently saw no one; they were too deeply occupied with each other. When they reached the low garden-wall they stood a moment looking off at the great flat-topped pine-clusters of the Villa Borghese; then Giovanelli seated himself familiarly upon the broad ledge of the wall. The western sun in the opposite sky sent out a brilliant shaft through a couple of cloud-bars, whereupon Daisy's companion took her parasol out of her hands and opened it. She came a little nearer, and he held the parasol over her; then, still holding it, he let it rest upon her shoulder, so that both of their heads were hidden from Winterbourne. This young man lingered a moment, then he began to walk. But he walked—not towards the couple with the parasol—towards the residence of his aunt, Mrs. Costello.

He flattered himself on the following day that there was no smiling among the servants when he, at least, asked for Mrs. Miller at her hotel. This lady and her daughter, however, were not at home; and on the next day after, repeating his visit, Winterbourne again had the misfortune not to find them. Mrs. Walker's party took place on the evening of the third day, and, in spite of the frigidity of his last interview with the hostess, Winterbourne was among the guests. Mrs. Walker was one of those American ladies who, while residing abroad, make a point, in their own phrase, of studying European society; and she had on this occasion collected several specimens of her diversely-born fellow-mortals to serve, as it were, as text-books. When Winterbourne arrived, Daisy Miller was not there, but in a few moments he saw her mother come in alone, very shyly and ruefully. Mrs. Miller's hair above her exposed-looking temples was more frizzled than ever. As she approached Mrs. Walker, Winterbourne also drew near.

"You see I've come all alone," said poor Mrs. Miller. "I'm so frightened I don't know what to do. It's the first time I've ever been to a party alone, especially in this country. I wanted to bring Randolph, or Eugenio, or some one, but Daisy just pushed me off by myself. I ain't used to going round alone."

"And does not your daughter intend to favour us with her society?" demanded Mrs. Walker, impressively.

"Well, Daisy's all dressed," said Mrs. Miller, with that accent of the dispassionate, if not of the philosophic, historian with which she always recorded the current incidents of her daughter's career. "She got dressed on purpose before dinner. But she's got a friend of hers there; that gentleman—the Italian—that she wanted to bring. They've got going at the piano; it seems as if they couldn't leave off. Mr. Giovanelli sings splendidly. But I guess they'll come before very long," concluded Mrs. Miller, hopefully.

"I'm sorry she should come—in that way," said Mrs. Walker.

"Well, I told her that there was no use in her getting dressed before dinner if she was going to wait three hours," responded Daisy's mamma. "I didn't see the use of her putting on such a dress as that to sit round with Mr. Giovanelli."

"This is most horrible!" said Mrs. Walker, turning away and addressing herself to Winterbourne. "*Elle s'affiche.*[11] It's her revenge for my having ventured to remonstrate with her. When she comes I shall not speak to her."

Daisy came after eleven o'clock; but she was not, on such an occasion, a young lady to wait to be spoken to. She rustled forward in radiant loveliness, smiling and chattering, carrying a large bouquet, and attended by Mr. Giovanelli. Every one stopped talking, and turned and looked at her. She came straight to Mrs. Walker.

"I'm afraid you thought I never was coming, so I sent mother off to tell you. I wanted to make Mr. Giovanelli practise some things before he came; you know he sings beautifully, and I want you to ask him to sing. This is Mr. Giovanelli; you know I introduced him to you; he's got the most lovely voice, and he knows the most charming set of songs. I made him go over them this evening on purpose; we had the greatest time at the hotel." Of all this Daisy delivered herself with the sweetest, brightest audibleness, looking now at her hostess and now round the room, while she gave a series of little pats round her shoulders to the edges of her dress. "Is there any one I know?" she asked.

"I think every one knows you!" said Mrs. Walker, pregnantly, and she gave a very cursory greeting to Mr. Giovanelli. This gentleman bore himself gallantly. He smiled and bowed, and showed his white teeth; he curled his moustaches and rolled his eyes, and performed all the proper functions of a handsome Italian at an evening party. He sang very prettily half-a-dozen songs, though Mrs. Walker afterwards declared that she had been quite unable to find out who asked him. It was apparently not Daisy who had given him his orders. Daisy sat at a distance from the piano; and though she had publicly, as it were, professed a high admiration for his singing, talked, not inaudibly, while it was going on.

"It's a pity these rooms are so small; we can't dance," she said to Winterbourne, as if she had seen him five minutes before.

"I am not sorry we can't dance," Winterbourne answered; "I don't dance."

"Of course you don't dance; you're too stiff," said Miss Daisy. "I hope you enjoyed your drive with Mrs. Walker!"

"No, I didn't enjoy it; I preferred walking with you."

"We paired off; that was much better," said Daisy. "But did you ever hear anything so cool as Mrs. Walker's wanting me

---

[11] She seeks notoriety.

to get into her carriage and drop poor Mr. Giovanelli, and under the pretext that it was proper? People have different ideas! It would have been most unkind; he had been talking about that walk for ten days."

"He should not have talked about it at all," said Winterbourne; "he would never have proposed to a young lady of this country to walk about the streets with him."

"About the streets?" cried Daisy, with her pretty stare. "Where, then, would he have proposed to her to walk? The Pincio is not the streets, either; and I, thank goodness, am not a young lady of this country. The young ladies of this country have a dreadfully poky time of it, so far as I can learn; I don't see why I should change my habits for *them*."

"I am afraid your habits are those of a flirt," said Winterbourne, gravely.

"Of course they are," she cried, giving him her little smiling stare again. "I'm a fearful, frightful flirt! Did you ever hear of a nice girl that was not? But I suppose you will tell me now that I am not a nice girl."

"You're a very nice girl; but I wish you would flirt with me, and me only," said Winterbourne.

"Ah! thank you—thank you very much; you are the last man I should think of flirting with. As I have had the pleasure of informing you, you are too stiff."

"You say that too often," said Winterbourne.

Daisy gave a delighted laugh. "If I could have the sweet hope of making you angry, I should say it again."

"Don't do that; when I am angry I'm stiffer than ever. But if you won't flirt with me, do cease, at least, to flirt with your friend at the piano; they don't understand that sort of thing here."

"I thought they understood nothing else!" exclaimed Daisy.

"Not in young unmarried women."

"It seems to me much more proper in young unmarried women than in old married ones," Daisy declared.

"Well," said Winterbourne, "when you deal with natives you must go by the custom of the place. Flirting is a purely American custom; it doesn't exist here. So when you show yourself in public with Mr. Giovanelli, and without your mother—"

"Gracious! poor mother!" interposed Daisy.

"Though you may be flirting, Mr. Giovanelli is not; he means something else."

"He isn't preaching, at any rate," said Daisy with vivacity. "And if you want very much to know, we are neither of us flirting; we are too good friends for that; we are very intimate friends."

"Ah!" rejoined Winterbourne, "if you are in love with each other it is another affair."

She had allowed him up to this point to talk so frankly that he had no expectation of shocking her by this ejaculation; but she immediately got up, blushing visibly, and leaving him to exclaim mentally that little American flirts were the queerest creatures in the world. "Mr. Giovanelli, at least," she said, giving her interlocutor a single glance, "never says such very disagreeable things to me."

Winterbourne was bewildered; he stood staring. Mr. Giovanelli had finished singing; he left the piano and came over to Daisy. "Won't you come into the other room and have some tea?" he asked, bending before her with his ornamental smile.

Daisy turned to Winterbourne, beginning to smile again. He was still more perplexed, for this inconsequent smile made nothing clear, though it seemed to prove, indeed, that she had a sweetness and softness that reverted instinctively to the pardon of offences. "It has never occurred to Mr. Winterbourne to offer me any tea," she said, with her little tormenting manner.

"I have offered you advice," Winterbourne rejoined.

"I prefer weak tea!" cried Daisy, and she went off with the brilliant Giovanelli. She sat with him in the adjoining room, in the embrasure of the window, for the rest of the evening. There was an interesting performance at the piano, but neither of these young people gave heed to it. When Daisy came to take leave of Mrs. Walker, this lady conscientiously repaired the weakness of which she had been guilty at the moment of the young girl's arrival. She turned her back straight upon Miss Miller and left her to depart with what grace she might. Winterbourne was standing near the door; he saw it all. Daisy turned very pale and looked at her mother, but Mrs. Miller was humbly unconscious of any violation of the usual social forms. She appeared, indeed, to have felt an incongruous impulse to draw attention to her own striking observance of them. "Goodnight, Mrs. Walker," she said; "we've had a beautiful evening. You see, if I let Daisy come to parties without me, I don't want her to go away without me." Daisy turned away, looking with a pale, grave face at the circle near the door; Winterbourne saw that, for the first moment, she was too much shocked and puzzled even for indignation. He on his side was greatly touched.

"That was very cruel," he said to Mrs. Walker.

"She never enters my drawing-room again!" replied his hostess.

Since Winterbourne was not to meet her in Mrs. Walker's drawing-room, he went as often as possible to Mrs. Miller's hotel. The ladies were rarely at home; but when he found them the devoted Giovanelli was always present. Very often the brilliant little Roman was in the drawing-room with Daisy alone, Mrs. Miller being apparently constantly of the opinion that discretion is the better part of surveillance. Winterbourne noted, at first with surprise, that Daisy on these occasions was never embarrassed or annoyed by his own entrance; but he very presently began to feel that she had no more surprises for him; the unexpected in her behaviour was the only thing to expect. She showed no displeasure at her *tête-à-tête* with Giovanelli being interrupted; she could chatter as freshly and freely with two gentlemen as with one; there was always, in her conversation, the

same odd mixture of audacity and puerility. Winterbourne remarked to himself that if she was seriously interested in Giovanelli, it was very singular that she should not take more trouble to preserve the sanctity of their interviews; and he liked her the more for her innocent-looking indifference and her apparently inexhaustible good humour. He could hardly have said why, but she seemed to him a girl who would never be jealous. At the risk of exciting a somewhat derisive smile on the reader's part, I may affirm that with regard to the women who had hitherto interested him, it very often seemed to Winterbourne among the possibilities that, given certain contingencies, he should be afraid—literally afraid—of these ladies; he had a pleasant sense that he should never be afraid of Daisy Miller. It must be added that this sentiment was not altogether flattering to Daisy; it was part of his conviction, or rather of his apprehension, that she would prove a very light young person.

But she was evidently very much interested in Giovanelli. She looked at him whenever he spoke; she was perpetually telling him to do this and to do that; she was constantly "chaffing" and abusing him. She appeared completely to have forgotten that Winterbourne had said anything to displease her at Mrs. Walker's little party. One Sunday afternoon, having gone to St. Peter's with his aunt, Winterbourne perceived Daisy strolling about the great church in company with the inevitable Giovanelli. Presently he pointed out the young girl and her cavalier to Mrs. Costello. This lady looked at them a moment through her eyeglass, and then she said,

"That's what makes you so pensive in these days, eh?"

"I had not the least idea I was pensive," said the young man.

"You are very much pre-occupied; you are thinking of something."

"And what is it," he asked, "that you accuse me of thinking of?"

"Of that young lady's—Miss Baker's, Miss Chandler's—what's her name?—Miss

Miller's intrigue with that little barber's block."

"Do you call it an intrigue," Winterbourne asked—"an affair that goes on with such peculiar publicity?"

"That's their folly," said Mrs. Costello, "it's not their merit."

"No," rejoined Winterbourne, with something of that pensiveness to which his aunt had alluded. "I don't believe that there is anything to be called an intrigue."

"I have heard a dozen people speak of it; they say she is quite carried away by him."

"They are certainly very intimate," said Winterbourne.

Mrs. Costello inspected the young couple again with her optical instrument. "He is very handsome. One easily sees how it is. She thinks him the most elegant man in the world, the finest gentleman. She has never seen anything like him; he is better even than the courier. It was the courier, probably, who introduced him; and if he succeeds in marrying the young lady, the courier will come in for a magnificent commission."

"I don't believe she thinks of marrying him," said Winterbourne, "and I don't believe he hopes to marry her."

"You may be very sure she thinks of nothing. She goes on from day to day, from hour to hour, as they did in the Golden Age. I can imagine nothing more vulgar. And at the same time," added Mrs. Costello, "depend upon it that she may tell you any moment that she is 'engaged.'"

"I think that is more than Giovanelli expects," said Winterbourne.

"Who is Giovanelli?"

"The little Italian. I have asked questions about him and learned something. He is apparently a perfectly respectable little man. I believe he is, in a small way, a *cavaliere avvocato*.[12] But he doesn't move in what are called the first circles. I think it is really not absolutely impossible that the courier introduced him. He is evidently immensely charmed with Miss Miller. If she thinks him the finest gentleman in the

world, he, on his side, has never found himself in personal contact with such splendour, such opulence, such expensiveness, as this young lady's. And then she must seem to him wonderfully pretty and interesting. I rather doubt that he dreams of marrying her. That must appear to him too impossible a piece of luck. He has nothing but his handsome face to offer, and there is a substantial Mr. Miller in that mysterious land of dollars. Giovanelli knows that he hasn't a title to offer. If he were only a count or a *marchese*! He must wonder at his luck, at the way they have taken him up."

"He accounts for it by his handsome face, and thinks Miss Miller a young lady *qui se passe ses fantaisies!*"[13] said Mrs. Costello.

"It is very true," Winterbourne pursued, "that Daisy and her mamma have not yet risen to that stage of—what shall I call it? —of culture, at which the idea of catching a count or a *marchese* begins. I believe that they are intellectually incapable of that conception."

"Ah! but the *avvocato* can't believe it," said Mrs. Costello.

Of the observation excited by Daisy's "intrigue," Winterbourne gathered that day at St. Peter's sufficient evidence. A dozen of the American colonists in Rome came to talk with Mrs. Costello, who sat on a little portable stool at the base of one of the great pilasters. The vesper service was going forward in splendid chants and organtones in the adjacent choir, and meanwhile, between Mrs. Costello and her friends, there was a great deal said about poor little Miss Miller's going really "too far." Winterbourne was not pleased with what he heard; but when, coming out upon the great steps of the church, he saw Daisy, who had emerged before him, get into an open cab with her accomplice and roll away through the cynical streets of Rome, he could not deny to himself that she was

---

[12] A lawyer.
[13] Who enjoys her caprices.

going very far indeed. He felt very sorry for her—not exactly that he believed that she had completely lost her head, but because it was painful to hear so much that was pretty, and undefended, and natural, assigned to a vulgar place among the categories of disorder. He made an attempt after this to give a hint to Mrs. Miller. He met one day in the Corso [14] a friend—a tourist like himself, who had just come out of the Doria Palace, where he had been walking through the beautiful gallery. His friend talked for a moment about the superb portrait of Innocent X., by Velasquez, which hangs in one of the cabinets of the palace, and then said, "And in the same cabinet, by-the-way, I had the pleasure of contemplating a picture of a different kind—that pretty American girl whom you pointed out to me last week." In answer to Winterbourne's inquiries, his friend narrated that the pretty American girl—prettier than ever—was seated with a companion in the secluded nook in which the great papal portrait was enshrined.

"Who was her companion?" asked Winterbourne.

"A little Italian with a bouquet in his button-hole. The girl is delightfully pretty; but I thought I understood from you the other day that she was a young lady *du meilleur monde.*" [15]

"So she is!" answered Winterbourne; and having assured himself that his informant had seen Daisy and her companion but five minutes before, he jumped into a cab and went to call on Mrs. Miller. She was at home; but she apologized to him for receiving him in Daisy's absence.

"She's gone out somewhere with Mr. Giovanelli," said Mrs. Miller. "She's always going round with Mr. Giovanelli."

"I have noticed that they are very intimate," Winterbourne observed.

"Oh, it seems as if they couldn't live without each other!" said Mrs. Miller. "Well, he's a real gentleman, anyhow. I keep telling Daisy she's engaged!"

"And what does Daisy say?"

"Oh, she says she isn't engaged. But she

might as well be!" this impartial parent resumed. "She goes on as if she was. But I've made Mr. Giovanelli promise to tell me, if *she* doesn't. I should want to write to Mr. Miller about it—shouldn't you?"

Winterbourne replied that he certainly should; and the state of mind of Daisy's mamma struck him as so unprecedented in the annals of parental vigilance that he gave up as utterly irrelevant the attempt to place her upon her guard.

After this Daisy was never at home, and Winterbourne ceased to meet her at the houses of their common acquaintance because, as he perceived, these shrewd people had quite made up their minds that she was going too far. They ceased to invite her, and they intimated that they desired to express to observant Europeans the great truth that, though Miss Daisy Miller was a young American lady, her behaviour was not representative—was regarded by her compatriots as abnormal. Winterbourne wondered how she felt about all the cold shoulders that were turned towards her, and sometimes it annoyed him to suspect that she did not feel at all. He said to himself that she was too light and childish, too uncultivated and unreasoning, too provincial, to have reflected upon her ostracism, or even to have perceived it. Then at other moments he believed that she carried about in her elegant and irresponsible little organism a defiant, passionate, perfectly observant consciousness of the impression she produced. He asked himself whether Daisy's defiance came from the consciousness of innocence, or from her being, essentially, a young person of the reckless class. It must be admitted that holding one's self to a belief in Daisy's "innocence" came to seem to Winterbourne more and more a matter of fine-spun gallantry. As I have already had occasion to relate, he was angry at finding himself reduced to chopping logic about this young lady; he was vexed at his want of instinctive certitude as to

---

[14] Important Roman thoroughfare.
[15] Of the higher class.

how far her eccentricities were generic, national, and how far they were personal. From either view of them he had somehow missed her, and now it was too late. She was "carried away" by Mr. Giovanelli.

A few days after his brief interview with her mother, he encountered her in that beautiful abode of flowering desolation known as the Palace of the Caesars. The early Roman spring had filled the air with bloom and perfume, and the rugged surface of the Palatine [16] was muffled with tender verdure. Daisy was strolling along the top of one of those great mounds of ruin that are embanked with mossy marble and paved with monumental inscriptions. It seemed to him that Rome had never been so lovely as just then. He stood looking off at the enchanting harmony of line and colour that remotely encircles the city, inhaling the softly humid odours, and feeling the freshness of the year and the antiquity of the place reaffirm themselves in mysterious interfusion. It seemed to him, also, that Daisy had never looked so pretty; but this had been an observation of his whenever he met her. Giovanelli was at her side, and Giovanelli, too, wore an aspect of even unwonted brilliancy.

"Well," said Daisy, "I should think you would be lonesome!"

"Lonesome?" asked Winterbourne.

"You are always going round by yourself. Can't you get any one to walk with you?"

"I am not so fortunate," said Winterbourne, "as your companion."

Giovanelli, from the first, had treated Winterbourne with distinguished politeness; he listened with a deferential air to his remarks; he laughed, punctiliously, at his pleasantries; he seemed disposed to testify to his belief that Winterbourne was a superior young man. He carried himself in no degree like a jealous wooer; he had obviously a great deal of tact; he had no objection to your expecting a little humility of him. It even seemed to Winterbourne at times that Giovanelli would find a cer-

tain mental relief in being able to have a private understanding with him—to say to him, as an intelligent man, that, bless you, *he* knew how extraordinary was this young lady, and didn't flatter himself with delusive—or, at least, *too* delusive—hopes of matrimony and dollars. On this occasion he strolled away from his companion to pluck a sprig of almond-blossom, which he carefully arranged in his button-hole.

"I know why you say that," said Daisy, watching Giovanelli. "Because you think I go round too much with *him*." And she nodded at her attendant.

"Every one thinks so—if you care to know," said Winterbourne.

"Of course I care to know!" Daisy exclaimed, seriously. "But I don't believe it. They are only pretending to be shocked. They don't really care a straw what I do. Besides, I don't go round so much."

"I think you will find they do care. They will show it—disagreeably."

Daisy looked at him a moment. "How—disagreeably?"

"Haven't you noticed anything?" Winterbourne asked.

"I have noticed you. But I noticed you were as stiff as an umbrella the first time I saw you."

"You will find I am not so stiff as several others," said Winterbourne, smiling.

"How shall I find it?"

"By going to see the others."

"What will they do to me?"

"They will give you the cold shoulder. Do you know what that means?"

Daisy was looking at him intently; she began to colour. "Do you mean as Mrs. Walker did the other night?"

"Exactly!" said Winterbourne.

She looked away at Giovanelli, who was decorating himself with his almond-blossom. Then, looking back at Winterbourne, "I shouldn't think you would let people be so unkind!" she said.

---

[16] One of Rome's seven hills.

"How can I help it?" he asked.

"I should think you would say something."

"I did say something;" and he paused a moment. "I say that your mother tells me that she believes you are engaged."

"Well, she does," said Daisy very simply.

Winterbourne began to laugh. "And does Randolph believe it?" he asked.

"I guess Randolph doesn't believe anything," said Daisy. Randolph's scepticism excited Winterbourne to further hilarity, and he observed that Giovanelli was coming back to them. Daisy, observing it too, addressed herself again to her countryman. "Since you have mentioned it," she said, "I *am* engaged." . . . Winterbourne looked at her; he had stopped laughing. "You don't believe it!" she added.

He was silent a moment; and then, "Yes, I believe it," he said.

"Oh, no, you don't!" she answered. "Well, then—I am not!"

The young girl and her cicerone were on their way to the gate of the enclosure, so that Winterbourne, who had but lately entered, presently took leave of them. A week afterwards he went to dine at a beautiful villa on the Caelian Hill, and, on arriving, dismissed his hired vehicle. The evening was charming, and he promised himself the satisfaction of walking home beneath the Arch of Constantine and past the vaguely-lighted monuments of the Forum. There was a waning moon in the sky, and her radiance was not brilliant, but she was veiled in a thin cloud-curtain which seemed to diffuse and equalize it. When, on his return from the villa (it was eleven o'clock), Winterbourne approached the dusky circle of the Colosseum, it occurred to him, as a lover of the picturesque, that the interior, in the pale moonshine, would be well worth a glance. He turned aside and walked to one of the empty arches, near which, as he observed, an open carriage—one of the little Roman street-cabs —was stationed. Then he passed in, among the cavernous shadows of the great struc-

ture, and emerged upon the clear and silent arena. The place had never seemed to him more impressive. One-half of the gigantic circus was in deep shade; the other was sleeping in the luminous dusk. As he stood there he began to murmur Byron's famous lines, out of "Manfred"; [17] but before he had finished his quotation he remembered that if nocturnal meditations in the Colosseum are recommended by the poets, they are deprecated by the doctors. The historic atmosphere was there, certainly; but the historic atmosphere, scientifically considered, was no better than a villainous miasma. Winterbourne walked to the middle of the arena, to take a more general glance, intending thereafter to make a hasty retreat. The great cross in the centre was covered with shadow; it was only as he drew near it that he made it out distinctly. Then he saw that two persons were stationed upon the low steps which formed its base. One of these was a woman, seated; her companion was standing in front of her.

Presently the sound of the woman's voice came to him distinctly in the warm night-air. "Well, he looks at us as one of the old lions or tigers may have looked at the Christian martyrs!" These were the words he heard, in the familiar accent of Miss Daisy Miller.

"Let us hope he is not very hungry," responded the ingenious Giovanelli. "He will have to take me first; you will serve for dessert!"

Winterbourne stopped, with a sort of horror; and, it must be added, with a sort of relief. It was as if a sudden illumination had been flashed upon the ambiguity of Daisy's behaviour, and the riddle had become easy to read. She was a young lady whom a gentleman need no longer be at pains to respect. He stood there looking at her—looking at her companion, and not reflecting that though he saw them vaguely, he himself must have been more brightly

---

[17] See Act III, sc. iv, lines 270 ff.

visible. He felt angry with himself that he had bothered so much about the right way of regarding Miss Daisy Miller. Then, as he was going to advance again, he checked himself; not from the fear that he was doing her injustice, but from the sense of the danger of appearing unbecomingly exhilarated by this sudden revulsion from cautious criticism. He turned away towards the entrance of the place; but, as he did so, he heard Daisy speak again.

"Why, it was Mr. Winterbourne! He saw me—and he cuts me!"

What a clever little reprobate she was, and how smartly she played at injured innocence! But he wouldn't cut her. Winterbourne came forward again, and went towards the great cross. Daisy had got up; Giovanelli lifted his hat. Winterbourne had now begun to think simply of the craziness, from a sanitary point of view, of a delicate young girl lounging away the evening in this nest of malaria. What if she *were* a clever little reprobate? that was no reason for her dying of the *perniciosa*.[18] "How long have you been here?" he asked, almost brutally.

Daisy, lovely in the flattering moonlight, looked at him a moment. Then—"All the evening," she answered, gently. . . . "I never saw anything so pretty."

"I am afraid," said Winterbourne, "that you will not think Roman fever very pretty. This is the way people catch it. I wonder," he added, turning to Giovanelli, "that you, a native Roman, should countenance such a terrible indiscretion."

"Ah," said the handsome native, "for myself I am not afraid."

"Neither am I—for you! I am speaking for this young lady."

Giovanelli lifted his well-shaped eyebrows and showed his brilliant teeth. But he took Winterbourne's rebuke with docility. "I told the signorina it was a grave indiscretion; but when was the signorina ever prudent?"

"I never was sick, and I don't mean to be!" the signorina declared. "I don't look

like much, but I'm healthy! I was bound to see the Colosseum by moonlight; I shouldn't have wanted to go home without that; and we have had the most beautiful time, haven't we, Mr. Giovanelli? If there has been any danger, Eugenio can give me some pills. He has got some splendid pills."

"I should advise you," said Winterbourne, "to drive home as fast as possible and take one!"

"What you say is very wise," Giovanelli rejoined. "I will go and make sure the carriage is at hand." And he went forward rapidly.

Daisy followed with Winterbourne. He kept looking at her; she seemed not in the least embarrassed. Winterbourne said nothing; Daisy chattered about the beauty of the place. "Well, I *have* seen the Colosseum by moonlight!" she exclaimed. "That's one good thing." Then, noticing Winterbourne's silence, she asked him why he didn't speak. He made no answer; he only began to laugh. They passed under one of the dark archways; Giovanelli was in front with the carriage. Here Daisy stopped a moment, looking at the young American. "*Did* you believe I was engaged the other day?" she asked.

"It doesn't matter what I believed the other day," said Winterbourne, still laughing.

"Well, what do you believe now?"

"I believe that it makes very little difference whether you are engaged or not!"

He felt the young girl's pretty eyes fixed upon him through the thick gloom of the archway; she was apparently going to answer. But Giovanelli hurried her forward. "Quick! quick!" he said; "if we get in by midnight we are quite safe."

Daisy took her seat in the carriage, and the fortunate Italian placed himself beside her. "Don't forget Eugenio's pills!" said Winterbourne, as he lifted his hat.

"I don't care," said Daisy, in a little

---

[18] Malaria.

strange tone, "whether I have Roman fever or not!" Upon this the cab-driver cracked his whip, and they rolled away over the desultory patches of the antique pavement.

Winterbourne—to do him justice, as it were—mentioned to no one that he had encountered Miss Miller, at midnight, in the Colosseum with a gentleman; but, nevertheless, a couple of days later, the fact of her having been there under these circumstances was known to every member of the little American circle, and commented accordingly. Winterbourne reflected that they had of course known it at the hotel, and that, after Daisy's return, there had been an exchange of remarks between the porter and the cab-driver. But the young man was conscious, at the same moment, that it had ceased to be a matter of serious regret to him that the little American flirt should be "talked about" by low-minded menials. These people, a day or two later, had serious information to give: the little American flirt was alarmingly ill. Winterbourne, when the rumour came to him, immediately went to the hotel for more news. He found that two or three charitable friends had preceded him, and that they were being entertained in Mrs. Miller's salon by Randolph.

"It's going round at night," said Randolph—"that's what made her sick. She's always going round at night. I shouldn't think she'd want to—it's so plaguy dark. You can't see anything here at night, except when there's a moon! In America there's always a moon!" Mrs. Miller was invisible; she was now, at least, giving her daughter the advantage of her society. It was evident that Daisy was dangerously ill.

Winterbourne went often to ask for news of her, and once he saw Mrs. Miller, who, though deeply alarmed, was—rather to his surprise—perfectly composed, and, as it appeared, a most efficient and judicious nurse. She talked a good deal about Dr. Davis, but Winterbourne paid her the compliment of saying to himself that she was not,

after all, such a monstrous goose. "Daisy spoke of you the other day," she said to him. "Half the time she doesn't know what she's saying, but that time I think she did. She gave me a message; she told me to tell you—she told me to tell you that she never was engaged to that handsome Italian. I am sure I am very glad; Mr. Giovanelli hasn't been near us since she was taken ill. I thought he was so much of a gentleman; but I don't call that very polite! A lady told me that he was afraid I was angry with him for taking Daisy round at night. Well, so I am; but I suppose he knows I'm a lady. I would scorn to scold him. Anyway, she says she's not engaged. I don't know why she wanted you to know; but she said to me three times, 'Mind you tell Mr. Winterbourne.' And then she told me to ask if you remembered the time you went to that castle in Switzerland. But I said I wouldn't give any such messages as that. Only, if she is not engaged, I'm sure I'm glad to know it."

But, as Winterbourne had said, it mattered very little. A week after this the poor girl died; it had been a terrible case of the fever. Daisy's grave was in the little Protestant cemetery, in an angle of the wall of imperial Rome, beneath the cypresses and the thick spring-flowers. Winterbourne stood there beside it, with a number of other mourners—a number larger than the scandal excited by the young lady's career would have led you to expect. Near him stood Giovanelli, who came nearer still before Winterbourne turned away. Giovanelli was very pale; on this occasion he had no flower in his button-hole; he seemed to wish to say something. At last he said, "She was the most beautiful young lady I ever saw, and the most amiable." And then he added in a moment, "and she was the most innocent."

Winterbourne looked at him, and presently repeated his words, "And the most innocent?"

"The most innocent!"

Winterbourne felt sore and angry. "Why

the devil," he asked, "did you take her to that fatal place?"

Mr. Giovanelli's urbanity was apparently imperturbable. He looked on the ground a moment, and then he said, "For myself, I had no fear; and she wanted to go."

"That was no reason!" Winterbourne declared.

The subtle Roman again dropped his eyes. "If she had lived, I should have got nothing. She would never have married me, I am sure."

"She would never have married you?"

"For a moment I hoped so. But no, I am sure."

Winterbourne listened to him; he stood staring at the raw protuberance among the April daisies. When he turned away again, Mr. Giovanelli with his light, slow step, had retired.

Winterbourne almost immediately left Rome; but the following summer he again met his aunt, Mrs. Costello, at Vevey. Mrs. Costello was fond of Vevey. In the interval Winterbourne had often thought of Daisy Miller and her mystifying manners. One day he spoke of her to his aunt—said it was on his conscience that he had done her injustice.

"I am sure I don't know," said Mrs. Costello. "How did your injustice affect her?"

"She sent me a message before her death which I didn't understand at the time. But I have understood it since. She would have appreciated one's esteem."

"Is that a modest way," asked Mrs. Costello, "of saying that she would have reciprocated one's affection?"

Winterbourne offered no answer to this question; but he presently said, "You were right in that remark that you made last summer. I was booked to make a mistake. I have lived too long in foreign parts."

Nevertheless, he went back to live at Geneva, whence there continue to come the most contradictory accounts of his motives of sojourn: a report that he is "studying" hard—an intimation that he is much interested in a very clever foreign lady.

THE LESSON OF THE MASTER
[1892 (1888)]

I

HE HAD BEEN told the ladies were at church, but this was corrected by what he saw from the top of the steps—they descended from a great height in two arms, with a circular sweep of the most charming effect—at the threshold of the door which, from the long bright gallery, overlooked the immense lawn. Three gentlemen, on the grass, at a distance, sat under the great trees, while the fourth figure showed a crimson dress that told as a "bit of color" amid the fresh rich green. The servant had so far accompanied Paul Overt as to introduce him to this view, after asking him if he wished first to go to his room. The young man declined that privilege, conscious of no disrepair from so short and easy a journey and always liking to take at once a general perceptive possession of a new scene. He stood there a little with his eyes on the group and on the admirable picture, the wide grounds of an old country house near London—that only made it better—on a splendid Sunday in June. "But that lady, who's *she?*" he said to the servant before the man left him.

"I think she's Mrs. St. George, sir."

"Mrs. St. George, the wife of the distinguished——" Then Paul Overt checked himself, doubting if a footman would know.

"Yes, sir—probably, sir," said his guide, who appeared to wish to intimate that a person staying at Summersoft would naturally be, if only by alliance, distinguished. His tone, however, made poor Overt himself feel for the moment scantly so.

"And the gentlemen?" Overt went on.

"Well, sir, one of them's General Fancourt."

"Ah, yes, I know; thank you." General Fancourt was distinguished, there was no doubt of that, for something he had done, or perhaps even hadn't done—the young man couldn't remember which—some years before in India. The servant went away, leaving the glass doors open into the gallery, and Paul Overt remained at the head of the wide double staircase, saying to himself that the place was sweet and promised a pleasant visit, while he leaned on the balustrade of fine old iron-work which, like all the other details, was of the same period as the house. It all went together and spoke in one voice—a rich English voice of the early part of the eighteenth century. It might have been church time on a summer's day in the reign of Queen Anne: the stillness was too perfect to be modern, the nearness counted so as distance, and there was something so fresh and sound in the originality of the large smooth house, the expanse of beautiful brickwork that showed for pink rather than red and that had been kept clear of messy creepers by the law under which a woman with a rare complexion disdains a veil. When Paul Overt became aware that the people under the trees had noticed him, he turned back through the open doors into the great gallery which was the pride of the place. It marched across from end to end and seemed—with its bright colors, its high paneled windows, its faded flowered chintzes, its quickly recognized portraits and pictures, the blue-and-white china of its cabinets and the attenuated festoons and rosettes of its ceiling—a cheerful, upholstered avenue into the other century.

Our friend was slightly nervous; that went with his character as a student of fine prose, went with the artist's general disposition to vibrate; and there was a particular thrill in the idea that Henry St. George might be a member of the party. For the young aspirant he had remained a high literary figure, in spite of the lower range of production to which he had fallen after his three first great successes, the comparative absence of quality in his later work. There had been moments when Paul Overt almost shed tears for this; but now that he was near him—he had never met him—he was conscious only of the fine original source and of his own immense debt. After he had taken a turn or two up and down the gallery, he came out again and descended the steps. He was but slenderly supplied with a certain social boldness—it was really a weakness in him —so that, conscious of a want of acquaintance with the four persons in the distance, he gave way to motions recommended by their not committing him to a positive approach. There was a fine English awkwardness in this—he felt that too as he sauntered vaguely and obliquely across the lawn, taking an independent line. Fortunately there was an equally fine English directness in the way one of the gentlemen presently rose and made as if to "stalk" him, though with an air of conciliation and reassurance. To this demonstration Paul Overt instantly responded, even if the gentleman were not his host. He was tall, straight, and elderly and had, like the great house itself, a pink, smiling face, and into the bargain a white mustache. Our young man met him halfway while he laughed and said: "Er—Lady Watermouth told us you were coming; she asked me just to look after you." Paul Overt thanked him, liking him on the spot, and turned round with him to walk toward the others. "They've all gone to church— all except us," the stranger continued as they went; "we're just sitting here—it's so jolly." Overt pronounced it jolly indeed: it was such a lovely place. He mentioned that he was having the charming impression for the first time.

"Ah, you've not been here before?" said his companion. "It's a nice little place— not much to *do*, you know." Overt wondered what he wanted to "do"—he felt that he himself was doing so much. By the time they came to where the others sat he had recognized his initiator for a military man and—such was the turn of Overt's imagination—had found him thus still more sympathetic. He would naturally have a need for action, for deeds at variance with the pacific pastoral scene. He was evidently so good-natured, however, that he accepted the inglorious hour for what it was worth. Paul Overt shared it with him and with his companions for the next twenty minutes; the latter looked at him and he looked at them without knowing much who they were, while the talk went on without much telling him even what it meant. It seemed indeed to mean nothing in particular; it wandered, with casual pointless pauses and short terrestrial flights, amid names of persons and places—names which, for our friend, had no great power of evocation. It was all sociable and slow, as was right and natural of a warm Sunday morning. His first attention was given to the question, privately considered, of whether one of the two younger men would be Henry St. George. He knew many of his distinguished contemporaries by their photographs, but had never, as happened, seen a portrait of the great misguided novelist. One of the gentlemen was unimaginable—he was too young; and the other scarcely looked clever enough, with such mild, undiscriminating eyes. If those eyes were St. George's the problem presented by the ill-matched parts of his genius would be still more difficult of solution. Besides, the deportment of their proprietor was not, as regards the lady in the red dress, such as could be natural, toward the wife of his bosom, even to a writer accused by several critics of sacrificing too much to manner. Lastly, Paul Overt had a vague sense that if the gentleman with the expressionless eyes bore the name that had set his heart beating faster (he also had contradictory, conventional whiskers—the young admirer of the celebrity had never in a mental vision seen *his* face in so vulgar a frame) he would have given him a sign of recognition or of friendliness, would have heard of him a little, would know something about *Ginistrella,* would have an impression of how that fresh fiction had caught the eye of real criticism. Paul Overt had a dread of being grossly proud, but even morbid modesty might view the authorship of *Ginistrella* as constituting a degree of identity. His soldierly friend became clear enough: he was "Fancourt," but was also "the General"; and he mentioned to the new visitor in the course of a few moments that he had but lately returned from twenty years' service abroad.

"And now you remain in England?" the young man asked.

"Oh, yes; I've bought a small house in London."

"And I hope you like it," said Overt, looking at Mrs. St. George.

"Well, a little house in Manchester Square—there's a limit to the enthusiasm *that* inspires."

"Oh, I meant being at home again—being back in Piccadilly."

"My daughter likes Piccadilly—that's the main thing. She's very fond of art and music and literature and all that kind of thing. She missed it in India and she finds it in London, or she hopes she'll find it. Mr. St. George has promised to help her—he has been awfully kind to her. She has gone to church—she's fond of that too—but they'll all be back in a quarter of an hour. You must let me introduce you to her—she'll be so glad to know you. I daresay she has read every blest word you've written."

"I shall be delighted—I haven't written so very many," Overt pleaded, feeling, and without resentment, that the General at least was vagueness itself about that. But he wondered a little why, expressing this friendly disposition, it didn't occur to the doubtless eminent soldier to pronounce the word that would put him in relation with Mrs. St. George. If it was a question of introductions Miss Fancourt—apparently as yet unmarried—was far away, while the wife of his illustrious confrere was almost between them. This lady struck Paul Overt as altogether pretty, with a surprising juvenility and a high smartness of aspect, something that—he could scarcely have said why—served for mystification. St. George certainly had every right to a charming wife, but he himself would never have imagined the important little woman in the aggressively Parisian dress the partner for life, the *alter ego,* of a man of letters. That partner in general, he knew, that second self, was far from presenting herself in a single type: observation had taught him that she was not inveterately, not necessarily plain. But he had never before seen her look so much as if her prosperity had deeper foundations than an ink-spotted study table littered with proof sheets. Mrs. St. George might have been the wife of a gentleman who "kept" books rather than wrote them, who carried on great affairs in the City and made better bargains than those that poets mostly make with publishers. With this she hinted at a success more personal—a success peculiarly stamping the age in which society, the world of conversation, is a great drawing room with the City for its antechamber. Overt numbered her years at first as some thirty, and then ended by believing that she might approach her fiftieth. But she somehow in this case juggled away the excess and the difference—you only saw them in a rare glimpse, like the rabbit in the conjuror's sleeve. She was extraordinarily white, and her every element and item was pretty; her eyes, her ears, her hair, her voice, her hands, her feet—to which her relaxed attitude in her wicker chair gave a great publicity—and the numerous ribbons and trinkets with which she was bedecked. She looked as if she had put on her best clothes to go to church and then had decided they were too good for that and had stayed at home. She told a story of some length about the shabby way Lady Jane had treated the Duchess, as well as an anecdote in relation to a purchase she had made in Paris—on her way back from Cannes; made for Lady Egbert, who had never refunded the money. Paul Overt suspected her of a tendency to figure great people as larger than life, until he noticed the manner in which she handled Lady Egbert, which was so sharply mutinous that it reassured him. He felt he should have understood her better if he might have met her eye; but she scarcely so much as glanced at him. "Ah, here they come—all the good ones!" she said at last; and Paul Overt admired at his distance the

return of the churchgoers—several persons, in couples and threes, advancing in a flicker of sun and shade at the end of a large green vista formed by the level grass and the overarching boughs.

"If you mean to imply that *we're* bad, I protest," said one of the gentlemen—"after making oneself agreeable all the morning!"

"Ah, if they've found you agreeable ——!" Mrs. St. George gaily cried. "But if we're good the others are better."

"They must be angels then," said the amused General.

"Your husband was an angel, the way he went off at your bidding," the gentleman who had first spoken declared to Mrs. St. George.

"At my bidding?"

"Didn't you make him go to church?"

"I never made him do anything in my life but once—when I made him burn up a bad book. That's all!" At her "That's all!" our young friend broke into an irrepressible laugh; it lasted only a second, but it drew her eyes to him. His own met them, though not long enough to help him to understand her; unless it were a step towards this that he saw on the instant how the burnt book—the way she alluded to it!—would have been one of her husband's finest things.

"A bad book?" her interlocutor repeated.

"I didn't like it. He went to church because your daughter went," she continued to General Fancourt. "I think it my duty to call your attention to his extraordinary demonstrations to your daughter."

"Well, if you don't mind them I don't!" the General laughed.

"*Il s'attache à ses pas.*[1] But I don't wonder—she's so charming."

"I hope she won't make him burn any books!" Paul Overt ventured to exclaim.

"If she'd make him write a few it would be more to the purpose," said Mrs. St. George. "He has been of a laziness of late——!"

Our young man stared—he was so struck

---

[1] He dogs her steps.

with the lady's phraseology. Her "Write a few" seemed to him almost as good as her "That's all." Didn't she, as the wife of a rare artist, know what it was to produce *one* perfect work of art? How in the world did she think they were turned off? His private conviction was that, admirably as Henry St. George wrote, he had written for the last ten years, and especially for the last five, only too much, and there was an instant during which he felt inwardly solicited to make this public. But before he had spoken, a diversion was effected by the return of the absentees. They strolled up dispersedly—there were eight or ten of them—and the circle under the trees rearranged itself as they took their place in it. They made it much larger, so that Paul Overt could feel—he was always feeling that sort of thing, as he said to himself— that, if the company had already been interesting to watch, the interest would now become intense. He shook hands with his hostess, who welcomed him without many words, in the manner of a woman able to trust him to understand and conscious that so pleasant an occasion would in every way speak for itself. She offered him no particular facility for sitting by her, and when they had all subsided again he found himself still next General Fancourt, with an unknown lady on his other flank.

"That's my daughter—that one opposite," the General said to him without loss of time. Overt saw a tall girl, with magnificent red hair, in a dress of a pretty gray-green tint and of a limp silken texture, a garment that clearly shirked every modern effect. It had therefore somehow the stamp of the latest thing, so that our beholder quickly took her for nothing if not contemporaneous.

"She's very handsome—very handsome," he repeated while he considered her. There was something noble in her head, and she appeared fresh and strong.

Her good father surveyed her with complacency, remarking soon: "She looks too hot—that's her walk. But she'll be all right presently. Then I'll make her come over and speak to you."

"I should be sorry to give you that trouble. If you were to take me over *there*——!" the young man murmured.

"My dear sir, do you suppose I put myself out that way? I don't mean for you, but for Marian," the General added.

"*I* would put myself out for her soon enough," Overt replied; after which he went on: "Will you be so good as to tell me which of those gentlemen is Henry St. George?"

"The fellow talking to my girl. By Jove, he *is* making up to her—they're going off for another walk."

"Ah, is that he—really?" Our friend felt a certain surprise, for the personage before him seemed to trouble a vision which had been vague only while not confronted with the reality. As soon as the reality dawned, the mental image, retiring with a sigh, became substantial enough to suffer a slight wrong. Overt, who had spent a considerable part of his short life in foreign lands, made now, but not for the first time, the reflection that whereas in those countries he had almost always recognized the artist and the man of letters by his personal "type," the mold of his face, the character of his head, the expression of his figure, and even the indications of his dress, so in England this identification was as little as possible a matter of course, thanks to the greater conformity, the habit of sinking the profession instead of advertising it, the general diffusion of the air of the gentleman—the gentleman committed to no particular set of ideas. More than once, on returning to his own country, he had said to himself about people met in society: "One sees them in this place and that, and one even talks with them; but to find out what they *do* one would really have to be a detective." In respect to several individuals whose work he was the opposite of "drawn to"—perhaps he was wrong—he found himself adding, "No wonder they conceal it—when it's so bad!" He noted that oftener than in France and in Germany his artist looked like a gentleman—that is, like an English one—while, certainly outside a few exceptions, his gentleman didn't look like an artist. St. George was not one of the exceptions; that circumstance he definitely apprehended before the great man had turned his back to walk off with Miss Fancourt. He certainly looked better behind than any foreign man of letters—showed for beautifully correct in his tall black hat and his superior frock coat. Somehow, all the same, these very garments—he wouldn't have minded them so much on a weekday—were disconcerting to Paul Overt, who forgot for the moment that the head of the profession was not a bit better dressed than himself. He had caught a glimpse of a regular face, a fresh color, a brown mustache, and a pair of eyes surely never visited by a fine frenzy, and he promised himself to study these denotements on the first occasion. His superficial sense was that their owner might have passed for a lucky stockbroker—a gentleman driving eastward every morning from a sanitary suburb in a smart dogcart. That carried out the impression already derived from his wife. Paul's glance, after a moment, traveled back to this lady, and he saw how her own had followed her husband as he moved off with Miss Fancourt. Overt permitted himself to wonder a little if she were jealous when another woman took him away. Then he made out that Mrs. St. George wasn't glaring at the indifferent maiden. Her eyes rested but on her husband, and with unmistakable serenity. That was the way she wanted him to be—she liked his conventional uniform. Overt longed to hear more about the book she had induced him to destroy.

II

As they all came out from luncheon General Fancourt took hold of him with an "I say, I want you to know my girl!" as

if the idea had just occurred to him and he hadn't spoken of it before. With the other hand he possessed himself all paternally of the young lady. "You know all about him. I've seen you with his books. She reads everything — everything!" he went on to Paul. The girl smiled at him and then laughed at her father. The General turned away and his daughter spoke—"Isn't papa delightful?"

"He is indeed, Miss Fancourt."

"As if I read you because I read 'everything'!"

"Oh, I don't mean for saying that," said Paul Overt. "I liked him from the moment he began to be kind to me. Then he promised me this privilege."

"It isn't for you he means it—it's for me. If you flatter yourself that he thinks of anything in life but me you'll find you're mistaken. He introduces everyone. He thinks me insatiable."

"You speak just like him," laughed our youth.

"Ah, but sometimes I want to"—and the girl colored. "I don't read everything—I read very little. But I have read you."

"Suppose we go into the gallery," said Paul Overt. She pleased him greatly, not so much because of this last remark—though that of course was not too disconcerting—as because, seated opposite to him at luncheon, she had given him for half an hour the impression of her beautiful face. Something else had come with it—a sense of generosity, of an enthusiasm which, unlike many enthusiasms, was not all manner. That was not spoiled for him by his seeing that the repast had placed her again in familiar contact with Henry St. George. Sitting next her this celebrity was also opposite our young man, who had been able to note that he multiplied the attentions lately brought by his wife to the General's notice. Paul Overt had gathered as well that this lady was not in the least discomposed by these fond excesses and that she gave every sign of an unclouded spirit. She had Lord Masham on one side of her and on the other the accomplished Mr. Mulliner, editor of the new high-class lively evening paper which was expected to meet a want felt in circles increasingly conscious that Conservatism must be made amusing, and unconvinced when assured by those of another political color that it was already amusing enough. At the end of an hour spent in her company Paul Overt thought her still prettier than at the first radiation, and if her profane allusions to her husband's work had not still rung in his hears he should have liked her—so far as it could be a question of that in connection with a woman to whom he had not yet spoken and to whom probably he should never speak if it were left to her. Pretty women were a clear need to this genius, and for the hour it was Miss Fancourt who supplied the want. If Overt had promised himself a closer view the occasion was now of the best, and it brought consequences felt by the young man as important. He saw more in St. George's face, which he liked the better for its not having told its whole story in the first three minutes. That story came out as one read, in short installments—it was excusable that one's analogies should be somewhat professional—and the text was a style considerably involved, a language not easy to translate at sight. There were shades of meaning in it and a vague perspective of history which receded as you advanced. Two facts Paul had particularly heeded. The first of these was that he liked the measured mask much better at inscrutable rest than in social agitation; its almost convulsive smile above all displeased him (as much as any impression from that source could), whereas the quiet face had a charm that grew in proportion as stillness settled again. The change to the expression of gaiety excited, he made out, very much the private protest of a person sitting gratefully in the twilight when the lamp is brought in too soon. His second reflection was that, though generally averse to the flagrant use of ingratiating arts by a man of age "making up" to a pretty girl, he

was not in this case too painfully affected: which seemed to prove either that St. George had a light hand or the air of being younger than he was, or else that Miss Fancourt's own manner somehow made everything right.

Overt walked with her into the gallery, and they strolled to the end of it, looking at the pictures, the cabinets, the charming vista, which harmonized with the prospect of the summer afternoon, resembling it by a long brightness, with great divans and old chairs that figured hours of rest. Such a place as that had the added merit of giving those who came into it plenty to talk about. Miss Fancourt sat down with her new acquaintance on a flowered sofa, the cushions of which, very numerous, were tight ancient cubes of many sizes, and presently said: "I'm so glad to have a chance to thank you."

"To thank me——?" He had to wonder.

"I liked your book so much. I think it splendid."

She sat there smiling at him, and he never asked himself which book she meant; for after all he had written three or four. That seemed a vulgar detail, and he wasn't even gratified by the idea of the pleasure she told him—her handsome bright face told him—he had given her. The feeling she appealed to, or at any rate the feeling she excited, was something larger, something that had little to do with any quickened pulsation of his own vanity. It was responsive admiration of the life she embodied, the young purity and richness of which appeared to imply that real success was to resemble *that,* to live, to bloom, to present the perfection of a fine type, not to have hammered out headachy fancies with a bent back at an ink-stained table. While her gray eyes rested on him—there was a widish space between these, and the division of her rich-colored hair, so thick that it ventured to be smooth, made a free arch above them—he was almost ashamed of that exercise of the pen which it was her present inclination to commend. He was conscious he should have liked better to please her in some other way. The lines of her face were those of a woman grown, but the child lingered on in her complexion and in the sweetness of her mouth. Above all she was natural—that was indubitable now; more natural than he had supposed at first, perhaps on account of her aesthetic toggery, which was conventionally unconventional, suggesting what he might have called a tortuous spontaneity. He had feared that sort of thing in other cases, and his fears had been justified; for, though he was an artist to the essence, the modern reactionary nymph, with the brambles of the woodland caught in her folds and a look as if the satyrs had toyed with her hair, made him shrink, not as a man of starch and patent leather, but as a man potentially himself a poet or even a faun. The girl was really more candid than her costume, and the best proof of it was her supposing her liberal character suited by any uniform. This was a fallacy, since if she was draped as a pessimist he was sure she liked the taste of life. He thanked her for her appreciation—aware at the same time that he didn't appear to thank her enough and that she might think him ungracious. He was afraid she would ask him to explain something he had written, and he always winced at that—perhaps too timidly—for to his own ear the explanation of a work of art sounded fatuous. But he liked her so much as to feel a confidence that in the long run he should be able to show her he wasn't rudely evasive. Moreover, she surely wasn't quick to take offense, wasn't irritable; she could be trusted to wait. So when he said to her, "Ah, don't talk of anything I've done, don't talk of it *here;* there's another man in the house who's the actuality!"—when he uttered this short sincere protest it was with the sense that she would see in the words neither mock humility nor the impatience of a successful man bored with praise.

"You mean Mr. St. George—isn't he delightful?"

Paul Overt met her eyes, which had a cool morning light that would have half broken his heart if he hadn't been so young. "Alas, I don't know him. I only admire him at a distance."

"Oh, you *must* know him—he wants so to talk to you," returned Miss Fancourt, who evidently had the habit of saying the things that, by her quick calculation, would give people pleasure. Paul saw how she would always calculate on everything's being simple between others.

"I shouldn't have supposed he knew anything about me," he professed.

"He does then—everything. And if he didn't I should be able to tell him."

"To tell him everything?" our friend smiled.

"You talk just like the people in your book," she answered.

"Then they must all talk alike."

She thought a moment, not a bit disconcerted. "Well, it must be so difficult. Mr. St. George tells me it *is*—terribly. I've tried too—and I find it so. I've tried to write a novel."

"Mr. St. George oughtn't to discourage you," Paul went so far as to say.

"You do much more—when you wear that expression."

"Well, after all, why try to be an artist?" the young man pursued. "It's so poor—so poor!"

"I don't know what you mean," said Miss Fancourt, who looked grave.

"I mean as compared with being a person of action—as living your works."

"But what's art but an intense life—if it be real?" she asked. "I think it's the only one—everything else is so clumsy!" Her companion laughed, and she brought out with her charming serenity what next struck her. "It's so interesting to meet so many celebrated people."

"So I should think—but surely it isn't new to you."

"Why, I've never seen anyone—anyone: living always in Asia."

The way she talked of Asia somehow enchanted him. "But doesn't that continent swarm with great figures? Haven't you administered provinces in India and had

captive rajahs and tributary princes
chained to your car?"

It was as if she didn't care even *should*
he amuse himself at her cost. "I was with
my father, after I left school to go out
there. It was delightful being with him—
we're alone together in the world, he and
I—but there was none of the society I like
best. One never heard of a picture—never
of a book, except bad ones."

"Never of a picture? Why, wasn't all
life a picture?"

She looked over the delightful place
where they sat. "Nothing to compare to
this. I adore England!" she cried.

It fairly stirred in him the sacred chord.
"Ah, of course I don't deny that we must
do something with her, poor old dear, yet!"

"She hasn't been touched, really," said
the girl.

"Did Mr. St. George say that?"

There was a small and, as he felt, harmless spark of irony in his question; which,
however, she answered very simply, not
noticing the insinuation. "Yes, he says England hasn't been touched—not considering
all there is," she went on eagerly. "He's so
interesting about our country. To listen to
him makes one want to do something."

"It would make *me* want to," said Paul
Overt, feeling strongly, on the instant, the
suggestion of what she said and that of the
emotion with which she said it, and well
aware of what an incentive, on St. George's
lips, such a speech might be.

"Oh, you—as if you hadn't! I should
like so to hear you talk together," she added
ardently.

"That's very genial of you; but he'd
have it all his own way. I'm prostrate before him."

She had an air of earnestness. "Do you
think, then, he's so perfect?"

"Far from it. Some of his later books
seem to me of a queerness——!"

"Yes, yes—he knows that."

Paul Overt stared. "That they seem to
me of a queerness——?"

"Well, yes, or at any rate that they're
not what they should be. He told me he

didn't esteem them. He has told me such
wonderful things—he's so interesting."

There was a certain shock for Paul Overt
in the knowledge that the fine genius they
were talking of had been reduced to so
explicit a confession and had made it, in
his misery, to the first comer; for though
Miss Fancourt was charming what was she
after all but an immature girl encountered
at a country house? Yet precisely this was
part of the sentiment he himself had just
expressed: he would make way completely
for the poor peccable great man, not because he didn't read him clear, but altogether because he did. His consideration
was half composed of tenderness for superficialities which he was sure their perpe-
trator judged privately, judged more ferociously than anyone, and which represented
some tragic intellectual secret. He would
have his reasons for his psychology *à
fleur de peau*,[2] and these reasons could only
be cruel ones, such as would make him
dearer to those who already were fond of
him. "You excite my envy. I have my
reserves, I discriminate—but I love him,"
Paul said in a moment. "And seeing him
for the first time this way is a great event
for me."

"How momentous—how magnificent!"
cried the girl. "How delicious to bring you
together!"

"*Your* doing it—that makes it perfect,"
our friend returned.

"He's as eager as you," she went on.
"But it's so odd you shouldn't have met."

"It's not really so odd as it strikes you.
I've been out of England so much—made
repeated absences all these last years."

She took this in with interest. "And yet
you write of it as well as if you were always here."

"It's just the being away perhaps. At
any rate the best bits, I suspect, are those
that were done in dreary places abroad."

"And why were they dreary?"

"Because they were health resorts—where
my poor mother was dying."

---

[2] Ready to burst out.

"Your poor mother?"—she was all sweet wonder.

"We went from place to place to help her to get better. But she never did. To the deadly Riviera (I hate it!), to the high Alps, to Algiers, and far away—a hideous journey—to Colorado."

"And she isn't better?" Miss Fancourt went on.

"She died a year ago."

"Really?—like mine! Only that's years since. Some day you must tell me about your mother," she added.

He could at first, on this, only gaze at her. "What right things you say! If you say them to St. George I don't wonder he's in bondage."

It pulled her up for a moment. "I don't know what you mean. He doesn't make speeches and professions at all—he isn't ridiculous."

"I'm afraid you consider, then, that I am."

"No, I don't"—she spoke it rather shortly. And then she added: "He understands —understands everything."

The young man was on the point of saying jocosely: "And I don't—is that it?" But these words, in time, changed themselves to others slightly less trivial. "Do you suppose he understands his wife?"

Miss Fancourt made no direct answer, but after a moment's hesitation put it: "Isn't she charming?"

"Not in the least!"

"Here he comes. Now you must know him," she went on. A small group of visitors had gathered at the other end of the gallery and had been there overtaken by Henry St. George, who strolled in from a neighboring room. He stood near them a moment, not falling into the talk but taking up an old miniature from a table and vaguely regarding it. At the end of a minute he became aware of Miss Fancourt and her companion in the distance; whereupon, laying down his miniature, he approached them with the same procrastinating air, his hands in his pockets and his eyes turned, right and left, to the pictures.

The gallery was so long that this transit took some little time, especially as there was a moment when he stopped to admire the fine Gainsborough. "He says Mrs. St. George has been the making of him," the girl continued in a voice slightly lowered.

"Ah, he's often obscure!" Paul laughed.

"Obscure?" she repeated as if she heard it for the first time. Her eyes rested on her other friend, and it wasn't lost upon Paul that they appeared to send out great shafts of softness. "He's going to speak to us!" she fondly breathed. There was a sort of rapture in her voice, and our friend was startled. "Bless my soul, does she care for him like *that?*—is she in love with him?" he mentally inquired. "Didn't I tell you he was eager?" she had meanwhile asked of him.

"It's eagerness dissimulated," the young man returned as the subject of their observation lingered before his Gainsborough. "He edges toward us shyly. Does he mean that she saved him by burning that book?"

"That book? what book did she burn?" The girl quickly turned her face to him.

"Hasn't he told you, then?"

"Not a word."

"Then he doesn't tell you everything!" Paul had guessed that she pretty much supposed he did. The great man had now resumed his course and come nearer; in spite of which his more qualified admirer risked a profane observation. "St. George and the Dragon is what the anecdote suggests!"

His companion, however, didn't hear it; she smiled at the dragon's adversary. "He *is* eager—he is!" she insisted.

"Eager for you—yes."

But meanwhile she had called out: "I'm sure you want to know Mr. Overt. You'll be great friends, and it will always be delightful to me to remember I was here when you first met and that I had something to do with it."

There was a freshness of intention in the words that carried them off; nevertheless our young man was sorry for Henry St. George, as he was sorry at any time for any person publicly invited to be responsive and delightful. He would have been so touched to believe that a man he deeply admired should care a straw for him that he wouldn't play with such a presumption if it were possibly vain. In a single glance of the eye of the pardonable master he read—having the sort of divination that belonged to his talent—that this personage had ever a store of friendly patience, which was part of his rich outfit, but was versed in no printed page of a rising scribbler. There was even a relief, a simplification, in that: liking him so much already for what he had done, how could one have liked him any more for a perception which must at the best have been vague? Paul Overt got up, trying to show his compassion, but at the same instant he found himself encompassed by St. George's happy personal art—a manner of which it was the essence to conjure away false positions. It all took place in a moment. Paul was conscious that he knew him now, conscious of his handshake and of the very quality of his hand; of his face, seen nearer and consequently seen better, of a general fraternizing assurance, and in particular of the circumstance that St. George didn't dislike him (as yet at least) for being imposed by a charming but too gushing girl, attractive enough without such danglers. No irritation at any rate was reflected in the voice with which he questioned Miss Fancourt as to some project of a walk— a general walk of the company round the park. He had soon said something to Paul about a talk—"We must have a tremendous lot of talk; there are so many things, aren't there?"—but our friend could see this idea wouldn't in the present case take very immediate effect. All the same he was extremely happy, even after the matter of the walk had been settled—the three presently passed back to the other part of the gallery, where it was discussed with several members of the party; even when, after they had all gone out together, he found himself for half an hour conjoined with Mrs. St. George. Her husband had

taken the advance with Miss Fancourt, and this pair were quite out of sight. It was the prettiest of rambles for a summer afternoon—a grassy circuit, of immense extent, skirting the limit of the park within. The park was completely surrounded by its old mottled but perfect red wall, which, all the way on their left, constituted in itself an object of interest. Mrs. St. George mentioned to him the surprising number of acres thus enclosed, together with numerous other facts relating to the property and the family, and the family's other properties: she couldn't too strongly urge on him the importance of seeing their other houses. She ran over the names of these and rang the changes on them with the facility of practice, making them appear an almost endless list. She had received Paul Overt very amiably on his breaking ground with her by the mention of his joy in having just made her husband's acquaintance, and struck him as so alert and so accommodating a little woman that he was rather ashamed of his *mot* about her to Miss Fancourt; though he reflected that a hundred other people, on a hundred occasions, would have been sure to make it. He got on with Mrs. St. George, in short, better than he expected; but this didn't prevent her suddenly becoming aware that she was faint with fatigue and must take her way back to the house by the shortest cut. She professed that she hadn't the strength of a kitten and was a miserable wreck; a character he had been too preoccupied to discern in her while he wondered in what sense she could be held to have been the making of her husband. He had arrived at a glimmering of the answer when she announced that she must leave him, though this perception was of course provisional. While he was in the very act of placing himself at her disposal for the return, the situation underwent a change; Lord Masham had suddenly turned up, coming back to them, overtaking them, emerging from the shrubbery—Overt could scarcely have said how he appeared—and

Mrs. St. George had protested that she wanted to be left alone and not to break up the party. A moment later she was walking off with Lord Masham. Our friend fell back and joined Lady Watermouth, to whom he presently mentioned that Mrs. St. George had been obliged to renounce the attempt to go further.

"She oughtn't to have come out at all," her ladyship rather grumpily remarked.

"Is she so very much of an invalid?"

"Very bad indeed." And his hostess added with still greater austerity: "She oughtn't really to come to one!" He wondered what was implied by this, and presently gathered that it was not a reflection on the lady's conduct or her moral nature: it only represented that her strength was not equal to her aspirations.

III

The smoking room at Summersoft was on the scale of the rest of the place—high, light, commodious, and decorated with such refined old carvings and moldings that it seemed rather a bower for ladies who should sit at work at fading crewels than a parliament of gentlemen smoking strong cigars. The gentlemen mustered there in considerable force on the Sunday evening, collecting mainly at one end, in front of one of the cool, fair fireplaces of white marble, the entablature of which was adorned with a delicate little Italian "subject." There was another in the wall that faced it, and, thanks to the mild summer night, a fire in neither; but a nucleus for aggregation was furnished on one side by a table in the chimney corner laden with bottles, decanters, and tall tumblers. Paul Overt was a faithless smoker; he would puff a cigarette for reasons with which tobacco had nothing to do. This was particularly the case on the occasion of which I speak; his motive was the vision of a little direct talk with Henry St. George. The "tremendous" communion of which the great man had held out hopes to him earlier

in the day had not yet come off, and this saddened him considerably, for the party was to go its several ways immediately after breakfast on the morrow. He had, however, the disappointment of finding that apparently the author of *Shadowmere* was not disposed to prolong his vigil. He wasn't among the gentlemen assembled when Paul entered, nor was he one of those who turned up, in bright habiliments, during the next ten minutes. The young man waited a little, wondering if he had only gone to put on something extraordinary; this would account for his delay as well as contribute further to Overt's impression of his tendency to do the approved superficial thing. But he didn't arrive—he must have been putting on something more extraordinary than was probable. Our hero gave him up, feeling a little injured, a little wounded, at this loss of twenty coveted words. He wasn't angry, but he puffed his cigarette sighingly, with the sense of something rare possibly missed. He wandered away with his regret and moved slowly round the room, looking at the old prints on the walls. In this attitude he presently felt a hand on his shoulder and a friendly voice in his ear: "This is good. I hoped I should find you. I came down on purpose." St. George was there without a change of dress and with a fine face—his graver one —to which our young man all in a flutter responded. He explained that it was only for the Master—the idea of a little talk— that he had sat up, and that, not finding him, he had been on the point of going to bed.

"Well, you know, I don't smoke—my wife doesn't let me," said St. George, looking for a place to sit down. "It's very good for me—very good for me. Let us take that sofa."

"Do you mean smoking's good for you?"

"No, no—her not letting me. It's a great thing to have a wife who's so sure of all the things one can do without. One might never find them out oneself. She doesn't allow me to touch a cigarette." They took possession of a sofa at a distance from the group of smokers, and St. George went on: "Have you got one yourself?"

"Do you mean a cigarette?"

"Dear no—a wife!"

"No; and yet I'd give up my cigarette for one."

"You'd give up a good deal more than that," St. George returned. "However, you'd get a great deal in return. There's a something to be said for wives," he added, folding his arms and crossing his outstretched legs. He declined tobacco altogether and sat there without returning fire. His companion stopped smoking, touched by his courtesy; and after all they were out of the fumes, their sofa was in a faraway corner. It would have been a mistake, St. George went on, a great mistake for them to have separated without a little chat; "for I know all about you," he said, "I know you're very remarkable. You've written a very distinguished book."

"And how do you know it?" Paul asked.

"Why, my dear fellow, it's in the air, it's in the papers, it's everywhere." St. George spoke with the immediate familiarity of a confrere—a tone that seemed to his neighbor the very rustle of the laurel. "You're on all men's lips and, what's better, on all women's. And I've just been reading your book."

"Just? You hadn't read it this afternoon," said Overt.

"How do you know that?"

"I think you should know how I know it," the young man laughed.

"I suppose Miss Fancourt told you."

"No indeed—she led me rather to suppose you had."

"Yes—that's much more what she'd do. Doesn't she shed a rosy glow over life? But you didn't believe her?" asked St. George.

"No, not when you came to us there."

"Did I pretend? did I pretend badly?" But without waiting for an answer to this St. George went on: "You ought always to believe such a girl as that—always, always. Some women are meant to be taken with

allowances and reserves; but you must take *her* just as she is."

"I like her very much," said Paul Overt.

Something in his tone appeared to excite on his companion's part a momentary sense of the absurd; perhaps it was the air of deliberation attending this judgment. St. George broke into a laugh to reply. "It's the best thing you can do with her. She's a rare young lady! In point of fact, however, I confess I hadn't read you this afternoon."

"Then you see how right I was in this particular case not to believe Miss Fancourt."

"How right? how can I agree to that when I lost credit by it?"

"Do you wish to pass exactly for what she represents you? Certainly you needn't be afraid," Paul said.

"Ah, my dear young man, don't talk about passing—for the likes of me! I'm passing away—nothing else than that. She has a better use for her young imagination (isn't it fine?) than in 'representing' in any way such a weary wasted used-up animal!" The Master spoke with a sudden sadness that produced a protest on Paul's part; but before the protest could be uttered he went on, reverting to the latter's striking novel: "I had no idea you were so good—one hears of so many things. But you're surprisingly good."

"I'm going to be surprisingly better," Overt made bold to reply.

"I see that, and it's what fetches me. I don't see so much else—as one looks about —that's going to be surprisingly better. They're going to be consistently worse— most of the things. It's so much easier to be worse—heaven knows I've found it so. I'm not in a great glow, you know, about what's breaking out all over the place. But you *must* be better, you really must keep it up. I haven't, of course. It's very difficult—that's the devil of the whole thing, keeping it up. But I see you'll be able to. It will be a great disgrace if you don't."

"It's very interesting to hear you speak

of yourself; but I don't know what you mean by your allusions to your having fallen off," Paul Overt observed with pardonable hypocrisy. He liked his companion so much now that the fact of any decline of talent or of care had ceased for the moment to be vivid to him.

"Don't say that—don't say that," St. George returned gravely, his head resting on the top of the sofa back and his eyes on the ceiling. "You know perfectly what I mean. I haven't read twenty pages of your book without seeing that you can't help it."

"You make me very miserable," Paul ecstatically breathed.

"I'm glad of that, for it may serve as a kind of warning. Shocking enough it must be, especially to a young fresh mind, full of faith—the spectacle of a man meant for better things sunk at my age in such dishonor." St. George, in the same contemplative attitude, spoke softly but deliberately, and without perceptible emotion. His tone indeed suggested an impersonal lucidity that was practically cruel—cruel to himself—and made his young friend lay an argumentative hand on his arm. But he went on while his eyes seemed to follow the graces of the eighteenth-century ceiling: "Look at me well, take my lesson to heart—for it *is* a lesson. Let that good come of it at least that you shudder with your pitiful impression, and that this may help to keep you straight in the future. Don't become in your old age what I have in mine—the depressing, the deplorable illustration of the worship of false gods!"

"What do you mean by your old age?" the young man asked.

"It has made me old. But I like your youth."

Paul answered nothing—they sat for a minute in silence. They heard the others going on about the governmental majority. Then "What do you mean by false gods?" he inquired.

His companion had no difficulty whatever in saying, "The idols of the market; money and luxury and 'the world'; placing one's children and dressing one's wife; everything that drives one to the short and easy way. Ah, the vile things they make one do!"

"But surely one's right to want to place one's children."

"One has no business to have any children," St. George placidly declared. "I mean, of course, if one wants to do anything good."

"But aren't they an inspiration—an incentive?"

"An incentive to damnation, artistically speaking."

"You touch on very deep things—things I should like to discuss with you," Paul said. "I should like you to tell me volumes about yourself. This is a great feast for *me!*"

"Of course it is, cruel youth. But to show you I'm still not incapable, degraded as I am, of an act of faith, I'll tie my vanity to the stake for you and burn it to ashes. You must come and see me—you must come and see us," the Master quickly substituted. "Mrs. St. George is charming; I don't know whether you've had any opportunity to talk with her. She'll be delighted to see you; she likes great celebrities, whether incipient or predominant. You must come and dine—my wife will write you. Where are you to be found?"

"This is my little address"—and Overt drew out his pocketbook and extracted a visiting card. On second thoughts, however, he kept it back, remarking that he wouldn't trouble his friend to take charge of it but would come and see him straightway in London and leave it at his door if he should fail to obtain entrance.

"Ah, you'll probably fail; my wife's always out—or when she isn't out is knocked up from having *been* out. You must come and dine—though that won't do much good either, for my wife insists on big dinners." St. George turned it over further, but then went on: "You must come down and see us in the country, that's the best way; we've plenty of room and it isn't bad."

"You've a house in the country?" Paul asked enviously.

"Ah, not like this! But we have a sort of place we go to—an hour from Euston. That's one of the reasons."

"One of the reasons?"

"Why my books are so bad."

"You must tell me all the others!" Paul longingly laughed.

His friend made no direct rejoinder to this, but spoke again abruptly. "Why have I never seen you before?"

The tone of the question was singularly flattering to our hero, who felt it to imply the great man's now perceiving he had for years missed something. "Partly, I suppose, because there has been no particular reason why you should see me. I haven't lived in the world—in your world. I've spent many years out of England, in different places abroad."

"Well, please don't do it any more. You must do England—there's such a lot of it."

"Do you mean I must write about it?" —and Paul struck the note of the listening candor of a child.

"Of course you must. And tremendously well, do you mind? That takes off a little of my esteem for this thing of yours—that it goes on abroad. Hang 'abroad'! Stay at home and do things here—do subjects we can measure."

"I'll do whatever you tell me," Overt said, deeply attentive. "But pardon me if I say I don't understand how you've been reading my book," he added. "I've had you before me all the afternoon, first in that long walk, then at tea on the lawn, till we went to dress for dinner, and all the evening at dinner and in this place."

St. George turned his face about with a smile. "I gave it but a quarter of an hour."

"A quarter of an hour's immense, but I don't understand where you put it in. In the drawing room after dinner you weren't reading—you were talking to Miss Fancourt."

"It comes to the same thing, because we talked about *Ginistrella*. She described it to me—she lent me her copy."

"Lent it to you?"

"She travels with it."

"It's incredible," Paul blushed.

"It's glorious for you, but it also turned out very well for me. When the ladies went off to bed she kindly offered to send the book down to me. Her maid brought it to me in the hall, and I went to my room with it. I hadn't thought of coming here, I do that so little. But I don't sleep early, I always have to read an hour or two. I sat down to your novel on the spot, without undressing, without taking off anything but my coat. I think that's a sign my curiosity had been strongly aroused about it. I read a quarter of an hour, as I tell you, and even in a quarter of an hour I was greatly struck."

"Ah, the beginning isn't very good—it's the whole thing!" said Overt, who had listened to this recital with extreme interest. "And you laid down the book and came after me?" he asked.

"That's the way it moved me. I said to myself, 'I see it's off his own bat, and he's there, by the way, and the day's over, and I haven't said twenty words to him.' It occurred to me that you'd probably be in the smoking room and that it wouldn't be too late to repair my omission. I wanted to do something civil to you, so I put on my coat and came down. I shall read your book again when I go up."

Our friend faced round in his place— he was touched as he had scarce ever been by the picture of such a demonstration in his favor. "You're really the kindest of men. *Cela s'est passé comme ça?* [3]—and I've been sitting here with you all this time and never apprehended it and never thanked you!"

"Thank Miss Fancourt—it was she who wound me up. She has made me feel as if I had read your novel."

"She's an angel from heaven!" Paul declared.

---

[3] Hasn't it been so?

"She is indeed. I've never seen anyone like her. Her interest in literature's touching—something quite peculiar to herself; she takes it all so seriously. She feels the arts and she wants to feel them more. To those who practice them it's almost humiliating—her curiosity, her sympathy, her good faith. How can anything be as fine as she supposes it?"

"She's a rare organization," the younger man sighed.

"The richest I've ever seen—an artistic intelligence really of the first order. And lodged in such a form!" St. George exclaimed.

"One would like to represent such a girl as that," Paul continued.

"Ah, there it is—there's nothing like life!" said his companion. "When you're finished, squeezed dry and used up and you think the sack's empty, you're still appealed to, you still get touches and thrills, the idea springs up—out of the lap of the actual—and shows you there's always something to be done. But I shan't do it—she's not for me!"

"How do you mean, not for you?"

"Oh, it's all over—she's for you, if you like."

"Ah, much less!" said Paul. "She's not for a dingy little man of letters; she's for the world, the bright, rich world of bribes and rewards. And the world will take hold of her—it will carry her away."

"It will try—but it's just a case in which there may be a fight. It would be worth fighting, for a man who had it in him, with youth and talent on his side."

These words rang not a little in Paul Overt's consciousness—they held him briefly silent. "It's a wonder she has remained as she is; giving herself away so—with so much to give away."

"Remaining, you mean, so ingenuous—so natural? Oh, she doesn't care a straw—she gives away because she overflows. She has her own feelings, her own standards; she doesn't keep remembering that she must be proud. And then she hasn't been here long enough to be spoiled; she has picked up a fashion or two, but only the amusing ones. She's a provincial—a provincial of genius," St. George went on; "her very blunders are charming, her mistakes are interesting. She has come back from Asia with all sorts of excited curiosities and unappeased appetites. She's first rate herself and she expends herself on the second rate. She's life herself and she takes a rare interest in imitations. She mixes all things up, but there are none in regard to which she hasn't perceptions. She sees things in a perspective—as if from the top of the Himalayas—and she enlarges everything she touches. Above all she exaggerates—to herself, I mean. She exaggerates you and me!"

There was nothing in that description to allay the agitation caused in our younger friend by such a sketch of a fine subject. It seemed to him to show the art of St. George's admired hand, and he lost himself in gazing at the vision—this hovered there before him—of a woman's figure which should be part of the glory of a novel. But at the end of a moment the thing had turned into smoke, and out of the smoke—the last puff of a big cigar—proceeded the voice of General Fancourt, who had left the others and come and planted himself before the gentlemen on the sofa. "I suppose that when you fellows get talking you sit up half the night."

"Half the night?—*jamais de la vie!*[4] I follow a hygiene"—and St. George rose to his feet.

"I see—you're hothouse plants," laughed the General. "That's the way you produce your flowers."

"I produce mine between ten and one every morning—I bloom with a regularity!" St. George went on.

"And with a splendor!" added the polite General, while Paul noted how little the author of *Shadowmere* minded, as he phrased it to himself, when addressed as a celebrated storyteller. The young man had an idea *he* should never get used to

---

4 Never in my life!

that; it would always make him uncomfortable—from the suspicion that people would think they had to—and he would want to prevent it. Evidently his great colleague had toughened and hardened—had made himself a surface. The group of men had finished their cigars and taken up their bedroom candlesticks; but before they all passed out Lord Watermouth invited the pair of guests who had been so absorbed together to "have" something. It happened that they both declined; upon which General Fancourt said: "Is that the hygiene? You don't water the flowers?"

"Oh, I should drown them!" St. George replied; but, leaving the room still at his young friend's side, he added whimsically, for the latter's benefit, in a lower tone: "My wife doesn't let me."

"Well, I'm glad I'm not one of you fellows!" the General richly concluded.

The nearness of Summersoft to London had this consequence, chilling to a person who had had a vision of sociability in a railway carriage, that most of the company, after breakfast, drove back to town, entering their own vehicles, which had come out to fetch them, while their servants returned by train with their luggage. Three or four young men, among whom was Paul Overt, also availed themselves of the common convenience; but they stood in the portico of the house and saw the others roll away. Miss Fancourt got into a victoria with her father after she had shaken hands with our hero and said, smiling in the frankest way in the world, "I *must* see you more. Mrs. St. George is so nice; she has promised to ask us both to dinner together." This lady and her husband took their places in a perfectly appointed brougham—she required a closed carriage—and as our young man waved his hat to them in response to their nods and flourishes he reflected that, taken together, they were an honorable image of success, of the material rewards and the social credit of literature. Such things were not the full measure, but he nevertheless felt a little proud for literature.

IV

Before a week had elapsed he met Miss Fancourt in Bond Street, at a private view of the works of a young artist in "black-and-white" who had been so good as to invite him to the stuffy scene. The drawings were admirable, but the crowd in the one little room was so dense that he felt himself up to his neck in a sack of wool. A fringe of people at the outer edge endeavored by curving forward their backs and presenting, below them, a still more convex surface of resistance to the pressure of the mass, to preserve an interval between their noses and the glazed mounts of the pictures; while the central body, in the comparative gloom projected by a wide horizontal screen hung under the skylight and allowing only a margin for the day, remained upright, dense, and vague, lost in the contemplation of its own ingredients. This contemplation sat especially in the sad eyes of certain female heads, surmounted with hats of strange convolution and plumage, which rose on long necks above the others. One of the heads, Paul perceived, was much the most beautiful of the collection, and his next discovery was that it belonged to Miss Fancourt. Its beauty was enhanced by the glad smile she sent him across surrounding obstructions, a smile that drew him to her as fast as he could make his way. He had seen for himself at Summersoft that the last thing her nature contained was an affectation of indifference; yet even with this circumspection he took a fresh satisfaction in her not having pretended to await his arrival with composure. She smiled as radiantly as if she wished to make him hurry, and as soon as he came within earshot she broke out in her voice of joy: "He's here—he's here; he's coming back in a moment!"

"Ah, your father?" Paul returned as she offered him her hand.

"Oh, dear no, this isn't in my poor father's line. I mean Mr. St. George. He has just left me to speak to someone—he's coming back. It's he who brought me—wasn't it charming?"

"Ah that gives him a pull over me—I couldn't have 'brought' you, could I?"

"If you had been so kind as to propose it—why not you as well as he?" the girl returned with a face that, expressing no cheap coquetry, simply affirmed a happy fact.

"Why he's a *père de famille*.[5] They've privileges," Paul explained. And then quickly: "Will you go to see places with *me?*" he asked.

"Anything you like," she smiled. "I know what you mean, that girls have to have a lot of people——!" Then she broke off: "I don't know; I'm free. I've always been like that—I can go about with any-one. I'm so glad to meet you," she added with a sweet distinctness that made those near her turn round.

"Let me at least repay that speech by taking you out of this squash," her friend said. "Surely people aren't happy here!"

"No, they're awfully *mornes*,[6] aren't they? But I'm very happy indeed and I promised Mr. St. George to remain on this spot till he comes back. He's going to take me away. They send him invitations for things of this sort—more than he wants. It was so kind of him to think of me."

"They also send me invitations of this kind—more than *I* want. And if thinking of *you* will do it——!" Paul went on.

"Oh, I delight in them—everything that's life, everything that's London!"

"They don't have private views in Asia, I suppose," he laughed. "But what a pity that for this year, even in this gorged city, they're pretty well over."

"Well, next year will do, for I hope you believe we're going to be friends always. Here he comes!" Miss Fancourt continued before Paul had time to respond.

He made out St. George in the gaps of the crowd, and this perhaps led to his hurrying a little to say: "I hope that doesn't mean I'm to wait till next year to see you."

"No, no—aren't we to meet at dinner on the twenty-fifth?" she panted with an eagerness as happy as his own.

"That's almost next year. Is there no means of seeing you before?"

She stared with all her brightness. "Do you mean you'd *come?*"

"Like a shot, if you'll be so good as to ask me!"

"On Sunday then—this next Sunday?"

"What have I done that you should doubt it?" the young man asked with delight.

Miss Fancourt turned instantly to St. George, who had now joined them, and announced triumphantly: "He's coming on Sunday—this next Sunday!"

"Ah, my day—my day too!" said the famous novelist, laughing, to their companion.

"Yes, but not yours only. You shall meet in Manchester Square; you shall talk—you shall be wonderful!"

"We don't meet often enough," St. George allowed, shaking hands with his disciple. "Too many things—ah, too many things! But we must make it up in the country in September. You won't forget you've promised me that?"

"Why, he's coming on the twenty-fifth—you'll see him then," said the girl.

"On the twenty-fifth?" St. George asked vaguely.

"We dine with you; I hope you haven't forgotten. He's dining out that day," she added gaily to Paul.

"Oh, bless me, yes—that's charming! And you're coming? My wife didn't tell me," St. George said to him. "Too many things—too many things!" he repeated.

"Too many people—too many people!" Paul exclaimed, giving ground before the penetration of an elbow.

"You oughtn't to say that. They all read you."

"Me? I should like to see them! Only two or three at most," the young man returned.

"Did you ever hear anything like that? He knows, haughtily, how good he is!" St.

---

[5] A family man or father of a family.
[6] Gloomy or dull.

George declared, laughing, to Miss Fancourt. "They read *me*, but that doesn't make me like them any better. Come away from them, come away!" And he led the way out of the exhibition.

"He's going to take me to the Park," Miss Fancourt observed to Overt with elation as they passed along the corridor that led to the street.

"Ah, does he go there?" Paul asked, taking the fact for a somewhat unexpected illustration of St. George's *mœurs*.[7]

"It's a beautiful day—there'll be a great crowd. We're going to look at the people, to look at types," the girl went on. "We shall sit under the trees; we shall walk by the Row."

"I go once a year—on business," said St. George, who had overheard Paul's question.

"Or with a country cousin, didn't you tell me? I'm the country cousin!" she continued over her shoulder to Paul as their friend drew her toward a hansom to which he had signaled. The young man watched them get in; he returned, as he stood there, the friendly wave of the hand with which, ensconced in the vehicle beside her, St. George took leave of him. He even lingered to see the vehicle start away and lose itself in the confusion of Bond Street. He followed it with his eyes; it put to him embarrassing things. "She's not for *me*!" the great novelist had said emphatically at Summersoft; but his manner of conducting himself toward her appeared not quite in harmony with such a conviction. How could he have behaved differently if she *had* been for him? An indefinite envy rose in Paul Overt's heart as he took his way on foot alone; a feeling addressed alike, strangely enough, to each of the occupants of the hansom. How much he should like to rattle about London with such a girl! How much he should like to go and look at "types" with St. George! The next Sunday at four o'clock he called in Manchester Square, where his secret wish was gratified by his finding Miss Fancourt alone. She was in a large, bright, friendly, occupied room, which was painted red all over, draped with the quaint, cheap, florid stuffs that are represented as coming from southern and eastern countries, where they are fabled to serve as the counterpanes of the peasantry, and bedecked with pottery of vivid hues, ranged on casual shelves, and with many watercolor drawings from the hand (as the visitor learned) of the young lady herself, commemorating with a brave breadth the sunsets, the mountains, the temples, and palaces of India. He sat an hour—more than an hour, two hours—and all the while no one came in. His hostess was so good as to remark, with her liberal humanity, that it was delightful they weren't interrupted: it was so rare in London, especially at that season, that people got a good talk. But luckily now, of a fine Sunday, half the world went out of town, and that made it better for those who didn't go, when these others were in sympathy. It was the defect of London—one of two or three, the very short list of those she recognized in the teeming world city she adored—that there were too few good chances for talk: you never had time to carry anything far.

"Too many things, too many things!" Paul said, quoting St. George's exclamation of a few days before.

"Ah, yes, for him there are too many—his life's too complicated."

"Have you seen it *near*? That's what I should like to do; it might explain some mysteries," her visitor went on. She asked him what mysteries he meant, and he said · "Oh, peculiarities of his work, inequalities, superficialities. For one who looks at it from the artistic point of view it contains a bottomless ambiguity."

She became at this, on the spot, all intensity. "Ah, do describe that more—it's so interesting. There are no such suggestive questions. I'm so fond of them. He thinks he's a failure—fancy!" she beautifully wailed.

"That depends on what his ideal may have been. With his gifts it ought to have

---

[7] Habits.

been high. But till one knows what he really proposed to himself——! Do *you* know by chance?" the young man broke off.

"Oh, he doesn't talk to me about himself. I can't make him. It's too provoking."

Paul was on the point of asking what, then, he did talk about, but discretion checked it and he said instead: "Do you think he's unhappy at home?"

She seemed to wonder. "At home?"

"I mean in his relations with his wife. He has a mystifying little way of alluding to her."

"Not to me," said Marian Fancourt with her clear eyes. "That wouldn't be right, would it?" she asked gravely.

"Not particularly; so I'm glad he doesn't mention her to you. To praise her might bore you, and he has no business to do anything else. Yet he knows you better than me."

"Ah, but he respects *you!*" the girl cried as with envy.

Her visitor stared a moment, then broke into a laugh. "Doesn't he respect you?"

"Of course, but not in the same way. He respects what you've done—he told me so the other day."

Paul drank it in, but retained his faculties. "When you went to look at types?"

"Yes—we found so many: he has such an observation of them! He talked a great deal about your book. He says it's really important."

"Important! Ah the grand creature!"— and the author of the work in question groaned for joy.

"He was wonderfully amusing, he was inexpressibly droll, while we walked about. He sees everything; he has so many comparisons and images, and they're always exactly right. *C'est d'un trouvé,*[s] as they say!"

"Yes, with his gifts, such things as he ought to have done!" Paul sighed.

"And don't you think he *has* done them?"

Ah, it was just the point. "A part of them, and of course even that part's immense. But he might have been one of the greatest. However, let us not make this an

hour of qualifications. Even as they stand," our friend earnestly concluded, "his writings are a mine of gold."

To this proposition she ardently responded, and for half an hour the pair talked over the Master's principal productions. She knew them well—she knew them even better than her visitor, who was struck with her critical intelligence and with something large and bold in the movement in her mind. She said things that startled him and that evidently had come to her directly; they weren't picked-up phrases—she placed them too well. St. George had been right about her being first rate, about her not being afraid to gush, not remembering that she must be proud. Suddenly something came back to her, and she said: "I recollect that he did speak of Mrs. St. George to me once. He said, apropos of something or other, that she didn't care for perfection."

"That's a great crime in an artist's wife," Paul returned.

"Yes, poor thing!" and the girl sighed with a suggestion of many reflections, some of them mitigating. But she presently added: "Ah perfection, perfection—how one ought to go in for it! I wish *I* could."

"Everyone can in his way," her companion opined.

"In *his* way, yes—but not in hers. Women are so hampered—so condemned! Yet it's a kind of dishonor if you don't, when you want to *do* something, isn't it?" Miss Fancourt pursued, dropping one train in her quickness to take up another, an accident that was common with her. So these two young persons sat discussing high themes in their eclectic drawing room, in their London "season"—discussing, with extreme seriousness, the high theme of perfection. It must be said in extenuation of this eccentricity that they were interested in the business. Their tone had truth and their emotion beauty; they weren't posturing for each other or for someone else.

---

[s] It is felicitous.

The subject was so wide that they found themselves reducing it; the perfection to which for the moment they agreed to confine their speculations was that of the valid, the exemplary work of art. Our young woman's imagination, it appeared, had wandered far in that direction, and her guest had the rare delight of feeling in their conversation a full interchange. This episode will have lived for years in his memory and even in his wonder; it had the quality that fortune distills in a single drop at a time—the quality that lubricates many ensuing frictions. He still, whenever he likes, has a vision of the room, the bright, red, sociable, talkative room with the curtains that, by a stroke of successful audacity, had the note of vivid blue. He remembers where certain things stood, the particular book open on the table and the almost intense odor of the flowers placed, at the left, somewhere behind him. These facts were the fringe, as it were, of a fine special agitation which had its birth in those two hours and of which perhaps the main sign was in its leading him inwardly and repeatedly to breathe, "I had no idea there was anyone like this—I had no idea there was anyone like this!" Her freedom amazed him and charmed him—it seemed so to simplify the practical question. She was on the footing of an independent personage—a motherless girl who had passed out of her teens and had a position and responsibilities, who wasn't held down to the limitations of a little miss. She came and went with no dragged duenna, she received people alone, and, though she was totally without hardness, the question of protection or patronage had no relevancy in regard to her. She gave such an impression of the clear and the noble combined with the easy and the natural that in spite of her eminent modern situation she suggested no sort of sisterhood with the "fast" girl. Modern she was indeed, and made Paul Overt, who loved old color, the golden glaze of time, think with some alarm of the muddled palette of the future. He couldn't get used to her interest in the

arts he cared for; it seemed too good to be real—it was so unlikely an adventure to tumble into such a well of sympathy. One might stray into the desert easily—that was on the cards and that was the law of life; but it was too rare an accident to stumble on a crystal well. Yet if her aspirations seemed at one moment too extravagant to be real they struck him at the next as too intelligent to be false. They were both high and lame, and, whims for whims, he preferred them to any he had met in a like relation. It was probable enough she would leave them behind—exchange them for politics or "smartness" or mere prolific maternity, as was the custom of scribbling, daubing, educated, flattered girls in an age of luxury and a society of leisure. He noted that the water colors on the walls of the room she sat in had mainly the quality of being naïves, and reflected that naïveté in art is like a zero in a number: its importance depends on the figure it is united with. Meanwhile, however, he had fallen in love with her. Before he went away, at any rate, he said to her: "I thought St. George was coming to see you today, but he doesn't turn up."

For a moment he supposed she was going to cry "Comment donc? [9] Did you come here only to meet him?" But the next he became aware of how little such a speech would have fallen in with any note of flirtation he had as yet perceived in her. She only replied: "Ah, yes, but I don't think he'll come. He recommended me not to expect him." Then she gaily but all gently added: "He said it wasn't fair to you. But I think I could manage two."

"So could I," Paul Overt returned, stretching the point a little to meet her. In reality his appreciation of the occasion was so completely an appreciation of the woman before him that another figure in the scene, even so esteemed a one as St. George, might for the hour have appealed to him vainly. He left the house wondering what the great man had meant

---

[9] How's that? What, then?

by its not being fair to him; and, still more than that, whether he had actually stayed away from the force of that idea. As he took his course through the Sunday solitude of Manchester Square, swinging his stick and with a good deal of emotion fermenting in his soul, it appeared to him he was living in a world strangely magnanimous. Miss Fancourt had told him it was possible she should be away, and that her father should be, on the following Sunday, but that she had the hope of a visit from him in the other event. She promised to let him know should their absence fail, and then he might act accordingly. After he had passed into one of the streets that open from the Square he stopped, without definite intentions, looking skeptically for a cab. In a moment he saw a hansom roll through the place from the other side and come a part of the way toward him. He was on the point of hailing the driver when he noticed a "fare" within; then he waited, seeing the man prepare to deposit his passenger by pulling up at one of the houses. The house was apparently the one he himself had just quitted; at least he drew that inference as he recognized Henry St. George in the person who stepped out of the hansom. Paul turned off as quickly as if he had been caught in the act of spying. He gave up his cab—he preferred to walk; he would go nowhere else. He was glad St. George hadn't renounced his visit altogether—that would have been too absurd. Yes, the world was magnanimous, and even he himself felt so as, on looking at his watch, he noted but six o'clock, so that he could mentally congratulate his successor on having an hour still to sit in Miss Fancourt's drawing room. He himself might use that hour for another visit, but by the time he reached the Marble Arch the idea of such a course had become incongruous to him. He passed beneath that architectural effort and walked into the Park till he had got upon the spreading grass. Here he continued to walk; he took his way across the elastic turf and came out by the

Serpentine. He watched with a friendly eye the diversions of the London people, he bent a glance almost encouraging on the young ladies paddling their sweethearts about the lake and the guardsmen tickling tenderly with their bearskins the artificial flowers in the Sunday hats of their partners. He prolonged his meditative walk; he went into Kensington Gardens, he sat upon the penny chairs, he looked at the little sailboats launched upon the round pond and was glad he had no engagement to dine. He repaired for this purpose, very late, to his club, where he found himself unable to order a repast and told the waiter to bring whatever there was. He didn't even observe what he was served with, and he spent the evening in the library of the establishment, pretending to read an article in an American magazine. He failed to discover what it was about; it appeared in a dim way to be about Marian Fancourt.

Quite late in the week she wrote to him that she was not to go into the country—it had only just been settled. Her father, she added, would never settle anything, but put it all on her. She felt her responsibility—she had to—and since she was forced this was the way she had decided. She mentioned no reasons, which gave our friend all the clearer field for bold conjecture about them. In Manchester Square on this second Sunday he esteemed his fortune less good, for she had three or four other visitors. But there were three or four compensations; perhaps the greatest of which was that, learning how her father had after all, at the last hour, gone out of town alone, the bold conjecture I just now spoke of found itself becoming a shade more bold. And then her presence was her presence, and the personal red room was there and was full of it, whatever phantoms passed and vanished, emitting incomprehensible sounds. Lastly, he had the resource of staying till everyone had come and gone and of believing this grateful to her, though she gave no particular sign. When they were alone together he came to his point. "But St. George did come—last Sunday. I saw him as I looked back."

"Yes, but it was the last time."

"The last time?"

"He said he would never come again."

Paul Overt stared. "Does he mean he wishes to cease to see you?"

"I don't know what he means," the girl bravely smiled. "He won't at any rate see me here."

"And pray why not?"

"I haven't the least idea," said Marian Fancourt, whose visitor found her more perversely sublime than ever yet as she professed this clear helplessness.

V

"Oh, I say, I want you to stop a little," Henry St. George said to him at eleven o'clock the night he dined with the head of the profession. The company—none of it indeed *of* the profession—had been numerous and was taking its leave; our young man, after bidding good night to his hostess, had put out his hand in farewell to the master of the house. Besides drawing from the latter the protest I have cited, this movement provoked a further priceless word about their chance now to have a talk, their going into his room, his having still everything to say. Paul Overt was all delight at this kindness; nevertheless he mentioned in weak, jocose qualification the bare fact that he had promised to go to another place which was at a considerable distance.

"Well, then, you'll break your promise, that's all. You quite awful humbug!" St. George added in a tone that confirmed our young man's ease.

"Certainly I'll break it—but it was a real promise."

"Do you mean to Miss Fancourt? You're following her?" his friend asked.

He answered by a question. "Oh, is *she* going?"

"Base impostor!" his ironic host went on. "I've treated you handsomely on the article of that young lady: I won't make

another concession. Wait three minutes— I'll be with you." He gave himself to his departing guests, accompanied the long-trained ladies to the door. It was a hot night, the windows were open, the sound of the quick carriages and of the linkmen's call came into the house. The affair had rather glittered; a sense of festal things was in the heavy air: not only the influence of that particular entertainment, but the suggestion of the wide hurry of pleasure which in London on summer nights fills so many of the happier quarters of the complicated town. Gradually Mrs. St. George's drawing room emptied itself; Paul was left alone with his hostess, to whom he explained the motive of his waiting. "Ah, yes, some intellectual, some *professional*, talk," she leered; "at this season doesn't one miss it? Poor dear Henry, I'm so glad!" The young man looked out of the window a moment, at the called hansoms that lurched up, at the smooth broughams that rolled away. When he turned round Mrs. St. George had disappeared; her husband's voice rose to him from below—he was laughing and talking, in the portico, with some lady who awaited her carriage. Paul had solitary possession, for some minutes, of the warm deserted rooms where the covered tinted lamplight was soft, the seats had been pushed about, and the odor of flowers lingered. They were large, they were pretty, they contained objects of value; everything in the picture told of a "good house." At the end of five minutes a servant came in with a request from the Master that he would join him downstairs; upon which, descending, he followed his conductor through a long passage to an apartment thrown out, in the rear of the habitation, for the special requirements, as he guessed, of a busy man of letters.

St. George was in his shirt sleeves in the middle of a large high room—a room without windows, but with a wide skylight at the top, that of a place of exhibition. It was furnished as a library, and the serried bookshelves rose to the ceiling, a surface of incomparable tone produced by dimly gilt "backs" interrupted here and there by the suspension of old prints and drawings. At the end furthest from the door of admission was a tall desk, of great extent, at which the person using it could write only in the erect posture of a clerk in a countinghouse; and stretched from the entrance to this structure was a wide plain band of crimson cloth, as straight as a garden path and almost as long, where, in his mind's eye, Paul at once beheld the Master pace to and fro during vexed hours—hours, that is, of admirable composition. The servant gave him a coat, an old jacket with a hang of experience, from a cupboard in the wall, retiring afterwards with the garment he had taken off. Paul Overt welcomed the coat; it was a coat for talk, it promised confidences—having visibly received so many—and had tragic literary elbows. "Ah, we're practical—we're practical!" St. George said as he saw his visitor look the place over. "Isn't it a good big cage for going round and round? My wife invented it and she locks me up here every morning."

Our young man breathed—by way of tribute—with a certain oppression. "You don't miss a window—a place to look out?"

"I did at first awfully; but her calculation was just. It saves time, it has saved me many months in these ten years. Here I stand, under the eye of day—in London of course, very often, it's rather a bleared old eye—walled in to my trade. I can't get away—so the room's a fine lesson in concentration. I've learnt the lesson, I think; look at that big bundle of proof and acknowledge it." He pointed to a fat roll of papers, on one of the tables, which had not been undone.

"Are you bringing out another——?" Paul asked in a tone the fond deficiencies of which he didn't recognize till his companion burst out laughing, and indeed scarce even then.

"You humbug, you humbug!" — St. George appeared to enjoy caressing him, as it were, with that opprobrium. "Don't I know what you think of them?" he asked, standing there with his hands in his pockets and with a new kind of smile. It was as if he were going to let his young votary see him all now.

"Upon my word in that case you know more than I do!" the latter ventured to respond, revealing a part of the torment of being able neither clearly to esteem nor distinctly to renounce him.

"My dear fellow," said the more and more interesting Master, "don't imagine I talk about my books specifically; they're not a decent subject—*il ne manquerait plus que ça!* [10] I'm not so bad as you may apprehend. About myself, yes, a little, if you like; though it wasn't for that I brought you down here. I want to ask you something—very much indeed; I value this chance. Therefore sit down. We're practical, but there *is* a sofa, you see—for she does humor my poor bones so far. Like all really great administrators and disciplinarians she knows when wisely to relax." Paul sank into the corner of a deep leathern couch, but his friend remained standing and explanatory. "If you don't mind, in this room, this is my habit. From the door to the desk and from the desk to the door. That shakes up my imagination gently; and don't you see what a good thing it is that there's no window for her to fly out of? The eternal standing as I write (I stop at that bureau and put it down, when anything comes, and so we go on) was rather wearisome at first, but we adopted it with an eye to the long run: you're in better order—if your legs don't break down!—and you can keep it up for more years. Oh, we're practical—we're practical!" St. George repeated, going to the table and taking up all mechanically the bundle of proofs. But, pulling off the wrapper, he had a change of attention that appealed afresh to our hero. He lost himself a moment, examining the sheets of his new book, while the younger man's eyes wandered over the room again.

[10] That (subject) would be the last straw!

"Lord, what good things I should do if I had such a charming place as this to do them in!" Paul reflected. The outer world, the world of accident and ugliness, was so successfully excluded, and within the rich protecting square, beneath the patronizing sky, the dream-figures, the summoned company, could hold their particular revel. It was a fond prevision of Overt's rather than an observation on actual data, for which occasions had been too few, that the Master thus more closely viewed would have the quality, the charming gift, of flashing out, all surprisingly, in personal intercourse and at moments of suspended or perhaps even of diminished expectation. A happy relation with him would be a thing proceeding by jumps, not by traceable stages.

"Do you read them—really?" he asked, laying down the proofs on Paul's inquiring of him how soon the work would be published. And when the young man answered, "Oh, yes, always," he was moved to mirth again by something he caught in his manner of saying that. "You go to see your grandmother on her birthday—and very proper it is, especially as she won't last forever. She has lost every faculty and every sense; she neither sees, nor hears, nor speaks; but all customary pieties and kindly habits are respectable. Only you're strong if you *do* read 'em! *I* couldn't, my dear fellow. You *are* strong, I know; and that's just a part of what I wanted to say to you. You're very strong indeed. I've been going into your other things—they've interested me immensely. Someone ought to have told me about them before—someone I could believe. But whom can one believe? You're wonderfully on the right road—it's awfully decent work. Now do you mean to keep it up?—that's what I want to ask you."

"Do I mean to do others?" Paul asked, looking up from his sofa at his erect inquisitor and feeling partly like a happy little boy when the schoolmaster is gay, and partly like some pilgrim of old who might have consulted a world-famous oracle. St. George's own performance had been infirm, but as an adviser he would be infallible.

"Others—others? Ah, the number won't matter; one other would do, if it were really a further step—a throb of the same effort. What I mean is, have you it in your heart to go in for some sort of decent perfection?"

"Ah, decency, ah, perfection——!" the young man sincerely sighed. "I talked of them the other Sunday with Miss Fancourt."

It produced on the Master's part a laugh of odd acrimony. "Yes, they'll 'talk' of them as much as you like! But they'll do little to help one to them. There's no obligation of course; only you strike me as capable," he went on. "You must have thought it all over. I can't believe you're without a plan. That's the sensation you give me, and it's so rare that it really stirs one up—it makes you remarkable. If you haven't a plan, if you *don't* mean to keep it up, surely you're within your rights; it's nobody's business, no one can force you, and not more than two or three people will notice you don't go straight. The others—*all* the rest, every blest soul in England, will think you do—will think you *are* keeping it up: upon my honor they will! I shall be one of the two or three who know better. Now the question is whether you can do it for two or three. Is that the stuff you're made of?"

It locked his guest a minute as in closed throbbing arms. "I could do it for one, if you were the one."

"Don't say that; I don't deserve it; it scorches me," he protested with eyes suddenly grave and glowing. "The 'one' is of course oneself, one's conscience, one's idea, the singleness of one's aim. I think of that pure spirit as a man thinks of a woman he has in some detested hour of his youth loved and forsaken. She haunts him with reproachful eyes, she lives forever before him. As an artist, you know, I've married for money." Paul stared and even blushed a little, confounded by this avowal; whereupon his host, observing the expression of his face, dropped a quick laugh and pursued: "You don't follow my figure. I'm not speaking of my dear wife, who had a small fortune—which, however, was not my bribe. I fell in love with her, as many other people have done. I refer to the mercenary muse whom I led to the altar of literature. Don't, my boy, put your nose into *that* yoke. The awful jade will lead you a life!"

Our hero watched him, wondering and deeply touched. "Haven't you been happy!"

"Happy? It's a kind of hell."

"There are things I should like to ask you," Paul said after a pause.

"Ask me anything in all the world. I'd turn myself inside out to save you."

"To 'save' me?" he quavered.

"To make you stick to it—to make you see it through. As I said to you the other night at Summersoft, let my example be vivid to you."

"Why, your books are not so bad as that," said Paul, fairly laughing and feeling that if ever a fellow had breathed the air of art——!

"So bad as what?"

"Your talent's so great that it's in everything you do, in what's less good as well as in what's best. You've some forty volumes to show for it—forty volumes of wonderful life, of rare observation, of magnificent ability."

"I'm very clever, of course I know that"—but it was a thing, in fine, this author made nothing of. "Lord, what rot they'd all be if I hadn't been! I'm a successful charlatan," he went on—"I've been able to pass off my system. But do you know what it is? It's *carton-pierre.*"

"*Carton-pierre?*" Paul was struck, and gaped.

"Lincrusta-Walton!" [11]

"Ah, don't say such things—you make me bleed!" the younger man protested. "I see you in a beautiful, fortunate home, living in comfort and honor."

"Do you call it honor?"—his host took him up with an intonation that often comes back to him. "That's what I want *you* to go in for. I mean the real thing. This is brummagem."

"Brummagem?" Paul ejaculated while his eyes wandered, by a movement natural at the moment, over the luxurious room.

"Ah, they make it so well today—it's wonderfully deceptive!"

Our friend thrilled with the interest and perhaps even more with the pity of it. Yet he wasn't afraid to seem to patronize when he could still so far envy. "Is it deceptive that I find you living with every appearance of domestic felicity—blest with a devoted, accomplished wife, with children whose acquaintance I haven't yet had the pleasure of making, but who *must* be delightful young people, from what I know of their parents?"

St. George smiled as for the candor of his question. "It's all excellent, my dear fellow—heaven forbid I should deny it. I've made a great deal of money; my wife has known how to take care of it, to use it without wasting it, to put a good bit of it by, to make it fructify. I've got a loaf on the shelf; I've got everything in fact but the great thing."

"The great thing?" Paul kept echoing.

"The sense of having done the best—the sense which is the real life of the artist and the absence of which is his death, of having drawn from his intellectual instrument the finest music that nature had hidden in it, of having played it as it should be played. He either does that or he doesn't—and if he doesn't he isn't worth speaking of. Therefore, precisely, those who really know *don't* speak of him. He may still hear a great chatter, but what he hears most is the incorruptible silence of Fame. I've squared her, you may say, for my little hour—but what's my little hour? Don't imagine for a moment," the Master pursued, "that I'm such a cad as to have

[11] The references are to statuary pasteboard and to a canvas fabric for ceilings that bore the trademark Lincrusta-Walton; St. George, in other words, is calling his achievement papier-maché or sham.

brought you down here to abuse or to complain of my wife to you. She's a woman of distinguished qualities, to whom my obligations are immense; so that, if you please, we'll say nothing about her. My boys—my children are all boys—are straight and strong, thank God, and have no poverty of growth about them, no penury of needs. I receive periodically the most satisfactory attestation from Harrow, from Oxford, from Sandhurst—oh, we've done the best for them!—of their eminence as living, thriving, consuming organisms."

"It must be delightful to feel that the son of one's loins is at Sandhurst," Paul remarked enthusiastically.

"It is—it's charming. Oh, I'm a patriot!"

The young man then could but have the greater tribute of questions to pay. "Then what did you mean—the other night at Summersoft—by saying that children are a curse?"

"My dear youth, on what basis are we talking?" and St. George dropped upon the sofa at a short distance from him. Sitting a little sideways he leaned back against the opposite arm with his hands raised and interlocked behind his head. "On the supposition that a certain perfection's possible and even desirable—isn't it so? Well, all I say is that one's children interfere with perfection. One's wife interferes. Marriage interferes."

"You think, then, the artist shouldn't marry?"

"He does so at his peril—he does so at his cost."

"Not even when his wife's in sympathy with his work?"

"She never is—she can't be! Women haven't a conception of such things."

"Surely they on occasion work themselves," Paul objected.

"Yes, very badly indeed. Oh, of course, often, they think they understand, they think they sympathize. Then it is they're most dangerous. Their idea is that you shall do a great lot and get a great lot of money. Their great nobleness and virtue, their exemplary conscientiousness as Brit-

ish females, is in keeping you up to that. My wife makes all my bargains with my publishers for me, and has done so for twenty years. She does it consummately well—that's why I'm really pretty well off. Aren't you the father of their innocent babes, and will you withhold from them their natural sustenance? You asked me the other night if they're not an immense incentive. Of course they are—there's no doubt of that!"

Paul turned it over: it took, from eyes he had never felt open so wide, so much looking at. "For myself I've an idea I need incentives."

"Ah, well, then, *n'en parlons plus!*" [12] his companion handsomely smiled.

"*You* are an incentive, I maintain," the young man went on. "You don't affect me in the way you'd apparently like to. Your great success is what I see—the pomp of Ennismore Gardens!"

"Success?"—St. George's eyes had a cold, fine light. "Do you call it success to be spoken of as you'd speak of me if you were sitting here with another artist—a young man intelligent and sincere like yourself? Do you call it success to make you blush—as you *would* blush!—if some foreign critic (some fellow, of course I mean, who should know what he was talking about and should have shown you he did, as foreign critics like to show it) were to say to you: 'He's the one, in this country, whom they consider the most perfect, isn't he?' Is it success to be the occasion of a young Englishman's having to stammer as you would have to stammer at such a moment for old England? No, no; success is to have made people wriggle to another tune. Do try it!"

Paul continued all gravely to glow. "Try what?"

"Try to do some really good work."

"Oh, I want to, heaven knows!"

"Well, you can't do it without sacrifices —don't believe that for a moment," the Master said. "I've made none. I've had

---

[12] Let's say no more about it!

everything. In other words, I've missed everything."

'You've had the full, rich, masculine, human, general life, with all the responsibilities and duties and burdens and sorrows and joys—all the domestic and social initiations and complications. They must be immensely suggestive, immensely amusing," Paul anxiously submitted.

"Amusing?"

"For a strong man—yes."

"They've given me subjects without number, if that's what you mean; but they've taken away at the same time the power to use them. I've touched a thousand things, but which one of them have I turned into gold? The artist has to do only with that —he knows nothing of any baser metal. I've led the life of the world, with my wife and my progeny; the clumsy, conventional, expensive, materialized, vulgarized, brutalized life of London. We've got everything handsome, even a carriage—we're perfect Philistines and prosperous, hospitable, eminent people. But, my dear fellow, don't try to stultify yourself and pretend you don't know what we *haven't* got. It's bigger than all the rest. Between artists—come!" the Master wound up. "You know as well as you sit there that you'd put a pistol ball into your brain if you had written my books!"

It struck his listener that the tremendous talk promised by him at Summersoft had indeed come off, and with a promptitude, a fullness, with which the latter's young imagination had scarcely reckoned. His impression fairly shook him and he throbbed with the excitement of such deep soundings and such strange confidences. He throbbed indeed with the conflict of his feelings—bewilderment and recognition and alarm, enjoyment and protest and assent, all commingled with tenderness (and a kind of shame in the participation) for the sores and bruises exhibited by so fine a creature, and with a sense of the tragic secret nursed under his trappings. The idea of *his*, Paul Overt's, becoming the occasion of such an act of humility made him

flush and pant, at the same time that his consciousness was in certain directions too much alive not to swallow—and not intensely to taste—every offered spoonful of the revelation. It had been his odd fortune to blow upon the deep waters, to make them surge and break in waves of strange eloquence. But how couldn't he give out a passionate contradiction of his host's last extravagance, how couldn't he enumerate to him the parts of his work he loved, the splendid things he had found in it, beyond the compass of any other writer of the day? St. George listened a while, courteously; then he said, laying his hand on his visitor's: "That's all very well; and if your idea's to do nothing better, there's no reason you shouldn't have as many good things as I—as many human and material appendages, as many sons or daughters, a wife with as many gowns, a house with as many servants, a stable with as many horses, a heart with as many aches." The Master got up when he had spoken thus— he stood a moment—near the sofa, looking down on his agitated pupil. "Are you possessed of any property?" it occurred to him to ask.

"None to speak of."

"Oh, well then there's no reason why you shouldn't make a goodish income—if you set about it the right way. Study *me* for that—study me well. You may really have horses."

Paul sat there some minutes without speaking. He looked straight before him —he turned over many things. His friend had wandered away, taking up a parcel of letters from the table where the roll of proofs had lain. "What was the book Mrs. St. George made you burn—the one she didn't like?" our young man brought out.

"The book she made me burn—how did you know that?" The Master looked up from his letters quite without the facial convulsion the pupil had feared.

"I heard her speak of it at Summersoft."

"Ah, yes—she's proud of it. I don't know —it was rather good."

"What was it about?"

"Let me see." And he seemed to make an effort to remember. "Oh, yes—it was about myself." Paul gave an irrepressible groan for the disappearance of such a production, and the elder man went on: "Oh, but *you* should write it—*you* should do me." And he pulled up—from the restless motion that had come upon him; his fine smile a generous glare. "There's a subject, my boy: no end of stuff in it!"

Again Paul was silent, but it was all tormenting. "Are there no women who really understand—who can take part in a sacrifice?"

"How can they take part? They themselves are the sacrifice. They're the idol and the altar and the flame."

"Isn't there even *one* who sees further?" Paul continued.

For a moment St. George made no answer; after which, having torn up his letters, he came back to the point all ironic. "Of course I know the one you mean. But not even Miss Fancourt."

"I thought you admired her so much."

"It's impossible to admire her more. Are you in love with her?" St. George asked.

"Yes," Paul Overt presently said.

"Well, then, give it up."

Paul stared. "Give up my 'love'?"

"Bless me, no. Your idea." And then as our hero but still gazed: "The one you talked with her about. The idea of a decent perfection."

"She'd help it—she'd help it!" the young man cried.

"For about a year—the first year, yes. After that she'd be as a millstone round its neck."

Paul frankly wondered. "Why, she has a passion for the real thing, for good work—for everything you and I care for most."

"'You and I' is charming, my dear fellow!" his friend laughed. "She has it indeed, but she'd have a still greater passion for her children—and very proper too. She'd insist on everything's being made comfortable, advantageous, propitious for them. That isn't the artist's business."

"The artist—the artist! Isn't he a man all the same?"

St. George had a grand grimace. "I mostly think not. You know as well as I what he has to do: the concentration, the finish, the independence he must strive for from the moment he begins to wish his work really decent. Ah, my young friend, his relation to women, and especially to the one he's most intimately concerned with, is at the mercy of the damning fact that whereas he can in the nature of things have but one standard, they have about fifty. That's what makes them so superior," St. George amusingly added. "Fancy an artist with a change of standards as you'd have a change of shirts or of dinner plates. To *do* it—to do it and make it divine—is the only thing he has to think about. 'Is it done or not?' is his only question. Not 'Is it done as well as a proper solicitude for my dear little family will allow?' He has nothing to do with the relative—he has only to do with the absolute; and a dear little family may represent a dozen relatives."

"Then you don't allow him the common passions and affections of men?" Paul asked.

"Hasn't he a passion, an affection, which includes all the rest? Besides, let him have all the passions he likes—if he only keeps his independence. He must be able to be poor."

Paul slowly got up. "Why, then, did you advise me to make up to her?"

St. George laid a hand on his shoulder. "Because she'd make a splendid wife! And I hadn't read you then."

The young man had a strained smile. "I wish you had left me alone!"

"I didn't know that that wasn't good enough for you," his host returned.

"What a false position, what a condemnation of the artist, that he's a mere disfranchised monk and can produce his effect only by giving up personal happiness. What an arraignment of art!" Paul went on with a trembling voice.

"Ah, you don't imagine by chance that I'm defending art? 'Arraignment'—I should think so! Happy the societies in which it hasn't made its appearance, for from the moment it comes they have a consuming ache, they have an incurable corruption, in their breast. Most assuredly is the artist in a false position! But I thought we were taking him for granted. Pardon me," St. George continued: "*Ginistrella* made me!"

Paul stood looking at the floor—one o'clock struck, in the stillness, from a neighboring church tower. "Do you think she'd ever look at me?" he put to his friend at last.

"Miss Fancourt — as a suitor? Why shouldn't I think it? That's why I've tried to favor you—I've had a little chance or two of bettering your opportunity."

"Forgive my asking you, but do you mean by keeping away yourself?" Paul said with a blush.

"I'm an old idiot—my place isn't there," St. George stated gravely.

"I'm nothing yet, I've no fortune; and there must be so many others," his companion pursued.

The Master took this considerably in, but made little of it. "You're a gentleman and a man of genius. I think you might do something."

"But if I must give that up — the genius?"

"Lots of people, you know, think I've kept mine," St. George wonderfully grinned.

"You've a genius for mystification!" Paul declared, but grasping his hand gratefully in attenuation of this judgment.

"Poor, dear boy, I do worry you! But try, try, all the same. I think your chances are good and you'll win a great prize."

Paul held fast the other's hand a minute; he looked into the strange deep face. "No, I *am* an artist—I can't help it!"

"Ah, show it then!" St. George pleadingly broke out. "Let me see before I die the thing I most want, the thing I yearn for: a life in which the passion—ours—

is really intense. If you can be rare don't fail of it! Think what it is—how it counts —how it lives!"

They had moved to the door and he had closed both his hands over his companion's. Here they paused again and our hero breathed deep. "I want to live!"

"In what sense?"

"In the greatest."

"Well, then, stick to it—see it through."

"With your sympathy—your help?"

"Count on that—you'll be a great figure to me. Count on my highest appreciation, my devotion. You'll give me satisfaction— if that has any weight with you!" After which, as Paul appeared still to waver, his host added: "Do you remember what you said to me at Summersoft?"

"Something infatuated, no doubt!"

"'I'll do anything in the world you tell me.' You said that."

"And you hold me to it?"

"Ah, what am I?" the Master expressively sighed.

"Lord, what things I shall have to do!" Paul almost moaned as he departed.

VI

"It goes on too much abroad—hang abroad!" These or something like them had been the Master's remarkable words in relation to the action of *Ginistrella;* and yet, though they had made a sharp impression on the author of that work, like almost all spoken words from the same source, he a week after the conversation I have noted left England for a long absence and full of brave intentions. It is not a perversion of the truth to pronounce that encounter the direct cause of his departure. If the oral utterance of the eminent writer had the privilege of moving him deeply, it was especially on his turning it over at leisure, hours and days later, that it appeared to yield him its full meaning and exhibit its extreme importance. He spent the summer in Switzerland and, having in September begun a new task, determined not to cross the Alps till he should have made a good start. To this end he returned to a quiet corner he knew well, on the edge of the Lake of Geneva and within sight of the towers of Chillon: a region and a view for which he had an affection that sprang from old associations and was capable of mysterious revivals and refreshments. Here he lingered late, till the snow was on the nearer hills, almost down to the limit to which he could climb when his stint, on the shortening afternoons, was performed. The autumn was fine, the lake was blue, and his book took form and direction. These felicities, for the time, embroidered his life, which he suffered to cover him with its mantle. At the end of six weeks he felt he had learnt St. George's lesson by heart, had tested and proved its doctrine. Nevertheless he did a very inconsistent thing: before crossing the Alps he wrote to Marian Fancourt. He was aware of the perversity of this act, and it was only as a luxury, an amusement, the reward of a strenuous autumn, that he justified it. She had asked of him no such favor when, shortly before he left London, three days after their dinner in Ennismore Gardens, he went to take leave of her. It was true she had had no ground—he hadn't named his intention of absence. He had kept his counsel for want of due assurance: it was that particular visit that was, the next thing, to settle the matter. He had paid the visit to see how much he really cared for her, and quick departure, without so much as an explicit farewell, was the sequel to this inquiry, the answer to which had created within him a deep yearning. When he wrote her from Clarens he noted that he owed her an explanation (more than three months after!) for not having told her what he was doing.

She replied now briefly but promptly, and gave him a striking piece of news: that of the death, a week before, of Mrs. St. George. This exemplary woman had succumbed, in the country, to a violent attack of inflammation of the lungs—he would remember that for a long time she had been delicate. Miss Fancourt added that she believed her husband was overwhelmed by the blow; he would miss her too terribly—she had been everything in life to him. Paul Overt, on this, immediately wrote to St. George. He would from the day of their parting have been glad to remain in communication with him, but had hitherto lacked the right excuse for troubling so busy a man. Their long nocturnal talk came back to him in every detail, but this was no bar to an expression of proper sympathy with the head of the profession, for hadn't that very talk made it clear that the late accomplished lady was the influence that ruled his life? What catastrophe could be more cruel than the extinction of such an influence? This was to be exactly the tone taken by St. George in answering his young friend upwards of a month later. He made no allusion of course to their important discussion. He spoke of his wife as frankly and generously as if he had quite forgotten that occasion, and the feeling of deep bereavement was visible in his words. "She took everything off my hands—off my mind. She carried on our life with the greatest art, the rarest devotion, and I was free, as few men can have been, to drive my pen, to shut myself up with my trade. This was a rare service—the highest she could have rendered me. Would I could have acknowledged it more fitly!"

A certain bewilderment, for our hero, disengaged itself from these remarks: they struck him as a contradiction, a retractation, strange on the part of a man who hadn't the excuse of witlessness. He had certainly not expected his correspondent to rejoice in the death of his wife, and it was perfectly in order that the rupture of a tie of more than twenty years should have left him sore. But if she had been so clear a blessing what in the name of consistency had the dear man meant by turning *him* upside down that night—by dosing him to that degree, at the most sensitive hour of his life, with the doctrine of renunciation? If Mrs. St. George was an irreparable loss then her husband's inspired advice had been a bad joke and renunciation was a mistake. Overt was on the point of rushing back to London to show that, for his part, he was perfectly willing to consider it so, and he went so far as to take the manuscript of the first chapters of his new book out of his table drawer and insert it into a pocket of his portmanteau. This led to his catching a glimpse of certain pages he hadn't looked at for months, and that accident, in turn, to his being struck with the high promise they revealed—a rare result of such retrospections, which it was his habit to avoid as much as possible: they usually brought home to him that the glow of composition might be a purely subjective and misleading emotion. On this occasion a certain belief in himself disengaged itself whimsically from the serried erasures of his first draft, making him think it best after all to pursue his present trial to the end. If he could write so well under the rigor of privation it might be a mistake to change the conditions before that spell had spent itself. He would go back to London of course, but he would go back only when he should have finished his book. This was the vow he privately made, restoring his manuscript to the table drawer. It may be added that it took him a long time to finish his book, for the subject was as difficult as it was fine, and he was literally embarrassed by the fullness of his notes. Something within him warned him he must make it supremely good— otherwise he should lack, as regards his private behavior, a handsome excuse. He had a horror of this deficiency and found himself as firm as need be on the question of the lamp and the file. He crossed the Alps at last and spent the winter, the spring, the ensuing summer, in Italy, where still, at the end of a twelvemonth, his task was unachieved. "Stick to it — see it through": this general injunction of St. George's was good also for the particular case. He applied it to the utmost, with the result that when in its slow order the summer had come round again he felt he had given all that was in him. This time

he put his papers into his portmanteau, with the address of his publisher attached, and took his way northward.

He had been absent from London for two years; two years which, seeming to count as more, had made such a difference in his own life—through the production of a novel far stronger, he believed, than *Ginistrella*—that he turned out into Piccadilly, the morning after his arrival, with a vague expectation of changes, of finding great things had happened. But there were few transformations in Piccadilly—only three or four big red houses where there had been low black ones—and the brightness of the end of June peeped through the rusty railings of the Green Park and glittered in the varnish of the rolling carriages as he had seen it in other, more cursory Junes. It was a greeting he appreciated; it seemed friendly and pointed, added to the exhilaration of his finished book, of his having his own country and the huge oppressive amusing city that suggested everything, that contained everything, under his hand again. "Stay at home and do things here—do subjects we can measure," St. George had said; and now it struck him he should ask nothing better than to stay at home forever. Late in the afternoon he took his way to Manchester Square, looking out for a number he hadn't forgotten. Miss Fancourt, however, was not at home, so that he turned rather dejectedly from the door. His movement brought him face to face with a gentleman just approaching it and recognized on another glance as Miss Fancourt's father. Paul saluted this personage, and the General returned the greeting with his customary good manner—a manner so good, however, that you could never tell whether it meant he placed you. The disappointed caller felt the impulse to address him; then, hesitating, became both aware of having no particular remark to make, and convinced that though the old soldier remembered him he remembered him wrong. He therefore went his way without computing the irresistible effect his own evident recognition would have on the General, who never neglected a chance to gossip. Our young man's face was expressive, and observation seldom let it pass. He hadn't taken ten steps before he heard himself called after with a friendly semi-articulate "Er—I beg your pardon!" He turned round and the General, smiling at him from the porch, said: "Won't you come in? I won't leave you the advantage of me!" Paul declined to come in, and then felt regret, for Miss Fancourt, so late in the afternoon, might return at any moment. But her father gave him no second chance; he appeared mainly to wish not to have struck him as ungracious. A further look at the visitor had recalled something, enough at least to enable him to say: "You've come back, you've come back?" Paul was on the point of replying that he had come back the night before, but he suppressed, the next instant, this strong light on the immediacy of his visit and, giving merely a general assent, alluded to the young lady he deplored not having found. He had come late in the hope she would be in. "I'll tell her—I'll tell her," said the old man; and then he added quickly, gallantly: "You'll be giving us something new? It's a long time, isn't it?" Now he remembered him right.

"Rather long. I'm very slow," Paul explained. "I met you at Summersoft a long time ago."

"Oh, yes—with Henry St. George. I remember very well. Before his poor wife——" General Fancourt paused a moment, smiling a little less. "I daresay you know."

"About Mrs. St. George's death? Certainly—I heard at the time."

"Oh, no, I mean—I mean he's to be married."

"Ah, I've not heard that!" But just as Paul was about to add "To whom?" the General crossed his intention.

"When did you come back? I know you've been away—by my daughter. She was very sorry. You ought to give her something new."

"I came back last night," said our young man, to whom something had occurred which made his speech for the moment a little thick.

"Ah, most kind of you to come so soon. Couldn't you turn up at dinner?"

"At dinner?" Paul just mechanically repeated, not liking to ask whom St. George was going to marry, but thinking only of that.

"There are several people, I believe. Certainly St. George. Or afterwards if you like better. I believe my daughter expects——" He appeared to notice something in the visitor's raised face (on his steps he stood higher) which led him to interrupt himself, and the interruption gave him a momentary sense of awkwardness, from which he sought a quick issue. "Perhaps, then, you haven't heard she's to be married."

Paul gaped again. "To be married?"

"To Mr. St. George—it has just been settled. Odd marriage, isn't it?" Our listener uttered no opinion on this point: he only continued to stare. "But I daresay it will do—she's so awfully literary!" said the General.

Paul had turned very red. "Oh, it's a surprise—very interesting, very charming! I'm afraid I can't dine—so many thanks!"

"Well, you must come to the wedding!" cried the General. "Oh, I remember that day at Summersoft. He's a great man, you know."

"Charming—charming!" Paul stammered for retreat. He shook hands with the General and got off. His face was red and he had the sense of its growing more and more crimson. All the evening at home—he went straight to his rooms and remained there dinnerless—his cheek burned at intervals as if it had been smitten. He didn't understand what had happened to him, what trick had been played him, what treachery practiced. "None, none," he said to himself. "I've nothing to do with it. I'm out of it—it's none of my business." But that bewildered murmur was followed again and again by the incongruous ejaculation: "Was it a plan—was it a plan?" Sometimes he cried to himself, breathless, "Have

I been duped, sold, swindled?" If at all, he was an absurd, an abject victim. It was as if he hadn't lost her till now. He had renounced her, yes; but that was another affair—that was a closed but not a locked door. Now he seemed to see the door quite slammed in his face. Did he expect her to wait—was she to give him his time like that: two years at a stretch? He didn't know what he had expected—he only knew what he hadn't. It wasn't this—it wasn't this. Mystification, bitterness, and wrath rose and boiled in him when he thought of the deference, the devotion, the credulity with which he had listened to St. George. The evening wore on and the light was long; but even when it had darkened he remained without a lamp. He had flung himself on the sofa, where he lay through the hours with his eyes either closed or gazing at the gloom, in the attitude of a man teaching himself to bear something, to bear having been made a fool of. He had made it too easy—that idea passed over him like a hot wave. Suddenly, as he heard eleven o'clock strike, he jumped up, remembering what General Fancourt had said about his coming after dinner. He'd go— he'd see her at least; perhaps he should see what it meant. He felt as if some of the elements of a hard sum had been given him and the others were wanting: he couldn't do his sum till he had got all his figures.

He dressed and drove quickly, so that by half-past eleven he was at Manchester Square. There were a good many carriages at the door—a party was going on; a circumstance which at the last gave him a slight relief, for now he would rather see her in a crowd. People passed him on the staircase; they were going away, going "on" with the hunted herdlike movement of London society at night. But sundry groups remained in the drawing room, and it was some minutes, as she didn't hear him announced, before he discovered and spoke to her. In this short interval he had seen St. George talking to a lady before the fireplace; but he at once looked away, feeling unready for an encounter, and

therefore couldn't be sure the author of *Shadowmere* noticed him. At all events he didn't come over; though Miss Fancourt did as soon as she saw him—she almost rushed at him, smiling, rustling, radiant, beautiful. He had forgotten what her head, what her face offered to the sight; she was in white, there were gold figures on her dress and her hair was a casque of gold. He saw in a single moment that she was happy, happy with an aggressive splendor. But she wouldn't speak to him of that, she would speak only of himself.

"I'm so delighted; my father told me. How kind of you to come!" She struck him as so fresh and brave, while his eyes moved over her, that he said to himself irresistibly: "Why to *him*, why not to youth, to strength, to ambition, to a future? Why, in her rich young force, to failure, to abdication, to superannuation?" In his thought at that sharp moment he blasphemed even against all that had been left of his faith in the peccable master. "I'm so sorry I missed you," she went on. "My father told me. How charming of you to have come so soon!"

"Does that surprise you?" Paul Overt asked.

"The first day? No, from you—nothing that's nice." She was interrupted by a lady who bade her good night, and he seemed to read that it cost her nothing to speak to him in that tone; it was her old liberal, lavish way, with a certain added amplitude that time had brought; and if this manner began to operate on the spot, at such a juncture in her history, perhaps in the other days too it had meant just as little or as much—a mere mechanical charity, with the difference now that she was satisfied, ready to give but in want of nothing. Oh, she was satisfied—and why shouldn't she be? Why shouldn't she have been surprised at his coming the first day —for all the good she had ever got from him? As the lady continued to hold her attention Paul turned from her with a strange irritation in his complicated artistic soul and a sort of disinterested disappointment. She was so happy that it was almost stupid—a disproof of the extraordinary intelligence he had formerly found in her. Didn't she know how bad St. George could be, hadn't she recognized the awful thinness——? If she didn't she was nothing, and if she did why such an insolence of serenity? This question expired as our young man's eyes settled at last on the genius who had advised him in a great crisis. St. George was still before the chimney piece, but now he was alone—fixed, waiting, as if he meant to stop after everyone—and he met the clouded gaze of the young friend so troubled as to the degree of his right (the right his resentment would have enjoyed) to regard himself as a victim. Somehow the ravage of the question was checked by the Master's radiance. It was as fine in its way as Marian Fancourt's, it denoted the happy human being; but also it represented to Paul Overt that the author of *Shadowmere* had now definitely ceased to count—ceased to count as a writer. As he smiled a welcome across the place he was almost *banal*, was almost smug. Paul fancied that for a moment he hesitated to make a movement, as if, for all the world, he *had* his bad conscience; then they had already met in the middle of the room and had shaken hands—expressively, cordially on St. George's part. With which they had passed back together to where the elder man had been standing, while St. George said: "I hope you're never going away again. I've been dining here; the General told me." He was handsome, he was young, he looked as if he had still a great fund of life. He bent the friendliest, most unconfessing eyes on his disciple of a couple of years before; asked him about everything, his health, his plans, his late occupations, the new book. "When will it be out—soon, soon, I hope? Splendid, eh? That's right; you're a comfort, you're a luxury! I've read you all over again these last six months." Paul waited to see if he'd tell him what the General had told him in the afternoon and what Miss Fancourt, verbally at least, of course hadn't. But as

it didn't come out he at last put the question, "Is it true, the great news I hear— that you're to be married?"

"Ah, you *have* heard it, then?"

"Didn't the General tell you?" Paul asked.

The Master's face was wonderful. "Tell me what?"

"That he mentioned it to me this afternoon?"

"My dear fellow, I don't remember. We've been in the midst of people. I'm sorry, in the case, that I lose the pleasure, myself, of announcing to you a fact that touches me so nearly. It *is* a fact, strange as it may appear. It has only just become one. Isn't it ridiculous?" St. George made this speech without confusion, but on the other hand, so far as our friend could judge, without latent impudence. It struck his interlocutor that, to talk so comfortably and coolly, he must simply have forgotten what had passed between them. His next words, however, showed he hadn't, and they produced, as an appeal to Paul's own memory, an effect which would have been ludicrous if it hadn't been cruel. "Do you recall the talk we had at my house that night, into which Miss Fancourt's name entered? I've often thought of it since."

"Yes; no wonder you said what you did"—Paul was careful to meet his eyes.

"In the light of the present occasion? Ah, but there was no light then. How could I have foreseen this hour?"

"Didn't you think it probable?"

"Upon my honor, no," said Henry St. George. "Certainly I owe you that assurance. Think how my situation has changed."

"I see—I see," our young man murmured.

His companion went on as if, now that the subject had been broached, he was, as a person of imagination and tact, quite ready to give every satisfaction—being both by his genius and his method so able to enter into everything another might feel. "But it's not only that; for honestly, at my age, I never dreamed—a widower with big boys and with so little else! It has turned out differently from anything one could have dreamed, and I'm fortunate beyond all measure. She has been so free, and yet she consents. Better than anyone else perhaps—for I remember how you liked her before you went away, and how she liked you—you can intelligently congratulate me."

"She has been so free!" Those words made a great impression on Paul Overt, and he almost writhed under that irony in them as to which it so little mattered whether it was designed or casual. Of course she had been free, and appreciably perhaps by his own act; for wasn't the Master's allusion to her having liked him a part of the irony too? "I thought that by your theory you disapproved of a writer's marrying."

"Surely—surely. But you don't call me a writer?"

"You ought to be ashamed," said Paul.

"Ashamed of marrying again?"

"I won't say that—but ashamed of your reasons."

The elder man beautifully smiled. "You must let me judge of them, my good friend."

"Yes; why not? For you judged wonderfully of mine."

The tone of these words appeared suddenly, for St. George, to suggest the unsuspected. He stared as if divining a bitterness. "Don't you think I've been straight?"

"You might have told me at the time perhaps."

"My dear fellow, when I say I couldn't pierce futurity——!"

"I mean afterwards."

The Master wondered. "After my wife's death?"

"When this idea came to you."

"Ah, never, never! I wanted to save you, rare and precious as you are."

Poor Overt looked hard at him. "Are you marrying Miss Fancourt to save me?"

"Not absolutely, but it adds to the pleasure. I shall be the making of you," St. George smiled. "I was greatly struck, after

our talk, with the brave, devoted way you quitted the country, and still more perhaps with your force of character in remaining abroad. You're very strong—you're wonderfully strong."

Paul tried to sound his shining eyes; the strange thing was that he seemed sincere—not a mocking fiend. He turned away, and as he did so heard the Master say something about his giving them all the proof, being the joy of his old age. He faced him again, taking another look. "Do you mean to say you've stopped writing?"

"My dear fellow, of course I have. It's too late. Didn't I tell you?"

"I can't believe it!"

"Of course you can't—with your own talent! No, no; for the rest of my life I shall only read you."

"Does she know that—Miss Fancourt?"

"She will—she will." Did he mean this, our young man wondered, as a covert intimation that the assistance he should derive from that young lady's fortune, moderate as it was, would make the difference of putting it in his power to cease to work ungratefully an exhausted vein? Somehow, standing there in the ripeness of his successful manhood, he didn't suggest that any of his veins were exhausted. "Don't you remember the moral I offered myself to you that night as pointing?" St. George continued. "Consider at any rate the warning I am at present."

This was too much—he *was* the mocking fiend. Paul turned from him with a mere nod for good night and the sense in a sore heart that he might come back to him and his easy grace, his fine way of arranging things, sometime in the far future, but couldn't fraternize with him now. It was necessary to his soreness to believe for the hour in the intensity of his grievance—all the more cruel for its not being a legal one. It was doubtless in the attitude of hugging this wrong that he descended the stairs without taking leave of Miss Fancourt, who hadn't been in view at the moment he quitted the room. He was glad to get out into the honest, dusky, unsophisticating night, to move fast, to take his way home on foot. He walked a long time, going astray, paying no attention. He was thinking of too many other things. His steps recovered their direction, however, and at the end of an hour he found himself before his door in the small, inexpensive, empty street. He lingered, questioning himself still before going in, with nothing around and above him but moonless blackness, a bad lamp or two, and a few far-away dim stars. To these last faint features he raised his eyes; he had been saying to himself that he should have been "sold" indeed, diabolically sold, if now, on his new foundation, at the end of a year, St. George were to put forth something of his prime quality—something of the type of *Shadowmere* and finer than his finest. Greatly as he admired his talent Paul literally hoped such an incident wouldn't occur; it seemed to him just then that he shouldn't be able to bear it. His late adviser's words were still in his ears—"You're very strong, wonderfully strong." Was he really? Certainly he would have to be, and it might a little serve for revenge. *Is* he? the reader may ask in turn, if his interest has followed the perplexed young man so far. The best answer to that perhaps is that he's doing his best, but that it's too soon to say. When the new book came out in the autumn Mr. and Mrs. St. George found it really magnificent. The former still has published nothing, but Paul doesn't even yet feel safe. I may say for him, however, that if this event were to occur he would really be the very first to appreciate it: which is perhaps a proof · that the Master was essentially right and that nature had dedicated him to intellectual, not to personal passion.

FLICKERBRIDGE
[1903 (1902)]

I

FRANK GRANGER had arrived from Paris to paint a portrait—an order given

him, as a young compatriot with a future, whose early work would some day have a price, by a lady from New York, a friend of his own people and also, as it happened, of Addie's, the young woman to whom it was publicly both affirmed and denied that he was engaged. Other young women in Paris—fellow-members there of the little tight transpontine world of art-study—professed to know that the pair had been "several times" over so closely contracted. This, however, was their own affair; the last phase of the relation, the last time of the times, had passed into vagueness; there was perhaps even an impression that if they were inscrutable to their friends they were not wholly crystalline to each other and themselves. What had occurred for Granger, at all events, in connection with the portrait was that Mrs. Bracken, his intending model, whose return to America was at hand, had suddenly been called to London by her husband, occupied there with pressing business, but had yet desired that her displacement should not interrupt her sittings. The young man, at her request, had followed her to England and profited by all she could give him, making shift with a small studio lent him by a London painter whom he had known and liked, a few years before, in the French *atelier* that then cradled, and that continued to cradle, so many of their kind.

The British capital was a strange, grey world to him, where people walked, in more ways than one, by a dim light; but he was happily of such a turn that the impression, just as it came, could nowhere ever fail him, and even the worst of these things was almost as much an occupation —putting it only at that—as the best. Mrs. Bracken, moreover, passed him on, and while the darkness ebbed a little in the April days he found himself consolingly committed to a couple of fresh subjects. This cut him out work for more than another month, but meanwhile, as he said, he saw a lot—a lot that, with frequency and with much expression, he wrote about to Addie. She also wrote to her absent friend, but in briefer snatches, a meagreness to her reasons for which he had long since assented. She had other play for her pen, as well as, fortunately, other remuneration; a regular correspondence for a "prominent Boston paper," fitful connections with public sheets perhaps also, in cases, fitful, and a mind, above all, engrossed at times, to the exclusion of everything else, with the study of the short story. This last was what she had mainly come out to go into, two or three years after he had found himself engulfed in the mystery of Carolus.[1] She was indeed, on her own deep sea, more engulfed than he had ever been, and he had grown to accept the sense that, for progress too, she sailed under more canvas. It had not been particularly present to him till now that he had in the least got on, but the way in which Addie had—and evidently, still more, would—was the theme, as it were, of every tongue. She had thirty short stories out and nine descriptive articles. His three or four portraits of fat American ladies— they were all fat, all ladies and all American—were a poor show compared with these triumphs; especially as Addie had begun to throw out that it was about time they should go home. It kept perpetually coming up in Paris, in the transpontine world, that, as the phrase was, America had grown more interesting since they left. Addie was attentive to the rumour, and, as full of conscience as she was of taste, of patriotism as of curiosity, had often put it to him frankly, with what he, who was of New York, recognised as her New England emphasis: "I'm not sure, you know, that we do *real* justice to our country." Granger felt he would do it on the day—if the day ever came—he should irrevocably marry her. No other country could possibly have produced her.

II

But meanwhile it befell, in London, that he was stricken with influenza and with subsequent sorrow. The attack was short but sharp—had it lasted Addie would certainly have come to his aid; most of a blight, really, in its secondary stage. The good ladies his sitters—the ladies with the frizzled hair, with the diamond earrings, with the chins tending to the massive— left for him, at the door of his lodgings, flowers, soup and love, so that with their assistance he pulled through; but his convalescence was slow and his weakness out of proportion to the muffled shock. He came out, but he went about lame; it tired him to paint—he felt as if he had been ill for a month. He strolled in Kensington Gardens when he should have been at work; he sat long on penny chairs and helplessly mused and mooned. Addie desired him to return to Paris, but there were chances under his hand that he felt he had just wit enough left not to relinquish. He would have gone for a week to the sea—he would have gone to Brighton; but Mrs. Bracken had to be finished—Mrs. Bracken was so soon to sail. He just managed to finish her in time—the day before the date fixed for his breaking ground on a greater business still, the circumvallation of Mrs. Dunn. Mrs. Dunn duly waited on him, and he sat down before her, feeling, however, ere he rose, that he must take a long breath before the attack. While asking himself that night, therefore, where he should best replenish his lungs, he received from Addie, who had had from Mrs. Bracken a poor report of him, a communication which, besides being of sudden and startling interest, applied directly to his case.

His friend wrote to him under the lively emotion of having from one day to another become aware of a new relative, an ancient cousin, a sequestered gentlewoman, the sole survival of "the English branch of

---

[1] The art of portrait-painting, so called after "Carolus" or "Carolus-Duran," the name adopted by the French portrait-painter Charles Auguste Emile Durand (1837-1917), head of one of the principal studios in Paris and famous for his teaching.

the family," still resident, at Flickerbridge, in the "old family home," and with whom, that he might immediately betake himself to so auspicious a quarter for change of air, she had already done what was proper to place him, as she said, in touch. What came of it all, to be brief, was that Granger found himself so placed almost as he read: he was in touch with Miss Wenham of Flickerbridge, to the extent of being in correspondence with her, before twenty-four hours had sped. And on the second day he was in the train, settled for a five-hours' run to the door of this amiable woman, who had so abruptly and kindly taken him on trust and of whom but yesterday he had never so much as heard. This was an oddity—the whole incident was —of which, in the corner of his compartment, as he proceeded, he had time to take the size. But the surprise, the incongruity, as he felt, could but deepen as he went. It was a sufficiently queer note, in the light, or the absence of it, of his late experience, that so complex a product as Addie should have *any* simple insular tie; but it was a queerer note still that she should have had one so long only to remain unprofitably unconscious of it. Not to have done something with it, used it, worked it, talked about it at least, and perhaps even written—these things, at the rate she moved, represented a loss of opportunity under which, as he saw her, she was peculiarly formed to wince. She was at any rate, it was clear, doing something with it now; using it, working it, certainly, already talking—and, yes, quite possibly writing—about it. She was, in short, smartly making up what she had missed, and he could take such comfort from his own action as he had been helped to by the rest of the facts, succinctly reported from Paris on the very morning of his start.

It was the singular story of a sharp split —in a good English house—that dated now from years back. A worthy Briton, of the best middling stock, had, early in the forties, as a very young man, in Dresden, whither he had been despatched to qualify in German for a stool in an uncle's counting-house, met, admired, wooed and won an American girl, of due attractions, domiciled at that period with her parents and a sister, who was also attractive, in the Saxon capital. He had married her, taken her to England, and there, after some years of harmony and happiness, lost her. The sister in question had, after her death, come to him, and to his young child, on a visit, the effect of which, between the pair, eventually defined itself as a sentiment that was not to be resisted. The bereaved husband, yielding to a new attachment and a new response, and finding a new union thus prescribed, had yet been forced to reckon with the unaccommodating law of the land. Encompassed with frowns in his own country, however, marriages of this particular type were wreathed in smiles in his sister's-in-law, so that his remedy was not forbidden. Choosing between two allegiances he had let the one go that seemed the least close, and had, in brief, transplanted his possibilities to an easier air. The knot was tied for the couple in New York, where, to protect the legitimacy of such other children as might come to them, they settled and prospered. Children came, and one of the daughters, growing up and marrying in her turn, was, if Frank rightly followed, the mother of his own Addie, who had been deprived of the knowledge of her indeed, in childhood, by death, and been brought up, though without undue tension, by a stepmother— a character thus, in the connection, repeated.

The breach produced in England by the invidious action, as it was there held, of the girl's grandfather, had not failed to widen—all the more that nothing had been done on the American side to close it. Frigidity had settled, and hostility had only been arrested by indifference. Darkness, therefore, had fortunately supervened, and a cousinship completely divided. On either side of the impassable gulf, of the impenetrable curtain, each branch had put forth its leaves—a foliage wanting, in the

American quarter, it was distinct enough to Granger, in no sign or symptom of climate and environment. The graft in New York had taken, and Addie was a vivid, an unmistakable flower. At Flickerbridge, or wherever, on the other hand, strange to say, the parent stem had had a fortune comparatively meagre. Fortune, it was true, in the vulgarest sense, had attended neither party. Addie's immediate belongings were as poor as they were numerous, and he gathered that Miss Wenham's pretensions to wealth were not so marked as to expose the claim of kinship to the imputation of motive. To this lady's single identity, at all events, the original stock had dwindled, and our young man was properly warned that he should find her shy and solitary. What was singular was that, in these conditions, she should desire, she should endure, to receive him. But that was all another story, lucid enough when mastered. He kept Addie's letters, exceptionally copious, in his lap; he conned them at intervals; he held the threads.

He looked out between whiles at the pleasant English land, an April *aquarelle* [2] washed in with wondrous breadth. He knew the French thing, he knew the American, but he had known nothing of this. He saw it already as the remarkable Miss Wenham's setting. The doctor's daughter at Flickerbridge, with nippers on her nose, a palette on her thumb and innocence in her heart, had been the miraculous link. She had become aware, even there, in our world of wonders, that the current fashion for young women so equipped was to enter the Parisian lists. Addie had accordingly chanced upon her, on the slopes of Montparnasse, as one of the English girls in one of the thorough-going sets. They had met in some easy collocation and had fallen upon common ground; after which the young woman, restored to Flickerbridge for an interlude and retailing there her adventures and impressions, had mentioned to Miss Wenham, who had known and protected her from babyhood, that that lady's own name of Adelaide was, as well as the

surname conjoined with it, borne, to her knowledge, in Paris, by an extraordinary American specimen. She had then recrossed the Channel with a wonderful message, a courteous challenge, to her friend's duplicate, who had in turn granted through her every satisfaction. The duplicate had, in other words, bravely let Miss Wenham know exactly who she was. Miss Wenham, in whose personal tradition the flame of resentment appeared to have been reduced by time to the palest ashes—for whom, indeed, the story of the great schism was now but a legend only needing a little less dimness to make it romantic—Miss Wenham had promptly responded by a letter fragrant with the hope that old threads might be taken up. It was a relationship that they must puzzle out together, and she had earnestly sounded the other party to it on the subject of a possible visit. Addie had met her with a definite promise; she would come soon, she would come when free, she would come in July; but meanwhile she sent her deputy. Frank asked himself by what name she had described, by what character introduced him to Flickerbridge. He felt mainly, on the whole, as if he were going there to find out if he were engaged to her. He was at sea, really, now, as to which of the various views Addie herself took of it. To Miss Wenham she must definitely have taken one, and perhaps Miss Wenham would reveal it. This expectation was really his excuse for a possible indiscretion.

III

He was indeed to learn on arrival to what he had been committed; but that was for a while so much a part of his first general impression that the fact took time to detach itself, the first general impression demanding verily all his faculties of response. He almost felt, for a day or two, the victim of a practical joke, a gross abuse of confidence. He had presented him-

---

[2] Water-color.

self with the moderate amount of flutter involved in a sense of due preparation; but he had then found that, however primed with prefaces and prompted with hints, he had not been prepared at all. How *could* he be, he asked himself, for anything so foreign to his experience, so alien to his proper world, so little to be preconceived in the sharp north light of the newest impressionism, and yet so recognised, after all, really, in the event, so noted and tasted and assimilated? It was a case he would scarce have known how to describe—could doubtless have described best with a full, clean brush, supplemented by a play of gesture; for it was always his habit to see an occasion, of whatever kind, primarily as a picture, so that he might get it, as he was wont to say, so that he might keep it, well together. He had been treated of a sudden, in this adventure, to one of the sweetest, fairest, coolest impressions of his life—one, moreover, visibly, from the start, complete and homogeneous. Oh, it was *there*, if that was all one wanted of a thing! It was so "there" that, as had befallen him in Italy, in Spain, confronted at last, in dusky side-chapel or rich museum, with great things dreamed of or with greater ones unexpectedly presented, he had held his breath for fear of breaking the spell; had almost, from the quick impulse to respect, to prolong, lowered his voice and moved on tiptoe. Supreme beauty suddenly revealed is apt to strike us as a possible illusion, playing with our desire—instant freedom with it to strike us as a possible rashness.

This fortunately, however—and the more so as his freedom for the time quite left him—didn't prevent his hostess, the evening of his advent and while the vision was new, from being exactly as queer and rare and *impayable*,[3] as improbable, as impossible, as delightful at dinner at eight (she appeared to keep these immense hours) as she had overwhelmingly been at tea at five. She was in the most natural way in the world one of the oddest apparitions, but that the particular means to such an end

could be natural was an inference difficult to make. He failed in fact to make it for a couple of days; but then—though then only—he made it with confidence. By this time indeed he was sure of everything, including, luckily, himself. If we compare his impression, with slight extravagance, to some of the greatest he had ever received, this is simply because the image before him was so rounded and stamped. It expressed with pure perfection, it exhausted its character. It was so absolutely and so unconsciously what it was. He had been floated by the strangest of chances out of the rushing stream into a clear, still backwater—a deep and quiet pool in which objects were sharply mirrored. He had hitherto in life known nothing that was old except a few statues and pictures; but here everything was old, was immemorial, and nothing so much so as the very freshness itself. Vaguely to have supposed there were such nooks in the world had done little enough, he now saw, to temper the glare of their opposites. It was the fine touches that counted, and these had to be seen to be believed.

Miss Wenham, fifty-five years of age, and unappeasably timid, unaccountably strange, had, on her reduced scale, an almost Gothic grotesqueness; but the final effect of one's sense of it was an amenity that accompanied one's steps like wafted gratitude. More flurried, more spasmodic, more apologetic, more completely at a loss at one moment and more precipitately abounding at another, he had never before in all his days seen any maiden lady; yet for no maiden lady he had ever seen had he so promptly conceived a private enthusiasm. Her eyes protruded, her chin receded and her nose carried on in conversation a queer little independent motion. She wore on the top of her head an upright circular cap that made her resemble a caryatid disburdened, and on other parts of her person strange combinations of colours, stuffs, shapes, of metal, mineral

---

[3] Priceless.

and plant. The tones of her voice rose and fell, her facial convulsions, whether tending—one could scarce make out—to expression or *re*pression, succeeded each other by a law of their own; she was embarrassed at nothing and at everything, frightened at everything and at nothing, and she approached objects, subjects, the simplest questions and answers and the whole material of intercourse, either with the indirectness of terror or with the violence of despair. These things, none the less, her refinements of oddity and intensities of custom, her suggestion at once of conventions and simplicities, of ease and of agony, her roundabout, retarded suggestions and perceptions, still permitted her to strike her guest as irresistibly charming. He didn't know what to call it; she was a fruit of time. She had a queer distinction. She had been expensively produced, and there would be a good deal more of her to come.

The result of the whole quality of her welcome, at any rate, was that the first evening, in his room, before going to bed, he relieved his mind in a letter to Addie, which, if space allowed us to embody it in our text, would usefully perform the office of a "plate." It would enable us to present ourselves as profusely illustrated. But the process of reproduction, as we say, costs. He wished his friend to know how grandly their affair turned out. She had put him in the way of something absolutely special —an old house untouched, untouchable, indescribable, an old corner such as one didn't believe existed, and the holy calm of which made the chatter of studios, the smell of paint, the slang of critics, the whole sense and sound of Paris, come back as so many signs of a huge monkey-cage. He moved about, restless, while he wrote; he lighted cigarettes and, nervous and suddenly scrupulous, put them out again; the night was mild and one of the windows of his large high room, which stood over the garden, was up. He lost himself in the things about him, in the type of the room, the last century with not a chair moved, not a point stretched. He hung over the

objects and ornaments, blissfully few and adorably good, perfect pieces all, and never one, for a change, French. The scene was as rare as some fine old print with the best bits down in the corners. Old books and old pictures, allusions remembered and aspects conjectured, reappeared to him; he knew now what anxious islanders had been trying for in their backward hunt for the homely. But the homely at Flickerbridge was all style, even as style at the same time was mere honesty. The larger, the smaller past—he scarce knew which to call it—was at all events so hushed to sleep round him as he wrote that he had almost a bad conscience about having come. How one might love it, but how one might spoil it! To look at it too hard was positively to make it conscious, and to make it conscious was positively to wake it up. Its only safety, of a truth, was to be left still to sleep—to sleep in its large, fair chambers, and under its high, clean canopies.

He added thus restlessly a line to his letter, maundered round the room again, noted and fingered something else, and then, dropping on the old flowered sofa, sustained by the tight cubes of its cushions, yielded afresh to the cigarette, hesitated, stared, wrote a few words more. He wanted Addie to know, that was what he most felt, unless he perhaps felt more how much she herself would want to. Yes, what he supremely saw was all that Addie would make of it. Up to his neck in it there he fairly turned cold at the sense of suppressed opportunity, of the outrage of privation, that his correspondent would retrospectively and, as he even divined with a vague shudder, almost vindictively nurse. Well, what had happened was that the acquaintance had been kept for her, like a packet enveloped and sealed for delivery, till her attention was free. He saw her there, heard her and felt her—felt how she would feel and how she would, as she usually said, "rave." Some of her young compatriots called it "yell," and in the reference itself, alas! illustrated their meaning.

She would understand the place, at any rate, down to the ground; there wasn't the slightest doubt of that. Her sense of it would be exactly like his own, and he could see, in anticipation, just the terms of recognition and rapture in which she would abound. He knew just what she would call quaint, just what she would call bland, just what she would call weird, just what she would call wild. She would take it all in with an intelligence much more fitted than his own, in fact, to deal with what he supposed he must regard as its literary relations. She would have read the obsolete, long-winded memoirs and novels that both the figures and the setting ought clearly to remind one of; she would know about the past generations—the lumbering county magnates and their turbaned wives and round-eyed daughters, who, in other days, had treated the ruddy, sturdy, tradeless town, the solid square houses and wide, walled gardens, the streets to-day all grass and gossip, as the scene of a local "season." She would have warrant for the assemblies, dinners, deep potations; for the smoked sconces in the dusky parlours; for the long, muddy century of family coaches, "holsters," highwaymen. She would put a finger, in short, just as he had done, on the vital spot—the rich humility of the whole thing, the fact that neither Flickerbridge in general nor Miss Wenham in particular, nor anything nor anyone concerned, had a suspicion of their character and their merit. Addie and he would have to come to let in light.

He let it in then, little by little, before going to bed, through the eight or ten pages he addressed to her; assured her that it was the happiest case in the world, a little picture—yet full of "style" too—absolutely composed and transmitted, with tradition, and tradition only, in every stroke, tradition still noiselessly breathing and visibly flushing, marking strange hours in the tall mahogany clocks that were never wound up and that yet audibly ticked on. All the elements, he was sure he should see, would hang together with a charm, present-

ing his hostess—a strange iridescent fish for the glazed exposure of an aquarium—as floating in her native medium. He left his letter open on the table, but, looking it over next morning, felt of a sudden indisposed to send it. He would keep it to add more, for there would be more to know; yet when three days had elapsed he had still not sent it. He sent instead, after delay, a much briefer report, which he was moved to make different and, for some reason, less vivid. Meanwhile he learned from Miss Wenham how Addie had introduced him. It took time to arrive with her at that point, but after the Rubicon was crossed they went far afield.

IV

"Oh yes, she said you were engaged. That was why—since I *had* broken out so —she thought I would like to see you; as I assure you I've been so delighted to. But *aren't* you?" the good lady asked as if she saw in his face some ground for doubt.

"Assuredly—if she says so. It may seem very odd to you, but I haven't known, and yet I've felt that, being nothing whatever to you directly, I need some warrant for consenting thus to be thrust on you. We *were,*" the young man explained, "engaged a year ago; but since then (if you don't mind my telling you such things; I feel now as if I could tell you anything!) I haven't quite known how I stand. It hasn't seemed that we were in a position to marry. Things are better now, but I haven't quite known how she would see them. They were so bad six months ago that I understood her, I thought, as breaking off. I haven't broken; I've only accepted, for the time—because men must be easy with women—being treated as 'the best of friends.' Well, I try to be. I wouldn't have come here if I hadn't been. I thought it would be charming for her to know you—when I heard from her the extraordinary way you had dawned upon her, and charming therefore if I could help her to it. And if I'm help-

ing you to know *her*," he went on, "isn't
that charming too?"

"Oh, I so want to!" Miss Wenham murmured, in her unpractical, impersonal way.
"You're so different!" she wistfully declared.

"It's *you*, if I may respectfully, ecstatically say so, who are different. That's the
point of it all. I'm not sure that anything
so terrible really ought to happen to you
as to know us."

"Well," said Miss Wenham, "I do know
you a little, by this time, don't I? And I
don't find it terrible. It's a delightful
change for me."

"Oh, I'm not sure you ought to have a
delightful change!"

"Why not—if you do?"

"Ah, I can bear it. I'm not sure that
you can. I'm too bad to spoil—I *am*
spoiled. I'm nobody, in short; I'm nothing. I've no type. You're *all* type. It has
taken long, delicious years of security and
monotony to produce you. You fit your
frame with a perfection only equalled by
the perfection with which your frame fits
you. So this admirable old house, all time-
softened white within and time-faded red
without, so everything that surrounds you
here and that has, by some extraordinary
mercy, escaped the inevitable fate of exploitation: so it all, I say, is the sort
of thing that, if it were the least bit
to fall to pieces, could never, ah, never
more, be put together again. I have, dear
Miss Wenham," Granger went on, happy
himself in his extravagance, which was yet
all sincere, and happier still in her deep,
but altogether pleased mystification—"I've
found, do you know, just the thing one has
ever heard of that you most resemble.
You're the Sleeping Beauty in the wood."

He still had no compunction when he
heard her bewilderedly sigh: "Oh, you're
too delightfully droll!"

"No, I only put things just as they are,
and as I've also learned a little, thank
heaven, to see them—which isn't, I quite
agree with you, at all what anyone does.
You're in the deep doze of the spell that

has held you for long years, and it would
be a shame, a crime, to wake you up. Indeed I already feel, with a thousand scru-
ples, that I'm giving you the fatal shake.
I say it even though it makes me sound a
little as if I thought myself the fairy
prince."

She gazed at him with her queerest, kindest look, which he was getting used to, in
spite of a faint fear, at the back of his
head, of the strange things that sometimes
occurred when lonely ladies, however mature, began to look at interesting young
men from over the seas as if the young
men desired to flirt. "It's so wonderful,"
she said, "that you should be so very odd
and yet so very good-natured." Well, it
all came to the same thing—it was so wonderful that *she* should be so simple and yet
so little of a bore. He accepted with gratitude the theory of his languor—which
moreover was real enough and partly perhaps why he was so sensitive; he let himself go as a convalescent, let her insist on
the weakness that always remained after
fever. It helped him to gain time, to preserve the spell even while he talked of
breaking it; saw him through slow strolls
and soft sessions, long gossips, fitful, hopeless questions—there was so much more to
tell than, by any contortion, she *could*—
and explanations addressed gallantly and
patiently to her understanding, but not, by
good fortune, really reaching it. They were
perfectly at cross-purposes, and it was
all the better, and they wandered together
in the silver haze with all communication
blurred.

When they sat in the sun in her formal
garden he was quite aware that the tender-
est consideration failed to disguise his
treating her as the most exquisite of curiosities. The term of comparison most present to him was that of some obsolete musical instrument. The old-time order of her
mind and her air had the stillness of a
painted spinnet that was duly dusted,
gently rubbed, but never tuned nor played
on. Her opinions were like dried rose-
leaves; her attitudes like British sculpture;

her voice was what he imagined of the possible tone of the old gilded, silver-stringed harp in one of the corners of the drawing-room. The lonely little decencies and modest dignities of her life, the fine grain of its conservatism, the innocence of its ignorance, all its monotony of stupidity and salubrity, its cold dulness and dim brightness, were there before him. Meanwhile, within him, strange things took place. It was literally true that his impression began again, after a lull, to make him nervous and anxious, and for reasons peculiarly confused, almost grotesquely mingled, or at least comically sharp. He was distinctly an agitation and a new taste—that he could see; and he saw quite as much therefore the excitement she already drew from the vision of Addie, an image intensified by the sense of closer kinship and presented to her, clearly, with various erratic enhancements, by her friend the doctor's daughter. At the end of a few days he said to her: "Do you know she wants to come without waiting any longer? She wants to come while I'm here. I received this morning her letter proposing it, but I've been thinking it over and have waited to speak to you. The thing is, you see, that if she writes to *you* proposing it——"

"Oh, I shall be so particularly glad!"

V

They were, as usual, in the garden, and it had not yet been so present to him that if he were only a happy cad there would be a good way to protect her. As she wouldn't hear of his being yet beyond precautions she had gone into the house for a particular shawl that was just the thing for his knees, and, blinking in the watery sunshine, had come back with it across the fine little lawn. He was neither fatuous nor asinine, but he had almost to put it to himself as a small task to resist the sense of his absurd advantage with her. It filled him with horror and awkwardness, made him think of he didn't know what, re-

called something of Maupassant's—the smitten "Miss Harriet" and her tragic fate.[4] There was a preposterous possibility—yes, he held the strings quite in his hands—of keeping the treasure for himself. That was the art of life—what the real artist would consistently do. He would close the door on his impression, treat it as a private museum. He would see that he could lounge and linger there, live with wonderful things there, lie up there to rest and refit. For himself he was sure that after a little he should be able to paint there—do things in a key he had never thought of before. When she brought him the rug he took it from her and made her sit down on the bench and resume her knitting; then, passing behind her with a laugh, he placed it over her own shoulders; after which he moved to and fro before her, his hands in his pockets and his cigarette in his teeth. He was ashamed of the cigarette—a villainous false note; but she allowed, liked, begged him to smoke, and what he said to her on it, in one of the pleasantries she benevolently missed, was that he did so for fear of doing worse. That only showed that the end was really in sight. "I dare say it will strike you as quite awful, what I'm going to say to you, but I can't help it. I speak out of the depths of my respect for you. It will seem to you horrid disloyalty to poor Addie. Yes—there we are; there *I* am, at least, in my naked monstrosity." He stopped and looked at her till she might have been almost frightened. "Don't let her come. Tell her not to. I've tried to prevent it, but she suspects."

The poor woman wondered. "Suspects?"

"Well, I drew it, in writing to her, on reflection, as mild as I could—having been visited, in the watches of the night, by the instinct of what might happen. Something told me to keep back my first letter—in which, under the first impression, I myself rashly 'raved'; and I concocted instead of it

---

[4] This story by Guy de Maupassant, first published as "Miss Hastings" in 1883, was the title story of the volume *Miss Harriet*, Paris, 1884.

an insincere and guarded report. But guarded as I was I clearly didn't keep you 'down,' as we say, enough. The wonder of your colour—daub you over with grey as I might—must have come through and told the tale. She scents battle from afar—by which I mean she scents 'quaintness.' But keep her off. It's hideous, what I'm saying —but I owe it to you. I owe it to the world. She'll kill you."

"You mean I sha'n't get on with her?"

"Oh, fatally! See how *I* have. She's intelligent, remarkably pretty, remarkably good. And she'll adore you."

"Well then?"

"Why, that will be just how she'll do for you."

"Oh, I can hold my own!" said Miss Wenham with the head-shake of a horse making his sleigh-bells rattle in frosty air.

"Ah, but you can't hold hers! She'll rave about you. She'll write about you. You're Niagara before the first white traveller— and you know, or rather you can't know, what Niagara became *after* that gentleman. Addie will have discovered Niagara. She will understand you in perfection; she will feel you down to the ground; not a delicate shade of you will she lose or let anyone else lose. You'll be too weird for words, but the words will nevertheless come. You'll be too exactly the real thing and to be left too utterly just as you are, and all Addie's friends and all Addie's editors and contributors and readers will cross the Atlantic and flock to Flickerbridge, so, unanimously, universally, vociferously, to leave you. You'll be in the magazines with illustrations; you'll be in the papers with headings; you'll be everywhere with everything. You don't understand—you think you do, but you don't. Heaven forbid you *should* understand! That's just your beauty—your 'sleeping' beauty. But you needn't. You can take me on trust. Don't have her. Say, as a pretext, as a reason, anything in the world you like. Lie to her—scare her away. I'll go away and give you up—I'll sacrifice everything myself." Granger pursued his exhortation,

convincing himself more and more. "If I saw my way out, my way completely through, *I* would pile up some fabric of fiction for her—I should only want to be sure of its not tumbling down. One would have, you see, to keep the thing up. But I would throw dust in her eyes. I would tell her that you don't do at all—that you're not, in fact, a desirable acquaintance. I'd tell her you're vulgar, improper, scandalous; I'd tell her you're mercenary, designing, dangerous; I'd tell her the only safe course is immediately to let you drop. I would thus surround you with an impenetrable legend of conscientious misrepresentation, a circle of pious fraud, and all the while privately keep you for myself."

She had listened to him as if he were a band of music and she a small shy garden-party. "I shouldn't like you to go away. I shouldn't in the least like you not to come again."

"Ah, there it is!" he replied. "How can I come again if Addie ruins you?"

"But how will she ruin me—even if she does what you say? I know I'm too old to change and really much too queer to please in any of the extraordinary ways you speak of. If it's a question of quizzing me I don't think my cousin, or anyone else, will have quite the hand for it that *you* seem to have. So that if *you* haven't ruined me——!"

"But I *have*—that's just the point!" Granger insisted. "I've undermined you at least. I've left, after all, terribly little for Addie to do."

She laughed in queer tones. "Well, then, we'll admit that you've done everything but frighten me."

He looked at her with surpassing gloom. "No—that again is one of the most dreadful features. You'll positively like it— what's to come. You'll be caught up in a chariot of fire like the prophet—wasn't there, was there, one?—of old. That's exactly why—if one could but have done it —you would have been to be kept ignorant and helpless. There's something or other in Latin that says that it's the finest things that change the most easily for the worse. You already enjoy your dishonour and revel in your shame. It's too late—you're lost!"

VI

All this was as pleasant a manner of passing the time as any other, for it didn't prevent his old-world corner from closing round him more entirely, nor stand in the way of his making out, from day to day, some new source, as well as some new effect, of its virtue. He was really scared at moments at some of the liberties he took in talk—at finding himself so familiar; for the great note of the place was just that a certain modern ease had never crossed its threshold, that quick intimacies and quick oblivions were a stranger to its air. It had known, in all its days, no rude, no loud invasion. Serenely unconscious of most contemporary things, it had been so of nothing so much as of the diffused social practice of running in and out. Granger held his breath, on occasions, to think how Addie would run. There were moments when, for some reason, more than at others, he heard her step on the stair-case and her cry in the hall. If he played freely, none the less, with the idea with which we have shown him as occupied, it was not that in every measurable way he didn't sacrifice, to the utmost, to stillness. He only hovered, ever so lightly, to take up again his thread. She wouldn't hear of his leaving her, of his being in the least fit again, as she said, to travel. She spoke of the journey to London—which was in fact a matter of many hours—as an experiment fraught with lurking complications. He added then day to day, yet only hereby, as he reminded her, giving other complications a larger chance to multiply. He kept it before her, when there was nothing else to do, that she must consider; after which he had his times of fear that she perhaps really would make for him this sacrifice.

He knew that she had written again to Paris, and knew that he must himself again write—a situation abounding for each in the elements of a quandary. If he stayed so long, why then he wasn't better, and if he wasn't better Addie might take it into her head——! They must make it clear that he *was* better, so that, suspicious, alarmed at what was kept from her, she shouldn't suddenly present herself to nurse him. If he was better, however, why did he stay so long? If he stayed only for the attraction the sense of the attraction might be contagious. This was what finally grew clearest for him, so that he had for his mild disciple hours of still sharper prophecy. It consorted with his fancy to represent to her that their young friend had been by this time unsparingly warned; but nothing could be plainer than that this was ineffectual so long as he himself resisted the ordeal. To plead that he remained because he was too weak to move was only to throw themselves back on the other horn of their dilemma. If he was too weak to move Addie would bring him her strength—of which, when she got there, she would give them specimens enough. One morning he broke out at breakfast with an intimate conviction. They would see that she was actually starting—they would receive a wire by noon. They didn't receive it, but by his theory the portent was only the stronger. It had, moreover, its grave as well as its gay side, for Granger's paradox and pleasantry were only the most convenient way for him of saying what he felt. He literally heard the knell sound, and in expressing this to Miss Wenham with the conversational freedom that seemed best to pay his way he the more vividly faced the contingency. He could never return, and though he announced it with a despair that did what might be to make it pass as a joke, he saw that, whether or no she at last understood, she quite at last believed him. On this, to his knowledge, she wrote again to Addie, and the contents of her letter excited his curiosity. But that sentiment, though not assuaged, quite dropped when, the day after, in the evening, she let him know that she had had, an hour before, a telegram.

"She comes Thursday."

He showed not the least surprise. It was the deep calm of the fatalist. It *had* to be. "I must leave you then to-morrow."

She looked, on this, as he had never seen her; it would have been hard to say whether what was in her face was the last failure to follow or the first effort to meet. "And really not to come back?"

"Never, never, dear lady. Why should I come back? You can never be again what you *have* been. I shall have seen the last of you."

"Oh!" she touchingly urged.

"Yes, for I should next find you simply brought to self-consciousness. You'll be exactly what you are, I charitably admit—nothing more or less, nothing different. But you'll be it all in a different way. We live in an age of prodigious machinery, all organised to a single end. That end is publicity—a publicity as ferocious as the appetite of a cannibal. The thing therefore is not to have any illusions—fondly to flatter yourself, in a muddled moment, that the cannibal will spare you. He spares nobody. He spares nothing. It will be all right. You'll have a lovely time. You'll be only just a public character—blown about the world for all you are and proclaimed for all you are on the housetops. It will be for *that,* mind, I quite recognise—because Addie is superior—as well as for all you aren't. So good-bye."

He remained, however, till the next day, and noted at intervals the different stages of their friend's journey; the hour, this time, she would really have started, the hour she would reach Dover, the hour she would get to town, where she would alight at Mrs. Dunn's. Perhaps she would bring Mrs. Dunn, for Mrs. Dunn would swell the chorus. At the last, on the morrow, as if in anticipation of this, stillness settled between them; he became as silent as his hostess. But before he went she brought out, shyly and anxiously, as an appeal, the question that, for hours, had clearly been giving her thought. "Do you meet her then to-night in London?"

"Dear, no. In what position am I, alas! to do that? When can I *ever* meet her again?" He had turned it all over. "If I could meet Addie after this, you know, I could meet *you.* And if I do meet Addie," he lucidly pursued, "what will happen, by the same stroke, is that I *shall* meet you. And that's just what I've explained to you that I dread."

"You mean that she and I will be inseparable?"

He hesitated. "I mean that she'll tell me all about you. I can hear her, and her ravings, now."

She gave again—and it was infinitely sad—her little whinnying laugh. "Oh, but if what you say is true, you'll know."

"Ah, but Addie won't! Won't, I mean, know that *I* know—or at least won't believe it. Won't believe that anyone knows. Such," he added, with a strange, smothered sigh, "*is* Addie. Do you know," he wound up, "that what, after all, has most definitely happened is that you've made me see her as I've never done before?"

She blinked and gasped, she wondered and despaired. "Oh, no, it will be *you.* I've had nothing to do with it. Everything's *all* you!"

But for all it mattered now! "You'll see," he said, "that she's charming. I shall go, for to-night, to Oxford. I shall almost cross her on the way."

"Then, if she's charming, what am I to tell her from you in explanation of such strange behaviour as your flying away just as she arrives?"

"Ah, you needn't mind about that—you needn't tell her anything."

She fixed him as if as never again. "It's none of my business, of course I feel; but isn't it a little cruel if you're engaged?"

Granger gave a laugh almost as odd as one of her own. "Oh, you've cost me that!" and he put out his hand to her.

She wondered while she took it. "Cost you——?"

"We're not engaged. Good-bye."

THE BEAST IN THE JUNGLE
[1903]

I

WHAT determined the speech that startled him in the course of their encounter
scarcely matters, being probably but some
words spoken by himself quite without intention—spoken as they lingered and slowly moved together after their renewal of
acquaintance. He had been conveyed by
friends, an hour or two before, to the
house at which she was staying; the party
of visitors at the other house, of whom he
was one, and thanks to whom it was his
theory, as always, that he was lost in the
crowd, had been invited over to luncheon.
There had been after luncheon much dis-
persal, all in the interest of the original
motive, a view of Weatherend itself and
the fine things, intrinsic features, pictures,
heirlooms, treasures of all the arts, that
made the place almost famous; and the
great rooms were so numerous that guests
could wander at their will, hang back from
the principal group, and, in cases where
they took such matters with the last seriousness, give themselves up to mysterious
appreciations and measurements. There
were persons to be observed, singly or in
couples, bending toward objects in out-of-
the-way corners with their hands on their
knees and their heads nodding quite as with
the emphasis of an excited sense of smell.
When they were two they either mingled
their sounds of ecstasy or melted into
silences of even deeper import, so that
there were aspects of the occasion that
gave it for Marcher much the air of the
"look round," previous to a sale highly
advertised, that excites or quenches, as may
be, the dream of acquisition. The dream of
acquisition at Weatherend would have had
to be wild indeed, and John Marcher found
himself, among such suggestions, discon-
certed almost equally by the presence of
those who knew too much and by that of
those who knew nothing. The great rooms
caused so much poetry and history to

press upon him that he needed to wander
apart to feel in a proper relation with
them, though his doing so was not, as
happened, like the gloating of some of
his companions, to be compared to the
movements of a dog sniffing a cupboard.
It had an issue promptly enough in a direction that was not to have been calculated.

It led, in short, in the course of the
October afternoon, to his closer meeting
with May Bartram, whose face, a reminder,
yet not quite a remembrance, as they sat,
much separated, at a very long table, had
begun merely by troubling him rather
pleasantly. It affected him as the sequel of
something of which he had lost the beginning. He knew it, and for the time quite
welcomed it, as a continuation, but didn't
know what it continued, which was an
interest, or an amusement, the greater as
he was also somehow aware—yet without
a direct sign from her—that the young
woman herself had not lost the thread.
She had not lost it, but she wouldn't give it
back to him, he saw, without some putting
forth of his hand for it; and he not only
saw that, but saw several things more,
things odd enough in the light of the fact
that at the moment some accident of group-
ing brought them face to face he was
still merely fumbling with the idea that
any contact between them in the past
would have had no importance. If it had
had no importance he scarcely knew why
his actual impression of her should so
seem to have so much; the answer to
which, however, was that in such a life as
they all appeared to be leading for the
moment one could but take things as they
came. He was satisfied, without in the
least being able to say why, that this young
lady might roughly have ranked in the
house as a poor relation; satisfied also that
she was not there on a brief visit, but was
more or less a part of the establishment—
almost a working, a remunerated part.
Didn't she enjoy at periods a protection
that she paid for by helping, among other
services, to show the place and explain it,

deal with the tiresome people, answer questions about the dates of the buildings, the styles of the furniture, the authorship of the pictures, the favourite haunts of the ghost? It wasn't that she looked as if you could have given her shillings—it was impossible to look less so. Yet when she finally drifted toward him, distinctly handsome, though ever so much older—older than when he had seen her before—it might have been as an effect of her guessing that he had, within the couple of hours, devoted more imagination to her than to all the others put together, and had thereby penetrated to a kind of truth that the others were too stupid for. She *was* there on harder terms than anyone; she was there as a consequence of things suffered, in one way and another, in the interval of years; and she remembered him very much as she was remembered—only a good deal better.

By the time they at last thus came to speech they were alone in one of the rooms —remarkable for a fine portrait over the chimney-place—out of which their friends had passed, and the charm of it was that even before they had spoken they had practically arranged with each other to stay behind for talk. The charm, happily, was in other things too; it was partly in there being scarce a spot at Weatherend without something to stay behind for. It was in the way the autumn day looked into the high windows as it waned; in the way the red light, breaking at the close from under a low, sombre sky, reached out in a long shaft and played over old wainscots, old tapestry, old gold, old colour. It was most of all perhaps in the way she came to him as if, since she had been turned on to deal with the simpler sort, he might, should he choose to keep the whole thing down, just take her mild attention for a part of her general business. As soon as he heard her voice, however, the gap was filled up and the missing link supplied; the slight irony he divined in her attitude lost its advantage. He almost jumped at it to get there before her. "I met you years and years ago in Rome. I remember all about it." She confessed to disappointment —she had been so sure he didn't; and to prove how well he did he began to pour forth the particular recollections that popped up as he called for them. Her face and her voice, all at his service now, worked the miracle—the impression operating like the torch of a lamplighter who touches into flame, one by one, a long row of gas jets. Marcher flattered himself that the illumination was brilliant, yet he was really still more pleased on her showing him, with amusement, that in his haste to make everything right he had got most things rather wrong. It hadn't been at Rome—it had been at Naples; and it hadn't been seven years before—it had been more nearly ten. She hadn't been either with her uncle and aunt, but with her mother and her brother; in addition to which it was not with the Pembles that *he* had been, but with the Boyers, coming down in their company from Rome—a point on which she insisted, a little to his confusion, and as to which she had her evidence in hand. The Boyers she had known, but she didn't know the Pembles, though she had heard of them, and it was the people he was with who had made them acquainted. The incident of the thunderstorm that had raged round them with such violence as to drive them for refuge into an excavation—this incident had not occurred at the Palace of the Cæsars, but at Pompeii, on an occasion when they had been present there at an important find.

He accepted her amendments, he enjoyed her corrections, though the moral of them was, she pointed out, that he *really* didn't remember the least thing about her; and he only felt it as a drawback that when all was made conformable to the truth there didn't appear much of anything left. They lingered together still, she neglecting her office—for from the moment he was so clever she had no proper right to him—and both neglecting the house, just waiting as to see if a memory or two more wouldn't again breathe upon them. It had not taken them many minutes, after all, to put down on the table, like the cards of a pack, those that constituted their respective hands; only what came out was that the pack was unfortunately not perfect—that the past, invoked, invited, encouraged, could give them, naturally, no more than it had. It had made them meet—her at twenty, him at twenty-five; but nothing was so strange, they seemed to say to each other, as that, while so occupied, it hadn't done a little more for them. They looked at each other as with the feeling of an occasion missed; the present one would have been so much better if the other, in the far distance, in the foreign land, hadn't been so stupidly meagre. There weren't, apparently, all counted, more than a dozen little old things that had succeeded in coming to pass between them; trivialities of youth, simplicities of freshness, stupidities of ignorance, small possible germs, but too deeply buried —too deeply (didn't it seem?) to sprout after so many years. Marcher said to himself that he ought to have rendered her some service—saved her from a capsized boat in the Bay, or at least recovered her dressing-bag, filched from her cab, in the streets of Naples, by a lazzarone with a stiletto. Or it would have been nice if he could have been taken with fever, alone, at his hotel, and she could have come to look after him, to write to his people, to drive him out in convalescence. *Then* they would be in possession of the something or other that their actual show seemed to lack. It yet somehow presented itself, this show, as too good to be spoiled; so that they were reduced for a few minutes more to wondering a little helplessly why—since they seemed to know a certain number of the same people—their reunion had been so long averted. They didn't use that name for it, but their delay from minute to minute to join the others was a kind of confession that they didn't quite want it to be a failure. Their attempted supposition of reasons for their not having met but showed how little they knew of each other. There came in fact a moment when Marcher

felt a positive pang. It was vain to pretend she was an old friend, for all the communities were wanting, in spite of which it was as an old friend that he saw she would have suited him. He had new ones enough —was surrounded with them, for instance, at that hour at the other house; as a new one he probably wouldn't have so much as noticed her. He would have liked to invent something, get her to make-believe with him that some passage of a romantic or critical kind *had* originally occurred. He was really almost reaching out in imagination—as against time—for something that would do, and saying to himself that if it didn't come this new incident would simply and rather awkwardly close. They would separate, and now for no second or for no third chance. They would have tried and not succeeded. Then it was, just at the turn, as he afterwards made it out to himself, that, everything else failing, she herself decided to take up the case and, as it were, save the situation. He felt as soon as she spoke that she had been consciously keeping back what she said and hoping to get on without it; a scruple in her that immensely touched him when, by the end of three or four minutes more, he was able to measure it. What she brought out, at any rate, quite cleared the air and supplied the link—the link it was such a mystery he should frivolously have managed to lose.

"You know you told me something that I've never forgotten and that again and again has made me think of you since; it was that tremendously hot day when we went to Sorrento, across the bay, for the breeze. What I allude to was what you said to me, on the way back, as we sat, under the awning of the boat, enjoying the cool. Have you forgotten?"

He had forgotten, and he was even more surprised than ashamed. But the great thing was that he saw it was no vulgar reminder of any "sweet" speech. The vanity of women had long memories, but she was making no claim on him of a compliment or a mistake. With another woman, a totally different one, he might have feared the recall possibly even of some imbecile "offer." So, in having to say that he had indeed forgotten, he was conscious rather of a loss than of a gain; he already saw an interest in the matter of her reference. "I try to think—but I give it up. Yet I remember the Sorrento day."

"I'm not very sure you do," May Bartram after a moment said; "and I'm not very sure I ought to want you to. It's dreadful to bring a person back, at any time, to what he was ten years before. If you've lived away from it," she smiled, "so much the better."

"Ah, if you haven't why should I?" he asked.

"Lived away, you mean, from what I myself was?"

"From what I was. I was of course an ass," Marcher went on; "but I would rather know from you just the sort of ass I was than—from the moment you have something in your mind—not know anything."

Still, however, she hesitated. "But if you've completely ceased to be that sort——?"

"Why, I can then just so all the more bear to know. Besides, perhaps I haven't."

"Perhaps. Yet if you haven't," she added, "I should suppose you would remember. Not indeed that I in the least connect with my impression the invidious name you use. If I had only thought you foolish," she explained, "the thing I speak of wouldn't so have remained with me. It was about yourself." She waited, as if it might come to him; but as, only meeting her eyes in wonder, he gave no sign, she burnt her ships. "Has it ever happened?"

Then it was that, while he continued to stare, a light broke for him and the blood slowly came to his face, which began to burn with recognition. "Do you mean I told you——?" But he faltered, lest what came to him shouldn't be right, lest he should only give himself away.

"It was something about yourself that it was natural one shouldn't forget—that is if one remembered you at all. That's

why I ask you," she smiled, "if the thing you then spoke of has ever come to pass?"

Oh, then he saw, but he was lost in wonder and found himself embarrassed. This, he also saw, made her sorry for him, as if her allusion had been a mistake. It took him but a moment, however, to feel that it had not been, much as it had been a surprise. After the first little shock of it her knowledge on the contrary began, even if rather strangely, to taste sweet to him. She was the only other person in the world then who would have it, and she had had it all these years, while the fact of his having so breathed his secret had unaccountably faded from him. No wonder they couldn't have met as if nothing had happened. "I judge," he finally said, "that I know what you mean. Only I had strangely enough lost the consciousness of having taken you so far into my confidence."

"Is it because you've taken so many others as well?"

"I've taken nobody. Not a creature since then."

"So that I'm the only person who knows?"

"The only person in the world."

"Well," she quickly replied, "I myself have never spoken. I've never, never repeated of you what you told me." She looked at him so that he perfectly believed her. Their eyes met over it in such a way that he was without a doubt. "And I never will."

She spoke with an earnestness that, as if almost excessive, put him at ease about her possible derision. Somehow the whole question was a new luxury to him—that is, from the moment she was in possession. If she didn't take the ironic view she clearly took the sympathetic, and that was what he had had, in all the long time, from no one whomsoever. What he felt was that he couldn't at present have begun to tell her and yet could profit perhaps exquisitely by the accident of having done so of old. "Please don't then. We're just right as it is."

"Oh, I am," she laughed, "if you are!" To which she added: "Then you do still feel in the same way?"

It was impossible to him not to take to himself that she was really interested, and it all kept coming as a sort of revelation. He had thought of himself so long as abominably alone, and, lo, he wasn't alone a bit. He hadn't been, it appeared, for an hour—since those moments on the Sorrento boat. It was *she* who had been, he seemed to see as he looked at her—she who had been made so by the graceless fact of his lapse of fidelity. To tell her what he had told her—what had it been but to ask something of her? something that she had given, in her charity, without his having, by a remembrance, by a return of the spirit, failing another encounter, so much as thanked her. What he had asked of her had been simply at first not to laugh at him. She had beautifully not done so for ten years, and she was not doing so now. So he had endless gratitude to make up. Only for that he must see just how he had figured to her. "What, exactly, was the account I gave——?"

"Of the way you did feel? Well, it was very simple. You said you had had from your earliest time, as the deepest thing within you, the sense of being kept for something rare and strange, possibly prodigious and terrible, that was sooner or later to happen to you, that you had in your bones the foreboding and the conviction of, and that would perhaps overwhelm you."

"Do you call that very simple?" John Marcher asked.

She thought a moment. "It was perhaps because I seemed, as you spoke, to understand it."

"You do understand it?" he eagerly asked.

Again she kept her kind eyes on him. "You still have the belief?"

"Oh!" he exclaimed helplessly. There was too much to say.

"Whatever it is to be," she clearly made out, "it hasn't yet come."

He shook his head in complete surrender now. "It hasn't yet come. Only, you know, it isn't anything I'm to *do*, to achieve in the world, to be distinguished or admired for. I'm not such an ass as *that*. It would be much better, no doubt, if I were."

"It's to be something you're merely to suffer?"

"Well, say to wait for—to have to meet, to face, to see suddenly break out in my life; possibly destroying all further consciousness, possibly annihilating me; possibly, on the other hand, only altering everything, striking at the root of all my world and leaving me to the consequences, however they shape themselves."

She took this in, but the light in her eyes continued for him not to be that of mockery. "Isn't what you describe perhaps but the expectation—or, at any rate, the sense of danger, familiar to so many people—of falling in love?"

John Marcher thought. "Did you ask me that before?"

"No—I wasn't so free-and-easy then. But it's what strikes me now."

"Of course," he said after a moment, "it strikes you. Of course it strikes *me*. Of course what's in store for me may be no more than that. The only thing is," he went on, "that I think that if it had been that, I should by this time know."

"Do you mean because you've *been* in love?" And then as he but looked at her in silence: "You've been in love, and it hasn't meant such a cataclysm, hasn't proved the great affair?"

"Here I am, you see. It hasn't been overwhelming."

"Then it hasn't been love," said May Bartram.

"Well, I at least thought it was. I took it for that—I've taken it till now. It was agreeable, it was delightful, it was miserable," he explained. "But it wasn't strange. It wasn't what *my* affair's to be."

"You want something all to yourself—something that nobody else knows or *has* known?"

"It isn't a question of what I 'want'—

God knows I don't want anything. It's only a question of the apprehension that haunts me—that I live with day by day."

He said this so lucidly and consistently that, visibly, it further imposed itself. If she had not been interested before she would have been interested now. "Is it a sense of coming violence?"

Evidently now too, again, he liked to talk of it. "I don't think of it as—when it does come—necessarily violent. I only think of it as natural and as of course, above all, unmistakable. I think of it simply as *the* thing. *The* thing will of itself appear natural."

"Then how will it appear strange?"

Marcher bethought himself. "It won't—to *me*."

"To whom then?"

"Well," he replied, smiling at last, "say to you."

"Oh then, I'm to be present?"

"Why, you *are* present—since you know."

"I see." She turned it over. "But I mean at the catastrophe."

At this, for a minute, their lightness gave way to their gravity; it was as if the long look they exchanged held them together. "It will only depend on yourself—if you'll watch with me."

"Are you afraid?" she asked.

"Don't leave me *now*," he went on.

"Are you afraid?" she repeated.

"Do you think me simply out of my mind?" he pursued instead of answering. "Do I merely strike you as a harmless lunatic?"

"No," said May Bartram. "I understand you. I believe you."

"You mean you feel how my obsession —poor old thing!—may correspond to some possible reality?"

"To some possible reality."

"Then you *will* watch with me?"

She hesitated, then for the third time put her question. "Are you afraid?"

"Did I tell you I was—at Naples?"

"No, you said nothing about it."

"Then I don't know. And I should *like* to know," said John Marcher. "You'll tell me yourself whether you think so. If you'll watch with me you'll see."

"Very good then." They had been moving by this time across the room, and at the door, before passing out, they paused as if for the full wind-up of their understanding. "I'll watch with you," said May Bartram.

II

The fact that she "knew"—knew and yet neither chaffed him nor betrayed him—had in a short time begun to constitute between them a sensible bond, which became more marked when, within the year that followed their afternoon at Weatherend, the opportunities for meeting multiplied. The event that thus promoted these occasions was the death of the ancient lady, her great-aunt, under whose wing, since losing her mother, she had to such an extent found shelter, and who, though but the widowed mother of the new successor to the property, had succeeded—thanks to a high tone and a high temper—in not forfeiting the supreme position at the great house. The deposition of this personage arrived but with her death, which, followed by many changes, made in particular a difference for the young woman in whom Marcher's expert attention had recognised from the first a dependent with a pride that might ache though it didn't bristle. Nothing for a long time had made him easier than the thought that the aching must have been much soothed by Miss Bartram's now finding herself able to set up a small home in London. She had acquired property, to an amount that made that luxury just possible, under her aunt's extremely complicated will, and when the whole matter began to be straightened out, which indeed took time, she let him know that the happy issue was at last in view. He had seen her again before that day, both because she had more than once accompanied the ancient lady to town and because he had paid another visit to the friends who so conveniently made of Weatherend one of the charms of their own hospitality. These friends had taken him back there; he had achieved there again with Miss Bartram some quiet detachment; and he had in London succeeded in persuading her to more than one brief absence from her aunt. They went together, on these latter occasions, to the National Gallery and the South Kensington Museum, where, among vivid reminders, they talked of Italy at large—not now attempting to recover, as at first, the taste of their youth and their ignorance. That recovery, the first day at Weatherend, had served its purpose well, had given them quite enough; so that they were, to Marcher's sense, no longer hovering about the head-waters of their stream, but had felt their boat pushed sharply off and down the current.

They were literally afloat together; for our gentleman this was marked, quite as marked as that the fortunate cause of it was just the buried treasure of her knowledge. He had with his own hands dug up this little hoard, brought to light—that is to within reach of the dim day constituted by their discretions and privacies—the object of value the hiding-place of which he had, after putting it into the ground himself, so strangely, so long forgotten. The exquisite luck of having again just stumbled on the spot made him indifferent to any other question; he would doubtless have devoted more time to the odd accident of his lapse of memory if he had not been moved to devote so much to the sweetness, the comfort, as he felt, for the future, that this accident itself had helped to keep fresh. It had never entered into his plan that anyone should "know," and mainly for the reason that it was not in him to tell anyone. That would have been impossible, since nothing but the amusement of a cold world would have waited on it. Since, however, a mysterious fate had opened his mouth in youth, in spite of him, he would count that a compensation and profit by it to the utmost. That the right person *should* know tempered the

asperity of his secret more even than his shyness had permitted him to imagine; and May Bartram was clearly right, because—well, because there she was. Her knowledge simply settled it; he would have been sure enough by this time had she been wrong. There was that in his situation, no doubt, that disposed him too much to see her as a mere confidant, taking all her light for him from the fact—the fact only—of her interest in his predicament, from her mercy, sympathy, seriousness, her consent not to regard him as the funniest of the funny. Aware, in fine, that her price for him was just in her giving him this constant sense of his being admirably spared, he was careful to remember that she had, after all, also a life of her own, with things that might happen to *her,* things that in friendship one should likewise take account of. Something fairly remarkable came to pass with him, for that matter, in this connection—something represented by a certain passage of his consciousness, in the suddenest way, from one extreme to the other.

He had thought himself, so long as nobody knew, the most disinterested person in the world, carrying his concentrated burden, his perpetual suspense, ever so quietly, holding his tongue about it, giving others no glimpse of it nor of its effect upon his life, asking of them no allowance and only making on his side all those that were asked. He had disturbed nobody with the queerness of having to know a haunted man, though he had had moments of rather special temptation on hearing people say that they were "unsettled." If they were as unsettled as he was—he who had never been settled for an hour in his life—they would know what it meant. Yet it wasn't, all the same, for him to make them, and he listened to them civilly enough. This was why he had such good—though possibly such rather colourless—manners; this was why, above all, he could regard himself, in a greedy world, as decently—as, in fact, perhaps even a little sublimely—unselfish. Our point is accordingly that he valued this character quite sufficiently to measure his present danger of letting it lapse, against which he promised himself to be much on his guard. He was quite ready, none the less, to be selfish just a little, since, surely, no more charming occasion for it had come to him. "Just a little," in a word, was just as much as Miss Bartram, taking one day with another, would let him. He never would be in the least coercive, and he would keep well before him the lines on which consideration for her—the very highest—ought to proceed. He would thoroughly establish the heads under which her affairs, her requirements, her peculiarities—he went so far as to give them the latitude of that name—would come into their intercourse. All this naturally was a sign of how much he took the intercourse itself for granted. There was nothing more to be done about *that*. It simply existed; had sprung into being with her first penetrating question to him in the autumn light there at Weatherend. The real form it should have taken on the basis that stood out large was the form of their marrying. But the devil in this was that the very basis itself put marrying out of the question. His conviction, his apprehension, his obsession, in short, was not a condition he could invite a woman to share; and that consequence of it was precisely what was the matter with him. Something or other lay in wait for him, amid the twists and the turns of the months and the years, like a crouching beast in the jungle. It signified little whether the crouching beast were destined to slay him or to be slain. The definite point was the inevitable spring of the creature; and the definite lesson from that was that a man of feeling didn't cause himself to be accompanied by a lady on a tiger-hunt. Such was the image under which he had ended by figuring his life.

They had at first, none the less, in the scattered hours spent together, made no allusion to that view of it; which was a sign he was handsomely ready to give that he didn't expect, that he in fact didn't care always to be talking about it. Such a feature in one's outlook was really like a hump on one's back. The difference it made every minute of the day existed quite independently of discussion. One discussed, of course, *like* a hunchback, for there was always, if nothing else, the hunchback face. That remained, and she was watching him; but people watched best, as a general thing, in silence, so that such would be predominantly the manner of their vigil. Yet he didn't want, at the same time, to be solemn; solemn was what he imagined he too much tended to be with other people. The thing to be, with the one person who knew, was easy and natural—to make the reference rather than be seeming to avoid it, to avoid it rather than be seeming to make it, and to keep it, in any case, familiar, facetious even, rather than pedantic and portentous. Some such consideration as the latter was doubtless in his mind, for instance, when he wrote pleasantly to Miss Bartram that perhaps the great thing he had so long felt as in the lap of the gods was no more than this circumstance, which touched him so nearly, of her acquiring a house in London. It was the first allusion they had yet again made, needing any other hitherto so little; but when she replied, after having given him the news, that she was by no means satisfied with such a trifle, as the climax to so special a suspense, she almost set him wondering if she hadn't even a larger conception of singularity for him than he had for himself. He was at all events destined to become aware little by little, as time went by, that she was all the while looking at his life, judging it, measuring it, in the light of the thing she knew, which grew to be at last, with the consecration of the years, never mentioned between them save as "the real truth" about him. That had always been his own form of reference to it, but she adopted the form so quietly that, looking back at the end of a period, he knew there was no moment at which it was traceable that she had, as he might say, got inside his condition, or exchanged the attitude of beautifully indulging for that of still more beautifully believing him.

It was always open to him to accuse her of seeing him but as the most harmless of maniacs, and this, in the long run—since it covered so much ground—was his easiest description of their friendship. He had a screw loose for her, but she liked him in spite of it, and was practically, against the rest of the world, his kind, wise keeper, unremunerated, but fairly amused and, in the absence of other near ties, not disreputably occupied. The rest of the world of course thought him queer, but she, she only, knew how, and above all why, queer; which was precisely what enabled her to dispose the concealing veil in the right folds. She took his gaiety from him—since it had to pass with them for gaiety —as she took everything else; but she certainly so far justified by her unerring touch his finer sense of the degree to which he had ended by convincing her. *She* at least never spoke of the secret of his life except as "the real truth about you," and she had in fact a wonderful way of making it seem, as such, the secret of her own life too. That was in fine how he so constantly felt her as allowing for him; he couldn't on the whole call it anything else. He allowed for himself, but she, exactly, allowed still more; partly because, better placed for a sight of the matter, she traced his unhappy perversion through portions of its course into which he could scarce follow it. He knew how he felt, but, besides knowing that, she knew how he *looked* as well; he knew each of the things of importance he was insidiously kept from doing, but she could add up the amount they made, understand how much, with a lighter weight on his spirit, he might have done, and thereby establish how, clever as he was, he fell short. Above all she was in the secret of the difference between the forms he went through—those of his little office under Government, those of caring for his modest patrimony, for his library, for his garden in the country, for the people in London whose invitations he

accepted and repaid—and the detachment that reigned beneath them and that made of all behaviour, all that could in the least be called behaviour, a long act of dissimulation. What it had come to was that he wore a mask painted with the social simper, out of the eye-holes of which there looked eyes of an expression not in the least matching the other features. This the stupid world, even after years, had never more than half discovered. It was only May Bartram who had, and she achieved, by an art indescribable, the feat of at once —or perhaps it was only alternately— meeting the eyes from in front and mingling her own vision, as from over his shoulder, with their peep through the apertures.

So, while they grew older together, she did watch with him, and so she let this association give shape and colour to her own existence. Beneath *her* forms as well detachment had learned to sit, and behaviour had become for her, in the social sense, a false account of herself. There was but one account of her that would have been true all the while, and that she could give, directly, to nobody, least of all to John Marcher. Her whole attitude was a virtual statement, but the perception of that only seemed destined to take its place for him as one of the many things necessarily crowded out of his consciousness. If she had, moreover, like himself, to make sacrifices to their real truth, it was to be granted that her compensation might have affected her as more prompt and more natural. They had long periods, in this London time, during which, when they were together, a stranger might have listened to them without in the least pricking up his ears; on the other hand, the real truth was equally liable at any moment to rise to the surface, and the auditor would then have wondered indeed what they were talking about. They had from an early time made up their mind that society was, luckily, unintelligent, and the margin that this gave them had fairly become one of their commonplaces. Yet there were still moments when the situation turned almost fresh—usually under the effect of some expression drawn from herself. Her expressions doubtless repeated themselves, but her intervals were generous. "What saves us, you know, is that we answer so completely to so usual an appearance: that of the man and woman whose friendship has become such a daily habit, or almost, as to be at last indispensable." That, for instance, was a remark she had frequently enough had occasion to make, though she had given it at different times different developments. What we are especially concerned with is the turn it happened to take from her one afternoon when he had come to see her in honour of her birthday. This anniversary had fallen on a Sunday, at a season of thick fog and general outward gloom; but he had brought her his customary offering, having known her now long enough to have established a hundred little customs. It was one of his proofs to himself, the present he made her on her birthday, that he had not sunk into real selfishness. It was mostly nothing more than a small trinket, but it was always fine of its kind, and he was regularly careful to pay for it more than he thought he could afford. "Our habit saves you, at least, don't you see? because it makes you, after all, for the vulgar, indistinguishable from other men. What's the most inveterate mark of men in general? Why, the capacity to spend endless time with dull women—to spend it, I won't say without being bored, but without minding that they are, without being driven off at a tangent by it; which comes to the same thing. I'm your dull woman, a part of the daily bread for which you pray at church. That covers your tracks more than anything."

"And what covers yours?" asked Marcher, whom his dull woman could mostly to this extent amuse. "I see of course what you mean by your saving me, in one way and another, so far as other people are concerned—I've seen it all along. Only, what is it that saves you? I often think, you know, of that."

She looked as if she sometimes thought of that too, but in rather a different way. "Where other people, you mean, are concerned?"

"Well, you're really so in with me, you know—as a sort of result of my being so in with yourself. I mean of my having such an immense regard for you, being so tremendously grateful for all you've done for me. I sometimes ask myself if it's quite fair. Fair I mean to have so involved and —since one may say it—interested you. I almost feel as if you hadn't really had time to do anything else."

"Anything else but be interested?" she asked. "Ah, what else does one ever want to be? If I've been 'watching' with you, as we long ago agreed that I was to do, watching is always in itself an absorption."

"Oh, certainly," John Marcher said, "if you hadn't had your curiosity——! Only, doesn't it sometimes come to you, as time goes on, that your curiosity is not being particularly repaid?"

May Bartram had a pause. "Do you ask that, by any chance, because you feel at all that yours isn't? I mean because you have to wait so long."

Oh, he understood what she meant. "For the thing to happen that never does happen? For the beast to jump out? No, I'm just where I was about it. It isn't a matter as to which I can *choose*, I can decide for a change. It isn't one as to which there *can* be a change. It's in the lap of the gods. One's in the hands of one's law—there one is. As to the form the law will take, the way it will operate, that's its own affair."

"Yes," Miss Bartram replied; "of course one's fate is coming, of course it *has* come, in its own form and its own way, all the while. Only, you know, the form and the way in your case were to have been—well, something so exceptional and, as one may say, so particularly *your* own."

Something in this made him look at her with suspicion. "You say 'were to *have* been,' as if in your heart you had begun to doubt."

"Oh!" she vaguely protested.

"As if you believed," he went on, "that nothing will now take place."

She shook her head slowly, but rather inscrutably. "You're far from my thought."

He continued to look at her. "What then is the matter with you?"

"Well," she said after another wait, "the matter with me is simply that I'm more sure than ever my curiosity, as you call it, will be but too well repaid."

They were frankly grave now; he had got up from his seat; had turned once more about the little drawing-room to which, year after year, he brought his inevitable topic; in which he had, as he might have said, tasted their intimate community with every sauce, where every object was as familiar to him as the things of his own house and the very carpets were worn with his fitful walk very much as the desks in old counting-houses are worn by the elbows of generations of clerks. The generations of his nervous moods had been at work there, and the place was the written history of his whole middle life. Under the impression of what his friend had just said he knew himself, for some reason, more aware of these things, which made him, after a moment, stop again before her. "Is it, possibly, that you've grown afraid?"

"Afraid?" He thought, as she repeated the word, that his question had made her, a little, change colour; so that, lest he should have touched on a truth, he explained very kindly. "You remember that that was what you asked *me* long ago—that first day at Weatherend."

"Oh yes, and you told me you didn't know—that I was to see for myself. We've said little about it since, even in so long a time."

"Precisely," Marcher interposed—"quite as if it were too delicate a matter for us to make free with. Quite as if we might find, on pressure, that I *am* afraid. For then," he said, "we shouldn't, should we? quite know what to do."

She had for the time no answer to this question. "There have been days when I

thought you were. Only, of course," she added, "there have been days when we have thought almost anything."

"Everything. Oh!" Marcher softly groaned as with a gasp, half spent, at the face, more uncovered just then than it had been for a long while, of the imagination always with them. It had always had its incalculable moments of glaring out, quite as with the very eyes of the very Beast, and, used as he was to them, they could still draw from him the tribute of a sigh that rose from the depths of his being. All that they had thought, first and last, rolled over him; the past seemed to have been reduced to mere barren speculation. This in fact was what the place had just struck him as so full of—the simplification of everything but the state of suspense. That remained only by seeming to hang in the void surrounding it. Even his original fear, if fear it had been, had lost itself in the desert. "I judge, however," he continued, "that you see I'm not afraid now."

"What I see is, as I make it out, that you've achieved something almost unprecedented in the way of getting used to danger. Living with it so long and so closely, you've lost your sense of it; you know it's there, but you're indifferent, and you cease even, as of old, to have to whistle in the dark. Considering what the danger is," May Bartram wound up, "I'm bound to say that I don't think your attitude could well be surpassed."

John Marcher faintly smiled. "It's heroic?"

"Certainly—call it that."

He considered. "I *am*, then, a man of courage?"

"That's what you were to show me."

He still, however, wondered. "But doesn't the man of courage know what he's afraid of—or *not* afraid of? I don't know *that*, you see. I don't focus it. I can't name it. I only know I'm exposed."

"Yes, but exposed—how shall I say?—so directly. So intimately. That's surely enough."

"Enough to make you feel, then—as what we may call the end of our watch—that I'm not afraid?"

"You're not afraid. But it isn't," she said, "the end of our watch. That is, it isn't the end of yours. You've everything still to see."

"Then why haven't *you?*" he asked. He had had, all along, to-day, the sense of her keeping something back, and he still had it. As this was his first impression of that, it made a kind of date. The case was the more marked as she didn't at first answer; which in turn made him go on. "You know something I don't." Then his voice, for that of a man of courage, trembled a little. "You know what's to happen." Her silence, with the face she showed, was almost a confession—it made him sure. "You know, and you're afraid to tell me. It's so bad that you're afraid I'll find out."

All this might be true, for she did look as if, unexpectedly to her, he had crossed some mystic line that she had secretly drawn round her. Yet she might, after all, not have worried; and the real upshot was that he himself, at all events, needn't. "You'll never find out."

III

It was all to have made, none the less, as I have said, a date; as came out in the fact that again and again, even after long intervals, other things that passed between them wore, in relation to this hour, but the character of recalls and results. Its immediate effect had been indeed rather to lighten insistence—almost to provoke a reaction; as if their topic had dropped by its own weight and as if moreover, for that matter, Marcher had been visited by one of his occasional warnings against egotism. He had kept up, he felt, and very decently on the whole, his consciousness of the importance of not being selfish, and it was true that he had never sinned in that direction without promptly enough trying to press the scales the other way. He often

repaired his fault, the season permitting, by inviting his friend to accompany him to the opera; and it not infrequently thus happened that, to show he didn't wish her to have but one sort of food for her mind, he was the cause of her appearing there with him a dozen nights in the month. It even happened that, seeing her home at such times, he occasionally went in with her to finish, as he called it, the evening, and, the better to make his point, sat down to the frugal but always careful little supper that awaited his pleasure. His point was made, he thought, by his not eternally insisting with her on himself; made for instance, at such hours, when it befell that, her piano at hand and each of them familiar with it, they went over passages of the opera together. It chanced to be on one of these occasions, however, that he reminded her of her not having answered a certain question he had put to her during the talk that had taken place between them on her last birthday. "What is it that saves *you?*"—saved her, he meant, from that appearance of variation from the usual human type. If he had practically escaped remark, as she pretended, by doing, in the most important particular, what most men do—find the answer to life in patching up an alliance of a sort with a woman no better than himself—how had she escaped it, and how could the alliance, such as it was, since they must suppose it had been more or less noticed, have failed to make her rather positively talked about?

"I never said," May Bartram replied, "that it hadn't made me talked about."

"Ah well then, you're not 'saved.'"

"It has not been a question for me. If you've had your woman, I've had," she said, "my man."

"And you mean that makes you all right?"

She hesitated. "I don't know why it shouldn't make me—humanly, which is what we're speaking of—as right as it makes you."

"I see," Marcher returned. " 'Humanly,'

no doubt, as showing that you're living for something. Not, that is, just for me and my secret."

May Bartram smiled. "I don't pretend it exactly shows that I'm not living for you. It's my intimacy with you that's in question."

He laughed as he saw what she meant. "Yes, but since, as you say, I'm only, so far as people make out, ordinary, you're —aren't you?—no more than ordinary either. You help me to pass for a man like another. So if I *am*, as I understand you, you're not compromised. Is that it?"

She had another hesitation, but she spoke clearly enough. "That's it. It's all that concerns me—to help you to pass for a man like another."

He was careful to acknowledge the remark handsomely. "How kind, how beautiful, you are to me! How shall I ever repay you?"

She had her last grave pause, as if there might be a choice of ways. But she chose. "By going on as you are."

It was into this going on as he was that they relapsed, and really for so long a time that the day inevitably came for a further sounding of their depths. It was as if these depths, constantly bridged over by a structure that was firm enough in spite of its lightness and of its occasional oscillation in the somewhat vertiginous air, invited on occasion, in the interest of their nerves, a dropping of the plummet and a measurement of the abyss. A difference had been made moreover, once for all, by the fact that she had, all the while, not appeared to feel the need of rebutting his charge of an idea within her that she didn't dare to express, uttered just before one of the fullest of their later discussions ended. It had come up for him then that she "knew" something and that what she knew was bad—too bad to tell him. When he had spoken of it as visibly so bad that she was afraid he might find it out, her reply had left the matter too equivocal to be let alone and yet, for Marcher's special sensibility, almost too formidable again to

touch. He circled about it at a distance that alternately narrowed and widened and that yet was not much affected by the consciousness in him that there was nothing she could "know," after all, any better than he did. She had no source of knowledge that he hadn't equally—except of course that she might have finer nerves. That was what women had where they were interested; they made out things, where people were concerned, that the people often couldn't have made out for themselves. Their nerves, their sensibility, their imagination, were conductors and revealers, and the beauty of May Bartram was in particular that she had given herself so to his case. He felt in these days what, oddly enough, he had never felt before, the growth of a dread of losing her by some catastrophe—some catastrophe that yet wouldn't at all be *the* catastrophe: partly because she had, almost of a sudden, begun to strike him as useful to him as never yet, and partly by reason of an appearance of uncertainty in her health, coincident and equally new. It was characteristic of the inner detachment he had hitherto so successfully cultivated and to which our whole account of him is a reference, it was characteristic that his complications, such as they were, had never yet seemed so as at this crisis to thicken about him, even to the point of making him ask himself if he were, by any chance, of a truth, within sight or sound, within touch or reach, within the immediate jurisdiction of the thing that waited.

When the day came, as come it had to, that his friend confessed to him her fear of a deep disorder in her blood, he felt somehow the shadow of a change and the chill of a shock. He immediately began to imagine aggravations and disasters, and above all to think of her peril as the direct menace for himself of personal privation. This indeed gave him one of those partial recoveries of equanimity that were agreeable to him—it showed him that what was still first in his mind was the loss she herself might suffer. "What if she should have to die before knowing, before seeing——?" It would have been brutal, in the early stages of her trouble, to put that question to her; but it had immediately sounded for him to his own concern, and the possibility was what most made him sorry for her. If she did "know," moreover, in the sense of her having had some—what should he think? —mystical, irresistible light, this would make the matter not better, but worse, in-asmuch as her original adoption of his own curiosity had quite become the basis of her life. She had been living to see what would *be* to be seen, and it would be cruel to her to have to give up before the accomplish-ment of the vision. These reflections, as I say, refreshed his generosity; yet, make them as he might, he saw himself, with the lapse of the period, more and more discon-certed. It lapsed for him with a strange, steady sweep, and the oddest oddity was that it gave him, independently of the threat of much inconvenience, almost the only positive surprise his career, if career it could be called, had yet offered him. She kept the house as she had never done; he had to go to her to see her—she could meet him nowhere now, though there was scarce a corner of their loved old London in which she had not in the past, at one time or another, done so; and he found her always seated by her fire in the deep, old-fash-ioned chair she was less and less able to leave. He had been struck one day, after an absence exceeding his usual measure, with her suddenly looking much older to him than he had ever thought of her be-ing; then he recognised that the sudden-ness was all on his side—he had just been suddenly struck. She looked older because inevitably, after so many years, she *was* old, or almost; which was of course true in still greater measure of her companion. If she was old, or almost, John Marcher as-suredly was, and yet it was her showing of the lesson, not his own, that brought the truth home to him. His surprises began here; when once they had begun they multiplied; they came rather with a rush: it was as if, in the oddest way in the world, they had all been kept back, sown in a thick cluster, for the late afternoon of life, the time at which, for people in general, the unexpected has died out.

One of them was that he should have caught himself—for he *had* so done—*really* wondering if the great accident would take form now as nothing more than his being condemned to see this charming woman, this admirable friend, pass away from him. He had never so unreservedly qualified her as while confronted in thought with such a possibility; in spite of which there was small doubt for him that as an answer to his long riddle the mere effacement of even so fine a feature of his situation would be an abject anticlimax. It would repre-sent, as connected with his past attitude, a drop of dignity under the shadow of which his existence could only become the most grotesque of failures. He had been far from holding it a failure—long as he had waited for the appearance that was to make it a success. He had waited for a quite other thing, not for such a one as that. The breath of his good faith came short, however, as he recognised how long he had waited, or how long, at least, his companion had. That she, at all events, might be recorded as having waited in vain —this affected him sharply, and all the more because of his at first having done little more than amuse himself with the idea. It grew more grave as the gravity of her condition grew, and the state of mind it produced in him, which he ended by watching, himself, as if it had been some definite disfigurement of his outer person, may pass for another of his surprises. This conjoined itself still with another, the really stupefying consciousness of a ques-tion that he would have allowed to shape itself had he dared. What did everything mean—what, that is, did *she* mean, she and her vain waiting and her probable death and the soundless admonition of it all—unless that, at this time of day, it was simply, it was overwhelmingly too late? He had never, at any stage of his queer consciousness, admitted the whisper of such a correction; he had never, till within these last few months, been so false to his conviction as not to hold that what was to come to him had time, whether *he* struck himself as having it or not. That at last, at last, he certainly hadn't it, to speak of, or had it but in the scantiest measure—such, soon enough, as things went with him, became the inference with which his old obsession had to reckon: and this it was not helped to do by the more and more confirmed appearance that the great vagueness casting the long shadow in which he had lived had, to attest itself, almost no margin left. Since it was in Time that he was to have met his fate, so it was in Time that his fate was to have acted; and as he waked up to the sense of no longer being young, which was exactly the sense of being stale, just as that, in turn, was the sense of being weak, he waked up to another matter beside. It all hung together; they were subject, he and the great vagueness, to an equal and indivisible law. When the possibilities themselves had, accordingly, turned stale, when the secret of the gods had grown faint, had perhaps even quite evaporated, that, and that only, was failure. It wouldn't have been failure to be bankrupt, dishonoured, pilloried, hanged; it was failure not to be anything. And so, in the dark valley into which his path had taken its unlooked-for twist, he wondered not a little as he groped. He didn't care what awful crash might overtake him, with what ignominy or what monstrosity he might yet be associated—since he wasn't, after all, too utterly old to suffer—if it would only be decently proportionate to the posture he had kept, all his life, in the promised presence of it. He had but one desire left—that he shouldn't have been "sold."

IV

Then it was that one afternoon, while the spring of the year was young and new, she met, all in her own way, his frankest betrayal of these alarms. He had gone in late to see her, but evening had not settled, and she was presented to him in that long, fresh light of waning April days which affects us often with a sadness sharper than the greyest hours of autumn. The week had been warm, the spring was supposed to have begun early, and May Bartram sat, for the first time in the year, without a fire, a fact that, to Marcher's sense, gave the scene of which she formed part a smooth and ultimate look, an air of knowing, in its immaculate order and its cold, meaningless cheer, that it would never see a fire again. Her own aspect—he could scarce have said why—intensified this note. Almost as white as wax, with the marks and signs in her face as numerous and as fine as if they had been etched by a needle, with soft white draperies relieved by a faded green scarf, the delicate tone of which had been consecrated by the years, she was the picture of a serene, exquisite, but impenetrable sphinx, whose head, or indeed all whose person, might have been powdered with silver. She was a sphinx, yet with her white petals and green fronds she might have been a lily too—only an artificial lily, wonderfully imitated and constantly kept, without dust or stain, though not exempt from a slight droop and a complexity of faint creases, under some clear glass bell. The perfection of household care, of high polish and finish, always reigned in her rooms, but they especially looked to Marcher at present as if everything had been wound up, tucked in, put away, so that she might sit with folded hands and with nothing more to do. She was "out of it," to his vision; her work was over; she communicated with him as across some gulf, or from some island of rest that she had already reached, and it made him feel strangely abandoned. Was it—or, rather, wasn't it—that if for so long she had been watching with him the answer to their question had swum into her ken and taken on its name, so that her occupation was verily gone? He had as much as charged her with this in saying to her, many months before, that she even then knew something she was keeping from him. It was a point he had never since ventured to press, vaguely fearing, as he did, that it might become a difference, perhaps a disagreement, between them. He had in short, in this later time, turned nervous, which was what, in all the other years, he had never been; and the oddity was that his nervousness should have waited till he had begun to doubt, should have held off so long as he was sure. There was something, it seemed to him, that the wrong word would bring down on his head, something that would so at least put an end to his suspense. But he wanted not to speak the wrong word; that would make everything ugly. He wanted the knowledge he lacked to drop on him, if drop it could, by its own august weight. If she was to forsake him it was surely for her to take leave. This was why he didn't ask her again, directly, what she knew; but it was also why, approaching the matter from another side, he said to her in the course of his visit: "What do you regard as the very worst that, at this time of day, *can* happen to me?"

He had asked her that in the past often enough; they had, with the odd, irregular rhythm of their intensities and avoidances, exchanged ideas about it and then had seen the ideas washed away by cool intervals, washed like figures traced in sea-sand. It had ever been the mark of their talk that the oldest allusions in it required but a little dismissal and reaction to come out again, sounding for the hour as new. She could thus at present meet his inquiry quite freshly and patiently. "Oh, yes, I've repeatedly thought, only it always seemed to me of old that I couldn't quite make up my mind. I thought of dreadful things, between which it was difficult to choose; and so must you have done."

"Rather! I feel now as if I had scarce done anything else. I appear to myself to have spent my life in thinking of nothing

but dreadful things. A great many of them I've at different times named to you, but there were others I couldn't name."

"They were too, too dreadful?"

"Too, too dreadful—some of them."

She looked at him a minute, and there came to him as he met it an inconsequent sense that her eyes, when one got their full clearness, were still as beautiful as they had been in youth, only beautiful with a strange, cold light—a light that somehow was a part of the effect, if it wasn't rather a part of the cause, of the pale, hard sweetness of the season and the hour. "And yet," she said at last, "there are horrors we have mentioned."

It deepened the strangeness to see her, as such a figure in such a picture, talk of "horrors," but she was to do, in a few minutes, something stranger yet—though even of this he was to take the full measure but afterwards—and the note of it was already in the air. It was, for the matter of that, one of the signs that her eyes were having again such a high flicker of their prime. He had to admit, however, what she said. "Oh yes, there were times when we did go far." He caught himself in the act, speaking as if it all were over. Well, he wished it were; and the consummation depended, for him, clearly, more and more on his companion.

But she had now a soft smile. "Oh, far——!"

It was oddly ironic. "Do you mean you're prepared to go further?"

She was frail and ancient and charming as she continued to look at him, yet it was rather as if she had lost the thread. "Do you consider that we went so far?"

"Why, I thought it the point you were just making—that we *had* looked most things in the face."

"Including each other?" She still smiled. "But you're quite right. We've had together great imaginations, often great fears; but some of them have been unspoken."

"Then the worst—we haven't faced that.

I *could* face it, I believe, if I knew what you think it. I feel," he explained, "as if I had lost my power to conceive such things." And he wondered if he looked as blank as he sounded. "It's spent."

"Then why do you assume," she asked, "that mine isn't?"

"Because you've given me signs to the contrary. It isn't a question for you of conceiving, imagining, comparing. It isn't a question now of choosing." At last he came out with it. "You know something that I don't. You've showed me that before."

These last words affected her, he could see ·in a moment, remarkably, and she spoke with firmness. "I've shown you, my dear, nothing."

He shook his head. "You can't hide it."

"Oh, oh!" May Bartram murmured over what she couldn't hide. It was almost a smothered groan.

"You admitted it months ago, when I spoke of it to you as of something you were afraid I would find out. Your answer was that I couldn't, that I wouldn't, and I don't pretend I have. But you had something therefore in mind, and I see now that it must have been, that it still is, the possibility that, of all possibilities, has settled itself for you as the worse. This," he went on, "is why I appeal to you. I'm only afraid of ignorance now—I'm not afraid of knowledge." And then as for a while she said nothing: "What makes me sure is that I see in your face and feel here, in this air and amid these appearances, that you're out of it. You've done. You've had your experience. You leave me to my fate."

Well, she listened, motionless and white in her chair, as if she had in fact a decision to make, so that her whole manner was a virtual confession, though still with a small, fine, inner stiffness, an imperfect surrender. "It *would* be the worst," she finally let herself say. "I mean the thing that I've never said."

It hushed him a moment. "More mon-strous than all the monstrosities we've named?"

"More monstrous. Isn't that what you sufficiently express," she asked, "in calling it the worst?"

Marcher thought. "Assuredly—if you mean, as I do, something that includes all the loss and all the shame that are think-able."

"It would if it *should* happen," said May Bartram. "What we're speaking of, remember, is only my idea."

"It's your belief," Marcher returned. "That's enough for me. I feel your beliefs are right. Therefore if, having this one, you give me no more light on it, you abandon me."

"No, no!" she repeated. "I'm with you—don't you see?—still." And as if to make it more vivid to him she rose from her chair—a movement she seldom made in these days—and showed herself, all draped and all soft, in her fairness and slimness. "I haven't forsaken you."

It was really, in its effort against weakness, a generous assurance, and had the success of the impulse not, happily, been great, it would have touched him to pain more than to pleasure. But the cold charm in her eyes had spread, as she hovered before him, to all the rest of her person, so that it was, for the minute, almost like a recovery of youth. He couldn't pity her for that; he could only take her as she showed—as capable still of helping him. It was as if, at the same time, her light might at any instant go out; wherefore he must make the most of it. There passed before him with intensity the three or four things he wanted most to know; but the question that came of itself to his lips really covered the others. "Then tell me if I shall consciously suffer."

She promptly shook her head. "Never!"

It confirmed the authority he imputed to her, and it produced on him an extraordinary effect. "Well, what's better than that? Do you call that the worst?"

"You think nothing is better?" she asked.

She seemed to mean something so special that he again sharply wondered, though still with the dawn of a prospect of relief. "Why not, if one doesn't *know?*" After which, as their eyes, over his question, met in a silence, the dawn deepened and something to his purpose came, prodigiously, out of her very face. His own, as he took it in, suddenly flushed to the forehead, and he gasped with the force of a perception to which, on the instant, everything fitted. The sound of his gasp filled the air; then he became articulate. "I see—if I don't suffer!"

In her own look, however, was doubt. "You see what?"

"Why, what you mean—what you've always meant."

She again shook her head. "What I mean isn't what I've always meant. It's different."

"It's something new?"

She hesitated. "Something new. It's not what you think. I see what you think."

His divination drew breath then; only her correction might be wrong. "It isn't that I *am* a donkey?" he asked between faintness and grimness. "It isn't that it's all a mistake?"

"A mistake?" she pityingly echoed. *That* possibility, for her, he saw, would be monstrous; and if she guaranteed him the immunity from pain it would accordingly not be what she had in mind. "Oh, no," she declared; "it's nothing of that sort. You've been right."

Yet he couldn't help asking himself if she weren't, thus pressed, speaking but to save him. It seemed to him he should be most lost if his history should prove all a platitude. "Are you telling me the truth, so that I sha'n't have been a bigger idiot than I can bear to know? I *haven't* lived with a vain imagination, in the most besotted illusion? I haven't waited but to see the door shut in my face?"

She shook her head again. "However the case stands *that* isn't the truth. Whatever the reality, it *is* a reality. The door isn't shut. The door's open," said May Bartram.

"Then something's to come?"

She waited once again, always with her cold, sweet eyes on him. "It's never too late." She had, with her gliding step, diminished the distance between them, and she stood nearer to him, close to him, a minute, as if still full of the unspoken. Her movement might have been for some finer emphasis of what she was at once hesitating and deciding to say. He had been standing by the chimney-piece, fireless and sparely adorned, a small, perfect old French clock and two morsels of rosy Dresden constituting all its furniture; and her hand grasped the shelf while she kept him waiting, grasped it a little as for support and encouragement. She only kept him waiting, however; that is, he only waited. It had become suddenly, from her movement and attitude, beautiful and vivid to him that she had something more to give him; her wasted face delicately shone with it, and it glittered, almost as with the white lustre of silver, in her expression. She was right, incontestably, for what he saw in her face was the truth, and strangely, without consequence, while their talk of it as dreadful was still in the air, she appeared to present it as inordinately soft. This, prompting bewilderment, made him but gape the more gratefully for her revelation, so that they continued for some minutes silent, her face shining at him, her contact imponderably pressing, and his stare all kind, but all expectant. The end, none the less, was that what he had expected failed to sound. Something else took place instead, which seemed to consist at first in the mere closing of her eyes. She gave way at the same instant to a slow, fine shudder, and though he remained staring—though he stared, in fact, but the harder—she turned off and regained her chair. It was the end of what she had been intending, but it left him thinking only of that.

"Well, you don't say——?"

She had touched in her passage a bell

near the chimney and had sunk back, strangely pale. "I'm afraid I'm too ill."

"Too ill to tell me?" It sprang up sharp to him, and almost to his lips, the fear that she would die without giving him light. He checked himself in time from so expressing his question, but she answered as if she had heard the words.

"Don't you know—now?"

" 'Now'——?" She had spoken as if something that had made a difference had come up within the moment. But her maid, quickly obedient to her bell, was already with them. "I know nothing." And he was afterwards to say to himself that he must have spoken with odious impatience, such an impatience as to show that, supremely disconcerted, he washed his hands of the whole question.

"Oh!" said May Bartram.

"Are you in pain?" he asked, as the woman went to her.

"No," said May Bartram.

Her maid, who had put an arm round her as if to take her to her room, fixed on him eyes that appealingly contradicted her; in spite of which, however, he showed once more his mystification. "What then has happened?"

She was once more, with her companion's help, on her feet, and, feeling withdrawal imposed on him, he had found, blankly, his hat and gloves and had reached the door. Yet he waited for her answer. "What *was* to," she said.

V

He came back the next day, but she was then unable to see him, and as it was literally the first time this had occurred in the long stretch of their acquaintance he turned away, defeated and sore, almost angry—or feeling at least that such a break in their custom was really the beginning of the end—and wandered alone with his thoughts, especially with one of them that he was unable to keep down. She was dying, and he would lose her; she was dying, and his life would end. He stopped in the park, into which he had passed, and stared before him at his recurrent doubt. Away from her the doubt pressed again; in her presence he had believed her, but as he felt his forlornness he threw himself into the explanation that, nearest at hand, had most of a miserable warmth for him and least of a cold torment. She had deceived him to save him—to put him off with something in which he should be able to rest. What could the thing that was to happen to him be, after all, but just this thing that had begun to happen? Her dying, her death, his consequent solitude—*that* was what he had figured as the beast in the jungle, that was what had been in the lap of the gods. He had had her word for it as he left her; for what else, on earth, could she have meant? It wasn't a thing of a monstrous order; not a fate rare and distinguished; not a stroke of fortune that overwhelmed and immortalised; it had only the stamp of the common doom. But poor Marcher, at this hour, judged the common doom sufficient. It would serve his turn, and even as the consummation of infinite waiting he would bend his pride to accept it. He sat down on a bench in the twilight. He hadn't been a fool. Something had *been*, as she had said, to come. Before he rose indeed it had quite struck him that the final fact really matched with the long avenue through which he had had to reach it. As sharing his suspense, and as giving herself all, giving her life, to bring it to an end, she had come with him every step of the way. He had lived by her aid, and to leave her behind would be cruelly, damnably to miss her. What could be more overwhelming than that?

Well, he was to know within the week, for though she kept him a while at bay, left him restless and wretched during a series of days on each of which he asked about her only again to have to turn away, she ended his trial by receiving him where she had always received him. Yet she had been brought out at some hazard into the presence of so many of the things that were, consciously, vainly, half their past, and there was scant service left in the gentleness of her mere desire, all too visible, to check his obsession and wind up his long trouble. That was clearly what she wanted; the one thing more, for her own peace, while she could still put out her hand. He was so affected by her state that, once seated by her chair, he was moved to let everything go; it was she herself therefore who brought him back, took up again, before she dismissed him, her last word of the other time. She showed how she wished to leave their affair in order. "I'm not sure you understood. You've nothing to wait for more. It *has* come."

Oh, how he looked at her! "Really?"

"Really."

"The thing that, as you said, *was* to?"

"The thing that we began in our youth to watch for."

Face to face with her once more he believed her; it was a claim to which he had so abjectly little to oppose. "You mean that it has come as a positive, definite occurrence, with a name and a date?"

"Positive. Definite. I don't know about the 'name,' but, oh, with a date!"

He found himself again too helplessly at sea. "But come in the night—come and passed me by?"

May Bartram had her strange, faint smile. "Oh no, it hasn't passed you by!"

"But if I haven't been aware of it, and it hasn't touched me——?"

"Ah, your not being aware of it," and she seemed to hesitate an instant to deal with this—"your not being aware of it is the strangeness *in* the strangeness. It's the wonder *of* the wonder." She spoke as with the softness almost of a sick child, yet now at last, at the end of all, with the perfect straightness of a sybil. She visibly knew that she knew, and the effect on him was of something co-ordinate, in its high character, with the law that had ruled him. It was the true voice of the law; so on her lips would the law itself have sounded. "It *has* touched you," she went on. "It has done its office. It has made you all its own."

"So utterly without my knowing it?"

"So utterly without your knowing it." His hand, as he leaned to her, was on the arm of her chair, and, dimly smiling always now, she placed her own on it. "It's enough if *I* know it."

"Oh!" he confusedly sounded, as she herself of late so often had done.

"What I long ago said is true. You'll never know now, and I think you ought to be content. You've *had* it," said May Bartram.

"But had what?"

"Why, what was to have marked you out. The proof of your law. It has acted. I'm too glad," she then bravely added, "to have been able to see what it's *not*."

He continued to attach his eyes to her, and with the sense that it was all beyond him, and that *she* was too, he would still have sharply challenged her, had he not felt it an abuse of her weakness to do more than take devoutly what she gave him, take it as hushed as to a revelation. If he did speak, it was out of the foreknowledge of his loneliness to come. "If you're glad of what it's 'not,' it might then have been worse?"

She turned her eyes away, she looked straight before her; with which, after a moment: "Well, you know our fears."

He wondered. "It's something then we never feared?"

On this, slowly, she turned to him. "Did we ever dream, with all our dreams, that we should sit and talk of it thus?"

He tried for a little to make out if they had; but it was as if their dreams, numberless enough, were in solution in some thick, cold mist, in which thought lost itself. "It might have been that we couldn't talk?"

"Well"—she did her best for him—"not from this side. This, you see," she said, "is the *other* side."

"I think," poor Marcher returned, "that all sides are the same to me." Then, however, as she softly shook her head in correction: "We mightn't, as it were, have got across——?"

"To where we are—no. We're *here*"—she made her weak emphasis.

"And much good does it do us!" was her friend's frank comment.

"It does us the good it can. It does us the good that *it* isn't here. It's past. It's behind," said May Bartram. "Before——" but her voice dropped.

He had got up, not to tire her, but it was hard to combat his yearning. She after all told him nothing but that his light had failed—which he knew well enough without her. "Before——?" he blankly echoed.

"Before, you see, it was always to *come*. That kept it present."

"Oh, I don't care what comes now! Besides," Marcher added, "it seems to me I liked it better present, as you say, than I can like it absent with *your* absence."

"Oh, mine!"—and her pale hands made light of it.

"With the absence of everything." He had a dreadful sense of standing there before her for—so far as anything but this proved, this bottomless drop was concerned—the last time of their life. It rested on him with a weight he felt he could scarce bear, and this weight it apparently was that still pressed out what remained in him of speakable protest. "I believe you; but I can't begin to pretend I understand. *Nothing,* for me, is past; nothing *will* pass until I pass myself, which I pray my stars may be as soon as possible. Say, however," he added, "that I've eaten my cake, as you contend to the last crumb—how can the thing I've never felt at all be the thing I was marked out to feel?"

She met him, perhaps, less directly, but she met him unperturbed. "You take your 'feelings' for granted. You were to suffer your fate. That was not necessarily to know it."

"How in the world—when what is such knowledge but suffering?"

She looked up at him a while, in silence. "No—you don't understand."

"I suffer," said John Marcher.

"Don't, don't!"

"How can I help at least *that?*"

"*Don't!*" May Bartram repeated.

She spoke it in a tone so special, in spite of her weakness, that he stared an instant—stared as if some light, hitherto hidden, had shimmered across his vision. Darkness again closed over it, but the gleam had already become for him an idea. "Because I haven't the right——?"

"Don't *know*—when you needn't," she mercifully urged. "You needn't—for we shouldn't."

"Shouldn't?" If he could but know what she meant!

"No—it's too much."

"Too much?" he still asked—but with a mystification that was the next moment, of a sudden, to give way. Her words, if they meant something, affected him in this light—the light also of her wasted face—as meaning *all*, and the sense of what knowledge had been for herself came over him with a rush which broke through into a question. "Is it of that, then, you're dying?"

She but watched him, gravely at first, as if to see, with this, where he was, and she might have seen something, or feared something, that moved her sympathy. "I would live for you still—if I could." Her eyes closed for a little, as if, withdrawn into herself, she were, for a last time, trying. "But I can't!" she said as she raised them again to take leave of him.

She couldn't indeed, as but too promptly and sharply appeared, and he had no vision of her after this that was anything but darkness and doom. They had parted forever in that strange talk; access to her chamber of pain, rigidly guarded, was almost wholly forbidden him; he was feeling now moreover, in the face of doctors, nurses, the two or three relatives attracted doubtless by the presumption of what she had to "leave," how few were the rights, as they were called in such cases, that he had to put forward, and how odd it might even seem that their intimacy shouldn't have given him more of them. The stupidest fourth cousin had more, even though she had been nothing in such a person's life. She had been a feature of features in *his,* for what else was it to have been so indispensable? Strange beyond saying were the ways of existence, baffling for him the anomaly of his lack, as he felt it to be, of producible claim. A woman might have been, as it were, everything to him, and it might yet present him in no connection that anyone appeared obliged to recognise. If this was the case in these closing weeks it was the case more sharply on the occasion of the last offices rendered, in the great grey London cemetery, to what had been mortal, to what had been precious, in his friend. The concourse at her grave was not numerous, but he saw himself treated as scarce more nearly concerned with it than if there had been a thousand others. He was in short from this moment face to face with the fact that he was to profit extraordinarily little by the interest May Bartram had taken in him. He couldn't quite have said what he expected, but he had somehow not expected this approach to a double privation. Not only had her interest failed him, but he seemed to feel himself unattended—and for a reason he couldn't sound—by the distinction, the dignity, the propriety, if nothing else, of the man markedly bereaved. It was as if, in the view of society, he had not *been* markedly bereaved, as if there still failed some sign or proof of it, and as if, none the less, his character could never be affirmed, nor the deficiency ever made up. There were moments, as the weeks went by, when he would have liked, by some almost aggressive act, to take his stand on the intimacy of his loss, in order that it *might* be questioned and his retort, to the relief of his spirit, so recorded; but the moments of an irritation more helpless followed fast on these, the moments during which, turning things over with a good conscience but with a bare horizon, he found himself wondering if he oughtn't to have begun, so to speak, further back.

He found himself wondering indeed at many things, and this last speculation had others to keep it company. What could he have done, after all, in her lifetime, without giving them both, as it were, away? He couldn't have made it known she was watch-

ing him, for that would have published the superstition of the Beast. This was what closed his mouth now—now that the Jungle had been threshed to vacancy and that the Beast had stolen away. It sounded too foolish and too flat; the difference for him in this particular, the extinction in his life of the element of suspense, was such in fact as to surprise him. He could scarce have said what the effect resembled; the abrupt cessation, the positive prohibition, of music perhaps, more than anything else, in some place all adjusted and all accustomed to sonoriety and to attention. If he could at any rate have conceived lifting the veil from his image at some moment of the past (what had he done, after all, if not lift it to *her?*) so to do this to-day, to talk to people at large of the Jungle cleared and confide to them that he now felt it as safe, would have been not only to see them listen as to a goodwife's tale, but really to hear himself tell one. What it presently came to in truth was that poor Marcher waded through his beaten grass, where no life stirred, where no breath sounded, where no evil eye seemed to gleam from a possible lair, very much as if vaguely looking for the Beast, and still more as if missing it. He walked about in an existence that had grown strangely more spacious, and, stopping fitfully in places where the undergrowth of life struck him as closer, asked himself yearningly, wondered secretly and sorely, if it would have lurked here or there. It would have at all events *sprung;* what was at least complete was his belief in the truth itself of the assurance given him. The change from his old sense to his new was absolute and final: what was to happen *had* so absolutely and finally happened that he was as little able to know a fear for his future as to know a hope; so absent in short was any question of anything still to come. He was to live entirely with the other question, that of his unidentified past, that of his having to see his fortune impenetrably muffled and masked.

The torment of this vision became then his occupation; he couldn't perhaps have

consented to live but for the possibility of
guessing. She had told him, his friend, not
to guess; she had forbidden him, so far
as he might, to know, and she had even in
a sort denied the power in him to learn:
which were so many things, precisely, to
deprive him of rest. It wasn't that he
wanted, he argued for fairness, that anything that had happened to him should
happen over again; it was only that he
shouldn't, as an anticlimax, have been
taken sleeping so sound as not to be able
to win back by an effort of thought the
lost stuff of consciousness. He declared to
himself at moments that he would either
win it back or have done with consciousness
for ever; he made this idea his one motive,
in fine, made it so much his passion that
none other, to compare with it, seemed ever
to have touched him. The lost stuff of
consciousness became thus for him as a
strayed or stolen child to an unappeasable
father; he hunted it up and down very
much as if he were knocking at doors and
inquiring of the police. This was the
spirit in which, inevitably, he set himself
to travel; he started on a journey that was
to be as long as he could make it; it danced
before him that, as the other side of the
globe couldn't possibly have less to say to
him, it might, by a possibility of suggestion, have more. Before he quitted London,
however, he made a pilgrimage to May
Bartram's grave, took his way to it through
the endless avenues of the grim suburban
necropolis, sought it out in the wilderness
of tombs, and, though he had come but
for the renewal of the act of farewell,
found himself, when he had at last stood
by it, beguiled into long intensities. He
stood for an hour, powerless to turn away
and yet powerless to penetrate the darkness
of death; fixing with his eyes her inscribed
name and date, beating his forehead against
the fact of the secret they kept, drawing
his breath, while he waited as if, in pity
of him, some sense would rise from the
stones. He kneeled on the stones, however,
in vain; they kept what they concealed;
and if the face of the tomb did become a

face for him it was because her two names
were like a pair of eyes that didn't know
him. He gave them a last long look, but no
palest light broke.

VI

He stayed away, after this, for a year;
he visited the depths of Asia, spending
himself on scenes of romantic interest, of
superlative sanctity; but what was present
to him everywhere was that for a man who
had known what *he* had known the world
was vulgar and vain. The state of mind in
which he had lived for so many years shone
out to him, in reflection, as a light that
coloured and refined, a light beside which
the glow of the East was garish, cheap and
thin. The terrible truth was that he had
lost—with everything else—a distinction as
well; the things he saw couldn't help being
common when he had become common to
look at them. He was simply now one of
them himself—he was in the dust, without
a peg for the sense of difference; and there
were hours when, before the temples of
gods and the sepulchres of kings, his spirit
turned, for nobleness of association, to the
barely discriminated slab in the London
suburb. That had become for him, and more
intensely with time and distance, his one
witness of a past glory. It was all that was
left to him for proof or pride, yet the past
glories of Pharaohs were nothing to him as
he thought of it. Small wonder then that he
came back to it on the morrow of his return. He was drawn there this time as irresistibly as the other, yet with a confidence, almost, that was doubtless the effect
of the many months that had elapsed. He
had lived, in spite of himself, into his
change of feeling, and in wandering over
the earth had wandered, as might be said,
from the circumference to the centre of his
desert. He had settled to his safety and
accepted perforce his extinction; figuring
to himself, with some colour, in the likeness
of certain little old men he remembered to
have seen, of whom, all meagre and wizened as they might look, it was related that

they had in their time fought twenty duels or been loved by ten princesses. They indeed had been wondrous for others, while he was but wondrous for himself; which, however, was exactly the cause of his haste to renew the wonder by getting back, as he might put it, into his own presence. That had quickened his steps and checked his delay. If his visit was prompt it was because he had been separated so long from the part of himself that alone he now valued.

It is accordingly not false to say that he reached his goal with a certain elation, and stood there again with a certain assurance. The creature beneath the sod *knew* of his rare experience, so that, strangely now, the place had lost for him its mere blankness of expression. It met him in mildness—not, as before, in mockery; it wore for him the air of conscious greeting that we find, after absence, in things that have closely belonged to us and which seem to confess of themselves to the connection. The plot of ground, the graven tablet, the tended flowers affected him so as belonging to him that he quite felt for the hour like a contented landlord reviewing a piece of property. Whatever had happened—well, had happened. He had not come back this time with the vanity of that question, his former worrying, "What, *what?*" now practically so spent. Yet he would, none the less, never again so cut himself off from the spot; he would come back to it every month, for if he did nothing else by its aid he at least held up his head. It thus grew for him, in the oddest way, a positive resource; he carried out his idea of periodical returns, which took their place at last among the most inveterate of his habits. What it all amounted to, oddly enough, was that, in his now so simplified world, this garden of death gave him the few square feet of earth on which he could still most live. It was as if, being nothing anywhere else for anyone, nothing even for himself, he were just everything here, and if not for a crowd of witnesses, or indeed for any witness but John Marcher, then by clear right

of the register that he could scan like an open page. The open page was the tomb of his friend, and *there* were the facts of the past, there the truth of his life, there the backward reaches in which he could lose himself. He did this, from time to time, with such effect that he seemed to wander through the old years with his hand in the arm of a companion who was, in the most extraordinary manner, his other, his younger self; and to wander, which was more extraordinary yet, round and round a third presence—not wandering she, but stationary, still, whose eyes, turning with his revolution, never ceased to follow him, and whose seat was his point, so to speak, of orientation. Thus in short he settled to live —feeding only on the sense that he once *had* lived, and dependent on it not only for a support but for an identity.

It sufficed him, in its way, for months, and the year elapsed; it would doubtless even have carried him further but for an accident, superficially slight, which moved him, in a quite other direction, with a force beyond any of his impressions of Egypt or of India. It was a thing of the merest chance—the turn, as he afterwards felt, of a hair, though he was indeed to live to believe that if light hadn't come to him in this particular fashion it would still have come in another. He was to live to believe this, I say, though he was not to live, I may not less definitely mention, to do much else. We allow him at any rate the benefit of the conviction, struggling up for him at the end, that, whatever might have happened or not happened, he would have come round of himself to the light. The incident of an autumn day had put the match to the train laid from of old by his misery. With the light before him he knew that even of late his ache had only been smothered. It was strangely drugged, but it throbbed; at the touch it began to bleed. And the touch, in the event, was the face of a fellow-mortal. This face, one grey afternoon when the leaves were thick in the alleys, looked into Marcher's own, at the cemetery, with an expression like the

cut of a blade. He felt it, that is, so deep
down that he winced at the steady thrust.
The person who so mutely assaulted him
was a figure he had noticed, on reaching his
own goal, absorbed by a grave a short distance away, a grave apparently fresh, so
that the emotion of the visitor would probably match it for frankness. This fact
alone forbade further attention, though
during the time he stayed he remained
vaguely conscious of his neighbour, a middle-aged man apparently, in mourning,
whose bowed back, among the clustered
monuments and mortuary yews, was constantly presented. Marcher's theory that
these were elements in contact with which
he himself revived, had suffered, on this
occasion, it may be granted, a sensible
though inscrutable check. The autumn day
was dire for him as none had recently been,
and he rested with a heaviness he had not
yet known on the low stone table that bore
May Bartram's name. He rested without
power to move, as if some spring in him,
some spell vouchsafed, had suddenly been
broken forever. If he could have done that
moment as he wanted he would simply
have stretched himself on the slab that was
ready to take him, treating it as a place
prepared to receive his last sleep. What in
all the wide world had he now to keep
awake for? He stared before him with the
question, and it was then that, as one of
the cemetery walks passed near him, he
caught the shock of the face.

His neighbour at the other grave had
withdrawn, as he himself, with force in
him to move, would have done by now, and
was advancing along the path on his way
to one of the gates. This brought him near,
and his pace was slow, so that—and all
the more as there was a kind of hunger in
his look—the two men were for a minute
directly confronted. Marcher felt him on
the spot as one of the deeply stricken—a
perception so sharp that nothing else in the
picture lived for it, neither his dress, his
age, nor his presumable character and
class; nothing lived but the deep ravage of
the features that he showed. He *showed*

them—that was the point; he was moved, as
he passed, by some impulse that was either
a signal for sympathy or, more possibly,
a challenge to another sorrow. He might
already have been aware of our friend,
might, at some previous hour, have noticed
in him the smooth habit of the scene, with
which the state of his own senses so scantly
consorted, and might thereby have been
stirred as by a kind of overt discord. What
Marcher was at all events conscious of was,
in the first place, that the image of
scarred passion presented to him was conscious too—of something that profaned the
air; and, in the second, that, roused, startled, shocked, he was yet the next moment
looking after it, as it went, with envy. The
most extraordinary thing that had happened to him—though he had given that
name to other matters as well—took place,
after his immediate vague stare, as a consequence of this impression. The stranger
passed, but the raw glare of his grief remained, making our friend wonder in pity
what wrong, what wound it expressed,·
what injury not to be healed. What had
the man *had* to make him, by the loss of
it, so bleed and yet live?

Something—and this reached him with
a pang—that *he*, John Marcher, hadn't;
the proof of which was precisely John
Marcher's arid end. No passion had ever
touched him, for this was what passion
meant; he had survived and maundered
and pined, but where had been *his* deep
ravage? The extraordinary thing we speak
of was the sudden rush of the result of
this question. The sight that had just met
his eyes named to him, as in letters of
quick flame, something he had utterly, in-
sanely missed, and what he had missed
made these things a train of fire, made them
mark themselves in an anguish of inward
throbs. He had seen *outside* of his life,
not learned it within, the way a woman was
mourned when she had been loved for herself; such was the force of his conviction
of the meaning of the stranger's face, which
still flared for him like a smoky torch. It
had not come to him, the knowledge, on the

wings of experience; it had brushed him, jostled him, upset him, with the disrespect of chance, the insolence of an accident. Now that the illumination had begun, however, it blazed to the zenith, and what he presently stood there gazing at was the sounded void of his life. He gazed, he drew breath, in pain; he turned in his dismay, and, turning, he had before him in sharper incision than ever the open page of his story. The name on the table smote him as the passage of his neighbour had done, and what it said to him, full in the face, was that *she* was what he had missed. This was the awful thought, the answer to all the past, the vision at the dread clearness of which he turned as cold as the stone beneath him. Everything fell together, confessed, explained, overwhelmed; leaving him most of all stupefied at the blindness he had cherished. The fate he had been marked for he had met with a vengeance—he had emptied the cup to the lees; he had been the man of his time, *the* man, to whom nothing on earth was to have happened. That was the rare stroke—that was his visitation. So he saw it, as we say, in pale horror, while the pieces fitted and fitted. So *she* had seen it, while he didn't, and so she served at this hour to drive the truth home. It was the truth, vivid and monstrous, that all the while he had waited the wait was itself his portion. This the companion of his vigil had at a given moment perceived, and she had then offered him the chance to baffle his doom. One's doom, however, was never baffled, and on the day she had told him that his own had come down she had seen him but stupidly stare at the escape she offered him.

The escape would have been to love her; then, *then* he would have lived. *She* had lived—who could say now with what passion?—since she had loved him for himself; whereas he had never thought of her (ah, how it hugely glared at him!) but in the chill of his egotism and the light of her use. Her spoken words came back to him, and the chain stretched and stretched. The beast had lurked indeed, and the beast, at its hour, had sprung; it had sprung in that twilight of the cold April when, pale, ill, wasted, but all beautiful, and perhaps even then recoverable, she had risen from her chair to stand before him and let him imaginably guess. It had sprung as he didn't guess; it had sprung as she hopelessly turned from him, and the mark, by the time he left her, had fallen where it *was* to fall. He had justified his fear and achieved his fate; he had failed, with the last exactitude, of all he was to fail of; and a moan now rose to his lips as he remembered she had prayed he mightn't know. This horror of waking—*this* was knowledge, knowledge under the breath of which the very tears in his eyes seemed to freeze. Through them, none the less, he tried to fix it and hold it; he kept it there before him so that he might feel the pain. That at least, belated and bitter, had something of the taste of life. But the bitterness suddenly sickened him, and it was as if, horribly, he saw, in the truth, in the cruelty of his image, what had been appointed and done. He saw the Jungle of his life and saw the lurking Beast; then, while he looked, perceived it, as by a stir of the air, rise, huge and hideous, for the leap that was to settle him. His eyes darkened —it was close; and, instinctively turning, in his hallucination, to avoid it, he flung himself, on his face, on the tomb.

BOOK IV

American Literature 1900 to the Present

I

PERSPECTIVES IN PHILOSOPHY AND CRITICISM

II

DIRECTIONS IN FICTION

III

DIRECTIONS IN POETRY

IV

WORLD WAR II AND AFTER

BOOK IV

AMERICAN LITERATURE SINCE 1900

I

LITERARY production in the United States since 1900—the contemporary period, in the sense that many of its most important writers are still producing—has been characterized by profusion and diversity. The student is confronted by claims to his attention on the part of a multitude of writers, and by a bewildering variety in the materials chosen by these writers, in their methods, and in their purposes. Before the Japanese attack at Pearl Harbor brought the United States into the Second World War, however, certain broad outlines of direction and developing emphasis in this voluminous literature could be discerned; and since the atomic bomb ended that war, the whole period from 1900 to 1940 can be viewed in the perspective of what already seems no little historical distance, its character in some degree can be determined, and its achievement may be tentatively assayed.

Certain new or newly important factors emerge at once as influential in the literature of the period. Fundamental in any consideration is recognition of the swift broadening, in these decades, of the base on which the whole literary process rests—the increase in the number of readers and in the market for magazines and books. This increase resulted in part from the rapid development of advertising, both as a means of making magazines pay and as a method of making books sell; in part from mechanical improvements in printing and commercial innovations in distribution; in part from the extension of public library facilities; in large part, surely, from the vast multiplication of the number of persons receiving high school and college training. This swiftly expanding market for the printed word had pronounced effects on both book and magazine publishing.

The principle of development of American magazines in the twentieth century was that of descent from the ivory tower into the marketplace. Functionally more popular than library books, the "quality magazines" had nevertheless kept rather aloof from the sweat and noise of immediate social and political conflict. But the rude incursion of the ten-cent magazines in the mid-nineties not only had jarred the complacency of the older journals but bade fair to ruin them. The low price of the newcomers had brought unheard-of circulations and a consequent rich harvest of advertising; but still worse was the undeniable fact that the cheap magazines had a real "quality" of their own and at the same time made a contribution to market-place debate that got them

561

talked about, while the *Atlantic, Harper's, Century, Scribner's,* and *Forum* were shoved to one side.

The "muckraking" crusade in the first decade of the new century was a case in point. This was really a group of journalistic crusades led by some of the new magazines against abuses in municipal government, "big business," adulterated drugs and foods, and so on. *McClure's* was a leader in such crusades, with a carefully planned and well executed series of articles, until the leading members of its staff seceded in 1906 and bought the *American Magazine,* which had been founded in 1876 as *Frank Leslie's Popular Magazine* and which was now revolutionized by its new owners. Other leaders were *Everybody's* (1899-1929), *Collier's Weekly* (1888-   ), and the less popular *Arena* (1889-1909).

The *Atlantic* and *Harper's* saved themselves by going modern, while their fellows of the old "quality" group died. The *Atlantic* was brought into the market-place by Walter Hines Page during his short editorship in 1898-1899. *Harper's* put the old style behind it in 1925. Both of these old magazines retained a respect for good writing and for the thoughtful, stimulating essay.

The function performed in earlier decades by such magazines as *Atlantic Monthly* and *Harper's* was in some degree taken over between 1900 and 1940 by the "little magazines" and quarterly reviews: periodicals which fought against the current of commercialism, depending on subscriptions or endowment rather than on advertising for support. They welcomed to their pages young and unknown writers, and sought literary excellence in the work they published, rather than broad popular appeal. *Poetry* (1911-   ), founded and for many years edited by Harriet Monroe, is clearly the most important of these magazines. Others which made substantial contributions were *Little Review* (1914-1929), the *Dial* in its New York series (1916-1929), *New Masses* (1926-   ), and *transition* (1927-1938), which were international in scope; *Southwest Review* (1915-   ), *Midland* (1915-1933), *Frontier* (1920-1939), *Prairie Schooner* (1927-   ), and *Southern Review* (1935-1942), all primarily regional in emphasis; *Partisan Review* (1934-   ), *Kenyon Review* (1939-   ), and *Accent* (1940-   ). Such iconoclastic, "sophisticated" magazines as *The Smart Set* (1912-1923), *The American Mercury* (1924-   ), and *The New Yorker* (1925-   ) exploited some phases of the culture and ideas best represented by the "little magazines."

Some of these "little magazines" and the quarterly reviews allied with them were avowedly and even ostentatiously esoteric—militantly not for the masses. These emphasized a schismatic differentiation characteristic of the literature of the period, in part a reaction against the commercial power of the popular—a distinction between writing for the few, the intellectually élite or elect, and writing for the many. Certain creative writers, notably of poetry, and certain critics, have so cultivated this distinction that their work has become unintelligible to all but a tiny minority of American readers. Such differentiation has existed before in American literature, of course—Emerson and Whitman were denounced by contemporaries as unintelligible, for example— but never before has the gulf been so wide.

Meantime book publishing had followed the general tendency of specialization and had separated itself not only from magazine production but even from printing. Yet book publishing, too, was responsive to the principle by which literature pushed its way into the arena of popular discussion, and great numbers of topical books were issued during the depression decade of the thirties, to be followed by long lists of books by correspondents and fighting men during the second World War.

Despite paper shortages caused by the war, publishers' total production of books soared to unprecedented heights during the 1940's. The American people were buying books as never before. Two new methods of distribution contributed to this expansion. One of these was the book club. The Book-of-the-Month Club was founded in 1926, launching a movement which by 1945 numbered twenty-five clubs, the two largest of which had about a million members each. Book clubs in the United States sold in the neighborhood of 75,000,000 books in 1945. The other factor was the sale of very inexpensive books in drug stores, news stands, and department stores, to the extent of many millions yearly. As with the cheap series of the eighties, many of these books were trash, but many also were of high quality; and the "pocket book" libraries helped teach Americans to own the books they read and thus take more pride in their readership. The two movements together brought a new era in book publishing through a popularization of books unparalleled in history.

The increase in popular consumption of the printed word in this period has been matched and indeed far outstripped by the rise to enormous popularity of two new forms of communication, the motion picture and the radio. Specific influences of both on literary development are readily apparent. Talented writers of fiction have deserted literature temporarily or permanently for the salaries of Hollywood. Others obviously have striven to fashion their books for the motion picture audience as well as for the reader. Writers of integrity and distinction have given thoughtful attention to both forms—notably Ben Hecht, Ernest Hemingway, William Faulkner, and John Steinbeck to the motion picture, Archibald MacLeish and Stephen Vincent Benét to radio. By reason of its special technical demands, however, radio is rapidly producing, in the work of such writers as Norman Corwin and Arch Oboler, a distinguished literature of its own. More diffused relationships to both the motion picture and radio may be less clearly recognized—in the structure of novels and short stories, perhaps, and in the use of dialogue.

New developments in older arts have their place among the forces which have shaped American fiction and poetry since 1900. Most important among them is the revitalized theatre, with its emphasis on authentic regionalism and on social criticism, and its experimentation in the projection of inner experience. The student will find, also, in the work of some contemporary American writers, significant analogies and relationships to modern developments in music, painting, and photography.

Contact with the thought and artistic production current on the European continent, fruitful in American literature since the days of Irving and Emerson, was a third major factor in the period from 1900 to 1940. Its force was greatly augmented by America's participation in the First World War, and the subsequent temporary or sustained residence in Europe of many American writers. Few Europeans have had so wide an influence on American letters as Sigmund Freud. His findings and even his methods are widely exemplified in the work of American writers—novelists, short story writers, even poets. The Freudian novel, having as its primary purpose the interpretation of individual experience in terms of psychoanalysis, and following in some degree the work of D. H. Lawrence and May Sinclair, both widely read in America, has attained the status of a definite phase of our literary development. Even more powerful has been the impact of the work of James Joyce, especially *Ulysses,* with the "stream of consciousness" novel as another clearly marked result of influence from across the Atlantic. Marcel Proust, Thomas Mann and other European writers of fiction have also exerted measurable influence. Late in the period the proletarian movement emerged as another distinct phase, fostering fiction, drama, poetry and criticism written by more or less consistent adherents of Karl Marx, and stimulated by the progress of Soviet Russia and by the breakdown of capitalist economy in the depression of the 1930's. In poetry certain other European influences have been especially potent. Since the days of Amy Lowell, American writers of verse have studied modern French poetry to marked effect. They have not neglected Rilke, Yeats, or Gerard Manley Hopkins, and have maintained a degree of literary reciprocity with the younger British school of W. H. Auden, C. Day-Lewis and their contemporaries and successors. In the field of ideas, even such a seemingly indigenous movement as Southern agrarianism bears a closer relationship to British distributism than has been generally recognized. All in all, the contemporary impulses from abroad hold place with the increasing popular demand for the printed word, and with the development of other forms of communication, as among the more potent forces which have shaped literary production in the United States in the period from 1900 to 1940.

II

It is no less important, however, for the student to recognize the continuity of our literary development, the organic relationship of the production of the decades from 1900 to 1940 with that of the preceding periods. The writers of the new century inherited more than they invented or acquired. They inherited, most notably, a maturing critical realism in fiction—directly from Norris and Crane, from Garland and Howells, from Henry James; indirectly from the great French and Russian realists of the 19th century. This realism, protean in method and material, sometimes restrained and decorous, sometimes boldly naturalistic, treated in this period every geographical and social area of the country and examined every aspect of American life, public or private. For a generation realism has dominated the realm of serious fiction, has invaded the provinces of poetry and drama. In this pervasive aspect of their work, the American writers of the 20th century are clearly indebted to their immediate predecessors.

They inherited, further—most significantly from Henry James and Stephen Crane—the heightening interest in literary technique which has found expression in much of the most characteristic writing of the period, in diverse and often fruitful innovation and experimentation in both fiction and poetry.

They inherited—from Whitman and again from Henry James—a dawning consciousness of the world community; but they did little with it, preoccupied for the most part with the rich diversity of national scenes and themes, until the rise of fascism, its ominous victories in the Ethiopian War and the Spanish Civil War, and the outbreak of the Second World War toward the end of the period aroused some of the more alert of American writers to vigorous proclamation of the common interests of all mankind.

Still another heritage from American writers of the 19th century to their 20th century descendants remains to be discussed. Though less tangible than those already mentioned, it has perhaps been more significant and far-reaching in its effects than any of them. Briefly stated, this heritage was the problem of resolving fundamental conflicts between the sciences, on the one hand, and such humane disciplines as religion, philosophy, and literature, on the other.

It was a problem chiefly for professional philosophers who could write with some charm of style and for literary critics who had something to say about first principles. To deal with this problem at all effectively necessitated considerable thought concerning what has come to be known as "the place of value in a world of facts." It was a problem that such seminal and synthesizing minds as Emerson and John Fiske in the United States, Matthew Arnold and Herbert Spencer in England, had dealt with profoundly and at length without ever solving, since its terms were being constantly altered by the steady advance of the sciences. In the 20th Century this advance became even more rapid and bewildering, as physics provided the basis for a philosophical indeterminism quite different from the determinism so confidently erected on the findings of 19th Century biology, and as psychology, sociology, and anthropology opened up new areas of fascinating but sometimes none too exact knowledge. The atomic bomb, of course, has given the problem a new and sinister urgency.

III

On May 4, 1907, William James wrote a long letter to his younger brother, Henry. After criticizing Henry's *The American Scene,* William commented as follows on his own latest brain-child: "I have just finished the proofs of a little book called 'Pragmatism' which even you *may* enjoy reading. It is a very 'sincere' and, from the point of view of ordinary philosophy-professorial manners, a very unconventional utterance, not particularly original at any one point, yet, in the midst of the literature of the way of thinking which it represents, with just that amount of squeak or shrillness in the voice that enables one book to *tell,* when others don't, to supersede its brethren, and be treated later as 'representative.' I shouldn't be surprised if ten years hence it should be rated as 'epoch-making,' for of the definitive triumph of that general way of thinking I can entertain no doubt whatever—I believe it to be something quite like the protestant reformation."

James' pragmatic way of thinking, which he first advanced in 1898 in an address entitled "Philosophical Conceptions and Practical Results," and for which, according to his own acknowledgment, he was most indebted to the American Charles Saunders Peirce and the Englishman Shadworth Hodgson, has not of course triumphed as broadly as did the protestant reformation. But it did establish a method acceptable to many scientists as a criterion for the truth of general propositions and hypotheses. And it did succeed in using this method to salvage many older theological and ethical conceptions as workable beliefs or useful myths and symbols. F. C. S. Schiller in England and John Dewey in the United States collaborated with James to spread the good work of pragmatism as a unifying cultural agent, although James developed perspectives which he labelled "Radical Empiricism" and "Pluralism," Schiller christened his approach "Humanism," and Dewey called his "Instrumentalism." Writing in 1910, one of their followers, H. Heath Bawden, observed: "These three leading exponents of pragmatism may be regarded as meeting the objections to philosophy urged, respectively, by the man of affairs, by the mystical religious man, and by the man of science."

The wandering Scottish philosopher, Thomas Davidson, who did so much for the cause of philosophical study in the United States in the last decades of the 19th Century, wrote to his young protégé, Morris R. Cohen, on May 14, 1899: "There is not the slightest need for skepticism, dogmatism, or 'will to believe.' These are merely the refuges of sluggish and inaccurate thinking. The human mind is quite capable of solving all its own problems, and reaching truth and joy. But before such solutions can have a value for humanity, or be the means of doing away with the injustice which so tries your soul, there must be a new apostolate, a new race of prophets. . . ."

Davidson could take so affirmative a stand because he had faith in human reason, or what he liked to speak of as "intellectual piety." This faith he transmitted to Cohen, whose *Reason and Nature* (1931) has been called by Huntington Cairns "one of the few inexhaustible philosophical volumes written in America." Asserting that distrust and neglect of the reason are the main errors of our time and are partly to blame for the fact that "from Moscow to the Mediterranean there reigns a pathetic faith in salvation through brutality," Cohen analyzes such rivals and substitutes for the rational process as authority, pure experience, intuition, and the creative imagination, and finds each of them inadequate to serve as a chief guide to the good life or a principal criterion of truth. He then corrects the misconception that reason is neither a central nor a necessary aspect of the scientific method and defines the uses of reason in both the natural and the social sciences, including a consideration of ethics as a possible science. The burden of his whole argument is that some philosophies developed out of the pragmatic way of thinking have undertaken to reconcile the sciences and the humanities in a wrong and dangerous way, by betraying human reason and its ordered and traditional values to the flux of existence with all its chaotic and novel ambiguities.

In the preface to Cohen's *Reason and Nature* appears the following passage: "My debt to George Santayana's *Life of Reason* might have been much greater if I had not arrived at my fundamental positions by a road which I imagine to be altogether different from his own. Only after the essentials of this book were worked out in my own mind did I begin to appreciate the profound insight with which naturalism and spirituality are united in the latter parts of the *Life of Reason*. I mention this not for the sake of any vain claims to originality but in the hope that my readers may be led to a greater appreciation of the richest philosophic classic produced on this side of the Atlantic."

Not content with the synthesis which he had achieved in *The Life of Reason* (1905-1906), Santayana, after leaving Harvard to reside abroad, began with *Scepticism and Animal Faith* (1923) to give his "system" a final and thoroughly elaborated form. With the gathering of his four separate works, *The Realm of Essence, The Realm of Matter, The Realm of Truth,* and *The Realm of Spirit* into one omnibus volume entitled *Realms of Being* (1942), this "system" stood complete and readily accessible. Believing that "a philosopher to-day would be ridiculous and negligible who had not strained his dogmas through the utmost rigours of scepticism," Santayana none the less arrived at a point far beyond doubt or negation. Although he seems to regard his "system" as in effect providing a broader basis of rationalization than has heretofore existed for the familiar assumptions of that animal faith which is often called common sense, he makes so much of "essences" that his ultimate position may be defined as an "aesthetic mysticism" that permits the most ineffable values to flourish serenely in a world of the most brutal facts. *Realms of Being* is an

American "testament of beauty" written, not in the discursive blank verse of Robert Bridges' long philosophical poem bearing that title, but in a prose that is plated, sonorous, and image-strewn.

Despite the literary merit or aesthetic quality found often in the writing of William James or Morris Cohen and almost never absent from that of Santayana, who has likewise distinguished himself as a poet, a novelist, and a belletristic essayist, a considerable gap has existed in present-day America between philosophy as a professional activity and criticism of literature and the arts. This gap has been partly bridged by such aestheticians as Theodore Meyer Greene, in his *The Arts and the Art of Criticism* (1940), Stephen C. Pepper, in his *The Basis of Criticism in the Arts* (1945), and John Hospers, in his *Meaning and Truth in the Arts* (1947).

Furthermore, a considerable number of literary critics, coalescing into schools that have followed each other with a bewildering rapidity, have sought, despite their frequent philosophical naiveté or pretentiousness and their propensity for faddism, to perform the function which Matthew Arnold prescribed for their clan, i.e., "to make an intellectual situation of which the creative power can profitably avail itself" or "to establish an order of ideas, if not absolutely true, yet true by comparison with that which it displaces; to make the best ideas prevail." In adjusting or opposing their ideas to the advance of the sciences, they have often been trapped into the pitfalls that lurk for amateur philosophers, but their maneuvering in such circumstances has usually been interesting to observe for its bounce or fence, its liveliness or ingenuity.

Four main schools of these critics may be distinguished from the welter of minor ones. They are the Iconoclasts or Nihilists, who swarmed in the 1920's and whose leader was H. L. Mencken; the Neo-Humanists, whom they derided and whose most aggressive personality was Irving Babbitt; the Historical Analysts, who have been active all during the period and among whom may be placed Edmund Wilson; and the Ex-Agrarian Ontological Aesthetes, who have been responsible in the late 1930's and the 1940's for a quiet revolution in academic circles and whose leader is John Crowe Ransom.

The main contribution of the Nihilists was that they brought a hard-boiled journalistic materialism, borrowed from Nietzsche, from Shaw, and from a native tradition of cynical humor, to bear on the sentimentality, venalities, hypocrisies, and pretensions of American mores, thought, and letters. They looked to the sciences, especially to biology, chemistry, physics, and psychology, for the accomplishment of a transvaluation of values and a total redirection of creative writing. Yet they grimly opined that many important social problems were insoluble because of the common man's inherent and incurable stupidity. The notion of the critic as artist, revamped from Oscar Wilde, was most acceptable to them because it absolved criticism of any responsibility to established ethical, social, intellectual, and aesthetic norms. Mencken, with his unique exuberance and impudence, was as much of a stimulus in the world of letters as William James had been in the worlds of philosophy and science. But Mencken's friend, James Branch Cabell, after ranking him in *Some of Us* (1930) as a force "somewhere between electricity and influenza," went on to remark: "The superb glow of Mencken also has had its sad aftermath, in the form of very many disciples whom one can but describe as the debunkers, the Mencken-oids."

The main contribution of the Neo-Humanists was that they reformulated a conception of the good life derived from Plato, Aristotle, and a select group of writers through the ages, and used this conception to determine whether important minds, books, and ideas praised for their "modernity" were making for man's spiritual health or decline. They were opposed to all forms of "naturalism," under which term they comprehended two main converging streams of tendency—a scientific materialism that Babbitt traced back to Bacon, and a sentimental humanitarianism that he believed Rousseau had done much to swell to a flood. Insistence that the creative artist should discipline his imagination, that the critic should be rational in procedure rather than authoritarian or impressionistic, and that democracy was doomed unless it diminished its anti-intellectualism under the leadership of an intellectual élite, made Babbitt's position in his field roughly analogous to that of Cohen among professional philosophers. From the beginning Babbitt had one major ally, Paul Elmer More, who wrote two of the most impressive prose works of our time, each in many volumes—*The Shelburne Essays* (1904-1936), and *The Greek Tradition* (1917-1931). Their ablest disciple, Stuart P. Sherman, deserted them in the early 1920's, although he continued for a while to do battle with their mutual foe, H. L. Mencken. With the onset of the depression, the tribe of Neo-Humanists increased. In 1930 they issued a symposium, *Humanism and America,* which provoked an anti-Humanist symposium and a controversy that raged for months and still has occasional repercussions. No heir of Babbitt or More, however, has approached either master in learning, profundity, and rhetorical skill.

The main contribution of the Historical Analysts has been that they have interpreted writers and their works by relating them fully to the contextual patterns—economic, cultural, ideological, biographical, and the like—that have helped produce them. From such sources as Taine, Sainte-Beuve, Marx, Freud, Trotsky, and Spengler they have developed their various analyses. They have brought literary criticism so closely into rapport with the sciences, particularly the social sciences and psychology, that one of their number, Herbert J. Muller, has seen fit to write a pioneer study entitled *Science and Criticism* (1943), assessing the resources which the former field holds for the latter.

One of the most persistent members of this school has been Van Wyck Brooks, but from *America's Coming-of-Age* (1915) to *The Times of Melville and Whitman* (1947), he has so altered his basic hypotheses that he has incurred the charge of using the past merely as a pasture for his own subjectivism. In the 1930's many critics of this school were converted to Marxism, which is as notable for its program of revolution as for its philosophy of history. In consequence their historical analyses were often marred by carping at writers who had not expressed sympathy with the plight of the worker in their day or had failed ignominiously to perform the feat of anticipating the very latest changes in the Stalinist party line. V. F. Calverton and Granville Hicks produced Marxist histories of American literature to supplement V. L. Parrington's monumental *Main Currents in American Thought,* and Bernard Smith wrote a Marxist history of American literary criticism. In *Axel's Castle* (1931), *The Triple Thinkers* (1938), and *The Wound and the Bow* (1941), Edmund Wilson has proved himself the sanest, the most versatile, and the most erudite critic employing historical analysis, and his *To the Finland Station* (1940) is a brilliant interpretation of the development of Marxist thought. Such disciplines as semantics, in which Alfred Korzybski and Kenneth Burke have pioneered, and the history of ideas, as conceived by A. O. Lovejoy and his followers, have added to the scientific techniques at the disposal of the historically minded critic, but as yet these techniques have not been brought fully into play.

The main contribution of the Ex-Agrarian Ontological Aesthetes has been exposition and illustration of the doctrine that literature affords a kind of knowledge, insight into the "realms of being," that is just as valid and as real as scientific knowledge and insight. John Crowe Ransom and his close friend, Allen Tate, have parted company with all the other schools or critics that have been discussed here. They have put themselves poles asunder from the Nihilists by their championship of orthodox religion. It is noteworthy that Ransom's *God Without Thunder,* subtitled *An Unorthodox Defense of Orthodoxy,* appeared in the same year, 1930, as Mencken's militantly atheistic *Treatise on the Gods.* Although recognizing much value in the Neo-Humanist approach, Ransom and Tate have condemned it on several counts, particularly for its overemphasis on ethics for the sake of ethics and its aesthetic inadequacy. "The obtuseness of the Neo-Humanists with respect to technical effects," Ransom has written, "is like that of story-book puritans with respect to a beautiful woman. They inquire at once about her character and state of grace; saying to themselves that men have been fooled so often, by women who were beautiful but sinful, and even more by women who were beautiful but dumb. They should not forget to remark after all that the woman is beautiful; that is a good deal. There are categories of beauty to be discussed, and techniques of beauty; for beauty is comparatively rare, and probably it is achieved and maintained often with heroic pains. It has the same right to its connoisseurs that moral character has."

Above all, Ransom and Tate have challenged the Historical Analysts of all types. Against the Marxists' critique of capitalist economy they opposed, at an earlier stage of their argument, an agrarian critique of industrial economy. In this view, Communism and Fascism were the twin evils to which industrialism led, unless its progress could be arrested by decentralization and the redistribution of the means of production to the people through individual ownership of small farms and community ownership of small factories.

The historical approach to literature, they are convinced, is inadequate, no matter what technique of interpretation is used. The causes that have made a piece of writing what it is are irrelevant to the process of judging it as a work of art. This process is best carried out by isolating the poem or the novel or the play from any context or milieu or corpus of abstractions and examining it as a whole composed of parts with its central and its tangential meaning self-contained within the compass of its structure and texture. Exercise in this process has given them a liking for a poetry where image and statement are fully related, as in the work of Donne and his fellow 17th Century Metaphysicals. Tate has gathered his best critical writing into *Reactionary Essays on Poetry and Ideas* (1936), and *Reason in Madness* (1941); Ransom his into *The World's Body* (1938), and *The New Criticism* (1941). These volumes owe much to the Arnoldian manner and post-Arnoldian matter of T. S. Eliot's critical essays, from *The Sacred Wood* (1920) to *After Strange Gods* (1934), though Ransom has classified Eliot as an "historical critic" and chided him for his "theoretical innocence" and "no great philosophical habit."

IV

American fiction of the period from 1900 to 1940 reflected and in some degree expressed the search for values apparent in the philosophy and criticism of the period. As the Freudian novel, the stream-of-consciousness novel, the Marxist novel contended for pre-eminence, as form in both the novel and the short story underwent vigorous experimentation, as regional fiction and historical fiction adopted new purposes and techniques and revealed new emphases, the field appeared confused and indeed chaotic. In the perspective of the years which follow the second world war, however, it is possible to discern in the fiction of the first four decades of the century not only response to the philosophical problems of the period and adherence to the points of view of the major schools of criticism, but an underlying pattern.

Beneath all the varied and often conflicting and contrasting phases of literary development in these decades there was a slow and powerful general movement from negative emphasis in the critical examination of American life and of modern society as a whole to positive revaluation of the same materials, and ultimately to affirmation. A few writers attained a positive viewpoint early in the period and in their careers. A larger number retained the negative, or exhibited in their work only peripheral and partial response to the general movement. But among the American writers of eminence and influence in these years are many whose individual development corresponded to the general pattern. The character of the ultimate affirmation varied widely. The findings included positive values in democracy, in internationalism, in the common man, in religion, in man's relation to the earth, in human life as a whole. It is true that, as the young poet Karl Shapiro observed in his *Essay on Rime* (1945),

> So various
> And multifoliate are our breeds of faith
> That we could furnish a herbarium
> With the American specimens alone.
> A choice anthology of a few of these
> Made its appearance just before the war;
> It is an album of philosophies
> Called *I Believe*. The essays it contains
> Have nothing in common but proximity.

But in relation to the prevailing attitudes of the earlier decades of the period the fact of faith—of any faith—marks change.

The productive career of Theodore Dreiser spanned the whole period. Indeed, his first novel, *Sister Carrie* (1900), was written before the turn of the century; his last two, *The Bulwark* and *The Stoic,* were published after the end of the second world war. In study of the fiction of the period his work is of primary importance. No American novelist of the times had greater influence on his contemporaries. None is more clearly representative of the general pattern of literary development.

Dreiser began his work in fiction as a disciple of Frank Norris and Zola, as a naturalist in philosophy and a negative critic of society in intention. In *Sister Carrie* and again in *Jennie Gerhardt* he singled out the institution of marriage and the conventions of sexual morality for special emphasis, though in both novels there is ample evidence of his awareness of deeper flaws in the social structure as a whole. In *The Financier* and *The Titan* he traced in exhaustive detail the rise to wealth and power of an unscrupulous "captain of industry." In *The Genius* he attacked with equal vehemence moral conventions, as thwarting and distorting the development of the artist, and commercialism, as destructive of his integrity. In autobiographical books and essays written for the most part in the second decade of the century he announced his adherence to a mechanistic and nihilistic philosophy.

By this time Dreiser had attained a commanding position in serious American fiction. He was generally recognized by critics and younger novelists— in spite of the heaviness and clumsiness of much of his writing—as the pioneer and foremost exponent of literary naturalism. Sherwood Anderson spoke for a generation in his tribute to Dreiser in his *Horses and Men* (1919): "O, those who follow him shall have many things that Dreiser does not have. That is a part of the wonder and beauty of Theodore Dreiser, the things that others shall have, because of him." Dreiser's place of leadership was secured and his influence attained its height with the publication of *An American Tragedy* (1925). In the pages of this massive novel he broadened his indictment of a materialistic, money-worshipping society to include far-ranging and diverse aspects of American conduct and aspiration. This novel affirms the sacredness of human life, and contemplates with profound sympathy the weaknesses and failures of human beings. But its general emphasis, like that of almost all of Dreiser's work which had preceded it, is overwhelmingly negative. In *An American Tragedy* Dreiser was still the militant naturalist and the destructive critic of American life.

There followed in Dreiser's career a long period of relative silence. He devoted himself to active participation in social and economic crusades, wrote and published little. More than two decades separated *An American Tragedy* and his next major novel. Only after his death, with the publication of *The Bulwark* in 1946, was it possible to assess the distance he had traversed in the interval. In this novel of Dreiser's last years the emphasis had shifted, the essential philosophy had changed. There was still the scornful hatred of all that dwarfs and distorts the human person, still the profound tenderness for weakness and suffering. But there was a new affirmation of positive values in human experience, a wistful approach to religious faith. Dreiser did not abandon his vision of the evil and failure in American life, but he transcended it. In *The Bulwark* he achieved a positive statement of character and experience, a work of matured and balanced critical realism. In *The Stoic* (1947), also published after his death, Dreiser had carried further the story of Frank Cowperwood, the central figure of *The Financier* and *The Titan*. Here again Dreiser recognized the need—in the words of one of his characters—"To think earnestly and seekingly for some reason or excuse for life!"

A comparable pattern is discoverable in the work of other major writers of fiction in the period from 1900 to 1940. Sometimes clearly, sometimes obscurely, many of these writers have expressed in their fiction their personal advance from destructive criticism to positive evaluation, from negation to affirmation. Sherwood Anderson's memorable early short stories in *Winesburg, Ohio* (1919), and other volumes, some of which stand among the finest creative expressions of the time, are concerned almost exclusively with individual maladjustments and frustrations. In the best of his novels, *Poor White* (1920) and *Dark Laughter* (1925), he voiced a broader and more searching indictment of American life, stressing especially the effect of the separation of the workman from the rewards of the craftsman in modern industry; but he could offer for the individual no solution to the problem thus posed save a personal and primitive hedonism. In his later work, however, especially in his *Memoirs*

(1942) and such descriptive comments on the American scene as *Hello, Towns* (1929), a positive element is increasingly evident. He still saw with characteristic tenderness and insight the failures and sorrows of men; but his whole vision of American life moved toward affirmation.

Ernest Hemingway's reputation and influence rose in the 1920's on the basis of his strongly negative studies of mutilation and distortion. In *The Sun Also Rises* (1926) he achieved a definitive statement of the effect of the first world war and its aftermath on both American and European intellectuals. His *A Farewell to Arms* (1929) was the most striking of the many anti-war novels of the decade. His innovations in form and style were widely influential, especially in the short story. In harmony with the nihilistic philosophy which underlay his fiction, he moved to intensified glorification of the physical and an accompanying strong suggestion of the will to death—elements both strongly exemplified in the novel *To Have and Have Not* (1937). But with the rise of fascism and the outbreak of the war in Spain—a country he knew well and loved —Hemingway experienced a relatively sudden discovery of positive values. In *For Whom The Bell Tolls* (1940) he achieved the period's most notable affirmation of the interdependence of humanity in transcendence of national boundaries.

John Steinbeck's *The Grapes of Wrath* (1939) showed increased and positive emphasis on elements previously present in his work. In *Tortilla Flat* (1935) he had viewed the lives of the poor and the dispossessed with amused and somewhat ironic sympathy. *In Dubious Battle* (1936) was marked by an almost clinical detachment, with social and economic conflict viewed objectively. In *Of Mice and Men* (1937), however, Steinbeck moved through a confused sentimentalism and nihilism toward the passionate affirmation of the worth and dignity of the common man which gave *The Grapes of Wrath* a clearly positive meaning in spite of its bitter attack on capitalistic injustice. This view received moving statement in *The Moon Is Down* (1942). His more recent work has been largely ambiguous in intention and relatively feeble in effect.

Thomas Wolfe's vision of American life, marked throughout his work by an intense and clouded energy, always included response to elements of beauty and nobility in the American scene. The gradual growth in human meaning of the characters centrally portrayed in his fiction reflected his own philosophical progress toward a positive resolution, intimated in the democratic faith of *You Can't Go Home Again* (1940), but left tragically incomplete by his early death.

Many American writers of fiction between 1900 and 1940 limited their presentation of American life to distinct regions of the country. Regional fiction is an important part of the achievement of the period. In the work of most of the regional writers the student may discover relation to the philosophical and critical conflicts of the times. Willa Cather's first novel, the international *Alexander's Bridge* (1912), is essentially a study in frustration and futility, strongly influenced by the subject-matter and technique of Henry James. When she turned to the materials of middle western farm and village life which she used in *O Pioneers!* (1913) and *My Antonia* (1918), she revealed from the outset the strong sense of place, the recognition of the meaning of the earth to men and of the goodness of life lived in harmony with it, which has been a distinguishing characteristic of her work as a whole. Repeatedly in her work, as in the fine early stories and later novels of another midwestern regionalist, Ruth Suckow, the familiar regional theme of "escape from the village" was tempered and balanced by emphasis on the positive and durable satisfactions of rural life. Ellen Glasgow was one of the most important Southern contributors to the regional fiction of the period. After her early "problem" and historical novels she turned to realistic treatment of the contemporary scene in her own region, and portrayed with increasing effectiveness in a series of novels from *Barren Ground* (1925) to *Vein of Iron* (1935) and *In This Our Life* (1941) the conflict between social decay and personal strength and integrity. The distinguished novels of Elizabeth Madox Roberts and Caroline Gordon possess comparable meaning. William Faulkner's innovations in fictional technique from *Soldiers' Pay* (1926) to *Intruder in the Dust* (1948) gave added importance to his powerful studies of a narrow field in Southern life. In his later work, however, he rather intensified his involvement in the confusion and violence of this narrow world of his creation than achieved fresh perspective in relation to it. A similar observation applies to the fiction of Erskine Caldwell.

Historical fiction showed interesting response to the dominant ideas of these decades. Though many popular historical novels of the period have had little motivation beyond the provision of entertainment for the reader—in some cases, for the motion picture audience—and have small significance for the student, there has been definite development in this field of fiction. It has included emphasis on historical and biographical accuracy and has presented in some cases interpretations of characters and events contrary to the generally accepted impressions—as in Kenneth Roberts' treatment of the Revolutionary War in *Oliver Wiswell* (1940) and Howard Fast's interpretation of the Reconstruction in *Freedom Road* (1944). James Boyd and Walter D. Edmonds were pioneers in the general effort to present in fiction a broader and sounder reading of American history.

There remain those writers of fiction whose work is expressive of one or another mood of the period but whose development shows only peripheral or partial relationship to the general philosophical movement. Sinclair Lewis caught most precisely the spirit of the times in his vigorous negative criticism of Amercan life in *Main Street* (1920) and *Babbitt* (1922), incidentally projecting a picture of America which was eminently acceptable in Europe. But his later work shows no growth in vision or understanding, and a diminution of creative power. John Dos Passos experimented significantly in the technique of fiction, especially in the far-ranging survey from many points of view in the trilogy *U. S. A.* (1930-1936). The implications of *U. S. A.* are prevailingly negative; but in his studies in American biography in *The Ground We Stand On* (1941) Dos Passos announced a positive faith in democracy and an affirmative vision of American life with which his subsequently published work has seemed not fully consistent. In his brief creative career F. Scott Fitzgerald moved very definitely from the brittle sophistication of *The Beautiful and Damned* (1922) to a far deeper and broader creative understanding in *The Great Gatsby* (1925) and *Tender is the Night* (1934). James Branch Cabell early perfected a method of satirical romance as a vehicle for his negative criticism of contemporary life, and in *Jurgen* (1919), *Figures of Earth* (1921), and other novels composing his vast cycle of the *Biography of the Life* (i.e., descendants) *of Manuel,* this method enjoyed wide popularity. In *Beyond Life* (1919) he formulated his aesthetic philosophy, asserting a pragmatic value for romance as opposed to realism, because "men play the ape to their dreams," but denying the artist's obligation to do more than amuse himself—a denial which, of course, he did not intend to be taken literally. He continued to write through the remaining decades of the period with no marked change in method or purpose, to a much reduced audience. James T. Farrell was one of the most consistent of the fiction writers of the period from 1900 to 1940. With a lucid objectivity he has sought to reproduce aspects of metropolitan life. His vast mural consists of two main panoramas—that of the Studs Lonigan trilogy (1932-1935) and that of the Danny O'Neill tetralogy (1936-1943), with such brilliant side panels as *Gas-House McGinty* (1933), *Ellen Rogers* (1941) and *Bernard Clare* (1946). Antipodal to Cabell in every aspect of his fiction, Farrell is like the older writer only in one way—consistent, pertinacious retention of an established purpose and method.

V

The poetry of the years from 1900 to 1940 as a whole reflected and expressed, as did the fiction, the general movement of thought in the period. The student will discover, however, most marked diversity in the kinds of affirmation at which individual poets arrived. He will find that of four writers beginning their work in a common attitude of skepticism or even nihilism, one may arrive at a position of orthodox religious faith; a second at affirmation of values in democracy and the life of the common man; a third at an assertion of intrinsic and sufficient meaning in poetry itself—a positive aesthetic philosophy; while a fourth may retain his skepticism.

Both Edwin Arlington Robinson and Robert Frost began their work as poets before the end of the 19th century. Frost's creative production spanned the whole period from 1900 to 1940, Robinson's more than three-fourths of it. The two writers had in common elements of the New England background, both material and intellectual. Robinson's unsatisfied search for philosophical truth and a meaning in life was early expressed in the long poem *Captain Craig* (1902), and in one of his most self-revealing poems, *The Man Against the Sky* (1916), he approached a positive solution in a characteristically indirect and tentative way. But his long Arthurian poems—the first two written under the shadow of the first world war—are filled with rich images of decay and disintegration, of the death of a world; and in the long psychological studies of contemporary life and character to which he devoted much of the creative effort of his later years the negative elements outweigh the positive.

Frost found from the first affirmative values in contact with the earth and in the living tissue of experience. The books on which his wide fame was first based, *North of Boston* (1914) and *Mountain Interval* (1916), stressed elements of bleakness and harshness in New England rural life, and were read by contemporaries as a part of the period's critical indictment of American life as a whole. But these books contained also many poems in which soundness and goodness in men and things found appreciative expression. Frost's later volumes were marked by increasing mellowness and deepening assurance, though he retained much of a healthy and often playful skepticism.

The most characteristic of Carl Sandburg's *Chicago Poems* (1916) were definitely in harmony with the critical spirit of his times, in their vigorous indictment of a heartless and inhuman materialism. But Sandburg, like Whitman, found much to admire in the vigor and color of American life, and expressed in his second volume, *Cornhuskers* (1918), an especially strong enjoyment of the midwestern landscape. From the social concern manifested in *Chicago Poems* his was a characteristic advance to the broad and positive democratic vision expressed in *The People, Yes* (1938). Of two other noteworthy poets who appeared in the middle west in the same decade with Sandburg, Vachel Lindsay espoused from the first a deep and indeed religious faith in the goodness of American life, though he did not ignore evidences of evil. Edgar Lee Masters, on the other hand, rarely deviated from the bitter negativism which, voiced freshly and powerfully, made *Spoon River Anthology* (1915) one of the characteristic books of its generation. In the work of the California poet, Robinson Jeffers, from *Flagons and Apples* (1912) to *The Double Axe* (1948), all the attitudes of Nietzschean nihilism have found unique expression.

The career of T. S. Eliot is one of the most significant of the period, and his work holds more enduring interest for the student and for other writers than that of most poets who began their production in the second decade of the century. His early poems, centering about the characteristic "Love Song of J. Alfred Prufrock," displayed intellectual arrogance and exploited to the fullest degree the period's sharply critical attitude toward American life. He advanced to the broadened and deepened recognition of the whole tragic dilemma of his time which made *The Waste Land* (1922) a landmark in the literature of negation. But already present in this poem were indications of the direction in which Eliot was to go. Rather swiftly he moved to a positive position far beyond that attained by most of his contemporaries, in his adherence to an orthodox and dogmatic religious faith. Eliot's acute and widely influential critical writing reflected and paralleled his development as a poet.

The early writing of Stephen Vincent Benét in both poetry and fiction followed largely the negative conventions of the thought of the early 1920's. But with the writing of the long historical poem, *John Brown's Body* (1928), he applied a fresh and positive approach to the whole American tradition. Perhaps more widely read than the work of any American poet since Longfellow, this book contributed materially to the general revaluation of American life which emerged in the literary production of the later years of the period. In both his subsequent poetry and in fiction Benét shared significantly in this revaluation. In general outline the poetic development of Archibald MacLeish, from early emphasis on negative elements in thought and in personal experience to a vigorous affirmation of a positive democratic faith, parallels that of Stephen Vincent Benét. The chief achievement of Hart Crane's brief creative life, the long poem *The Bridge* (1930), embraced in a single sweeping vision, in dynamic relationship and significant perspective, the greatness and the failure of America.

Among the numerous poets of importance who have adopted more or less completely, and illustrated or expressed in their work, the critical doctrine advocated by John Crowe Ransom, Wallace Stevens is one of the most noteworthy. In poems throughout his career, and directly in the brilliant essay, "The Noble Rider and the Sound of Words," in the symposium *The Language of Poetry* (1942), he has maintained the autonomy and the intrinsic positive value of the poet's art. The work of many of the most accomplished younger poets at the end of the period shows similar emphasis.

As the second world war set a boundary to a period, and our national literature rounded out its third half-century, many American writers were addressing themselves to the same problems that had seemed primary and immediate to the founders of that literature: the definition of function and character for American writing, the formulation of the meaning of American life. The prevailingly negative generations since the Civil War had not worked in vain. They had cleared ground, laid foundations on which in a changed world a new literature might be built.

VI

Ultimately this literature will have to stand or fall, not alone on the richness and range of its ideas, its affirmations and negations, but equally on its more purely aesthetic values. How will it meet the test of a criticism which asks of a novel or a story or a poem not only what it means but what it is? What has been gained by the technical innovations and experiments that have been so marked a feature of modern American writing?

In fiction there has been a real gain in the sensuous immediacy of the experience presented. This kind of immediacy makes for a firmer, a more intense illusion of life. In general this immediacy has been achieved by two quite different procedures.

One procedure, best illustrated in Gertrude Stein's stories in *Three Lives* (1909) and in her novel, *The Making of Americans* (1925), and in the work of Sherwood Anderson and Ernest Hemingway, has involved a simplification of narrative style. "Fine writing" has been scrupulously avoided; the quest has been for the plainest, shortest words; rhythmic repetition of phrase has been exploited fully as a prose device. In Hemingway the "scene" has been reduced to sharp notation of what characters did and said and sensed, and this notation has been permitted to speak altogether for itself.

The other procedure, best illustrated in the work of William Faulkner, John Dos Passos and Thomas Wolfe, has involved a complication of narrative structure or "point of view" or both that has resulted in a corresponding complication of style. In order to emphasize inner as opposed to outer experience, to convey the persistence of the past in the present of consciousness, and to give dramatic focus and tension to a story covering considerable time and concerning numerous characters, Faulkner has experimented brilliantly with the cutback, as in *Light in August* (1932), or with the patterned shifting from one "point of view" to another in the monologues composing *As I Lay Dying* (1930), or with both devices bizarrely linked, as in *The Sound and the Fury* (1929). To bring home to his readers the interrelatedness of individual destinies in a metropolitan environment, as in *Manhattan Transfer* (1925), or in the complex semi-barbaric "civilization" of modern industrial capitalism, as in *U.S.A.*, Dos Passos has developed a structure that has been described as "collective." This consists of a kaleidoscope of episodes in the discontinuous biographies of a host of fictitious characters. In *U.S.A.* these episodes are substantial rather than fragmentary and are interlarded with stylized, impressionistic sketches of historical personages, with short pastiches of stockmarket reports, headlines, quotations from popular songs, and the like called "newsreels," and with bits of stream-of-consciousness monologue labeled "the camera eye." In the novels of

Thomas Wolfe, musical structure, involving the interweaving of themes and symbols, has been attempted on an elaborate scale.

In poetry there has been a real gain in the concentration, fusion, and inclusiveness of the experience presented. These qualities are essential differentia of poetry from prose. They have been most notably achieved by those poets who, in turning to varying traditions in the poetry of the past, have practiced a scholarly and a critical eclecticism.

Inclusiveness of the experience presented was one of the features of Whitman's poetry that made it an important influence on the New Poetry movement, on the work of Carl Sandburg, Vachel Lindsay, Robinson Jeffers, and Hart Crane among others. *Leaves of Grass* embraced an extraordinary range of concepts, emotions, and sensations. But these elements were seldom adequately fused; they were too often merely juxtaposed; and the long lines, the endless catalogues, the loose, oceanic, symphonic structures made for diffuseness rather than concentration.

Hence other traditions were revived to modify the heritage of technique from Whitman. One of these was the tradition of the English Metaphysicals, who had relied on the "conceit" to fuse and concentrate concepts, emotions, and sensations and to achieve irony and tension. Another was the tradition of the French Symbolists, who had followed Poe more than Whitman in relying on suggestive imagery and tone-color to convey meaning and emotional nuances with a minimum of verbalism. And a third was the dramatic monologue of Browning with its use of characters and crucial moments in their experience to serve as "objective correlatives" by which the poet might express indirectly his sense of an age or of the nature of reality or his emotional responses to diverse aspects of life. All these traditions may be found operative in the technique of T. S. Eliot, and they have been reflected, likewise, in various combinations and with other garnerings, in the work of John Crowe Ransom, Allen Tate and Wallace Stevens.

The aesthetic gains of both fiction and poetry in our time have not been possible without corresponding losses. Perhaps the most objectionable of these, for the ordinary reader, has been the loss of clarity, of explicitness, in communication. But the answer can be made that these are the virtues of science, which imposes its conceptual formulas on the buzzing immediacy of experience and seeks to exclude from its characteristic statements the blurs of meaning that occur when words are used emotively and sensuously. In an age so oppressively dominated by scientific abstractionism as our own, it may be that literature must restore man to what has been termed the existential, to direct contact with the world's body and the soul's fire, and thus keep him human.

Volumes XI and XII in the series, *A History of American Life*—Harold U. Faulkner's *The Quest for Social Justice 1898-1914* (New York, 1931) and Preston W. Slosson's *The Great Crusade and After 1914-1928* (New York, 1928)—are good reading for the social and historical backgrounds of the literature, as is also Charles and Mary Beard's *America in Midpassage* (New York, 1939). C. C. Regier's *The Era of the Muckrakers* (Chapel Hill, 1932) is helpful for the social and intellectual history of the years before World War I; F. L. Allen's *Only Yesterday* (New York, 1931) and *Since Yesterday* (New York, 1940), Leo Gurko's *The Angry Decade* (New York, 1947), and Dixon Wecter's *The Age of the Great Depression* (New York, 1948) deal vividly with aspects of American social and intellectual history in the period between the wars. R. H. Gabriel's *The Course of American Democratic Thought* and Merle Curti's *The Growth of American Thought*, already listed, carry forward the history of ideas; the two symposia edited by H. E. Stearns, *Civilization in the United States* (New York, 1922) and *America Now* (New York, 1938), offer comprehensive exhibits of the state of culture in the 1920's and the 1930's. The most valable studies in the literary history of the period are Alfred Kazin's *On Native Grounds* (New York, 1942) for prose and Horace Gregory and Marya Zaturenska's *A History of American Poetry 1900-1940* (New York, 1946). The latter volume should be supplemented by Louis Untermeyer's anthology, *Modern American Poetry* (New York, 1936 and 1942) and Oscar Williams' anthology, *The War Poets* (New York, 1945). F. L. Pattee's *The New American Literature 1890-1930* (New York, 1930) and Vernon Loggins' *I Hear America: Literature in the United States Since 1900* (New York, 1937) are pedestrian but informative. For the impact of literary and ideological tendencies from abroad, consult Oscar Cargill's *Intellectual America: Ideas on the March* (New York, 1941), the first volume of a work still in preparation, the second volume of which is to deal with *Ideas in Conflict*. Aside from the general studies of fiction by Quinn and Van Doren, already cited, there are several able special studies of American fiction in the 20th Century—Harry Hartwick's *The Foreground of American Fiction* (New York, 1934); Harlan Hatcher's *Creating the Modern American Novel* (New York, 1935); Percy Boynton's *America in Contemporary Fiction* (Chicago, 1940); Joseph Warren Beach's *American Fiction 1920-1940* (New York, 1941); and Maxwell Geismar's *Writers in Crisis: the American Novel between Two Wars* (Boston, 1942) and *The Last of the Provincials: The American Novel, 1915-1925* (Boston, 1947). American drama has been the subject of four comprehensive studies —J. W. Krutch's *The American Drama Since 1918* (New York, 1939), F. H. O'Hara's *Today in American Drama* (Chicago, 1939), Eleanor Flexner's *American Playwrights 1918-1938* (New York, 1938), and Edmond M. Gagey's *Revolution in Amercian Drama* (New York, 1947)—each written from a different critical point of view. Such more general studies as Cleanth Brooks' *Modern Poetry and the Tradition* (Chapel Hill, 1939) and H. W. Wells' *New Poets from Old* (New York, 1940) establish valuable perspectives for the study of modern American poetry, as do J. W. Beach's *The Twentieth Century Novel* (New York, 1932) and Cleanth Brooks and Robert Penn Warren's *Understanding Fiction* (New York, 1943) for the study of modern American fiction and Eric Bentley's *The Playwright as Thinker* (New York, 1946) for the study of modern American drama. Harry Slochower's *No Voice is Wholly Lost* (New York, 1945) includes some American writers in its stimulating and often profound analysis of philosophical attitudes in modern writing. The symposium, *After the Genteel Tradition,* ed. Malcolm Cowley (New York, 1936) and J. Donald Adams' *The Shape of Books to Come* (New York, 1944) are interesting attempts to define the tendencies and drifts in modern American writing. The most comprehensive shorter analysis of all aspects of this writing is the 204-page "Critical Survey" in Fred B. Millett's bio-bibliographical compilation, *Contemporary American Authors* (New York, 1940), which will soon be due for a revision to bring it up to date. Floyd Stovall's *American Idealism* (Norman, Okla., 1943) has some penetrating analyses. F. J. Hoffman, Charles Allen, and Carolyn F. Ulrich have produced a valuable history and bibliography in *The Little Magazine* (Princeton, 1946). Arthur E. Murphy's *The Uses of Reason* (New York, 1943), the symposium *Naturalism and the Human Spirit,* ed. Y. H. Krikorian (New York, 1944), and Edgar Sheffield Brightman's *Nature and Values* (Nashville, 1945) will acquaint the student with issues in recent philosophical discussion in America; likewise helpful are the later introductions and selections in the anthology edited by W. G. Muelder and L. Sears, *The Development of American Philosophy* (Boston, 1940). Bernard Smith's *Forces in American Criticism,* already listed, has good chapters on the 20th Century, but Morton D. Zabel's anthology, *Literary Opinion in America* (New York, 1937) is an indispensable supplement, while John Crowe Ransom's *The New Criticism* (Norfolk, Conn., 1941), Yvor Winters' *The Anatomy of Nonsense* (Norfolk, Conn., 1943), Henry Peyre's *Writers and Their Critics* (Ithaca, N. Y., 1944), James T. Farrell's *A Note on Literary Criticism* (New York, 1936) and *The League of Frightened Philistines* (New York, 1945), and Stanley Hyman's *The Armed Vision* (New York, 1948), contain some illuminating chapters. Of the various schools of critics, the Neo-Humanists have received most attention in such volumes as Gorham B. Munson's *The Dilemma of the Liberated* (New York, 1930); Louis J. Mercier's *The Challenge of Humanism* (New York, 1933) and *American Humanism and the New Age* (Minneapolis, 1948); G. R. Elliott's *Humanism and Imagination* (Chapel Hill, 1938); Robert Shafer's *Paul Elmer More and American Criticism* (New York, 1935).

American Literature 1900 to the Present

I

PERSPECTIVES IN PHILOSOPHY AND CRITICISM

American Literature 1900 to the Present

I

PERSPECTIVES IN PHILOSOPHY AND CRITICISM

1842 ∾ *William James* ∾ *1910*

BORN in New York City, William James acquired from his theologically
minded father, the wealthy Henry James, Sr., an insatiable curiosity.
He was subjected to somewhat the same cosmopolitan and highly experimental
early education that his younger brother, Henry, was. His later education
stressed painting and biology, included residence in Germany and France, and
brought him a medical degree from Harvard in 1869. He began his teaching
in physiology at Harvard, gave the first laboratory course in psychology ever
offered there, and found himself ultimately in the department of philosophy.

From 1880 to his retirement in 1907 James was an unusually busy academi-
cian, lecturing at California and Edinburgh, conducting his Harvard classes,
assuming leadership in such organizations as the Society for Psychical Research,
the American Psychological Association, and the American Philosophical Association, and keeping up a steady output of books, articles, reviews, and correspondence. He was an inspiring teacher because he took to heart his own
advice: "Prepare yourself in the subject so well that it shall be always on tap:
then in the class-room trust your spontaneity and fling away all further care."

Yet James liked research better than teaching, as these remarks on his
retirement in a letter to Henry suggest: "You can't tell how happy I am at
having thrown off the nightmare of my 'professorship.' As a 'professor' I
always felt myself a sham, with its chief duties of being a walking encyclopedia
of erudition. I am now at liberty to be a *reality,* and the comfort is unspeakable
—literally unspeakable, to be my own man after 35 years of being owned by
others. I can now live for truth pure and simple, instead of for truth accommodated to the most unheard-of requirements set by others. . . ." His major
books were *The Principles of Psychology,* 2 vols. (1890), one of the most important pioneer contributions to the subject; *The Will to Believe* (1897); *The
Varieties of Religious Experience* (1902); *Pragmatism* (1907); *The Meaning of
Truth* (1909); *A Pluralistic Universe* (1909); *Memories and Studies* (1911);
and *Essays in Radical Empiricism* (1912).

[The foremost work on James is Ralph Barton Perry's *The Thought and
Character of William James,* 2 vols. (Boston, 1935) re-issued in a condensed
version (Boston, 1948). Older works include T. Flournoy's *The Philosophy
of William James* (New York, 1917), H. V. Knox's *Philosophy of William
James* (London, 1914), and Josiah Royce's *William James and Other Essays
on the Philosophy of Life* (New York, 1911).]

From
PRAGMATISM
[1907]

What Pragmatism Means

SOME YEARS AGO, being with a camping party in the mountains, I returned from a solitary ramble to find every one engaged in a ferocious metaphysical dispute. The *corpus* of the dispute was a squirrel—a live squirrel supposed to be clinging to one side of a tree-trunk; while over against the tree's opposite side a human being was imagined to stand. This human witness tries to get sight of the squirrel by moving rapidly round the tree, but no matter how fast he goes, the squirrel moves as fast in the opposite direction, and always keeps the tree between himself and the man, so that never a glimpse of him is caught. The resultant metaphysical problem now is this: *Does the man go round the squirrel or not?* He goes round the tree, sure enough, and the squirrel is on the tree; but does he go round the squirrel? In the unlimited leisure of the wilderness, discussion had been worn threadbare. Every one had taken sides, and was obstinate; and the numbers on both sides were even. Each side, when I appeared, therefore appealed to me to make it a majority. Mindful of the scholastic adage that whenever you meet a contradiction you must make a distinction, I immediately sought and found one, as follows: "Which party is right," I said, "depends on what you *practically mean* by 'going round' the squirrel. If you mean passing from the north of him to the east, then to the south, then to the west, and then to the north of him again, obviously the man does go round him, for he occupies these successive positions. But if on the contrary you mean being first in front of him, then on the right of him, then behind him, then on his left, and finally in front again, it is quite as obvious that the man fails to go round him, for by the compensating movements the squirrel makes, he keeps his belly turned towards the man all the time, and his back turned away. Make the distinction, and there is no occasion for any farther dispute. You are both right and both wrong according as you conceive the verb 'to go round' in one practical fashion or the other."

Although one or two of the hotter disputants called my speech a shuffling evasion, saying they wanted no quibbling or scholastic hairsplitting, but meant just plain honest English 'round,' the majority seemed to think that the distinction had assuaged the dispute.

I tell this trivial anecdote because it is a peculiarly simple example of what I wish now to speak of as *the pragmatic method.* The pragmatic method is primarily a method of settling metaphysical disputes that otherwise might be interminable. Is the world one or many?—fated or free?—material or spiritual?—here are notions either of which may or may not hold good of the world; and disputes over such notions are unending. The pragmatic method in such cases is to try to interpret each notion by tracing its respective practical consequences. What difference would it practically make to any one if this notion rather than that notion were true? If no practical difference whatever can be traced, then the alternatives mean practically the same thing, and all dispute is idle. Whenever a dispute is serious, we ought to be able to show some practical difference that must follow from one side or the other's being right.

A glance at the history of the idea will show you still better what pragmatism means. The term is derived from the same Greek word πράγμα meaning action, from which our words 'practice' and 'practical' come. It was first introduced into philosophy by Mr. Charles Peirce in 1878. In an article entitled 'How to Make Our Ideas Clear,' in the 'Popular Science Monthly' for January of that year Mr. Peirce, after pointing out that our beliefs are really rules for action, said that, to develop a thought's meaning, we need only determine what conduct it is fitted to produce: that conduct is for us its sole significance. And the tangible fact at the root of all our thought-distinctions, however subtle, is that there is no one of them so fine as to consist in anything but a possible difference of practice. To attain perfect clearness in our thoughts of an object, then, we need only consider what conceivable effects of a practical kind the object may involve—what sensations we are to expect from it, and what reactions we must prepare. Our conception of these effects, whether immediate or remote, is then for us the whole of our conception of the object, so far as that conception has positive significance at all.

This is the principle of Peirce, the principle of pragmatism. It lay entirely unnoticed by any one for twenty years, until I, in an address before Professor Howison's philosophical union at the University of California,[1] brought it forward again and made a special application of it to religion. By that date (1898) the times seemed ripe for its reception. The word 'pragmatism' spread, and at present it fairly spots the pages of the philosophic journals. On all hands we find the 'pragmatic movement' spoken of, sometimes with respect, sometimes with contumely, seldom with clear understanding. It is evident that the term applies itself conveniently to a number of tendencies that hitherto have lacked a collective name, and that it has 'come to stay.'

To take in the importance of Peirce's principle, one must get accustomed to applying it to concrete cases. I found a few years ago that Ostwald,[2] the illustrious Leipzig chemist, had been making perfectly distinct use of the principle of pragmatism in his lectures on the philosophy of science, though he had not called it by that name. "All realities influence our practice," he wrote me, "and that influence is their meaning for us. I am accustomed to put questions to my classes in this way: In what respects would the world be different if this alternative or that were true? If I can find nothing that would become different, then the alternative has no sense."

That is, the rival views mean practically the same thing, and meaning, other than practical, there is for us none. Ostwald in a published lecture gives this example of what he means. Chemists have long wrangled over the inner constitution of certain bodies called 'tautomerous.' Their properties seemed equally consistent with the notion that an instable hydrogen atom oscillates inside of them, or that they are instable mixtures of two bodies. Controversy raged, but never was decided. "It would never have begun," says Ostwald, "if the combatants had asked themselves what particular experimental fact could have been made different by one or the other view being correct. For it would then have appeared that no difference of fact could possibly ensue; and the quarrel was as unreal as if, theorizing in primitive times about the raising of dough by yeast, one party should have invoked a 'brownie,' while another insisted on an 'elf' as the true cause of the phenomenon."

It is astonishing to see how many philosophical disputes collapse into insignificance the moment you subject them to this simple test of tracing a concrete consequence. There can *be* no difference anywhere that doesn't *make* a difference elsewhere—no difference in abstract truth that doesn't express itself in a difference in concrete fact and in conduct consequent upon that fact, imposed on somebody, somehow, somewhere, and somewhen. The whole function of philosophy ought to be to find out what definite difference it will make to you and me at definite instants of our life, if this world-formula or that world-formula be the true one.

There is absolutely nothing new in the pragmatic method. Socrates was an adept at it. Aristotle used it methodically. Locke, Berkeley, and Hume made momentous contributions to truth by its means. Shadworth Hodgson keeps insisting that realities are only what they are 'known as.' But

[1] George Holmes Howison (1834-1916).
[2] Wilhelm Ostwald (1853-1932), who taught at Harvard in 1905.

these forerunners of pragmatism used it in fragments: they were preluders only. Not until in our time has it generalized itself, become conscious of a universal mission, pretended to a conquering destiny. I believe in that destiny, and I hope I may end by inspiring you with my belief.

Pragmatism represents a perfectly familiar attitude in philosophy, the empiricist attitude, but it represents it, as it seems to me, both in a more radical and in a less objectionable form than it has ever yet assumed. A pragmatist turns his back resolutely and once for all upon a lot of inveterate habits dear to professional philosophers. He turns away from abstraction and insufficiency, from verbal solutions, from bad *a priori* reasons, from fixed principles, closed systems, and pretended absolutes and origins. He turns towards concreteness and adequacy, towards facts, towards action and towards power. That means the empiricist temper regnant and the rationalist temper sincerely given up. It means the open air and possibilities of nature, as against dogma, artificiality, and the pretense of finality in truth.

At the same time it does not stand for any special results. It is a method only. But the general triumph of that method would mean an enormous change in what I called in my last lecture the 'temperament' of philosophy. Teachers of the ultra-rationalistic type would be frozen out, much as the courtier type is frozen out in republics, as the ultramontane type of priest is frozen out in protestant lands. Science and metaphysics would come much nearer together, would in fact work absolutely hand in hand.

Metaphysics has usually followed a very primitive kind of quest. You know how men have always hankered after unlawful magic, and you know what a great part in magic *words* have always played. If you have his name, or the formula of incantation that binds him, you can control the spirit, genie, afrite, or whatever the power may be. Solomon knew the names of all the spirits, and having their names, he held them subject to his will. So the universe has always appeared to the natural mind as a kind of enigma, of which the key must be sought in the shape of some illuminating or power-bringing word or name. That word names the universe's *principle*, and to possess it is after a fashion to possess the universe itself. 'God,' 'Matter,' 'Reason,' 'the Absolute,' 'Energy,' are so many solving names. You can rest when you have them. You are at the end of your metaphysical quest.

But if you follow the pragmatic method, you cannot look on any such word as closing your quest. You must bring out of each word its practical cash-value, set it at work within the stream of your experience. It appears less as a solution, then, than as a program for more work, and more particularly as an indication of the ways in which existing realities may be *changed*.

Theories thus become instruments, not answers to enigmas, in which we can rest. We don't lie back upon them, we move forward, and, on occasion, make nature over again by their aid. Pragmatism unstiffens all our theories, limbers them up and sets each one at work. Being nothing essentially new, it harmonizes with many ancient philosophic tendencies. It agrees with nominalism for instance, in always appealing to particulars; with utilitarianism in emphasizing practical aspects; with positivism in its disdain for verbal solutions, useless questions and metaphysical abstractions.

All these, you see, are *anti-intellectualist* tendencies. Against rationalism as a pretension and a method pragmatism is fully armed and militant. But, at the outset, at least, it stands for no particular results. It has no dogmas, and no doctrines save its method. As the young Italian pragmatist Papini has well said,[3] it lies in the midst of our theories, like a corridor in a hotel. Innumerable chambers open out of it. In one you may find a man writing an atheistic volume; in the next some one on his

---

[3] Giovanni Papini (1881-   ).

knees praying for faith and strength; in a third a chemist investigating a body's properties. In a fourth a system of idealistic metaphysics is being excogitated; in a fifth the impossibility of metaphysics is being shown. But they all own the corridor, and all must pass through it if they want a practicable way of getting into or out of their respective rooms.

No particular results then, so far, but only an attitude of orientation, is what the pragmatic method means. The *attitude of looking away from first things, principles, 'categories,' supposed necessities; and of looking towards last things, fruits, consequences, facts.*

So much for the pragmatic method! You may say that I have been praising it rather than explaining it to you, but I shall presently explain it abundantly enough by showing how it works on some familiar problems. Meanwhile the word pragmatism has come to be used in a still wider sense, as meaning also a certain *theory of truth.* I mean to give a whole lecture to the statement of that theory, after first paving the way, so I can be very brief now. But brevity is hard to follow, so I ask for your redoubled attention for a quarter of an hour. If much remains obscure, I hope to make it clearer in the later lectures.

One of the most successfully cultivated branches of philosophy in our time is what is called inductive logic, the study of the conditions under which our sciences have evolved. Writers on this subject have begun to show a singular unanimity as to what the laws of nature and elements of fact mean, when formulated by mathematicians, physicists and chemists. When the first mathematical, logical, and natural uniformities, the first *laws,* were discovered, men were so carried away by the clearness, beauty and simplification that resulted, that they believed themselves to have deciphered authentically the eternal thoughts of the Almighty. His mind also thundered and reverberated in syllogisms. He also thought in conic sections, squares and roots and ratios, and geometrized like Euclid. He

made Kepler's laws for the planets to follow; he made velocity increase proportionally to the time in falling bodies; he made the law of the sines for light to obey when refracted; he established the classes, orders, families and genera of plants and animals, and fixed the distances between them. He thought the archetypes of all things, and devised their variation; and when we rediscover any one of these his wondrous institutions, we seize his mind in its very literal intention.

But as the sciences have developed farther, the notion has gained ground that most, perhaps all, of our laws are only approximations. The laws themselves, moreover, have grown so numerous that there is no counting them; and so many rival formulations are proposed in all the branches of science that investigators have become accustomed to the notion that no theory is absolutely a transcript of reality, but that any one of them may from some point of view be useful. Their great use is to summarize old facts and to lead to new ones. They are only a man-made language, a conceptual short-hand, as some one calls them, in which we write our reports of nature; and languages, as is well known, tolerate much choice of expression and many dialects.

Thus human arbitrariness has driven divine necessity from scientific logic. If I mention the names of Sigwart, Mach, Ostwald, Pearson, Milhaud, Poincaré, Duhem, Ruyssen, those of you who are students will easily identify the tendency I speak of, and will think of additional names.[4]

Riding now on the front of this wave of scientific logic Messrs. Schiller and

[4] Christoph von Sigwart (1830-1894), German logician; Ernst Mach (1838-1916), Austrian physicist and psychologist; Karl Pearson (1857-1936), English eugenicist; Gaston Milhaud (1858-1918), French philosopher and historian of science; Jules-Henri Poincaré (1854-1912), French physicist and mathematician; Pierre-Maurice Duhem (1861-1916), French physicist and mathematician; and Théodore Ruyssen (1868-   ), French philosopher.

Dewey appear with their pragmatistic account of what truth everywhere signifies. Everywhere, these teachers say, 'truth' in our ideas and beliefs means the same thing that it means in science. It means, they say, nothing but this, *that ideas (which themselves are but parts of our experience) become true just in so far as they help us to get into satisfactory relation with other parts of our experience,* to summarize them and get about them by conceptual short-cuts instead of following the interminable succession of particular phenomena. Any idea upon which we can ride, so to speak; any idea that will carry us prosperously from any one part of our experience to any other part, linking things satisfactorily, working securely, simplifying, saving labor; is true for just so much, true in so far forth, true *instrumentally.* This is the 'instrumental' view of truth taught so successfully at Chicago, the view that truth in our ideas means their power to 'work,' promulgated so brilliantly at Oxford.[5]

Messrs. Dewey, Schiller and their allies, in reaching this general conception of all truth, have only followed the example of geologists, biologists and philologists. In the establishment of these other sciences, the successful stroke was always to take some simple process actually observable in operation—as denudation by weather, say, or variation from parental type, or change of dialect by incorporation of new words and pronunciations—and then to generalize it, making it apply to all times, and produce great results by summating its effects through the ages.

The observable process which Schiller and Dewey particularly singled out for generalization is the familiar one by which any individual settles into *new opinions.* The process here is always the same. The individual has a stock of old opinions already, but he meets a new experience that puts them to a strain. Somebody contradicts them; or in a reflective moment he discovers that they contradict each other;

or he hears of facts with which they are incompatible; or desires arise in him which they cease to satisfy. The result is an inward trouble to which his mind till then had been a stranger, and from which he seeks to escape by modifying his previous mass of opinions. He saves as much of it as he can, for in this matter of belief we are all extreme conservatives. So he tries to change first this opinion, and then that (for they resist change very variously), until at last some new idea comes up which he can graft upon the ancient stock with a minimum of disturbance of the latter, some idea that mediates between the stock and the new experience and runs them into one another most felicitously and expediently.

This new idea is then adopted as the true one. It preserves the older stock of truths with a minimum of modification, stretching them just enough to make them admit the novelty, but conceiving that in ways as familiar as the case leaves possible. An *outrée* explanation, violating all our preconceptions, would never pass for a true account of a novelty. We should scratch round industriously till we found something less excentric. The most violent revolutions in an individual's beliefs leave most of his old order standing. Time and space, cause and effect, nature and history, and one's own biography remain untouched. New truth is always a go-between, a smoother-over of transitions. It marries old opinion to new fact so as ever to show a minimum of jolt, a maximum of continuity. We hold a theory true just in proportion to its success in solving this 'problem of maxima and minima.'[6] But success in solving this problem is eminently a matter of approximation. We say this theory solves it on the whole more satisfactorily than that theory; but that means more satisfactorily to ourselves, and individuals will emphasize their points of satisfaction differently. To a cer-

---

[5] John Dewey, now at Columbia, was at Chicago at this time; F. C. S. Schiller was at Oxford.

[6] Concepts in mathematics.

tain degree, therefore, everything here is plastic.

The point I now urge you to observe particularly is the part played by the older truths. Failure to take account of it is the source of much of the unjust criticism levelled against pragmatism. Their influence is absolutely controlling. Loyalty to them is the first principle—in most cases it is the only principle; for by far the most usual way of handling phenomena so novel that they would make for a serious rearrangement of our preconception is to ignore them altogether, or to abuse those who bear witness for them.

You doubtless wish examples of this process of truth's growth, and the only trouble is their superabundance. The simplest case of new truth is of course the mere numerical addition of new kinds of facts, or of new single facts of old kinds, to our experience—an addition that involves no alteration in the old beliefs. Day follows day, and its contents are simply added. The new contents themselves are not true, they simply *come* and *are*. Truth is *what we say about* them, and when we say that they have come, truth is satisfied by the plain additive formula.

But often the day's contents oblige a rearrangement. If I should now utter piercing shrieks and act like a maniac on this platform, it would make many of you revise your ideas as to the probable worth of my philosophy. 'Radium' came the other day as part of the day's content, and seemed for a moment to contradict our ideas of the whole order of nature, that order having come to be identified with what is called the conservation of energy. The mere sight of radium paying heat away indefinitely out of its own pocket seemed to violate that conservation. What to think? If the radiations from it were nothing but an escape of unsuspected 'potential' energy, pre-existent inside of the atoms, the principle of conservation would be saved. The discovery of 'helium' as the radiation's outcome, opened a way to this

belief. So Ramsay's view is generally held to be true, because, although it extends our old ideas of energy, it causes a minimum of alteration in their nature.[7]

I need not multiply instances. A new opinion counts as 'true' just in proportion as it gratifies the individual's desire to assimilate the novel in his experience to his beliefs in stock. It must both lean on old truth and grasp new fact; and its success (as I said a moment ago) in doing this, is a matter for the individual's appreciation. When old truth grows, then, by new truth's addition, it is for subjective reasons. We are in the process and obey the reasons. That new idea is truest which performs most felicitously its function of satisfying our double urgency. It makes itself true, gets itself classed as true, by the way it works; grafting itself then upon the ancient body of truth, which thus grows much as a tree grows by the activity of a new layer of cambium.

Now Dewey and Schiller proceed to generalize this observation and to apply it to the most ancient parts of truth. They also once were plastic. They also were called true for human reasons. They also mediated between still earlier truths and what in those days were novel observations. Purely objective truth, truth in whose establishment the function of giving human satisfaction in marrying previous parts of experience with newer parts played no rôle whatever, is nowhere to be found. The reason why we call things true is the reason why they *are* true, for 'to be true' *means* only to perform this marriage-function.

The trail of the human serpent is thus over everything. Truth independent; truth that we *find* merely; truth no longer malleable to human needs; truth incorrigible, in a word; such truth exists indeed superabundantly—or is supposed to exist by

---

[7] Sir William Ramsay (1852-1916), British chemist, discovered argon in 1894 and helium in 1895 and was an exponent of the transmutation theory.

rationalistically minded thinkers; but then it means only the dead heart of the living tree, and its being there means only that truth also has its paleontology, and its 'prescription,' and may grow stiff with years of veteran service and petrified in men's regard by sheer antiquity. But how plastic even the oldest truths nevertheless really are has been vividly shown in our day by the transformation of logical and mathematical ideas, a transformation which seems even to be invading physics. The ancient formulas are reinterpreted as special expressions of much wider principles, principles that our ancestors never got a glimpse of in their present shape and formulation.

Mr. Schiller still gives to all this view of truth the name of 'Humanism,' but, for this doctrine too, the name of pragmatism seems fairly to be in the ascendant, so I will treat it under the name of pragmatism in these lectures.

Such then would be the scope of pragmatism—first, a method; and second, a genetic theory of what is meant by truth. And these two things must be our future topics.

What I have said of the theory of truth will, I am sure, have appeared obscure and unsatisfactory to most of you by reason of its brevity. I shall make amends for that hereafter. In a lecture on 'common sense' I shall try to show what I mean by truths grown petrified by antiquity. In another lecture I shall expatiate on the idea that our thoughts become true in proportion as they successfully exert their go-between function. In a third I shall show how hard it is to discriminate subjective from objective factors in Truth's development. You may not follow me wholly in these lectures; and if you do, you may not wholly agree with me. But you will, I know, regard me at least as serious, and treat my effort with respectful consideration.

You will probably be surprised to learn, then, that Messrs. Schiller's and Dewey's theories have suffered a hailstorm of contempt and ridicule. All rationalism has risen against them. In influential quarters Mr. Schiller, in particular, has been treated like an impudent schoolboy who deserves a spanking. I should not mention this, but for the fact that it throws so much side-light upon that rationalistic temper to which I have opposed the temper of pragmatism. Pragmatism is uncomfortable away from facts. Rationalism is comfortable only in the presence of abstractions. This pragmatist talk about truths in the plural, about their utility and satisfactoriness, about the success with which they 'work,' etc., suggests to the typical intellectualist mind a sort of coarse lame second-rate makeshift article of truth. Such truths are not real truth. Such tests are merely subjective. As against this, objective truth must be something non-utilitarian, haughty, refined, remote, august, exalted. It must be an absolute correspondence of our thoughts with an equally absolute reality. It must be what we *ought* to think unconditionally. The conditioned ways in which we *do* think are so much irrelevance and matter for psychology. Down with psychology, up with logic, in all this question!

See the exquisite contrast of the types of mind! The pragmatist clings to facts and concreteness, observes truth at its work in particular cases, and generalizes. Truth, for him, becomes a class-name for all sorts of definite working-values in experience. For the rationalist it remains a pure abstraction, to the bare name of which we must defer. When the pragmatist undertakes to show in detail just *why* we must defer, the rationalist is unable to recognize the concretes from which his own abstraction is taken. He accuses us of *denying* truth; whereas we have only sought to trace exactly why people follow it. Your typical ultra abstractionist fairly shudders at concreteness: other things equal, he positively prefers the pale and spectral. If the two universes were offered, he would always choose the skinny outline rather than the rich thicket of reality. It is so much purer, clearer, nobler.

I hope that as these lectures go on, the

concreteness and closeness to facts of the pragmatism which they advocate may be what approves itself to you as its most satisfactory peculiarity. It only follows here the example of the sister-sciences, interpreting the unobserved by the observed. It brings old and new harmoniously together. It converts the absolutely empty notion of a static relation of 'correspondence' (what that may mean we must ask later) between our minds and reality, into that of a rich and active commerce (that any one may follow in detail and understand) between particular thoughts of ours, and the great universe of other experiences in which they play their parts and have their uses.

But enough of this at present! The justification of what I say must be postponed. I wish now to add a word in further explanation of the claim I made at our last meeting, that pragmatism may be a happy harmonizer of empiricist ways of thinking with the more religious demands of human beings.

Men who are strongly of the fact-loving temperament, you may remember me to have said, are liable to be kept at a distance by the small sympathy with facts which that philosophy from the present-day fashion of idealism offers them. It is far too intellectualistic. Old-fashioned theism was bad enough, with its notion of God as an exalted monarch, made up of a lot of unintelligible or preposterous 'attributes'; but, so long as it held strongly by the argument from design, it kept some touch with concrete realities. Since, however, darwinism has once for all displaced design from the minds of the 'scientific,' theism has lost that foothold; and some kind of an immanent or pantheistic deity working *in* things rather than above them is, if any, the kind recommended to our contemporary imagination. Aspirants to a philosophic religion turn, as a rule, more hopefully nowadays towards idealistic pantheism than towards the older dualistic theism, in spite of the fact that the latter still counts able defenders.

But, as I said in my first lecture, the brand of pantheism offered is hard for them to assimilate if they are lovers of facts, or empirically minded. It is the absolutistic brand, spurning the dust and reared upon pure logic. It keeps no connexion whatever with concreteness. Affirming the Absolute Mind, which is its substitute for God, to be the rational presupposition of all particulars of fact, whatever they may be, it remains supremely indifferent to what the particular facts in our world actually are. Be they what they may, the Absolute will father them. Like the sick lion in Esop's fable, all footprints lead into his den, but *nulla vestigia retrorsum.*[8] You cannot redescend into the world of particulars by the Absolute's aid, or deduce any necessary consequences of detail important for your life from your idea of his nature. He gives you indeed the assurance that all is well with *Him,* and for his eternal way of thinking; but thereupon he leaves you to be finitely saved by your own temporal devices.

Far be it from me to deny the majesty of this conception, or its capacity to yield religious comfort to a most respectable class of minds. But from the human point of view, no one can pretend that it doesn't suffer from the faults of remoteness and abstractness. It is eminently a product of what I have ventured to call the rationalistic temper. It disdains empiricism's needs. It substitutes a pallid outline for the real world's richness. It is dapper, it is noble in the bad sense, in the sense in which to be noble is to be inapt for humble service. In this real world of sweat and dirt, it seems to me that when a view of things is 'noble,' that ought to count as a presumption against its truth, and as a philosophic disqualification. The prince of darkness may be a gentleman, as we are told he is, but whatever the God of earth and heaven is, he can surely be no gentleman. His menial services are needed in the dust of our human trials, even more than

---

[8] No footsteps back.

his dignity is needed in the empyrean.

Now pragmatism, devoted though she be to facts, has no such materialistic bias as ordinary empiricism labors under. Moreover, she has no objection whatever to the realizing of abstractions, so long as you get about among particulars with their aid and they actually carry you somewhere. Interested in no conclusions but those which our minds and our experiences work out together, she has no *a priori* prejudices against theology. *If theological ideas prove to have a value for concrete life, they will be true, for pragmatism, in the sense of being good for so much. For how much more they are true, will depend entirely on their relations to the other truths that also have to be acknowledged.*

What I said just now about the Absolute, of transcendental idealism, is a case in point. First, I called it majestic and said it yielded religious comfort to a class of minds, and then I accused it of remoteness and sterility. But so far as it affords such comfort, it surely is not sterile; it has that amount of value; it performs a concrete function. As a good pragmatist, I myself ought to call the Absolute true 'in so far forth,' then; and I unhesitatingly now do so.

But what does *true in so far forth* mean in this case? To answer, we need only apply the pragmatic method. What do believers in the Absolute mean by saying that their belief affords them comfort? They mean that since, in the Absolute finite evil is 'overruled' already, we may, therefore, whenever we wish, treat the temporal as if it were potentially the eternal, be sure that we can trust its outcome, and, without sin, dismiss our fear and drop the worry of our finite responsibility. In short, they mean that we have a right ever and anon to take a moral holiday, to let the world wag in its own way, feeling that its issues are in better hands than ours and are none of our business.

The universe is a system of which the individual members may relax their anxieties occasionally, in which the don't-care

mood is also right for men, and moral holidays in order,—that, if I mistake not, is part, at least, of what the Absolute is 'known-as,' that is the great difference in our particular experiences which his being true makes, for us, that is his cash-value when he is pragmatically interpreted. Farther than that the ordinary lay-reader in philosophy who thinks favorably of absolute idealism does not venture to sharpen his conceptions. He can use the Absolute for so much, and so much is very precious. He is pained at hearing you speak incredulously of the Absolute, therefore, and disregards your criticisms because they deal with aspects of the conception that he fails to follow.

If the Absolute means this, and means no more than this, who can possibly deny the truth of it? To deny it would be to insist that men should never relax, and that holidays are never in order.

I am well aware how odd it must seem to some of you to hear me say that an idea is 'true' so long as to believe it is profitable to our lives. That it is *good,* for as much as it profits, you will gladly admit. If what we do by its aid is good, you will allow the idea itself to be good in so far forth, for we are the better for possessing it. But is it not a strange misuse of the word 'truth,' you will say, to call ideas also 'true' for this reason?

To answer this difficulty fully is impossible at this stage of my account. You touch here upon the very central point of Messrs. Schiller's, Dewey's and my own doctrine of truth, which I can not discuss with detail until my sixth lecture. Let me now say only this, that truth is *one species of good,* and not, as is usually supposed, a category distinct from good, and co-ordinate with it. *The true is the name of whatever proves itself to be good in the way of belief, and good, too, for definite, assignable reasons.* Surely you must admit this, that if there were *no* good for life in true ideas, or if the knowledge of them were positively disadvantageous and false ideas the only useful ones, then the current notion that **truth** is divine and precious, and its pursuit a duty, could never have grown up or become a dogma. In a world like that, our duty would be to *shun* truth, rather. But in this world, just as certain foods are not only agreeable to our taste, but good for our teeth, our stomach, and our tissues; so certain ideas are not only agreeable to think about, or agreeable as supporting other ideas that we are fond of, but they are also helpful in life's practical struggles. If there be any life that it is really better we should lead, and if there be any idea which, if believed in, would help us to lead that life, then it would be really *better for us* to believe in that idea, *unless, indeed, belief in it incidentally clashed with other greater vital benefits.*

'What would be better for us to believe'! This sounds very like a definition of truth. It comes very near to saying 'what we *ought* to believe': and in *that* definition none of you would find any oddity. Ought we ever not to believe what it is *better for us* to believe? And can we then keep the notion of what is better for us, and what is true for us, permanently apart?

Pragmatism says no, and I fully agree with her. Probably you also agree, so far as the abstract statement goes, but with a suspicion that if we practically did believe everything that made for good in our own personal lives, we should be found indulging all kinds of fancies about this world's affairs, and all kinds of sentimental superstitions about a world hereafter. Your suspicion here is undoubtedly well founded, and it is evident that something happens when you pass from the abstract to the concrete that complicates the situation.

I said just now that what is better for us to believe is true *unless the belief incidentally clashes with some other vital benefit.* Now in real life what vital benefits is any particular belief of ours most liable to clash with? What indeed except the vital benefits yielded by *other beliefs* when these prove incompatible with the first ones? In other words, the greatest enemy of any one of our truths may be the rest of our truths. Truths have once for all this desperate instinct of self-preservation and of desire to extinguish whatever contradicts them. My belief in the Absolute, based on the good it does me, must run the gauntlet of all my other beliefs. Grant that it may be true in giving me a moral holiday. Nevertheless, as I conceive it,—and let me speak now confidentially, as it were, and merely in my own private person,—it clashes with other truths of mine whose benefits I hate to give up on its account. It happens to be associated with a kind of logic of which I am the enemy, I find that it entangles me in metaphysical paradoxes that are inacceptable, etc., etc. But as I have enough trouble in life already without adding the trouble of carrying these intellectual inconsistencies, I personally just give up the Absolute. I just *take* my moral holidays; or else as a professional philosopher, I try to justify them by some other principle.

If I could restrict my notion of the Absolute to its bare holiday-giving value, it wouldn't clash with my other truths. But we can not easily thus restrict our hypotheses. They carry supernumerary features, and these it is that clash so. My disbelief in the Absolute means then disbelief in those other supernumerary features, for I fully believe in the legitimacy of taking moral holidays.

You see by this what I meant when I called pragmatism a mediator and reconciler and said, borrowing the word from Papini, that she 'unstiffens' our theories. She has in fact no prejudices whatever, no obstructive dogmas, no rigid canons of what shall count as proof. She is completely genial. She will entertain any hypothesis, she will consider any evidence. It follows that in the religious field she is at a great advantage both over positivistic empiricism, with its anti-theological bias, and over religious rationalism, with its exclusive interest in the remote, the noble, the simple, and the abstract in the way of conception.

In short, she widens the field of search

for God. Rationalism sticks to logic and the empyrean. Empiricism sticks to the external senses. Pragmatism is willing to take anything, to follow either logic or the senses and to count the humblest and most personal experiences. She will count mystical experiences if they have practical consequences. She will take a God who lives in the very dirt of private fact—if that should seem a likely place to find him.

Her only test of probable truth is what works best in the way of leading us, what fits every part of life best and combines with the collectivity of experience's demands, nothing being omitted. If theological ideas should do this, if the notion of God, in particular, should prove to do it, how could pragmatism possibly deny God's existence? She could see no meaning in treating as 'not true' a notion that was pragmatically so successful. What other kind of truth could there be, for her, than all this agreement with concrete reality?

In my last lecture I shall return again to the relations of pragmatism with religion. But you see already how democratic she is. Her manners are as various and flexible, her resources as rich and endless, and her conclusions as friendly as those of mother nature.

George Santayana
1863

O F SPANISH parentage, George Santayana was born in Madrid and came to the United States at the age of eight. He was educated in Boston schools and at Harvard, where he was a student of Josiah Royce and William James. After his graduation in 1886, he studied for two years at the University of Berlin, his chief mentor in philosophy being Friedrich Paulsen.

Santayana taught philosophy at Harvard from 1889 to 1912 with interludes of study at Cambridge University and of lecturing at the Sorbonne and Oxford. Among Harvard students who came under his influence were the poets Conrad Aiken and T. S. Eliot. Fond of teaching, he disliked what passed for scholarly research in America. An inheritance enabled him to resign his professorship and to go abroad to live—first at Oxford, then at Paris after World War I, and finally at Rome, where he remained all during World War II. Invading American troops found him at the Convent of the Blue Nuns, serene, somewhat cynical toward man as a political animal, and not unwilling to be interviewed.

Aside from his two philosophical masterpieces, *The Life of Reason* (1905-1906) and *Realms of Being* (1927-1942), with its introduction, *Scepticism and Animal Faith* (1923), Santayana has written several volumes of poems, the best of which is his *Sonnets and Other Verses* (1884), and one novel, *The Last Puritan* (1935), which became a best-seller. *The Sense of Beauty* (1896) was a major contribution to aesthetic theory. Among his volumes of essays have been *Interpretations of Poetry and Religion* (1900); *Three Philosophical Poets* (1910); *Winds of Doctrine* (1913); *Egotism in German Philosophy* (1916); *Character and Opinion in the United States* (1920); *Soliloquies in England* (1922); *Dialogues in Limbo* (1925); *Platonism and the Spiritual Life* (1927);

The Genteel Tradition at Bay (1931); and *Some Turns of Thought in Modern Philosophy* (1933). He has capped a prolific writing career with his autobiography, *Persons and Places,* of which two installments, *Background of My Life* (1944) and *The Middle Span* (1945), have thus far appeared, and a contribution to the philosophy of religion, *The Idea of Christ in the Gospels or God in Man: A Critical Essay* (1946).

[Most valuable works on Santayana and his thought are G. W. Howgate's *George Santayana* (Philadelphia, 1938) and a symposium edited by P. A. Schlipp and entitled *The Philosophy of George Santayana* (Evanston and Chicago, 1940.)]

PREFACE TO REALMS OF BEING
[1927]

THE WORLD is old, and can have changed but little since man arose in it, else man himself would have perished. Why, then, should he still live without a sure and sufficient philosophy? The equivalent of such a philosophy is probably hereditary in sundry animals not much older than man. They have had time to take the measure of life, and have settled down to a routine of preferences and habits which keeps their heads, as a race, above water; and they are presumaby visited at appropriate seasons by magic images, which are symbols to them for the world or for the cycles of their destiny. Among groups of men an equilibrium of this moral sort has been sometimes approached—in India, in China, under the Moslem or the Catholic regimens; and if socialist or other panaceas now exercise such a strange influence over men's hearts, it is perhaps because they are impatient of being so long the sport of divers ignorant dogmas and chance adventures, and aspire to live in a stable harmony with nature.

In fact, beneath these various complete systems which have professed but failed to be universal, there is actually a dumb human philosophy, incomplete but solid, prevalent among all civilised peoples. They all practise agriculture, commerce, and mechanical arts, with artificial instruments lately very much complicated; and they necessarily possess, with these arts, a modicum of sanity, morality, and science req-uisite for carrying them on, and tested by success in doing so. Is not this human competence philosophy enough? Is it not at least the nucleus of all sound philosophy? In spite of the superficial confusion reigning in the world, is not the universal wisdom of the future actually gathering about this human competence in engineering, in chemistry, in medicine, in war?

The Realm of Matter

It might seem so, since the sort of knowledge involved in the arts, though it may not go very far, is compulsory so far as it goes, and being sanctioned by success, it ought to be permanent and progressive. There is indeed a circle of material events called nature, to which all minds belonging to the same society are responsive in common. Not to be responsive to these facts is simply to be stupid and backward in the arts; those who explore and master their environment cannot help learning what it is. In this direction competence involves enlightenment. Among minds forming a moral society, and able to compare their several opinions, this enlightenment in the expert is coercive over the layman also, because the same facts confront them both. Did not the same facts confront them, communication would be impossible between them, or if communication was reputed to exist by magic there would be no possible conflict or progress among their opinions, because they would not refer to the same events. Even if each declared himself competent and prosperous in his own world, ne would know nothing of the world of his neighbours. Their several minds would simply be variously or similarly brilliant, like jewels, signifying nothing to one another.

If any mind hopes to address another (or even itself) persuasively, as I now wish to address the reader and my own thoughts, it must assume a single system of events to which both minds are responsive, and which includes their respective bodies and actions. Assuming such a common world, it is easy to see how animals may acquire knowledge of it and may communicate it. Material events will arouse in them intuitions conformable to their several stations, faculties, and passions; and their active nature (since they are animals, not plants) will compel them to regard many of the essences so given in intuition as signs for the environment in which they move, modifying this environment and affected by it. This assumption justifies itself at every turn in practice, and establishes in the habits of all men, in proportion to their competence, an appropriate adjustment to the REALM OF MATTER, and in their imagination a suitable picture of the same.

The Realm of Essence

Nevertheless, since the station, faculties, and passions of all men are not identical, these pictures will not be similar. Different observers may be addressed to different regions of nature, or sensitive to different elements in the same region; thus dwellers in distinct planets must evidently have distinct geographies, and the same battle in the clouds will be known to the deaf only as lightning and to the blind only as thunder, each responding to a different constituent of the total event, and not simultaneously. So an eclipse—itself but one aspect of a constellation of events in the heavens—may be known in various entirely different terms; by calculation before it occurs, by sense when it is occurring, by memory immediately afterwards, and by reports to posterity. All these indications are entirely inadequate to the facts they reveal in the realm of matter, and qualitatively unlike those facts; they are a set of variegated symbols by which sensitive animals can designate them. Of course, the existence and use of such languages is an added fact in nature—a fact so important and close to the egotism of the animals themselves as perhaps to obscure all else in their eyes. Their instinct, indeed, keeps their attention stretched upon the material world that actually surrounds them; but sometimes sensation and language, instead of being passed over like the ticking of the telegraph, may become objects in themselves, in all their absolute musical insignificance; and then animals become idealists. The terms in which they describe things, unlike the things they meant to describe, are purely specious, arbitrary, and ideal; whether visual, tactile, auditory, or conceptual these terms are essentially *words*. They possess intrinsically, in their own ontological plane, only logical or aesthetic being; and this contains no indication whatever of the material act of speaking, touching, or looking which causes them to appear. All possible terms in mental discourse are essences existing nowhere; visionary equally, whether the faculty that discovers them be sense or thought or the most fantastic fancy.

Such diversity in animal experience taken in itself exhibits sundry qualities or forms of being, a part of the infinite multitude of distinguishable ideal terms which (whether ever revealed to anybody or not) I call the REALM OF ESSENCE. Pure intuition, in its poetic ecstasy, would simply drink in such of these essences as happened to present themselves; but for a wakeful animal they are signals. They report to his spirit, in very summary and uncertain images, the material events which surround him and which concern his welfare. They may accordingly become terms in knowledge if interpreted judiciously, and if interpreted injudiciously they may become illusions.

All Mental Discourse Is More or Less Significant Poetry

The dumb philosophy of the human animal, by which he rears his family and practices the arts and finds his way home, might take definite shape and establish a healthy routine in all his dealings with matter (which includes society), and yet his imaginative experience might retain all its specious originality. The control which the environment exercises over the structure and conduct of animals is decidedly loose. They can live dragging a long chain of idle tricks, diseases, and obsolete organs; and even this loose control fails almost entirely in the case of alternative senses or languages, one of which may serve as well as another. Many species survive together, many rival endowments and customs and religions. And the same control fails altogether in regard to the immaterial essences which those senses or languages call up before the mind's eye. Adaptation is physical, and it is only the material operation in sensation or speech that can possibly be implicated in the clockwork of nature. The choice of those visionary essences which meantime visit the mind, though regular, is free; they are the transcript of life into discourse, the rhetorical and emotional rendering of existence, which when deepened and purified, becomes poetry or music. There can be no reason why differences in these spheres, even among men of the same race, should not be perpetual. It would be mere sluggishness and egotism to regret it. Such differences are not merely added like a vain luxury to a sane recognition, in other conscious terms, of the facts of nature. The "sane" response to nature is by action only and by an economy which nature can accept and weave into her own material economy; but as to the terms of sense and discourse, they are all from the very beginning equally arbitrary, poetical, and (if you choose) mad; yet all equally symptomatic. They vary initially and intangibly from mind to mind, even in expressing the same routine of nature. The imagination which eventually runs to fine art or religion is the same faculty which, under a more direct control of external events, yields vulgar perception. The promptings and the control exercised by matter are continuous in both cases; the dream requires a material dreamer as much as the waking sensation, and the latter is a transcript of his bodily condition just as directly as the dream. Poetic, creative, original fancy is not a secondary form of sensibility, but its first and only form. The same manual restlessness and knack which makes man a manufacturer of toys makes him, when by chance his toys prove useful, a manufacturer of implements. Fine art is thus older than servile labour, and the poetic quality of experience is more fundamental than its scientific value. Existence may revert at any moment to play, or may run down in idleness; but it is impossible that any work or discovery should ever come about without the accompaniment of pure contemplation, if there is consciousness at all; so that the inherent freedom of the spirit can never be stamped out, so long as spirit endures.

The Realm of Spirit

Nor is it safe to imagine that inspired people, because they dream awake in their philosophy, must come to grief in the real world. The great religious and political systems which I mentioned above have had brilliant careers. Their adepts have been far from making worse soldiers than sceptics make, or worse workmen than materialists; nor have they committed suicide or been locked up in the madhouse more often than exact philosophers. Nature drives with a loose rein, and vitality of any sort, even if expressed in fancy, can blunder through many a predicament in which reason would despair. And if the mythical systems decline at last, it is not so much by virtue of the maladjustments underlying their speculative errors—for their myths as a whole are wisely contrived—as because imagination in its freedom abandons these errors for others simply because the prevalent mood of mankind has changed, and it begins dreaming in a different key. Spirit bloweth where it listeth, and continually undoes its own work. This world of free expression, this drift of sensations, passions, and ideas, perpetually kindled and fading in the light of consciousness, I call the REALM OF SPIRIT. It is only for the sake of this free life that material competence and knowledge of fact are worth attaining. Facts for a living creature are only instruments; his play-life is his true life. On his working days, when he is attentive to matter, he is only his own servant, preparing the feast. He becomes his own master in his holidays and in his sportive passions. Among these must be counted literature and philosophy, and so much of love, religion, and patriotism as is not an effort to survive materially. In such enthusiasms there is much asseveration; but what they attest is really not the character of the external facts concerned, but only the spiritual uses to which the spirit turns them.

The Range of Reasonable Curiosity

A philosopher cannot wish to be deceived. His philosophy is a declaration of policy in the presence of the facts; and therefore his first care must be to ascertain and heartily to acknowledge all such facts as are relevant to his action or sentiment— not less, and not necessarily more. The pursuit of truth is a form of courage, and a philosopher may well love truth for its own sake, in that he is disposed to confront destiny, whatever it may be, with zest when possible, with resignation when necessary, and not seldom with amusement. The facts to which it is prudent and noble in him to bare his bosom are the morally relevant facts, such as touch his fortunes or his heart, or such as he can alter by his efforts; nor can he really discover other facts. Intuition, or absolute apprehension without

media or doubt, is proper to spirit perusing essences; it is impossible to animals confronting facts. Animals know things by exploration, reaction, and prophetic fancy; they therefore can know only such parts and depths of nature as they explore materially and respond to vitally. The brave impulse to search may, indeed, become eager and may wish to recognise no limits; and there may be spirits so utterly practical and serious that the pursuit of material facts absorbs them altogether, to the exclusion of all play of mind. Yet such hectic exactitude is an expression of fear, and automatic rather than rational. Curiosity in an animal always has limits which it is foolish to transgress, because beyond them theory insensibly lapses into verbal myths, and if still taken for true knowledge defeats the honest curiosity that inspired it. What renders knowledge true is fidelity to the object; but in the conduct and fancy of an animal this fidelity can be only rough, summary, dramatic; too much refinement renders it subjective, as does too much haste. This is true of mathematical refinements no less than of verbal pedantries. The realm of matter can never be disclosed either to hypothesis or to sensation in its presumable inmost structure and ultimate extent: the garment of appearance must always fit loosely and drape it in alien folds, because appearance is essentially an adaptation of facts to the scale and faculty of the observer.

There are also moral limits to seriousness and utter literalness in thought. The tragic compulsion to honour the facts is imposed on man by the destiny of his body, to which that of his mind is attached. But his destiny is not the only theme possible to his thought, nor the most congenial. The best part of this destiny is that he may often forget it; and existence would not be worth preserving if it had to be spent exclusively in anxiety about existence.

Relativity of Knowledge

It follows from all this that knowledge

of facts merely because they are facts cannot be the ultimate object of a philosopher, although he must wish to know the whole unvarnished truth about relevant matters. A liberal mind must live on its own terms, and think in them; it is not inferior to what surrounds it; fact-worship on its part would accordingly be a fault in taste and in morals. What is the function of philosophy? To disclose the absolute truth? But is it credible that the absolute truth should descend into the thoughts of a mortal creature, equipped with a few special senses and with a biased intellect, a man lost amidst millions of his fellows and a prey to the epidemic delusions of the race? Possession of the absolute truth is not merely by accident beyond the range of particular minds; it is incompatible with being alive, because it excludes any particular station, organ, interest, or date of survey; the absolute truth is undiscoverable just because it is not a perspective. Perspectives are essential to animal apprehension; an observer, himself a part of the world he observes, must have a particular station in it; he cannot be equally near to everything, nor internal to anything but himself; of the rest he can only take views, abstracted according to his sensibility and foreshortened according to his interests. Those animals which I was supposing endowed with an adequate philosophy surely do not posses the absolute truth. They read nature in their private idioms. Their imagination, like the human, is doubtless incapable of coping with all things at once, or even with the whole of anything natural. Mind was not created for the sake of discovering the absolute truth. The absolute truth has its own intangible reality, and scorns to be known. The function of mind is rather to increase the wealth of the universe in the spiritual dimension, by adding appearance to substance and passion to necessity, and by creating all those private perspectives, and those emotions of wonder, adventure, curiosity, and laughter which omniscience would exclude. If omniscience were alone respect-

able, creation would have been a mistake. The single duty of all creatures would then be to repair that creative error, by abolishing their several senses and desires and becoming indistinguishable from one another and from nothing at all; and if all creation could attain to this sort of salvation, the absolute substance, in whose honour all else had been abandoned, would become unconscious. The time will doubtless come for each of us, if not for the universe at large, to cease from care; but our passage through life will have added a marvellous episode to the tale of things; and our distinction and glory, as well as our sorrow, will have lain in being something in particular, and in knowing what it is.

Thus if there is a sense in which all special and separable existence is illusion, there is another sense in which illusion is itself a special and separable existence; and if this be condemned for not being absolute truth, it may also be prized for these very reasons. Sensation is true enough. All experience yields some acquaintance with the realm of essence, and some perspective of the material world; and this would always be a true perspective (since things seen at that angle and with that organ really look like that) if the appearance were not stretched to cover more than it covers in reality. Of such true perspectives the simplest and most violently foreshortened may be as good as the most complicated, the most poetical or pictorial as good as the most scientific, not only aesthetically but even cognitively; because it may report the things concerned on that human scale on which we need to measure them, and in this relation may report them correctly. Nor is the error which such very partial knowledge may breed, when inflated by precipitate judgments and vanity, altogether unavoidable. The variety of senses in man, the precarious rule of his instincts, and the range of his memory and fancy, give rise in him eventually to some sense of error and even of humour. He is almost able to pierce the illusions of his animal dogmatism, to surrender the claim to inspiration, and in one sense to transcend the relativity of his knowledge and the flightiness of his passions by acknowledging them with a good grace.

The Realm of Truth

This relativity does not imply that there is no absolute truth. On the contrary, if there were no absolute truth, all-inclusive and eternal, the desultory views taken from time to time by individuals would themselves be absolute. They would be irrelevant to one another, and incomparable in point of truth, each being without any object but the essence which appeared in it. If views can be more or less correct, and perhaps complementary to one another, it is because they refer to the same system of nature, the complete description of which, covering the whole past and the whole future, would be the absolute truth. This absolute truth is no living view, no actual judgment, but merely that segment of the realm of essence which happens to be illustrated in existence. The question whether a given essence belongs to this segment or not—that is, whether a suggested idea is or is not true—has a tragic importance for an animal intent on discovering and describing what exists, or has existed, or is destined to exist in his world. He seldom has leisure to dwell on essences apart from their presumable truth; even their beauty and dialectical pattern seem to him rather trivial, unless they are significant of facts in the realm of matter, controlling human destiny. I therefore give a special name to this tragic segment of the realm of essence and call it the REALM OF TRUTH.

Human Values of Knowledge

The knowledge of relevant truth, while it has this fundamental moral importance, is far from being our only concern in the life of reason. It comes in only incidentally, in so far as a staunch and comprehensive knowledge of things makes a man master of things, and independent of them in a great

measure. The business of a philosopher is rather to be a good shepherd of his thoughts. The share of attention and weight which he gives to physical speculation or to history or to psychology will express his race and disposition, or the spirit of his times; everyone is free to decide how far material arts and sciences are worth pursuing, and with what free creations they shall be surrounded. Young and ardent minds, and races without accumulated possessions, tend to poetry and metaphysics; they neglect or falsify the truth in the heat of their imaginative passion. Old men, old nations, incline to mix their wine with larger dilutions of reality; and they prefer history, biography, politics, and humorous fictions; because in all these, while the facts are neither conceived nor tested scientifically, the savour of earth and of experience remains dominant.

By the philosopher, however, both the homeliest brew and the most meticulous science are only relished as food for the spirit. Even if defeated in the pursuit of truth, the spirit may be victorious in self-expression and self-knowledge; and if a philosopher could be nothing else, he might still be a moralist and a poet. He will do well to endow his vision of things with all the force, colour, and scope of which his soul is capable. Then if he misses the truth of nature, as in many things is probable, he will at least have achieved a work of imagination. In such a case the universe, without being mapped as a whole in the fancy, will be enriched at one point, by the happy life enacted there, in one human focus of art and vision. The purer and more distinct the spirit which a philosopher can bring to light in his thoughts, the greater the intellectual achievement; and the greater the moral achievement also, if the policy so set forth is actually carried out in his whole life and conversation.

Legitimate Variety in Speculation

As for me, in stretching my canvas and taking up my palette and brush, I am not vexed that masters should have painted before me in styles which I have no power and no occasion to imitate; nor do I expect future generations to be satisfied with always repainting my pictures. Agreement is sweet, being a form of friendship; it is also a stimulus to insight, and helpful, as contradiction is not; and I certainly hope to find agreement in some quarters. Yet I am not much concerned about the number of those who may be my friends in the spirit, nor do I care about their chronological distribution, being as much pleased to discover one intellectual kinsman in the past as to imagine two in the future. That in the world at large alien natures should prevail, innumerable and perhaps infinitely various, does not disturb me. On the contrary, I hope fate may manifest to them such objects as they need and can love; and although my sympathy with them cannot be so vivid as with men of my own mind, and in some cases may pass into antipathy, I do not conceive that they are wrong or inferior for being different from me, or from one another. If God and nature can put up with them, why should I raise an objection? But let them take care; for if they have sinned against the facts (as I suspect is often the case) and are kicking against the pricks of matter, they must expect to be brought to confusion on the day of doom, or earlier. Not only will their career be brief and troubled, which is the lot of all flesh, but their faith will be stultified by events, which is a needless and eternal ignominy for the spirit. But if somehow, in their chosen terms, they have balanced their accounts with nature, they are to be heartily congratulated on their moral diversity. It is pleasant to think that the fertility of spirit is inexhaustible, if matter only gives it a chance, and that the worst and most successful fanaticism cannot turn the moral world permanently into a desert.

The pity of it is only that contrary souls should often fight for the same bodies, natural or political, as if space and matter in the universe were inadequate (as on earth indeed they are) for every essence in its own time to see the sun. But existence is precipitate and blind; it cannot bide its time; and the seeds of form are often so wantonly and thickly scattered that they strangle one another, call one another weeds and tares, and can live only in the distracted effort to keep others from living. Seldom does any soul live through a single and lovely summer in its native garden, suffered and content to bloom. Philosophers and nations cannot be happy unless separate; then they may be single-minded at home and tolerant abroad. If they have a spirit in them which is worth cultivating (which is not always the case) they need to entrench it in some consecrated citadel, where it may come to perfect expression. Human beings allowed to run loose are vowed to perdition, since they are too individual to agree and too gregarious to stand alone. Hence the rareness of any polity founded on wisdom, like that of which ancient Greece affords some glimpses, and the equal rareness of a pure and complete philosophy, such as that of Dante or of Spinoza, conceived in some moment of wonderful unanimity or of fortunate isolation.

The Temper of This System

My own philosophy, I venture to think, is well-knit in the same sense, in spite of perhaps seeming eclectic and of leaving so many doors open both in physics and in morals. My eclecticism is not helplessness before sundry influences; it is detachment and firmness in taking each thing simply for what it is. Openness, too, is a form of architecture. The doctrine that all moralities equally are but expressions of animal life is a tremendous dogma, at once blessing and purging all mortal passions; and the conviction that there can be no knowledge save animal faith positing external facts, and that this natural science is but a human symbol for those facts, also has an immense finality: the renunciation and the assurance in it are both radical and both invincible.

In confessing that I have merely touched the hem of nature's garment, I feel that virtue from her has passed into me, and made me whole. There is no more bewitching moment in childhood than when the boy, to whom someone is slyly propounding some absurdity, suddenly looks up and smiles. The brat has understood. A thin deception was being practised on him, in the hope that he might not be deceived, but by deriding it might prove he had attained to a man's stature and a man's wit. It was but banter prompted by love. So with this thin deception practised upon me by nature. The great Sphinx in posing her riddle and looking so threatening and mysterious is secretly hoping that I may laugh. She is not a riddle but a fact; the words she whispers are not oracles but prattle.

Why take her residual silence, which is inevitable, for a challenge or a menace? She does not know how to speak more plainly. Her secret is as great a secret to herself as to me. If I perceive it, and laugh, instantly she draws in her claws. A tremor runs through her enigmatical body; and if she were not of stone she would embrace her boyish discoverer, and yield herself to him altogether. It is so simple to exist, to be what one is for no reason, to engulf all questions and answers in the rush of being that sustains them. Henceforth nature and spirit can play together like mother and child, each marvellously pleasant to the other, yet deeply unintelligible; for as she created him she knew not how, merely by smiling in her dreams, so in awaking and smiling back he somehow understands her; at least he is all the understanding she has of herself.

1880 ∞ *Morris Raphael Cohen* ∞ 1947

A NATIVE of Minsk, Russia, Morris Raphael Cohen came to the United States at the age of twelve. He took his B.S. degree at the College of the City of New York in 1900 and his Ph.D. at Harvard six years later, being a student of both Josiah Royce and William James. His apprenticeship as a teacher was in history at the Educational Alliance, at the Davidson Collegiate Institute, and in the New York public schools. He also taught mathematics at City College and was professor of philosophy there from 1912 to 1938, when he retired with the rank of professor emeritus and accepted a special professorship at the University of Chicago. He gave lectures at Columbia, the New School for Social Research, and Cornell, and held visiting professorships at Johns Hopkins, St. John's College, Yale, Harvard, and Stanford.

Cohen concerned himself with three main fields of inquiry—the interrelations of philosophy and science, the philosophy of law, and the social history and problems of the Jews. He edited some of the papers of Charles Saunders Peirce, wrote the comprehensive chapter on "Later Philosophy" in the last volume of *The Cambridge History of American Literature,* and served as associate editor of the *Journal of the History of Ideas.* In the April and June, 1940, issues of this journal are the documents in his spirited controversy with the literary critic Bernard Smith over the legitimacy of the Marxist approach to literary history.

[His books include *Reason and Nature* (1931); *Law and the Social Order* (1933); *Introduction to Logic and Scientific Method,* with Ernest Nagel (1934); *A Preface to Logic* (1944); *The Faith of a Liberal* (1946); and *The Meaning of Human History* (1948).]

From
REASON AND NATURE
[1932]

IN DISPRAISE OF LIFE, EXPERIENCE,
AND REALITY

IN SPEAKING of the new philosophic movement which began with the present century, William James remarked: "It lacks logical rigour, but it has the tang of life." It is strikingly significant of the temper of our age that this was intended and has generally been taken as praise of the new philosophy. To any of the classical philosophers, to whom not life, but the good life was the object of rational effort, James's dictum would have sounded as a condemnation. For life devoid of logic is confused, unenlightened, and often brutish. Indeed the new philosophy itself maintains that it is precisely because unreflective life is so unsatisfactory that it gives rise to logic. Why then should the word *life* itself be a term of praise except to those who prefer the primitive and dislike intellectual effort?

I can imagine that a classical philosopher living long enough amongst us to penetrate some of our bewildering ways might conclude that our worship of mere life, rather than the good or rational life, reflects the temper of an acquisitive society, feverishly intent on mere accumulation, and mortally afraid to stop to discriminate between what is worth while and what is not. The same preference for terms of promiscuous all-inclusiveness, rather than for those that involve the discrimination essential to philosophic clarity, shows itself also in the use of the terms *experience* and *reality*. It is of course true that surface clarity can

readily be obtained by ignoring fundamental difficulties, and that we cannot dispense with terms indicating the unlimited immensities of which our little formulated systems are but infinitesimal selections. But if the world contains many things and therefore distinctions between them, ignoring these distinctions is not the same as profundity. The honourific use of non-discriminating terms can only serve to darken counsel. That this has actually been the case in ethics and in theories of knowledge, in religion and in art, is the burden of this brief epilogue.

That the continuance of mere physical life is an absolute moral good seems to be axiomatic in current ethics. It serves as a basis for the unqualified moral condemnation of all forms of suicide and euthanasia. Now I do not wish to question the biologic proposition that there are forces which make the organism continue to function after we have lost all specifically human goods, such as honour and reason. What I do wish to point out is that this setting up of mere life as an absolute moral good, apart from all its social conditions, is inconsistent with the moral approval of the hero or the martyr who throws away life for the sake of honour or conscience. It would be pathetically absurd to praise the abandoning of life by John Huss or Giordano Bruno on the ground that it increased or prolonged the total amount of life. Indiscriminate increase of population beyond any definite limit is of very doubtful moral value—despite the arguments of those who oppose all forms of birth control. We must not lose sight of the fact that life always carries with it not only the seeds of disease and inevitable death, but also the roots of all that is vicious and hideous in human conduct. We cannot, therefore, dispense with the classical problem of defining the good and discriminating it from the evil of life—a difficult and baffling problem, to be sure; but those who find it profitless are under no obligation to pursue moral philosophy.

The confusion of moral theory by the eulogistic use of the word *life* can be readily seen in the Nietzschean ethics—all the more instructive because Nietzsche himself starts from the classical perception of the inadequacy of ordinary utilitarianism in face of the moral values of heroism. The good life involves the sacrifice of ease and comfort, the receiving as well as the giving of hard blows. But just because Nietzsche is impatient of definition he falls into the easy error of sharply opposing the pursuit of life to the pursuit of knowledge—witness his essay on History. But the pursuit of knowledge is itself a form of life. This fact cannot be obscured by rhetorical contrasts between the life of the closet philosopher and the open-air or what is euphemistically called *real* life. To the eye of philosophic reflection the scholar or persistent thinker shows as much life or vitality as those who have to cover their naked restlessness by a gospel of strenuous but aimless perpetual motion—in no particular direction. This is not the occasion to sing the praises of the intellect and what it has done to humanize life. We may grant that the distaste for arduous intellectual tasks is natural, blameless, and in some cases even providential. But when such distaste sets itself up as a philosophy of life it is only ridiculous.

This brings us to our second point, the vitalistic theory of knowledge—or perhaps we should refer to it as the theory of a vitalistic intuition superior to knowledge —I mean the widespread notion that by mere living we get an insight superior to that of the intellect operative in mathematical and natural science. To prevent misunderstanding, let me say that I am not referring here to genuine mysticism which asserts that all intellection and language

move in the mist of appearances and cannot reach the ineffable reality. Genuine mysticism always holds fast to the idea that the substance of reality is altogether beyond the power of language, and hence it does not use language to describe this reality. It holds that language can at best only indicate its own shortcomings and thus point the way beyond itself. When, however, as in the Bergsonian theory, the claim of the scientific intellect is set aside for an instinctive intuition, and when this is held to provide a superior explanation of empirical phenomena like the formation of the eye of the scallop, it seems to me that philosophy is then not far from glorified quackery where the philosopher's stone is expected to remove the effects of the evil eye or cure toothaches and other empirical ailments. We may grant that biology as a natural science does not carry us very far into the mystery of life. But it does not follow that our ignorance can be cured in any other way. The fallibility of scientific reasoning is best corrected only by definite experiments and the critical reasoning of science itself. When men despair of solving theoretic problems and appeal to undefined words like *life* they show themselves devoid of intellectual stamina. It is doubtless true that in the process of living our ideas develop, mature, and receive a solid amplitude through an enriched content. Time tests our judgments and eliminates clever, plausible sophistries. But it is also true that the older a lamb grows the more sheepish he gets. Nothing seems so solidly established by anthropology and history as that men will not learn from what has actually happened to them unless they have developed the power of reflection. The idea that experience alone will teach everybody is a thin optimistic illusion.

The use of the word *experience* without any ascertainable meaning is perhaps the outstanding scandal of recent philosophy. In its original sense, which it still retains in ordinary, intelligible discourse, and from which we cannot altogether liberate ourselves in philosophy, experience denotes conscious feeling or something which happens to us personally. Thus I make my meaning clear when I say, "I did not experience any pain during an operation," or, "I have never experienced what it is to be struck by lightning." I may also speak of not having experienced the panic of 1872 or the other side of the moon. The absence of such experience need not, however, prevent me from knowing a good deal about the operation, the lightning, the panic of 1872, and the other side of the moon—more indeed than about many of my own experiences. For experience in this personal and ordinary sense is but an infinitesimal portion of what is going on in the world of time and space, and even a small part of the world of ordinary human affairs. To identify the substance of the world with the fact of our experience of some part of it is to set up an anthropocentric universe, compared to which the mediaeval one is sane and respectable. For the mediaeval one rebuked the silly and arrogant pretensions of humanity by setting against it the great glory of God.

The absurdity of identifying the whole realm of nature with our little human experience of it is obscured in two ways—to wit, (1) by confusing the nature of possible experience, and (2) by stretching the word *experience* until it *excludes* nothing and therefore includes no definite meaning.

That things known are all objects of a conceivable possible experience to some possible being more or less like us need not be denied. But the object of a possible experience is a matter of intellectual consideration, not the object of actual personal experience. If, on the other hand, we stretch the meaning of the word *experience* and make it include everything that we can think about, e.g. the state of the earth before the advent of life, then there remains no difference between an object considered and an object experienced, and the proposition that knowledge rests on experience ceases to have significance. It is vain to define words so as to deny the fact that

we know many things to be beyond our experience. In general, the term *experience* either means something personal and therefore limited, or it becomes so promiscuously all-inclusive that it ceases to have any intelligible negative. Without an alternative term to denote what is not experience it cannot have any pragmatic meaning. With characteristic sensitiveness to the difficulties of his own account, Professor Dewey has realized something of this dilemma in which the use of the term *experience* involves him. He has tried to defend it by the analogy of the use of the terms *zero* and *infinity*. But zero and infinity indicate at least definite directions. They indicate which of two definite terms is to the left or right of the other in a series. The term *experience*, however, in Professor Dewey's thought is equally applicable to everything that is an object of consideration. I cannot therefore see that it serves any definite intellectual function beyond carrying the faint aroma of praise.

In general, when familiar words are stretched and put to new uses, confusion is bound to result. For the meaning we attach to words is based on habits which arbitrary resolutions cannot readily change, and we invariably drag the old meaning into the new context.

An instructive instance of the confusing use of the term *experience* is the current phrase *religious experience,* used by those who regard it as a substitute for rational theology. Here again, I have no quarrel with any one who claims to have had the beatific vision of God or a special revelation of the truths of religion. One who makes such a claim puts himself beyond argument except when he asks others to believe what he believes. Then the doubt which Tennyson applied to his own vision certainly becomes relevant. Nor is my quarrel with those who assume the truths of their religion on the authority of an historic church or revelation fortified by the necessary truths of reason. The current fashion which talks about religious experience distrusts the great streams of historic tradition as it does the claims of systematic theology—witness James's *Varieties of Religious Experience,* in which none of the great historic religions receives any attention. He thinks he can establish "piecemeal supernaturalism" by the methods of natural science and the rules of empirical evidence. An elementary consideration, however, of the logic of induction shows the impossibility of proving the existence of miraculous or supernatural interventions on the basis of the postulate of the uniformity of nature involved in induction. Indeed, the naturalist can well maintain that as instances of mystic experiences have their parallel in the effects of drugs, starvation, etc., the naturalistic explanation of them is the only one that is scientifically worth investigating. In any case, the spiritualistic hypothesis does not lend itself to the crucial test of affording us verifiable predictions. Not only a scientist but even a court of law would be derelict if it accepted as proved anything which rests on no better evidence than that offered by abnormal psychology for a finite, personal God and the immortality of the individual soul.

It is of course true that most people do not hold these beliefs as scientific hypotheses at all. Indeed, most people regard the cold, logical analysis of their religion with a horror like that which would be evoked by a funeral orator who proceeded to give a scientific examination of the character of the deceased. We come to mourn and praise our friend, not to hear him psychoanalyzed. But all this is irrelevant in moments of reflection or when our beliefs are challenged by the contrary beliefs of others. One may say: I hold these truths and the faith in them strengthens my life. But such assertions cannot keep out the lurking doubt that it is the psychologic attitude rather than the truth of what is assumed that produces the practical effects. The pragmatic glorification of belief contains the deep poison of scepticism as to what really exists, and this like a Nessus shirt will destroy any religious belief that puts

it on. Religion may begin in ritual and conduct, but it inevitably goes on to reflective belief that must submit to the canons of logic. The popular and superficial contrast between religion and theology ignores the fact that where a diversity of religion exists it is impossible to stop a process of reflection as to which of two conflicting claims is true. In such a society, religious creed or theology (including the possibility of a negative or atheistic theory) becomes inescapable. Hazy talk about religious experience will not adequately meet the difficulties.

If terms that have no genuine negatives are to be condemned as devoid of significance, the word *reality* should head the list. I am not unmindful of the many attempts to define the unreal. But the question is: What corresponds to these definitions? The Hindoo mystic is deeply irritated when the wise Chinaman suggests that the realm of Maya or illusion does not really exist, or that it is not worth while worrying about it. The reality of illusion is the emphatic centre of the Hindoo's philosophy, and similarly, of all those who sharply contrast reality and appearance. The difficulty here is classic. What I am more especially concerned about, however, is to call attention to the fact that the word *reality* maintains itself as a term of praise rather than of description. To be "in touch with reality" is our way of expressing what our less sophisticated brothers and sisters do by the phrase "in tune with the infinite." It is an expression which carries an agreeable afflatus without dependence on any definite meaning. Such edification is pleasing and would be harmless if it did not also cause intellectual confusion. This the eulogistic use of the word *reality* certainly does in the theory of art, especially in its realistic and expressionistic form.

Professor Neilson defined [1] the realistic motive, in poetry and art generally, as the

---

[1] A reference to W. A. Neilson's *Essentials of Poetry* (1911).

sense of fact. But whatever else art may involve, the process of selection is certainly essential to it in all its forms, useful as well as ornamental. Hence, the honourific use of a non-discriminating term like *reality* undoubtedly tends to justify the introduction of the inept and the ugly, which certainly cannot be denied to have real existence. But it is not only realism that is thus encouraged to escape or confuse the fundamental problem of what is relevant, fitting, or beautiful in representation and ornament. Expressionistic theories glorify the same lack of discrimination between the beautiful and the ugly. For expressionism is but a subjective realism. This becomes clear when we reflect that the real denotes, first, human affairs, then physical things, and now vivid impressions or emotions, so that abstractions are not real to us. The praise of reality, therefore, now has as its core the glorification of vivid impressions or violent expressions, regardless of fitness or coherence. This shows itself in an indiscriminate admiration for the breaking of all hitherto accepted rules of art—as if all rules were necessarily hindrances. But rules of art like the so-called rules of nature are at bottom only statements of what is relevant and what irrelevant to any given case. Hence it is doubtless true that new situations in art cannot always be profitably decided by old rules. But this again is a question of specific fitness, not to be disposed of by the violent assertion that the expression of inner reality is inconsistent with all rules.

It is doubtful, for instance, whether such a convention as the rules of the sonnet ever hindered a great poet from expressing himself, though it doubtless has aided many minor ones, perhaps unduly so.

To conclude, we cannot praise life without including in our praise moral and physical evil, corruption and death. As experience certainly includes error and illusion, we cannot praise it indiscriminately as a support of truth. Finally, as reality undoubtedly includes the useless and the ugly, its praise cannot but confuse the arts.

Instead of life we want the good life. Instead of accepting experience science discriminates between the experience of truth and the experience of illusion. Not all reality, but only a reality free from ugliness and confusing incoherence is the aim of art. Conduct, science, and art thus depend on rational discrimination. Rational philosophy tries to meet this need by defining the good, the true, and the beautiful. The essence of the romantic use of the terms *life, experience,* and *reality* is that it avoids this necessary task, and is therefore flattering to those to whom the use of reason is irksome. But the way to serenity and happiness through wisdom is more arduous and requires a purified vision into our hearts as well as courage to face the abysmal mystery of existence.

1865 ∽ *Irving Babbitt* ∽ 1933

THAT Irving Babbitt was born in Dayton, Ohio, that he received both his A.B., 1889, and his M.A., 1893, from Harvard, and that he studied at the Sorbonne 1891-92 are all facts that find reflection in what may be called the provincially tinged cosmopolitan traditionalism of his critical writing. His real passion was for the ancient languages and literatures, particularly Greek and Latin. It was largely because of the lack of demand for teachers in these fields of diminishing student interest that he became a teacher of French, first at Williams, then at Harvard, where he was made instructor in 1894, assistant professor in 1902, and full professor in 1912.

Recognized by his better students as a master of comparative literature, he soon gained a wide reputation, and young men interested in the history of ideas, the threat of modernism to civilization, and the philosophy of literary criticism were drawn to his classes. He gave guest lectures at Kenyon, Yale, Stanford, Amherst, Toronto, and the Sorbonne. It was in 1892 that he met Paul Elmer More, when they found themselves the only two students in a class in Sanskrit at Harvard. They became as inseparably linked in friendship and general critical attitudes as Mencken and Nathan, or Ransom and Tate.

One of Babbitt's first students, Van Wyck Brooks, was finally to revert, in *The Opinions of Oliver Allston* (1941), to his old master's contentious conservatism. Another of his students, G. R. Elliott, author of *The Cycle of Modern Poetry* (1929) and *Humanism and Imagination* (1938), regarded Babbitt and Emerson as two of America's greatest spiritual heroes. One of the more tangible results of Babbitt's influence was Norman Foerster's School of Letters at the University of Iowa. Babbitt wrote *Literature and the American College* (1908); *The New Laokoon* (1910); *The Masters of Modern French Criticism* (1912); *Rousseau and Romanticism* (1919); *Democracy and Leadership* (1924); *On Being Creative, and Other Essays* (1932); and *Spanish Character, and Other Essays* (1940).

[See the symposium edited by F. Manchester and O. Shepard, *Irving Babbitt, Man and Teacher* (New York, 1941).]

From
DEMOCRACY AND LEADERSHIP
[1924]

INTRODUCTION

ACCORDING to Mr. Lloyd George,[1] the future will be even more exclusively taken up than is the present with the economic problem, especially with the relations between capital and labor. In that case, one is tempted to reply, the future will be very superficial. When studied with any degree of thoroughness, the economic problem will be found to run into the political problem, the political problem in turn into the philosophical problem, and the philosophical problem itself to be almost indissolubly bound up at last with the religious problem. This book is only one of a series in which I have been trying to bring out these deeper implications of the modern movement. Though devoted to different topics, the volumes of the series are yet bound together by their common preoccupation with the naturalistic trend, which goes back in some of its main aspects at least as far as the Renaissance, but which won its decisive triumphs over tradition in the eighteenth century. Among the men of the eighteenth century who prepared the way for the world in which we are now living I have, here as elsewhere in my writing, given a preëminent place to Rousseau. It is hard for any one who has investigated the facts to deny him this preëminence, even though one should not go so far as

---

[1] Prime minister of England and First Lord of the treasury (1916-22).

to say with Lord Acton [2] that "Rousseau produced more effect with his pen than Aristotle, or Cicero, or Saint Augustine, or Saint Thomas Aquinas, or any other man who ever lived." The great distinction of Rousseau in the history of thought, if my own analysis be correct, is that he gave the wrong answers to the right questions. It is no small distinction even to have asked the right questions.

Rousseau has at all events suggested to me the terms in which I have treated my present topic. He is easily first among the theorists of radical democracy. He is also the most eminent of those who have attacked civilization. Moreover, he has brought his advocacy of democracy and his attack on civilization into a definite relationship with one another. Herein he seems to go deeper than those who relate democracy, not to the question of civilization versus barbarism, but to the question of progress versus reaction. For why should men progress unless it can be shown that they are progressing towards civilization; or of what avail, again, is progress if barbarism is, as Rousseau affirms, more felicitous? If we thought clearly enough, we should probably dismiss as somewhat old-fashioned, as a mere survivor of the nineteenth century, the man who puts his primary emphasis on the contrast between the progressive and the reactionary, and turn our attention to the more essential contrast between the civilized man and the barbarian. The man of the nineteenth century was indeed wont to take for granted that the type of progress he sought to promote was a progress towards civilization. Some persons began to have doubts on this point even before the War, others had their doubts awakened by the War itself, and still others have been made doubtful by the peace. An age that thought it was progressing towards a "far-off divine event," [3] and turned out instead to be progressing towards Armageddon, suffered, one cannot help surmising, from some fundamental confusion in its notions of progress. One

may be aided in detecting the nature of this confusion by the Emersonian distinction of which I have made considerable use in my previous writing—the distinction, namely, between a "law for man" and a "law for thing." [4] The special praise that Confucius bestowed on his favorite disciple was that he was "always progressing and never came to a standstill." What Confucius plainly had in mind was progress according to the human law. What the man of the nineteenth century meant as a rule by the term was no less plainly material progress. He seems to have assumed, so far as he gave the subject any thought at all, that moral progress would issue almost automatically from material progress. In view of the duality of human experience, the whole question is, however, vastly more complex than the ordinary progressive has ever suspected. Progress according to the natural law must, if it is to make for civilization, be subordinated to some adequate end; and the natural law does not in itself supply this end. As a result of the neglect of this truth, we have the type of man who deems himself progressive and is yet pursuing power and speed for their own sake, the man who does not care where he is going, as some one has put it, provided only he can go there faster and faster.

If progress and civilization do not mean more than this, one might be justified in sharing Rousseau's predilection for barbarism. The reason he gives for preferring the barbaric to the civilized state is in itself extremely weighty: the barbaric state is, he maintains, the more fraternal. The fraternal spirit is the fine flower, not merely of genuine philosophy, but of genuine religion. One should be ready to make almost any sacrifice in order to attain it. My endeavor has, however, been to show

[2] British historian (1834-1902).
[3] Quoted from the last stanza of Tennyson's *In Memoriam*.
[4] These phrases are from Emerson's "Ode Inscribed to W. H. Channing."

that Rousseau's fraternity is only a sentimental dream. The psychic impossibility involved in this dream is obvious, one may even say, glaring. For example, Walt Whitman, one of the chief of Rousseau's American followers, preaches universal brotherhood among men each one of whom is, like himself, to "permit to speak at every hazard, Nature without check with original energy";[5] in other words, Whitman proposes to base brotherhood, a religious virtue, on expansive appetite.

I have tried here and elsewhere to show that democratic fraternity, as a Rousseau and a Whitman conceive it, and progress, as the utilitarian conceives it, are, however much they may clash at certain points, nevertheless only different aspects of the same naturalistic movement. This movement may be defined in its totality as humanitarianism. I ventured the assertion several years ago that something is omitted in this movement, and that the something may turn out to be the keystone of the arch. The error that results from this central omission assumes many forms. I choose almost at random a very crude form—the form in which it is finally reaching the man in the street. A writer in a widely circulated magazine, "Photoplay," devotes several editorial paragraphs to denouncing the people who say "don't"; they are, he complains, mere destroyers, the enemies of every generous creative impulse. Only in so far as one gets rid of the don'ts does one fulfil the saying of the Teacher, "I am come that ye shall have life, and that ye shall have it more abundantly." Mr. Henry Ford would no doubt dismiss such utterances as part of the great Jewish plot to destroy Gentile civilization.[6] It was not, however, a Jew, but Madame de Staël,[7] who declared that everything expansive in human nature is divine. This notion of a divine expansiveness has a long history in the Occident anterior to Madame de Stael, a history that in some of its phases goes at least as far back as the Neoplatonists.

In any case the assertion that one attains to more abundant life (in the religious sense) by getting rid of the don'ts sums up clearly, even though in an extreme form, the side of the modern movement with which I am taking issue. This book in particular is devoted to the most unpopular of all tasks—a defence of the veto power. Not the least singular feature of the singular epoch in which we are living is that the very persons who are least willing to hear about the veto power are likewise the persons who are most certain that they stand for the virtues that depend upon its exercise—for example, peace and brotherhood. As against the expansionists of every kind, I do not hesitate to affirm that what is specifically human in man and ultimately divine is a certain quality of will, a will that is felt in its relation to his ordinary self as a will to refrain. The affirmation of this quality of will is nothing new: it is implied in the Pauline opposition between a law of the spirit and a law of the members. In general, the primacy accorded to will over intellect is Oriental. The idea of humility, the idea that man needs to defer to a higher will, came into Europe with an Oriental religion, Christianity. This idea has been losing ground in almost exact ratio to the decline of Christianity. Inasmuch as the recognition of the supremacy of will seems to me imperative in any wise view of life, I side in important respects with the Christian against those who have in the Occident, whether in ancient or modern times, inclined to give the first place either to the intellect or the emotions. I differ from the Christian, however, in that my interest in the higher will and the power of veto it exercises over man's expansive desires is humanistic rather than religious. I am

[5] Quoted from the first section of Whitman's "Song of Myself."

[6] Because of articles printed in the Ford-controlled *Dearborn* (Mich.) *Independent* on the spurious *Protocols of the Elders of Zion*, Henry Ford gained a reputation for anti-Semitism, which he later repudiated.

[7] Anne Louise Germaine, Baronne de Staël-Holstein (1766-1817), French romantic writer and arbiter of taste.

concerned, in other words, less with the meditation in which true religion always culminates, than in the mediation or observance of the law of measure that should govern man in his secular relations. Moreover, I am for coming at my humanism in a positive and critical rather than in a merely traditional manner. To this extent I am with the naturalists, who have from the start been rejecting outer authority in favor of the immediate and experimental. One should have only respect for the man of science in so far as he deals in this critical fashion with the natural law— and no small part of human nature itself comes under the natural law. The error begins when an attempt is made to extend this law to cover the whole of human nature. This is to deny not merely outer authority, but something that is a matter of immediate experience, the opposition, namely, of which the individual is conscious in himself, between a law of the spirit and a law of the members. Deny or dissimulate this opposition and the inner life tends in the same measure to disappear. Carlyle's contrast between the Rousseauism of the French Revolution and true Christianity is also the contrast between humanitarianism in general, in either its sentimental or its utilitarian form, and any doctrine that affirms the higher will. "Alas, no, M. Roux!" Carlyle exclaims. "A Gospel of Brotherhood not according to any of the four old Evangelists and calling on men to repent, and amend *each his own* wicked existence, that they might be saved; but a Gospel rather, as we often hint, according to a new fifth Evangelist Jean-Jacques, calling on men to amend *each the whole world's* wicked existence and be saved by making the Constitution. A thing different and distant *toto cælo*." [8]

My own objection to this substitution of social reform for self-reform is that it involves the turning away from the more immediate to the less immediate. In general I have sought in my attack on the utilitarian-sentimental movement to avoid metaphysical and theological assumptions,

and to rely on psychological analysis supported by an immense and growing body of evidence. My humanism is in this sense not only positive and critical, but, what will be found to come to the same thing, individualistic. Under existing conditions, the significant struggle seems to me to be not that between the unsound individualist and the traditionalist, nor again, as is currently assumed, that between the unsound individualist and the altruist, but that between the sound and the unsound individualist. To be a sound individualist, one needs, as I take it, to retain one's hold on the truths of the inner life, even though breaking more or less completely with the past.

It may help to a fuller understanding of my present attempt to deal in a fashion at once critical and humanistic with the problem of the will in its bearing on the political problem if I say a few words at this point about certain previous stages in my argument. In the opening chapters of "Literature and the American College" I seek to discriminate between the humanist and the humanitarians of either the utilitarian or the sentimental brand. These two sides of the movement I sometimes term the Baconian and the Rousseauistic after the names of the men who seem to me to have prefigured them most completely in their writings and personalities. The humanitarian is not, I pointed out, primarily concerned, like the humanist, with the individual and his inner life, but with the welfare and progress of mankind in the lump. His favorite word is "service." The current tendency to regard humanism simply as an abbreviated and more convenient form for humanitarianism can only be the source of the most vicious confusions.

In "The Masters of Modern French Criticism" I attempt to carry a stage farther my defence of a critical humanism. Though the basis of the inner life is the opposition between a lower and a higher will, the

---

[8] Quoted from Carlyle's *The French Revolution* (1837); as much as possible.

higher will cannot, after all, act at random. It must have standards. Formerly the standards were supplied by tradition. The man who accepted Christian tradition, for example, was in no doubt as to the kind and degree of discipline he needed to impose on his lower nature. He thus achieved some measure of moral unity with himself and also with other men who accepted the same discipline. If the individualist, on the other hand, is to have standards, he must rely on the critical spirit in direct ratio to the completeness of his break with the traditional unifications of life. He is confronted at the outset with the most difficult of philosophical problems—that of the One and the Many. For it is obvious that standards cannot exist unless there is an element of oneness somewhere with which to measure the infinite otherwiseness of things. The special theme of "The Masters" is the problem of the One and the Many and the failure of Sainte-Beuve and other eminent French individualists to deal with it adequately and so to achieve standards in a modern fashion. The results of the critical endeavor of the past century may be summed up most completely, perhaps, in the word relativity. The failure of criticism to attain to any centre of judgment set above the shifting impressions of the individual and the flux of phenomenal nature is a defeat for civilization itself, if it be true, as I have tried to show, that civilization must ultimately depend on the maintenance of standards. In "The New Laokoon" I have sought to exhibit the anarchy that has supervened in literature and the arts with the progressive decline of standards. Superficially, this anarchy seems above all an anarchy of the emotions. On closer scrutiny, however, emotional anarchy itself turns out to be only a sign of something subtler and more dangerous—anarchy of the imagination. In "Rousseau and Romanticism," a book that is closely connected in argument with "The New Laokoon," the problem of the imagination receives special treatment. I come here to another distinctive feature of the type of

humanism I am defending. I not only have more to say of will and less of reason than the humanist in the Graeco-Roman tradition, but I also grant a most important role to imagination. If one does not, like Diderot,[9] dismiss as "artificial" the conflict between a natural or expansive will and a specifically human will or will to refrain, if, on the contrary, one insists on this conflict as a primordial fact of consciousness, one will be led, I believe, to the further conclusion that the outcome of this "civil war in the cave" will be determined by the attitude of the imagination; that the imagination, in other words, holds the balance of power between the higher and the lower nature of man. In the light of history (one need not go any farther back than the Great War) man's pretence to be governed by reason in any ordinary sense of the word seems a bad jest. The critical observer is forced to agree with Napoleon that, not reason, but "imagination governs mankind." It does not follow that mankind need be governed, as it has been very largely during the past century, by the Napoleonic quality of imagination.

The complaint has been made that the word imagination has been used in so many senses that it has ceased to have any meaning. My own understanding of the term may perhaps be made clearer by a brief historical survey. The Latin word (imaginatio) from which our word is derived is itself a rendering of the Greek phantasy or fancy (φαντασία). Fancy means literally "what appears"; in other words, either the various impressions of sense, or else a faculty that stores up these impressions and is therefore closely related to memory. Greek philosophy gave a rather low rating to "fancy" or appearance in comparison with reality, which it inclined to identify with reason or mind. To the Stoic in particular it seemed both feasible and imperative that reason should hold sway over all the impressions that

---

[9] Denis Diderot (1713-1784), French Encyclopedist.

beat upon the gateway of the senses and make a severe selection among them. "How easy a thing it is," says Marcus Aurelius,[10] "to put away and blot out every 'fancy' (i.e., impression) that is disturbing or alien, and to be at once in perfect peace." The disparagement of fancy in this sense is already found in Plato. He hopes to attain a truth that is "firm and not pulled around this way and that by our 'fancy.'" A chief source of Christian humility, on the other hand, was the conviction that man is unable by his own resources to achieve any such truth, the conviction, above all, that mere reason cannot prevail over the deceits of the senses. Pascal,[11] for example, gives to the word imagination about the same meaning that the Stoic gave either to it or its Greek equivalent, and like the Stoic he disparages imagination; only to this disparagement he adds the disparagement of reason. What he opposes to an imagination that is only a "mistress of error" and to a reason that is impotent to resist this error is the "heart," by which he means the illumination of the higher will in the form of grace. This inner revelation has itself the support of outer revelation. Here, he holds, one may find at last a firm footing of truth and reality. He does not admit that imagination has any part either in outer revelation or in the life of the "heart." He has this much at least in common with Plato that he believes it possible to draw a firm and fast line between imagination (or mere appearance) and reality. Strict psychology, however, scarcely warrants any such sharp discrimination between the true and the illusory. It forces one rather to conclude with Joubert,[12] that "illusion is an integral part of reality." This conclusion, however damaging it may be to mere dogma, does not force one to forego standards. But in that case one needs to attend to another possible meaning of the word imagination, the second main meaning, one is tempted to say, that the word has actually had in Occidental thought. The word in this other meaning stands less for what one perceives, either

inwardly or outwardly, than for what one conceives. Conceit, it should be remembered, was in older English usage not only a complimentary term, but one of the synonyms of imagination. The process by which the term has come to have its present unfavorable meaning of vain imagining has its adequate historical explanation into which I need not here enter. Now to "conceive" is, in an almost etymological sense, to gather things together, to see likenesses and analogies and in so far to unify what were else mere heterogeneity. The imagination, says Coleridge somewhat pedantically, is the "esemplastic" power—the power, that is, that fashions things into one. The passages in which Coleridge expounds this view of the imagination afford, perhaps, the best example in English of what I have called the second main meaning of the word.[13] For an instance of the other main meaning we may turn to Addison's papers on the imagination in the "Spectator."[14] Addison not only tends to reduce imagination to outer perception, but, encouraged by the Latin rendering of the Greek "fancy," to narrow outer perception itself to visual perception.

If we mean by imagination not merely what we perceive, but what we conceive, it follows inevitably that the problem of the imagination is closely bound up with that of the One and the Many and therefore with the problem of standards; for it is impossible, let me repeat, to achieve standards, at least along critical lines, unless one can discover in life somewhere an abiding unity with which to measure its mere variety and change. Because "illusion is an integral part of reality," we are not justified in assuming that every unity that

---

[10] Roman emperor and stoic philosopher (121-180).

[11] Blaise Pascal (1623-1662), French philosopher and mathematician.

[12] Joseph Joubert (1754-1824), French essayist.

[13] See Coleridge's *Biographia Literaria* (1817), ch. xiii.

[14] Nos. 411-21 discuss the Pleasures of the Imagination.

the imagination may conceive must therefore be dismissed as illusory. A somewhat paradoxical person might indeed affirm that, even though one did not raise directly the question of reality at all, it would still be possible to have standards; that one might measure men accurately enough for most practical purposes simply by the quality of their illusions—and their disillusions. However, in spite of the fact that absolute unity and reality must ever elude us and that the absolute in general must be dismissed as a metaphysical dream, we may still determine on experimental grounds to what degree any particular view of life is sanctioned or repudiated by the nature of things and rate it accordingly as more or less real. God, according to Synesius,[15] communicates with man through the imagination. Unfortunately the devil communicates with him in the same way and the test of these communications is not, strictly speaking, in the imagination itself. To determine the quality of our imaginings, we need to supplement the power in man that perceives and the power that conceives with a third power—that which discriminates. All divisions of man into powers or faculties are, I am aware, more or less arbitrary, but, though arbitrary, they are inevitable, if only as instruments of thought; and the threefold division I am here employing will, I believe, be found practically one of the most helpful.

In emphasizing the importance of the power in man that discriminates, I mean this power, working not abstractly, but on the actual material of experience. I may perhaps best sum up my whole point of view by saying that the only thing that finally counts in this world is a concentration, at once imaginative and discriminating, on the facts. Now the facts that one may perceive and on which one may concentrate are not only infinite in number, but of entirely different orders. This is one reason why material progress, so far from assuring moral progress, is, on the contrary, extremely difficult to combine with it. This progress has been won by an al-

most tyrannical concentration on the facts of the natural law. Man's capacity for concentration is limited, so that the price he has paid for material progress has been an increasing inattention to facts of an entirely different order—those, namely, of the human law. The resulting spiritual blindness has been an invitation to Nemesis. One may have some inkling of the nature of this Nemesis from the Great War and other similar symptoms that have been multiplying of late in our Western societies.

It goes without saying that the partisans of "progress" have not admitted their spiritual blindness. They have accepted as valid substitutes for the traditional standards and the moral unity that these standards tended to promote certain new unifications of life that display great imagination, indeed, but an imagination that has not been sufficiently tested from the point of view of reality. These new schemes for unifying men flourished especially in connection with the so-called romantic movement. It is therefore no small matter that the leaders of this movement can be shown to have erected deliberately a cult of the creative imagination on the ruins of discrimination. Any one who takes seriously the creations of this type of imagination, an imagination that is not disciplined to either the natural or the human law, but is, in Young's phrase, free to wander wild in its own realm of chimeras,[16] falls into mere conceit or vain imagining. Conceit has always been the specifically human malady, but never, perhaps, more so than to-day. The outstanding trait of the men of our period may seem in retrospect to have been the facility with which they put forth untried conceits as "ideals." We have all grown familiar with the type of person who is in his own conceit a lofty "idealist,"

---

[15] Greek neoplatonist philosopher (c. 370-430).

[16] The phrase is taken from *Conjectures on Original Composition* (1759) by Edward Young (1683-1765), famous for his poem, *Night Thoughts* (1742-5).

but when put to the test has turned out to be only a disastrous dreamer.

Though man is governed by imagination, fortunately it does not follow that he must be governed by conceit. There remains the distinction between the mere visionary and the man of vision. This distinction acquires its full importance only when related to the question of leadership. A main purpose of my present argument is to show that genuine leaders, good or bad, there will always be, and that democracy becomes a menace to civilization when it seeks to evade this truth. The notion in particular that a substitute for leadership may be found in numerical majorities that are supposed to reflect the "general will" is only a pernicious conceit. In the long run democracy will be judged, no less than other forms of government, by the quality of its leaders, a quality that will depend in turn on the quality of their vision. Where there is no vision, we are told, the people perish; but where there is sham vision, they perish even faster. The worst difficulties of the present time arise, I am sometimes tempted to think, even less from lack of vision than from sham vision. Otherwise stated, what is disquieting about the time is not so much its open and avowed materialism as what it takes to be its spirituality.

Among the visionaries who have usurped the credit that belongs only to the man of vision, Rousseau seems to me to have been, at least in these recent ages of the world, the most conspicuous. The Nature to which he invites us to return is only a conceit. This conceit encourages one to substitute for the vital control, which is the true voice of man's higher self, expansive emotion. Ideally this substitution is to be marked by a triumph of the fraternal spirit. Actually, as I have sought to prove, the outcome of yielding to a mere expansive conceit of the emotions is not fraternity, but a decadent imperialism. I have made a considerable use of the word imperialism in this work and in a somewhat broader sense than is familiar to English and American readers. My justification lies in the fact that one finds behind every other form of imperialism the imperialism or push for power of the individual. In this respect, at least, I am in accord with Bergson, who declares that "imperialism is, as it were, inherent in the vital urge. It is at the bottom of the soul of individuals as well as of the soul of peoples." By his cult of *élan vital* Bergson is in the direct line of descent from Rousseau. One must note, however, an important divergence between master and disciple that is all to the advantage of the latter. Bergson does not hope to base on *élan vital* a fraternity that must be sought rather in the exercise of *frein vital*.[17] On the contrary, *élan vital* is, he avows frankly, imperialistic. According to the new Bergsonian beatitude, not the meek in spirit, but those who have the most vigorous vital urge are to inherit the earth. It is hard to overlook the affinity between this world-famed philosophy, as interpreted by its author, and the vulgar admiration for "punch."

My application of the epithet decadent to the type of imperialism that has been promoted by the glorification of instinct from Rousseau to Bergson calls for a word of comment. That there are various types of imperialism, even if we use the word, not in the psychological, but in the more familiar political sense, appears evident. For example, the imperialism that made the Romans masters of the world is not of the same kind as that which prevailed when they cringed beneath a Tiberius or a Nero. Yet it is possible to trace the process by which the older imperialism finally took on a decadent cast. The critical moment for Rome was the moment of triumph when the leaders of the State no longer felt the restraining influence of dangerous rivals like Carthage. At the same time they were beginning to grow individualistic in the sense that they were beginning to throw off the traditional controls. As a result of

[17] Babbitt here contrasts his own will-to-refrain (*frein vital*) with Bergson's life-force (*élan vital*).

all this emancipation, "men's desires," in Montesquieu's phrase, "became immense." [18] It has been usual to regard as the most significant symptom of this inordinateness the growth of luxury. "Luxury," says Juvenal,[19] "more cruel than the foeman's arms, fell upon us, and is avenging the conquered world." A still graver symptom, however, was the appearance of leaders who were ever more and more ruthless in the pursuit either of their personal advantage or that of some class or faction. The new spirit that was undermining the Roman constitution manifested itself even less, as Cicero notes, in acts of injustice and cruelty to the vanquished peoples than in the rage of civil strife. It can scarcely be maintained of the Romans who thus precipitated the decadence that they exercised to any serious degree their *frein vital,* or will to refrain. The right opponents of these anarchical individualists, one may venture to affirm, were not the mere traditionalists, but the individualists who had qualified for true leadership by setting bounds to their expansive lusts, especially the lust of domination. Rome declined because she failed to produce individualists of this type in sufficient numbers. Certain analogies may be discovered between this Roman dilemma and the dilemma with which we are now confronted in America. We, too, seem to be reaching the acme of our power and are at the same time discarding the standards of the past. This emancipation has been accompanied by an extraordinary increase in luxury and self-indulgence. Persons who postpone everything else to their "comfort" and to commercial prosperity are probably more numerous in America to-day than they were in ancient Rome. Disturbing as this symptom may be, it is less so than the increasing role played in our national life by "blocs" with highly unethical leaders— leaders who seek to advance the material interests of some special group at the expense of the whole community. The actual gravity of this symptom may perhaps be exaggerated; if it should prove, however,

to be something more than a passing phase, it portends the end of our constitutional liberties and the rise of a decadent imperialism. The more one ponders either the modern American or the ancient Roman situation, the more surely will one be led from imperialism in the political, to imperialism in the psychological sense. In other words, one will be forced, if one wishes to get at the root of the matter, to turn from the merely peripheral manifestations of the push for power to the inner life of the individual.

My views as to the relation between the Rousseauistic movement and imperialism may perhaps be still further elucidated by a comparison with the views on the same subject of two recent European writers, the German, Oswald Spengler, and the Frenchman, Ernest Seillière. Spengler has developed in his chief work, "The Downfall of the Occident," [20] the thesis that the Western world, especially Western European "culture," is now engaged in a sort of rake's progress that starts with Rousseau and his return to nature. The goal of this decadence, as Spengler describes it, is not unlike what I have termed a decadent imperialism. Moreover, we are not only on a descending curve, but it is a fatal curve. He has actually appended to the first volume of his book a table exhibiting the degree of degeneracy that the Occident will have attained about the year 2000. The whole conception not only implies a philosophy of history, but a philosophy of history that has, in my judgment, gone mad. This conception is based in any case on an utter denial of the quality of will in man on which I myself put supreme emphasis. In spite therefore of certain superficial resemblances in our respective views,

---

[18] Baron de Montesquieu (1689-1755), French philosopher and jurist, author of *The Spirit of the Laws* (1748).

[19] Roman satirist (c. 60-140).

[20] Better known as *The Decline of the West,* title of the only English translation of the work originally published in 1918.

Spengler and I are at the opposite poles of human thought. My own attitude is one of extreme unfriendliness to every possible philosophy of history (in the more technical sense of the term), whether it be the older type found in a Saint Augustine or a Bossuet,[21] which tends to make of man the puppet of God, or the newer type which tends in all its varieties to make of man the puppet of nature. "The Downfall of the Occident" seems to me a fairly complete repertory of the naturalistic fallacies of the nineteenth century; it is steeped throughout in the special brand of fatalism in which these fallacies culminate, and as a result of which the Occident is actually threatened with "downfall." One is justified in my opinion in dismissing Spengler as a charlatan, even though one be forced to add that he is a charlatan of genius. The immense sale of his books in Germany, if it is indicative of a real influence, is a depressing symptom.

The second writer I have mentioned, M. Seillière, merits a very different judgment. In about a score of volumes he has been tracing with great psychological finesse the influence of Rousseau on the literature and life of the past century. This influence he associates with what he calls an irrational imperialism. In short, the results of his survey are on the negative side very similar to my own. On the positive or constructive side, on the other hand, M. Seillière and I diverge sharply. What he opposes to an irrational imperialism is a rational imperialism; by which he means "the social army on the march towards the conquest of power by the coordination of individual efforts." In his general position, as revealed in such utterances, he seems to me to strike back through the utilitarians to Hobbes and ultimately, in some respects, to Machiavelli. The essential contrast for me is not, as for M. Seillière, that between a rational and an irrational imperialism, but between imperialism and that quality of will in man which is, in every possible sense of the word, anti-imperialistic. M. Seillière, again,

seems as much bent on running together Stoical and Christian ethics as I am on separating them and insisting on their final incompatibility. Stoicism in both its ancient and modern forms I regard, at least in its total trend, as false and impossible; whereas I hold that at the heart of genuine Christianity are certain truths which have already once saved Western civilization and, judiciously employed, may save it again.

I wish also to say a few words at the outset regarding certain possible misapprehensions of my method. The most serious of these misapprehensions may arise if one looks either in this volume or in the previous volumes of the series (with the partial exception of "The Masters of Modern French Criticism") for rounded estimates of individuals. I have not attempted such estimates. Still less have I attempted rounded estimates of historical epochs— for example, of the nineteenth century. It is even less sensible, perhaps, to indict a whole century than it is, according to Burke, to indict a whole people. I am attacking, not the nineteenth century in general, but the naturalistic nineteenth century and its prolongation into the twentieth century, along with the tendencies in the previous centuries, from the Renaissance down, that prepared the way for naturalism. My treatment of this whole naturalistic trend has seemed, even to critics who are not altogether unfriendly, to be negative, extreme, and one-sided. I hope I may be pardoned if I reply briefly to each of these three charges.

As to the charge that my treatment of naturalism is one-sided, there is a sense, it must be admitted, in which it is not only one-sided, but one-sided to the last degree. There is, however, a humanistic intention even in the one-sidedness. I dwell persistently on the aspect of human nature that the naturalists have no less persistently neglected in the hope that the way may

---

[21] Jacques Bénigne Bossuet (1627-1704), French bishop and orator.

thus be opened for a more balanced view. Moreover, what the naturalists have neglected is not something that is on the fringe or outer rim of human experience, but something, on the contrary, that is very central. The naturalistic effort during the past century or more has resulted in an immense and bewildering peripheral enrichment of life—in short, in what we are still glorifying under the name of progress. I have no quarrel with this type of progress in itself, I merely maintain that no amount of peripheral enrichment of life can atone for any lack at the centre. Furthermore, though I assail the naturalists for what seems to me a vital oversight, I have, let me repeat, at least one trait in common with them—I desire to be experimental. I seek to follow out the actual consequences of this oversight, to deal with it, not abstractly, but in its fruits. If certain readers have persisted in seeing in my books something that I myself have not sought to put there, namely, rounded estimates of individuals and historic epochs, the misapprehension has no doubt arisen from the very abundance of my concrete illustrations.

As to the charge that I am negative, I have already said that the element in man that has been overlooked by naturalistic psychology is felt in relation to his ordinary self negatively. If instead of taking the point of view of one's ordinary self, one heeds the admonitions of the inner monitor, the result is two of the most positive of all things: character and happiness. This is the great paradox of life itself. For being negative in this sense I am not in the least apologetic. There is, however, another sense in which I may seem negative and about this I feel differently. The type of criticism that prevailed about the beginning of the nineteenth century proposed to substitute the "fruitful criticism of beauties for the barren criticism of faults." I may be accused of reversing too sharply this maxim even by some who admit that the proper remedy for the lax appreciativeness of the modern movement is a criticism

that displays a tonic astringency. I am constantly calling attention to the defects of certain eminent personalities, it may be urged, and at the same time have little or nothing to say of their virtues. My method is even in this respect, I believe, legitimate, provided that it be properly understood, though I myself cannot help regretting that it should make me appear so constantly unamiable.

The charge that I am extreme touches me even more nearly than the charge that I am negative and one-sided; for I aim to be a humanist and the essence of humanism is moderation. There is, however, much confusion on the subject of moderation. A man's moderation is measured by his success in mediating between some sound general principle and the infinitely various and shifting circumstances of actual life. The man who is thus rightly mediatory attains to one of the most precious of virtues—urbanity; though one must add that probably no virtue has been more frequently counterfeited. When an intellectually and spiritually indolent person has to choose between two conflicting views he often decides to "split the difference" between truth and error, or between two errors. In any case, he must dispose of the question of truth or error before he can properly begin to mediate at all. Otherwise he will run the risk of resembling the English statesman of whom it was said that he never deviated from the straight and narrow path between right and wrong. Some of the casuists whom Pascal attacked had managed to assume a moderate attitude towards murder! One may fancy oneself urbane when in reality one is in danger of being numbered with the immense multitude that Dante saw in the vestibule of Hell—the multitude of those who are equally "displeasing to God and to the enemies of God." To be sure, it is not always easy in any particular instance to distinguish between the humanist and the mere Laodicean. Thus Luther denounced Erasmus as a Laodicean, whereas to us he seems rather to have shown real poise and urbanity in his dealings with the religious and other extremists of his time.

At all events the differences of doctrine I debate in the following pages are of a primary nature and so not subject to mediation. Between the man who puts his main emphasis on the inner life of the individual and the man who puts this emphasis on something else—for example, the progress and service of humanity—the opposition is one of first principles. The question I raise, therefore, is not whether one should be a moderate humanitarian, but whether one should be a humanitarian at all. In general I commit myself to the position that we are living in a world that in certain important respects has gone wrong on first principles; which will be found to be only another way of saying that we are living in a world that has been betrayed by its leaders. On the appearance of leaders who have recovered in some form the truths of the inner life and repudiated the errors of naturalism may depend the very survival of Western civilization. The truths of the inner life may be proclaimed in various forms, religious and humanistic, and have actually been so proclaimed in the past and justified in each case by their fruits in life and conduct. It is because I am unable to discover these truths in any form in the philosophies now fashionable that I have been led to prefer to the wisdom of the age the wisdom of the ages.

Henry Louis Mencken
1880

JOHANN BURKHARD MENCKEN, 1674-1732, wrote a treatise attacking the charlatanry of the learned; he was one of the German forbears of the subject of this sketch. H. L. Mencken was born in Baltimore. His father, a cigar manufacturer, wanted him to be an engineer, but after attending the Baltimore Polytechnic Institute young Henry became a newspaper reporter, and in 1903 further proclaimed his independence by having printed a thin volume entitled *Ventures into Verse*. In 1906 he joined the staff of the Baltimore *Evening Sun*, wrote for it until 1941, and is still a stockholder and a director of the corporation publishing it. In 1930 Mencken married the novelist Sarah Haardt, who died in 1935.

As literary critic of the *Smart Set* and later its co-editor, and as co-editor and later editor of the *American Mercury* from 1924 to 1933, Mencken built up a nation-wide and even international reputation as an iconoclast. George Jean Nathan, whom he first met in 1907 and who was to become America's leading critic of the theatre, was associated with him on both periodicals and has remained one of his closest friends. Nathan burlesqued their relationship in the characters of Morton and Norton in his raffish pseudo-novel, *Monks are Monks,* 1929. Carrying on the impressionistic tradition in literary criticism established in America by Lewis E. Gates, Percival Pollard, and James Huneker, Mencken championed such writers as Dreiser, Cabell, Lewis, Ben Hecht, and

Ruth Suckow, and engaged in a memorable controversy with Stuart P. Sherman, almost until the latter's death in 1926. The issues were the merits of Dreiser, the wisdom of our participation in World War I, the values of the American tradition, the function of criticism, and the responsibilities of the writer.

Always railing at demagoguery in the tradition of James Fenimore Cooper's *The American Democrat,* which he edited in 1931, Mencken could never stomach the New Deal, prophesied it would end in "the bum's rush," and came out for Alf Landon. He thus swept into the void his already ebbed influence as an iconoclast. Thereafter he gave his attention increasingly to the philological labors involved in supplementing his pioneer and already much revised *The American Language* (fourth edition, 1936), which is now regarded as epoch-making. As one critic has said, "The scholars have learned from Mencken, and Mencken has learned from the scholars."

Breaking a long silence on public questions in a lengthy interview for *Life* magazine for August 5, 1946, Mencken was still the hard-boiled, Anglophobic, Roosevelt-hating Cassandra of yesteryear, with even his previous faith in science destroyed by the atomic bomb. But his wit was still bitingly alive. This wit can best be enjoyed in such of his books as *George Bernard Shaw, His Plays* (1905); *The Philosophy of Friedrich Nietzsche* (1908); *A Book of Prefaces* (1917); *In Defense of Women* (1918); the six series of *Prejudices* (1919-1927); *Notes on Democracy* (1926); *Treatise on the Gods* (1930); *Treatise on Right and Wrong* (1934); and the three autobiographical volumes, *Happy Days* (1940), *Newspaper Days* (1941), and *Heathen Days* (1943), re-issued in one volume as *The Days of H. L. Mencken* (1948).

[Besides the autobiographical volumes and a copious Menckeniana in the magazines and journals, the student may consult Isaac Goldberg's *The Man Mencken* (New York, 1925) and Benjamin De Casseres' *Mencken and Shaw* (New York, 1930).]

FOOTNOTE ON CRITICISM
[1922]

NEARLY all the discussions of criticism that I am acquainted with start off with a false assumption, to wit, that the primary motive of the critic, the impulse which makes a critic of him instead of, say, a politician, or a stockbroker, is pedagogical —that he writes because he is possessed by a passion to advance the enlightenment, to put down error and wrong, to disseminate some specific doctrine: psychological, epistemological, historical, or aesthetic. This is true, it seems to me, only of bad critics, and its degree of truth increases in direct ratio to their badness. The motive of the critic who is really worth reading—the only critic of whom, indeed, it may be said truthfully that it is at all possible to read him, save as an act of mental discipline— is something quite different. That motive is not the motive of the pedagogue, but the motive of the artist. It is no more and no less than the simple desire to function freely and beautifully, to give outward and objective form to ideas that bubble inwardly and have a fascinating lure in them, to get rid of them dramatically and make an articulate noise in the world. It was for this reason that Plato wrote the "Republic," and for this reason that Beethoven wrote the Ninth Symphony, and it is for this reason, to drop a million miles, that I am writing the present essay. Everything else is afterthought, mock-modesty, messianic delusion—in brief, affectation and folly. Is the contrary conception of criticism widely cherished? Is it almost universally held that the thing is a brother to jurisprudence, advertising, laparotomy, chautauqua lecturing and the art of the schoolmarm? Then certainly the fact that it is so held should be sufficient to set up an overwhelming probability of its lack of truth and sense.. If I speak with some heat, it is as one who has suffered. When, years ago, I devoted myself diligently to critical pieces upon the writings of Theodore Dreiser, I found that practically every one who took any notice of my proceedings at all fell into either one of two assumptions about my underlying purpose: (a) that I had a fanatical devotion for Mr. Dreiser's ideas and desired to propagate them, or (b) that I was an ardent patriot, and yearned to lift up American literature. Both assumptions were false. I had then, and I have now, very little interest in many of Mr. Dreiser's main ideas; when we meet, in fact, we usually quarrel about them. And I am wholly devoid of public spirit, and haven't the least lust to improve American literature; if it ever came to what I regard as perfection my job would be gone. What, then, was my motive in writing about Mr. Dreiser so copiously? My motive, well known to Mr. Dreiser himself and to every one else who knew me as intimately as he did, was simply and solely to sort out and give coherence to the ideas of Mr. Mencken, and to put them into suave and ingratiating terms, and to discharge them with a flourish, and maybe with a phrase of pretty song, into the dense fog that blanketed the Republic.

The critic's choice of criticism rather than of what is called creative writing is chiefly a matter of temperament—perhaps, more accurately of hormones—with accidents of education and environment to help. The feelings that happen to be dominant in him at the moment the scribbling frenzy seizes him are feelings inspired, not directly by life itself, but by books, pictures, music, sculpture, architecture, religion, philosophy —in brief, by some other man's feelings about life. They are thus, in a sense, secondhand, and it is no wonder that creative artists so easily fall into the theory that they are also second-rate. Perhaps they usually are. If, indeed, the critic continues on this plane—if he lacks the intellectual agility and enterprise needed to make the leap from the work of art to the vast and mysterious complex of phenomena behind it—then they *always* are, and he remains no more than a fugelman or policeman to his betters. But if a genuine artist is concealed within him—if his feelings are in any sense profound and original, and his capacity for self-expression is above the average of educated men—then he moves inevitably from the work of art to life itself, and begins to take on a dignity that he formerly lacked. It is impossible to think of a man of any actual force and originality, universally recognized as having those qualities, who spent his whole life appraising and describing the work of other men. Did Goethe, or Carlyle, or Matthew Arnold, or Sainte-Beuve, or Macaulay, or even, to come down a few pegs, Lewes,[1] or Lowell, or Hazlitt? Certainly not. The thing that becomes most obvious about the writings of all such men, once they are examined carefully, is that the critic is always being swallowed up by the creative artist—that what starts out as the review of a book, or a play, or other work of art, usually develops very quickly into an independent essay upon the theme of that work of art, or upon some theme that it suggests—in a word, that it becomes a fresh work of art, and only indirectly related to the one that suggested it. This fact, indeed, is so plain that it scarcely needs statement. What the pedagogues always object to in, for example, the *Quarterly*

---

[1] G. H. Lewes (1817-1878), British philosopher, literary critic, and lover of George Eliot.

reviewers is that they forgot the books they were supposed to review, and wrote long papers—often, in fact, small books —expounding ideas suggested (or not suggested) by the books under review. Every critic who is worth reading falls inevitably into the same habit. He cannot stick to his task: what is before him is always infinitely less interesting to him than what is within him. If he is genuinely first-rate—if what is within him stands the test of type, and wins an audience, and produces the reactions that every artist craves—then he usually ends by abandoning the criticism of specific works of art altogether, and setting up shop as a merchant in general ideas, *i.e.*, as an artist working in the materials of life itself.

Mere reviewing, however conscientiously and competently it is done, is plainly a much inferior business. Like writing poetry, it is chiefly a function of intellectual immaturity. The young literatus just out of the university, having as yet no capacity for grappling with the fundamental mysteries of existence, is put to writing reviews of books, or plays, or music, or painting. Very often he does it extremely well; it is, in fact, not hard to do well, for even decayed pedagogues often do it, as such graves of the intellect as the New York *Times* bear witness. But if he continues to do it, whether well or ill, it is a sign to all the world that his growth ceased when they made him *Artium Baccalaureus*. Gradually he becomes, whether in or out of the academic grove, a professor, which is to say, a man devoted to diluting and retailing the ideas of his superiors—not an artist, not even a bad artist, but almost the antithesis of an artist. He is learned, he is sober, he is painstaking and accurate— but he is as hollow as a jug. Nothing is in him save the ghostly echoes of other men's thoughts and feelings. If he were a genuine artist he would have thoughts and feelings of his own, and the impulse to give them objective form would be irresistible. An artist can no more withstand that impulse than a politician can withstand the

temptations of a job. There are no mute, inglorious Miltons, save in the hallucinations of poets. The one sound test of a Milton is that he functions as a Milton. His difference from other men lies precisely in the superior vigor of his impulse to self-expression, not in the superior beauty and loftiness of his ideas. Other men, in point of fact, often have the same ideas, or perhaps even loftier ones, but they are able to suppress them, usually on grounds of decorum, and so they escape being artists, and are respected by right-thinking persons, and die with money in the bank, and are forgotten in two weeks.

Obviously, the critic whose performance we are commonly called upon to investigate is a man standing somewhere along the path leading from the beginning that I have described to the goal. He has got beyond being a mere cataloguer and valuer of other men's ideas, but he has not yet become an autonomous artist—he is not yet ready to challenge attention with his own ideas alone. But it is plain that his motion, in so far as he is moving at all, must be in the direction of that autonomy— that is, unless one imagines him sliding backward into senile infantilism: a spectacle not unknown to literary pathology, but too pathetic to be discussed here. Bear this motion in mind, and the true nature of his aims and purposes becomes clear; more, the incurable falsity of the aims and purposes usually credited to him becomes equally clear. He is not actually trying to perform an impossible act of arctic justice upon the artist whose work gives him a text. He is not trying with mathematical passion to find out exactly what was in that artist's mind at the moment of creation, and to display it precisely and in an ecstasy of appreciation. He is not trying to bring the work discussed into accord with some transient theory of aesthetics, or ethics, or truth, or to determine its degree of departure from that theory. He is not trying to lift up the fine arts, or to defend democracy against sense, or to promote happiness at the domestic hearth, or to convert sophomores into right-thinkers, or to serve God. He is not trying to fit a group of novel phenomena into the orderly process of history. He is not even trying to discharge the catalytic office that I myself, in a romantic moment, once sought to force upon him. He is, first and last, simply trying to express himself. He is trying to arrest and challenge a sufficient body of readers, to make them pay attention to him, to impress them with the charm and novelty of his ideas, to provoke them into an agreeable (or shocked) awareness of him, and he is trying to achieve thereby for his own inner ego the grateful feeling of a function performed, a tension relieved, a *katharsis* attained which Wagner achieved when he wrote "Die Walküre," [2] and a hen achieves every time she lays an egg.

Joseph Conrad is moved by that necessity to write romances; Bach was moved to write music; poets are moved to write poetry; critics are moved to write criticism. The form is nothing; the only important thing is the motive power, and it is the same in all cases. It is the pressing yearning of every man who has ideas in him to empty them upon the world, to hammer them them into plausible and ingratiating shapes, to compel the attention and respect of his equals, to lord it over his inferiors. So seen, the critic becomes a far more transparent and agreeable fellow than ever he was in the discourses of the psychologists who sought to make him a mere appraiser in an intellectual customs house, a gauger in a distillery of the spirit, a just and infallible judge upon the cosmic bench. Such offices, in point of fact, never fit him. He always bulges over their confines. So labelled and estimated, it inevitably turns out that the specific critic under examination is a very bad one, or no critic at all. But when he is thought of, not as pedagogue, but as artist, then he begins to take on reality, and, what is more, dignity. Carlyle was surely no just and infallible judge; on the contrary, he was full of prejudices, biles, naïvetés, humors. Yet he is read, consulted, attended

to. Macaulay was unfair, inaccurate, fanciful, lyrical—yet his essays live. Arnold had his faults too, and so did Sainte-Beuve, and so did Goethe, and so did many another of that line—and yet they are remembered today, and all the learned and conscientious critics of their time, laboriously concerned with the precise intent of the artists under review, and passionately determined to set it forth with god-like care and to relate it exactly to this or that great stream of ideas —all these pedants are forgotten. What saved Carlyle, Macaulay and company is as plain as day. They were first-rate artists. They could make the thing charming, and that is always a million times more important than making it true.

Truth, indeed, is something that is believed in completely only by persons who have never tried personally to pursue it to its fastnesses and grab it by the tail. It is the adoration of second-rate men—men who always receive it at secondhand. Pedagogues believe in immutable truths and spend their lives trying to determine them and propagate them; the intellectual progress of man consists largely of a concerted effort to block and destroy their enterprise. Nine times out of ten, in the arts as in life, there is actually no truth to be discovered; there is only error to be exposed. In whole departments of human inquiry it seems to me quite unlikely that the truth ever *will* be discovered. Nevertheless, the rubber stamp thinking of the world always makes the assumption that the exposure of an error is identical with the discovery of the truth—that error and truth are simple opposites. They are nothing of the sort. What the world turns to when it has been cured of one error, is usually simply another error, and maybe one worse than the first one. This is the whole history of the intellect in brief. The average man of today does not believe in precisely the same imbecilities that the Greek of the fourth century before Christ believed in, but the

---

[2] Second of the series of the Niebelung Ring, this music drama by Richard Wagner was first produced in Munich in 1870.

things that he *does* believe in are often quite as idiotic. Perhaps this statement is a bit too sweeping. There is, year by year, a gradual accumulation of what may be called, provisionally, truths—there is a slow accretion of ideas that somehow manage to meet all practicable human tests, and so survive. But even so, it is risky to call them absolute truths. All that one may safely say of them is that no one, as yet, has demonstrated that they are errors. Soon or late, if experience teaches us anything, they are likely to succumb too. The profoundest truths of the Middle Ages are now laughed at by schoolboys. The profoundest truths of democracy will be laughed at, a few centuries hence, even by schoolteachers.

In the department of aesthetics, wherein critics mainly disport themselves, it is almost impossible to think of a so-called truth that shows any sign of being permanently true. The most profound of principles begins to fade and quiver almost as soon as it is stated. But the work of art, as opposed to the theory behind it, has a longer life, particularly if that theory be obscure and questionable, and so cannot be determined accurately. "Hamlet," the Mona Lisa, "Faust," "Dixie," "Parsifal," "Mother Goose," "Annabel Lee," "Huckleberry Finn"—these things, so baffling to pedagogy, so contumacious to the categories, so mysterious in purpose and utility—these things live. And why? Because there is in them the flavor of salient, novel and attractive personality, because the quality that shines from them is not that of correct demeanor but that of creative passion, because they pulse and breathe and speak, because they are genuine works of art. So with criticism. Let us forget all the heavy effort to make a science of it; it is a fine art, or nothing. If the critic, retiring to his cell to concoct his treatise upon a book or play or what-not, produces a piece of writing that shows sound structure, and brilliant color, and the flash of new and persuasive ideas, and civilized manners, and the charm of an uncommon personality in free func-

tion, then he has given something to the world that is worth having, and sufficiently justified his existence. Is Carlyle's "Frederick" true? [3] Who cares? As well ask if the Parthenon is true, or the C Minor Symphony,[4] or "Wiener Blut."[5] Let the critic who is an artist leave such necropsies to professors of aesthetics, who can no more determine the truth than he can, and will infallibly make it unpleasant and a bore.

It is, of course, not easy to practice this abstention. Two forces, one within and one without, tend to bring even a Hazlitt or a Huneker [6] under the campus pump. One is the almost universal human susceptibility to messianic delusions—the irresistible tendency of practically every man, once he finds a crowd in front of him, to strut and roll his eyes. The other is the public demand, born of such long familiarity with pedagogical criticism that no other kind is readily conceivable, that the critic teach something as well as say something—in the popular phrase, that he be constructive. Both operate powerfully against his free functioning, and especially the former. He finds it hard to resist the flattery of his customers, however little he may actually esteem it. If he knows anything at all, he knows that his following, like that of every other artist in ideas, is chiefly made up of the congenitally subaltern type of man and woman—natural converts, lodge joiners, me-toos, stragglers after circus parades. It is precious seldom that he ever gets a positive idea out of them; what he usually gets is mere unintelligent ratification. But this troop, despite its obvious failings, corrupts him in various ways. For one thing, it enormously reënforces his belief in his own

[3] Carlyle's *Frederick the Great* appeared in six volumes between 1858 and 1865.
[4] Johannes Brahms' Symphony No. 1 in C Minor was first performed at Carlsruhe in 1876.
[5] Operetta by Johann Strauss (1825-1899).
[6] James Gibbons Huneker (1860-1920), cosmopolitan American literary, music, and art critic.

ideas, and so tends to make him stiff and dogmatic—in brief, precisely everything that he ought not to be. And for another thing, it tends to make him (by a curious contradiction) a bit pliant and politic: he begins to estimate new ideas, not in proportion as they are amusing or beautiful, but in proportion as they are likely to please. So beset, front and rear, he sometimes sinks supinely to the level of a professor, and his subsequent proceedings are interesting no more. The true aim of a critic is certainly not to make converts. He must know that very few of the persons who are susceptible to conversion are worth converting. Their minds are intrinsically flabby and parasitical, and it is certainly not sound sport to agitate minds of that sort. Moreover, the critic must always harbor a grave doubt about most of the ideas that they lap up so greedily—it must occur to him not infrequently, in the silent watches of the night, that much that he writes is sheer buncombe. As I have said, I can't imagine any idea—that is, in the domain of aesthetics—that is palpably and incontrovertibly sound. All that I am familiar with, and in particular all that I announce most vociferously, seem to me to contain a core of quite obvious nonsense. I thus try to avoid cherishing them too lovingly, and it always gives me a shiver to see any one else gobble them at one gulp. Criticism, at bottom, is indistinguishable from skepticism. Both launch themselves, the one by aesthetic presentations and the other by logical presentations, at the common human tendency to accept whatever is approved, to take in ideas ready-made, to be responsive to mere rhetoric and gesticulation. A critic who believes in anything absolutely is bound to that something quite as helplessly as a Christian is bound to the Freudian garbage in the Book of Revelation. To that extent, at all events, he is unfree and unintelligent, and hence a bad critic.

The demand for "constructive" criticism is based upon the same false assumption that immutable truths exist in the arts, and that the artist will be improved by being made aware of them. This notion, whatever the form it takes, is always absurd—as much so, indeed, as its brother delusion that the critic, to be competent, must be a practitioner of the specific art he ventures to deal with, i.e., that a doctor, to cure a belly-ache, must have a belly-ache. As practically encountered, it is disingenuous as well as absurd, for it comes chiefly from bad artists who tire of serving as performing monkeys, and crave the greater ease and safety of sophomores in class. They demand to be taught in order to avoid being knocked about. In their demand is the theory that instruction, if they could get it, would profit them—that they are capable of doing better work than they do. As a practical matter, I doubt that this is ever true. Bad poets never actually grow any better; they invariably grow worse and worse. In all history there has never been, to my knowledge, a single practitioner of any art who, as a result of "constructive" criticism, improved his work. The curse of all the arts, indeed, is the fact that they are constantly invaded by persons who are not artists at all—persons whose yearning to express their ideas and feelings is unaccompanied by the slightest capacity for charming expression—in brief, persons with absolutely nothing to say. This is particularly true of the art of letters, which interposes very few technical obstacles to the vanity and garrulity of such invaders. Any effort to teach them to write better is an effort wasted, as every editor discovers for himself; they are as incapable of it as they are of jumping over the moon. The only sort of criticism that can deal with them to any profit is the sort that employs them frankly as laboratory animals. It cannot cure them, but it can at least make an amusing and perhaps edifying show of them. It is idle to argue that the good in them is thus destroyed with the bad. The simple answer is that there *is* no good in them. Suppose Poe had wasted his time trying to dredge good work out of Rufus Dawes, author of "Geraldine." [7] He would have failed miserably—and spoiled a capital essay, still diverting after three quarters of a century. Suppose Beethoven, dealing with Gottfried Weber, had tried laboriously to make an intelligent music critic of him. How much more apt, useful and durable the simple note: "Arch-ass! Double-barrelled ass!" Here was absolutely sound criticism. Here was a judgment wholly beyond challenge. Moreover, here was a small but perfect work of art.

Upon the low practical value of so-called constructive criticism I can offer testimony out of my own experience. My books are commonly reviewed at great length, and many critics devote themselves to pointing out what they conceive to be my errors, both of fact and of taste. Well, I cannot recall a case in which any suggestion offered by a constructive critic has helped me in the slightest, or even actively interested me. Every such wet-nurse of letters has sought fatuously to make me write in a way differing from that in which the Lord God Almighty, in His infinite wisdom, impels me to write—that is, to make me write stuff which, coming from me, would be as false as an appearance of decency in a Congressman. All the benefits I have ever got from the critics of my work have come from the destructive variety. A hearty slating always does me good, particularly if it be well written. It begins by enlisting my professional respect; it ends by making me examine my ideas coldly in the privacy of my chamber. Not, of course, that I usually revise them, but I at least examine them. If I decide to hold fast to them, they are all the dearer to me thereafter, and I expound them with a new passion and plausibility. If, on the contrary, I discern holes in them, I shelve them in a *pianissimo* manner, and set about hatching new ones to take their place. But constructive criticism irritates me. I do not object to being denounced, but I can't abide being schoolmastered, especially by men I regard as imbeciles.

I find, as a practicing critic, that very few men who write books are even as tolerant as I am—that most of them, soon or late, show signs of extreme discomfort under criticism, however polite its terms. Perhaps this is why enduring friendships between authors and critics are so rare. All artists, of course, dislike one another more or less, but that dislike seldom rises to implacable enmity, save between opera singer and opera singer, and creative author and critic. Even when the latter two keep up an outward show of good-will, there is always bitter antagonism under the surface. Part of it, I daresay, arises out of the impossible demands of the critic, particularly if he be tinged with the constructive madness. Having favored an author with his good opinion, he expects the poor fellow to live up to that good opinion without the slightest compromise or faltering, and this is commonly beyond human power. He feels that any let-down compromises *him* —that his hero is stabbing him in the back, and making him ridiculous—and this feeling rasps his vanity. The most bitter of all literary quarrels are those between critics and creative artists, and most of them arise in just this way. As for the creative artist, he on his part naturally resents the critic's air of pedagogical superiority and he resents it especially when he has an uneasy feeling that he has fallen short of his best work, and that the discontent of the critic is thus justified. Injustice is relatively easy to bear; what stings is justice. Under it all, of course, lurks the fact that I began with: the fact that the critic is himself an artist, and that his creative impulse, soon or late, is bound to make him neglect the punctilio. When he sits down to compose his criticism, his artist ceases to be a friend, and becomes mere raw material for his work of

[7] *Geraldine, Athenia of Damascus, and Miscellaneous Poems* (New York, 1839), by the minor American poetaster, Rufus Dawes (1803-1859), was the subject of one of Poe's most violent critical onslaughts.

art. It is my experience that artists invariably resent this cavalier use of them. They are pleased so long as the critic confines himself to the modest business of interpreting them—preferably in terms of their own estimate of themselves—but the moment he proceeds to adorn their theme with variations of his own, the moment he brings new ideas to the enterprise and begins contrasting them with their ideas, that moment they grow restive. It is precisely at this point, of course, that criticism becomes genuine criticism; before that it was mere reviewing. When a critic passes it he loses his friends. By becoming an artist, he becomes the foe of all other artists.

But the transformation, I believe, has good effects upon him: it makes him a better critic. Too much *Gemütlichkeit* [8] is as fatal to criticism as it would be to surgery or politics. When it rages unimpeded it leads inevitably either to a dull professorial sticking on of meaningless labels or to log-rolling, and often it leads to both. One of the most hopeful symptoms of the new *Aufklärung* [9] in the Republic is the revival of acrimony in criticism—the renaissance of the doctrine that aesthetic matters are important, and that it is worth the while of a healthy male to take them seriously, as he takes business, sport and amour. In the days when American literature was showing its first vigorous growth, the native criticism was extraordinarily violent and even vicious; in the days when American literature swooned upon the tomb of the Puritan *Kultur* it became flaccid and childish. The typical critic of the first era was Poe, as the typical critic of the second was Howells. Poe carried on his critical jehads with such ferocity that he often got into law-suits, and sometimes ran no little risk of having his head cracked. He regarded literary questions as exigent and momentous. The lofty aloofness of the don was simply not in him. When he encountered a book that seemed to him to be bad, he attacked it almost as sharply as a Chamber of Commerce would attack a fanatic preaching free speech, or the corporation of Trinity Church would attack Christ. His opponents replied in the same Berserker manner. Much of Poe's surviving ill-fame, as a drunkard and dead-beat, is due to their inordinate denunciations of him. They were not content to refute him; they constantly tried to dispose of him altogether. The very ferocity of that ancient row shows that the native literature, in those days, was in a healthy state. Books of genuine value were produced. Literature always thrives best, in fact, in an atmosphere of hearty strife. Poe, surrounded by admiring professors, never challenged, never aroused to the emotions of revolt, would probably have written poetry indistinguishable from the hollow stuff of, say, Prof. Dr. George E. Woodberry.[10] It took the persistent (and often grossly unfair and dishonorable) opposition of Griswold *et al* to stimulate him to his highest endeavors. He needed friends, true enough, but he also needed enemies.

Today, for the first time in years, there is strife in American criticism, and the Paul Elmer Mores and Hamilton Wright Mabies [11] are no longer able to purr in peace. The instant they fall into stiff professorial attitudes they are challenged, and often with anything but urbanity. The *ex cathedra* manner thus passes out, and free discussion comes in. Heretics lay on boldly, and the professors are forced to make some defense. Often, going further, they attempt counter-attacks. Ears are bitten off. Noses are bloodied. There are wallops both above and below the belt. I am, I need not say, no believer in any magical merit in debate, no matter how free it may be. It certainly does not necessarily establish the truth; both sides, in fact, may be wrong, and they often are. But it at least accomplishes two important effects. On the one hand, it ex-

[8] Good nature.
[9] Enlightenment.
[10] American critic and teacher, 1855-1930.
[11] Whereas Hamilton Wright Mabie (1845-1916) was truly a "genteel" literary critic, More, as Mencken acknowledged in an essay in his *Prejudices: Third Series*, was a more formidable conservative.

poses all the cruder fallacies to hostile examination, and so disposes of many of them. And on the other hand, it melodramatizes the business of the critic, and so convinces thousands of bystanders, otherwise quite inert, that criticism is an amusing and instructive art, and that the problems it deals with are important. What men will fight for seems to be worth looking into.

Edmund Wilson

1895

EDMUND WILSON was born in Red Bank, New Jersey, of a prosperous bourgeois family, his father being a prominent lawyer and politician. He attended Princeton, where he was a good friend of F. Scott Fitzgerald, and was graduated in 1916, after considerable experience in college journalism. Leaving a job as reporter on the New York *Evening Sun,* he saw two years of army service in World War I, first in a hospital unit in France and later in the Intelligence Corps.

Back from the war, he worked on *Vanity Fair* and became its managing editor. From 1926 to 1931 he was associate editor of the *New Republic.* As a frequent contributor to this periodical and the *Atlantic Monthly* and as book critic for the *New Yorker,* Wilson has won a wide following. Guggenheim fellowships in 1935 and 1939 enabled him to travel and to complete some of his more ambitious writing projects. He has attempted several literary forms, having among his many publications a volume of poems, two volumes of plays, one novel, and one volume of short-stories. Of these, only the last, *Memoirs of Hecate County* (1946), has had any great vogue.

Wilson has written two accounts of economic and social conditions observed in travel—*The American Jitters* (1932), a picture of depression America, and *Travels in Two Democracies* (1936), a contrast between Soviet Russia and the United States. His most impressive work thus far has been his history of Marxism, *To the Finland Station* (1940). One of his books, *Note-books of Night* (1943), may best be described as an autobiographical mélange. His literary criticism is gathered into *Axel's Castle* (1931); *The Triple Thinkers* (1938); *The Boys in the Back Room* (1941), and *The Wound and the Bow* (1941). He has edited important documents in the history of criticism in *The Shock of Recognition* (1943) and the papers of F. Scott Fitzgerald in *The Crack-Up* (1945). "The Historical Interpretation of Literature" was contributed to the symposium, *The Intent of the Critic,* ed. Donald A. Stauffer (New Haven, 1941).

[Stanley Hyman's *The Armed Vision* (New York, 1948) contains a challenging essay on Wilson.]

THE HISTORICAL INTERPRETATION OF LITERATURE
[1941]

I WANT to talk about the historical interpretation of literature—that is, about the interpretation of literature in its social, economic and political aspects.

To begin with, it will be worth while to say something about the kind of criticism which seems to be furthest removed from this. There is a kind of comparative criticism which tends to be non-historical. The essays of T. S. Eliot, which have had such an immense influence in our time, are, for example, fundamentally non-historical. Eliot sees, or tries to see, the whole of literature, so far as he is acquainted with it, spread out before him under the aspect of eternity. He then compares the work of different periods and countries, and tries to draw from it general conclusions about what literature ought to be. He understands, of course, that our point of view in connection with literature changes, and he has what seems to me a very sound conception of the whole body of writing of the past as something to which new works are continually being added, and which is not merely increased in bulk thereby but modified as a whole—so that Sophocles is no longer precisely what he was for Aristotle, or Shakespeare what he was for Ben Jonson or for Dryden or for Dr. Johnson, on account of all the later literature that has intervened between them and us. Yet at every point of this continual accretion, the whole field may be surveyed, as it were, spread out before the critic. The critic tries to see it as God might: he calls the books to a Day of Judgment. And looking at things in this way, he may arrive at interesting and valuable conclusions which could hardly be reached by approaching them in any other way. Eliot was able to see, for example—what I believe had never been noticed before—that the French symbolist poetry of the nineteenth century had certain fundamental resemblances to the English poetry of the age of Donne. Another kind of critic would draw certain historical conclusions from these purely esthetic findings, as the Russian D. S. Mirsky [1] did; but Eliot does not draw them.

Another example of this kind of non-historical criticism, in a somewhat different way and on a somewhat different plane, is the work of the late George Saintsbury. Saintsbury was a connoisseur of wines, he wrote an entertaining book on the subject.[2] And his attitude toward literature, too, was that of the connoisseur. He tastes the authors and tells you about the vintages; he distinguishes the qualities of the various wines. His palate was as fine as could be, and he possessed the great qualification that he knew how to take books on their own terms and was thus able to appreciate a very large variety of different kinds of writing. He was a man of strong social prejudices and peculiarly intransigent political views, but, so far as it is humanly possible, he kept them out of his literary criticism. The result is one of the most agreeable commentaries on literature that have ever been written. Most scholars who have read as much as Saintsbury don't have Saintsbury's discriminating taste. Saintsbury has been over the whole ground like any academic historian, but his account of it is not merely a chronology: it is a record of fastidious enjoyment. Since enjoyment is the only thing he is looking for, he does not need to know the causes of things, and the historical background of literature does not interest him very much.

There is, however, another tradition of criticism that dates from the beginning of the eighteenth century. In 1725, the Neapolitan philosopher Vico published *La Scienza Nuova*, a revolutionary work on the philosophy of history, in which he as-

[1] Contemporary historian of Russian literature (1890-   ).

[2] *Notes in a Wine-Cellar* is one of the more personal productions of George Edward Bateman Saintsbury (1845-1933), one of the most prolific of modern English literary critics and historians.

serted for the first time that *the social world* was *certainly the work of man,* and attempted what is, so far as I know, the first social interpretation of a work of literature. This is what Vico says about Homer: "Homer composed the *Iliad in his youth*—that is, in the youth of Greece. Greece was then all aflame with sublime passions, with pride, anger and vengeance. These sentiments are incompatible with dissimulation and do not exclude generosity; Greece admired Achilles, *the hero of force.* Homer composed the *Odyssey* when he was *old,* when the passions of the Greeks were beginning to be cooled by reflection, the mother of prudence. In the time of Homer's youth, the pride of Agamemnon, the insolence and barbarity of Achilles, were what was pleasing to the peoples of Greece. In the time of its old age, they already liked the luxury of Alcinoüs, the delights of Calypso, the sensuous pleasures of Circe, the songs of the sirens, and the pastimes of the lovers of Penelope. How could one possibly assign to the same age manners so completely dissimilar? Plato is so much impressed by this difficulty that, not knowing how to resolve it, he pretends that in his divine transports of poetic enthusiasm, Homer was able to foresee the effeminate and dissolute life of the future. But isn't this to attribute the height of imprudence to him whom he presents as the founder of Greek civilization? To publish an account of such manners before they existed, even though one condemned them at the same time, wouldn't this be to teach people to imitate them? Let us agree rather that the author of the *Iliad* must have long preceded the author of the *Odyssey*—that the former, who came from the northeastern part of Greece, sang of the Trojan War, which had taken place in his part of the country; whereas the latter, who had been born in the southeastern part, celebrated Ulysses, who reigned in that part of the world."

You see that Vico has here explained Homer in terms both of historical period and of geographical origin. The idea that

human arts and institutions were to be studied and elucidated as the products of the geographical and climatic conditions in which the people who created them lived and of the phase of their social development through which they were passing at the moment, made great progress during the eighteenth century. There are traces of it even in Dr. Johnson, that most orthodox and classical of critics—as, for example, when he accounts for certain characteristics of Shakespeare by the relative barbarity of the age in which he lived, pointing out just as Vico had done that "nations, like individuals, have their infancy." And by the eighties of the eighteenth century Herder,[3] in his *Ideas on the Philosophy of History,* was writing of poetry that it was a kind of "Proteus among the people, which is always changing its form in response to the languages, manners and habits, to the temperaments and climates, nay, even to the accents of different nations." He said —what could still seem startling even so late as that—that "language was not a divine communication, but something men had produced themselves." In the lectures on the philosophy of history that Hegel delivered in Berlin in 1822-1823, he discussed the national literatures as expressions of the societies which had produced them—societies which he conceived as great organisms continually transforming themselves under the propulsion of a succession of dominant ideas.

In the field of literary criticism, this historical point of view came to its first complete flower in the work of the French critic Taine, in the middle of the nineteenth century. The whole school of historian-critics to which he belonged—Michelet, Renan,[4] Sainte-Beuve—had been occupied in interpreting books in terms of their historical origins. But Taine was the first

---

[3] Johann Gottfried von Herder (1744-1803), German philosopher, poet, and critic.

[4] Jules Michelet (1798-1874), historian of the French Revolution, and Ernst Renan (1823-1892), biographer of Christ.

to try to apply these principles systematically and on a large scale to a work devoted exclusively to literature. In the Introduction to his *History of English Literature*, published in 1863, he made his famous pronouncement that works of literature were to be understood as the upshot of three interfusing factors: *the moment, the race, and the milieu*. Taine thought he was a scientist and a mechanist who was examining works of literature from the same point of view as the chemist in experimenting with chemical compounds. But the difference between the critic and the chemist is that the critic cannot first combine his elements and then watch to see what they will do: he can only examine phenomena which have already taken place. What Taine actually does is pretend to set the stage for the experiment by describing the moment, the race and the milieu; and then say, "Such a situation demands such a kind of writer." He now goes on to describe the kind of writer that the situation demands, and at the end of the description we discover that we are confronted with Shakespeare or Milton or Byron, or whoever the great figure is—who turns out to prove the accuracy of Taine's prognosis by precisely fitting the description.

There is thus an element of imposture in Taine; but it is a lucky thing that there is. If he had really been the mechanist that he thought he was, his work on literature would have had little value. The truth was that Taine loved literature for its own sake —he was at his best an excellent artist himself—and that he had very strong moral convictions which give his writing emotional power. His mind, to be sure, was an analytic one, and his analysis, though terribly oversimplified, does have an explanatory value. Yet his work was what we call creative. Whatever he may say about chemical experiments, it is evident when he writes of a great writer that the moment, the race and the milieu have combined, like the three sounds of the chord in Browning's poem about Abt Vogler, to produce not a fourth sound but a star.

To Taine's set of elements was added, dating from the middle of the century, a new element, the economic, which was introduced into the discussion of historical phenomena mainly by Marx and Engels.[5] The non-Marxist critics themselves were at the time already taking into account the influence of the social classes. In his chapters on the Norman conquest of England, Taine shows that the difference between the literatures produced respectively by the Normans and the Saxons was partly the difference between a ruling class, on the one hand, and a vanquished and oppressed class, on the other. And Michelet in his volume on the Regency, which was finished the same year that the *History of English Literature* appeared, studies *Manon Lescaut*[6] as a document representing the point of view of the small gentry before the French Revolution. But Marx and Engels derived the social classes from the ways that people made or got their livings— from what they called the *methods of production;* and they tended to regard these economic processes as fundamental to civilization.

The Dialectical Materialism of Marx and Engels was not really so materialistic as it sounds. There was in it a large element of the Hegelian idealism that Marx and Engels thought they had gotten rid of. At no time did they take so mechanistic a view of things as Taine began by professing; and their theory of the relation of works of literature to what they called the *economic base* was a good deal less simple than Taine's theory of the moment, the race and the milieu. They thought that art, politics, religion, philosophy and literature belonged to what they called the *super-structure* of human activity; but they saw that the practitioners of these various departments tended also to constitute social groups, and

---

[5] The first volume of Karl Marx' *Das Kapital* appeared in 1867; it was completed by Friedrich Engels in 1885 and 1895.

[6] A novel (1753) by the Abbé Prévost (1697-1763).

634   E D M U N D   W I L S O N

that they were always pulling away from the kind of solidarity based on economic classes in order to establish a professional solidarity of their own. Furthermore, the activities of the superstructure could influence one another, and they could influence the economic base. It may be said of Marx and Engels in general that, contrary to the popular impression, they were modest, confused and groping, where a materialist like Taine was cocksure. Marx once made an attempt to explain why the poems of Homer were so good when the society that produced them was from his point of view—that is, from the industrial point of view—so primitive; and this gave him a good deal of trouble. If we compare his discussion of this problem with Vico's discussion of Homer, we see that the explanation of literature in terms of a philosophy of social history is becoming, instead of simpler and easier, more difficult and complex.

Marx and Engels were deeply imbued, moreover, with the German admiration for literature which they had learned from the age of Goethe. It would never have occurred to either of them that *der Dichter*[7] was not one of the noblest and most beneficent of humankind. When Engels writes about Goethe, he presents him as a man equipped for "practical life," whose career was frustrated by the "misery" of the historical situation in Germany in his time, and reproaches him for allowing himself to lapse into the "cautious, smug and narrow" philistinism of the class from which he came; but Engels regrets this because it interfered with the development of the "mocking, defiant, world-despising genius," *"der geniale Dichter," "der gewaltige Poet,"*[8] of whom Engels would not even, he says, have asked that he should have been a political liberal if he had not sacrificed to his bourgeois shrinkings his truer esthetic sense. And the great critics who were trained on Marx—Franz Mehring[9] and Bernard Shaw—had all this reverence for the priesthood of literature. Shaw deplores the lack of political philosophy and what

he regards as the middle-class snobbery in Shakespeare; but he celebrates Shakespeare's poetry and his dramatic imagination almost as enthusiastically as Swinburne did, describing even those pot-boiling comedies—*Twelfth Night* and *As You Like It*—the themes of which seem to him most contemptible, as "the Crown Jewels of English dramatic poetry."[10] Such a critic may do more for a writer by showing him a real man in a real world at a definite moment of time than the impressionist critic of Swinburne's type who flourished in the same period of the late nineteenth century. The purely impressionist critic approaches the whole of literature as an exhibit of bellettristic jewels, and he can only write a rhapsodic catalogue. But when Shaw turned his spotlight on Shakespeare as a figure in the Shavian drama of history, he invested him with a new interest as perhaps no other English critic had done.

The insistence that the man of letters should play a political rôle, the disparagement of works of art in comparison with political action, were thus originally no part of Marxism. They only became associated with it later. This happened by way of Russia, and it was due to special tendencies in that country that date from long before the Revolution or the promulgation of Marxism itself. In Russia there have been very good reasons why the political implications of literature should particularly occupy the critics. The art of Pushkin[11] itself, with its marvellous power of implication, had certainly been partly created by the censorship of Nicholas I, and Pushkin set the tradition for most of the

---

[7] The poet.

[8] These phrases mean "the ingenious poet" and "the powerful poet."

[9] This German critic (1846-1919), was Marx' biographer and editor.

[10] For an account of Shaw's criticism of Shakespeare, see Archibald Henderson, *George Bernard Shaw, His Life and Works* (Cincinnati, 1911), pp. 262 *et seq.*

[11] Aleksandr Sergyeevich Pushkin (1799-1837), Russian romantic poet.

great Russian writers that followed him. Every play, every poem, every story, must be a parable of which the moral is implied. If it were stated, the censor would suppress the book, as he tried to do with *The Bronze Horseman* of Pushkin, where it was merely a question of the packed implications protruding a little too plainly. Right down through the writings of Chekhov and up almost to the Revolution, the imaginative literature of Russia presents the peculiar paradox of an art which is technically objective and yet charged with dynamic social messages. In Russia under the Tsar, all social criticism was necessarily political because the most urgent need from the point of view of the intelligentsia was to get rid of the Tsarist régime. Even the neo-Christian moralist Tolstoy, who pretends to be non-political, is as political in his implications as any because his preaching will inevitably embroil him with the Church, and the Church is an integral part of the tsardom. His pamphlet called *What Is Art?*, in which he throws overboard Shakespeare and a large part of modern literature, including his own novels, in the interests of his intransigent morality, is the example which is most familiar to us of the moralizing Russian criticism; but it was only the most sensational expression of a kind of approach which had been prevalent since Belinsky and Chernyshevsky [12] in the early part of the century. The critics, who were usually journalists writing in exile or in a contraband press, were always tending to demand of the imaginative writers that they should illustrate bolder morals.

After the Revolution occurred, this situation did not change. The old habits of censorship persisted in the new socialist society of the Soviets, which was necessarily made up of people who had been stamped by the die of the old despotism. We find the peculiar phenomenon of a series of literary groups attempting one after another to obtain official recognition or to make themselves sufficiently powerful so that they could establish themselves as arbiters of literature. Lenin and Trotsky and Lunacharsky [13] had the sense to oppose these attempts: the comrade-dictators of Proletcult or Lev or Rapp [14] would certainly have been just as bad as the Count Benckendorf who made Pushkin miserable, and when the Stalin bureaucracy, after the death of Gorky, got control of this department as of everything else, they instituted a system of repression that made Benckendorf and Nicholas I look like Lorenzo de' Medici. In the meantime, Trotsky, himself a great political writer who had always had an interest in belles-lettres, attempted in 1924, apropos of one of these movements, to clarify the situation. He wrote a brilliant and important book called *Literature and Revolution,* in which he explained the aims of the government, analysed the work of the Russian writers, and praised or rebuked the latter as they seemed to him in harmony or in conflict with the former. Trotsky is intelligent, sympathetic; it is evident that he is really fond of literature and that he knows that a work of art does not fulfil its function in terms of the formulas of party propaganda. But Mayakovsky, the Soviet poet,[15] whom Trotsky had praised with reservations, expressed himself in a famous joke when he was asked what he thought about Trotsky's book—a pun which implied that a Commissar turned critic was unmistakably a Commissar still; and what a foreigner cannot accept in Trotsky is his assumption that it is the duty of the government to take a hand in the direction of literature.

This point of view, indigenous to Russia, has been imported to other countries through the permeation of Communist influence. The Communist press and its literary followers have reflected the con-

---

[12] V. G. Belinsky (1811-1848) and N. G. Chernyshevsky (1828-1889), arbiters of Russian literary taste.

[13] A. V. Lunacharsky (1876-1933), Russian revolutionary dramatist noted for his symbolism and fantasy.

[14] Soviet writers' organizations.

[15] V. V. Mayakovsky (1894-1930).

trol of the Kremlin in all the phases through which it has passed, down to the wholesale imprisonment of Soviet writers which has been taking place since 1935. But it has never been a part of the American system that our Republican or Democratic administration should lay down a political line for the guidance of the national literature. A gesture in this direction lately on the part of Archibald MacLeish, who seems a little carried away by the eminence of his position as Librarian of Congress, was anything but cordially received by serious American writers. And so long as the United States happily remains a non-totalitarian country, we can very well do without this aspect of the historical criticism of literature.

Another element of a different order has, however, since Marx's time been added to the historical study of the origins of works of literature. I mean the psychoanalysis of Freud. This appears as an extension of something which had already got well started before, which had figured even in Johnson's *Lives of the Poets,* and of which the great exponent had been Sainte-Beuve: the interpretation of works of literature in the light of the personalities behind them. But the Freudians made this interpretation more exact and more systematic. The great example of the psychoanalysis of an artist is Freud's own essay on Leonardo da Vinci; but this is pretty much an attempt to reconstruct a straight case history. The best example I know of the application of Freudian analysis to literature is in Van Wyck Brooks's book, *The Ordeal of Mark Twain,* in which Brooks uses an incident of Mark Twain's boyhood as a key to his whole career. He has been loudly attacked for this by Bernard de Voto,[16] and he has himself since repudiated the general method on the ground that nobody but an analyst can ever know enough about a writer to make a valid psychoanalytic diagnosis. This is true, of course, and the method has led to bad results where the critic has built a Freudian mechanism out of very slender evidence, and then given us merely a ro-

mance based on the supposed working of this mechanism instead of a genuine study of the writer's life and work. But I believe that Brooks had hold of something when he fixed upon that incident of which Mark Twain gave so vivid an account to his biographer—that scene at the deathbed of his father when his mother made him promise that he would not break her heart. If it was not one of those crucial happenings which are supposed to determine the complexes of Freud, it has certainly a typical significance in relation to Mark Twain's whole psychology. The stories that people tell about their childhood are likely to be profoundly symbolic even when they have been partly or wholly made up in the light of later experience. And the attitudes, the compulsions, the emotional "patterns" that recur in the work of a writer are of great interest to the historical critic.

These attitudes and patterns are embedded in the community and the historical moment, and they may indicate its ideals and its diseases as the cell shows the condition of the tissue. The recent scientific experimentation in the combining of Freudian with Marxist method, and of psychoanalysis with anthropology, has had its parallel development in criticism. And there is thus another element added to our equipment for analyzing literary works, and the problem grows still more complex.

The analyst, however, is of course not concerned with the comparative values of his patients any more than the surgeon is. He cannot tell you why the neurotic Dostoevsky produces work of immense value to his fellows, while another man with the same neurotic pattern would become a public menace. Freud himself emphatically states in his study of Leonardo that his method does not make any attempt to account for Leonardo's genius. The problems of comparative value remain after we have investigated the Freudian psychological factor just as they do after we have given

[16] A reference to De Voto's *Mark Twain's America* (Boston, 1932).

due attention to the Marxist economic factor and the racial and geographical factors. No matter how thorough and complete our explanations of works of literature may be from the historical and biographical points of view, we must be ready to try to estimate the relative degrees of success attained by the products of the various periods and the various personalities in some such way as Eliot and Saintsbury do. We must be able to tell good from bad, the first-rate from the second-rate. We shall not otherwise write literary criticism at all, but merely social or political history as reflected in literary texts, or psychological case histories from past eras, or, to take the historical point of view in its simplest and most academic form, merely chronologies of books that have been published.

And now how, in these matters of literary art, do we tell the good art from the bad? Norman Kemp Smith, the Kantian philosopher, whose courses I was fortunate enough to take at Princeton twenty-five years ago, used to tell us that this recognition was based primarily on an emotional reaction. For purposes of practical criticism this is a safe assumption to go on. It is possible to discriminate in a variety of ways the elements that in any given department go to make a successful work of literature. Different schools have at different times demanded different things of literature: *unity, symmetry, universality, originality, vision, inspiration, strangeness, suggestiveness, improving morality, socialist realism,* etc. But you could have any set of these qualities that any school of writing demanded and still not have a good play, a good novel, a good poem, a good history. If you identify the essence of good literature with any one of these elements or with any combination of them, you simply shift the emotional reaction to the recognition of the elements. Or if you add to your other demands the demand that the writer must have *talent,* you simply shift this recognition to the talent. Once people find some grounds of agreement in the coincidence of their emotional reactions to

books, they may be able to discuss these elements profitably; but if they do not have this basic agreement, the discussion will make no sense.

How, you may ask, are we to distinguish this élite who know what they are talking about? They are self-appointed and self-perpetuating, and they will compel you to accept their authority. Impostors may try to put themselves over, but these impostors will not last. The position of the people who understand writing (as is also the case in every other art) is simply that they know what they know, and that they are determined to impose their opinions by main force of eloquence or assertion on the people who do not know.

But what is the *cause* of this emotional reaction which is the critic's divining-rod? This question has long been an object of study by the branch of philosophy called esthetics, and it has recently been made a subject of scientific experimentation. Both these kinds of investigation of literature are likely to be prejudiced in the eyes of the critic by the fact that they are often carried on by persons who are themselves obviously deficient in literary taste. Yet one should not deny the possible value of explorations in this domain by men of acute minds who take as their given data the esthetic emotions of other men.

Almost everybody interested in literature has tried to explain these emotions to himself; and I of course have my own explanation.

In my view, all our intellectual activity, in whatever field it takes place, is an attempt to give a meaning to our experience —that is, to make life more practicable; for by understanding things we make it easier to survive and get around among them. Euclid, working in a convention of abstractions, shows us relations between the distances of our unwieldy and cluttered-up environment upon which we are able to count. A drama of Sophocles also indicates relations between the various human impulses, which appear so confused and dangerous, and brings out a certain justice of Fate—that is to say, of the way in which the interaction of these impulses is seen in the long run to work out—upon which we can also depend. The kinship from this point of view of the purposes of science and art appears particularly clearly with the Greeks, because not only do both Euclid and Sophocles satisfy us by making patterns, but they make very much the same kind of patterns. Euclid's *Elements* takes simple theorems and by a series of logical operations builds them up to a climax in the square on the hypotenuse. A typical drama of Sophocles makes much the same kind of pattern.

Some writers (as well as some scientists) have a more specific message: not content with such an effort as that of Sophocles to make life appear more sensible, and hence to make it more bearable, they try, like Plato, to explain the conditions for making it something different and better. Other kinds of literature, such as Sappho's lyrics, have less philosophical content than Sophocles. A lyric gives us nothing but a pattern imposed on the expression of a feeling; but this pattern of metrical qualities and of balancing consonants and vowels has the effect of reducing the feeling, however unruly or painful it may seem when we experience it in the course of our lives, to something orderly, symmetrical and pleasing. It also relates it to the more comprehensive scheme, works it into the larger texture, of the body of poetic art. The discord has been resolved, the anomaly subjected to discipline. And this control of his emotion by the poet has the effect at second-hand of making it easier for the reader to manage his own emotions. (Why certain sounds and rhythms gratify us more than others and how they are related

to the ideas which they are selected as appropriate for conveying, are questions that may be passed on to the scientist.)

And this brings us back to the historical point of view. The experience of mankind is always changing; and the writer who is to be anything more than an echo of his predecessors must always find expression for something which has not yet been expressed, must master new phenomena which have never yet been mastered. With each such victory of the human intellect, whether in the language of philosophy or the language of poetry, we experience a deep satisfaction: we have been cured of some ache of disorder, relieved of some oppressive burden of uncomprehended events.

This relief that brings the sense of power, and with the sense of power, joy, is the emotion which tells us when we are in the presence of a first-rate piece of literature. But, you may at this point object, are not people often solaced and rejoiced by literature of the trashiest kind? They are: crude and limited people do certainly feel such emotions in connection with work that is limited and crude. The man who is more highly organized and has a wider intellectual range will feel it in connection with work that is finer and more complex. The difference between the emotion of the more highly organized man and the emotion of the less highly organized one is merely a matter of gradation. You sometimes encounter books that seem to mark precisely the borderline between work that is definitely superior and work that is definitely bad—the novels of John Steinbeck, for example. When I was speaking a little while back of the experts who establish the standards of taste, I meant the people who can distinguish Grade A and who prefer it to the other grades.

John Crowe Ransom

1888

JOHN CROWE RANSOM was born in Pulaski, Tennessee, of a Scotch-Irish family thoroughly imbued with the traditions of the Old South. His father was a clergyman. Ransom completed his undergraduate work at Vanderbilt University and then went to Oxford as a Rhodes Scholar, specializing in classics and mathematics. From 1914 to 1937 he was a member of the English department at Vanderbilt, with two periods abroad—one during World War I, when he served as first lieutenant in the field artillery and taught in an artillery school in France, and the other in 1931-32, when he held a Guggenheim fellowship and taught at the University of the Southwest at Exeter.

While at Vanderbilt he was the leader of the famous *Fugitive* group. This group was composed of intellectuals of Nashville and environs who met informally to read and discuss their ventures into poetry. Between 1922 and 1925 they published the best of these in the little magazine, the *Fugitive*. The group included poets of the stature of Allen Tate, Donald Davidson, Merrill Moore, and Robert Penn Warren.

During the depression years Ransom also became the moving spirit of a critical group that drew its members from the Southern intelligentsia at large—the so-called Southern Agrarians. Their official manifesto, *I'll Take My Stand,* appeared in 1930.

Going to Kenyon College, in Gambier, Ohio, as professor of English in 1937, Ransom became founder and editor of the *Kenyon Review* in 1938. Although its appeal has been limited to an intellectual élite, it must be ranked as one of the most influential literary quarterlies of our time. Ransom's volumes of poetry include *Poems about God* (1919); *Chills and Fever* (1924); *Grace After Meat* (1924); *Two Gentlemen in Bonds* (1927); and *Selected Poems* (1946). His best prose is gathered into *God Without Thunder* (1930); *The World's Body* (1938); and *The New Criticism* (1941).

[*The Sewanee Review,* LXI (Summer, 1948), 367-476, contains a series of essays in homage to Ransom; a less sympathetic study appears in Yvor Winters' *The Anatomy of Nonsense* (Norfolk, Conn., 1943), reprinted in his *In Defense of Reason* (New York, 1947).]

From
THE WORLD'S BODY
[1938]

Poets Without Laurels

THE POETS I refer to in the title are the "moderns": those whom a small company of adept readers enjoys, perhaps enormously, but the general public detests; those in whose hands poetry as a living art has lost its public support.

Consequently I do not refer to such poets as Edna St. Vincent Millay and

Robert Frost, who are evidently influenced by modernism without caring to "go modern" in the sense of joining the revolution; which is very much as if they had stopped at a mild or parlor variety of socialism, when all about them the brave, or at least the doctrinaire, were marching under the red banner. Probably they are wise in their time; they have laurels deservedly and wear them gracefully. But they do not define the issue which I wish to discuss. And still less do I refer to poets like E. A. Robinson, Sturge Moore,[1] and John Masefield, who are even less modern; though I have no intention of questioning their laurels either. I refer to poets with no laurels.

I do not wish to seem to hold the public responsible for their condition, as if it had suddenly become phlegmatic, cruel, and philistine. The poets have certainly for their part conducted themselves peculiarly. They could not have estranged the public more completely if they had tried; and smart fellows as they are, they know very well what they have been doing, and what they are still stubborn in doing, and what the consequences are.

For they have failed more and more flagrantly, more and more deliberately, to identify themselves with the public interests, as if expressly to renounce the kind affections which poets had courted for centuries. Accordingly, they do not only encounter public indifference, they sometimes encounter active hostility. A Pulitzer committeeman, I hear, says about some modernist poet whose book is up for judgment: "He will never get the award except over my dead body." The violence of the remark seems to exceed the occasion, but it is not exceptional.

Poets used to be bards and patriots, priests and prophets, keepers of the public conscience, and, naturally, men of public importance. Society crowned them with wreaths of laurel, according to the tradition which comes to us from the Greeks and is perpetuated by official custom in England—and in Oklahoma. Generally the favor must have been gratefully received. But modern poets are of another breed. It is as if all at once they had lost their prudence as well as their piety, and formed a compact to unclasp the chaplet from their brows, inflicting upon themselves the humility of delaureation, and retiring from public responsibility and honors. It is this phenomenon which has thrown critical theory into confusion.

Sir Philip Sidney made the orthodox defense of poetry on the ground of the poet's service to patriotism and virtue:

> He doth not only show the way, but giveth so sweet a prospect into the way, as will entice any man to enter into it.

And what was the technique of enticement?

> With a tale forsooth he cometh unto you, with a tale which holdeth children from play, and old men from the chimney corner.

The poets, therefore, told entrancing tales, which had morals. But the fact was, also, that the poets were not always content to win to virtue by indirection, or enticement, but were prepared to preach with almost no disguise, and to become sententious and repetitious, and the literature which they created is crowded with precise maxims for the moralists. There it stands on the shelves now. Sometimes the so-called poet has been only a moralist with a poetic manner. And all the poets famous in our tradition, or very nearly all, have been poets of a powerful moral cast.

So I shall try a preliminary definition of the poet's traditional function on behalf of society: he proposed to make virtue delicious. He compounded a moral effect with an aesthetic effect. The total effect was not a pure one, but it was rich, and relished highly. The name of the moral effect was goodness; the name of the aesthetic effect was beauty. Perhaps these

---

[1] Thomas Sturge Moore (1870-1944), minor British poet, dramatist, and aesthetician, whose collected *Poems* appeared in four volumes, 1931-33.

did not have to coexist, but the planners of society saw to it that they should; they called upon the artists to reinforce morality with charm. The artists obliged.

When they had done so, the public did not think of attempting to distinguish in its experience as reader the glow which was aesthetic from the glow which was moral. Most persons probably could not have done this; many persons cannot do it today. There is yet no general recognition of the possibility that an aesthetic effect may exist by itself, independent of morality or any other useful set of ideas. But the modern poet is intensely concerned with this possibility, and he has disclaimed social responsibility in order to secure this pure aesthetic effect. He cares nothing, professionally, about morals, or God, or native land. He has performed a work of dissociation and purified his art.

There are distinct styles of "modernity," but I think their net results, psychologically, are about the same. I have in mind what might be called the "pure" style and what might be called the "obscure" style.

A good "pure" poem is Wallace Stevens' "Sea Surface Full of Clouds"—famous perhaps, but certainly not well known. I shall have to deal with it summarily. Time and place, "In that November off Tehuantepec." The poem has five uniform stanzas, presenting as many surface effects beheld at breakfast time "after the slopping of the sea by night grew still." The first surface made one think of rosy chocolate and gilt umbrellas; the second, of chophouse chocolate and sham umbrellas; the third, of porcelain chocolate and pied umbrellas; the fourth, of musky chocolate and frail umbrellas; the fifth, of Chinese chocolate and large umbrellas. Nothing could be more discriminating than these details, which induct us respectively into the five fields of observation. The poem has a calculated complexity, and its technical competence is so high that to study it, if you do that sort of thing, is to be happy. That it has not been studied by a

multitude of persons is due to a simple consideration which strikes us at once: the poem has no moral, political, religious, or sociological values. It is not about "res publica," the public thing. The subject matter is trifling.

Poetry of this sort, as it was practised by some French poets of the nineteenth century, and as it is practised by many British and American poets now, has been called pure poetry, and the name is accurate. It is nothing but poetry; it is poetry for poetry's sake, and you cannot get a moral out of it. But it was to be expected that it would never win the public at large. The impulse which led readers to the old poetry was at least as much moral as it was aesthetic, while the new poetry cannot count on any customers except those specializing in strict aesthetic effects. But the modern poets intend to rate only as poets, and would probably think it meretricious to solicit patronage by making moral overtures.

As an example of "obscure" poetry, though not the most extreme one, I cite Allen Tate's "Death of Little Boys." Here are some of its verses:

Then you will touch at the bedside, torn
    in two,
Gold curls now deftly intricate with gray
As the windowpane extends a fear to you
From one peeled aster drenched with the
    wind all day. . . .

Till all the guests, come in to look, turn
    down
Their palms; and delirium assails the cliff
Of Norway where you ponder, and your
    little town
Reels like a sailor drunk in his rotten skiff.

There is evidently a wide difference between Stevens and Tate, as poets. Tate has an important subject, and his poem is a human document, with a contagious fury about it: Stevens, pursuing purity, does not care to risk such a subject. But Tate, as if conscious that he is close to moralizing and sententiousness, builds up deliberately, I imagine, an effect of obscurity; for example, he does not care to explain the private meaning of his windowpane and his Norwegian cliff; or else, by some feat, he permits these bright features to belong to his total image without permitting them to reveal any precise meaning, either for himself or for his reader. Stevens, however, is objective from beginning to end; he completes all his meanings, knowing these will have little or no moral importance.

Pure or obscure, the modern poet manages not to slip into the old-fashioned moral-beautiful compound. If pure, he will not consider a subject which lends itself to moralization; that is, a subject of practical interest. It is his chief problem to find then a subject which has any interest at all. If, however, he prefers the other road, he may take the subject nearest his own humanity, a subject perhaps of terrifying import; but in treating it will stop short of all moral or theoretical conclusions, and confuse his detail to the point where it leaves no positive implications.

To be more technical: it is as if the pure poet presented a subject and declined to make any predication about it or even to start predication; and as if the obscure poet presented a subject in order to play with a great deal of important predication without ever completing any.

Personally, I prefer the rich obscure poetry to the thin pure poetry. The deaths of little boys are more exciting than the sea surfaces. It may be that the public preference, however, is otherwise. The public is inclined simply to ignore the pure poetry, because it lacks practical usefulness; but to hate the obscure poetry, because it looks important enough to attend to, and yet never yields up any specific fruit. Society, through its spokesmen the dozens of social-minded critics, who talk about the necessity of "communication," is now raging with indignation, or it may be with scorn, against the obscure poetry which this particular generation of poets has deposited. Nevertheless, both types of poetry, obscure as well as pure, aim at

poetic autonomy; that is, speaking roughly, at purity.

Modern poetry in this respect is like modern painting. European painting used to be nearly as social a thing as poetry. It illustrated the sacred themes prescribed by the priests, whether popularly (Raphael) or esoterically and symbolically (Michelangelo); did the portraits of kings and cardinals, and the scenes of battles and great occasions; worked up allegorical and sentimental subjects. But more or less suddenly it asserted its independence. So we find Impressionists, doing the most innocent tricks with landscapes and mere objects; and we find Cézanne, painting so many times and so lovingly his foolish little bowl of fruits. The procedure was a strange one for the moral laity, who could detect nothing of importance there; and indeed nothing of public importance was there, only matters of technical interest to painters, and to persons who found painting sufficient. Later, and today, we find painters taking up the most heroic human material again in the most promising manner, yet arriving at no explicit meaning and, on the whole, simply playing with its powerful symbols. (Not all painters, of course.)

Apostate, illaureate, and doomed to outlawry the modern poets may be. I have the feeling that modernism is an unfortunate road for them to have taken. But it was an inevitable one. It is not hard to defend them from imputations against their honor and their logic. It is probably a question of whether we really know them, and understand their unusual purpose, and the powerful inhibitions they impose upon themselves.

But let us approach the matter from a slightly different angle. Poets have had to become modern because the age is modern. Its modernism envelops them like a sea, or an air. Nothing in their thought can escape it.

Modern poetry is pure poetry. The motive behind it cannot be substantially different from the motive behind the other modern activities, which is certainly the driving force of all our modernism. What is its name? "Purism" would be exact, except that it does not have the zealous and contriving sound we want. "Platonism" would do, provided there were time to come to an agreement about the essential meaning of Plato's act. I think the name "Puritanism" will describe this motive, if I may extend a little a term whose application in history has been mostly religious and moral.

Our period differs outwardly from other periods because it first differs inwardly. Its spiritual temper is puritanical; that is, it craves to perfect the parts of experience separately or in their purity, and is a series of isolated perfections. These have often been brilliant. But perhaps the modern program, on the whole, is not the one under which men maintain their best health and spirits. A little fear to that effect is beginning to cloud the consciousness of the brilliant moderns.

And here I conclude my defense of the modern poet. He is a good workman, and his purpose is really quite orthodox in its modernism. But it is no better.

The development of modern civilization has been a grand progression in which Puritanism has invaded first one field and then another.

The first field perhaps was religion. The religious impulse used to join to itself and dominate and hold together nearly all the fields of human experience; politics, science, art, and even industry, and by all means moral conduct. But Puritanism came in the form of the Protestant Reformation and separated religion from all its partners. Perhaps the most important of these separations was that which lopped off from religion the aesthetic properties which simple-hearted devotees and loving artists had given it. The aesthetic properties constituted the myth, which to the temperamental Protestants became superstition, and the ceremonial, which became idolatry.

Under the progressive zeal of the Reformation the being of God has become rarefied in the degree that it has been purified, until we find difficulty in grasping it, and there are people who tell me, just as there are people who tell the reader, that religion as a living force here in the Western world is spent. Theology is purer or more abstract than ever before, but it would seem to belong exclusively to theologians, and it cannot by itself assemble together all those who once delighted in the moral precepts, the music and the pomp, the social communion, and the concrete Godhead, of the synthetic institution which was called religion.

Next, or perhaps at the same time, Puritanism applied itself to morality. Broad as the reach of morality may be, it is distinct enough as an experience to be capable of purification. We may say that its destiny was to become what we know as sociology, a body of positivistic science. It had to be emancipated from its religious overlords, whose authority, after all, was not a moral one. Then it had to be emancipated from the dictates of taste, or aesthetic, and this latter emancipation was the harder, and perhaps the more needless. The Greeks, though they were incipient Puritans, scarcely attempted it. They had a compound phrase meaning "beautiful-good," which even their philosophers used habitually as the name of something elemental and indissoluble. Suspicion was aroused in Greeks by a goodness which could not produce beauty, just as to a man like Spenser the idea of virtue was incomplete until it flowered into poetic form, and just as to the sympathetic French artist our new American liberty was not quite won until identifiable with an able-bodied demi-goddess lifting a torch. The splitting up of the moral-beautiful compound for the sake of the pure moral article is visibly at work in the New Testament, and in the bourgeois cult of plainness in seventeenth-century England, and in the finicky private life of a Puritan moralist like Kant, and today in moral or sociological treatises (and authors) which neither exhibit nor discuss charm. Now, it is true that we moralize with "maximum efficiency" when we do it technically, or abstractly, but when that comes to be the rule we no longer approach a moral discussion with anything but a moral interest. To be moral is no longer to be "decent," and it looks as if moral appeal had become something less wide and less instant than it was.

Then Puritanism worked upon politics. I am not prepared to go deeply into this, but it is evident that purification consisted in taking the state away from the church, from the monarch, from the feudal aristocracy, from any other concrete attachments, in order that it might propel itself by the force of pure statecraft. Progress in this direction meant constitutionalism, parliamentarianism, republicanism. A modern state like ours is transparent in the perfection of its logic. But that does not make it the more realistic. It is obliged to count upon a universal and continuous will on the part of the citizens to accept an abstract formula of political action. But such a will may not be there. The population, not being composed exclusively of politicians, is inclined to delegate statecraft to those who profess it. The old mixed states had a greater variety of loyalties to appeal to.

Puritanism is an ideal which not all persons are strong enough to realize, but only those with great power of concentration. Its best chance of success lies in individual projects. Accordingly, Puritanism fairly came into its own in the vast multitude of private enterprises which go together to make modern science. Galileo and Kepler found science captive to religious dogma. America, the paradise of Puritanism, was not yet in being, but England was; and there presently, while other Puritanisms were going on, Lord Bacon was able to anticipate the complete emancipation of science by virtue of its adoption of the pure experimental method. Now, there have been other incubi besides religion resting upon science at one time or another; and chiefly the tendency of poetry to haunt its deliberations. Poetry is a figurative way of expression, science is a technical or abstract way; but since science employs language, the figurative associations are hard to keep out. In earlier days poetry kept close to science, and it did not seem strange if Lucretius wanted to set forth the body of accepted science in verse. But poetry now cannot attend science into its technical labyrinth. The result is greater success for scientists, but not necessarily their greater happiness as men; and the general understanding on our part that we will follow science if we are scientists, but otherwise will leave it to the scientists.

It was but one step that Puritanism had to go from there into the world of business, where the material sciences are systematically applied. The rise of the modern business world is a development attendant upon the freedom which it has enjoyed; upon business for business' sake, or pure business, or "laissez faire," with such unconditioned principles as efficiency, technological improvement, and maximum productivity. If I wished to attack the record of business, I should by now have been long anticipated. It is common opinion that business as a self-contained profession has created business men who are defective in their humanity; that the conduct of business has made us callous to personal relations and to social justice; and that many of the occupations which business has devised are, in the absence of aesthetic standards, servile.

All these exclusions and specializations, and many more, have been making modern life what it is. It is significant that every specialization on the list has had to resist the insidious charms of aesthetic experience before its own perfection could arise. (Evidently the aesthetic interest is remarkably catholic among our faculties in its affinities; ready to attach itself easily to almost any sort of moment; a ubiquitous element in experience, it might be thought, which it would be unhealthy to cast out.) But the energy of so deep an impulse as Puritanism had to flow through all the channels, and to come to its last outlet in a pure art, a pure poetry. Those who have not observed the necessity may choose to hold its pre-destined agents the poets in contempt, or in amazement. The poets are in the spirit of their time. On the one hand, they have been pushed out of their old attachments, whereby they used to make themselves use-ful to public causes, by the specialists who did not want the respective causes to be branded with amateurism. On the other hand, they are moved by a universal tend-ency into their own appropriate kind of specialization, which can be, as they have been at pains to show, as formidable as any other.

Considerations of this kind, I feel sure, have been more or less precisely within the intuition of all modern poets, and have motivated their performance. Technically, they are quite capable of writing the old compound poetry, but they cannot bring themselves to do it; or rather, when they have composed it in unguarded moments, as modern poets still sometimes do, they are under the necessity of destroying it immediately. There is no baffling degree of virtuosity in the old lines,

Roll on, thou deep and dark blue Ocean, roll!
Ten thousand fleets sweep over thee in vain:
Man marks the earth with ruin, his control
Stops with the shore.[2]

The modern poet can accomplish just as elegant a rumination as this; but thinks it would commit him to an anachronism, for this is the style of an older period. In that period, though it was a comparatively late one, and though this poet thought he was in advance of it, the prophets of so-ciety were still numbering and tuning their valuable reflections before they saw fit to release them; and morality, philosophy, re-ligion, science, and art could still meet comfortably in one joint expression, though perhaps not with the same distinc-tion they might have gained if they had had their pure and several expressions. A passage of Byron's if sprung upon an unsuspecting modern would be felt imme-diately as "dating"; it would be felt as something that did very well for those dark ages before the modern mind achieved its own disintegration and perfected its faculties serially.

Even as readers, we must testify readily to the force of this time-principle. We sometimes pore over an old piece of poetry for so long that we fall under its spell and forget that its spirit is not our spirit. But we began to read it in a pe-culiar manner; by saying to ourselves, This is early Greek epic, This is seventeenth century English drama. By means of one of the ripest and subtlest powers in us, that is, the historical sense, we made an adapta-tion of our minds to its mind, and were able to suspend those centuries which had intervened. Those centuries had made our minds much more knowing and at the same time, it is to be feared, much less sug-gestible. Yet it is not exactly with our own minds that we are reading the old poetry; otherwise we could not read it. For when we come back to our own world there be-gins to function in us a different style of consciousness altogether. And if we had begun to read a poetry of this old sort by saying, This was written last night by the poet around the corner, we could not have put up with it. If we throw away impa-tiently a contemporaneous poetry which displays archaisms of diction, what will we do with that which displays archaisms of temper? It looks spurious; for we require our art, and the living artists require it too, to be as contemporaneous as our bank-ing or our locomotion.

What, then, is the matter with a pure poetry? The question is really more the-oretical than practical. A school, an age,

[2] Quoted from Byron's *Childe Harold's Pilgrimage* (1812).

is involved by such a question, not merely some small poem or poet. And there is nothing the matter with this particular branch of purity which is not the matter with our other modern activities. All are affected by Puritanism, just as the vegetation is affected, generally and indifferently, by the climate.

It is impossible to answer the question categorically because the items are intangible. But we find ourselves reasoning about it as well as we can, which is as follows.

You may dissociate the elements of experience and exploit them separately. But then at the best you go on a schedule of small experiences, taking them in turn, and trusting that when the rotation is complete you will have missed nothing. And at the worst you will become so absorbed in some one small experience that you will forget to go on and complete the schedule; in that case you will have missed something. The theory that excellence lies in the perfection of the single functions, and that society should demand that its members be hard specialists, assumes that there is no particular harm in missing something. But I do not see why. A maniac with a fixed idea is a variety of specialist, and an absorbing specialty is a small mania.

As for poetry, it seems to me a pity that its beauty should have to be cloistered and conventual, if it is "pure," or teasing and evasive, if it is "obscure." The union of beauty with goodness and truth has been common enough to be regarded as natural. It is the dissociation which is unnatural and painful.

But when we talk about simple and compound experiences, we are evidently employing a chemical mode of speech to represent something we cannot quite make out. Units of consciousness are hard to handle scientifically; it takes more science than we have. Max Eastman thinks the future of literary criticism is bound up with the future of psychology and very likely it is; but it is difficult to share his sanguine expectations of that science.[3]

It cannot become as effective a science as chemistry.

Nevertheless, I shall make a tentative argument from the analogy of chemistry. Lemonade is only a mechanical mixture, not very interesting to chemists. Aside from the water, a drop of lemonade contains lemon and sugar in no standard proportions. If it tastes too sour, add sugar, and if it tastes too sweet, add lemon. (And do not forget to stir the mixture.) No matter what the final proportions, you can still detect in the lemonade the sweet taste and the sour; though this is too abstract a matter to bother about if the lemonade is satisfactory, for in that case you simply drink it.

Table salt, however, is a true chemical compound; a molecule of it is $NaCl$. Understanding this, you do not claim to know the taste either of sodium or of chlorine when you say you are acquainted with the taste of salt. Whatever the Na was and however it tasted by itself, it gave up that identity when it compounded with Cl; and vice versa.

$NaCl$ is found in the state of nature, where it is much commoner than either of its constituents. But suppose the chemists decided to have nothing to do with $NaCl$ because of its compoundness, and undertook to extract from it the pure Na and Cl to serve on the table. Suppose they made war on all the natural compounds, broke them down into the hundred or so atomic elements, and asked us to live on these alone. The beneficiaries would regard this service as well-meaning but mistaken.

But we provide the necessities for our minds and affections with more harshness than we dare use on our stomachs and bodies—so inferior in precision is our knowledge of minds to our knowledge of bodies. Poets are now under the influence of a perfectly arbitrary theory which I

[3] Max Eastman's *The Literary Mind, Its Place in an Age of Science* (1931) and *Art and the Life of Action* (1934) contain his most provocative discussions of literary criticism.

have called Puritanism. They pursue A, an aesthetic element thought always to have the same taste and to be the one thing desirable for poets. They will not permit the presence near it of M, the moral element, because that will produce the lemonade MA, and they do not approve of lemonade. In lemonade the A gets itself weakened and neutralized by the M.

But it is possible that MA is not a drop of lemonade after all, but a true molecule, into which the separate M and the separate A have disappeared and out of which an entirely new taste is born. The effects which we attribute to a poet like Virgil, or Milton, are on the following order: pious, philosophical, imaginative, sonorous, and the like. But perhaps the effect which we actually receive from the poetry is not that of an aggregate or series or mechanical mixture of distinct properties but only the single effect of a compound. In that event the properties will exist separate only in our minds, by a later act of qualitative analysis, and they will not really be in the poetry in their own identities.

Is the old-fashioned full poetry a mechanical mixture like lemonade or a chemical compound like table salt? That is probably the most important question which the modern critics have opened up to speculation. There are many corollary questions along with it, like these: When does the display of doctrine in poetry in-cur the charge of didacticism? And must the poet also bear arms—that is, like the economist and the social reformer, view his performance in the light of a utility rather than an end?

Now some poetry, so-called, is not even lemonade, for the ingredients have not been mixed, much less compounded. Lumps of morality and image lie side by side, and are tasted in succession. T. S. Eliot thinks that this has been the character of a great deal of English poetry since the age of Dryden. Such poetry occupies some of the best room in the library, and takes up some of the best time of the earnest student of literature. It is decidedly one of the causes of that revulsion of feeling on the part of the modern poet which drives him away from the poetic tradition.

When our critical theory is complete, perhaps we shall be able to distinguish various combinations of elements passing for poetry; thus, poetry by assemblage, poetry by mixture, and poetry by composition. The last of these sounds the best.

I suggest that critics and philosophers fix their most loving attention upon certain natural compounds in human experience. But I say so diffidently, and not too hopefully. It will take a long time to change the philosophical set which has come over the practice of the poets. The intellectual climate in which they live will have to be altered first.

American Literature 1900 to the Present

II
DIRECTIONS IN FICTION

1871 ∾ *Theodore Dreiser* ∾ 1945

THEODORE DREISER'S father was a native of southern Germany, a strict Catholic, and a failure in his business enterprises in America. His mother was a member of a prosperous Moravian family in Ohio. Theodore, born at Terre Haute, was the twelfth of thirteen children. His training in parochial and public schools, frequently interrupted as the family moved from one Indiana town to another, and his one year at the University of Indiana, contributed less directly to his preparation for the writing he was to do than did his experience in various jobs in Chicago, where he was supporting himself before he was twenty, and his subsequent newspaper work in Chicago, St. Louis, and Pittsburgh.

Dreiser's first novel, *Sister Carrie* (1900), was published on the editorial recommendation of Frank Norris, but was withdrawn from sale by the publishers because of its frankness. Dreiser continued his work as a journalist, becoming editor of *Broadway Magazine* (1906-7) and then editor-in-chief of *Delineator* and other Butterick periodicals, until the publication of his second novel, *Jennie Gerhardt* (1911), when he resigned to give his full time to writing. His fifth novel, *The "Genius"* (1915), was temporarily suppressed by its publisher because of threatened action by the New York Society for the Suppression of Vice.

After the appearance of *An American Tragedy* (1925), Dreiser took an increasingly active part in social movements. He was arrested while participating in a civil liberties investigation in Harlan County, Kentucky, and made a visit to the Soviet Union which he reported in *Dreiser Looks at Russia* (1928). From 1932 to 1934 he was one of the editors of the *American Spectator*. In 1939 he edited *Living Thoughts of Thoreau*. From 1894 on Dreiser spent most of his life in New York City, which he described in *The Color of a Great City* (1923) and other books. But in his last years he settled in California, where he died shortly after completing his first novel in twenty years, *The Bulwark* (1946). In addition to the novels mentioned above, Dreiser wrote *The Financier* (1912), *The Titan* (1914) and the posthumous and incomplete *The Stoic* (1948). *Twelve Men* (1919) is a collection of brief and personal biographical sketches, including one of Dreiser's brother Paul (who spelled their name "Dresser"), a successful writer of popular songs, who gave Theodore encouragement and material assistance during his early years as a writer.

Dreiser's short stories were collected in *Free and Other Stories* (1918) and *Chains* (1927). His frank and detailed autobiographical writings include *A Traveller at Forty* (1913); *A Hoosier Holiday* (1916); *A Book About Myself*

(1922); and *Dawn* (1931). *Tragic America* (1932) and *America Is Worth Saving* (1941) present aspects of his social philosophy.

[Dreiser has been much discussed in magazines and journals. His autobiographical books are helpful, as well as Dorothy Dudley's *Forgotten Frontiers: Dreiser and the Land of the Free* (New York, 1932). H. L. Mencken's *A Book of Prefaces* (New York, 1917) and S. P. Sherman's *On Contemporary Literature* (New York, 1917) present opposing points of view regarding Dreiser.]

OLD ROGAUM AND HIS THERESA
[1918]

IN ALL Bleecker Street was no more comfortable doorway than that of the butcher Rogaum, even if the first floor was given over to meat market purposes. It was to one side of the main entrance, which gave ingress to the butcher shop, and from it led up a flight of steps, at least five feet wide, to the living rooms above. A little portico stood out in front of it, railed on either side, and within was a second or final door, forming, with the outer or storm door, a little area, where Mrs. Rogaum and her children frequently sat of a summer's evening. The outer door was never locked, owing to the inconvenience it would inflict on Mr. Rogaum, who had no other way of getting upstairs. In winter, when all had gone to bed, there had been cases in which belated travelers had taken refuge there from the snow or sleet. One or two newsboys occasionally slept there, until routed out by Officer Maguire, who, seeing it half open one morning at two o'clock, took occasion to look in. He jogged the newsboys sharply with his stick, and then, when they were gone, tried the inner door, which was locked.

"You ought to keep that outer door locked, Rogaum," he observed to the phlegmatic butcher the next evening, as he was passing, "people might get in. A couple o' kids was sleepin' in there last night."

"Ach, dot iss no difference," answered Rogaum pleasantly. "I haf der inner door locked, yet. Let dem sleep. Dot iss no difference."

"Better lock it," said the officer, more to vindicate his authority than anything else. "Something will happen there yet."

The door was never locked, however, and now of a summer evening Mrs. Rogaum and the children made pleasant use of its recess, watching the rout of street cars and occasionally belated trucks go by. The children played on the sidewalk, all except the budding Theresa (eighteen just turning), who, with one companion of the neighborhood, the pretty Kenrihan girl, walked up and down the block, laughing, glancing, watching the boys. Old Mrs. Kenrihan lived in the next block, and there, sometimes, the two stopped. There, also, they most frequently pretended to be when talking with the boys in the intervening side street. Young "Connie" Almerting and George Goujon were the bright particular mashers who held the attention of the maidens in this block. These two made their acquaintance in the customary bold, boyish way, and thereafter the girls had an urgent desire to be out in the street together after eight, and to linger where the boys could see and overtake them.

Old Mrs. Rogaum never knew. She was a particularly fat, old German lady, completely dominated by her liege and portly lord, and at nine o'clock regularly, as he had long ago deemed meet and fit, she was wont to betake her way upward and so to bed. Old Rogaum himself, at that hour, closed the market and went to his chamber.

Before that all the children were called sharply, once from the doorstep below Rogaum did it first and Rogaum last. It had come, because of a shade of lenience, and once from the window above, only Mrs.

not wholly apparent in the father's nature, that the older of the children needed two callings and sometimes three. Theresa, now that she had "got in" with the Kenrihan maiden, needed that many calls and even more.

She was just at that age for which mere thoughtless, sensory life holds its greatest charm. She loved to walk up and down in the as yet bright street where were voices and laughter, and occasionally moonlight streaming down. What a nuisance it was to be called at nine, anyhow. Why should one have to go in then, anyhow. What old fogies her parents were, wishing to go to bed so early. Mrs. Kenrihan was not so strict with her daughter. It made her pettish when Rogaum insisted, calling as he often did, in German, "Come you now," in a very hoarse and belligerent voice.

She came, eventually, frowning and wretched, all the moonlight calling her, all the voices of the night urging her to come back. Her innate opposition due to her urgent youth made her coming later and later, however, until now, by August of this, her eighteenth year, it was nearly ten when she entered, and Rogaum was almost invariably angry.

"I vill lock you oudt," he declared, in strongly accented English, while she tried to slip by him each time. "I vill show you. Du sollst come ven I say, yet. Hear now."

"I'll not," answered Theresa, but it was always under her breath.

Poor Mrs. Rogaum trembled at hearing the wrath in her husband's voice. It spoke of harder and fiercer times which had been with her. Still she was not powerful enough in the family councils to put in a weighty word. So Rogaum fumed unrestricted.

There were other nights, however, many of them, and now that the young sparks of the neighborhood had enlisted the girls' attention, it was a more trying time than ever. Never did a street seem more beautiful. Its shabby red walls, dusty pavements and protruding store steps and iron railings seemed bits of the ornamental paraphernalia of heaven itself. These lights, the cars,

the moon, the street lamps! Theresa had a tender eye for the dashing Almerting, a young idler and loafer of the district, the son of a stationer farther up the street. What a fine fellow he was, indeed! What a handsome nose and chin! What eyes! What authority! His cigarette was always cocked at a high angle, in her presence, and his hat had the least suggestion of being set to one side He had a shrewd way of winking one eye, taking her boldly by the arm, hailing her as "Hey, Pretty!" and was strong and athletic, and worked (when he worked) in a tobacco factory. His was a trade, indeed, nearly acquired, as he said, and his jingling pockets attested that he had money of his own· Altogether he was very captivating.

"Aw, whaddy ya want to go in for?" he used to say to her, tossing his head gayly on one side to listen and holding her by the arm, as old Rogaum called. "Tell him yuh didn't hear."

"No, I've got to go," said the girl, who was soft and plump and fair—a Rhine maiden type.

"Well, yuh don't have to go just yet. Stay another minute. George, what was that fellow's name that tried to sass us the other day?"

"Theresa!" roared old Rogaum forcefully. "If you do not now come! Ve vill see!"

"I've got to go," repeated Theresa with a faint effort at starting. "Can't you hear? Don't hold me. I haf to."

"Aw, whaddy ya want to be such a coward for? Y' don't have to go. He won't do nothin' tuh yuh. My old man was always hollerin' like that up tuh a coupla years ago. Let him holler! Say, kid, but yuh got sweet eyes! They're as blue! An' your mouth——"

"Now stop! You hear me!" Theresa would protest softly, as, swiftly, he would slip an arm about her waist and draw her to him, sometimes in a vain, sometimes in a successful effort to kiss her.

As a rule she managed to interpose an elbow between her face and his, but even then he would manage to touch an ear or a cheek or her neck—sometimes her mouth, full and warm—before she would develop sufficient energy to push him away and herself free. Then she would protest mock earnestly or sometimes run away.

"Now, I'll never speak to you any more, if that's the way you're going to do. My father don't allow me to kiss boys, anyhow," and then she would run, half a-shamed, half smiling herself as he would stare after her, or if she lingered, develop a kind of anger and even rage.

"Aw, cut it! Whaddy ya want to be so shy for? Don'tcha like me? What's gettin' into yuh, anyhow? Hey?"

In the meantime George Goujon and Myrtle Kenrihan, their companions, might be sweeting and going through a similar contest, perhaps a hundred feet up the street or near at hand. The quality of old Rogaum's voice would by now have become so raucous, however, that Theresa would have lost all comfort in the scene and, becoming frightened, hurry away. Then it was often that both Almerting and Goujon as well as Myrtle Kenrihan would follow her to the corner, almost in sight of the irate old butcher.

"Let him call," young Almerting would insist, laying a final hold on her soft white fingers and causing her to quiver thereby.

"Oh, no," she would gasp nervously. "I can't."

"Well, go on, then," he would say, and with a flip of his heel would turn back, leaving Theresa to wonder whether she had alienated him forever or no. Then she would hurry to her father's door.

"Muss ich all my time spenden calling, mit you on de streeds oudt?" old Rogaum would roar wrathfully, the while his fat hand would descend on her back. "Take dot now. Vy don't you come ven I call? In now. I vill show you. Und come you yussed yunce more at dis time—ve vill see if I am boss in my own house, aber! Komst du vun minute nach ten to-morrow und you vill see vot you vill get. I vill der door lock. Du sollst not in kommen. Mark! Oudt

sollst du stayen—oudt!" and he would glare wrathfully at her retreating figure.

Sometimes Theresa would whimper, sometimes cry or sulk. She almost hated her father for his cruelty, "the big, fat, rough thing," and just because she wanted to stay out in the bright streets, too! Because he was old and stout and wanted to go to bed at ten, he thought every one else did. And outside was the dark sky with its stars, the street lamps, the cars, the tinkle and laughter of eternal life!

"Oh!" she would sigh as she undressed and crawled into her small neat bed. To think that she had to live like this all her days! At the same time old Rogaum was angry and equally determined. It was not so much that he imagined that his Theresa was in bad company as yet, but he wished to forefend against possible danger. This was not a good neighborhood by any means. The boys around here were tough. He wanted Theresa to pick some nice sober youth from among the other Germans he and his wife knew here and there—at the Lutheran Church, for instance. Otherwise she shouldn't marry. He knew she only walked from his shop to the door of the Kenrihans and back again. Had not his wife told him so? If he had thought upon what far pilgrimage her feet had already ventured, or had even seen the dashing Almerting hanging near, then had there been wrath indeed. As it was, his mind was more or less at ease.

On many, many evenings it was much the same. Sometimes she got in on time, sometimes not, but more and more "Connie" Almerting claimed her for his "steady," and bought her ice-cream. In the range of the short block and its confining corners it was all done, lingering by the curbstone and strolling a half block either way in the side streets, until she had offended seriously at home, and the threat was repeated anew. He often tried to persuade her to go on picnics or outings of various kinds, but this, somehow, was not to be thought of at her age—at least with him. She knew her father would never endure the thought, and never even had the courage to mention it, let alone run away. Mere lingering with him at the adjacent street corners brought stronger and stronger admonishments—even more blows and the threat that she should not get in at all.

Well enough she meant to obey, but on one radiant night late in June the time fled too fast. The moon was so bright, the air so soft. The feel of far summer things was in the wind and even in this dusty street. Theresa, in a newly starched white summer dress, had been loitering up and down with Myrtle when as usual they encountered Almerting and Goujon. Now it was ten, and the regular calls were beginning.

"Aw, wait a minute," said "Connie." "Stand still. He won't lock yuh out."

"But he will, though," said Theresa. "You don't know him."

"Well, if he does, come on back to me. I'll take care of yuh. I'll be here. But he won't though. If you stayed out a little while he'd letcha in all right. That's the way my old man used to try to do me but it didn't work with me. I stayed out an' he let me in, just the same. Don'tcha let him kidja." He jingled some loose change in his pocket.

Never in his life had he had a girl on his hands at any unseasonable hour, but it was nice to talk big, and there was a club to which he belonged, the Varick Street Roosters, and to which he had a key. It would be closed and empty at this hour, and she could stay there until morning, if need be, or with Myrtle Kenrihan. He would take her there if she insisted. There was a sinister grin on the youth's face.

By now Theresa's affections had carried her far. This youth with his slim body, his delicate strong hands, his fine chin, straight mouth and hard dark eyes—how wonderful he seemed. He was but nineteen to her eighteen but cold, shrewd, daring. Yet how tender he seemed to her, how well worth having! Always, when he kissed her now, she trembled in the balance. There was something in the iron grasp of his fingers that went through her like fire. His glance

held hers at times when she could scarcely endure it.

"I'll wait, anyhow," he insisted.

Longer and longer she lingered, but now for once no voice came.

She began to feel that something was wrong—a greater strain than if old Rogaum's voice had been filling the whole neighborhood.

"I've got to go," she said.

"Gee, but you're a coward, yuh are!" said he derisively. "What'r yuh always so scared about? He always says he'll lock yuh out, but he never does."

"Yes, but he will," she insisted nervously. "I think he has this time. You don't know him. He's something awful when he gets real mad. Oh, Connie, I must go!" For the sixth or seventh time she moved, and once more he caught her arm and waist and tried to kiss her, but she slipped away from him.

"Ah, yuh!" he exclaimed. "I wish he would lock yuh out!"

At her own doorstep she paused momentarily, more to soften her progress than anything. The outer door was open as usual, but not the inner. She tried it, but it would not give. It was locked! For a moment she paused, cold fear racing over her body, and then knocked.

No answer.

Again she rattled the door this time nervously, and was about to cry out.

Still no answer.

At last she heard her father's voice, hoarse and indifferent, not addressed to her at all, but to her mother.

"Let her go, now," it said savagely, from the front room where he supposed she could not hear. "I vill her a lesson teach."

"Hadn't you better let her in now, yet?" pleaded Mrs. Rogaum faintly.

"No," insisted Mr. Rogaum. "Nefer! Let her go now. If she vill alvays stay oudt, let her stay now. Ve vill see how she likes dot."

His voice was rich in wrath; and he was saving up a good beating for her into the bargain, that she knew. She would have to wait and wait and plead, and when she was thoroughly wretched and subdued he would let her in and beat her—such a beating as she had never received in all her born days.

Again the door rattled, and still she got no answer. Not even her call brought a sound.

Now, strangely, a new element, not heretofore apparent in her nature, but nevertheless wholly there, was called into life, springing to action as Diana, full formed. Why should he always be so harsh? She hadn't done anything but stay out a little later than usual. He was always so anxious to keep her in and subdue her. For once the cold chill of her girlish fears left her, and she wavered angrily.

"All right," she said, some old German stubbornness springing up, "I don't knock. You don't need to let me in, then."

A suggestion of tears was in her eyes, but she backed firmly out onto the stoop and sat down, hesitating. Old Rogaum saw her, lowering down from the lattice, but said nothing! He would teach her for once what were proper hours!

At the corner, standing, Almerting also saw her. He recognized the simple white dress, and paused steadily, a strange thrill racing over him. Really they had locked her out! Gee, this was new. It was great in a way. There she was, white, quiet, shut out, waiting at her father's doorstep.

Sitting thus, Theresa pondered a moment, her girlish rashness and anger dominating her. Her pride was hurt and she felt revengeful. They would shut her out, would they? All right, she would go out and they should look to it how they would get her back—the old curmudgeons. For the moment the home of Myrtle Kenrihan came to her as a possible refuge, but she decided that she need not go there yet. She had better wait about awhile and see—or walk and frighten them. He would beat her, would he? Well, maybe he would and maybe he wouldn't. She might come back, but still that was a thing afar off. Just now it didn't matter so much. "Connie" was still there on the corner. He loved her dearly. She felt it.

Getting up, she stepped to the now quiet-

ing sidewalk and strolled up the street. It was a rather nervous procedure, however. There were street cars still, and stores lighted and people passing, but soon these would not be, and she was locked out. The side streets were already little more than long silent walks and gleaming rows of lamps.

At the corner her youthful lover almost pounced upon her.

"Locked out, are yuh?" he asked, his eyes shining.

For the moment she was delighted to see him, for a nameless dread had already laid hold of her. Home meant so much. Up to now it had been her whole life.

"Yes," she answered feebly.

"Well, let's stroll on a little," said the boy. He had not as yet quite made up his mind what to do, but the night was young. It was so fine to have her with him—his.

At the farther corner they passed Officers Maguire and Delehanty, idly swinging their clubs and discussing politics.

" 'Tis a shame," Officer Delehanty was saying, "the way things are run now," but he paused to add, "Ain't that old Rogaum's girl over there with young Almerting?"

"It is," replied Maguire, looking after.

"Well, I'm thinkin' he'd better be keepin' an eye on her," said the former. "She's too young to be runnin' around with the likes o' him."

Maguire agreed. "He's a young tough," he observed. "I never liked him. He's too fresh. He works over here in Myer's tobacco factory, and belongs to the Roosters. He's up to no good, I'll warrant that."

"Teach 'em a lesson, I would," Almerting was saying to Theresa as they strolled on. "We'll walk around a while an' make 'em think yuh mean business. They won't lock yuh out any more. If they don't let yuh in when we come back I'll find yuh a place, all right."

His sharp eyes were gleaming as he looked around into her own. Already he had made up his mind that she should not go back if he could help it. He knew a better place than home for this night, anyhow—

the club room of the Roosters, if nowhere else. They could stay there for a time, anyhow.

By now old Rogaum, who had seen her walking up the street alone, was marveling at her audacity, but thought she would soon come back. It was amazing that she should exhibit such temerity, but he would teach her! Such a whipping! At half-past ten, however, he stuck his head out of the open window and saw nothing of her. At eleven, the same. Then he walked the floor.

At first wrathful, then nervous, then nervous and wrathful, he finally ended all nervous, without a scintilla of wrath. His stout wife sat up in bed and began to wring her hands.

"Lie down!" he commanded. "You make me sick. I know vot I am doing!"

"Is she still at der door?" pleaded the mother.

"No," he said. "I don't tink so. She should come ven I call."

His nerves were weakening, however, and now they finally collapsed.

"She vent de stread up," he said anxiously after a time. "I vill go after."

Slipping on his coat, he went down the stairs and out into the night. It was growing late, and the stillness and gloom of midnight were nearing. Nowhere in sight was his Theresa. First one way and then another he went, looking here, there, everywhere, finally groaning.

"Ach, Gott!" he said, the sweat bursting out on his brow, "vot in Teufel's name iss dis?"

He thought he would seek a policeman, but there was none. Officer Maguire had long since gone for a quiet game in one of the neighboring saloons. His partner had temporarily returned to his own beat. Still old Rogaum hunted on, worrying more and more.

Finally he bethought him to hasten home again, for she must have got back. Mrs. Rogaum, too, would be frantic if she had not. If she were not there he must go to the police. Such a night! and his Theresa—— This thing could not go on.

As he turned into his own corner he almost ran, coming up to the little portico wet and panting. At a puffing step he turned, and almost fell over a white body at his feet, a prone and writhing woman.

"Ach, Gott!" he cried aloud, almost shouting in his distress and excitement. "Theresa, vot iss dis? Wilhelmina, a light now. Bring a light now, I say for himmel's sake! Theresa hat sich *umgebracht*. Help!"

He had fallen to his knees and was turning over the writhing, groaning figure. By the pale light of the street, however, he could make out that it was not his Theresa, fortunately, as he had at first feared, but another, and yet there was something very like her in the figure.

"Um!" said the stranger weakly. "Ah!"

The dress was gray, not white as was his Theresa's, but the body was round and plump. It cut the fiercest cords of his intensity, this thought of death to a young woman, but there was something else about the situation which made him forget his own troubles.

Mrs. Rogaum, loudly admonished, almost tumbled down the stairs. At the foot she held the light she had brought—a small glass oil-lamp—and then nearly dropped it. A fairly attractive figure, more girl than woman, rich in all the physical charms that characterize a certain type, lay near to dying. Her soft hair had fallen back over a good forehead, now quite white. Her pretty hands, well decked with rings, were clutched tightly in an agonized grip. At her neck a blue silk shirtwaist and light lace collar were torn away where she had clutched herself, and on the white flesh was a yellow stain as of one who had been burned. A strange odor reeked in the area, and in one corner was a spilled bottle.

"Ach, Gott!" exclaimed Mrs. Rogaum. "It iss a vooman! She haf herself gekilt. Run for der police! Oh, my! Oh, my!"

Rogaum did not kneel for more than a moment. Somehow, this creature's fate seemed in some psychic way identified with that of his own daughter. He bounded up, and jumping out his front door, began to call lustily for the police. Officer Maguire, at his social game nearby, heard the very first cry and came running.

"What's the matter here, now?" he exclaimed, rushing up full and ready for murder, robbery, fire, or, indeed, anything in the whole roster of human calamities.

"A vooman!" said Rogaum excitedly. "She haf herself *umgebracht*. She iss dying. Ach, Gott! in my own doorstep, yet!"

"Vere iss der hospital?" put in Mrs. Rogaum, thinking clearly of an ambulance, but not being able to express it. "She iss gekilt, sure. Oh! Oh!" and bending over her the poor old motherly soul stroked the tightened hands, and trickled tears upon the blue shirtwaist. "Ach, vy did you do dot?" she said. "Ach, for vy?"

Officer Maguire was essentially a man of action. He jumped to the sidewalk, amid the gathering company, and beat loudly with his club upon the stone flagging. Then he ran to the nearest police phone, returning to aid in any other way he might. A milk wagon passing on its way from the Jersey ferry with a few tons of fresh milk aboard, he held it up and demanded a helping.

"Give us a quart there, will you?" he said authoritatively. "A woman's swallowed acid in here."

"Sure," said the driver, anxious to learn the cause of the excitement. "Got a glass, anybody?"

Maguire ran back and returned, bearing a measure. Mrs. Rogaum stood looking nervously on, while the stocky officer raised the golden head and poured the milk.

"Here, now, drink this," he said. "Come on. Try an' swallow it."

The girl, a blonde of the type the world too well knows, opened her eyes, and looked, groaning a little.

"Drink it," shouted the officer fiercely. "Do you want to die? Open your mouth!"

Used to a fear of the law in all her days, she obeyed now, even in death. The lips parted, the fresh milk was drained to the end, some spilling on neck and cheek.

While they were working old Rogaum came back and stood looking on, by the side of his wife. Also Officer Delahanty, having heard the peculiar wooden ring of the stick upon the stone in the night, had come up.

"Ach, ach," exclaimed Rogaum rather distractedly, "und she is oudt yet. I could not find her. Oh! Oh!"

There was a clang of a gong up the street as the racing ambulance turned rapidly in. A young hospital surgeon dismounted, and seeing the woman's condition, ordered immediate removal. Both officers and Rogaum, as well as the surgeon, helped place her in the ambulance. After a moment the lone bell, ringing wildly in the night, was all the evidence remaining that a tragedy had been here.

"Do you know how she came here?" asked Officer Delahanty, coming back to get Rogaum's testimony for the police.

"No, no," answered Rogaum wretchedly. "She vass here alretty. I vass for my daughter loog. Ach, himmel, I haf my daughter lost. She iss avay."

Mrs. Rogaum also chattered, the significance of Theresa's absence all the more painfully emphasized by this.

The officer did not at first get the import of this. He was only interested in the facts of the present case.

"You say she was here when you come? Where was you?"

"I say I vass for my daughter loog. I come here, und der vooman vass here now alretty."

"Yes. What time was this?"

"Only now yet. Yussed a half-hour."

Officer Maguire had strolled up, after chasing away a small crowd that had gathered with fierce and unholy threats. For the first time now he noticed the peculiar perturbation of the usually placid German couple.

"What about your daughter?" he asked, catching a word as to that.

Both old people raised their voices at once.

"She haf gone. She haf run avay. Ach, himmel, ve must for her loog. Quick—she could not get in. Ve haf der door shut."

"Locked her out, eh?" inquired Maguire after a time, hearing much of the rest of the story.

"Yes," exclaimed Rogaum. "It vass to schkare her a liddle. She vould not come ven I called."

"Sure, that's the girl we saw walkin' with young Almerting, do ye mind? The one in the white dress," said Delahanty to Maguire.

"White dress, yah!" echoed Rogaum, and then the fact of her walking with some one came home like a blow.

"Did you hear dot?" he exclaimed even as Mrs. Rogaum did likewise. *Mein Gott, hast du das gehoert?*"

He fairly jumped as he said it. His hands flew up to his stout and ruddy head.

"Whaddy ya want to let her out for nights?" asked Maguire roughly, catching the drift of the situation. "That's no time for young girls to be out, anyhow, and with these toughs around here. Sure, I saw her, nearly two hours ago."

"Ach," groaned Rogaum. "Two hours yet. Ho, ho, ho!" His voice was quite hysteric.

"Well, go on in," said Officer Delahanty. "There's no use yellin' out here. Give us a description of her an' we'll send out an alarm. You won't be able to find her walkin' around."

Her parents described her exactly. The two men turned to the nearest police box and then disappeared, leaving the old German couple in the throes of distress. A timeworn old church-clock nearby now chimed out one and then two. The notes cut like knives. Mrs. Rogaum began fearfully to cry. Rogaum walked and blustered to himself.

"It's a queer case, that," said Officer Delahanty to Maguire after having reported the matter of Theresa, but referring solely to the outcast of the doorway so recently sent away and in whose fate they were much more interested. She being a part of the commercialized vice of the city, they were curious as to the cause of her suicide. "I think I know that woman. I think I

know where she came from. You do, too—Adele's around the corner, eh? She didn't come into that doorway by herself, either. She was put there. You know how they do."

"You're right," said Maguire. "She was put there, all right, and that's just where she come from, too."

The two of them now tipped up their noses and cocked their eyes significantly.

"Let's go around," added Maguire.

They went, the significant red light over the transom at 68 telling its own story. Strolling leisurely up, they knocked. At the very first sound a painted denizen of the half-world opened the door.

"Where's Adele?" asked Maguire as the two, hats on as usual, stepped in.

"She's gone to bed."

"Tell her to come down."

They seated themselves deliberately in the gaudy mirrored parlor and waited, conversing between themselves in whispers. Presently a sleepy-looking woman of forty in a gaudy robe of heavy texture, and slippered in red, appeared.

"We're here about that suicide case you had tonight. What about it? Who was she? How'd she come to be in that doorway around the corner? Come, now," Maguire added, as the madam assumed an air of mingled injured and ignorant innocence, "you know. Can that stuff! How did she come to take poison?"

"I don't know what you're talking about," said the woman with the utmost air of innocence. "I never heard of any suicide."

"Aw, come now," insisted Delahanty, "the girl around the corner. You know. We know you've got a pull, but we've got to know about this case, just the same. Come across now. It won't be published. What made her take the poison?"

Under the steady eyes of the officers the woman hesitated, but finally weakened.

"Why—why—her lover went back on her—that's all. She got so blue we just couldn't do anything with her. I tried to, but she wouldn't listen."

"Lover, eh?" put in Maguire as though that were the most unheard-of-thing in the world. "What was his name?"

"I don't know. You never can tell that."

"What was her name—Annie?" asked Delahanty wisely, as though he knew but was merely inquiring for form's sake.

"No—Emily."

"Well, how did she come to get over there, anyhow?" inquired Maguire most pleasantly.

"George took her," she replied, referring to a man-of-all-work about the place.

Then little by little as they sat there the whole miserable story came out, miserable as all the wilfulness and error and suffering of the world.

"How old was she?"

"Oh, twenty-one."

"Well, where'd she come from?"

"Oh, here in New York. Her family locked her out one night, I think."

Something in the way the woman said this last brought old Rogaum and his daughter back to the policemen's minds. They had forgotten all about her by now, although they had turned in an alarm. Fearing to interfere too much with this well-known and politically controlled institution, the two men left, but outside they fell to talking of the other case.

"We ought to tell old Rogaum about her some time," said Maguire to Delahanty cynically. "He locked his kid out to-night."

"Yes, it might be a good thing for him to hear that," replied the other. "We'd better go round there an' see if his girl's back yet. She may be back by now," and so they returned but little disturbed by the joint miseries.

At Rogaum's door they once more knocked loudly.

"Is your daughter back again?" asked Maguire when a reply was had.

"Ach, no," replied the hysterical Mrs. Rogaum, who was quite alone now. "My husband he haf gone oudt again to loog vunce more. Oh, my! Oh, my!"

"Well, that's what you get for lockin' her out," returned Maguire loftily, the

other story fresh in his mind. "That other girl downstairs here tonight was locked out too, once." He chanced to have a girl-child of his own and somehow he was in the mood for pointing a moral. "You oughtn't to do anything like that. Where d'yuh expect she's goin' to if you lock her out?"

Mrs. Rogaum groaned. She explained that it was not her fault, but anyhow it was carrying coals to Newcastle to talk to her so. The advice was better for her husband.

The pair finally returned to the station to see if the call had been attended to.

"Sure," said the sergeant, "certainly. Whaddy ya think?" and he read from the blotter before him:

"'Look out for girl, Theresa Rogaum. Aged 18; height, about 5, 3; light hair, blue eyes, white cotton dress, trimmed with blue ribbon. Last seen with lad named Almerting, about 19 years of age, about 5, 9; weight, 135 pounds.'"

There were other details even more pointed and conclusive. For over an hour now, supposedly, policemen from the Battery to Harlem, and far beyond had been scanning long streets and dim shadows for a girl in a white dress with a youth of nineteen,—supposedly.

Officer Halsey, another of this region, which took in a portion of Washington Square, had seen a good many couples this pleasant summer evening since the description of Theresa and Almerting had been read to him over the telephone, but none that answered to these. Like Maguire and Delahanty, he was more or less indifferent to all such cases, but idling on a corner near the park at about three a. m., a brother officer, one Paisly by name, came up and casually mentioned the missing pair also.

"I bet I saw that couple, not over an hour ago. She was dressed in white, and looked to me as if she didn't want to be out. I didn't happen to think at the time, but now I remember. They acted sort o' funny. She did, anyhow. They went in this park down at the Fourth Street end there."

"Supposing we beat it, then," suggested Halsey, weary for something to do.

"Sure," said the other quickly, and together they began a careful search, kicking around in the moonlight under the trees. The moon was leaning moderately toward the west, and all the branches were silvered with light and dew. Among the flowers, past clumps of bushes, near the fountain, they searched, each one going his way alone. At last, the wandering Halsey paused beside a thick clump of flaming bushes, ruddy, slightly, even in the light. A murmur of voices greeted him, and something very much like the sound of a sob.

"What's that?" he said mentally, drawing near and listening.

"Why don't you come on now?" said the first of the voices heard. "They won't let you in any more. You're with me, ain't you? What's the use cryin'?"

No answer to this, but no sobs. She must have been crying silently.

"Come on. I can take care of yuh. We can live in Hoboken. I know a place where we can go to-night. That's all right."

There was a movement as if the speaker were patting her on the shoulder.

"What's the use cryin'? Don't you believe I love yuh?"

The officer who had stolen quietly around to get a better view now came closer. He wanted to see for himself. In the moonlight, from a comfortable distance, he could see them seated. The tall bushes were almost all about the bench. In the arms of the youth was the girl in white, held very close. Leaning over to get a better view, he saw him kiss her and hold her—hold her in such a way that she could but yield to him, whatever her slight disinclination.

It was a common affair at earlier hours, but rather interesting now. The officer was interested. He crept nearer.

"What are you two doin' here?" he suddenly inquired, rising before them, as though he had not seen.

The girl tumbled out of her compromising position, speechless and blushing violently. The young man stood up, nervous, but still defiant.

"Aw, we were just sittin' here," he replied.

"Yes? Well, say, what's your name? I think we're lookin' for you two, anyhow. Almerting?"

"That's me," said the youth.

"And yours?" he added, addressing Theresa.

"Theresa Rogaum," replied the latter brokenly, beginning to cry.

"Well, you two'll have to come along with me," he added laconically. "The Captain wants to see both of you," and he marched them solemnly away.

"What for?" young Almerting ventured to inquire after a time, blanched with fright.

"Never mind," replied the policeman irritably. "Come along, you'll find out at the station-house. We want you both. That's enough."

At the other end of the park Paisly joined them, and, at the station-house, the girl was given a chair. She was all tears and melancholy with a modicum possibly of relief at being thus rescued from the world. Her companion, for all his youth, was defiant if circumspect, a natural animal defeated of its aim.

"Better go for her father," commented the sergeant, and by four in the morning old Rogaum, who had still been up and walking the floor, was rushing stationward. From an earlier rage he had passed to an almost killing grief, but now at the thought that he might possibly see his daughter alive and well once more he was overflowing with a mingled emotion which contained rage, fear, sorrow, and a number of other things. What should he do to her if she were alive? Beat her? Kiss her? Or what? Arrived at the station, however, and seeing his fair Theresa in the hands of the police, and this young stranger lingering near, also detained, he was beside himself with fear, rage, affection.

"You! You!" he exclaimed at once, glaring at the imperturbable Almerting, when told that this was the young man who was found with his girl. Then, seized with a sudden horror, he added, turning to Theresa, "Vot haf you done? Oh, oh! You! You!" he repeated again to Almerting angrily, now that he felt that his daughter was safe. "Come not near my tochter any more! I vill preak your effery pone, du teufel, du!"

He made a move toward the incarcerated lover, but here the sergeant interfered.

"Stop that, now," he said calmly. "Take your daughter out of here and go home, or I'll lock you both up. We don't want any fighting in here. D'ye hear? Keep your daughter off the streets hereafter, then she won't get into trouble. Don't let her run around with such young toughs as this." Almerting winced. "Then there won't anything happen to her. We'll do whatever punishing's to be done."

"Aw, what's eatin' him!" commented Almerting dourly, now that he felt himself reasonably safe from a personal encounter. "What have I done? He locked her out, didn't he? I was just keepin' her company till morning."

"Yes, we know all about that," said the sergeant, "and about you, too. You shut up, or you'll go down town to Special Sessions. I want no guff out o' you." Still he ordered the butcher angrily to be gone.

Old Rogaum heard nothing. He had his daughter. He was taking her home. She was not dead—not even morally injured in so far as he could learn. He was a compound of wondrous feelings. What to do was beyond him.

At the corner near the butcher shop they encountered the wakeful Maguire, still idling, as they passed. He was pleased to see that Rogaum had his Theresa once more. It raised him to a high, moralizing height.

"Don't lock her out any more," he called significantly. "That's what brought the other girl to your door, you know!"

"Vot iss dot?" said Rogaum.

"I say the other girl was locked out. That's why she committed suicide."

"Ach, I know," said the husky German under his breath, but he had no intention of locking her out. He did not know what he would do until they were in the presence of his crying wife, who fell upon Theresa, weeping. Then he decided to be reasonably lenient.

"She vass like you," said the old mother to the wondering Theresa, ignorant of the seeming lesson brought to their very door. "She vass loog like you."

"I vill not vip you now," said the old butcher solemnly, too delighted to think of punishment after having feared every horror under the sun, "aber, go not oudt any more. Keep off de streads so late. I von't haf it. Dot loafer, aber—let him yussed come here some more! I fix him!"

"No, no," said the fat mother tearfully, smoothing her daughter's hair. "She vouldn't run avay no more yet, no, no." Old Mrs. Rogaum was all mother.

"Well, you wouldn't let me in," insisted Theresa, "and I didn't have any place to go. What do you want me to do? I'm not going to stay in the house all the time."

"I fix him!" roared Rogaum, unloading all his rage now on the recreant lover freely. "Yussed let him come some more! Der penitentiary he should haf!"

"Oh, he's not so bad," Theresa told her mother, almost a heroine now that she was home and safe. "He's Mr. Almerting, the stationer's boy. They live here in the next block."

"Don't you ever bother that girl again," the sergeant was saying to young Almerting as he turned him loose an hour later. "If you do, we'll get you, and you won't get off under six months. Y' hear me, do you?"

"Aw, I don't want 'er," replied the boy truculently and cynically. "Let him have his old daughter. What's he want to lock 'er out for? They'd better not lock 'er out again though, that's all I say. I don't want 'er."

"Beat it!" replied the sergeant, and away he went.

1876 ∽ *Willa Cather* ∽ 1947

WILLA CATHER'S girlhood in Virginia, her youth on the Nebraska prairie, her years at the University of Nebraska, and her mature life in great American cities have all contributed to her fiction. Born on a farm near Winchester, Virginia, at the age of nine she went with her family to a ranch near Red Cloud, Nebraska. She began writing at the University of Nebraska; after graduation she worked on a newspaper in Pittsburgh and later taught English in high schools there, at the same time continuing her work with stories and poems.

Her ability impressed S. S. McClure, publisher of *McClure's Magazine,* and in 1906 she joined his editorial staff. In 1911 she resigned her position in order to give all her time to writing. Her first novel, *Alexander's Bridge* (1912), resembled those of Henry James in scenes and characters; but with *O Pioneers!* (1913) she found the field of her first individual achievement, that of the farm and small town life of Nebraska and neighboring states. Later treatments of this material include the novels *My Antonia* (1918) and *A Lost Lady* (1923), and the long stories of *Obscure Destinies* (1932).

Metropolitan life, especially of musicians, is portrayed in *The Song of the Lark* (1915) and *Lucy Gayheart* (1935), and university faculty life in *The Professor's House* (1925). The powerful impression made on Miss Cather by the American Southwest, in travel and temporary residence, found reflection in her historical novel of Sante Fé, *Death Comes to the Archbishop* (1927), and similar experience of French Canada in *Shadows on the Rock* (1931). She returned to the scenes of her Virginia childhood for *Sapphira and the Slave Girl* (1940), also historical. A small group of her essays was collected in *Not Under Forty* (1936). Her last stories were collected in a volume published after her death, *The Old Beauty and Others* (1948).

[See R. Rapin's *Willa Cather* (New York, 1930), Carl Van Doren's *The American Novel* (New York, 1940), G. Snell's *The Shapers of American Fiction* (New York, 1947), and Maxwell Geismar's *The Last of the Provincials* (Boston, 1947).]

NEIGHBOUR ROSICKY
[1932 (1930)]

I

WHEN Doctor Burleigh told Neighbour Rosicky he had a bad heart, Rosicky protested.

"So? No, I guess my heart was always pretty good. I got a little asthma, maybe. Just a awful short breath when I was pitchin' hay last summer, dat's all."

"Well now, Rosicky, if you know more about it than I do, what did you come to me for? It's your heart that makes you short of breath, I tell you. You're sixty-five years old, and you've always worked hard, and your heart's tired. You've got to be careful from now on, and you can't do heavy work any more. You've got five boys at home to do it for you."

The old farmer looked up at the Doctor with a gleam of amusement in his queer triangular-shaped eyes. His eyes were large and lively, but the lids were caught up in the middle in a curious way, so that they formed a triangle. He did not look like a sick man. His brown face was creased but not wrinkled, he had a ruddy colour in his smooth-shaven cheeks and in his lips, under his long brown moustache. His hair was thin and ragged around his ears, but very little grey. His forehead, naturally high and crossed by deep parallel lines, now ran all the way up to his pointed crown. Rosicky's face had the habit of looking interested,—suggested a contented disposition and a reflective quality that was gay rather than grave. This gave him a certain detachment, the easy manner of an onlooker and observer.

"Well, I guess you ain't got no pills fur a bad heart, Doctor Ed. I guess the only thing is fur me to git me a new one."

Doctor Burleigh swung round in his desk-chair and frowned at the old farmer. "I think if I were you I'd take a little care of the old one, Rosicky."

Rosicky shrugged. "Maybe I don't know how. I expect you mean fur me not to drink my coffee no more."

"I wouldn't in your place. But you'll do as you choose about that. I've never yet been able to separate a Bohemian from his coffee or his pipe. I've quit trying. But the sure thing is you've got to cut out farm work. You can feed the stock and do chores about the barn, but you can't do anything in the fields that makes you short of breath."

"How about shelling corn?"

"Of course not!"

Rosicky considered with puckered brows.

"I can't make my heart go no longer'n it wants to, can I, Doctor Ed?"

"I think it's good for five or six years yet, maybe more, if you'll take the strain off it. Sit around the house and help Mary. If I had a good wife like yours, I'd want to stay around the house."

His patient chuckled. "It ain't no place fur a man. I don't like no old man hanging round the kitchen too much. An' my wife, she's a awful hard worker her own self."

"That's it; you can help her a little. My Lord, Rosicky, you are one of the few men I know who has a family he can get some comfort out of; happy dispositions, never quarrel among themselves, and they treat you right. I want to see you live a few years and enjoy them."

"Oh, they're good kids, all right," Rosicky assented.

The Doctor wrote him a prescription and asked him how his oldest son, Rudolph, who had married in the spring, was getting on. Rudolph had struck out for himself, on rented land. "And how's Polly? I was afraid Mary mightn't like an American daughter-in-law, but it seems to be working out all right."

"Yes, she's a fine girl. Dat widder woman bring her daughters up very nice. Polly got lots of spunk, an' she got some style, too. Da's nice, for young folks to have some style." Rosicky inclined his head gallantly. His voice and his twinkly smile were an affectionate compliment to his daughter-in-law.

"It looks like a storm, and you'd better be getting home before it comes. In town in the car?" Doctor Burleigh rose.

"No, I'm in de wagon. When you got five boys, you ain't got much chance to ride round in de Ford. I ain't much for cars, noway."

"Well, it's a good road out to your place; but I don't want you bumping around in a wagon much. And never again on a hay-rake, remember!"

Rosicky placed the Doctor's fee delicately behind the desk-telephone, looking the other way, as if this were an absent-minded gesture. He put on his plush cap and his corduroy jacket with a sheepskin collar, and went out.

The Doctor picked up his stethoscope and frowned at it as if he were seriously annoyed with the instrument. He wished it had been telling tales about some other man's heart, some old man who didn't look the Doctor in the eye so knowingly, or hold out such a warm brown hand when he said good-bye. Doctor Burleigh had been a poor boy in the country before he went away to medical school; he had known Rosicky almost ever since he could remember, and he had a deep affection for Mrs. Rosicky.

Only last winter he had had such a good breakfast at Rosicky's, and that when he needed it. He had been out all night on a long, hard confinement case at Tom Marshall's, a big rich farm where there was plenty of stock and plenty of feed and a great deal of expensive farm machinery of the newest model, and no comfort whatever. The woman had too many children and too much work, and she was no manager. When the baby was born at last, and handed over to the assisting neighbour woman, and the mother was properly attended to, Burleigh refused any breakfast in that slovenly house, and drove his buggy—the snow was too deep for a car— eight miles to Anton Rosicky's place. He didn't know another farm-house where a man could get such a warm welcome, and such good strong coffee with rich cream. No wonder the old chap didn't want to give up his coffee!

He had driven in just when the boys had come back from the barn and were washing up for breakfast. The long table, covered with a bright oilcloth, was set out with dishes waiting for them, and the warm kitchen was full of the smell of coffee and hot biscuit and sausage. Five big handsome boys, running from twenty to twelve, all with what Burleigh called natural good manners—they hadn't a bit of the painful self-consciousness he himself had to struggle with when he was a lad. One ran to put his horse away, another helped him off with

his fur coat and hung it up, and Josephine, the youngest child and the only daughter, quickly set another place under her mother's direction.

With Mary, to feed creatures was the natural expression of affection,—her chickens, the calves, her big hungry boys. It was a rare pleasure to feed a young man whom she seldom saw and of whom she was as proud as if he belonged to her. Some country housekeepers would have stopped to spread a white cloth over the oilcloth, to change the thick cups and plates for their best china, and the wooden-handled knives for plated ones. But not Mary.

"You must take us as you find us, Doctor Ed. I'd be glad to put out my good things for you if you was expected, but I'm glad to get you any way at all."

He knew she was glad,—she threw back her head and spoke out as if she were announcing him to the whole prairie. Rosicky hadn't said anything at all; he merely smiled his twinkling smile, put some more coal on the fire, and went into his own room to pour the Doctor a little drink in a medicine glass. When they were all seated, he watched his wife's face from his end of the table and spoke to her in Czech.[1] Then, with the instinct of politeness which seldom failed him, he turned to the Doctor and said slyly; "I was just tellin' her not to ask you no questions about Mrs. Marshall till you eat some breakfast. My wife, she's terrible fur to ask questions."

The boys laughed, and so did Mary. She watched the Doctor devour her biscuit and sausage, too much excited to eat anything herself. She drank her coffee and sat taking in everything about her visitor. She had

---

[1] Czech is the national language of Bohemia, Rosicky's native land. Bohemia was an ancient kingdom and later a part successively of Poland, Hungary, Austria, and Germany. It is now the western province of Czechoslovakia. There was a large emigration to the United States 1894-1914.

known him when he was a poor country boy, and was boastfully proud of his success, always saying: "What do people go to Omaha for, to see a doctor, when we got the best one in the State right here?" If Mary liked people at all, she felt physical pleasure in the sight of them, personal exultation in any good fortune that came to them. Burleigh didn't know many women like that, but he knew she was like that.

When his hunger was satisfied, he did, of course, have to tell them about Mrs. Marshall, and he noticed what a friendly interest the boys took in the matter.

Rudolph, the oldest one (he was still living at home then), said: "The last time I was over there, she was lifting them big heavy milk-cans and I knew she oughtn't to be doing it."

"Yes, Rudolph told me about that when he come home, and I said it wasn't right," Mary put in warmly. "It was all right for me to do them things up to the last, for I was terrible strong, but that woman's weakly. And do you think she'll be able to nurse it, Ed?" She sometimes forgot to give him the title she was so proud of. "And to think of your being up all night and then not able to get a decent breakfast! I don't know what's the matter with such people."

"Why, Mother," said one of the boys, "if Doctor Ed had got breakfast there, we wouldn't have him here. So you ought to be glad."

"He knows I'm glad to have him, John, any time. But I'm sorry for that poor woman, how bad she'll feel the Doctor had to go away in the cold without his breakfast."

"I wish I'd been in practice when these were getting born." The doctor looked down the row of close-clipped heads. "I missed some good breakfasts by not being."

The boys began to laugh at their mother because she flushed so red, but she stood her ground and threw up her head. "I don't care, you wouldn't have got away from this house without breakfast. No doctor ever did. I'd have had something

ready fixed that Anton could warm up for you."

The boys laughed harder than ever, and exclaimed at her: "I'll bet you would!" "She would, that!"

"Father, did you get breakfast for the doctor when we were born?"

"Yes, and he used to bring me my breakfast, too, mighty nice. I was always awful hungry!" Mary admitted with a guilty laugh.

While the boys were getting the Doctor's horse, he went to the window to examine the house plants. "What do you do to your geraniums to keep them blooming all winter, Mary? I never pass this house that from the road I don't see your windows full of flowers."

She snapped off a dark red one, and a ruffled new green leaf, and put them in his buttonhole. "There, that looks better. You look too solemn for a young man, Ed. Why don't you git married? I'm worried about you. Settin' at breakfast, I looked at you real hard, and I seen you've got some grey hairs already."

"Oh, yes! They're coming. Maybe they'd come faster if I married."

"Don't talk so. You'll ruin your health eating at the hotel. I could send your wife a nice loaf of nut bread, if you only had one. I don't like to see a young man getting grey. I'll tell you something, Ed; you make some strong black tea and keep it handy in a bowl, and every morning just brush it into your hair, an' it'll keep the grey from showin' much. That's the way I do!"

Sometimes the Doctor heard the gossipers in the drug-store wondering why Rosicky didn't get on faster. He was industrious, and so were his boys, but they were rather free and easy, weren't pushers, and they didn't always show good judgment. They were comfortable, they were out of debt, but they didn't get much ahead. Maybe, Doctor Burleigh reflected, people as generous and warm-hearted and affectionate as the Rosickys never got ahead much; maybe you couldn't enjoy your life and put it into the bank, too.

II

When Rosicky left Doctor Burleigh's office he went into the farm-implement store to light his pipe and put on his glasses and read over the list Mary had given him. Then he went into the general merchandise place next door and stood about until the pretty girl with the plucked eyebrows, who always waited on him, was free. Those eyebrows, two thin India-ink strokes, amused him, because he remembered how they used to be. Rosicky always prolonged his shopping by a little joking; the girl knew the old fellow admired her, and she liked to chaff with him.

"Seems to me about every other week you buy ticking, Mr. Rosicky, and always the best quality," she remarked as she measured off the heavy bolt with red stripes.

"You see, my wife is always makin' goose-fedder pillows, an' de thin stuff don't hold in dem little down-fedders."

"You must have lots of pillows at your house."

"Sure. She makes quilts of dem, too. We sleeps easy. Now she's makin' a fedder quilt for my son's wife. You know Polly, that married my Rudolph. How much my bill, Miss Pearl?"

"Eight eighty-five."

"Chust make it nine, and put in some candy fur de women."

"As usual. I never did see a man buy so much candy for his wife. First thing you know, she'll be getting too fat."

"I'd like dat. I ain't much fur all dem slim women like what de style is now."

"That's one for me, I suppose, Mr. Bohunk!" Pearl sniffed and elevated her India-ink strokes.

When Rosicky went out to his wagon, it was beginning to snow,—the first snow of the season, and he was glad to see it. He rattled out of town and along the highway through a wonderfully rich stretch of country, the finest farms in the county. He admired this High Prairie, as it was called, and always liked to drive through it. His own place lay in a rougher territory, where there was some clay in the soil and it was not so productive. When he bought his land, he hadn't the money to buy on High Prairie; so he told his boys, when they grumbled, that if their land hadn't some clay in it, they wouldn't own it at all. All the same, he enjoyed looking at these fine farms, as he enjoyed looking at a prize bull.

After he had gone eight miles, he came to the graveyard, which lay just at the edge of his own hay-land. There he stopped his horses and sat still on his wagon seat, looking about at the snowfall. Over yonder on the hill he could see his own house, crouching low, with the clump of orchard behind and the windmill before, and all down the gentle hill-slope the rows of pale gold cornstalks stood out against the white field. The snow was falling over the corn-field and the pasture and the hay-land, steadily, with very little wind,—a nice dry snow. The graveyard had only a light wire fence about it and was all overgrown with long red grass. The fine snow, settling into this red grass and upon the few little evergreens and the headstones, looked very pretty.

It was a nice graveyard, Rosicky reflected, sort of snug and homelike, not cramped or mournful,—a big sweep all round it. A man could lie down in the long grass and see the complete arch of the sky over him, hear the wagons go by; in summer the mowing-machine rattled right up to the wire fence. And it was so near home. Over there across the cornstalks his own roof and windmill looked so good to him that he promised himself to mind the Doctor and take care of himself. He was awful fond of his place, he admitted. He wasn't anxious to leave it. And it was a comfort to think that he would never have to go farther than the edge of his own hayfield. The snow, falling over his barn-yard and the graveyard, seemed to draw things together like. And they were all old neighbours in the graveyard, most of them friends; there was nothing to feel awkward or embarrassed about. Embarrassment was the most disagreeable feeling Rosicky knew. He didn't often have it,— only with certain people whom he didn't understand at all.

Well, it was a nice snowstorm; a fine sight to see the snow falling so quietly and graciously over so much open country. On his cap and shoulders, on the horses' backs and manes, light, delicate, mysterious it fell; and with it a dry cool fragrance was released into the air. It meant rest for vegetation and men and beasts, for the ground itself; a season of long nights for sleep, leisurely breakfasts, peace by the fire. This and much more went through Rosicky's mind, but he merely told himself that winter was coming, clucked to his horses, and drove on.

When he reached home, John, the youngest boy, ran out to put away his team for him, and he met Mary coming up from the outside cellar with her apron full of carrots. They went into the house together. On the table, covered with oilcloth figured with clusters of blue grapes, a place was set, and he smelled hot coffee-cake of some kind. Anton never lunched in town; he thought that extravagant, and anyhow he didn't like the food. So Mary always had something ready for him when he got home.

After he was settled in his chair, stirring his coffee in a big cup, Mary took out of the oven a pan of *kolache* stuffed with apricots, examined them anxiously to see whether they had got too dry, put them beside his plate, and then sat down opposite him.

Rosicky asked her in Czech if she wasn't going to have any coffee.

She replied in English, as being somehow the right language for transacting business: "Now what did Doctor Ed say, Anton? You tell me just what."

"He said I was to tell you some compliments, but I forgot 'em." Rosicky's eyes twinkled.

"About you, I mean. What did he say about your asthma?"

"He says I ain't got no asthma." Rosicky took one of the little rolls in his broad brown fingers. The thickened nail of his right thumb told the story of his past.

"Well, what is the matter? And don't try to put me off."

"He don't say nothing much, only I'm a little older, and my heart ain't so good like it used to be."

Mary started and brushed her hair back from her temples with both hands as if she were a little out of her mind. From the way she glared, she might have been in a rage with him.

"He says there's something the matter with your heart? Doctor Ed says so?"

"Now don't yell at me like I was a hog in de garden, Mary. You know I always did like to hear a woman talk soft. He didn't say anything de matter wid my heart, only it ain't so young like it used to be, an' he tell me not to pitch hay or run de corn-sheller."

Mary wanted to jump up, but she sat still. She admired the way he never under any circumstances raised his voice or spoke roughly. He was city-bred, and she was country-bred; she often said she wanted her boys to have their papa's nice ways.

"You never have no pain there, do you? It's your breathing and your stomach that's been wrong. I wouldn't believe nobody but Doctor Ed about it. I guess I'll go see him myself. Didn't he give you no advice?"

"Chust to take it easy like, an' stay round de house dis winter. I guess you got some carpenter work for me to do. I kin make some new shelves for you, and I want dis long time to build a closet in de boys' room and make dem two little fellers keep dere clo'es hung up."

Rosicky drank his coffee from time to time, while he considered. His moustache was of the soft long variety and came down over his mouth like the teeth of a buggy-rake over a bundle of hay. Each time he put down his cup, he ran his blue handkerchief over his lips. When he took a drink of water, he managed very neatly with the back of his hand.

Mary sat watching him intently, trying to find any change in his face. It is hard to see anyone who has become like your own body to you. Yes, his hair had got thin, and his high forehead had deep lines running from left to right. But his neck, always clean shaved except in the busiest seasons, was not loose or baggy. It was burned a dark reddish brown, and there were deep creases in it, but it looked firm and full of blood. His cheeks had a good colour. On either side of his mouth there was a half-moon down the length of his cheek, not wrinkles, but two lines that had come there from his habitual expression. He was shorter and broader than when she married him; his back had grown broad and curved, a good deal like the shell of an old turtle, and his arms and legs were short.

He was fifteen years older than Mary, but she had hardly ever thought about it before. He was her man, and the kind of man she liked. She was rough, and he was gentle,—city-bred, as she always said. They had been shipmates on a rough voyage and had stood by each other in trying times. Life had gone well with them because, at bottom, they had the same ideas about life. They agreed, without discussion, as to what was most important and what was secondary. They didn't often exchange opinions, even in Czech,—it was as if they had thought the same thought together. A good deal had to be sacrificed and thrown overboard in a hard life like theirs, and they had never disagreed as to the things that could go. It had been a hard life, and a soft life, too. There wasn't anything brutal in the short, broad-backed man with the three-cornered eyes and the forehead that went on to the top of his skull. He was a city man, a gentle man, and though he had married a rough farm girl, he had never touched her without gentleness.

They had been at one accord not to hurry through life, not to be always skimping and saving. They saw their neighbours buy more land and feed more stock than they did, without discontent. Once when the creamery agent came to the Rosickys to persuade them to sell him their cream, he told them how much money the Fasslers, their nearest neighbours, had made on their cream last year.

"Yes," said Mary, "and look at them Fassler children! Pale, pinched little things, they look like skimmed milk. I'd rather put some colour into my children's faces than put money into the bank."

The agent shrugged and turned to Anton. "I guess we'll do like she says," said Rosicky.

III

Mary very soon got into town to see Doctor Ed, and then she had a talk with her boys and set a guard over Rosicky. Even John, the youngest, had his father on his mind. If Rosicky went to throw hay down from the loft, one of the boys ran up the ladder and took the fork from him. He sometimes complained that though he was getting to be an old man, he wasn't an old woman yet.

That winter he stayed in the house in the afternoons and carpentered, or sat in the chair between the window full of plants and the wooden bench where the two pails of drinking-water stood. This spot was called "Father's corner," though it was not a corner at all. He had a shelf there, where he kept his Bohemian papers and his pipes and tobacco, and his shears and needles and thread and tailor's thimble. Having been a tailor in his youth, he couldn't bear to see a woman patching at his clothes, or at the boys'. He liked tailoring, and always patched all the overalls and jackets and work shirts. Occasionally he made over a pair of pants one of the older boys had outgrown, for the little fellow.

While he sewed, he let his mind run

back over his life. He had a good deal to remember, really; life in three countries. The only part of his youth he didn't like to remember was the two years he had spent in London, in Cheapside, working for a German tailor who was wretchedly poor. Those days, when he was nearly always hungry, when his clothes were dropping off him for dirt, and the sound of a strange language kept him in continual bewilderment, had left a sore spot in his mind that wouldn't bear touching.

He was twenty when he landed at Castle Garden in New York, and he had a protector who got him work in a tailor shop in Vesey Street, down near the Washington Market. He looked upon that part of his life as very happy. He became a good workman, he was industrious, and his wages were increased from time to time. He minded his own business and envied nobody's good fortune. He went to night school and learned to read English. He often did overtime work and was well paid for it, but somehow he never saved anything. He couldn't refuse a loan to a friend, and he was self-indulgent. He liked a good dinner, and a little went for beer, a little for tobacco; a good deal went to the girls. He often stood through an opera on Saturday nights; he could get standing-room for a dollar. Those were the great days of opera in New York, and it gave a fellow something to think about for the rest of the week. Rosicky had a quick ear, and a childish love of all the stage splendour; the scenery, the costumes, the ballet. He usually went with a chum, and after the performance they had beer and maybe some oysters somewhere. It was a fine life; for the first five years or so it satisfied him completely. He was never hungry or cold or dirty, and everything amused him: a fire, a dog fight, a parade, a storm, a ferry ride. He thought New York the finest, richest, friendliest city in the world.

Moreover, he had what he called a happy home life. Very near the tailor shop was a small furniture-factory, where an old Austrian, Loeffler, employed a few skilled men and made unusual furniture, most of it to order, for the rich German housewives up-town. The top floor of Loeffler's five-storey factory was a loft, where he kept his choice lumber and stored the odd pieces of furniture left on his hands. One of the young workmen he employed was a Czech, and he and Rosicky became fast friends. They persuaded Loeffler to let them have a sleeping-room in one corner of the loft. They bought good beds and bedding and had their pick of the furniture kept up there. The loft was low-pitched, but light and airy, full of windows, and good-smelling by reason of the fine lumber put up there to season. Old Loeffler used to go down to the docks and buy wood from South America and the East from the sea captains. The young men were as foolish about their house as a bridal pair. Zichec, the young cabinet-maker, devised every sort of convenience, and Rosicky kept their clothes in order. At night and on Sundays, when the quiver of machinery underneath was still, it was the quietest place in the world, and on summer nights all the sea winds blew in. Zichec often practised on his flute in the evening. They were both fond of music and went to the opera together. Rosicky thought he wanted to live like that for ever.

But as the years passed, all alike, he began to get a little restless. When spring came round, he would begin to feel fretted, and he got to drinking. He was likely to drink too much of a Saturday night. On Sunday, he was languid and heavy, getting over his spree. On Monday he plunged into work again. So he never had time to figure out what ailed him, though he knew something did. When the grass turned green in Park Place, and the lilac hedge at the back of Trinity churchyard put out its blossoms, he was tormented by a longing to run away. That was why he drank too much; to get a temporary illusion of freedom and wide horizons.

Rosicky, the old Rosicky, could remember as if it were yesterday the day when the young Rosicky found out what was the matter with him. It was on a Fourth of July afternoon, and he was sitting in Park Place in the sun. The lower part of New York was empty. Wall Street, Liberty Street, Broadway, all empty. So much stone and asphalt with nothing going on, so many empty windows. The emptiness was intense, like the stillness in a great factory when the machinery stops and the belts and bands cease running. It was too great a change, it took all the strength out of one. Those blank buildings, without the stream of life pouring through them, were like empty jails. It struck young Rosicky that this was the trouble with big cities; they built you in from the earth itself, cemented you away from any contact with the ground. You lived in an unnatural world, like the fish in an aquarium, who were probably much more comfortable than they ever were in the sea.

On that very day he began to think seriously about the articles he had read in the Bohemian papers, describing prosperous Czech farming communities in the West. He believed he would like to go out there as a farm hand; it was hardly possible that he could ever have land of his own. His people had always been workmen; his father and grandfather had worked in shops. His mother's parents had lived in the country, but they rented their farm and had a hard time to get along. Nobody in his family had ever owned any land,—that belonged to a different station of life altogether. Anton's mother died when he was little, and he was sent into the country to her parents. He stayed with them until he was twelve, and formed these ties with the earth and the farm animals and growing things which are never made at all unless they are made early. After his grandfather died, he went back to live with his father and step-mother, but she was very hard on him, and his father helped him to get passage to London.

After that Fourth of July day in Park Place, the desire to return to the country never left him. To work on another man's farm would be all he asked; to see the sun

rise and set and to plant things and watch them grow. He was a very simple man. He was like a tree that has not many roots, but one tap-root that goes down deep. He subscribed for a Bohemian paper printed in Chicago, then for one printed in Omaha. His mind got farther and farther west. He began to save a little money to buy his liberty. When he was thirty-five, there was a great meeting in New York of Bohemian athletic societies, and Rosicky left the tailor shop and went home with the Omaha delegates to try his fortune in another part of the world.

IV

Perhaps the fact that his own youth was well over before he began to have a family was one reason why Rosicky was so fond of his boys. He had almost a grandfather's indulgence for them. He had never had to worry about any of them—except, just now, a little about Rudolph.

On Saturday night the boys always piled into the Ford, took little Josephine, and went to town to the moving-picture show. One Saturday morning they were talking at the breakfast table about starting early that evening, so that they would have an hour or so to see the Christmas things in the stores before the show began. Rosicky looked down the table.

"I hope you boys ain't disappointed, but I want you to let me have de car tonight. Maybe some of you can go in with de neighbours."

Their faces fell. They worked hard all week, and they were still like children. A new jackknife or a box of candy pleased the older ones as much as the little fellow.

"If you and Mother are going to town," Frank said, "maybe you could take a couple of us along with you anyway."

"No, I want to take de car down to Rudolph's, and let him an' Polly go in to de show. She don't git into town enough, an' I'm afraid she's gettin' lonesome, an' he can't afford no car yet."

That settled it. The boys were a good deal dashed. Their father took another piece of apple-cake and went on: "Maybe next Saturday night de two little fellers can go along wid dem."

"Oh, is Rudolph going to have the car every Saturday night?"

Rosicky did not reply at once; then he began to speak seriously: "Listen, boys; Polly ain't lookin' so good. I don't like to see nobody lookin' sad. It comes hard fur a town girl to be a farmer's wife. I don't want no trouble to start in Rudolph's family. When it starts, it ain't so easy to stop. An American girl don't git used to our ways all at once. I like to tell Polly she and Rudolph can have the car every Saturday night till after New Year's, if it's all right with you boys."

"Sure it's all right, Papa," Mary cut in. "And it's good you thought about that. Town girls is used to more than country girls. I lay awake nights, scared she'll make Rudolph discontented with the farm."

The boys put as good a face on it as they could. They surely looked forward to their Saturday nights in town. That evening Rosicky drove the car the half-mile down to Rudolph's new, bare little house.

Polly was in a short-sleeved gingham dress, clearing away the supper dishes. She was a trim, slim little thing, with blue eyes and shingled yellow hair, and her eyebrows were reduced to a mere brush-stroke, like Miss Pearl's.

"Good evening, Mr. Rosicky. Rudolph's at the barn, I guess." She never called him father, or Mary mother. She was sensitive about having married a foreigner. She never in the world would have done it if Rudolph hadn't been such a handsome, persuasive fellow and such a gallant lover. He had graduated in her class in the high school in town, and their friendship began in the ninth grade.

Rosicky went in, though he wasn't exactly asked. "My boys ain't goin' to town tonight, an' I brought de car over fur you two to go in to de picture show."

Polly, carrying dishes to the sink, looked over her shoulder at him. "Thank you. But I'm late with my work tonight, and pretty tired. Maybe Rudolph would like to go in with you."

"Oh, I don't go to de shows! I'm too old-fashioned. You won't feel so tired after you ride in de air a ways. It's a nice clear night, an' it ain't cold. You go an' fix yourself up, Polly, an' I'll wash de dishes an' leave everything nice fur you."

Polly blushed and tossed her bob. "I couldn't let you do that, Mr. Rosicky. I wouldn't think of it."

Rosicky said nothing. He found a bib apron on a nail behind the kitchen door. He slipped it over his head and then took Polly by her two elbows and pushed her gently toward the door of her own room. "I washed up de kitchen many times for my wife, when de babies was sick or somethin'. You go an' make yourself look nice. I like you to look prettier'n any of dem town girls when you go in. De young folks must have some fun, an' I'm goin' to look out fur you, Polly."

That kind, reassuring grip on her elbows, the old man's funny bright eyes, made Polly want to drop her head on his shoulders for a second. She restrained herself, but she lingered in his grasp at the door of her room, murmuring tearfully: "You always lived in the city when you were young, didn't you? Don't you ever get lonesome out here?"

As she turned round to him, her hand fell naturally into his, and he stood holding it and smiling into her face with his peculiar, knowing, indulgent smile without a shadow of reproach in it. "Dem big cities is all right fur de rich, but dey is terrible hard fur de poor."

"I don't know. Sometimes I think I'd like to take a chance. You lived in New York, didn't you?"

"An' London. Da's bigger still. I learned my trade dere. Here's Rudolph comin', you better hurry."

"Will you tell me about London some time?"

"Maybe. Only I ain't no talker, Polly. Run an' dress yourself up."

The bedroom door closed behind her, and Rudolph came in from the outside, looking anxious. He had seen the car and was sorry any of his family should come just then. Supper hadn't been a very pleasant occasion. Halting in the doorway, he saw his father in a kitchen apron, carrying dishes to the sink. He flushed crimson and something flashed in his eye. Rosicky held up a warning finger.

"I brought de car over fur you an' Polly to go to de picture show, an' I made her let me finish here so you won't be late. You go put on a clean shirt, quick!"

"But don't the boys want the car, Father?"

"Not tonight dey don't." Rosicky fumbled under his apron and found his pants pocket. He took out a silver dollar and said in a hurried whisper: "You go an' buy dat girl some ice cream an' candy tonight, like you was courtin'. She's awful good friends wid me."

Rudolph was very short of cash, but he took the money as if it hurt him. There had been a crop failure all over the county. He had more than once been sorry he'd married this year.

In a few minutes the young people came out, looking clean and a little stiff. Rosicky hurried them off, and then he took his own time with the dishes. He scoured the pots and pans and put away the milk and swept the kitchen. He put some coal in the stove and shut off the draughts, so the place would be warm for them when they got home late at night. Then he sat down and had a pipe and listened to the clock tick.

Generally speaking, marrying an American girl was certainly a risk. A Czech should marry a Czech. It was lucky that Polly was the daughter of a poor widow woman; Rudolph was proud, and if she had a prosperous family to throw up at him, they could never make it go. Polly was one of four sisters, and they all worked; one was book-keeper in the bank, one taught music, and Polly and her younger sister had been clerks, like Miss Pearl. All four of them were musical, had pretty voices, and sang in the Methodist choir, which the eldest sister directed.

Polly missed the sociability of a store position. She missed the choir, and the company of her sisters. She didn't dislike housework, but she disliked so much of it. Rosicky was a little anxious about this pair. He was afraid Polly would grow so discontented that Rudy would quit the farm and take a factory job in Omaha. He had worked for a winter up there, two years ago, to get money to marry on. He had done very well, and they would always take him back at the stockyards. But to Rosicky that meant the end of everything for his son. To be a landless man was to be a wage-earner, a slave, all your life; to have nothing, to be nothing.

Rosicky thought he would come over and do a little carpentering for Polly after the New Year. He guessed she needed jollying. Rudolph was a serious sort of chap, serious in love and serious about his work.

Rosicky shook out his pipe and walked home across the fields. Ahead of him the lamplight shone from his kitchen windows. Suppose he were still in a tailor shop on Vesey Street, with a bunch of pale, narrow-chested sons working on machines, all coming home tired and sullen to eat supper in a kitchen that was a parlour also; with another crowded, angry family quarrelling just across the dumb-waiter shaft, and squeaking pulleys at the windows where dirty washings hung on dirty lines above a court full of old brooms and mops and ash-cans. . . .

He stopped by the windmill to look up at the frosty winter stars and draw a long breath before he went inside. That kitchen with the shining windows was dear to him; but the sleeping fields and bright stars and the noble darkness were dearer still.

V

On the day before Christmas the weather set in very cold; no snow, but a bitter, biting wind that whistled and sang over the flat land and lashed one's face like fine wires. There was baking going on in the Rosicky kitchen all day, and Rosicky sat inside, making over a coat that Albert had outgrown into an overcoat for John. Mary had a big red geranium in bloom for Christmas, and a row of Jerusalem cherry trees, full of berries. It was the first year she had ever grown these; Doctor Ed brought her the seeds from Omaha when he went to some medical convention. They reminded Rosicky of plants he had seen in England; and all afternoon, as he stitched, he sat thinking about those two years in London, which his mind usually shrank from even after all this while.

He was a lad of eighteen when he dropped down into London, with no money and no connexions except the address of a cousin who was supposed to be working at a confectioner's. When he went to the pastry shop, however, he found that the cousin had gone to America. Anton tramped the streets for several days, sleeping in doorways and on the Embankment, until he was in utter despair. He knew no English and the sound of the strange language all about him confused him. By chance he met a poor German tailor who had learned his trade in Vienna, and could speak a little Czech. This tailor, Lifschnitz, kept a repair shop in a Cheapside basement, underneath a cobbler. He didn't much need an apprentice, but he was sorry for the boy and took him in for no wages but his keep and what he could pick up. The pickings were supposed to be coppers given you when you took work home to a customer. But most of the customers called for their clothes themselves, and the coppers that came Anton's way were very few. He had, however, a place to sleep. The tailor's family lived upstairs in three rooms; a kitchen, a bedroom, where Lifschnitz and his wife and five children slept, and a living-room. Two corners of this living-room were curtained off for lodgers; in one Rosicky slept on an old horsehair sofa, with a feather quilt to wrap himself in. The other corner

was rented to a wretched, dirty boy, who was studying the violin. He actually practised there. Rosicky was dirty, too. There was no way to be anything else. Mrs. Lifschnitz got the water she cooked and washed with from a pump in a brick court, four flights down. There were bugs in the place, and multitudes of fleas, though the poor woman did the best she could. Rosicky knew she often went empty to give another potato or a spoonful of dripping to the two hungry, sad-eyed boys who lodged with her. He used to think he would never get out of there, never get a clean shirt to his back again. What would he do, he wondered, when his clothes actually dropped to pieces and the worn cloth wouldn't hold patches any longer?

It was still early when the old farmer put aside his sewing and his recollections. The sky had been a dark grey all day, with not a gleam of sun, and the light failed at four o'clock. He went to shave and change his shirt while the turkey was roasting. Rudolph and Polly were coming over for supper.

After supper they sat round in the kitchen, and the younger boys were saying how sorry they were it hadn't snowed. Everybody was sorry. They wanted a deep snow that would lie long and keep the wheat warm, and leave the ground soaked when it melted.

"Yes, sir!" Rudolph broke out fiercely; "if we have another dry year like last year, there's going to be hard times in this country."

Rosicky filled his pipe. "You boys don't know what hard times is. You don't owe nobody, you got plenty to eat an' keep warm, an' plenty water to keep clean. When you got them, you can't have it very hard."

Rudolph frowned, opened and shut his big right hand, and dropped it clenched upon his knee. "I've got to have a good deal more than that, Father, or I'll quit this farming gamble. I can always make good wages railroading, or at the packing house, and be sure of my money."

"Maybe so," his father answered dryly.

Mary, who had just come in from the pantry and was wiping her hands on the roller towel, thought Rudy and his father were getting too serious. She brought her darning-basket and sat down in the middle of the group.

"I ain't much afraid of hard times, Rudy," she said heartily. "We've had a plenty, but we've always come through. Your father wouldn't never take nothing very hard, not even hard times. I got a mind to tell you a story on him. Maybe you boys can't hardly remember the year we had that terrible hot wind, that burned everything up on the Fourth of July? All the corn an' the gardens. An' that was in the days when we didn't have alfalfa yet,— I guess it wasn't invented.

"Well, that very day your father was out cultivatin' corn, and I was here in the kitchen makin' plum preserves. We had bushels of plums that year. I noticed it was terrible hot, but it's always hot in the kitchen when you're preservin', an' I was too busy with my plums to mind. Anton come in from the field about three o'clock, an' I asked him what was the matter.

" 'Nothin',' he says, 'but it's pretty hot, an' I think I won't work no more today.' He stood round for a few minutes, an' then he says: 'Ain't you near through? I want you should git up a nice supper for us to-night. It's Fourth of July.'

"I told him to git along, that I was right in the middle of preservin', but the plums would taste good on hot biscuit. 'I'm goin' to have fried chicken, too,' he says, and he went off an' killed a couple. You three oldest boys was little fellers, playin' round outside, real hot an' sweaty, an' your father took you to the horse tank down by the windmill an' took off your clothes an' put you in. Them two box-elder trees was little then, but they made shade over the tank. Then he took off all his own clothes, an' got in with you. While he was playin' in the water with you, the Methodist preacher drove into our place to say how all the neighbours was goin' to meet at the school-house that night, to pray for rain. He drove right to the windmill, of course, and there was your father and you three with no clothes on. I was in the kitchen door, an' I had to laugh, for the preacher acted like he ain't never seen a naked man before. He surely was embarrassed, an' your father couldn't git to his clothes; they was all hangin' up on the windmill to let the sweat dry out of 'em. So he laid in the tank where he was, an' put one of you boys on top of him to cover him up a little, an' talked to the preacher.

"When you got through playin' in the water, he put clean clothes on you and a clean shirt on himself, an' by that time I'd begun to get supper. He says: 'It's too hot in here to eat comfortable. Let's have a picnic in the orchard. We'll eat our supper behind the mulberry hedge, under them linden trees.'

"So he carried our supper down, an' a bottle of my wild-grape wine, an' everything tasted good, I can tell you. The wind got cooler as the sun was goin' down, and it turned out pleasant, only I noticed how the leaves was curled up on the linden trees. That made me think, an' I asked your father if that hot wind all day hadn't been terrible hard on the gardens an' the corn.

" 'Corn,' he says, 'there ain't no corn.'

" 'What you talkin' about?' I said. 'Ain't we got forty acres?'

" 'We ain't got an ear,' he says, 'nor nobody else ain't got none. All the corn in this country was cooked by three o'clock today, like you'd roasted it in an oven.'

" 'You mean you won't get no crop at all?' I asked him. I couldn't believe it, after he'd worked so hard.

" 'No crop this year,' he says. 'That's why we're havin' a picnic. We might as well enjoy what we got.'

"An' that's how your father behaved, when all the neighbours was so discouraged they couldn't look you in the face. An' we enjoyed ourselves that year, poor as we was, an' our neighbours wasn't a bit better off for bein' miserable.

Some of 'em grieved till they got poor digestions and couldn't relish what they did have."

The younger boys said they thought their father had the best of it. But Rudolph was thinking that, all the same, the neighbours had managed to get ahead more, in the fifteen years since that time. There must be something wrong about his father's way of doing things. He wished he knew what was going on in the back of Polly's mind. He knew she liked his father, but he knew, too, that she was afraid of something. When his mother sent over coffee-cake or prune tarts or a loaf of fresh bread, Polly seemed to regard them with a certain suspicion. When she observed to him that his brothers had nice manners, her tone implied that it was remarkable they should have. With his mother she was stiff and on her guard. Mary's hearty frankness and gusts of good humour irritated her. Polly was afraid of being unusual or conspicuous in any way, of being "ordinary," as she said!

When Mary had finished her story, Rosicky laid aside his pipe.

"You boys like me to tell you about some of dem hard times I been through in London?" Warmly encouraged, he sat rubbing his forehead along the deep creases. It was bothersome to tell a long story in English (he nearly always talked to the boys in Czech), but he wanted Polly to hear this one.

"Well, you know about dat tailor shop I worked in in London? I had one Christmas dere I ain't never forgot. Times was awful bad before Christmas; de boss ain't got much work, an' have it awful hard to pay his rent. It ain't so much fun, bein' poor in a big city like London, I'll say! All de windows is full of good t'ings to eat, an' all de pushcarts in de streets is full, an' you smell 'em all de time, an' you ain't got no money,—not a damn bit. I didn't mind de cold so much, though I didn't have no overcoat, chust a short jacket I'd outgrowed so it wouldn't meet on me, an' my hands was chapped raw.

But I always had a good appetite, like you all know, an' de sight of dem pork pies in de windows was awful fur me!

"Day before Christmas was terrible foggy dat year, an' dat fog gits into your bones and makes you all damp like. Mrs. Lifschnitz didn't give us nothin' but a little bread an' drippin' for supper, because she was savin' to try for to give us a good dinner on Christmas Day. After supper de boss say I can go an' enjoy myself, so I went into de streets to listen to de Christmas singers. Dey sing old songs an' make very nice music, an' I run round after dem a good ways, till I got awful hungry. I t'ink maybe if I go home, I can sleep till morning an' forgit my belly.

"I went into my corner real quiet, and roll up in my fedder quilt. But I ain't got my head down, till I smell somet'ing good. Seem like it git stronger an' stronger, an' I can't git to sleep noway. I can't understand dat smell. Dere was a gas light in a hall across de court, dat always shine in at my window a little. I got up an' look around. I got a little wooden box in my corner fur a stool, 'cause I ain't got no chair. I picks up dat box, and under it dere is a roast goose on a platter! I can't believe my eyes. I carry it to de window where de light comes in, an' touch it and smell it to find out, an' den I taste it to be sure. I say, I will eat chust one little bite of dat goose, so I can go to sleep, and tomorrow I won't eat none at all. But I tell you, boys, when I stop, one half of dat goose was gone!"

The narrator bowed his head, and the boys shouted. But little Josephine slipped behind his chair and kissed him on the neck beneath his ear.

"Poor little Papa, I don't want him to be hungry!"

"Da's long ago, child. I ain't never been hungry since I had your mudder to cook fur me."

"Go on and tell us the rest, please," said Polly.

"Well, when I come to realize what I

done, of course, I felt terrible. I felt better in de stomach, but very bad in de heart. I set on my bed wid dat platter on my knees, an' it all come to me; how hard dat poor woman save to buy dat goose, and how she get some neighbour to cook it dat got more fire, an' how she put it in my corner to keep it away from dem hungry children. Dey was a old carpet hung up to shut my corner off, an' de children wasn't allowed to go in dere. An' I know she put it in my corner because she trust me more'n she did de violin boy. I can't stand it to face her after I spoil de Christmas. So I put on my shoes and go out into de city. I tell myself I better throw myself in de river; but I guess I ain't dat kind of a boy.

"It was after twelve o'clock, an' terrible cold, an' I start out to walk about London all night. I walk along de river awhile, but dey was lots of drunks all along; men, and women too. I chust move along to keep away from de police. I git onto de Strand, an' den over to New Oxford Street, where dere was a big German restaurant on de ground floor, wid big windows all fixed up fine, an' I could see de people havin' parties inside. While I was lookin' in, two men and two ladies come out, laughin' and talkin' and feelin' happy about all dey been eatin' an' drinkin', and dey was speakin' Czech,—not like de Austrians, but like de home folks talk it.

"I guess I went crazy, an' I done what I ain't never done before nor since. I went right up to dem gay people an' begun to beg dem: 'Fellow-countrymen, for God's sake give me money enough to buy a goose!'

"Dey laugh, of course, but de ladies speak awful kind to me, an' dey take me back into de restaurant and give me hot coffee and cakes, an' make me tell all about how I happened to come to London, an' what I was doin' dere. Dey take my name and where I work down on paper, an' both of dem ladies give me ten shillings.

"De big market at Covent Garden ain't very far away, an' by dat time it was open. I go dere an' buy a big goose an' some pork

pies, an' potatoes and onions, an' cakes an' oranges fur de children,—all I could carry! When I git home, everybody is still asleep. I pile all I bought on de kitchen table, an' go in an' lay down on my bed, an' I ain't waken up till I hear dat woman scream when she come out into her kitchen. My goodness, but she was surprise! She laugh an' cry at de same time, an' hug me and waken all de children. She ain't stop fur no breakfast; she git de Christmas dinner ready dat morning, and we all sit down an' eat all we can hold. I ain't never seen dat violin boy have all he can hold before.

"Two three days after dat, de two men come to hunt me up, an' dey ask my boss, and he give me a good report an' tell dem I was a steady boy all right. One of dem Bohemians was very smart an' run a Bohemian newspaper in New York, an' de odder was a rich man, in de importing business, an' dey been travelling togedder. Dey told me how t'ings was easier in New York, an' offered to pay my passage when dey was goin' home soon on a boat. My boss say to me: 'You go. You ain't got no chance here, an' I like to see you git ahead, fur you always been a good boy to my woman, and fur dat fine Christmas dinner you give us all.' An' da's how I got to New York."

That night when Rudolph and Polly, arm in arm, were running home across the fields with the bitter wind at their backs, his heart leaped for joy when she said she thought they might have his family come over for supper on New Year's Eve. "Let's get up a nice supper, and not let your mother help at all; make her be company for once."

"That would be lovely of you, Polly," he said humbly. He was a very simple, modest boy, and he, too, felt vaguely that Polly and her sisters were more experienced and worldly than his people.

VI

The winter turned out badly for farmers. It was bitterly cold, and after the first light snows before Christmas there was no snow at all,—and no rain. March was as bitter as February. On those days when the wind fairly punished the country, Rosicky sat by his window. In the fall he and the boys had put in a big wheat planting, and now the seed had frozen in the ground. All that land would have to be ploughed up and planted over again, planted in corn. It had happened before, but he was younger then, and he never worried about what had to be. He was sure of himself and of Mary; he knew they could bear what they had to bear, that they would always pull through somehow. But he was not so sure about the young ones, and he felt troubled because Rudolph and Polly were having such a hard start.

Sitting beside his flowering window while the panes rattled and the wind blew in under the door, Rosicky gave himself to reflection as he had not done since those Sundays in the loft of the furniture-factory in New York, long ago. Then he was trying to find what he wanted in life for himself; now he was trying to find what he wanted for his boys, and why it was he so hungered to feel sure they would be here, working this very land, after he was gone.

They would have to work hard on the farm, and probably they would never do much more than make a living. But if he could think of them as staying here on the land, he wouldn't have to fear any great unkindness for them. Hardships, certainly; it was a hardship to have the wheat freeze in the ground when seed was so high; and to have to sell your stock because you had no feed. But there would be other years when everything came along right, and you caught up. And what you had was your own. You didn't have to choose between bosses and strikers, and go wrong either way. You didn't have to do with dishonest and cruel people. They were the only things in his experience he had found terrifying and horrible; the look in the eyes of a dishonest and crafty man, of a scheming and rapacious woman.

In the country, if you had a mean neighbour, you could keep off his land and make him keep off yours. But in the city, all the foulness and misery and brutality of your neighbours was part of your life. The worst things he had come upon in his journey through the world were human,—depraved and poisonous specimens of man. To this day he could recall certain terrible faces in the London streets. There were mean people everywhere, to be sure, even in their own country town here. But they weren't tempered, hardened, sharpened, like the treacherous people in cities who live by grinding or cheating or poisoning their fellow-men. He had helped to bury two of his fellow-workmen in the tailoring trade, and he was distrustful of the organized industries that see one out of the world in big cities. Here, if you were sick, you had Doctor Ed to look after you; and if you died, fat Mr. Haycock, the kindest man in the world, buried you.

It seemed to Rosicky that for good, honest boys like his, the worst they could do on the farm was better than the best they would be likely to do in the city. If he'd had a mean boy, now, one who was crooked and sharp and tried to put anything over on his brothers, then town would be the place for him. But he had no such boy. As for Rudolph, the discontented one, he would give the shirt off his back to anyone who touched his heart. What Rosicky really hoped for his boys was that they could get through the world without ever knowing much about the cruelty of human beings. "Their mother and me ain't prepared them for that," he sometimes said to himself.

These thoughts brought him back to a grateful consideration of his own case. What an escape he had had, to be sure! He, too, in his time, had had to take money for repair work from the hand of a hungry child who let it go so wistfully; because it was money due his boss. And now, in all these years, he had never had to take a cent from anyone in bitter need,—never had to look at the face of a woman become like a wolf's from struggle and famine. When he thought of these things, Rosicky would put on his cap and jacket and slip down to the barn and give his work-horses a little extra oats, letting them eat it out of his hand in their slobbery fashion. It was his way of expressing what he felt, and made him chuckle with pleasure.

The spring came warm, with blue skies, —but dry, dry as a bone. The boys began ploughing up the wheat-fields to plant them over in corn. Rosicky would stand at the fence corner and watch them, and the earth was so dry it blew up in clouds of brown dust that hid the horses and the sulky plough and the driver. It was a bad outlook.

The big alfalfa-field that lay between the home place and Rudolph's came up green, but Rosicky was worried because during that open windy winter a great many Russian thistle plants had blown in there and lodged. He kept asking the boys to rake them out; he was afraid their seed would root and "take the alfalfa." Rudolph said that was nonsense. The boys were working so hard planting corn, their father felt he couldn't insist about the thistles, but he set great store by that big alfalfa field. It was a feed you could depend on,— and there was some deeper reason, vague, but strong. The peculiar green of that clover woke early memories in old Rosicky, went back to something in his childhood in the old world. When he was a little boy, he had played in fields of that strong blue-green colour.

One morning, when Rudolph had gone to town in the car, leaving a work-team idle in his barn, Rosicky went over to his son's place, put the horses to the buggy-rake, and set about quietly raking up those thistles. He behaved with guilty caution, and rather enjoyed stealing a march on Doctor Ed, who was just then taking his first vacation in seven years of practice and was attending a clinic in Chicago. Rosicky got the thistles raked up, but did not stop to burn them. That would take some time, and his breath was pretty short,

so he thought he had better get the horses back to the barn.

He got them into the barn and to their stalls, but the pain had come on so sharp in his chest that he didn't try to take the harness off. He started for the house, bending lower with every step. The cramp in his chest was shutting him up like a jack-knife. When he reached the windmill, he swayed and caught at the ladder. He saw Polly coming down the hill, running with the swiftness of a slim greyhound. In a flash she had her shoulder under his armpit.

"Lean on me, Father, hard! Don't be afraid. We can get to the house all right."

Somehow they did, though Rosicky became blind with pain; he could keep on his legs, but he couldn't steer his course. The next thing he was conscious of was lying on Polly's bed, and Polly bending over him wringing out bath towels in hot water and putting them on his chest. She stopped only to throw coal into the stove, and she kept the tea-kettle and the black pot going. She put these hot applications on him for nearly an hour, she told him afterwards, and all that time he was drawn up stiff and blue, with the sweat pouring off him.

As the pain gradually loosed its grip, the stiffness went out of his jaws, the black circles round his eyes disappeared, and a little of his natural colour came back. When his daughter-in-law buttoned his shirt over his chest at last, he sighed.

"Da's fine, de way I feel now, Polly. It was a awful bad spell, an' I was so sorry it all come on you like it did."

Polly was flushed and excited. "Is the pain really gone? Can I leave you long enough to telephone over to your place?"

Rosicky's eyelids fluttered. "Don't telephone, Polly. It ain't no use to scare my wife. It's nice and quiet here, an' if I ain't too much trouble to you, just let me lay still till I feel like myself. I ain't got no pain now. It's nice here."

Polly bent over him and wiped the moisture from his face. "Oh, I'm so glad it's over!" she broke out impulsively. "It just broke my heart to see you suffer so, Father."

Rosicky motioned her to sit down on the chair where the tea-kettle had been, and looked up at her with that lively affectionate gleam in his eyes. "You was awful good to me, I won't never forget dat. I hate it to be sick on you like dis. Down at de barn I say to myself, dat young girl ain't had much experience in sickness, I don't want to scare her, an' maybe she's got a baby comin' or somet'ing."

Polly took his hand. He was looking at her so intently and affectionately and confidingly; his eyes seemed to caress her face, to regard it with pleasure. She frowned with her funny streaks of eyebrows, and then smiled back at him.

"I guess maybe there is something of that kind going to happen. But I haven't told anyone yet, not my mother or Rudolph. You'll be the first to know."

His hand pressed hers. She noticed that it was warm again. The twinkle in his yellow-brown eyes seemed to come nearer.

"I like mighty well to see dat little child, Polly," was all he said. Then he closed his eyes and lay half-smiling. But Polly sat still, thinking hard. She had a sudden feeling that nobody in the world, not her mother, not Rudolph, or anyone, really loved her as much as old Rosicky did. It perplexed her. She sat frowning and trying to puzzle it out. It was as if Rosicky had a special gift for loving people, something that was like an ear for music or an eye for colour. It was quiet, unobtrusive; it was merely there. You saw it in his eyes,—perhaps that was why they were merry. You felt it in his hands, too. After he dropped off to sleep, she sat holding his warm, broad, flexible brown hand. She had never seen another in the least like it. She wondered if it wasn't a kind of gypsy hand, it was so alive and quick and light in its communications,—very strange in a farmer. Nearly all the farmers she knew had huge lumps of fists, like mauls, or they were knotty and bony

and uncomfortable-looking, with stiff fingers. But Rosicky's was like quicksilver, flexible, muscular, about the colour of a pale cigar, with deep, deep creases across the palm. It wasn't nervous, it wasn't a stupid lump; it was a warm brown human hand, with some cleverness in it, a great deal of generosity, and something else which Polly could only call "gypsy-like," —something nimble and lively and sure, in the way that animals are.

Polly remembered that hour long afterwards; it had been like an awakening to her. It seemed to her that she had never learned so much about life from anything as from old Rosicky's hand. It brought her to herself; it communicated some direct and untranslatable message.

When she heard Rudolph coming in the car, she ran out to meet him.

"Oh, Rudy, your father's been awful sick! He raked up those thistles he's been worrying about, and afterwards he could hardly get to the house. He suffered so I was afraid he was going to die."

Rudolph jumped to the ground. "Where is he now?"

"On the bed. He's asleep. I was terribly scared, because, you know, I'm so fond of your father." She slipped her arm through his and they went into the house. That afternoon they took Rosicky home and put him to bed, though he protested that he was quite well again.

The next morning he got up and dressed and sat down to breakfast with his family. He told Mary that his coffee tasted better than usual to him, and he warned the boys not to bear any tales to Doctor Ed when he got home. After breakfast he sat down by his window to do some patching and asked Mary to thread several needles for him before she went to feed her chickens,—her eyes were better than his, and her hands steadier. He lit his pipe and took up John's overalls. Mary had been watching him anxiously all morning, and as she went out of the door with her bucket of scraps, she saw that he was smiling. He was thinking, indeed, about Polly, and how he might never have known what a tender heart she had if he hadn't got sick over there. Girls nowadays didn't wear their heart on their sleeve. But now he knew Polly would make a fine woman after the foolishness wore off. Either a woman had that sweetness at her heart or she hadn't. You couldn't always tell by the look of them; but if they had that, everything came out right in the end.

After he had taken a few stitches, the cramp began in his chest, like yesterday. He put his pipe cautiously down on the window-sill and bent over to ease the pull. No use,—he had better try to get to his bed if he could. He rose and groped his way across the familiar floor, which was rising and falling like the deck of a ship. At the door he fell. When Mary came in, she found him lying there, and the moment she touched him she knew that he was gone.

Doctor Ed was away when Rosicky died, and for the first few weeks after he got home he was hard driven. Every day he said to himself that he must get out to see that family that had lost their father. One soft, warm moonlight night in early summer he started for the farm. His mind was on other things, and not until his road ran by the graveyard did he realize that Rosicky wasn't over there on the hill where the red lamplight shone, but here, in the moonlight. He stopped his car, shut off the engine, and sat there for a while.

A sudden hush had fallen on his soul. Everything here seemed strangely moving and significant, though signifying what, he did not know. Close by the wire fence stood Rosicky's mowing-machine, where one of the boys had been cutting hay that afternoon; his own work-horses had been going up and down there. The new-cut hay perfumed all the night air. The moonlight silvered the long, billowy grass that grew over the graves and hid the fence; the few little evergreens stood out black in it, like shadows in a pool. The sky was very blue and soft, the stars rather faint because the moon was full.

For the first time it struck Doctor Ed that this was really a beautiful graveyard. He thought of city cemeteries; acres of shrubbery and heavy stone, so arranged and lonely and unlike anything in the living world. Cities of the dead, indeed; cities of the forgotten, of the "put away." But this was open and free, this little square of long grass which the wind for ever stirred. Nothing but the sky overhead, and the many-coloured fields running on until they met that sky. The horses worked here in summer; the neighbours passed on their way to town; and over yonder, in the cornfield, Rosicky's own cattle would be eating fodder as winter came on. Nothing could be more undeathlike than this place; nothing could be more right for a man who had helped to do the work of great cities and had always longed for the open country and had got to it at last. Rosicky's life seemed to him complete and beautiful.

James Branch Cabell

1879

JAMES BRANCH CABELL was born in Virginia and has spent most of his life there. He was graduated at William and Mary College, where he taught Greek and French; he later worked on newspapers in New York City and Richmond. After the publication of his first novel, *The Eagle's Shadow,* in 1904, he devoted most of his time to the writing of fiction. With his irony, satire, concern for style, and anti-realism, Cabell brought the 1890's into the 1920's. Exoneration of his *Jurgen* (1919) at a famous censorship trial in 1922 made his works so popular that they were issued in an 18-volume definitive edition at the end of the decade. Thereafter he wrote three trilogies under the name of Branch Cabell, finally restoring the James with *There Were Two Pirates* (1946) and *Let Me Lie* (1947). *The Line of Love,* a collection repeatedly revised, is the source of the following story. [See W. A. McNeill's *Cabellian Harmonics* (New York, 1928), C. Van Doren's *James Branch Cabell* (New York, 1932), and E. Wagenknecht's "Cabell: A Reconsideration" in *College English,* IX (February, 1948), 238-46.]

THE WEDDING JEST
[1921 (1919)]

I. Concerning Several Compacts

IT IS a tale which they narrate in Poictesme, telling how love began between Florian de Puysange and Adelaide de la Forêt. They tell also how young Florian had earlier fancied other women for one reason or another; but that this, he knew, was the great love of his life, and a love which would endure unchanged as long as his life lasted.

And the tale tells how the Comte de la Forêt stroked a gray beard, and said, "Well, after all, Puysange is a good fief—"

"As if that mattered!" cried his daughter, indignantly. "My father, you are a deplorably sordid person."

"My dear," replied old Perion of the Forest, "it does matter. Fiefs last."

So he gave his consent to the match, and the two young people were married on Walburga's Eve, on the day that ends April.

And they narrate how Florian de Puysange was vexed by a thought that was in his mind. He did not know what this thought was. But something he had overlooked; something there was he had meant to do, and had not done: and a troubling consciousness of this lurked at the back of his mind like a small formless cloud. All day, while bustling about other matters, he had groped toward this unapprehended thought.

Now he had it: Tiburce.

The young Vicomte de Puysange stood in the doorway, looking back into the bright hall where they of Storisende were dancing at his marriage feast. His wife, for a whole half-hour his wife, was dancing with handsome Etienne de Nérac. Her glance met Florian's, and Adelaide flashed him an especial smile. Her hand went out as though to touch him, for all that the width of the hall severed them.

Florian remembered presently to smile back at her. Then he went out of the castle into a starless night that was as quiet as an unvoiced menace. A small and hard and gnarled-looking moon ruled over the dusk's secrecy. The moon this night, afloat in a luminous gray void, somehow reminded Florian of a glistening and unripe huge apple.

The foliage about him moved at most as a sleeper breathes, while Florian descended eastward through walled gardens, and so came to the graveyard. White mists were rising, such mists as the witches of Amneran notoriously evoked in these parts on each Walburga's Eve to purchase recreations which squeamishness leaves undescribed.

For five years now Tiburce d'Arnaye had lain there. Florian thought of his dead comrade and of the love which had been between them,—a love more perfect and deeper and higher than commonly exists between men,—and the thought came to Florian, and was petulantly thrust away, that Adelaide loved ignorantly where Tiburce d'Arnaye had loved with comprehension. Yes, he had known almost the worst of Florian de Puysange, this dear lad who, none the less, had flung himself between Black Torrismond's sword and the breast of Florian de Puysange. And it seemed to

Florian unfair that all should prosper with him, and Tiburce lie there imprisoned in dirt which shut away the color and variousness of things and the drollness of things, wherein Tiburce d'Arnaye had taken such joy. And Tiburce, it seemed to Florian—for this was a strange night,—was struggling futilely under all that dirt, which shut out movement, and clogged the mouth of Tiburce, and would not let him speak; and was struggling to voice a desire which was unsatisfied and hopeless.

"O comrade dear," said Florian, "you who loved merriment, there is a feast afoot on this strange night, and my heart is sad that you are not here to share the feasting. Come, come, Tiburce, a right trusty friend you were to me; and, living or dead, you should not fail to make merry at my wedding."

Thus he spoke. White mists were rising, and it was Walburga's Eve.

So a queer thing happened, and it was that the earth upon the grave began to heave and to break in fissures, as when a mole passes through the ground. And other queer things happened after that, and presently Tiburce d'Arnaye was standing there, gray and vague in the moonlight as he stood there brushing the mold from his brows, and as he stood there blinking bright wild eyes. And he was not greatly changed, it seemed to Florian; only, the brows and nose of Tiburce cast no shadows upon his face, nor did his moving hand cast any shadow there, either, though the moon was naked overhead.

"You had forgotten the promise that was between us," said Tiburce; and his voice had not changed, much, though it was smaller.

"It is true. I had forgotten. I remember now." And Florian shivered a little, not with fear, but with distaste.

"A man prefers to forget these things when he marries. It is natural enough. But are you not afraid of me who come from yonder?"

"Why should I be afraid of you, Tiburce, who gave your life for mine?"

"I do not say. But we change yonder."

"And does love change, Tiburce? For surely love is immortal."

"Living or dead, love changes. I do not say love dies in us who may hope to gain nothing more from love. But each lies alone, in the quiet clay. And there is nothing to do, as yet, there is not anything to do in that dark place save only to think of what life was, and of what sunlight was, and of what we sang and whispered in dark places when we had lips; and of how young grass and murmuring waters and the winds of April and the high stars beget fine follies even now; and to think of how merry our loved ones still contrive to be, even now, with their new playfellows. Such reflections are not always conducive to philanthropy."

Then Florian asked concerning the old compact between these two.

"Oh, but assuredly," replied Tiburce d'Arnaye. He now discoursed of curious matters; and, as he talked, the mists about the graveyard thickened. "And so," Tiburce said, in concluding his tale, "it is not permitted that I make merry at your wedding after the fashion of those who are still in the warm flesh. But, now that you recall our ancient compact, it is permitted I have my peculiar share in the merriment, and I may drink with you to the bride's welfare."

"I drink," said Florian, as he took the proffered cup, "to the welfare of my beloved Adelaide, whom alone of women I have really loved, and whom I shall love always."

"I perceive," replied the other, "that you must still be having your joke."

Then Florian drank, and after him Tiburce. And Florian said,—

"But it is a strange drink, Tiburce, and now that you have tasted it you are changed."

"You have not changed, at least," Tiburce answered; and for the first time he smiled, a little perturbingly by reason of the change in him.

"Tell me," said Florian, "of how you fare yonder."

So Tiburce told him of yet more curious matters. Now the augmenting mists had shut off all the rest of the world. Florian could see only vague rolling graynesses and a gray and changed Tiburce sitting there, with bright wild eyes, and discoursing in a small chill voice. The appearance of a woman came, and sat beside him on the right. She, too, was gray, as became Eve's senior: and she made a sign which Florian remembered, and it troubled him.

Tiburce said then, "And now, young Florian, you who were once so dear to me, it is to your welfare I drink."

"I drink to yours, Tiburce."

Tiburce drank first: and Florian, having drunk in turn, cried out,—

"You have changed beyond recognition!"

"You have not changed," Tiburce d'Arnaye replied again. "Now let me tell you of our pastimes yonder."

With that he talked of exceedingly curious matters. And Florian began to grow dissatisfied, for Tiburce was no longer recognizable, and Tiburce whispered things uncomfortable to believe; and other eyes, as wild as his, but lit with red flarings from behind, like a beast's eyes, showed in the mists to this side and to that side, for unhappy beings were passing through the mists upon secret errands which they discharged unwillingly. Then, too, the appearance of a gray man now sat to the left of that which had been Tiburce d'Arnaye, and this newcomer was marked so that all might know who he was: and Florian's heart was troubled to note how handsome and how admirable was that desecrated face even now.

"But I must go," said Florian, "lest they miss me at Storisende, and Adelaide be worried."

"Surely it will not take long to toss off a third cup. Nay, comrade, who were once so dear, let us two now drink our last toast together. Then go, in Sclaug's name, and celebrate your marriage. But before that let us drink to the continuance of human mirth-making everywhere."

Florian drank first. Then Tiburce took his turn, looking at Florian as Tiburce drank slowly. As he drank, Tiburce d'Arnaye was changed even more, and the shape of him altered, and the shape of him trickled as though Tiburce were builded of sliding fine white sand. So Tiburce d'Arnaye returned to his own place. The appearances that had sat to his left and to his right were no longer there to trouble Florian with memories. And Florian saw that the mists of Walburga's Eve had departed, and that the sun was rising, and that the graveyard was all overgrown with nettles and tall grass.

He had not remembered the place being thus, and it seemed to him the night had passed with unnatural quickness. But he thought more of the fact that he had been beguiled into spending his wedding-night in a graveyard, in such questionable company, and of what explanation he could make to Adelaide.

II. OF YOUNG PERSONS IN MAY

The tale tells how Florian de Puysange came in the dawn through flowering gardens, and heard young people from afar, already about their maying. Two by two he saw them from afar as they went with romping and laughter into the tall woods behind Storisende to fetch back the Maypole with dubious old rites. And as they went they sang, as was customary, that song which Raimbaut de Vaqueiras made in the ancient time in honor of May's ageless triumph, and with which Florian's reputed father also had been familiar when a strange magic had made Jurgen young again in the world's annually recaptured youth.

Sang they:

"May shows with godlike showing
To-day for each that sees
May's magic overthrowing
All musty memories
In him whom May decrees

To be love's own. He saith,
'I wear love's liveries
Until released by death.'

"Thus all we laud May's sowing,
Nor heed how harvests please
When nowhere grain worth growing
Greets autumn's questing breeze,
And garnerers garner these—
Vain words and wasted breath
And spilth and tasteless lees,—
Until released by death.

"Unwillingly foreknowing
That love with May-time flees,
We take this day's bestowing,
And feed on fantasies
Such as love lends for ease
Where none but travaileth,
With lean infrequent fees,
Until released by death."

And Florian shook his sleek black head. "A very foolish and pessimistical old song, a superfluous song, and a song that is particularly out of place in the loveliest spot in the loveliest of all possible worlds."

Yet Florian took no inventory of the gardens. There was but a happy sense of green and gold, with blue topping all; of twinkling, fluent, tossing leaves and of the gray under-side of elongated, straining leaves; a sense of pert bird noises, and of a longer shadow than usual slanting before him, and a sense of youth and well-being everywhere. Certainly it was not a morning wherein pessimism might hope to flourish.

Instead, it was of Adelaide that Florian thought: of the tall, impulsive, and yet timid, fair girl who was both shrewd and innocent, and of her tenderly colored loveliness, and of his abysmally unmerited felicity in having won her. Why, but what, he reflected, grimacing—what if he had too hastily married somebody else? For he had earlier fancied other women for one reason or another: but this, he knew, was the great love of his life, and a love which would endure unchanged as long as his life lasted.

III. What Comes of Marrying Happily

The tale tells how Florian de Puysange found Adelaide in the company of two ladies who were unknown to him. One of these was very old, the other an imposing matron in middle life. The three were pleasantly shaded by young oak-trees; beyond was a tall hedge of clipped yew. The older women were at chess, while Adelaide bent her meek golden head to some of that fine needlework in which the girl delighted. And beside them rippled a small sunlit stream, which babbled and gurgled with silver flashes. Florian hastily noted these things as he ran laughing to his wife.

"Heart's dearest—!" he cried. And he saw, perplexed, that Adelaide had risen with a faint wordless cry, and was gazing at him as though she were puzzled and alarmed a very little.

"Such an adventure as I have to tell you of!" says Florian then.

"But, hey, young man, who are you that would seem to know my daughter so well?" demands the lady in middle life, and she rose majestically from her chess-game.

Florian stared, as he well might. "Your daughter, madame! But you are not Dame Melicent—"

At this the old, old woman raised her nodding head. "Dame Melicent? And was it I you were seeking, sir?"

Now Florian looked from one to the other of these incomprehensible strangers, bewildered: and his eyes came back to his lovely wife, and his lips smiled irresolutely. "Is this some jest to punish me, my dear?"

But then a new and graver trouble kindled in his face, and his eyes narrowed, for there was something odd about his wife also.

"I have been drinking in queer company," he said. "It must be that my head is not yet clear. Now certainly it seems to me that you are Adelaide de la Forêt, and certainly it seems to me that you are not Adelaide."

The girl replied, "Why, no, messire; I am Sylvie de Nointel."

"Come, come," says the middle-aged lady, briskly, "let us make an end to this play-acting, and, young fellow, let us have a sniff at you. No, you are not tipsy, after all. Well, I am glad of that. So let us get to the bottom of this business. What do they call you when you are at home?"

"Florian de Puysange," he answered, speaking meekly enough. This capable large person was to the young man rather intimidating.

"La!" said she. She looked at him very hard. She nodded gravely two or three times, so that her double chin opened and shut. "Yes, and you favor him. How old are you?"

He told her twenty-four.

She said, inconsequently: "So I was a fool, after all. Well, young man, you will never be as good-looking as your father, but I trust you have an honester nature. However, bygones are bygones. Is the old rascal still living? and was it he that had the impudence to send you to me?"

"My father, madame, was slain at the battle of Marchfeld—"

"Some fifty years ago! And you are twenty-four. Young man, your parentage had unusual features, or else we are at cross-purposes. Let us start at the beginning of this. You tell us that you are called Florian de Puysange and that you have been drinking in queer company. Now let us have the whole story."

So Florian told her of last night's happenings, with no more omissions than seemed desirable with feminine auditors.

Then the old woman said: "I think this is a true tale, my daughter, for the witches of Amneran contrive strange things, with mists to aid them, and with Lilith and Sclaug to abet. There was your own husband's grandfather, whom Sclaug held imprisoned for twenty years in the Well of Ogde—"

"But, if you come to that, Mother, the men of his family always did tell the most improbable lies, as I can very well remember—"

"—Yes, and before old Kerin's time this fate had fallen to men who were over-friendly with the dead—"

"Stuff and nonsense!" said the stout lady.

"But, no, my daughter. Thus seven persons slept at Ephesus, from the time of Decius to the time of Theodosius—"

"Still, Mother—"

"—And the proof of it is that they were called Constantine and Dionysius and John and Malchus and Marcian and Maximian and Serapion. They were duly canonized. You cannot deny that this thing happened without asserting no less than seven blessed saints to have been unprincipled liars, and that would be a very horrible heresy—"

"Yet, Mother, you know as well as I do—"

"—And thus Epimenides, another excellently spoken-of saint, slept at Athens for fifty-seven years. Thus Charlemagne slept in the Untersberg, and will sleep until the ravens of Miramon Lluagor have left his mountain. Thus Rhyming Thomas in the Eildon Hills, thus Ogier in Avalon, thus Oisin—"

The old lady bade fair to go on interminably in her gentle resolute piping old voice, but the other interrupted.

"Well, Mother, do not excite yourself about it, for it only makes your asthma worse, and does no especial good to anybody. Things may be as you say. Certainly I intended nothing irreligious. Yet these extended naps, appropriate enough for saints and emperors, are out of place in one's own family. So, if it is not stuff and nonsense, it ought to be. And that I stick to."

"But we forget the boy, my dear," said the old lady. "Now listen, Florian de Puysange. Thirty years ago last night, to the month and the day, it was that you vanished from our knowledge, leaving my daughter a forsaken bride. For I am what the years have made of Dame Melicent, and this is my daughter Adelaide, and yonder is her daughter Sylvie de Nointel."

"La, Mother," observed the stout lady, "but are you certain it was the last of April? I had been thinking it was some time in June. And I protest it could not have been all of thirty years. Let me see now, Sylvie, how old is your brother Richard? Twenty-eight, you say. Well, Mother, I always said you had a marvelous memory for things like that, and I often envy you. But how does time fly, to be sure!"

And Florian was perturbed. "For this is an awkward thing, and Tiburce has played me an unworthy trick. He never did know when to leave off joking; but such posthumous frivolity is past endurance. For, see now, in what a pickle it has landed me! I have outlived my friends, I may encounter difficulty in regaining my fiefs, and certainly I have lost the fairest wife man ever had. Oh, can it be, madame, that you are indeed my Adelaide!"

"Yes, every pound of me, poor boy, and that says much."

"—And that you have been untrue to the eternal fidelity which you vowed to me here by this very stream! Oh, but I cannot believe it was thirty years ago, for not a grass-blade or a pebble has been altered; and I perfectly remember the lapping of water under those lichened rocks, and that continuous file of ripples yonder, which are shaped like arrowheads."

Adelaide rubbed her nose. "Did I promise eternal fidelity? I can hardly remember that far back. But I remember I wept a great deal, and my parents assured me you were either dead or a rascal, so that tears could not help, either way. Then Ralph de Nointel came along, good man, and made me a fair husband, as husbands go—"

"As for that stream," then said Dame Melicent, "it is often I have thought of that stream, sitting here with my grandchildren where I once sat with gay young men whom nobody remembers now save me. Yes, it is strange to think that instantly, and within the speaking of any simple word, no

drop of water retains the place it had before the word was spoken: and yet the stream remains unchanged, and stays as it was when I sat here with those young men who are gone. Yes, that is a strange thought, and it is a sad thought, too, for those of us who are old."

"But, Mother, of course the stream remains unchanged," agreed Dame Adelaide. "Streams always do except after heavy rains. Everybody knows that, and I can see nothing very remarkable about it. As for you, Florian, if you stickle for love's being an immortal affair," she added, with a large twinkle, "I would have you know I have been a widow for three years. So the matter might be arranged."

Florian looked at her sadly. To him the situation was incongruous with the terrible archness of a fat woman. "But, madame, you are no longer the same person."

She patted him upon the shoulder. "Come, Florian, there is some sense in you, after all. Console yourself, lad, with the reflection that if you had stuck manfully by your wife instead of mooning about graveyards, I would still be just as I am to-day, and you would be tied to me. Your friend probably knew what he was doing when he drank to our welfare, for we would never have suited each other, as you can see for yourself. Well, Mother, many things fall out queerly in this world, but with age we learn to accept what happens without flustering too much over it. What are we to do with this resurrected old lover of mine?"

It was horrible to Florian to see how prosaically these women dealt with his unusual misadventure. Here was a miracle occurring virtually before their eyes, and these women accepted it with maddening tranquillity as an affair for which they were not responsible. Florian began to reflect that elderly persons were always more or less unsympathetic and inadequate.

"First of all," says Dame Melicent, "I would give him some breakfast. He must be hungry after all these years. And you could put him in Adhelmar's room—"

"But," Florian said wildly, to Dame Adelaide, "you have committed the crime of bigamy, and you are, after all, my wife!"

She replied, herself not untroubled: "Yes, but, Mother, both the cook and the butler are somewhere in the bushes yonder, up to some nonsense that I prefer to know nothing about. You know how servants are, particularly on holidays. I could scramble him some eggs, though, with a rasher. And Adhelmar's room it had better be, I suppose, though I had meant to have it turned out. But, as for bigamy and being your wife," she concluded more cheerfully, "it seems to me the least said, the soonest mended. It is to nobody's interest to rake up those foolish bygones, so far as I can see."

"Adelaide, you profane equally love, which is divine, and marriage, which is a holy sacrament."

"Florian, do you really love Adelaide de Nointel?" asked this terrible woman. "And now that I am free to listen to your proposals, do you wish to marry me?"

"Well, no," said Florian: "for, as I have just said, you are no longer the same person."

"Why, then, you see for yourself! So do you quit talking nonsense about immortality and sacraments."

"But, still," cried Florian, "love is immortal. Yes, I repeat to you, precisely as I told Tiburce, love is immortal."

Then says Dame Melicent, nodding her shriveled old head: "When I was young, and was served by nimbler senses and desires, and was housed in brightly colored flesh, there were a host of men to love me. Minstrels yet tell of the men that loved me, and of how many tall men were slain because of their love for me, and of how in the end it was Perion who won me. For the noblest and the most faithful of all my lovers was Perion of the Forest, and through tempestuous years he sought me with a love that conquered time and chance: and so he won me. Thereafter he made me a fair husband, as husbands go. But I might not stay the girl he had loved, nor might he remain the lad that Melicent had dreamed of, with dreams bedrugging the long years in which Demetrios held Melicent a prisoner, and youth went away from her. No, Perion and I could not do that, any more than might two drops of water there retain their place in the stream's flowing. So Perion and I grew old together, friendlily enough; and our senses and our desires began to serve us more drowsily, so that we did not greatly mind the falling away of youth, nor greatly mind to note what shriveled hands now moved before us, performing common tasks; and we were content enough. But of the high passion that had wedded us there was no trace, and of little senseless human bickerings there were a great many. For one thing,"—and the old lady's voice was changed,—"for one thing, he was foolishly particular about what he would eat and what he would not eat, and that upset my housekeeping, and I had never any patience with such nonsense."

"Well, but even if this was the ending of a world-famous romance," said Florian, "it is not quite nice of you to acknowledge it."

Then said Dame Adelaide: "That is a true word, Mother. All men get finicky about their food, and think they are the only persons to be considered, and there is no end to it if once you begin to humor them. So there has to be a stand made. Well, and indeed my poor Ralph, too, was all for kissing and pretty talk at first, and I accepted it willingly enough. You know how girls are. They like to be made much of, and it is perfectly natural. But that leads to children. And when the children began to come, I had not much time to bother with him: and Ralph had his farming and his warfaring to keep him busy. A man with a growing family cannot afford to neglect his affairs. And certainly, not being blind, he began to notice that girls here and there had brighter eyes and trimmer waists than I had. I do not know what such observations may have led to when Ralph was away from me: I never inquired into it, because in such matters all men are fools. But I put up with no nonsense at home, and he made me a fair husband, as husbands go. That much I will say for him gladly: and if any widow says more than that, Florian, do you beware of her, for she is an untruthful woman."

"Be that as it may," replied Florian, "it is not quite becoming to speak thus of your dead husband. No doubt you speak the truth: there is no telling what sort of person you may have married in what still seems to me unseemly haste to provide me with a successor: but, even so, a little charitable prevarication would be far more edifying."

He spoke with such earnestness that there fell a silence. The women seemed to pity him. And in the silence Florian heard from afar young persons returning from the woods behind Storisende, and bringing with them the May-pole. They were still singing.

Sang they:

"Unwillingly foreknowing
That love with May-time flees,
We take this day's bestowing,
And feed on fantasies—"

IV. Youth Solves It

The tale tells how lightly and sweetly, and compassionately, too, then spoke young Sylvie de Nointel, to Florian in his vexed loneliness. For the girl now cried out:

"Ah, but, assuredly, Messire Florian, you do not argue with my pets quite seriously! Old people always have some such queer notions. Of course love all depends upon what sort of person you are. Now, as I see it, Mama and Grandmama are not the sort of persons who have real love-affairs. Devoted as I am to both of them, I cannot but perceive they are lacking in real depth of sentiment. They simply do not understand or care about such matters.

They are fine, straightforward, practical persons, poor dears, and always have been, of course, for in things like that one does not change, as I have often noticed. And Father, and Grandfather Perion, too, as I remember him, was kindhearted and admirable and all that, but nobody could ever have expected him to be a satisfactory lover. Why, he was bald as an egg, the poor pet!"

And Sylvie laughed again at the preposterous notions of old people. She flashed an especial smile at Florian. Her hand went out as though to touch him, in an unforgotten gesture.

"Old people do not understand," said Sylvie de Nointel, in tones which took this handsome young fellow ineffably into confidence.

"Mademoiselle," said Florian, with a sigh that is part relief and all approval, "it is you who speak the truth; and your elders here have fallen victims to the cynicism of a crassly material age. Love is immortal when it is really love and when one is the right sort of person. There is the love—known to how few, alas! and a passion of which I regret to find your mother incapable,—which defies every accident of time and chance, and which endures unchanged until the end of life."

"I am so glad you think so, Messire Florian," she answered demurely.

"And do you not think so, mademoiselle?"

"How should I know," she asked him, "as yet?" He noted she had incredibly long lashes.

"Thrice happy is he that convinces you!" says Florian.

And about them, who were young in the world's recaptured youth, spring triumphed with an ageless rural pageant, and birds cried to their mates. He noted the red brevity of her lips and their probable softness.

Meanwhile the elder women regarded each other.

"It is the season of May. They are young and they are together. Poor children!" said

Dame Melicent. "Youth cries to youth for the toys of youth, and saying, 'Lo, I cry with the voice of a great god!'"

"Still," said Madame Adelaide, "Puysange is a good fief—"

"As if that mattered!" cried her daughter, indignantly. "My mother, you are a deplorably sordid person."

And Florian also did not heed his elders with any real attention as he stood there by the sunlit stream, in which no drop of water retained its place for a moment, and which yet did not alter in appearance at all. He did not heed his elders for the excellent reason that Sylvie de Nointel was now

about to speak again; and he preferred to listen to her.

For, this girl, he knew, was lovelier than any other person had ever been since Eve first raised just such admiring, innocent, and venturesome eyes to inspect what must have seemed to her the quaintest of all animals, called man. So it was with a shrug that Florian remembered how he had earlier fancied other women for one reason or another; since this, as he now knew—for the tenth time or, it might be, for the eleventh, —was the great love of his life, and a love which would, quite certainly, endure unchanged as long as Florian's life lasted.

Sinclair Lewis
1885

SINCLAIR LEWIS' father, of Welsh descent and New England background, was a physician at Sauk Center, Minnesota. Lewis attended the Sauk Center high school and then entered Yale, where he did much writing and helped to edit a literary magazine. His college career was interrupted by his conversion to Socialism and a period spent (as janitor) at Upton Sinclair's Helicon Hall. After graduation in 1907 he held for brief periods many journalistic jobs and minor editorial posts, while he acquired competence and a limited reputation as a writer of entertaining fiction.

Lewis's first serious novel, *Main Street* (1920), published by a new firm after many rejections, was conspicuously popular in the America of the early 1920's, and was translated into many European languages. In 1930 Lewis was awarded a Nobel Prize in literature; he was the first American to be so honored. In the 1930's Lewis became strongly interested in the theatre, both as writer and as actor.

In addition to *Main Street*, Lewis' novels include *Our Mr. Wrenn* (1914); *The Job* (1917); *Babbitt* (1922); *Arrowsmith* (1925); *Elmer Gantry* (1927); *Dodsworth* (1929); *Ann Vickers* (1933); *Work of Art* (1934); *It Can't Happen Here* (1935); *The Prodigal Parents* (1938); *Bethel Merriday* (1940); *Gideon Planish* (1943); *Cass Timberlane* (1945); and *Kingsblood Royal* (1947).

[See Carl Van Doren's *Sinclair Lewis* (New York, 1933) and Warren Beck's "How Good Is Sinclair Lewis?" in *College English*, IX (January, 1948), 173-180.]

From
BABBITT
[1922]

CHAPTER I

I

THE TOWERS of Zenith aspired above the morning mist; austere towers of steel and cement and limestone, sturdy as cliffs and delicate as silver rods. They were neither citadels nor churches, but frankly and beautifully office-buildings.

The mist took pity on the fretted structures of earlier generations: the Post Office with its shingle-tortured mansard, the red brick minarets of hulking old houses, factories with stingy and sooted windows, wooden tenements colored like mud. The city was full of such grotesqueries, but the clean towers were thrusting them from the business center, and on the farther hills were shining new houses, homes—they seemed—for laughter and tranquillity.

Over a concrete bridge fled a limousine of long sleek hood and noiseless engine. These people in evening clothes were returning from an all-night rehearsal of a Little Theater play, an artistic adventure considerably illuminated by champagne. Below the bridge curved a railroad, a maze of green and crimson lights. The New York Flyer boomed past, and twenty lines of polished steel leaped into the glare.

In one of the skyscrapers the wires of the Associated Press were closing down. The telegraph operators wearily raised their celluloid eye-shades after a night of talking with Paris and Peking. Through the building crawled the scrubwomen, yawning, their old shoes slapping. The dawn mist spun away. Cues of men with lunch-boxes clumped toward the immensity of new factories, sheets of glass and hollow tile, glittering shops where five thousand men worked beneath one roof, pouring out the honest wares that would be sold up the Euphrates and across the veldt. The whistles rolled out in greeting a chorus cheerful as the April dawn; the song of labor in a city built—it seemed—for giants.

II

There was nothing of the giant in the aspect of the man who was beginning to awaken on the sleeping-porch of a Dutch Colonial house in that residential district of Zenith known as Floral Heights.

His name was George F. Babbitt. He was forty-six years old now, in April 1920, and he made nothing in particular, neither butter nor shoes nor poetry, but he was nimble in the calling of selling houses for more than people could afford to pay.

His large head was pink, his brown hair thin and dry. His face was babyish in slumber, despite his wrinkles and the red spectacle-dents on the slopes of his nose. He was not fat but he was exceedingly well fed; his cheeks were pads, and the unroughened hand which lay helpless upon the khaki-colored blanket was slightly puffy. He seemed prosperous, extremely married and unromantic; and altogether unromantic appeared this sleeping-porch, which looked on one sizable elm, two respectable grass-plots, a cement driveway, and a corrugated iron garage. Yet Babbitt was again dreaming of the fairy child, a dream more romantic than scarlet pagodas by a silver sea.

For years the fairy child had come to him. Where others saw but Georgie Babbitt, she discerned gallant youth. She waited for him, in the darkness beyond mysterious groves. When at last he could slip away from the crowded house he darted to her. His wife, his clamoring friends, sought to follow, but he escaped, the girl fleet beside him, and they crouched together on a shadowy hillside. She was so slim, so white, so eager! She cried that he was gay and valiant, that she would wait for him, that they would sail—

Rumble and bang of the milk-truck.

Babbitt moaned, turned over, struggled back toward his dream. He could see only her face now, beyond misty waters. The furnace-man slammed the basement door. A dog barked in the next yard. As Babbitt sank blissfully into a dim warm tide, the paper-carrier went by whistling, and the rolled-up *Advocate* thumped the front door. Babbitt roused, his stomach constricted with alarm. As he relaxed, he was pierced by the familiar and irritating rattle of someone cranking a Ford: snap-ah-ah, snap-ah-ah, snap-ah-ah. Himself a pious motorist, Babbitt cranked with the unseen driver, with him waited through taut hours for the roar of the starting engine, with him agonized as the roar ceased and again began the infernal patient snap-ah-ah—a round, flat sound, a shivering cold-morning sound, a sound infuriating and inescapable. Not till the rising voice of the motor told him that the Ford was moving was he released from the panting tension. He glanced once at his favorite tree, elm twigs against the gold patina of sky, and fumbled for sleep as for a drug. He who had been a boy very credulous of life was no longer greatly interested in the possible and improbable adventures of each new day.

He escaped from reality till the alarm-clock rang, at seven-twenty.

III

It was the best of nationally advertised and quantitatively produced alarm-clocks, with all modern attachments, including cathedral chime, intermittent alarm, and a phosphorescent dial. Babbitt was proud of being awakened by such a rich device. Socially it was almost as creditable as buying expensive cord tires.

He sulkily admitted now that there was no more escape, but he lay and detested the grind of the real-estate business, and disliked his family, and disliked himself for disliking them. The evening before, he had played poker at Vergil Gunch's till midnight, and after such holidays he was irritable before breakfast. It may have been the tremendous home-brewed beer of the prohibition-era and the cigars to which that beer enticed him; it may have been

resentment of return from this fine, bold man-world to a restricted region of wives and stenographers, and of suggestions not to smoke so much.

From the bedroom beside the sleeping-porch, his wife's detestably cheerful "Time to get up, Georgie boy," and the itchy sound, the brisk and scratchy sound, of combing hairs out of a stiff brush.

He grunted; he dragged his thick legs, in faded baby-blue pajamas, from under the khaki blanket; he sat on the edge of the cot, running his fingers through his wild hair, while his plump feet mechanically felt for his slippers. He looked regretfully at the blanket—forever a suggestion to him of freedom and heroism. He had bought it for a camping trip which had never come off. It symbolized gorgeous loafing, gorgeous cursing, virile flannel shirts.

He creaked to his feet, groaning at the waves of pain which passed behind his eyeballs. Though he waited for their scorching recurrence, he looked blurrily out at the yard. It delighted him, as always; it was the neat yard of a successful business man of Zenith, that is, it was perfection, and made him also perfect. He regarded the corrugated iron garage. For the three-hundred-and-sixty-fifth time in a year he reflected, "No class to that tin shack. Have to build me a frame garage. But by golly it's the only thing on the place that isn't up-to-date!" While he stared he thought of a community garage for his acreage development, Glen Oriole. He stopped puffing and jiggling. His arms were akimbo. His petulant, sleep-swollen face was set in harder lines. He suddenly seemed capable, an official, a man to contrive, to direct, to get things done.

On the vigor of his idea he was carried down the hard, clean, unused-looking hall into the bathroom.

Though the house was not large it had, like all houses on Floral Heights, an altogether royal bathroom of porcelain and glazed tile and metal sleek as silver. The towel-rack was a rod of clear glass set in nickel. The tub was long enough for a Prussian Guard, and above the set bowl was a sensational exhibit of tooth-brush holder, shaving-brush holder, soap-dish, sponge-dish, and medicine-cabinet, so glittering and so ingenious that they resembled an electrical instrument-board. But the Babbitt whose god was Modern Appliances was not pleased. The air of the bathroom was thick with the smell of a heathen tooth-paste. "Verona been at it again! 'Stead of sticking to Lilidol, like I've re-peat-ed-ly asked her, she's gone and gotten some confounded stinkum stuff that makes you sick!"

The bath-mat was wrinkled and the floor was wet. (His daughter Verona eccentrically took baths in the morning, now and then.) He slipped on the mat, and slid against the tub. He said "Damn!" Furiously he snatched up his tube of shaving-cream, furiously he lathered, with a belligerent slapping of the unctuous brush, furiously he raked his plump cheeks with a safety-razor. It pulled. The blade was dull. He said, "Damn—oh—oh—damn it!"

He hunted through the medicine-cabinet for a packet of new razor-blades (reflecting, as invariably, "Be cheaper to buy one of these dinguses and strop your own blades") and when he discovered the packet, behind the round box of bicarbonate of soda, he thought ill of his wife for putting it there and very well of himself for not saying "Damn." But he did say it, immediately afterward, when with wet and soap-slippery fingers he tried to remove the horrible little envelope and crisp clinging oiled paper from the new blade.

Then there was the problem, oft-pondered, never solved, of what to do with the old blade, which might imperil the fingers of his young. As usual, he tossed it on top of the medicine-cabinet, with a mental note that some day he must remove the fifty or sixty other blades that were also temporarily piled up there. He finished his shaving in a growing testiness increased by his spinning headache and by the emptiness in his stomach. When he was done, his round face smooth and streamy and his eyes stinging from soapy water, he reached for a towel. The family towels were wet, wet and clammy and vile, all of them wet, he found, as he blindly snatched them—his own face-towel, his wife's, Verona, Ted's, Tinka's, and the lone bath-towel with the huge welt of initial. Then George F. Babbitt did a dismaying thing. He wiped his face on the guest-towel! It was a pansy-embroidered trifle which always hung there to indicate that the Babbitts were in the best Floral Heights society. No one had ever used it. No guest had ever dared to. Guests secretively took a corner of the nearest regular towel.

He was raging, "By golly, here they go and use up all the towels, every doggone one of 'em, and they use 'em and get 'em all wet and sopping, and never put out a dry one for me—of course, I'm the goat!—and then I want one and—I'm the only person in the doggone house that's got the slightest doggone bit of consideration for other people and thoughtfulness and consider there may be others that may want to use the doggone bathroom after me and consider—"

He was pitching the chill abominations into the bath-tub, pleased by the vindictiveness of that desolate flapping sound; and in the midst his wife serenely trotted in, observed serenely, "Why Georgie dear, what are you doing? Are you going to wash out the towels? Why, you needn't wash out the towels. Oh, Georgie, you didn't go and use the guest-towel, did you?"

It is not recorded that he was able to answer.

For the first time in weeks he was sufficiently roused by his wife to look at her.

IV

Myra Babbitt—Mrs. George F. Babbitt —was definitely mature. She had creases from the corners of her mouth to the bottom of her chin, and her plump neck bagged. But the thing that marked her as having passed the line was that she no longer had reticences before her husband, and no longer worried about not having reticences. She was in a petticoat now, and corsets which bulged, and unaware of being seen in bulgy corsets. She had become so dully habituated to married life that in her full matronliness she was as sexless as an anemic nun. She was a good woman, a kind woman, a diligent woman, but no one, save perhaps Tinka her ten-year-old, was at all interested in her or entirely aware that she was alive.

After a rather thorough discussion of all the domestic and social aspects of towels she apologized to Babbitt for his having an alcoholic headache; and he recovered enough to endure the search for a B.V.D. undershirt which had, he pointed out, malevolently been concealed among his clean pajamas.

He was fairly amiable in the conference on the brown suit.

"What do you think, Myra?" He pawed at the clothes hunched on a chair in their bedroom, while she moved about mysteriously adjusting and patting her petticoat and, to his jaundiced eye, never seeming to get on with her dressing. "How about it? Shall I wear the brown suit another day?"

"Well, it looks awfully nice on you."

"I know, but gosh, it needs pressing."

"That's so. Perhaps it does."

"It certainly could stand being pressed, all right."

"Yes, perhaps it wouldn't hurt it to be pressed."

"But gee, the coat doesn't need pressing. No sense in having the whole darn suit pressed, when the coat doesn't need it."

"That's so."

"But the pants certainly need it, all right. Look at them—look at those wrinkles—the pants certainly do need pressing."

"That's so. Oh, Georgie, why couldn't you wear the brown coat with the blue trousers we were wondering what we'd do with them?"

"Good Lord! Did you ever in all my life know me to wear the coat of one suit and the pants of another? What do you think I am? A busted bookkeeper?"

"Well, why don't you put on the dark gray suit to-day, and stop in at the tailor and leave the brown trousers?"

"Well, they certainly need—Now where the devil is that gray suit? Oh, yes, here we are."

He was able to get through the other crises of dressing with comparative resoluteness and calm.

His first adornment was the sleeveless dimity B.V.D. undershirt, in which he resembled a small boy humorlessly wearing a cheesecloth tabard at a civic pageant. He never put on B.V.D.'s without thanking the God of Progress that he didn't wear tight, long, old-fashioned undergarments, like his father-in-law and partner, Henry Thompson. His second embellishment was combing and slicking back his hair. It gave him a tremendous forehead, arching up two inches beyond the former hair-line. But most wonder-working of all was the donning of his spectacles.

There is character in spectacles—the pretentious tortoise-shell, the meek pince-nez of the school teacher, the twisted silver-framed glasses of the old villager. Babbitt's spectacles had huge, circular, frameless lenses of the very best glass; the ear-pieces were thin bars of gold. In them he was the modern business man; one who gave orders to clerks and drove a car and played occasional golf and was scholarly in regard to Salesmanship. His head suddenly appeared not babyish but weighty, and you noted his heavy, blunt nose, his straight mouth and thick, long upper lip, his chin over-fleshy but strong; with respect you beheld him put on the rest of his uniform as a Solid Citizen.

The gray suit was well cut, well made,

and completely undistinguished. It was a standard suit. White piping on the V of the vest added a flavor of law and learning. His shoes were black laced boots, good boots, honest boots, standard boots, extraordinarily uninteresting boots. The only frivolity was in his purple knitted scarf. With considerable comment on the matter to Mrs. Babbitt (who, acrobatically fastening the back of her blouse to her skirt with a safety-pin, did not hear a word he said), he chose between the purple scarf and a tapestry effect with stringless brown harps among blown palms, and into it he thrust a snake-head pin with opal eyes.

A sensational event was changing from the brown suit to the gray the contents of his pockets. He was earnest about these objects. They were of eternal importance, like baseball or the Republican Party. They included a fountain pen and a silver pencil (always lacking a supply of new leads) which belonged in the righthand upper vest pocket. Without them he would have felt naked. On his watch-chain were a gold penknife, silver cigar-cutter, seven keys (the use of two of which he had forgotten), and incidentally a good watch. Depending from the chain was a large, yellowish elk's-tooth—proclamation of his membership in the Benevolent and Protective Order of Elks. Most significant of all was his loose-leaf pocket note-book, that modern and efficient note-book which contained the addresses of people whom he had forgotten, prudent memoranda of postal money-orders which had reached their destinations months ago, stamps which had lost their mucilage, clippings of verses by T. Cholmondeley Frink and of the newspaper editorials from which Babbitt got his opinions and his polysyllables, notes to be sure and do things which he did not intend to do, and one curious inscription—D.S.S.D.M.Y.P.D.F.

But he had no cigarette-case. No one had ever happened to give him one, so he hadn't the habit, and people who carried cigarette-cases he regarded as effeminate.

Last, he stuck in his lapel the Boosters' Club button. With the conciseness of great art the button displayed two words: "Boosters—Pep!" It made Babbitt feel loyal and important. It associated him with Good Fellows, with men who were nice and human, and important in business circles. It was his V.C., his Legion of Honor ribbon, his Phi Beta Kappa key.

With the subtleties of dressing ran other complex worries. "I feel kind of punk this morning," he said. "I think I had too much dinner last evening. You oughtn't to serve those heavy banana fritters."

"But you asked me to have some."

"I know, but—I tell you, when a fellow gets past forty he has to look after his digestion. There's a lot of fellows that don't take proper care of themselves. I tell you at forty a man's a fool or his doctor—I mean, his own doctor. Folks don't give enough attention to this matter of dieting. Now I think—Course a man ought to have a good meal after the day's work, but it would be a good thing for both of us if we took lighter lunches."

"But Georgie, here at home I always do have a light lunch."

"Mean to imply I make a hog of myself, eating down-town? Yes, sure! You'd have a swell time if you had to eat the truck that new steward hands out to us at the Athletic Club! But I certainly do feel out of sorts, this morning. Funny, got a pain down here on the left side—but no, that wouldn't be appendicitis, would it? Last night, when I was driving over to Verg Gunch's, I felt a pain in my stomach, too. Right here it was—kind of a sharp shooting pain. I—Where'd that dime go to? Why don't you serve more prunes at breakfast? Of course I eat an apple every evening—an apple a day keeps the doctor away—but still, you ought to have more prunes, and not all these fancy doo-dads."

"The last time I had prunes you didn't eat them."

"Well, I didn't feel like eating 'em, I suppose. Matter of fact, I think I did eat some of 'em. Anyway—I tell you it's mighty important to—I was saying to Verg Gunch, just last evening, most people don't take sufficient care of their diges—"

"Shall we have the Gunches for our dinner, next week?"

"Why sure; you bet."

"Now see here, George: I want you to put on your nice dinner-jacket that evening."

"Rats! The rest of 'em won't want to dress."

"Of course they will. You remember when you didn't dress for the Littlefields' supper-party, and all the rest did, and how embarrassed you were."

"Embarrassed, hell! I wasn't embarrassed. Everybody knows I can put on as expensive a Tux. as anybody else, and I should worry if I don't happen to have it on sometimes. All a darn nuisance, anyway. All right for a woman, that stays around the house all the time, but when a fellow's worked like the dickens all day, he doesn't want to go and hustle his head off getting into the soup-and-fish for a lot of folks that he's seen in just reg'lar ordinary clothes that same day."

"You know you enjoy being seen in one. The other evening you admitted you were glad I'd insisted on your dressing. You said you felt a lot better for it. And oh, Georgie, I do wish you wouldn't say 'Tux.' It's 'dinner-jacket.'"

"Rats, what's the odds?"

"Well, it's what all the nice folks say. Suppose Lucile McKelvey heard you calling it a 'Tux.'"

"Well, that's all right now! Lucile McKelvey can't pull anything on me! Her folks are common as mud, even if her husband and her dad are millionaires! I suppose you're trying to rub in your exalted social position! Well, let me tell you that your revered paternal ancestor, Henry T., doesn't even call it a 'Tux.'! He calls it a 'bobtail jacket for a ringtail monkey,' and you couldn't get him into one unless you chloroformed him!"

"Now don't be horrid, George."

"Well, I don't want to be horrid, but Lord! you're getting as fussy as Verona. Ever since she got out of college she's been too rambunctious to live with—doesn't know what she wants—well, I know what she wants!—all she wants is to marry a millionaire, and live in Europe, and hold some preacher's hand, and simultaneously at the same time stay right here in Zenith and be some blooming kind of a socialist agitator or boss charity-worker or some damn thing! Lord, and Ted is just as bad! He wants to go to college, and he doesn't want to go to college. Only one of the three that knows her own mind is Tinka. Simply can't understand how I ever came to have a pair of shillyshallying children like Rone and Ted. I may not be any Rockefeller or James J. Shakespeare, but I certainly do know my own mind, and I do keep right on plugging along in the office and—Do you know the latest? Far as I can figure out, Ted's new bee is he'd like to be a movie actor and—and here I've told him a hundred times, if he'll go to college and law-school and make good, I'll set him up in business and—Verona's just exactly as bad. Doesn't know what she wants. Well, well, come on! Aren't you ready yet? The girl rang the bell three minutes ago."

V

Before he followed his wife, Babbitt stood at the westernmost window of their room. This residential settlement, Floral Heights, was on a rise; and though the center of the city was three miles away—Zenith had between three and four hundred thousand inhabitants now—he could see the top of the Second National Tower, an Indiana limestone building of thirty-five stories.

Its shining walls rose against April sky to a simple cornice like a streak of white fire. Integrity was in the tower, and decision. It bore its strength lightly as a tall soldier. As Babbitt stared, the nervousness was soothed from his face, his slack chin lifted in reverence. All he articulated was "That's one lovely sight!" but he was inspired by the rhythm of the city; his love of it renewed. He beheld the tower as a temple-spire of the religion of business, a faith passionate, exalted, surpassing common men; and as he clumped down to breakfast he whistled the ballad "Oh, by gee, by gosh, by jingo" as though it were a hymn melancholy and noble.

1876 ∽ *Sherwood Anderson* ∽ 1942

A NDERSON came to writing late, after widely varied experience in business, especially in advertising. A precarious childhood in small Ohio towns, reflected to some extent in his first novel, *Windy McPherson's Son* (1916), qualified him for the profoundly sympathetic understanding of unhappy and ill-adjusted human beings which is revealed in all his works. It was in Chicago that he began writing fiction. He lived for a time in New York, but in 1925 bought a farm near Marion, Virginia, and spent most of the rest of his life there. For a time he owned and edited both of Marion's local newspapers. Anderson's finest achievements in fiction are among his short stories collected in *Winesburg, Ohio* (1919); *The Triumph of the Egg* (1921); *Horses and Men* (1923); and *Death in the Woods* (1933). His most important novels, *Poor White* (1920) and *Dark Laughter* (1925), deal in part with the effect of industrialism on human personality. His poems in *Mid-American Chants* (1918) and *A New Testament* (1927) show the influence of Whitman in both form and ideas. Among his autobiographical books are *A Story-Teller's Story* (1924), *Sherwood Anderson's Notebook* (1926), *Hello Towns* (1929), and *Sherwood Anderson's Memoirs* (1942).

[See N. B. Fagan's *The Phenomenon of Sherwood Anderson* (New York, 1927), Harry Hartwick's *The Foreground of American Fiction* (New York, 1934), and M. Geismar's *The Last of the Provincials* (Boston, 1947).]

DEATH IN THE WOODS
[1933 (1926)]

SHE WAS an old woman and lived on a farm near the town in which I lived. All country and small-town people have seen such old women, but no one knows much about them. Such an old woman comes into town driving an old worn-out horse or she comes afoot carrying a basket. She may own a few hens and have eggs to sell. She brings them in a basket and takes them to a grocer. There she trades them in. She gets some salt pork and some beans. Then she gets a pound or two of sugar and some flour.

Afterward she goes to the butcher's and asks for some dog meat. She may spend ten or fifteen cents, but when she does she asks for something. In my day the butchers gave liver to anyone who wanted to carry it away. In our family we were always having it. Once one of my brothers got a whole cow's liver at the slaughter-house near the fair-grounds. We had it until we were sick of it. It never cost a cent. I have hated the thought of it ever since.

The old farm woman got some liver and a soup bone. She never visited with any-one, and as soon as she got what she wanted she lit out for home. It made quite a load for such an old body. No one gave her a lift. People drive right down a road and never notice an old woman like that.

There was such an old woman used to come into town past our house one sum-mer and fall when I was sick with what was called inflammatory rheumatism. She went home later carrying a heavy pack on her back. Two or three large gaunt-look-ing dogs followed at her heels.

The old woman was nothing special. She was one of the nameless ones that hardly anyone knows, but she got into my thoughts. I have just suddenly now, after all these years, remembered her and what happened. It is a story. Her name was, I think, Grimes, and she lived with her husband and son in a small unpainted house on the bank of a small creek four miles from town.

The husband and son were a tough lot. Although the son was but twenty-one, he had already served a term in jail. It was whispered about that the woman's husband stole horses and ran them off to some other county. Now and then, when a horse turned up missing, the man had also disappeared. No one ever caught him. Once, when I was loafing at Tom White-head's livery barn, the man came there and sat on the bench in front. Two or three other men were there, but no one spoke to him. He sat for a few minutes and then got up and went away. When he was leaving he turned around and stared at the men. There was a look of defiance in his eyes. "Well, I have tried to be friendly. You don't want to talk to me.

It has been so wherever I have gone in this town. If, some day, one of your fine horses turns up missing, well, then what?" He did not say anything actually. "I'd like to bust one of you on the jaw," was about what his eyes said. I remember how the look in his eyes made me shiver.

The old man belonged to a family that had had money once. His name was Grimes, Jake Grimes. It all comes back clearly now. His father, John Grimes, had owned a sawmill when the country was new and had made money. Then he got to drinking and running after women. When he died, there wasn't much left.

Jake blew in the rest. Pretty soon there wasn't any more lumber to cut and his land was nearly all gone.

He got his wife off a German farmer, for whom he went to work one June day in the wheat harvest. She was a young thing then and scared to death. You see, the farmer was up to something with the girl —she was, I think, a bound girl, and his wife had her suspicions. She took it out on the girl when the man wasn't around. Then, when the wife had to go off to town for supplies, the farmer got after her. She told young Jake that nothing really ever happened, but he didn't know whether to believe it or not.

He got her pretty easy himself, the first time he was out with her. He wouldn't have married her if the German farmer hadn't tried to tell him where to get off. He got her to go riding with him in his buggy one night when he was threshing on the place, and then he came for her the next Sunday night.

She managed to get out of the house without her employer's seeing, but when she was getting into the buggy he showed up. It was almost dark, and he just popped up suddenly at the horse's head. He grabbed the horse by the bridle and Jake got out his buggy whip.

They had it out all right! The German was a tough one. Maybe he didn't care whether his wife knew or not. Jake hit him over the face and shoulders with the buggy whip, but the horse got to acting up and he had to get out.

Then the two men went for it. The girl didn't see it. The horse started to run away and went nearly a mile down the road before the girl got him stopped. Then she managed to tie him to a tree beside the road. (I wonder how I know all this. It must have stuck in my mind from small-town tales when I was a boy.) Jake found her there after he got through with the German. She was huddled up in the buggy seat, crying, scared to death. She told Jake a lot of stuff, how the German had tried to get her, how he chased her once into the barn, how another time, when they happened to be alone in the barn together, he tore her dress open clear down the front. The German, she said, might have got her that time if he hadn't heard his old woman drive in at the gate. She had been off to town for supplies. Well, she would be putting the horse in the barn. The German managed to sneak off to the fields without his wife seeing. He told the girl he would kill her if she told. What could she do? She told a lie about ripping her dress in the barn when she was feeding the stock. I remember now that she was a bound girl and did not know where her father and mother were. Maybe she did not have any father. You know what I mean.

II

She married Jake and had a son and daughter but the daughter died.

Then she settled down to feed stock. That was her job. At the German's place she had cooked the food for the German and his wife. The wife was a strong woman with big hips and worked most of the time in the fields with her husband. She fed them and fed the cows in the barn, fed the pigs, the horses, and the chickens. Every moment of every day as a young girl was spent feeding something.

Then she married Jake Grimes and he had to be fed. She was a slight thing, and when she had been married for three or four years, and after the two children were born, her slender shoulders became stooped.

Jake always had a lot of big dogs around the house, that stood near the unused sawmill near the creek. He was always trading horses when he wasn't stealing something, and had a lot of poor bony ones about. Also, he kept three or four pigs and a cow. They were all pastured in the few acres left of the Grimes place and Jake did little.

He went into debt for a threshing outfit and ran it for several years, but it did not pay. People did not trust him. They were afraid he would steal the grain at night. He had to go a long way off to get work, and it cost too much to get there. In the winter he hunted and cut a little firewood, to be sold in some near-by town. When the boy grew up he was just like his father. They got drunk together. If there wasn't anything to eat in the house when they came home the old man gave his old woman a cut over the head. She had a few chickens of her own and had to kill one of them in a hurry. When they were all killed she wouldn't have any eggs to sell when she went to town, and then what would she do?

She had to scheme all her life about getting things fed, getting the pigs fed so they would grow fat and could be butchered in the fall. When they were butchered her husband took most of the meat off to town and sold it. If he did not do it first the boy did. They fought sometimes and when they fought the old woman stood aside trembling.

She had got the habit of silence anyway—that was fixed. Sometimes, when she began to look old—she wasn't forty yet—and when the husband and son were both off, trading horses or drinking or hunting or stealing, she went around the house and the barnyard muttering to herself.

How was she going to get everything fed?—that was her problem. The dogs had to be fed. There wasn't enough hay in the barn for the cow and the horses. If she didn't feed the chickens how could they lay eggs? Without eggs to sell how could she get things in town, things she had to have to keep the life of the farm going? Thank heaven, she did not have to feed her husband—in a certain way. That hadn't lasted long after their marriage and after the babies came. Where he went on his long trips she did not know. Sometimes he was gone from home for weeks, and after the boy grew up they went off together.

They left everything at home for her to manage and she had no money. She knew no one. No one ever talked to her in town. When it was winter she had to gather sticks of wood for her fire, had to try to keep the stock fed with very little grain.

The stock in the barn cried to her hungrily, the dogs followed her about. In the winter the hens laid few enough eggs. They huddled in the corners of the barn and she kept watching them. If a hen lays an egg in the barn in the winter and you do not find it, it freezes and breaks.

One day in winter the old woman went off to town with a few eggs and the dogs followed her. She did not get started until nearly three o'clock and the snow was heavy. She hadn't been feeling very well for several days and so she went muttering along, scantily clad, her shoulders stooped. She had an old grain bag in which she carried her eggs, tucked away down in the bottom. There weren't many of them, but in winter the price of eggs is up. She would get a little meat for the eggs, some salt pork, a little sugar, and some coffee, perhaps. It might be the butcher would give her a piece of liver.

When she had got to town and was trading in her eggs the dogs lay by the door outside. She did pretty well, got the things she needed, more than she had hoped. Then she went to the butcher and he gave her some liver and some dog meat.

It was the first time anyone had spoken to her in a friendly way for a long time. The butcher was alone in his shop when she went in and was annoyed by the thought of such a sick-looking old woman out on such a day. It was bitter cold and the snow, that had let up during the afternoon, was falling again. The butcher said something about her husband and her son, swore at them, and the old woman stared at him, a look of mild surprise in her eyes as he talked. He said that if either the husband or the son were going to get any of the liver or the heavy bones with scraps of meat hanging to them that he had put into the grain bag, he'd see him starve first.

Starve, eh? Well, things had to be fed. Men had to be fed, and the horses that weren't any good but maybe could be traded off, and the poor thin cow that hadn't given any milk for three months.

Horses, cows, pigs, dogs, men.

III

The old woman had to get back before darkness came if she could. The dogs followed at her heels, sniffing at the heavy grain bag she had fastened on her back. When she got to the edge of town she stopped by a fence and tied the bag on her back with a piece of rope she had carried in her dress pocket for just that purpose. That was an easier way to carry it. Her arms ached. It was hard when she had to crawl over fences, and once she fell over and landed in the snow. The dogs went frisking about. She had to struggle to get to her feet again, but she made it. The point of climbing over the fences was that there was a short cut over a hill and through a wood. She might have gone around by the road, but it was a mile farther that way. She was afraid she couldn't make it. And then, besides, the stock had to be fed. There was a little hay left, a little corn. Perhaps her husband and son would bring some home when they came. They had driven off in the only buggy the Grimes family had, a rickety thing, a rickety horse hitched to the buggy, two other rickety horses led by halters. They were going to trade horses, get a little money if they could. They might come home drunk. It would be well to have something in the house when they came back.

The son had an affair on with a woman at the county seat, fifteen miles away. She was a bad woman, a tough one. Once, in the summer, the son had brought her to the house. Both she and the son had been drinking. Jake Grimes was away and the son and his woman ordered the old woman about like a servant. She didn't mind much; she was used to it. Whatever happened, she never said anything. That was her way of getting along. She had managed that way when she was a young girl at the German's and ever since she had married Jake. That time her son brought his woman to the house they stayed all night, sleeping together just as though they were married. It hadn't shocked the old woman, not much. She had got past being shocked early in life.

With the pack on her back she went painfully along across an open field, wading in the deep snow, and got into the woods.

There was a path, but it was hard to follow. Just beyond the top of the hill, where the wood was thickest, there was a small clearing. Had someone once thought of building a house there? The clearing was as large as a building lot in town, large enough for a house and a garden. The path ran along the side of the clearing and when she got there the old woman sat down to rest at the foot of a tree.

It was a foolish thing to do. When she got herself placed, the pack against the tree's trunk, it was nice, but what about getting up again? She worried about that for a moment and then quietly closed her eyes.

She must have slept for a time. When you are about so cold you can't get any colder. The afternoon grew a little warmer and the snow came thicker than ever. Then after a time the weather cleared. The moon even came out.

There were four Grimes dogs that had followed Mrs. Grimes into town, all tall gaunt fellows. Such men as Jake Grimes and his son always keep just such dogs. They kick and abuse them, but they stay. The Grimes dogs, in order to keep from starving, had to do a lot of foraging for themselves, and they had been at it while the old woman slept with her back to the tree at the side of the clearing. They had been chasing rabbits in the woods and in adjoining fields, and in their ranging had picked up three other farm dogs.

After a time all the dogs came back to the clearing. They were excited about something. Such nights, cold and clear and with a moon, do things to dogs. It may be that some old instinct, come down from the time when they were wolves and ranged the woods in packs on winter nights, comes back into them.

The dogs in the clearing, before the old woman, had caught two or three rabbits and their immediate hunger had been satisfied. They began to play, running in circles in the clearing. Round and round they ran, each dog's nose at the tail of the next dog. In the clearing, under the snow-laden trees and under the wintry moon they made a strange picture, running thus silently, in a circle their running had beaten in the soft snow. The dogs made no sound. They ran around and around in the circle.

It may have been that the old woman saw them doing that before she died. She may have awakened once or twice and looked at the strange sight with dim old eyes.

She wouldn't be very cold now, just drowsy. Life hangs on a long time. Perhaps the old woman was out of her head. She may have dreamed of her girlhood, at the German's, and before that, when she was a child and before her mother lit out and left her.

Her dreams couldn't have been very pleasant. Not many pleasant things had happened to her. Now and then one of the Grimes dogs left the running circle and came to stand before her. The dog thrust his face close to her face. His red tongue was hanging out.

The running of the dogs may have been a kind of death ceremony. It may have been that the primitive instinct of the wolf, having been aroused in the dogs by the night and the running, made them somehow afraid.

"Now we are no longer wolves. We are dogs, the servants of men. Keep alive, man! When man dies we become wolves again."

When one of the dogs came to where the old woman sat with her back against the tree and thrust his nose close to her face he seemed satisfied and went back to run with the pack. All the Grimes dogs did it at some time during the evening, before she died. I knew all about it afterward, when I grew to be a man, because once in a wood on another winter night I saw a pack of dogs act just like that. The dogs were waiting for me to die as they had waited for the old woman that night when I was a child, but when it happened to me I was a young man and had no intention whatever of dying.

The old woman died softly and quietly. When she was dead and when one of the Grimes dogs had come to her and had found her dead all the dogs stopped running.

They gathered about her.

Well, she was dead now. She had fed the Grimes dogs when she was alive, what about now?

There was the pack on her back, the grain bag containing the piece of salt pork, the liver the butcher had given her, the dog meat, the soup bones. The butcher in town, having been suddenly overcome with a feeling of pity, had loaded her grain bag heavily. It had been a big haul for the old woman.

A big haul for the dogs now.

IV

One of the Grimes dogs sprang suddenly out from among the others and began worrying the pack on the old woman's back. Had the dogs really been wolves that one would have been the leader of the pack. What he did, all the others did.

All of them sank their teeth into the grain bag the old woman had fastened with ropes to her back.

They dragged the old woman's body out into the open clearing. The worn-out dress was quickly torn from her shoulders. When she was found, a day or two later, the dress had been torn from her body clear to the hips but the dogs had not touched her body. They had got the meat out of the grain bag, that was all. Her body was frozen stiff when it was found and the shoulders were so narrow and the body so slight that in death it looked like the body of some charming young girl.

Such things happened in towns of the Middle West, on farms near town, when I was a boy. A hunter out after rabbits found the old woman's body and did not touch it. Something, the beaten round path in the little snow-covered clearing, the silence of the place, the place where the dogs had worried the body trying to pull the grain bag away or tear it open— something startled the man and he hurried off to town.

I was in Main Street with one of my brothers, who was taking the afternoon papers to the stores. It was almost night.

The hunter came into a grocery and told his story. Then he went to a hardware shop and into a drug store. Men began to gather on the sidewalks. Then they started out along the road to the place in the wood.

My brother should have gone on about his business of distributing papers, but he didn't. Everyone was going to the woods. The undertaker went and the town marshal. Several men got on a dray and rode out to where the path left the road and went into the woods, but the horses weren't very sharply shod and slid about on the slippery roads. They made no better time than those of us who walked.

The town marshal was a large man whose leg had been injured in the Civil War. He carried a heavy cane and limped rapidly along the road. My brother and I followed at his heels, and as we went other men and boys joined the crowd.

It had grown dark by the time we got to where the old woman had left the road, but the moon had come out. The marshal was thinking there might have been a murder. He kept asking the hunter questions. The hunter went along with his gun across his shoulders, a dog following at his heels. It isn't often a rabbit hunter has a chance to be so conspicuous. He was taking full advantage of it, leading the procession with the town marshal. "I didn't see any wounds. She was a beautiful young girl. Her face was buried in the snow. No, I didn't know her." As a matter of fact, the hunter had not looked closely at the body. He had been frightened. She might have been murdered and someone might spring out from behind a tree and murder him too. In a woods, in the late afternoon, when the trees are all bare and there is white snow on the ground, when all is silent, something creepy steals over the mind and body. If something strange or uncanny has happened in the neighbourhood, all you think about is getting away from there as fast as you can.

The crowd of men and boys had got to where the old woman crossed the field, and went, following the marshal and the hunter, up the slight incline and into the woods.

My brother and I were silent. He had his bundle of papers in a bag slung across his shoulder. When he got back to town he would have to go on distributing his papers before he went home to supper. If I went along, as he had no doubt already

determined I should, we would both be late. Either Mother or our younger sister would have to warm our supper.

Well, we would have something to tell. A boy did not get such a chance very often. It was lucky we just happened to go into the grocery when the hunter came in. The hunter was a country fellow. Neither of us had ever seen him before.

Now the crowd of men and boys had got to the clearing. Darkness comes quickly on such winter nights, but the full moon made everything clear. My brother and I stood near the trees beneath which the old woman had died.

She did not look old, lying there frozen in that light. One of the men turned her over in the snow and I saw everything. My body trembled with some strange mystical feeling, and so did my brother's. It might have been the cold.

Neither of us had ever seen a woman's body before. It may have been the snow, clinging to the frozen flesh, that made it look so white and lovely, so like marble. No woman had come with the party from town, but one of the men, he was the town blacksmith, took off his overcoat and spread it over her. Then he gathered her into his arms and started off to town, all the others following silently. At that time no one knew who she was.

V

I had seen everything, had seen the oval in the snow, like a miniature race track, where the dogs had run, had seen how the men were mystified, had seen the white, bare, young-looking shoulders, had heard the whispered comments of the men.

The men were simply mystified. They took the body to the undertaker's, and when the blacksmith, the hunter, the marshal, and several others had got inside, they closed the door. If Father had been there, perhaps he could have got in, but we boys couldn't.

I went with my brother to distribute the rest of his papers, and when we got home it was my brother who told the story.

I kept silent and went to bed early. It may have been I was not satisfied with the way he told it.

Later, in the town, I must have heard other fragments of the old woman's story. She was recognized the next day and there was an investigation.

The husband and son were found somewhere and brought to town, and there was an attempt to connect them with the woman's death, but it did not work. They had perfect enough alibis.

However, the town was against them. They had to get out. Where they went, I never heard.

I remember only the picture there in the forest, the men standing about, the naked, girlish-looking figure, face down in the snow, the tracks made by the running dogs, and the clear, cold winter sky above. White fragments of clouds were drifting across the sky. They went racing across the little open space among the trees.

The scene in the forest had become for me, without my knowing it, the foundation for the real story I am now trying to tell. The fragments, you see, had to be picked up slowly, long afterward.

Things happened. When I was a young man I worked on the farm of a German. The hired girl was afraid of her employer. The farmer's wife hated her.

I saw things at that place. Once, later, I had a half-uncanny, mystical sort of adventure with dogs in a forest on a clear, moonlit winter night. When I was a schoolboy, and on a summer day, I went with a boy friend out along a creek some miles from town and came to the house where the old woman had lived. No one had lived in the house since her death. The doors were broken from the hinges, the window lights were all broken. As the boy and I stood in the road outside, two dogs, just roving farm dogs, no doubt, came running around the corner of the house. The dogs were tall, gaunt fellows and came down to the fence and glared through at us, standing in the road.

The whole thing, the story of the old woman's death, was to me, as I grew older, like music heard from far off. The notes had to be picked up slowly one at a time. Something had to be understood.

The woman who died was one destined to feed animal life. Anyway, that is all she ever did. She was feeding animal life before she was born, as a child, as a young woman working on the farm of the German, after she married, when she grew old, and when she died. She fed animal life in cows, in chickens, in pigs, in horses, in dogs, in men. Her daughter had died in childhood, and with her one son she had no articulate relations. On the night when she died she was hurrying homeward, bearing on her body food for animal life.

She died in the clearing in the woods, and even after her death continued feeding animal life.

You see it is likely that, when my brother told the story, that night when we got home and my mother and sister sat listening, I did not think he got the point. He was too young and so was I. A thing so complete has its own beauty.

I shall not try to emphasize the point. I am only explaining why I was dissatisfied then, and have been ever since. I speak of that only that you may understand why I have been impelled to try to tell the simple story over again.

1885 ∽ *Ring Lardner* ∽ 1933

FROM the public schools of Niles, Michigan, the small town where he was born, Lardner went for two years to the Armour Institute of Technology in Chicago. He devoted most of the rest of his life to newspaper work, as a sports writer and columnist. *You Know Me, Al* (1917), stories in baseball vernacular, first made him widely known. His best stories were collected in *Round Up* (1929). [See M. Geismar's *Writers in Crisis* (Boston, 1942).]

EX PARTE

MOST ALWAYS when a man leaves his wife, there's no excuse in the world for him. She may have made whoop-whoop-whoopee with the whole ten commandments, but if he shows his disapproval to the extent of walking out on her, he will thereafter be a total stranger to all his friends excepting the two or three bums who will tour the night clubs with him so long as he sticks to his habits of paying for everything.

When a woman leaves her husband, she must have good and sufficient reasons. He drinks all the time, or he runs around, or he doesn't give her any money, or he uses her as the heavy bag in his home gymnasium work. No more is he invited to his former playmates' houses for dinner and bridge. He is an outcast just the same as if he had done the deserting. Whichever way it happens, it's his fault. He can state his side of the case if he wants to, but there is nobody around listening.

Now I claim to have a little chivalry in me, as well as a little pride. So in spite of the fact that Florence has broadcast her grievances over the red and blue network both, I intend to keep mine to myself till death do me part.

But after I'm gone, I want some of my old pals to know that this thing wasn't as lopsided as she has made out, so I will write the true story, put it in an envelope with my will and appoint Ed Osborne executor. He used to be my best friend and

would be yet if his wife would let him. He'll have to read all my papers, including this, and he'll tell everybody else about it and maybe they'll be a little sorry that they treated me like an open manhole.

(Ed, please don't consider this an attempt to be literary. You know I haven't written for publication since our days on "The Crimson and White," and I wasn't so hot then. Just look on it as a statement of facts. If I were still alive, I'd take a bible oath that nothing herein is exaggerated. And whatever else may have been my imperfections, I never lied save to shield a woman or myself.)

Well, a year ago last May I had to go to New York. I called up Joe Paxton and he asked me out to dinner. I went, and met Florence. She and Marjorie Paxton had been at school together and she was there for a visit. We fell in love with each other and got engaged. I stopped off in Chicago on the way home, to see her people. They liked me all right, but they hated to have Florence marry a man who lived so far away. They wanted to postpone her leaving home as long as possible and they made us wait till April this year.

I had a room at the Belden and Florence and I agreed that when we were married, we would stay there awhile and take our time about picking out a house. But the last day of March, two weeks before the date of our wedding, I ran into Jeff Cooper and he told me his news, that the Standard Oil was sending him to China in some big job that looked permanent.

"I'm perfectly willing to go," he said. "So is Bess. It's a lot more money and we think it will be an interesting experience. But here I am with a brand-new place on my hands that cost me $45,000, including the furniture, and no chance to sell it in a hurry except at a loss. We were just beginning to feel settled. Otherwise we would have no regrets about leaving this town. Bess hasn't any real friends here and you're the only one I can claim."

"How much would you take for your house, furniture and all?" I asked him.

"I'd take a loss of $5,000," he said. "I'd take $40,000 with the buyer assuming my mortgage of $15,000, held by the Phillips Trust and Mortgage Company in Seattle."

I asked him if he would show me the place. They had only been living there a month and I hadn't had time to call. He said, what did I want to look at it for and I told him I would buy it if it looked o.k. Then I confessed that I was going to be married; you know I had kept it a secret around here.

Well, he took me home with him and he and Bess showed me everything, all new and shiny and a bargain if you ever saw one. In the first place, there's the location, on the best residential street in town, handy to my office and yet with a whole acre of ground, and a bed of cannas coming up in the front yard that Bess had planted when they bought the property last fall. As for the house, I always liked stucco, and this one is built! You could depend on old Jeff to see to that.

But the furniture was what decided me. Jeff had done the smart thing and ordered the whole works from Wolfe Brothers, taking their advice on most of the stuff, as neither he nor Bess knew much about it. Their total bill, furnishing the entire place, rugs, beds, tables, chairs, everything, was only $8,500, including a mahogany upright player-piano that they ordered from Seattle. I had my mother's old mahogany piano in storage and I kind of hoped Jeff wouldn't want me to buy this, but it was all or nothing, and with a bargain like

that staring me in the face, I didn't stop to argue, not when I looked over the rest of the furniture and saw what I was getting.

The living-room had, and still has, three big easy chairs and a couch, all over-stuffed, as they call it, to say nothing of an Oriental rug that alone had cost $500. There was a long mahogany table behind the couch, with lamps at both ends in case you wanted to lie down and read. The dining-room set was solid mahogany—a table and eight chairs that had separated Jeff from $1,000.

The floors downstairs were all oak parquet. Also he had blown himself to an oak mantelpiece and oak woodwork that must have run into heavy dough. Jeff told me what it cost him extra, but I don't recall the amount.

The Coopers were strong for mahogany and wanted another set for their bedroom, but Jake Wolfe told them it would get monotonous if there was too much of it. So he sold them five pieces—a bed, two chairs, a chiffonier and a dresser—of some kind of wood tinted green, with flowers painted on it. This was $1,000 more, but it certainly was worth it. You never saw anything prettier than that bed when the lace spreads were on.

Well, we closed the deal and at first I thought I wouldn't tell Florence, but would let her believe we were going to live at the Belden and then give her a surprise by taking her right from the train to our own home. When I got to Chicago, though, I couldn't keep my mouth shut. I gave it away and it was I, not she, that had the surprise.

Instead of acting tickled to death, as I figured she would, she just looked kind of funny and said she hoped I had as good taste in houses as I had in clothes. She tried to make me describe the house and the furniture to her, but I wouldn't do it. To appreciate a layout like that, you have to see it for yourself.

We were married and stopped in Yellowstone for a week on our way here. That was the only really happy week we had together. From the minute we arrived home till she left for good, she was a different woman than the one I thought I knew. She never smiled and several times I caught her crying. She wouldn't tell me what ailed her and when I asked if she was just home-sick, she said no and choked up and cried some more.

You can imagine that things were not as I expected they would be. In New York and in Chicago and Yellowstone, she had had more life than any girl I ever met. Now she acted all the while as if she were playing the title role at a funeral.

One night late in May the telephone rang. It was Mrs. Dwan and she wanted Florence. If I had known what this was going to mean, I would have slapped the receiver back on the hook and let her keep on wanting.

I had met Dwan a couple of times and had heard about their place out on the Turnpike. But I had never seen it or his wife either.

Well, it developed that Mildred Dwan had gone to school with Florence and Marjorie Paxton, and she had just learned from Marjorie that Florence was my wife and living here. She said she and her hus-band would be in town and call on us the next Sunday afternoon.

Florence didn't seem to like the idea and kind of discouraged it. She said we would drive out and call on them instead. Mrs. Dwan said no, that Florence was the new-comer and it was her (Mrs. Dwan's) first move. So Florence gave in.

They came and they hadn't been in the house more than a minute when Florence began to cry. Mrs. Dwan cried, too, and Dwan and I stood there first on one foot and then the other, trying to pretend we didn't know the girls were crying. Finally, to relieve the tension, I invited him to come and see the rest of the place. I showed him all over and he was quite enthusiastic. When we returned to the living-room, the girls had dried their eyes and were back in school together.

Florence accepted an invitation for one-o'clock dinner a week from that day. I told her, after they had left, that I would go along only on condition that she and our hostess would both control their tear-ducts. I was so accustomed to solo sobbing that I didn't mind it any more, but I couldn't stand a duet of it either in harmony or unison.

Well, when we got out there and had driven down their private lane through the trees and caught a glimpse of their house, which people around town had been talking about as something wonderful, I laughed harder than any time since I was single. It looked just like what it was, a reorganized barn. Florence asked me what was funny, and when I told her, she pulled even a longer face than usual.

"I think it's beautiful," she said.

Tie that!

I insisted on her going up the steps alone. I was afraid if the two of us stood on the porch at once, we'd fall through and maybe founder before help came. I warned her not to smack the knocker too hard or the door might crash in and frighten the horses.

"If you make jokes like that in front of the Dwans," she said, "I'll never speak to you again."

"I'd forgotten you ever did," said I.

I was expecting a hostler to let us in, but Mrs. Dwan came in person.

"Are we late?" said Florence.

"A little," said Mrs. Dwan, "but so is dinner. Helga didn't get home from church till half past twelve."

"I'm glad of it," said Florence, "I want you to take me all through this beautiful, beautiful house right this minute."

Mrs. Dwan called her husband and in-sisted that he stop in the middle of mixing a cocktail so he could join us in a tour of the beautiful, beautiful house.

"You wouldn't guess it," said Mrs. Dwan, "but it used to be a barn."

I was going to say I had guessed it. Florence gave me a look that changed my mind.

"When Jim and I first came here," said Mrs. Dwan, "we lived in an ugly little rented house on Oliver Street. It was only temporary, of course; we were just waiting till we found what we really wanted. We used to drive around the country Saturday afternoons and Sundays, hoping we would run across the right sort of thing. It was in the late fall when we first saw this place. The leaves were off the trees and it was visible from the Turnpike.

"'Oh, Jim!' I exclaimed. 'Look at that simply gorgeous old barn! With those wide shingles! And I'll bet you it's got handhewn beams in that middle, main section,' Jim bet me I was wrong, so we left the car, walked up the driveway, found the door open and came brazenly in. I won my bet as you can see."

She pointed to some dirty old rotten beams that ran across the living-room ceiling and looked as if five or six generations of rats had used them for gnawing practise.

"They're beautiful!" said Florence.

"The instant I saw them," said Mrs. Dwan, "I knew this was going to be our home!"

"I can imagine!" said Florence.

"We made inquiries and learned that the place belonged to a family named Taylor," said Mrs. Dwan. "The house had burned down and they had moved away. It was suspected that they had started the fire themselves, as they were terribly hard up and it was insured. Jim wrote to old Mr. Taylor in Seattle and asked him to set a price on the barn and the land, which is about four acres. They exchanged several letters and finally Mr. Taylor accepted Jim's offer. We got it for a song."

"Wonderful!" said Florence.

"And then, of course," Mrs. Dwan continued, "we engaged a house-wrecking company to tear down the other four sections of the barn—the stalls, the cow-shed, the tool-shed, and so forth—and take them away, leaving us just this one room. We had a man from Seattle come and put in these old pine walls and the flooring, and plaster the ceiling. He was recommended by a friend of Jim's and he certainly knew his business."

"I can see he did," said Florence.

"He made the hay-loft over for us, too, and we got the wings built by day-labor, with Jim and me supervising. It was so much fun that I was honestly sorry when it was finished."

"I can imagine!" said Florence.

Well, I am not very well up in Early American, which was the name they had for pretty nearly everything in the place, but for the benefit of those who are not on terms with the Dwans I will try and describe from memory the objets d'art they bragged of the most and which brought forth the loudest squeals from Florence.

The living-room walls were brown bare boards without a picture or scrap of wall-paper. On the floor were two or three "hooked rugs," whatever that means, but they needed five or six more of them, or one big carpet, to cover up all the knots in the wood. There was a maple "low-boy"; a "dough-trough" table they didn't have space for in the kitchen; a pine "stretcher" table with sticks connecting the four legs near the bottom so you couldn't put your feet anywhere; a "Dutch" chest that looked as if it had been ordered from the under-taker by one of Singer's Midgets, but he got well; and some "Windsor" chairs in which the only position you could get comfortable was to stand up behind them and lean your elbows on their back.

Not one piece that matched another, and not one piece of mahogany anywhere. And the ceiling, between the beams, had apparently been plastered by a workman who was that way, too.

"Some day soon I hope to have a piano," said Mrs. Dwan. "I can't live much longer without one. But so far I haven't been able to find one that would fit in."

"Listen," I said. "I've got a piano in storage that belonged to my mother. It's a mahogany upright and not so big that it wouldn't fit in this room, especially when you get that 'trough' table out. It isn't doing me any good, and I'll sell it to you for $250. Mother paid $1,250 for it new."

"Oh, I couldn't think of taking it!" said Mrs. Dwan.

"I'll make it $200 even just because you're a friend of Florence's," I said.

"Really, I couldn't!" said Mrs. Dwan.

"You wouldn't have to pay for it all at once," I said.

"Don't you see," said Florence, "that a mahogany upright piano would be a perfect horror in here? Mildred wouldn't have it as a gift, let alone buy it. It isn't in the period."

"She could get it tuned," I said.

The answer to this was, "I'll show you the up-stairs now and we can look at the dining-room later on."

We were led to the guest-chamber. The bed was a maple four-poster, with pine-apple posts, and a "tester" running from pillar to post. You would think a "tester" might be a man that went around trying out beds, but it's really a kind of frame that holds a canopy over the bed in case it rains and the roof leaks. There was a quilt made by Mrs. Dwan's great-grand-mother, Mrs. Anthony Adams, in 1859, at Lowell, Mass. How is that for a memory?

"This used to be the hay-loft," said Mrs. Dwan.

"You ought to have left some of the hay so the guests could hit it," I said.

The dressers, or chests of drawers, and the chairs were all made of maple. And the same in the Dwans' own room; everything maple.

"If you had maple in one room and mahogany in the other," I said, "people wouldn't get confused when you told them that so and so was up in Maple's room."

Dwan laughed, but the women didn't.

The maid hollered up that dinner was ready.

"The cocktails aren't ready," said Dwan.

"You will have to go without them," said Mrs. Dwan. "The soup will be cold."

This put me in a great mood to admire the "sawbuck" table and the "slat back" chairs, which were evidently the chef-d'oeuvre and the piece de resistance of the chez Dwan.

"It came all the way from Pennsylvania," said Mildred, when Florence's outcries, brought on by her first look at the table, had died down. "Mother picked it up at a little place near Stroudsburg and sent it to me. It only cost $550, and the chairs were $45 apiece."

"How reasonable!" exclaimed Florence.

That was before she had sat in one of them. Only one thing was more unreasonable than the chairs, and that was the table itself, consisting of big planks nailed together and laid onto a railroad tie, supported underneath by a whole forest of cross-pieces and beams. The surface was as smooth on top as the trip to Catalina Island and all around the edges, great big divots had been taken out with some blunt instrument, probably a bayonet. There were stains and scorch marks that Florence fairly crowed over, but when I tried to add to the general ensemble by laying a lighted cigaret right down beside my soup-plate, she and both the Dwans yelled murder and made me take it off.

They planted me in an end seat, a location just right for a man who had stretched himself across a railway track and had both legs cut off at the abdomen. Not being that kind of man, I had to sit so far back that very few of my comestibles carried more than half-way to their target.

After dinner I was all ready to go home and get something to eat, but it had been darkening up outdoors for half an hour and now such a storm broke that I knew it was useless trying to persuade Florence to make a start.

"We'll play some bridge," said Dwan, and to my surprise he produced a card-table that was nowhere near "in the period."

At my house there was a big center chandelier that lighted up a bridge game no matter in what part of the room the table was put. But here we had to waste forty minutes moving lamps and wires and stands and when they were all fixed, you could tell a red suit from a black suit, but not a spade from a club. Aside from that and the granite-bottomed "Windsor" chairs and the fact that we played "families" for a cent a point and Florence and I won $12 and I didn't get paid, it was one of the pleasantest afternoons I ever spent gambling.

The rain stopped at five o'clock and as we splashed through the puddles of Dwan's driveway, I remarked to Florence that I had never known she was such a kidder.

"What do you mean?" she asked me.

"Why, your pretending to admire all that junk," I said.

"Junk!" said Florence. "That is one of the most beautifully furnished homes I have ever seen!"

And so far as I can recall, that was her last utterance in my presence for six nights and five days.

At lunch on Saturday I said: "You know I like the silent drama one evening a week, but not twenty-four hours a day every day. What's the matter with you? If it's laryngitis, you might write me notes."

"I'll tell you what's the matter!" she burst out. "I hate this house and everything in it! It's too new! Everything shines! I loathe new things! I want a home like Mildred's, with things in it that I can look at without blushing for shame. I can't invite anyone here. It's too hideous. And I'll never be happy here a single minute as long as I live!"

Well, I don't mind telling that this kind of got under my skin. As if I hadn't intended to give her a pleasant surprise! As if Wolfe Brothers, in business thirty years, didn't know how to furnish a home complete! I was pretty badly hurt, but I choked it down and said, as calmly as I could:

"If you'll be a little patient, I'll try to sell this house and its contents for what I paid for it and them. It oughtn't to be much trouble; there are plenty of people around who know a bargain. But it's too bad you didn't confess your barn complex to me long ago. Only last February, old Ken Garrett had to sell his establishment

and the men who bought it turned it into a garage. It was a livery-stable which I could have got for the introduction of a song, or maybe just the vamp. And we wouldn't have had to spend a nickel to make it as nice and comfortable and homey as your friend Mildred's dump."

Florence was on her way upstairs before I had finished my speech.

I went down to Earl Benham's to see if my new suit was ready. It was and I put it on and left the old one to be cleaned and pressed.

On the street I met Harry Cross.

"Come up to my office," he said. "There's something in my desk that may interest you."

I accepted his invitation and from three different drawers he pulled out three different quart bottles of Early American rye.

Just before six o'clock I dropped in Kane's store and bought myself a pair of shears, a blow torch and an ax. I started home, but stopped among the trees, inside my front gate and cut big holes in my coat and trousers. Alongside the path to the house was a sizable mud puddle. I waded in it. And I bathed my gray felt hat.

Florence was sitting on the floor of the living-room, reading. She seemed a little upset by my appearance.

"Good heavens! What's happened?"

"Nothing much," said I. "I just didn't want to look too new."

"What are those things you're carrying?"

"Just a pair of shears, a blow torch and an ax. I'm going to try and antique this place and I think I'll begin on the dining-room table."

Florence went into her scream, dashed upstairs and locked herself in. I went about my work and had the dinner-table looking pretty Early when the maid smelled fire and rushed in. She rushed out again and came back with a pitcher of water. But using my vest as a snuffer, I had had the flames under control all the while and there was nothing for her to do.

"I'll just nick it up a little with this ax," I told her, "and by the time I'm through, dinner ought to be ready."

"It will never be ready as far as I'm concerned," she said. "I'm leaving just as soon as I can pack."

And Florence had the same idea—vindicating the old adage about great minds.

I heard the front door slam and the back door slam, and I felt kind of tired and sleepy, so I knocked off work and went up to bed.

That's my side of the story, Eddie, and it's true so help me my bootlegger. Which reminds me that the man who sold Harry the rye makes this town once a week, or did when this was written. He's at the Belden every Tuesday from nine to six and his name is Mike Farrell.

1896 ∾ *F. Scott Fitzgerald* ∾ *1940*

FITZGERALD was born at St. Paul, Minnesota. He attended private schools and spent four years at Princeton University, but left without taking a degree, in 1917, to enter the United States army. After the war he worked for an advertising agency in New York City. He soon became one of the most popular fiction writers of his time. His novels of the jazz age, *This Side of Paradise* (1920) and *The Beautiful and Damned* (1922), were followed by more searching studies of contemporary life in *The Great Gatsby* (1925) and *Tender Is the Night* (1934). Fitzgerald's short stories were collected in *Tales of the Jazz Age* (1922), *All the Sad Young Men* (1926), and *Taps at Reveille* (1935). He spent the last three years of his life in Hollywood. His incomplete novel, *The Last Tycoon* (1941), was published posthumously.

BABYLON REVISITED

"AND WHERE'S Mr. Campbell?" Charlie asked.

"Gone to Switzerland. Mr. Campbell's a pretty sick man, Mr. Wales."

"I'm sorry to hear that. And George Hardt?" Charlie inquired.

"Back in America, gone to work."

"And where is the Snow Bird?"

"He was in here last week. Anyway, his friend, Mr. Schaeffer, is in Paris."

Two familiar names from the long list of a year and a half ago. Charlie scribbled an address in his notebook and tore out the page.

"If you see Mr. Schaeffer, give him this," he said. "It's my brother-in-law's address.

I haven't settled on a hotel yet."

He was not really disappointed to find Paris was so empty. But the stillness in the Ritz bar was strange and portentous. It was not an American bar any more—he felt polite in it, and not as if he owned it. It had gone back into France. He felt the stillness from the moment he got out of the taxi and saw the doorman, usually in a frenzy of activity at this hour, gossiping with a *chausseur* by the servants' entrance.

Passing through the corridor, he heard only a single, bored voice in the once-clamorous women's room. When he turned into the bar he travelled the twenty feet of green carpet with his eyes fixed straight ahead by old habit; and then, with his foot firmly on the rail, he turned and surveyed the room, encountering only a single pair of eyes that fluttered up from a newspaper in the corner. Charlie asked for the head barman, Paul, who in the latter days of the bull market had come to work in his own custom-built car—disembarking, however, with due nicety at the nearest corner. But Paul was at his country house today and Alix giving him information.

"No, no more," Charlie said. "I'm going slow these days."

Alix congratulated him: "You were going pretty strong a couple of years ago."

"I'll stick to it all right," Charlie assured him. "I've stuck to it for over a year and a half now."

"How do you find conditions in America?"

"I haven't been to America for months. I'm in business in Prague, representing a couple of concerns there. They don't know about me down there."

Alix smiled.

"Remember the night of George Hardt's bachelor dinner here?" said Charlie. "By the way, what's become of Claude Fessenden?"

Alix lowered his voice confidentially: "He's in Paris, but he doesn't come here any more. Paul doesn't allow it. He ran up a bill of thirty thousand francs, charging all his drinks and his lunches, and usually his dinner, for more than a year. And when Paul finally told him he had to pay, he gave him a bad check."

Alix shook his head sadly.

"I don't understand it, such a dandy fellow. Now he's all bloated up—" He made a plump apple of his hands.

Charlie watched a group of strident queens installing themselves in a corner.

"Nothing affects them," he thought. "Stocks rise and fall, people loaf or work, ·but they go on forever." The place oppressed him. He called for the dice and shook with Alix for the drink.

"Here for long, Mr. Wales?"

"I'm here for four or five days to see my little girl."

"Oh-h! You have a little girl?"

Outside, the fire-red, gas-blue, ghost-green signs shone smokily through the tranquil rain. It was late afternoon and the streets were in movement; the *bistros* gleamed. At the corner of the Boulevard des Capucines he took a taxi. The Place de la Concorde moved by in pink majesty; they crossed the logical Seine, and Charlie felt the sudden provincial quality of the left bank.

Charlie directed his taxi to the Avenue de l'Opéra, which was out of his way. But he wanted to see the blue hour spread over the magnificent façade, and imagine that the cab horns, playing endlessly the first few bars of *La Pluie que Lent*, were the trumpets of the Second Empire. They were closing the iron grill in front of Brentano's Bookstore, and people were already at dinner behind the trim little bourgeois hedge of Duval's. He had never eaten at a really cheap restaurant in Paris. Five-course dinner, four francs fifty, eighteen cents, wine included. For some odd reason he wished that he had.

As they rolled on to the Left Bank and he felt its sudden provincialism, he thought, "I spoiled this city for myself. I didn't realize it, but the days came along one after another, and then two years were gone, and everything was gone, and I was gone."

He was thirty-five, and good to look at. The Irish mobility of his face was sobered by a deep wrinkle between his eyes. As he rang his brother-in-law's bell in the Rue Palatine, the wrinkle deepened till it pulled down his brows; he felt a cramping sensation in his belly. From behind the maid who opened the door darted a lovely little girl of nine, who shrieked "Daddy!" and flew up, struggling like a fish, into his arms. She pulled his head around by one ear and set her cheek against his.

"My old pie," he said.

"Oh, daddy, daddy, daddy, daddy, dads, dads, dads!"

She drew him into the salon, where the family waited, a boy and girl his daughter's age, his sister-in-law and her husband. He greeted Marion with his voice pitched carefully to avoid either feigned enthusiasm or dislike, but her response was more frankly tepid, though she minimized her expression of unalterable distrust by directing her regard toward his child. The two men clasped hands in a friendly way and Lincoln Peters rested his for a moment on Charlie's shoulder.

The room was warm and comfortably American. The three children moved intimately about, playing through the yellow oblongs that led to other rooms; the cheer of six o'clock spoke in the eager smacks of the fire and the sounds of French activity in the kitchen. But Charlie did not relax; his heart sat up rigidly in his body and he drew confidence from his daughter, who from time to time came close to him, holding in her arms the doll he had brought.

"Really extremely well," he declared in answer to Lincoln's question. "There's a lot of business there that isn't moving at all, but we're doing even better than ever. In fact, damn well. I'm bringing my sister over from America next month to keep house for me. My income last year was bigger than it was when I had money. You see, the Czechs——"

His boasting was for a specific purpose; but after a moment, seeing a faint restiveness in Lincoln's eye, he changed the subject:

"Those are fine children of yours, well brought up, good manners."

"We think Honoria's a great little girl too."

Marion Peters came back from the kitchen. She was a tall woman with worried eyes, who had once possessed a fresh American loveliness. Charlie had never been sensitive to it and was always surprised when people spoke of how pretty she had been. From the first there had been an instinctive antipathy between them.

"Well, how do you find Honoria?" she asked.

"Wonderful. I was astonished how much she's grown in ten months. All the children are looking well."

"We haven't had a doctor for a year. How do you like being back in Paris?"

"It seems very funny to see so few Americans around."

"I'm delighted," Marion said vehemently. "Now at least you can go into a store without their assuming you're a millionaire. We've suffered like everybody, but on the whole it's a good deal pleasanter."

"But it was nice while it lasted," said Charlie. "We were a sort of royalty, almost infallible, with a sort of magic around us. In the bar this afternoon"—he stumbled, seeing his mistake—"there wasn't a man I knew."

She looked at him keenly. "I should think you'd have had enough of bars."

"I only stayed a minute. I take one drink every afternoon, and no more."

"Don't you want a cocktail before dinner?" Lincoln asked.

"I take only one drink every afternoon, and I've had that."

"I hope you keep to it," said Marion.

Her dislike was evident in the coldness with which she spoke, but Charlie only smiled; he had larger plans. Her very aggressiveness gave him an advantage, and he knew enough to wait. He wanted them to initiate the discussion of what they knew had brought him to Paris.

At dinner he couldn't decide whether Honoria was most like him or her mother. Fortunate if she didn't combine the traits of both that had brought them to disaster. A great wave of protectiveness went over him. He thought he knew what to do for her. He believed in character; he wanted to jump back a whole generation and trust in character again as the eternally valuable element. Everything else wore out.

He left soon after dinner, but not to go home. He was curious to see Paris by night with clearer and more judicious eyes than those of other days. He bought a *strapontin* for the Casino and watched Josephine Baker go through her chocolate arabesques.

After an hour he left and strolled toward Montmartre, up the Rue Pigalle into the Place Blanche. The rain had stopped and there were a few people in evening clothes disembarking from taxis in front of cabarets, and *cocottes* prowling singly or in pairs, and many Negroes. He passed a lighted door from which issued music, and stopped with the sense of familiarity; it was Bricktop's, where he had parted with so many hours and so much money. A few doors farther on he found another ancient rendezvous and incautiously put his head inside. Immediately an eager orchestra burst into sound, a pair of professional dancers leaped to their feet and a maître d'hôtel swooped toward him, crying, "Crowd just arriving, sir!" But he withdrew quickly.

"You have to be damn drunk," he thought.

Zelli's was closed, the bleak and sinister cheap hotels surrounding it were dark; up in the Rue Blanche there was more light and a local, colloquial French crowd. The Poet's Cave had disappeared, but the two great mouths of the Café of Heaven and the Café of Hell still yawned—even devoured, as he watched, the meager contents of a tourist bus—a German, a Japanese, and an American couple who glanced at him with frightened eyes.

So much for the effort and ingenuity of Montmartre. All the catering to vice and waste was on an utterly childish scale, and he suddenly realized the meaning of the world "dissipate"—to dissipate into thin air; to make nothing out of something. In the little hours of the night every move from place to place was an enormous human jump, an increase of paying for the privilege of slower and slower motion.

He remembered thousand-franc notes given to an orchestra for playing a single number, hundred-franc notes tossed to a doorman for calling a cab.

But it hadn't been given for nothing.

It had been given, even the most wildly squandered sum, as an offering to destiny that he might not remember the things most worth remembering, the things that now he would always remember—his child taken from his control, his wife escaped to a grave in Vermont.

In the glare of a *brasserie* a woman spoke to him. He bought her some eggs and coffee, and then, eluding her encouraging stare, gave her a twenty-franc note and took a taxi to his hotel.

II

He woke up on a fine fall day—football weather. The depression of yesterday was gone and he liked the people on the streets. At noon he sat opposite Honoria at Le Grand Vatel, the only restaurant he could think of not reminiscent of champagne dinners and long luncheons that began at two and ended in a blurred and vague twilight.

"Now, how about vegetables? Oughtn't you to have some vegetables?"

"Well, yes."

"Here's *épinards* and *chou-fleur* and carrots and *haricots*."

"I'd like *chou-fleur*."

"Wouldn't you like to have two vegetables?"

"I usually have only one at lunch."

The waiter was pretending to be inordinately fond of children. *"Qu'elle est mignonne la petite? Elle parle exactement comme une française."*

"How about dessert? Shall we wait and see?"

The waiter disappeared. Honoria looked at her father expectantly.

"What are we going to do?"

"First, we're going to that toy store in the Rue Saint-Honoré and buy you anything you like. And then we're going to the vaudeville at the Empire."

She hesitated. "I like it about the vaudeville, but not the toy store."

"Why not?"

"Well, you brought me this doll." She had it with her. "And I've got lots of things. And we're not rich any more, are we?"

"We never were. But today you are to have anything you want."

"All right," she agreed resignedly.

When there had been her mother and a French nurse he had been inclined to be strict; now he extended himself, reached out for a new tolerance; he must be both parents to her and not shut any of her out of communication.

"I want to get to know you," he said gravely. "First let me introduce myself. My name is Charles J. Wales, of Prague."

"Oh, daddy!" her voice cracked with laughter.

"And who are you, please?" he persisted, and she accepted a rôle immediately: "Honoria Wales, Rue Palatine, Paris."

"Married or single?"

"No, not married. Single."

He indicated the doll. "But I see you have a child, madame."

Unwilling to disinherit it, she took it to her heart and thought quickly: "Yes, I've been married, but I'm not married now. My husband is dead."

He went on quickly, "And the child's name?"

"Simone. That's after my best friend at school."

"I'm very pleased that you're doing so well at school."

"I'm third this month," she boasted. "Elsie"—that was her cousin—"is only about eighteenth, and Richard is about at the bottom."

"You like Richard and Elsie, don't you?"

"Oh, yes. I like them all right."

Cautiously and casually he asked: "And Aunt Marion and Uncle Lincoln—which do you like best?"

"Oh, Uncle Lincoln, I guess."

He was increasingly aware of her presence. As they came in, a murmur of ". . . adorable" followed them, and now the people at the next table bent all their silences upon her, staring as if she were something no more conscious than a flower.

"Why don't I live with you?" she asked suddenly. "Because mamma's dead?"

"You must stay here and learn more French. It would have been hard for daddy to take care of you so well."

"I don't really need much taking care of any more. I do everything for myself."

Going out of the restaurant, a man and a woman unexpectedly hailed him.

"Well, the old Wales!"

"Hello there, Lorraine . . . Dunc."

Sudden ghosts out of the past: Duncan Schaeffer, a friend from college. Lorraine Quarles, a lovely, pale blonde of thirty; one of a crowd who had helped them make months into days in the lavish times of three years ago.

"My husband couldn't come this year," she said, in answer to his question. "We're poor as hell. So he gave me two hundred a month, and told me I could do my worst on that. . . . This your little girl?"

"What about coming back and sitting down?" Duncan asked.

"Can't do it." He was glad for an excuse. As always, he felt Lorraine's passionate, provocative attraction, but his own rhythm was different now.

"Well, how about dinner?" she asked.

"I'm not free. Give me your address and let me call you."

"Charlie, I believe you're sober," she said judicially. "I honestly believe he's sober, Dunc. Pinch him and see if he's sober."

Charlie indicated Honoria with his head. They both laughed.

"What's your address?" said Duncan skeptically.

He hesitated, unwilling to give the name of his hotel.

"I'm not settled yet. I'd better call you. We're going to see the vaudeville at the Empire."

"There! That's what I want to do," Lorraine said. "I want to see some clowns and acrobats and jugglers. That's just what we'll do, Dunc."

"We've got to do an errand first," said Charlie. "Perhaps we'll see you there."

"All right, you snob. . . . Good-by, beautiful little girl."

"Good-by."

Honoria bobbed politely.

Somehow, an unwelcome encounter. They liked him because he was functioning, because he was serious; they wanted to see him, because he was stronger than they were now, because they wanted to draw a certain sustenance from his strength.

At the Empire, Honoria proudly refused to sit upon her father's folded coat. She was already an individual with a code of her own, and Charlie was more and more absorbed by the desire of putting a little of himself into her before she crystallized utterly. It was hopeless to try to know her in so short a time.

Between the acts they came upon Duncan and Lorraine in the lobby where the band was playing.

"Have a drink?"

"All right, but not up at the bar. We'll take a table."

"The perfect father."

Listening abstractedly to Lorraine, Charlie watched Honoria's eyes leave their table, and he followed them wistfully about the room, wondering what they saw. He met her glance and she smiled.

"I liked that lemonade," she said.

What had she said? What had he expected? Going home in a taxi afterward, he pulled her over until her head rested against his chest.

"Darling, do you ever think about your mother?"

"Yes, sometimes," she answered vaguely.

"I don't want you to forget her. Have you got a picture of her?"

"Yes, I think so. Anyhow, Aunt Marion has. Why don't you want me to forget her?"

"She loved you very much."

"I loved her too."

They were silent for a moment.

"Daddy, I want to come and live with you," she said suddenly.

His heart leaped; he had wanted it to come like this.

"Aren't you perfectly happy?"

"Yes, but I love you better than anybody. And you love me better than anybody, don't you, now that mummy's dead?"

"Of course I do. But you won't always like me best, honey. You'll grow up and meet somebody your own age and go marry him and forget you ever had a daddy."

"Yes, that's true," she agreed tranquilly.

He didn't go in. He was coming back at nine o'clock and he wanted to keep himself fresh and new for the thing he must say then.

"When you're safe inside, just show yourself in that window."

"All right. Good-by, dads, dads, dads, dads."

He waited in the dark street until she appeared, all warm and glowing, in the window above and kissed her fingers out into the night.

III

They were waiting. Marion sat behind the coffee service in a dignified black dinner dress that just faintly suggested mourning. Lincoln was walking up and down with the animation of one who had already been talking. They were as anxious as he was to get into the question. He opened it almost immediately:

"I suppose you know what I want to see you about—why I really came to Paris."

Marion played with the black stars on her necklace and frowned.

"I'm awfully anxious to have a home," he continued. "And I'm awfully anxious to have Honoria in it. I appreciate your taking in Honoria for her mother's sake, but things have changed now"—he hesitated and then continued more forcibly—"changed radically with me, and I want to ask you to reconsider the matter. It would be silly for me to deny that about three years ago I was acting badly——"

Marion looked up at him with hard eyes.

"—But all that's over. As I told you, I haven't had more than a drink a day for over a year, and I take that drink deliberately, so that the idea of alcohol won't get too big in my imagination. You see the idea?"

"No," said Marion succinctly.

"It's a sort of stunt I set myself. It keeps the matter in proportion."

"I get you," said Lincoln. "You don't want to admit it's got any attraction for you."

"Something like that. Sometimes I forget and don't take it. But I try to take it. Anyhow, I couldn't afford to drink in my position. The people I represent are more than satisfied with what I've done, and I'm bringing my sister over from Burlington to keep house for me, and I want awfully to have Honoria too. You know that even when her mother and I weren't getting along well we never let anything that happened touch Honoria. I know she's fond of me and I know I'm able to take care of her—well, there you are. How do you feel about it?"

He knew that now he would have to take a beating. It would last an hour or two hours, and it would be difficult, but if he modulated his inevitable resentment to the chastened attitude of the reformed sinner, he might win his point in the end.

Keep your temper, he told himself. You don't want to be justified. You want Honoria.

Lincoln spoke first: "We've been talking it over ever since we got your letter last month. We're happy to have Honoria here. She's a dear little thing, and we're glad to be able to help her, but of course that isn't the question——"

Marion interrupted suddenly. "How long are you going to stay sober, Charlie?" she asked.

"Permanently, I hope."

"How can anybody count on that?"

"You know I never did drink heavily until I gave up business and came over here with nothing to do. Then Helen and I began to run around with——"

"Please leave Helen out of it. I can't bear to hear you talk about her like that."

He stared at her grimly; he had never been certain how fond of each other the sisters were in life.

"My drinking only lasted about a year and a half—from the time we came over until I—collapsed."

"It was time enough."

"It was time enough," he agreed.

"My duty is entirely to Helen," she said. "I try to think what she would have wanted me to do. Frankly, from the night you did that terrible thing you haven't really existed for me. I can't help that. She was my sister."

"Yes."

"When she was dying she asked me to look out for Honoria. If you hadn't been in a sanitarium then, it might have helped matters."

He had no answer.

"I'll never in my life be able to forget the morning when Helen knocked at my door, soaked to the skin and shivering, and said you'd locked her out."

Charlie gripped the sides of the chair. This was more difficult than he expected: he wanted to launch out into a long expostulation and explanation, but he only said: "The night I locked her out—" and she interrupted, "I don't feel up to going over that again."

After a moment's silence Lincoln said: "We're getting off the subject. You want Marion to set aside her legal guardianship and give you Honoria. I think the main point for her is whether she has confidence in you or not."

"I don't blame Marion," Charlie said slowly, "but I think she can have entire confidence in me. I had a good record up to three years ago. Of course, it's within human possibilities I may go wrong again. But if we wait much longer I'll lose Honoria's childhood and my chance for a home." He shook his head. "I'll simply lose her, don't you see?"

"Yes, I see," said Lincoln.

"Why didn't you think of all this before?" Marion asked.

"I suppose I did, from time to time, but Helen and I were getting along badly. When I consented to the guardianship, I was flat on my back in a sanitarium, and the market had cleaned me out. I knew

I'd acted badly, and I thought if it would bring any peace to Helen, I'd agree to anything. But now it's different. I'm functioning, I'm behaving damn well, so far as——"

"Please don't swear at me," Marion said.

He looked at her, startled. With each remark the force of her dislike became more and more apparent. She had built up all her fear of life into one wall and faced it toward him. This trivial reproof was possibly the result of some trouble with the cook several hours before. Charlie became increasingly alarmed at leaving Honoria in this atmosphere of hostility against himself; sooner or later it would come out, in a word here, a shake of the head there, and some of that distrust would be irrevocably implanted in Honoria. But he pulled his temper down out of his face and shut it up inside him; he had won a point, for Lincoln realized the absurdity of Marion's remark, and asked her lightly since when she had objected to the word "damn."

"Another thing," Charlie said: "I'm able to give her certain advantages now. I'm going to take a French governess to Prague with me. I've got a lease on a new apartment——"

He stopped, realizing that he was blundering. They couldn't be expected to accept with equanimity the fact that his income was again twice as large as their own.

"I suppose you can give her more luxuries than we can," said Marion. "When you were throwing away money we were living along watching every ten francs. . . . I suppose you'll start doing it again."

"Oh, no," he said. "I've learned. I worked hard for ten years, you know—until I got lucky in the market, like so many people. Terribly lucky. It didn't seem any use working any more, so I quit. It won't happen again."

There was a long silence. All of them felt their nerves straining, and for the first time in a year Charlie wanted a drink.

He was sure now that Lincoln Peters wanted him to have his child.

Marion shuddered suddenly; part of her saw that Charlie's feet were planted on the earth now, and her own maternal feeling recognized the naturalness of his desire; but she had lived for a long time with a prejudice—a prejudice founded on a curious disbelief in her sister's happiness, which, in the shock of one terrible night, had turned to hatred for him. It had all happened at a point in her life where the discouragement of ill health and adverse circumstances made it necessary for her to believe in tangible villainy and a tangible villain.

"I can't help what I think!" she cried out suddenly. "How much you were responsible for Helen's death, I don't know. It's something you'll have to square with your own conscience."

An electric current of agony surged through him; for a moment he was almost on his feet, an unuttered sound echoing in his throat. He hung on to himself for a moment, another moment.

"Hold on there," said Lincoln uncomfortably. "I never thought you were responsible for that."

"Helen died of heart trouble," Charlie said dully.

"Yes, heart trouble." Marion spoke as if the phrase had another meaning for her.

Then, in the flatness that followed her outburst, she saw him plainly and she knew he had somehow arrived at control over the situation. Glancing at her husband, she found no help from him, and as abruptly as if it were a matter of no importance, she threw up the sponge.

"Do what you like!" she cried, springing up from her chair. "She's your child. I'm not the person to stand in your way. I think if it were my child I'd rather see her—" She managed to check herself. "You two decide it. I can't stand this. I'm sick. I'm going to bed."

She hurried from the room; after a moment Lincoln said:

"This has been a hard day for her. You know how strongly she feels—" His voice was almost apologetic: "When a woman gets an idea in her head."

"Of course."

"It's going to be all right. I think she sees now that you—can provide for the child, and so we can't very well stand in your way or Honoria's way."

"Thank you, Lincoln."

"I'd better go along and see how she is."

"I'm going."

He was still trembling when he reached the street, but a walk down the Rue Bonaparte to the quais set him up, and as he crossed the Seine, fresh and new by the quai lamps, he felt exultant. But back in his room he couldn't sleep. The image of Helen haunted him. Helen whom he had loved so until they had senselessly begun to abuse each other's love, tear it into shreds. On that terrible February night that Marion remembered so vividly, a slow quarrel had gone on for hours. There was a scene at the Florida, and then he attempted to take her home, and then she kissed young Webb at a table; after that there was what she had hysterically said. When he arrived home alone he turned the key in the lock in wild anger. How could he know she would arrive an hour later alone, that there would be a snowstorm in which she wandered about in slippers, too confused to find a taxi? Then the aftermath, her escaping pneumonia by a miracle, and all the attendant horror. They were "reconciled," but that was the beginning of the end, and Marion, who had seen with her own eyes and who imagined it to be one of many scenes from her sister's martyrdom, never forgot.

Going over it again brought Helen nearer, and in the white, soft light that steals upon half sleep near morning he found himself talking to her again. She said that he was perfectly right about Honoria and that she wanted Honoria to be with him. She said she was glad he was being good and doing better. She said a lot of other things—very friendly things—but she was in a swing in a white dress, and swinging faster and faster all the time, so that at the end he could not hear clearly all that she said.

IV

He woke up feeling happy. The door of the world was open again. He made plans, vistas, futures for Honoria and himself, but suddenly he grew sad, remembering all the plans he and Helen had made. She had not planned to die. The present was the thing—work to do, and some one to love. But not to love too much, for he knew the injury that a father can do to a daughter or a mother to a son by attaching them too closely; afterward, out in the world, the child would seek in the marriage partner the same blind tenderness and, failing probably to find it, turn against love and life.

It was another bright, crisp day. He called Lincoln Peters at the bank where he worked and asked if he could count on taking Honoria when he left for Prague. Lincoln agreed that there was no reason for delay. One thing—the legal guardianship. Marion wanted to retain that a while longer. She was upset by the whole matter, and it would oil things if she felt that the situation was still in her control for another year. Charlie agreed, wanting only the tangible, visible child.

Then the question of a governess. Charlie sat in a gloomy agency and talked to a cross Bernaise and to a buxom Breton peasant, neither of whom he could have endured. There were others whom he would see tomorrow.

He lunched with Lincoln Peters at Griffons, trying to keep down his exultation.

"There's nothing quite like your own child," Lincoln said. "But you understand how Marion feels too."

"She's forgotten how hard I worked for seven years there," Charlie said. "She just remembers one night."

"There's another thing," Lincoln hesitated. "While you and Helen were tearing around Europe throwing money away, we were just getting along. I didn't touch any of the prosperity because I never got ahead enough to carry anything but my insurance. I think Marion felt there was some kind of injustice in it—you not even working toward the end, and getting richer and richer."

"It went just as quick as it came," said Charlie.

"Yes, a lot of it stayed in the hands of *chasseurs* and saxophone players and maîtres d'hôtel—well, the big party's over now. I just said that to explain Marion's feeling about those crazy years. If you drop in about six o'clock tonight before Marion's too tired, we'll settle the details on the spot."

Back at his hotel, Charlie found a *pneumatique* that had been redirected from the Ritz bar where Charlie had left his address for the purpose of finding a certain man.

Dear Charlie: You were so strange when we saw you the other day that I wondered if I did something to offend you. If so, I'm not conscious of it. In fact, I have thought about you too much for the last year, and it's always been in the back of my mind that I might see you if I came over here. We *did* have such good times that crazy spring, like the night you and I stole the butcher's tricycle, and the time we tried to call on the president and you had the old derby rim and the wire cane. Everybody seems so old lately, but I don't feel old a bit. Couldn't we get together some time today for old time's sake? I've got a vile hang-over for the moment, but will be feeling better this afternoon and will look for you about five in the sweetshop at the Ritz.

Always devotedly,
Lorraine.

His first feeling was one of awe that he had actually, in his mature years, stolen a tricycle and pedalled Lorraine all over the Étoile between the small hours and dawn. In retrospect it was a nightmare. Locking out Helen didn't fit in with any other act of his life, but the tricycle incident did—it was one of many. How many weeks or months of dissipation to arrive at that condition of utter irresponsibility?

He tried to picture how Lorraine had appeared to him then—very attractive; Helen was unhappy about it, though she said nothing. Yesterday, in the restaurant, Lorraine had seemed trite, blurred, worn away. He emphatically did not want to see her, and he was glad Alix had not given away his hotel address. It was a relief to think, instead, of Honoria, to think of Sundays spent with her and of saying good morning to her and of knowing she was there in his house at night, drawing her breath in the darkness.

At five he took a taxi and bought presents for all the Peters—a piquant cloth doll, a box of Roman soldiers, flowers for Marion, big linen handkerchiefs for Lincoln.

He saw, when he arrived in the apartment, that Marion had accepted the inevitable. She greeted him now as though he were a recalcitrant member of the family, rather than a menacing outsider. Honoria had been told she was going; Charlie was glad to see that her tact made her conceal her excessive happiness. Only on his lap did she whisper her delight and the question "When?" before she slipped away with the other children.

He and Marion were alone for a minute in the room, and on an impulse he spoke out boldly:

"Family quarrels are bitter things. They don't go according to any rules. They're not like aches or wounds; they're more like splits in the skin that won't heal because there's not enough material. I wish you and I could be on better terms."

"Some things are hard to forget," she answered. "It's a question of confidence." There was no answer to this and presently she asked, "When do you propose to take her?"

"As soon as I can get a governess. I hoped the day after tomorrow."

"That's impossible. I've got to get her things in shape. Not before Saturday."

He yielded. Coming back into the room, Lincoln offered him a drink.

"I'll take my daily whisky," he said.

It was warm here, it was a home, people together by a fire. The children felt very safe and important; the mother and father were serious, watchful. They had things to do for the children more important than his visit here. A spoonful of medicine was, after all, more important than the strained relations between Marion and himself. They were not dull people, but they were very much in the grip of life and circumstances. He wondered if he couldn't do something to get Lincoln out of his rut at the bank.

A long peal at the door-bell; the *bonne à tout faire* passed through and went down the corridor. The door opened upon another long ring, and then voices, and the three in the salon looked up expectantly; Richard moved to bring the corridor within his range of vision, and Marion rose. Then the maid came back along the corridor, closely followed by the voices, which developed under the light into Duncan Schaeffer and Lorraine Quarles.

They were gay, they were hilarious, they were roaring with laughter. For a moment Charlie was astounded; unable to understand how they had ferreted out the Peters' address.

"Ah-h-h!" Duncan wagged his finger roguishly at Charlie. "Ah-h-h!"

They both slid down another cascade of laughter. Anxious and at a loss, Charlie shook hands with them quickly and presented them to Lincoln and Marion. Marion nodded, scarcely speaking. She had drawn back a step toward the fire; her little girl stood beside her, and Marion put an arm about her shoulder.

With growing annoyance at the intrusion, Charlie waited for them to explain themselves. After some concentration Duncan said:

"We came to invite you out to dinner. Lorraine and I insist that all this shishi business 'bout your address got to stop."

Charlie came closer to them, as if to force them backward down the corridor.

"Sorry, but I can't. Tell me where you'll be and I'll phone you in half an hour."

This made no impression. Lorraine sat down suddenly on the side of a chair, and focussing her eyes on Richard, cried, "Oh, what a nice little boy! Come here, little boy." Richard glanced at his mother, but did not move. With a perceptible shrug of her shoulders, Lorraine turned back to Charlie:

"Come and dine. Sure your cousins won' mine. See you so sel'om. Or solemn."

"I can't," said Charlie sharply. "You two have dinner and I'll phone you."

Her voice became suddenly unpleasant. "All right, we'll go. But I remember once when you hammered on my door at four A.M. I was enough of a good sport to give you a drink. Come on, Dunc."

Still in slow motion, with blurred, angry faces, with uncertain feet, they retired along the corridor.

"Good night," Charlie said.

"Good night!" responded Lorraine emphatically.

When he went back into the salon Marion had not moved, only now her son was standing in the circle of her other arm. Lincoln was still swinging Honoria back and forth like a pendulum from side to side.

"What an outrage!" Charlie broke out. "What an absolute outrage!"

Neither of them answered. Charlie dropped into an armchair, picked up his drink, set it down again and said:

"People I haven't seen for two years having the colossal nerve——"

He broke off. Marion had made the sound "Oh!" in one swift, furious breath, turned her body from him with a jerk and left the room.

Lincoln set down Honoria carefully.

"You children go in and start your soup," he said, and when they obeyed, he said to Charlie:

"Marion's not well and she can't stand shocks. That kind of people make her really physically sick."

"I didn't tell them to come here. They wormed your name out of somebody. They deliberately——"

"Well, it's too bad. It doesn't help matters. Excuse me a minute."

Left alone, Charlie sat tense in his chair. In the next room he could hear the children eating, talking in monosyllables, already oblivious to the scene between their elders. He heard a murmur of conversation from a farther room and then the ticking bell of a telephone receiver picked up, and in a panic he moved to the other side of the room and out of earshot.

In a minute Lincoln came back. "Look here, Charlie. I think we'd better call off dinner for tonight. Marion's in bad shape."

"Is she angry with me?"

"Sort of," he said, almost roughly. "She's not strong and——"

"You mean she's changed her mind about Honoria."

"She's pretty bitter right now. I don't know. You phone me at the bank tomorrow."

"I wish you'd explain to her I never dreamed these people would come here. I'm just as sore as you are."

"I couldn't explain anything to her now."

Charlie got up. He took his coat and hat and started down the corridor. Then he opened the door of the dining room and said in a strange voice, "Good night, children."

Honoria rose and ran around the table to hug him.

"Good night, sweetheart," he said vaguely, and then trying to make his voice more tender, trying to conciliate something, "Good night, dear children."

V

Charlie went directly to the Ritz bar with the furious idea of finding Lorraine and Duncan, but they were not there,

and he realized that in any case there was nothing he could do. He had not touched his drink at the Peters', and now he ordered a whisky-and-soda. Paul came over to say hello.

"It's a great change," he said sadly. "We do about half the business we did. So many fellows I hear about back in the States lost everything, maybe not in the first crash, but then in the second. Your friend George Hardt lost every cent, I hear. Are you back in the States?"

"No. I'm in business in Prague."

"I heard that you lost a lot in the crash."

"I did," and he added grimly, "but I lost everything I wanted in the boom."

"Selling short?"

"Something like that."

Again the memory of those days swept over him like a nightmare—the people they had met travelling; the people who couldn't add a row of figures or speak a coherent sentence. The little man Helen had consented to dance with at the ship's party, who had insulted her ten feet from the table; the women and girls carried screaming with drink or drugs out of public places . . . the men who locked their wives out in the snow, because the snow of '29 wasn't real snow. If you didn't want it to be snow, you just paid some money.

He went to the phone and called the Peters apartment; Lincoln answered.

"I called up because this thing is on my mind. Has Marion said anything definite?"

"Marion's sick," Lincoln answered shortly. "I know this thing isn't altogether your fault, but I can't have her go to pieces about it. I'm afraid we'll have to let it slide for six months; I can't take the chance of working her up to this state again."

"I see."

"I'm sorry, Charlie."

He went back to his table. His whisky glass was empty, but he shook his head when Alix looked at it questioningly. There wasn't much he could do now except send Honoria some things; he would send her a lot of things tomorrow. He thought rather angrily that this was just money—he had given so many people money. . . .

"No, no more," he said to another waiter. "What do I owe you?"

He would come back some day; they couldn't make him pay forever. But he wanted his child, and nothing was much good now, beside that fact. He wasn't young any more, with a lot of nice thoughts and dreams to have by himself. He was absolutely sure Helen wouldn't have wanted him to be so alone.

John Dos Passos
1896

DOS PASSOS was born in Chicago. His early experience included travel in Mexico and Belgium and some years on a farm in Virginia. He attended private schools and Harvard University, graduating in 1916. After service in an ambulance corps with the French army, he enlisted in the medical corps of the American army in 1918. His first novels, *One Man's Initiation—1917* (1920) and *Three Soldiers* (1921), were based on his war experience. He lived for a time in Paris in the early 1920's, but returned to the United States, to work at Provincetown, Massachusetts, and to travel frequently throughout the country. *Manhattan Transfer* (1925) increased his literary reputation. The technical experimentation and the social criticism of this novel were elaborated in the loosely related books which make up the trilogy *U.S.A.*, published in 1938: *The 42nd Parallel* (1930); *1919* (1932); and *The Big Money* (1936), source of the following selections. Among his later works, *The Ground We Stand On* (1941), essays on early Americans, and *Number One* (1943), a novel about demagoguery, are the most significant. [See J. W. Beach, *American Fiction 1920-1940* (New York, 1941).]

TIN LIZZIE

"MR. FORD the automobileer," the featurewriter wrote in 1900,

"Mr. Ford the automobileer began by giving his steed three or four sharp jerks with the lever at the righthand side of the seat; that is, he pulled the lever up and down sharply in order, as he said, to mix air with gasoline and drive the charge into the exploding cylinder. . . . Mr. Ford slipped a small electric switch handle and there followed a puff, puff, puff. . . . The puffing of the machine assumed a higher key. She was flying along about eight miles an hour. The ruts in the road were deep, but the machine certainly went with a dreamlike smoothness. There was none of the bumping common even to a streetcar. . . . By this time the boulevard had been reached, and the automobileer, letting a lever fall a little, let her out. Whiz! She picked up speed with infinite rapidity. As she ran on there was a clattering behind, the new noise of the automobile.

For twenty years or more, ever since he'd left his father's farm when he was sixteen to get a job in a Detroit machineshop, Henry Ford had been nuts about machinery. First it was watches, then he designed a steamtractor, then he built a horseless carriage with an engine adapted from the Otto gasengine he'd read about in *The World of Science*, then a mechanical buggy with a onecylinder fourcycle motor, that would run forward but not back;

at last, in ninetyeight, he felt he was far enough along to risk throwing up his job with the Detroit Edison Company, where he'd worked his way up from night fireman to chief engineer, to put all his time into working on a new gasoline engine,

(in the late eighties he'd met Edison at a meeting of electriclight employees in Atlantic City. He'd gone up to Edison after Edison had delivered an address and asked him if he thought gasoline was practical as a motor fuel. Edison had said yes. If Edison said it, it was true. Edison was the great admiration of Henry Ford's life);

and in driving his mechanical buggy, sitting there at the lever jauntily dressed in a tightbuttoned jacket and a high collar and a derby hat, back and forth over the level illpaved streets of Detroit,

scaring the big brewery horses and the skinny trotting horses and the sleekrumped pacers with the motor's loud explosions,

looking for men scatterbrained enough to invest money in a factory for building automobiles.

He was the eldest son of an Irish immigrant who during the Civil War had married the daughter of a prosperous Pennsylvania Dutch farmer and settled down to farming near Dearborn in Wayne County, Michigan;

like plenty of other Americans, young Henry grew up hating the endless sogging through the mud about the chores, the hauling and pitching manure, the kerosene lamps to clean, the irk and sweat and solitude of the farm.

He was a slender, active youngster, a good skater, clever with his hands; what he liked was to tend the machinery and let the others do the heavy work. His mother had told him not to drink, smoke, gamble or go into debt, and he never did.

When he was in his early twenties his father tried to get him back from Detroit, where he was working as mechanic and repairman for the Drydock Engine Company that built engines for steamboats, by giving him forty acres of land.

Young Henry built himself an uptodate square white dwellinghouse with a false mansard roof and married and settled down on the farm,

but he let the hired men do the farming;

he bought himself a buzzsaw and rented a stationary engine and cut the timber off the woodlots.

He was a thrifty young man who never drank or smoked or gambled or coveted his neighbor's wife, but he couldn't stand living on the farm.

He moved to Detroit, and in the brick barn behind his house tinkered for years in his spare time with a mechanical buggy that would be light enough to run over the clayey wagonroads of Wayne County, Michigan.

By 1900 he had a practicable car to promote.

He was forty years old before the Ford Motor Company was started and production began to move.

Speed was the first thing the early automobile manufacturers went after. Races advertised the makes of cars.

Henry Ford himself hung up several records at the track at Grosse Pointe and on the ice on Lake St. Clair. In his 999 he did the mile in thirtynine and fourfifths seconds.

But it had always been his custom to hire others to do the heavy work. The speed he was busy with was speed in production, the records records in efficient output. He hired Barney Oldfield, a stunt bicyclerider from Salt Lake City, to do the racing for him.

Henry Ford had ideas about other things than the designing of motors, carburetors, magnetos, jigs and fixtures, punches and dies; he had ideas about sales,

that the big money was in economical quantity production, quick turnover, cheap interchangeable easilyreplaced standardized parts;

it wasn't until 1909, after years of arguing with his partners, that Ford put out the first Model T.

Henry Ford was right.

That season he sold more than ten thousand tin lizzies, ten years later he was selling almost a million a year.

In these years the Taylor Plan was stirring up plantmanagers and manufacturers all over the country. Efficiency was the word. The same ingenuity that went into improving the performance of a machine could go into improving the performance of the workmen producing the machine.

In 1913 they established the assemblyline at Ford's. That season the profits were something like twentyfive million dollars, but they had trouble in keeping the men on the job, machinists didn't seem to like it at Ford's.

Henry Ford had ideas about other things than production.

He was the largest automobile manufacturer in the world; he paid high wages; maybe if the steady workers thought they were getting a cut (a very small cut) in the profits, it would give trained men an inducement to stick to their jobs,

wellpaid workers might save enough money to buy a tin lizzie; the first day Ford's announced that cleancut properlymarried American workers who wanted jobs had a chance to make five bucks a day (of course it turned out that there were strings to it; always there were strings to it)

such an enormous crowd waited outside the Highland Park plant

all through the zero January night

that there was a riot when the gates were opened; cops broke heads, jobhunters threw bricks; property, Henry Ford's own property, was destroyed. The company dicks had to turn on the firehose to beat back the crowd.

The American Plan; automotive prosperity seeping down from above; it turned out there were strings to it.

But that five dollars a day
paid to good, clean American workmen
who didn't drink or smoke cigarettes or read or think,
and who didn't commit adultery
and whose wives didn't take in boarders,
made America once more the Yukon of the sweated workers of the world;
made all the tin lizzies and the automotive age, and incidentally,
made Henry Ford the automobileer, the admirer of Edison, the birdlover,
the great American of his time.

But Henry Ford had ideas about other things besides assemblylines and the livinghabits of his employees. He was full of ideas. Instead of going to the city to make his fortune, here was a country boy who'd made his fortune by bringing the city out to the farm. The precepts he'd learned out of McGuffey's Reader, his mother's prejudices and preconceptions, he had preserved clean and unworn as freshprinted bills in the safe in a bank.

He wanted people to know about his ideas, so he bought the *Dearborn Independent* and started a campaign against cigarettesmoking.

When war broke out in Europe, he had ideas about that too. (Suspicion of armymen and soldiering were part of the midwest farm tradition, like thrift, stickativeness, temperance and sharp practice in money matters.) Any intelligent American mechanic could see that if the Europeans hadn't been a lot of ignorant underpaid foreigners who drank, smoked, were loose about women and wasteful in their methods of production, the war could never have happened.

When Rosika Schwimmer broke through the stockade of secretaries and servicemen who surrounded Henry Ford and suggested to him that he could stop the war,

he said sure they'd hire a ship and go over and get the boys out of the trenches by Christmas.

He hired a steamboat, the *Oscar II*, and filled it up with pacifists and socialworkers,

to go over to explain to the princelings of Europe

that what they were doing was vicious and silly.

It wasn't his fault that Poor Richard's commonsense no longer rules the world and that most of the pacifists were nuts,

goofy with headlines.

When William Jennings Bryan went over to Hoboken to see him off, somebody handed William Jennings Bryan a squirrel in a cage; William Jennings Bryan made a speech with the squirrel under his arm. Henry Ford threw American Beauty roses to the crowd. The band played *I Didn't Raise My Boy to Be a Soldier.* Practical jokers let loose more squirrels. An eloping couple was married by a platoon of ministers in the saloon, and Mr. Zero, the flophouse humanitarian, who reached the dock too late to sail,

dove into the North River and swam after the boat.

The *Oscar II* was described as a floating Chautauqua; Henry Ford said it felt like a middlewestern village, but by the time they reached Christiansand in Norway, the reporters had kidded him so that he had gotten cold feet and gone to bed. The world was too crazy outside of Wayne County, Michigan. Mrs. Ford and the management sent an Episcopal dean after him who brought him home under wraps,

and the pacifists had to speechify without him.

Two years later Ford's was manufacturing munitions, Eagle boats; Henry Ford was planning oneman tanks, and oneman submarines like the one tried out in the Revolutionary War. He announced to the press that he'd turn over his war profits to the government,

but there's no record that he ever did.

One thing he brought back from his trip was the Protocols of the Elders of Zion.

He started a campaign to enlighten the world in the *Dearborn Independent;* the Jews were why the world wasn't like Wayne County, Michigan, in the old horse and buggy days;

the Jews had started the war, Bolshevism, Darwinism, Marxism, Nietzsche, short skirts and lipstick. They were behind Wall Street and the international bankers, and the whiteslave traffic and the movies and the Supreme Court and ragtime and the illegal liquor business.

Henry Ford denounced the Jews and ran for senator and sued the *Chicago Tribune* for libel,

and was the laughingstock of the kept metropolitan press;

but when the metropolitan bankers tried to horn in on his business

he thoroughly outsmarted them.

In 1918 he had borrowed on notes to buy out his minority stockholders for the picayune sum of seventyfive million dollars.

In February, 1920, he needed cash to pay off some of these notes that were coming due. A banker is supposed to have called on him and offered him every facility if the bankers' representative could be made a member of the board of directors. Henry Ford handed the banker his hat,

and went about raising the money in his own way:

he shipped every car and part he had in his plant to his dealers and demanded immediate cash payment. Let the other fellow do the borrowing had always been a cardinal principle. He shut down production and canceled all orders from the supplyfirms. Many dealers were ruined, many supplyfirms failed, but when he reopened his plant,

he owned it absolutely,

the way a man owns an unmortgaged farm with the taxes paid up.

In 1922 there started the Ford boom for President (high wages, waterpower, industry scattered to the small towns) that was skillfully pricked behind the scenes

by another crackerbarrel philosopher,

Calvin Coolidge;

but in 1922 Henry Ford sold one million three hundred and thirtytwo thousand two hundred and nine tin lizzies; he was the richest man in the world.

Good roads had followed the narrow ruts made in the mud by the Model T. The great automotive boom was on. At Ford's production was improving all the time; less waste, more spotters, strawbosses, stoolpigeons (fifteen minutes for lunch, three minutes to go to the toilet, the Taylorized speedup everywhere, reach under, adjust washer, screw down bolt, shove in cotterpin, reachunder adjustwasher, screwdown bolt, reachunderadjustscrewdownreachunderadjust until every ounce of life was sucked off into production and at night the workmen went home grey shaking husks).

Ford owned every detail of the process from the ore in the hills until the car rolled off the end of the assemblyline under its own power, the plants were rationalized to the last tenthousandth of an inch as measured by the Johansen scale;

in 1926 the production cycle was reduced to eightyone hours from the ore in the mine to the finished salable car proceeding under its own power,

but the Model T was obsolete.

New Era prosperity and the American Plan

(there were strings to it, always there were strings to it)

had killed Tin Lizzie.

Ford's was just one of many automobile plants.

When the stockmarket bubble burst,

Mr. Ford the crackerbarrel philosopher said jubilantly,

"I told you so.

Serves you right for gambling and getting in debt.

The country is sound."

But when the country on cracked shoes, in frayed trousers, belts tightened over hollow bellies,

idle hands cracked and chapped with the cold of that coldest March day of 1932,

started marching from Detroit to Dearborn, asking for work and the American Plan, all they could think of at Ford's was machineguns.

The country was sound, but they mowed the marchers down.

They shot four of them dead.

Henry Ford as an old man

is a passionate antiquarian,

(lives besieged on his father's farm embedded in an estate of thousands of millionaire acres, protected by an army of servicemen, secretaries, secret agents, dicks under orders of an English exprizefighter,

always afraid of the feet in broken shoes on the roads, afraid the gangs will kidnap his grandchildren,

that a crank will shoot him,

that Change and the idle hands out of work will break through the gates and the high fences;

protected by a private army against

the new America of starved children and hollow bellies and cracked shoes stamping on souplines,

that has swallowed up the old thrifty farmlands

of Wayne County, Michigan,

as if they had never been).

Henry Ford as an old man

is a passionate antiquarian.

He rebuilt his father's farmhouse and put it back exactly in the state he remembered it in as a boy. He built a village of museums for buggies, sleighs, coaches, old plows, waterwheels, obsolete models of mo-

torcars. He scoured the country for fiddlers
to play oldfashioned squaredances.

Even old taverns he bought and put back
into their original shape, as well as Thomas
Edison's early laboratories.

When he bought the Wayside Inn near
Sudbury, Massachusetts, he had the new
highway where the newmodel cars roared
and slithered and hissed oilily past *(the
new noise of the automobile)*,

    moved away from the door,

    put back the old bad road,

    so that everything might be

    the way it used to be,

    in the days of horses and buggies.

THE CAMERA EYE (50)

they have clubbed us off the streets
they are stronger   they are rich   they
hire and fire the politicians the newspaper-
editors the old judges the small men with
reputations the collegepresidents the ward-
heelers (listen businessmen collegepresidents judges   America will not forget her
betrayers) they hire the men with guns
the uniforms the policecars the patrol-
wagons

all right you have won   you will kill
the brave men our friends tonight

there is nothing left to do   we are beaten
we the beaten crowd together in these old
dingy schoolrooms on Salem Street shuffle
up and down the gritty creaking stairs sit
hunched with bowed heads on benches and
hear the old words of the haters of oppression   made new in sweat and agony to-
night

our work is over   the scribbled phrases
the nights typing releases the smell of the
printshop the sharp reek of newprinted
leaflets the rush for Western Union string-
ing words into wires the search for stinging words to make you feel who are your
oppressors America

America our nation has been beaten by
strangers who have turned our language
inside out who have taken the clean words
our fathers spoke and made them slimy and
foul

their hired men sit on the judge's bench
they sit back with their feet on the tables
under the dome of the State House they
are ignorant of our beliefs they have the
dollars the guns the armed forces the
powerplants

they have built the electricchair and hired
the executioner to throw the switch

all right we are two nations

America our nation has been beaten by
strangers who have bought the laws and
fenced off the meadows and cut down the
woods for pulp and turned our pleasant
cities into slums and sweated the wealth out
of our people and when they want to they
hire the executioner to throw the switch

but do they know that the old words of
the immigrants are being renewed in
blood and agony tonight do they know
that the old American speech of the haters
of oppression is new tonight in the mouth
of an old woman from Pittsburgh of a
husky boilermaker from Frisco who hopped
freights clear from the Coast to come
here in the mouth of a Back Bay social-
worker in the mouth of an Italian printer
of a hobo from Arkansas   the language
of the beaten nation is not forgotten in
our ears tonight

the men in the deathhouse made the old
words new before they died

*If it had not been for these things, I
might have lived out my life talking at
streetcorners to scorning men. I might have
died unknown, unmarked, a failure. This is
our career and our triumph. Never in our
full life can we hope to do such work for
tolerance, for justice, for man's understanding of man as how we do by an accident.*

now their work is over   the immigrants
haters of oppression lie quiet in black suits
in the little undertaking parlor in the
North End   the city is quiet the men of
the conquering nation are not to be seen
on the streets

they have won why are they scared to
be seen on the streets? on the streets
you see only the downcast faces of the

beaten the streets belong to the beaten nation all the way to the cemetery where the bodies of the immigrants are to be burned we line the curbs in the drizzling rain we crowd the wet sidewalks elbow to elbow silent pale looking with scared eyes at the coffins

we stand defeated America

NEWSREEL LXVII

when things are upset, there's always chaos, said Mr. Ford. Work can accomplish wonders and overcome chaotic conditions. When the Russian masses will learn to want more than they have, when they will want white collars, soap, better clothes, better shoes, better housing, better living conditions

I lift up my finger and I say
tweet tweet
shush shush
now now
come come

REPUBLIC-TRUMBULL STEEL MERGER VOTED

There along the dreamy Amazon
We met upon the shore
Tho' the love I knew is ever gone

WHEAT OVERSOLD REACHES NEW HIGH

Dreams linger on

the first thing the volunteer firefighters did was to open the windows to let the smoke out. This created a draft and the fire with a good thirty mile wind right from the ocean did the rest

RECORD TURNOVER IN INSURANCE SHARES AS TRADING PROGRESSES

outside the scene was a veritable bedlam. Well-dressed women walked up and down wringing their hands, helpless to save their belongings, while from the windows of the

upper stories there rained a shower of trunks, suitcases and clothing hurled out indiscriminately. Jewelry and bricabrac valued at thousands was picked up by the spectators from the lawn, who thrust the objects under their coats and disappeared

BROKERS LOANS HIT NEW HIGH

Change all of your gray skies
Turn them into gay skies
And keep sweeping the cobwebs off the
moon

MARKETS OPTIMISTIC

learn new uses for cement. How to develop profitable concrete business. How to judge materials. How to figure jobs. How to reinforce concrete. How to build forms, roads, sidewalks, floors, foundations, culverts, cellars

And even tho' the Irish and the Dutch
Say it don't amount to much
Fifty million Frenchmen can't be
wrong

STARSPANGLED BANDIT GANG ROBS DINERS

MURDER BARES QUAKER STATE FANTASIES

Poker Slayer Praised

Poor little Hollywood Rose
so all alone
No one in Hollywood knows
how sad she's grown

FIVE HUNDRED MILLIONS IN BANK DEAL

Sure I love the dear silver that shines in
your hair
And the brow that's all furrowed
And wrinkled with care
I kiss the dear fingers so toil worn
for me

CARBONIC BUYS IN DRY ICE

GAB MARATHON RUN FOR GOLD ON BROADWAY

the broad advertising of the bull markets, the wide extension of the ticker services, the equipping of branch brokerage offices with tickers, transparent, magnified translux stockquotation rolls· have had the natural result of stirring up nation-wide interest in the stockmarket

VAG

The young man waits at the edge of the concrete, with one hand he grips a rubbed suitcase of phony leather, the other hand almost making a fist, thumb up

that moves in ever so slight an arc when a car slithers past, a truck roars clatters; the wind of cars passing ruffles his hair, slaps grit in his face.

Head swims, hunger has twisted the belly tight,

he has skinned a heel through the torn sock, feet ache in the broken shoes, under the threadbare suit carefully brushed off with the hand, the torn drawers have a crummy feel, the feel of having slept in your clothes; in the nostrils lingers the staleness of discouraged carcasses crowded into a transient camp, the carbolic stench of the jail, on the taut cheeks the shamed flush from the boring eyes of cops and deputies, railroadbulls (they eat three squares a day, they are buttoned into wellmade clothes, they have wives to sleep with, kids to play with after supper, they work for the big men who buy their way, they stick their chests out with the sureness of power behind their backs). Git the hell out, scram. Know what's good for you, you'll make yourself scarce. Gittin' tough, eh? Think you kin take it, eh?

The punch in the jaw, the slam on the head with the nightstick, the wrist grabbed and twisted behind the back, the big knee brought up sharp into the crotch,

the walk out of town with sore feet to stand and wait at the edge of the hissing speeding string of cars where the reek of ether and lead and gas melts into the silent grassy smell of the earth.

Eyes black with want seek out the eyes of the drivers, a hitch, a hundred miles down the road.

Overhead in the blue a plane drones. Eyes follow the silver Douglas that flashes once in the sun and bores its smooth way out of sight into the blue.

(The transcontinental passengers sit pretty, big men with bankaccounts, highlypaid jobs, who are saluted by doormen; telephonegirls say goodmorning to them. Last night after a fine dinner, drinks with friends, they left Newark. Roar of climbing motors slanting up into the inky haze. Lights drop away. An hour staring along a silvery wing at a big lonesome moon hurrying west through curdling scum. Beacons flash in a line across Ohio.

At Cleveland the plane drops banking in a smooth spiral, the string of lights along the lake swings in a circle. Climbing roar of the motors again; slumped in the soft seat drowsing through the flat moonlight night.

Chi. A glimpse of the dipper. Another spiral swoop from cool into hot air thick with dust and the reek of burnt prairies.

Beyond the Mississippi dawn creeps up behind through the murk over the great plains. Puddles of mist go white in the Iowa hills, farms, fences, silos, steel glint from a river. The blinking eyes of the beacons reddening into day. Watercourses vein the eroded hills.

Omaha. Great cumulus clouds, from coppery churning to creamy to silvery white, trail brown skirts of rain over the hot plains. Red and yellow badlands, tiny horned shapes of cattle.

Cheyenne. The cool high air smells of sweetgrass.

The tightbaled clouds to westward burst and scatter in tatters over the strawcolored hills. Indigo mountains jut rimrock. The plane breasts a huge crumbling cloudbank and toboggans over bumpy air across green and crimson slopes into the sunny dazzle of Salt Lake.

The transcontinental passenger thinks contracts, profits, vacationtrips, mighty continent between Atlantic and Pacific, power, wires humming dollars, cities jammed, hills empty, the indiantrail leading into the wagonroad, the macadamed pike, the concrete skyway; trains, planes: history the billiondollar speedup,

and in the bumpy air over the desert ranges towards Las Vegas

sickens and vomits into the carton container the steak and mushrooms he ate in New York. No matter, silver in the pocket, greenbacks in the wallet, drafts, certified checks, plenty restaurants in L. A.)

The young man waits on the side of the road; the plane has gone; thumb moves in a small arc when a car tears hissing past. Eyes seek the driver's eyes. A hundred miles down the road. Head swims, belly tightens, wants crawl over his skin like ants:

went to school, books said opportunity, ads promised speed, own your home, shine bigger than your neighbor, the radiocrooner whispered girls, ghosts of platinum girls coaxed from the screen, millions in winnings were chalked up on the boards in the offices, paychecks were for hands willing to work, the cleared desk of an executive with three telephones on it;

waits with swimming head, needs knot the belly, idle hands numb, beside the speeding traffic.

A hundred miles down the road.

Ernest Hemingway

1898

DURING his boyhood Ernest Hemingway spent long vacations in Northern Michigan with his father, a physician at Oak Park, Illinois, and an ardent hunter and fisherman. He did not attend college, but worked as a farmhand, sparring partner, and reporter on the Kansas City *Star* before volunteering in an American ambulance unit at the outbreak of the first world war. He later joined the Italian army, and was wounded and decorated. After the war he did newspaper work in Europe, figured prominently in the group of American expatriates in Paris, and became especially interested in Spain.

Hemingway's first book, *Three Stories and Ten Poems*, was published in Paris, in 1923. *The Sun Also Rises* (1926) and *A Farewell to Arms* (1929) gave him popular as well as critical reputation. In 1927 he returned to the United States, and in 1930 bought a house at Key West, Florida. An expedition after big game in Africa yielded the material of the autobiographical *Green Hills of Africa* (1935), and a sustained and almost professional interest in bullfighting that of *Death in the Afternoon* (1932).

In 1936 Hemingway returned to Spain at the beginning of the Spanish Civil War. He wrote the text and assisted in the production of the documentary motion picture, *The Spanish Earth,* and supported the Loyalist cause in other ways. His novel of the Spanish Civil War, *For Whom the Bell Tolls,* appeared in 1940. A play also dealing with the Spanish War appeared in 1938, with a collection of Hemingway's short stories from earlier volumes, under the title *The Fifth Column and the First Forty-nine Stories.*

[See E. B. Burgum's *The Novel and the World's Dilemma* (New York, 1947) and R. B. West's essay in *Forms of Modern Fiction,* ed. W. Van O'Connor (Minneapolis, 1948).]

BIG TWO-HEARTED RIVER: PART I
[1925]

THE TRAIN went on up the track out of sight, around one of the hills of burnt timber. Nick sat down on the bundle of canvas and bedding the baggage man had pitched out of the door of the baggage car. There was no town, nothing but the rails and the burned-over country. The thirteen saloons that had lined the one street of Seney had not left a trace. The foundations of the Mansion House hotel stuck up above the ground. The stone was chipped and split by the fire. It was all that was left of the town of Seney. Even the surface had been burned off the ground.

Nick looked at the burned-over stretch of hillside, where he had expected to find the scattered houses of the town, and then walked down the railroad track to the bridge over the river. The river was there. It swirled against the log spiles of the bridge. Nick looked down into the clear, brown water, colored from the pebbly bottom, and watched the trout keeping themselves steady in the current with wavering fins. As he watched them they changed their positions by quick angles, only to hold steady in the fast water again. Nick watched them a long time.

He watched them holding themselves with their noses into the current, many trout in deep, fast moving water, slightly distorted as he watched far down through the glassy convex surface of the pool, its surface pushing and swelling smooth against the resistance of the log-driven piles of the bridge. At the bottom of the pool were the big trout. Nick did not see them at first. Then he saw them at the bottom of the pool, big trout looking to hold themselves on the gravel bottom in a varying mist of gravel and sand, raised in spurts by the current.

Nick looked down into the pool from the bridge. It was a hot day. A kingfisher flew up the stream. It was a long time since Nick had looked into a stream and seen trout. They were very satisfactory. As the shadow of the kingfisher moved up the stream, a big trout shot upstream in a long angle, only his shadow marking the angle, then lost his shadow as he came through the surface of the water, caught the sun, and then, as he went back into the stream under the surface, his shadow seemed to float down the stream with the current, unresisting, to his post under the bridge where he tightened facing up into the current.

Nick's heart tightened as the trout moved. He felt all the old feeling.

He turned and looked down the stream. It stretched away, pebbly-bottomed with shallows and big boulders and a deep pool as it curved away around the foot of a bluff.

Nick walked back up the ties to where his pack lay in the cinders beside the railway track. He was happy. He adjusted the pack harness around the bundle, pulling straps tight, slung the pack on his back, got his arms through the shoulder straps and took some of the pull off his shoulders by leaning his forehead against the wide band of the tump-line. Still, it was too heavy. It was much too heavy. He had his leather rod-case in his hand and leaning forward to keep the weight of the pack high on his shoulders he walked along the road that paralleled the railway track, leaving the burned town behind in the heat, and then turned off around a hill with a high, fire-scarred hill on either side onto a road that went back into the country. He walked along the road feeling the ache from the pull of the heavy pack. The road climbed steadily. It was hard work walking up-hill. His muscles ached and the day was hot, but Nick felt happy. He felt he had left everything behind, the need for thinking, the need to write, other needs. It was all back of him.

From the time he had gotten down off the train and the baggage man had thrown his pack out of the open car door things had been different. Seney was burned, the country was burned over and changed, but it did not matter. It could not all be burned. He knew that. He hiked along the road, sweating in the sun, climbing to cross the range of hills that separated the railway from the pine plains.

The road ran on, dipping occasionally, but always climbing. Nick went on up. Finally the road after going parallel to the burnt hillside reached the top. Nick leaned back against a stump and slipped out of the pack harness. Ahead of him, as far as he could see, was the pine plain. The burned country stopped off at the left with the range of hills. On ahead islands of dark pine trees rose out of the plain. Far off to the left was the line of the river. Nick followed it with his eye and caught glints of the water in the sun.

There was nothing but the pine plain ahead of him, until the far blue hills that marked the Lake Superior height of land. He could hardly see them, faint and far away in the heat-light over the plain. If he looked too steadily they were gone. But if he only half-looked they were there, the far-off hills of the height of land.

Nick sat down against the charred stump and smoked a cigarette. His pack balanced on the top of the stump, harness holding ready, a hollow molded in it from his back. Nick sat smoking, looking out over the country. He did not need to get his map out. He knew where he was from the position of the river.

As he smoked, his legs stretched out in front of him, he noticed a grasshopper walk along the ground and up onto his woolen sock. The grasshopper was black. As he had walked along the road, climbing, he had started many grasshoppers from the dust. They were all black. They were not the big grasshoppers with yellow and black or red and black wings whirring out from their black wing sheathing as they fly up. These were just ordinary hoppers, but all a sooty black in color. Nick had wondered about them as he walked, without really thinking about them. Now, as he watched the black hopper that was nibbling at the wool of his sock with its fourway lip, he realized that they had all turned black from living in the burned-over land. He realized that the fire must have come the year before, but the grasshoppers were all black now. He wondered how long they would stay that way.

Carefully he reached his hand down and took hold of the hopper by the wings. He turned him up, all his legs walking in the air, and looked at his jointed belly. Yes, it was black too, iridescent where the back and head were dusty.

"Go on, hopper," Nick said, speaking out loud for the first time. "Fly away somewhere."

He tossed the grasshopper up into the air and watched him sail away to a charcoal stump across the road.

Nick stood up. He leaned his back against the weight of his pack where it rested upright on the stump and got his arms through the shoulder straps. He stood with the pack on his back on the brow of the hill looking out across the country, toward the distant river, and then struck down the hillside away from the road. Underfoot the ground was good walking. Two hundred yards down the hillside the fire line stopped. Then it was sweet fern, growing ankle high, to walk through, and clumps of jack pines; a long undulating country with frequent rises and descents, sandy underfoot and the country alive again.

Nick kept his direction by the sun. He knew where he wanted to strike the river and he kept on through the pine plain, mounting small rises to see other rises ahead of him and sometimes from the top of a rise a great solid island of pines off to his right or his left. He broke off some sprigs of the heathery sweet fern, and put them under his pack straps. The chafing crushed it and he smelled it as he walked.

He was tired and very hot, walking across the uneven, shadeless pine plain. At any time he knew he could strike the river by turning off to his left. It could not be more than a mile away. But he kept on toward the north to hit the river as far upstream as he could go in one day's walking.

For some time as he walked Nick had been in sight of one of the big islands of pine standing out above the rolling high ground he was crossing. He dipped down and then as he came slowly up to the crest of the bridge he turned and made toward the pine trees.

There was no underbrush in the island of pine trees. The trunks of the trees went straight up or slanted toward each other. The trunks were straight and brown without branches. The branches were high above. Some interlocked to make a solid shadow on the brown forest floor. Around the grove of trees was a bare space. It was brown and soft underfoot as Nick walked on it. This was the over-lapping of the pine needle floor, extending out beyond the width of the high branches. The trees had grown tall and the branches moved high, leaving in the sun this bare space they had once covered with shadow. Sharp at the edge of this extension of the forest floor commenced the sweet fern.

Nick slipped off his pack and lay down in the shade. He lay on his back and looked up into the pine trees. His neck and back and the small of his back rested as he stretched. The earth felt good against his

back. He looked up at the sky, through the branches, and then shut his eyes. He opened them and looked up again. There was a wind high up in the branches. He shut his eyes again and went to sleep.

Nick woke stiff and cramped. The sun was nearly down. His pack was heavy and the straps painful as he lifted it on. He leaned over with the pack on and picked up the leather rod-case and started out from the pine trees across the sweet fern swale, toward the river. He knew it could not be more than a mile.

He came down a hillside covered with stumps into a meadow. At the edge of the meadow flowed the river. Nick was glad to get to the river. He walked upstream through the meadow. His trousers were soaked with the dew as he walked. After the hot day, the dew had come quickly and heavily. The river made no sound. It was too fast and smooth. At the edge of the meadow, before he mounted to a piece of high ground to make camp, Nick looked down the river at the trout rising. They were rising to insects come from the swamp on the other side of the stream when the sun went down. The trout jumped out of water to take them. While Nick walked through the little stretch of meadow alongside the stream, trout had jumped high out of water. Now as he looked down the river, the insects must be settling on the surface, for the trout were feeding steadily all down the stream. As far down the long stretch as he could see, the trout were rising, making circles all down the surface of the water, as though it were starting to rain.

The ground rose, wooded and sandy, to overlook the meadow, the stretch of river and the swamp. Nick dropped his pack and rod-case and looked for a level piece of ground. He was very hungry and he wanted to make his camp before he cooked. Between two jack pines, the ground was quite level. He took the ax out of the pack and chopped out two projecting roots. That leveled a piece of ground large enough to sleep on. He smoothed out the sandy soil with his hand and pulled all the sweet fern bushes by their roots. His hands smelled good from the sweet fern. He smoothed the uprooted earth. He did not want anything making lumps under the blankets. When he had the ground smooth, he spread his three blankets. One he folded double, next to the ground. The other two he spread on top.

With the ax he slit off a bright slab of pine from one of the stumps and split it into pegs for the tent. He wanted them long and solid to hold in the ground. With the tent unpacked and spread on the ground, the pack, leaning against a jack-pine, looked much smaller. Nick tied the rope that served the tent for a ridge-pole to the trunk of one of the pine trees and pulled the tent up off the ground with the other end of the rope and tied it to the other pine. The tent hung on the rope like a canvas blanket on a clothesline. Nick poked a pole he had cut up under the back peak of the canvas and then made it a tent by pegging out the sides. He pegged the sides out taut and drove the pegs deep, hitting them down into the ground with the flat of the ax until the rope loops were buried and the canvas was drum tight.

Across the open mouth of the tent Nick fixed cheesecloth to keep out mosquitoes. He crawled inside under the mosquito bar with various things from the pack to put at the head of the bed under the slant of the canvas. Inside the tent the light came through the brown canvas. It smelled pleasantly of canvas. Already there was something mysterious and homelike. Nick was happy as he crawled inside the tent. He had not been unhappy all day. This was different though. Now things were done. There had been this to do. Now it was done. It had been a hard trip. He was very tired. That was done. He had made his camp. He was settled. Nothing could touch him. It was a good place to camp. He was there, in the good place. He was in his home where he had made it. Now he was hungry.

He came out, crawling under the cheese-cloth. It was quite dark outside. It was lighter in the tent.

Nick went over to the pack and found, with his fingers, a long nail in a paper sack of nails, in the bottom of the pack. He drove it into the pine tree, holding it close and hitting it gently with the flat of the ax. He hung the pack up on the nail. All his supplies were in the pack. They were off the ground and sheltered now.

Nick was hungry. He did not believe he had ever been hungrier. He opened and emptied a can of pork and beans and a can of spaghetti into the frying pan.

"I've got a right to eat this kind of stuff, if I'm willing to carry it," Nick said. His voice sounded strange in the darkening woods. He did not speak again.

He started a fire with some chunks of pine he got with the ax from a stump. Over the fire he stuck a wire grill, pushing the four legs down into the ground with his boot. Nick put the frying pan on the grill over the flames. He was hungrier. The beans and spaghetti warmed. Nick stirred them and mixed them together. They began to bubble, making little bubbles that rose with difficulty to the surface. There was a good smell. Nick got out a bottle of tomato catchup and cut four slices of bread. The little bubbles were coming faster now. Nick sat down beside the fire and lifted the frying pan off. He poured about half the contents out into the tin plate. It spread slowly on the plate. Nick knew it was too hot. He poured on some tomato catchup. He knew the beans and spaghetti were still too hot. He looked at the fire, then at the tent, he was not going to spoil it all by burning his tongue. For years he had never enjoyed fried bananas because he had never been able to wait for them to cool. His tongue was very sensitive. He was very hungry. Across the river in the swamp, in the almost dark, he saw a mist rising. He looked at the tent once more. All right. He took a full spoonful from the plate.

"Chrise," Nick said, "Geezus Chrise," he said happily.

He ate the whole plateful before he remembered the bread. Nick finished the second plateful with the bread, mopping the plate shiny. He had not eaten since a cup of coffee and a ham sandwich in the station restaurant at St. Ignace. It had been a very fine experience. He had been that hungry before, but had not been able to satisfy it. He could have made camp hours before if he had wanted to. There were plenty of good places to camp on the river. But this was good.

Nick tucked two big chips of pine under the grill. The fire flared up. He had forgotten to get water for the coffee. Out of the pack he got a folding canvas bucket and walked down the hill, across the edge of the meadow, to the stream. The other bank was in the white mist. The grass was wet and cold as he knelt on the bank and dipped the canvas bucket into the stream. It bellied and pulled hard in the current. The water was ice cold. Nick rinsed the bucket and carried it full up to the camp. Up away from the stream it was not so cold.

Nick drove another big nail and hung up the bucket full of water. He dipped the coffee pot half full, put some more chips under the grill onto the fire and put the pot on. He could not remember which way he made coffee. He could remember an argument about it with Hopkins, but not which side he had taken. He decided to bring it to a boil. He remembered now that was Hopkins's way. He had once argued about everything with Hopkins. While he waited for the coffee to boil, he opened a small can of apricots. He liked to open cans. He emptied the can of apricots out into a tin cup. While he watched the coffee on the fire, he drank the juice syrup of the apricots, carefully at first to keep from spilling, then meditatively, sucking the apricots down. They were better than fresh apricots.

The coffee boiled as he watched. The lid came up and coffee and grounds ran down the side of the pot. Nick took it off the grill.

It was a triumph for Hopkins. He put sugar in the empty apricot cup and poured some of the coffee out to cool. It was too hot to pour and he used his hat to hold the handle of the coffee pot. He would not let it steep in the pot at all. Not the first cup. It should be straight Hopkins all the way. Hop deserved that. He was a very serious coffee drinker. He was the most serious man Nick had ever known. Not heavy, serious. That was a long time ago. Hopkins spoke without moving his lips. He had played polo. He made millions of dollars in Texas. He had borrowed carfare to go to Chicago, when the wire came that his first big well had come in. He could have wired for money. That would have been too slow. They called Hop's girl the Blonde Venus. Hop did not mind because she was not his real girl. Hopkins said very confidently that none of them would make fun of his real girl. He was right. Hopkins went away when the telegram came. That was on the Black River. It took eight days for the telegram to reach him. Hopkins gave away his .22 caliber Colt automatic pistol to Nick. He gave his camera to Bill. It was to remember him always by. They were all going fishing again next summer. The Hop Head was rich. He would get a yacht and they would all cruise along the north shore of Lake Superior. He was excited but serious. They said good-bye and all felt bad. It broke up the trip. They never saw Hopkins again. That was a long time ago on the Black River.

Nick drank the coffee, the coffee according to Hopkins. The coffee was bitter. Nick laughed. It made a good ending to the story. His mind was starting to work. He knew he could choke it because he was tired enough. He spilled the coffee out of the pot and shook the grounds loose into the fire. He lit a cigarette and went inside the tent. He took off his shoes and trousers, sitting on the blankets, rolled the shoes up inside the trousers for a pillow and got in between the blankets.

Out through the front of the tent he

watched the glow of the fire, when the night wind blew on it. It was a quiet night. The swamp was perfectly quiet. Nick stretched under the blanket comfortably. A mosquito hummed close to his ear. Nick sat up and lit a match. The mosquito was on the canvas, over his head. Nick moved the match quickly up to it. The mosquito made a satisfactory hiss in the flame. The match went out. Nick lay down again under the blanket. He turned on his side and shut his eyes. He was sleepy. He felt sleep coming. He curled up under the blanket and went to sleep.

BIG TWO-HEARTED RIVER: PART II

IN THE morning the sun was up and the tent was starting to get hot. Nick crawled out under the mosquito netting stretched across the mouth of the tent, to look at the morning. The grass was wet on his hands as he came out. He held his trousers and his shoes in his hands. The sun was just up over the hill. There was the meadow, the river and the swamp. There were birch trees in the green of the swamp on the other side of the river.

The river was clear and smoothly fast in the early morning. Down about two hundred yards were three logs all the way across the stream. They made the water smooth and deep above them. As Nick watched, a mink crossed the river on the logs and went into the swamp. Nick was excited. He was excited by the early morning and the river. He was really too hurried to eat breakfast, but he knew he must. He built a little fire and put on the coffee pot.

While the water was heating in the pot he took an empty bottle and went down over the edge of the high ground to the meadow. The meadow was wet with dew and Nick wanted to catch grasshoppers for bait before the sun dried the grass. He found plenty of good grasshoppers. They were at the base of the grass stems. Sometimes they clung to a grass stem. They were cold and wet with the dew, and could not jump until the sun warmed them. Nick picked them up, taking only the medium-sized brown ones, and put them into the bottle. He turned over a log and just under the shelter of the edge were several hundred hoppers. It was a grasshopper lodging house. Nick put about fifty of the medium browns into the bottle. While he was picking up the hoppers the others warmed in the sun and commenced to hop away. They flew when they hopped. At first they made one flight and stayed stiff when they landed, as though they were dead.

Nick knew that by the time he was through with breakfast they would be as lively as ever. Without dew in the grass it would take him all day to catch a bottle full of good grasshoppers and he would have to crush many of them, slamming at them with his hat. He washed his hands at the stream. He was excited to be near it. Then he walked up to the tent. The hoppers were already jumping stiffly in the grass. In the bottle, warmed by the sun, they were jumping in a mass. Nick put in a pine stick as a cork. It plugged the mouth of the bottle enough, so the hoppers could not get out and left plenty of air passage.

He had rolled the log back and knew he could get grasshoppers there every morning.

Nick laid the bottle full of jumping grasshoppers against a pine trunk. Rapidly he mixed some buckwheat flour with water and stirred it smooth, one cup of flour, one cup of water. He put a handful of coffee in the pot and dipped a lump of grease out of a can and slid it sputtering across the hot skillet. On the smoking skillet he poured smoothly the buckwheat batter. It spread like lava, the grease spitting sharply. Around the edges the buckwheat cake began to firm, then brown, then crisp. The surface was bubbling slowly to porousness. Nick pushed under the browned under surface with a fresh pine chip. He shook the skillet sideways and the cake was loose on the surface. I won't try and flop it, he thought. He slid the chip of clean wood all the way under the cake, and flopped it over onto its face. It sputtered in the pan.

When it was cooked Nick regreased the skillet. He used all the batter. It made another big flapjack and one smaller one.

Nick ate a big flapjack and a smaller one, covered with apple butter. He put apple butter on the third cake, folded it over twice, wrapped it in oiled paper and put it in his shirt pocket. He put the apple butter jar back in the pack and cut bread for two sandwiches.

In the pack he found a big onion. He sliced it in two and peeled the silky outer skin. Then he cut one half into slices and made onion sandwiches. He wrapped them in oiled paper and buttoned them in the other pocket of his khaki shirt. He turned the skillet upside down on the grill, drank the coffee, sweetened and yellow brown with the condensed milk in it, and tidied up the camp. It was a good camp.

Nick took his fly rod out of the leather rod-case, jointed it, and shoved the rod-case back into the tent. He put on the reel and threaded the line through the guides. He had to hold it from hand to hand, as he threaded it, or it would slip back through its own weight. It was a heavy, double tapered fly line. Nick had paid eight dollars for it a long time ago. It was made heavy to lift back in the air and come forward flat and heavy and straight to make it possible to cast a fly which has no weight. Nick opened the aluminum leader box. The leaders were coiled between the damp flannel pads. Nick had wet the pads at the water cooler on the train up to St. Ignace. In the damp pads the gut leaders had softened and Nick unrolled one and tied it by a loop at the end to the heavy fly line. He fastened a hook on the end of the leader. It was a small hook; very thin and springy.

Nick took it from his hook book, sitting with the rod across his lap. He tested the knot and the spring of the rod by pulling the line taut. It was a good feeling. He was careful not to let the hook bite into his finger.

He started down to the stream, holding his rod, the bottle of grasshoppers hung from his neck by a thong tied in half hitches around the neck of the bottle. His landing net hung by a hook from his belt. Over his shoulder was a long flour sack tied at each corner into an ear. The cord went over his shoulder. The sack flapped against his legs.

Nick felt awkward and professionally happy with all his equipment hanging from him. The grasshopper bottle swung against his chest. In his shirt the breast pockets bulged against him with the lunch and his fly book.

He stepped into the stream. It was a shock. His trousers clung tight to his legs. His shoes felt the gravel. The water was a rising cold shock.

Rushing, the current sucked against his legs. Where he stepped in, the water was over his knees. He waded with the current. The gravel slid under his shoes. He looked down at the swirl of water below each leg and tipped up the bottle to get a grasshopper.

The first grasshopper gave a jump in the neck of the bottle and went out into the water. He was sucked under in the whirl by Nick's right leg and came to the surface a little way down stream. He floated rapidly, kicking. In a quick circle, breaking the smooth surface of the water, he disappeared. A trout had taken him.

Another hopper poked his face out of the bottle. His antennæ wavered. He was getting his front legs out of the bottle to jump. Nick took him by the head and held him while he threaded the slim hook under his chin, down through his thorax and into the last segments of his abdomen. The grasshopper took hold of the hook with his front feet, spitting tobacco juice on it. Nick dropped him into the water.

Holding the rod in his right hand he let out line against the pull of the grasshopper in the current. He stripped off line from the reel with his left hand and let it run free. He could see the hopper in the little waves of the current. It went out of sight.

There was a tug on the line. Nick pulled against the taut line. It was his first strike. Holding the now living rod across the current, he brought in the line with his left hand. The rod bent in jerks, the trout pumping against the current. Nick knew it was a small one. He lifted the rod straight up in the air. It bowed with the pull.

He saw the trout in the water jerking with his head and body against the shifting tangent of the line in the stream.

Nick took the line in his left hand and pulled the trout, thumping tiredly against the current, to the surface. His back was mottled the clear, water-over-gravel color, his side flashing in the sun. The rod under his right arm, Nick stooped, dipping his right hand into the current. He held the trout, never still, with his moist right hand, while he unhooked the barb from his mouth, then dropped him back into the stream.

He hung unsteadily in the current, then settled to the bottom beside a stone. Nick reached down his hand to touch him, his arm to the elbow under water. The trout was steady in the moving stream, resting on the gravel, beside a stone. As Nick's fingers touched him, touched his smooth, cool, underwater feeling he was gone, gone in a shadow across the bottom of the stream.

He's all right, Nick thought. He was only tired.

He had wet his hand before he touched the trout, so he would not disturb the delicate mucus that covered him. If a trout was touched with a dry hand, a white fungus attacked the unprotected spot. Years before when he had fished crowded streams, with fly fishermen ahead of him and behind him, Nick had again and again come on dead trout, furry with white fungus, drifted against a rock, or floating belly up in some pool. Nick did not like to fish with other men on the river. Unless they were of your party, they spoiled it.

He wallowed down the stream, above his knees in the current, through the fifty yards of shallow water above the pile of logs that crossed the stream. He did not rebait his hook and held it in his hand as he waded. He was certain he could catch small trout in the shallows, but he did not want them. There would be no big trout in the shallows this time of day.

Now the water deepened up his thighs sharply and coldly. Ahead was the smooth dammed-back flood of water above the logs. The water was smooth and dark; on the left, the lower edge of the meadow; on the right the swamp.

Nick leaned back against the current and took a hopper from the bottle. He threaded the hopper on the hook and spat on him for good luck. Then he pulled several yards of line from the reel and tossed the hopper out ahead onto the fast, dark water. It floated down towards the logs, then the weight of the line pulled the bait under the surface. Nick held the rod in his right hand, letting the line run out through his fingers.

There was a long tug. Nick struck and the rod came alive and dangerous, bent double, the line tightening, coming out of water, tightening, all in a heavy, dangerous, steady pull. Nick felt the moment when the leader would break if the strain increased and let the line go.

The reel ratcheted into a mechanical shriek as the line went out in a rush. Too fast. Nick could not check it, the line rushing out, the reel note rising as the line ran out.

With the core of the reel showing, his heart feeling stopped with the excitement, leaning back against the current that mounted icily his thighs, Nick thumbed the reel hard with his left hand. It was awkward getting his thumb inside the fly reel frame.

As he put on pressure the line tightened into sudden hardness and beyond the logs a huge trout went high out of water. As he jumped, Nick lowered the tip of the rod. But he felt, as he dropped the tip to ease the strain, the moment when the strain was too great; the hardness too tight. Of course, the leader had broken. There was no mistaking the feeling when all spring left the line and it became dry and hard. Then it went slack.

His mouth dry, his heart down, Nick reeled in. He had never seen so big a trout. There was a heaviness, a power not to be held, and then the bulk of him, as he jumped. He looked as broad as a salmon.

Nick's hand was shaky. He reeled in slowly. The thrill had been too much. He felt, vaguely, a little sick, as though it would be better to sit down.

The leader had broken where the hook was tied to it. Nick took it in his hand. He thought of the trout somewhere on the bottom, holding himself steady over the gravel, far down below the light, under the logs, with the hook in his jaw. Nick knew the trout's teeth would cut through the snell of the hook. The hook would imbed itself in his jaw. He'd bet the trout was angry. Anything that size would be angry. That was a trout. He had been solidly hooked. Solid as a rock. He felt like a rock, too, before he started off. By God, he was a big one. By God, he was the biggest one I ever heard of.

Nick climbed out onto the meadow and stood, water running down his trousers and out of his shoes, his shoes squlchy. He went over and sat on the logs. He did not want to rush his sensations any.

He wriggled his toes in the water, in his shoes, and got out a cigarette from his breast pocket. He lit it and tossed the match into the fast water below the logs. A tiny trout rose at the match, as it swung around in the fast current. Nick laughed. He would finish the cigarette.

He sat on the logs, smoking, drying in the sun, the sun warm on his back, the river shallow ahead entering the woods, curving into the woods, shallows, light glittering, big water-smooth rocks, cedars along the bank and white birches, the logs warm in the sun, smooth to sit on, without bark, gray to the touch; slowly the feeling of disappointment left him. It went away slowly, the feeling of disappointment that came sharply after the thrill that made his shoulders ache. It was all right now. His rod lying out on the logs, Nick tied a new hook on the leader, pulling the gut tight until it grimped into itself in a hard knot.

He baited up, then picked up the rod and walked to the far end of the logs to get into the water, where it was not too deep. Under and beyond the logs was a deep pool. Nick walked around the shallow shelf near the swamp shore until he came out on the shallow bed of the stream.

On the left, where the meadow ended and the woods began, a great elm tree was uprooted. Gone over in a storm, it lay back into the woods, its roots clotted with dirt, grass growing in them, rising a solid bank beside the stream. The river cut to the edge of the uprooted tree. From where Nick stood he could see deep channels, like ruts, cut in the shallow bed of the stream by the flow of the current. Pebbly where he stood and pebbly and full of boulders beyond; where it curved near the tree roots, the bed of the stream was marly and between the ruts of deep water green weed fronds swung in the current.

Nick swung the rod back over his shoulder and forward, and the line, curving forward, laid the grasshopper down on one of the deep channels in the weeds. A trout struck and Nick hooked him.

Holding the rod far out toward the uprooted tree and sloshing backward in the current, Nick worked the trout, plunging, the rod bending alive, out of the danger of the weeds into the open river. Holding the rod, pumping alive against the current, Nick brought the trout in. He rushed, but always came, the spring of the rod yielding to the rushes, sometimes jerking under water, but always bringing him in. Nick eased downstream with the rushes.

The rod above his head he led the trout over the net, then lifted.

The trout hung heavy in the net, mottled trout back and silver sides in the meshes. Nick unhooked him; heavy sides, good to hold, big undershot jaw, and slipped him, heaving and big sliding, into the long sack that hung from his shoulders in the water.

Nick spread the mouth of the sack against the current and it filled, heavy with water. He held it up, the bottom in the stream, and the water poured out through the sides. Inside at the bottom was the big trout, alive in the water.

Nick moved downstream. The sack out ahead of him sunk heavy in the water, pulling from his shoulders.

It was getting hot, the sun hot on the back of his neck.

Nick had one good trout. He did not care about getting many trout. Now the stream was shallow and wide. There were trees along both banks. The trees of the left bank made short shadows on the current in the forenoon sun. Nick knew there were trout in each shadow. In the afternoon, after the sun had crossed toward the hills, the trout would be in the cool shadows on the other side of the stream.

The very biggest ones would lie up close to the bank. You could always pick them up there on the Black. When the sun was down they all moved out into the current. Just when the sun made the water blinding in the glare before it went down, you were liable to strike a big trout anywhere in the current. It was almost impossible to fish then, the surface of the water was blinding as a mirror in the sun. Of course, you could fish upstream, but in a stream like the Black, or this, you had to wallow against the current and in a deep place, the water piled up on you. It was no fun to fish upstream with this much current.

Nick moved along through the shallow stretch watching the banks for deep holes. A beech tree grew close beside the river, so that the branches hung down into the water. The stream went back in under the leaves. There were always trout in a place like that.

Nick did not care about fishing that hole. He was sure he would get hooked in the branches.

It looked deep though. He dropped the grasshopper so the current took it under water, back in under the overhanging branch. The line pulled hard and Nick struck. The trout threshed heavily, half out of water in the leaves and branches. The line was caught. Nick pulled hard and the trout was off. He reeled in and holding the hook in his hand, walked down the stream.

Ahead, close to the left bank, was a big log. Nick saw it was hollow; pointing up river the current entered it smoothly, only a little ripple spread each side of the log. The water was deepening. The top of the hollow log was gray and dry. It was partly in the shadow.

Nick took the cork out of the grasshopper bottle and a hopper clung to it. He picked him off, hooked him and tossed him out. He held the rod far out so that the hopper on the water moved into the current flowing into the hollow log. Nick lowered the rod and the hopper floated in. There was a heavy strike. Nick swung the rod against the pull. It felt as though he were hooked into the log itself, except for the live feeling.

He tried to force the fish out into the current. It came, heavily.

The line went slack and Nick thought the trout was gone. Then he saw him, very near, in the current, shaking his head, trying to get the hook out. His mouth was clamped shut. He was fighting the hook in the clear flowing current.

Looping in the line with his left hand, Nick swung the rod to make the line taut and tried to lead the trout toward the net, but he was gone, out of sight, the line pumping. Nick fought him against the current, letting him thump in the water against the spring of the rod. He shifted the rod to his left hand, worked the trout upstream, holding his weight, fighting on the rod, and then let him down into the net. He lifted him clear of the water, a heavy half circle in the net, the net dripping, unhooked him and slid him into the sack.

He spread the mouth of the sack and looked down in at the two big trout alive in the water.

Through the deepening water, Nick waded over to the hollow log. He took the sack off, over his head, the trout flopping as it came out of water, and hung it so the trout were deep in the water. Then he pulled himself up on the log and sat, the water from his trousers and boots running down into the stream. He laid his rod down, moved along to the shady end of the log and took the sandwiches out of his pocket. He dipped the sandwiches in the cold water. The current carried away the crumbs. He ate the sandwiches and dipped his hat full of water to drink, the water running out through his hat just ahead of his drinking.

It was cool in the shade, sitting on the log. He took a cigarette out and struck a match to light it. The match sunk into the gray wood, making a tiny furrow. Nick leaned over the side of the log, found a hard place and lit the match. He sat smoking and watching the river.

Ahead the river narrowed and went into a swamp. The river became smooth and deep and the swamp looked solid with cedar trees, their trunks close together, their branches solid. It would not be possible to walk through a swamp like that. The branches grew so low. You would have to keep almost level with the ground to move at all. You could not crash through the branches. That must be why the animals that lived in swamps were built the way they were, Nick thought.

He wished he had brought something to read. He felt like reading. He did not feel like going on into the swamp. He looked down the river. A big cedar slanted all the way across the stream. Beyond that the river went into the swamp.

Nick did not want to go in there now. He felt a reaction against deep wading with the water deepening up under his armpits, to hook big trout in places impossible to land them. In the swamp the banks were bare, the big cedars came together overhead, the sun did not come through, except in patches; in the fast deep water, in the half light, the fishing would be tragic. In the swamp fishing was a tragic adventure. Nick did not want it. He did not want to go down the stream any further today.

He took out his knife, opened it and stuck it in the log. Then he pulled up the sack, reached into it and brought out one of the trout. Holding him near the tail, hard to hold, alive, in his hand, he whacked him against the log. The trout quivered, rigid. Nick laid him on the log in the shade and broke the neck of the other fish the same way. He laid them side by side on the log. They were fine trout.

Nick cleaned them, slitting them from the vent to the tip of the jaw. All the insides and the gills and tongue came out in one piece. They were both males; long gray-white strips of milt, smooth and clean. All the insides clean and compact, coming out all together. Nick tossed the offal ashore for the minks to find.

He washed the trout in the stream. When he held them back up in the water they looked like live fish. Their color was not gone yet. He washed his hands and dried them on the log. Then he laid the trout on the sack spread out on the log, rolled them up in it, tied the bundle and put it in the landing net. His knife was still standing, blade stuck in the log. He cleaned it on the wood and put it in his pocket.

Nick stood up on the log, holding his rod, the landing net hanging heavy, then stepped into the water and splashed ashore. He climbed the bank and cut up into the woods, toward the high ground. He was going back to camp. He looked back. The river just showed through the trees. There were plenty of days coming when he could fish the swamp.

A DAY'S WAIT
[1933]

HE CAME into the room to shut the windows while we were still in bed and I saw he looked ill. He was shivering, his face was white, and he walked slowly as though it ached to move.

"What's the matter, Schatz?"

"I've got a headache."

"You better go back to bed."

"No. I'm all right."

"You go to bed. I'll see you when I'm dressed."

But when I came downstairs he was dressed, sitting by the fire, looking a very sick and miserable boy of nine years. When I put my hand on his forehead I knew he had a fever.

"You go up to bed," I said, "you're sick."

"I'm all right," he said.

When the doctor came he took the boy's temperature.

"What is it?" I asked him.

"One hundred and two."

Downstairs, the doctor left three different medicines in different colored capsules with instructions for giving them. One was to bring down the fever, another a purgative, the third to overcome an acid condition. The germs of influenza can only exist in an acid condition, he explained. He seemed to know all about influenza and said there was nothing to worry about if the fever did not go above one hundred and four degrees. This was a light epidemic of flu and there was no danger if you avoided pneumonia.

Back in the room I wrote the boy's temperature down and made a note of the time to give the various capsules.

"Do you want me to read to you?"

"All right. If you want to," said the boy. His face was very white and there were dark areas under his eyes. He lay still in the bed and seemed very detached from what was going on.

I read aloud from Howard Pyle's *Book of Pirates;* but I could see he was not following what I was reading.

"How do you feel, Schatz?" I asked him.

"Just the same, so far," he said.

I sat at the foot of the bed and read to myself while I waited for it to be time to give another capsule. It would have been natural for him to go to sleep, but when I looked up he was looking at the foot of the bed, looking very strangely.

"Why don't you try to go to sleep? I'll wake you up for the medicine."

"I'd rather stay awake."

After a while he said to me, "You don't have to stay in here with me, Papa, if it bothers you."

"It doesn't bother me."

"No, I mean you don't have to stay if it's going to bother you."

I thought perhaps he was a little lightheaded and after giving him the prescribed capsules at eleven o'clock I went out for a while.

It was a bright, cold day, the ground covered with a sleet that had frozen so that it seemed as if all the bare trees, the bushes, the cut brush and all the grass and the bare ground had been varnished with ice. I took the young Irish setter for a little walk up the road and along a frozen creek, but it was difficult to stand or walk on the glassy surface and the red dog slipped and slithered and I fell twice, hard, once dropping my gun and having it slide away over the ice.

We flushed a covey of quail under a high clay bank with overhanging brush and I killed two as they went out of sight over the top of the bank. Some of the covey lit in trees, but most of them scattered into brush piles and it was necessary to jump on the ice-coated mounds of brush several times before they would flush. Coming out while you were poised unsteadily on the icy, springy brush they made difficult shooting and I killed two, missed five, and started back pleased to have found a covey close to the house and happy there were so many left to find on another day.

At the house they said the boy had refused to let any one come into the room.

"You can't come in," he said. "You mustn't get what I have."

I went up to him and found him in exactly the position I had left him, white-faced, but with the tops of his cheeks flushed by the fever, staring still, as he had stared, at the foot of the bed.

I took his temperature.

"What is it?"

"Something like a hundred," I said. It was one hundred and two and four tenths.

"It was a hundred and two," he said.

"Who said so?"

"The doctor."

"Your temperature is all right," I said. "It's nothing to worry about."

"I don't worry," he said, "but I can't keep from thinking."

"Don't think," I said. "Just take it easy."

"I'm taking it easy," he said and looked straight ahead. He was evidently holding tight onto himself about something.

"Take this with water."

"Do you think it will do any good?"

"Of course it will."

I sat down and opened the *Pirate* book and commenced to read, but I could see he was not following, so I stopped.

"About what time do you think I'm going to die?" he asked.

"What?"

"About how long will it be before I die?"

"You aren't going to die. What's the matter with you?"

"Oh, yes, I am. I heard him say a hundred and two."

"People don't die with a fever of one hundred and two. That's a silly way to talk."

"I know they do. At school in France the boys told me you can't live with forty-four degrees. I've got a hundred and two."

He had been waiting to die all day, ever since nine o'clock in the morning.

"You poor Schatz," I said. "Poor old Schatz. It's like miles and kilometers. You aren't going to die. That's a different thermometer. On that thermometer thirty-seven

is normal. On this kind it's ninety-eight."

"Are you sure?"

"Absolutely," I said. "It's like miles and kilometers. You know, like how many kilometers we make when we do seventy miles in the car?"

"Oh," he said.

But his gaze at the foot of the bed relaxed slowly. The hold over himself relaxed too, finally, and the next day it was very slack and he cried very easily at little things that were of no importance.

From

FOR WHOM THE BELL TOLLS
[1940]

CHAPTER XXVII

EL SORDO was making his fight on a hilltop. He did not like this hill and when he saw it he thought it had the shape of a chancre. But he had had no choice except this hill and he had picked it as far away as he could see it and galloped for it, the automatic rifle heavy on his back, the horse laboring, barrel heaving between his thighs, the sack of grenades swinging against one side, the sack of automatic rifle pans banging against the other, and Joaquín and Ignacio halting and firing, halting and firing to give him time to get the gun in place.

There had still been snow then, the snow that had ruined them, and when his horse was hit so that he wheezed in a slow, jerking, climbing stagger up the last part of the crest, splattering the snow with a bright, pulsing jet, Sordo had hauled him along by the bridle, the reins over his shoulder as he climbed. He climbed as hard as he could with the bullets spatting on the rocks, with the two sacks heavy on his shoulders, and then, holding the horse by the mane, had shot him quickly, expertly, and tenderly just where he had needed him, so that the horse pitched, head forward down to plug a gap between two rocks. He had gotten the gun to firing over the horse's back and he fired two pans, the gun clattering, the empty shells pitching into the snow, the smell of burnt hair from the burnt hide where the hot muzzle rested, him firing at what came up to the hill, forcing them to scatter for cover, while all the time there was a chill in his back from not knowing what was behind him. Once the last of the five men had reached the hilltop the chill went out of his back and he had saved the pans he had left until he would need them.

There were two more horses dead along the slope and three more were dead here on the hilltop. He had only succeeded in stealing three horses last night and one had bolted when they tried to mount him bareback in the corral at the camp when the first shooting had started.

Of the five men who had reached the hilltop three were wounded. Sordo was wounded in the calf of his leg and in two places in his left arm. He was very thirsty, his wounds had stiffened, and one of the wounds in his left arm was very painful. He also had a bad headache and as he lay waiting for the planes to come he thought of a joke in Spanish. It was, *"Hay que tomar la muerte como si fuera aspirina,"* which means, "You will have to take death as an aspirin." But he did not make the joke aloud. He grinned somewhere inside the pain in his head and inside the nausea that came whenever he moved his arm and looked around at what there was left of his band.

The five men were spread out like the points of a five-pointed star. They had dug with their knees and hands and made mounds in front of their heads and shoulders with the dirt and piles of stones. Using this cover, they were linking the individual mounds up with stones and dirt. Joaquín, who was eighteen years old, had a steel helmet that he dug with and he passed dirt in it.

He had gotten this helmet at the blowing up of the train. It had a bullet hole through it and every one had always joked at him for keeping it. But he had hammered the jagged edges of the bullet hole smooth and driven a wooden plug into it and then cut the plug off and smoothed it even with the metal inside the helmet.

When the shooting started he had clapped this helmet on his head so hard it banged his head as though he had been hit with a casserole and, in the last lung-aching, leg-dead, mouth-dry, bullet-spatting, bullet-cracking, bullet-singing run up the final slope of the hill after his horse was killed, the helmet had seemed to weigh a great amount and to ring his bursting forehead with an iron band. But he had kept it. Now he dug with it in a steady, almost machinelike desperation. He had not yet been hit.

"It serves for something finally," Sordo said to him in his deep, throaty voice.

"Resistir y fortificar es vencer," Joaquín said, his mouth stiff with the dryness of fear which surpassed the normal thirst of battle. It was one of the slogans of the Communist party and it meant, "Hold out and fortify, and you will win."

Sordo looked away and down the slope at where a cavalryman was sniping from behind a boulder. He was very fond of this boy and he was in no mood for slogans.

"What did you say?"

One of the men turned from the building that he was doing. This man was lying flat on his face, reaching carefully up with his hands to put a rock in place while keeping his chin flat against the ground.

Joaquín repeated the slogan in his dried-up boy's voice without checking his digging for a moment.

"What was the last word?" the man with his chin on the ground asked.

"Vencer," the boy said. "Win."

"Mierda," the man with his chin on the ground said.

"There is another that applies to here," Joaquín said, bringing them out as though they were talismans, "Pasionaria says it is better to die on your feet than to live on your knees."

"Mierda again," the man said and another man said, over his shoulder, "We're on our bellies, not our knees."

"Thou. Communist. Do you know your

Pasionaria has a son thy age in Russia since the start of the movement?"

"It's a lie," Joaquín said.

"*Qué va,* it's a lie," the other said. "The dynamiter with the rare name told me. He was of thy party, too. Why should he lie?"

"It's a lie," Joaquín said. "She would not do such a thing as keep a son hidden in Russia out of the war."

"I wish I were in Russia," another of Sordo's men said. "Will not thy Pasionaria send me now from here to Russia, Communist?"

"If thou believest so much in thy Pasionaria, get her to get us off this hill," one of the men who had a bandaged thigh said.

"The fascists will do that," the man with his chin in the dirt said.

"Do not speak thus," Joaquín said to him.

"Wipe the pap of your mother's breasts off thy lips and give me a hatful of that dirt," the man with his chin on the ground said. "No one of us will see the sun go down this night."

El Sordo was thinking: It is shaped like a chancre. Or the breast of a young girl with no nipple. Or the top cone of a volcano. You have never seen a volcano, he thought. Nor will you ever see one. And this hill is like a chancre. Let the volcanos alone. It's late now for the volcanos.

He looked very carefully around the withers of the dead horse and there was a quick hammering of firing from behind a boulder well down the slope and he heard the bullets from the submachine gun thud into the horse. He crawled along behind the horse and looked out of the angle between the horse's hindquarters and the rock. There were three bodies on the slope just below him where they had fallen when the fascists had rushed the crest under cover of the automatic rifle and submachine gunfire and he and the others had broken down the attack by throwing and rolling down hand grenades. There were other bodies that he could not see on the other sides of the hill crest. There was no

dead ground by which attackers could approach the summit and Sordo knew that as long as his ammunition and grenades held out and he had as many as four men they could not get him out of there unless they brought up a trench mortar. He did not know whether they had sent to La Granja for a trench mortar. Perhaps they had not, because surely, soon, the planes would come. It had been four hours since the observation plane had flown over them.

This hill is truly like a chancre, Sordo thought, and we are the very pus of it. But we killed many when they made that stupidness. How could they think that they would take us thus? They have such modern armament that they lose all their sense with overconfidence. He had killed the young officer who had led the assault with a grenade that had gone bouncing and rolling down the slope as they came up it, running, bent half over. In the yellow flash and gray roar of smoke he had seen the officer dive forward to where he lay now like a heavy, broken bundle of old clothing marking the farthest point that the assault had reached. Sordo looked at this body and then, down the hill, at the others.

They are brave but stupid people, he thought. But they have sense enough now not to attack us again until the planes come. Unless, of course, they have a mortar coming. It would be easy with a mortar. The mortar was the normal thing and he knew that they would die as soon as a mortar came up, but when he thought of the planes coming up he felt as naked on that hilltop as though all of his clothing and even his skin had been removed. There is no nakeder thing than I feel, he thought. A flayed rabbit is as well covered as a bear in comparison. But why should they bring planes? They could get us out of here with a trench mortar easily. They are proud of their planes, though, and they will probably bring them. Just as they were so proud of their automatic weapons that they made that stupidness. But undoubtedly they must have sent for a mortar, too.

One of the men fired. Then jerked the bolt and fired again, quickly.

"Save thy cartridges," Sordo said.

"One of the sons of the great whore tried to reach that boulder," the man pointed.

"Did you hit him?" Sordo asked, turning his head with difficulty.

"Nay," the man said. "The fornicator ducked back."

"Who is a whore of whores is Pilar," the man with his chin in the dirt said. "That whore knows we are dying here."

"She could do no good," Sordo said. The man had spoken on the side of his good ear and he had heard him without turning his head. "What could she do?"

"Take these sluts from the rear."

"*Qué va*," Sordo said. "They are spread around a hillside. How would she come on them? There are a hundred and fifty of them. Maybe more now."

"But if we hold out until dark," Joaquín said.

"And if Christmas comes on Easter," the man with his chin on the ground said.

"And if thy aunt had *cojones* she would be thy uncle," another said to him. "Send for thy Pasionaria. She alone can help us."

"I do not believe that about the son," Joaquín said. "Or if he is there he is training to be an aviator or something of that sort."

"He is hidden there for safety," the man told him.

"He is studying dialectics. Thy Pasionaria has been there. So have Lister and Modesto and others. The one with the rare name told me."

"That they should go to study and return to aid us," Joaquín said.

"That they should aid us now," another man said. "That all the cruts of Russian sucking swindlers should aid us now." He fired and said, "*Me cago en tal;* I missed him again."

"Save thy cartridges and do not talk so much or thou wilt be very thirsty," Sordo said. "There is no water on this hill."

"Take this," the man said and rolling on his side he pulled a wineskin that he wore slung from his shoulder over his head and handed it to Sordo. "Wash thy mouth out, old one. Thou must have much thirst with thy wounds."

"Let all take it," Sordo said.

"Then I will have some first," the owner said and squirted a long stream into his mouth before he handed the leather bottle around.

"Sordo, when thinkest thou the planes will come?" the man with his chin in the dirt asked.

"Any time," said Sordo. "They should have come before."

"Do you think these sons of the great whore will attack again?"

"Only if the planes do not come."

He did not think there was any need to speak about the mortar. They would know it soon enough when the mortar came.

"God knows they've enough planes with what we saw yesterday."

"Too many," Sordo said.

His head hurt very much and his arm was stiffening so that the pain of moving it was almost unbearable. He looked up at the bright, high, blue early summer sky as he raised the leather wine bottle with his good arm. He was fifty-two years old and he was sure this was the last time he would see that sky.

He was not at all afraid of dying but he was angry at being trapped on this hill which was only utilizable as a place to die. If we could have gotten clear, he thought. If we could have made them come up the long valley or if we could have broken loose across the road it would have been all right. But this chancre of a hill. We must use it as well as we can and we have used it very well so far.

If he had known how many men in history have had to use a hill to die on it would not have cheered him any for, in the moment he was passing through, men are not impressed by what has happened to other men in similar circumstances any more than a widow of one day is helped by the knowledge that other loved husbands have died. Whether one has fear of it or not, one's death is difficult to accept. Sordo had accepted it but there was no sweetness in its acceptance even at fifty-two, with three wounds and him surrounded on a hill.

He joked about it to himself but he looked at the sky and at the far mountains and he swallowed the wine and he did not want it. If one must die, he thought, and clearly one must, I can die. But I hate it.

Dying was nothing and he had no picture of it nor fear of it in his mind. But living was a field of grain blowing in the wind on the side of a hill. Living was a hawk in the sky. Living was an earthen jar of water in the dust of the threshing with the grain flailed out and the chaff blowing. Living was a horse between your legs and a carbine under one leg and a hill and a valley and a stream with trees along it and the far side of the valley and the hills beyond.

Sordo passed the wine bottle back and nodded his head in thanks. He leaned forward and patted the dead horse on the shoulder where the muzzle of the automatic rifle had burned the hide. He could still smell the burnt hair. He thought how he had held the horse there, trembling, with the fire around them, whispering and cracking, over and around them like a curtain, and had carefully shot him just at the intersection of the cross-lines between the two eyes and the ears. Then as the horse pitched down he had dropped down behind his warm, wet back to get the gun to going as they came up the hill.

"*Eras mucho caballo,*" he said, meaning, "Thou wert plenty of horse."

El Sordo lay now on his good side and looked up at the sky. He was lying on a heap of empty cartridge hulls but his head was protected by the rock and his body lay in the lee of the horse. His wounds had stiffened badly and he had much pain and he felt too tired to move.

"What passes with thee, old one?" the man next to him asked.

"Nothing. I am taking a little rest."

"Sleep," the other said. "*They* will wake us when they come."

Just then some one shouted from down the slope.

"Listen, bandits!" the voice came from behind the rocks where the closest automatic rifle was placed. "Surrender now before the planes blow you to pieces."

"What is it he says?" Sordo asked.

Joaquín told him. Sordo rolled to one side and pulled himself up so that he was crouched behind the gun again.

"Maybe the planes aren't coming," he said. "Don't answer them and do not fire. Maybe we can get them to attack again."

"If we should insult them a little?" the man who had spoken to Joaquín about La Pasionaria's son in Russia asked.

"No," Sordo said. "Give me thy big pistol. Who has a big pistol?"

"Here."

"Give it to me." Crouched on his knees he took the big 9 mm. Star and fired one shot into the ground beside the dead horse, waited, then fired again four times at irregular intervals. Then he waited while he counted sixty and then fired a final shot directly into the body of the dead horse. He grinned and handed back the pistol.

"Reload it," he whispered, "and that every one should keep his mouth shut and no one shoot."

"*Bandidos!*" the voice shouted from behind the rocks.

No one spoke on the hill.

"*Bandidos!* Surrender now before we blow thee to little pieces."

"They're biting," Sordo whispered happily.

As he watched, a man showed his head over the top of the rocks. There was no shot from the hilltop and the head went down again. El Sordo waited, watching, but nothing more happened. He turned his head and looked at the others who were all watching down their sectors of the slope. As he looked at them the others shook their heads.

"Let no one move," he whispered.

"Sons of the great whore," the voice

came now from behind the rocks again.

"Red swine. Mother rapers. Eaters of the milk of thy fathers."

Sordo grinned. He could just hear the bellowed insults by turning his good ear. This is better than the aspirin, he thought. How many will we get? Can they be that foolish?

The voice had stopped again and for three minutes they heard nothing and saw no movement. Then the sniper behind the boulder a hundred yards down the slope exposed himself and fired. The bullet hit a rock and ricocheted with a sharp whine. Then Sordo saw a man, bent double, run from the shelter of the rocks where the automatic rifle was across the open ground to the big boulder behind which the sniper was hidden. He almost dove behind the boulder.

Sordo looked around. They signalled to him that there was no movement on the other slopes. El Sordo grinned happily and shook his head. This is ten times better than the aspirin, he thought, and he waited, as happy as only a hunter can be happy.

Below on the slope the man who had run from the pile of stones to the shelter of the boulder was speaking to the sniper.

"Do you believe it?"

"I don't know," the sniper said.

"It would be logical," the man, who was the officer in command, said. "They are surrounded. They have nothing to expect but to die."

The sniper said nothing.

"What do you think?" the officer asked.

"Nothing," the sniper said.

"Have you seen any movement since the shots?"

"None at all."

The officer looked at his wrist watch. It was ten minutes to three o'clock.

"The planes should have come an hour ago," he said. Just then another officer flopped in behind the boulder. The sniper moved over to make room for him.

"Thou, Paco," the first officer said. "How does it seem to thee?"

The second officer was breathing heavily from his sprint up and across the hillside from the automatic rifle position.

"For me it is a trick," he said.

"But if it is not? What a ridicule we make waiting here and laying siege to dead men."

"We have done something worse than ridiculous already," the second officer said. "Look at that slope."

He looked up the slope to where the dead were scattered close to the top. From where he looked the line of the hilltop showed the scattered rocks, the belly, projecting legs, shod hooves jutting out, of Sordo's horse, and the fresh dirt thrown up by the digging.

"What about the mortars?" asked the second officer.

"They should be here in an hour. If not before."

"Then wait for them. There has been enough stupidity already."

"*Bandidos!*" the first officer shouted suddenly, getting to his feet and putting his head well up above the boulder so that the crest of the hill looked much closer as he stood upright. "Red swine! Cowards!"

The second officer looked at the sniper and shook his head. The sniper looked away but his lips tightened.

The first officer stood there, his head all clear of the rock and with his hand on his pistol butt. He cursed and vilified the hilltop. Nothing happened. Then he stepped clear of the boulder and stood there looking up the hill.

"Fire, cowards, if you are alive," he shouted. "Fire on one who has no fear of any Red that ever came out of the belly of the great whore."

This last was quite a long sentence to shout and the officer's face was red and congested as he finished.

The second officer, who was a thin sunburned man with quiet eyes, a thin, long-lipped mouth and a stubble of beard over his hollow cheeks, shook his head again. It was this officer who was shouting who had ordered the first assault. The young lieutenant who was dead up the slope had been the best friend of this other lieutenant who was named Paco Berrendo and who was listening to the shouting of the captain, who was obviously in a state of exaltation.

"Those are the swine who shot my sister and my mother," the captain said. He had a red face and a blond, British-looking moustache and there was something wrong about his eyes. They were a light blue and the lashes were light, too. As you looked at them they seemed to focus slowly. Then "Reds," he shouted. "Cowards!" and commenced cursing again.

He stood absolutely clear now and, sighting carefully, fired his pistol at the only target that the hilltop presented: the dead horse that had belonged to Sordo. The bullet threw up a puff of dirt fifteen yards below the horse. The captain fired again. The bullet hit a rock and sung off.

The captain stood there looking at the hilltop. The Lieutenant Berrendo was looking at the body of the other lieutenant just below the summit. The sniper was looking at the ground under his eyes. Then he looked up at the captain.

"There is no one alive up there," the captain said. "Thou," he said to the sniper, "go up there and see."

The sniper looked down. He said nothing.

"Don't you hear me?" the captain shouted at him.

"Yes, my captain," the sniper said, not looking at him.

"Then get up and go." The captain still had his pistol out. "Do you hear me?"

"Yes, my captain."

"Why don't you go, then?"

"I don't want to, my captain."

"You don't *want* to?" The captain pushed the pistol against the small of the man's back. "You don't *want* to?"

"I am afraid, my captain," the soldier said with dignity.

Lieutenant Berrendo, watching the captain's face and his odd eyes, thought he was going to shoot the man then.

"Captain Mora," he said.

"Lieutenant Berrendo?"

"It is possible the soldier is right."

"That he is right to say he is afraid? That he is right to say he does not *want* to obey an order?"

"No. That he is right that it is a trick."

"They are all dead," the captain said. "Don't you hear me say they are all dead?"

"You mean our comrades on the slope?" Berrendo asked him. "I agree with you."

"Paco," the captain said, "don't be a fool. Do you think you are the only one who cared for Julián? I tell you the Reds are dead. Look!"

He stood up, then put both hands on top of the boulder and pulled himself up, kneeing-up awkwardly, then getting on his feet.

"Shoot," he shouted, standing on the gray granite boulder and waved both his arms. "Shoot me! Kill me!"

On the hilltop El Sordo lay behind the dead horse and grinned.

What a people, he thought. He laughed, trying to hold it in because the shaking hurt his arm.

"Reds," came the shout from below. "Red canaille. Shoot me! Kill me!"

Sordo, his chest shaking, barely peeped past the horse's crupper and saw the captain on top of the boulder waving his arms. Another officer stood by the boulder. The sniper was standing at the other side. Sordo kept his eye where it was and shook his head happily.

"Shoot me," he said softly to himself. "Kill me!" Then his shoulders shook again. The laughing hurt his arm and each time he laughed his head felt as though it would burst. But the laughter shook him again like a spasm.

Captain Mora got down from the boulder. "Now do you believe me, Paco?" he questioned Lieutenant Berrendo.

"No," said Lieutenant Berrendo.

"*Cojones!*" the captain said. "Here there is nothing but idiots and cowards."

The sniper had gotten carefully behind the boulder again and Lieutenant Berrendo was squatting beside him.

The captain, standing in the open beside

the boulder, commenced to shout filth at the hilltop. There is no language so filthy as Spanish. There are words for all the vile words in English and there are other words and expressions that are used only in countries where blasphemy keeps pace with the austerity of religion. Lieutenant Berrendo was a very devout Catholic. So was the sniper. They were Carlists from Navarra and while both of them cursed and blasphemed when they were angry they regarded it as a sin which they regularly confessed.

As they crouched now behind the boulder watching the captain and listening to what he was shouting, they both disassociated themselves from him and what he was saying. They did not want to have that sort of talk on their consciences on a day in which they might die. Talking thus will not bring luck, the sniper thought. Speaking thus of the *Virgen* is bad luck. This one speaks worse than the Reds.

Julián is dead, Lieutenant Berrendo was thinking. Dead there on the slope on such a day as this is. And this foul mouth stands there bringing more ill fortune with his blasphemies.

Now the captain stopped shouting and turned to Lieutenant Berrendo. His eyes looked stranger than ever.

"Paco," he said, happily, "you and I will go up there."

"Not me."

"What?" The captain had his pistol out again.

I hate these pistol brandishers, Berrendo was thinking. They cannot give an order without jerking a gun out. They probably pull out their pistols when they go to the toilet and order the move they will make.

"I will go if you order me to. But under protest," Lieutenant Berrendo told the captain.

"Then I will go alone," the captain said. "The smell of cowardice is too strong here."

Holding his pistol in his right hand, he strode steadily up the slope. Berrendo and the sniper watched him. He was making no attempt to take any cover and he was looking straight ahead of him at the rocks, the dead horse, and the fresh-dug dirt of the hilltop.

El Sordo lay behind the horse at the corner of the rock, watching the captain come striding up the hill.

Only one, he thought. We get only one. But from his manner of speaking he is *caza mayor*.[1] Look at him walking. Look what an animal. Look at him stride forward. This one is for me. This one I take with me on the trip. This one coming now makes the same voyage I do. Come on, Comrade Voyager. Come striding. Come right along. Come along to meet it. Come on. Keep on walking. Don't slow up. Come right along. Come as thou art coming. Don't stop and look at those. That's right. Don't even look down. Keep on coming with your eyes forward. Look, he has a moustache. What do you think of that? He runs to a moustache, the Comrade Voyager. He is a captain. Look at his sleeves. I said he was *caza mayor*. He has the face of an *Inglés*.[2] Look. With a red face and blond hair and blue eyes. With no cap on and his moustache is yellow. With blue eyes. With pale blue eyes. With pale blue eyes with something wrong with them. With pale blue eyes that don't focus. Close enough. Too close. Yes, Comrade Voyager. Take it, Comrade Voyager.

He squeezed the trigger of the automatic rifle gently and it pounded back three times against his shoulder with the slippery jolt the recoil of a tripoded automatic weapon gives.

The captain lay on his face on the hillside. His left arm was under him. His right arm that had held the pistol was stretched forward of his head. From all down the slope they were firing on the hill crest again.

Crouched behind the boulder, thinking that now he would have to sprint across that open space under fire, Lieutenant

---

[1] Big game—a hunting term.

[2] Englishman.

Berrendo heard the deep hoarse voice of Sordo from the hilltop.

"Bandidos!" the voice came. *"Bandidos!* Shoot me! Kill me!"

On the top of the hill El Sordo lay behind the automatic rifle laughing so that his chest ached, so that he thought the top of his head would burst.

"Bandidos," he shouted again happily. "Kill me, *bandidos!"* Then he shook his head happily. We have lots of company for the Voyage, he thought.

He was going to try for the other officer with the automatic rifle when he would leave the shelter of the boulder. Sooner or later he would have to leave it. Sordo knew that he could never command from there and he thought he had a very good chance to get him.

Just then the others on the hill heard the first sound of the coming of the planes.

El Sordo did not hear them. He was covering the down-slope edge of the boulder with his automatic rifle and he was thinking: when I see him he will be running already and I will miss him if I am not careful. I could shoot behind him all across that stretch. I should swing the gun with him and ahead of him. Or let him start and then get on him and ahead of him. I will try to pick him up there at the edge of the rock and swing just ahead of him. Then he felt a touch on his shoulder and he turned and saw the gray, fear-drained face of Joaquín and he looked where the boy was pointing and saw the three planes coming.

At this moment Lieutenant Berrendo broke from behind the boulder and, with his head bent and his legs plunging, ran down and across the slope to the shelter of the rocks where the automatic rifle was placed.

Watching the planes, Sordo never saw him go.

"Help me to pull this out," he said to Joaquín and the boy dragged the automatic rifle clear from between the horse and the rock.

The planes were coming on steadily. They were in echelon and each second they grew larger and their noise was greater. "Lie on your backs to fire at them," Sordo said. "Fire ahead of them as they come."

He was watching them all the time. *"Cabrones! Hijos de puta!"* he said rapidly.

"Ignacio!" he said. "Put the gun on the shoulder of the boy. Thou!" to Joaquín, "Sit there and do not move. Crouch over. More. No. More."

He lay back and sighted with the automatic rifle as the planes came on steadily.

"Thou, Ignacio, hold me the three legs of that tripod." They were dangling down the boy's back and the muzzle of the gun was shaking from the jerking of his body that Joaquín could not control as he crouched with bent head hearing the droning roar of their coming.

Lying flat on his belly and looking up into the sky watching them come, Ignacio gathered the legs of the tripod into his two hands and steadied the gun.

"Keep thy head down," he said to Joaquín. "Keep thy head forward."

"Pasionaria says 'Better to die on thy—'" Joaquín was saying to himself as the drone came nearer them. Then he shifted suddenly into "Hail Mary, full of grace, the Lord is with thee; Blessed art thou among women and Blessed is the fruit of thy womb, Jesus. Holy Mary, Mother of God, pray for us sinners now and at the hour of our death. Amen. Holy Mary, Mother of God," he started, then he remembered quickly as the roar came now unbearably and started an act of contrition racing in it, "Oh my God, I am heartily sorry for having offended thee who art worthy of all my love——"

Then there were the hammering explosions past his ears and the gun barrel hot against his shoulder. It was hammering now again and his ears were deafened by the muzzle blast. Ignacio was pulling down hard on the tripod and the barrel was burning his back. It was hammering now in the roar and he could not remember the act of contrition.

All he could remember was at the hour of our death. Amen. At the hour of our death. Amen. At the hour. At the hour. Amen. The others all were firing. Now and at the hour of our death. Amen.

Then, through the hammering of the gun, there was the whistle of the air splitting apart and then in the red black roar the earth rolled under his knees and then waved up to hit him in the face and then dirt and bits of rock were falling all over and Ignacio was lying on him and the gun was lying on him. But he was not dead because the whistle came again and the earth rolled under him with the roar. Then it came again and the earth lurched under his belly and one side of the hilltop rose into the air and then fell slowly over them where they lay.

The planes came back three times and bombed the hilltop but no one on the hilltop knew it. Then the planes machine-gunned the hilltop and went away. As they dove on the hill for the last time with their machine guns hammering, the first plane pulled up and winged over and then each plane did the same and they moved from echelon to V-formation and went away into the sky in the direction of Segovia.

Keeping a heavy fire on the hilltop, Lieutenant Berrendo pushed a patrol up to one of the bomb craters from where they could throw grenades onto the crest. He was taking no chances of any one being alive and waiting for them in the mess that was up there and he threw four grenades into the confusion of dead horses, broken and split rocks, and torn yellow-stained explosive-stinking earth before he climbed out of the bomb crater and walked over to have a look.

No one was alive on the hilltop except the boy Joaquín, who was unconscious under the dead body of Ignacio. Joaquín was bleeding from the nose and from the ears. He had known nothing and had no feeling since he had suddenly been in the very heart of the thunder and the breath had been wrenched from his body when the one bomb struck so close and Lieutenant Berrendo made the sign of the cross and then shot him in the back of the head, as quickly and as gently, if such an abrupt movement can be gentle, as Sordo had shot the wounded horse.

Lieutenant Berrendo stood on the hilltop and looked down the slope at his own dead and then across the country seeing where they had galloped before Sordo had turned at bay here. He noticed all the dispositions that had been made of the troops and then he ordered the dead men's horses to be brought up and the bodies tied across the saddles so that they might be packed in to La Granja.

"Take that one, too," he said. "The one with his hands on the automatic rifle. That should be Sordo. He is the oldest and it was he with the gun. No. Cut the head off and wrap it in a poncho." He considered a minute. "You might as well take all the heads. And of the others below on the slope and where we first found them. Collect the rifles and pistols and pack that gun on a horse."

Then he walked down to where the lieutenant lay who had been killed in the first assault. He looked down at him but did not touch him.

"Qué cosa más mala es la guerra," he said to himself, which meant, "What a bad thing war is."

Then he made the sign of the cross again and as he walked down the hill he said five Our Fathers and five Hail Marys for the repose of the soul of his dead comrade. He did not wish to stay to see his orders being carried out.

William Faulkner

1897

W ILLIAM FAULKNER, descendant of a distinguished Mississippi family, was born at New Albany, Mississippi. He attended the University of Mississippi, and has lived most of his life on a plantation near Oxford, Mississippi. He served with the Royal Air Force as a volunteer during the first World War.

Faulkner's early poems and stories were published in the 1920's in *The Double Dealer,* a New Orleans regional magazine, but he did not obtain wide recognition until the appearance of the novels *As I Lay Dying* (1930) and *Sanctuary* (1931). *The Hamlet* (1940) and *These Thirteen* (1931) are the respective sources of the following selections. [See Malcolm Cowley, *The Portable Faulkner* (New York, 1946) and R. P. Warren in *Forms of Modern Fiction,* ed. W. Van O'Connor (Minneapolis, 1948).]

SPOTTED HORSES

[1940]

YES, SIR. Flem Snopes has filled that whole country full of spotted horses. You can hear folks running them all day and all night, whooping and hollering, and the horses running back and forth across them little wooden bridges ever now and then kind of like thunder. Here I was this morning pretty near half way to town, with the team ambling along and me setting in the buckboard about half asleep, when all of a sudden something come swurging up outen the bushes and jumped the road clean, without touching hoof to it. It flew right over my team, big as a billboard and flying through the air like a hawk. It taken me thirty minutes to stop my team and untangle the harness and the buckboard and hitch them up again.

That Flem Snopes. I be dog if he ain't a case, now. One morning about ten years ago, the boys was just getting settled down on Varner's porch for a little talk and tobacco, when here come Flem out from behind the counter, with his coat off and his hair all parted, like he might have been clerking for Varner for ten years already. Folks all knowed him; it was a big family of them about five miles down the bottom. That year, at least. Sharecropping. They never stayed on any place over a year. Then they would move on to another place, with the chap or maybe the twins of that year's litter. It was a regular nest of them. But Flem. The rest of them stayed tenant farmers, moving ever year, but here come Flem one day, walking out from behind Jody Varner's counter like he owned it. And he wasn't there but a year or two before folks knowed that, if him and Jody was both still in that store in ten years more, it would be Jody clerking for Flem Snopes. Why, that fellow could make a nickel where it wasn't but four cents to begin with. He skun me in two trades, myself, and the fellow that can do that, I just hope he'll get rich before I do; that's all.

All right. So here Flem was, clerking at Varner's, making a nickel here and there and not telling nobody about it. No, sir. Folks never knowed when Flem got the better of somebody lessen the fellow he beat told it. He'd just set there in the store-chair, chewing his tobacco and keeping his own business to hisself, until about a week later we'd find out it was somebody else's business he was keeping to hisself—provided the fellow he trimmed was mad enough to tell it. That's Flem.

We give him ten years to own ever thing Jody Varner had. But he never waited no ten years. I reckon you-all know that gal of Uncle Billy Varner's, the youngest one; Eula. Jody's sister. Ever Sunday ever yellow-wheeled buggy and curried riding horse in that country would be hitched to Bill Varner's fence, and the young bucks setting on the porch, swarming around Eula like bees around a honey pot. One of these here kind of big, soft-looking gals that could giggle richer than plowed new-ground. Wouldn't none of them leave before the others, and so they would set there on the porch until time to go home, with some of them with nine and ten miles to ride and then get up to-morrow and go back to the field. So they would all leave together and they would ride in a clump down to the creek ford and hitch them curried horses and yellow-wheeled buggies and get out and fight one another. Then they would get in the buggies again and go on home.

Well, one day about a year ago, one of them yellow-wheeled buggies and one of them curried saddle-horses quit this country. We heard they was heading for Texas. The next day Uncle Billy and Eula and Flem come into town in Uncle Bill's surrey, and when they come back, Flem and Eula was married. And on the next day we heard that two more of them yellow-wheeled buggies had left the country. They mought have gone to Texas, too. It's a big place.

Anyway, about a month after the wedding, Flem and Eula went to Texas, too. They was gone pretty near a year. Then one day last month, Eula come back, with a baby. We figgered up, and we decided that it was as well-growed a three-months-old baby as we ever see. It can already pull up on a chair. I reckon Texas makes big

men quick, being a big place. Anyway, if it keeps on like it started, it'll be chewing tobacco and voting time it's eight years old.

And so last Friday here come Flem himself. He was on a wagon with another fellow. The other fellow had one of these two-gallon hats and a ivory-handled pistol and a box of gingersnaps sticking out of his hind pocket, and tied to the tail-gate of the wagon was about two dozen of them Texas ponies, hitched to one another with barbed wire. They was colored like parrots and they was quiet as doves, and ere a one of them would kill you quick as a rattlesnake. Nere a one of them had two eyes the same color, and nere a one of them had ever seen a bridle, I reckon; and when that Texas man got down offen the wagon and walked up to them to show how gentle they was, one of them cut his vest clean offen him, same as with a razor.

Flem had done already disappeared; he had went on to see his wife, I reckon, and to see if that ere baby had done gone on to the field to help Uncle Billy plow, maybe. It was the Texas man that taken the horses on to Mrs. Littlejohn's lot. He had a little trouble at first, when they come to the gate, because they hadn't never see a fence before, and when he finally got them in and taken a pair of wire cutters and unhitched them and got them into the barn and poured some shell corn into the trough, they durn nigh tore down the barn. I reckon they thought that shell corn was bugs, maybe. So he left them in the lot and he announced that the auction would begin at sunup to-morrow.

That night we was setting on Mrs. Littlejohn's porch. You-all mind the moon was nigh full that night, and we could watch them spotted varmints swirling along the fence and back and forth across the lot same as minnows in a pond. And then now and then they would all kind of huddle up against the barn and rest themselves by biting and kicking one another. We would hear a squeal, and then a set of hoofs would go Bam! against the barn, like a pistol. It sounded just like a fellow with a pistol, in a nest of cattymounts, taking his time.

It wasn't ere a man knowed yet if Flem owned them things or not. They just knowed one thing: that they wasn't never going to know for sho if Flem did or not, or if maybe he didn't just get on that wagon at the edge of town, for the ride or not. Even Eck Snopes didn't know, Flem's own cousin. But wasn't nobody surprised at that. We knowed that Flem would skin Eck quick as he would ere a one of us.

They was there by sunup next morning, some of them come twelve and sixteen miles, with seed-money tied up in tobacco sacks in their overalls, standing along the fence, when the Texas man come out of Mrs. Littlejohn's after breakfast and clumb onto the gate post with that ere white pistol butt sticking outen his hind pocket. He taken a new box of gingersnaps outen his pocket and bit the end offen it like a cigar and spit out the paper, and said the auction was open. And still they was coming up in wagons and a horse- and mule-back and hitching the teams across the road and coming to the fence. Flem wasn't nowhere in sight.

But he couldn't get them started. He begun to work on Eck, because Eck holp him last night to get them into the barn and feed them that shell corn. Eck got out just in time. He come outen that barn like a chip on the crest of a busted dam of water, and clumb into the wagon just in time.

He was working on Eck when Henry Armstid come up in his wagon. Eck was saying he was skeered to bid on one of them, because he might get it, and the Texas man says, "Them ponies? Them little horses?" He clumb down offen the gate post and went toward the horses. They broke and run, and him following them, kind of chirping to them, with his hand out like he was fixing to catch a fly, until he got three or four of them cornered. Then he jumped into them, and then we

couldn't see nothing for a while because of the dust. It was a big cloud of it, and them blare-eyed, spotted things swoaring outen it twenty foot to a jump, in forty directions without counting up. Then the dust settled and there they was, that Texas man and the horse. He had its head twisted clean around like a owl's head. Its legs was braced and it was trembling like a new bride and groaning like a saw mill, and him holding its head wrung clean around on its neck so it was snuffing sky. "Look it over," he says, with his heels dug too and that white pistol sticking outen his pocket and his neck swole up like a spreading adder's until you could just tell what he was saying, cussing the horse and talking to us all at once: "Look him over, the fiddle-headed son of fourteen fathers. Try him, buy him; you will get the best—" Then it was all dust again, and we couldn't see nothing but spotted hide and mane, and that ere Texas man's boot-heels like a couple of walnuts on two strings, and after a while that two-gallon hat come sailing out like a fat old hen crossing a fence.

When the dust settled again, he was just getting outen the far fence corner, brushing himself off. He come and got his hat and brushed it off and come and clumb onto the gate post again. He was breathing hard. He taken the gingersnap box outen his pocket and et one, breathing hard. The hammerhead horse was still running round and round the lot like a merry-go-round at a fair. That was when Henry Armstid come shoving up to the gate in them patched overalls and one of them dangle-armed shirts of hisn. Hadn't nobody noticed him until then. We was all watching the Texas man and the horses. Even Mrs. Littlejohn; she had done come out and built a fire under the wash-pot in her back yard, and she would stand at the fence a while and then go back into the house and come out again with a arm full of wash and stand at the fence again. Well, here come Henry shoving up, and then we see Mrs. Armstid right behind him, in that ere faded wrapper and sunbonnet and them tennis shoes. "Git on back to that wagon," Henry says.

"Henry," she says.

"Here, boys," the Texas man says; "make room for missus to git up and see. Come on, Henry," he says; "here's your chance to buy that saddle-horse missus has been wanting. What about ten dollars, Henry?"

"Henry," Mrs. Armstid says. She put her hand on Henry's arm. Henry knocked her hand down.

"Git on back in that wagon, like I told you," he says.

Mrs. Armstid never moved. She stood behind Henry, with her hands rolled into her dress, not looking at nothing. "He hain't no more despair than to buy one of them things," she says. "And us not five dollars ahead of the pore house, he hain't no more despair." It was the truth, too. They ain't never made more than a bare living offen that place of theirs, and them with four chaps and the very clothes they wears she earns by weaving by the firelight at night while Henry's asleep.

"Shut your mouth and git on back to that wagon," Henry says. "Do you want I taken a wagon stake to you here in the big road?"

Well, that Texas man taken one look at her. Then he begun on Eck again, like Henry wasn't even there. But Eck was skeered. "I can git me a snapping turtle or a water moccasin for nothing. I ain't going to buy none."

So the Texas man said he would give Eck a horse. "To start the auction, and because you holp me last night. If you'll start the bidding on the next horse," he says, "I'll give you that fiddle-head horse."

I wish you could have seen them, standing there with their seed-money in their pockets, watching that Texas man give Eck Snopes a live horse, all fixed to call him a fool if he taken it or not. Finally Eck says he'll take it. "Only I just starts the bidding," he says. "I don't have to buy the next one lessen I ain't overtopped." The Texas man said all right, and Eck bid a

dollar on the next one, with Henry Armstid standing there with his mouth already open, watching Eck and the Texas man like a mad-dog or something. "A dollar," Eck says.

The Texas man looked at Eck. His mouth was already open too, like he had started to say something and what he was going to say had up and died on him. "A dollar?" he says. "One dollar? You mean, one dollar, Eck?"

"Durn it," Eck says; "two dollars, then."

Well, sir, I wish you could a seen that Texas man. He taken out that gingersnap box and held it up and looked into it, careful, like it might have been a diamond ring in it, or a spider. Then he throwed it away and wiped his face with a bandanna. "Well," he says. "Well. Two dollars. Two dollars. Is your pulse all right, Eck?" he says. "Do you have ager-sweats at night, maybe?" he says. "Well," he says, "I got to take it. But are you boys going to stand there and see Eck get two horses at a dollar a head?"

That done it. I be dog if he wasn't nigh as smart as Flem Snopes. He hadn't no more than got the words outen his mouth before here was Henry Armstid, waving his hand. "Three dollars" Henry says. Mrs. Armstid tried to hold him again. He knocked her hand off, shoving up to the gate post.

"Mister," Mrs. Armstid says, "we got chaps in the house and not corn to feed the stock. We got five dollars I earned my chaps a-weaving after dark, and him snoring in the bed. And he hain't no more despair."

"Henry bids three dollars," the Texas man says. "Raise him a dollar, Eck, and the horse is yours."

"Henry," Mrs. Armstid says.

"Raise him, Eck," the Texas man says.

"Four dollars," Eck says.

"Five dollars," Henry says, shaking his fist. He shoved up right under the gate post. Mrs. Armstid was looking at the Texas man too.

"Mister," she says, "if you take that

five dollars I earned my chaps a-weaving for one of them things, it'll be a curse onto you and yourn during all the time of man."

But it wasn't no stopping Henry. He had shoved up, waving his fist at the Texas man. He opened it; the money was in nickels and quarters, and one dollar bill that looked like a cow's cud. "Five dollars," he says. "And the man that raises it'll have to beat my head off, or I'll beat hisn."

"All right," the Texas man says. "Five dollars is bid. But don't you shake your hand at me."

It taken till nigh sundown before the last one was sold. He got them hotted up once and the bidding got up to seven dollars and a quarter, but most of them went around three or four dollars, him setting on the gate post and picking the horses out one at a time by mouth-word, and Mrs. Littlejohn pumping up and down at the tub and stopping and coming to the fence for a while and going back to the tub again. She had done got done too, and the wash was hung on the line in the back yard, and we could smell supper cooking. Finally they was all sold; he swapped the last two and the wagon for a buckboard.

We was all kind of tired, but Henry Armstid looked more like a mad-dog than ever. When he bought, Mrs. Armstid had went back to the wagon, setting in it behind them two rabbit-sized, bone-pore mules, and the wagon itself looking like it would fall all to pieces soon as the mules moved. Henry hadn't even waited to pull it outen the road; it was still in the middle of the road and her setting in it, not looking at nothing, ever since this morning.

Henry was right up against the gate. He went up to the Texas man. "I bought a horse and I paid cash," Henry says. "And yet you expect me to stand around here until they are all sold before I can get my horse. I'm going to take my horse outen that lot."

The Texas man looked at Henry. He talked like he might have been asking for a cup of coffee at the table. "Take your horse," he says.

Then Henry quit looking at the Texas man. He begun to swallow, holding onto the gate. "Ain't you going to help me?" he says.

"It ain't my horse," the Texas man says.

Henry never looked at the Texas man again, he never looked at nobody. "Who'll help me catch my horse?" he says. Never nobody said nothing. "Bring the plowline," Henry says. Mrs. Armstid got outen the wagon and brought the plowline. The Texas man got down offen the post. The woman made to pass him, carrying the rope.

"Don't you go in there, missus," the Texas man says.

Henry opened the gate. He didn't look back. "Come on here," he says.

"Don't you go in there, missus," the Texas man says.

Mrs. Armstid wasn't looking at nobody, neither, with her hands across her middle, holding the rope. "I reckon I better," she says. Her and Henry went into the lot. The horses broke and run. Henry and Mrs. Armstid followed.

"Get him into the corner," Henry says. They got Henry's horse cornered finally, and Henry taken the rope, but Mrs. Armstid let the horse get out. They hemmed it up again, but Mrs. Armstid let it get out again, and Henry turned and hit her with the rope. "Why didn't you head him back?" Henry says. He hit her again. "Why didn't you?" It was about that time I looked around and see Flem Snopes standing there.

It was the Texas man that done something. He moved fast for a big man. He caught the rope before Henry could hit the third time, and Henry whirled and made like he would jump at the Texas man. But he never jumped. The Texas man went and taken Henry's arm and led him outen the lot. Mrs. Armstid come behind them and the Texas man taken some money outen his pocket and he give it into Mrs. Armstid's hand. "Get him into the wagon and take him on home," the Texas man says, like he might have been telling them he enjoyed his supper.

Then here comes Flem. "What's that for, Buck?" Flem says.

"Thinks he bought one of them ponies," the Texas man says. "Get him on away, missus."

But Henry wouldn't go. "Give him back that money," he says. "I bought that horse and I aim to have him if I have to shoot him."

And there was Flem, standing there with his hands in his pockets, chewing, like he had just happened to be passing.

"You take your money and I take my horse," Henry says. "Give it back to him," he says to Mrs. Armstid.

"You don't own no horse of mine," the Texas man says. "Get him on home, missus."

Then Henry seen Flem. "You got something to do with these horses," he says. "I bought one. Here's the money for it." He taken the bill outen Mrs. Armstid's hand. He offered it to Flem. "I bought one. Ask him. Here. Here's the money," he says, giving the bill to Flem.

When Flem taken the money, the Texas man dropped the rope he had snatched outen Henry's hand. He had done sent Eck Snopes's boy up to the store for another box of gingersnaps, and he taken the box outen his pocket and looked into it. It was empty and he dropped it on the ground. "Mr. Snopes will have your money for you tomorrow," he says to Mrs. Armstid. "You can get it from him tomorrow. He don't own no horse. You get him into the wagon and get him on home." Mrs. Armstid went back to the wagon and got in. "Where's that ere buckboard I bought?" the Texas man says. It was after sundown then. And then Mrs. Littlejohn come out on the porch and rung the supper bell.

I come on in and et supper. Mrs. Little-

john would bring in a pan of bread or something, then she would go out to the porch a minute and come back and tell us. The Texas man had hitched his team to the buckboard he had swapped them last two horses for, and him and Flem had gone, and then she told that the rest of them that never had ropes had went back to the store with I. O. Snopes to get some ropes, and wasn't nobody at the gate but Henry Armstid, and Mrs. Armstid setting in the wagon in the road, and Eck Snopes and that boy of hisn. "I don't care how many of them fool men gets killed by them things," Mrs. Littlejohn says, "but I ain't going to let Eck Snopes take that boy into that lot again." So she went down to the gate, but she come back without the boy or Eck neither.

"It ain't no need to worry about that boy," I says. "He's charmed." He was right behind Eck last night when Eck went to help feed them. The whole drove of them jumped clean over that boy's head and never touched him. It was Eck that touched him. Eck snatched him into the wagon and taken a rope and frailed the tar outen him.

So I had done et and went to my room and was undressing, long as I had a long trip to make next day; I was trying to sell a machine to Mrs. Bundren up past Whiteleaf; when Henry Armstid opened that gate and went in by hisself. They couldn't make him wait for the balance of them to get back with their ropes. Eck Snopes said he tried to make Henry wait, but Henry wouldn't do it. Eck said Henry walked right up to them and that when they broke, they run clean over Henry like a hay-mow breaking down. Eck said he snatched that boy of hisn out of the way just in time and that them things went through that gate like a creek flood and into the wagons and teams hitched side the road, busting wagon tongues and snapping harness like it was fishing-line, with Mrs. Armstid still setting in their wagon in the middle of it like something carved outen wood. Then they scattered, wild horses and tame mules with pieces of harness and singletrees dangling offen them, both ways up and down the road.

"There goes ourn, paw!" Eck says his boy said. "There it goes, into Mrs. Little-john's house." Eck says it run right up the steps and into the house like a boarder late for supper. I reckon so. Anyway, I was in my room, in my underclothes, with one sock in my hand, leaning out the window when the commotion busted out, when I heard something run into the melodeon in the hall; it sounded like a railroad engine. Then the door to my room come sailing in like when you throw a tin bucket top into the wind and I looked over my shoulder and see something that looked like a fourteen-foot pinwheel a-blaring its eyes at me. It had to blare them fast, because I was already done jumped out the window.

I reckon it was anxious, too. I reckon it hadn't never seen underclothes before, or maybe it was a sewing-machine agent it hadn't never seen. Anyway, it swirled and turned to run back up the hall and outen the house, when it met Eck Snopes and that boy just coming in, carrying a rope. It swirled again and run down the hall and out the back door just in time to meet Mrs. Littlejohn. She had just gathered up the clothes she had washed, and she was coming onto the back porch with a armful of washing in one hand and a scrubbing-board in the other, when the horse skidded up to her, trying to stop and swirl again. It never taken Mrs. Little-john no time a-tall.

"Git outen here, you son," she says. She hit it across the face with the scrubbing-board; that ere scrubbing-board split as neat as ere a axe could have done it, and when the horse swirled to run back up the hall, she hit it again with what was left of the scrubbing-board, not on the head this time. "And stay out," she says.

Eck and that boy was half-way down the hall by this time. I reckon that horse looked like a pinwheel to Eck too. "Git to hell outen here, Ad!" Eck says. Only there

wasn't time. Eck dropped flat on his face, but the boy never moved. The boy was about a yard tall maybe, in overhalls just like Eck's; that horse swoared over his head without touching a hair. I saw that, because I was just coming back up the front steps, still carrying that ere sock and still in my underclothes, when the horse come onto the porch again. It taken one look at me and swirled again and run to the end of the porch and jumped the banisters and the lot fence like a hen-hawk and lit in the lot running and went out the gate again and jumped eight or ten upsidedown wagons and went on down the road. It was a full moon then. Mrs. Armstid was still setting in the wagon like she had done been carved outen wood and left there and forgot.

That horse. It never missed a lick. It was going about forty miles a hour when it come to the bridge over the creek. It would have had a clear road, but it so happened that Vernon Tull was already using the bridge when it got there. He was coming back from town; he hadn't heard about the auction; him and his wife and three daughters and Mrs. Tull's aunt, all setting in chairs in the wagon bed, and all asleep, including the mules. They waked up when the horse hit the bridge one time, but Tull said the first he knew was when the mules tried to turn the wagon around in the middle of the bridge and he seen that spotted varmint run right twixt the mules and run up the wagon tongue like a squirrel. He said he just had time to hit it across the face with his whipstock, because about that time the mules turned the wagon around on that ere one-way bridge and that horse clumb across one of the mules and jumped down onto the bridge again and went on, with Vernon standing up in the wagon and kicking at it.

Tull said the mules turned in the harness and clumb back into the wagon, too, with Tull trying to beat them out again, with the reins wrapped around his wrist. After that he says all he seen was overturned chairs and womenfolks' legs and white drawers shining in the moonlight, and his mules and that spotted horse going on up the road like a ghost.

The mules jerked Tull outen the wagon and drug him a spell on the bridge before the reins broke. They thought at first that he was dead, and while they was kneeling around him, picking the bridge splinters outen him, here come Eck and that boy, still carrying the rope. They was running and breathing a little hard. "Where'd he go?" Eck says.

I went back and got my pants and shirt and shoes on just in time to go and help get Henry Armstid outen the trash in the lot. I be dog if he didn't look like he was dead, with his head hanging back and his teeth showing in the moonlight, and a little rim of white under his eyelids. We could still hear them horses, here and there; hadn't none of them got more than four-five miles away yet, not knowing the country, I reckon. So we could hear them and folks yelling now and then: "Whooey. Head him."

We toted Henry into Mrs. Littlejohn's. She was in the hall; she hadn't put down the armful of clothes. She taken one look at us, and she laid down the busted scrubbing board and taken up the lamp and opened a empty door. "Bring him in here," she says.

We toted him in and laid him on the bed. Mrs. Littlejohn set the lamp on the dresser, still carrying the clothes. "I'll declare, you men," she says. Our shadows was way up the wall, tiptoeing too; we could hear ourselves breathing. "Better get his wife," Mrs. Littlejohn says. She went out, carrying the clothes.

"I reckon we had," Quick says. "Go get her, somebody."

"Whyn't you go?" Winterbottom says.

"Let Ernest git her," Durley says. "He lives neighbors with them."

Ernest went to fetch her. I be dog if Henry didn't look like he was dead. Mrs. Littlejohn come back, with a kettle and some towels. She went to work on Henry, and then Mrs. Armstid and Ernest come in. Mrs. Armstid come to the foot of the bed and stood there, with her hands rolled into her apron, watching what Mrs. Littlejohn was doing, I reckon.

"You men get outen the way," Mrs. Littlejohn says. "Go outside," she says. "See if you can't find something else to play with that will kill some more of you."

"Is he dead?" Winterbottom says.

"It ain't your fault if he ain't," Mrs. Littlejohn says. "Go tell Will Varner to come up here. I reckon a man ain't so different from a mule, come long come short. Except maybe a mule's got more sense."

We went to get Uncle Billy. It was a full moon. We could hear them, now and then, four mile away: "Whooey. Head him." The country was full of them, one on ever wooden bridge in the land, running across it like thunder: "Whooey. There he goes. Head him."

We hadn't got far before Henry begun to scream. I reckon Mrs. Littlejohn's water had brung him to; anyway, he wasn't dead. We went on to Uncle Billy's. The house was dark. We called to him, and after a while the window opened and Uncle Billy put his head out, peart as a peckerwood, listening. "Are they still trying to catch them durn rabbits?" he says.

He come down, with his britches on over his nightshirt and his suspenders dangling, carrying his horse-doctoring grip. "Yes, sir," he says, cocking his head like a woodpecker; "they're still a-trying."

We could hear Henry before we reached Mrs. Littlejohn's. He was going Ah-Ah-Ah. We stopped in the yard. Uncle Billy went on in. We could hear Henry. We stood in the yard, hearing them on the bridges, this-a-way and that: "Whooey. Whooey."

"Eck Snopes ought to caught hisn," Ernest says. "Looks like he ought," Winterbottom said.

Henry was going Ah-Ah-Ah steady in the house; then he begun to scream. "Uncle Billy's started," Quick says. We looked

into the hall. We could see the light where
the door was. Then Mrs. Littlejohn come
out.

"Will needs some help," she says. "You,
Ernest. You'll do." Ernest went into the
house.

"Hear them?" Quick said. "That one
was on Four-Mile Bridge." We could hear
them; it sounded like thunder a long way
off. It didn't last long:

"Whooey."

We could hear Henry: "Ah-Ah-Ah-Ah-
Ah."

"They are both started now," Winterbottom says. "Ernest too."

That was early in the night. Which was
a good thing, because it taken a long night
for folks to chase them things right and
for Henry to lay there and holler, being
Uncle Billy never had none of this here
chloryfoam to set Henry's leg with. So it
was considerate in Flem to get them
started early. And what do you reckon
Flem's com-ment was?

That's right. Nothing. Because he wasn't
there. Hadn't nobody see him since that
Texas man left.

That was Saturday night. I reckon Mrs.
Armstid got home about daylight, to see
about the chaps. I don't know where they
thought her and Henry was. But lucky the
oldest one was a gal, about twelve, big
enough to take care of the little ones.
Which she did for the next two days. Mrs.
Armstid would nurse Henry all night and
work in the kitchen for hern and Henry's
keep, and in the afternoon she would drive
home (it was about four miles) to see to
the chaps. She would cook up a pot of
victuals and leave it on the stove, and the
gal would bar the house and keep the little
ones quiet. I would hear Mrs. Littlejohn
and Mrs. Armstid talking in the kitchen.
"How are the chaps making out?" Mrs.
Littlejohn says.

"All right," Mrs. Armstid says.

"Don't they get skeered at night?" Mrs.
Littlejohn says.

"Ina May bars the door when I leave,"
Mrs. Armstid says. "She's got the axe in
bed with her. I reckon she can make out."

I reckon they did. And I reckon Mrs.
Armstid was waiting for Flem to come
back to town; hadn't nobody seen him until
this morning; to get her money the Texas
man said Flem was keeping for her. Sho.
I reckon she was.

Anyway, I heard Mrs. Armstid and Mrs.
Littlejohn talking in the kitchen this morn-
ing while I was eating breakfast. Mrs.
Littlejohn had just told Mrs. Armstid that
Flem was in town. "You can ask him for
that five dollars," Mrs. Littlejohn says.

"You reckon he'll give it to me?" Mrs.
Armstid says.

Mrs. Littlejohn was washing dishes,
washing them like a man, like they was
made out of iron. "No," she says. "But
asking him won't do no hurt. It might
shame him. I don't reckon it will, but it
might."

"If he wouldn't give it back, it ain't no
use to ask," Mrs. Armstid says.

"Suit yourself," Mrs. Littlejohn says.
"It's your money."

I could hear the dishes.

"Do you reckon he might give it back
to me?" Mrs. Armstid says. "That Texas
man said he would. He said I could get
it from Mr. Snopes later."

"Then go and ask him for it," Mrs.
Littlejohn says.

I could hear the dishes.

"He won't give it back to me," Mrs.
Armstid says.

"All right," Mrs. Littlejohn says. "Don't
ask him for it, then."

I could hear the dishes; Mrs. Armstid
was helping. "You don't reckon he would,
do you?" she says. Mrs. Littlejohn never
said nothing. It sounded like she was
throwing the dishes at one another. "Maybe I better go and talk to Henry about
it," Mrs. Armstid says.

"I would," Mrs. Littlejohn says. I be
dog if it didn't sound like she had two
plates in her hands, beating them together.

"Then Henry can buy another five-dollar horse with it. Maybe he'll buy one next time that will out and out kill him. If I thought that, I'd give you back the money, myself."

"I reckon I better talk to him first," Mrs. Armstid said. Then it sounded like Mrs. Littlejohn taken up all the dishes and throwed them at the cook-stove, and I come away.

That was this morning. I had been up to Bundren's and back, and I thought that things would have kind of settled down. So after breakfast, I went up to the store. And there was Flem, setting in the store chair and whittling, like he might not have ever moved since he came to clerk for Jody Varner. I. O. was leaning in the door, in his shirt sleeves and with his hair parted too, same as Flem was before he turned the clerking job over to I. O. It's a funny thing about them Snopes: they all look alike, yet there ain't ere a two of them that claims brothers. They're always just cousins, like Flem and Eck and Flem and I. O. Eck was there too, squatting against the wall, him and that boy, eating cheese and crackers outen a sack; they told me that Eck hadn't been home a-tall. And that Lon Quick hadn't got back to town, even. He followed his horse clean down to Samson's Bridge, with a wagon and a camp outfit. Eck finally caught one of hisn. It run into a blind lane at Freeman's, and Eck and the boy taken and tied their rope across the end of the lane, about three foot high. The horse come to the end of the lane and whirled and run back without ever stopping. Eck says it never seen the rope a-tall. He says it looked just like one of these here Christmas pinwheels. "Didn't it try to run again?" I says.

"No," Eck says, eating a bite of cheese offen his knife blade. "Just kicked some."

"Kicked some?" I says.

"It broke its neck," Eck says.

Well, they was squatting there, about six of them, talking, talking at Flem; never nobody knowed yet if Flem had ere a interest in them horses or not. So finally I come right out and asked him. "Flem's done skun all of us so much," I says, "that we're proud of him. Come on, Flem," I says, "how much did you and that Texas man make offen them horses? You can tell us. Ain't nobody here but Eck that bought one of them; the others ain't got back to town yet, and Eck's your own cousin; he'll be proud to hear, too. How much did you-all make?"

They was all whittling, not looking at Flem, making like they was studying. But you could a heard a pin drop. And I. O. He had been rubbing his back up and down on the door, but he stopped now, watching Flem like a pointing dog. Flem finished cutting the sliver offen his stick. He spit across the porch, into the road. "'Twarn't none of my horses," he says.

I. O. cackled, like a hen, slapping his legs with both hands. "You boys might just as well quit trying to get ahead of Flem," he said.

Well, about that time I see Mrs. Armstid come outen Mrs. Littlejohn's gate, coming up the road. I never said nothing. I says, "Well, if a man can't take care of himself in a trade, he can't blame the man that trims him."

Flem never said nothing, trimming at the stick. He hadn't seen Mrs. Armstid. "Yes, sir," I says. "A fellow like Henry Armstid ain't got nobody but hisself to blame."

"Course he ain't," I. O. says. He ain't seen her, neither. "Henry Armstid's a born fool. Always is been. If Flem hadn't a got his money, somebody else would."

We looked at Flem. He never moved. Mrs. Armstid come on up the road.

"That's right," I says. "But, come to think of it, Henry never bought no horse." We looked at Flem; you could a heard a match drop. "That Texas man told her to get that five dollars back from Flem next day. I reckon Flem's done already taken that money to Mrs. Littlejohn's and give it to Mrs. Armstid."

We watched Flem. I. O. quit rubbing his back against the door again. After a while Flem raised his head and spit across the porch, into the dust. I. O. cackled, just like a hen. "Ain't he a beating fellow, now?" I. O. says.

Mrs. Armstid was getting closer, so I kept on talking, watching to see if Flem would look up and see her. But he never looked up. I went on talking about Tull, about how he was going to sue Flem, and Flem setting there, whittling his stick, not saying nothing else after he said they wasn't none of his horses.

Then I. O. happened to look around. He seen Mrs. Armstid. "Psssst!" he says. Flem looked up. "Here she comes!" I. O. says. "Go out the back. I'll tell her you done went to town today."

But Flem never moved. He just set there, whittling, and we watched Mrs. Armstid come up onto the porch, in that ere faded sunbonnet and wrapper and them tennis shoes that made a kind of hissing noise on the porch. She come onto the porch and stopped, her hands rolled into her dress in front, not looking at nothing.

"He said Saturday," she says, "that he wouldn't sell Henry no horse. He said I could get the money from you."

Flem looked up. The knife never stopped. It went on trimming off a sliver same as if he was watching it. "He taken that money off with him when he left," Flem says.

Mrs. Armstid never looked at nothing. We never looked at her, neither, except that boy of Eck's. He had a half-et cracker in his hand, watching her, chewing.

"He said Henry hadn't bought no horse," Mrs. Armstid says. "He said for me to get the money from you today."

"I reckon he forgot about it," Flem said. "He taken that money off with him Saturday." He whittled again. I. O. kept on rubbing his back, slow. He licked his lips. After a while the woman looked up the road, where it went on up the hill, toward the graveyard. She looked up that way for

a while, with that boy of Eck's watching her and I. O. rubbing his back slow against the door. Then she turned back toward the steps.

"I reckon it's time to get dinner started," she says.

"How's Henry this morning, Mrs. Armstid?" Winterbottom says.

She looked at Winterbottom; she almost stopped. "He's resting, I thank you kindly," she says.

Flem got up, outen the chair, putting his knife away. He spit across the porch. "Wait a minute, Mrs. Armstid," he says. She stopped again. She didn't look at him. Flem went on into the store, with I. O. done quit rubbing his back now, with his head craned after Flem, and Mrs. Armstid standing there with her hands rolled into her dress, not looking at nothing. A wagon come up the road and passed; it was Freeman, on the way to town. Then Flem come out again, with I. O. still watching him. Flem had one of these little striped sacks of Jody Varner's candy; I bet he still owes Jody that nickel, too. He put the sack into Mrs. Armstid's hand, like he would have put it into a hollow stump. He spit again across the porch. "A little sweetening for the chaps," he says.

"You're right kind," Mrs. Armstid says. She held the sack of candy in her hand, not looking at nothing. Eck's boy was watching the sack, the half-et cracker in his hand; he wasn't chewing now. He watched Mrs. Armstid roll the sack into her apron. "I reckon I better get on back and help with dinner," she says. She turned and went back across the porch. Flem sat down in the chair again and opened his knife. He spit across the porch again, past Mrs. Armstid where she hadn't went down the steps yet. Then she went on, in that ere sunbonnet and wrapper all the same color, back down the road toward Mrs. Littlejohn's. You couldn't see her dress move, like a natural woman walking. She looked like a old snag still standing up and moving along on a high water. We watched her turn in at Mrs. Littlejohn's and go outen sight. Flem was whittling. I. O. begun to rub his back on the door. Then he begun to cackle, just like a durn hen.

"You boys might just as well quit trying," I. O. says. "You can't git ahead of Flem. You can't touch him. Ain't he a sight, now?"

I be dog if he ain't. If I had brung a herd of wild cattymounts into town and sold them to my neighbors and kinfolks, they would have lynched me. Yes, sir.

A ROSE FOR EMILY
[1931]

I

WHEN Miss Emily Grierson died, our whole town went to her funeral: the men through a sort of respectful affection for a fallen monument, the women mostly out of curiosity to see the inside of her house, which no one save an old man-servant—a combined gardener and cook—had seen in at least ten years.

It was a big, squarish frame house that had once been white, decorated with cupolas and spires and scrolled balconies in the heavily lightsome style of the Seventies, set on what had once been our most select street. But garages and cotton gins had encroached and obliterated even the august names of that neighborhood; only Miss Emily's house was left, lifting its stubborn and coquettish decay above the cotton wagons and the gasoline pumps—an eyesore among eyesores. And now Miss Emily had gone to join the representatives of those august names where they lay in the cedar-bemused cemetery among the ranked and anonymous graves of Union and Confederate soldiers who fell at the battle of Jefferson.

Alive, Miss Emily had been a tradition, a duty, and a care; a sort of hereditary obligation upon the town, dating from that day in 1894 when Colonel Sartoris, the mayor—he who fathered the edict that no Negro woman should appear on the streets without an apron—remitted her taxes, the dispensation dating from the death of her father on into perpetuity. Not that Miss Emily would have accepted charity. Colonel Sartoris invented an involved tale to the effect that Miss Emily's father had loaned money to the town, which the town, as a matter of business, preferred this way of repaying. Only a man of Colonel Sartoris' generation and thought could have invented it, and only a woman could have believed it.

When the next generation, with its more modern ideas, became mayors and aldermen, this arrangement created some little dissatisfaction. On the first of the year they mailed her a tax notice. February came, and there was no reply. They wrote her a formal letter, asking her to call at the sheriff's office at her convenience. A week later the mayor wrote her himself, offering to call or to send his car for her, and received in reply a note on paper of an archaic shape, in a thin, flowing calligraphy in faded ink, to the effect that she no longer went out at all. The tax notice was also enclosed, without comment.

They called a special meeting of the Board of Aldermen. A deputation waited upon her, knocked at the door through which no visitor had passed since she ceased giving china-painting lessons eight or ten years earlier. They were admitted by the old Negro into a dim hall from which a stairway mounted into still more shadow. It smelled of dust and disuse—a close, dank smell. The Negro led them into the parlor. It was furnished in heavy, leather-covered furniture. When the Negro opened the blinds of one window, they could see that the leather was cracked; and when they sat down, a faint dust rose sluggishly about their thighs, spinning with slow motes in the single sun-ray. On a tarnished gilt easel before the fireplace stood a crayon portrait of Miss Emily's father.

They rose when she entered—a small,

fat woman in black, with a thin gold chain descending to her waist and vanishing into her belt, leaning on an ebony cane with a tarnished gold head. Her skeleton was small and spare; perhaps that was why what would have been merely plumpness in another was obesity in her. She looked bloated, like a body long submerged in motionless water, and of that pallid hue. Her eyes, lost in the fatty ridges of her face, looked like two small pieces of coal pressed into a lump of dough as they moved from one face to another while the visitors stated their errand.

She did not ask them to sit. She just stood in the door and listened quietly until the spokesman came to a stumbling halt. Then they could hear the invisible watch ticking at the end of the gold chain.

Her voice was dry and cold. "I have no taxes in Jefferson. Colonel Sartoris explained it to me. Perhaps one of you can gain access to the city records and satisfy yourselves."

"But we have. We are the city authorities, Miss Emily. Didn't you get a notice from the sheriff, signed by him?"

"I received a paper, yes," Miss Emily said. "Perhaps he considers himself the sheriff . . . I have no taxes in Jefferson."

"But there is nothing on the books to show that, you see. We must go by the—"

"See Colonel Sartoris. I have no taxes in Jefferson."

"But, Miss Emily—"

"See Colonel Sartoris." (Colonel Sartoris had been dead almost ten years.) "I have no taxes in Jefferson. Tobe!" The Negro appeared. "Show these gentlemen out."

II

So she vanquished them, horse and foot, just as she had vanquished their fathers thirty years before about the smell. That was two years after her father's death and a short time after her sweetheart—the one we believed would marry her—had deserted her. After her father's death she went out very little; after her sweetheart went away, people hardly saw her at all. A few of the ladies had the temerity to call, but were not received, and the only sign of life about the place was the Negro man—a young man then—going in and out with a market basket.

"Just as if a man—any man—could keep a kitchen properly," the ladies said; so they were not surprised when the smell developed. It was another link between the gross, teeming world and the high and mighty Griersons.

A neighbor, a woman, complained to the mayor, Judge Stevens, eighty years old.

"But what will you have me do about it, madam?" he said.

"Why, send her word to stop it," the woman said. "Isn't there a law?"

"I'm sure that won't be necessary," Judge Stevens said. "It's probably just a snake or a rat that nigger of hers killed in the yard. I'll speak to him about it."

The next day he received two more complaints, one from a man who came in diffident deprecation. "We really must do something about it, Judge. I'd be the last one in the world to bother Miss Emily, but we've got to do something." That night the Board of Aldermen met—three graybeards and one younger man, a member of the rising generation.

"It's simple enough," he said. "Send her word to have her place cleaned up. Give her a certain time to do it in, and if she don't . . ."

"Dammit, sir," Judge Stevens said, "will you accuse a lady to her face of smelling bad?"

So the next night, after midnight, four men crossed Miss Emily's lawn and slunk about the house like burglars, sniffing along the base of the brickwork and at the cellar openings while one of them performed a regular sowing motion with his hand out of a sack slung from his shoulder. They broke open the cellar door and sprinkled lime there, and in all the outbuildings. As they recrossed the lawn, a window that had been dark was lighted and Miss Emily sat in it, the light behind her, and her upright torso motionless as that of an idol. They crept quietly across the lawn and into the shadow of the locusts that lined the street. After a week or two the smell went away.

That was when people had begun to feel really sorry for her. People in our town, remembering how Old Lady Wyatt, her great-aunt, had gone completely crazy at last, believed that the Griersons held themselves a little too high for what they really were. None of the young men was quite good enough for Miss Emily and such. We had long thought of them as a tableau: Miss Emily a slender figure in white in the background, her father a spraddled silhouette in the foreground, his back to her and clutching a horsewhip, the two of them framed by the back-flung front door. So when she got to be thirty and was still single, we were not pleased exactly, but vindicated; even with insanity in the family she wouldn't have turned down all of her chances if they had really materialized.

When her father died, it got about that the house was all that was left to her; and in a way, people were glad. At last they could pity Miss Emily. Being left alone, and a pauper, she had become humanized. Now she too would know the old thrill and the old despair of a penny more or less.

The day after his death all the ladies prepared to call at the house and offer condolence and aid, as is our custom. Miss Emily met them at the door, dressed as usual and with no trace of grief on her face. She told them that her father was not dead. She did that for three days, with the ministers calling on her, and the doctors, trying to persuade her to let them dispose of the body. Just as they were about to resort to law and force, she broke down, and they buried her father quickly.

We did not say she was crazy then. We believed she had to do that. We remem-bered all the young men her father had driven away, and we knew that with nothing left, she would have to cling to that which had robbed her, as people will.

III

She was sick for a long time. When we saw her again, her hair was cut short, making her look like a girl, with a vague resemblance to those angels in colored church windows—sort of tragic and serene.

The town had just let the contracts for paving the sidewalks, and in the summer after her father's death they began the work. The construction company came with niggers and mules and machinery, and a foreman named Homer Barron, a Yankee —a big, dark, ready man, with a big voice and eyes lighter than his face. The little boys would follow in groups to hear him cuss the niggers, and the niggers singing in time to the rise and fall of picks. Pretty soon he knew everybody in town. Whenever you heard a lot of laughing about the square, Homer Barron would be in the center of the group. Presently we began to see him and Miss Emily on Sunday afternoons driving in the yellow-wheeled buggy and the matched team of bays from the livery stable.

At first we were glad that Miss Emily would have an interest, because the ladies all said, "Of course a Grierson would not think seriously of a Northerner, a day laborer." But there were still others, older people, who said that even grief could not cause a real lady to forget noblesse oblige —without calling it noblesse oblige. They just said, "Poor Emily. Her kinsfolk should come to her." She had some kin in Alabama; but years ago her father had fallen out with them over the estate of Old Lady Wyatt, the crazy woman, and there was no communication between the two families. They had not even been represented at the funeral.

And as soon as the old people said, "Poor Emily," the whispering began. "Do you suppose it's really so?" they said to one another. "Of course it is. What else could . . ." This behind their hands; rustling of craned silk and satin behind jalousies closed upon the sun of Sunday afternoon as the thin, swift clop-clop-clop of the matched team passed: "Poor Emily."

She carried her head high enough—even when we believed that she was fallen. It was as if she demanded more than ever the recognition of her dignity as the last Grierson; as if it had wanted that touch of earthiness to reaffirm her imperviousness. Like when she bought the rat poison, the arsenic. That was over a year after they had begun to say "Poor Emily," and while the two female cousins were visiting her.

"I want some poison," she said to the druggist. She was over thirty then, still a slight woman, though thinner than usual, with cold, haughty black eyes in a face the flesh of which was strained across the temples and about the eye-sockets as you imagine a lighthouse-keeper's face ought to look. "I want some poison," she said.

"Yes, Miss Emily. What kind? For rats and such? I'd recom—"

"I want the best you have. I don't care what kind."

The druggist named several. "They'll kill anything up to an elephant. But what you want is—"

"Arsenic," Miss Emily said. "Is that a good one?"

"Is . . . . arsenic? Yes, ma'am. But what you want—"

"I want arsenic."

The druggist looked down at her. She looked back at him, erect, her face like a strained flag. "Why, of course," the druggist said. "If that's what you want. But the law requires you to tell what you are going to use it for."

Miss Emily just stared at him, her head tilted back in order to look him eye for eye, until he looked away and went and got the arsenic and wrapped it up. The Negro delivery boy brought her the package; the druggist didn't come back. When she opened the package at home there was written on the box, under the skull and bones: "For rats."

IV

So the next day we all said, "She will kill herself"; and we said it would be the best thing. When she had first begun to be seen with Homer Barron, we had said, "She will marry him." Then we said, "She will persuade him yet," because Homer himself had remarked—he liked men, and it was known that he drank with the younger men in the Elks' Club—that he was not a marrying man. Later we said, "Poor Emily" behind the jalousies as they passed on Sunday afternoon in the glittering buggy. Miss Emily with her head high and Homer Barron with his hat cocked and a cigar in his teeth, reins and whip in a yellow glove.

Then some of the ladies began to say that it was a disgrace to the town and a bad example to the young people. The men did not want to interfere, but at last the ladies forced the Baptist minister— Miss Emily's people were Episcopal—to call upon her. He would never divulge what happened during that interview, but he refused to go back again. The next Sunday they again drove about the streets, and the following day the minister's wife wrote to Miss Emily's relations in Alabama.

So she had blood-kin under her roof again and we sat back to watch developments. At first nothing happened. Then we were sure that they were to be married. We learned that Miss Emily had been to the jeweler's and ordered a man's toilet set in silver, with the letters H.B. on each piece. Two days later we learned that she had bought a complete outfit of men's clothing, including a nightshirt, and we said, "They are married." We were really glad. We were glad because the two female cousins were even more Grierson than Miss Emily had ever been.

So we were not surprised when Homer

Barron—the streets had been finished some time since—was gone. We were a little disappointed that there was not a public blowing-off, but we believed that he had gone on to prepare for Miss Emily's coming, or to give her a chance to get rid of the cousins. (By that time it was a cabal, and we were all Miss Emily's allies to help circumvent the cousins.) Sure enough, after another week they departed. And, as we had expected all along, within three days Homer Barron was back in town. A neighbor saw the Negro man admit him at the kitchen door at dusk one evening.

And that was the last we saw of Homer Barron. And of Miss Emily for some time. The Negro man went in and out with the market basket, but the front door remained closed. Now and then we would see her at a window for a moment, as the men did that night when they sprinkled the lime, but for almost six months she did not appear on the streets. Then we knew that this was to be expected too; as if that quality of her father which had thwarted her woman's life so many times had been too virulent and too furious to die.

When we next saw Miss Emily, she had grown fat and her hair was turning gray. During the next few years it grew grayer and grayer until it attained an even pepper-and-salt iron-gray, when it ceased turning. Up to the day of her death at seventy-four it was still that vigorous iron-gray, like the hair of an active man.

From that time on her front door remained closed, save for a period of six or seven years, when she was about forty, during which she gave lessons in china-painting. She fitted up a studio in one of the downstairs rooms, where the daughters and granddaughters of Colonel Sartoris' contemporaries were sent to her with the same regularity and in the same spirit that they were sent to church on Sundays with a twenty-five-cent piece for the collection plate. Meanwhile her taxes had been remitted.

Then the newer generation became the backbone and the spirit of the town, and the painting pupils grew up and fell away and did not send their children to her with boxes of color and tedious brushes and pictures cut from the ladies' magazines. The front door closed upon the last one and remained closed for good. When the town got free postal delivery, Miss Emily alone refused to let them fasten the metal numbers above her door and attach a mailbox to it. She would not listen to them.

Daily, monthly, yearly we watched the Negro grow grayer and more stooped, going in and out with the market basket. Each December we sent her a tax notice, which would be returned by the post office a week later, unclaimed. Now and then we would see her in one of the downstairs windows—she had evidently shut up the top floor of the house—like the carven torso of an idol in a niche, looking or not looking at us, we could never tell which. Thus she passed from generation to generation—dear, inescapable, impervious, tranquil, and perverse.

And so she died. Fell ill in the house filled with dust and shadows, with only a doddering Negro man to wait on her. We did not even know she was sick; we had long since given up trying to get any information from the Negro. He talked to no one, probably not even to her, for his voice had grown harsh and rusty, as if from disuse.

She died in one of the downstairs rooms, in a heavy walnut bed with a curtain, her gray head propped on a pillow yellow and moldy with age and lack of sunlight.

V

The Negro met the first of the ladies at the front door and let them in, with their hushed, sibilant voices and their quick, curious glances, and then he disappeared. He walked right through the house and out the back and was not seen again.

The two female cousins came at once. They held the funeral on the second day, with the town coming to look at Miss Emily beneath a mass of bought flowers, with the crayon face of her father musing profoundly above the bier and the ladies sibilant and macabre; and the very old men—some in their brushed Confederate uniforms—on the porch and the lawn, talking of Miss Emily as if she had been a contemporary of theirs, believing that they had danced with her and courted her perhaps, confusing time with its mathematical progression, as the old do, to whom all the past is not a diminishing road but, instead, a huge meadow which no winter ever quite touches, divided from them now by the narrow bottleneck of the most recent decade of years.

Already we knew that there was one room in that region above stairs which no one had seen in forty years, and which would have to be forced. They waited until Miss Emily was decently in the ground before they opened it.

The violence of breaking down the door seemed to fill this room with pervading dust. A thin, acrid pall as of the tomb seemed to lie everywhere upon this room decked and furnished as for a bridal: upon the valance curtains of faded rose color, upon the rose-shaded lights, upon the dressing table, upon the delicate array of crystal and the man's toilet things backed with tarnished silver, silver so tarnished that the monogram was obscured. Among them lay a collar and tie, as if they had just been removed, which, lifted, left upon the surface a pale crescent in the dust. Upon a chair hung the suit, carefully folded; beneath it the two mute shoes and the discarded socks.

The man himself lay in the bed.

For a long while we just stood there, looking down at the profound and fleshless grin. The body had apparently once lain in the attitude of an embrace, but now the long sleep that outlasts love, that conquers even the grimace of love, had cuckoled him. What was left of him, rotted beneath what was left of the nightshirt, had become inextricable from the bed in which he lay; and upon him and upon the pillow beside him lay that even coating of the patient and biding dust.

Then we noticed that in the second pillow was the indentation of a head. One of us lifted something from it, and leaning forward, that faint and invisible dust dry and acrid in the nostrils, we saw a long strand of iron-gray hair.

John Steinbeck
1902

JOHN STEINBECK was born at Salinas, California, where his father was for many years treasurer of the county. When he went from the Salinas high school to Stanford University he did not work for a degree, but spent four years taking courses of his own choosing, chiefly in biology and other sciences.

His early writing earned little money, and he supported himself with jobs of many kinds, including fruit-picking in California orchards as a migratory worker. In 1930 he married Carol Henning, and they lived for some time at Monterey on an income of not more than twenty-five dollars a month, getting much of their food from the ocean by fishing from their launch. It was not until the publication of his novel of the *paisanos* of Monterey, *Tortilla Flat*, in 1935 that Steinbeck won an audience and critical recognition.

In some of his short stories and in the widely read novels *Of Mice and Men* (1937) and *The Grapes of Wrath* (1939) Steinbeck has presented social conflict and agitation, stressing especially the problems of homeless migratory workers; but he has resisted classification in any specific radical group. The most direct statement of his personal philosophy is to be found in the introductory and narrative chapters of *Sea of Cortez* (1941), a volume which is also a scientific report of an expedition to study the marine biology of the Gulf of California.

Steinbeck's *Of Mice and Men* was highly successful as a play, and *Of Mice and Men, The Grapes of Wrath,* and *Tortilla Flat* were made into popular motion pictures. Steinbeck wrote the text for a documentary film of contemporary Mexico, *The Forgotten Village,* produced by Herbert Kline, described in Steinbeck's text as a story of "the long moment when the past slips reluctantly into the future." The text was published, with photographic illustrations from the film, in 1941. Later novels by Steinbeck are *The Moon is Down* (1942), *Cannery Row* (1945), and *The Wayward Bus* (1947). The following story is from *The Long Valley* (1938).

[See Henry T. Moore's *The Novels of John Steinbeck: A First Critical Study* (New York, 1939) and George Snell, *The Shapers of American Fiction* (New York, 1947).]

THE RAID
[1938]

IT WAS DARK in the little California town when the two men stepped from the lunch car and strode arrogantly through the back streets. The air was full of the sweet smell of fermenting fruit from the packing plants. High over the corners, blue arc lights swung in the wind and put moving shadows of telephone wires on the ground. The old wooden buildings were silent and resting. The dirty windows dismally reflected the street lights.

The two men were about the same size, but one was much older than the other. Their hair was cropped, they wore blue jeans. The older man had on a peajacket, while the younger wore a blue turtle-neck sweater. As they swung down the dark street, footsteps echoed back loudly from the wooden buildings. The younger man began to whistle *Come to Me My Melancholy Baby.* He stopped abruptly. "I wish

that damn tune would get out of my head. It's been going all day. It's an old tune, too."

His companion turned toward him. "You're scared, Root. Tell the truth. You're scared as hell."

They were passing under one of the blue street lights. Root's face put on its toughest look, the eyes squinted, the mouth went crooked and bitter. "No, I ain't scared." They were out of the light. His face relaxed again. "I wish I knew the ropes better. You been out before, Dick. You know what to expect. But I ain't ever been out."

"The way to learn is to do," Dick quoted sententiously. "You never really learn nothing from books."

They crossed a railroad track. A block tower up the line a little was starred with green lights. "It's awful dark," said Root. "I wonder if the moon will come up later. Usually does when it's so dark. You going to make the first speech, Dick?"

"No, you make it. I had more experience

than you. I'll watch them while you talk and then I can smack them where I know they bite. Know what you're going to say?"

"Sure I do. I got it all in my head, every word. I wrote it out and learned it. I heard guys tell how they got up and couldn't think of a thing to say, and then all of a sudden they just started in like it was somebody else, and the words came out like water out of a hydrant. Big Mike Sheane said it was like that with him. But I wasn't taking no chances, so I wrote it out."

A train hooted mournfully, and in a moment it rounded a bend and pushed its terrible light down the track. The lighted coaches rattled past. Dick turned to watch it go by. "Not many people on that one," he said with satisfaction. "Didn't you say your old man worked on the railroad?"

Root tried to keep the bitterness out of his voice. "Sure, he works on the road. He's a brakeman. He kicked me out when he found out what I was doing. He was scared he'd lose his job. He couldn't see. I talked to him, but he just couldn't see. He kicked me right out." Root's voice was lonely. Suddenly he realized how he had weakened and how he sounded homesick. "That's the trouble with them," he went on harshly. "They can't see beyond their jobs. They can't see what's happening to them. They hang on to their chains."

"Save it," said Dick. "That's good stuff. Is that part of your speech?"

"No, but I guess I'll put it in if you say it's good."

The street lights were fewer now. A line of locust trees grew along the road, for the town was beginning to thin and the country took control. Along the unpaved road there were a few little houses with ill-kept gardens.

"Jesus! It's dark," Root said again. "I wonder if there'll be any trouble. It's a good night to get away if anything happens."

Dick snorted into the collar of his pea-jacket. They walked along in silence for a while.

"Do you think you'd try to get away, Dick?" Root asked.

"No, by God! It's against orders. If anything happens we got to stick. You're just a kid. I guess you'd run if I let you!"

Root blustered: "You think you're hell on wheels just because you been out a few times. You'd think you was a hundred to hear you talk."

"I'm dry behind the ears, anyway," said Dick.

Root walked with his head down. He said softly, "Dick, are you sure you wouldn't run? Are you sure you could just stand there and take it?"

"Of course I'm sure. I've done it before. It's the orders, ain't it? Why, it's good publicity." He peered through the darkness at Root. "What makes you ask, kid? You scared you'll run? If you're scared you got no business here."

Root shivered. "Listen, Dick, you're a good guy. You won't tell nobody what I say, will you? I never been tried. How do I know what I'll do if somebody smacks me in the face with a club? How can anybody tell what he'd do? I don't think I'd run. I'd try not to run."

"All right, kid. Let it go at that. But you try running, and I'll turn your name in. We got no place for yellow bastards. You remember that, kid."

"Oh, lay off that kid stuff. You're running that in the ground."

The locust trees grew closer together as they went. The wind rustled gently in the leaves. A dog growled in one of the yards as the men went by. A light fog began to drift down through the air, and the stars were swallowed in it. "You sure you got everything ready?" Dick asked. "Got the lamps? Got the lit'ature? I left all that to you."

"I did it all this afternoon," said Root. "I didn't put the posters up yet, but I got them in a box out there."

"Got oil in the lamps?"

"They had plenty in. Say, Dick, I guess some bastard has squealed, don't you?"

"Sure. Somebody always squeals."

"Well, you didn't hear nothing about no raid, did you?"

"How the hell would I hear. You think they'd come and tell me they was going to knock my can off? Get hold of yourself, Root. You got the pants scared off you. You're going to make me nervous if you don't cut it out."

II

They approached a low, square building, black and heavy in the darkness. Their feet pounded on a wooden sidewalk. "Nobody here, yet," said Dick. "Let's open her up and get some light." They had come to a deserted store. The old show-windows were opaque with dirt. A Lucky Strike poster was stuck to the glass on one side while a big cardboard Coca-Cola lady stood like a ghost in the other. Dick threw open the double doors and walked in. He struck a match and lighted a kerosene lamp, got the chimney back in place, and set the lamp on an up-ended apple box. "Come on, Root, we got to get things ready."

The walls of the building were scabrous with streaked whitewash. A pile of dusty newspapers had been kicked into a corner. The two back windows were laced with cobwebs. Except for the three apple boxes, there was nothing at all in the store.

Root walked to one of the boxes and took out a large poster bearing a portrait of a man done in harsh reds and blacks. He tacked the portrait to the whitewashed wall behind the lamp. Then he tacked another poster beside it, a large red symbol on a white background. Last he up-ended another apple box and piled leaflets and little paper-bound books on it. His footsteps were loud on the bare wooden floor. "Light the other lamp, Dick! It's too damned dark in here."

"Scared of the dark, too, kid?"

"No. The men will be here pretty soon. We want to have more light when they come. What time is it?"

Dick looked at his watch. "Quarter to eight. Some of the guys ought to be here pretty soon now." He put his hands in the breast pockets of his peajacket and stood loosely by the box of pamphlets. There was nothing to sit on. The black and red portrait stared harshly out at the room. Root leaned against the wall.

The light from one of the lamps yellowed, and the flame slowly sank down. Dick stepped over to it. "I thought you said there was plenty of oil. This one's dry."

"I thought there was plenty. Look! The other one's nearly full. We can pour some of that oil in this lamp."

"How we going to do that? We got to put them both out to pour the oil. You got any matches?"

Root felt through his pockets. "Only two."

"Now, you see? We got to hold this meeting with only one lamp. I should've looked things over this afternoon. I was busy in town, though. I thought I could leave it to you."

"Maybe we could quick pour some of this oil in a can and then pour it into the other lamp."

"Yeah, and then set the joint on fire. You're a hell of a helper."

Root leaned back against the wall again. "I wish they'd come. What time is it, Dick?"

"Five after eight."

"Well, what's keeping them? What are they waiting for? Did you tell them eight o'clock?"

"Oh! Shut up, kid. You'll get my goat pretty soon. I don't know what's keeping them. Maybe they got cold feet. Now shut up for a little while." He dug his hands into the pockets of his jacket again. "Got a cigarette, Root?"

"No."

It was very still. Nearer the center of

the town, automobiles were moving; the mutter of their engines and an occasional horn sounded. A dog barked unexcitedly at one of the houses. The wind ruffled the locust trees in whishing gusts.

"Listen, Dick! Do you hear voices? I think they're coming." They turned their heads and strained to listen.

"I don't hear nothing. You just thought you heard it."

Root walked to one of the dirty windows and looked out. Coming back, he paused at the pile of pamphlets and straightened them neatly. "What time is it now, Dick?"

"Keep still, will you? You'll drive me nuts. You got to have guts for this job. For God's sake show some guts."

"Well, I never been out before, Dick."

"Do you think anybody couldn't tell that? You sure make it plain enough."

The wind gusted sharply in the locust trees. The front doors clicked and one of them opened slowly, squeaking a little at the hinges. The breeze came in, ruffled the pile of dusty newspapers in the corner and sailed the posters out from the wall like curtains.

"Shut the door, Root. . . . No, leave it open. Then we can hear them coming better." He looked at his watch. "It's nearly half-past eight."

"Do you think they'll come? How long we going to wait, if they don't show up?"

The older man stared at the open door. "We ain't going to leave here before nine-thirty at the earliest. We got orders to hold this meeting."

The night sounds came in more clearly through the open door—the dance of dry locust leaves on the road, the slow steady barking of the dog. On the wall the red and black portrait was menacing in the dim light. It floated out at the bottom again. Dick looked around at it. "Listen, kid," he said quietly. "I know you're scared. When you're scared, just take a look at him." He indicated the picture with his thumb. "He wasn't scared. Just remember about what he did."

The boy considered the portrait. "You suppose he wasn't ever scared?"

Dick reprimanded him sharply. "If he was, nobody ever found out about it. You take that for a lesson and don't go opening up for everybody to show them how you feel."

"You're a good guy, Dick. I don't know what I'll do when I get sent out alone."

"You'll be all right, kid. You got stuff in you. I can tell that. You just never been under fire."

Root glanced quickly at the door. "Listen! You hear somebody coming?"

"Lay off that stuff! When they get here, they'll get here."

"Well, let's close the door. It's kind of cold in here. Listen! There is somebody coming."

Quick footsteps sounded on the road, broke into a run and crossed the wooden sidewalk. A man in overalls and a painter's cap ran into the room. He was panting and winded. "You guys better scram," he said. "There's a raiding party coming. None of the boys is coming to the meeting. They was going to let you take it, but I wouldn't do that. Come on! Get your stuff together and get out. That party's on the way."

Root's face was pale and tight. He looked nervously at Dick. The older man shivered. He thrust his hands into his breast pockets and slumped his shoulders. "Thanks," he said. "Thanks for telling us. You run along. We'll be all right."

"The others was just going to leave you take it," the man said.

Dick nodded. "Sure, they can't see the future. They can't see beyond their nose. Run along now before you get caught."

"Well, ain't you guys coming? I'll help carry some of your stuff."

"We're going to stay," Dick said woodenly. "We got orders to stay. We got to take it."

The man was moving toward the door. He turned back. "Want me to stay with you?"

"No, you're a good guy. No need for you

III

to stay. We could maybe use you some other time."

"Well, I did what I could."

Dick and Root heard him cross the wooden sidewalk and trot off into the darkness. The night resumed its sounds. The dead leaves scraped along the ground. The motors hummed from the centre of the town.

Root looked at Dick. He could see that the man's fists were doubled up in his breast pockets. The face muscles were stiff, but he smiled at the boy. The posters drifted out from the wall and settled back again.

"Scared, kid?"

Root bristled to deny it, and then gave it up. "Yes, I'm scared. Maybe I won't be no good at this."

"Take hold, kid!" Dick said fiercely. "You take hold!"

Dick quoted to him, " 'The men of little spirit must have an example of stead-steadfastness. The people at large must have an example of injustice.' There it is, Root. That's orders." He relapsed into silence. The barking dog increased his tempo.

"I guess that's them," said Root. "Will they kill us, do you think?"

"No, they don't very often kill anybody."

"But they'll hit us and kick us, won't they? They'll hit us in the face with sticks and break our nose. Big Mike, they broke his jaw in three places."

"Take hold, kid! You take hold! And listen to me; if some one busts you, it isn't him that's doing it, it's the System. And it isn't you he's busting. He's taking a crack at the Principle. Can you remember that?"

"I don't want to run, Dick. Honest to God I don't. If I start to run, you hold me, will you?"

Dick walked near and touched him on the shoulder. "You'll be all right. I can tell a guy that will stick."

"Well, hadn't we better hide the lit'ature so it won't all get burned?"

"No—somebody might put a book in his pocket and read it later. Then it would be doing some good. Leave the books there. And shut up now! Talking only makes it worse."

The dog had gone back to his slow, spiritless barking. A rush of wind brought a scurry of dead leaves in the open door. The portrait poster blew out and came loose at one corner. Root walked over and pinned it back. Somewhere in the town, an automobile squealed its brakes.

"Hear anything, Dick? Hear them coming yet?"

"No."

"Listen, Dick. Big Mike lay two days with his jaw broke before anybody'd help him."

The older man turned angrily on him. One doubled fist came out of his peajacket pocket. His eyes narrowed as he looked at the boy. He walked close and put an arm about his shoulders. "Listen to me close, kid," he said. "I don't know much, but I been through this mill before. I can tell you this for sure. When it comes—it won't hurt. I don't know why, but it won't. Even if they kill you it won't hurt." He dropped his arm and moved toward the front door. He looked out and listened in two directions before he came back into the room.

"Hear anything?"

"No. Not a thing."

"What—do you think is keeping them?"

"How do you suppose I'd know?"

Root swallowed thickly. "Maybe they won't come. Maybe it was all a lie that fella told us, just a joke."

"Maybe."

"Well, are—we going to wait all night to get our cans knocked off?"

Dick mimicked him. "Yes, we're going to wait all night to get our cans knocked off."

The wind sounded in one big fierce gust and then dropped away completely. The dog stopped barking. A train screamed for the crossing and went crashing by, leaving the night more silent than before. In a house nearby, an alarm clock went off. Dick said, "Somebody goes to work early. Night watchman, maybe." His voice was too loud in the stillness. The front door squeaked slowly shut.

"What time is it now, Dick?"

"Quarter-past nine."

"Jesus! Only that? I thought it was about morning. . . . Don't you wish they'd come and get it over, Dick? Listen, Dick! —I thought I heard voices."

They stood stiffly, listening. Their heads were bent forward. "You hear voices, Dick?"

"I think so. Like they're talking low."

The dog barked again, fiercely this time. A little quiet murmur of voices could be heard. "Look, Dick! I thought I saw somebody out the back window."

The older man chuckled uneasily. "That's so we can't get away. They got the place surrounded. Take hold, kid! They're coming now. Remember about it's not them, it's the System."

There came a rushing clatter of footsteps. The doors burst open. A crowd of men thronged in, roughly dressed men, wearing black hats. They carried clubs and sticks in their hands. Dick and Root stood erect, their chins out, their eyes dropped and nearly closed.

Once inside, the raiders were uneasy. They stood in a half-circle about the two men, scowling, waiting for some one to move.

Young Root glanced sidewise at Dick and saw that the older man was looking at him coldly, critically, as though he judged his deportment. Root shoved his trembling hands in his pockets. He forced himself forward. His voice was shrill with fright. "Comrades," he shouted, "you're just men like we are. We're all brothers—" A piece of two-by-four lashed out and struck him on the side of the head with a fleshy thump. Root went down to his knees and steadied himself with his hands.

The men stood still, glaring.

Root climbed slowly to his feet. His split ear spilled a red stream down his neck. The side of his face was mushy and purple. He got himself erect again. His breath burst passionately. His hands were steady now, his voice sure and strong. His eyes were hot with an ecstasy. "Can't you see?" he shouted. "It's all for you. We're doing it for you. All of it. You don't know what you're doing."

"Kill the red rats!"

Some one giggled hysterically. And then the wave came. As he went down, Root caught a moment's glimpse of Dick's face smiling a tight, hard smile.

IV

He came near the surface several times, but didn't quite make it into consciousness. At last he opened his eyes and knew things. His face and head were heavy with bandages. He could only see a line of light between his puffed eyelids. For a time he lay, trying to think his way out. Then he heard Dick's voice near to him.

"You awake, kid?"

Root tried his voice and found that it croaked pretty badly. "I guess so."

"They sure worked out on your head. I thought you was gone. You was right about your nose. It ain't going to be very pretty."

"What'd they do to you, Dick?"

"Oh, they bust my arm and a couple of ribs. You got to learn to turn your face down to the ground. That saves your eyes." He paused and drew a careful breath. "Hurts some to breathe when you get a rib bust. We are lucky. The cops picked us up and took us in."

"Are we in jail, Dick?"

"Yeah! Hospital cell."

"What they got on the book?"

He heard Dick try to chuckle, and gasp when it hurt him. "Inciting to riot. We'll get six months, I guess. The cops got the lit'ature."

"You won't tell them I'm under age, will you, Dick?"

"No. I won't. You better shut up. Your voice don't sound so hot. Take it easy."

Root lay silent, muffled in a coat of dull pain. But in a moment he spoke again. "It didn't hurt, Dick. It was funny. I felt all full up—and good."

"You done fine, kid. You done as good as anybody I ever seen. I'll give you a blow to the committee. You just done fine."

Root struggled to get something straight in his head. "When they was busting me I wanted to tell them I didn't care."

"Sure, kid. That's what I told you. It wasn't them. It was the System. You don't want to hate them. They don't know no better."

Root spoke drowsily. The pain was muffling him under. "You remember in the Bible, Dick, how it says something like 'Forgive them because they don't know what they're doing'?"

Dick's reply was stern. "You lay off that religion stuff, kid." He quoted, " 'Religion is the opium of the people.' "

"Sure, I know," said Root. "But there wasn't no religion to it. It was just—I felt like saying that. It was just kind of the way I felt."

1900 ∾ *Thomas Wolfe* ∾ 1938

THOMAS WOLFE was born at Asheville, North Carolina, where he attended public schools. His father was a stonecutter, a man marked by an unusually retentive memory and by a love of poetry; his mother managed a boarding-house. Among his ancestors were Carolina frontiersmen, of English and Scotch-Irish origin; his father's mother belonged to a Dutch family which had settled in Pennsylvania. He wrote to his mother in 1930: "I am proud of my people, proud of my pioneer and mountaineer and Pennsylvania Dutch ancestry. . . . One half of me is great fields and mighty barns, and one half of me is the great hills of North Carolina."

Wolfe entered the University of Carolina at fifteen. He became student editor of the *Tar Heel* in his senior year, and as a member of Frederick H. Koch's Carolina Playmakers group he wrote and acted in plays. One of his plays, "The Return of Buck Gavin," was included in *Carolina Folk-Plays, Second Series* (1924). After graduation in 1920 he went to Harvard, where he continued his study of playwriting in George Pierce Baker's "47 Workshop" and took a master's degree. In 1924 he was appointed an instructor in English at New York University and taught until 1930, with intervals in Europe.

After the successful publication of his first novel, *Look Homeward, Angel,* in 1929, he devoted his full time to writing. He lived for a time in England and traveled in Germany, but did much of his later work in a basement room in South Brooklyn. In the preparation of his books for publication, the condensation and revision of his voluminous manuscripts, Wolfe owed much to the help of his editor, Maxwell Perkins, and in his last years to Edward C. Aswell. He died on a trip to the Pacific Northwest in 1938.

Only two of Wolfe's novels had been published before his death, *Look Homeward, Angel* and *Of Time and the River* (1935). He had collected a few shorter pieces of fiction in *From Death to Morning* (1935), and had discussed his purposes and methods as a writer, and his experiences in connection with the publication of *Look Homeward, Angel,* in *The Story of a Novel* (1936). Two more novels, *The Web and the Rock* (1939) and *You Can't Go Home Again* (1940), appeared after his death. *The Hills Beyond* (1941) is a collection of short stories and essays, with portions of an uncompleted novel.

[Appraisals by Bernard De Voto, in *Forays and Rebuttals* (New York, 1936), and R. P. Warren, in *Literary Opinion in America* (New York, 1937), ed. M. D. Zabel, were themselves analyzed by T. L. Collins in the *Sewanee Review* (Oct. 1942). M. Geismar's *Writers in Crisis* (Boston, 1942) contains a study of Wolfe; see also E. B. Burgum's *The Novel and the World's Dilemma* (New York, 1947).]

THE LOST BOY
[1941 (1937)]

I

LIGHT CAME and went and came again, the booming strokes of three o'clock beat out across the town in thronging bronze from the courthouse bell, light winds of April blew the fountain out in rainbow sheets, until the plume returned and pulsed, as Grover turned into the Square. He was a child, dark-eyed and grave, birthmarked upon his neck—a berry of warm brown— and with a gentle face, too quiet and too listening for his years. The scuffed boy's shoes, the thick-ribbed stockings gartered at the knees, the short knee pants cut straight with three small useless buttons at the side, the sailor blouse, the old cap battered out of shape, perched sideways up on top of the raven head, the old soiled canvas bag slung from the shoulder, empty now, but waiting for the crisp sheets of the afternoon—these friendly, shabby garments, shaped by Grover, uttered him. He turned and passed along the north side of the Square and in that moment saw the union of Forever and of Now.

Light came and went and came again, the great plume of the fountain pulsed and winds of April sheeted it across the Square in a rainbow gossamer of spray. The fire department horses drummed on the floors with wooden stomp, most casually, and with dry whiskings of their clean, coarse tails. The street cars ground into the Square from every portion of the compass and halted briefly like wound toys in their familiar quarter-hourly formula. A dray, hauled by a boneyard nag, rattled across the cobbles on the other side before his father's shop. The courthouse bell boomed out its solemn warning of immediate three, and everything was just the same as it had always been.

He saw that haggis of vexed shapes with quiet eyes—that hodgepodge of ill-sorted architectures that made up the Square, and he did not feel lost. For "Here," thought Grover, "here is the Square as it has always been—and papa's shop, the fire department and the City Hall, the fountain pulsing with its plume, the street cars coming in and halting at the quarter hour, the hardware store on the corner there, the row of old brick buildings on this side of the street, the people passing and the light that comes and changes and that always will come back again, and everything that comes and goes and changes in the Square, and yet will be the same again. And here," the boy thought, "is Grover with his paper bag. Here is old Grover, almost twelve years old. Here is the month of April, 1904. Here is the courthouse bell and three o'clock. Here is Grover on the Square that never changes. Here is Grover, caught upon this point of time."

It seemed to him that the Square, itself

the accidental masonry of many years, the chance agglomeration of time and of disrupted strivings, was the center of the universe. It was for him, in his soul's picture, the earth's pivot, the granite core of changelessness, the eternal place where all things came and passed, and yet abode forever and would never change.

He passed the old shack on the corner—the wooden fire-trap where S. Goldberg ran his wiener stand. Then he passed the Singer place next door, with its gleaming display of new machines. He saw them and admired them, but he felt no joy. They brought back to him the busy hum of housework and of women sewing, the intricacy of stitch and weave, the mystery of style and pattern, the memory of women bending over flashing needles, the pedaled tread, the busy whir. It was women's work: it filled him with unknown associations of dullness and of vague depression. And always, also, with a moment's twinge of horror, for his dark eye would always travel toward that needle stitching up and down so fast the eye could never follow it. And then he would remember how his mother once had told him she had driven the needle through her finger, and always, when he passed this place, he would remember it and for a moment crane his neck and turn his head away.

He passed on then, but had to stop again next door before the music store. He always had to stop by places that had shining perfect things in them. He loved hardware stores and windows full of accurate geometric tools. He loved windows full of hammers, saws, and planing boards. He liked windows full of strong new rakes and hoes, with unworn handles, of white perfect wood, stamped hard and vivid with the maker's seal. He loved to see such things as these in the windows of hardware stores. And he would fairly gloat upon them and think that some day he would own a set himself.

Also, he always stopped before the music and piano store. It was a splendid store. And in the window was a small white dog upon his haunches, with head cocked gravely to one side, a small white dog that never moved, that never barked, that listened attentively at the flaring funnel of a horn to hear "His Master's Voice"—a horn forever silent, and a voice that never spoke. And within were many rich and shining shapes of great pianos, an air of splendor and of wealth.

And now, indeed, he *was* caught, held suspended. A waft of air, warm, chocolate-laden, filled his nostrils. He tried to pass the white front of the little eight-foot shop; he paused, struggling with conscience; he could not go on. It was the little candy shop run by old Crocker and his wife. And Grover could not pass.

"Old stingy Crockers!" he thought scornfully. "I'll not go there any more. But—" as the maddening fragrance of rich cooking chocolate touched him once again—"I'll just look in the window and see what they've got." He paused a moment, looking with his dark and quiet eyes into the window of the little candy shop. The window, spotlessly clean, was filled with trays of fresh-made candy. His eyes rested on a tray of chocolate drops. Unconsciously he licked his lips. Put one of them upon your tongue and it just melted there, like honeydew. And then the trays full of rich homemade fudge. He gazed longingly at the deep body of the chocolate, reflectively at maple walnut, more critically, yet with longing, at the mints, the nougatines, and all the other dainties.

"Old stingy Crockers!" Grover muttered once again, and turned to go. "I wouldn't go in *there* again."

And yet he did not go away. "Old stingy Crockers" they might be; still, they did make the best candy in town, the best, in fact, that he had ever tasted.

He looked through the window back into the little shop and saw Mrs. Crocker there. A customer had gone in and had made a purchase, and as Grover looked he saw Mrs. Crocker, with her little wrenny face, her pinched features, lean over and peer primly at the scales. She had a piece of fudge in her clean, bony, little fingers, and as Grover looked, she broke it, primly, in her little bony hands. She dropped a morsel down into the scales. They weighted down alarmingly, and her thin lips tightened. She snatched the piece of fudge out of the scales and broke it carefully once again. This time the scales wavered, went down very slowly, and came back again. Mrs. Crocker carefully put the reclaimed piece of fudge back in the tray, dumped the remainder in a paper bag, folded it and gave it to the customer, counted the money carefully and doled it out into the till, the pennies in one place, the nickels in another.

Grover stood there, looking scornfully. "Old stingy Crocker—afraid that she might give a crumb away!"

He grunted scornfully and again he turned to go. But now Mr. Crocker came out from the little partitioned place where they made all their candy, bearing a tray of fresh-made fudge in his skinny hands. Old Man Crocker rocked along the counter to the front and put it down. He really rocked along. He was a cripple. And like his wife, he was a wrenny, wizened little creature, with bony hands, thin lips, a pinched and meager face. One leg was inches shorter than the other, and on this leg there was an enormous thick-soled boot, with a kind of wooden, rocker-like arrangement, six inches high at least, to make up for the deficiency. On this wooden cradle Mr. Crocker rocked along, with a prim and apprehensive little smile, as if he were afraid he was going to lose something.

"Old stingy Crocker!" muttered Grover. "Humph! He wouldn't give you anything!"

And yet—he did not go away. He hung there curiously, peering through the window, with his dark and gentle face now focused and intent, alert and curious, flattening his nose against the glass. Unconsciously he scratched the thick-ribbed fabric of one stockinged leg with the scuffed and worn toe of his old shoe. The fresh, warm odor of the new-made fudge was delicious. It was a little maddening. Half consciously he began to fumble in one trouser pocket,

and pulled out his purse, a shabby worn old black one with a twisted clasp. He opened it and prowled about inside.

What he found was not inspiring—a nickel and two pennies and—he had forgotten them—the stamps. He took the stamps out and unfolded them. There were five twos, eight ones, all that remained of the dollar-sixty-cents' worth which Reed, the pharmacist, had given him for running errands a week or two before.

"Old Crocker," Grover thought, and looked somberly at the grotesque little form as it rocked back into the shop again, around the counter, and up the other side. "Well—" again he looked indefinitely at the stamps in his hand—"he's had all the rest of them. He might as well take these."

So, soothing conscience with this sop of scorn, he went into the shop and stood looking at the trays in the glass case and finally decided. Pointing with a slightly grimy finger at the fresh-made tray of chocolate fudge, he said, "I'll take fifteen cents' worth of this, Mr. Crocker." He paused a moment, fighting with embarrassment, then he lifted his dark face and said quietly, "And please, I'll have to give you stamps again."

Mr. Crocker made no answer. He did not look at Grover. He pressed his lips together primly. He went rocking away and got the candy scoop, came back, slid open the door of the glass case, put fudge into the scoop, and, rocking to the scales, began to weigh the candy out. Grover watched him as he peered and squinted, he watched him purse and press his lips together, he saw him take a piece of fudge and break it in two parts. And then old Crocker broke two parts in two again. He weighed, he squinted, and he hovered, until it seemed to Grover that by calling *Mrs.* Crocker stingy he had been guilty of a rank injustice. But finally, to his vast relief, the job was over, the scales hung there, quivering apprehensively, upon the very hair-line of nervous balance, as if even the scales were afraid that one more move from Old Man Crocker and they would be undone.

Mr. Crocker took the candy then and dumped it in a paper bag and, rocking back along the counter toward the boy, he dryly said: "Where are the stamps?" Grover gave them to him. Mr. Crocker relinquished his clawlike hold upon the bag and set it down upon the counter. Grover took the bag and dropped it in his canvas sack, and then remembered. "Mr. Crocker —" again he felt the old embarrassment that was almost like strong pain—"I gave you too much," Grover said. "There were eighteen cents in stamps. You—you can just give me three ones back."

Mr. Crocker did not answer. He was busy with his bony little hands, unfolding the stamps and flattening them out on top of the glass counter. When he had done so, he peered at them sharply for a moment, thrusting his scrawny neck forward and running his eye up and down, like a bookkeeper who totes up rows of figures.

When he had finished, he said tartly: "I don't like this kind of business. If you want candy, you should have the money for it. I'm not a post office. The next time you come in here and want anything, you'll have to pay me money for it."

Hot anger rose in Grover's throat. His olive face suffused with angry color. His tarry eyes got black and bright. He was on the verge of saying: "Then why did you take my other stamps? Why do you tell me now, when you have taken all the stamps I had, that you don't want them?"

But he was a boy, a boy of eleven years, a quiet, gentle, gravely thoughtful boy, and he had been taught how to respect his elders. So he just stood there looking with his tar-black eyes. Old Man Crocker, pursing at the mouth a little, without meeting Grover's gaze, took the stamps up in his thin, parched fingers and, turning, rocked away with them down to the till.

He took the twos and folded them and laid them in one rounded scallop, then took the ones and folded them and put them in the one next to it. Then he closed the till and started to rock off, down toward the other end. Grover, his face now quiet and grave, kept looking at him, but Mr. Crocker did not look at Grover. Instead he began to take some stamped cardboard shapes and fold them into boxes.

In a moment Grover said, "Mr. Crocker, will you give me the three ones, please?"

Mr. Crocker did not answer. He kept folding boxes, and he compressed his thin lips quickly as he did so. But Mrs. Crocker, back turned to her spouse, also folding boxes with her birdlike hands, muttered tartly: "Hm! *I'd* give him nothing!"

Mr. Crocker looked up, looked at Grover, said, "What are you waiting for?"

"Will you give me the three ones, please?" Grover said.

"I'll give you nothing," Mr. Crocker said.

He left his work and came rocking forward along the counter. "Now you get out of here! Don't you come in here with any more of those stamps," said Mr. Crocker.

"I should like to know where he gets them—that's what *I* should like to know," said Mrs. Crocker.

She did not look up as she said these words. She inclined her head a little to the side, in Mr. Crocker's direction, and continued to fold the boxes with her bony fingers.

"You get out of here!" said Mr. Crocker. "And don't you come back here with any stamps. . . . Where did you get those stamps?" he said.

"That's just what *I've* been thinking," Mrs. Crocker said. "*I've* been thinking all along."

"You've been coming in here for the last two weeks with those stamps," said Mr. Crocker. "I don't like the look of it. Where did you get those stamps?" he said.

"That's what *I've* been thinking," said Mrs. Crocker, for a second time.

Grover had got white underneath his olive skin. His eyes had lost their luster. They looked like dull, stunned balls of tar. "From Mr. Reed," he said. "I got the stamps from Mr. Reed." Then he burst out desperately: "Mr. Crocker—Mr. Reed will tell you how I got the stamps. I did some work for Mr. Reed, he gave me those stamps two weeks ago."

"Mr. Reed," said Mrs. Crocker acidly. She did not turn her head. "I call it mighty funny."

"Mr. Crocker," Grover said, "if you'll just let me have three ones——"

"You get out of here!" cried Mr. Crocker, and he began rocking forward toward Grover. "Now don't you come in here again, boy! There's something funny about this whole business! I don't like the look of it," said Mr. Crocker. "If you can't pay as other people do, then I don't want your trade."

"Mr. Crocker," Grover said again, and underneath the olive skin his face was gray, "if you'll just let me have those three——"

"You get out of here!" Mr. Crocker cried, rocking down toward the counter's end. "If you don't get out, boy——"

"I'd call a policeman, that's what I'd do," Mrs. Crocker said.

Mr. Crocker rocked around the lower end of the counter. He came rocking up to Grover. "You get out," he said.

He took the boy and pushed him with his bony little hands, and Grover was sick and gray down to the hollow pit of his stomach.

"You've got to give me those three ones," he said.

"You get out of here!" shrilled Mr. Crocker. He seized the screen door, pulled it open, and pushed Grover out. "Don't you come back in here," he said, pausing for a moment, and working thinly at the lips. He turned and rocked back in the shop again. The screen door slammed behind him. Grover stood there on the pavement. And light came and went and came again into the Square.

The boy stood there, and a wagon rattled past. There were some people passing by, but Grover did not notice them. He stood there blindly, in the watches of the sun, feeling this was Time, this was the center of the universe, the granite core of changelessness, and feeling, this is Grover, this the Square, this is Now.

But something had gone out of day. He felt the overwhelming, soul-sickening guilt that all the children, all the good men of the earth, have felt since Time began. And even anger had died down, had been drowned out, in this swelling tide of guilt, and "This is the Square"—thought Grover as before—"This is Now. There is my father's shop. And all of it is as it has always been—save I."

And the Square reeled drunkenly around him, light went in blind gray motes before his eyes, the fountain sheeted out to rainbow iridescence and returned to its proud, pulsing plume again. But all the brightness had gone out of day, and "Here is the Square, and here is permanence, and here is Time—and all of it the same as it has always been, save I."

The scuffed boots of the lost boy moved and stumbled blindly. The numb feet crossed the pavement—reached the cobbled street, reached the plotted central square —the grass plots, and the flower beds, so soon to be packed with red geraniums.

"I want to be alone," thought Grover, "where I cannot go near him. . . . Oh God, I hope he never hears, that no one ever tells him——"

The plume blew out, the iridescent sheet of spray blew over him. He passed through, found the other side and crossed the street, and—"Oh God, if papa ever hears!" thought Grover, as his numb feet started up the steps into his father's shop.

He found and felt the steps—the width and thickness of old lumber twenty feet in length. He saw it all—the iron columns on his father's porch, painted with the dull anomalous black-green that all such columns in this land and weather come to; two angels, fly-specked, and the waiting stones. Beyond and all around, in the stonecutter's shop, cold shapes of white and marble, rounded stone, the languid angel with strong marble hands of love.

He went on down the aisle, the white shapes stood around him. He went on to the back of the workroom. This he knew— the little cast-iron stove in left-hand corner, caked, brown, heat-blistered, and the elbow of the long stack running out across the shop; the high and dirty window looking down across the Market Square toward Niggertown; the rude old shelves, plank-boarded, thick, the wood not smooth but pulpy, like the strong hair of an animal; upon the shelves the chisels of all sizes and a layer of stone dust; an emery wheel with pump tread; and a door that let out on the alleyway, yet the alleyway twelve feet below. Here in the room, two trestles of this coarse spiked wood upon which rested gravestones, and at one, his father at work.

The boy looked, saw the name was Creasman: saw the carved analysis of John, the symmetry of the s, the fine sentiment that was being polished off beneath the name and date: "John Creasman, November 7, 1903."

Gant looked up. He was a man of fifty-three, gaunt-visaged, mustache cropped, immensely long and tall and gaunt. He wore good dark clothes—heavy, massive—save he had no coat. He worked in shirt-sleeves with his vest on, a strong watch chain stretching across his vest, wing collar and black tie, Adam's apple, bony forehead, bony nose, light eyes, gray-green, undeep and cold, and, somehow, lonely-looking, a striped apron going up around his shoulders, and starched cuffs. And in one hand a tremendous rounded wooden mallet like a butcher's bole; and in his other hand, a strong cold chisel.

"How are you, son?"

He did not look up as he spoke. He spoke quietly, absently. He worked upon the chisel and the wooden mallet, as a jeweler might work on a watch, except that in the man and in the wooden mallet there was power too.

"What is it, son?" he said.

He moved around the table from the head, started up on "J" once again.

"Papa, I never stole the stamps," said Grover.

Gant put down the mallet, laid the chisel down. He came around the trestle.

"What?" he said.

As Grover winked his tar-black eyes, they brightened, the hot tears shot out. "I never stole the stamps," he said.

"Hey? What is this?" his father said. "What stamps?"

"That Mr. Reed gave me, when the other boy was sick and I worked there for three days. . . . And Old Man Crocker," Grover said, "he took all the stamps. And I told him Mr. Reed had given them to me. And now he owes me three ones—and Old Man Crocker says he don't believe that they were mine. He says—he says—that I must have taken them somewhere," Grover blurted out.

"The stamps that Reed gave you—hey?" the stonecutter said. "The stamps you had—" He wet his thumb upon his lips, threw back his head and slowly swung his gaze around the ceiling, then turned and strode quickly from his workshop out into the storeroom.

Almost at once he came back again, and as he passed the old gray painted-board partition of his office he cleared his throat and wet his thumb and said, "Now, I tell you——"

Then he turned and strode up toward the front again and cleared his throat and said, "I tell you now—" He wheeled about and started back, and as he came along the aisle between the marshaled rows of gravestones he said beneath his breath, "By God, now——"

He took Grover by the hand and they went out flying. Down the aisle they went by all the gravestones, past the fly-specked angels waiting there, and down the wooden steps and across the Square. The fountain pulsed, the plume blew out in sheeted iridescence, and it swept across them; an old gray horse, with a peaceful look about his torn lips, swucked up the cool mountain water from the trough as Grover and his father went across the Square, but they did not notice it.

They crossed swiftly to the other side in a direct line to the candy shop. Gant was still dressed in his long striped apron, and he was still holding Grover by the hand. He opened the screen door and stepped inside.

"Give him the stamps," Gant said.

Mr. Crocker came rocking forward behind the counter, with the prim and careful look that now was somewhat like a smile. "It was just—" he said.

"Give him the stamps," Gant said, and threw some coins down on the counter.

Mr. Crocker rocked away and got the stamps. He came rocking back. "I just didn't know—" he said.

The stonecutter took the stamps and gave them to the boy. And Mr. Crocker took the coins.

"It was just that—" Mr. Crocker began again, and smiled.

Gant cleared his throat: "You never were a father," he said. "You never knew the feelings of a father, or understood the feelings of a child; and that is why you acted as you did. But a judgment is upon you. God has cursed you. He has afflicted you. He has made you lame and childless as you are—and lame and childless, miserable as you are, you will go to your grave and be forgotten!"

And Crocker's wife kept kneading her bony little hands and said, imploringly, "Oh, no—oh don't say that, please don't say that."

The stonecutter, the breath still hoarse in him, left the store, still holding the boy tightly by the hand. Light came again into the day.

"Well, son," he said, and laid his hand on the boy's back. "Well, son," he said, "now don't you mind."

They walked across the Square, the sheeted spray of iridescent light swept out on them, the horse swizzled at the watertrough, and "Well, son," the stonecutter said.

And the old horse sloped down, ringing with his hoofs upon the cobblestones.

"Well, son," said the stonecutter once again, "be a good boy."

And he trod his own steps then with his great stride and went back again into his shop.

The lost boy stood upon the Square, hard by the porch of his father's shop.

"This is Time," thought Grover. "Here is the Square, here is my father's shop, and here am I."

And light came and went and came again—but now not quite the same as it had done before. The boy saw the pattern of familiar shapes and knew that they were just the same as they had always been. But something had gone out of day, and something had come in again. Out of the vision of those quiet eyes some brightness had gone, and into their vision had come some deeper color. He could not say, he did not know through what transforming shadows life had passed within that quarter hour. He only knew that something had been lost—something forever gained.

Just then a buggy curved out through the Square, and fastened to the rear end was a poster, and it said "St. Louis" and "Excursion" and "The Fair."

II—THE MOTHER

As we went down through Indiana—you were too young, child, to remember it—but I always think of all of you the way you looked that morning, when we went down through Indiana, going to the Fair. All of the apple trees were coming out, and it was April; it was the beginning of spring in southern Indiana and everything was getting green. Of course we don't have farms at home like those in Indiana. The childern had never seen such farms as those, and I reckon, kidlike, they had to take it in.

So all of them kept running up and down the aisle—well, no, except for you and Grover. *You* were too young, Eugene. You were just three, I kept you with me. As for Grover—well, I'm going to tell you about that.

But the rest of them kept running up and down the aisle and from one window to another. They kept calling out and hollering to each other every time they saw something new. They kept trying to look out on all sides, in every way at once, as if they wished they had eyes at the back of their heads. It was the first time any of them had ever been in Indiana, and I reckon that it all seemed strange and new.

And so it seemed they couldn't get enough. It seemed they never could be still. They kept running up and down and back and forth, hollering and shouting to each other, until—"I'll vow! You childern! I never saw the beat of you!" I said. "The way that you keep running up and down and back and forth and never can be quiet for a minute beats all I ever saw," I said.

You see, they were excited about going to St. Louis, and so curious over everything they saw. They couldn't help it, and they wanted to see everything. But—"I'll vow!" I said. "If you childern don't sit down and rest you'll be worn to a frazzle before we ever get to see St. Louis and the Fair!"

Except for Grover! He—no, sir! not him. Now, boy, I want to tell you—I've raised the lot of you—and if I do say so, there wasn't a numbskull in the lot. But *Grover!* Well, you've all grown up now, all of you have gone away, and none of you are childern any more. . . . And of course, I hope that, as the fellow says, you have reached the dignity of man's estate. I suppose you have the judgment of grown men. . . . But *Grover! Grover* had it even then!

Oh, even as a child, you know—at a time when I was almost afraid to trust the rest of you out of my sight—I could depend on Grover. He could go anywhere, I could send him anywhere, and I'd always know he'd get back safe, and do exactly what I told him to!

Why, I didn't even have to tell him. You could send that child to market and tell him what you wanted, and he'd come home with *twice* as much as you could get yourself for the same money!

Now you know, I've always been considered a good trader. But *Grover!*—why, it got so finally that I wouldn't even tell him. Your papa said to me: "You'd be better off if you'd just tell him what you want

and leave the rest to him. For," your papa says, "damned if I don't believe he's a better trader than you are. He gets more for the money than anyone I ever saw."

Well, I had to admit it, you know. I had to own up then. Grover, even as a child, was a far better trader than I was. . . . Why, yes, they told it on him all over town, you know. They said all of the market men, all of the farmers, knew him. They'd begin to laugh when they saw him coming—they'd say: "Look out! Here's Grover! Here's one trader you're not going to fool!"

And they were right! *That* child! I'd say, "Grover, suppose you run uptown and see if they've got anything good to *eat* today"—and I'd just wink at him, you know, but he'd know what I meant. I wouldn't let on that I *wanted* anything exactly, but I'd say, "Now it just occurs to me that some good fresh stuff may be coming in from the country, so suppose you take this dollar and just see what you can do with it."

Well, sir, that was all that was needed. The minute you told that child that you depended on his judgment, he'd have gone to the ends of the earth for you—and, let me tell you something, he wouldn't *miss*, either!

His eyes would get as black as coals—oh! the way that child would look at you, the intelligence and sense in his expression. He'd say: "Yes, *ma'am!* Now don't you worry, mama. You leave it all to me—and I'll do *good!*" said Grover.

And he'd be off like a streak of lightning and—oh Lord! As your father said to me, "I've been living in this town for almost thirty years," he said—"I've seen it grow up from a crossroads village, and I thought I knew everything there was to know about it—but that child—" your papa says—"he knows places that I never heard of!" . . . Oh, he'd go right down there to that place below your papa's shop where the draymen and the country people used to park their wagons—or he'd go down there to those old lots on Concord

Street where the farmers used to keep their wagons. And, child that he was, he'd go right in among them, sir—*Grover* would! —go right in and barter with them like a grown man!

And he'd come home with things he'd bought that would make your eyes stick out. . . . Here he comes one time with another boy, dragging a great bushel basketful of ripe termaters between them. "Why, Grover!" I says. "How on earth are we ever going to use them? Why they'll go bad on us before we're half way through with them." "Well, mama," he says, "I know—" oh, just as solemn as a judge— "but they were the last the man had," he says, "and he wanted to go home, and so I got them for ten cents," he says. "They were so cheap," said Grover, "I thought it was a shame to let 'em go, and I figgered that what we couldn't eat—why," says Grover, "you could *put up!*" Well, the way he said it—so earnest and so serious—I had to laugh. "But I'll vow!" I said. "If you don't beat all!" . . . But that was *Grover!*—the way he was in *those* days! As everyone said, boy that he was, he had the sense and judgment of a grown man. . . . Child, child, I've seen you all grow up, and all of you were bright enough. There were no half-wits in *my* family. But for all-round intelligence, judgment, and general ability, Grover surpassed the whole crowd. I've never seen his equal, and everyone who knew him as a child will say the same.

So that's what I tell them now when they ask me about all of you. I have to tell the truth. I always said that *you* were smart enough, Eugene—but when they come around and brag to me about you, and about how you have got on and have a kind of name—I don't let on, you know. I just sit there and let them talk. I don't brag on you—if *they* want to brag on you, that's *their* business. I never bragged on one of my own childern in my life. When father raised us up, we were all brought up to believe that it was not good breeding to brag about your kin. "If the others want

to do it," father said, "well, let *them* do it. Don't ever let on by a word or sign that you know what they are talking about. Just let *them* do the talking, and say nothing."

So when they come around and tell me all about the things *you've* done—I don't let on to them, I never say a word. Why yes!—why, here, you know—oh, along about a month or so ago, this feller comes —a well-dressed man, you know—he looked intelligent, a good substantial sort of person. He said he came from New Jersey, or somewhere up in that part of the country, and he began to ask me all sorts of questions—what you were like when you were a boy, and all such stuff as that.

I just pretended to study it all over and then I said, "Well, yes"—real serious-like, you know—"well, yes—I reckon I ought to know a little something about him. Eugene was my child, just the same as all the others were. I brought him up just the way I brought up all the others. And," I says—oh, just as solemn as you please— "he wasn't a *bad* sort of a boy. Why," I says, "up to the time that he was twelve years old he was just about the same as any other boy—a good, average, normal sort of fellow."

"Oh," he says. "But didn't you notice something? Wasn't there something kind of strange?" he says—"something different from what you noticed in the other childern?"

I didn't let on, you know—I just took it all in and looked as solemn as an owl— I just pretended to study it all over, just as serious as you please.

"Why no," I says, real slow-like, after I'd studied it all over. "As I remember it, he was a good, ordinary, normal sort of boy, just like all the others."

"Yes," he says—oh, all excited-like, you know— "But didn't you notice how brilliant he was? Eugene must have been more brilliant than the rest!"

"Well, now," I says, and pretended to study that all over too. "Now let me see. . . . Yes," I says—I just looked him in the eye, as solemn as you please—"he did pretty well. . . . Well, yes," I says, "I guess he was a fairly bright sort of a boy. I never had no complaints to make of him on that score. He was bright enough," I says. "The only trouble with him was that he was lazy."

"Lazy!" he says—oh, you should have seen the look upon his face, you know—he jumped like someone had stuck a pin in him. "Lazy!" he says. "Why, you don't mean to tell me——"

"Yes," I says—oh, I never cracked a smile—"I was telling him the same thing myself the last time that I saw him. I told him it was a mighty lucky thing for him that he had the gift of gab. Of course, he went off to college and read a lot of books, and I reckon that's where he got this flow of language they say he has. But as I said to him the last time that I saw him: 'Now look a-here,' I said. 'If you can earn your living doing a light, easy class of work like this you do,' I says, 'you're mighty lucky, because none of the rest of your people,' I says, 'had any such luck as that. They had to work hard for a living.' "

Oh, I told him, you know. I came right out with it. I made no bones about it. And I tell you what—I wish you could have seen his face. It was a study.

"Well," he says, at last, "you've got to admit this, haven't you—he was the brightest boy you had, now wasn't he?"

I just looked at him a moment. I had to tell the truth. I couldn't fool him any longer. "No," I says. "He was a good, bright boy—I got no complaint to make about him on that score—but the brightest boy I had, the one that surpassed all the rest of them in sense, and understanding, and in judgment—the best boy I had—the smartest boy I ever saw—was—well, it wasn't Eugene," I said. "It was another one."

He looked at me a moment, then he said, "Which boy was that?"

Well, I just looked at him, and smiled. I shook my head, you know. I wouldn't tell him. "I never brag about my own," I said.

"You'll have to find out for yourself."

But—I'll have to tell *you*—and you know yourself, I brought the whole crowd up, I knew you all. And you can take my word for it—the best one of the lot was —*Grover!*

And when I think of Grover as he was along about that time, I always see him sitting there, so grave and earnest-like, with his nose pressed to the window, as we went down through Indiana in the morning, to the Fair.

All through that morning we were going down along beside the Wabash River—the Wabash River flows through Indiana, it is the river that they wrote the song about—so all that morning we were going down along the river. And I sat with all you childern gathered about me as we went down through Indiana, going to St. Louis, to the Fair.

And Grover sat there, so still and earnest-like, looking out the window, and he didn't move. He sat there like a man. He was just eleven and a half years old, but he had more sense, more judgment, and more understanding than any child I ever saw.

So here he sat beside this gentleman and looked out the window. I never knew the man—I never asked his name—but I tell you what! He was certainly a fine-looking, well-dressed, good, substantial sort of man, and I could see that he had taken a great liking to Grover. And Grover sat there looking out, and then turned to this gentleman, as grave and earnest as a grown-up man, and says, "What kind of crops grow here, sir?" Well, this gentleman threw his head back and just hah-hahed. "Well, I'll see if I can tell you," says this gentleman, and then, you know, he talked to him, they talked together, and Grover took it all in, as solemn as you please, and asked this gentleman every sort of question—what the trees were, what was growing there, how big the farms were—all sorts of questions, which this gentleman would answer, until I said: "Why, I'll vow, Grover! You shouldn't ask so many questions. You'll bother the very life out of this gentleman."

The gentleman threw his head back and laughed right out. "Now you leave that boy alone. He's all right," he said. "He doesn't bother me a bit, and if I know the answers to his questions I will answer him. And if I don't know, why, then, I'll tell him so. But he's *all right*," he said, and put his arm round Grover's shoulders. "You leave him alone. He doesn't bother me a bit."

And I can still remember how he looked that morning, with his black eyes, his black hair, and with the birthmark on his neck —so grave, so serious, so earnest-like—as he sat by the train window and watched the apple trees, the farms, the barns, the houses, and the orchards, taking it all in, I reckon, because it was strange and new to him.

It was so long ago, but when I think of it, it all comes back, as if it happened yesterday. Now all of you have either died or grown up and gone away, and nothing is the same as it was then. But all of you were there with me that morning and I guess I should remember how the others looked, but somehow I don't. Yet I can still see Grover just the way he was, the way he looked that morning when we went down through Indiana, by the river, to the Fair.

III—THE SISTER

Can you remember, Eugene, how Grover used to look? I mean the birthmark, the black eyes, the olive skin. The birthmark always showed because of those open sailor blouses kids used to wear. But I guess you must have been too young when Grover died. . . . I was looking at that old photograph the other day. You know the one I mean—that picture showing mama and papa and all of us children before the house on Woodson Street. *You* weren't there, Eugene. *You* didn't get in. *You* hadn't arrived when that was taken. . . . You remember how mad you used to get when we'd tell you that you were only a dishrag hanging out in Heaven when something happened?

You were the baby. That's what you get for being the baby. You don't get in the picture, do you? . . . I was looking at that old picture just the other day. There we were. And, my God, what is it all about? I mean, when you see the way we were— Daisy and Ben and Grover, Steve and all of us—and then how everyone either dies or grows up and goes away—and then— look at us now! Do you ever get to feeling funny? You know what I mean—do you ever get to feeling *queer*—when you try to figure these things out? You've been to college and you ought to know the answer —and I wish you'd tell me if you know.

My Lord, when I think sometimes of the way I used to be—the dreams I used to have. Playing the piano, practicing seven hours a day, thinking that some day I would be a great pianist. Taking singing lessons from Aunt Nell because I felt that some day I was going to have a great career in opera. . . . Can you beat it now? Can you imagine it? *Me!* In grand opera! . . . Now I want to ask you. I'd like to know.

My Lord! When I go uptown and walk down the street and see all these funny-looking little boys and girls hanging around the drug store—do you suppose any of them have ambitions the way we did? Do you suppose any of these funny-looking little girls are thinking about a big career in opera? . . . Didn't you ever see that picture of us? I was looking at it just the other day. It was made before the old house down on Woodson Street, with papa standing there in his swallow-tail, and mama there beside him—and Grover, and Ben, and Steve, and Daisy, and myself, with our feet upon our bicycles. Luke, poor kid, was only four or five. *He* didn't have a bicycle like us. But there he was. And there were all of us together.

Well, there I was, and my poor old skinny legs and long white dress, and two pigtails hanging down my back. And all the funny-looking clothes we wore, with the doo-lolley business on them. . . . But I guess you can't remember. You weren't born.

But, well, we were a right nice-looking

set of people, if I do say so. And there was "86" the way it used to be, with the front porch, the grape vines, and the flower beds before the house—and "Miss Eliza" standing there by papa, with a watch charm pinned upon her waist. . . . I shouldn't laugh, but "Miss Eliza"—well, mama was a pretty woman then. Do you know what I mean? "Miss Eliza" was a right good-looking woman, and papa in his swallowtail was a good-looking man. Do you remember how he used to get dressed up on Sunday? And how grand we thought he was? And how he let me take his money out and count it? And how rich we all thought he was? And how wonderful that dinkey little shop on the Square looked to us? . . . Can you beat it, now? Why, we thought that papa was the biggest man in town and—oh, you can't tell me! You can't tell me! He had his faults, but papa was a wonderful man. You know he was!

And there was Steve and Ben and Grover, Daisy, Luke, and me lined up there before the house with one foot on our bicycles. And I got to thinking back about it all. It all came back.

Do you remember anything about St. Louis? You were only three or four years old then, but you must remember something. . . . Do you remember how you used to bawl when I would scrub you? How you'd bawl for Grover? Poor kid, you used to yell for Grover every time I'd get you in the tub. . . . He was a sweet kid and he was crazy about you—he almost brought you up.

That year Grover was working at the Inside Inn out on the Fair Grounds. Do you remember the old Inside Inn? That big old wooden thing inside the Fair? And how I used to take you there to wait for Grover when he got through working? And old fat Billy Pelham at the newsstand—how he always used to give you a stick of chewing gum?

They were all crazy about Grover. Everybody liked him. . . . And how proud Grover was of you! Don't you remember how he used to show you off? How he used to

take you around and make you talk to Billy Pelham? And Mr. Curtis at the desk? And how Grover would try to make you talk and get you to say "Grover"? and you couldn't say it—you couldn't pronounce the "r." You'd say "Gova." Have you forgotten that? You shouldn't forget *that*, because—you were a *cute* kid, then— Ho-ho-ho-ho-ho—I don't know where it's gone to, but you were a big hit in those days. . . . I tell you, boy, you were Somebody back in those days.

And I was thinking of it all the other day when I was looking at that photograph. How we used to go and meet Grover there, and how he'd take us to the Midway. Do you remember the Midway? The Snake-Eater and the Living Skeleton, the Fat Woman and the Chute-the-chute, the Scenic Railway and the Ferris Wheel? How you bawled the night we took you up on the Ferris Wheel? You yelled your head off —I tried to laugh it off, but I tell you, I was scared myself. Back in those days, that was Something. And how Grover laughed at us and told us there was no danger. . . . My lord! poor little Grover. He wasn't quite twelve years old at the time, but he seemed so grown up to us. I was two years older, but I thought he knew it all.

It was always that way with him. Looking back now, it sometimes seems that it was Grover who brought us up. He was always looking after us, telling us what to do, bringing us something—some ice cream or some candy, something he had bought out of the poor little money he'd gotten at the Inn.

Then I got to thinking of the afternoon we sneaked away from home. Mama had gone out somewhere. And Grover and I got on the street car and went downtown. And my Lord, we thought that we were going Somewhere. In those days, that was what we called a *trip*. A ride in the street car was something to write home about in those days. . . . I hear that it's all built up around there now.

So we got on the car and rode the whole way down into the business section of St.

Louis. We got out on Washington Street and walked up and down. And I tell you, boy, we thought that that was Something. Grover took me into a drug store and set me up to soda water. Then we came out and walked around some more, down to the Union Station and clear over to the river. And both of us half scared to death at what we'd done and wondering what mama would say if she found out.

We stayed down there till it was getting dark, and we passed by a lunchroom—an old one-armed joint with one-armed chairs and people sitting on stools and eating at the counter. We read all the signs to see what they had to eat and how much it cost, and I guess nothing on the menu was more than fifteen cents, but it couldn't have looked grander to us if it had been Delmonico's. So we stood there with our noses pressed against the window, looking in. Two skinny little kids, both of us scared half to death, getting the thrill of a lifetime out of it. You know what I mean? And smelling everything with all our might and thinking how good it all smelled. . . . Then Grover turned to me and whispered: "Come on, Helen. Let's go in. It says fifteen cents for pork and beans. And I've got the money," Grover said. "I've got sixty cents."

I was so scared I couldn't speak. I'd never been in a place like that before. But I kept thinking, "Oh Lord, if mama should find out!" I felt as if we were committing some big crime. . . . Don't you know how it is when you're a kid? It was the thrill of a lifetime. . . . I couldn't resist. So we both went in and sat down on those high stools before the counter and ordered pork and beans and a cup of coffee. I suppose we were too frightened at what we'd done really to enjoy anything. We just gobbled it all up in a hurry, and gulped our coffee down. And I don't know whether it was the excitement—I guess the poor kid was already sick when we came in there and didn't know it. But I turned and looked at him, and he was white as death. . . . And when I asked him what was the matter, he wouldn't tell me. He was too proud. He

said he was all right, but I could see that he was sick as a dog. . . . So he paid the bill. It came to forty cents—I'll never forget *that* as long as I live. . . . And sure enough, we no more than got out the door —he hardly had time to reach the curb— before it all came up.

And the poor kid was so scared and so ashamed. And what scared him so was not that he had gotten sick, but that he had spent all that money and it had come to nothing. And mama would find out. . . . Poor kid, he just stood there looking at me and he whispered: "Oh Helen, don't tell mama. She'll be mad if she finds out." Then we hurried home, and he was still white as a sheet when we got there.

Mama was waiting for us. She looked at us—you know how "Miss Eliza" looks at you when she thinks you've been doing something that you shouldn't. Mama said, "Why, where on earth have you two children been?" I guess she was all set to lay us out. Then she took one look at Grover's face. That was enough for her. She said, "Why, child, what in the world!" She was white as a sheet herself. . . . And all that Grover said was—"Mama, I feel sick."

He was sick as a dog. He fell over on the bed, and we undressed him and mama put her hand upon his forehead and came out in the hall—she was so white you could have made a black mark on her face with chalk—and whispered to me, "Go get the doctor quick, he's burning up."

And I went chasing up the street, my pigtails flying, to Dr. Packer's house. I brought him back with me. When he came out of Grover's room he told mama what to do but I don't know if she even heard him.

Her face was white as a sheet. She looked at me and looked right through me. She never saw me. And oh, my Lord, I'll never forget the way she looked, the way my heart stopped and came up in my throat. I was only a skinny little kid of fourteen. But she looked as if she was dying right before my eyes. And I knew that if anything happened to him, she'd never get over it if she lived to be a hundred.

Poor old mama. You know, he always was her eyeballs—you know that, don't you?—not the rest of us!—no, sir! I know what I'm talking about. It always has been Grover—she always thought more of him than she did of any of the others. And—poor kid!—he was a sweet kid. I can still see him lying there, and remember how sick he was, and how scared I was! I don't know why I was so scared. All we'd done had been to sneak away from home and go into a lunchroom—but I felt guilty about the whole thing, as if it was my fault.

It all came back to me the other day when I was looking at that picture, and I thought, my God, we were two kids together, and I was only two years older than Grover was, and now I'm forty-six. . . . Can you believe it? Can you figure it out—the way we grow up and change and go away? . . . And my Lord, Grover seemed so grown-up to me. He was such a quiet kid—I guess that's why he seemed older than the rest of us.

I wonder what Grover would say now if he could see that picture. All my hopes and dreams and big ambitions have come to nothing, and it's all so long ago, as if it happened in another world. Then it comes back, as if it happened yesterday. . . . Sometimes I lie awake at night and think of all the people who have come and gone, and how everything is different from the way we thought that it would be. Then I go out on the street next day and see the faces of the people that I pass. . . . Don't they look strange to you? Don't you see something funny in people's eyes, as if all of them were puzzled about something? As if they were wondering what had happened to them since they were kids? Wondering what it is that they have lost? . . . Now am I crazy, or do you know what I mean? You've been to college, Gene, and I want you to tell me if you know the answer. Now do they look that way to you? I never noticed that look in people's eyes when I was a kid—did you?

My God, I wish I knew the answer to these things. I'd like to find out what is wrong—what has changed since then—and if we have the same queer look in our eyes, too. Does it happen to us all, to everyone? . . . Grover and Ben, Steve, Daisy, Luke, and me—all standing there before that house on Woodson Street in Altamont—there we are, and you see the way we were—and how it all gets lost. What is it, anyway, that people lose?

How is it that nothing turns out the way we thought it would be? It all gets lost until it seems that it has never happened—that it is something we dreamed somewhere. . . . You see what I mean? . . . It seems that it must be something we heard somewhere—that it happened to someone else. And then it all comes back again.

And suddenly you remember just how it was, and see again those two funny, frightened, skinny little kids with their noses pressed against the dirty window of that lunchroom thirty years ago. You remember the way it felt, the way it smelled, even the strange smell in the old pantry in that house we lived in then. And the steps before the house, the way the rooms looked. And those two little boys in sailor suits who used to ride up and down before the house on tricycles. . . . And the birthmark on Grover's neck. . . . The Inside Inn. . . . St. Louis, and the Fair.

It all comes back as if it happened yesterday. And then it goes away again, and seems farther off and stranger than if it happened in a dream.

IV—THE BROTHER

"*This* is King's Highway," the man said.

And then Eugene looked and saw that it was just a street. There were some big new buildings, a large hotel, some restaurants and "bar-grill" places of the modern kind, the livid monotone of neon lights, the ceaseless traffic of motor cars—all this was new, but it was just a street.

And he knew that it had always been just a street, and nothing more—but somehow—well, he stood there looking at it, wondering what else he had expected to find.

The man kept looking at him with inquiry in his eyes, and Eugene asked him if the Fair had not been out this way.

"Sure, the Fair was out beyond here," the man said. "Out where the park is now. But this street you're looking for—don't you remember the name of it or nothing?" the man said.

Eugene said he thought the name of the street was Edgemont, but that he wasn't sure. Anyhow it was something like that. And he said the house was on the corner of that street and of another street.

Then the man said: "What was that other street?"

Eugene said he did not know, but that King's Highway was a block or so away, and that an interurban line ran past about half a block from where he once had lived.

"What line was this?" the man said, and stared at him.

"The interurban line," Eugene said.

Then the man stared at him again, and finally, "I don't know no interurban line," he said.

Eugene said it was a line that ran behind some houses, and that there were board fences there and grass beside the tracks. But somehow he could not say that it was summer in those days and that you could smell the ties, a wooden, tarry smell, and feel a kind of absence in the afternoon after the car had gone. He only said the interurban line was back behind somewhere between the backyards of some houses and some old board fences, and that King's Highway was a block or two away.

He did not say that King's Highway had not been a street in those days but a kind of road that wound from magic out of some dim and haunted land, and that along the way it had got mixed in with Tom the Piper's son, with hot cross buns, with all the light that came and went, and with coming down through Indiana in the morning, and the smell of engine smoke, the Union Station, and most of all with voices lost and far and long ago that said "King's Highway."

He did not say these things about King's Highway because he looked about him and he saw what King's Highway was. All he could say was that the street was near King's Highway, and was on the corner, and that the interurban trolley line was close to there. He said it was a stone house, and that there were stone steps before it, and a strip of grass. He said he thought the house had had a turret at one corner, he could not be sure.

The man looked at him again, and said, "This is King's Highway, but I never heard of any street like that."

Eugene left him then, and went on till he found the place. And so at last he turned into the street, finding the place where the two corners met, the huddled block, the turret, and the steps, and paused a moment, looking back, as if the street were Time.

For a moment he stood there, waiting—for a word, and for a door to open, for the child to come. He waited, but no words were spoken; no one came.

Yet all of it was just as it had always been, except that the steps were lower, the porch less high, the strip of grass less wide, than he had thought. All the rest of it was as he had known it would be. A graystone front, three-storied, with a slant slate roof, the side red brick and windowed, still with the old arched entrance in the center for the doctor's use.

There was a tree in front, and a lamp post; and behind and to the side, more trees than he had known there would be. And all the slatey turret gables, all the slatey window gables, going into points, and the two arched windows, in strong stone, in the front room.

It was all so strong, so solid, and so ugly—and all so enduring and so good, the way he had remembered it, except he did not smell the tar, the hot and caulky dryness of the old cracked ties, the boards of backyard fences and the coarse and sultry grass, and absence in the afternoon when the street car had gone, and the twins, sharp-visaged in their sailor suits, pumping with furious shrillness on tricycles up and down before the house, and the feel of the hot afternoon, and the sense that everyone was absent at the Fair.

Except for this, it all was just the same; except for this and for King's Highway, which was now a street; except for this, and for the child that did not come.

It was a hot day. Darkness had come. The heat rose up and hung and sweltered like a sodden blanket in St. Louis. It was wet heat, and one knew that there would be no relief or coolness in the night. And when one tried to think of the time when the heat would go away, one said: "It cannot last. It's bound to go away," as we always say it in America. But one did not believe it when he said it. The heat soaked down and men sweltered in it; the faces of the people were pale and greasy with the heat. And in their faces was a patient wretchedness, and one felt the kind of desolation that one feels at the end of a hot day in a great city in America—when one's home is far away, across the continent, and he thinks of all that distance, all that heat, and feels, "Oh God! but it's a big country!"

And he feels nothing but absence, absence, and the desolation of America, the loneliness and sadness of the high, hot skies, and evening coming on across the Middle West, across the sweltering and heat-sunken land, across all the lonely little towns, the farms, the fields, the oven swelter of Ohio, Kansas, Iowa, and Indiana at the close of day, and voices, casual in the heat, voices at the little stations, quiet, casual, somehow faded into that enormous vacancy and weariness of heat, of space, and of the immense, the sorrowful, the most high and awful skies.

Then he hears the engine and the wheel again, the wailing whistle and the bell, the sound of shifting in the sweltering yard, and walks the street, and walks the street, beneath the clusters of hard lights, and by the people with sagged faces, and is drowned in desolation and in no belief.

He feels the way one feels when one comes back, and knows that he should not have come, and when he sees that, after all, King's Highway is—a street; and St. Louis—the enchanted name—a big, hot, common town upon the river, sweltering in wet, dreary heat, and not quite South, and nothing else enough to make it better.

It had not been like this before. He could remember how it would get hot, and how good the heat was, and how he would lie out in the backyard on an airing mattress, and how the mattress would get hot and dry and smell like a hot mattress full of sun, and how the sun would make him want to sleep, and how, sometimes, he would go down into the basement to feel coolness, and how the cellar smelled as cellars always smell—a cool, stale smell, the smell of cobwebs and of grimy bottles. And he could remember, when you opened the door upstairs, the smell of the cellar would come up to you—cool, musty, stale and dank and dark—and how the thought of the dark cellar always filled him with a kind of numb excitement, a kind of visceral expectancy.

He could remember how it got hot in the afternoons, and how he would feel a sense of absence and vague sadness in the afternoons, when everyone had gone away. The house would seem so lonely, and sometimes he would sit inside, on the second step of the hall stairs, and listen to the sound of silence and of absence in the afternoon. He could smell the oil upon the floor and on the stairs, and see the sliding doors with their brown varnish and the beady chains across the door, and thrust his hands among the beady chains, and gather them together in his arms, and let them clash, and swish with light beady swishings all around him. He could feel darkness, absence, varnished darkness, and stained light within the house, through the stained glass of the window on the stairs, through the small stained glasses by the door, stained light and absence, silence and the smell of floor oil and vague sadness in the house on a hot mid-afternoon. And all these things themselves would have a kind of life: would seem to wait attentively, to be most living and most still.

He would sit there and listen. He could hear the girl next door practice her piano lessons in the afternoon, and hear the street car coming by between the backyard fences, half a block away, and smell the dry and sultry smell of backyard fences, the smell of coarse hot grasses by the car tracks in the afternoon, the smell of tar, of dry caulked ties, the smell of bright worn flanges, and feel the loneliness of backyards in the afternoon and the sense of absence when the car was gone.

Then he would long for evening and return, the slant of light, and feet along the street, the sharp-faced twins in sailor suits upon their tricycles, the smell of supper and the sound of voices in the house again, and Grover coming from the Fair.

That is how it was when he came into the street, and found the place where the two corners met, and turned at last to see if Time was there. He passed the house: some lights were burning, the door was open, and a woman sat upon the porch. And presently he turned, came back, and stopped before the house again. The corner light fell blank upon the house. He stood looking at it, and put his foot upon the step.

Then he said to the woman who was sitting on the porch: "This house—excuse me—but could you tell me, please, who lives here in this house?"

He knew his words were strange and hollow, and he had not said what he wished to say. She stared at him a moment, puzzled.

Then she said: "I live here. Who are you looking for?"

He said, "Why, I am looking for——"

And then he stopped, because he knew he could not tell her what it was that he was looking for.

"There used to be a house—" he said.

The woman was now staring at him hard. He said, "I think I used to live here." She said nothing.

In a moment he continued, "I used to live here in this house," he said, "when I was a little boy."

She was silent, looking at him, then she said: "Oh. Are you sure this was the house? Do you remember the address?"

"I have forgotten the address," he said, "but it was Edgemont Street, and it was on the corner. And I know this is the house."

"This isn't Edgemont Street," the woman said. "The name is Bates."

"Well, then, they changed the name of the street," he said, "but this is the same house. It hasn't changed."

She was silent a moment, then she nodded: "Yes. They did change the name of the street. I remember when I was a child they called it something else," she said. "But that was a long time ago. When was it that you lived here?"

"In 1904."

Again she was silent, looking at him. Then presently: "Oh. That was the year of the Fair. You were here then?"

"Yes." He now spoke rapidly, with more confidence. "My mother had the house, and we were here for seven months. And the house belonged to Dr. Packer," he went on. "We rented it from him."

"Yes," the woman said, and nodded, "this was Dr. Packer's house. He's dead now, he's been dead for many years. But this was the Packer house, all right."

"That entrance on the side," he said, "where the steps go up, that was for Dr. Packer's patients. That was the entrance to his office."

"Oh," the woman said, "I didn't know that. I've often wondered what it was. I didn't know what it was for."

"And this big room in front here," he continued, "that was the office. And there were sliding doors, and next to it, a kind of alcove for his patients——"

"Yes, the alcove is still there, only all

of it has been made into one room now—and I never knew just what the alcove was for."

"And there were sliding doors on this side, too, that opened on the hall—and a stairway going up upon this side. And halfway up the stairway, at the landing, a little window of colored glass—and across the sliding doors here in the hall, a kind of curtain made of strings of beads."

She nodded, smiling. "Yes, it's just the same—we still have the sliding doors and the stained glass window on the stairs. There's no bead curtain any more," she said, "but I remember when people had them. I know what you mean."

"When we were here," he said, "we used the doctor's office for a parlor—except later on—the last month or two—and then we used it for—a bedroom."

"It is a bedroom now," she said. "I run the house—I rent rooms—all of the rooms upstairs are rented—but I have two brothers and they sleep in this front room."

Both of them were silent for a moment, then Eugene said, "My brother stayed there too."

"In the front room?" the woman said.

He answered, "Yes."

She paused, then said: "Won't you come in? I don't believe it's changed much. Would you like to see?"

He thanked her and said he would, and he went up the steps. She opened the screen door to let him in.

Inside it was just the same—the stairs, the hallway, the sliding doors, the window of stained glass upon the stairs. And all of it was just the same, except for absence, the stained light of absence in the afternoon, and the child who once had sat there, waiting on the stairs.

It was all the same except that as a child he had sat there feeling things were *Somewhere*—and now he *knew*. He had sat there feeling that a vast and sultry river was somewhere—and now he knew! He had sat there wondering what King's Highway was, where it began, and where it ended—

now he knew! He had sat there haunted by the magic word "downtown"—now he knew!—and by the street car, after it had gone—and by all things that came and went and came again, like the cloud shadows passing in a wood, that never could be captured.

And he felt that if he could only sit there on the stairs once more, in solitude and absence in the afternoon, he would be able to get it back again. Then would he be able to remember all that he had seen and been—the brief sum of himself, the universe of his four years, with all the light of Time upon it—that universe which was so short to measure, and yet so far, so endless, to remember. Then would he be able to see his own small face again, pooled in the dark mirror of the hall, and peer once more into the grave eyes of the child that he had been, and discover there in his quiet three-years' self the lone integrity of "I," knowing: "Here is the House, and here House listening; here is Absence, Absence in the afternoon; and here in this House, this Absence, is my core, my kernel—here am I!"

But as he thought it, he knew that even if he could sit here alone and get it back again, it would be gone as soon as seized, just as it had been then—first coming like the vast and drowsy rumors of the distant and enchanted Fair, then fading like cloud shadows on a hill, going like faces in a dream—coming, going, coming, possessed and held but never captured, like lost voices in the mountains long ago—and like the dark eyes and quiet face of the dark, lost boy, his brother, who, in the mysterious rhythms of his life and work, used to come into this house, then go, and then return again.

The woman took Eugene back into the house and through the hall. He told her of the pantry, told her where it was and pointed to the place, but now it was no longer there. And he told her of the back-yard, and of the old board fence around the yard. But the old board fence was gone. And he told her of the carriage house, and told her it was painted red. But now there was a small garage. And the backyard was still there, but smaller than he thought, and now there was a tree.

"I did not know there was a tree," he said. "I do not remember any tree."

"Perhaps it was not there," she said. "A tree could grow in thirty years." And then they came back through the house again and paused at the sliding doors.

"And could I see this room?" he said.

She slid the doors back. They slid open smoothly, with a rolling heaviness, as they used to do. And then he saw the room again. It was the same. There was a window at the side, the two arched windows at the front, the alcove and the sliding doors, the fireplace with the tiles of mottled green, the mantle of dark mission wood, the mantel posts, a dresser and a bed, just where the dresser and the bed had been so long ago.

"Is this the room?" the woman said. "It hasn't changed?"

He told her that it was the same.

"And your brother slept here where my brothers sleep?"

"This is his room," he said.

They were silent. He turned to go, and said, "Well, thank you. I appreciate your showing me."

She said that she was glad and that it was no trouble. "And when you see your family, you can tell them that you saw the house," she said. "My name is Mrs. Bell. You can tell your mother that a Mrs. Bell has the house now. And when you see your brother, you can tell him that you saw the room he slept in, and that you found it just the same."

He told her then that his brother was dead.

The woman was silent for a moment. Then she looked at him and said: "He died here, didn't he? In this room?"

He told her that it was so.

"Well, then," she said, "I knew it. I don't know how. But when you told me he was here, I knew it."

He said nothing. In a moment the woman said, "What did he die of?"

"Typhoid."

She looked shocked and troubled, and said involuntarily, "My two brothers——"

"That was a long time ago," he said. "I don't think you need to worry now."

"Oh, I wasn't thinking about that," she said. "It was just hearing that a little boy—your brother—was—was in this room that my two brothers sleep in now——"

"Well, maybe I shouldn't have told you then. But he was a good boy—and if you'd known him you wouldn't mind."

She said nothing, and he added quickly: "Besides, he didn't stay here long. This wasn't really his room—but the night he came back with my sister he was so sick—they didn't move him."

"Oh," the woman said, "I see." And then: "Are you going to tell your mother you were here?"

"I don't think so."

"I—I wonder how she feels about this room."

"I don't know. She never speaks of it."

"Oh. . . . How old was he?"

"He was twelve."

"You must have been pretty young yourself."

"I was not quite four."

"And—you just wanted to see the room, didn't you? That's why you came back."

"Yes."

"Well—" indefinitely—"I guess you've seen it now."

"Yes, thank you."

"I guess you don't remember much about him, do you? I shouldn't think you would."

"No, not much."

The years dropped off like fallen leaves: the face came back again—the soft dark oval, the dark eyes, the soft brown berry on the neck, the raven hair, all bending down, approaching—the whole appearing to him ghost-wise, intent and instant.

"Now say it—*Grover!*"

"Gova."

"No—not Gova—*Grover!* . . . Say it!"

"Gova."

"Ah-h—you didn't say it. You said Gova. *Grover*—now say it!"

"Gova."

"Look, I tell you what I'll do if you say it right. Would you like to go down to King's Highway? Would you like Grover to set you up? All right, then. If you say Grover and say it right, I'll take you to King's Highway and set you up to ice cream. Now say it right—*Grover!*"

"Gova."

"Ah-h, you-u. You're the craziest little old boy I ever did see. Can't you even say Grover?"

"Gova."

"Ah-h, you-u. Old Tongue-Tie, that's what you are. . . . Well, come on, then, I'll set you up anyway."

It all came back, and faded, and was lost again. Eugene turned to go, and thanked the woman and said good-bye.

"Well, then, good-bye," the woman said, and they shook hands. "I'm glad if I could show you. I'm glad if—" She did not finish, and at length she said: "Well, then, that was a long time ago. You'll find everything changed now, I guess. It's all built up around here now—and way out beyond here, out beyond where the Fair Grounds used to be. I guess you'll find it changed."

They had nothing more to say. They just stood there for a moment on the steps, and then shook hands once more.

"Well, good-bye."

And again he was in the street, and found the place where the corners met, and for the last time turned to see where Time had gone.

And he knew that he would never come again, and that lost magic would not come again. Lost now was all of it—the street, the heat, King's Highway, and Tom the Piper's son, all mixed in with the vast and drowsy murmur of the Fair, and with the sense of absence in the afternoon, and the

house that waited, and the child that dreamed. And out of the enchanted wood, that thicket of man's memory, Eugene knew that the dark eye and the quiet face of his friend and brother—poor child, life's stranger, and life's exile, lost like all of us, a cipher in blind mazes, long ago—the lost boy was gone forever, and would not return.

From

YOU CAN'T GO HOME AGAIN
[1940]

Chapter XXVII

THE LOCUSTS HAVE NO KING

THE TRAGIC LIGHT of evening falls upon the huge and rusty jungle of South Brooklyn. It falls without glare or warmth upon the faces of all the men with dead eyes and flesh of tallow-grey as they lean upon their window sills at the sad, hushed end of day.

If at such a time you walk down this narrow street, between the mean and shabby houses, past the eyes of all the men who lean there quietly at their open windows in their shirt-sleeves, and turn in at the alley here and follow the two-foot strip of broken concrete pavement that skirts the alley on one side, and go to the very last shabby house down at the end, and climb up the flight of worn steps to the front entrance, and knock loudly at the door with your bare knuckles (the bell is out of order), and then wait patiently until someone comes, and ask whether Mr. George Webber lives here, you will be informed that he most certainly does, and that if you will just come in and go down this stairway to the basement and knock at the door there on your right, you will probably find him in. So you go down the stairway to the damp and gloomy basement hall, thread your way between the dusty old boxes, derelict furniture, and other lumber stored there in the passage, rap on the door that has been indicated to you, and Mr. Webber himself will open it and usher you right into his room, his home, his castle.

The place may seem to you more like a dungeon than a room that a man would voluntarily elect to live in. It is long and narrow, running parallel to the hall from front to rear, and the only natural light that enters it comes through two small windows rather high up in the wall, facing each other at the opposite ends, and these are heavily guarded with iron bars, placed there by some past owner of the house to keep the South Brooklyn thugs from breaking in.

The room is furnished adequately but not so luxuriously as to deprive it of a certain functional and Spartan simplicity. In the back half there is an iron bed with sagging springs, a broken-down dresser with a cracked mirror above it, two kitchen chairs, and a steamer trunk and some old suitcases that have seen much use. At the front end, under the yellow glow of an electric light suspended from the ceiling by a cord, there is a large desk, very much scarred and battered, with the handles missing on most of the drawers, and in front of it there is a straight-backed chair made out of some old, dark wood. In the center, ranged against the walls, where they serve to draw the two ends of the room together into æsthetic unity, stand an ancient gate-legged table, so much of its dark green paint flaked off that the dainty pink complexion of its forgotten youth shows through all over, a tier of bookshelves, unpainted, and two large crates or packing cases, their thick top boards pried off to reveal great stacks of ledgers and of white and yellow manuscript within. On top of the desk, on the table, on the bookshelves, and all over the floor are scattered, like fallen leaves in autumn woods, immense masses of loose paper with writing on every sheet, and everywhere are books, piled up on their sides or leaning crazily against each other.

This dark cellar is George Webber's abode and working quarters. Here, in winter, the walls, which sink four feet below the level of the ground, sweat continuously with clammy drops of water. Here, in summer, it is he who does the sweating.

His neighbors, he will tell you, are for the most part Armenians, Italians, Spaniards, Irishmen, and Jews—in short, Americans. They live in all the shacks, tenements, and slums in all the raw, rusty streets and alleys of South Brooklyn.

And what is that you smell?

Oh, that! Well, you see, he shares impartially with his neighbors a piece of public property in the vicinity; it belongs to all of them in common, and it gives to South Brooklyn its own distinctive atmosphere. It is the old Gowanus Canal, and that aroma you speak of is nothing but the huge symphonic stink of it, cunningly compacted of unnumbered separate putrefactions. It is interesting sometimes to try to count them. There is in it not only the noisome stenches of a stagnant sewer, but also the smells of melted glue, burned rubber, and smoldering rags, the odors of a boneyard horse, long dead, the incense of putrefying offal, the fragrance of deceased decaying cats, old tomatoes, rotten cabbage, and prehistoric eggs.

And how does he stand it?

Well, one gets used to it. One can get used to anything, just as all these other people do. They never think of the smell, they never speak of it, they'd probably miss it if they moved away.

To this place, then, George Webber has come, and here "holed in" with a kind of dogged stubbornness touched with desperation. And you will not be far wrong if you surmise that he has come here deliberately, driven by a resolution to seek out the most forlorn and isolated hiding spot that he could find. . . .

Slowly the years crept by and George lived alone in Brooklyn. They were hard years, desperate years, lonely years, years of interminable writing and experimentation, years of exploration and discovery, years of grey timelessness, weariness, exhaustion, and self-doubt. He had reached the wilderness period of his life and was hacking his way through the jungles of experience. He had stripped himself down to the brutal facts of self and work. These were all he had.

He saw himself more clearly now than he had ever done before, and, in spite of living thus alone, he no longer thought of himself as a rare and special person who was doomed to isolation, but as a man who worked and who, like other men, was a part of life. He was concerned passionately with reality. He wanted to see things whole, to find out everything he could, and then to create out of what he knew the fruit of his own vision.

One criticism that had been made of his first book still rankled in his mind. An unsuccessful scribbler turned critic had simply dismissed the whole book as a "barbaric yawp," accusing Webber of getting at things with his emotions rather than with his brains, and of being hostile toward the processes of the intellect and "the intellectual point of view." These charges, if they had any truth in them, seemed to George to be the kind of lifeless half-truth that was worse than no truth at all. The trouble with the so-called "intellectuals" was that they were not intellectual enough, and their point of view more often than not had no point, but was disparate, arbitrary, sporadic, and confused.

To be an "intellectual" was, it seemed, a vastly different thing from being intelligent. A dog's nose would usually lead him toward what he wished to find, or away from what he wished to avoid: this was intelligent. That is, the dog had the sense of reality in his nose. But the "intellectual" usually had no nose, and was lacking in the sense of reality. The most striking difference between Webber's mind and the mind of the average "intellectual" was that Webber absorbed experience like a sponge, and made use of everything that he absorbed. He really learned constantly from experience. But the "intellectuals" of his

acquaintance seemed to learn nothing. They had no capacity for rumination and digestion. They could not reflect.

He thought over a few of them that he had known:

There was Haythorpe, who when George first knew him was an æsthete of the late baroque in painting, writing, all the arts, author of one-act costume plays—"Gesmonder! Thy hands pale chalices of hot desire!" Later he became an æsthete of the primitives—the Greek, Italian, and the German; then æsthete of the nigger cults—the wood sculptures, coon songs, hymnals, dances, and the rest; still later, æsthete of the comics—of cartoons, Chaplin, and the Brothers Marx; then of Expressionism; then of the Mass; then of Russia and the Revolution; at length, æsthete of homosexuality; and finally, death's æsthete—suicide in a graveyard in Connecticut.

There was Collingswood, who, fresh out of Harvard, was not so much the æsthete of the arts as of the mind. First, a Bolshevik from Beacon Hill, practitioner of promiscuous, communal love as the necessary answer to "bourgeois morality"; then back to Cambridge for post-graduate study at the feet of Irving Babbitt[1]—Collingswood is now a Humanist, the bitter enemy of Rousseau, Romanticism, and of Russia (which is, he now thinks, Rousseau in modern form); the playwright, next—New Jersey, Beacon Hill, or Central Park seen in the classic unities of the Greek drama; at length, disgusted realist—"all that's good in modern art or letters is to be found in advertisements"; then a job as a scenario writer and two years in Hollywood—all now is the moving picture, with easy money, easy love affairs, and drunkenness; and finally, back to Russia, but with his first love lacking—no sex triflings now, my comrades—we who serve the Cause and wait upon the day lead lives of Spartan abstinence—what was the free life, free love, enlightened pleasure of the proletariat ten years ago is now despised as the con-

---

[1] See pp. 609-610 of this volume.

temptible debauchery of "bourgeois decadence."

There was Spurgeon from the teaching days at the School for Utility Cultures—good Spurgeon—Chester Spurgeon of the Ph. D.—Spurgeon of "the great tradition"—thin-lipped Spurgeon, ex-student of Professor Stuart Sherman,[2] and bearer-onward of the Master's Torch. Noble-hearted Spurgeon, who wrote honeyed flatteries of Thornton Wilder and his *Bridge* [3]—"The tradition of the Bridge is Love, just as the tradition of America and of Democracy is Love. Hence—" Spurgeon hences—Love grows Wilder as the years Bridge on across America. Oh, where now, good Spurgeon, "intellectual" Spurgeon—Spurgeon whose thin lips and narrowed eyes were always so glacial prim on Definitions? Where now, brave intellect, by passion uninflamed? Spurgeon of the flashing mind, by emotion unimpulsed, is now a devoted leader of the intellectual Communists (See Spurgeon's article entitled, "Mr. Wilder's Piffle," in the *New Masses*).— So, Comrade Spurgeon, hail! Hail, Comrade Spurgeon—and most heartily, my bright-eyed Intellectual, farewell!

Whatever George Webber was, he knew he was not an "intellectual." He was just an American who was looking hard at the life around him, and sorting carefully through all the life he had ever seen and known, and trying to extract some essential truth out of this welter of his whole experience. But, as he said to his friend and editor, Fox Edwards:

"What *is* truth? No wonder jesting Pilate turned away. The truth, it has a thousand faces—show only one of them, and the *whole* truth flies away! But how to show the whole? That's the question. . . .

"Discovery in itself is not enough. It's not enough to find out what things are. You've also got to find out where they come from, where each brick fits in the wall."

He always came back to the wall.

"I think it's like this," he said. "You see a wall, you look at it so much and so hard that one day you see clear through

it. Then, of course, it's not just one wall any longer. It's every wall that ever was."

He was still spiritually fighting out the battle of his first book, and all the problems it had raised. He was still searching for a way. At times he felt that his first book had taught him nothing—not even confidence. His feelings of hollow desperation and self-doubt seemed to grow worse instead of better, for he had now torn himself free from almost every personal tie which had ever bound him, and which formerly had sustained him in some degree with encouragement and faith. He was left, therefore, to rely almost completely on his own resources.

There was also the insistent, gnawing consciousness of work itself, the necessity of turning toward the future and the completion of a new book. He was feeling, now as never before, the inexorable pressure of time. In writing his first book, he had been unknown and obscure, and there had been a certain fortifying strength in that, for no one had expected anything of him. But now the spotlight of publication had been turned upon him, and he felt it beating down with merciless intensity. He was pinned beneath the light—he could not crawl out of it. Though he had not won fame, still he was known now. He had been examined, probed, and talked about. He felt that the world was looking at him with a critic eye.

It had been easy in his dreams to envision a long and fluent sequence of big books, but now he was finding it a different matter to accomplish them. His first book had been more an act of utterance than an act of labor. It was an impassioned expletive of youth—something that had been pent up in him, something felt and seen and imagined and put down at white-hot heat. The writing of it had been a process of spiritual and emotional evacuation. But that was behind him now, and he knew he should never try to repeat it.

---

[2] Prominent American critic of the 1920's.

[3] Thornton Wilder's *The Bridge of San Luis Rey* was published in 1927.

Henceforth his writing would have to come from unending labor and preparation.

In his effort to explore his experience, to extract the whole, essential truth of it, and to find a way to write about it, he sought to recapture every particle of the life he knew down to its minutest details. He spent weeks and months trying to put down on paper the exactitudes of countless fragments—what he called, "the dry, caked colors of America"—how the entrance to a subway looked, the design and webbing of the elevated structure, the look and feel of an iron rail, the particular shade of rusty green with which so many things are painted in America. Then he tried to pin down the foggy color of the brick of which so much of London is constructed, the look of an English doorway, of a French window, of the roofs and chimney pots of Paris, of a whole street in Munich—and each of these foreign things he then examined in contrast to its American equivalent.

It was a process of discovery in its most naked, literal, and primitive terms. He was just beginning really to see thousands of things for the first time, to see the relations between them, to see here and there whole series and systems of relations. He was like a scientist in some new field of chemistry who for the first time realizes that he has stumbled upon a vast new world, and who will then pick out identities, establish affiliations, define here and there the outlines of sub-systems in crystalline union, without yet being aware what the structure of the whole is like, or what the final end will be.

The same processes now began to inform his direct observation of the life around him. Thus, on his nocturnal ramblings about New York, he would observe the homeless men who prowled in the vicinity of restaurants, lifting the lids of garbage cans and searching around inside for morsels of rotten food. He saw them everywhere, and noticed how their numbers increased during the hard and desperate days of 1932. He knew what kind of men they were, for he talked to many of them; he knew what

they had been, where they had come from, and even what kind of scraps they could expect to dig out of the garbage cans. He found out the various places all over the city where such men slept at night. A favorite rendezvous was a corridor of the subway station at Thirty-third Street and Park Avenue in Manhattan. There one night he counted thirty-four huddled together on the cold concrete, wrapped up in sheathings of old newspaper.

It was his custom almost every night, at one o'clock or later, to walk across the Brooklyn Bridge, and night after night, with a horrible fascination, he used to go to the public latrine or "comfort station" which was directly in front of the New York City Hall. One descended to this place down a steep flight of stairs from the street, and on bitter nights he would find the place crowded with homeless men who had sought refuge there. Some were those shambling hulks that one sees everywhere, in Paris as well as New York, in good times as well as bad—old men, all rags and bags and long white hair and bushy beards stained dirty yellow, wearing tattered overcoats in the cavernous pockets of which they carefully stored away all the little rubbish they lived on and spent their days collecting in the streets—crusts of bread, old bones with rancid shreds of meat still clinging to them, and dozens of cigarette butts. Some were the "stumble bums" from the Bowery, criminal, fumed with drink or drugs, or half insane with "smoke." But most of them were just flotsam of the general ruin of the time—honest, decent, middle-aged men with faces seamed by toil and want, and young men, many of them mere boys in their teens, with thick, unkempt hair. These were the wanderers from town to town, the riders of freight trains, the thumbers of rides on highways, the uprooted, unwanted male population of America. They drifted across the land and gathered in the big cities when winter came, hungry, defeated, empty, hopeless, restless, driven by they knew not what, always on the move, looking everywhere for work, for the bare crumbs to support their miserable lives, and finding neither work nor crumbs. Here in New York, to this obscene meeting place, these derelicts came, drawn into a common stew of rest and warmth and a little surcease from their desperation.

George had never before witnessed anything to equal the indignity and sheer animal horror of the scene. There was even a kind of devil's comedy in the sight of all these filthy men squatting upon those open, doorless stools. Arguments and savage disputes and fights would sometimes break out among them over the possession of these stools, which all of them wanted more for rest than for necessity. The sight was revolting, disgusting, enough to render a man forever speechless with very pity.

He would talk to the men and find out all he could about them, and when he could stand it no more he would come out of this hole of filth and suffering, and there, twenty feet above it, he would see the giant hackles of Manhattan shining coldly in the cruel brightness of the winter night. The Woolworth Building was not fifty yards away, and a little farther down were the silvery spires and needles of Wall Street, great fortresses of stone and steel that housed enormous banks. The blind injustice of this contrast seemed the most brutal part of the whole experience, for there, all around him in the cold moonlight, only a few blocks away from this abyss of human wretchedness and misery, blazed the pinnacles of power where a large portion of the entire world's wealth was locked in mighty vaults. . . .

The lives of men who have to live in our great cities are often tragically lonely. In many more ways than one, these dwellers in the hive are modern counterparts of Tantalus.[4] They are starving to death in the midst of abundance. The crystal stream flows near their lips but always falls away when they try to drink of it. The vine, richweighted with its golden fruit, bends down, comes near, but springs back when they reach to touch it.

Melville, at the beginning of his great fable, *Moby Dick*,[5] tells how the city people of his time would, on every occasion that was afforded them, go down to the dock, to the very edges of the wharf, and stand there looking out to sea. In the great city of today, however, there is no sea to look out to, or, if there is, it is so far away, so inaccessible, walled in behind such infinite ramifications of stone and steel, that the effort to get to it is disheartening. So now, when the city man looks out, he looks out on nothing but crowded vacancy.

Does this explain, perhaps, the desolate emptiness of city youth—those straggling bands of boys of sixteen or eighteen that one can always see at night or on a holiday, going along a street, filling the air with raucous jargon and senseless cries, each trying to outdo the others with joyless catcalls and mirthless quips and jokes which are so feeble, so stupidly inane, that one hears them with strong mixed feelings of pity and of shame? Where here, among these lads, is all the merriment, high spirits, and spontaneous gayety of youth? These creatures, millions of them, seem to have been born but half made up, without innocence, born old and stale and dull and empty.

Who can wonder at it? For what a world it is that most of them were born into! They were suckled on darkness, and weaned on violence and noise. They had to try to draw out moisture from the cobblestones, their true parent was a city street, and in that barren universe no urgent sails swelled out and leaned against the wind, they rarely knew the feel of earth beneath their feet and no birds sang, their youthful eyes grew hard, unseeing, from being stopped forever by a wall of masonry.

In other times, when painters tried to paint a scene of awful desolation, they chose the desert or a heath of barren rocks,

---

[4] A mythological king who was punished by being placed close to water and food which receded whenever he attempted to drink or eat.

[5] See Vol. I, pp. 998-1000.

and there would try to picture man in his great loneliness—the prophet in the desert, Elijah being fed by ravens on the rocks.[6] But for a modern painter, the most desolate scene would be a street in almost any one of our great cities on a Sunday afternoon.

Suppose a rather drab and shabby street in Brooklyn, not quite tenement perhaps, and lacking therefore even the gaunt savagery of poverty, but a street of cheap brick buildings, warehouses, and garages, with a cigar store or a fruit stand or a barber shop on the corner. Suppose a Sunday afternoon in March—bleak, empty, slaty grey. And suppose a group of men, Americans of the working class, dressed in their "good" Sunday clothes—the cheap machine-made suits, the new cheap shoes, the cheap felt hats stamped out of universal grey. Just suppose this, and nothing more. The men hang around the corner before the cigar store or the closed barber shop, and now and then, through the bleak and empty street, a motor car goes flashing past, and in the distance they hear the cold rumble of an elevated train. For hours they hang around the corner, waiting—waiting—waiting——

For what?

Nothing. Nothing at all. And that is what gives the scene its special quality of tragic loneliness, awful emptiness, and utter desolation. Every modern city man is familiar with it.

And yet—and yet——

It is also true—and this is a curious paradox about America—that these same men who stand upon the corner and wait around on Sunday afternoons for nothing are filled at the same time with an almost quenchless hope, an almost boundless optimism, an almost indestructible belief that something is bound to turn up, something is sure to happen. This is a peculiar quality of the American soul, and it contributes largely to the strange enigma of our life, which is so incredibly mixed of harshness and of tenderness, of innocence and of crime, of loneliness and of good fellowship, of deso-

lation and of exultant hope, of terror and of courage, of nameless fear and of soaring conviction, of brutal, empty, naked, bleak, corrosive ugliness, and of beauty so lovely and so overwhelming that the tongue is stopped by it, and the language for it has not yet been uttered.

How explain this nameless hope that seems to lack all reasonable foundation? I cannot. But if you were to go up to this fairly intelligent-looking truck driver who stands and waits there with his crowd, and if you put to him your question, and if he understood what you were talking about (he wouldn't), and if he were articulate enough to frame in words the feelings that are in him (he isn't)—he might answer you with something such as this:

"Now is duh mont' of March, duh mont' of March—now it is Sunday afternoon in Brooklyn in duh mont' of March, an' we stand upon cold corners of duh day. It's funny dat dere are so many corners in duh mont' of March, here in Brooklyn where no corners are. Jesus! On Sunday in duh mont' of March we sleep late in duh mornin', den we get up an' read duh papers—duh funnies an' duh sportin' news. We eat some chow. An' den we dress up in duh afternoon, we leave our wives, we leave duh funnies littered on duh floor, an' go outside in Brooklyn in duh mont' of March an' stand around upon ten t'ousand corners of duh day. We need a corner in duh mont' of March, a wall to stand to, a shelter an' a door. Dere must be *some* place inside in duh mont' of March, but we never found it. So we stand around on corners where duh sky is cold an' ragged still wit' winter, in our good clothes we stand around wit' a lot of udder guys we know, before duh barber shop, just lookin' for a door."

Ah, yes, for in summer:

It is so cool and sweet tonight, a million feet are walking here across the jungle web of Brooklyn in the dark, and it's so hard now to remember that it ever was the month of March in Brooklyn and that we

---

[6] I Kings, 17:6.

couldn't find a door. There are so many million doors tonight. There's a door for everyone tonight, all's open to the air, all's interfused tonight: remote the thunder of the elevated trains on Fulton Street, the rattling of the cars along Atlantic Avenue, the glare of Coney Island seven miles away, the mob, the racket, and the barkers shouting, the cars swift-shuttling through the quiet streets, the people swarming in the web, lit here and there with livid blurs of light, the voices of the neighbors leaning at their windows, harsh, soft, all interfused. All's illusive in the liquid air tonight, all mixed in with the radios that blare from open windows. And there is something over all tonight, something fused, remote, and trembling, made of all of this, and yet not of it, upon the huge and weaving ocean of the night in Brooklyn—something that we had almost quite forgotten in the month of March. What's this?—a sash raised gently? —a window?—a near voice on the air?— something swift and passing, almost captured, there below?—there in the gulf of night the mournful and yet thrilling voices of the tugs?—the liner's blare? Here—there —some otherwhere—was it a whisper?—a woman's call?—a sound of people talking behind the screens and doors in Flatbush? It trembles in the air throughout the giant web tonight, as fleeting as a step—near— as soft and sudden as a woman's laugh. The liquid air is living with the very whisper of the thing that we are looking for tonight throughout America—the very thing that seemed so bleak, so vast, so cold, so hopeless, and so lost as we waited in our good clothes on ten thousand corners of the day in Brooklyn in the month of March.

If George Webber had never gone beyond the limits of the neighborhood in which he lived, the whole chronicle of the earth would have been there for him just the same. South Brooklyn was a universe.

The people in the houses all around him, whose lives in the cold, raw days of winter always seemed hermetic, sterile, and remote, as shut out from him as though they were something sealed up in a tin, became in spring and summer so real to him it seemed that he had known them from his birth. For, as the days and nights grew warmer, everybody kept their windows open, and all the dwellers in these houses conducted their most intimate affairs in loud and raucous voices which carried to the street and made the casual passer-by a confidant of every family secret.

God knows he saw squalor and filth and misery and despair enough, violence and cruelty and hate enough, to crust his lips forever with the hard and acrid taste of desolation. He found a sinister and demented Italian grocer whose thin mouth writhed in a servile smile as he cringed before his customers, and the next moment was twisted in a savage snarl as he dug his clawlike fingers into the arm of his wretched little son. And on Saturdays the Irishmen would come home drunk, and then would beat their wives and cut one another's throats, and the whole course and progress of their murderous rages would be published nakedly from their open windows with laugh, shout, scream, and curse.

But he found beauty in South Brooklyn, too. There was a tree that leaned over into the narrow alley where he lived, and George could stand at his basement window and look up at it and watch it day by day as it came into its moment's glory of young and magic green. And then toward sunset, if he was tired, he could lie down to rest a while upon his iron bed and listen to the dying birdsong in the tree. Thus, each spring, in that one tree, he found all April and the earth. He also found devotion, love, and wisdom in a shabby little Jewish tailor and his wife, whose dirty children were always tumbling in and out of the dingy suffocation of his shop.

In the infinite variety of such common, accidental, oft-unheeded things one can see the web of life as it is spun. Whether we wake at morning in the city, or lie at night in darkness in the country towns, or walk the streets of furious noon in all the dusty, homely, and enduring lights of present time, the universe around us is the same. Evil lives forever—so does good. Man alone has knowledge of these two, and he is such a little thing.

For what is man?

First, a child, soft-boned, unable to support itself on its rubbery legs, befouled with its excrement, that howls and laughs by turns, cries for the moon but hushes when it gets its mother's teat; a sleeper, eater, guzzler, howler, laugher, idiot, and a chewer of its toe; a little tender thing all blubbered with its spit, a reacher into fires, a beloved fool.

After that, a boy, hoarse and loud before his companions, but afraid of the dark; will beat the weaker and avoid the stronger; worships strength and savagery, loves tales of war and murder, and violence done to others; joins gangs and hates to be alone; makes heroes out of soldiers, sailors, prize fighters, football players, cowboys, gunmen, and detectives; would rather die than not out-try and out-dare his companions, wants to beat them and always to win, shows his muscle and demands that it be felt, boasts of his victories and will never own defeat.

Then the youth: goes after girls, is foul behind their backs among the drugstore boys, hints at a hundred seductions, but gets pimples on his face; begins to think about his clothes, becomes a fop, greases his hair, smokes cigarettes with a dissipated air, reads novels, and writes poetry on the sly. He sees the world now as a pair of legs and breasts; he knows hate, love, and jealousy; he is cowardly and foolish, he cannot endure to be alone; he lives in a crowd, thinks with the crowd, is afraid to be marked off from his fellows by an eccentricity. He joins clubs and is afraid of ridicule; he is bored and unhappy and wretched most of the time. There is a great cavity in him, he is dull.

Then the man: he is busy, he is full of plans and reasons, he has work. He gets children, buys and sells small packets of everlasting earth, intrigues against his rivals, is exultant when he cheats them. He wastes his little three score years and ten

in spendthrift and inglorious living; from his cradle to his grave he scarcely sees the sun or moon or stars; he is unconscious of the immortal sea and earth; he talks of the future and he wastes it as it comes. If he is lucky, he saves money. At the end his fat purse buys him flunkeys to carry him where his shanks no longer can; he consumes rich food and golden wine that his wretched stomach has no hunger for; his weary and lifeless eyes look out upon the scenery of strange lands for which in youth his heart was panting. Then the slow death, prolonged by costly doctors, and finally the graduate undertakers, the perfumed carrion, the suave ushers with palms outspread to leftwards, the fast motor hearses, and the earth again.

This is man: a writer of books, a putterdown of words, a painter of pictures, a maker of ten thousand philosophies. He grows passionate over ideas, he hurls scorn and mockery at another's work, he finds the one way, the true way, for himself, and calls all others false—yet in the billion books upon the shelves there is not one that can tell him how to draw a single fleeting breath in peace and comfort. He makes histories of the universe, he directs the destiny of nations, but he does not know his own history, and he cannot direct his own destiny with dignity or wisdom for ten consecutive minutes.

This is man: for the most part a foul, wretched, abominable creature, a packet of decay, a bundle of degenerating tissues, a creature that gets old and hairless and has a foul breath, a hater of his kind, a cheater, a scorner, a mocker, a reviler, a thing that kills and murders in a mob or in the dark, loud and full of brag surrounded by his fellows, but without the courage of a rat alone. He will cringe for a coin, and show his snarling fangs behind the giver's back; he will cheat for two sous, and kill for forty dollars, and weep copiously in court to keep another scoundrel out of jail.

This is man, who will steal his friend's woman, feel the leg of his host's wife below the table cloth, dump fortunes on his whores, bow down in worship before charlatans, and let his poets die. This is man, who swears he will live only for beauty, for art, for the spirit, but will live only for fashion, and will change his faith and his convictions as soon as fashion changes. This is man, the great warrior with the flaccid gut, the great romantic with the barren loins, the eternal knave devouring the eternal fool, the most glorious of all the animals, who uses his brain for the most part to make himself a stench in the nostrils of the Bull, the Fox, the Dog, the Tiger, and the Goat.

Yes, this is man, and it is impossible to say the worst of him, for the record of his obscene existence, his baseness, lust, cruelty, and treachery, is illimitable. His life is also full of toil, tumult, and suffering. His days are mainly composed of a million idiot repetitions—in goings and comings along hot streets, in sweatings and freezings, in the senseless accumulation of fruitless tasks, in decaying and being patched, in grinding out his life so that he may buy bad food, in eating bad food so that he may grind his life out in distressful defecations. He is the dweller in that ruined tenement who, from one moment's breathing to another, can hardly forget the bitter weight of his uneasy flesh, the thousand diseases and distresses of his body, the growing incubus of his corruption. This is man, who, if he can remember ten golden moments of joy and happiness out of all his years, ten moments unmarked by care, unseamed by aches or itches, has power to lift himself with his expiring breath and say: "I have lived upon this earth and known glory!"

This is man, and one wonders why he wants to live at all. A third of his life is lost and deadened under sleep; another third is given to a sterile labor; a sixth is spent in all his goings and his comings, in the moil and shuffle of the streets, in thrusting, shoving, pawing. How much of him is left, then, for a vision of the tragic stars? How much of him is left to look upon the everlasting earth? How much of him is left for glory and the making of great

songs? A few snatched moments only from the barren glut and suck of living.

Here, then, is man, this moth of time, this dupe of brevity and numbered hours, this travesty of waste and sterile breath. Yet if the gods could come here to a desolate, deserted earth where only the ruin of man's cities remained, where only a few marks and carvings of his hand were legible upon his broken tablets, where only a wheel lay rusting in the desert sand, a cry would burst out of their hearts and they would say: "He lived, and he was here!"

Behold his works:

He needed speech to ask for bread—and he had Christ! He needed songs to sing in battle—and he had Homer! He needed words to curse his enemies—and he had Dante, he had Voltaire, he had Swift! He needed cloth to cover up his hairless, puny flesh against the seasons—and he wove the robes of Solomon, he made the garments of great kings, he made the samite for the young knights! He needed walls and a roof to shelter him—and he made Blois! He needed a temple to propitiate his God—and he made Chartres and Fountains Abbey! He was born to creep upon the earth—and he made great wheels, he sent great engines thundering down the rails, he launched great wings into the air, he put great ships upon the angry sea!

Plagues wasted him, and cruel wars destroyed his strongest sons, but fire, flood, and famine could not quench him. No, nor the inexorable grave—his sons leaped shouting from his dying loins. The shaggy bison with his thews of thunder died upon the plains; the fabled mammoths of the unrecorded ages are vast scaffoldings of dry, insensate loam; the panthers have learned caution and move carefully among tall grasses to the water hole; and man lives on amid the senseless nihilism of the universe.

For there is one belief, one faith, that is man's glory, his triumph, his immortality —and that is his belief in life. Man loves life, and, loving life, hates death, and because of this he is great, he is glorious, he is beautiful, and his beauty is everlasting.

He lives below the senseless stars and writes his meanings in them. He lives in fear, in toil, in agony, and in unending tumult, but if the blood foamed bubbling from his wounded lungs at every breath he drew, he would still love life more dearly than an end of breathing. Dying, his eyes burn beautifully, and the old hunger shines more fiercely in them—he has endured all the hard and purposeless suffering, and still he wants to live.

Thus it is impossible to scorn this creature. For out of his strong belief in life, this puny man made love. At his best, he *is* love. Without him there can be no love, no hunger, no desire.

So this is man—the worst and best of him—this frail and petty thing who lives his day and dies like all the other animals, and is forgotten. And yet, he is immortal, too, for both the good and evil that he does live after him. Why, then, should any living man ally himself with death, and, in his greed and blindness, batten on his brother's blood?

James T. Farrell

1904

FARRELL was born on Chicago's South Side and attended parochial schools there; later he took courses at De Paul University and the University of Chicago. He began writing as a student and in 1932 published his first novel, *Young Lonigan, A Boyhood in Chicago Streets*. This and succeeding novels formed the trilogy *Studs Lonigan* (1935), which established Farrell's reputation. His later novels include *A World I Never Made* (1936) and *Father and Son* (1940). The collected *Short Stories of James T. Farrell* appeared in 1937. His critical essays appear in *The League of Frightened Philistines* (1945) and other volumes. [See J. W. Beach, *American Fiction 1920-1940* (New York, 1941).]

THE ORATORY CONTEST

[1937]

I

FACING the bathroom mirror, Gerry O'Dell practiced for the contest, and he imagined the thunder of applause that would greet him at the conclusion of his oration. His mother called him, and he said that he was coming. He met his dad in the hallway, and Mr. O'Dell looked at his narrow-faced, small, sixteen-year-old son with a mingling of pride and humility.

"Well, Gerry, how do you feel? The old soupbone in your throat loosened up?" the father asked.

"Yes, Dad," Gerry nervously answered.

"Gerry, your mother and I are mighty proud of you, and we'll be giving you all the . . . the moral support we can tonight. Don't get worried because you're speaking in public, or because of the size of the crowd. Ah, anyway, Gerry, oratory is certainly a great gift for a boy to have," the father said, putting his hairy hands into his blue trouser pockets and rocking backward on his heels. "Gerry, if a man has the makings of a great orator in him, he need have no fears of getting ahead in life."

"George, don't be making the boy nervous. Gerald, supper is ready," the mother called.

"Martha, I was only explaining to him," the father apologetically explained.

"Father, you mustn't be saying any more now," she said in a nagging tone.

The father followed his son into the dining room, and he seemed to have been hurt as the family sat down for supper.

"Well, Sis, how did school go today?" the father asked, cutting into his lamb chop and looking at his pig-tailed daughter while Gerry talked with his brother, Michael, about Sister Sylvester, the eighth-grade teacher at Saint Catherine's grammar school.

"I was spelled down," Ellen said.

"What word did you miss, Sis?"

"Interest, Daddy."

"Maybe you'll do better the next time."

"But, gee, Daddy, I tried so hard. I could have cried right then and there like a baby," she said.

"That's just too bad! Too bad that you couldn't show off before Georgie Schaeffer," Michael said, making a wry face at his sister.

"Is that so!"

Mrs. O'Dell told her younger children to stop arguing and eat their supper. It was no time to be disturbing Gerald. The family ate, and the father cast continued glances of approval and pride at his oldest son.

"Gerry, where did you learn the things you're talking about tonight? You must certainly have studied a lot to learn them," the father said.

"I read the Constitution, and the editorials on it that have been printed recently in *The Chicago Questioner*. And then, of course, there was my civics course, and Father Robert gave me lots of suggestions, and he spent an awful lot of time helping me rehearse my speech. He helped me get it written and to get my delivery set in my mind," Gerry said.

"Gerry, when I heard you give your oration at the semi-finals, I was a mighty proud father, I was."

Gerry smiled self-consciously.

"After you finish high school, you'll have to go to college. I want you to get a fine education."

"But, Dad, how can I?" Gerry said, looking hopefully at his father.

"You ought to be able to get a job and study law in the evenings downtown at Saint Vincent's."

"That's what I'll have to do," Gerry said disconsolately.

"Of course, something might turn up," the father said.

"George, that is what you've been saying for twenty years," Mrs. O'Dell said sarcastically.

"Martha, you can't say that I ain't tried. I've provided for you and the children as well as I could, and I always brought my pay home to you untouched. I don't see where you have any right to complain when a man has always done his best."

"George, I'm not complaining. It's just that after all these years I'm tired out. Look how long we're married, and we don't even own our own home."

"We will yet. I mean it! I swear we will! A fellow at the barns was telling me yesterday that he can get a ticket on the English Sweepstakes. Now suppose I should win that! One hundred thousand dollars! Say, we'd be rolling in wealth. You know, Martha, you never can tell what will happen in life. Now last year, I remember reading in the papers where some foreigner, a cook in some New York hotel, won over a hundred thousand dollars on a sweepstakes ticket."

"And you're not that cook. You've been talking yourself blue in the face about winning in baseball pools almost as long as I can remember. And what have you won? What?"

"Didn't I win twenty-five dollars on a baseball pool last year?"

"Yes, and how much did you spend buying tickets during the year?"

"Gee, give a man a chance."

"Give you a chance! That's all I've ever given you."

"Have it your way then. But three years ago Tom Foley, who runs a car on Western Avenue, won five hundred, didn't he? If he can have luck like that, what's to stop me from having it?"

"You're not Tom Foley."

"Aw, Ma!" O'Dell whined, causing Gerry to glance at him quickly in disgust.

"I can't be listening to all your nonsense, George. I got to see that the boys get ready for tonight," she said when they had finished their tea and dessert.

"Gee, Ma, are you sure you can't come?" Gerry said as she arose from the table, a small, broad, fat-cheeked woman in her forties whose stomach was swollen out.

"Gerald, your mother isn't feeling up to snuff this evening. But I'll be thinking of you, speaking, and saying a little prayer to the Lord that you'll win the prize. Your mother knows that her son is going to take the prize, and she'll be just as happy whether she hears you or not, just as long as you telephone me the minute you get out of the hall," the mother said.

"Ma, can I go?" the sister asked.

"You got to stay home with your mother," the father said while Gerry kissed Mrs. O'Dell goodbye and left.

II

Mrs. O'Dell sat knitting baby socks in the dining room, and the daughter was bent over her school books at the table. The father entered the cramped room and asked his wife for some money. She slowly arose and waddled to their bedroom. She drew a two-dollar bill from a large leather pocketbook and handed it to him.

"George, I get spells. I'm afraid," she said.

"Don't worry, Martha. Gerry is a chip off the old block, and he has the makings of a fine orator. Why, he already orates better than a lot of lawyers and politicians I've heard," he said.

"It's not that, George. I'm too old now and this one is going to be a harder ordeal than when I was younger and had the others. Oh, George, I'm afraid! I can't bear to think of leaving you and the children without their mother."

Worried, he gently patted her back, ten-derly caressed her unkempt black hair.

"I feel as if I can't carry the load inside of me. And my back gets so sore. I had a dream last night, and it's a premonition. I fear I shan't be pulling through. Oh, George, hold me, kiss me like you used to a long time ago! I can't bear it, the thought of dying and leaving you with an infant baby."

She sobbed in his arms. Holding her, he felt as if paralyzed. He sensed in her the mystery of woman which enabled them to bring forth a man's child. He was filled with respect, awed into speechlessness. He kissed her, clasped her tightly, his feelings reverential. He thought of how they were going along now, and of how they were past knowing and feeling again what they had known and felt in those first burning days of their marriage. Now it was just having sympathy with each other, being used to one another, having their family, their duties, and the obligations which they had to meet together, the feeling of liking, more than loving, each other, and wanting to be proud of their kids. He kissed her again.

Michael called his dad from the doorway. The parents blushed with embarrassment. They turned their heads aside. The father gruffly told his son that he was coming. He kissed his wife a final goodbye.

III

It was a muggy, misty March evening. Walking to the street-car line with his son, O'Dell turned memories of other times over and over in his mind. He remembered his courtship and the days when he was younger and had worked nights, and of how at this time, on this kind of a night, he would be driving his car along Ashland Avenue. He wished that it were still those days and that he were young instead of a motorman rapidly getting old as his family was beginning to grow up. It was strange now to think of himself in other days, to think of what he had been, to realize how he had not at all known what life had in store for himself and his young bride. And now they both knew. And just to think that there had been a time when this boy, Michael, beside him had not been born, and neither had Gerry. Gerry had once been in his mother's womb just as the latest newcomer was at this very moment. He remembered the coming of his three children, Martha's shrieks and agonies, his own apprehensions and worries, the helpless feeling that had come over him, the drowsy tiredness on Martha's face after each delivery. He was afraid for it to happen all over again, afraid that this new one was going to mean trouble. *Death!* He wished that it were over with. Yes, and he wished that he were a young motorman again, instead of being pretty close on toward the declining years of middle age. He shook his head wistfully, thinking of how now, for years, day after day, he had driven street-cars. And he had been driving them before the boy at his side was born, and even before Gerry had been on the way. Gerry had turned out fine, but not just exactly what he had imagined Gerry would be. Ah, nothing in life turned out just as a man imagined that it would turn out. And this new one? When it would be Gerry's age, he and Martha, if the Lord spared them both, they would be old. He trembled at the thought of this new one, and it turned his mind to thoughts of the years, of death, the end of them both.

"Mickey, you always want to be good to your mother. Help her all you can while you've got her, because you'll never realize how much she means to you until she's gone," he said.

"Yes, Dad," the boy dutifully replied, the father's words merely giving him the feeling that the old man was just preaching a little in order to hear himself talk.

"You won't have her with you always, you know."

They boarded a street-car and stood on the rear platform talking with the conductor who was a friend of Mr. O'Dell's.

O'Dell told his friend where they were going and why. The conductor told O'Dell that one of his girls was a smart one like that, too, and she had just won a prize button in school for writing. But anyway, that girl of his, she was a great kid, and a smart one, too. Then they had to get off at Sixty-third Street and change for an eastbound car.

IV

O'Dell became increasingly timid as the car approached the school auditorium of Mary Our Mother. He tried to force a feeling of reassurance upon himself, thinking that he was just as good as any man, telling himself that he was a free-born American who earned his living by honest work. He had just as much right as any man to come to this contest and hear his own boy whom he was educating out of his hard-earned money. He was an honest man, and work was honorable, and what if he was a motorman and some of the fathers of Gerry's classmates were higher up on the ladder than he? No, there was no need of his being ashamed. America was a democratic country. Still, he was shy. He knew that he would feel out of place. But he was proud of his son, and he knew that Gerry was going to win out over the sons of richer fathers, and . . . he felt that he just wouldn't be in place, and that maybe he shouldn't have come.

And he realized that Gerry, instead of waiting for him and Michael, had gone ahead. Gerry, he suddenly felt, was ashamed of him. He argued with himself that the boy had had to get there early, and that, anyway, he had been nervous about the contest and restless, like a colt before the start of a race. But still, no, he could not rid his mind of that thought.

He noticed other people on the sidewalk, walking in the same direction as he, and he heard them talking. Some of them sounded like parents, and he was sure that many of them must be the fathers and mothers of boys who went to Mary Our

Mother. Did any of them, he wondered, have thoughts such as he? Well, before this evening was over they were all going to know about Gerald O'Dell.

And at home, there was Martha, her body big and swollen. He wished that she had come along. And she was at home, knitting away. He was responsible for her condition, and if he had curbed himself, well, they wouldn't be having this worry and this danger, and all the expense and sacrifice that it would involve, and she would be at his side, and they would both be so proud and happy, hearing Gerry win with his oration. How good it would be to have Martha at his side, both of them hearing the whole auditorium applaud her boy, her own flesh and blood. And she would not be granted this pleasure. He could just see her at home, knitting, silent, afraid. And she was going to be hurt, and this new child was going to be, maybe, so hard at her age, and oh, God forbid that she should die.

In front of the auditorium, he saw boys of varying ages, some only a year or so older than his Michael, other lads of seventeen and eighteen in long pants. He looked about to see if Gerry were among them, but he wasn't. He would like to tell them who he was, the father of Gerry O'Dell.

"Mike, here we are," he said in an attempt to be whimsical.

He handed two complimentary tickets to the lad collecting them at the door, and in a humble mood he followed the usher to seats in the center of the auditorium. He looked shyly about the lighted hall, seeing a confusion of strange faces, the people moving down the aisles to seats, and he was excited and expectant. He wanted it to begin. He glanced up toward the stage, with the stand and a row of chairs in front of the drawn red curtain. The boys, judges and the honored guests, including a number of priests, some of whom might be Gerry's teachers, would all sit in those chairs. And again he felt out of place, humbly so. He felt that in the auditorium there must be the fathers of many of

Gerry's classmates, men who had gone so much further in the world than he had, men who could afford to send their sons to good colleges.

He remembered the sight of the lads outside, and it caused him to think of how Gerry must have an entire life closed out to his father and mother, a life they could never get their little fingers on. He glanced sidewise at Michael, who was awkwardly twisting in his seat and looking about at faces with a boy's alive and curious eyes. And what did he see? What? Michael, too, and the girl, they had their lives that were closed to their father and mother, and as they grew older they would both drift further and further away.

"Like it, Mickey?" he asked, wanting to get close to his son, to be like a pal with him.

Michael smiled, muttered an absorbed uhuh.

"Some day you'll be going to the school here, too, and maybe, like Gerry, you'll be winning oratorical contests and prizes."

"I'd rather be on the football team."

"Maybe you can do both."

Michael smiled frankly, and the father suddenly found his mood dissipating under the smile. He did not feel himself to be such a stranger to Michael.

V

He was conscious of the movement of people, priests in the rear, the hall filling up, and he guessed that it was going to start. Suddenly the orchestra began a scratchy prelude, and O'Dell told himself that it must be fine music. Like those around him, he sat quiet, a little hushed. Glad, too, that it was starting. He waited, entertained but anxious, through the elocution contests, when first-year students recited pieces. The junior contest followed, and four boys delivered famous orations. O'Dell thought that the tall boy who delivered a speech of Senator Hoar's defending the retention of the Philippine Islands, had been the best. All of them had been good, but his boy would be better. And that was what he was waiting for.

He heard more music, idly reflecting that the priests here at Mary Our Mother must be giving the boys a good education. Anxiety was working within him like a pump. Right after the music Gerry would speak. He gripped and clasped his hands. Michael stirred. He tapped him, whispering to be quiet and to act well-mannered. The music, carried through by violins, seemed like the distant sounds of a waterfall, and they lulled within him. Dreamily he visualized Gerry speaking, imagined the lad's future as a great lawyer, and he thought of how boys in oratorical contests such as this one would, in years to come, be delivering the famous speeches and orations of Senator Gerald O'Dell. Gerald O'Dell, his son, the boy whose education had cost him sacrifices.

And now Gerry, small and freckled, was on the platform. He seemed so calm, as if there was not a worry in his head. He stood there, straight, dignified, and, ah, but wouldn't he be a pride to his father in the years to come. He was speaking. O'Dell leaned forward, listening attentively as his son's deep and full voice carried down the auditorium.

So the first step is, what is the Constitution?

O'Dell was in a spell, completely under the sway of his son's words, and he nodded his head as Gerry's voice rose in the final introductory statement which suggested that the United States and the Constitution are inseparable, and that without one there could not be the other.

And to all of us who are true Americans, our Constitution is sacred, the creed of those rights which are guaranteed to every one of us as an enduring pledge of our liberties.

Gerry spoke without halt, retaining not only the absorbed attention of his father but also of nearly everyone in the auditorium. He continued, declaiming that the defense of the Constitution, and of the principles which it embodied, was a sacred duty to be held inviolable, and that he who

did not, nor would not, uphold these principles did not deserve to be called an American. He added that he who holds public office and willingly betrays his trust cannot be called an American. But in his talk he was not primarily interested in such men, even though they wantonly betrayed their public trust. He was concerned with something more vital, the betrayal of the fundamental principles on which the Constitution was founded, that of state's rights, individual liberty. And men, men in public affairs, were, because of ignorance or perversity or even malice, seeking to destroy that principle by advocating the passage of a Federal Maternity Act and a law establishing a Federal Educational Department. These men wanted to abolish child labor by an act of Congress, even though the Constitution did not grant this prerogative to Congress.

O'Dell smiled when the boy quoted the late Champ Clark.

If the groups seeking Federal assistance would put their burdens on the state legislatures where they belong, Congress would have time for the work which, under the Constitution, belongs to Congress.

Continuing, Gerry referred to this tendency toward centralization, seeking to prove that it was unjustified. And then, with cleanly contrived gestures and a rising voice, he concluded:

Should we allow our rights to be taken from us? No! Wherever this tendency to centralization shows its serpentine head, we shall fight it, because it is a menace to us, to everyone who is a liberty-loving American, and we must fight this menace. And defending our liberties, we shall take a slogan from some recent words of a Cabinet member, Herbert Hoover: "It is time to decentralize." Our forefathers, Washington, Jefferson, and Madison, fought to give us our rights. Shall we let them be stripped away from us? Never! We will defend our rights. We will raise our voices until we are heard and our voices resound. Yes, we will even shout: It is time to decentralize.

Gerry O'Dell bowed to the audience. He turned and walked to his place among the others on the stage, while the applause thundered. The father clapped himself weary, restraining strong impulses to shout and stamp his feet. Tears welled in his eyes. He smiled with a simple and child-like joy. Unable to check himself, he turned to the man on his left and said:

"That's my boy."

"Smart lad."

The remaining speeches in the senior oratorical contest seemed dull and uninteresting to him. His boy had it all over these other lads. And he felt himself justified in these impressions when the judges announced their decision, and amid a second strong burst of clapping Gerald O'Dell was announced the winner of the gold medal in the Senior Oratorical Contest. O'Dell rushed out to a drugstore to telephone the news to Martha. Then he and Michael went back. The tag end of the crowd was filtering out. Boys were coming out in groups, standing, talking, dispers-ing with the crowd. He searched for Gerry. Gerry would certainly have waited. A boy came out. It was Gerry. No! He searched again. Gerry must be inside, being congratulated. He went in, but found the stage empty. Gerry must have gone. He told himself that Gerry had known that his father would wait to see him, congratulate him, buy him a treat, and that then they would go home together. And Gerry had not waited. He still looked anxiously about at the disappearing faces. Where was he? He asked a boy in a lingering group of students if any of them had seen Gerald O'Dell. They hadn't. He said that he was Gerald's father. They said Gerald had spoken well and deserved his victory. He stood with Michael. Only a few scattered groups remained in front of the hall. Feeling blank, he told himself, yes, Gerry had gone. He solemnly led Michael away, both of them silent. He asked himself why Gerry hadn't waited, and he knew the answer to his question.

Katherine Anne Porter

1894

MISS PORTER was born in Texas and attended convent schools in the South. She has lived in France, Mexico, and New York City, but has spent most of her life in the southern United States. Her stories published in the 1920's were collected in 1930 in the volume *Flowering Judas*. Subsequent collections include *Pale Horse, Pale Rider* (1939) and *The Leaning Tower* (1944).

THE JILTING OF GRANNY WEATHERALL

[1930]

SHE flicked her wrist neatly out of Doctor Harry's pudgy careful fingers and pulled the sheet up to her chin. The brat ought to be in knee breeches. Doctoring around the country with spectacles on his nose! "Get along now, take your school-books and go. There's nothing wrong with me."

Doctor Harry spread a warm paw like

a cushion on her forehead where the forked green vein danced and made her eyelids twitch. "Now, now, be a good girl, and we'll have you up in no time."

"That's no way to speak to a woman nearly eighty years old just because she's down. I'd have you respect your elders, young man."

"Well, Missy, excuse me." Doctor Harry patted her cheek. "But I've got to warn you, haven't I? You're a marvel, but you must be careful or you're going to be good and sorry."

"Don't tell me what I'm going to be. I'm on my feet now, morally speaking. It's Cornelia. I had to go to bed to get rid of her."

Her bones felt loose, and floated around in her skin, and Doctor Harry floated like a balloon around the foot of the bed. He floated and pulled down his waistcoat and swung his glasses on a cord. "Well, stay where you are, it certainly can't hurt you."

"Get along and doctor your sick," said Granny Weatherall. "Leave a well woman alone. I'll call for you when I want you. . . . Where were you forty years ago when I pulled through milk-leg and double pneumonia? You weren't even born. Don't let Cornelia lead you on," she shouted, because Doctor Harry appeared to float up to the ceiling and out. "I pay my own bills, and I don't throw my money away on nonsense!"

She meant to wave good-by, but it was too much trouble. Her eyes closed of themselves, it was like a dark curtain drawn around the bed. The pillow rose and floated under her, pleasant as a hammock in a light wind. She listened to the leaves rustling outside the window. No, somebody was swishing newspapers: no, Cornelia and Doctor Harry were whispering together. She leaped broad awake, thinking they whispered in her ear.

"She was never like this, never like this!" "Well, what can we expect?" "Yes, eighty years old. . . ."

Well, and what if she was? She still had ears. It was like Cornelia to whisper around doors. She always kept things secret in such a public way. She was always being tactful and kind. Cornelia was dutiful; that was the trouble with her. Dutiful and good: "So good and dutiful," said Granny, "that I'd like to spank her." She saw herself spanking Cornelia and making a fine job of it.

"What'd you say, Mother?"

Granny felt her face tying up in hard knots.

"Can't a body think, I'd like to know?"

"I thought you might want something."

"I do. I want a lot of things. First off, go away and don't whisper."

She lay and drowsed, hoping in her sleep that the children would keep out and let her rest a minute. It had been a long day. Not that she was tired. It was always pleasant to snatch a minute now and then. There was always so much to be done, let me see: tomorrow.

Tomorrow was far away and there was nothing to trouble about. Things were finished somehow when the time came; thank God there was always a little margin over for peace: then a person could spread out the plan of life and tuck in the edges orderly. It was good to have everything clean and folded away, with the hair brushes and tonic bottles sitting straight on the white embroidered linen: the day started without fuss and the pantry shelves laid out with rows of jelly glasses and brown jugs and white stone-china jars with blue whirligigs and words painted on them: coffee, tea, sugar, ginger, cinnamon, all-spice: and the bronze clock with the lion on top nicely dusted off. The dust that lion could collect in twenty-four hours! The box in the attic with all those letters tied up, well, she'd have to go through that to-morrow. All those letters—George's letters and John's letters and her letters to them both—lying around for the children to find afterwards made her uneasy. Yes, that would be tomorrow's business. No use to let them know how silly she had been once.

While she was rummaging around she found death in her mind and it felt clammy and unfamiliar. She had spent so much time preparing for death there was no need for bringing it up again. Let it take care of itself now. When she was sixty she had felt very old, finished, and went around making farewell trips to see her children and grandchildren, with a secret in her mind: This is the very last of your mother, children! Then she made her will and came down with a long fever. That was all just a notion like a lot of other things, but it was lucky too, for she had once for all got over the idea of dying for a long time. Now she couldn't be worried. She hoped she had better sense now. Her father had lived to be one hundred and two years old and had drunk a noggin of strong hot toddy on his last birthday. He told the reporters it was his daily habit, and he owed his long life to that. He had made quite a scandal and was very pleased about it. She believed she'd just plague Cornelia a little.

"Cornelia! Cornelia!" No footsteps, but a sudden hand on her cheek. "Bless you, where have you been?"

"Here, mother."

"Well, Cornelia, I want a noggin of hot toddy."

"Are you cold, darling?"

"I'm chilly, Cornelia. Lying in bed stops the circulation. I must have told you that a thousand times."

Well, she could just hear Cornelia telling her husband that Mother was getting a little childish and they'd have to humor her. The thing that most annoyed her was that Cornelia thought she was deaf, dumb, and blind. Little hasty glances and tiny gestures tossed around her and over her head saying, "Don't cross her, let her have her way, she's eighty years old," and she sitting there as if she lived in a thin glass cage. Sometimes Granny almost made up her mind to pack up and move back to her own house where nobody could remind her every minute that she was old. Wait, wait, Cornelia, till your own children whisper behind your back!

In her day she had kept a better house and had got more work done. She wasn't too old yet for Lydia to be driving eighty miles for advice when one of the children jumped the track, and Jimmy still dropped in and talked things over: "Now, Mammy, you've a good business head, I want to know what you think of this? . . ." Old. Cornelia couldn't change the furniture around without asking. Little things, little things! They had been so sweet when they were little. Granny wished the old days were back again with the children young and everything to be done over. It had been a hard pull, but not too much for her. When she thought of all the food she had cooked, and all the clothes she had cut and sewed, and all the gardens she had made—well, the children showed it. There they were, made out of her, and they couldn't get away from that. Sometimes she wanted to see John again and point to them and say, Well, I didn't do so badly, did I? But that would have to wait. That was for tomorrow. She used to think of him as a man, but now all the children were older than their father, and he would be a child beside her if she saw him now. It seemed strange and there was something wrong in the idea. Why, he couldn't possibly recognize her. She had fenced in a hundred acres once, digging the post holes herself and clamping the wires with just a negro boy to help. That changed a woman. John would be looking for a young woman with the peaked Spanish comb in her hair and the painted fan. Digging post holes changed a woman. Riding country roads in the winter when women had their babies was another thing: sitting up nights with sick horses and sick negroes and sick children and hardly ever losing one. John, I hardly ever lost one of them! John would see that in a minute, that would be something he could understand, she wouldn't have to explain anything!

It made her feel like rolling up her sleeves and putting the whole place to rights again. No matter if Cornelia was determined to be everywhere at once, there were a great many things left undone on this place. She would start tomorrow and do them. It was good to be strong enough for everything, even if all you made melted and changed and slipped under your hands, so that by the time you finished you almost forgot what you were working for. What was it I set out to do? she asked herself intently, but she could not remember. A fog rose over the valley, she saw it marching across the creek swallowing the trees and moving up the hill like an army of ghosts. Soon it would be at the near edge of the orchard, and then it was time to go in and light the lamps. Come in, children, don't stay out in the night air.

Lighting the lamps had been beautiful. The children huddled up to her and breathed like little calves waiting at the bars in the twilight. Their eyes followed the match and watched the flame rise and settle in a blue curve, then they moved away from her. The lamp was lit, they didn't have to be scared and hang on to mother any more. Never, never, never more. God, for all my life I thank Thee. Without Thee, my God, I could never have done it. Hail, Mary, full of grace.

I want you to pick all the fruit this year and see that nothing is wasted. There's always someone who can use it. Don't let good things rot for want of using. You waste life when you waste good food. Don't let things get lost. It's bitter to lose things. Now, don't let me get to thinking, not when I am tired and taking a little nap before supper. . . .

The pillow rose about her shoulders and pressed against her heart and the memory was being squeezed out of it: oh, push down the pillow, somebody: it would smother her if she tried to hold it. Such a fresh breeze blowing and such a green day with no threats in it. But he had not come, just the same. What does a woman do when she has put on the white veil and set out the white cake for a man and he doesn't come? She tried to remember. No, I swear he never harmed me but in that. He never harmed me but in that . . . and

what if he did? There was the day, the day, but a whirl of dark smoke rose and covered it, crept up and over into the bright field where everything was planted so carefully in orderly rows. That was hell, she knew hell when she saw it. For sixty years she had prayed against remembering him and against losing her soul in the deep pit of hell, and now the two things were mingled in one and the thought of him was a smoky cloud from hell that moved and crept in her head when she had just got rid of Doctor Harry and was trying to rest a minute. Wounded vanity, Ellen, said a sharp voice in the top of her mind. Don't let your wounded vanity get the upper hand of you. Plenty of girls get jilted. You were jilted, weren't you? Then stand up to it. Her eyelids wavered and let in streamers of blue-gray light like tissue paper over her eyes. She must get up and pull the shades down or she'd never sleep. She was in bed again and the shades were not down. How could that happen? Better turn over, hide from the light, sleeping in the light gave you nightmares. "Mother, how do you feel now?" and a stinging wetness on her forehead. But I don't like having my face washed in cold water!

Hapsy? George? Lydia? Jimmy? No, Cornelia, and her features were swollen and full of little puddles. "They're coming, darling, they'll all be here soon." Go wash your face, child, you look funny.

Instead of obeying, Cornelia knelt down and put her head on the pillow. She seemed to be talking but there was no sound. "Well, are you tongue-tied? Whose birthday is it? Are you going to give a party?"

Cornelia's mouth moved urgently in strange shapes. "Don't do that, you bother me, daughter."

"Oh, no, Mother. Oh, no. . . ."

Nonsense. It was strange about children. They disputed your every word. "No what, Cornelia?"

"Here's Doctor Harry."

"I won't see that boy again. He just left five minutes ago."

"That was this morning, Mother. It's night now. Here's the nurse."

"This is Doctor Harry, Mrs. Weatherall. I never saw you look so young and happy!"

"Ah, I'll never be young again—but I'd be happy if they'd let me lie in peace and get rested."

She thought she spoke up loudly, but no one answered. A warm weight on her forehead, a warm bracelet on her wrist, and a breeze went on whispering, trying to tell her something. A shuffle of leaves in the everlasting hand of God, He blew on them and they danced and rattled. "Mother, don't mind, we're going to give you a little hypodermic." "Look here, daughter, how do ants get in this bed? I saw sugar ants yesterday." Did you send for Hapsy too?

It was Hapsy she really wanted. She had to go a long way back through a great many rooms to find Hapsy standing with a baby on her arm. She seemed to herself to be Hapsy also, and the baby on Hapsy's arm was Hapsy and himself and herself, all at once, and there was no surprise in the meeting. Then Hapsy melted from within and turned flimsy as gray gauze and the baby was a gauzy shadow, and Hapsy came up close and said, "I thought you'd never come," and looked at her very searchingly and said, "You haven't changed a bit!" They leaned forward to kiss, when Cornelia began whispering from a long way off, "Oh, is there anything you want to tell me? Is there anything I can do for you?"

Yes, she had changed her mind after sixty years and she would like to see George. I want you to find George. Find him and be sure to tell him I forgot him. I want him to know I had my husband just the same and my children and my house like any other woman. A good house too and a good husband that I loved and fine children out of him. Better than I hoped for even. Tell him I was given back everything he took away and more. Oh, no, oh, God, no, there was something else besides the house and the man and the

children. Oh, surely they were not all? What was it? Something not given back. . . . Her breath crowded down under her ribs and grew into a monstrous frightening shape with cutting edges; it bored up into her head, and the agony was unbelievable: Yes, John, get the Doctor now, no more talk, my time has come.

When this one was born it should be the last. The last. It should have been born first, for it was the one she had truly wanted. Everything came in good time. Nothing left out, left over. She was strong, in three days she would be as well as ever. Better. A woman needed milk in her to have her full health.

"Mother, do you hear me?"

"I've been telling you—"

"Mother, Father Connolly's here."

"I went to Holy Communion only last week. Tell him I'm not so sinful as all that."

"Father just wants to speak to you."

He could speak as much as he pleased. It was like him to drop in and inquire about her soul as if it were a teething baby, and then stay on for a cup of tea and a round of cards and gossip. He always had a funny story of some sort, usually about an Irishman who made his little mistakes and confessed them, and the point lay in some absurd thing he would blurt out in the confessional showing his struggles between native piety and original sin. Granny felt easy about her soul. Cornelia, where are your manners? Give Father Connolly a chair. She had her secret comfortable understanding with a few favorite saints who cleared a straight road to God for her. All as surely signed and sealed as the papers for the new Forty Acres. Forever . . . heirs and assigns forever. Since the day the wedding cake was not cut, but thrown out and wasted. The whole bottom dropped out of the world, and there she was blind and sweating with nothing under her feet and the walls falling away. His hand had caught her under the breast, she had not fallen, there was the freshly polished floor with the green rug on it, just as before. He had cursed like a sailor's parrot and said, "I'll kill him for you." Don't lay a hand on him, for my sake leave something to God. "Now, Ellen, you must believe what I tell you. . . ."

So there was nothing, nothing to worry about any more, except sometimes in the night one of the children screamed in a nightmare, and they both hustled out shaking and hunting for the matches and calling, "There, wait a minute, here we are!" John, get the doctor now, Hapsy's time has come. But there was Hapsy standing by the bed in a white cap. "Cornelia, tell Hapsy to take off her cap. I can't see her plain."

Her eyes opened very wide and the room stood out like a picture she had seen somewhere. Dark colors with the shadows rising towards the ceiling in long angles. The tall black dresser gleamed with nothing on it but John's picture, enlarged from a little one, with John's eyes very black when they should have been blue. You never saw him, so how do you know how he looked? But the man insisted the copy was perfect, it was very rich and handsome. For a picture, yes, but it's not my husband. The table by the bed had a linen cover and a candle and a crucifix. The light was blue from Cornelia's silk lampshades. No sort of light at all, just frippery. You had to live forty years with kerosene lamps to appreciate honest electricity. She felt very strong and she saw Doctor Harry with a rosy nimbus around him.

"You look like a saint, Doctor Harry, and I vow that's as near as you'll ever come to it."

"She's saying something."

"I heard you, Cornelia. What's all this carrying-on?"

"Father Connolly's saying—"

Cornelia's voice staggered and bumped like a cart in a bad road. It rounded corners and turned back again and arrived nowhere. Granny stepped up in the cart very lightly and reached for the reins, but a man sat beside her and she knew him by his hands, driving the cart. She did not look in his face, for she knew without seeing, but looked instead down the road where the trees leaned over and bowed to each other and a thousand birds were singing a Mass. She felt like singing too, but she put her hand in the bosom of her dress and pulled out a rosary, and Father Connolly murmured Latin in a very solemn voice and tickled her feet. My God, will you stop that nonsense? I'm a married woman. What if he did run away and leave me to face the priest by myself? I found another a whole world better. I wouldn't have exchanged my husband for anybody except St. Michael himself, and you may tell him that for me with a thank you in the bargain.

Light flashed on her closed eyelids, and a deep roaring shook her. Cornelia, is that lightning? I hear thunder. There's going to be a storm. Close all the windows. Call the children in. . . . "Mother, here we are, all of us." "Is that you, Hapsy?" "Oh, no, I'm Lydia. We drove as fast as we could." Their faces drifted above her, drifted away. The rosary fell out of her hands and Lydia put it back. Jimmy tried to help, their hands fumbled together, and Granny closed two fingers around Jimmy's thumb. Beads wouldn't do, it must be something alive. She was so amazed her thoughts ran round and round. So, my dear Lord, this is my death and I wasn't even thinking about it. My children have come to see me die. But I can't, it's not time. Oh, I always hated surprises. I wanted to give Cornelia the amethyst set —Cornelia, you're to have the amethyst set, but Hapsy's to wear it when she wants, and, Doctor Harry, do shut up. Nobody sent for you. Oh, my dear Lord, do wait a minute. I meant to do something about the Forty Acres, Jimmy doesn't need it and Lydia will later on, with that worthless husband of hers. I meant to finish the altar cloth and send six bottles of wine to Sister Borgia for her dyspepsia. I want to send six bottles of wine to Sister Borgia, Father Connolly, now don't let me forget.

Cornelia's voice made short turns and tilted over and crashed. "Oh, Mother, oh, Mother, oh, Mother. . . ."

"I'm not going, Cornelia. I'm taken by surprise. I can't go."

You'll see Hapsy again. What about her? "I thought you'd never come." Granny made a long journey outward, looking for Hapsy. What if I don't find her? What then? Her heart sank down and down, there was no bottom to death, she couldn't come to the end of it. The blue light from Cornelia's lampshade drew into a tiny point in the center of her brain, it flickered and winked like an eye, quietly it fluttered and dwindled. Granny lay curled down within herself, amazed and watchful, staring at the point of light that was herself; her body was now only a deeper mass of shadow in an endless darkness and this darkness would curl around the light and swallow it up. God, give a sign!

For the second time there was no sign. Again no bridegroom and the priest in the house. She could not remember any other sorrow because this grief wiped them all away. Oh, no, there's nothing more cruel than this—I'll never forgive it. She stretched herself with a deep breath and blew out the light.

Cornelia's voice made short turns and tilted over and crashed. "Oh, Mother, oh, Mother, oh, Mother. . . ."

"I'm not going, Cornelia. I'm taken by surprise. I can't go."

You'll see Hapsy again. What about her? "I thought you'd never come." Granny made a long journey outward, looking for Hapsy. What if I don't find her? What then? Her heart sank down, she could not come to the bottom of it. The blue light from Cornelia's lampshade drew into a tiny point in the center of her brain, it flickered and winked like an eye, quietly it fluttered and

and dwindled. Granny lay curled down within herself, amazed and watchful, staring at the point of light that was herself; her body was now only a deeper mass of shadow in an endless darkness and this darkness would curl around the light and swallow it up. God, give a sign!

For the second time there was no sign. Again no bridegroom and the priest in the house. She could not remember any other sorrow because this grief wiped them all away. Oh, no, there's nothing more cruel than this—I'll never forgive it. She stretched herself with a deep breath and blew out the light.

American Literature 1900 to the Present

III
DIRECTIONS IN POETRY

1869 ∾ *Edwin Arlington Robinson* ∾ 1935

EDWIN ARLINGTON ROBINSON was born at the village of Head Tide, Maine, but in his infancy his parents moved to Gardiner in the same state, where he spent his boyhood and attended high school. His father, a retired shipbuilder and merchant, encouraged his early interest in poetry. He went to Harvard in 1891, but left after two years because of his father's death and his own poverty. He remained for two years at home, working chiefly at his poetry. In 1896 he published at his own expense the three hundred paper-bound copies of his first book, *The Torrent and The Night Before,* having failed to find another publisher. In that same year his mother died, and he went to New York to live. Thereafter he returned to Gardiner only three times: for the funerals of his two brothers, and to receive an honorary degree from Bowdoin College in 1925.

In New York Robinson supported himself precariously for several years, resorting at times to labor for which his body was ill-suited. In 1905 Theodore Roosevelt became interested in Robinson's work, and through Roosevelt's influence he obtained a position in the New York Custom House which he held until 1910. After 1911 he did most of his writing at the McDowell colony at Peterborough, New Hampshire, where he was a regular and favored guest.

Robinson's eminence among contemporary American poets was not generally recognized until the appearance of his *Collected Poems* in 1922. Of his later books *Tristram* (1927) was conspicuously successful. A complete edition of the *Collected Poems* was published in 1937.

[Robinson and his work have been discussed in Herman Hagedorn's *Edwin Arlington Robinson* (New York, 1938), E. Kaplan's *Philosophy in the Poetry of Edwin Arlington Robinson* (New York, 1940), Emery Neff's *Edwin Arlington Robinson* (New York, 1938), and numerous other books.]

JOHN EVERELDOWN
[1896]

"Where are you going to-night, to-night,—
　Where are you going, John Evereldown?
There's never the sign of a star in sight,
　Nor a lamp that's nearer than Tilbury
　　Town.
Why do you stare as a dead man might? 5
Where are you pointing away from the
　light?

And where are you going to-night, to-night,—
　Where are you going, John Evereldown?"

"Right through the forest, where none can
　see,
　There's where I'm going, to Tilbury
　　Town.
The men are asleep,—or awake, may be,— 10

But the women are calling John Everel-
    down.
Ever and ever they call for me,
And while they call can a man be free?
So right through the forest, where none can
    see,
    That's where I'm going, to Tilbury
      Town."   15

"But why are you going so late, so late,—
    Why are you going, John Evereldown?
Though the road be smooth and the way be
    straight,
    There are two long leagues to Tilbury
      Town.   20
Come in by the fire, old man, and wait!
Why do you chatter out there by the gate?
And why are you going so late, so late,—
    Why are you going, John Evereldown?"

"I follow the women wherever they
    call,—   25
    That's why I'm going to Tilbury Town.
God knows if I pray to be done with it all,
    But God is no friend to John Everel-
      down.
So the clouds may come and the rain may
    fall,
The shadows may creep and the dead men
    crawl,—   30
But I follow the women wherever they call,
    And that's why I'm going to Tilbury
      Town."

LUKE HAVERGAL
[1896]

Go to the western gate, Luke Havergal,
There where the vines cling crimson on the
    wall,
And in the twilight wait for what will
    come.
The leaves will whisper there of her, and
    some,
Like flying words, will strike you as they
    fall;   5
But go, and if you listen she will call.
Go to the western gate, Luke Havergal—
Luke Havergal.

No, there is not a dawn in eastern skies
To rift the fiery night that's in your
    eyes;   10
But there, where western glooms are gath-
    ering,
The dark will end the dark, if anything:
God slays Himself with every leaf that flies,
And hell is more than half of paradise.
No, there is not a dawn in eastern
    skies—   15
In eastern skies.

Out of a grave I come to tell you this,
Out of a grave I come to quench the kiss
That flames upon your forehead with a
    glow
That blinds you to the way that you must
    go.   20
Yes, there is yet one way to where she is,
Bitter, but one that faith may never miss.
Out of a grave I come to tell you this—
To tell you this.

There is the western gate, Luke
    Havergal,   25
There are the crimson leaves upon the wall.
Go, for the winds are tearing them away,—
Nor think to riddle the dead words they
    say,
Nor any more to feel them as they fall;
But go, and if you trust her she will call. 30
There is the western gate, Luke Havergal—
Luke Havergal.

RICHARD CORY
[1897]

Whenever Richard Cory went down town,
We people on the pavement looked at him:
He was a gentleman from sole to crown,
Clean favored, and imperially slim.

And he was always quietly arrayed,   5
And he was always human when he talked;
But still he fluttered pulses when he said,
'Good-morning,' and he glittered when he
    walked.

And he was rich—yes, richer than a king—
And admirably schooled in every grace: 10

In fine, we thought that he was everything
To make us wish that we were in his place.

So on we worked, and waited for the light,
And went without the meat, and cursed the
　　　　bread;
And Richard Cory, one calm summer
　　　　night,　　　　　　　　　　　　　15
Went home and put a bullet through his
　　　　head.

THE HOUSE ON THE HILL
[1896]

They are all gone away,
　　The House is shut and still,
There is nothing more to say.

Through broken walls and gray
　　The winds blow bleak and shrill:　5
They are all gone away.

Nor is there one to-day
　　To speak them good or ill:
There is nothing more to say.

Why is it then we stray　　　　　　10
　　Around that sunken sill?
They are all gone away,

And our poor fancy-play
　　For them is wasted skill:
There is nothing more to say.　　　15

There is ruin and decay
　　In the House on the Hill:
They are all gone away,
There is nothing more to say.

AN OLD STORY
[1896]

Strange that I did not know him then,
　　That friend of mine!
I did not even show him then
　　One friendly sign;

But cursed him for the ways he had　5
　　To make me see
My envy of the praise he had
　　For praising me.

I would have rid the earth of him
　　Once, in my pride. . . . .　　　10
I never knew the worth of him
　　Until he died.

SONNET
[1897]

Oh for a poet—for a beacon bright
To rift this changeless glimmer of dead
　　　　gray;
To spirit back the Muses, long astray,
And flush Parnassus with a newer light;
To put these little sonnet-men to flight　5
Who fashion, in a shrewd mechanic way,
Songs without souls, that flicker for a day,
To vanish in irrevocable night.

What does it mean, this barren age of ours?
Here are the men, the women, and the
　　　　flowers,　　　　　　　　　　　10
The seasons, and the sunset, as before.
What does it mean? Shall there not one
　　　　arise
To wrench one banner from the western
　　　　skies,
And mark it with his name forevermore?

THE MASTER
(LINCOLN)
[1910 (1909)]

A flying word from here and there
Had sown the name at which we sneered,
But soon the name was everywhere,
To be reviled and then revered:
A presence to be loved and feared,　　5
We cannot hide it, or deny
That we, the gentlemen who jeered,
May be forgotten by and by.

He came when days were perilous
And hearts of men were sore beguiled;　10
And having made his note of us,
He pondered and was reconciled.

Was ever master yet so mild
As he, and so untamable?
We doubted, even when he smiled,   15
Not knowing what he knew so well.

He knew that undeceiving fate
Would shame us whom he served unsought;
He knew that he must wince and wait—
The jest of those for whom he fought; 20
He knew devoutly what he thought
Of us and of our ridicule;
He knew that we must all be taught
Like little children in a school.

We gave a glamour to the task   25
That he encountered and saw through,
But little of us did he ask,
And little did we ever do.
And what appears if we review
The season when we railed and chaffed? 30
It is the face of one who knew
That we were learning while we laughed.

The face that in our vision feels
Again the venom that we flung,
Transfigured to the world reveals   35
The vigilance to which we clung.
Shrewd, hallowed, harassed, and among
The mysteries that are untold,
The face we see was never young
Nor could it wholly have been old.   40

For he, to whom we had applied
Our shopman's test of age and worth,
Was elemental when he died,
As he was ancient at his birth:
The saddest among kings of earth,   45
Bowed with a galling crown, this man
Met rancor with a cryptic mirth,
Laconic—and Olympian.

The love, the grandeur, and the fame
Are bounded by the world alone;   50
The calm, the smouldering, and the flame
Of awful patience were his own:
With him they are forever flown
Past all our fond self-shadowings,
Wherewith we cumber the Unknown   55
As with inept, Icarian wings.

For we were not as other men:
'Twas ours to soar and his to see;
But we are coming down again,
And we shall come down pleasantly;   60
Nor shall we longer disagree
On what it is to be sublime,
But flourish in our perigee
And have one Titan at a time.

THE TOWN DOWN THE RIVER
[1910 (1908)]

I

Said the Watcher by the Way
To the young and the unladen,
To the boy and to the maiden,
"God be with you both to-day.
First your song came ringing,   5
Now you come, you two,—
Knowing naught of what you do,
Or of what your dreams are bringing.

"O you children who go singing
To the Town down the River,   10
Where the millions cringe and shiver,
Tell me what you know to-day;
Tell me how far you are going,
Tell me how you find your way.
O you children who go dreaming,   15
Tell me what you dream to-day."

"He is old and we have heard him,"
Said the boy then to the maiden;
"He is old and heavy laden
With a load we throw away.   20
Care may come to find us,
Age may lay us low;
Still, we seek the light we know,
And the dead we leave behind us.

"Did he think that he would blind us 25
Into such a small believing
As to live without achieving,
When the lights have led so far?
Let him watch or let him wither,—
Shall he tell us where we are?   30
We know best who go together,
Downward, onward, and so far."

II

Said the Watcher by the Way
To the fiery folk that hastened,
To the loud and the unchastened,   35
"You are strong, I see, to-day.
Strength and hope may lead you
To the journey's end,—
Each to be the other's friend
If the Town should fail to need you.   40

"And are ravens there to feed you
In the Town down the River,
Where the gift appalls the giver
And youth hardens day by day?
O you brave and you unshaken,   45
Are you truly on your way?
And are sirens in the River,
That you come so far to-day?"

"You are old, and we have listened,"
Said the voice of one who halted;   50
"You are sage and self-exalted,
But your way is not our way.
You that cannot aid us
Give us words to eat.
Be assured that they are sweet,   55
And that we are as God made us.

"Not in vain have you delayed us,
Though the River still be calling
Through the twilight that is falling
And the Town be still so far.   60
By the whirlwind of your wisdom
Leagues are lifted as leaves are;
But a king without a kingdom
Fails us, who have come so far."

III

Said the Watcher by the Way   65
To the slower folk who stumbled,
To the weak and the world-humbled,
"Tell me how you fare to-day.
Some with ardor shaken,
All with honor scarred,   70
Do you falter, finding hard
The far chance that you have taken?"

"You speak well of what you know not,"
Muttered one; and then a second:
"You have begged and you have
          beckoned,   75
But you see us on our way.
Who are you to scold us,
Knowing what we know?
Jeremiah, long ago,
Said as much as you have told us.   80

"As we are, then, you behold us:
Derelicts of all conditions,
Poets, rogues, and sick physicians,
Plodding forward from afar;
Forward now into the darkness   85
Where the men before us are;
Forward, onward, out of grayness,
To the light that shone so far."

IV

Said the Watcher by the Way
To some aged ones who lingered,   90
To the shrunken, the claw-fingered,
"So you come for me to-day."—
"Yes, to give you warning;
You are old," one said;
"You have old hairs on your head,   95
Fit for laurel, not for scorning.

"From the first of early morning
We have toiled along to find you;
We, as others, have maligned you,
But we need your scorn to-day.   100
By the light that we saw shining,
Let us not be lured alway;
Let us hear no River calling
When to-morrow is to-day."

"But your lanterns are unlighted   105
And the Town is far before you:
Let us hasten, I implore you,"
Said the Watcher by the Way.
"Long have I waited,
Longer have I known   110
That the Town would have its own,
And the call be for the fated."

"In the name of all created,
Let us hear no more, my brothers;
Are we older than all others?   115
Are the planets in our way?"—
"Hark," said one; "I hear the River,
Calling always, night and day."—
"Forward, then! The lights are shining,"
Said the Watcher by the Way.   120

"Or, do you at length awaken
To an antic retribution,
Goading to a new confusion
The drugged hopes of yesterday?
O you poor mad men that hobble,   125
Will you not return, or stay?
Do you trust, you broken people,
To a dawn without the day?"

EXIT
[1910]

For what we owe to other days,
Before we poisoned him with praise,
May we who shrank to find him weak
Remember that he cannot speak.

For envy that we may recall,   5
And for our faith before the fall,
May we who are alive be slow
To tell what we shall never know.

For penance he would not confess,
And for the fateful emptiness   10
Of early triumph undermined,
May we now venture to be kind.

UNCLE ANANIAS
[1910 (1905)]

His words were magic and his heart was
    true,
    And everywhere he wandered he was
    blessed.
Out of all ancient men my childhood knew
    I choose him and I mark him for the best.
Of all authoritative liars, too,   5
    I crown him loveliest.

How fondly I remember the delight
    That always glorified him in the spring;
The joyous courage and the benedight
    Profusion of his faith in everything!   10
He was a good old man, and it was right
    That he should have his fling.

And often, underneath the apple-trees,
    When we surprised him in the summer
    time,
With what superb magnificence and ease   15
    He sinned enough to make the day
    sublime!
And if he liked us there about his knees,
    Truly it was no crime.

All summer long we loved him for the same
    Perennial inspiration of his lies;   20
And when the russet wealth of autumn
    came,
    There flew but fairer visions to our
    eyes—
Multiple, tropical, winged with a feathery
    flame,
    Like birds of paradise.

So to the sheltered end of many a year   25
    He charmed the seasons out with
    pageantry
Wearing upon his forehead, with no fear,
    The laurel of approved iniquity.
And every child who knew him, far or near,
    Did love him faithfully.   30

ALMA MATER
[1910]

He knocked, and I beheld him at the door—
    A vision for the gods to verify.
"What battered ancientry is this,"
    thought I,
"And when, if ever, did we meet before?"
But ask him as I might, I got no more   5
For answer than a moaning and a cry:
Too late to parley, but in time to die,
He staggered, and lay shapeless on the
    floor.

When had I known him? And what brought
   him here?
Love, warning, malediction, hunger,
   fear?   10
Surely I never thwarted such as he?—
Again, what soiled obscurity was this:
Out of what scum, and up from what abyss,
Had they arrived—these rags of memory?

FOR A DEAD LADY
[1910 (1909)]

No more with overflowing light
Shall fill the eyes that now are faded,
Nor shall another's fringe with night
Their woman-hidden world as they did.
No more shall quiver down the days   5
The flowing wonder of her ways,
Whereof no language may requite
The shifting and the many-shaded.

The grace, divine, definitive,
Clings only as a faint forestalling;   10
The laugh that love could not forgive
Is hushed, and answers to no calling;
The forehead and the little ears
Have gone where Saturn keeps the years;
The breast where roses could not live   15
Has done with rising and with falling.

The beauty, shattered by the laws
That have creation in their keeping,
No longer trembles at applause,
Or over children that are sleeping;   20
And we who delve in beauty's lore
Know all that we have known before
Of what inexorable cause
Makes Time so vicious in his reaping.

TWO GARDENS IN LINNDALE
[1910]

Two brothers, Oakes and Oliver,
Two gentle men as ever were,
Would roam no longer, but abide
In Linndale, where their fathers died,
And each would be a gardener.   5

"Now first we fence the garden through,
With this for me and that for you,"
Said Oliver.—"Divine!" said Oakes,
"And I, while I raise artichokes,
Will do what I was born to do."   10

"But this is not the soil, you know,"
Said Oliver, "to make them grow:
The parent of us, who is dead,
Compassionately shook his head
Once on a time and told me so."   15

"I hear you, gentle Oliver,"
Said Oakes, "and in your character
I find as fair a thing indeed
As ever bloomed and ran to seed
Since Adam was a gardener.   20

"Still, whatsoever I find there,
Forgive me if I do not share
The knowing gloom that you take on
Of one who doubted and is done:
For chemistry meets every prayer."   25

"Sometimes a rock will meet a plough,"
Said Oliver; "but anyhow
'Tis here we are, 'tis here we live,
With each to take and each to give:
There's no room for a quarrel now.   30

"I leave you in all gentleness
To science and a ripe success.
Now God be with you, brother Oakes,
With you and with your artichokes:
You have the vision, more or less."   35
"By fate, that gives to me no choice,
I have the vision and the voice:
Dear Oliver, believe in me,
And we shall see what we shall see;
Henceforward let us both rejoice."   40

"But first, while we have joy to spare
We'll plant a little here and there;
And if you be not in the wrong,
We'll sing together such a song
As no man yet sings anywhere."   45

They planted and with fruitful eyes
Attended each his enterprise.

"Now days will come and days will go,
And many a way be found, we know,"
Said Oakes, "and we shall sing, like-
    wise."   50

"The days will go, the years will go,
And many a song be sung, we know,"
Said Oliver; "and if there be
Good harvesting for you and me,
Who cares if we sing loud or low?"   55

They planted once, and twice, and thrice,
Like amateurs in paradise;
And every spring, fond, foiled, elate,
Said Oakes, "We are in tune with Fate:
One season longer will suffice."   60

Year after year 'twas all the same:
With none to envy, none to blame,
They lived along in innocence,
Nor ever once forgot the fence,
Till on a day the Stranger came.   65

He came to greet them where they were,
And he too was a Gardener:
He stood between these gentle men,
He stayed a little while, and then
The land was all for Oliver.   70

'Tis Oliver who tills alone
Two gardens that are now his own;
'Tis Oliver who sows and reaps
And listens, while the other sleeps,
For songs undreamed of and unknown.   75

'Tis he, the gentle anchorite,
Who listens for them day and night;
But most he hears them in the dawn,
When from his trees across the lawn
Birds ring the chorus of the light.   80

He cannot sing without the voice,
But he may worship and rejoice
For patience in him to remain,
The chosen heir of age and pain,
Instead of Oakes—who had no choice.   85

'Tis Oliver who sits beside
The other's grave at eventide,
And smokes, and wonders what new race

Will have two gardens, by God's grace,
In Linndale, where their fathers died.   90

And often, while he sits and smokes,
He sees the ghost of gentle Oakes
Uprooting, with a restless hand,
Soft, shadowy flowers in a land
Of asphodels and artichokes.   95

EROS TURANNOS [1]
[1916 (1914)]

She fears him, and will always ask
    What fated her to choose him;
She meets in his engaging mask
    All reasons to refuse him;
But what she meets and what she fears   5
Are less than are the downward years,
Drawn slowly to the foamless weirs
    Of age, were she to lose him.

Between a blurred sagacity
    That once had power to sound him,   10
And Love, that will not let him be
    The Judas that she found him,
Her pride assuages her almost,
As if it were alone the cost.—
He sees that he will not be lost,   15
    And waits and looks around him.

A sense of ocean and old trees
    Envelops and allures him;
Tradition, touching all he sees,
    Beguiles and reassures him;   20
And all her doubts of what he says
Are dimmed with what she knows of days—
Till even prejudice delays
    And fades, and she secures him.

The falling leaf inaugurates   25
    The reign of her confusion;
The pounding wave reverberates
    The dirge of her illusion;
And home, where passion lived and died,
Becomes a place where she can hide,   30
While all the town and harbor side
    Vibrate with her seclusion.

[1] Love the Tyrant.

We tell you, tapping on our brows,
  The story as it should be,—
As if the story of a house   35
  Were told, or ever could be;
We'll have no kindly veil between
Her visions and those we have seen,—
As if we guessed what hers have been,
  Or what they are or would be.   40

Meanwhile we do no harm; for they
  That with a god have striven,
Not hearing much of what we say,
  Take what the god has given;
Though like waves breaking it may be, 45
Or like a changed familiar tree,
Or like a stairway to the sea
  Where down the blind are driven.

BEWICK FINZER
[1916]

Time was when his half million drew
  The breath of six per cent;
But soon the worm of what-was-not
  Fed hard on his content;
And something crumbled in his brain   5
  When his half million went.

Time passed, and filled along with his
  The place of many more;
Time came, and hardly one of us
  Had credence to restore,   10
From what appeared one day, the man
  Whom we had known before.

The broken voice, the withered neck,
  The coat worn out with care,
The cleanliness of indigence,   15
  The brilliance of despair,
The fond imponderable dreams
  Of affluence,—all were there.

Poor Finzer, with his dreams and schemes,
  Fares hard now in the race,   20
With heart and eye that have a task
  When he looks in the face
Of one who might so easily
  Have been in Finzer's place.

He comes unfailing for the loan   25
  We give and then forget;
He comes, and probably for years
  Will he be coming yet,—
Familiar as an old mistake,
  And futile as regret.   30

THE MAN AGAINST THE SKY
[1916]

Between me and the sunset, like a dome
Against the glory of a world on fire,
Now burned a sudden hill,
Bleak, round, and high, by flame-lit height
      made higher,
With nothing on it for the flame to kill 5
Save one who moved and was alone up
      there
To loom before the chaos and the glare
As if he were the last god going home
Unto his last desire.

Dark, marvelous, and inscrutable he moved
      on   10
Till down the fiery distance he was gone,
Like one of those eternal, remote things
That range across a man's imaginings
When a sure music fills him and he knows
What he may say thereafter to few
      men,—   15
The touch of ages having wrought
An echo and a glimpse of what he thought
A phantom or a legend until then;
For whether lighted over ways that save,
Or lured from all repose,   20
If he go on too far to find a grave,
Mostly alone he goes.

Even he, who stood where I had found him,
On high with fire all round him,
Who moved along the molten west,   25
And over the round hill's crest
That seemed half ready with him to go
      down,
Flame-bitten and flame-cleft,
As if there were to be no last thing left
Of a nameless · unimaginable town,— 30
Even he who climbed and vanished may
      have taken

Down to the perils of a depth not known,
From death defended though by men
    forsaken,
The bread that every man must eat alone;
He may have walked while others hardly
    dared   35
Look on to see him stand where many fell;
And upward out of that, as out of hell,
He may have sung and striven
To mount where more of him shall yet be
    given,
Bereft of all retreat,   40
To sevenfold heat,—
As on a day when three in Dura shared
The furnace,[2] and were spared
For glory by that king of Babylon
Who made himself so great that God, who
    heard,   45
Covered him with long feathers, like a
    bird.[3]

Again, he may have gone down easily,
By comfortable altitudes, and found,
As always, underneath him solid ground
Whereon to be sufficient and to stand   50
Possessed already of the promised land,
Far stretched and fair to see:
A good sight, verily,
And one to make the eyes of her who bore
    him
Shine glad with hidden tears.   55
Why question of his ease of who before
    him,
In one place or another where they left
Their names as far behind them as their
    bones,
And yet by dint of slaughter, toil and theft,
And shrewdly sharpened stones,   60
Carved hard the way for his ascendency
Through deserts of lost years?
Why trouble him now who sees and hears
No more than what his innocence requires,
And therefore to no other height aspires 65
Than one at which he neither quails nor
    tires?
He may do more by seeing what he sees
Than others eager for iniquities;
He may, by seeing all things for the best,
Incite futurity to do the rest.   70

Or with an even likelihood,
He may have met with atrabilious eyes
The fires of time on equal terms and passed
Indifferently down, until at last
His only kind of grandeur would have
    been,   75
Apparently, in being seen.
He may have had for evil or for good
No argument; he may have had no care
For what without himself went anywhere
To failure or to glory, and least of all 80
For such a stale, flamboyant miracle;
He may have been the prophet of an art
Immovable to old idolatries;
He may have been a player without a part,
Annoyed that even the sun should have the
    skies   85
For such a flaming way to advertise;
He may have been a painter sick at heart
With Nature's toiling for a new surprise;
He may have been a cynic, who now, for all
Of anything divine that his effete   90
Negation may have tasted,
Saw truth in his own image, rather small,
Forbore to fever the ephemeral,
Found any barren height a good retreat
From any swarming street,   95
And in the sun saw power superbly wasted;
And when the primitive old-fashioned stars
Came out again to shine on joys and wars
More primitive, and all arrayed for doom,
He may have proved a world a sorry
    thing   100
In his imagining,
And life a lighted highway to the tomb,

Or, mounting with infirm unsearching
    tread,
His hopes to chaos led,
He may have stumbled up there from the
    past,   105
And with an aching strangeness viewed the
    last
Abysmal conflagration of his dreams,—
A flame where nothing seems
To burn but flame itself, by nothing fed;

---

[2] Daniel 3.
[3] Daniel 4:33.

And while it all went out,   110
Not even the faint anodyne of doubt
May then have eased a painful going down
From pictured heights of power and lost
    renown,
Revealed at length to his outlived endeavor
Remote and unapproachable forever;   115
And at his heart there may have gnawed
Sick memories of a dead faith foiled and
    flawed
And long dishonored by the living death
Assigned alike by chance
To brutes and hierophants;   120
And anguish fallen on those he loved
    around him
May once have dealt the last blow to
    confound him,
And so have left him as death leaves a
    child,
Who sees it all too near;
And he who knows no young way to
    forget   125
May struggle to the tomb unreconciled.
Whatever suns may rise or set
There may be nothing kinder for him here
Than shafts and agonies;
And under these   130
He may cry out and stay on horribly;
Or, seeing in death too small a thing to
    fear,
He may go forward like a stoic Roman
Where pangs and terrors in his pathway
    lie,—
Or, seizing the swift logic of a woman, 135
Curse God and die.[4]

Or maybe there, like many another one
Who might have stood aloft and looked
    ahead,
Black-drawn against wild red,
He may have built, unawed by fiery
    gules   140
That in him no commotion stirred,
A living reason out of molecules
Why molecules occurred,
And one for smiling when he might have
    sighed
Had he seen far enough,   145
And in the same inevitable stuff

Discovered an odd reason too for pride
In being what he must have been by laws
Infrangible and for no kind of cause.
Deterred by no confusion or surprise   150
He may have seen with his mechanic eyes
A world without a meaning, and had room,
Alone amid magnificence and doom,
To build himself an airy monument
That should, or fail him in his vague
    intent,   155
Outlast an accidental universe—
To call it nothing worse—
Or, by the burrowing guile
Of Time disintegrated and effaced,
Like once-remembered mighty trees go
    down   160
To ruin, of which by man may now be
    traced
No part sufficient even to be rotten,
And in the book of things that are
    forgotten
Is entered as a thing not quite worth while.
He may have been so great   165
That satraps would have shivered at his
    frown,
And all he prized alive may rule a state
No larger than a grave that holds a clown;
He may have been a master of his fate,
And of his atoms,—ready as another   170
In his emergence to exonerate
His father and his mother;
He may have been a captain of a host,
Self-eloquent and ripe for prodigies,
Doomed here to swell by dangerous
    degrees,   175
And then give up the ghost.
Nahum's great grasshoppers [5] were such as
    these,
Sun-scattered and soon lost.

Whatever the dark road he may have
    taken,
This man who stood on high   180
And faced alone the sky,
Whatever drove or lured or guided him,—
A vision answering a faith unshaken,

---

[4] Job 2:9.
[5] Nahum 3:17.

An easy trust assumed by easy trials,
A sick negation born of weak denials, 185
A crazed abhorrence of an old condition,
A blind attendance on a brief ambition,—
Whatever stayed him or derided him,
His way was even as ours;
And we, with all our wounds and all our
    powers, 190
Must each await alone at his own height
Another darkness or another light;
And there, of our poor self dominion reft,
If inference and reason shun
Hell, Heaven, and Oblivion, 195
May thwarted will (perforce precarious,
But for our conservation better thus)
Have no misgiving left
Of doing yet what here we leave undone?
Or if unto the last of these we cleave, 200
Believing or protesting we believe
In such an idle and ephemeral
Florescence of the diabolical,—
If, robbed of two fond old enormities,
Our being had no onward auguries, 205
What then were this great love of ours to
    say
For launching other lives to voyage again
A little farther into time and pain,
A little faster in a futile chase
For a kingdom and a power and a Race 210
That would have still in sight
A manifest end of ashes and eternal night?
Is this the music of the toys we shake
So loud,—as if there might be no mistake
Somewhere in our indomitable will? 215
Are we no greater than the noise we make
Along one blind atomic pilgrimage
Whereon by crass chance billeted we go
Because our brains and bones and cartilage
Will have it so? 220
If this we say, then let us all be still
About our share in it, and live and die
More quietly thereby.

Where was he going, this man against the
    sky?
You know not, nor do I. 225
But this we know, if we know anything:
That we may laugh and fight and sing
And of our transcience here make offering
To an orient Word that will not be erased,

Or, save in incommunicable gleams 230
Too permanent for dreams,
Be found or known.
No tonic and ambitious irritant
Of increase or of want
Has made an otherwise insensate waste 235
Of ages overthrown
A ruthless, veiled, implacable foretaste
Of other ages that are still to be
Depleted and rewarded variously
Because a few, by fate's economy, 240
Shall seem to move the world the way it
    goes;
No soft evangel of equality,
Safe-cradled in a communal repose
That huddles into death and may at last
Be covered well with equatorial
    snows— 245
And all for what, the devil only knows—
Will aggregate an inkling to confirm
The credit of a sage or of a worm,
Or tell us why one man in five
Should have a care to stay alive 250
While in his heart he feels no violence
Laid on his humor and intelligence
When infant Science makes a pleasant face
And waves again that hollow toy, the Race;
No planetary trap where souls are
    wrought 255
For nothing but the sake of being caught
And sent again to nothing will attune
Itself to any key of any reason
Why man should hunger through another
    season
To find out why 'twere better late than
    soon 260
To go away and let the sun and moon
And all the silly stars illuminate
A place for creeping things,
And those that root and trumpet and have
    wings,
And herd and ruminate, 265
Or dive and flash and poise in rivers and
    seas,
Or by their loyal tails in lofty trees
Hang screeching lewd victorious derision
Of man's immortal vision.
Shall we, because Eternity records 270
Too vast an answer for the time-born
    words

We spell, whereof so many are dead that
    once
In our capricious lexicons
Were so alive and final, hear no more
The Word itself, the living word   275
That none alive has ever heard
Or ever spelt,
And few have ever felt
Without the fears and old surrenderings
And terrors that began   280
When Death let fall a feather from his
    wings
And humbled the first men?
Because the weight of our humility,
Wherefrom we gain
A little wisdom and much pain,   285
Falls here too sore and there too tedious,
Are we in anguish or complacency,
Not looking far enough ahead
To see by what mad couriers we are led
Along the roads of the ridiculous,   290
To pity ourselves and laugh at faith
And while we curse life bear it?
And if we see the soul's dead end in death,
Are we to fear it?
What folly is here that has not yet a
    name   295
Unless we say outright that we are liars?
What have we seen beyond our sunset fires
That lights again the way by which we
    came?
Why pay we such a price, and one we give
So clamoringly, for each racked empty
    day   300
That leads one more last human hope away,
As quiet fiends would lead past our crazed
    eyes
Our children to an unseen sacrifice?
If after all that we have lived and thought,
All comes to Nought,—   305
If there be nothing after Now,
And we be nothing anyhow,
And we know that,—why live?
'Twere sure but weaklings' vain distress
To suffer dungeons where so many
    doors   310
Will open on the cold eternal shores
That look sheer down
To the dark tideless floods of Nothingness
Where all who know may drown.

MR. FLOOD'S PARTY

[1929 (1920)]

Old Eben Flood, climbing alone one night
Over the hill between the town below
And the forsaken upland hermitage
That held as much as he should ever know
On earth again of home, paused warily. 5
The road was his with not a native near;
And Eben, having leisure, said aloud,
For no man else in Tilbury Town to hear:

"Well, Mr. Flood, we have the harvest
    moon
Again, and we may not have many
    more;   10
The bird is on the wing, the poet says,
And you and I have said it here before.
Drink to the bird." He raised up to the
    light
The jug that he had gone so far to fill,
And answered huskily: "Well, Mr.
    Flood,   15
Since you propose it, I believe I will."

Alone, as if enduring to the end
A valiant armor of scarred hopes outworn,
He stood there in the middle of the road
Like Roland's ghost winding a silent
    horn.   20
Below him, in the town among the trees,
Where friends of other days had honored
    him,
A phantom salutation of the dead
Rang thinly till old Eben's eyes were dim.

Then, as a mother lays her sleeping
    child   25
Down tenderly, fearing it may awake,
He set the jug down slowly at his feet
With trembling care, knowing that most
    things break;
And only when assured that on firm earth
It stood, as the uncertain lives of men 30
Assuredly did not, he paced away,
And with his hand extended paused again:

"Well, Mr. Flood, we have not met like this
In a long time; and many a change has
    come

To both of us, I fear, since last it was   35
We had a drop together. Welcome home!"
Convivially returning with himself,
Again he raised the jug up to the light;
And with an acquiescent quaver said:
"Well, Mr. Flood, if you insist, I might.   40

"Only a very little, Mr. Flood—
For auld lang syne. No more, sir; that
    will do."
So, for the time, apparently it did,
And Eben evidently thought so too;
For soon amid the silver loneliness   45
Of night he lifted up his voice and sang,
Secure, with only two moons listening,

Until the whole harmonious landscape
    rang—

"For auld lang syne." The weary throat
    gave out,
The last word wavered; and the song being
    done,   50
He raised again the jug regretfully
And shook his head, and was again alone.
There was not much that was ahead of him,
And there was nothing in the town below—
Where strangers would have shut the many
    doors   55
That many friends had opened long ago.

Robert Frost

1875

R OBERT FROST, poet of New England, was born in San Francisco and
   spent the first years of his life there. His father, a New Englander who
was active in San Francisco politics, died when the boy was ten. His mother
was a Scotch woman who had been a schoolteacher. She moved with her son
to Lawrence, Massachusetts, where he attended high school. He spent a year at
Dartmouth College and later two years at Harvard, but did not graduate. At
twenty he married Eleanor Miriam White.

Convinced since he had studied Virgil in high school that he wanted to
be a poet, Frost was able to sell only occasional poems to *The Youth's Companion, The Independent,* and other magazines. He worked as mill hand, as
country schoolteacher, as cobbler, as country editor, and finally and most persistently as farmer, buying and cultivating for eleven years an isolated farm
near Derry, N. H.

At his wife's suggestion, Frost took his family to England in 1912. There
he found the encouragement so long withheld in his own country. He became
the friend of Edward Thomas, William Wilfrid Gibson, and other British
poets, and published in England his first books, *A Boy's Will* (1913) and *North
of Boston* (1914). Belated recognition greeted him on his return to America in
1915, and since that time he has been generally regarded as a writer of the first
rank in his generation.

For thirty years Frost has devoted much of his time and energy to teaching.
He has taught at Amherst, the University of Michigan, and Harvard, and
regularly at the Breadloaf School of Middlebury College since he helped to

establish that School in 1920. For many years he traveled widely through the country as a lecturer, by preference talking informally with small groups of students. Most of his writing he has done in intervals of farming in New Hampshire and Vermont.

Frost's *Collected Poems* (1939) include the volumes *A Boy's Will, North of Boston, Mountain Interval, New Hampshire, West-Running Brook,* and *A Further Range.* Since 1939 he has published *The Witness Tree* (1942), *A Masque of Reason* (1945), *Steeple Bush* (1947), and *A Masque of Mercy* (1947).

[Studies of Frost and his work are found in a symposium edited by Richard Thornton under the title *Recognition of Robert Frost* (New York, 1937), C. Ford's *The Less Traveled Road: A Study of Robert Frost* (Cambridge, 1935), L. R. Thompson's *Fire and Ice* (New York, 1942), and R. P. T. Coffin's *New Poetry of New England: Frost and Robinson* (Baltimore, 1938).]

INTO MY OWN
[1913 (1909)]

One of my wishes is that those dark trees,
So old and firm they scarcely show the
    breeze,
Were not, as 'twere, the merest mask of
    gloom,
But stretched away unto the edge of doom.

I should not be withheld but that some
    day   5
Into their vastness I should steal away,
Fearless of ever finding open land,
Or highway where the slow wheel pours the
    sand.

I do not see why I should e'er turn back,
Or those should not set forth upon my
    track   10
To overtake me, who should miss me here
And long to know if still I held them dear.

They would not find me changed from him
    they knew—
Only more sure of all I thought was true.

MOWING
[1913]

There was never a sound beside the wood
    but one,

And that was my long scythe whispering
    to the ground.
What was it it whispered? I knew not well
    myself;
Perhaps it was something about the heat
    of the sun,
Something, perhaps, about the lack of
    sound—   5
And that was why it whispered and did not
    speak.
It was no dream of the gift of idle hours,
Or easy gold at the hand of fay or elf:
Anything more than the truth would have
    seemed too weak
To the earnest love that laid the swale in
    rows,   10
Not without feeble-pointed spikes of
    flowers
(Pale orchises), and scared a bright green
    snake.
The fact is the sweetest dream that labor
    knows.
My long scythe whispered and left the hay
    to make.

HOME BURIAL
[1914]

He saw her from the bottom of the stairs
Before she saw him. She was starting down,
Looking back over her shoulder at some
    fear.

She took a doubtful step and then undid it
To raise herself and look again. He spoke 5
Advancing toward her: 'What is it you
      see
From up there always—for I want to
      know.'
She turned and sank upon her skirts at
      that,
And her face changed from terrified to
      dull.
He said to gain time: 'What is it you
      see,'   10
Mounting until she cowered under him.
'I will find out now—you must tell me,
      dear.'
She, in her place, refused him any help
With the least stiffening of her neck and
      silence.
She let him look, sure that he wouldn't
      see,   15
Blind creature; and a while he didn't see.
But at last he murmured, 'Oh,' and again,
      'Oh.'

'What is it—what?' she said.

                              'Just that I see.'

'You don't,' she challenged. 'Tell me what
      it is.'   20

'The wonder is I didn't see at once.
I never noticed it from here before.
I must be wonted to it—that's the reason.
The little graveyard where my people are!
So small the window frames the whole of
      it.   25
Not so much larger than a bedroom, is it?
There are three stones of slate and one of
      marble,
Broad-shouldered little slabs there in the
      sunlight
On the sidehill. We haven't to mind those.
But I understand: it is not the stones, 30
But the child's mound—'

      'Don't, don't, don't, don't,' she cried.

She withdrew shrinking from beneath his
      arm

That rested on the banister, and slid
      downstairs;
And turned on him with such a daunting
      look,   35
He said twice over before he knew himself:
'Can't a man speak of his own child he's
      lost?'

'Not you! Oh, where's my hat? Oh, I don't
      need it!
I must get out of here. I must get air.
I don't know rightly whether any man
      can.'   40

'Amy! Don't go to someone else this time.
Listen to me. I won't come down the stairs.'
He sat and fixed his chin between his fists.
'There's something I should like to ask you,
      dear.'

'You don't know how to ask it.'   45

                              'Help me, then.'

Her fingers moved the latch for all reply.

'My words are nearly always an offence.
I don't know how to speak of anything
So as to please you. But I might be
      taught   50
I should suppose. I can't say I see how.
A man must partly give up being a man
With women-folk. We could have some
      arrangement
By which I'd bind myself to keep hands
      off
Anything special you're a-mind to name. 55
Though I don't like such things 'twixt
      those that love.
Two that don't love can't live together
      without them.
But two that do can't live together with
      them.'
She moved the latch a little. 'Don't—don't
      go.
Don't carry it to someone else this time. 60
Tell me about it if it's something human.
Let me into your grief. I'm not so much
Unlike other folks as your standing there

Apart would make me out. Give me my
    chance.
I do think, though, you overdo it a little. 65
What was it brought you up to think it the
    thing
To take your mother-loss of a first child
So inconsolably—in the face of love.
You'd think his memory might be
    satisfied——'

'There you go sneering now!'   70

       'I'm not, I'm not!
You make me angry. I'll come down to you.
God, what a woman! And it's come to this,
A man can't speak of his own child that's
    dead.'

'You can't because you don't know how. 75
If you had any feelings, you that dug
With your own hand—how could you?—his
    little grave;
I saw you from that very window there,
Making the gravel leap and leap in air,
Leap up, like that, like that, and land so
    lightly   80
And roll back down the mound beside the
    hole.
I thought, Who is that man? I don't know
    you.
And I crept down the stairs and up the
    stairs
To look again, and still your spade kept
    lifting.
Then you came in. I heard your rumbling
    voice   85
Out in the kitchen, and I don't know why,
But I went near to see with my own eyes.
You could sit there with the stains on your
    shoes
Of the fresh earth from your own baby's
    grave
And talk about your everyday concerns. 90
You had stood the spade up against the
    wall
Outside there in the entry, for I saw it.'

'I shall laugh the worst laugh I ever
    laughed.

I'm cursed. God, if I don't believe I'm
    cursed.'

'I can repeat the very words you were
    saying.   95
"Three foggy mornings and one rainy day
Will rot the best birch fence a man can
    build."
Think of it, talk like that at such a time!
What had how long it takes a birch to rot
To do with what was in the darkened
    parlour.   100
You *couldn't* care! The nearest friends can
    go
With anyone to death, comes so far short
They might as well not try to go at all.
No, from the time when one is sick to
    death,
One is alone, and he dies more alone. 105
Friends make pretence of following to the
    grave,
But before one is in it, their minds are
    turned
And making the best of their way back
    to life
And living people, and things they
    understand.
But the world's evil. I won't have grief
    so   110
If I can change it. Oh, I won't, I won't!'

'There, you have said it all and you feel
    better.
You won't go now. You're crying. Close the
    door.
The heart's gone out of it: why keep it up.
Amy! There's someone coming down the
    road!'   115

'*You*—oh, you think the talk is all. I
    must go—
Somewhere out of this house. How can I
    make you——'

'If—you—do!' She was opening the door
    wider.
'Where do you mean to go? First tell me
    that.
I'll follow and bring you back by force. I
    will!—'   120

THE CODE
[1914]

There were three in the meadow by the
    brook
Gathering up windrows, piling cocks of
    hay,
With an eye always lifted toward the west
Where an irregular sun-bordered cloud
Darkly advanced with a perpetual dagger 5
Flickering across its bosom. Suddenly
One helper, thrusting pitchfork in the
    ground,
Marched himself off the field and home. One
    stayed.
The town-bred farmer failed to understand.

'What is there wrong?'   10

    'Something you just now said.'

'What did I say?'

    'About our taking pains.'

'To cock the hay?—because it's going to
    shower?
I said that more than half an hour ago. 15
I said it to myself as much as you.'

'You didn't know. But James is one big
    fool.
He thought you meant to find fault with his
    work.
That's what the average farmer would have
    meant.
James would take time, of course, to chew
    it over   20
Before he acted: he's just got round to
    act.'

'He is a fool if that's the way he takes
    me.'

'Don't let it bother you. You've found out
    something.
The hand that knows his business won't
    be told
To do work better or faster—those two
    things.   25
I'm as particular as anyone:

Most likely I'd have served you just the
    same.
But I know you don't understand our ways.
You were just talking what was in your
    mind,
What was in all our minds, and you weren't
    hinting.   30
Tell you a story of what happened once:
I was up here in Salem at a man's
Named Sanders with a gang of four or five
Doing the haying. No one liked the boss.
He was one of the kind sports call a
    spider,   35
All wiry arms and legs that spread out
    wavy
From a humped body nigh as big's a
    biscuit.
But work! that man could work, especially
If by so doing he could get more work
Out of his hired help. I'm not denying 40
He was hard on himself. I couldn't find
That he kept any hours—not for himself.
Daylight and lantern-light were one to him:
I've heard him pounding in the barn all
    night.
But what he liked was someone to
    encourage.   45
Them that he couldn't lead he'd get behind
And drive, the way you can, you know, in
    mowing—
Keep at their heels and threaten to mow
    their legs off.
I'd seen about enough of his bulling tricks
(We call that bulling). I'd been watching
    him.   50
So when he paired off with me in the
    hayfield
To load the load, thinks I, Look out for
    trouble.
I built the load and topped it off; old
    Sanders
Combed it down with a rake and says,
    "O.K."
Everything went well till we reached the
    barn   55
With a big jag to empty in a bay.
You understand that meant the easy job
For the man up on top of throwing *down*
The hay and rolling it off wholesale,

Where on a mow it would have been slow
    lifting.
You wouldn't think a fellow'd need much
    urging   65
Under these circumstances, would you now?
But the old fool seizes his fork in both
    hands,
And looking up bewhiskered out of the pit,
Shouts like an army captain. "Let her
    come!"
Thinks I, d'ye mean it? "What was that
    you said?"   70
I asked out loud, so's there'd be no mistake.
"Did you say, let her come?" "Yes, let her
    come."
He said it over, but he said it softer.
Never you say a thing like that to a man,
Not if he values what he is. God, I'd as
    soon   75
Murdered him as left out his middle name.
I'd built the load and knew just where to
    find it.
Two or three forkfuls I picked lightly
    round for,
Like meditating, and then I just dug in
And dumped the rackful on him in ten
    lots.   80
I looked over the side once in the dust
And caught sight of him treading-water-
    like,
Keeping his head above. "Damn ye," I
    says,
"That gets ye!" He squeaked like a
    squeezed rat.
That was the last I saw or heard of
    him.   85
I cleaned the rack and drove out to cool
    off.
As I sat mopping the hayseed from my
    neck,
And sort of waiting to be asked about it,
One of the boys sings out, "Where's the old
    man?"
"I left him in the barn, under the hay. 90
If ye want him ye can go and dig him out."
They realized, from the way I swobbed my
    neck
More than was needed, something must be
    up.

They headed for the barn—I stayed where
    I was.
They told me afterward: First they forked
    hay,   95
A lot of it, out into the barn floor.
Nothing! They listened for him. Not a
    rustle!
I guess they thought I'd spiked him in the
    temple
Before I buried him, or I couldn't have
    managed.
They excavated more. "Go keep his wife 100
Out of the barn."
          Some one looked in a window;
And curse me, if he wasn't in the kitchen,
Slumped way down in a chair, with both his
    feet
Stuck in the oven, the hottest day that
    summer.
He looked so clean disgusted from
    behind   105
There was no one that dared to stir him up
Or let him know that he was being looked
    at.
Apparently I hadn't buried him
(I may have knocked him down); but my
    just trying
To bury him had hurt his dignity.   110
He had gone to the house so's not to meet
    me.
He kept away from us all afternoon.
We tended to his hay. We saw him out
After a while picking peas in his garden:
He couldn't keep away from doing
    something.'   115

'Weren't you relieved to find he wasn't
    dead?'

'No!—and yet I don't know—it's hard
    to say.
I went about to kill him fair enough.'

'You took an awkward way. Did he
    discharge you?'

'Discharge me? No! He knew I did just
    right.'   120

AN OLD MAN'S WINTER NIGHT
[1916]

All out-of-doors looked darkly in at him
Through the thin frost, almost in separate
    stars,
That gathers on the pane in empty rooms.
What kept his eyes from giving back the
    gaze
Was the lamp tilted near them in his
    hand.   5
What kept him from remembering what it
    was
That brought him to that creaking room
    was age.
He stood with barrels round him—at a
    loss;
And having scared the cellar under him
In clomping there, he scared it once
    again   10
In clomping off; and scared the outer
    night,
Which has its sounds, familiar, like the
    roar
Of trees and crack of branches—common
    things,
But nothing so like beating on a box.
A light he was to no one but himself   15
Where now he sat, concerned with he knew
    what;
A quiet light, and then not even that.
He consigned to the moon, such as she was,
So late-arising, to the broken moon—
As better than the sun in any case   20
For such a charge—his snow upon the roof,
His icicles along the wall to keep;
And slept. The log that shifted with a jolt
Once in the stove, disturbed him and he
    shifted,
And eased his heavy breathing; but still
    slept.   25
One aged man—one man—can't fill a house,
A farm, a countryside; or if he can,
It's thus he does it of a winter night.

HYLA BROOK
[1916]

By June our brook's run out of song and
    speed.

Sought for much after that, it will be
    found
Either to have gone groping underground
(And taken with it all the Hyla breed
That shouted in the mist a month ago, 5
Like ghost of sleigh-bells in a ghost of
    snow)—
Or flourished and come up in jewel-weed,
Weak foliage that is blown upon and bent
Even against the way its waters went.
Its bed is left a faded paper sheet   10
Of dead leaves stuck together by the heat—
A brook to none but who remember long.
This as it will be seen is other far
Than with brooks taken otherwhere in song.
We love the things we love for what they
    are.   15

THE COW IN APPLE TIME
[1916 (1914)]

Something inspires the only cow of late
To make no more of a wall than an open
    gate,
And think no more of wall-builders than
    fools.
Her face is flecked with pomace and she
    drools
A cider syrup. Having tasted fruit,   5
She scorns a pasture withering to the root.
She runs from tree to tree where lie and
    sweeten
The windfalls spiked with stubble and
    worm-eaten.
She leaves them bitten when she has to fly.
She bellows on a knoll against the sky. 10
Her udder shrivels and the milk goes dry.

'OUT, OUT—'
[1916]

The buzz-saw snarled and rattled in the
    yard
And made dust and dropped stove-length
    sticks of wood,
Sweet-scented stuff when the breeze drew
    across it.
And from there those that lifted eyes could
    count

Five mountain ranges one behind the
    other   5
Under the sunset far into Vermont.
And the saw snarled and rattled, snarled
    and rattled,
As it ran light, or had to bear a load.
And nothing happened: day was all but
    done.
Call it a day, I wish they might have
    said   10
To please the boy by giving him the half
    hour
That a boy counts so much when saved
    from work.
His sister stood beside them in her apron
To tell them 'Supper.' At the word, the
    saw,
As if to prove saws knew what supper
    meant,   15
Leaped out at the boy's hand, or seemed to
    leap—
He must have given the hand. However it
    was,
Neither refused the meeting. But the hand!
The boy's first outcry was a rueful laugh.
As he swung toward them holding up the
    hand   20
Half in appeal, but half as if to keep
The life from spilling. Then the boy saw
    all—
Since he was old enough to know, big boy
Doing a man's work, though a child at
    heart—
He saw all spoiled. 'Don't let him cut my
    hand off—   25
The doctor, when he comes. Don't let him,
    sister!'
So. But the hand was gone already.
The doctor put him in the dark of ether.
He lay and puffed his lips out with his
    breath.
And then—the watcher at his pulse took
    fright.   30
No one believed. They listened at his heart.
Little—less—nothing!—and that ended it.
No more to build on there. And they, since
    they
Were not the one dead, turned to their
    affairs.

BROWN'S DESCENT
OR
THE WILLY-NILLY SLIDE
[1916]

Brown lived at such a lofty farm
    That everyone for miles could see
His lantern when he did his chores
    In winter after half-past three.

And many must have seen him make   5
    His wild descent from there one night,
'Cross lots, 'cross walls, 'cross everything,
    Describing rings of lantern light.

Between the house and barn the gale
    Got him by something he had on   10
And blew him out on the icy crust
    That cased the world, and he was gone!

Walls were all buried, trees were few:
    He saw no stay unless he stove
A hole in somewhere with his heel.   15
    But though repeatedly he strove

And stamped and said things to himself,
    And sometimes something seemed to
        yield,
He gained no foothold, but pursued
    His journey down from field to field. 20

Sometimes he came with arms outspread
    Like wings, revolving in the scene
Upon his longer axis, and
    With no small dignity of mien.

Faster or slower as he chanced,   25
    Sitting or standing as he chose,
According as he feared to risk
    His neck, or thought to spare his clothes,

He never let the lantern drop.
    And some exclaimed who saw afar 30
The figures he described with it,
    'I wonder what those signals are

Brown makes at such an hour of night!
    He's celebrating something strange.
I wonder if he's sold his farm,   35
    Or been made Master of the Grange.'

He reeled, he lurched, he bobbed, he
    checked;
He fell and made the lantern rattle
(But saved the light from going out.)
    So half-way down he fought the
      battle,   40

Incredulous of his own bad luck.
And then becoming reconciled
To everything, he gave it up
    And came down like a coasting child.

'Well—I—be—' that was all he said,   45
    As standing in the river road,
He looked back up the slippery slope
    (Two miles it was) to his abode.

Sometimes as an authority
    On motor-cars, I'm asked if I   50
Should say our stock was petered out,
    And this is my sincere reply:

Yankees are what they always were.
    Don't think Brown ever gave up hope
Of getting home again because   55
    He couldn't climb that slippery slope;

Or even thought of standing there
    Until the January thaw
Should take the polish off the crust.
    He bowed with grace to natural law, 60

And then went round it on his feet,
    After the manner of our stock;
Not much concerned for those to whom,
    At that particular time o'clock,

It must have looked as if the course   65
    He steered was really straight away
From that which he was headed for—
    Not much concerned for them, I say;

No more so than became a man—
    And politician at odd seasons.   70
I've kept Brown standing in the cold
    While I invested him with reasons;

But now he snapped his eyes three times;
    Then shook his lantern, saying, 'Ile's

'Bout out!' and took the long way
    home   75
    By road, a matter of several miles.

STOPPING BY WOODS ON A SNOWY EVENING
[1923]

Whose woods these are I think I know.
His house is in the village though;
He will not see me stopping here
To watch his woods fill up with snow.

My little horse must think it queer   5
To stop without a farmhouse near
Between the woods and frozen lake
The darkest evening of the year.

He gives his harness bells a shake
To ask if there is some mistake.   10
The only other sound's the sweep
Of easy wind and downy flake.

The woods are lovely, dark and deep,
But I have promises to keep,
And miles to go before I sleep,   15
And miles to go before I sleep.

TO EARTHWARD
[1923]

Love at the lips was touch
As sweet as I could bear;
And once that seemed too much;
I lived on air

That crossed me from sweet things,   5
The flow of—was it musk
From hidden grapevine springs
Down hill at dusk?

I had the swirl and ache
From sprays of honeysuckle   10
That when they're gathered shake
Dew on the knuckle.

I craved strong sweets, but those
Seemed strong when I was young;
The petal of the rose   15
It was that stung.

Now no joy but lacks salt
That is not dashed with pain
And weariness and fault;
I crave the stain   20

Of tears, the aftermark
Of almost too much love,
The sweet of bitter bark
And burning clove.

When stiff and sore and scarred   25
I take away my hand
From leaning on it hard
In grass and sand,

The hurt is not enough:
I long for weight and strength   30
To feel the earth as rough
To all my length.

ONCE BY THE PACIFIC
[1928 (1926)]

The shattered water made a misty din.
Great waves looked over others coming in,
And thought of doing something to the
    shore
That water never did to land before.
The clouds were low and hairy in the
    skies,   5
Like locks blown forward in the gleam of
    eyes.
You could not tell, and yet it looked as if
The shore was lucky in being backed by
    cliff,
The cliff in being backed by continent;
It looked as if a night of dark intent 10
Was coming, and not only a night, an age.
Someone had better be prepared for rage.
There would be more than ocean-water
    broken
Before God's last *Put out the Light* was
    spoken.

A DRUMLIN WOODCHUCK
[1936]

One thing has a shelving bank,
Another a rotting plank,
To give it cozier skies
And make up for its lack of size.

My own strategic retreat   5
Is where two rocks almost meet,
And still more secure and snug,
A two-door burrow I dug.

With those in mind at my back
I can sit forth exposed to attack   10
As one who shrewdly pretends
That he and the world are friends.

All we who prefer to live
Have a little whistle we give,
And flash, at the least alarm   15
We dive down under the farm.

We allow some time for guile
And don't come out for a while
Either to eat or drink.
We take occasion to think.   20

And if after the hunt goes past
And the double-barrelled blast
(Like war and pestilence
And the loss of common sense),

If I can with confidence say   25
That still for another day,
Or even another year,
I will be there for you, my dear,

It will be because, though small
As measured against the All,   30
I have been so instinctively thorough
About my crevice and burrow.

A LEAF TREADER
[1936 (1935)]

I have been treading on leaves all day
    until I am autumn-tired.

God knows all the color and form of leaves
  I have trodden on and mired.
Perhaps I have put forth too much strength
  and been too fierce from fear.
I have safely trodden underfoot the leaves
  of another year.

All summer long they were over head, more
  lifted up than I.   5
To come to their final place in earth they
  had to pass me by.
All summer long I thought I heard them
  threatening under their breath.
And when they came it seemed with a will
  to carry me with them to death.

They spoke to the fugitive in my heart as
  if it were leaf to leaf.
They tapped at my eyelids and touched my
  lips with an invitation to grief.   10
But it was no reason I had to go because
  they had to go.
Now up my knee to keep on top of another
  year of snow.

COME IN
[1943 (1941)]

As I came to the edge of the woods,
Thrush music—hark!
Now if it was dusk outside,
Inside it was dark.

Too dark in the woods for a bird   5
By sleight of wing
To better its perch for the night,
Though it still could sing.

The last of the light of the sun
That had died in the west   10
Still lived for one song more
In a thrush's breast.

Far in the pillared dark
Thrush music went—
Almost like a call to come in   15
To the dark and lament.

But no, I was out for stars:
I would not come in.
I mean not even if asked,
And I hadn't been.   20

Carl Sandburg
1878

CARL SANDBURG'S parents were born in Sweden. During Carl's boyhood his father worked on the railroad near Galesburg, Illinois, and Carl as he grew up held transient jobs and did common labor. While serving as an enlisted man in the Spanish-American War he became convinced of his need of further education, and on his return he worked his way through four years at Lombard College at Galesburg, though he did not take a degree. For the next fifteen years he was active in the cause of labor in the Middle West, as a journalist and organizer. For a time he was secretary to the Socialist mayor of Milwaukee. In Milwaukee he met and married Lillian Steichen, a sister of the photographer, Edward Steichen. After holding other journalistic jobs in Chicago, he joined the staff of the Chicago *Daily News* in 1917. He continued to work for the *Daily News* until 1933; for some years he wrote a column of motion picture criticism. He travelled widely throughout the country as an informal lecturer and ballad singer. In 1933 he retired to a small farm near Harbert, Michigan; in 1946 he moved to North Carolina.

Sandburg had long outgrown the conventionality of his early verses (of which a small volume had been published in 1904 with the help of one of his teachers at Lombard College) when he submitted "Chicago" and similar poems to Harriet Monroe for the still youthful magazine *Poetry*. Her acceptance and publication of his work in 1914 proved beneficial both to Sandburg and to the magazine. With the publication of *Chicago Poems* in 1916 and succeeding volumes Sandburg was generally recognized as one of the important poets of the period.

Early and deeply interested in another man of the common people of Illinois, Sandburg has devoted the major sustained effort of his life to the production of a monumental biography of Abraham Lincoln. The two volumes of the earlier portion, *Abraham Lincoln: The Prairie Years,* appeared in 1926 and won wide approval, both critical and popular. A dozen years of research went into the making of the immensely detailed account of Lincoln's presidency, *Abraham Lincoln: The War Years* (4 vols., 1939). A special phase of the Lincoln story was treated in *Mary Lincoln, Wife and Widow* (1932), written with Paul M. Angle.

Sandburg's interest in folklore and the songs of the people found expression in a collection called *The American Songbag* (1927) and in many of the sections of the long poem *The People, Yes* (1936). He wrote imaginative tales for children in *Rootabaga Stories* (1922) and other volumes. His books of poems, in addition to those mentioned, are *Cornhuskers* (1918); *Smoke and Steel* (1920); *Slabs of the Sunburnt West* (1922); and *Good Morning, America* (1928). His novel, *Remembrance Rock,* appeared in 1948.

[Karl Detzer's *Carl Sandburg, A Study in Personality and Background* (New York, 1941) is helpful. An interesting early view is found in Amy Lowell's *Tendencies in Modern American Poetry* (Boston, 1917).]

A FENCE
[1916]

Now the stone house on the lake front is finished and the workmen are beginning the fence.
The palings are made of iron bars with steel points that can stab the life out of any man who falls on them.
As a fence, it is a masterpiece, and will shut off the rabble and all vagabonds and hungry men and all wandering children looking for a place to play.

Passing through the bars and over the steel points will go nothing except Death and the Rain and To-morrow.

CHICAGO
[1916 (1914)]

Hog-butcher for the world,
Tool-maker, Stacker of Wheat,
Player with Railroads and the Nation's Freight-handler;
Stormy, husky, brawling,
City of the Big Shoulders:

They tell me you are wicked and I believe
  them, for I have seen your painted
  women under the gas lamps luring
  the farm boys.
And they tell me you are crooked, and I
  answer: Yes, it is true I have seen
  the gunman kill and go free to kill
  again.
And they tell me you are brutal and my
  reply is: On the faces of women and
  children I have seen the marks of
  wanton hunger.
And having answered so I turn once more
  to those who sneer at this my city,
  and I give them back the sneer and
  say to them:
Come and show me another city with
  lifted head singing so proud to be
  alive and coarse and strong and cunning.
Flinging magnetic curses amid the toil of
  piling job on job, here is a tall bold
  slugger set vivid against the little
  soft cities;
Fierce as a dog with tongue lapping for
  action, cunning as a savage pitted
  against the wilderness,
      Bareheaded,
      Shoveling,
      Wrecking,
      Planning,
    Building, breaking, rebuilding,
Under the smoke, dust all over his mouth,
  laughing with white teeth,
Under the terrible burden of destiny laughing as a young man laughs,
Laughing even as an ignorant fighter
  laughs who has never lost a battle,
Bragging and laughing that under his wrist
  is the pulse, and under his ribs the
  heart of the people.
      Laughing!
Laughing the stormy, husky, brawling
  laughter of youth; half-naked, sweating, proud to be Hog-butcher, Tool-
  maker, Stacker of Wheat, Player
  with Railroads, and Freight-handler
  to the Nation.

THE POOR
[1916]

Among the mountains I wandered and saw
  blue haze and red crag and was
  amazed;
On the beach where the long push under
  the endless tide maneuvers, I stood
  silent;
Under the stars on the prairie watching the
  Dipper slant over the horizon's
  grass, I was full of thoughts.
Great men, pageants of war and labor,
  soldiers and workers, mothers lifting
  their children—these all I touched,
  and felt the solemn thrill of them.
And then one day I got a true look at the
  Poor, millions of the Poor, patient
  and toiling; more patient than crags,
  tides, and stars; innumerable, patient as the darkness of night—and
  all broken humble ruins of nations.

PRAIRIE WATERS BY NIGHT
[1918 (1917)]

Chatter of birds two by two raises a night
  song joining a litany of running
  water—sheer waters showing the
  russet of old stones remembering
  many rains.

And the long willows drowse on the
  shoulders of the running water,
  and sleep from much music; joined
  songs of day-end, feathery throats
  and stony waters, in a choir chanting
  new psalms.

It is too much for the long willows when
  low laughter of a red moon comes
  down; and the willows drowse and
  sleep on the shoulders of the running
  water.

COOL TOMBS
[1918 (1916)]

When Abraham Lincoln was shoveled into

the tombs, he forgot the copperheads
and the assassin . . in the dust, in
the cool tombs.

And Ulysses Grant lost all thought of con
    men and Wall Street, cash and col-
    lateral turned ashes . . . in the dust,
    in the cool tombs.

Pocahontas' body, lovely as a poplar, sweet
    as a red haw in November or a
    pawpaw in May—did she wonder?
    does she remember? . . . in the
    dust, in the cool tombs?

Take any streetful of people buying clothes
    and groceries, cheering a hero or
    throwing confetti and blowing tin
    horns . . tell me if the lovers are
    losers . . tell me if any get more
    than the lovers . . . in the dust . . .
    in the cool tombs.

FOUR PRELUDES ON PLAYTHINGS
OF THE WIND
[1921 (1920)]
"The past is a bucket of ashes."

I

The woman named Tomorrow
Sits with a hairpin in her teeth
And takes her time,
And does her hair the way she wants it,
And fastens at last the last braid and
    coil,   5
And puts the hairpin where it belongs,
And turns and drawls: "Well, what of it?
My grandmother, Yesterday, is gone.
What of it? Let the dead be dead."

II

The doors were cedar   10
And the panels strips of gold;
And the girls were golden girls,
And the panels read and the girls chanted:
    "We are the greatest city,

the greatest nation;
nothing like us ever was."
The doors are twisted on broken hinges.
Sheets of rain swish through on the wind
    where the golden girls ran and the
    panels read:
    "We are the greatest city,
    the greatest nation;
    nothing like us ever was."   15

III

It has happened before.
Strong men put up a city and got
    a nation together,
And paid singers to sing and women
    to warble: "We are the greatest city,
    the greatest nation;
    nothing like us ever was."

And while the singers sang,
And the strong men listened   20
And paid the singers well
And felt good about it all,
    there were rats and lizards who
    listened . . .
    and the only listeners left now . . .
    are . . . the rats . . . and the
    lizards.

And there are black crows
Crying, "Caw, caw,"
Bringing mud and sticks,   25
Building a nest
Over the words carved
On the doors where the panels were cedar
And the strips on the panels were gold,
And the golden girls came singing:
    "We are the greatest city,
    the greatest nation:
    nothing like us ever was."   30

The only singers now are crows crying,
    "Caw, caw;"
And the sheets of rain whine in the wind
    and doorways.
And the only listeners now are . . . the
    rats . . . and the lizards.

IV

The feet of the rats
Scribble on the door-sills;   35
The hieroglyphs of the rat footprints
Chatter the pedigrees of the rats,
And babble of the blood
And gabble of the breed
Of the grandfathers and the great-grand-
         fathers   40
Of the rats.

And the wind shifts,
And the dust on the door-sill shifts,
And even the writing of the rat footprints
Tells us nothing, nothing at all   45
About the greatest city, the greatest nation,
Where the strong men listened
And the women warbled: "Nothing like us
         ever was."

From
THE PEOPLE, YES
[1936]

The people will live on.
The learning and blundering people will
         live on.
    They will be tricked and sold and again
         sold
And go back to the nourishing earth for
         rootholds,
    The people so peculiar in renewal and
         comeback,   5
    You can't laugh off their capacity to
         take it.
The mammoth rests between his cyclonic
         dramas.

The   people   so   often   sleepy,   weary,
         enigmatic,
is a vast huddle with many units saying:
    "I earn my living.   10
    I make enough to get by
and it takes all my time.
    If I had more time
    I could do more for myself
and maybe for others.   15
    I could read and study

and talk things over
and find out about things.
    It takes time.
    I wish I had the time."   20

The people is a tragic and comic two-
face: hero and hoodlum: phantom and
gorilla twisting to moan with a gargoyle
mouth: "They buy me and sell me . . .
it's a game . . . sometime I'll break
loose . . ."   25

    Once having marched
Over the margins of animal necessity,
Over the grim line of sheer subsistence
    Then man came
To the deeper rituals of his bones,   30
To the lights lighter than any bones,
To the time for thinking things over,
To the dance, the song, the story,
Or the hours given over to dreaming,
    Once having so marched.   35

Between the finite limitations of the five
         senses
and the endless yearnings of man for the
         beyond
the people hold to the humdrum bidding
         of work and food
while reaching out when it comes their way
for lights beyond the prison of the five
         senses,   40
for keepsakes lasting beyond any hunger
         or death.
    This reaching is alive.
The panderers and liars have violated and
         smutted it.
    Yet this reaching is alive yet
for lights and keepsakes.   45

    The people know the salt of the sea
    and the strength of the winds
    lashing the corners of the earth.
    The people take the earth
    as a tomb of rest and a cradle of
         hope.   50
    Who else speaks for the Family of
         Man?
    They are in tune and step
    with constellations of universal law.

The people is a polychrome,
a spectrum and a prism   55
held in a moving monolith,
a console organ of changing themes,
a clavilux [1] of color poems
wherein the sea offers fog
and the fog moves off in rain   60
and the labrador sunset shortens
to a nocturne of clear stars
serene over the shot spray
of northern lights.

The steel mill sky is alive.   65
The fire breaks white and zigzag
shot on a gun-metal gloaming.
Man is a long time coming.
Man will yet win.
Brother may yet line up with
brother: 70

This old anvil laughs at many broken
    hammers.
There are men who can't be bought.
The fireborn are at home in fire.
The stars make no noise.
You can't hinder the wind from
    blowing.   75
Time is a great teacher.
Who can live without hope?

In the darkness with a great bundle of
    grief
    the people march.
In the night, and overhead a shovel of stars
    for keeps, the people march:
        "Where to? what next?" 80

---

[1] Color organ.

T. S. Eliot

1888

THOMAS STEARNS ELIOT was born at St. Louis and spent the first eighteen years of his life there. Both his father and his mother were members of old New England families distinguished by strong intellectual and religious interests. The poet's grandfather, The Rev. William Greenleaf Eliot, D.D., a graduate of Harvard Divinity School (1834), established the first Unitarian church at St. Louis and was instrumental in founding Washington University.

After preparatory work at Smith Academy in St. Louis and at Milton, Eliot entered Harvard in 1906. He completed his undergraduate work in three years and took his M.A. in the fourth, edited the *Harvard Advocate* (1909-10), and was Class Odist. Among his teachers were Irving Babbitt and George Santayana. After a year of study at the Sorbonne, Eliot returned to Harvard for graduate work in philosophy, completing his doctoral dissertation but not taking his degree. He traveled in Germany before the first world war, studied at Oxford, and in 1915 married an English girl. Rejected by the United States Navy because of poor health, he remained in England, teaching, working at Lloyds Bank, and serving as literary editor for a British publisher. In 1927 he became a British citizen.

Eliot's first books were *Prufrock and Other Observations* (1917) and a critical study of the poetry of Ezra Pound. In 1922 he founded *The Criterion,* a critical magazine which he edited for seventeen years. Publication of *The Waste Land* in the same year established his position as one of the most influential and representative writers of his time. This poem won a $2000 *Dial* award, and was translated into six languages, attaining especially wide circulation in France, Germany and Spain. In the introduction to a small volume of essays, *For Lancelot Andrewes* (1929), Eliot remarked that his "general point of view may be described as classicist in literature, royalist in politics, and anglo-Catholic in religion." His religious convictions were expressed in the pageant play *The Rock* (1934) and the poetic drama *Murder in the Cathedral* (1935), and were fully stated in the long essay *The Idea of a Christian Society* (1940).

Eliot's *Collected Poems,* 1909-1935, appeared in 1936, to be followed by *Four Quartets* in 1943, bringing together long poems already issued separately in 1940 and 1941. His early critical essays appeared in *The Sacred Wood* (1920). In 1932 he published *Selected Essays,* 1917-1932, and *John Dryden;* in 1933, *The Use of Poetry and the Use of Criticism* and *After Strange Gods;* in 1934 *Elizabethan Essays,* and in 1936 *Essays Ancient and Modern.*

[Most valuable of the discussions of Eliot's work is F. O. Matthiessen's *The Achievement of T. S. Eliot* (New York, 1940).]

THE LOVE SONG OF
J. ALFRED PRUFROCK
[1917 (1915)]

S'io credesse che mia risposta fosse
A persona che mai tornasse al mondo,
Questa fiamma staria senza piu scosse.
Ma perciocche giammai di questo fondo
Non torno vivo alcun s'i'odo il vero,
Senza tema d'infamia ti rispondo.[1]

Let us go then, you and I,
When the evening is spread out against the
      sky
Like a patient etherized upon a table;
Let us go, through certain half-deserted
      streets,
The muttering retreats   5
Of restless nights in one-night cheap
      hotels
And sawdust restaurants with oyster-
      shells:
Streets that follow like a tedious argument
Of insidious intent

To lead you to an overwhelming
      question. . . .   10
Oh, do not ask, "What is it?"
Let us go and make our visit.
In the room the women come and go
Talking of Michelangelo.

The yellow fog that rubs its back upon the
      window-panes,   15
The yellow smoke that rubs its muzzle on
      the window-panes,
Licked its tongue into the corners of the
      evening,
Lingered upon the pools that stand in
      drains,

---

[1] "If I could believe that my answer might be to a person who should ever return into the world, this flame would stand without more quiverings [i.e., I would not answer]; but inasmuch as, if I hear the truth, never from this depth did any living man return, without fear of infamy I answer thee."—From Dante's *Inferno,* XXVII:61-66 (Charles Eliot Norton's translation).

Let fall upon its back the soot that falls
    from chimneys,
Slipped by the terrace, made a sudden
    leap, 20
And seeing that it was a soft October
    night,
Curled once about the house, and fell
    asleep.

And indeed there will be time
For the yellow smoke that slides along the
    street,
Rubbing its back upon the window-
    panes; 25
There will be time, there will be time
To prepare a face to meet the faces that
    you meet;
There will be time to murder and create,
And time for all the works and days of
    hands
That lift and drop a question on your
    plate; 30
Time for you and time for me,
And time yet for a hundred indecisions,
And for a hundred visions and revisions,
Before the taking of a toast and tea.
In the room the women come and go 35
Talking of Michelangelo.

And indeed there will be time
To wonder, "Do I dare?" and, "Do I dare?"
Time to turn back and descend the stair,
With a bald spot in the middle of my
    hair— 40
(They will say: "How his hair is growing
    thin!")
My morning coat, my collar mounting
    firmly to the chin,
My necktie rich and modest, but asserted
    by a simple pin—
(They will say: "But how his arms and
    legs are thin!")
Do I dare 45
Disturb the universe?
In a minute there is time
For decisions and revisions which a minute
    will reverse.

For I have known them all already, known
    them all:

Have known the evenings, mornings,
    afternoons, 50
I have measured out my life with coffee
    spoons;
I know the voices dying with a dying
    fall
Beneath the music from a farther room.
    So how should I presume?

And I have known the eyes already, known
    them all— 55
The eyes that fix you in a formulated
    phrase,
And when I am formulated, sprawling on a
    pin,
When I am pinned and wriggling on the
    wall,
Then how should I begin
To spit out all the butt-ends of my days
    and ways? 60
    And how should I presume?

And I have known the arms already, known
    them all—
Arms that are braceleted and white and
    bare
(But in the lamplight, downed with light
    brown hair!)
Is it perfume from a dress 65
That makes me so digress?
Arms that lie along a table, or wrap about
    a shawl.
    And should I then presume?
    And how should I begin?

.   .   .   .

Shall I say, I have gone at dusk through
    narrow streets 70
And watched the smoke that rises from the
    pipes
Of lonely men in shirt-sleeves, leaning out
    of windows? . . .
I should have been a pair of ragged claws
Scuttling across the floors of silent seas.

And the afternoon, the evening, sleeps so
    peacefully! 75
Smoothed by long fingers,
Asleep . . . tired . . . or it malingers,
Stretched on the floor, here beside you and
    me.

Should I, after tea and cakes and ices,
Have the strength to force the moment to
  its crisis?　　　　80
But though I have wept and fasted, wept
  and prayed,
Though I have seen my head (grown
  slightly bald) brought in upon a
  platter,
I am no prophet—and here's no great
  matter;
I have seen the moment of my greatness
  flicker,
And I have seen the eternal Footman hold
  my coat, and snicker,　　　　85
And in short, I was afraid.

And would it have been worth it, after all,
After the cups, the marmalade, the tea,
Among the porcelain, among some talk of
  you and me,
Would it have been worth while,　　　　90
To have bitten off the matter with a smile,
To have squeezed the universe into a ball
To roll it toward some overwhelming
  question,
To say: "I am Lazarus, come from the
  dead,
Come back to tell you all, I shall tell you
  all"—　　　　95
If one, settling a pillow by her head,
  Should say: "That was not what I meant
    at all;
  That is not it, at all."

And would it have been worth it, after all,
Would it have been worth while,　　　　100
After the sunsets and the dooryards and the
  sprinkled streets,
After the novels, after the teacups, after
  the skirts that trail along the floor—
And this, and so much more?—
It is impossible to say just what I mean!
But as if a magic lantern threw the nerves
  in patterns on a screen:　　　　105
Would it have been worth while
If one, settling a pillow or throwing off a
  shawl,
And turning toward the window, should
  say:

"That is not it at all,
  That is not what I meant, at all."　　　　110

. . . .

No! I am not Prince Hamlet, nor was
  meant to be;
Am an attendant lord, one that will do
To swell a progress, start a scene or two,
Advise the prince; no doubt, an easy tool,
Deferential, glad to be of use,　　　　115
Politic, cautious, and meticulous;
Full of high sentence, but a bit obtuse;
At times, indeed, almost ridiculous—
Almost, at times, the Fool.

I grow old . . . I grow old . . .　　　　120
I shall wear the bottoms of my trousers
  rolled.

Shall I part my hair behind? Do I dare to
  eat a peach?
I shall wear white flannel trousers, and
  walk upon the beach.
I have heard the mermaids singing, each
  to each.

I do not think that they will sing to
  me.　　　　125

I have seen them riding seaward on the
  waves
Combing the white hair of the waves blown
  back
When the wind blows the water white and
  black.

We have lingered in the chambers of the
  sea
By sea-girls wreathed with seaweed red
  and brown　　　　130
Till human voices wake us, and we drown.

SWEENEY AMONG THE NIGHTINGALES
[1920]

Why should I speak of the nightingale?
The nightingale sings of adulterous
wrong.

Apeneck Sweeney spreads his knees
Letting his arms hang down to laugh,
The zebra stripes along his jaw
Swelling to maculate giraffe.

The circles of the stormy moon   5
Slide westward to the River Plate,
Death and the Raven drift above
And Sweeney guards the hornèd gate.

Gloomy Orion and the Dog
Are veiled; and hushed the shrunken
    seas;   10
The person in the Spanish cape
Tries to sit on Sweeney's knees

Slips and pulls the table cloth
Overturns a coffee cup,
Reorganized upon the floor   15
She yawns and draws a stocking up;

The silent man in mocha brown
Sprawls at the window-sill and gapes;
The waiter brings in oranges,
Bananas, figs and hot-house grapes; 20

The silent vertebrate exhales,
Contracts and concentrates, withdraws;
Rachel *née* Rabinovitch
Tears at the grapes with murderous paws;

She and the lady in the cape   25
Are suspect, thought to be in league;
Therefore the man with heavy eyes
Declines the gambit, shows fatigue,

Leaves the room and reappears
Outside the window, leaning in,   30
Branches of wistaria
Circumscribe a golden grin;

The host with someone indistinct
Converses at the door apart,
The nightingales are singing near   35
The Convent of the Sacred Heart,

And sang within the bloody wood
When Agamemnon cried aloud,
And let their liquid siftings fall
To stain the stiff dishonoured shroud. 40

THE HOLLOW MEN
[1925]

A penny for the Old Guy.
MISTAH KURTZ—HE DEAD.[1]

I

We are the hollow men
We are the stuffed men
Leaning together
Headpiece filled with straw. Alas!
Our dried voices, when   5
We whisper together
Are quiet and meaningless
As wind in dry grass
Or rats' feet over broken glass
In our dry cellar   10

Shape without form, shade without colour,
Paralysed force, gesture without motion;

Those who have crossed
With direct eyes, to death's other Kingdom
Remember us—if at all—not as lost   15
Violent souls, but only
As the hollow men
The stuffed men.

II

Eyes I dare not meet in dreams
In death's dream kingdom   20
These do not appear:
There, the eyes are
Sunlight on a broken column
There, is a tree swinging
And voices are   25
In the wind's singing
More distant and more solemn
Than a fading star.

Let me be no nearer
In death's dream kingdom   30
Let me also wear
Such deliberate disguises
Rat's coat, crowskin, crossed staves

[1] See Joseph Conrad's story, "Heart of Darkness."

In a field
Behaving as the wind behaves　　　　　35
No nearer—

Not that final meeting
In the twilight kingdom

III

This is the dead land
This is cactus land　　　　　　　　　40
Here the stone images
Are raised, here they receive
The supplication of a dead man's hand
Under the twinkle of a fading star.

Is it like this　　　　　　　　　　45
In death's other kingdom
Waking alone
At the hour when we are
Trembling with tenderness
Lips that would kiss　　　　　　　50
Form prayers to broken stone.

IV

The eyes are not here
There are no eyes here
In this valley of dying stars
In this hollow valley　　　　　　55
This broken jaw of our lost kingdoms

In this last of meeting places
We grope together
And avoid speech
Gathered on this beach of the tumid
　　　river　　　　　　　　　　60

Sightless, unless
The eyes reappear
As the perpetual star
Multifoliate rose
Of death's twilight kingdom　　　65
The hope only
Of empty men.

V

Here we go round the prickly pear
Prickly pear, prickly pear

Here we go round the prickly pear　70
At five o'clock in the morning.

Between the idea
And the reality
Between the motion
And the act　　　　　　　　　　75
Falls the Shadow
　　　　For Thine is the Kingdom

Between the conception
And the creation
Between the emotion　　　　　　80
And the response
Falls the Shadow
　　　　Life is very long

Between the desire
And the spasm　　　　　　　　85
Between the potency
And the existence
Between the essence
And the descent
Falls the Shadow　　　　　　　90
　　　　For Thine is the Kingdom

For Thine is
Life is
For Thine is the

This is the way the world ends　95
This is the way the world ends
This is the way the world ends
Not with a bang but a whimper.

JOURNEY OF THE MAGI
[1928]

'A cold coming we had of it,
Just the worst time of the year
For a journey, and such a long journey:
The ways deep and the weather sharp,
The very dead of winter.'　　　　5
And the camels galled, sore-footed,
　　　refractory,
Lying down in the melting snow.
There were times we regretted
The summer palaces on slopes, the terraces,
And the silken girls bringing sherbet.　10
Then the camel men cursing and grumbling

And running away, and wanting their
    liquor and women,
And the night-fires going out, and the lack
    of shelters,
And the cities hostile and the towns
    unfriendly
And the villages dirty and charging high
    prices: 15
A hard time we had of it.
At the end we preferred to travel all
    night,
Sleeping in snatches,
With the voices singing in our ears, saying
That this was all folly.   20

Then at dawn we came down to a
    temperate valley,
Wet, below the snow line, smelling of
    vegetation;
With a running stream and a water-mill
    beating the darkness,
And three trees on the low sky,
And an old white horse galloped away in
    the meadow.   25
Then we came to a tavern with vine-leaves
    over the lintel,
Six hands at an open door dicing for
    pieces of silver,
And feet kicking the empty wine-skins.
But there was no information, and so we
    continued
And arrived at evening, not a moment too
    soon   30
Finding the place; it was (you may say)
    satisfactory.

All this was a long time ago, I remember,
And I would do it again, but set down
This set down
This: were we led all that way for   35
Birth or Death? There was a Birth,
    certainly,
We had evidence and no doubt. I had seen
    birth and death,
But had thought they were different; this
    Birth was
Hard and bitter agony for us, like Death,
    our death.
We returned to our places, these
    Kingdoms,   40

But no longer at ease here, in the old
    dispensation,
With an alien people clutching their gods.
I should be glad of another death.

ANIMULA

[1929]

'Issues from the hand of God, the simple
    soul'
To a flat world of changing lights and
    noise,
To light, dark, dry or damp, chilly or
    warm;
Moving between the legs of tables and of
    chairs,
Rising or falling, grasping at kisses and
    toys,   5
Advancing boldly, sudden to take alarm,
Retreating to the corner of arm and knee,
Eager to be reassured, taking pleasure
In the fragrant brilliance of the Christmas
    tree,
Pleasure in the wind, the sunlight and the
    sea;   10
Studies the sunlit pattern on the floor
And running stags around a silver tray;
Confounds the actual and the fanciful,
Content with playing-cards and kings and
    queens,
What the fairies do and what the servants
    say.   15
The heavy burden of the growing soul
Perplexes and offends more, day by day;
Week by week, offends and perplexes more
With the imperatives of 'is and seems'
And may and may not, desire and
    control.   20
The pain of living and the drug of dreams
Curl up the small soul in the window seat
Behind the *Encyclopædia Britannica*.
Issues from the hand of time the simple
    soul
Irresolute and selfish, misshapen, lame,
Unable to fare forward or retreat,
Fearing the warm reality, the offered good,
Denying the importunity of the blood,
Shadow of its own shadows, spectre in its
    own gloom,
Leaving disordered papers in a dusty
    room;   30

Living first in the silence after the
    viaticum.

Pray for Guiterriez, avid of speed and
    power,
For Boudin, blown to pieces,
For this one who made a great fortune,
And that one who went his own way. 35
Pray for Floret, by the boarhound slain
    between the yew trees,
Pray for us now and at the hour of our
    birth.

From
THE ROCK
[1934]

X

You have seen the house built, you have
    seen it adorned
By one who came in the night, it is now
    dedicated to GOD.
It is now a visible church, one more light
    set on a hill
In a world confused and dark and
    disturbed by portents of fear.
And what shall we say of the future? Is
    one church all we can build? 5
Or shall the Visible Church go on to
    conquer the World?

The great snake lies ever half awake, at the
    bottom of the pit of the world,
    curled
In folds of himself until he awakens in
    hunger and moving his head to right
    and to left prepares for his hour to
    devour.
But the Mystery of Iniquity is a pit too
    deep for mortal eyes to plumb. Come
Ye out from among those who prize the
    serpent's golden eyes,   10
The worshippers, self-given sacrifice of the
    snake. Take
Your way and be ye separate.
Be not too curious of Good and Evil;
Seek not to count the future waves of
    Time;
But be ye satisfied that you have light 15
Enough to take your step and find your
    foothold.

O Light Invisible, we praise Thee!
Too bright for mortal vision.
O Greater Light, we praise Thee for the
    less;
The eastern light our spires touch at
    morning,   20
The light that slants upon our western
    doors at evening,
The twilight over stagnant pools at bat-
    flight,
Moon light and star light, owl and moth
    light,
Glow-worm glowlight on a grassblade.
O Light Invisible, we worship Thee!   25

We thank Thee for the lights that we have
    kindled,
The light of altar and of sanctuary;
Small lights of those who meditate at
    midnight
And lights directed through the coloured
    panes of windows
And light reflected from the polished
    stone,   30
The gilded carven wood, the coloured
    fresco.
Our gaze is submarine, our eyes look
    upward
And see the light that fractures through
    unquiet water.
We see the light but see not whence it
    comes.
O Light Invisible, we glorify Thee!   35

In our rhythm of earthly life we tire of
    light.
We are glad when the day ends, when
    the play ends; and ecstasy is too
    much pain.
We are children quickly tired: children
    who are up in the night and fall
    asleep as the rocket is fired; and the
    day is long for work or play.
We tire of distraction or concentration, we
    sleep and are glad to sleep,
Controlled by the rhythm of blood and the
    day and the night and the seasons. 40
And we must extinguish the candle, put out
    the light and relight it;
Forever must quench, forever relight the
    flame.

Therefore we thank Thee for our little
   light, that is dappled with shadow.
We thank Thee who hast moved us to
   building, to finding, to forming at
   the ends of our fingers and beams of
   our eyes.
And when we have built an altar to the

Invisible Light, we may set thereon
   the little lights for which our bodily
   vision is made.   45
And we thank Thee that darkness reminds
   us of light.
O Light Invisible, we give Thee thanks for
   Thy great glory!

Edna St. Vincent Millay
1892

EDNA MILLAY was born at Rockland, Maine. Her first book of poems, *Renascence* (1917), appeared while she was a student at Vassar. The lively and quotable personal poems of *A Few Figs from Thistles* (1920) and *Second April* (1921) made her widely popular in the 1920's. She stated a philosophy of life and art in the sonnet sequence of *Fatal Interview* (1931), and expressed her active interest in the problems of her time in the narrative *Conversation at Midnight* (1937). She has written plays in verse, among them *Aria da Capo* (1920) and *The Lamp and the Bell* (1921), and the libretto for an opera composed by Deems Taylor, *The King's Henchman* (1927). Other books by Miss Millay include *Wine from These Grapes* (1934); *Huntsman, What Quarry?* (1939); *Make Bright the Arrows* (1940); *There Are No Islands, Any More* (1940); *Collected Sonnets* (1941); and *Collected Lyrics* (1943). [See Elizabeth Atkins, *Edna St. Vincent Millay and Her Times* (New York, 1936).]

From
CONVERSATION AT MIDNIGHT
[1937]

I—SOME OF THE DRAMATIS PERSONAE [1]

MERTON is a distinguished-looking man of sixty-eight, a stock-broker, very wealthy. He has travelled extensively, and collected some famous and valuable paintings. He does not care for music, but loves poerty, of which in his opinion little has been written since Tennyson wrote *In Memoriam*. He is interested in the breeding and training of thoroughbreds, and owns a racing-stable. He has liked and admired Ricardo since the evening they first met, when Ricardo proceeded to outbid him at a private sale of old Dutch tiles. He is frequently a dinner-guest at Ricardo's house, but has long ago given up inviting Ricardo to dinner at his own house on Park Avenue, Ricardo having several times replied to such invitations by saying that he never does what he does not enjoy doing, and that he enjoys neither contract bridge nor the conversation of women. Merton is of Protestant stock, and accompanies his wife to church. He is a conservative, and votes Republican.

JOHN is a painter, a man considered by his fellow-artists to be exceptionally gifted, but who is financially unsuccess-

---

[1] Title supplied by the present editors.

ful. He makes his living now by painting portraits. The best work he ever did is a painting of Merton; but Merton does not like the portrait, and it has never been shown. John is by nature a religious man, and is deeply troubled by the fact that he can find nothing in which he can whole-heartedly believe. He met Ricardo several years ago, when he came to the house in Tenth Street to request the loan for exhibition of one of his early paintings, which Ricardo had bought from the gallery at the close of John's first show. John is forty-five, thin and very tall. He is not much interested in politics, but votes, when not too disheartened to vote at all, Democrat.

The name PYGMALION is a nickname. Pygmalion is a writer of short stories for popular magazines, financially very successful. He is forty years old, good-looking, though not so slender as he would like to be, very well-dressed, extremely attractive to women, gay, thoroughly disillusioned, making the most out of life for himself, not bothering to vote at all.

CARL is forty-three, somewhat under medium height, physically agile and graceful, plays an excellent game of tennis; . . . Carl is a communist. He is a poet, and has published three volumes of poetry, two written before he was thirty-five, which both Merton and Ricardo greatly admired, one written recently, which Merton finds incomprehensible and infuriating, but which amuses and rather fascinates Ricardo. Carl and Ricardo first met several years ago on board the *Cabo Tortosa,* a cargo-boat bound from New York to Barcelona. They were the only passengers, and avoided each other for ten days. On the eleventh they got into an argument as to the difference between dolphins and porpoises, and for the remainder of the voyage talked unintermittently. Carl and Pygmalion were class-mates at Harvard.

RICARDO is forty-three years old. He is the son of an Italian petty nobleman and an American woman. Both his parents are dead. He has inherited from his mother, along with a considerable fortune, the house in Tenth Street in which his mother was born, a handsome estate in the country known as Black Hall, and a gentle and affectionate nature. He has inherited from his father a striking physical beauty and an aristocratic and subtle mind. He is a liberal, and an agnostic.

II—SOME OF THE CONVERSATION [2]

TIME: The present.
PLACE: New York.
SCENE: The drawing room of Ricardo's house, a fine old house in Tenth Street, just west of Fifth Avenue.

CARL

Why, if you really are opposed to *anything* beyond personal discomfort
    and loss of property,—*why,*
If you really are distressed by the prospect
    of another war,
Don't you do something about it?—all you
    do is wring your hands and cry!
Why don't you consider by whom these
    wars are waged, and what for?
Then fight all future war by fighting the
    fascist state?—   5
It is that, particularly, it seems to me,
    that you all hate.

MERTON

It is that among other things, not particularly, that we propose, if we
    cannot curb it, at least to isolate.
"War and Fascism" are not Siamese twins,
    in spite of your clever slogan.
    Imagine, if you can,
What will happen when Russia, whose
    birth-rate is rapidly increasing,
    becomes as crowded as Japan.

---

[2] Title supplied by the present editors.

CARL (to Merton)

Even on your own terms, even with
everything your own way, you've
made a mess of things.   10
You can't any longer even support your
slaves in the slavery
To which they are accustomed. You are
unfit to rule.

Your economics is a make-shift, hit-or-
miss-assembled, third-degree, defen-
sive war, offensive peace,
Stuffed eagle, eye for a tooth, compulsory
school,

Lynch-law, plate-glass, red-plush, chro-
mium, hennaed horse-hair,   15
Cellophane-wrapped what-not; a hand-to-
mouth—
Septic-hand-to-sterilized-mouth affair.
It belongs in a side-show, along with all
the other obese
Two-headed monstrosities. And don't
worry, it will soon be there.

RICARDO

It is a pity these communists feel called
upon to imbibe not only their
morals   20
But also their manners, from Marx;
The grandfather of present-day communism
regrettably has stamped his progeny
Not only (and this only on occasion) with
the broad philosophical brow,
But also with the narrow humourless vanity and the shrill spite
That marred somewhat his articulation
then as now.   25

He was a talented, intolerant, jealous,
nasty old man.

It was the essential vulgarity of his mind
that at length betrayed him,
Despite his abstruse and admirable works,
into the arms of the vulgar.
Arrogance, abuse, bad temper, jealousy,
spleen,
Are medicines easy for the mob to swallow,
no capsules   30

Are required to disguise these tastes, they
are licked from the spoon.

Few people, comparatively speaking, have
read *Das Kapital;* those who say
they have read it
Include, among others, earnest workers,
who earnestly intend
To read it, but who, of course, work hard
and have not the time.

I, who have infinite leisure to read, being
a rich man   35
Uninterested in becoming any richer, and
interested in books,
Have read it. It is a fascinating and a
repulsive work;
Interminable, never for a moment brilliant, often profound,
Profound for pages, then suddenly infantile; best
When coldest, when most detached; it is a
great work, truly,   40
But marred by jealousies, by hatred of a
class which should have been—
By an economist, by a philosopher—considered only as one
Phenomenon in an anachronistic system
about to fall.

CARL

And having said that, what, precisely,
have you said?
You've informed us that you've read   45
Das Kapital, and that according to you
Marx was talking through his whisk-
ers; O.K.
Never mind how he said it; the point is:
what did he *say?*
And speaking of "vulgarity," isn't it just
a little bit cheap
To set the flaws of a great work—and you
admit it to be a great work—in the
front window; and try to keep
Its greatness in the back-lot?   50

RICARDO

I was using the world "vulgar" in the
Latin sense.

CARL
You most decidedly were not.

MERTON (to Carl)
Oppressed you *may* be, overworked or
    unemployed you *may* be,
But your Cause has been nursed and fos-
    tered in the generous lap
Of a liberal capitalistic state; you're an
    incubator baby,   55
Too weak to live in a draught, and accept-
    ing your pap
As your rightful due, and yelling for more,
    and not even a thank-you
To the system to which you owe your life,
    and which you mean to destroy
The moment you can stand on your feet!
    By God, *I'd* yank you
Out into the world—and you wouldn't
    have a printing-press for a toy   60
Either, or a nation-wide hook-up for a red
    tin horn,
If I had my say-so! But the government's
    a soft old fool,
Always getting all het up about the pre-
    maturely born,
And spending millions to cart a lot of
    queer-shaped heads to school.
You're pretty well off, I can tell you, in the
    U.S.A.   65
Think of me, when you're feeling home-
    sick for the good old times some
    day.

CARL
Don't worry, there'll be plenty of people
    thinking of you
When the moment's ripe. You might even
    get a post-card saying, "Dear
Merton, Cross marks modest apartment in
    the new
State Penitentiary. Wishing you were
    here."   70

MERTON
Why, that's no news! Do you think I don't
    know that?
That's what I've been saying all along. Do
    you think I don't know

That with *you* in power I wouldn't stand
    the chance of a rat
In a research laboratory?— Yet here you
    come and go
Unmolested, and shoot off your mouth, and
    publish the Daily Worker, and in-
    sist   75
On your rights under a liberal Constitu-
    tion! Tell me, would you care
To try publishing in Moscow today a paper
    called the Daily Capitalist?
Or preach the blessings of the profit-system
    to a crowd in the Red Square?

CARL
That's a quite different matter. Look here,
    even to your warped vision isn't it
    plain
That there's a difference between over-
    throwing a tyrannical government
    that is oppressing the majority of
    the people,   80
And scheming to undermine a government
    of the people for private gain?

MERTON
Certainly there's a difference. But suppose
    it were my honest conviction
That society from the bottom up is better
    off when divided into classes?
Suppose it were my impartial judgment
    that the amount of enslavement and
    affliction
Among the poor is less in a capitalist state
    than under a dictator-for-life chosen
    by the masses?   85
Should I be allowed to express that point
    of view or not?

CARL
In the first place, you'd be crazy . . . !

PYGMALION
And in the second place, you'd be shot.

RICARDO
Don't let it excite you, Merton. By the time
    we get communism here,
It will have grown so bourgeois that you'll

hardly notice the difference. Tammany Hall has already begun to appear 90
In Russia. Give a Comrade the chance
To hand out jobs, and he hands them to the boys from the home town, and to his sisters and his cousins and his aunts.

CARL

All that's being changed!

RICARDO

Things have been changed here, too,
When under pressure it seemed the expedient thing to do. 95

MERTON (to Carl)

In order to build new factories, in order even
To putty new window-panes into cobwebbed factory-windows, in order to repair
Old machinery, to say nothing of buying new; in order to procure
The raw materials of production; in order to be free to drill
The well that may not gush; to plant the acres that may be scorched or drowned 100
Before the season of the harvest; in order to risk great loss, and even in the good times
To wait for years before the enterprise begins to pay even its initial cost,—
You must have capital.
Your proletarian state will be a proletarian state only in the morning,
While it labours for its daily bread and shelter and shoes; 105
In the afternoon, that state will become a capitalist
Or it will cease to exist.

The surplus value that today, unjustly or justly,
Is taken over by the individual factory-owner to re-invest
In implements and materials, or to speculate with, or to fritter away, 110

Will be seized by the State, less adroitly but more ruthlessly even,
To be dispensed as the State sees fit, for sound or injudicious purchasing,
For uniforms, for statutes, for obsolete or unproven and impracticable machinery, or for efficient machinery;
For war, or for peace,—probably for both, as is the case today.
The worker will be quite as helpless then as now: he will earn a living of sorts, and the rest will go to his employer, that is, the State, and he will have nothing to say. 115

CARL

Don't worry, we can work it out, we're quite as brainy as you,
And we've no mental alimony to pay to an incompatible Ideal!—
That saps a man's resources.
A class that must daily construe
Its evil deeds in terms of righteousness has a part-time job to do 120
That will eventually exhaust it for the day.
The class that need not conceal
Either from the world or from itself what is its real
Objective, proceeds at once from the will to the deed, with no terrain
Of hilly evasion and swampy compromise to cross before it gain 125
Its goal.
Split men go forth to war in vain
Against the undivided. The flawed cannot defeat the whole.

MERTON

Interesting, of course, if true; but if true, then as true
Of the Hitlerite, and of the termite, as of you. 130

RICARDO

If, however, singleness of purpose and direct approach could contend
With deviousness and guile, we should not be here, my friend.

Sealed in Jurassic mortar the just bones
    repose
Of many a race that knew what it wanted
    and followed its nose.

CARL

Precisely. And today it's the capitalistic
    system that's so over-weight it can
    hardly waddle.   135
          If you have tears
For a prehistoric monster prepare to shed
    them now, for it's about to croak.
Oh, it can feed itself still by grabbing
    everything in reach for another
    few years
Perhaps; but there are conditions under
    which to be a stick-in-the-mud ceases
    to be a joke.

MERTON

The fittest to survive may well derive some
    satisfaction,   140
But should refrain from finding cause for
    pride, in that:
The value of a life is not determined by
    that life's protraction:
The fittest to survive in a sewer, is a
    sewer-rat.

PYGMALION (as if to himself)

The world stinks. It stinks like a dead cat
    under a doorstep. It stinks to hell.
Wherever I step I have to hold my nose,
    the world stinks so.   145
I can't get to windward of the stink, there's
    not a breath of air
Stirring, just a big stink squatting under
    the hot sky.

JOHN

Pgy, you're drunk.

PYGMALION

You bet I'm drunk. Do you think I don't
    know
Which side my gin is bittered on? Have
    you had a good whiff   150
Of this stinking world, and still you want
    to stay sober?

RICARDO

If you do not believe in God it is a good
    thing
To believe in Communism. There is much
    comfort,
As I observe, when lowering into an oblong
    hole a much prized object,
In the reflection that it is either (a) safe
    in the arms of Jesus, or (b)   155
Only a cog in a wheel and that the wheel
    continues to revolve and that that is
    the important thing.

If you do not believe in God and cannot
    bring yourself
To believe in Communism, then, I may say,
    you are in a singularly
Unprotected position.
You have not so much as a last year's
    mullein-stalk to set your back
    against; all winds blow upon you. 160
As for myself, I do not believe in God
    and I do not care for
The society of people.

I am willing to give them my coat, but I
    am not willing
To lend them my coat and have them wear
    it and return it.
I am willing to give them my loaf, but I
    am not willing   165
To sit and share it with them.
I do not wish to die, but I would rather
    die
Than have for my daily horizon year
    in-year-out—and sing Huzza! into
    the bargain—
The hairs on the backs of the necks of
    other people.
And I would rather stand with my back
    against an icy, unintelligible void 170
Than be steamed upon from behind by the
    honest breaths of many well-wishers.

      . . . . . .

CARL

You talk too well.
And you talk too god-damned much.
What about an adolescent stutter, just for
    a change,

And a sturdy, inarticulate GOOD
    IDEA? 175

RICARDO

It is difficult to dramatize the liberal at-
    titude; therefore we have no fol-
    lowing. Our flag,
Unless it flap at half-mast, floats too high
For the crude of vision to perceive.
We weave
No pattern of uniformed men in the shape
    of our emblem; we sing no lusty
    song; we have no battle-cry. 180
Bright colour and insistent noise attract
The multitude, without whose perilous
    favour
We may exist, but cannot act.
The simple man wants food, and wants to
    fight and sing.
How shall the thoughtful, the unshouted
    thing 185
Prevail with him? Though it should feed
    him better than ever he was fed
    before,
Offering no outlet for his intense but sim-
    ple spirit's need, no marching,
Monotonous, . . . hypnotic; no dances
    easy to learn;
It offers him food, and nothing more.

Only by self-defilement could a liberal
    party earn 190
A place among the branded herds; and to
    return
From shoddy years, from Avernus, is not
    easy.
Caught
In the amorphous amber of vulgarity would
    sit at length,

Helpless and fossilized, the winged, the
    noble thought.
Vulgarity alone has strength. 195

JOHN

If that were true,
Ricardo—and you will bear with me, for I
    am quoting you—
We should not now be here.
Not through the headlong, indiscriminate
    advance
Of unicellular minds, nor yet through the
    adroit 200
Juxtapositions of sardonic Chance
Do those great miracles appear
Which all men use, and better their condi-
    tion by; and though they are un-
    aware
To what extent superior is that egregious
    force, or with characteristic debonair
Assurance give it no thought at all, yet the
    egregious force is there,— 205
Feeding the herd that otherwise would go,
Starving, in search of grass in exhausted
    pastures where it has ceased to
    grow.
The liberal, the deliberate, the low of
    voice
Might well adopt by choice
And charter what is their fitting and
    historic rôle: 210
These are the whisperers-together, these
    from all time
Have been the angelic spies in the loud
    councils of the confident lost,
The insidious lobby, plausibly in terms of
    saving and cost
Planting the untemporal seed; the insistent
    leaven
That leavens the reluctant whole. 215

Wallace Stevens

1879

WALLACE STEVENS studied at Harvard, then entered a law school and was admitted to the bar in New York City in 1904. He became a member of the legal department of an insurance company at Hartford, Connecticut, in 1916, and was made vice-president of the company in 1934. His books of poems include *Harmonium* (1923, revised edition 1931); *Ideas of Order* (1936); *Owl's Clover* (1936); *The Man with the Blue Guitar* (1937); *Parts of a World* (1942); *Notes Toward a Supreme Fiction* (1942); *Transport to Summer* (1947); and *Three Academic Pieces* (1948). [See Hi Simons' "The Genre of Wallace Stevens" in *The Sewanee Review* (Autumn, 1945).]

ANOTHER WEEPING WOMAN
[1923]

Pour the unhappiness out
From your too bitter heart,
Which grieving will not sweeten.

Poison grows in this dark.
It is in the water of tears   5
Its black blooms rise.

The magnificent cause of being,
The imagination, the one reality
In this imagined world

Leaves you   10
With him for whom no phantasy moves,
And you are pierced by a death.

THE WORMS AT HEAVEN'S GATE
[1923]

Out of the tomb, we bring Badroulbadour,
Within our bellies, we her chariot.
Here is an eye. And here are, one by one,
The lashes of that eye and its white lid.
Here is the cheek on which that lid declined,   5
And, finger after finger, here, the hand,
The genius of that cheek. Here are the lips,
The bundle of the body and the feet.

. . . .

Out of the tomb we bring Badroulbadour.

A HIGH-TONED OLD CHRISTIAN WOMAN
[1923]

Poetry is the supreme fiction, madame.
Take the moral law and make a nave of it
And from the nave build haunted heaven. Thus,
The conscience is converted into palms,
Like windy citherns hankering for hymns. 5
We agree in principle. That's clear. But take
The opposing law and make a peristyle,
And from the peristyle project a masque
Beyond the planets. Thus, our bawdiness,
Unpurged by epitaph, indulged at last, 10
Is equally converted into palms,
Squiggling like saxophones. And palm for palm,
Madame, we are where we began. Allow,
Therefore, that in the planetary scene
Your disaffected flagellants, well-stuffed, 15
Smacking their muzzy bellies in parade,
Proud of such novelties of the sublime,
Such tink and tank and tunk-a-tunk-tunk,
May, merely may, madame, whip from themselves
A jovial hullabaloo among the spheres. 20
This will make widows wince. But fictive things
Wink as they will. Wink most when widows wince.

ANECDOTE OF THE JAR
[1923]

I placed a jar in Tennessee,
And round it was, upon a hill.
It made the slovenly wilderness
Surround that hill.

The wilderness rose up to it,   5
And sprawled around, no longer wild.
The jar was round upon the ground
And tall and of a port in air.

It took dominion everywhere.
The jar was gray and bare.   10
It did not give of bird or bush,
Like nothing else in Tennessee.

ARCHITECTURE [1]
[1923]

I

What manner of building shall we build?
Let us design a chastel de chasteté.
De pensée. . . .
Never cease to deploy the structure.
Keep the laborers shouldering plinths.   5
Pass the whole of life earing the clink of
    the
Chisels of the stone-cutters cutting the
    stones.

II

In this house, what manner of utterance
    shall there be?
What heavenly dithyramb
And cantilene?   10
What niggling forms of gargoyle patter?
Of what shall the speech be,
In that splay of marble
And of obedient pillars?

III

And how shall those come vested that
    come there?   15
In their ugly reminders?
Or gaudy as tulips?
As they climb the stairs
To the group of Flora Coddling Hecuba?

As they climb the flights   20
To the closes
Overlooking whole seasons?

IV

Let us build the building of light.
Push up the towers
To the cock-tops.   25
These are the pointings of our edifice,
Which, like a gorgeous palm,
Shall tuft the commonplace.
These are the window-sill
On which the quiet moonlight lies.   30

V

How shall we hew the sun,
Split it and make blocks
To build a ruddy palace?
How carve the violet moon
To set in nicks?   35
Let us fix portals, east and west,
Abhorring green-blue north and blue-green
    south.
Our chiefest dome a demoiselle of gold.
Pierce the interior with pouring shafts,
In diverse chambers.   40
Pierce, too, with buttresses of coral air
And purple timbers,
Various argentines,
Embossings of the sky.

VI

And, finally, set guardians in the
    grounds,   45
Gray, gruesome grumblers.
For no one proud, nor stiff,
No solemn one, nor pale,
No chafferer, may come
To sully the begonias, nor vex   50
With holy or sublime ado
The kremlin of kermess.

VII

Only the lusty and the plenteous
Shall walk
The bronze-filled plazas   55
And the nut-shell esplanades.

---

[1] This poem was omitted from the revised
edition of *Harmonium* (1931).

THE IDEA OF ORDER AT KEY WEST
[1935]

She sang beyond the genius of the sea.
The water never formed to mind or voice,
Like a body wholly body, fluttering
Its empty sleeves; and yet its mimic motion
Made constant cry, caused constantly a
    cry,   5
That was not ours although we understood,
Inhuman, of the veritable ocean.

The sea was not a mask. No more was she.
The song and water were not medleyed
    sound,
Even if what she sang was what she
    heard,   10
Since what she sang was uttered word by
    word.
It may be that in all her phrases stirred
The grinding water and the gasping wind;
But it was she and not the sea we heard.

For she was the maker of the song she
    sang.   15
The ever-hooded, tragic-gestured sea
Was merely a place by which she walked
    to sing.
Whose spirit is this? we said, because we
    knew
It was the spirit that we sought and knew
That we should ask this often as she
    sang.   20

If it was only the dark voice of the sea
That rose, or even colored by many waves;
If it was only the outer voice of sky
And cloud, of the sunken coral water-
    walled,
However clear, it would have been deep
    air,   25
The heaving speech of air, a summer sound
Repeated in a summer without end
And sound alone. But it was more than
    that,
More even than her voice, and ours, among
The meaningless plungings of water and
    the wind,   30
Theatrical distances, bronze shadows
    heaped

On high horizons, mountainous atmospheres
Of sky and sea.

                It was her voice that made
The sky acutest at its vanishing.   35
She measured to the hour its solitude.
She was the single artificer of the world
In which she sang. And when she sang, the
    sea,
Whatever self it had, became the self
That was her song, for she was the maker.
    Then we,   40
As we beheld her striding there alone,
Knew that there never was a world for her
Except the one she sang and, singing, made.

Ramon Fernandez, tell me, if you know,
Why, when the singing ended and we
    turned   45
Toward the town, tell why the glassy lights,
The lights in the fishing boats at anchor
    there,
As the night descended, tilting in the air,
Mastered the night and portioned out the
    sea,
Fixing emblazoned zones and fiery poles, 50
Arranging, deepening, enchanting night.

Oh! Blessed rage for order, pale Ramon,
The maker's rage to order words of the sea,
Words of the fragrant portals, dimly-
    starred,
And of ourselves and of our origins,   55
In ghostlier demarcations, keener sounds.

SOLDIER, THERE IS A WAR [1]
[1942]

Soldier, there is a war between the mind
And sky, between thought and day and
    night. It is
For that the poet is always in the sun,

Patches the moon together in his room
To his Virgilian cadences, up down,   5
Up down. It is a war that never ends.

---

[1] This is the final poem of the group
entitled "Notes Toward a Supreme Fiction," published separately (1942) and included in *Transport to Summer* (1947).

Yet it depends on yours. The two are one.
They are a plural, a right and left, a pair,
Two parallels that meet if only in

The meeting of their shadows or that
    meet   10
In a book in a barrack, a letter from Malay.
But your war ends. And after it you
    return

With six meats and twelve wines or else
    without
To walk another room . . . Monsieur and
    comrade,

The soldier **is poor without the** poet's
    lines,   15

His petty syllabi, the sounds that stick,
Inevitably modulating, in the blood.
And war for war, each has its gallant kind.

How simply the fictive hero becomes the
    real;
How gladly with proper words the soldier
    dies,   20
If he must, or lives on the bread of faith-
    ful speech.

1899 ∾ *Hart Crane* ∾ 1932

HAROLD HART CRANE was born in Garettsville, Ohio, the son of parents of pioneer stock. His father eventually removed to Cleveland and there became a wealthy candy manufacturer. The boy was a poet from childhood, wrote creditable verse at thirteen, and continued to develop as artist and mystic in spite of his father's desire that he should enter business. His parents were divorced during his childhood.

Young Crane visited his mother at the Isle of Pines in 1916, and in the next year spent some time in Paris and New York; thus he became acquainted by the time he was eighteen with both the sea and the city—two major influences upon him. The generosity of Otto Kahn, the banker, rescued him from an advertising career, and made it possible for him to devote himself to poetry. His poem "The Bridge," published in 1930, received the Helen Haire Levinson prize from *Poetry,* and the next year he was awarded a Guggenheim fellowship for writing to be done in Mexico. On his way home to New York from Mexico, he leaped from the boat and perished.

Crane's first volume was a collection of imagist verse, *White Buildings* (1926). His *Collected Poems* were published in 1933.

[P. Horton's *Hart Crane: The Life of an American Poet* (New York, 1937), and Brom Weber's *Hart Crane* (New York, 1948), are both biographical and critical. Critical introductions appear in both *White Buildings* and *Collected Poems;* they are supplied by Allen Tate and Waldo Frank respectively.]

From
THE BRIDGE
[1929]

CAPE HATTERAS

> *The seas all crossed,*
> *weathered the capes, the voyage done* [1] *...*
> —*Walt Whitman*

Imponderable the dinosaur
    sinks slow,
        the mammoth saurian
        ghoul, the eastern
        Cape ...
While rises in the west the coastwise range,
    slowly the hushed land—
Combustion at the astral core—the dorsal
    change
Of energy—convulsive shift of sand ...
But we, who round the capes, the prom-
    ontories   5
Where strange tongues vary messages of
    surf
Below grey citadels, repeating to the stars
The ancient names—return home to our
    own
Hearths, there to eat an apple and recall
The songs that gypsies dealt us at Mar-
    seille   10
Or how the priests walked—slowly through
    Bombay—
Or to read you, Walt,—knowing us in
    thrall
To that deep wonderment, our native clay
Whose depth of red, eternal flesh of
    Pocahontas—
Those continental folded aeons, sur-
    charged   15
With sweetness below derricks, chimneys,
    tunnels—
Is veined by all that time has really
    pledged us ...
And from above, thin squeaks of radio
    static,
The captured fume of space foams in our
    ears—
What whisperings of far watches on the
    main   20
Relapsing into silence, while time clears
Our lenses, lifts a focus, resurrects

A periscope to glimpse what joys or pain
Our eyes can share or answer—then de-
    flects
Us, shunting to a labyrinth submersed 25
Where each sees only his dim past re-
    versed ...

But that star-glistered salver of infinity,
The circle, blind crucible of endless space,
Is sluiced by motion,—subjugated never.
Adam and Adam's answer in the forest 30
Left Hesperus mirrored in the lucid pool.
Now the eagle dominates our days, is
    jurist
Of the ambiguous cloud. We know the
    strident rule
Of wings imperious ... Space, instanta-
    neous,
Flickers a moment, consumes us in its
    smile: 35
A flash over the horizon—shifting gears—
And we have laughter, or more sudden
    tears.
Dream cancels dream in this new realm of
    fact
From which we wake into the dream of
    act;
Seeing himself an atom in a shroud— 40
Man hears himself an engine in a cloud!

"—Recorders ages hence" [2]—ah, syllables
    of faith!
Walt, tell me, Walt Whitman, if infinity
Be still the same as when you walked the
    beach
Near Paumanok—your lone patrol—and
    heard the wraith   45
Through surf, its bird note there a long
    time falling [3] ...
For you, the panoramas and this breed of
    towers,
Of you—the theme that's statured in the
    cliff,
O Saunterer on free ways still ahead!

---

[1] The quotation is from Whitman's poem
"Passage to India." See pp. 103-109.

[2] The title of one of Whitman's shorter
poems.

[3] See Whitman's poem, "Out of the
Cradle Endlessly Rocking," pp. 83-87.

Not this our empire yet, but labyrinth 50
Wherein your eyes, like the Great Navigator's without ship,
Gleam from the great stones of each prison crypt
Of canyoned traffic . . . Confronting the Exchange,
Surviving in a world of stocks,—they also range
Across the hills where second timber strays 55
Back over Connecticut farms, abandoned pastures,—
Sea eyes and tidal, undenying, bright with myth!

The nasal whine of power whips a new universe . . .
Where spouting pillars spoor the evening sky,
Under the looming stacks of the gigantic power house 60
Stars prick the eyes with sharp ammoniac proverbs,
New verities, new inklings in the velvet hummed
Of dynamos, where hearing's leash is strummed . . .
Power's script,—wound, bobbin-bound, refined—
Is stropped to the slap of belts on booming spools, spurred 65
Into the bulging bouillon, harnessed jelly of the stars.
Towards what? The forked crash of split thunder parts
Our hearing momentwise; but fast in whirling armatures,
As bright as frogs' eyes, giggling in the girth
Of steely gizzards—axle-bound, confined 70
In coiled precision, bunched in mutual glee
The bearings glint,—O murmurless and shined
In oilrinsed circles of blind ecstasy!

Stars scribble on our eyes the frosty sagas,
The gleaming cantos of unvanquished space . . . 75

O sinewy silver biplane, nudging the wind's withers!
There, from Kill Devils Hill at Kitty Hawk
Two brothers in their twinship left the dune; [4]
Warping the gale, the Wright windwrestlers veered
Capeward, then blading the wind's flank, banked and spun 80
What ciphers risen from prophetic script,
What marathons new-set between the stars!
The soul, by naphtha fledged into new reaches,
Already knows the closer clasp of Mars,—
New latitudes, unknotting, soon give place 85
To what fierce schedules, rife of doom apace!

Behold the dragon's covey—amphibian, ubiquitous
To hedge the seaboard, wrap the headland, ride
The blue's cloud-templed districts unto ether . . .
While Iliads glimmer through eyes raised in pride 90
Hell's belt springs wider into heaven's plumed side.
O bright circumferences, heights employed to fly
War's fiery kennel masked in downy offings,—
This tournament of space, the threshed and chiselled height,
Is baited by marauding circles, bludgeon flail 95
Of rancorous grenades whose screaming petals carve us
Wounds that we wrap with theorems sharp as hail!

Wheeled swiftly, wings emerge from larval-silver hangars.
Taut motors surge, space-gnawing, into flight;

---

[4] The Wright brothers, Orville and Wilbur, made the first successful airplane flights, near Cape Hatteras, on Dec. 17, 1903.

Through sparkling visibility, outspread,
   unsleeping,   100
Wings clip the last peripheries of light . . .
Tellurian wind-sleuths on dawn patrol,
Each plane a hurtling javelin of winged
   ordinance,
Bristle the heights above a screeching gale
   to hover;
Surely no eye that Sunward Escadrille
   can cover!   105
There, meaningful, fledged as the Pleiades
With razor sheen they zoom each rapid
   helix!
Up-chartered choristers of their own speed-
   ing
They, cavalcade on escapade, shear Cu-
   mulus—
Lay siege and hurdle Cirrus down the
   skies!   110
While Cetus-like,[5] O thou Dirigible, enor-
   mous Lounger
Of pendulous auroral beaches,—satellited
   wide
By convoy planes, moonferrets that rejoin
   thee
On fleeing balconies as thou dost glide,
—Hast splintered space!

       Low, shadowed of the Cape, 115
Regard the moving turrets! From grey
   decks
See scouting griffons rise through gaseous
   crepe
Hung low . . . until a conch of thunder
   answers
Cloud-belfries, banging, while searchlights,
   like fencers,
Slit the sky's pancreas of foaming anthra-
   cite   120
Toward thee, O Corsair of the typhoon,—
   pilot, hear!
Thine eyes bicarbonated white by speed, O
   Skygak, see
How from thy path above the levin's
   lance
Thou sowest doom thou hast nor time nor
   chance
To reckon—as thy stilly eyes partake 125
What alcohol of space . . . ! Remember,
   Falcon-Ace,

Thou hast there in thy wrist a Sanskrit
   charge
To conjugate infinity's dim marge—
Anew . . .!

       But first, here at this height receive
The benediction of the shell's deep, sure
   reprieve!   130
Lead-perforated fuselage, escutcheoned
   wings
Lift agonized quittance, tilting from the
   invisible brink
Now eagle-bright, now
             quarry-hid, twist-
           -ing, sink with
Enormous repercussive list-
           -ings down
Giddily spiralled
     gauntlets, upturned, unlooping 135
In guerrilla sleights, trapped in combus-
         tion gyr-
Ing, dance the curdled depth
           down whizzing
Zodiacs, dashed
   (now nearing fast the Cape!)
       down gravitation's
          vortex into crashed
. . . dispersion . . . into mashed and
   shapeless débris. . . .
By Hatteras bunched the beached heap of
   high bravery!   140

The stars have grooved our eyes with old
   persuasions
Of love and hatred, birth,—surcease of
   nations . . .
But who has held the heights more sure
   than thou,
O Walt!—Ascensions of thee hover in me
   now
As thou at junctions elegiac, there, of
   speed   145
With vast eternity, dost wield the rebound
   seed!
The competent loam, the probable grass,—
   travail
Of tides awash the pedestal of Everest,
   fail

---

[5] Cetus, the Whale, is the name of a constellation.

Not less than thou in pure impulse inbred
To answer deepest soundings! O, upward
    from the dead   150
Thou bringest tally, and a pact, new
    bound,
Of living brotherhood!

            Thou, there beyond—
Glacial sierras and the flight of ravens,
Hermetically past condor zones, through
    zenith havens
Past where the albatross has offered up 155
His last wing-pulse, and downcast as a
    cup
That's drained, is shivered back to earth—
    thy wand
Has beat a song, O Walt,—there and
    beyond!
And this, thine other hand, upon my heart
Is plummet ushered of those tears that
    start   160
What memories of vigils, bloody, by that
    Cape,—
Ghoul-mound of man's perversity at balk
And fraternal massacre! Thou, pallid there
    as chalk
Hast kept of wounds, O Mourner, all that
    sum
That then from Appomattox stretched to
    Somme![6]   165
Cowslip and shad-blow, flaked like tethered
    foam
Around bared teeth of stallions, bloomed
    that spring
When first I read thy lines, rife as the
    loam
Of prairies, yet like breakers cliffward
    leaping!
O, early following thee, I searched the
    hill   170
Blue-writ and odor-firm with violets, 'til
With June the mountain laurel broke
    through green
And filled the forest with what Clustrous
    sheen!
Potomac lilies,—then the Pontiac rose,
And Klondike edelweiss of occult
    snows!   175
White banks of moonlight came descending
    valleys—

How speechful on oak-vizored palisades,
As vibrantly I following down Sequoia
    alleys
Heard thunder's eloquence through green
    arcades
Set trumpets breathing in each clump
    and grass tuft—'til   180
Gold autumn, captured, crowned the trem-
    bling hill!

Panis Angelicus![7] Eyes tranquil with the
    blaze
Of love's own diametric gaze, of love's
    amaze!
Not greatest, thou,—not first, nor last,—
    but near
And onward yielding past my utmost
    year.   185
Familiar, thou, as mendicants in public
    places;
Evasive—too—as dayspring's spreading arc
    to trace is:—
Our Meistersinger, thou set breath in
    steel;
And it was thou who on the boldest heel
Stood up and flung the span on even
    wing   190
Of that great Bridge, our Myth, whereof I
    sing!

Years of the Modern! Propulsions toward
    what capes?
But thou, *Panis Angelicus,* hast thou not
    seen
And passed that Barrier that none es-
    capes—
But knows it leastwise as death-strife?—
    O, something green,   195
Beyond all sesames of science was thy
    choice
Wherewith to bind us throbbing with one
    voice,
New integers of Roman, Viking, Celt—

---

[6] Especially bloody battles of the Civil
War and the First World War, respectively.

[7] Angelic bread. The phrase appears in
the hymn for matins of Corpus Christi
and of the Votive Office of the Most
Blessed Sacrament, composed by St.
Thomas Aquinas.

Thou, Vedic Caesar, to the greensward
    knelt!

And now, as launched in abysmal cupolas
    of space,   200
Toward endless terminals, Easters of speed-
    ing light—
Vast engines outward veering with seraphic
    grace
On clarion cylinders pass out of sight
To course that span of consciousness thou'st
    named
The Open Road [8]—thy vision is re-
    claimed!   205
What heritage thou'st signalled to our
    hands!

And see! the rainbow's arch—how shim-
    meringly stands

Above the Cape's ghoul-mound, O joyous
    seer!
Recorders ages hence, yes, they shall hear
In their own veins uncancelled thy sure
    tread   210
And read thee by the aureole 'round thy
    head
Of pasture-shine, *Panis Angelicus!*
                    Yes, Walt,
Afoot again, and onward without halt,—
Not soon, nor suddenly,—No, never to let
    go
My Hand
    in yours,
             Walt Whitman—
                  so— 215

---

[8] A reference to Whitman's poem, "Song of the Open Road."

1898 ∼ *Stephen Vincent Benét* ∼ 1943

STEPHEN VINCENT BENÉT began his writing during his boyhood, which was spent at army posts in California and Georgia; both his father and his paternal grandfather were army officers. He published his first book of poems, *Five Men and Pompey*, in 1915, the year he entered Yale. He published a second book of poems during his college years, edited the *Yale Literary Magazine*, and took his bachelor's degree in 1919 and a master's in 1920. Doing further graduate study at the Sorbonne, he met in Paris Rosemary Carr, a member of the staff of the Paris edition of the Chicago *Tribune*, whom he married in 1921. Thereafter, Benét earned his living by writing, in the early years chiefly by selling light stories to popular magazines. In 1926, with the assistance of a Guggenheim fellowship, he went to southern France, where he remained for two years and wrote *John Brown's Body* (1928). Immediately successful and awarded a Pulitzer prize, this poem became one of the most widely read of the period.

During the 1930's Benét wrote the poems of *Burning City* (1936), and the short stories collected in *Thirteen O'Clock* (1937) (among these the immediately famous tale of "The Devil and Daniel Webster") and *Tales Before Midnight* (1939). He edited the Yale Series of Younger Poets, was a member of the staff of the *Saturday Review of Literature*, and an editor of the Rivers of America series. He was one of the first of American writers to recognize clearly the threat to this country involved in the rise of fascism. He worked earnestly to enlist support for the Loyalist cause during the Civil War in Spain. After Pearl Harbor he devoted his strength and ability unstintingly to the war effort, writing pamphlets and radio plays and encouraging and assisting other writers. *Western Star* (1944) is a completed portion of a second long poetic narrative of American history which he left unfinished at his death.

[See symposium on Benét in *Saturday Review of Literature,* March 27, 1943.]

From
JOHN BROWN'S BODY
[1928]
INVOCATION

American muse, whose strong and diverse
    heart
So many men have tried to understand
But only made it smaller with their art,
Because you are as various as your land,

As mountainous-deep, as flowered with
    blue rivers,   5
Thirsty with deserts, buried under snows,
As native as the shape of Navajo quivers,
And native, too, as the sea-voyaged rose.

Swift runner, never captured or subdued,
Seven-branched elk beside the mountain
    stream,   10
That half a hundred hunters have pursued
But never matched their bullets with the
    dream,

Where the great huntsmen failed, I set my
    sorry
And mortal snare for your immortal
    quarry.

You are the buffalo ghost, the broncho-
    ghost   15
With dollar-silver in your saddle-horn,
The cowboys riding in from Painted Post,
The Indian arrow in the Indian corn,

And you are the clipped velvet of the
    lawns
Where Shropshire grows from Massachu-
    setts' sods,   20
The grey Maine rocks—and the war-
    painted dawns
That break above the Garden of the Gods.

The prairie-schooners crawling toward the
    ore
And the cheap car, parked by the station-
    door.

Where the skyscrapers lift their foggy
    plumes   25
Of stranded smoke out of a stony mouth
You are that high stone and its arrogant
    fumes,
And you are ruined gardens in the South

And bleak New England farms, so winter-
    white
Even their roofs look lonely, and the
    deep   30
The middle grainland where the wind of
    night
Is like all blind earth sighing in her sleep.

A friend, an enemy, a sacred hag
With two tied oceans in her medicine-bag.

They tried to fit you with an English
    song   35
And clip your speech into the English tale.
But, even from the first, the words went
    wrong,
The catbird pecked away the nightingale.

The homesick men begot high-cheekboned
    things
Whose wit was whittled with a different
    sound   40
And Thames and all the rivers of the kings
Ran into Mississippi and were drowned.

They planted England with a stubborn
    trust.
But the cleft dust was never English dust.

Stepchild of every exile from content   45
And all the disavouched, hard-bitten pack
Shipped overseas to steal a continent
With neither shirts nor honor to their back.

Pimping grandee and rump-faced regicide,
Apple-cheeked younkers from a windmill-
      square,   50
Puritans stubborn as the nails of Pride,
Rakes from Versailles and thieves from
      County Clare,

The black-robed priests who broke their
      hearts in vain
To make you God and France or God and
      Spain.

These were your lovers in your buckskin-
      youth.   55
And each one married with a dream so
      proud
He never knew it could not be the truth
And that he coupled with a girl of cloud.

And now to see you is more difficult yet
Except as an immensity of wheel   60
Made up of wheels, oiled with inhuman
      sweat
And glittering with the heat of ladled steel.

All these you are, and each is partly you,
And none is false, and none is wholly true.

So how to see you as you really are,   65
So how to suck the pure, distillate, stored
Essence of essence from the hidden star
And make it pierce like a riposting sword.

For, as we hunt you down, you must es-
      cape
And we pursue a shadow of our own   70
That can be caught in a magician's cape
But has the flatness of a painted stone.

Never the running stag, the gull at wing,
The pure elixir, the American thing.

And yet, at moments when the mind was
      hot   75
With something fiercer than joy or grief,

When each known spot was an eternal
      spot
And every leaf was an immortal leaf,

I think that I have seen you, not as one,
But clad in diverse semblances and pow-
      ers,   80
Always the same, as light falls from the
      sun,
And always different, as the differing hours.

Yet, through each altered garment that
      you wore
The naked body, shaking the heart's core.

All day the snow fell on that Eastern
      town   85
With its soft, pelting, little, endless sigh
Of infinite flakes that brought the tall
      sky down
Till I could put my hands in the white sky

And taste cold scraps of heaven on my
      tongue
And walk in such a changed and luminous
      light   90
As gods inhabit when the gods are young.
All day it fell. And when the gathered
      night

Was a blue shadow cast by a pale glow
I saw you then, snow-image, bird of the
      snow.

And I have seen and heard you in the
      dry   95
Close-huddled furnace of the city street
When the parched moon was planted in
      the sky
And the limp air hung dead against the
      heat.

I saw you rise, red as that rusty plant,
Dizzied with lights, half-mad with senseless
      sound,   100
Enormous metal, shaking to the chant
Of a triphammer striking iron ground.

Enormous power, ugly to the fool,
And beautiful as a well-handled tool.

These, and the memory of that windy
day   105
On the bare hills, beyond the last barbed
wire,
When all the orange poppies bloomed one
way
As if a breath would blow them into fire,

I keep forever, like the sea-lion's tusk
The broken sailor brings away to land, 110
But when he touches it, he smells the
musk,
And the whole sea lies hollow in his hand.

So, from a hundred visions, I make one,
And out of darkness build my mocking
sun.

And should that task seem fruitless in the
eyes   115
Of those a different magic sets apart
To see through the ice-crystal of the wise
No nation but the nation that is Art,

Their words are just. But when the birch-
bark-call
Is shaken with the sound that hunters
make   120
The moose comes plunging through the
forest-wall
Although the rifle waits beside the lake.

Art has no nations—but the mortal sky
Lingers like gold in immortality.

This flesh was seeded from no foreign
grain   125
But Pennsylvania and Kentucky wheat,
And it has soaked in California rain
And five years tempered in New England
sleet [1]

To strive at last, against an alien proof
And by the changes of an alien moon, 130
To build again that blue, American roof
Over a half-forgotten battle-tune

And call unsurely, from a haunted ground,
Armies of shadows and the shadow-sound.

In your Long House [2] there is an attic-
place   135
Full of dead epics and machines that rust,
And there, occasionally, with casual face,
You come awhile to stir the sleepy dust;

Neither in pride nor mercy, but in vast
Indifference at so many gifts unsought, 140
The yellowed satins, smelling of the past,
And all the loot the lucky pirates brought.

I only bring a cup of silver air,
Yet, in your casualness, receive it there.

Receive the dream too haughty for the
breast,   145
Receive the words that should have walked
as bold
As the storm walks along the mountain-
crest
And are like beggars whining in the cold.

The maimed presumption, the unskilful
skill,
The patchwork colors, fading from the
first,   150
And all the fire that fretted at the will
With such a barren ecstasy of thirst.

Receive them all—and should you choose
to touch them
With one slant ray of quick, American
light,
Even the dust will have no power to smutch
them,   155
Even the worst will glitter in the night.

If not—the dry bones littered by the way
May still point giants toward their golden
prey.

---

[1] See biographical headnote, p. 874.
[2] Ceremonial building of the Indians of
the Five Nations.

ODE TO WALT WHITMAN
(May 31, 1819—March 26, 1892)
[1936 (1935)]

Now comes Fourth Month and the early
    buds on the trees
By the roads of Long Island, the forsythia
    has flowered,
In the North, the cold will be breaking;
    even in Maine
The cold will be breaking soon; the young,
    bull-voiced freshets
Roar from green mountains, gorging the
    chilly brooks   5
With the brown, trout-feeding waters, the
    unlocked springs;
Now Mississippi stretches with the Spring
    rains. . . .

It is forty years and more,
The time of the ripeness and withering of
    a man,
Since you lay in the house in Camden [1] and
    heard, at last,   10
The great, slow footstep, splashing the
    Third Month snow
In the little, commonplace street
—Town snow, already trampled and grow-
    ing old,
Soot-flecked and dingy, patterned with
    passing feet,
The bullet-pocks of rain, the strong urine
    of horses,   15
The slashing, bright steel runners of small
    boys' sleds
Hitching on behind the fast cutters.
They dragged their sleds to the tops of
    the hills and yelled
The Indian yell of all boyhood, for pure
    joy
Of the cold and the last gold light and the
    swift rush down   20
Belly-flopping into darkness, into bedtime.
You saw them come home, late, hungry
    and burning-cheeked,
The boys and girls, the strong children,
Dusty with snow, their mittens wet with
    the silver drops of thawed snow.

All winter long, you had heard their sharp
    footsteps passing,   25
The skating crunch of their runners,
An old man, tied to a house, after many
    years,
An old man with his rivery, clean white
    hair,
His bright eyes, his majestic poverty,
His fresh pink skin like the first straw-
    berry-bloom,   30
His innocent, large, easy old man's clothes
—Brown splotches on the hands of clean
    old men
At County Farms or sitting on warm
    park-benches
Like patient flies, talking of their good
    sons,
"Yes, my son's good to me"—   35
An old man, poor, without sons, waiting
    achingly
For spring to warm his lameness,
For spring to flourish,
And yet, when the eyes glowed, neither
    old nor tied.

All winter long there had been footsteps
    passing,   40
Steps of postmen and neighbors, quick
    steps of friends,
All winter long you had waited that great,
    snow-treading step
The enemy, the vast comrade,
The step behind, in the wards, [2] when the
    low lamp flickered
And the sick boy gasped for breath,   45
"Lean on me! Lean upon my shoulder!
    By God, you shall not die!"
The step ahead, on the long, wave-thun-
    dering beaches of Paumanok,
Invisible, printless, weighty,
The shape half-seen through the wet, sweet
    sea-fog of youth,
Night's angel and the dark Sea's,   50

---

[1] Whitman spent his last years in a
small house at 328 (now 330) Mickle
Street, Camden, New Jersey. The house is
now a Whitman museum.

[2] See Whitman's accounts of his experiences in military hospitals in Washington
during the Civil War, pp. 89, 136.

The grand, remorseless treader,
Magnificent Death.

"Let me taste all, my flesh and my fat are
    sweet,
My body hardy as lilac, the strong flower.
I have tasted the calamus; I can taste the
    nightbane." 55

Always the water about you since you
    were born,
The endless lapping of water, the strong
    motion,
The gulls by the ferries knew you, and the
    wild sea-birds,
The sandpiper, printing the beach with
    delicate prints.

At last, old, wheeled to the wharf, you
    still watched the water, 60
The tanned boys, flat-bodied, diving, the
    passage of ships,
The proud port, distant, the people, the
    work of harbors. . . .

"I have picked out a bit of hill with a
    southern exposure.
I like to be near the trees. I like to be near
The water-sound of the trees." 65

Now, all was the same in the cluttered,
    three-windowed room,
Low-ceiled, getting the sun like a schooner's
    cabin,
The crowding photos hiding the ugly wall-
    paper.
The floor-litter, the strong chair, timbered
    like a ship,
The hairy black-and-silver of the old
    wolfskin; 70
In the back-yard, neither lilac nor pear
    yet bloomed
But the branch of the lilac swelling with
    first sap;
And there, in the house, the figures, the
    nurse, the woman,
The passing doctor, the friends, the little
    clan,
The disciple with the notebook who's
    always there. 75

All these and the pain and the water-bed
    to ease you
And you said it rustled of oceans and were
    glad
And the pain shut and relaxed and shut
    once more.

"Old body, counsellor, why do you thus
    torment me?
Have we not been friends from our
    youth?" 80

But now it came,
Slow, perceived by no others,
The splashing step through the grey, soft,
    Saturday rain,
Inexorable footstep of the huge friend.
"Are you there at last, fine enemy? 85
Ah, haste, friend, hasten, come closer!
Breathe upon me with your grave, your
    releasing lips!
I have heard and spoken; watched the
    bodies of boys
Flash in the copper sun and dive to green
    waters,
Seen the fine ships and the strong matrons
    and the tall axemen, 90
The young girls, free, athletic; the drunk-
    ard, retching
In his poor dream; the thief taken by
    officers;
The President, calm, grave, advising the
    nation;
The infant, with milk-wet lips in his
    bee-like slumber.
They are mine; all, all are mine; must
    I leave them, truly? 95
I have cherished them in my veins like
    milk and fruit.
I have warmed them at my bare breast
    like the eggs of pigeons.
The great plains of the buffalo are mine,
    the towns, the hills, the ship-bearing
    waters.
These States are my wandering sons.
I had them in my youth; I cannot desert
    them. 100
The green leaf of America is printed on
    my heart forever."

Now it entered the house, it marched upon
 the stair.
By the bedside the faces dimmed, the huge
 shoulder blotting them,
—It is so they die on the plains, the
 great, old buffalo,
The herd-leaders, the beasts with the kingly
 eyes, 105
Innocent, curly-browed,
They sink to the earth like mountains,
 hairy and silent,
And their tongues are cut by the hunter.
  Oh, singing tongue!
Great tongue of bronze and salt and the
 free grasses, 110
Tongue of America, speaking for the first
 time,
Must the hunter have you at last?
Now, face to face, you saw him
And lifted the right arm once, as a pilot
 lifts it,
Signalling with the bell, 115
In the passage at night, on the river known
 yet unknown,
—Perhaps to touch his shoulder, perhaps
 in pain—
Then the rain fell on the roof and the
 twilight darkened
And they said that in death you looked
 like a marvelous old, wise child.

2

It is Fourth Month now and spring in
 another century, 120
Let us go to the hillside and ask; he will
 like to hear us;
"Is it good, the sleep?"

 "It is good, the sleep and the waking.
I have picked out a bit of hill where the
 south sun warms me.
I like to be near the trees." 125

Nay, let him ask, rather.
"Is it well with you, comrades?
The cities great, portentous, humming with
 action?
The bridges mightily spanning wide-
 breasted rivers?

The great plains growing the wheat, the
 old lilac hardy, well-budded? 130
Is it well with these States?"

"The cities are great, portentous, a world-
 marvel,
The bridges arched like the necks of
 beautiful horses.
We had made the dry land bloom and the
 dead land blossom."

"Is it well with these States?" 135

"The old wound of your war is healed
 and we are one nation.
We have linked the whole land with the
 steel and the hard highways.
We have fought new wars and won them.
 In the French field
There are bones of Texarkana and Little
 Falls,
Aliens; our own; in the low-flying Belgian
 ground; 140
In the cold sea of the English; in dark-
 faced islands.
Men speak of them well or ill; they
 themselves are silent."

"Is it well with these States?"

"We have made many, fine new toys.
 We—
There is a rust on the land. 145
A rust and a creeping blight and a scaled
 evil,
For six years eating, yet deeper than those
 six years,
Men labor to master it but it is not
 mastered.
There is the soft, grey, foul tent of the
 hatching worm
Shrouding the elm, the chestnut, the
 Southern cypress. 150
There is shadow in the bright sun, there
 is shadow upon the streets.
They burn the grain in the furnace while
 men go hungry.
They pile the cloth of the looms while
 men go ragged.
We walk naked in our plenty."

"My tan-faced children?" [3]   155

"These are your tan-faced children.
These skilled men, idle, with the holes in
   their shoes.
These drifters from State to State, these
   wolvish, bewildered boys
Who ride the blinds and the box-cars
   from jail to jail,
Burnt in their youth like cinders of hot
   smokestacks,   160
Learning the thief's crouch and the cadger's
   whine,
Dishonored, abandoned, disinherited.
These, dying in the bright sunlight they
   cannot eat,
Or the strong men, sitting at home, their
   hands clasping nothing,
Looking at their lost hands.   165
These are your tan-faced children, the
   parched young,
The old man rooting in waste-heaps, the
   family rotting
In the flat, before eviction,
With the toys of plenty about them,
The shiny toys making ice and music and
   light,   170
But no price for the shiny toys and the
   last can empty.
The sleepers in blind corners of the night.
The women with dry breasts and phantom
   eyes.
The walkers upon nothing, the four
   million.
These are your tan-faced children."   175

                    "But the land?"

"Over the great plains of the buffalo-land,
The dust-storm blows, the choking, sifting,
   small dust.
The skin of that land is ploughed by the
   dry, fierce wind
And blown away, like a torrent;   180
It drifts foot-high above the young sprouts
   of grain
And the water fouls, the horses stumble
   and sicken,
The wash-board cattle stagger and die of
   drought.

We tore the buffalo's pasture with the steel
   blade.
We made the waste land blossom and it
   has blossomed.   185
That was our fate; now that land takes
   its own revenge,
And the giant dust-flower blooms above
   five States."

"But the gains of the years, who got
   them?"

                    "Many, great gains.
Many, yet few; they robbed us in the broad
   daylight,   190
Saying, 'Give us this and that; we are
   kings and titans;
We know the ropes; we are solid; we are
   hard-headed;
We will build you cities and railroads.'
   —as if they built them!
They, the preying men, the men whose
   hearts were like engines,
Gouging the hills for gold, laying waste
   the timber,   195
The men like band-saws, moving over the
   land.
And, after them, the others,
Soft-bodied, lacking even the pirate's
   candor,
Men of paper, robbing by paper, with
   paper faces,
Rustling like frightened paper when the
   storm broke.   200
The men with the jaws of moth and aphis
   and beetle,
Boring the dusty, secret hole in the corn,
Fixed, sucking the land, with neither wish
   nor pride
But the wish to suck and continue.
They have been sprayed, a little.   205
But they say they will have the land back
   again, these men."

"There were many such in my time.
I have seen the rich arrogant and the
   poor oppressed.

---

[3] From the first line of Whitman's poem,
"Pioneers! O Pioneers!" See p. 99. Other
phrases of Whitman's appear frequently
in Benét's poem.

I have seen democracy, also. I have seen
The good man slain, the knave and the
    fool in power,   210
The democratic vista botched by the peo-
    ple,
Yet not despaired, loving the giant land,
Though I prophesied to these States."

"Now they say we must have one tyranny
    or another
And a dark bell rings in our hearts."   215

"Was the blood spilt for nothing, then?"

3

Under dry winter
Arbutus grows.
It is careless of man.
It is careless of man.   220

Man can tear it,
Crush it, destroy it;
Uproot the trailers,
The thumb-shaped leafings.

A man in gray clothes   225
May come there also,
Lie all day there
In weak spring sunlight.

White, firm-muscled,
The flesh of his body;   230
Wind, sun, earth
In him, possessing him.

In his heart
A flock of birds crying.
In his belly   235
The new grass growing.

In his skull
Sunlight and silence,
Like a vast room
Full of sunlight and silence.   240

In the lines of his palms
The roads of America,
In the knots of his hands
The anger of America.

In the sweat of his flesh   245
The sorrows of America,
In the seed of his loins
The glory of America.

The sap of the birch-tree
Is in his pelt,   250
The maple, the red-bud
Are his nails and parings.

He grows through the earth and is part of
    it like the roots of new grass.

Little arbutus
Delicate, tinted,   255
Tiny, tender,
Fragile, immortal.

If you can grow,
A man can grow
Not like others   260
But like a man.

Man is a bull
But he has not slain you
And this man lies
Like a lover beside you.   265

Beside the arbutus,
The green-leaved Spring,
He lies like a lover
By his young bride,
In the white hour,   270
The white, first waking.

4

They say, they say, they say and let them
    say.
Call you a revolutionist—you were one—
A nationalist—you were one—a man of
    peace,
A man describing battles, an old
    fraud,   275
A Charlus,[4] an adept self-advertiser,
A "good, gray poet"—oh, God save us
    all!

---

[4] A charlatan.

God save us from the memoirs and the
   memories!
And yet, they count. They have to. If they
   didn't
There'd be no Ph.Ds. And each
   disciple   280
Jealously guards his own particular store
Of acorns fallen from the oak's abundance
And spits and scratches at the other
   gatherers.
"I was there when he died!"
   "He was not there when he died!"   285
"It was me he trusted, me! X got on his
   nerves!
He couldn't stand X in the room!"
                     "Y's well-intentioned
But a notorious liar—and, as for Z . . ."

So all disciples, always and forever.   290
—And the dire court at Longwood,[5] those
   last years,
The skull of Sterne, grinning at the
   anatomists,[6]
Poe's hospital-bed,[7] the madness of the
   Dean,[8]
The bright, coughing blood Keats[9] wrote
   in to the girl,
The terrible corpse of France,[10] shrunk,
   naked and solitary—   295
Oh, yes, you were spared some things.
Though why did Mrs. Davis[11] sue the estate
And what did you mean when you said—
                     And who cares?
You're still the giant lode we quarry   300
For gold, fools' gold and all the earthy
   metals,
The matchless mine.
Still the trail-breaker, still the rolling
   river.

You and your land, your turbulent, seeking
   land
Where anything can grow.   305

And they have wasted the pasture and the
   fresh valley,
Stunk the river, shot the ten thousand sky-
   darkening pigeon
To build sham castles for imitation Medici

And the rugged sons of the rugged sons of
   death.
The slum, the sharecropper's cabin, the
   senseless tower,   310
The factory town with the dirty stoops of
   twilight,
The yelling cheapness, the bitter want
   among plenty,
But never Monticello,[12] never again.
And there are many years in the dust of
   America
And they are not ended yet.   315

Far north, far north are the sources of
   the great river,
The headwaters, the cold lakes,
By the little sweet-tasting brooks of the
   blond country,
The country of snow and wheat,
Or west among the black mountains, the
   glacial springs.   320

---

[5] Farmhouse on the island of St. Helena
where Napoleon was imprisoned. A few
friends stayed with him.

[6] According to contemporary report, the
body of Laurence Sterne (1713-1768),
English novelist, was stolen by grave-rob-
bers, sold to an anatomist at Cambridge,
and recognized in the course of dissection.
See *The Life and Times of Laurence
Sterne* (New Haven, 3rd edit., 1929), by
Wilbur L. Cross, pp. 491-493.

[7] See the essay on Poe, vol. I, pp. 433-
447.

[8] Jonathan Swift (1667-1745), English
writer and Dean of St. Patrick's Cathedral,
Dublin, was adjudged "unsound of mind
and memory" three years before his death.
See *Swift* (New York, 1930) by Carl Van
Doren, pp. 262-268.

[9] John Keats (1795-1821), English poet,
died of tuberculosis.

[10] One legend has it that Roland, French
National hero, was not killed at the battle
of Roncesvalles, but died of thirst in the
Pyrenees.

[11] Mrs. Mary Davis, widow of a sea-
captain, befriended Whitman when he was
in great need and later became his housekeeper. When his will gave her only $500,
she sued his estate for $5000. The court
awarded her an additional $500.

[12] Home of Thomas Jefferson, designed
and built by him.

Far north and west they lie and few come
to them, few taste them,
But, day and night, they flow south,
By the French grave and the Indian,
steadily flowing,
By the forgotten camps of the broken
heart,
By the countries of black earth, fertile,
and yellow earth and red earth, 325
A growing, a swelling torrent:
Rivers meet it, and tiny rivulets,
Meet it, stain it,
Great rivers, rivers of pride, come bowing
their watery heads
Like muddy gift-bearers, bringing their
secret burdens, 330
Rivers from the high horse-plains and
the deep, green Eastern pastures
Sink into it and are lost and rejoice and
shout with it, shout within it,
They and their secret gifts,
A fleck of gold from Montana, a sliver of
steel from Pittsburgh,
A wheat-grain from Minnesota, an apple-
blossom from Tennessee, 335
Roiled, mixed with the mud and earth of
the changing bottoms
In the vast, rending floods,
But rolling, rolling from Arkansas, Kan-
sas, Iowa,
Rolling from Ohio, Wisconsin, Illinois,
Rolling and shouting: 340
Till, at last, it is Mississippi,
The Father of Waters; the matchless; the
great flood
Dyed with the earth of States; with the
dust and the sun and the seed of
half the States;
The huge heart-vein, pulsing and pulsing;
gigantic; ever broader, ever mightier;
It rolls past broken landings and camellia-
smelling woods; strange birds fly
over it: 345
It rolls through the tropic magic, the al-
most-jungle, the warm darkness
breeding the warm, enormous stars;
It rolls to the blue Gulf; ocean; and the
painted birds fly.

The grey moss mixes with it, the hawk's
feather has fallen in it,
The cardinal feather, the feather of the
small thrush
Singing spring to New England, 350
The apple-pip and the pepper-seed and
the checkerberry,
And always the water flowing, earthy, ma-
jestic,
Fed with snow and heat, dew and moon-
light,
Always the wide, sure water,
Over the rotted deer-horn 355
The gold, Spanish money,
The long-rusted iron of many undertak-
ings,
Over DeSoto's bones and Joliet's wonder,
And the long forest-years before them, the
brief years after,
The broad flood, the eternal motion, the
restless-hearted 360
Always, forever, Mississippi, the god.

NIGHTMARE, WITH ANGELS
[1936]

An angel came to me and stood by my
bedside,
Remarking in a professorial-historical-eco-
nomic and irritated voice,
"If the Romans had only invented a decent
explosion-engine!
Not even the best, not even a Ford V-8
But, say, a Model T or even an early
Napier, 5
They'd have built good enough roads for
it (they knew how to build roads)
From Cape Wrath to Cape St. Vincent,
Susa, Babylon and Moscow,
And the motorized legions never would
have fallen,
And peace, in the shape of a giant eagle,
would brood over the entire Western
World!"
He changed his expression, looking now
like a combination of Gilbert Mur-
ray, Hilaire Belloc and a dozen
other scientists, writers, and proph-
ets, 10

And continued, in angelic tones,
"If the Greeks had known how to coöp-
      erate, if there'd never been a Ref-
      ormation,
If Sparta had not been Sparta, and the
      Church had been the Church of the
      saints,
The Argive peace like a free-blooming
      olive-tree, the peace of Christ (who
      loved peace) like a great, beautiful
      vine enwrapping the spinning earth!
Take it nearer home," he said.   15
"Take these Mayans and their star-clocks,
      their carvings and their great cities.
Who sacked them out of their cities,
      drowned the cities with a green
      jungle?
A plague? A change of climate? A queer
      migration?
Certainly they were skilful, certainly they
      created.
And, in Tenochtitlan, the dark obsidian
      knife and the smoking heart on
      the stone but a fair city,   20
And the Incas had it worked out beau-
      tifully till Pizarro smashed them.
The collectivist state was there, and the
      ladies very agreeable.
They lacked steel, alphabet and gunpowder
      and they had to get married when
      the government said so.
They also lacked unemployment and over-
      production.
For that matter," he said, "take the Cro-
      Magnons,   25
The fellows with the big skulls, the hand-
      some folk, the excellent scribers of
      mammoths,
Physical gods and yet with the sensitive
      brain (they drew the fine, running
      reindeer).

What stopped them? What kept us all
      from being Apollos and Aphrodites
Only with a new taste to the nectar,
The laughing gods, not the cruel, the gods
      of song, not of war?   30
Supposing Aurelius, Confucius, Napoleon,
      Plato, Gautama, Alexander—
Just to take half a dozen—
Had ever realized and stabilized the full
      dream?
How long, O Lord God in the highest?
      How long, what now, perturbed
      spirit?"

He turned blue at the wingtips and dis-
      appeared as another angel ap-
      proached me.   35
This one was quietly but appropriately
      dressed in cellophane, synthetic rub-
      ber and stainless steel,
But his mask was the blind mask of Ares,
      snouted for gasmasks.
He was neither soldier, sailor, farmer, dic-
      tator nor munitions-manufacturer.
Nor did he have much conversation, except
      to say,
"You will not be saved by General Motors
      or the prefabricated house.   40
You will not be saved by dialectic mate-
      rialism or the Lambeth Conference.
You will not be saved by Vitamin D or
      the expanding universe.
In fact, you will not be saved."
Then he showed his hand:
In his hand was a woven, wire basket, full
      of seeds, small metallic and shining
      like the seeds of portulaca;   45
Where he sowed them, the green vine
      withered, and the smoke and the
      armies sprang up.

American Literature 1900 to the Present

IV
WORLD WAR II AND AFTER

E. B. White

1899

E. B. WHITE was born at Mt. Vernon, New York, and attended Cornell University, graduating in 1921 after interrupting his college course to serve as a private during the first world war. He worked as a reporter and in an advertising agency before becoming a member of the editorial staff of the *New Yorker*. Much of his writing was done for the "Talk of the Town" column of that magazine, and in small part collected in *Every Day Is Saturday* (1934) and *Quo Vadimus* (1939). In 1929 he married Katharine Sergeant Angell, also a *New Yorker* editor. From their Maine farm he wrote for a department in *Harper's* called "One Man's Meat" his observations of contemporary America and the onset of the Second World War; these essays and sketches were collected in 1942 and again in 1944 under the same title. He has published two volumes of poems, *The Lady Is Cold* (1929) and *The Fox of Peapack* (1938), and has edited, with his wife, Katherine S. White, *A Subtreasury of American Humor* (1941).

[See James Thurber's appreciation of White in *Saturday Review of Literature* (Oct. 15, 1938).]

From
ONE MAN'S MEAT

WALDEN
[1942 (1939)]

MISS NIMS, take a letter to Henry David Thoreau. Dear Henry: I thought of you the other afternoon as I was approaching Concord doing fifty on Route 62. That is a high speed at which to hold a philosopher in one's mind, but in this century we are a nimble bunch.

On one of the lawns in the outskirts of the village a woman was cutting the grass with a motorized lawn mower. What made me think of you was that the machine had rather got away from her, although she was game enough, and in the brief glimpse I had of the scene it appeared to me that the lawn was mowing the lady. She kept a tight grip on the handles, which throbbed violently with every explosion of the one-cylinder motor, and as she sheered around bushes and lurched along at a reluctant trot behind her impetuous servant, she looked like a puppy who had grabbed something that was too much for him. Concord hasn't changed much, Henry; the farm implements and the animals still have the upper hand.

I may as well admit that I was journeying to Concord with the deliberate intention of visiting your woods; for although I have never knelt at the grave of a philosopher nor placed wreaths on moldy poets, and have often gone a mile out of my way to avoid some place of historical interest, I have always wanted to see Walden Pond. The account which you left of your sojourn there is, you will be amused to learn, a document of increasing pertinence; each year it seems to gain a little headway, as the world loses ground. We may all be transcendental yet, whether we like it or not. As our common complexities increase, any tale of individual simplicity (and yours is the best written and the cockiest) acquires a new fascination; as our goods accumulate, but not our well-being, your report of an existence without material adornment takes on a certain awkward credibility.

My purpose in going to Walden Pond, like yours, was not to live cheaply or to live dearly there, but to transact some private business with the fewest obstacles. Approaching Concord, doing forty, doing forty-five, doing fifty, the steering wheel held snug in my palms, the highway held grimly in my vision, the crown of the road now serving me (on the righthand curves), now defeating me (on the lefthand curves), I began to rouse myself from the stupefaction which a day's motor journey induces. It was a delicious evening, Henry, when the whole body is one sense, and imbibes delight through every pore, if I may coin a phrase. Fields were richly brown where the harrow, drawn by the stripped Ford, had lately sunk its teeth; pastures were green; and overhead the sky had that same everlasting great look which you will find on Page 144 of the Oxford pocket edition. I could feel the road entering me, through tire, wheel, spring, and cushion; shall I not have intelligence with earth too? Am I not partly leaves and vegetable mold myself?—a man of infinite horsepower, yet partly leaves.

Stay with me on 62 and it will take you into Concord. As I say, it was a delicious evening. The snake had come forth to die in a bloody S on the highway, the wheel upon its head, its bowels flat now and exposed. The turtle had come up too to cross the road and die in the attempt, its hard shell smashed under the rubber blow, its intestinal yearning (for the other side of the road) forever squashed. There was a sign by the wayside which announced that the road had a "cotton surface." You wouldn't know what that is, but neither, for that matter, did I. There is a cryptic

ingredient in many of our modern improvements—we are awed and pleased without knowing quite what we are enjoying. It is something to be traveling on a road with a cotton surface.

The civilization round Concord today is an odd distillation of city, village, farm, and manor. The houses, yards, fields look not quite suburban, not quite rural. Under the bronze beech and the blue spruce of the departed baron grazes the milch goat of the heirs. Under the porte-cochère stands the reconditioned station wagon; under the grape arbor sit the puppies for sale. (But why do men degenerate ever? What makes families run out?)

It was June and everywhere June was publishing her immemorial stanza; in the lilacs, in the syringa, in the freshly edged paths and the sweetness of moist beloved gardens, and the little wire wickets that preserve the tulips' front. Farmers were already moving the fruits of their toil into their yards, arranging the rhubarb, the asparagus, the strictly fresh eggs on the painted stands under the little shed roofs with the patent shingles. And though it was almost a hundred years since you had taken your ax and started cutting out your home on Walden Pond, I was interested to observe that the philosophical spirit was still alive in Massachusetts: in the center of a vacant lot some boys were assembling the framework of the rude shelter, their whole mind and skill concentrated in the rather inauspicious helter-skeleton of studs and rafters. They too were escaping from town, to live naturally, in a rich blend of savagery and philosophy.

That evening, after supper at the inn, I strolled out into the twilight to dream my shapeless transcendental dreams and see that the car was locked up for the night (first open the right front door, then reach over, straining, and pull up the handles of the left rear and the left front till you hear the click, then the handle of the right rear, then shut the right front but open it again, remembering that the key is still in the ignition switch, remove the key, shut the right front again with a bang, push the tiny keyhole cover to one side, insert key, turn, and withdraw). It is what we all do, Henry. It is called locking the car. It is said to confuse thieves and keep them from making off with the laprobe. Four doors to lock behind one robe. The driver himself never uses a laprobe, the free movement of his legs being vital to the operation of the vehicle; so that when he locks the car it is a pure and unselfish act. I have in my life gained very little essential heat from laprobes, yet I have ever been at pains to lock them up.

The evening was full of sounds, some of which would have stirred your memory. The robins still love the elms of New England villages at sundown. There is enough of the thrush in them to make song inevitable at the end of day, and enough of the tramp to make them hang round the dwellings of men. A robin, like many another American, dearly loves a white house with green blinds. Concord is still full of them.

Your fellow-townsmen were stirring abroad—not many afoot, most of them in their cars; and the sound which they made in Concord at evening was a rustling and a whispering. The sound lacks steadfastness and is wholly unlike that of a train. A train, as you know who lived so near the Fitchburg line, whistles once or twice sadly and is gone, trailing a memory in smoke, soothing to ear and mind. Automobiles, skirting a village green, are like flies that have gained the inner ear—they buzz, cease, pause, start, shift, stop, halt, brake, and the whole effect is a nervous polytone curiously disturbing.

As I wandered along, the toc toc of ping pong balls drifted from an attic window. In front of the Reuben Brown house a Buick was drawn up. At the wheel, motionless, his hat upon his head, a man sat, listening to Amos and Andy on the radio (it is a drama of many scenes and without an end). The deep voice of Andrew Brown, emerging from the car, although it originated more than two hundred miles away, was unstrained by distance. When you used

to sit on the shore of your pond on Sunday morning, listening to the church bells of Acton and Concord, you were aware of the excellent filter of the intervening atmosphere. Science has attended to that, and sound now maintains its intensity without regard for distance. Properly sponsored, it goes on forever.

A fire engine, out for a trial spin, roared past Emerson's house, hot with readiness for public duty. Over the barn roofs the martins dipped and chittered. A swarthy daughter of an asparagus grower, in culottes, shirt, and bandanna, pedalled past on her bicycle. It was indeed a delicious evening, and I returned to the inn (I believe it was your house once) to rock with the old ladies on the concrete veranda.

Next morning early I started afoot for Walden, out Main Street and down Thoreau, past the depot and the Minuteman Chevrolet Company. The morning was fresh, and in a bean field along the way I flushed an agriculturalist, quietly studying his beans. Thoreau Street soon joined Number 126, an artery of the State. We number our highways nowadays, our speed being so great we can remember little of their quality or character and are lucky to remember their number. (Men have an indistinct notion that if they keep up this activity long enough all will at length ride somewhere, in next to no time.) Your pond is on 126.

I knew I must be nearing your woodland retreat when the Golden Pheasant lunchroom came into view—Sealtest ice cream, toasted sandwiches, hot frankfurters, waffles, tonics, and lunches. Were I the proprietor, I should add rice, Indian meal, and molasses—just for old time's sake. The Pheasant, incidentally, is for sale: a chance for some nature lover who wishes to set himself up beside a pond in the Concord atmosphere and live deliberately, fronting only the essential facts of life on Number 126. Beyond the Pheasant was a place called Walden Breezes, an oasis whose porch pillars were made of old green shutters sawed into lengths. On the porch was a distorting mirror, to give the traveler a comical image of himself, who had miraculously learned to gaze in an ordinary glass without smiling. Behind the Breezes, in a sun-parched clearing, dwelt your philosophical descendants in their trailers, each trailer the size of your hut, but all grouped together for the sake of congeniality. Trailer people leave the city, as you did, to discover solitude and in any weather, at any hour of the day or night, to improve the nick of time; but they soon collect in villages and get bogged deeper in the mud than ever. The camp behind Walden Breezes was just rousing itself to the morning. The ground was packed hard under the heel, and the sun came through the clearing to bake the soil and enlarge the wry smell of cramped housekeeping. Cushman's bakery truck had stopped to deliver an early basket of rolls. A camp dog, seeing me in the road, barked petulantly. A man emerged from one of the trailers and set forth with a bucket to draw water from some forest tap.

Leaving the highway I turned off into the woods toward the pond, which was apparent through the foliage. The floor of the forest was strewn with dried old oak leaves and *Transcripts*. From beneath the flattened popcorn wrapper (*granum explosum*) peeped the frail violet. I followed a footpath and descended to the water's edge. The pond lay clear and blue in the morning light, as you have seen it so many times. In the shallows a man's waterlogged shirt undulated gently. A few flies came out to greet me and convoy me to your cove, past the No Bathing signs on which the fellows and the girls had scrawled their names. I felt strangely excited sudddenly to be snooping around your premises, tiptoeing along watchfully, as though not to tread by mistake upon the intervening century. Before I got to the cove I heard something which seemed to me quite wonderful: I heard your frog, a full, clear *troonk,* guiding me, still hoarse and solemn, bridging the years as the robins had bridged them in the sweetness of the vil-

lage evening. But he soon quit, and I came on a couple of young boys throwing stones at him.

Your front yard is marked by a bronze tablet set in a stone. Four small granite posts, a few feet away, show where the house was. On top of the tablet was a pair of faded blue bathing trunks with a white stripe. Back of it is a pile of stones, a sort of cairn, left by your visitors as a tribute I suppose. It is a rather ugly little heap of stones, Henry. In fact the hillside itself seems faded, browbeaten; a few tall skinny pines, bare of lower limbs, a smattering of young maples in suitable green, some birches and oaks, and a number of trees felled by the last big wind. It was from the bole of one of these fallen pines, torn up by the roots, that I extracted the stone which I added to the cairn—a sentimental act in which I was interrupted by a small terrier from a nearby picnic group, who confronted me and wanted to know about the stone.

I sat down for a while on one of the posts of your house to listen to the bluebottles and the dragonflies. The invaded glade sprawled shabby and mean at my feet, but the flies were tuned to the old vibration. There were the remains of a fire in your ruins, but I doubt that it was yours; also two beer bottles trodden into the soil and become part of earth. A young oak had taken root in your house, and two or three ferns, unrolling like the ticklers at a banquet. The only other furnishings were a DuBarry pattern sheet, a page torn from a picture magazine, and some crusts in wax paper.

Before I quit I walked clear round the pond and found the place where you used to sit on the northeast side to get the sun in the fall, and the beach where you got sand for scrubbing your floor. On the eastern side of the pond, where the highway borders it, the State has built dressing rooms for swimmers, a float with diving towers, drinking fountains of porcelain, and rowboats for hire. The pond is in fact a State Preserve, and carries a twenty-

dollar fine for picking wild flowers, a decree signed in all solemnity by your fellow-
citizens Walter C. Wardwell, Erson B.
Barlow, and Nathaniel I. Bowditch. There
was a smell of creosote where they had
been building a wide wooden stairway to
the road and the parking area. Swimmers
and boaters were arriving; bodies plunged
vigorously into the water and emerged wet
and beautiful in the bright air. As I left,
a boatload of town boys were splashing
about in mid-pond, kidding and fooling,
the young fellows singing at the tops of
their lungs in a wild chorus:

*Amer-ica, Amer-ica, God shed his grace on
    thee,*
And crown thy good with brotherhood
From sea to shi-ning sea!

I walked back to town along the railroad,
following your custom. The rails were expanding noisily in the hot sun, and on the
slope of the roadbed the wild grape and
the blackberry sent up their creepers to
the track.

The expense of my brief sojourn in
Concord was:

Canvas shoes	$1.95
* Baseball bat	.25
* Left-handed fielder's glove	1.25
Hotel and meals	4.25
	———
In all	$7.70

* gifts to take back to a boy

As you see, this amount was almost what
you spent for food for eight months. I cannot defend the shoes or the expenditure for
shelter and food: they reveal a meanness
and grossness in my nature which you
would find contemptible. The baseball
equipment, however, is the kind of impedi-
ment with which you were never on even
terms. You must remember that the house
where you practiced the sort of economy
which I respect was haunted only by mice
and squirrels. You never had to cope with
a shortstop.

FREEDOM
[1942 (1940)]

I HAVE often noticed on my trips up to
the city that people have recut their clothes
to follow the fashion. On my last trip,
however, it seemed to me that people had
remodeled their ideas too—taken in their
convictions a little at the waist, shortened
the sleeves of their resolve, and fitted themselves out in a new intellectual ensemble
copied from a smart design out of the very
latest page of history. It seemed to me they
had strung along with Paris a little too
long.

I confess to a disturbed stomach. I feel
sick when I find anyone adjusting his mind
to the new tyranny which is succeeding
abroad. Because of its fundamental stric-
tures, fascism does not seem to me to admit of any compromise or any rationalization, and I resent the patronizing air of
persons who find in my plain belief in
freedom a sign of immaturity. If it is
boyish to believe that a human being
should live free, then I'll gladly arrest my
development and let the rest of the world
grow up.

I shall report some of the strange remarks I heard in New York. One man told
me that he thought perhaps the Nazi ideal
was a sounder ideal than our constitutional
system "because have you ever noticed
what fine alert young faces the young German soldiers have in the newsreel?" He
added: "Our American youngsters spend
all their time at the movies—they're a
mess." That was his summation of the case,
his interpretation of the new Europe. Such
a remark leaves me pale and shaken. If it
represents the peak of our intelligence,
then the steady march of despotism will not
receive any considerable setback at our
shores.

Another man informed me that our democratic notion of popular government was
decadent and not worth bothering about—
"because England is really rotten and the
industrial towns there are a disgrace."
That was the only reason he gave for the

hopelessness of democracy; and he seemed mightily pleased with himself, as though he were more familiar than most with the anatomy of decadence, and had detected subtler aspects of the situation than were discernible to the rest of us.

Another man assured me that anyone who took *any* kind of government seriously was a gullible fool. You could be sure, he said, that there is nothing but corruption "because of the way Clemenceau acted at Versailles." He said it didn't make any difference really about this war. It was just another war. Having relieved himself of this majestic bit of reasoning, he subsided.

Another individual, discovering signs of zeal creeping into my blood, berated me for having lost my detachment, my pure skeptical point of view. He announced that he wasn't going to be swept away by all this nonsense, but would prefer to remain in the role of innocent bystander, which he said was the duty of any intelligent person. (I noticed, however, that he phoned later to qualify his remark, as though he had lost some of his innocence in the cab on the way home.)

Those are just a few samples of the sort of talk that seemed to be going round— talk which was full of defeatism and disillusion and sometimes of a too studied innocence. Men are not merely annihilating themselves at a great rate these days, but they are telling one another enormous lies, grandiose fibs. Such remarks as I heard are fearfully disturbing in their cumulative effect. They are more destructive than dive bombers and mine fields, for they challenge not merely one's immediate position but one's main defenses. They seemed to me to issue either from persons who could never have really come to grips with freedom, so as to understand her, or from renegades. Where I expected to find indignation, I found paralysis, or a sort of dim acquiescence, as in a child who is dully swallowing a distasteful pill. I was advised of the growing anti-Jewish sentiment by a man who seemed to be watching the

phenomenon of intolerance not through tears of shame but with a clear intellectual gaze, as through a well-ground lens.

The least a man can do at such a time is to declare himself and tell where he stands. I believe in freedom with the same burning delight, the same faith, the same intense abandon which attended its birth on this continent more than a century and a half ago. I am writing my declaration rapidly, much as though I were shaving to catch a train. Events abroad give a man a feeling of being pressed for time. Actually I do not believe I am pressed for time, and I apologize to the reader for a false impression that may be created. I just want to tell, before I get slowed down, that I am in love with freedom and that it is an affair of long standing and that it is a fine state to be in, and that I am deeply suspicious of people who are beginning to adjust to fascism and dictators merely because they are succeeding in war. From such adaptable natures a smell rises. I pinch my nose.

For as long as I can remember I have had a sense of living somewhat freely in a natural world. I don't mean I enjoyed freedom of action, but my existence seemed to have the quality of free-ness. I traveled with secret papers pertaining to a divine conspiracy. Intuitively I've always been aware of the vitally important pact which a man has with himself, to be all things to himself, and to be identified with all things, to stand self-reliant, taking advantage of his haphazard connection with a planet, riding his luck, and following his bent with the tenacity of a hound. My first and greatest love affair was with this thing we call freedom, this lady of infinite allure, this dangerous and beautiful and sublime being who restores and supplies us all.

It began with the haunting intimation (which I presume every child receives) of his mystical inner life; of God in man; of nature publishing herself through the "I." This elusive sensation is moving and memorable. It comes early in life: a boy, we'll say, sitting on the front steps on a summer night, thinking of nothing in particular, suddenly hearing as with a new perception and as though for the first time the pulsing sound of crickets, overwhelmed with the novel sense of identification with the natural company of insects and grass and night, conscious of a faint answering cry to the universal perplexing question: "What is 'I'?" Or a little girl, returning from the grave of a pet bird leaning with her elbows on the windowsill, inhaling the unfamiliar draught of death, suddenly seeing herself as part of the complete story. Or to an older youth, encountering for the first time a great teacher who by some chance word or mood awakens something and the youth beginning to breathe as an individual and conscious of strength in his vitals. I think the sensation must develop in many men as a feeling of identity with God—an eruption of the spirit caused by allergies and the sense of divine existence as distinct from mere animal existence. This is the beginning of the affair with freedom.

But a man's free condition is of two parts: the instinctive free-ness he experiences as an animal dweller on a planet, and the practical liberties he enjoys as a privileged member of human society. The latter is, of the two, more generally understood, more widely admired, more violently challenged and discussed. It is the practical and apparent side of freedom. The United States, almost alone today, offers the liberties and the privileges and the tools of freedom. In this land the citizens are still invited to write their plays and books, to paint their pictures, to meet for discussion, to dissent as well as to agree, to mount soapboxes in the public square, to enjoy education in all subjects without censorship, to hold court and judge one another, to compose music, to talk politics with their neighbors without wondering whether the secret police are listening, to exchange ideas as well as goods, to kid the government when it needs kidding, and to read real news of real events instead of phony

news manufactured by a paid agent of the state. This is a fact and should give every person pause.

To be free, in a planetary sense, is to feel that you belong to earth. To be free, in a social sense, is to feel at home in a democratic framework. In Adolf Hitler, although he is a freely flowering individual, we do not detect either type of sensibility. From reading his book I gather that his feeling for earth is not a sense of communion but a driving urge to prevail. His feeling for men is not that they co-exist, but that they are capable of being arranged and standardized by a superior intellect— that their existence suggests not a fulfillment of their personalities but a submersion of their personalities in the common racial destiny. His very great absorption in the destiny of the German people somehow loses some of its effect when you discover, from his writings, in what vast contempt he holds *all* people. "I learned," he wrote, ". . . to gain an insight into the unbelievably primitive opinions and arguments of the people." To him the ordinary man is a primitive, capable only of being used and led. He speaks continually of people as sheep, halfwits, and impudent fools —the same people from whom he asks the utmost in loyalty, and to whom he promises the ultimate in prizes.

Here in America, where our society is based on belief in the individual, not contempt for him, the free principle of life has a chance of surviving. I believe that it must and will survive. To understand freedom is an accomplishment which all men may acquire who set their minds in that direction; and to love freedom is a tendency which many Americans are born with. To live in the same room with freedom, or in the same hemisphere, is still a profoundly shaking experience for me.

One of the earliest truths (and to him most valuable) that the author of *Mein Kampf* discovered was that it is not the written word, but the spoken word, which in heated moments moves great masses of people to noble or ignoble action. The written word, unlike the spoken word, is something which every person examines privately and judges calmly by his own intellectual standards, not by what the man standing next to him thinks. "I know," wrote Hitler, "that one is able to win people far more by the spoken than by the written word. . . ." Later he adds contemptuously: "For let it be said to all knights of the pen and to all the political dandies, especially of today: the greatest changes in this world have never yet been brought about by a goose quill! No, the pen has always been reserved to motivate these changes theoretically."

Luckily I am not out to change the world—that's being done for me, and at a great clip. But I know that the free spirit of man is persistent in nature; it recurs, and has never successfully been wiped out, by fire or flood. I set down the above remarks merely (in the words of Mr. Hitler) to motivate that spirit, theoretically. Being myself a knight of the goose quill, I am under no misapprehension about "winning people"; but I am inordinately proud these days of the quill, for it has shown itself, historically, to be the hypodermic which inoculates men and keeps the germ of freedom always in circulation, so that there are individuals in every time in every land who are the carriers, the Typhoid Mary's, capable of infecting others by mere contact and example. These persons are feared by every tyrant—who shows his fear by burning the books and destroying the individuals. A writer goes about his task today with the extra satisfaction which comes from knowing that he will be the first to have his head lopped off—even before the political dandies. In my own case this is a double satisfaction, for if freedom were denied me by force of earthly circumstance, I am the same as dead and would infinitely prefer to go into fascism without my head than with it, having no use for it any more and not wishing to be saddled with so heavy an encumbrance.

CIVILIAN DEFENSE [1]
[1942]

THIS WEEK in our county the two leading topics are deer-slaying and civilian defense. Our best defenders are off in the woods, sharpening their aim and laying up protein reserves. The rest of us attend the meetings and listen to the speakers; in our minds we rebuild, with the volunteer bricklayers, the still unruined cities. On the way home we pass the cars of the hunters and note that they are wearing antlers. If Hitler had ever spent a fall in a New England village, watching the bucks go by on the running boards, he never would have dared reoccupy the Rhineland.

Everyone is excited about the local defense program, and there is a pleasing confusion in all quarters—the sort of confusion which makes a democracy so lovable and so frightening. The absence of the tangible foe, the unlikelihood of his soon appearing in military guise, these give the whole thing a certain incredibility without lessening its intensity. In a day or two a registrar will be around to find out whether I want to join a demolition squad or learn tap dancing to amuse the draftees. In scope, the co-ordinating program is quite amazing—a curious blend of rather elusive vitamins for school-children and protection against even more elusive poison gas for adults. At the moment its advantage to the cause, I suspect, is glandular: it will release in many people, including myself, a pent-up desire to serve their country in this fight. Its disadvantage is that sheer activity often creates the illusion of accomplishment; people's gaze will be diverted from the theater of war to the theater of defense, and a sense of invincibility not in accord with the facts will be developed. In a military way America is about as invincible

[1] This title, for a portion of an essay called "Coon Hunt," has been supplied by the present editors.

as anyone could wish, but in other ways I believe she is in immediate peril.

A few days before the defense meeting, where the civilians gathered to raise their barricades against the invader, the enemy slipped into town and out again, and I think there were hardly a dozen people who caught a glimpse of his coat tails. The populace was watching for planes in the sky—but when the enemy came he came in the curious shape of certain old boxes and hencoops and logs and odds and ends of rubbish that the town boys piled up, on Halloween, against the door of the Jewish merchant, the unpopular storekeeper who had been too grasping. It was a passing visit. The next day the hencoops were rolled away. The dummy which dangled in a noose from the elm tree, with the legend "This is what happens to you if you trade at——'s," was cut down. Bystanders laughed to see such fun, a few of the elders complimented the boys on the job, and the town settled in to its stride. People got ready to attend the defense meeting where they could volunteer to serve democracy by organizing a motor corps and preparing surgical dressings. The enemy had disappeared, virtually unnoticed, and all that remained were the fame of his European successes and the shadow of distant wings. Only a few people had felt his hot breath in the branches of the elm.

There would never be a moment, in war or in peace, when I wouldn't trade all the patriots in the county for one tolerant man. Or when I wouldn't swap the vitamins in a child's lunchbox for a jelly glass of magnanimity.

Karl Shapiro
1904

KARL SHAPIRO'S earlier work in poetry received the recognition of the Levinson prize and wide publication and comment; but it was his interpretation of experience in the Second World War which established his position in the front rank of the younger American poets. He served in the South Pacific with the United States Army from 1942 until the spring of 1945. His volume *V-Letter* was awarded the Pulitzer prize in poetry in 1944. His *Essay on Rime*, a comprehensive study of modern poetry and of the work of many important poets (among them Whitman, Joyce, Yeats and T. S. Eliot) was written while he was still in the Army and was published in the fall of 1945. Soon after his discharge he was appointed custodian of poetry at the Library of Congress. His *Trial of a Poet* appeared in 1947.

From
V-LETTER AND OTHER POEMS

TROOP TRAIN
[1944 (1943)]

It stops the town we come through.
    Workers raise

Their oily arms in good salute and grin.
Kids scream as at a circus. Business men
Glance hopefully and go their measured
    way.
And women standing at their dumbstruck
    door   5
More slowly wave and seem to warn us
    back,

As if a tear blinding the course of war
Might once dissolve our iron in their sweet
    wish.

Fruit of the world, O clustered on our-
    selves
We hang as from a cornucopia   10
In total friendliness, with faces bunched
To spray the streets with catcalls and with
    leers.
A bottle smashes on the moving ties
And eyes fixed on a lady smiling pink
Stretch like a rubber-band and snap and
    sting   15
The mouth that wants the drink-of-water
    kiss.

And on through crummy continents and
    days,
Deliberate, grimy, slightly drunk we crawl,
The good-bad boys of circumstance and
    chance,
Whose bucket-helmets bang the empty
    wall   20
Where twist the murdered bodies of our
    packs
Next to the guns that only seem themselves.
And distance like a strap adjusted shrinks,
Tightens across the shoulder and holds
    firm.

Here is a deck of cards; out of this
    hand   25
Dealer, deal me my luck, a pair of bulls,
The right draw to a flush, the one-eyed
    jack.
Diamonds and hearts are red but spades
    are black,
And spades are spades and clubs are clo-
    vers—black.
But deal me winners, souvenirs of
    peace.   30
This stands to reason and arithmetic,
Luck also travels and not all come back.

Trains lead to ships and ships to death or
    trains,
And trains to death or trucks, and trucks
    to death,

Or trucks lead to the march, the march to
    death,   35
Or that survival which is all our hope;
And death leads back to trucks and trains
    and ships,
But life leads to the march, O flag! at last
The place of life found after trains and
    death
—Nightfall of nations brilliant after
    war.   40

THE GUN
[1944 (1943)]

You were angry and manly to shatter the
    sleep of your throat;
The kiss of your blast is upon me, O
    friend of my fear,
And I savour your breath like a perfume
    as salt and austere
As the scent of the thunder of heaven that
    brims in the moat!

I grip you. We lie on the ground in the
    thongs of our clasp   5
And we stare like the hunter who starts
    at a tenuous cry;
We have wounded the wind with a wire and
    stung in the sky
A white hole that is small and unseen
    as the bite of the asp.

The smooth of your cheek—Do you sight
    from the depth of your eye
More faultless than vision, more true than
    the aiming of stars?   10
Is the heart of your hatred the target of
    redness of Mars
Or the roundness of heart of the one who
    must stumble and die?

O the valley is silent and shocked. I absolve
    from your name
The exaction of murder, my gun. It is I
    who have killed.
It is I whose enjoyment of horror is
    fine and fulfilled.   15
You are only the toy of my terror, my
    emblem of blame.

Come with me. We shall creep for his eyes
    like the sweat of my skin,
For the wind is repaired and the fallen is
    calling for breath.
You are only the means of the practical
    humor of death
Which is savage to punish the dead for
    the sake of my sin!   20

SUNDAY: NEW GUINEA
[1944 (1943)]

The bugle sounds the measured call to
    prayers,
The band starts bravely with a clarion
    hymn,
From every side, singly, in groups, in
    pairs,
Each to his kind of service comes to
    worship Him.

Our faces washed, our hearts in the
    right place,   5
We kneel or stand or listen from our
    tents;
Half-naked natives with their kind of
    grace

Move down the road with balanced staffs
    like mendicants.

And over the hill the guns bang like a
    door
And planes repeat their mission in the
    heights.   10
The jungle outmaneuvers creeping war
And crawls within the circle of our sacred
    rites.

I long for our dishevelled Sundays
    home,
Breakfast, the comics, news of latest
    crimes,
Talk without reference, and palin-
    dromes,[1]   15
Sleep and the Philharmonic and the pon-
    derous *Times*.

I long for lounging in the afternoons
Of clean intelligent warmth, my brother's
    mind,
Books and thin plates and flowers and
    shining spoons,
And your love's presence, snowy, beautiful,
    and kind.   20

----

[1] Word squares; cross-word puzzles.

From

ESSAY ON RIME:
THE CONFUSION IN BELIEF
[1945]
Personal Systems

POETRY OF
DISBELIEF

By nineteen twenty the thin ice of belief
Had cracked and given way. The figure-skater
Of rime had sunk beneath the lake, and art
Took on a deep and submarine aspect.
The corpse, the crawling rat, the bones, the wraith   5
Arrived in sequence; a whole world lay wrecked
And inundated. Prufrock[1] filled with grief
And whimsical mockery walked along the beach,
Envied the crab and heard the mermaid sing.
He toyed with death by drowning, fascinated   10

----

[1] See pp. 852-854.

Like Arnold by the ebbing Sea of Faith.[2]
Nor did the watcher understand his plight
In its true character, for *The Hollow Men,*
The Waste Land and *The Hippopotamus*
All seemed the obituary of the spirit   15
For whose demise the worldly celebrants
Made this macabre music. What we know
In retrospect is that the prophet's eyes
Were turned toward the cathedral and the past
As toward a promise. But in the interim   20
Between his deep and masterly despair
And the overt fulfillment of his faith
His word was our poetic law. It is
Ironical that the monsters of his pen,
Sweeney[3] and the young man carbuncular,   25
Should have enhanced our widespread disbelief
In one another. The younger men who saw
A theological Anglican emerge
From the familiar cracked sarcophagus
Thought it a yogi or a New England witch.   30
A dirge for him was sounded from the left;
All thought it hollow to pursue the strange
Pied Piper of despair to church. Besides,
There were brave kids to follow to the grave
In Austria and Spain. The pain of death   35
Was in that hour decorous and more sweet
Than life lived on the plane of accident,
Stagnation and the conspiracy of power.

THE WAR POET   So went a long procession to the war
In thirty-six, and left a leader home.   40
The choice of art for action was the last
Heroic stand of poetry in our time,
For in the final year of that decade
When the great war began, our poets were past
A reconciliation with the event,   45
Dumb-struck to realize the tragic fall
Of their belief. Scarcely a one remained
Who could with conscience answer the first call
Of his own country. Those who went abroad
And those who slept in tunnels dropped the pen.   50
The rime produced by soldiers of our war
Is the most sterile of the century.
Here I would like to interject the point
That poetry insofar as it depends
Upon belief succeeds in ratio   55
To the success of the belief itself.

---

[2] See Matthew Arnold's poem, "Dover Beach."
[3] See p. 854.

If we consider this tautology
In the light of modern rime we can see why
So many poets lie dead upon the shelf.
I do not speak of truth; the artist may   60
Adjure the six heads of the Hindu lady,
The Blessed Virgin or the Greek Aphrodite,
But once the reader questions the integrity
Of the believer, the game is up; because
Foremost we take for granted that the poem,   65
Though gravely false according to our lights,
Is given in good faith. Nor do we pause
To wonder if Shakespeare believed in sprites.
Yet in our day such is the anarchy
Of personal conviction and belief   70
That one cannot determine when the poem

THE CONFUSION Is fantasy, dream-symbolism, fact,
OF BELIEF Or merely nonsense. Yeats,[4] so we are told,
AND FANTASY Invented a toy universe with gyres
And spooky fires. We do not think that he   75
Believed in fairies and the pot of gold,
But what are we to say to his concern
With table-rapping and the great Blavatsky?[5]
Rilke[6] constructed a cosmography
For his own use in the Duino poems;   80
The chances are it was a Xanadu
And not a real belief, and yet who knows?
MacLeish[7] once wrote a serious review
Of a great contribution to philosophy
Which never existed. Why the practical joke,   85
The personal rearrangement of the stars,
The love, yet the contempt, for mysticism?
Dante believed in Hell, but the details
Which he legitimately conceived to fill
His page were the acknowledged images   90
Of art. Nor did the reader then confuse
The poet's belief with his imagination.
It is a condition of appreciation
That we accept the artist's premises
Wherever possible. When the Marxist muse   95
Was queen, this was the simple thing to do,
But when the Marxist poet fell out with Marx
The system as a vehicle for its culture
Collapsed. In our own life-time we have seen

---

[4] William Butler Yeats (1865-1939), Irish poet and dramatist.

[5] Elena Petrovna Blavatsky (1831-1891), Russian-born leader in the theosophical movement.

[6] Rainer Maria Rilke (1875-1926), German writer, born in Prague. Among his books of poems is *Duino Elegies*.

[7] Archibald MacLeish, contemporary American poet and essayist.

The biological cycle of an art   100
Complete itself and come to history.

Belief, it may be, is fortuitous
In rime; there are perhaps as many poets
Who shrug their shoulders at the word as there
Are those who clutch it like a talisman.   105
Shakespeare, we think, believed in God and country
And the nobility of man. What else?
The greatest poet has left us no account
BELIEF AND   Of his theology or his metaphysics;
POETRY   This in our day is almost tantamount   110
To calling him a fool or a barbarian.
Certain it is that we regard belief
As the tap-root of art. So various
And multifoliate are our breeds of faith
That we could furnish a herbarium   115
With the American specimens alone.
A choice anthology of a few of these
Made its appearance just before the war;
AN ALBUM OF   It is an album of philosophies
BELIEFS   Called *I Believe*. The essays it contains   120
Have nothing in common but proximity.

                    Dialectic and Criticism

The bedlam of persuasions, personal creeds,
Opposing forms, methods of dialectics,
And their subjoined esthetics might be classed
CRITICISM   Together under the heading *Criticism*.   125
AS A COMPLEX   By criticism I do not mean the art
OF MIND   Of judging art, but the complex of mind
Which has beset the modern writer, that
Which is expressed through self-dependent pride
In thought, act and invention. Commonly   130
We call this Objectivity, though Locke [8]
In a less positive age referred to it
As Prudence. Love of evidence and fact
Has narrowed vision and imagination
In poetry to the vanishing-point. Our moral   135
Self-reliance in art disclaims the worth
And even the use of art. The frenzied poet
Exhausted in the half-lit cage of science,
Pretending faith and weak identity
With his subjective soul is not the Faust   140
Who stormed the door of Hell and roused the Devil.
Alas for us, the structural universe
Has neither good nor evil but only true

---

[8] John Locke (1632-1704), English philosopher.

And false; we have the legend in reverse:
Satan calls *us* to save him from ennui   145
And to display our knowledge of the earth.

<table>
<tr><td>THE QUEST
FOR VALUES</td><td>

The triumph of criticism is seen at last
In our alchemic search for what we call
The criterion and the value. Man as a spirit
Having been laid to rest by Sociology,   150
Psychoanalysis and Economics, seeks
That to which substance can hold fast and yet
Be free as substance. In our neutrality
Of spirit we cannot countenance the soul
Or treat with it except as ectoplasm,   155
That is with humor and sophistication.
Yet curiously we note a chronic spasm
Of guilt in rime suggesting that morality
As the conflict of inborn good and evil
In human nature is still a force. We play   160
Semantically upon these attributes
Which once were the omnipotent and perfect
Prongs of the magnet of all life and death,
And holding to this neutral course we claim
The discovery of a science in behavior,   165
Our talk of which dilates on right and wrong,
Values in point-of-view, criteria
In taste, and criticism in everything.

One need but ask Where is the literature
Of nature, where the love poem and the plain   170
Statement of feeling? How and when and why
Did we conceive our horror for emotion,
Our fear of beauty? Whence the isolation
And proud withdrawal of the intellectual</td></tr>
</table>

One need but ask Where is the literature
Of nature, where the love poem and the plain   170
Statement of feeling? How and when and why
Did we conceive our horror for emotion,
Our fear of beauty? Whence the isolation
And proud withdrawal of the intellectual

THE POETRY
OF IDEAS
Into the cool control-room of the brain?   175
At what point in the history of art
Has such a cleavage between audience
And poet existed? When before has rime
Relied so heavily on the interpreter,
The analyst and the critic? Finally how   180
Has poetry as the vision of the soul
Descended to the poetry of sensation,
And that translated to the perceptive kind,
Evolved into the poetry of ideas?

THE POETRY
OF VISION
Perhaps it is that Poe was the last poet   185
In the classic signification of the word;
Europe was quick to claim the furniture
Of his rich vision (and the sticks and props
With which he stuffed his mansion) but the bird,
The princess, Helen herself, were dead.   190
Recumbent Poe before the deep backdrops

Became the Lenin of the Symbolists;
The yeast of criticism worked, and rime
Declined to verbiage, decomposed to forms.
The greatest of the logical suicides   195
During that century of fermenting art
Witnessed the great confusion and vowed silence;
This was Rimbaud, [9] in whom the broken cry
To purify the word echoes the prayer
Of Baudelaire [10] to purify the heart.   200

Nor is it any accident that Emerson
Anointed Whitman and not Poe. The nation

THE POETRY OF
THE SYNTHETIC
MYTH

A hundred years ago was real estate
For the synthetic myth and poetry
On the grand national-international scale.   205
I do not think that I exaggerate
In saying that our period has produced
More poems conceived as epics, large and small,
Than has the entire history of rime!
The bulk of those fall from the sanguine pens   210
Of Emersonian and Whitmanian bards;
These in their works, as if to justify
And prove our transcendental unity,
Recite the whole geography and construct
A gigantic stage perennially set   215
For some Siegfried who never comes. How odd
That Sandburg turning from the likely god
Of this mythology deserts his rime
And turns to monumental scholarship
For his interpretation. [11] The poet himself   220
Observes the overall imperative
Of criticism; poetry must wait on fact.
And we have seen that when the hero lifts
The vizor of his helmet to the gaze
Of the ecstatic myth-mad populace   225
That it is nothing but a shell, a voice
Without a face, a brash and neutral horn
That amplifies our disappointed hopes
And sends them crashing broadcast in the city
With deafening demolition; [12] air-raid, panic   230

DEATH OF
THE HERO

And fall, on these discords this music ends.
Thus our instinct for heroism gropes
Like a blinded Samson [13] in captivity

[9] Arthur Rimbaud (1854-1891), French poet.
[10] Pierre Charles Baudelaire (1821-1867), French poet.
[11] See biographical headnote on Carl Sandburg, p. xxx.
[12] A reference to a poetic drama for radio, "The Fall of the City," by Archibald MacLeish. Other radio plays by MacLeish are entitled "Air-Raid" and "Panic."
[13] Judges 16:23-30.

Only to pull the roof down on our heads
And by the inherent potency of belief 235
To wreck the temple, Dagon [14] and ourselves.
Our unifying manic myth persists
To tempt the ambitious nevertheless and pledge
To art the quantum and the formula
Of a world-faith. Rime at the ragged edge 240
Of civilization weeps among the facts.

[14] Chief god of the Philistines, captors of Samson.

Robert Penn Warren

1905

ROBERT PENN WARREN was a member of the "Fugitive" group of young writers at Vanderbilt University, where he graduated in 1925. He studied later at the University of California, Yale, and Oxford, and has taught at Vanderbilt, Louisiana State University, the University of Iowa, and the University of Minnesota. He has won prizes for poetry and, in 1947, won the Pulitzer prize for fiction; he has twice held Guggenheim fellowships. Warren was one of the founders and editors of *The Southern Review* (1935-1942). With Jack Purser and Cleanth Brooks, he edited *An Approach to Literature* (1936, 1938), and with Cleanth Brooks *Understanding Poetry* (1938) and *Understanding Fiction* (1943). He has written *John Brown: The Making of a Martyr* (1929); *Thirty-six Poems* (1936); *Eleven Poems on the Same Theme* (1942); *Selected Poems* (1944); and the novels *Night Rider* (1939), *At Heaven's Gate* (1943), and *All the King's Men* (1946). The selection which follows is from *The Circus in the Attic and Other Stories* (1947).

THE PATENTED GATE AND THE MEAN HAMBURGER
[1947]

YOU HAVE seen him a thousand times. You have seen him standing on the street corner on Saturday afternoon, in the little county-seat towns. He wears blue jean pants, or overalls washed to a pale pastel blue like the color of sky after a shower in spring, but because it is Saturday he has on a wool coat, an old one, perhaps the coat left from the suit he got married in a long time back. His long wrist bones hang out from the sleeves of the coat, the tendons showing along the bone like the dry twist

of grapevine still corded on the stove-length of a hickory sapling you would find in his wood box beside his cookstove among the split chunks of gum and red oak. The big hands, with the knotted, cracked joints and the square, horn-thick nails, hang loose off the wrist bone like clumsy, home-made tools hung on the wall of a shed after work. If it is summer, he wears a straw hat with a wide brim, the straw fraying loose around the edge. If it is winter, he wears a felt hat, black once, but now weathered with streaks of dark gray and dull purple in the sunlight. His face is long and bony, the jawbone long under the drawn-in cheeks. The flesh along the jawbone is nicked in a couple of places where the unaccustomed razor has been drawn over the leather-coarse skin. A tiny bit of blood crusts brown where the nick is. The color of the face is red, a dull red like the red clay mud or clay dust which clings to the bottom of his pants and to the cast-iron-looking brogans on his feet, or a red like the color of a piece of hewed cedar which has been left in the weather. The face does not look alive. It seems to be molded from the clay or hewed from the cedar. When the jaw moves, once, with its deliberate, massive motion on the quid of tobacco, you are still not convinced. That motion is but the cunning triumph of a mechanism concealed within.

But you see the eyes. You see that the eyes are alive. They are pale blue or gray, set back under the deep brows and thorny eyebrows. They are not wide, but are squinched up like eyes accustomed to wind or sun or to measuring the stroke of the ax or to fixing the object over the rifle sights. When you pass, you see that the eyes are alive and are warily and dispassionately estimating you from the ambush of the thorny brows. Then you pass on, and he stands there in that stillness which is his gift.

With him may be standing two or three others like himself, but they are still, too. They do not talk. The young men, who will be like these men when they get to be fifty or sixty, are down at the beer parlor, carousing and laughing with a high, whickering laugh. But the men on the corner are long past all that. They are past many things. They have endured and will endure in their silence and wisdom. They will stand on the street corner and reject the world which passes under their level gaze as a rabble passes under the guns of a rocky citadel around whose base a slatternly town has assembled.

I had seen Jeff York a thousand times, or near, standing like that on the street corner in town, while the people flowed past him, under the distant and wary and dispassionate eyes in ambush. He would be waiting for his wife and the three towheaded children who were walking around the town looking into store windows and at the people. After a while they would come back to him, and then, wordlessly, he would lead them to the store where they always did their trading. He would go first, marching with a steady bent-kneed stride, setting the cast-iron brogans down deliberately on the cement; then his wife, a small woman with covert, sidewise, curious glances for the world, would follow, and behind her the towheads bunched together in a dazed, glory-struck way. In the store, when their turn came, Jeff York would move to the counter, accept the clerk's greeting, and then bend down from his height to catch the whispered directions of his wife. He would straighten up and say, "Gimme a sack of flahr, if'n you please." Then when the sack of flour had been brought, he would lean again to his wife for the next item. When the stuff had all been bought and paid for with the grease-thick, wadded dollar bills which he took from an old leather coin purse with a metal catch to it, he would heave it all together into his arms and march out, his wife and towheads behind him and his eyes fixed level over the heads of the crowd. He would march down the street and around to the hitching lot where the wagons were, and put his stuff into his wagon and cover it with an old quilt to wait till he got ready to drive out to his place.

For Jeff York had a place. That was what made him different from the other men who looked like him and with whom he stood on the street corner on Saturday afternoon. They were croppers, but he, Jeff York, had a place. But he stood with them because his father had stood with their fathers and his grandfathers with their grandfathers, or with men like their fathers and grandfathers, in other towns, in settlements in the mountains, in towns beyond the mountains. They were the great-great-great-grandsons of men who, half woodsmen and half farmers, had been shoved into the sand hills, into the limestone hills, into the barrens, two hundred, two hundred and fifty years before and had learned there the way to grabble a life out of the sand and the stone. And when the soil had leached away into the sand or burnt off the stone, they went on west, walking with the bent-kneed stride over the mountains, their eyes squinching warily in the gaunt faces, the rifle over the crooked arm, hunting a new place.

But there was a curse on them. They only knew the life they knew, and that life did not belong to the fat bottom lands, where the cane was head-tall, and to the grassy meadows and the rich swale. So they passed those places by and hunted for the place which was like home and where they could pick up the old life, with the same feel in the bones and the squirrel's bark sounding the same after first light. They had walked a long way, to the sand hills of Alabama, to the red country of North Mississippi and Louisiana, to the Barrens of Tennessee, to the Knobs of Kentucky and the scrub country of West Kentucky, to the Ozarks. Some of them had stopped in Cobb County, Tennessee, in the hilly eastern part of the county, and had built their cabins and dug up the ground for the corn patch. But the land had washed away there, too, and in the end they had come down out of the high land into the bottoms—for half of Cobb County is a rich, swelling country—where the corn was good and the tobacco unfurled a leaf like a yard of green velvet and the white houses stood among the cedars and tulip trees and maples. But they were not to live in the white houses with the limestone chimneys set strong at the end of each gable. No, they were to live in the shacks on the back of the farms, or in cabins not much different from the cabins they had once lived in two hundred years before over the mountains or, later, in the hills of Cobb County. But the shacks and the cabins now stood on somebody else's ground, and the curse which they had brought with them over the mountain trail, more precious than the bullet mold or grandma's quilt, the

curse which was the very feeling in the bones and the habit in the hand, had come full circle.

Jeff York was one of those men, but he had broken the curse. It had taken him more than thirty years to do it, from the time when he was nothing but a big boy until he was fifty. It had taken him from sun to sun, year in and year out, and all the sweat in his body, and all the power of rejection he could muster, until the very act of rejection had become a kind of pleasure, a dark, secret, savage dissipation, like an obsessing vice. But those years had given him his place, sixty acres with a house and barn.

When he bought the place, it was not very good. The land was run-down from years of neglect and abuse. But Jeff York put brush in the gullies to stop the wash and planted clover on the run-down fields. He mended the fences, rod by rod. He patched the roof on the little house and propped up the porch, buying the lumber and shingles almost piece by piece and one by one as he could spare the sweat-bright and grease-slick quarters and half-dollars out of his leather purse. Then he painted the house. He painted it white, for he knew that that was the color you painted a house sitting back from the road with its couple of maples, beyond the clover field.

Last, he put up the gate. It was a patented gate, the kind you can ride up to and open by pulling on a pull rope without getting off your horse or out of your buggy or wagon. It had a high pair of posts, well braced and with a high cross-bar between, and the bars for the opening mechanism extending on each side. It was painted white, too. Jeff was even prouder of the gate than he was of the place. Lewis Simmons, who lived next to Jeff's place, swore he had seen Jeff come out after dark on a mule and ride in and out of that gate, back and forth, just for the pleasure of pulling on the rope and making the mechanism work. The gate was the seal Jeff York had put on all the years of sweat and rejection. He could sit on his porch on a Sunday afternoon in summer, before milking time, and look down the rise, down the winding dirt track, to the white gate beyond the clover, and know what he needed to know about all the years passed.

Meanwhile Jeff York had married and had had the three towheads. His wife was twenty years or so younger than he, a small, dark woman, who walked with her head bowed a little and from that humble and unprovoking posture stole sidewise, secret glances at the world from eyes which were brown or black—you never could tell which because you never remembered having looked her straight in the eye—and which were surprisingly bright in that sidewise, secret flicker, like the eyes of a small, cunning bird which surprise you from the brush. When they came to town she moved along the street, with a child in her arms or later with the three trailing behind her, and stole her looks at the world. She wore a calico dress, dun-colored, which hung loose to conceal whatever shape her thin body had, and in winter over the dress a brown wool coat with a scrap of fur at the collar which looked like some tattered growth of fungus feeding on old wood. She wore black high-heeled shoes, slippers of some kind, which she kept polished and which surprised you under that dress and coat. In the slippers she moved with a slightly limping, stealthy gait, almost sliding them along the pavement, as though she had not fully mastered the complicated trick required to use them properly. You knew that she wore them only when she came to town, that she carried them wrapped up in a piece of newspaper until their wagon had reached the first house on the outskirts of town, and that, on the way back, at the same point, she would take them off and wrap them up again and hold the bundle in her lap until she got home. If the weather happened to be bad, or if it was winter, she would have a pair of old brogans under the wagon seat.

It was not that Jeff York was a hard man and kept his wife in clothes that were as bad as those worn by the poorest of the women of the croppers. In fact, some of the cropper women, poor or not, black or white, managed to buy dresses with some color in them and proper hats, and went to the moving picture show on Saturday afternoon. But Jeff still owed a little money on his place, less than two hundred dollars, which he had had to borrow to rebuild his barn after it was struck by lightning. He had, in fact, never been entirely out of debt. He had lost a mule which had got out on the highway and been hit by a truck. That had set him back. One of his tow-heads had been sickly for a couple of winters. He had not been in deep, but he was not a man, with all those years of rejection behind him, to forget the meaning of those years. He was good enough to his family. Nobody ever said the contrary. But he was good to them in terms of all the years he had lived through. He did what he could afford. He bought the towheads a ten-cent bag of colored candy every Saturday afternoon for them to suck on during the ride home in the wagon, and the last thing before they left town, he always took the lot of them over to the dogwagon to get hamburgers and orange pop.

The towheads were crazy about hamburgers. And so was his wife, for that matter. You could tell it, even if she didn't say anything, for she would lift her bowed-forward head a little, and her face would brighten, and she would run her tongue out to wet her lips just as the plate with the hamburger would be set on the counter before her. But all those folks, like Jeff York and his family, like hamburgers, with pickle and onions and mustard and tomato catsup, the whole works. It is something different. They stay out in the country and eat hog-meat, when they can get it, and greens and corn bread and potatoes, and nothing but a pinch of salt to brighten it on the tongue, and when they get to town and get hold of beef and wheat bread and all the stuff to jack up the flavor, they have to swallow to keep the mouth from flooding before they even take the first bite.

So the last thing every Saturday, Jeff

York would take his family over to Slick Hardin's *Dew Drop Inn Diner* and give them the treat. The diner was built like a railway coach, but it was set on a concrete foundation on a lot just off the main street of town. At each end the concrete was painted to show wheels. Slick Hardin kept the grass just in front of the place pretty well mowed and one or two summers he even had a couple of flower beds in the middle of that shirttail-size lawn. Slick had a good business. For a few years he had been a prelim fighter over in Nashville and had got his name in the papers a few times. So he was a kind of hero, with the air of romance about him. He had been born, however, right in town and, as soon as he had found out he wasn't ever going to be good enough to be a real fighter, he had come back home and started the dog-wagon, the first one ever in town. He was a slick-skinned fellow, about thirty-five, prematurely bald, with his head slick all over. He had big eyes, pale blue and slick looking like agates. When he said something that he thought smart, he would roll his eyes around, slick in his head like marbles, to see who was laughing. Then he'd wink. He had done very well with his business, for despite the fact that he had picked up city ways and a lot of city talk, he still remembered enough to deal with the country people, and they were the ones who brought the dimes in. People who lived right there in town, except for school kids in the afternoon and the young toughs from the pool room or men on the night shift down at the railroad, didn't often get around to the dogwagon.

Slick Hardin was perhaps trying to be smart when he said what he did to Mrs. York. Perhaps he had forgotten, just for that moment, that people like Jeff York and his wife didn't like to be kidded, at least not in that way. He said what he did, and then grinned and rolled his eyes around to see if some of the other people present were thinking it was funny.

Mrs. York was sitting on a stool in front of the counter, flanked on one side by Jeff York and on the other by the three tow-heads. She had just sat down to wait for the hamburger—there were several orders in ahead of the York order—and had been watching in her sidewise fashion every move of Slick Hardin's hands as he patted the pink meat onto the hot slab and wiped the split buns over the greasy iron to make them ready to receive it. She always watched him like that, and when the hamburger was set before her she would wet her lips with her tongue.

That day Slick set the hamburger down in front of Mrs. York, and said, "Anybody likes hamburger much as you, Mrs. York, ought to git him a hamburger stand."

Mrs. York flushed up, and didn't say anything, staring at her plate. Slick rolled his eyes to see how it was going over, and somebody down the counter snickered. Slick looked back at the Yorks, and if he had not been so encouraged by the snicker he might, when he saw Jeff York's face, have hesitated before going on with his kidding. People like Jeff York are touchous, and they are especially touchous about the women-folks, and you do not make jokes with or about their women-folks unless it is perfectly plain that the joke is a very special kind of friendly joke. The snicker down the counter had defined the joke as not entirely friendly. Jeff was looking at Slick, and something was growing slowly in that hewed-cedar face, and back in the gray eyes in the ambush of thorny brows.

But Slick did not notice. The snicker had encouraged him, and so he said, "Yeah, if I liked them hamburgers much as you, I'd buy me a hamburger stand. Fact, I'm selling this one. You want to buy it?"

There was another snicker, louder, and Jeff York, whose hamburger had been about half way to his mouth for another bite, laid it down deliberately on his plate. But whatever might have happened at that moment did not happen. It did not happen because Mrs. York lifted her flushed face, looked straight at Slick Hardin, swallowed hard to get down a piece of the hamburger or to master her nerve, and said in a sharp, strained voice, "You sellen this place?"

There was complete silence. Nobody had expected her to say anything. The chances were she had never said a word in that diner in the couple of hundred times she had been in it. She had come in with Jeff York and, when a stool had come vacant, had sat down, and Jeff had said, "Gimme five hamburgers, if'n you please, and make 'em well done, and five bottles of orange pop." Then, after the eating was over, he had always laid down seventy-five cents on the counter—that is, after there were five hamburger-eaters in the family—and walked out, putting his brogans down slow, and his wife and kids following without a word. But now she spoke up and asked the question, in that strained, artificial voice, and everybody, including her husband, looked at her with surprise.

As soon as he could take it in, Slick Hardin replied, "Yeah, I'm selling it."

She swallowed hard again, but this time it could not have been hamburger, and demanded, "What you asken fer hit?"

Slick looked at her in the new silence, half shrugged, a little contemptuously, and said, "Fourteen hundred and fifty dollars."

She looked back at him, while the blood ebbed from her face. "Hit's a lot of money," she said in a flat tone, and returned her gaze to the hamburger on her plate.

"Lady," Slick said defensively, "I got that much money tied up here. Look at that there stove. It is a *Heat Master* and they cost. Them coffee urns, now. Money can't buy no better. And this here lot, lady, the diner sets on. Anybody knows I got that much money tied up here. I got more. This lot cost me more'n . . . ." He suddenly realized that she was not listening to him. And he must have realized, too, that she didn't have a dime in the world and couldn't buy his diner, and that he was making a fool of himself, defending his price. He stopped abruptly, shrugged his shoulders, and then swung his wide

gaze down the counter to pick out somebody to wink to.

But before he got the wink off, Jeff York had said, "Mr. Hardin."

Slick looked at him and asked, "Yeah?"

"She didn't mean no harm," Jeff York said. "She didn't mean to be messen in yore business."

Slick shrugged. "Ain't no skin off my nose," he said. "Ain't no secret I'm selling out. My price ain't no secret neither."

Mrs. York bowed her head over her plate. She was chewing a mouthful of her hamburger with a slow, abstracted motion of her jaw, and you knew that it was flavorless on her tongue.

That was, of course, on a Saturday. On Thursday afternoon of the next week Slick was in the diner alone. It was the slack time, right in the middle of the afternoon. Slick, as he told it later, was wiping off the stove and wasn't noticing. He was sort of whistling to himself, he said. He had a way of whistling soft through his teeth. But he wasn't whistling loud, he said, not so loud he wouldn't have heard the door open or the steps if she hadn't come gumshoeing in on him to stand there waiting in the middle of the floor until he turned round and was so surprised he nearly had heart failure. He had thought he was there alone, and there she was, watching every move he was making, like a cat watching a goldfish swim in a bowl.

"Howdy-do," he said, when he got his breath back.

"This place still fer sale?" she asked him.

"Yeah, lady," he said.

"What you asken fer hit?"

"Lady I done told you," Slick replied, "fourteen hundred and fifty dollars."

"Hit's a heap of money," she said.

Slick started to tell her how much money he had tied up there, but before he had got going, she had turned and slipped out of the door.

"Yeah," Slick said later to the men who came into the diner, "me like a fool starting to tell her how much money I got tied up here when I knowed she didn't have a dime. That woman's crazy. She must walked that five or six miles in here just to ask me something she already knowed the answer to. And then turned right round and walked out. But I am selling me this place. I'm tired of slinging hash to them hicks. I got me some connections over in Nashville and I'm gonna open me a place over there. A cigar stand and about three pool tables and maybe some beer. I'll have me a sort of club in the back. You know, membership cards to git in, where the boys will play a little game. Just sociable. I got good connections over in Nashville. I'm selling this place. But that woman, she ain't got a dime. She ain't gonna buy it."

But she did.

On Saturday Jeff York led his family over to the diner. They ate hamburgers without a word and marched out. After they had gone, Slick said, "Looks like she ain't going to make the invest-mint. Gonna buy a block of bank stock instead." Then he rolled his eyes, located a brother down the counter, and winked.

It was almost the end of the next week before it happened. What had been going on inside the white house out on Jeff York's place nobody knew or was to know. Perhaps she just starved him out, just not doing the cooking or burning everything. Perhaps she just quit attending to the children properly and he had to come back tired from work and take care of them. Perhaps she just lay in bed at night and talked and talked to him, asking him to buy it, nagging him all night long, while he would fall asleep and then wake up with a start to hear her voice still going on. Or perhaps she just turned her face away from him and wouldn't let him touch her. He was a lot older than she, and she was probably the only woman he had ever had. He had been too ridden by his dream and his passion for rejection during all the years before to lay even a finger on a wom-

an. So she had him there. Because he was a lot older and because he had never had another woman. But perhaps she used none of these methods. She was a small, dark, cunning woman, with a sidewise look from her lowered face, and she could have thought up ways of her own, no doubt.

Whatever she thought up, it worked. On Friday morning Jeff York went to the bank. He wanted to mortgage his place, he told Todd Sullivan, the president. He wanted fourteen hundred and fifty dollars, he said. Todd Sullivan would not let him have it. He already owed the bank one hundred and sixty dollars and the best he could get on a mortgage was eleven hundred dollars. That was in 1935 and then farmland wasn't worth much and half the land in the country was mortgaged anyway. Jeff York sat in the chair by Todd Sullivan's desk and didn't say anything. Eleven hundred dollars would not do him any good. Take off the hundred and sixty he owed and it wouldn't be but a little over nine hundred dollars clear to him. He sat there quietly for a minute, apparently turning that fact over in his head. Then Todd Sullivan asked him, "How much you say you need?"

Jeff York told him.

"What you want it for?" Todd Sullivan asked.

He told him that.

"I tell you," Todd Sullivan said, "I don't want to stand in the way of a man bettering himself. Never did. That diner ought to be a good proposition, all right, and I don't want to stand in your way if you want to come to town and better yourself. It will be a step up from that farm for you, and I like a man has got ambition. The bank can't lend you the money, not on that piece of property. But I tell you what I'll do. I'll buy your place. I got me some walking horses I'm keeping out on my father's place. But I could use me a little place of my own. For my horses. I'll give you seventeen hundred for it. Cash."

Jeff York did not say anything to that. He looked slow at Todd Sullivan as though he did not understand.

"Seventeen hundred," the banker repeated. "That's a good figure. For these times."

Jeff was not looking at him now. He was looking out the window, across the alleyway—Todd Sullivan's office was in the back of the bank. The banker, telling about it later when the doings of Jeff York had become for a moment a matter of interest, said, "I thought he hadn't even heard me. He looked like he was half asleep or something. I coughed to sort of wake him up. You know the way you do. I didn't want to rush him. You can't rush those people, you know. But I couldn't sit there all day. I had offered him a fair price."

It was, as a matter of fact, a fair price for the times, when the bottom was out of everything in the section.

Jeff York took it. He took the seventeen hundred dollars and bought the dogwagon with it, and rented a little house on the edge of town and moved in with his wife and the towheads. The first day after they got settled, Jeff York and his wife went over to the diner to get instructions from Slick about running the place. He showed Mrs. York all about how to work the coffee machine and the stove, and how to make up the sandwiches, and how to clean the place up after herself. She fried up hamburgers for all of them, herself, her husband, and Slick Hardin, for practice, and they ate the hamburgers while a couple of hangers-on watched them. "Lady," Slick said, for he had money in his pocket and was heading out for Nashville on the seven o'clock train that night, and was feeling expansive, "lady, you sure fling a mean hamburger."

He wiped the last crumbs and mustard off his lips, got his valise from behind the door, and said, "Lady, git in there and pitch. I hope you make a million hamburgers." Then he stepped out into the bright fall sunshine and walked away whistling up the street, whistling through

his teeth and rolling his eyes as though there were somebody to wink to. That was the last anybody in town ever saw of Slick Hardin.

The next day, Jeff York worked all day down at the diner. He was scrubbing up the place inside and cleaning up the trash which had accumulated behind it. He burned all the trash. Then he gave the place a good coat of paint outside, white paint. That took him two days. Then he touched up the counter inside with varnish. He straightened up the sign out front, which had begun to sag a little. He had that place looking spick and span.

Then on the fifth day after they got settled—it was Sunday—he took a walk in the country. It was along toward sun when he started out, not late, as a matter of fact, for by October the days are shortening up. He walked out the Curtisville pike and out the cut-off leading to his farm. When he entered the cut-off, about a mile from his own place, it was still light enough for the Bowdoins, who had a filling station at the corner, to see him plain when he passed.

The next time anybody saw him was on Monday morning about six o'clock. A man taking milk into town saw him. He was hanging from the main cross bar of the white patented gate. He had jumped off the gate. But he had propped the thing open so there wouldn't be any chance of clambering back up on it if his neck didn't break when he jumped and he should happen to change his mind.

But that was an unnecessary precaution, as it developed. Dr. Stauffer said that his neck was broken very clean. "A man who can break a neck as clean as that could make a living at it," Dr. Stauffer said. And added, "If he's damned sure it ain't ever his own neck."

Mrs. York was much cut up by her husband's death. People were sympathetic and helpful, and out of a mixture of sympathy and curiosity she got a good starting trade at the diner. And the trade kept right on. She got so she didn't hang her head and look sidewise at you and the world. She would look straight at you. She got so she could walk in high heels without giving the impression that it was a trick she was learning. She wasn't a bad-looking woman, as a matter of fact, once she had caught on how to fix herself up a little. The railroad men and the pool hall gang liked to hang out there and kid with her. Also, they said, she flung a mean hamburger.

Richard Wright

1908

RICHARD WRIGHT was born near Natchez, Mississippi. He began to earn his own living in Memphis at the age of fifteen; later he moved to Chicago. He was a member of the staff of the Federal Writers' Project in Chicago and in New York City, 1935-1937, and he held a Guggenheim fellowship in 1939. His books include *Uncle Tom's Children* (1938), a collection of stories; the novel *Native Son* (1940); *Twelve Million Black Voices* (1941); and the autobiography, *Black Boy* (1945), of which the following selection is Chapter XIII. The title has been supplied by the present editors.

From
BLACK BOY

DISCOVERY OF READING
[1945]

ONE MORNING I arrived early at work and went into the bank lobby where the Negro porter was mopping. I stood at a counter and picked up the Memphis *Commercial Appeal* and began my free reading of the press. I came finally to the editorial page and saw an article dealing with one H. L. Mencken. I knew by hearsay that he was the editor of the *American Mercury,* but aside from that I knew nothing about him. The article was a furious denunciation of Mencken, concluding with one, hot, short sentence: Mencken is a fool.

I wondered what on earth this Mencken had done to call down upon him the scorn of the South. The only people I had ever heard denounced in the South were Negroes, and this man was not a Negro. Then what ideas did Mencken hold that made a newspaper like the *Commercial Appeal* castigate him publicly? Undoubtedly he must be advocating ideas that the South did not like. Were there, then, people other than Negroes who criticized the South? I knew that during the Civil War the South had hated northern whites, but I had not encountered such hate during my life. Knowing no more of Mencken than I did at that moment, I felt a vague sympathy for him. Had not the South, which had assigned me the role of a non-man, cast at him its hardest words?

Now, how could I find out about this Mencken? There was a huge library near the riverfront, but I knew that Negroes were not allowed to patronize its shelves any more than they were the parks and playgrounds of the city. I had gone into the library several times to get books for the white men on the job. Which of them would now help me to get books? And how could I read them without causing concern to the white men with whom I worked? I had so far been successful in hiding my thoughts and feelings from them, but I knew that I would create hostility if I went about this business of reading in a clumsy way.

I weighed the personalities of the men on the job. There was Don, a Jew; but I distrusted him. His position was not much better than mine and I knew that he was uneasy and insecure; he had always treated me in an offhand, bantering way that barely concealed his contempt. I was afraid to ask him to help me to get books; his frantic desire to demonstrate a racial solidarity with the whites against Negroes might make him betray me.

Then how about the boss? No, he was a Baptist and I had the suspicion that he would not be quite able to comprehend why a black boy would want to read Mencken. There were other white men on the job whose attitudes showed clearly that they were Kluxers or sympathizers, and they were out of the question.

There remained only one man whose attitude did not fit into an anti-Negro category, for I had heard the white men refer to him as a "Pope lover." He was an Irish Catholic and was hated by the white Southerners. I knew that he read books, because I had got him volumes from the library several times. Since he, too, was an object of hatred, I felt that he might refuse me but would hardly betray me. I hesitated, weighing and balancing the imponderable realities.

One morning I paused before the Catholic fellow's desk.

"I want to ask you a favor," I whispered to him.

"What is it?"

"I want to read. I can't get books from the library. I wonder if you'd let me use your card?"

He looked at me suspiciously.

"My card is full most of the time," he said.

"I see," I said and waited, posing my question silently.

"You're not trying to get me into trouble, are you, boy?" he asked, staring at me.

"Oh, no, sir."

"What book do you want?"

"A book by H. L. Mencken."

"Which one?"

"I don't know. Has he written more than one?"

"He has written several."

"I didn't know that."

"What makes you want to read Mencken?"

"Oh, I just saw his name in the newspaper," I said.

"It's good of you to want to read," he said. "But you ought to read the right things."

I said nothing. Would he want to supervise my reading?

"Let me think," he said. "I'll figure out something."

I turned from him and he called me back. He stared at me quizzically.

"Richard, don't mention this to the other white men," he said.

"I understand," I said. "I won't say a word."

A few days later he called me to him.

"I've got a card in my wife's name," he said. "Here's mine."

"Thank you, sir."

"Do you think you can manage it?"

"I'll manage fine," I said.

"If they suspect you, you'll get in trouble," he said.

"I'll write the same kind of notes to the library that you wrote when you sent me for books," I told him. "I'll sign your name."

He laughed.

"Go ahead. Let me see what you get," he said.

That afternoon I addressed myself to forging a note. Now, what were the names of books written by H. L. Mencken? I did not know any of them. I finally wrote what I thought would be a foolproof note: *Dear Madam: Will you please let this nigger boy*—I used the word "nigger" to make the librarian feel that I could not possibly be the author of the note—*have some books by H. L. Mencken?* I forged the white man's name.

I entered the library as I had always done when on errands for whites, but I felt that I would somehow slip up and betray myself. I doffed my hat, stood a respectful distance from the desk, looked as unbookish as possible, and waited for the white patrons to be taken care of. When the desk was clear of people, I still waited. The white librarian looked at me.

"What do you want, boy?"

As though I did not possess the power of speech, I stepped forward and simply handed her the forged note, not parting my lips.

"What books by Mencken does he want?" she asked.

"I don't know, ma'am," I said, avoiding her eyes.

"Who gave you this card?"

"Mr. Falk," I said.

"Where is he?"

"He's at work, at the M—— Optical Company," I said. "I've been in here for him before."

"I remember," the woman said. "But he never wrote notes like this."

Oh, God, she's suspicious. Perhaps she would not let me have the books? If she had turned her back at that moment, I would have ducked out the door and never gone back. Then I thought of a bold idea.

"You can call him up, ma'am," I said, my heart pounding.

"You're not using these books, are you?" she asked pointedly.

"Oh, no, ma'am. I can't read."

"I don't know what he wants by Mencken," she said under her breath.

I knew now that I had won; she was thinking of other things and the race question had gone out of her mind. She went to the shelves. Once or twice she looked over her shoulder at me, as though she was still doubtful. Finally she came forward with two books in her hand.

"I'm sending him two books," she said. "But tell Mr. Falk to come in next time, or send me the names of the books he wants. I don't know what he wants to read."

I said nothing. She stamped the card and handed me the books. Not daring to glance at them, I went out of the library,

fearing that the woman would call me back for further questioning. A block away from the library I opened one of the books and read a title: *A Book of Prefaces*. I was nearing my nineteenth birthday and I did not know how to pronounce the word "preface." I thumbed the pages and saw strange words and strange names. I shook my head, disappointed. I looked at the other book; it was called *Prejudices*. I knew what that word meant; I had heard it all my life. And right off I was on guard against Mencken's books. Why would a man want to call a book *Prejudices?* The word was so stained with all my memories of racial hate that I could not conceive of anybody using it for a title. Perhaps I had made a mistake about Mencken? A man who had prejudices must be wrong.

When I showed the books to Mr. Falk, he looked at me and frowned.

"That librarian might telephone you," I warned him.

"That's all right," he said. "But when you're through reading those books, I want you to tell me what you get out of them."

That night in my rented room, while letting the hot water run over my can of pork and beans in the sink, I opened *A Book of Prefaces* and began to read. I was jarred and shocked by the style, the clear, clean, sweeping sentences. Why did he write like that? And how did one write like that? I pictured the man as a raging demon, slashing with his pen, consumed with hate, denouncing everything American, extolling everything European or German, laughing at the weaknesses of people, mocking God, authority. What was this? I stood up, trying to realize what reality lay behind the meaning of the words. . . . Yes, this man was fighting, fighting with words. He was using words as a weapon, using them as one would use a club. Could words be weapons? Well, yes, for here they were. Then, maybe, perhaps, I could use them as a weapon? No. It frightened me. I read on and what amazed me was not what he said, but how on earth anybody had the courage to say it.

Occasionally I glanced up to reassure myself that I was alone in the room. Who were these men about whom Mencken was talking so passionately? Who was Anatole France? Joseph Conrad? Sinclair Lewis, Sherwood Anderson, Dostoevski, George Moore, Gustave Flaubert, Maupassant, Tolstoy, Frank Harris, Mark Twain, Thomas Hardy, Arnold Bennett, Stephen Crane, Zola, Norris, Gorky, Bergson, Ibsen, Balzac, Bernard Shaw, Dumas, Poe, Thomas Mann, O. Henry, Dreiser, H. G. Wells, Gogol, T. S. Eliot, Gide, Baudelaire, Edgar Lee Masters, Stendhal, Turgenev, Huneker, Nietzsche, and scores of others? Were these men real? Did they exist or had they existed? And how did one pronounce their names?

I ran across many words whose meanings I did not know, and I either looked them up in a dictionary or, before I had a chance to do that, encountered the word in a context that made its meaning clear. But what strange world was this? I concluded the book with the conviction that I had somehow overlooked something terribly important in life. I had once tried to write, had once reveled in feeling, had let my crude imagination roam, but the impulse to dream had been slowly beaten out of me by experience. Now it surged up again and I hungered for books, new ways of looking and seeing. It was not a matter of believing or disbelieving what I read, but of feeling something new, of being affected by something that made the look of the world different.

As dawn broke I ate my pork and beans, feeling dopey, sleepy. I went to work, but the mood of the book would not die; it lingered, coloring everything I saw, heard, did. I now felt that I knew what the white men were feeling. Merely because I had read a book that had spoken of how they lived and thought, I identified myself with that book. I felt vaguely guilty. Would I, filled with bookish notions, act in a manner that would make the whites dislike me?

I forged more notes and my trips to the library became frequent. Reading grew into a passion. My first serious novel was Sinclair Lewis's *Main Street*. It made me see my boss, Mr. Gerald, and identify him as an American type. I would smile when I saw him lugging his golf bags into the office. I had always felt a vast distance separating me from the boss, and now I felt closer to him, though still distant. I felt now that I knew him, that I could feel the very limits of his narrow life. And this had happened because I had read a novel about a mythical man called George F. Babbitt.

The plots and stories in the novels did not interest me so much as the point of view revealed. I gave myself over to each novel without reserve, without trying to criticize it; it was enough for me to see and feel something different. And for me, everything was something different. Reading was like a drug, a dope. The novels created moods in which I lived for days. But I could not conquer my sense of guilt, my feeling that the white men around me knew that I was changing, that I had begun to regard them differently.

Whenever I brought a book to the job, I wrapped it in newspaper—a habit that was to persist for years in other cities and under other circumstances. But some of the white men pried into my packages when I was absent and they questioned me.

"Boy, what are you reading those books for?"

"Oh, I don't know, sir."

"That's deep stuff you're reading, boy."

"I'm just killing time, sir."

"You'll addle your brains if you don't watch out."

I read Dreiser's *Jennie Gerhardt* and *Sister Carrie* and they revived in me a vivid sense of my mother's suffering; I was overwhelmed. I grew silent, wondering about the life around me. It would have been impossible for me to have told anyone what I derived from these novels, for it was nothing less than a sense of life itself. All my life had shaped me for the realism, the naturalism of the modern novel, and I could not read enough of them.

Steeped in new moods and ideas, I bought a ream of paper and tried to write; but nothing would come, or what did come was flat beyond telling. I discovered that more than desire and feeling were necessary to write and I dropped the idea. Yet I still wondered how it was possible to know people sufficiently to write about them? Could I ever learn about life and people? To me, with my vast ignorance, my Jim Crow station in life, it seemed a task impossible of achievement. I now knew what being a Negro meant. I could endure the hunger. I had learned to live with hate. But to feel that there were feelings denied me, that the very breath of life itself was beyond my reach, that more than anything else hurt, wounded me. I had a new hunger.

In buoying me up, reading also cast me down, made me see what was possible, what I had missed. My tension returned, new, terrible, bitter, surging, almost too great to be contained. I no longer *felt* that the world about me was hostile, killing; I *knew* it. A million times I asked myself what I could do to save myself, and there were no answers. I seemed forever condemned, ringed by walls.

I did not discuss my reading with Mr. Falk, who had lent me his library card; it would have meant talking about myself and that would have been too painful. I smiled each day, fighting desperately to maintain my old behavior, to keep my disposition seemingly sunny. But some of the white men discerned that I had begun to brood.

"Wake up there, boy!" Mr. Olin said one day.

"Sir!" I answered for the lack of a better word.

"You act like you've stolen something," he said.

I laughed in the way I knew he expected me to laugh, but I resolved to be more conscious of myself, to watch my every act, to guard and hide the new knowledge that was dawning within me.

If I went north, would it be possible for me to build a new life then? But how could a man build a life upon vague, unformed yearnings? I wanted to write and I did not even know the English language. I bought English grammars and found them dull. I felt that I was getting a better sense of the language from novels than from grammars. I read hard, discarding a writer as soon as I felt that I had grasped his point of view. At night the printed page stood before my eyes in sleep.

Mrs. Moss, my landlady, asked me one Sunday morning:

"Son, what is this you keep on reading?"

"Oh, nothing. Just novels."

"What you get out of 'em?"

"I'm just killing time," I said.

"I hope you know your own mind," she said in a tone which implied that she doubted if I had a mind.

I knew of no Negroes who read the books I liked and I wondered if any Negroes ever thought of them. I knew that there were Negro doctors, lawyers, newspapermen, but I never saw any of them. When I read a Negro newspaper I never caught the faintest echo of my preoccupation in its pages. I felt trapped and occasionally, for a few days, I would stop reading. But a vague hunger would come over me for books, books that opened up new avenues of feeling and seeing, and again I would forge another note to the white librarian. Again I would read and wonder as only the naïve and unlettered can read and wonder, feeling that I carried a secret, criminal burden about with me each day.

That winter my mother and brother came and we set up housekeeping, buying furniture on the installment plan, being cheated and yet knowing no way to avoid it. I began to eat warm food and to my surprise found that regular meals enabled me to read faster. I may have lived through many illnesses and survived them, never suspecting that I was ill. My brother obtained a job and we began to save toward the trip north, plotting our time, setting tentative dates for departure. I told none of the white men on the job that I was planning to go north; I knew that the moment they felt I was thinking of the North they would change toward me. It would have made them feel that I did not like the life I was living, and because my life was completely conditioned by what they said or did, it would have been tantamount to challenging them.

I could calculate my chances for life in the South as a Negro fairly clearly now. I could fight the southern whites by organizing with other Negroes, as my grandfather had done. But I knew that I could never win that way; there were many whites and there were but few blacks. They were strong and we were weak. Outright black rebellion could never win. If I fought openly I would die and I did not want to die. News of lynchings were frequent.

I could submit and live the life of a genial slave, but that was impossible. All of my life had shaped me to live by my own feelings and thoughts. I could make up to Bess and marry her and inherit the house. But that, too, would be the life of a slave; if I did that, I would crush to death something within me, and I would hate myself as much as I knew the whites already hated those who had submitted. Neither could I ever willingly present myself to be kicked, as Shorty had done. I would rather have died than do that.

I could drain off my restlessness by fighting with Shorty and Harrison. I had seen many Negroes solve the problem of being black by transferring their hatred of themselves to others with a black skin and fighting them. I would have to be cold to do that, and I was not cold and I could never be.

I could, of course, forget what I had read, thrust the whites out of my mind, forget them; and find release from anxiety and longing in sex and alcohol. But the memory of how my father had conducted himself made that course repugnant. If I did not want others to violate my life, how could I voluntarily violate it myself?

I had no hope whatever of being a professional man. Not only had I been so conditioned that I did not desire it, but the fulfillment of such an ambition was beyond my capabilities. Well-to-do Negroes lived in a world that was almost as alien to me as the world inhabited by whites.

What, then, was there? I held my life in my mind, in my consciousness each day, feeling at times that I would stumble and drop it, spill it forever. My reading had created a vast sense of distance between me and the world in which I lived and tried to make a living, and that sense of distance was increasing each day. My days and nights were one long, quiet, continuously contained dream of terror, tension, and anxiety. I wondered how long I could bear it.

John Hersey

1914

JOHN HERSEY was born in China of missionary parents. He came to the United States as a child, graduated at Yale in 1936, and completed postgraduate work at Cambridge. In 1937 he became a member of the staff of *Time* magazine, and was sent to the Orient in 1939. As a correspondent for *Time* he covered the early phases of the Second World War in the Pacific; he wrote *Men on Bataan* (1942) and *Into the Valley* (1943), the latter based on direct observation of the fighting on Guadalcanal in 1942. In 1943 he was in the Mediterranean theatre of the war, and from this experience wrote the novel *A Bell for Adano* (1944). Both *Into the Valley* and *A Bell for Adano* were listed as "imperative" reading by the Council on Books in Wartime. *Hiroshima* first appeared in *The New Yorker* magazine for August 31, 1946, when the entire issue of the magazine was devoted to it.

HIROSHIMA
[1946]

I

A Noiseless Flash

At exactly fifteen minutes past eight in the morning, on August 6, 1945, Japanese time, at the moment when the atomic bomb flashed above Hiroshima, Miss Toshiko Sasaki, a clerk in the personnel department of the East Asia Tin Works, had just sat down at her place in the plant office and was turning her head to speak to the girl at the next desk. At that same moment, Dr. Masakazu Fujii was settling down cross-legged to read the Osaka *Asahi* on the porch of his private hospital, overhanging one of the seven deltaic rivers which divide Hiroshima; Mrs. Hatsuyo Nakamura, a tailor's widow, stood by the window of her kitchen, watching a neighbor tearing down his house because it lay in the path of an air-raid-defense fire lane; Father Wilhelm Kleinsorge, a German priest of the Society of Jesus, reclined in his underwear on a cot on the top floor of his order's three-story mission house, reading a Jesuit magazine, *Stimmen der Zeit;* Dr. Terufumi Sasaki, a young member of the surgical staff of the city's large, modern Red Cross Hospital, walked along one of the hospital corridors with a blood specimen for a Wassermann test in his hand; and the Reverend Mr. Kiyoshi Tanimoto, pastor of the Hiroshima Methodist Church, paused at the door of a rich man's house in Koi, the city's western suburb, and prepared to unload a handcart full of things he had evacuated from town in fear of the massive B-29 raid which everyone expected Hiroshima to suffer. A hundred thousand people were killed by the atomic bomb, and these six were among the survivors. They still wonder why they lived when so many others died. Each of them counts many small items of chance or volition—a step taken in time, a decision to go indoors, catching one streetcar instead of the next—that spared him. And now each knows that in the act of survival he lived a dozen lives and saw more death than he ever thought he would see. At the time, none of them knew anything.

The Reverend Mr. Tanimoto got up at five o'clock that morning. He was alone in the parsonage, because for some time his wife had been commuting with their year-old baby to spend nights with a friend in Ushida, a suburb to the north. Of all the important cities of Japan, only two, Kyoto and Hiroshima, had not been visited in strength by *B-san,* or Mr. B, as the Japanese, with a mixture of respect and unhappy familiarity, called the B-29; and Mr. Tanimoto, like all his neighbors and friends, was almost sick with anxiety. He had heard uncomfortably detailed accounts of mass raids on Kure, Iwakuni, Tokuyama, and other nearby towns; he was sure Hiroshima's turn would come soon. He had slept badly the night before, because there had been several air-raid warnings. Hiroshima had been getting such warnings almost every night for weeks, for at that time the B-29s were using Lake Biwa, northeast of Hiroshima, as a rendezvous point, and no matter what city the Americans planned to hit, the Superfortresses streamed in over the coast near Hiroshima. The frequency of the warnings and the continued abstinence of Mr. B with respect to Hiroshima had made its citizens jittery; a rumor was going around that the Americans were saving something special for the city.

Mr. Tanimoto is a small man, quick to talk, laugh, and cry. He wears his black hair parted in the middle and rather long; the prominence of the frontal bones just above his eyebrows and the smallness of his mustache, mouth, and chin give him a strange, old-young look, boyish and yet wise, weak and yet fiery. He moves nervously and fast, but with a restraint which suggests that he is a cautious, thoughtful man. He showed, indeed, just those qualities in the uneasy days before the bomb fell. Besides having his wife spend the nights in Ushida, Mr. Tanimoto had been carrying all the portable things from his church, in the close-packed residential district called Nagaragawa, to a house that belonged to a rayon manufacturer in Koi, two miles from the center of town. The rayon man, a Mr. Matsui, had opened his then unoccupied estate to a large number of his friends and acquaintances, so that they might evacuate whatever they wished to a safe distance from the probable target area. Mr. Tanimoto had had no difficulty in moving chairs, hymnals, Bibles, altar gear, and church records by pushcart himself, but the organ console and an upright piano required some aid. A friend of his named Matsuo had, the day before, helped him get the piano out to Koi; in return, he had promised this day to assist Mr. Matsuo in hauling out a daughter's belongings. That is why he had risen so early.

Mr. Tanimoto cooked his own breakfast. He felt awfully tired. The effort of moving the piano the day before, a sleepless night, weeks of worry and unbalanced diet, the cares of his parish—all combined to make him feel hardly adequate to the new day's work. There was another thing, too: Mr. Tanimoto had studied theology at Emory College, in Atlanta, Georgia; he had graduated in 1940; he spoke excellent English; he dressed in American clothes; he had corresponded with many American friends right up to the time the war began; and among a people obsessed with a fear of being spied upon—perhaps almost obsessed himself—he found himself growing increasingly uneasy. The police had questioned him several times, and just a few days before, he had heard that an influential acquaintance, a Mr. Tanaka, a retired officer of the Toyo Kisen Kaisha steamship line, an anti-Christian, a man famous in Hiroshima for his showy philanthropies and notorious for his personal tyrannies, had been telling people that Tanimoto should not be trusted. In compensation, to show himself publicly a good Japanese, Mr. Tanimoto had taken on the chairmanship of his local *tonarigumi,* or Neighborhood Association, and to his other duties and concerns this position had added the business of organizing air-raid defense for about twenty families.

Before six o'clock that morning, Mr. Tanimoto started for Mr. Matsuo's house. There he found that their burden was to be a *tansu,* a large Japanese cabinet, full of clothing and household goods. The two men set out. The morning was perfectly clear and so warm that the day promised to be uncomfortable. A few minutes after they started, the air-raid siren went off— a minute-long blast that warned of approaching planes but indicated to the people of Hiroshima only a slight degree of danger, since it sounded every morning at this time, when an American weather plane came over. The two men pulled and pushed the handcart through the city streets. Hiroshima was a fan-shaped city, lying mostly on the six islands formed by the seven estuarial rivers that branch out from the Ota River; its main commercial and residential districts, covering about four square miles in the center of the city, contained three-quarters of its population, which had been reduced by several evacuation programs from a wartime peak of 380,000 to about 245,000. Factories and other residential districts, or suburbs, lay compactly around the edges of the city. To the south were the docks, an airport, and the island-studded Inland Sea. A rim of mountains runs around the other three sides of the delta. Mr. Tanimoto and Mr. Matsuo took their way through the shopping center, already full of people, and across two of the rivers to the sloping streets of Koi, and up them to the outskirts and foothills. As they started up a valley away from the tight-ranked houses, the all-clear sounded. (The Japanese radar operators, detecting only three planes, supposed that they comprised a reconnaissance.) Pushing the handcart up to the rayon man's house was tiring, and the men, after they had maneuvered their load into the driveway and to the front steps, paused to rest awhile. They stood with a wing of the house between them and the city. Like most homes in this part of Japan, the house consisted of a wooden frame and wooden walls supporting a heavy tile roof. Its front hall, packed with rolls of bedding and clothing, looked like a cool cave full of fat cushions. Opposite the house, to the right of the front door, there was a large, finicky rock garden. There was no sound of planes. The morning was still; the place was cool and pleasant.

Then a tremendous flash of light cut across the sky. Mr. Tanimoto has a distinct recollection that it travelled from east to west, from the city toward the hills. It seemed a sheet of sun. Both he and Mr. Matsuo reacted in terror—and both had time to react (for they were 3,500 yards, or two miles, from the center of the explosion). Mr. Matsuo dashed up the front steps into the house and dived among the bedrolls and buried himself there. Mr. Tanimoto took four or five steps and threw himself between two big rocks in the garden. He bellied up very hard against one of them. As his face was against the stone, he did not see what happened. He felt a sudden pressure, and then splinters and pieces of board and fragments of tile fell on him. He heard no roar. (Almost no one in Hiroshima recalls hearing any noise of the bomb. But a fisherman in his sampan on the Inland Sea near Tsuzu, the man

with whom Mr. Tanimoto's mother-in-law and sister-in-law were living, saw the flash and heard a tremendous explosion; he was nearly twenty miles from Hiroshima, but the thunder was greater than when the B-29s hit Iwakuni, only five miles away.)

When he dared, Mr. Tanimoto raised his head and saw that the rayon man's house had collapsed. He thought a bomb had fallen directly on it. Such clouds of dust had risen that there was a sort of twilight around. In panic, not thinking for the moment of Mr. Matsuo under the ruins, he dashed out into the street. He noticed as he ran that the concrete wall of the estate had fallen over—toward the house rather than away from it. In the street, the first thing he saw was a squad of soldiers who had been burrowing into the hillside opposite, making one of the thousands of dugouts in which the Japanese apparently intended to resist invasion, hill by hill, life for life; the soldiers were coming out of the hole, where they should have been safe, and blood was running from their heads, chests, and backs. They were silent and dazed.

Under what seemed to be a local dust cloud, the day grew darker and darker.

At nearly midnight, the night before the bomb was dropped, an announcer on the city's radio station said that about two hundred B-29s were approaching southern Honshu and advised the population of Hiroshima to evacuate to their designated "safe areas." Mrs. Hatsuyo Nakamura, the tailor's widow, who lived in the section called Nobori-cho and who had long had a habit of doing as she was told, got her three children—a ten-year-old boy, Toshio, an eight-year-old girl, Yaeko, and a five-year-old girl, Myeko—out of bed and dressed them and walked with them to the military area known as the East Parade Ground, on the northeast edge of the city. There she unrolled some mats and the children lay down on them. They slept until about two, when they were awakened by the roar of the planes going over Hiroshima.

As soon as the planes had passed, Mrs.

Nakamura started back with her children. They reached home a little after two-thirty and she immediately turned on the radio, which, to her distress, was just then broadcasting a fresh warning. When she looked at the children and saw how tired they were, and when she thought of the number of trips they had made in past weeks, all to no purpose, to the East Parade Ground, she decided that in spite of the instructions on the radio, she simply could not face starting out all over again. She put the children in their bedrolls on the floor, lay down herself at three o'clock, and fell asleep at once, so soundly that when planes passed over later, she did not waken to their sound.

The siren jarred her awake at about seven. She arose, dressed quickly, and hurried to the house of Mr. Nakamoto, the head of her Neighborhood Association, and asked him what she should do. He said that she should remain at home unless an urgent warning—a series of intermittent blasts of the siren—was sounded. She returned home, lit the stove in the kitchen, set some rice to cook, and sat down to read that morning's Hiroshima *Chugoku*. To her relief, the all-clear sounded at eight o'clock. She heard the children stirring, so she went and gave each of them a handful of peanuts and told them to stay on their bedrolls, because they were tired from the night's walk. She had hoped that they would go back to sleep, but the man in the house directly to the south began to make a terrible hullabaloo of hammering, wedging, ripping, and splitting. The prefectural government, convinced, as everyone in Hiroshima was, that the city would be attacked soon, had begun to press with threats and warnings for the completion of wide fire lanes, which, it was hoped, might act in conjunction with the rivers to localize any fires started by an incendiary raid; and the neighbor was reluctantly sacrificing his home to the city's safety. Just the day before, the prefecture had ordered all able-bodied girls from the secondary schools to spend a few days helping to clear these lanes, and they started work soon after the all-clear sounded.

Mrs. Nakamura went back to the kitchen, looked at the rice, and began watching the man next door. At first, she was annoyed with him for making so much noise, but then she was moved almost to tears by pity. Her emotion was specifically directed toward her neighbor, tearing down his home, board by board, at a time when there was so much unavoidable destruction, but undoubtedly she also felt a generalized, community pity, to say nothing of self-pity. She had not had an easy time. Her husband, Isawa, had gone into the Army just after Myeko was born, and she had heard nothing from or of him for a long time, until, on March 5, 1942, she received a seven-word telegram: "Isawa died an honorable death at Singapore." She learned later that he had died on February 15th, the day Singapore fell, and that he had been a corporal. Isawa had been a not particularly prosperous tailor, and his only capital was a Sankoku sewing machine. After his death, when his allotments stopped coming, Mrs. Nakamura got out the machine and began to take in piecework herself, and since then had supported the children, but poorly, by sewing.

As Mrs. Nakamura stood watching her neighbor, everything flashed whiter than any white she had ever seen. She did not notice what happened to the man next door; the reflex of a mother set her in motion toward her children. She had taken a single step (the house was 1,350 yards, or three-quarters of a mile, from the center of the explosion) when something picked her up and she seemed to fly into the next room over the raised sleeping platform, pursued by parts of her house.

Timbers fell around her as she landed, and a shower of tiles pommelled her; everything became dark, for she was buried. The debris did not cover her deeply. She rose up and freed herself. She heard a child cry, "Mother, help me!" and saw her youngest—Myeko, the five-year-old—buried up to her breast and unable to move. As

Mrs. Nakamura started frantically to claw her way toward the baby, she could see or hear nothing of her other children.

In the days right before the bombing, Dr. Masakazu Fujii, being prosperous, hedonistic, and at the time not too busy, had been allowing himself the luxury of sleeping until nine or nine-thirty, but fortunately he had to get up early the morning the bomb was dropped to see a house guest off on a train. He rose at six, and half an hour later walked with his friend to the station, not far away, across two of the rivers. He was back home by seven, just as the siren sounded its sustained warning. He ate breakfast and then, because the morning was already hot, undressed down to his underwear and went out on the porch to read the paper. This porch—in fact, the whole building—was curiously constructed. Dr. Fujii was the proprietor of a peculiarly Japanese institution: a private, single-doctor hospital. This building, perched beside and over the water of the Kyo River, and next to the bridge of the same name, contained thirty rooms for thirty patients and their kinfolk—for, according to Japanese custom, when a person falls sick and goes to a hospital, one or more members of his family go and live there with him, to cook for him, bathe, massage, and read to him, and to offer incessant familial sympathy, without which a Japanese patient would be miserable indeed. Dr. Fujii had no beds—only straw mats—for his patients. He did, however, have all sorts of modern equipment: an X-ray machine, diathermy apparatus, and a fine tiled laboratory. The structure rested two-thirds on the land, one-third on piles over the tidal waters of the Kyo. This overhang, the part of the building where Dr. Fujii lived, was queer-looking, but it was cool in summer and from the porch, which faced away from the center of the city, the prospect of the river, with pleasure boats drifting up and down it, was always refreshing. Dr. Fujii had occasionally had anxious moments when the Ota and its mouth branches rose to flood, but the piling was apparently firm enough and the house had always held.

Dr. Fujii had been relatively idle for about a month because in July, as the number of untouched cities in Japan dwindled and as Hiroshima seemed more and more inevitably a target, he began turning patients away, on the ground that in case of a fire raid he would not be able to evacuate them. Now he had only two patients left—a woman from Yano, injured in the shoulder, and a young man of twenty-five recovering from burns he had suffered when the steel factory near Hiroshima in which he worked had been hit. Dr. Fujii had six nurses to tend his patients. His wife and children were safe; his wife and one son were living outside Osaka, and another son and two daughters were in the country on Kyushu. A niece was living with him, and a maid and a manservant. He had little to do and did not mind, for he had saved some money. At fifty, he was healthy, convivial, and calm, and he was pleased to pass the evenings drinking whiskey with friends, always sensibly and for the sake of conversation. Before the war, he had affected brands imported from Scotland and America; now he was perfectly satisfied with the best Japanese brand, Suntory.

Dr. Fujii sat down cross-legged in his underwear on the spotless matting of the porch, put on his glasses, and started reading the Osaka *Asahi*. He liked to read the Osaka news because his wife was there. He saw the flash. To him—faced away from the center and looking at his paper—it seemed a brilliant yellow. Startled, he began to rise to his feet. In that moment (he was 1,550 yards from the center), the hospital leaned behind his rising and, with a terrible ripping noise, toppled into the river. The Doctor, still in the act of getting to his feet, was thrown forward and around and over; he was buffeted and gripped; he lost track of everything, because things were so speeded up; he felt the water.

Dr. Fujii hardly had time to think that he was dying before he realized that he was alive, squeezed tightly by two long timbers

in a V across his chest, like a morsel suspended between two huge chopsticks—held
upright, so that he could not move, with
his head miraculously above water and his
torso and legs in it. The remains of his
hospital were all around him in a mad assortment of splintered lumber and materials
for the relief of pain. His left shoulder
hurt terribly. His glasses were gone.

FATHER WILHELM KLEINSORGE, of the Society of Jesus, was, on the morning of the
explosion, in rather frail condition. The
Japanese wartime diet had not sustained
him, and he felt the strain of being a foreigner in an increasingly xenophobic Japan; even a German, since the defeat of the
Fatherland, was unpopular. Father Kleinsorge had, at thirty-eight, the look of a
boy growing too fast—thin in the face, with
a prominent Adam's apple, a hollow chest,
dangling hands, big feet. He walked clumsily, leaning forward a little. He was tired
all the time. To make matters worse, he had
suffered for two days, along with Father
Cieslik, a fellow-priest, from a rather painful and urgent diarrhea, which they blamed
on the beans and black ration bread they
were obliged to eat. Two other priests then
living in the mission compound, which was
in the Nobori-cho section—Father Superior
LaSalle and Father Schiffer—had happily
escaped this affliction.

Father Kleinsorge woke up about six the
morning the bomb was dropped, and half
an hour later—he was a bit tardy because
of his sickness—he began to read Mass in
the mission chapel, a small Japanese-style
wooden building which was without pews,
since its worshippers knelt on the usual
Japanese matted floor, facing an altar
graced with splendid silks, brass, silver,
and heavy embroideries. This morning, a
Monday, the only worshippers were Mr.
Takemoto, a theological student living in
the mission house; Mr. Fukai, the secretary
of the diocese; Mrs. Murata, the mission's
devoutly Christian housekeeper; and his
fellow-priests. After Mass, while Father
Kleinsorge was reading the Prayers of

Thanksgiving, the siren sounded. He
stopped the service and the missionaries
retired across the compound to the bigger
building. There, in his room on the ground
floor, to the right of the front door, Father
Kleinsorge changed into a military uniform which he had acquired when he was
teaching at the Rokko Middle School in
Kobe and which he wore during air-raid
alerts.

After an alarm, Father Kleinsorge always went out and scanned the sky, and in
this instance, when he stepped outside, he
was glad to see only the single weather
plane that flew over Hiroshima each day
about this time. Satisfied that nothing
would happen, he went in and breakfasted
with the other Fathers on substitute coffee
and ration bread, which, under the circumstances, was especially repugnant to him.
The Fathers sat and talked awhile, until,
at eight, they heard the all-clear. They
went then to various parts of the building.
Father Schiffer retired to his room to do
some writing. Father Cieslik sat in his
room in a straight chair with a pillow over
his stomach to ease his pain, and read.
Father Superior LaSalle stood at the window of his room, thinking. Father Kleinsorge went up to a room on the third floor,
took off all his clothes except his underwear, and stretched out on his right side
on a cot and began reading his *Stimmen der
Zeit*.

After the terrible flash—which, Father
Kleinsorge later realized, reminded him of
something he had read as a boy about a
large meteor colliding with the earth—he
had time (since he was 1,400 yards from
the center) for one thought: A bomb has
fallen directly on us. Then, for a few
seconds or minutes, he went out of his
mind.

Father Kleinsorge never knew how he
got out of the house. The next things he
was conscious of were that he was wandering around in the mission's vegetable garden in his underwear, bleeding slightly
from small cuts along his left flank; that
all the buildings round about had fallen

down except the Jesuits' mission house, which had long before been braced and double-braced by a priest named Gropper, who was terrified of earthquakes; that the day had turned dark; and that Murata-*san*, the housekeeper, was nearby, crying over and over, *"Shu Jesusu, awaremi tamai! Our Lord Jesus, have pity on us!"*

ON THE TRAIN on the way into Hiroshima from the country, where he lived with his mother, Dr. Terufumi Sasaki, the Red Cross Hospital surgeon, thought over an unpleasant nightmare he had had the night before. His mother's home was in Mukai-hara, thirty miles from the city, and it took him two hours by train and tram to reach the hospital. He had slept uneasily all night and had wakened an hour earlier than usual, and, feeling sluggish and slightly feverish, had debated whether to go to the hospital at all; his sense of duty finally forced him to go, and he had started out on an earlier train than he took most mornings. The dream had particularly frightened him because it was so closely associated, on the surface at least, with a disturbing actuality. He was only twenty-five years old and had just completed his training at the Eastern Medical University, in Tsingtao, China. He was something of an idealist and was much distressed by the inadequacy of medical facilities in the country town where his mother lived. Quite on his own, and without a permit, he had begun visiting a few sick people out there in the evenings, after his eight hours at the hospital and four hours' commuting. He had recently learned that the penalty for practicing without a permit was severe; a fellow-doctor whom he had asked about it had given him a serious scolding. Nevertheless, he had continued to practice. In his dream, he had been at the bedside of a country patient when the police and the doctor he had consulted burst into the room, seized him, dragged him outside, and beat him up cruelly. On the train, he just about decided to give up the work in Mukaihara, since he felt it would be impossible to get a permit, because the authorities would hold that it would conflict with his duties at the Red Cross Hospital.

At the terminus, he caught a streetcar at once. (He later calculated that if he had taken his customary train that morning, and if he had had to wait a few minutes for the streetcar, as often happened, he would have been close to the center at the time of the explosion and would surely have perished.) He arrived at the hospital at seven-forty and reported to the chief surgeon. A few minutes later, he went to a room on the first floor and drew blood from the arm of a man in order to perform a Wassermann test. The laboratory containing the incubators for the test was on the third floor. With the blood specimen in his left hand, walking in a kind of distraction he had felt all morning, probably because of the dream and his restless night, he started along the main corridor on his way toward the stairs. He was one step beyond an open window when the light of the bomb was reflected, like a gigantic photographic flash, in the corridor. He ducked down on one knee and said to himself, as only a Japanese would, "Sasaki, *ganbare!* Be brave!" Just then (the building was 1,650 yards from the center), the blast ripped through the hospital. The glasses he was wearing flew off his face; the bottle of blood crashed against one wall; his Japanese slippers zipped out from under his feet—but otherwise, thanks to where he stood, he was untouched.

Dr. Sasaki shouted the name of the chief surgeon and rushed around to the man's office and found him terribly cut by glass. The hospital was in horrible confusion: heavy partitions and ceilings had fallen on patients, beds had overturned, windows had blown in and cut people, blood was spattered on the walls and floors, instruments were everywhere, many of the patients were running about screaming, many more lay dead. (A colleague working in the laboratory to which Dr. Sasaki had been walking was dead; Dr. Sasaki's patient, whom he had just left and who a few moments before had been dreadfully afraid of syphilis, was also dead.) Dr. Sasaki found himself the only doctor in the hospital who was unhurt.

Dr. Sasaki, who believed that the enemy had hit only the building he was in, got bandages and began to bind the wounds of those inside the hospital; while outside, all over Hiroshima, maimed and dying citizens turned their unsteady steps toward the Red Cross Hospital to begin an invasion that was to make Dr. Sasaki forget his private nightmare for a long, long time.

MISS TOSHIKO SASAKI, the East Asia Tin Works clerk, who is not related to Dr. Sasaki, got up at three o'clock in the morning on the day the bomb fell. There was extra housework to do. Her eleven-month-old brother, Akio, had come down the day before with a serious stomach upset; her mother had taken him to the Tamura Pediatric Hospital and was staying there with him. Miss Sasaki, who was about twenty, had to cook breakfast for her father, a brother, a sister, and herself, and—since the hospital, because of the war, was unable to provide food—to prepare a whole day's meals for her mother and the baby, in time for her father, who worked in a factory making rubber earplugs for artillery crews, to take the food by on his way to the plant. When she had finished and had cleaned and put away the cooking things, it was nearly seven. The family lived in Koi, and she had a forty-five-minute trip to the tin works, in the section of town called Kannonmachi. She was in charge of the personnel records in the factory. She left Koi at seven, and as soon as she reached the plant, she went with some of the other girls from the personnel department to the factory auditorium. A prominent local Navy man, a former employee, had committed suicide the day before by throwing himself under a train— a death considered honorable enough to warrant a memorial service, which was to

be held at the tin works at ten o'clock that morning. In the large hall, Miss Sasaki and the others made suitable preparations for the meeting. This work took about twenty minutes.

Miss Sasaki went back to her office and sat down at her desk. She was quite far from the windows, which were off to her left, and behind her were a couple of tall bookcases containing all the books of the factory library, which the personnel department had organized. She settled herself at her desk, put some things in a drawer, and shifted papers. She thought that before she began to make entries in her lists of new employees, discharges, and departures for the Army, she would chat for a moment with the girl at her right. Just as she turned her head away from the windows, the room was filled with a blinding light. She was paralyzed by fear, fixed still in her chair for a long moment (the plant was 1,600 yards from the center).

Everything fell, and Miss Sasaki lost consciousness. The ceiling dropped suddenly and the wooden floor above collapsed in splinters and the people up there came down and the roof above them gave way; but principally and first of all, the bookcases right behind her swooped forward and the contents threw her down, with her left leg horribly twisted and breaking underneath her. There, in the tin factory, in the first moment of the atomic age, a human being was crushed by books.

II

THE FIRE

IMMEDIATELY after the explosion, the Reverend Mr. Kiyoshi Tanimoto, having run wildly out of the Matsui estate and having looked in wonderment at the bloody soldiers at the mouth of the dugout they had been digging, attached himself sympathetically to an old lady who was walking along in a daze, holding her head with her left hand, supporting a small boy of three or four on her back with her right, and crying, "I'm hurt! I'm hurt! I'm hurt!" Mr. Tanimoto transferred the child to his own back and led the woman by the hand down the street, which was darkened by what seemed to be a local column of dust. He took the woman to a grammar school not far away that had previously been designated for use as a temporary hospital in case of emergency. By this solicitous behavior, Mr. Tanimoto at once got rid of his terror. At the school, he was much surprised to see glass all over the floor and fifty or sixty injured people already waiting to be treated. He reflected that, although the all-clear had sounded and he had heard no planes, several bombs must have been dropped. He thought of a hillock in the rayon man's garden from which he could get a view of the whole of Koi—of the whole of Hiroshima, for that matter—and he ran back up to the estate.

From the mound, Mr. Tanimoto saw an astonishing panorama. Not just a patch of Koi, as he had expected, but as much of Hiroshima as he could see through the clouded air was giving off a thick, dreadful miasma. Clumps of smoke, near and far, had begun to push up through the general dust. He wondered how such extensive damage could have been dealt out of a silent sky; even a few planes, far up, would have been audible. Houses nearby were burning, and when huge drops of water the size of marbles began to fall, he half thought that they must be coming from the hoses of firemen fighting the blazes. (They were actually drops of condensed moisture falling from the turbulent tower of dust, heat, and fission fragments that had already risen miles into the sky above Hiroshima.)

Mr. Tanimoto turned away from the sight when he heard Mr. Matsuo call out to ask whether he was all right. Mr. Matsuo had been safely cushioned within the falling house by the bedding stored in the front hall and had worked his way out. Mr. Tanimoto scarcely answered. He had thought

of his wife and baby, his church, his home, his parishioners, all of them down in that awful murk. Once more he began to run in fear—toward the city.

Mrs. Hatsuyo Nakamura, the tailor's widow, having struggled up from under the ruins of her house after the explosion, and seeing Myeko, the youngest of her three children, buried breast-deep and unable to move, crawled across the debris, hauled at timbers, and flung tiles aside, in a hurried effort to free the child. Then, from what seemed to be caverns far below, she heard two small voices crying, *"Tasukete! Tasukete! Help! Help!"*

She called the names of her ten-year-old son and eight-year-old daughter: "Toshio! Yaeko!"

The voices from below answered.

Mrs. Nakamura abandoned Myeko, who at least could breathe, and in a frenzy made the wreckage fly above the crying voices. The children had been sleeping nearly ten feet apart, but now their voices seemed to come from the same place. Toshio, the boy, apparently had some freedom to move, because she could feel him undermining the pile of wood and tiles as she worked from above. At last she saw his head, and she hastily pulled him out by it. A mosquito net was wound intricately, as if it had been carefully wrapped, around his feet. He said he had been blown right across the room and had been on top of his sister Yaeko under the wreckage. She now said, from underneath, that she could not move, because there was something on her legs. With a bit more digging, Mrs. Nakamura cleared a hole above the child and began to pull her arm. *"Itai!* It hurts!" Yaeko cried. Mrs. Nakamura shouted, "There's no time now to say whether it hurts or not," and yanked her whimpering daughter up. Then she freed Myeko. The children were filthy and bruised, but none of them had a single cut or scratch.

Mrs. Nakamura took the children out into the street. They had nothing on but underpants, and although the day was very hot, she worried rather confusedly about their being cold, so she went back into the wreckage and burrowed underneath and found a bundle of clothes she had packed for an emergency, and she dressed them in pants, blouses, shoes, padded-cotton air-raid helmets called *bokuzuki*, and even, irrationally, overcoats. The children were silent, except for the five-year-old, Myeko, who kept asking questions: "Why is it night already? Why did our house fall down? What happened?" Mrs. Nakamura, who did not know what had happened (had not the all-clear sounded?), looked around and saw through the darkness that all the houses in her neighborhood had collapsed. The house next door, which its owner had been tearing down to make way for a fire lane, was now very thoroughly, if crudely, torn down; its owner, who had been sacrificing his home for the community's safety, lay dead. Mrs. Nakamoto, wife of the head of the local air-raid-defense Neighborhood Association, came across the street with her head all bloody, and said that her baby was badly cut; did Mrs. Nakamura have any bandage? Mrs. Nakamura did not, but she crawled into the remains of her house again and pulled out some white cloth that she had been using in her work as a seamstress, ripped it into strips, and gave it to Mrs. Nakamoto. While fetching the cloth, she noticed her sewing machine; she went back in for it and dragged it out. Obviously, she could not carry it with her, so she unthinkingly plunged her symbol of livelihood into the receptacle which for weeks had been her symbol of safety—the cement tank of water in front of her house, of the type every household had been ordered to construct against a possible fire raid.

A nervous neighbor, Mrs. Hataya, called to Mrs. Nakamura to run away with her to the woods in Asano Park—an estate, by the Kyo River not far off, belonging to the wealthy Asano family, who once owned the Toyo Kisen Kaisha steamship line. The park had been designated as an evacuation area for their neighborhood. Seeing fire breaking out in a nearby ruin (except at the very center, where the bomb itself ignited some fires, most of Hiroshima's citywide conflagration was caused by inflammable wreckage falling on cookstoves and live wires), Mrs. Nakamura suggested going over to fight it. Mrs. Hataya said, "Don't be foolish. What if planes come and drop more bombs?" So Mrs. Nakamura started out for Asano Park with her children and Mrs. Hataya, and she carried her rucksack of emergency clothing, a blanket, an umbrella, and a suitcase of things she had cached in her air-raid shelter. Under many ruins, as they hurried along, they heard muffled screams for help. The only building they saw standing on their way to Asano Park was the Jesuit mission house, alongside the Catholic kindergarten to which Mrs. Nakamura had sent Myeko for a time. As they passed it, she saw Father Kleinsorge, in bloody underwear, running out of the house with a small suitcase in his hand.

RIGHT AFTER the explosion, while Father Wilhelm Kleinsorge, S. J., was wandering around in his underwear in the vegetable garden, Father Superior LaSalle came around the corner of the building in the darkness. His body, especially his back, was bloody; the flash had made him twist away from his window, and tiny pieces of glass had flown at him. Father Kleinsorge, still bewildered, managed to ask, "Where are the rest?" Just then, the two other priests living in the mission house appeared —Father Cieslik, unhurt, supporting Father Schiffer, who was covered with blood that spurted from a cut above his left ear and who was very pale. Father Cieslik was rather pleased with himself, for after the flash he had dived into a doorway, which he had previously reckoned to be the safest place inside the building, and when the blast came, he was not injured. Father LaSalle told Father Cieslik to take Father Schiffer to a doctor before he bled to death, and suggested either Dr. Kanda, who lived on the next corner, or Dr. Fujii, about six blocks away. The two men went out of the compound and up the street.

The daughter of Mr. Hoshijima, the mission catechist, ran up to Father Kleinsorge and said that her mother and sister were buried under the ruins of their house, which was at the back of the Jesuit compound, and at the same time the priests noticed that the house of the Catholic-kindergarten teacher at the front of the compound had collapsed on her. While Father LaSalle and Mrs. Murata, the mission housekeeper, dug the teacher out, Father Kleinsorge went to the catechist's fallen house and began lifting things off the top of the pile. There was not a sound underneath; he was sure the Hoshijima women had been killed. At last, under what had been a corner of the kitchen, he saw Mrs. Hoshijima's head. Believing her dead, he began to haul her out by the hair, but suddenly she screamed, "*Itai! Itai!* It hurts! It hurts!" He dug some more and lifted her out. He managed, too, to find her daughter in the rubble and free her. Neither was badly hurt.

A public bath next door to the mission house had caught fire, but since there the wind was southerly, the priests thought their house would be spared. Nevertheless, as a precaution, Father Kleinsorge went inside to fetch some things he wanted to save. He found his room in a state of weird and illogical confusion. A first-aid kit was hanging undisturbed on a hook on the wall, but his clothes, which had been on other hooks nearby, were nowhere to be seen. His desk was in splinters all over the room, but a mere papier-mâché suitcase, which he had hidden under the desk, stood handle-side up, without a scratch on it, in the doorway of the room, where he could not miss it. Father Kleinsorge later came to regard this as a bit of Providential interference, inasmuch as the suitcase contained his breviary, the account books for the whole diocese, and a considerable amount of paper money belonging to the mission, for which he was responsible. He

ran out of the house and deposited the suitcase in the mission air-raid shelter.

At about this time, Father Cieslik and Father Schiffer, who was still spurting blood, came back and said that Dr. Kanda's house was ruined and that fire blocked them from getting out of what they supposed to be the local circle of destruction to Dr. Fujii's private hospital, on the bank of the Kyo River.

DR. MASAKAZU FUJII'S hospital was no longer on the bank of the Kyo River; it was in the river. After the overturn, Dr. Fujii was so stupefied and so tightly squeezed by the beams gripping his chest that he was unable to move at first, and he hung there about twenty minutes in the darkened morning. Then a thought which came to him—that soon the tide would be running in through the estuaries and his head would be submerged—inspired him to fearful activity; he wriggled and turned and exerted what strength he could (though his left arm, because of the pain in his shoulder, was useless), and before long he had freed himself from the vise. After a few moments' rest, he climbed onto the pile of timbers and, finding a long one that slanted up to the river-bank, he painfully shinnied up it.

Dr. Fujii, who was in his underwear, was now soaking and dirty. His undershirt was torn, and blood ran down it from bad cuts on his chin and back. In this disarray, he walked out onto Kyo Bridge, beside which his hospital had stood. The bridge had not collapsed. He could see only fuzzily without his glasses, but he could see enough to be amazed at the number of houses that were down all around. On the bridge, he encountered a friend, a doctor named Machii, and asked in bewilderment, "What do you think it was?"

Dr. Machii said, "It must have been a *Molotoffano hanakago*"—a Molotov flower basket, the delicate Japanese name for the "bread basket," or self-scattering cluster of bombs.

At first, Dr. Fujii could see only two

fires, one across the river from his hospital
site and one quite far to the south. But at
the same time, he and his friend observed
something that puzzled them, and which,
as doctors, they discussed: although there
were as yet very few fires, wounded people
were hurrying across the bridge in an endless parade of misery, and many of them
exhibited terrible burns on their faces and
arms. "Why do you suppose it is?" Dr.
Fujii asked. Even a theory was comforting
that day, and Dr. Machii stuck to his.
"Perhaps because it was a Molotov flower
basket," he said.

There had been no breeze earlier in the
morning when Dr. Fujii had walked to
the railway station to see his friend off,
but now brisk winds were blowing every
which way; here on the bridge the wind
was easterly. New fires were leaping up,
and they spread quickly, and in a very
short time terrible blasts of hot air and
showers of cinders made it impossible to
stand on the bridge any more. Dr. Machii
ran to the far side of the river and along a
still unkindled street. Dr. Fujii went down
into the water under the bridge, where a
score of people had already taken refuge,
among them his servants, who had extri-
cated themselves from the wreckage. From
there, Dr. Fujii saw a nurse hanging in
the timbers of his hospital by her legs, and
then another painfully pinned across the
breast. He enlisted the help of some of the
others under the bridge and freed both of
them. He thought he heard the voice of his
niece for a moment, but he could not find
her; he never saw her again. Four of his
nurses and the two patients in the hospital
died, too. Dr. Fujii went back into the
water of the river and waited for the fire
to subside.

THE LOT of Drs. Fujii, Kanda, and Machii
right after the explosion—and, as these
three were typical, that of the majority of
the physicians and surgeons of Hiroshima
—with their offices and hospitals destroyed,
their equipment scattered, their own bod-

ies incapacitated in varying degrees, explained why so many citizens who were
hurt went untended and why so many who
might have lived died. Of a hundred and
fifty doctors in the city, sixty-five were already dead and most of the rest were
wounded. Of 1,780 nurses, 1,654 were dead
or too badly hurt to work. In the biggest
hospital, that of the Red Cross, only six
doctors out of thirty were able to function,
and only ten nurses out of more than two
hundred. The sole uninjured doctor on the
Red Cross Hospital staff was Dr. Sasaki.
After the explosion, he hurried to a storeroom to fetch bandages. This room, like
everything he had seen as he ran through
the hospital, was chaotic—bottles of medicines thrown off shelves and broken, salves
spattered on the walls, instruments strewn
everywhere. He grabbed up some bandages
and an unbroken bottle of mercurochrome,
hurried back to the chief surgeon, and
bandaged his cuts. Then he went out into
the corridor and began patching up the
wounded patients and the doctors and
nurses there. He blundered so without his
glasses that he took a pair off the face of
a wounded nurse, and although they only
approximately compensated for the errors
of his vision, they were better than nothing. (He was to depend on them for more
than a month.)

Dr. Sasaki worked without method, taking those who were nearest him first, and
he noticed soon that the corridor seemed
to be getting more and more crowded.
Mixed in with the abrasions and lacerations
which most people in the hospital had
suffered, he began to find dreadful burns.
He realized then that casualties were pouring in from outdoors. There were so many
that he began to pass up the lightly
wounded; he decided that all he could hope
to do was to stop people from bleeding to
death. Before long, patients lay and
crouched on the floors of the wards and
the laboratories and all the other rooms,
and in the corridors, and on the stairs, and
in the front hall, and under the porte-

cochère, and on the stone front steps, and in the driveway and courtyard, and for blocks each way in the streets outside. Wounded people supported maimed people; disfigured families leaned together. Many people were vomiting. A tremendous number of schoolgirls—some of those who had been taken from their classrooms to work outdoors, clearing fire lanes—crept into the hospital. In a city of two hundred and forty-five thousand, nearly a hundred thousand people had been killed or doomed at one blow; a hundred thousand more were hurt. At least ten thousand of the wounded made their way to the best hospital in town, which was altogether unequal to such a trampling, since it had only six hundred beds, and they had all been occupied. The people in the suffocating crowd inside the hospital wept and cried, for Dr. Sasaki to hear, "*Sensei!* Doctor!," and the less seriously wounded came and pulled at his sleeve and begged him to go to the aid of the worse wounded. Tugged here and there in his stockinged feet, bewildered by the numbers, staggered by so much raw flesh, Dr. Sasaki lost all sense of profession and stopped working as a skillful surgeon and a sympathetic man; he became an automaton, mechanically wiping, daubing, winding, wiping, daubing, winding.

SOME OF the wounded in Hiroshima were unable to enjoy the questionable luxury of hospitalization. In what had been the personnel office of the East Asia Tin Works, Miss Sasaki lay doubled over, unconscious, under the tremendous pile of books and plaster and wood and corrugated iron. She was wholly unconscious (she later estimated) for about three hours. Her first sensation was of dreadful pain in her left leg. It was so black under the books and debris that the borderline between awareness and unconsciousness was fine; she apparently crossed it several times, for the pain seemed to come and go. At the moments when it was sharpest, she felt that her leg had been cut off somewhere below

the knee. Later, she heard someone walking on top of the wreckage above her, and anguished voices spoke up, evidently from within the mess around her: "Please help! Get us out!"

FATHER KLEINSORGE stemmed Father Schiffer's spurting cut as well as he could with some bandage that Dr. Fujii had given the priests a few days before. When he finished, he ran into the mission house again and found the jacket of his military uniform and an old pair of gray trousers. He put them on and went outside. A woman from next door ran up to him and shouted that her husband was buried under her house and the house was on fire; Father Kleinsorge must come and save him.

Father Kleinsorge, already growing apathetic and dazed in the presence of the cumulative distress, said, "We haven't much time." Houses all around were burning, and the wind was now blowing hard. "Do you know exactly which part of the house he is under?" he asked.

"Yes, yes," she said. "Come quickly."

They went around to the house, the remains of which blazed violently, but when they got there, it turned out that the woman had no idea where her husband was. Father Kleinsorge shouted several times, "Is anyone there?" There was no answer. Father Kleinsorge said to the woman, "We must get away or we will all die." He went back to the Catholic compound and told the Father Superior that the fire was coming closer on the wind, which had swung around and was now from the north; it was time for everybody to go.

Just then, the kindergarten teacher pointed out to the priests Mr. Fukai, the secretary of the diocese, who was standing in his window on the second floor of the mission house, facing in the direction of the explosion, weeping. Father Cieslik, because he thought the stairs unusable, ran around to the back of the mission house to look for a ladder. There he heard people crying for help under a nearby fallen roof. He called to passers-by running away in the street to help him lift it, but nobody paid any attention, and he had to leave the buried ones to die. Father Kleinsorge ran inside the mission house and scrambled up the stairs, which were awry and piled with plaster and lathing, and called to Mr. Fukai from the doorway of his room.

Mr. Fukai, a very short man of about fifty, turned around slowly, with a queer look, and said, "Leave me here."

Father Kleinsorge went into the room and took Mr. Fukai by the collar of his coat and said, "Come with me or you'll die."

Mr. Fukai said, "Leave me here to die."

Father Kleinsorge began to shove and haul Mr. Fukai out of the room. Then the theological student came up and grabbed Mr. Fukai's feet, and Father Kleinsorge took his shoulders, and together they carried him downstairs and outdoors. "I can't walk!" Mr. Fukai cried. "Leave me here!" Father Kleinsorge got his paper suitcase with the money in it and took Mr. Fukai up pickaback, and the party started for the East Parade Ground, their district's "safe area." As they went out of the gate, Mr. Fukai, quite childlike now, beat on Father Kleinsorge's shoulders and said, "I won't leave. I won't leave." Irrelevantly, Father Kleinsorge turned to Father LaSalle and said, "We have lost all our possessions but not our sense of humor."

The street was cluttered with parts of houses that had slid into it, and with fallen telephone poles and wires. From every second or third house came the voices of people buried and abandoned, who invariably screamed, with formal politeness, *"Tasukete kure!* Help, if you please!" The priests recognized several ruins from which these cries came as the homes of friends, but because of the fire it was too late to help. All the way, Mr. Fukai whimpered, "Let me stay." The party turned right when they came to a block of fallen houses that was one flame. At Sakai Bridge, which would take them across to the East Parade Ground, they saw that the whole community on the opposite side of the river was a sheet of fire; they dared not cross and decided to take refuge in Asano Park, off to their left. Father Kleinsorge, who had been weakened for a couple of days by his bad case of diarrhea, began to stagger under his protesting burden, and as he tried to climb up over the wreckage of several houses that blocked their way to the park, he stumbled, dropped Mr. Fukai, and plunged down, head over heels, to the edge of the river. When he picked himself up, he saw Mr. Fukai running away. Father Kleinsorge shouted to a dozen soldiers, who were standing by the bridge, to stop him. As Father Kleinsorge started back to get Mr. Fukai, Father LaSalle called out, "Hurry! Don't waste time!" So Father Kleinsorge just requested the soldiers to take care of Mr. Fukai. They said they would, but the little, broken man got away from them, and the last the priests could see of him, he was running back toward the fire.

Mr. Tanimoto, fearful for his family and church, at first ran toward them by the shortest route, along Koi Highway. He was the only person making his way into the city; he met hundreds and hundreds who were fleeing, and every one of them seemed to be hurt in some way. The eyebrows of some were burned off and skin hung from their faces and hands. Others, because of pain, held their arms up as if carrying something in both hands. Some were vomiting as they walked. Many were naked or in shreds of clothing. On some undressed bodies, the burns had made patterns—of undershirt straps and suspenders and, on the skin of some women (since white repelled the heat from the bomb and dark clothes absorbed it and conducted it to the skin), the shapes of flowers they had had on their kimonos. Many, although injured themselves, supported relatives who were worse off. Almost all had their heads bowed, looked straight ahead, were silent, and showed no expression whatever.

After crossing Koi Bridge and Kannon Bridge, having run the whole way, Mr. Tanimoto saw, as he approached the center, that all the houses had been crushed and many were afire. Here the trees were bare and their trunks were charred. He tried at several points to penetrate the ruins, but the flames always stopped him. Under many houses, people screamed for help, but no one helped; in general, survivors that day assisted only their relatives or immediate neighbors, for they could not comprehend or tolerate a wider circle of misery. The wounded limped past the screams, and Mr. Tanimoto ran past them. As a Christian he was filled with compassion for those who were trapped, and as a Japanese he was overwhelmed by the shame of being unhurt, and he prayed as he ran, "God help them and take them out of the fire."

He thought he would skirt the fire, to the left. He ran back to Kannon Bridge and followed for a distance one of the rivers. He tried several cross streets, but all were blocked, so he turned far left and ran out to Yokogawa, a station on a railroad line that detoured the city in a wide semicircle, and he followed the rails until he came to a burning train. So impressed was he by this time by the extent of the damage that he ran north two miles to Gion, a suburb in the foothills. All the way, he overtook dreadfully burned and lacerated people, and in his guilt he turned to right and left as he hurried and said to some of them, "Excuse me for having no burden like yours." Near Gion, he began to meet country people going toward the city to help, and when they saw him, several exclaimed, "Look! There is one who is not wounded." At Gion, he bore toward the right bank of the main river, the Ota, and ran down it until he reached fire again. There was no fire on the other side of the river, so he threw off his shirt and shoes and plunged into it. In midstream, where the current was fairly strong, exhaustion and fear finally caught up with him—he had run nearly seven miles—and he became

limp and drifted in the water. He prayed, "Please, God, help me to cross. It would be nonsense for me to be drowned when I am the only uninjured one." He managed a few more strokes and fetched up on a spit downstream.

Mr. Tanimoto climbed up the bank and ran along it until, near a large Shinto shrine, he came to more fire, and as he turned left to get around it, he met, by incredible luck, his wife. She was carrying their infant son. Mr. Tanimoto was now so emotionally worn out that nothing could surprise him. He did not embrace his wife; he simply said, "Oh, you are safe." She told him that she had got home from her night in Ushida just in time for the explosion; she had been buried under the parsonage with the baby in her arms. She told how the wreckage had pressed down on her, how the baby had cried. She saw a chink of light, and by reaching up with a hand, she worked the hole bigger, bit by bit. After about half an hour, she heard the crackling noise of wood burning. At last the opening was big enough for her to push the baby out, and afterward she crawled out herself. She said she was now going to Ushida again. Mr. Tanimoto said he wanted to see his church and take care of the people of his Neighborhood Association. They parted as casually—as bewildered—as they had met.

Mr. Tanimoto's way around the fire took him across the East Parade Ground, which, being an evacuation area, was now the scene of a gruesome review: rank on rank of the burned and bleeding. Those who were burned moaned, *"Mizu, mizu!* Water, water!"* Mr. Tanimoto found a basin in a nearby street and located a water tap that still worked in the crushed shell of a house, and he began carrying water to the suffering strangers. When he had given drink to about thirty of them, he realized he was taking too much time. "Excuse me," he said loudly to those nearby who were reaching out their hands to him and crying their thirst. "I have many people to take care of." Then he ran away. He went to the river again, the basin in his hand, and jumped down onto a sandspit. There he saw hundreds of people so badly wounded that they could not get up to go farther from the burning city. When they saw a man erect and unhurt, the chant began again: *"Mizu, mizu, mizu."* Mr. Tanimoto could not resist them; he carried them water from the river—a mistake, since it was tidal and brackish. Two or three small boats were ferrying hurt people across the river from Asano Park, and when one touched the spit, Mr. Tanimoto again made his loud, apologetic speech and jumped into the boat. It took him across to the park. There, in the underbrush, he found some of his charges of the Neighborhood Association, who had come there by his previous instructions, and saw many acquaintances, among them Father Kleinsorge and the other Catholics. But he missed Fukai, who had been a close friend. "Where is Fukai-*san?*" he asked.

"He didn't want to come with us," Father Kleinsorge said. "He ran back."

WHEN MISS SASAKI heard the voices of the people caught along with her in the dilapidation at the tin factory, she began speaking to them. Her nearest neighbor, she discovered, was a high-school girl who had been drafted for factory work, and who said her back was broken. Miss Sasaki replied, "I am lying here and I can't move. My left leg is cut off."

Some time later, she again heard somebody walk overhead and then move off to one side, and whoever it was began burrowing. The digger released several people, and when he had uncovered the high-school girl, she found that her back was not broken, after all, and she crawled out. Miss Sasaki spoke to the rescuer, and he worked toward her. He pulled away a great number of books, until he had made a tunnel to her. She could see his perspiring face as he said, "Come out, Miss." She tried. "I can't move," she said. The man excavated some more and told her to try with all her strength to get out. But books

were heavy on her hips, and the man finally saw that a bookcase was leaning on the books and that a heavy beam pressed down on the bookcase. "Wait," he said. "I'll get a crowbar."

The man was gone a long time, and when he came back, he was ill-tempered, as if her plight were all her fault. "We have no men to help you!" he shouted in through the tunnel. "You'll have to get out by yourself."

"That's impossible," she said. "My left leg . . ." The man went away.

Much later, several men came and dragged Miss Sasaki out. Her left leg was not severed, but it was badly broken and cut and it hung askew below the knee. They took her out into a courtyard. It was raining. She sat on the ground in the rain. When the downpour increased, someone directed all the wounded people to take cover in the factory's air-raid shelters. "Come along," a torn-up woman said to her. "You can hop." But Miss Sasaki could not move, and she just waited in the rain. Then a man propped up a large sheet of corrugated iron as a kind of lean-to, and took her in his arms and carried her to it. She was grateful until he brought two horribly wounded people—a woman with a whole breast sheared off and a man whose face was all raw from a burn—to share the simple shed with her. No one came back. The rain cleared and the cloudy afternoon was hot; before nightfall the three grotesques under the slanting piece of twisted iron began to smell quite bad.

THE FORMER HEAD of the Nobori-cho Neighborhood Association to which the Catholic priests belonged was an energetic man named Yoshida. He had boasted, when he was in charge of the district air-raid defenses, that fire might eat away all of Hiroshima but it would never come to Nobori-cho. The bomb blew down his house, and a joist pinned him by the legs, in full view of the Jesuit mission house across the way and of the people hurrying along the street. In their confusion as they hurried past, Mrs. Nakamura, with her children, and Father Kleinsorge, with Mr. Fukai on his back, hardly saw him; he was just part of the general blur of misery through which they moved. His cries for help brought no response from them; there were so many people shouting for help that they could not hear him separately. They and all the others went along. Nobori-cho became absolutely deserted, and the fire swept through it. Mr. Yoshida saw the wooden mission house—the only erect building in the area—go up in a lick of flame, and the heat was terrific on his face. Then flames came along his side of the street and entered his house. In a paroxysm of terrified strength, he freed himself and ran down the alleys of Nobori-cho, hemmed in by the fire he had said would never come. He began at once to behave like an old man; two months later his hair was white.

As Dr. Fujii stood in the river up to his neck to avoid the heat of the fire, the wind blew stronger and stronger, and soon, even though the expanse of water was small, the waves grew so high that the people under the bridge could no longer keep their footing. Dr. Fujii went close to the shore, crouched down, and embraced a large stone with his usable arm. Later it became possible to wade along the very edge of the river, and Dr. Fujii and his two surviving nurses moved about two hundred yards upstream, to a sandspit near Asano Park. Many wounded were lying on the sand. Dr. Machii was there with his family; his daughter, who had been outdoors when the bomb burst, was badly burned on her hands and legs but fortunately not on her face. Although Dr. Fujii's shoulder was by now terribly painful, he examined the girl's burns curiously. Then he lay down. In spite of the misery all around, he was ashamed of his appearance, and he remarked to Dr. Machii that he looked like a beggar, dressed as he was in nothing but torn and bloody

underwear. Later in the afternoon, when the fire began to subside, he decided to go to his parental house, in the suburb of Nagatsuka. He asked Dr. Machii to join him, but the Doctor answered that he and his family were going to spend the night on the spit, because of his daughter's injuries. Dr. Fujii, together with his nurses, walked first to Ushida, where, in the partially damaged house of some relatives, he found first-aid materials he had stored there. The two nurses bandaged him and he them. They went on. Now not many people walked in the streets, but a great number sat and lay on the pavement, vomited, waited for death, and died. The number of corpses on the way to Nagatsuka was more and more puzzling. The Doctor wondered: Could a Molotov flower basket have done all this?

Dr. Fujii reached his family's house in the evening. It was five miles from the center of town, but its roof had fallen in and the windows were all broken.

ALL DAY, people poured into Asano Park. This private estate was far enough away from the explosion so that its bamboos, pines, laurel, and maples were still alive, and the green place invited refugees—partly because they believed that if the Americans came back, they would bomb only buildings; partly because the foliage seemed a center of coolness and life, and the estate's exquisitely precise rock gardens, with their quiet pools and arching bridges, were very Japanese, normal, secure; and also partly (according to some who were there) because of an irresistible, atavistic urge to hide under leaves. Mrs. Nakamura and her children were among the first to arrive, and they settled in the bamboo grove near the river. They all felt terribly thirsty, and they drank from the river. At once they were nauseated and began vomiting, and they retched the whole day. Others were also nauseated; they all thought (probably because of the strong odor of ionization, an "electric smell" given off by the bomb's fission) that they were sick from a gas the Americans had dropped. When Father Kleinsorge and the other priests came into the park, nodding to their friends as they passed, the Nakamuras were all sick and prostrate. A woman named Iwasaki, who lived in the neighborhood of the mission and who was sitting near the Nakamuras, got up and asked the priests if she should stay where she was or go with them. Father Kleinsorge said, "I hardly know where the safest place is." She stayed there, and later in the day, though she had no visible wounds or burns, she died. The priests went farther along the river and settled down in some underbrush. Father LaSalle lay down and went right to sleep. The theological student, who was wearing slippers, had carried with him a bundle of clothes, in which he had packed two pairs of leather shoes. When he sat down with the others, he found that the bundle had broken open and a couple of shoes had fallen out and now he had only two lefts. He retraced his steps and found one right. When he rejoined the priests, he said, "It's funny, but things don't matter any more. Yesterday, my shoes were my most important possessions. Today, I don't care. One pair is enough."

Father Cieslik said, "I know. I started to bring my books along, and then I thought, 'This is no time for books.'"

When Mr. Tanimoto, with his basin still in his hand, reached the park, it was very crowded, and to distinguish the living from the dead was not easy, for most of the people lay still, with their eyes open. To Father Kleinsorge, an Occidental, the silence in the grove by the river, where hundreds of gruesomely wounded suffered together, was one of the most dreadful and awesome phenomena of his whole experience. The hurt ones were quiet; no one wept, much less screamed in pain; no one complained; none of the many who died did so noisily; not even the children cried; very few people even spoke. And when Father Kleinsorge gave water to some whose faces had been almost blotted out by flash burns, they took their share and then raised themselves a little and bowed to him, in thanks.

Mr. Tanimoto greeted the priests and then looked around for other friends. He saw Mrs. Matsumoto, wife of the director of the Methodist School, and asked her if she was thirsty. She was, so he went to one of the pools in the Asanos' rock gardens and got water for her in his basin. Then he decided to try to get back to his church. He went into Nobori-cho by the way the priests had taken as they escaped, but he did not get far; the fire along the streets was so fierce that he had to turn back. He walked to the riverbank and began to look for a boat in which he might carry some of the most severely injured across the river from Asano Park and away from the spreading fire. Soon he found a good-sized pleasure punt drawn up on the bank, but in and around it was an awful tableau—five dead men, nearly naked, badly burned, who must have expired more or less all at once, for they were in attitudes which suggested that they had been working together to push the boat down into the river. Mr. Tanimoto lifted them away from the boat, and as he did so, he experienced such horror at disturbing the dead—preventing them, he momentarily felt, from launching their craft and going on their ghostly way—that he said out loud, "Please forgive me for taking this boat. I must use it for others, who are alive." The punt was heavy, but he managed to slide it into the water. There were no oars, and all he could find for propulsion was a thick bamboo pole. He worked the boat upstream to the most crowded part of the park and began to ferry the wounded. He could pack ten or twelve into the boat for each crossing, but as the river was too deep in the center to pole his way across, he had to paddle with the bamboo, and consequently each trip took a very long time. He worked several hours that way.

Early in the afternoon, the fire swept into the woods of Asano Park. The first

Mr. Tanimoto knew of it was when, returning in his boat, he saw that a great number of people had moved toward the riverside. On touching the bank, he went up to investigate, and when he saw the fire, he shouted, "All the young men who are not badly hurt come with me!" Father Kleinsorge moved Father Schiffer and Father LaSalle close to the edge of the river and asked people there to get them across if the fire came too near, and then joined Tanimoto's volunteers. Mr. Tanimoto sent some to look for buckets and basins and told others to beat the burning underbrush with their clothes; when utensils were at hand, he formed a bucket chain from one of the pools in the rock gardens. The team fought the fire for more than two hours, and gradually defeated the flames. As Mr. Tanimoto's men worked, the frightened people in the park pressed closer and closer to the river, and finally the mob began to force some of the unfortunates who were on the very bank into the water. Among those driven into the river and drowned were Mrs. Matsumoto, of the Methodist School, and her daughter.

When Father Kleinsorge got back after fighting the fire, he found Father Schiffer still bleeding and terribly pale. Some Japanese stood around and stared at him, and Father Schiffer whispered, with a weak smile, "It is as if I were already dead." "Not yet," Father Kleinsorge said. He had brought Dr. Fujii's first-aid kit with him, and he had noticed Dr. Kanda in the crowd, so he sought him out and asked him if he would dress Father Schiffer's bad cuts. Dr. Kanda had seen his wife and daughter dead in the ruins of his hospital; he sat now with his head in his hands. "I can't do anything," he said. Father Kleinsorge bound more bandage around Father Schiffer's head, moved him to a steep place, and settled him so that his head was high, and soon the bleeding diminished.

The roar of approaching planes was heard about this time. Someone in the crowd near the Nakamura family shouted, "It's some Grummans coming to strafe us!" A baker named Nakashima stood up and commanded, "Everyone who is wearing anything white, take it off." Mrs. Nakamura took the blouses off her children, and opened her umbrella and made them get under it. A great number of people, even badly burned ones, crawled into bushes and stayed there until the hum, evidently of a reconnaissance or weather run, died away.

It began to rain. Mrs. Nakamura kept her children under the umbrella. The drops grew abnormally large, and someone shouted, "The Americans are dropping gasoline. They're going to set fire to us!" (This alarm stemmed from one of the theories being passed through the park as to why so much of Hiroshima had burned: it was that a single plane had sprayed gasoline on the city and then somehow set fire to it in one flashing moment.) But the drops were palpably water, and as they fell, the wind grew stronger and stronger, and suddenly —probably because of the tremendous convection set up by the blazing city—a whirlwind ripped through the park. Huge trees crashed down; small ones were uprooted and flew into the air. Higher, a wild array of flat things revolved in the twisting funnel—pieces of iron roofing, papers, doors, strips of matting. Father Kleinsorge put a piece of cloth over Father Schiffer's eyes, so that the feeble man would not think he was going crazy. The gale blew Mrs. Murata, the mission housekeeper, who was sitting close by the river, down the embankment at a shallow, rocky place, and she came out with her bare feet bloody. The vortex moved out onto the river, where it sucked up a water-spout and eventually spent itself.

After the storm, Mr. Tanimoto began ferrying people again, and Father Kleinsorge asked the theological student to go across and make his way out to the Jesuit Novitiate at Nagatsuka, about three miles from the center of town, and to request the priests there to come with help for Fathers Schiffer and LaSalle. The student got into Mr. Tanimoto's boat and went off with him. Father Kleinsorge asked Mrs. Nakamura if she would like to go out to Nagatsuka with the priests when they came. She said she had some luggage and her children were sick—they were still vomiting from time to time, and so, for that matter, was she—and therefore she feared she could not. He said he thought the fathers from the Novitiate could come back the next day with a pushcart to get her.

Late in the afternoon, when he went ashore for a while, Mr. Tanimoto, upon whose energy and initiative many had come to depend, heard people begging for food. He consulted Father Kleinsorge, and they decided to go back into town to get some rice from Mr. Tanimoto's Neighborhood Association shelter and from the mission shelter. Father Cieslik and two or three others went with them. At first, when they got among the rows of prostrate houses, they did not know where they were; the change was too sudden, from a busy city of two hundred and forty-five thousand that morning to a mere pattern of residue in the afternoon. The asphalt of the streets was still so soft and hot from the fires that walking was uncomfortable. They encountered only one person, a woman, who said to them as they passed, "My husband is in those ashes." At the mission, where Mr. Tanimoto left the party, Father Kleinsorge was dismayed to see the building razed. In the garden, on the way to the shelter, he noticed a pumpkin roasted on the vine. He and Father Cieslik tasted it and it was good. They were surprised at their hunger, and they ate quite a bit. They got out several bags of rice and gathered up several other cooked pumpkins and dug up some potatoes that were nicely baked under the ground, and started back. Mr. Tanimoto rejoined them on the way. One of the people with him had some cooking utensils. In the park, Mr. Tanimoto organized the lightly wounded women of his neighborhood to cook. Father Kleinsorge offered the Nakamura family some

pumpkin, and they tried it, but they could not keep it on their stomachs. Altogether, the rice was enough to feed nearly a hundred people.

Just before dark, Mr. Tanimoto came across a twenty-year-old girl, Mrs. Kamai, the Tanimoto's next-door neighbor. She was crouching on the ground with the body of her infant daughter in her arms. The baby had evidently been dead all day. Mrs. Kamai jumped up when she saw Mr. Tanimoto and said, "Would you please try to locate my husband?"

Mr. Tanimoto knew that her husband had been inducted into the Army just the day before; he and Mrs. Tanimoto had entertained Mrs. Kamai in the afternoon, to make her forget. Kamai had reported to the Chugoku Regional Army Headquarters—near the ancient castle in the middle of town—where some four thousand troops were stationed. Judging by the many maimed soldiers Mr. Tanimoto had seen during the day, he surmised that the barracks had been badly damaged by whatever it was that had hit Hiroshima. He knew he hadn't a chance of finding Mrs. Kamai's husband, even if he searched, but he wanted to humor her. "I'll try," he said.

"You've got to find him," she said. "He loved our baby so much. I want him to see her once more."

III

DETAILS ARE BEING INVESTIGATED

EARLY IN THE evening of the day the bomb exploded, a Japanese naval launch moved slowly up and down the seven rivers of Hiroshima. It stopped here and there to make an announcement—alongside the crowded sandspits, on which hundreds of wounded lay; at the bridges, on which others were crowded; and eventually, as twilight fell, opposite Asano Park. A young officer stood up in the launch and shouted through a megaphone, "Be patient! A naval hospital ship is coming to take care of you!" The sight of the shipshape launch against the background of the havoc across the river; the unruffled young man in his neat uniform; above all, the promise of medical help—the first word of possible succor anyone had heard in nearly twelve awful hours—cheered the people in the park tremendously. Mrs. Nakamura settled her family for the night with the assurance that a doctor would come and stop their retching. Mr. Tanimoto resumed ferrying the wounded across the river. Father Kleinsorge lay down and said the Lord's Prayer and a Hail Mary to himself, and fell right asleep; but no sooner had he dropped off than Mrs. Murata, the conscientious mission housekeeper, shook him and said, "Father Kleinsorge! Did you remember to repeat your evening prayers?" He answered rather grumpily, "Of course," and he tried to go back to sleep but could not. This, apparently, was just what Mrs. Murata wanted. She began to chat with the exhausted priest. One of the questions she raised was when he thought the priests from the Novitiate, for whom he had sent a messenger in mid-afternoon, would arrive to evacuate Father Superior LaSalle and Father Schiffer.

THE MESSENGER Father Kleinsorge had sent—the theological student who had been living at the mission house—had arrived at the Novitiate, in the hills about three miles out, at half past four. The sixteen priests there had been doing rescue work in the outskirts; they had worried about their colleagues in the city but had not known how or where to look for them. Now they hastily made two litters out of poles and boards, and the student led half a dozen of them back into the devastated area. They worked their way along the Ota above the city; twice the heat of the fire forced them into the river. At Misasa Bridge, they encountered a long line of soldiers making a bizarre forced march away from the Chugoku Regional Army Headquarters in the center of the town. All were grotesquely burned, and they

supported themselves with staves or leaned on one another. Sick, burned horses, hanging their heads, stood on the bridge. When the rescue party reached the park, it was after dark, and progress was made extremely difficult by the tangle of fallen trees of all sizes that had been knocked down by the whirlwind that afternoon. At last—not long after Mrs. Murata asked her question—they reached their friends, and gave them wine and strong tea.

The priests discussed how to get Father Schiffer and Father LaSalle out to the Novitiate. They were afraid that blundering through the park with them would jar them too much on the wooden litters, and that the wounded men would lose too much blood. Father Kleinsorge thought of Mr. Tanimoto and his boat, and called out to him on the river. When Mr. Tanimoto reached the bank, he said he would be glad to take the injured priests and their bearers upstream to where they could find a clear roadway. The rescuers put Father Schiffer onto one of the stretchers and lowered it into the boat, and two of them went aboard with it. Mr. Tanimoto, who still had no oars, poled the punt upstream.

About half an hour later, Mr. Tanimoto came back and excitedly asked the remaining priests to help him rescue two children he had seen standing up to their shoulders in the river. A group went out and picked them up—two young girls who had lost their family and were both badly burned. The priests stretched them on the ground next to Father Kleinsorge and then embarked Father LaSalle. Father Cieslik thought he could make it out to the Novitiate on foot, so he went aboard with the others. Father Kleinsorge was too feeble; he decided to wait in the park until the next day. He asked the men to come back with a handcart, so that they could take Mrs. Nakamura and her sick children to the Novitiate.

Mr. Tanimoto shoved off again. As the boatload of priests moved slowly upstream, they heard weak cries for help. A woman's voice stood out especially: "There are peo-

ple here about to be drowned! Help us!
The water is rising!" The sounds came
from one of the sandspits, and those in
the punt could see, in the reflected light
of the still-burning fires, a number of
wounded people lying at the edge of the
river, already partly covered by the flooding tide. Mr. Tanimoto wanted to help
them, but the priests were afraid that
Father Schiffer would die if they didn't
hurry, and they urged their ferryman
along. He dropped them where he had put
Father Schiffer down and then started back
alone toward the sandspit.

THE NIGHT WAS hot, and it seemed even
hotter because of the fires against the sky,
but the younger of the two girls Mr. Tanimoto and the priests had rescued complained to Father Kleinsorge that she was
cold. He covered her with his jacket. She
and her older sister had been in the salt
water of the river for a couple of hours
before being rescued. The younger one
had huge, raw flash burns on her body;
the salt water must have been excruciatingly painful to her. She began to shiver
heavily, and again said it was cold. Father
Kleinsorge borrowed a blanket from someone nearby and wrapped her up, but she
shook more and more, and said again, "I
am so cold," and then she suddenly stopped
shivering and was dead.

MR. TANIMOTO found about twenty men
and women on the sandspit. He drove the
boat onto the bank and urged them to get
aboard. They did not move and he realized
that they were too weak to lift themselves.
He reached down and took a woman by the
hands, but her skin slipped off in huge,
glove-like pieces. He was so sickened by
this that he had to sit down for a moment. Then he got out into the water and,
though a small man, lifted several of the
men and women, who were naked, into his
boat. Their backs and breasts were clammy, and he remembered uneasily what the
great burns he had seen during the day
had been like: yellow at first, then red

and swollen, with the skin sloughed off,
and finally, in the evening, suppurated
and smelly. With the tide risen, his bamboo
pole was now too short and he had to paddle most of the way across with it. On the
other side, at a higher spit, he lifted the
slimy living bodies out and carried them
up the slope away from the tide. He had
to keep consciously repeating to himself.
"These are human beings." It took him
three trips to get them all across the
river. When he had finished, he decided
he had to have a rest, and he went back
to the park.

As Mr. Tanimoto stepped up the dark
bank, he tripped over someone, and someone else said angrily, "Look out! That's
my hand." Mr. Tanimoto, ashamed of
hurting wounded people, embarrassed at
being able to walk upright, suddenly
thought of the naval hospital ship, which
had not come (it never did), and he had
for a moment a feeling of blind, murderous
rage at the crew of the ship, and then at
all doctors. Why didn't they come to help
these people?

DR. FUJII lay in dreadful pain throughout
the night on the floor of his family's roof-
less house on the edge of the city. By the
light of a lantern, he had examined himself and found: left clavicle fractured;
multiple abrasions and lacerations of face
and body, including deep cuts on the chin,
back, and legs; extensive contusions on
chest and trunk; a couple of ribs possibly
fractured. Had he not been so badly hurt,
he might have been at Asano Park, assisting the wounded.

BY NIGHTFALL, ten thousand victims of
the explosion had invaded the Red Cross
Hospital, and Dr. Sasaki, worn out, was
moving aimlessly and dully up and down
the stinking corridors with wads of bandage and bottles of mercurochrome, still
wearing the glasses he had taken from
the wounded nurse, binding up the worst
cuts as he came to them. Other doctors
were putting compresses of saline solution

on the worst burns. That was all they could do. After dark, they worked by the light of the city's fires and by candles the ten remaining nurses held for them. Dr. Sasaki had not looked outside the hospital all day; the scene inside was too terrible and so compelling that it had not occurred to him to ask any questions about what had happened beyond the windows and doors. Ceilings and partitions had fallen; plaster, dust, blood, and vomit were everywhere. Patients were dying by the hundreds, but there was nobody to carry away the corpses. Some of the hospital staff distributed biscuits and rice balls, but the charnel-house smell was so strong that few were hungry. By three o'clock the next morning, after nineteen straight hours of his gruesome work, Dr. Sasaki was incapable of dressing another wound. He and some other survivors of the hospital staff got straw mats and went outdoors—thousands of patients and hundreds of dead were in the yard and on the driveway—and hurried around behind the hospital and lay down in hiding, to snatch some sleep. But within an hour wounded people had found them; a complaining circle formed around them: "Doctors! Help us! How can you sleep?" Dr. Sasaki got up again and went back to work. Early in the day, he thought for the first time of his mother, at their country home in Mukaihara, thirty miles from town. He usually went home every night. He was afraid she would think he was dead.

NEAR THE spot upriver to which Mr. Tanimoto had transported the priests, there sat a large case of rice cakes which a rescue party had evidently brought for the wounded lying thereabouts but hadn't distributed. Before evacuating the wounded priests, the others passed the cakes around and helped themselves. A few minutes later, a band of soldiers came up, and an officer, hearing the priests speaking a foreign language, drew his sword and hysterically asked who they were. One of the priests calmed him down and explained

that they were Germans—allies. The officer apologized and said that there were reports going around that American parachutists had landed.

The priests decided that they should take Father Schiffer first. As they prepared to leave, Father Superior LaSalle said he felt awfully cold. One of the Jesuits gave up his coat, another his shirt; they were glad to wear less in the muggy night. The stretcher bearers started out. The theological student led the way and tried to warn the others of obstacles, but one of the priests got a foot tangled in some telephone wire and tripped and dropped his corner of the litter. Father Schiffer rolled off, lost consciousness, came to, and then vomited. The bearers picked him up and went on with him to the edge of the city, where they had arranged to meet a relay of other priests, left him with them, and turned back and got the Father Superior.

The wooden litter must have been terribly painful for Father LaSalle, in whose back scores of tiny particles of window glass were embedded. Near the edge of town, the group had to walk around an automobile burned and squatting on the narrow road, and the bearers on one side, unable to see their way in the darkness, fell into a deep ditch. Father LaSalle was thrown onto the ground and the litter broke in two. One priest went ahead to get a handcart from the Novitiate, but he soon found one beside an empty house and wheeled it back. The priests lifted Father LaSalle into the cart and pushed him over the bumpy road the rest of the way. The rector of the Novitiate, who had been a doctor before he entered the religious order, cleaned the wounds of the two priests and put them to bed between clean sheets, and they thanked God for the care they had received.

THOUSANDS of people had nobody to help them. Miss Sasaki was one of them. Abandoned and helpless, under the crude lean-to in the courtyard of the tin factory, beside the woman who had lost a breast and the man whose burned face was scarcely a face any more, she suffered awfully that night from the pain in her broken leg. She did not sleep at all; neither did she converse with her sleepless companions.

IN THE PARK, Mrs. Murata kept Father Kleinsorge awake all night by talking to him. None of the Nakamura family were able to sleep, either; the children, in spite of being very sick, were interested in everything that happened. They were delighted when one of the city's gas-storage tanks went up in a tremendous burst of flame. Toshio, the boy, shouted to the others to look at the reflection in the river. Mr. Tanimoto, after his long run and his many hours of rescue work, dozed uneasily. When he awoke, in the first light of dawn, he looked across the river and saw that he had not carried the festered, limp bodies high enough on the sandspit the night before. The tide had risen above where he had put them; they had not had the strength to move; they must have drowned. He saw a number of bodies floating in the river.

EARLY THAT day, August 7th, the Japanese radio broadcast for the first time a succinct announcement that very few, if any, of the people most concerned with its content, the survivors in Hiroshima, happened to hear: "Hiroshima suffered considerable damage as the result of an attack by a few B-29s. It is believed that a new type of bomb was used. The details are being investigated." Nor is it probable that any of the survivors happened to be tuned in on a short-wave rebroadcast of an extraordinary announcement by the President of the United States, which identified the new bomb as atomic: "That bomb had more power than twenty thousand tons of TNT. It had more than two thousand times the blast power of the British Grand Slam, which is the largest bomb ever yet used in the history of warfare." Those victims who were able to worry at all about what

had happened thought of it and discussed it in more primitive, childish terms—gasoline sprinkled from an airplane, maybe, or some combustible gas, or a big cluster of incendiaries, or the work of parachutists; but, even if they had known the truth, most of them were too busy or too weary or too badly hurt to care that they were the objects of the first great experiment in the use of atomic power, which (as the voices on the short wave shouted) no country except the United States, with its industrial know-how, its willingness to throw two billion gold dollars into an important wartime gamble, could possibly have developed.

MR. TANIMOTO was still angry at doctors. He decided that he would personally bring one to Asano Park—by the scruff of the neck, if necessary. He crossed the river, went past the Shinto shrine where he had met his wife for a brief moment the day before, and walked to the East Parade Ground. Since this had long before been designated as an evacuation area, he thought he would find an aid station there. He did find one, operated by an Army medical unit, but he also saw that its doctors were hopelessly overburdened, with thousands of patients sprawled among corpses across the field in front of it. Nevertheless, he went up to one of the Army doctors and said, as reproachfully as he could, "Why have you not come to Asano Park? You are badly needed there."

Without even looking up from his work, the doctor said in a tired voice, "This is my station."

"But there are many dying on the riverbank over there."

"The first duty," the doctor said, "is to take care of the slightly wounded."

"Why—when there are many who are heavily wounded on the riverbank?"

The doctor moved to another patient. "In an emergency like this," he said, as if he were reciting from a manual, "the first task is to help as many as possible— to save as many lives as possible. There is no hope for the heavily wounded. They will die. We can't bother with them."

"That may be right from a medical standpoint—" Mr. Tanimoto began, but then he looked out across the field, where the many dead lay close and intimate with those who were still living, and he turned away without finishing his sentence, angry now with himself. He didn't know what to do; he had promised some of the dying people in the park that he would bring them medical aid. They might die feeling cheated. He saw a ration stand at one side of the field, and he went to it and begged some rice cakes and biscuits, and he took them back, in lieu of doctors, to the people in the park.

THE MORNING, again, was hot. Father Kleinsorge went to fetch water for the wounded in a bottle and a teapot he had borrowed. He had heard that it was possible to get fresh tap water outside Asano Park. Going through the rock gardens, he had to climb over and crawl under the trunks of fallen pine trees; he found he was weak. There were many dead in the gardens. At a beautiful moon bridge, he passed a naked, living woman who seemed to have been burned from head to toe and was red all over. Near the entrance to the park, an Army doctor was working, but the only medicine he had was iodine, which he painted over cuts, bruises, slimy burns, everything—and by now everything that he painted had pus on it. Outside the gate of the park, Father Kleinsorge found a faucet that still worked—part of the plumbing of a vanished house—and he filled his vessels and returned. When he had given the wounded the water, he made a second trip. This time, the woman by the bridge was dead. On his way back with the water, he got lost on a detour around a fallen tree, and as he looked for his way through the woods, he heard a voice ask from the underbrush, "Have you anything to drink?" He saw a uniform. Thinking there was just one soldier, he approached with the water. When he had penetrated

the bushes, he saw there were about twenty men, and they were all in exactly the same nightmarish state: their faces were wholly burned, their eyesockets were hollow, the fluid from their melted eyes had run down their cheeks. (They must have had their faces upturned when the bomb went off; perhaps they were anti-aircraft personnel.) Their mouths were mere swollen, pus-covered wounds, which they could not bear to stretch enough to admit the spout of the teapot. So Father Kleinsorge got a large piece of grass and drew out the stem so as to make a straw, and gave them all water to drink that way. One of them said, "I can't see anything." Father Kleinsorge answered, as cheerfully as he could, "There's a doctor at the entrance to the park. He's busy now, but he'll come soon and fix your eyes, I hope."

Since that day, Father Kleinsorge has thought back to how queasy he had once been at the sight of pain, how someone else's cut finger used to make him turn faint. Yet there in the park he was so benumbed that immediately after leaving this horrible sight he stopped on a path by one of the pools and discussed with a lightly wounded man whether it would be safe to eat the fat, two-foot carp that floated dead on the surface of the water. They decided, after some consideration, that it would be unwise.

Father Kleinsorge filled the containers a third time and went back to the riverbank. There, amid the dead and dying, he saw a young woman with a needle and thread mending her kimono, which had been slightly torn. Father Kleinsorge joshed her. "My, but you're a dandy!" he said. She laughed.

He felt tired and lay down. He began to talk with two engaging children whose acquaintance he had made the afternoon before. He learned that their name was Kataoka; the girl was thirteen, the boy five. The girl had been just about to set out for a barbershop when the bomb fell. As the family started for Asano Park, their mother decided to turn back for some food and extra clothing; they became separated from her in the crowd of fleeing people, and they had not seen her since. Occasionally they stopped suddenly in their perfectly cheerful playing and began to cry for their mother.

It was difficult for all the children in the park to sustain the sense of tragedy. Toshio Nakamura got quite excited when he saw his friend Seichi Sato riding up the river in a boat with his family, and he ran to the bank and waved and shouted, "Sato! Sato!"

The boy turned his head and shouted, "Who's that?"

"Nakamura."

"Hello, Toshio!"

"Are you all safe?"

"Yes. What about you?"

"Yes, we're all right. My sisters are vomiting, but I'm fine."

Father Kleinsorge began to be thirsty in the dreadful heat, and he did not feel strong enough to go for water again. A little before noon, he saw a Japanese woman handing something out. Soon she came to him and said in a kindly voice, "These are tea leaves. Chew them, young man, and you won't feel thirsty." The woman's gentleness made Father Kleinsorge suddenly want to cry. For weeks, he had been feeling oppressed by the hatred of foreigners that the Japanese seemed increasingly to show, and he had been uneasy even with his Japanese friends. This stranger's gesture made him a little hysterical.

Around noon, the priests arrived from the Novitiate with the handcart. They had been to the site of the mission house in the city and had retrieved some suitcases that had been stored in the air-raid shelter and had also picked up the remains of melted holy vessels in the ashes of the chapel. They now packed Father Kleinsorge's papier-mâché suitcase and the things belonging to Mrs. Murata and the Nakamuras into the cart, put the two Nakamura girls aboard, and prepared to start out. Then one of the Jesuits who had a practical turn of mind remembered that they had been notified some time before that if they suffered property damage at the hands of the enemy, they could enter a claim for compensation with the prefectural police. The holy men discussed this matter there in the park, with the wounded as silent as the dead around them, and decided that Father Kleinsorge, as a former resident of the destroyed mission, was the one to enter the claim. So, as the others went off with the handcart, Father Kleinsorge said goodbye to the Kataoka children and trudged to a police station. Fresh, clean-uniformed policemen from another town were in charge, and a crowd of dirty and disarrayed citizens crowded around them, mostly asking after lost relatives. Father Kleinsorge filled out a claim form and started walking through the center of the town on his way to Nagatsuka. It was then that he first realized the extent of the damage; he passed block after block of ruins, and even after all he had seen in the park, his breath was taken away. By the time he reached the Novitiate, he was sick with exhaustion. The last thing he did as he fell into bed was request that someone go back for the motherless Kataoka children.

ALTOGETHER, Miss Sasaki was left two days and two nights under the piece of propped-up roofing with her crushed leg and her two unpleasant comrades. Her only diversion was when men came to the factory air-raid shelters, which she could see from under one corner of her shelter, and hauled corpses up out of them with ropes. Her leg became discolored, swollen, and putrid. All that time, she went without food and water. On the third day, August 8th, some friends who supposed she was dead came to look for her body and found her. They told her that her mother, father, and baby brother, who at the time of the explosion were in the Tamura Pediatric Hospital, where the baby was a patient, had all been given up as certainly dead, since the hospital was totally destroyed. Her friends then left her to think that piece of news over. Later, some men picked her up by the arms and legs and carried her quite a distance to a truck. For about an hour, the truck moved over a bumpy road, and Miss Sasaki, who had become convinced that she was dulled to pain, discovered that she was not. The men lifted her out at a relief station in the section of Inokuchi, where two Army doctors looked at her. The moment one of them touched her wound, she fainted. She came to in time to hear them discuss whether or not to cut off her leg; one said there was gas gangrene in the lips of the wound and predicted she would die unless they amputated, and the other said that was too bad, because they had no equipment with which to do the job. She fainted again. When she recovered consciousness, she was being carried somewhere on a stretcher. She was put aboard a launch, which went to the nearby island of Ninoshima, and she was taken to a military hospital there. Another doctor examined her and said that she did not have gas gangrene, though she did have a fairly ugly compound fracture. He said quite coldly that he was sorry, but this was a hospital for operative surgical cases only, and because she had no gangrene, she would have to return to Hiroshima that night. But then the doctor took her temperature, and what he saw on the thermometer made him decide to let her stay.

THAT DAY, August 8th, Father Cieslik went into the city to look for Mr. Fukai, the Japanese secretary of the diocese, who had ridden unwillingly out of the flaming city on Father Kleinsorge's back and then had run back crazily into it. Father Cieslik started hunting in the neighborhood of Sakai Bridge, where the Jesuits had last seen Mr. Fukai; he went to the East Parade Ground, the evacuation area to which the secretary might have gone, and

looked for him among the wounded and dead there; he went to the prefectural police and made inquiries. He could not find any trace of the man. Back at the Novitiate that evening, the theological student, who had been rooming with Mr. Fukai at the mission house, told the priests that the secretary had remarked to him, during an air-raid alarm one day not long before the bombing, "Japan is dying. If there is a real air raid here in Hiroshima, I want to die with our country." The priests concluded that Mr. Fukai had run back to immolate himself in the flames. They never saw him again.

AT THE Red Cross Hospital, Dr. Sasaki worked for three straight days with only one hour's sleep. On the second day, he began to sew up the worst cuts, and right through the following night and all the next day he stitched. Many of the wounds were festered. Fortunately, someone had found intact a supply of *narucopon*, a Japanese sedative, and he gave it to many who were in pain. Word went around among the staff that there must have been something peculiar about the great bomb, because on the second day the vice-chief of the hospital went down in the basement to the vault where the X-ray plates were stored and found the whole stock exposed as they lay. That day, a fresh doctor and ten nurses came in from the city of Yamaguchi with extra bandages and antiseptics, and the third day another physician and a dozen more nurses arrived from Matsue—yet there were still only eight doctors for ten thousand patients. In the afternoon of the third day, exhausted from his foul tailoring, Dr. Sasaki became obsessed with the idea that his mother thought he was dead. He got permission to go to Mukaihara. He walked out to the first suburbs, beyond which the electric train service was still functioning, and reached home late in the evening. His mother said she had known he was all right all along; a wounded nurse had stopped by to tell her. He went to bed and slept for seventeen hours.

BEFORE DAWN on August 8th, someone entered the room at the Novitiate where Father Kleinsorge was in bed, reached up to the hanging light bulb, and switched it on. The sudden flood of light, pouring in on Father Kleinsorge's half sleep, brought him leaping out of bed, braced for a new concussion. When he realized what had happened, he laughed confusedly and went back to bed. He stayed there all day.

On August 9th, Father Kleinsorge was still tired. The rector looked at his cuts and said they were not even worth dressing, and if Father Kleinsorge kept them clean, they would heal in three or four days. Father Kleinsorge felt uneasy; he could not yet comprehend what he had been through; as if he were guilty of something awful, he felt he had to go back to the scene of the violence he had experienced. He got up out of bed and walked into the city. He scratched for a while in the ruins of the mission house, but he found nothing. He went to the sites of a couple of schools and asked after people he knew. He looked for some of the city's Japanese Catholics, but he found only fallen houses. He walked back to the Novitiate, stupefied and without any new understanding.

AT TWO minutes after eleven o'clock on the morning of August 9th, the second atomic bomb was dropped, on Nagasaki. It was several days before the survivors of Hiroshima knew they had company, because the Japanese radio and newspapers were being extremely cautious on the subject of the strange weapon.

ON AUGUST 9TH, Mr. Tanimoto was still working in the park. He went to the suburb of Ushida, where his wife was staying with friends, and got a tent which he had stored there before the bombing. He now took it to the park and set it up as a shelter for some of the wounded who could not move or be moved. Whatever he did in the park, he felt he was being watched by the twenty-year-old girl, Mrs. Kamai, his former neighbor, whom he had seen on the day the bomb exploded, with her dead baby daughter in her arms. She kept the small corpse in her arms for four days, even though it began smelling bad on the second day. Once, Mr. Tanimoto sat with her for a while, and she told him that the bomb had buried her under their house with the baby strapped to her back, and that when she had dug herself free, she had discovered that the baby was choking, its mouth full of dirt. With her little finger, she had carefully cleaned out the infant's mouth, and for a time the child had breathed normally and seemed all right; then suddenly it had died. Mrs. Kamai also talked about what a fine man her husband was, and again urged Mr. Tanimoto to search for him. Since Mr. Tanimoto had been all through the city the first day and had seen terribly burned soldiers from Kamai's post, the Chugoku Regional Army Headquarters, everywhere, he knew it would be impossible to find Kamai, even if he were living, but of course he didn't tell her that. Every time she saw Mr. Tanimoto, she asked whether he had found her husband. Once, he tried to suggest that perhaps it was time to cremate the baby, but Mrs. Kamai only held it tighter. He began to keep away from her, but whenever he looked at her, she was staring at him and her eyes asked the same question. He tried to escape her glance by keeping his back turned to her as much as possible.

THE JESUITS took about fifty refugees into the exquisite chapel of the Novitiate. The rector gave them what medical care he could—mostly just the cleaning away of pus. Each of the Nakamuras was provided with a blanket and a mosquito net. Mrs. Nakamura and her younger daughter had no appetite and ate nothing; her son and other daughter ate, and lost, each meal they were offered. On August 10th, a friend, Mrs. Osaki, came to see them and told them that her son Hideo had been burned alive in the factory where he worked. This Hideo had been a kind of hero to Toshio, who had often gone to the plant to watch him run his machine. That night, Toshio woke up screaming. He had dreamed that he had seen Mrs. Osaki coming out of an opening in the ground with her family, and then he saw Hideo at his machine, a big one with a revolving belt, and he himself was standing beside Hideo, and for some reason this was terrifying.

On August 10th, Father Kleinsorge, having heard from someone that Dr. Fujii had been injured and that he had eventually gone to the summer house of a friend of his named Okuma, in the village of Fukawa, asked Father Cieslik if he would go and see how Dr. Fugii was. Father Cieslik went to Misasa station, outside Hiroshima, rode for twenty minutes on an electric train, and then walked for an hour and a half in a terribly hot sun to Mr. Okuma's house, which was beside the Ota River at the foot of a mountain. He found Dr. Fujii sitting in a chair in a kimono, applying compresses to his broken collarbone. The Doctor told Father Cieslik about having lost his glasses and said that his eyes bothered him. He showed the priest huge blue and green stripes where beams had bruised him. He offered the Jesuit first a cigarette and then whiskey, though it was only eleven in the morning. Father Cieslik thought it would please Dr. Fujii if he took a little, so he said yes. A servant brought some Suntory whiskey, and the Jesuit, the Doctor, and the host had a very pleasant chat. Mr. Okuma had lived in Hawaii, and he told some things about Americans. Dr. Fujii talked a bit about the disaster. He said that Mr. Okuma and a nurse had gone into the ruins of his hospital and brought back a small safe which he had moved into his air-raid shelter. This contained some surgical instruments, and Dr. Fujii gave Father Cieslik

a few pairs of scissors and tweezers for the rector at the Novitiate. Father Cieslik was bursting with some inside dope he had, but he waited until the conversation turned naturally to the mystery of the bomb. Then he said he knew what kind of bomb it was; he had the secret on the best authority—that of a Japanese newspaperman who had dropped in at the Novitiate. The bomb was not a bomb at all; it was a kind of fine magnesium powder sprayed over the whole city by a single plane, and it exploded when it came into contact with the live wires of the city power system. "That means," said Dr. Fujii, perfectly satisfied, since after all the information came from a newspaperman, "that it can only be dropped on big cities and only in the daytime, when the tram lines and so forth are in operation."

After five days of ministering to the wounded in the park, Mr. Tanimoto returned, on August 11th, to his parsonage and dug around in the ruins. He retrieved some diaries and church records that had been kept in books and were only charred around the edges, as well as some cooking utensils and pottery. While he was at work, a Miss Tanaka came and said that her father had been asking for him. Mr. Tanimoto had reason to hate her father, the retired shipping-company official who, though he made a great show of his charity, was notoriously selfish and cruel, and who, just a few days before the bombing, had said openly to several people that Mr. Tanimoto was a spy for the Americans. Several times he had derided Christianity and called it un-Japanese. At the moment of the bombing, Mr. Tanaka had been walking in the street in front of the city's radio station. He received serious flash burns, but he was able to walk home. He took refuge in his Neighborhood Association shelter and from there tried hard to get medical aid. He expected all the doctors of Hiroshima to come to him, because he was so rich and so famous for giving his money away. When none of them came, he angrily set out to look for them; leaning on his daughter's arm, he walked from private hospital to private hospital, but all were in ruins, and he went back and lay down in the shelter again. Now he was very weak and knew he was going to die. He was willing to be comforted by any religion.

Mr. Tanimoto went to help him. He descended into the tomblike shelter and, when his eyes were adjusted to the darkness, saw Mr. Tanaka, his face and arms puffed up and covered with pus and blood, and his eyes swollen shut. The old man smelled very bad, and he moaned constantly. He seemed to recognize Mr. Tanimoto's voice. Standing at the shelter stairway to get light, Mr. Tanimoto read loudly from a Japanese-language pocket Bible: "For a thousand years in Thy sight are but as yesterday when it is past, and as a watch in the night. Thou carriest the children of men away as with a flood; they are as a sleep; in the morning they are like grass which groweth up. In the morning it flourisheth and groweth up; in the evening it is cut down, and withereth. For we are consumed by Thine anger and by Thy wrath are we troubled. Thou hast set our iniquities before Thee, our secret sins in the light of Thy countenance. For all our days are passed away in Thy wrath: we spend our years as a tale that is told. . . ."

Mr. Tanaka died as Mr. Tanimoto read the psalm.

ON AUGUST 11TH, word came to the Ninoshima Military Hospital that a large number of military casualties from the Chugoku Regional Army Headquarters were to arrive on the island that day, and it was deemed necessary to evacuate all civilian patients. Miss Sasaki, still running an alarmingly high fever, was put on a large ship. She lay out on deck, with a pillow under her leg. There were awnings over the deck, but the vessel's course put her in the sunlight. She felt as if she were under a magnifying glass in the sun.

Pus oozed out of her wound, and soon the whole pillow was covered with it. She was taken ashore at Hatsukaichi, a town several miles to the southwest of Hiroshima, and put in the Goddess of Mercy Primary School, which had been turned into a hospital. She lay there for several days before a specialist on fractures came from Kobe. By then her leg was red and swollen up to her hip. The doctor decided he could not set the breaks. He made an incision and put in a rubber pipe to drain off the putrescence.

AT THE NOVITIATE, the motherless Kataoka children were inconsolable. Father Cieslik worked hard to keep them distracted. He put riddles to them. He asked, "What is the cleverest animal in the world?," and after the thirteen-year-old girl had guessed the ape, the elephant, the horse, he said, "No, it must be the hippopotamus," because in Japanese that animal is *kaba,* the reverse of *baka,* stupid. He told Bible stories, beginning, in the order of things, with the Creation. He showed them a scrapbook of snapshots taken in Europe. Nevertheless, they cried most of the time for their mother.

Several days later, Father Cieslik started hunting for the children's family. First, he learned through the police that an uncle had been to the authorities in Kure, a city not far away, to inquire for the children. After that, he heard that an older brother had been trying to trace them through the post office in Ujina, a suburb of Hiroshima. Still later, he heard that the mother was alive and was on Goto Island, off Nagasaki. And at last, by keeping a check on the Ujina post office, he got in touch with the brother and returned the children to their mother.

ABOUT a week after the bomb dropped, a vague, incomprehensible rumor reached Hiroshima—that the city had been destroyed by the energy released when atoms were somehow split in two. The weapon was referred to in this word-of-mouth report as *genshi bakudan*—the root characters of which can be rtanslated as "original child bomb." No one understood the idea or put any more credence in it than in the powdered magnesium and such things. Newspapers were being brought in from other cities, but they were still confining themselves to extremely general statements, such as *Domei's* assertion on August 12th: "There is nothing to do but admit the tremendous power of this inhuman bomb." Already, Japanese physicists had entered the city with Lauritsen electroscopes and Neher electrometers; they understood the idea all too well.

ON AUGUST 12TH, the Nakamuras, all of them still rather sick, went to the nearby town of Kabe and moved in with Mrs. Nakamura's sister-in-law. The next day, Mrs. Nakamura, although she was too ill to walk much, returned to Hiroshima alone, by electric car to the outskirts, by foot from there. All week, at the Novitiate, she had worried about her mother, brother, and older sister, who had lived in the part of town called Fukuro, and besides, she felt drawn by some fascination, just as Father Kleinsorge had been. She discovered that her family were all dead. She went back to Kabe so amazed and depressed by what she had seen and learned in the city that she could not speak that evening.

A COMPARATIVE orderliness, at least, began to be established at the Red Cross Hospital. Dr. Sasaki, back from his rest, undertook to classify his patients (who were still scattered everywhere, even on the stairways). The staff gradually swept up the debris. Best of all, the nurses and attendants started to remove the corpses. Disposal of the dead, by decent cremation and enshrinement, is a greater moral responsibility to the Japanese than adequate care of the living. Relatives identified most of the first day's dead in and around the hospital. Beginning on the second day, whenever a patient appeared to be moribund, a piece of paper with his name on

it was fastened to his clothing. The corpse detail carried the bodies to a clearing outside, placed them on pyres of wood from ruined houses, burned them, put some of the ashes in envelopes intended for exposed X-ray plates, marked the envelopes with the names of the deceased, and piled them, neatly and respectfully, in stacks in the main office. In a few days, the envelopes filled one whole side of the impromptu shrine.

IN KABE, on the morning of August 15th, ten-year-old Toshio Nakamura heard an airplane overhead. He ran outdoors and identified it with a professional eye as a B-29. "There goes Mr. B!" he shouted.

One of his relatives called out to him, "Haven't you had enough of Mr. B?"

The question had a kind of symbolism. At almost that very moment, the dull, dispirited voice of Hirohito, the Emperor Tenno, was speaking for the first time in history over the radio: "After pondering deeply the general trends of the world and the actual conditions obtaining in Our Empire today, We have decided to effect a settlement of the present situation by resorting to an extraodinary measure. . . ."

Mrs. Nakamura had gone to the city again, to dig up some rice she had buried in her Neighborhood Association air-raid shelter. She got it and started back for Kabe. On the electric car, quite by chance, she ran into her younger sister, who had not been in Hiroshima the day of the bombing. "Have you heard the news?" her sister asked.

"What news?"

"The war is over."

"Don't say such a foolish thing, sister."

"But I heard it over the radio myself." And then, in a whisper, "It was the Emperor's voice."

"Oh," Mrs. Nakamura said (she needed nothing more to make her give up thinking, in spite of the atomic bomb, that Japan still had a chance to win the war), "in that case. . . ."

SOME time later, in a letter to an American, Mr. Tanimoto described the events of that morning. "At the time of the Post-War, the marvelous thing in our history happened. Our Emperor broadcasted his own voice through radio directly to us, common people of Japan. Aug. 15th we were told that some news of great importance could be heard & all of us should hear it. So I went to Hiroshima railway station. There sat a loud-speaker in the ruins of the station. Many civilians, all of them were in bound-age, some being helped by shoulder of their daughters, some sustaining their injured feet by sticks, they listened to the broadcast and when they came to realize the fact that it was the Emperor, they cried with full tears in their eyes, 'What a wonderful blessing it is that Tenno himself call on us and we can hear his own voice in person. We are thoroughly satisfied in such a great sacrifice.' When they came to know the war was ended—that is, Japan was de-feated, they, of course, were deeply dis-appointed, but followed after their Em-peror's commandment in calm spirit, making whole-hearted sacrifice for the ever-lasting peace of the world—and Japan started her new way."

IV

PANIC GRASS AND FEVERFEW

ON AUGUST 18TH, twelve days after the bomb burst, Father Kleinsorge set out on foot for Hiroshima from the Novitiate with his papier-mâché suitcase in his hand. He had begun to think that this bag, in which he kept his valuables, had a talis-manic quality, because of the way he had found it after the explosion, standing handle-side up in the doorway of his room, while the desk under which he had previously hidden it was in splinters all over the floor. Now he was using it to carry the yen belonging to the Society of Jesus to the Hiroshima branch of the Yokohama Specie Bank, already reopened in its half-ruined building. On the whole, he felt quite well that morning. It is true that the minor cuts he had received had not healed in three or four days, as the rector of the Novitiate, who had examined them, had positively promised they would, but Father Kleinsorge had rested well for a week and considered that he was again ready for hard work. By now he was accustomed to the terrible scene through which he walked on his way into the city: the large rice field near the Novitiate, streaked with brown; the houses on the outskirts of the city, standing but decrepit, with broken windows and dishevelled tiles; and then, quite suddenly, the beginning of the four square miles of reddish-brown scar, where nearly everything had been buffeted down and burned; range on range of col-lapsed city blocks, with here and there a crude sign erected on a pile of ashes and tiles ("Sister, where are you?" or "All safe and we live at Toyosaka"); naked trees and canted telephone poles; the few stand-ing, gutted buildings only accentuating the horizontality of everything else (the Museum of Science and Industry, with its dome stripped to its steel frame, as if for an autopsy; the modern Chamber of Com-merce Building, its tower as cold, rigid, and unassailable after the blow as before; the huge, low-lying, camouflaged city hall; the row of dowdy banks, caricaturing a shaken economic system); and in the streets a macabre traffic—hundreds of crumpled bicycles, shells of streetcars and automo-biles, all halted in mid-motion. The whole way, Father Kleinsorge was oppressed by the thought that all the damage he saw had been done in one instant by one bomb. By the time he reached the center of town, the day had become very hot. He walked to the Yokohama Bank, which was doing business in a temporary wooden stall on the ground floor of its building, de-posited the money, went by the mission compound just to have another look at the wreckage, and then started back to the Novitiate. About halfway there, he began to have peculiar sensations. The more or less magical suitcase, now empty, suddenly seemed terribly heavy. His knees grew weak. He felt excruciatingly tired. With a considerable expenditure of spirit, he managed to reach the Novitiate. He did not think his weakness was worth mentioning to the other Jesuits. But a couple of days later, while attempting to say Mass, he had an onset of faintness and even after three attempts was unable to go through with the service, and the next morning the rector, who had examined Father Kleinsorge's apparently negligible but unhealed cuts daily, asked in surprise, "What have you done to your wounds?" They had suddenly opened wider and were swollen and inflamed.

As she dressed on the morning of August 20th, in the home of her sister-in-law in Kabe, not far from Nagatsuka, Mrs. Nakamura, who had suffered no cuts or burns at all, though she had been rather nauseated all through the week she and her children had spent as guests of Father Kleinsorge and the other Catholics at the Novitiate, began fixing her hair and noticed, after one stroke, that her comb carried with it a whole handful of hair; the second time, the same thing happened, so she stopped combing at once. But in the next three or four days, her hair kept falling out of its own accord, until she was quite bald. She began living indoors, practically in hiding. On August 26th, both she and her younger daughter, Myeko, woke up feeling extremely weak and tired, and they stayed on their bedrolls. Her son and other daughter, who had shared every experience with her during and after the bombing, felt fine.

At about the same time—he lost track of the days, so hard was he working to set up a temporary place of worship in a private house he had rented in the outskirts—Mr. Tanimoto fell suddenly ill with a general malaise, weariness, and feverishness, and he, too, took to his bedroll on the floor of the half-wrecked house of a friend in the suburb of Ushida.

These four did not realize it, but they were coming down with the strange, capricious disease which came later to be known as radiation sickness.

MISS SASAKI lay in steady pain in the Goddess of Mercy Primary School, at Hatsukaichi, the fourth station to the southwest of Hiroshima on the electric train. An internal infection still prevented the proper setting of the compound fracture of her lower left leg. A young man who was in the same hospital and who seemed to have grown fond of her in spite of her unremitting preoccupation with her suffering, or else just pitied her because of it, lent her a Japanese translation of de Maupassant, and she tried to read the stories, but she could concentrate for only four or five minutes at a time.

The hospitals and aid stations around Hiroshima were so crowded in the first weeks after the bombing, and their staffs were so variable, depending on their health and on the unpredictable arrival of outside help, that patients had to be constantly shifted from place to place. Miss Sasaki, who had already been moved three times, twice by ship, was taken at the end of August to an engineering school, also at Hatsukaichi. Because her leg did not improve but swelled more and more, the doctors at the school bound it with crude splints and took her by car, on September 9th, to the Red Cross Hospital in Hiroshima. This was the first chance she had had to look at the ruins of Hiroshima; the last time she had been carried through the city's streets, she had been hovering on the edge of unconsciousness. Even though the wreckage had been described to her, and though she was still in pain, the sight horrified and amazed her, and there was something she noticed about it that particularly gave her the creeps. Over everything—up through the wreckage of the city, in gutters, along the riverbanks, tangled among tiles and tin roofing, climbing on charred tree trunks—was a blanket of fresh, vivid, lush, optimistic green; the verdancy rose even from the foundations of ruined houses. Weeds already hid the ashes, and wild flowers were in bloom among the city's bones. The bomb had not only left the underground organs of plants intact; it had stimulated them. Everywhere were bluets and Spanish bayonets, goosefoot, morning glories and day lilies, the hairy-fruited bean, purslane and clotbur and sesame and panic grass and feverfew. Especially in a circle at the center, sickle senna grew in extraordinary regeneration, not only standing among the charred remnants of the same plant but pushing up in new places, among bricks and through cracks in the asphalt. It actually seemed as if a load of sickle-senna seed had been dropped along with the bomb.

At the Red Cross Hospital, Miss Sasaki was put under the care of Dr. Sasaki. Now, a month after the explosion, something like order had been reëstablished in the hospital; which is to say that the patients who still lay in the corridors at least had mats to sleep on and that the supply of medicines, which had given out in the first few days, had been replaced, though inadequately, by contributions from other cities. Dr. Sasaki, who had had one seventeen-hour sleep at his home on the third night, had ever since then rested only about six hours a night, on a mat at the hospital; he had lost twenty pounds from his very small body; he still wore the borrowed glasses.

Since Miss Sasaki was a woman and was so sick (and perhaps, he afterward admitted, just a little bit because she was named Sasaki), Dr. Sasaki put her on a mat in a semi-private room, which at that time had only eight people in it. He questioned her and put down on her record card, in the correct, scrunched-up German in which he wrote all his records: "*Mittelgrosse Patientin in gutem Ernährungszustand. Fraktur am linken Unterschenkelknochen mit Wunde; Anschwellung in der linken Unterschenkelgegend. Haut und sichtbare Schleimhäute mässig durchblutet und kein Oedema,*" noting that she was a medium-sized female patient in good general health; that she had a compound fracture of the left tibia, with swelling of the left lower leg; that her skin and visible mucous membranes were heavily spotted with *petechiae,* which are hemorrhages about the size of grains of rice, or even as big as soybeans; and, in addition, that her head, eyes, throat, lungs, and heart were apparently normal; and that she had a fever. He wanted to set her fracture and put her leg in a cast, but he had run out of plaster of Paris long since, so he just stretched her out on a mat and prescribed aspirin for her fever, and glucose intravenously and diastase orally for her undernourishment (which he had not entered on her record because everyone suffered from it). She exhibited only one of the queer symptoms so many of his patients were just then beginning to show —the spot hemorrhages.

Dr. Fujii was still pursued by bad luck, which still was connected with rivers. Now he was living in the summer house of Mr. Okuma, in Fukawa. This house clung to the steep banks of the Ota River. Here his injuries seemed to make good progress, and he even began to treat refugees who came to him from the neighborhood, using medical supplies he had retrieved from a cache in the suburbs. He noticed in some of his patients a curious syndrome of symptoms that cropped out in the third and fourth weeks, but he was not able to do much more than swathe cuts and burns. Early in September, it began to rain, steadily and heavily. The river rose. On September 17th, there came a cloudburst and then a typhoon, and the water crept higher and higher up the bank. Mr. Okuma and Dr. Fujii became alarmed and scrambled up the mountain to a peasant's house. (Down in Hiroshima, the flood took up where the bomb had left off—swept away bridges that had survived the blast, washed out streets, undermined foundations of buildings that still stood—and ten miles to the west, the Ono Army Hospital, where a team of experts from Kyoto Imperial University was studying the delayed affliction of the patients, suddenly slid down a beautiful, pine-dark mountainside into the Inland Sea and drowned most of the investigators and their mysteriously diseased patients alike.) After the storm, Dr. Fujii and Mr. Okuma went down to the river and found that the Okuma house had been washed altogether away.

BECAUSE so many people were suddenly feeling sick nearly a month after the atomic bomb was dropped, an unpleasant rumor began to move around, and eventually it made its way to the house in Kabe where Mrs. Nakamura lay bald and ill. It was that the atomic bomb had deposited some sort of poison on Hiroshima which would give off deadly emanations for seven years; nobody could go there all that time. This especially upset Mrs. Nakamura, who remembered that in a moment of confusion on the morning of the explosion she had literally sunk her entire means of livelihood, her Sankoku sewing machine, in the small cement water tank in front of what was left of her house; now no one would be able to go and fish it out. Up to this time, Mrs. Nakamura and her relatives had been quite resigned and passive about the moral issue of the atomic bomb, but this rumor suddenly aroused them to more hatred and resentment of America than they had felt all through the war.

Japanese physicists, who knew a great deal about atomic fission (one of them owned a cyclotron), worried about lingering radiation at Hiroshima, and in mid-August, not many days after Presiden Truman's disclosure of the type of bomb that had been dropped, they entered the city to make investigations. The first thing they did was roughly to determine a center by observing the side on which telephone poles all around the heart of the town were scorched; they settled on the torii gateway of the Gokoku Shrine, right next to the parade ground of the Chugoku Regional Army Headquarters. From there, they worked north and south with Lauritsen

electroscopes, which are sensitive to both beta particles and gamma rays. These indicated that the highest intensity of radioactivity, near the torii, was 4.2 times the average natural "leak" of ultra-short waves for the earth of that area. The scientists noticed that the flash of the bomb had discolored concrete to a light reddish tint, had scaled off the surface of granite, and had scorched certain other types of building material, and that consequently the bomb had, in some places, left prints of the shadows that had been cast by its light. The experts found, for instance, a permanent shadow thrown on the roof of the Chamber of Commerce Building (220 yards from the rough center) by the structure's rectangular tower; several others in the lookout post on top of the Hypothec Bank (2,050 yards); another in the tower of the Chugoku Electric Supply Building (800 yards); another projected by the handle of a gas pump (2,630 yards); and several on granite tombstones in the Gokoku Shrine (385 yards). By triangulating these and other such shadows with the objects that formed them, the scientists determined that the exact center was a spot a hundred and fifty yards south of the torii and a few yards southeast of the pile of ruins that had once been the Shima Hospital. (A few vague human silhouettes were found, and these gave rise to stories that eventually included fancy and precise details. One story told how a painter on a ladder was monumentalized in a kind of bas-relief on the stone façade of a bank building on which he was at work, in the act of dipping his brush into his paint can; another, how a man and his cart on the bridge near the Museum of Science and Industry, almost under the center of the explosion, were cast down in an embossed shadow which made it clear that the man was about to whip his horse.) Starting east and west from the actual center, the scientists, in early September, made new measurements, and the highest radiation they found this time was 3.9 times the natural "leak." Since radiation of at least a thousand times the natural "leak" would be required to cause serious effects on the human body, the scientists announced that people could enter Hiroshima without any peril at all.

As soon as this reassurance reached the household in which Mrs. Nakamura was concealing herself—or, at any rate, within a short time, after her hair had started growing back again—her whole family relaxed their extreme hatred of America, and Mrs. Nakamura sent her brother-in-law to look for the sewing machine. It was still submerged in the water tank, and when he brought it home, she saw, to her dismay, that it was all rusted and useless.

BY THE END of the first week in September, Father Kleinsorge was in bed at the Novitiate with a fever of 102.2, and since he seemed to be getting worse, his colleagues decided to send him to the Catholic International Hospital in Tokyo. Father Cieslik and the rector took him as far as Kobe and a Jesuit from that city took him the rest of the way, with a message from a Kobe doctor to the Mother Superior of the International Hospital: "Think twice before you give this man blood transfusions, because with atomic-bomb patients we aren't at all sure that if you stick needles in them, they'll stop bleeding."

When Father Kleinsorge arrived at the hospital, he was terribly pale and very shaky. He complained that the bomb had upset his digestion and given him abdominal pains. His white blood count was three thousand (five to seven thousand is normal), he was seriously anemic, and his temperature was 104. A doctor who did not know much about these strange manifestations—Father Kleinsorge was one of a handful of atomic patients who had reached Tokyo—came to see him, and to the patient's face he was most encouraging. "You'll be out of here in two weeks," he said. But when the doctor got out in the corridor, he said to the Mother Superior, "He'll die. All these bomb people die— you'll see. They go along for a couple of weeks and then they die."

The doctor prescribed suralimentation for Father Kleinsorge. Every three hours, they forced some eggs or beef juice into him, and they fed him all the sugar he could stand. They gave him vitamins, and iron pills and arsenic (in Fowler's solution) for his anemia. He confounded both the doctor's predictions; he neither died nor got up in a fortnight. Despite the fact that the message from the Kobe doctor deprived him of transfusions, which would have been the most useful therapy of all, his fever and his digestive troubles cleared up fairly quickly. His white count went up for a while, but early in October it dropped again, to 3,600; then, in ten days, it suddenly climbed above normal, to 8,800; and it finally settled at 5,800. His ridiculous scratches puzzled everyone. For a few days, they would mend, and then, when he moved around, they would open up again. As soon as he began to feel well, he enjoyed himself tremendously. In Hiroshima he had been one of thousands of sufferers; in Tokyo he was a curiosity. American Army doctors came by the dozen to observe him. Japanese experts questioned him. A newspaper interviewed him. And once, the confused doctor came and shook his head and said, "Baffling cases, these atomic-bomb people."

MRS. NAKAMURA lay indoors with Myeko. They both continued sick, and though Mrs. Nakamura vaguely sensed that their trouble was caused by the bomb, she was too poor to see a doctor and so never knew exactly what the matter was. Without any treatment at all, but merely resting, they began gradually to feel better. Some of Myeko's hair fell out, and she had a tiny burn on her arm which took months to heal. The boy, Toshio, and the older girl, Yaeko, seemed well enough, though they, too, lost some hair and occasionally had bad headaches. Toshio was still having nightmares, always about the nineteen-year-old mechanic, Hideo Osaki, his hero, who had been killed by the bomb.

On HIS BACK with a fever of 104, Mr. Tanimoto worried about all the funerals he ought to be conducting for the deceased of his church. He thought he was just over-tired from the hard work he had done since the bombing, but after the fever had persisted for a few days, he sent for a doctor. The doctor was too busy to visit him in Ushida, but he dispatched a nurse, who recognized his symptoms as those of mild radiation disease and came back from time to time to give him injections of Vitamin B$_1$. A Buddhist priest with whom Mr. Tanimoto was acquainted called on him and suggested that moxibustion might give him relief; the priest showed the pastor how to give himself the ancient Japanese treatment, by setting fire to a twist of the stimulant herb moxa placed on the wrist pulse. Mr. Tanimoto found that each moxa treatment temporarily re-duced his fever one degree. The nurse had told him to eat as much as possible, and every few days his mother-in-law brought him vegetables and fish from Tsuzu, twenty miles away, where she lived. He spent a month in bed, and then went ten hours by train to his father's home in Shikoku. There he rested another month.

DR. SASAKI and his colleagues at the Red Cross Hospital watched the unprecedented disease unfold and at last evolved a theory about its nature. It had, they decided, three stages. The first stage had been all over before the doctors even knew they were dealing with a new sickness; it was the direct reaction to the bombardment of the body, at the moment when the bomb went off, by neutrons, beta particles, and gamma rays. The apparently uninjured people who had died so mysteriously in the first few hours or days had succumbed in this first stage. It killed ninety-five per cent of the people within a half mile of the center, and many thousands who were farther away. The doctors realized in retrospect that even though most of these dead had also suffered from burns and blast effects, they had absorbed enough

radiation to kill them. The rays simply destroyed body cells—caused their nuclei to degenerate and broke their walls. Many people who did not die right away came down with nausea, headache, diarrhea, malaise, and fever, which lasted several days. Doctors could not be certain whether some of these symptoms were the result of radiation or nervous shock. The second stage set in ten or fifteen days after the bombing. Its first symptom was falling hair. Diarrhea and fever, which in some cases went as high as 106, came next. Twenty-five to thirty days after the ex-plosion, blood disorders appeared: gums bled, the white-blood-cell count dropped sharply, and *petechiae* appeared on the skin and mucous membranes. The drop in the number of white blood corpuscles reduced the patient's capacity to resist infection, so open wounds were unusually slow in healing and many of the sick de-veloped sore throats and mouths. The two key symptoms, on which the doctors came to base their prognosis, were fever and the lowered white-corpuscle count. If fever re-mained steady and high, the patient's chances for survival were poor. The white count almost always dropped below four thousand; a patient whose count fell be-low one thousand had little hope of living. Toward the end of the second stage, if the patient survived, anemia, or a drop in the red blood count, also set in. The third stage was the reaction that came when the body struggled to compensate for its ills—when, for instance, the white count not only returned to normal but increased to much higher than normal levels. In this stage, many patients died of complications, such as infections in the chest cavity. Most burns healed with deep layers of pink, rubbery scar tissue, known as keloid tumors. The duration of the disease varied, depending on the patient's constitution and the amount of radiation he had received. Some victims recovered in a week; with others the disease dragged on for months.

As the symptoms revealed themselves, it became clear that many of them resembled the effects of overdoses of X-ray, and the doctors based their therapy on that likeness. They gave victims liver extract, blood transfusions, and vitamins, especially B_1. The shortage of supplies and instruments hampered them. Allied doctors who came in after the surrender found plasma and penicillin very effective. Since the blood disorders were, in the long run, the predominant factor in the disease, some of the Japanese doctors evolved a theory as to the seat of the delayed sickness. They thought that perhaps gamma rays, entering the body at the time of the explosion, made the phosphorus in the victims' bones radioactive, and that they in turn emitted beta particles, which, though they could no penetrate far through flesh, could enter the bone marrow, where blood is manufactured, and gradually tear it down. Whatever its source, the disease had some baffling quirks. Not all the patients exhibited all the main symptoms. People who suffered flash burns were protected, to a considerable extent, from radiation sickness. Those who had lain quietly for days or even hours after the bombing were much less liable to get sick than those who had been active. Gray hair seldom fell out. And, as if nature were protecting man against his own ingenuity, the reproductive processes were affected for a time; men became sterile, women had miscarriages, menstruation stopped.

FOR TEN DAYS after the flood, Dr. Fujii lived in the peasant's house on the mountain above the Ota. Then he heard about a vacant private clinic in Kaitaichi, a suburb to the east of Hiroshima. He bought it at once, moved there, and hung out a sign inscribed in English, in honor of the conquerors:

M. FUJII, M.D.
MEDICAL & VENEREAL

Quite recovered from his wounds, he soon built up a strong practice, and he was delighted, in the evenings, to receive members of the occupying forces, on whom he lavished whiskey and practiced English.

GIVING Miss Sasaki a local anaesthetic of procaine, Dr. Sasaki made an incision in her leg on October 23rd, to drain the infection, which still lingered on eleven weeks after the injury. In the following days, so much pus formed that he had to dress the opening each morning and evening. A week later, she complained of great pain, so he made another incision; he cut still a third, on November 9th, and enlarged it on the twenty-sixth. All this time, Miss Sasaki grew weaker and weaker, and her spirits fell low. One day, the young man who had lent her his translation of de Maupassant at Hatsukaichi came to visit her; he told her that he was going to Kyushu but that when he came back, he would like to see her again. She didn't care. Her leg had been so swollen and painful all along that the doctor had not even tried to set the fractures, and though an X-ray taken in November showed that the bones were mending, she could see under the sheet that her left leg was nearly three inches shorter than her right and that her left foot was turning inward. She thought often of the man to whom she had been engaged. Someone told her he was back from overseas. She wondered what he had heard about her injuries that made him stay away.

FATHER KLEINSORGE was discharged from the hospital in Tokyo on December 19th and took a train home. On the way, two days later, at Yokogawa, a stop just before Hiroshima, Dr. Fujii boarded the train. It was the first time the two men had met since before the bombing. They sat together. Dr. Fujii said he was going to the annual gathering of his family, on the anniversary of his father's death. When they started talking about their experiences, the Doctor was quite entertaining as he told how his places of residence kept falling into rivers. Then he asked Father Kleinsorge how he was, and the Jesuit talked about his stay in the hospital. "The doctors told me to be cautious," he said. "They ordered me to have a two-hour nap every afternoon."

Dr. Fujii said, "It's hard to be cautious in Hiroshima these days. Everyone seems to be so busy."

A NEW municipal government, set up under Allied Military Government direction, had gone to work at last in the city hall. Citizens who had recovered from various degrees of radiation sickness were coming back by the thousand—by November 1st, the population, mostly crowded into the outskirts, was already 137,000, more than a third of the wartime peak—and the government set in motion all kinds of projects to put them to work rebuilding the city. It hired men to clear the streets, and others to gather scrap iron, which they sorted and piled in mountains opposite the city hall. Some returning residents were putting up their own shanties and huts, and planting small squares of winter wheat beside them, but the city also authorized and built four hundred one-family "barracks." Utilities were repaired—electric lights shone again, trams started running, and employees of the waterworks fixed seventy thousand leaks in mains and plumbing. A Planning Conference, with an enthusiastic young Military Government officer, Lieutenant John D. Montgomery, of Kalamazoo, as its adviser, began to consider what sort of city the new Hiroshima should be. The ruined city had flourished—and had been an inviting target—mainly because it had been one of the most important military-command and communications centers in Japan, and would have become the Imperial headquarters had the islands been invaded and Tokyo been captured. Now there would be no huge military establishments to help revive the city. The Planning Conference, at a loss as to just what importance Hiroshima could have, fell back on rather vague cultural and paving projects. It drew maps with avenues a hundred yards wide and thought seriously of erecting a group of buildings as a monument to the disaster,

and naming them the Institute of International Amity. Statistical workers gathered what figures they could on the effects of the bomb. They reported that 78,150 people had been killed, 13,983 were missing, and 37,425 had been injured. No one in the city government pretended that these figures were accurate—though the Americans accepted them as official—and as the months went by and more and more hundreds of corpses were dug up from the ruins, and as the number of unclaimed urns of ashes at the Zempoji Temple in Koi rose into the thousands, the statisticians began to say that at least a hundred thousand people had lost their lives in the bombing. Since many people died of a combination of causes, it was impossible to figure exactly how many were killed by each cause, but the statisticians calculated that about twenty-five per cent had died of direct burns from the bomb, about fifty per cent from other injuries, and about twenty per cent as a result of radiation effects. The statisticians' figures on property damage were more reliable: sixty-two thousand out of ninety thousand buildings destroyed, and six thousand more damaged beyond repair. In the heart of the city, they found only five modern buildings that could be used again without major repairs. This small number was by no means the fault of flimsy Japanese construction. In fact, since the 1923 earthquake, Japanese building regulations had required that the roof of each large building be able to bear a minimum load of seventy pounds per square foot, whereas American regulations do not normally specify more than forty pounds per square foot.

Scientists swarmed into the city. Some of them measured the force that had been necessary to shift marble gravestones in the cemeteries, to knock over twenty-two of the forty-seven railroad cars in the yards at Hiroshima station, to lift and move the concrete roadway on one of the bridges, and to perform other noteworthy acts of strength, and concluded that the pressure exerted by the explosion varied from 5.3

to 8.0 tons per square yard. Others found that mica, of which the melting point is 900° C., had fused on granite gravestones three hundred and eighty yards from the center; that telephone poles of *Cryptomeria japonica,* whose carbonization temperature is 240° C., had been charred at forty-four hundred yards from the center; and that the surface of gray clay tiles of the type used in Hiroshima, whose melting point is 1,300° C., had dissolved at six hundred yards; and, after examining other significant ashes and melted bits, they concluded that the bomb's heat on the ground at the center must have been 6,000° C. And from further measurements of radiation, which involved, among other things, the scraping up of fission fragments from roof troughs and drainpipes as far away as the suburb of Takusu, thirty-three hundred yards from the center, they learned some far more important facts about the nature of the bomb. General MacArthur's headquarters systematically censored all mention of the bomb in Japanese scientific publications, but soon the fruit of the scientists' calculations became common knowledge among Japanese physicists, doctors, chemists, journalists, professors, and, no doubt, those statesmen and military men who were still in circulation. Long before the American public had been told, most of the scientists and lots of non-scientists in Japan knew—from the calculations of Japanese nuclear physicists—that a uranium bomb had exploded at Hiroshima and a more powerful one, of plutonium, at Nagasaki. They also knew that theoretically one ten times as powerful—or twenty—could be developed. The Japanese scientists thought they knew the exact height at which the bomb at Hiroshima was exploded and the approximate weight of the uranium used. They estimated that, even with the primitive bomb used at Hiroshima, it would require a shelter of concrete fifty inches thick to protect a human being entirely from radiation sickness. The scientists had these and other details which remained subject to security in the United States,

printed and mimeographed and bound into little books. The Americans knew of the existence of these, but tracing them and seeing that they did not fall into the wrong hands would have obliged the occupying authorities to set up, for this one purpose alone, an enormous police system in Japan. Altogether, the Japanese scientists were somewhat amused at the efforts of their conquerors to keep security on atomic fission.

Late in February, 1946, a friend of Miss Sasaki's called on Father Kleinsorge and asked him to visit her in the hospital. She had been growing more and more depressed and morbid; she seemed little interested in living. Father Kleinsorge went to see her several times. On his first visit, he kept the conversation general, formal, and yet vaguely sympathetic, and did not mention religion. Miss Sasaki herself brought it up the second time he dropped in on her. Evidently she had had some talks with a Catholic. She asked bluntly, "If your God is so good and kind, how can he let people suffer like this?" She made a gesture which took in her shrunken leg, the other patients in her room, and Hiroshima as a whole.

"My child," Father Kleinsorge said, "man is not now in the condition God intended. He has fallen from grace through sin." And he went on to explain all the reasons for everything.

It came to Mrs. Nakamura's attention that a carpenter from Kabe was building a number of wooden shanties in Hiroshima which he rented for fifty yen a month—$3.33, at the fixed rate of exchange. Mrs. Nakamura had lost the certificates for her bonds and other wartime savings, but fortunately she had copied off all the numbers just a few days before the bombing and had taken the list to Kabe, and so, when her hair had grown in enough for her to be presentable, she went to her bank in Hiroshima, and a clerk there told her that after checking her numbers against the records the bank would give her her money. As soon as she got it, she rented one of the carpenter's shacks. It was in Nobori-cho, near the site of her former house, and though its floor was dirt and it was dark inside, it was at least a home in Hiroshima, and she was no longer dependent on the charity of her in-laws. During the spring, she cleared away some nearby wreckage and planted a vegetable garden. She cooked with utensils and ate off plates she scavenged from the debris. She sent Myeko to the kindergarten which the Jesuits reopened, and the two older children attended Nobori-cho Primary School, which, for want of buildings, held classes out of doors. Toshio wanted to study to be a mechanic, like his hero, Hideo Osaki. Prices were high; by midsummer Mrs. Nakamura's savings were gone. She sold some of her clothes to get food. She had once had several expensive kimonos, but during the war one had been stolen, she had given one to a sister who had been bombed out in Tokuyama, she had lost a couple in the Hiroshima bombing, and now she sold her last one. It brought only a hundred yen, which did not last long. In June, she went to Father Kleinsorge for advice about how to get along, and in early August, she was still considering the two alternatives he suggested—taking work as a domestic for some of the Allied occupation forces, or borrowing from her relatives enough money, about five hundred yen, or a bit more than thirty dollars, to repair her rusty sewing machine and resume the work of a seamstress.

WHEN Mr. Tanimoto returned from Shikoku, he draped a tent he owned over the roof of the badly damaged house he had rented in Ushida. The roof still leaked, but he conducted services in the damp living room. He began thinking about raising money to restore his church in the city. He became quite friendly with Father Kleinsorge and saw the Jesuits often. He envied them their Church's wealth; they seemed to be able to do anything they wanted. He had nothing to work with except his own energy, and that was not what it had been.

THE SOCIETY of Jesus had been the first institution to build a relatively permanent shanty in the ruins of Hiroshima. That had been while Father Kleinsorge was in the hospital. As soon as he got back, he began living in the shack, and he and another priest, Father Laderman, who had joined him in the mission, arranged for the purchase of three of the standardized "barracks," which the city was selling at seven thousand yen apiece. They put two together, end to end, and made a pretty chapel of them; they ate in the third. When materials were available, they commissioned a contractor to build a three-story mission house exactly like the one that had been destroyed in the fire. In the compound, carpenters cut timbers, gouged mortises, shaped tenons, whittled scores of wooden pegs and bored holes for them, until all the parts for the house were in a neat pile; then, in three days, they put the whole thing together, like an Oriental puzzle, without any nails at all. Father Kleinsorge was finding it hard, as Dr. Fujii had suggested he would, to be cautious and to take his naps. He went out every day on foot to call on Japanese Catholics and prospective converts. As the months went by, he grew more and more tired. In June, he read an article in the Hiroshima *Chugoku* warning survivors against working too hard—but what could he do? By July, he was worn out, and early in August, almost exactly on the anniversary of the bombing, he went back to the Catholic International Hospital, in Tokyo, for a month's rest.

WHETHER or not Father Kleinsorge's answers to Miss Sasaki's questions about life were final and absolute truths, she seemed quickly to draw physical strength from them. Dr. Sasaki noticed it and congratulated Father Kleinsorge. By April 15th, her temperature and white count were normal and the infection in the wound was beginning to clear up. On the twentieth, there was almost no pus, and for the first time she jerked along a corridor on crutches. Five days later, the wound had begun to heal, and on the last day of the month she was discharged.

During the early summer, she prepared herself for conversion to Catholicism. In that period she had ups and downs. Her depressions were deep. She knew she would always be a cripple. Her fiancé never came to see her. There was nothing for her to do except read and look out, from her house on a hillside in Koi, across the ruins of the city where her parents and brother died. She was nervous, and any sudden noise made her put her hands quickly to her throat. Her leg still hurt; she rubbed it often and patted it, as if to console it.

It took six months for the Red Cross Hospital, and even longer for Dr. Sasaki, to get back to normal. Until the city restored electric power, the hospital had to limp along with the aid of a Japanese Army generator in its back yard. Operating tables, X-ray machines, dentist chairs, everything complicated and essential came in a trickle of charity from other cities. In Japan, face is important even to institutions, and long before the Red Cross Hospital was back to par on basic medical equipment, its directors put up a new yellow brick veneer façade, so the hospital became the handsomest building in Hiroshima —from the street. For the first four months, Dr. Sasaki was the only surgeon on the staff and he almost never left the building; then, gradually, he began to take an interest in his own life again. He got married in March. He gained back some of the weight he lost, but his appetite remained only fair; before the bombing, he used to eat four rice balls at every meal, but a year after it he could manage only two. He felt tired all the time. "But I have to realize," he said, "that the whole community is tired."

A YEAR after the bomb was dropped, Miss Sasaki was a cripple; Mrs. Nakamura was destitute; Father Kleinsorge was back in the hospital; Dr. Sasaki was not capable of the work he once could do; Dr. Fujii had lost the thirty-room hospital it took him many years to acquire, and had no prospects of rebuilding it; Mr. Tanimoto's church had been ruined and he no longer had his exceptional vitality. The lives of these six people, who were among the luckiest in Hiroshima, would never be the same. What they thought of their experiences and of the use of the atomic bomb was, of course, not unanimous. One feeling they did seem to share, however, was a curious kind of elated community spirit, something like that of the Londoners after their blitz—a pride in the way they and their fellow-survivors had stood up to a dreadful ordeal. Just before the anniversary, Mr. Tanimoto wrote in a letter to an American some words which expressed this feeling: "What a heartbreaking scene this was the first night! About midnight I landed on the riverbank. So many injured people lied on the ground that I made my way by striding over them. Repeating 'Excuse me,' I forwarded and carried a tub of water with me and gave a cup of water to each one of them. They raised their upper bodies slowly and accepted a cup of water with a bow and drunk quietly and, spilling any remnant, gave back a cup with hearty expression of their thankfulness, and said, 'I couldn't help my sister, who was buried under the house, because I had to take care of my mother who got a deep wound on her eye and our house soon set fire and we hardly escaped. Look, I lost my home, my family, and at last myself bitterly injured. But now I have gotted my mind to dedicate what I have and to complete the war for our country's sake.' Thus they pledged to me, even women and children did the same. Being entirely tired I lied down on the ground among them, but couldn't sleep at all. Next morning I found many men and women dead, whom I gave water last night. But, to my great

surprise, I never heard any one cried in disorder, even though they suffered in great
agony. They died in silence, with no
grudge, setting their teeth to bear it. All
for the country!

"Dr. Y. Hiraiwa, professor of Hiroshima
University of Literature and Science, and
one of my church members, was buried by
the bomb under the two storied house with
his son, a student of Tokyo University.
Both of them could not move an inch under
tremendously heavy pressure. And the
house already caught fire. His son said,
'Father, we can do nothing except make
our mind up to consecrate our lives for the
country. Let us give *Banzai* to our Emperor.' Then the father followed after his
son, '*Tenno-heika, Banzai, Banzai, Banzai!*'
In the result, Dr. Hiraiwa said, 'Strange to
say, I felt calm and bright and peaceful
spirit in my heart, when I chanted *Banzai*
to Tenno.' Afterward his son got out and
digged down and pulled out his father and
thus they were saved. In thinking of their
experience of that time Dr. Hiraiwa repeated, 'What a fortunate that we are
Japanese! It was my first time I ever
tasted such a beautiful spirit when I decided to die for our Emperor.'

"Miss Kayoko Nobutoki, a student of
girl's high school, Hiroshima Jazabuin, and
a daughter of my church member, was
taking rest with her friends beside the
heavy fence of the Buddhist Temple. At
the moment the atomic bomb was dropped,
the fence fell upon them. They could not
move a bit under such a heavy fence and
then smoke entered into even a crack and
choked their breath. One of the girls begun
to sing *Kimi ga yo*, national anthem, and
others followed in chorus and died. Meanwhile one of them found a crack and
struggled hard to get out. When she was
taken in the Red Cross Hospital she told
how her friends died, tracing back in her
memory to singing in chorus our national
anthem. They were just 13 years old.

"Yes, people of Hiroshima died manly in
the atomic bombing, believing that it was
for Emperor's sake."

A surprising number of the people of
Hiroshima remained more or less indifferent about the ethics of using the
bomb. Possibly they were too terrified by it
to want to think about it at all. Not many
of them even bothered to find out much
about what it was like. Mrs. Nakamura's
conception of it—and awe of it—was typical. "The atom bomb," she would say when
asked about it, "is the size of a matchbox.
The heat of it is six thousand times that
of the sun. It exploded in the air. There
is some radium in it. I don't know just
how it works, but when the radium is put
together, it explodes," As for the use of
the bomb, she would say, "It was war and
we had to expect it." And then she would
add, "*Shikata ga nai,*" a Japanese expression as common as, and corresponding to,
the Russian word "*nichevo*": "It can't be
helped. Oh, well. Too bad." Dr. Fujii said
approximately the same thing about the
use of the bomb to Father Kleinsorge one
evening, in German: "*Da ist nichts zu
machen.* There's nothing to be done about
it."

Many citizens of Hiroshima, however,
continued to feel a hatred for Americans
which nothing could possibly erase. "I
see," Dr. Sasaki once said, "that they are
holding a trial for war criminals in Tokyo
just now. I think they ought to try the
men who decided to use the bomb and they
should hang them all."

Father Kleinsorge and the other German
Jesuit priests, who, as foreigners, could be
expected to take a relatively detached view,
often discussed the ethics of using the
bomb. One of them, Father Siemes, who
was out at Nagatsuka at the time of the
attack, wrote in a report to the Holy See
in Rome: "Some of us consider the bomb
in the same category as poison gas and
were against its use on a civilian population. Others were of the opinion that in
total war, as carried on in Japan, there
was no difference between civilians and
soldiers, and that the bomb itself was an
effective force tending to end the bloodshed,
warning Japan to surrender and thus to

avoid total destruction. It seems logical that he who supports total war in principle cannot complain of a war against civilians. The crux of the matter is whether total war in its present form is justifiable, even when it serves a just purpose. Does it not have material and spiritual evil as its consequences which far exceed whatever good might result? When will our moralists give us a clear answer to this question?"

It would be impossible to say what horrors were embedded in the minds of the children who lived through the day of the bombing in Hiroshima. On the surface, their recollections, months after the disaster, were of an exhilarating adventure. Toshio Nakamura, who was ten at the time of the bombing, was soon able to talk freely, even gaily, about the experience, and a few weeks before the anniversary he

wrote the following matter-of-fact essay for his teacher at Nobori-cho Primary School: "The day before the bomb, I went for a swim. In the morning, I was eating peanuts. I saw a light. I was knocked to little sister's sleeping place. When we were saved, I could only see as far as the tram. My mother and I started to pack our things. The neighbors were walking around burned and bleeding. Hataya-*san* told me to run away with her. I said I wanted to wait for my mother. We went to the park. A whirlwind came. At night a gas tank burned and I saw the reflection in the river. We stayed in the park one night. Next day I went to Taiko Bridge and met my girl friends Kikuki and Murakami. They were looking for their mothers. But Kikuki's mother was wounded and Murakami's mother, alas was dead."

INDEX OF AUTHORS AND TITLES

[A]

"Abraham Lincoln," Walt Whitman, 135
Adams, Henry, 354
"Alma Mater," Edwin Arlington Robinson, 828
"And This of All My Hopes," Emily Dickinson, 233
Anderson, Sherwood, 697
"Anecdote of the Jar," Wallace Stevens, 867
"Animula," T. S. Eliot, 857
"Another Weeping Woman," Wallace Stevens, 866
"Apostate, The," Jack London, 401
"Appeal of Darwinism, The," Oliver Wendell Holmes, 202
"Architecture," Wallace Stevens, 867
"Art of Fiction, The," Henry James, 438
"As Toilsome I Wander'd Virginia's Woods," Walt Whitman, 90
"Autobiography," Abraham Lincoln, 15
Autobiography, Mark Twain, 311

[B]

Babbitt, Irving, 609
Babbitt, Sinclair Lewis, 691
"Babylon Revisited," F. Scott Fitzgerald, 711
"Ballad of Trees and the Master, A," Sidney Lanier, 144
"Battle of Bull Run, July, 1861," Walt Whitman, 133
"Beast in the Jungle, The," Henry James, 532
"Beat! Beat! Drums!" Walt Whitman, 88
"Bee, The," Emily Dickinson, 225
Benét, Stephen Vincent, 874
"Bewick Finzer," Edwin Arlington Robinson, 831
"Big Two-Hearted River," Ernest Hemingway, 732
Black Boy, Richard Wright, 913
"Blue Hotel, The," Stephen Crane, 369
"Boys in the Army," Walt Whitman, 136
"Brahmin Caste of New England, The," Oliver Wendell Holmes, 191
"Brain Within Its Groove, The," Emily Dickinson, 228
Bridge, The, Hart Crane, 870
"Broadway Sights," Walt Whitman, 132

"Brown's Descent," Robert Frost, 843
"Burial of the Guns, The," Thomas Nelson Page, 172
"Bustle in a House, The," Emily Dickinson, 232
"Butterfly's Assumption-Gown, The," Emily Dickinson, 231
"By the Bivouac's Fitful Flame," Walt Whitman, 89

[C]

Cabell, James Branch, 681
"Camera Eye (50), The," John Dos Passos, 728
"Cape Hatteras," Hart Crane, 870
Cather, Willa, 663
"Chanting the Square Deific," Walt Whitman, 97
"Chariot, The," Emily Dickinson, 226
"Chicago," Carl Sandburg, 847
"Civilian Defense," E. B. White, 896
"Code, The," Robert Frost, 840
Cohen, Morris Raphael, 604
"Come In," Robert Frost, 846
"Come Up From the Fields Father," Walt Whitman, 89
Conversation at Midnight, Edna St. Vincent Millay, 859
"Cool Tombs," Carl Sandburg, 848
"Corn," Sidney Lanier, 144
"Cow in Apple Time, The," Robert Frost, 842
Crane, Hart, 869
Crane, Stephen, 368
Criticism and Fiction, William Dean Howells, 335
"Crossing Brooklyn Ferry," Walt Whitman, 79
"Curious Republic of Gondour, The," Mark Twain, 268

[D]

Daisy Miller: A Study, Henry James, 451
"Day's Wait, A," Ernest Hemingway, 743
"Deacon's Masterpiece, The," Oliver Wendell Holmes, 189
"Death in the Woods," Sherwood Anderson, 697
"Death is a Dialogue," Emily Dickinson, 232

"Democracy and Leadership," Irving Babbitt, 610

Democratic Vistas, Walt Whitman, 119

Dickinson, Emily, 224

Dos Passos, John, 723

Dreiser, Theodore, 651

"Drumlin Woodchuck, A," Robert Frost, 845

Dunne, Finley Peter, 393

"Dying Fires," Frank Norris, 386

[E]

Education of Henry Adams, The, 355

Eliot, T. S., 851

Elsie Venner, Oliver Wendell Holmes, 191

"Eros Turannos," Edwin Arlington Robinson, 830

Essay on Rime, Karl Shapiro, 899

"Ex Parte," Ring Lardner, 705

"Exclusion," Emily Dickinson, 226

"Exit," Edwin Arlington Robinson, 828

[F]

"Farewell Address at Springfield, Illinois," Abraham Lincoln, 16

Farrell, James T., 807

Faulkner, William, 754

"Fence, A," Carl Sandburg, 847

Fitzgerald, F. Scott, 711

"Flickerbridge," Henry James, 520

"Footnote on Criticism," H. L. Mencken, 622

"For a Dead Lady," Edwin Arlington Robinson, 829

For Whom the Bell Tolls, Ernest Hemingway, 744

"Four Preludes on Playthings of the Wind," Carl Sandburg, 849

"Freedom," E. B. White, 893

Freeman, Mary E. Wilkins, 214

Frost, Robert, 836

[G]

Garland, Hamlin, 359

George, Henry, 345

"Gettysburg Address, The," Abraham Lincoln, 17

"Gloucester Moors," William Vaughn Moody, 419

"Goodbye My Fancy!" Walt Whitman, 114

"Grass, The," Emily Dickinson, 230

"Gun, The," Karl Shapiro, 898

[H]

Harte, Bret, 234

Hemingway, Ernest, 731

Hersey, John, 918

"High-Toned Old Christian Woman, A," Wallace Stevens, 866

"Hiltons' Holiday, The," Sarah Orne Jewett, 205

Hiroshima, John Hersey, 919

"Historical Interpretation of Literature, The," Edmund Wilson, 631

"Hollow Men, The," T. S. Eliot, 855

Holmes, Oliver Wendell, 185

"Home Burial," Robert Frost, 837

"House on the Hill, The," Edwin Arlington Robinson, 825

"How Modern Civilization May Decline," Henry George, 346

"How to Tell a Story," Mark Twain, 304

Howells, William Dean, 321

"Hyla Brook," Robert Frost, 842

[I]

"I Died for Beauty," Emily Dickinson, 226

"I Found the Phrase," Emily Dickinson, 233

"I Had Been Hungry," Emily Dickinson, 233

"I Had No Time to Hate," Emily Dickinson, 228

"I Never Lost as Much But Twice," Emily Dickinson, 233

"I Never Saw a Moor," Emily Dickinson, 232

"I Sit and Look Out," Walt Whitman, 88

"I Taste a Liquor Never Brewed," Emily Dickinson, 228

"Idea of Order at Key West, The," Wallace Stevens, 868

"If I Shouldn't Be Alive," Emily Dickinson, 233

"If You Were Coming in the Fall," Emily Dickinson, 228

"In a Library," Emily Dickinson, 227

"In Dispraise of Life, Experience, and Reality," Morris Raphael Cohen, 605

"In Vain," Emily Dickinson, 229

"Indian Summer," Emily Dickinson, 231

"Indignity Put Upon the Remains of George Holland by the Reverend Mr. Sabine, The," Mark Twain, 253

"Individual as Primitive Energy, The," Henry Adams, 355

"Into My Own," Robert Frost, 837

"Invocation," Stephen Vincent Benét, 875

"I've Seen a Dying Eye," Emily Dickinson, 232

[J]

James, Henry, 422

James, William, 585

Jewett, Sarah Orne, 204

"Jilting of Granny Weatherall, The," Katherine Anne Porter, 813

John Brown's Body, Stephen Vincent Benét, 875

"John Evereldown," Edwin Arlington Robinson, 823

"Journey of the Magi," T. S. Eliot, 856

[L]

Lanier, Sidney, 141

Lardner, Ring, 705

"Last Invocation, The," Walt Whitman, 102

"Last Leaf, The," Oliver Wendell Holmes, 187

"Last Night That She Lived, The," Emily Dickinson, 226

"Leaf Treader, A," Robert Frost, 845

"Letter to Mrs. Bixby," Abraham Lincoln, 17

"Lesson of the Master, The," Henry James, 484

Lewis, Sinclair, 690

"Life and Song," Sidney Lanier, 143

Line of Love, The, James Branch Cabell, 681

Lincoln, Abraham, 15

"Loafing in the Woods," Walt Whitman, 137

"Locusts Have No King, The," Thomas Wolfe, 797

London, Jack, 400

"Lonely House, The," Emily Dickinson, 227

"Lost Boy, The," Thomas Wolfe, 778

"Love Song of J. Alfred Prufrock, The," T. S. Eliot, 852

"Luke Havergal," Edwin Arlington Robinson, 824

[M]

"Man Against the Sky, The," Edwin Arlington Robinson, 831

"Marshes of Glynn, The," Sidney Lanier, 152

"Master, The," Edwin Arlington Robinson, 825

"Menagerie, The," William Vaughn Moody, 420

Mencken, Henry Louis, 621

Millay, Edna St. Vincent, 859

Moody, William Vaughn, 415

"Moral Teratology," Oliver Wendell Holmes, 198

"Mowing," Robert Frost, 837

"Mr. Flood's Party," Edwin Arlington Robinson, 835

"Much Madness Is Divinest Sense," Emily Dickinson, 227

"My Aunt," Oliver Wendell Holmes, 188

My Literary Passions, William Dean Howells, 338

"My Passion for Ferries," Walt Whitman, 132

My Year in a Log Cabin, William Dean Howells, 342

Mysterious Stranger, The, Mark Twain, 307

"Mystery of Pain, The," Emily Dickinson, 228

[N]

"Neighbour Rosicky," Willa Cather, 663

"New Feet Within My Garden Go," Emily Dickinson, 225

"Newsreel LXVII," John Dos Passos, 729

"Nightmare With Angels," Stephen Vincent Benét, 884

"Nine from Eight," Sidney Lanier, 142

"Noiseless Patient Spider, A," Walt Whitman, 102

"Non-Resistance," Oliver Wendell Holmes, 190

Norris, Frank, 385

[O]

"O Captain! My Captain!" Walt Whitman, 97

"Ode in Time of Hesitation, An," William Vaughn Moody, 415

"Ode to Walt Whitman," Stephen Vincent Benét, 878

"Old Man's Winter Night, An," Robert Frost, 842

"Old Rogaum and His Theresa," Theodore Dreiser, 652

"Old Story, An," Edwin Arlington Robinson, 825

"Old Times on the Mississippi," Mark Twain, 271

One Man's Meat, E. B. White, 889

"On the Decay of the Art of Lying," Mark Twain, 287

"Once by the Pacific," Robert Frost, 845

"Once I Pass'd Through a Populous City," Walt Whitman, 88

"Oratory Contest, The," James T. Farrell, 807

"Out of the Cradle Endlessly Rocking," Walt Whitman, 83

" 'Out, Out—,' " Robert Frost, 842

[P]

Page, Thomas Nelson, 171

"Passage to India," Walt Whitman, 103

"Patented Gate and the Mean Hamburger, The," Robert Penn Warren, 905

"Patroling Barnegat," Walt Whitman, 113

"Pedigree of Honey, The," Emily Dickinson, 230

People, Yes, The, Carl Sandburg, 850

Personal Recollections of Joan of Arc, Mark Twain, 290

"Pioneers! O Pioneers!" Walt Whitman, 99

Poet at the Breakfast-Table, The, Oliver Wendell Holmes, 194

"Poets Without Laurels," John Crowe Ransom, 639

"Poor, The," Carl Sandburg, 848

Porter, Katherine Anne, 813

Porter, William Sidney (O. Henry), 396

Pragmatism, William James, 586

"Prairie Waters by Night," Carl Sandburg, 848

"Prayer of Columbus," Walt Whitman, 110

"Preface to 1855 Edition of *Leaves of Grass,*" Walt Whitman, 114

Prejudices III, H. L. Mencken, 622

"Presentiment," Emily Dickinson, 231

Progress and Poverty, Henry George, 346

[R]

"Raid, The," John Steinbeck, 771

Ransom, John Crowe, 639

"Real," Emily Dickinson, 232

Realms of Being, Preface to, George Santayana, 597

Reason and Nature, Morris Raphael Cohen, 605

"Renunciation," Emily Dickinson, 229

"Revolt of 'Mother,' The," Mary E. Wilkins Freeman, 214

"Richard Cory," Edwin Arlington Robinson, 824

Robinson, Edwin Arlington, 823

Rock, The, T. S. Eliot, 858

"Rodman the Keeper," Constance Fenimore Woolson, 155

"Romance of Real Life, A," William Dean Howells, 324

"Rose for Emily, A," William Faulkner, 765

Roughing It, Mark Twain, 256

[S]

Sandburg, Carl, 846

Santayana, George, 596

"Scarabee, The," Oliver Wendell Holmes, 194

"Second Inaugural Address," Abraham Lincoln, 17

"Service of Song, A," Emily Dickinson, 230

"Setting Sail," Emily Dickinson, 232

Shapiro, Karl, 897

"Snake, The," Emily Dickinson, 225

"Soldier, There Is a War," Wallace Stevens, 868

"Somebody's Mother," William Dean Howells, 331

"Song of Myself," Walt Whitman, 30

"Song of the Broad-axe," Walt Whitman, 72

"Song of the Universal," Walt Whitman, 111

"Sonnet," Edwin Arlington Robinson, 825

Specimen Days and Collect, Walt Whitman, 132

"Speech on the Babies," Mark Twain, 285

"Spiritual Characters Among the Soldiers," Walt Whitman, 136

"Spotted Horses," William Faulkner, 754

Steinbeck, John, 770

Stevens, Wallace, 866

"Stopping by Woods on a Snowy Evening," Robert Frost, 844

"Success," Emily Dickinson, 225

"Summer's Armies," Emily Dickinson, 230

"Sunday: New Guinea," Karl Shapiro, 899

"Suspense," Emily Dickinson, 228

"Sweeney Among the Nightingales," T. S. Eliot, 854

"Symphony, The," Sidney Lanier, 147

[T]

"Tennessee's Partner," Bret Harte, 235

"There Was a Child Went Forth," Walt Whitman, 70

"There's a Certain Slant of Light," Emily Dickinson, 232

"Tin Lizzie," John Dos Passos, 723

"To an Insect," Oliver Wendell Holmes, 188

"To Earthward," Robert Frost, 844

"To Fight Aloud Is Very Brave," Emily Dickinson, 227

"To the Person Sitting in Darkness," Mark Twain, 294

"Tolstoy," William Dean Howells, 340

"Tourguenief," William Dean Howells, 338

"Town Down the River, The," Edwin Arlington Robinson, 826

"Troop Train," Karl Shapiro, 897

"Truth in Fiction," William Dean Howells, 335

Twain, Mark, 241

"Two Gardens in Linndale," Edwin Arlington Robinson, 829

"Two Streams, The," Oliver Wendell Holmes, 191

[U]

"Uncle Ananias," Edwin Arlington Robinson, 828

"Under the Lion's Paw," Hamlin Garland, 360